D0090429

J · F · K
RECKLESS YOUTH
·

RANDOM HOUSE
NEW YORK

J · F · K

RECKLESS YOUTH

·

NIGEL HAMILTON

The Kennedy family, 1934. From left: Pat, Joe Jr., Bobby,
Kathleen, Rose, Jack, Rosemary, Teddy, Joe Sr., Jean, Eunice
(Bachrach/John F. Kennedy Library)

Grateful acknowledgment is made to the following for permission to reprint previously published
material:
BERKLEY PUBLISHING GROUP: Excerpts from *The Search for JFK* by Joan and Clay Blair. Copyright
© 1976 by Joan and Clay Blair. Reprinted by permission of The Berkley Publishing Group.
COLUMBIA UNIVERSITY, ORAL HISTORY RESEARCH OFFICE: Excerpts from the reminiscences of Alan G.
Kirk in the Oral History Collection of Columbia University, hereafter COHC. Reprinted by
permission.
DOUBLEDAY, A DIVISION OF BANTAM DOUBLEDAY DELL PUBLISHING GROUP, INC.: Excerpts from *Times
to Remember* by Rose Fitzgerald Kennedy. Copyright © 1974 by The Joseph P. Kennedy, Jr.,
Foundation. Reprinted by permission of Doubleday, a division of Bantam Doubleday Dell
Publishing Group, Inc.
HARPERCOLLINS PUBLISHERS: Excerpts from the introduction by Henry Luce to *Why England Slept*
by John F. Kennedy. Reprinted by permission of HarperCollins Publishers.
HARVARD COLLEGE: Excerpts from the student file of John F. Kennedy. Reprinted by permission of
Harvard College.
LIDDELL HART CENTRE FOR MILITARY ARCHIVES AT KING'S COLLEGE, LONDON: Excerpts from papers
held at the Liddell Hart Centre for Military Archives. Reprinted by permission of The Trustees of
the Liddel Hart Centre for Military Archives.
MACMILLAN PUBLISHING COMPANY: Excerpts from *John Fitzgerald Kennedy: As We Remember Him*
by Goddard Lieberson and Joan Myers, editors. Copyright © 1965 by Columbia Records.
Reprinted by permission of Atheneum Publishers, an imprint of Macmillan Publishing Company.
SEELEY G. MUDD MANUSCRIPT LIBRARY AT PRINCETON UNIVERSITY: Excerpts from the James V.
Forrestal Papers, the John F. Kennedy student record file, and the Arthur Krock Papers.
Published with permission of Princeton University Libraries.
SIMON AND SCHUSTER, INC.: Excerpts from *The Fitzgeralds and The Kennedys* by Doris Kearns
Goodwin. Copyright © 1987 by Doris Kearns Goodwin. Reprinted by permission of Simon and
Schuster, Inc.

Library of Congress Cataloging-in-Publication Data
Hamilton, Nigel.
JFK, reckless youth / Nigel Hamilton.
p. cm.
Includes bibliographical references and index.
ISBN 0-679-41216-6
1. Kennedy, John F. (John Fitzgerald), 1917–1963—Childhood
and youth. 2. Presidents—United States—Biography. I. Title.
E842.H275 1992
973.922′092—dc20   92-8207
[B]

Manufactured in the United States of America
23456789
First Edition

Book design by Bernard Klein

For Outi

CONTENTS

Contents

PROLOGUE

The Birth of Camelot

At nine-thirty A.M. on November 25, 1963, the doors to the great rotunda of the U.S. Capitol were closed. Over a quarter of a million people had paid their last respects to the slain president, John F. Kennedy. At eleven o'clock the coffin, draped by the Stars and Stripes, would be carried outside and borne first to the White House, then to St. Matthew's Cathedral, and from there to Arlington Cemetery, the confiscated estate of the Confederate general Robert E. Lee, where a special underground vault had been prepared.

There had been much dispute about the burial site. "We're all going to be buried around Daddy in Boston," Eunice, sister of the dead president, had insisted. Her brother, the attorney general of the United States, had agreed, as had the Irish "mafia"—the thin-lipped contingent of hangers-on, bodyguards, pimps, and court jesters who had been paid over the years by the father of the slain president. Even the new president, Lyndon Johnson, had assumed the burial would be in Brookline, the suburb of Boston where Kennedy was born.

The secretary for defense, however, had favored Arlington: a national rather than a parochial resting place for the first president to be killed in office since President McKinley in 1901. Although Robert McNamara's suggestion was ridiculed by the White House staff, the State Department, and the dead president's immediate family, it was welcomed by the president's widow, Jackie. Unable to tame her husband's rampant sexual appetite in his lifetime, she was determined to shape his memory in death. Thus, at Jackie Kennedy's insistence, Arlington became the choice, com-

plete with a hastily assembled Eternal Flame copied from that of the
tomb of the Unknown Soldier beneath the Arc de triomphe.

Those who had thought the former First Lady, distraught beyond
words since her traumatic experience in Dallas the previous Friday,
would be unable to cope with her husband's funeral were very much
mistaken. Once, in tears at her inability to alter her husband's behavior
or his family's support for him no matter what he did, she'd sobbed,
"You can't beat the Kennedys!" In death, however, she could, steeling
her heart to make her husband's funeral the most memorable pageant in
modern American history.

Meanwhile, ex-ambassador Joseph P. Kennedy, architect of her husband's rise to political prominence, had been felled by a stroke in 1961, and
although he forced his nurse to dress him and take him to the airport at
Hyannis, he was not permitted to attend the funeral and was driven
home. "We have told him, but we don't think that he understands it,"
explained Rose Kennedy, having flown to Washington with thoughts
only of what she would wear at the funeral and bringing extra black
stockings for her daughters.

The two Mrs. Kennedys barely spoke to each other. Jackie had never
liked Rose Kennedy, whom she considered "a nobody," and she resented,
as she'd always resented, Rose Kennedy's presence in the White House.
The "compounds" at Palm Beach and Hyannis Port, where Jackie and
her husband had spent part of their time, were Kennedy homes, dating
back to the twenties and thirties. Surrendering the White House to the
new president and Mrs. Johnson, Jackie would soon, incredibly, have no
home to go to (Averell Harriman would wind up lending her his). For the
moment, however, the White House remained Jackie's home, and as long
as she remained there, she wished no one to forget it.

The funeral, at Jackie's prompting, was to be modeled not on Franklin
Roosevelt's—the most recent American president to be given a state
funeral—but on Abraham Lincoln's in 1865. In redecorating the White
House, Jackie had been impressed by engravings of Lincoln's end. Lincoln too had been slain in office; an inspiring moral leader, he too was a
victim of hate and a martyr to the oppressed. Returning from Texas with
the "stolen" corpse (Texas law forbade the removal of a body involved
in homicide without an autopsy), "Jackie had sent a message that she
wanted the President laid out as Lincoln had been," noted Arthur Schlesinger, a special counsel to the president, in his diary. Thus, while the naval
doctors at Bethesda covered up evidence of the late president's venereal
and Addison's diseases and dressed the corpse for public viewing, loyal
aides were sent to fetch books pertaining to Lincoln's funeral from the
Library of Congress. The black crepe, catafalque, caisson, and muffled
drums of the nation's tribute to Abraham Lincoln thus became the blue-

print for the world's farewell to John F. Kennedy, although the funeral was to be updated to include a display of the latest American military might: a flyover by fifty F-105 jet fighters, one for each state of the union. And television.

Jackie's performance as the grieving president's widow certainly surpassed that of Lincoln's widow. She chose her own appointees to give orations in St. Matthew's Cathedral and by the grave in Arlington (only one of these was given); meanwhile she herself acted her televised role with unbelievable aplomb. She had never possessed nor shown the meanest interest in politics, her husband's career, but despite the fact that her new Greek friend—and future husband—was staying as her personal guest in the White House, she now displayed a version of mourning that would have become Electra.

By her bearing the young widow imparted a classical quality to the proceedings, which themselves took on overtones similar to the burial of Caesar Augustus. Following the Senate, Supreme Court, and congressional eulogies in the rotunda (Senator Mansfield's speech, unlike Mark Antony's, being considered "absolutely appalling" by the British ambassador), Jackie led her daughter, Caroline, by the hand to the catafalque where the new president, Lyndon Johnson, had just laid a wreath. Before the cameras she whispered to Caroline, "We're going to say good-bye to Daddy, and we're going to kiss him good-bye, and tell Daddy how much we love him and how much we'll always miss him." The family's official literary eulogizer later recorded:

> Mother and daughter moved forward, the widow gracefully, the child watching carefully to do just as she did. Jacqueline Kennedy knelt. Caroline knelt. "You know. You just kiss," whispered Mrs. Kennedy. Eyes closed, they leaned over to brush their lips against the flag. Caroline's small gloved hand crept underneath, to be nearer, and in that single instant an entire nation was brought to its knees. The audience in the rotunda, the national audience, those who until now had been immune, those who had endured everything else were stricken in a fraction of a second. A chord deep in the hearts of men had been touched. . . . Still clutching Caroline, she rose and stepped toward the door with simple majesty. The others stumbled after her.

Although unwilling to take on the role of politician's wife, Jackie had transformed herself in 1961 into a charming and increasingly regal First Lady, particularly after the long frumpery of Mamie Eisenhower. Now in her final televised role as outgoing First Lady she instinctively knew it was her duty to canonize her husband's memory and bring his "reign" to a glorious close. A replica of Lincoln's catafalque had been located and taken to the rotunda; meanwhile the White House was draped in black and soon resembled "Versailles after the king had died," according to Jackie's brother-in-law, Prince Radziwill. Jackie remained "in her parlor behind shut doors," while another brother-in-law, Sargent Shriver, "composed and pale," attended to the organization of the funeral.

The artist Bill Walton, having hung the East Room in black crepe, peered into the coffin. He and Schlesinger advised Jackie to keep the casket closed. Morticians from Joe Gawler's had been secretly brought in to reconstruct the president's shattered skull, but "it was not a good job," Arthur Schlesinger noted at the time; "probably it could not have been with half his head blasted away. It was too waxen, too made up."

Jackie, on their advice, thus agreed to seal the casket rather than let the world gape at a wax effigy. Moreover, she declared, the usual trappings of an American death were to be strictly verboten. As she explained to Bunny Mellon, custodian of the White House Rose Garden, she didn't want St. Matthew's Cathedral "looking like Harlem or Coney Island." She wanted Arlington, too, to be decorated with taste. "Do one thing for me, Bunny," she directed Mrs. Mellon when considering the likely flood of wreaths, ribbons, and flowers from well-wishers. "Please see that they're put far, far from the grave."

Monday, November 25, 1963, was Jackie Kennedy's historic day. The night before she'd had a call from the wife of the columnist Joe Alsop, in whose house her husband had committed his first adultery as president of the United States, on the night of his inauguration. "Susan Mary Alsop called me to say how wonderful I have been," Jackie later remarked. "How did she expect me to behave?" As she followed on foot her husband's casket from the White House to St. Matthew's Cathedral, the crowds—later estimated at a million people—now "saw no one but her," wrote William Manchester, appointed by Jackie to chronicle her husband's death and burial. "Her impact on them was tremendous; in her bearing they saw a confirmation of her gallantry in the rotunda, a symbol of the national catharsis."

Manchester was not alone. The editor of *National Geographic,* watching from an upper window, later wrote, "Jacqueline Kennedy walked with a poise and grace that words cannot convey—as regal as any emperor, queen, or prince who followed her." A London-newspaper correspondent reported that Mrs. Kennedy had "given the American people from this day on the one thing they always lacked—majesty."

As tears flowed, the prose became ever more purple. Manchester's version, even three years later, was considered by his own editor to be embarrassingly puerile. Jack Kennedy had been transformed, in Manchester's prose, into the "child of [King] Arthur," while the portrait of Jackie was of a princess "born of elves in a fairy glade and dressed in such magic cloth of gold (chosen by Prince Jack) that the Texans in their polka dot dresses and bow ties are seen as newly arrived scum—plucked from the dung heap by magical Jack."

Certainly Jackie was determined to elbow off the stage the new president and his retinue of Texans. Johnson had not been consulted the previous day about the eulogies in the rotunda, and his presidential limousine, in the cavalcade of mourners making its way from St. Matthew's to the grave, was displaced by cars carrying the late president's personal lieutenants and hangers-on. The new president of the United States was not even given a place to stand near the widow at the graveside. The woman with the "whim of iron" (as McGeorge Bundy once put it) had willed the entire performance, from her own makeup and lace veil to the Highland bagpipers and Irish burial detail—even the famous salute her three-year-old son gave to the casket outside the cathedral.

What Jackie recognized was that the world demanded theater, and getting her children to perform alongside her was her intuitive contribution to this final act of her husband's administration. If in its calculated style it bore little relation to the fun-loving, woman-crazy, endlessly witty personality of the president when he was alive; if the Arlington master of ceremonies sweated lest the mourners arrive too early or the overhead jets too late or the specially rigged eternal flame not ignite, the actors were unconcerned. Buoyed by the prizeworthy performance of the widow—as if in her extraordinary self-possession she were single-handedly keeping the nation, even the world, together—they acted on. "I had never understood the function of a funeral before," Arthur Schlesinger later reflected. "Now I realized that it is to keep people from going to pieces."

John F. Kennedy, his coffin resting upon a caisson drawn by six gray horses, was no more. As the First Lady's social secretary would later comment:

> This was her last great tribute to him in her role, and just as he would have wanted it . . . not only a tribute to John F. Kennedy, the man, but also a tribute to the United States of America because in the eyes of the world we looked pretty shoddy, having our President assassinated in Dallas. But I think the way the funeral was handled, the way everybody acted, suddenly put America back up again in the minds of the people around the world.

This was no exaggeration. Despite insufficient time for issuing formal invitations, the funeral was attended by delegates from eighty-two countries, including eight heads of state, ten prime ministers, and a great number of the world's royalty. Hundreds of millions of people across the globe watched the funeral live; it was even aired on Soviet state television.

Photographs and journalists' descriptions flooded the front pages of the world's press, while the stream of obituaries, memorial services, and tributes continued unabated. Men and women from Massachusetts to Moscow wept openly. "It was like the fall of all the hopes of youth—as though youth had tried and been thwarted," Mrs. Mellon later recalled. "It seemed to me that this country had symbolically killed something."

But what? In the drama of the terrible assassination in Dallas, myths were spun that would take historians decades to defuse. John F. Kennedy had been president for only two years and ten months, after squeaking home in the most hotly contested presidential election in American history. How, in so short a time, had he become the most internationally popular American president in history? What had he really achieved?

Above all, who really *was* John F. Kennedy behind the winsome, orthodontically perfect smile? What was the truth behind rumors of his womanizing, his dalliances with gangster's molls, spies, and Hollywood stars from Grace Kelly to Marilyn Monroe? What inspired the tearful, wishful fictions surrounding his tragic death? Did he really possess a political conscience, or was he the playboy figurehead of a new generation of liberals? What was his true relation to that eminence grise, his father, whom liberals from Eleanor Roosevelt to Harry Truman despised? What hand had this father, though denied a place at his son's graveside, played in John F. Kennedy's apocalyptic life, beginning in a suburb of Boston and ending at the White House?

No writer has ever been able to penetrate the many myths and protective veils his family has woven since that painful day in November 1963 when the smiling, waving president of the United States fell victim to assassination. Perhaps it is only now, a quarter of a century since his death, that a truthful accounting can be made that is both scholarly and fresh.

To begin that undertaking, however, and in order to properly understand the family and the world that shaped John Fitzgerald Kennedy, we must go back to Boston and briefly examine the raucous, turn-of-the-century hustings dominated by his politician grandfather, John F. Fitzgerald, then move on to Joseph P. Kennedy—failed shipyard manager, failed Hollywood producer, failed diplomat, failed politician—but brilliantly successful Wall Street swindler and the strangest of fathers, without whom John Fitzgerald Kennedy could never have reached the White House at all.

PART

·1·

BOSTON
BEGINNINGS

Former congressman John F. Fitzgerald (right) on a Boston beach, circa 1901 (John F. Kennedy Library)

Boston Beginnings

Boston, established by Puritan immigrants as a small settlement on the New England coast in 1630, was in many ways America's most historic city. Its citizens marched at the forefront of the American Revolution, from the Boston Tea Party in 1773 to the evacuation of British soldiers in March 1775. Never again were enemy forces permitted to enter the port, which became the cradle of the U.S. Navy, symbolized by the preservation of "Old Ironsides," the wooden warship that won every sea battle against the British in the War of 1812. The city itself, meanwhile, became the capital of Massachusetts: one of the original thirteen states of the Union.

As America grew in the nineteenth century, however, Boston's relative importance declined. During the Civil War its vital sea commerce was paralyzed, while the advent of railways and heavy industries favored American cities farther west and south and with better communications inland: Pittsburgh, Chicago, New York, and Philadelphia. Absorbing great surges of immigration from Europe, Boston's population continued to grow, but the more adventurous moved across the continent, leaving Boston a relative backwater, where the poorer folk eked out livings as peddlers, stevedores, and small tradesmen by Boston's once-thriving harbor.

More than half these immigrant families were ones of Irish extraction whose parents or grandparents had fled the notorious Irish potato famines of the 1840s. Noted for gregariousness, sentimentality, and willingness to undertake hard labor, the Irish did not, in the main, make great entrepreneurs. For its wealth Boston therefore relied largely on invisible earnings—profits accruing from investments made by earlier settlers, scions, and traders: the Saltonstalls, Lowells, Cabots, Adamses, and other families, collectively known as the Boston Brahmins. Living in antique splendor on Beacon Hill and in Back Bay, these descendants of great professional, mercantile, and textile families had, since independence, contributed no fewer than three United States presidents; moreover, their religious fervor and passion for pedagogy had not only produced America's first public school and first college but would in time spawn nearly fifty universities in the Boston area.

With this profusion of colleges, universities, genteel families, fine residences, and great financial institutions, Boston thus exuded on the one hand an air of complacent distinction, mirrored in the respectable neoclassical architecture of Charles Bulfinch. On the other it bustled with the intimate familiarity of its predominately Irish-immigrant stock, whose political rhetoric echoed its growing stranglehold on Boston's Democratic party in an arcane system of local ward "bosses" who bartered municipal jobs and favors for electoral votes.

In 1887 Boston elected its first Irish-Catholic mayor. With his term in office a vast field of new patronage opened, encompassing jobs ranging from superintendants of city services to simple messengers, sewage contractors, and city suppliers. As the Irish Catholics tightened their grip on the Democratic-party machine in Boston in the 1890s, there seemed every chance they could, by sheer numbers, keep the mayoralty in their hands for decades to come.

It was this political opportunity, at a time when the Irish themselves were still struggling for home rule across the Atlantic, that would excite the ambitions of a young Boston Irish-Catholic: John F. Fitzgerald.

Fitzgerald's father had arrived in America a penniless immigrant during the 1840s. From humble peddler he'd gradually improved his lot, marrying a fellow Irish immigrant and becoming partner in a thriving grocery shop on Hanover Street in the North End. The Fitzgeralds were a potent couple, producing twelve children in twenty years. Because the store doubled in the evening as a private tavern, the children were raised in the easy atmosphere of Irish drinking patrons: evenings of gossip, bragging, reminiscences of the Emerald Isle, as well as Irish shanties, tearful ballads, rebel songs—and hard political bargaining.

John Francis Fitzgerald, born on February 11, 1863, was the Fitzgeralds' fourth son and had quickly become the star of the family. From the Eliot Grammar School he'd passed into the famous Boston Latin School, where he was not only "kingpin in school athletics" but captained the football squad, coached the baseball team (on which he played first base), and became sports editor of the school paper, the *Latin School Register*. Graduating with honors in Greek, Latin, French, and German as well as mathematics, physics, English, and history, he entered the city's Jesuit university, Boston College, in the South End. As *The Boston Daily Globe* later reported, "The young man was trying for an education of the most liberal kind, as it was his ambition to become a physician."

Having "graduated well up toward the head of his class," Fitzgerald entered the Harvard medical school"—a bravura performance for a child of immigrants who had not even been permitted to attend school in Ireland. His apprenticeship as a doctor, however, was not destined to last long.

A Political Debut

John Fitzgerald's mother had passed away when he was sixteen. Two weeks before the final exams at the end of his first year at Harvard Medical School, in 1885, came a second misfortune. "I had been there about nine months," Fitzgerald recalled, "when my father died." In his will Thomas Fitzgerald "left a few thousand," but with nine orphaned children in the family to feed and house, there was simply "not enough to educate me."

A fellow grocer who acted as the ward boss, or political chief, of the North End generously offered to finance "Little Fitzy's" further medical training. Fitzgerald's heart, however, was no longer in medicine. "For some reason or other," he related, "it used to be my trust to boss the family. I even washed the faces of the other boys every day and oftentimes dressed them, even the babies." Now, aged twenty-one, Fitzy became the family provider. "I thought my life belonged to my brothers and that I could do better outside the Medical School, so I gave it up and took the examination for a position in the Customs House. I came out somewhere near the top of the list and was appointed a clerk and served there three years or more." At home, meanwhile, "I took charge of the house. We had no sister, and we hired a housekeeper."

What Fitzgerald didn't say was that he much preferred politics to medicine. He was a born organizer: restless, energetic, social. He'd founded his own boat club, Neptune Associates, at age twenty-one. When it ran into financial difficulties after hiring Boston's Music Hall for a dance, he "was not worried," *The Boston Post* later chronicled. "He forced the merchants to advertise on his programme and made the politicians buy his tickets and adopted many other advertising schemes. On the night of the ball, after the guests had arrived, he turned off all the water in the building, and so forced them to drink tonics, which greatly assisted the treasury of the club."

"In those early days," *The Post* explained, "Fitz engineered Catholic sociables and originated the sunlight dances in Boston. He was the social leader among the Irish people. The boys consulted him on clothes, the girls on etiquette and dress."

Behind a mask of tireless socializer, however, Fitzgerald was already acting as political secretary to Matthew Keaney, the North End ward boss. In Keaney's back-room office the young customs-house clerk learned the lore and language of Boston-Irish Democratic politics. Noth-

ing was written, nothing sacrosanct. Funeral wakes were political platforms; nominations for office were rigged; elections were fiddled—using
"repeaters" to multiply votes and carpetbaggers to augment them, even
stand-ins for deceased voters. But if a Democrat cast his ballot for the
"wrong" candidate in a local Democratic-party election, he instantly
forfeited his privileges with the ward boss: representation in court, welfare for his family in hard times, help with marriage, baptism, funeral and
burial arrangements, as well as temporary and permanent jobs at City
Hall—a course few immigrants dared brave.

In the description of another newspaper, John F. Fitzgerald was "a
blend of audacity, vigor, force and perseverance." He managed a polo
team that competed across America. He read prolifically. He was seen
everywhere. In September 1889 he finally married his childhood sweetheart, Josie Hannon, but continued to support his seven remaining brothers at home, his treasury topped up by various financial perks and
backhanders associated with his political activities. At last, in 1891, at age
twenty-eight, "I went into the fire and life insurance business," he recalled, and he put himself forward for the lowest rung of the electoral
ladder: a seat on Boston's Common Council.

Becoming a three-hundred-dollar-a-year Boston city councillor only
whetted Fitzgerald's appetite for politics. In 1892 he set his heart on
becoming a state senator. His ward boss was discouraging. "Keaney was
of the old school, very conservative," Fitzgerald later remarked. In
Keaney's view, as long as the caucus was controlled by the two other
ward bosses for the district, Fitzgerald stood no chance of winning the
Democratic-party nomination.

Matthew Keaney, however, died suddenly in February 1892. Fitzgerald
himself became the new North End ward boss. "There was a combination
between Wards 7 and 8 which shut out Ward 6," he later recalled his
senatorial debut. "Ward 6 was left out, and had neither [state-senatorial
nor state-representative] office for 10 years. I knew the feeling at the North
End was very strong that somebody should make the fight, and I took up
the battle."

Fully expecting to be beaten, Little Fitzy learned at the last moment
that, thanks to a dispute between the other two ward bosses, "I was going
to get the nomination." In such an Irish-Democratic area, party nomination was tantamount to election, and on November 8, 1892, the twenty-
nine-year-old "Boy Wonder" from Boston's North End was elected a
Massachusetts state senator.

Beneath the great copper cupola of Bulfinch's statehouse on Beacon
Hill, John F. Fitzgerald took his seat on January 4, 1893, and it was there
he met for the first time his fellow Democrat, the state senator for East
Boston, Patrick J. Kennedy.

Congressman Fitzgerald

Five years older than Fitzgerald, Pat Kennedy, the boss of Ward 2, was a big, taciturn man with heavy moustaches but without gift of oratory or education. His father, also a penniless Irish immigrant, had died of cholera in Boston the year Pat was born. Pat had no brothers, only sisters, all of whom had helped their mother in her small notions store in East Boston—known in those days as Noddle's Island.

Pat had left school at fourteen to become a stevedore at the docks, but after serving in several harbor taverns he'd decided at age twenty-two to buy his own. By age twenty-six he had two drinking parlors and was inevitably drawn into the Boston-Irish political arena, winning election five times to the Massachusetts House of Representatives. In 1887 he'd married a wealthy spinster, Mary Hickey, by whom he'd had a son, Joseph, in 1888, and a second son, Francis, who died after three months in June 1891. In November 1891 he'd successfully stood for state senator, but he served only a single term concurrently with John Fitzgerald, ostensibly retiring at the end of 1893 to concentrate on his liquor and drinking-parlor businesses.

In fact Pat Kennedy—who in the summer of 1892 had been appointed one of Boston's Democratic delegates to the Chicago convention to help choose the party's presidential candidate—much preferred to manipulate Boston's Democratic party from behind the scenes. As a member of the party's so-called Strategy Board, which met each week at the Quincy Hotel in South Boston, he divided up the Democratic party's spoils. It was this secret council that, in 1894, became the bane of John Fitzgerald's political life, for scarcely had Fitzgerald won a second senatorial term in the autumn of that year than Little Fitzy announced that he wished to stand as candidate for Congress, directly challenging the Strategy Board's nominee, incumbent Congressman Joseph O'Neil.

To Pat Kennedy this was tantamount to a declaration of war. Orders were given out that votes cast for Fitzgerald at the party caucus in September were not to be counted, or were to be destroyed. As Fitzgerald himself recalled, "I had no show in the South End where the organization was bound up with O'Neil. I said to them frankly: 'What are my chances in Ward 7? Do I get the vote that will be cast for me?' They told me with brutal frankness that they were bound to carry the ward for O'Neil by hook or by crook."

Crook was the operative word. "This gives an example of the way politics were carried on in the city in the old days," Fitzgerald later explained. "Realizing that my time would be wasted in the South End, I took my volunteers and brought them to East Boston and Charlestown. . . . I had an army of young fellows who were friendly to me in the different sections of the city. When I was a boy growing up, I was president of the Neptune Associates of the North End, and I fraternized a great deal with the social organizations in the different sections of the city, which gave me a large acquaintanceship. Then my athletic abilities brought me into contact with boys and young men from all over the city, as did the fact that I had won out in the Senate fight after a year in the Common Council."

Throughout the summer of 1894 Little Fitzy thus mounted a series of barnstorming rallies, speeches, and public meetings that not only attracted huge audiences but seized the initiative by boldly setting campaign issues before the public. By the time O'Neil returned from Washington to meet Fitzgerald's growing challenge, he'd been forced onto the defensive. To the dismay of the Strategy Board, Fitzgerald publicly challenged Congressman O'Neil to an open debate with him— even hiring a number of possible halls where the debate could take place, and publishing in the Boston newspapers an open letter inviting O'Neil to appear with him.

O'Neil declined the invitation. Instead, he laboriously defended his record in front of "900 of the solid men of the ward" and read aloud laudatory telegrams from fellow congressmen. He played on his close ties with the current president of the United States, Grover Cleveland. As for the charge that he'd failed to get the Charlestown Navy Yard reopened after twenty-five years of shutdown, he was quite frank: "They say I haven't opened the navy yard. Well, [Senator] Henry Cabot Lodge tried that for four years without success. If I haven't opened the navy yard, certainly a new man in my place would hardly be able to do it."

The chairman of the meeting said, "They all felt sure that when the ballots were counted after the caucus it would be found that the citizens of the district had stood by such an honored and tried public servant as Mr. O'Neil." But, as *The Boston Globe* afterward acknowledged, "the prevailing opinion was that the congressman had been resting on his laurels too much," whereas the challenge of an electoral fight seemed to galvanize Fitzgerald's formidable energy and rhetoric. Though his votes in South Boston would have to be written off—since they would never be counted—Fitzgerald deliberately took the fight into the other strongholds of his opponent, such as Patrick Kennedy's Ward 2 in East Boston. There, in the Lyceum Hall, a crowd of two thousand people awaited him. The young state senator first excoriated O'Neil for failing to present himself to the voters in an open debate, then demolished his feeble congressional record, and finally brought the spotlight onto himself:

> My record in the common council and the state senate is before you all; the books are open and all you have to do is to read. I have all along fought the battles of the democracy and have always been true to my party and that is more than he can say.
>
> Do not be deceived by any side issues! The fight is between Mr. O'Neil and myself. If you want a man to think he has a mortgage on the office at stake, then vote for Mr. O'Neil, but if you want to give the young men of the party a chance, support me!

The next evening Fitzgerald was followed around Boston from stump to stump by a "torchlight procession of about 500 staunch supporters, carrying banners, drums and flags." Wherever he spoke, "the number of disenfranchised females in the audience was noticeable." In Ward 12 "the hall was packed, many women being in the gallery," the newspapers reported, and the crowd was "very enthusiastic." In Charlestown, where O'Neil had addressed the "solid" Democratic-party citizenry the night before, the crowds went wild. "Lexington Street was blocked with people in the vicinity of Armory Hall. Fireworks and red lights were set off in profusion, and when the carriages halted at the door the senator was taken on the shoulders of the crowd and carried to the platform."

No congressional primary in the history of Boston had ever aroused such anticipation, for this was the first to incorporate the "Australian" system of secret balloting, using centrally printed voting slips. The poll held in Kennedy's Ward 2 "eclipsed all previous ones in its history," *The Globe* reported. "There were more votes cast than ever before, and the interest was at fever heat. . . . At 4 o'clock the doors of the armory were thrown open, and then followed a grand rush to the rail. In less than 30 seconds the space was jammed with a struggling mass of humanity. . . . So great was the jam and the disturbance that to proceed with business was out of the question and Mr. Robinson [the polling warden] ordered the police to clear the room."

Pat Kennedy had hoped to rig the election as he had previous ones, but was soon thwarted. When it was found that no one was monitoring the poll on Fitzgerald's account—that only P. J. Kennedy's henchmen were there—"someone immediately telephoned to the city," and a Fitzgerald man was dispatched by hansom cab. "He was loudly applauded as he drove into Maverick Square. He proceeded at once to the ward room and had a consultation with Senator P. J. Kennedy." After discussions,

Kennedy reluctantly agreed to let three Fitzgerald men monitor proceedings. According to *The Globe:*

> There was a great jam throughout the evening; hundreds stood in
> line for over two hours at a time waiting their turn, and scores of
> henchmen of the two candidates importuned the voter to vote their
> ticket.
>   Senator P. J. Kennedy, who headed the O'Neil ticket, did most
> work in behalf of his candidate. He did not seem to have his forces
> well in hand, in fact, it was an open secret that he had been deserted
> by men whom he had depended upon. Nevertheless the Senator put
> up a great fight. By 6 o'clock Maverick Street was packed solid with
> men. It was almost impossible to get near the wardroom, and it was
> only by the efforts of a squad of police that the street was kept open.
> It seemed as if all the voters of ward 6 had come over to the island
> to shout for Fitzgerald, and this they did with a will. Impromptu
> rallies were held under every lamp within a radius of 200 yards of the
> wardroom, and when Senator Fitzgerald put in an appearance,
> shortly after 8 o'clock, for the second time, he received quite an
> ovation.

In one polling station after another the wardens reported "the largest
vote ever cast in a caucus." However, to secure outright nomination at
the Democratic congressional convention to be held a few days later, the
successful candidate had to win 82 of the 163 delegates. Tension mounted
as midnight approached. "People who never before attended a caucus"
turned out to cast their votes, and the result was close.

Delegates committed to O'Neil won in six of the twelve wards, without
a single Fitzgerald man being elected. In the major inner-city wards,
however, the opposite was true. To his chagrin, in his own East Boston
ward where he was undisputed party boss, only Pat Kennedy himself was
elected as a delegate to support O'Neil, the remaining eighteen delegates
being pledged to Fitzgerald. The offices of *The Boston Globe* acted as the
central newsroom, and outside the building in the early hours of the
morning two armies of supporters gathered to watch the results as they
were brought from the ward rooms and pinned to the bulletin board.
"They cheered, they smoked, they talked and in many instances they
lubricated their parched tongues at the barrooms" of School Street,
Washington Street and adjoining roads. When the figures for Kennedy's
East Boston ward arrived, O'Neil's supporters could scarcely believe their
eyes. OLD MACHINE MEN PARALYZED BY FITZGERALD'S BIG SCOOP, *The
Globe*'s headline ran, and the article that followed commented that

the defeat of their favorite was a great blow to the older men of the party in East Boston, and especially to those who have run the political machine for many years.

They could not realize it. They stood aghast when the figures were announced that Fitzgerald had gone out of the island with every delegate pledged to his support, with the exception of Senator P. J. Kennedy.

It was a regular Waterloo. . . . Calculations were knocked higher than a kite, and what is more they could not conceal their disappointment. It was an event totally unlooked for. . . . They knew it was going to be a hot fight, but they were totally unprepared for the onslaught that was made by the young men of the party, and the tactics and boldness of the latter were a surprise from which they did not recover until too late.

By early morning Fitzgerald's total nudged toward the vital eighty-two mark, and when the president of the Democratic-party committee in Boston, James Donovan, and Pat Kennedy—"two of O'Neil's most active lieutenants"—arrived to see for themselves *The Globe*'s bulletin board, they were mocked unmercifully. By six A.M. it was clear Fitzgerald had won. The final result was eighty-seven delegates pledged to Fitzgerald, seventy-six to O'Neil.

"The only topic of conversation among politicians yesterday was the defeat of Congressman O'Neil for a renomination," *The Globe* afterward recorded. "This furnished endless sources of conjecture not only for Democrats but also for Republicans. That such a man as Mr. O'Neil should be beaten by so young a statesman as Senator Fitzgerald could hardly have been believed a week ago, and the leaders of his party have not yet recovered from the surprise into which they were thrown by the returns of Friday night."

Meanwhile the young senator's house was besieged by well-wishers coming "from all parts of the city to the humble street near North Square" where Fitzgerald lived. Fitzgerald was quoted saying his house

wasn't large enough to accommodate my friends. My neighbors swarmed in to congratulate me. The people of the North End, where I was born and bred, and the spot I love more dearly than any other on earth, were wild with delight. Those who knew me as a boy and saw me grow to manhood know whether I deserved this tribute.

Fitzgerald had certainly brought a new form of young, enthusiastic, high-profile, populist campaigning to Boston politics. "With me was an army of young men," he announced after the primary result, "who when I announced my candidacy, came to my cause, and to them is due the victory. . . . The people of the district have expressed themselves in favor of me and I expect to be triumphantly elected. It shall be my endeavor to be a worthy successor to Mr. O'Neil in Congress."

John F. Fitzgerald was duly elected a congressman to the United States House of Representatives on November 6, 1894, by a margin of two thousand votes over his Republican rival, and a year later—as was the custom of the time—he took his seat in Washington as the only Democrat from Massachusetts.

Cause Célèbre

The story of how Fitzgerald fared as a congressman, and later as mayor of Boston, need not detain us here. What is important to note is Little Fitzy's remarkable energy and campaigning style, for it was these his grandson would one day inherit—honed, ironically, in bitter combat with Patrick J. Kennedy.

Kennedy never forgave Fitzgerald his victory over O'Neil, and though Fitzgerald was elected to three consecutive terms in Congress, in 1894, 1896, and 1898, Kennedy finally felled him in 1900. "As my father was ending his third term in Congress and expecting renomination and re-election," Fitzgerald's eldest daughter, Rose, recalled years later, "there were seismic movements, shifts, realignments. I had no idea at the time what it was all about. . . . P. J. Kennedy and the other Board members blocked his renomination."

In fact a bitter, five-day battle had taken place in the convention rooms of the Democratic party in mid-October 1900, with Kennedy the victor. For five long years Fitzgerald was cast into the wilderness until, in 1905, he once again challenged the Strategy Board—this time for the Boston mayoralty. "A busier, brighter Boston" became one of his slogans. But his cause célèbre was the fight against ward bossism itself. Under the headline DIRECT APPEALS TO THE PEOPLE *The Boston Globe* reported, on November 8, Fitzgerald's fighting words:

> This fight will settle for all time the fact whether the men who are ambitious to obtain public office in Boston must have the backing of the boss. When I made the announcement of my candidacy I was told on every side that I would not succeed because the chairmen of the Ward organizations and the members of the Ward and city

committees were almost solid against me. . . . I believe that in Boston the majority of people are honorable people. I do not believe that they want any such characterless domination of their public officials. This belief I have put into practice and I now appeal to the people of Boston over the heads of the bosses, and I know that you will not prove faithless.

Fitzgerald's helpers had distributed "small American flags to each person attending." The reason for the flags steadily became apparent, as his speech became more passionate:

> Of what use is popular suffrage if it can be bargained for and traded with? Under a system of this kind we will have no rights except what the bosses give us.
> If we permit boss rule to gain the ascendancy we deny our right to have government of the people, by the people and for the people.
> My friends, we are threatened with an administration of Boston which I firmly believe will never be tolerated. I am proud of the cause we battle for. It is the people's cause. I am proud of the people's friends. I am proud of the enemies who oppose us. They are the people's enemies. We will say with Lincoln: Let us have faith that right makes might and in that faith let us to the end dare to do our duty as we understand it.

To cheers and the chanting of "Down with the Czar" (i.e., Martin Lomasney, the Ward 8 boss), Fitzgerald sat down. He had turned the tables on the Strategy Board, gaining sympathy as the underdog and—as in 1894—the tactical initiative. Nor did he rely on the spoken word. Political election in a democracy was, he reasoned, a spectacle. The business of election represented democracy in action and was worthy of celebration. Torchlight parades, marching bands, flag-draped streets, and other methods were used to drum up public interest, for the public would decide Fitzgerald's fate. "Nobody in Boston had ever seen such a bustling campaign," his biographer, J. H. Cutler, recorded.

> It featured a snorting procession of speeding automobiles—the first time a fleet of horseless carriages had been mobilized in a Boston mayoral contest. Johnny Fitz and six supporters led the parade in a big red car, followed by two more containing stenographers and reporters. Squads of "Dearos" and Jefferson Club members rushed on electric trolleys from ward to ward to greet the Little General, and, cheering wildly, they carried him on their shoulders into auditoriums where rallies were scheduled. Young Napoleon's "lanc-

ers," as they were called by reporters, were always waiting, and were as carefully trained as a stage chorus. The squads of lancers knew their exit and entrance lines and had been trained to respond to signals. . . . Fitzgerald flashed as many "signs," it was noted, as a major league baseball manager. . . . He plastered the town with posters with his portrait in the center circled by screaming type that proclaimed: "The people, not the bosses, must rule. Bigger, Better, Busier Boston." Fitzgerald even used the originally derisive label of "Napoleon" to advantage, featuring it on buttons and posters. When a local cigarmaker brought out a "Napoleon" cigar, everyone knew who the Little Corporal was. If Mayor Collins had been Boston's most revered politician, Fitzgerald was easily the most colorful. He whipped crowds into a frenzy of delight as he shouted: "I am making my contest single-handed against the machine, the bosses and the corporations."

Pat Kennedy's choice of an ailing street commissioner, Ned Donovan, as the Strategy Board's candidate proved a disastrous misjudgment. It permitted Fitzgerald to not only excoriate Donovan's lack of credentials, but to expose the conspiracy of Kennedy, Lomasney, and the Boston "machine" behind Donovan. "You remember the fable of the lamb and the wolf?" Fitzgerald cried before a vast audience at a rally on November 14, 1905. "Under the wool of Edward Donovan, the candidate, look sharp and you will find the hide and claws of Mr. Lomasney the boss!"

Issue by issue Fitzgerald laid out his rival's past performance and asked his famous "public questions," beginning, "I have charged you with having voted—" and ending, "Why don't you answer this charge? Why don't you answer, Mr. Donovan?" He charged Kennedy and the consuls with forcing Ned Donovan to stand at all, by threatening to have him sacked as superintendant of streets, drawing a salary of $7,500 per annum, if he did not; he charged that when a handful of men got together in back rooms and chose "a candidate for mayor for 50,000 democrats without any authority whatever from them, we are obliged to rub our eyes and ask if this is really a free country after all. Let us stand firmly for our rights as citizens, before it is too late. Let every man who calls himself a democrat go to the primaries Thursday, whether or not he ever went there before, and contribute his effort to the prevention of an odious political despotism in our fair city."

The 1905 campaign for the Democratic nomination became a fight no one in Boston would ever forget—least of all Pat Kennedy. At six A.M. on November 16, balloting began throughout the primary wards of Boston. It was "one of the most hotly contested in the history of the city." Such was the level of excitement that money had begun to change hands in startling amounts. "Conservative estimates place the amount of money tied up in this way as approaching $100,000," *The Globe* recorded—far exceeding the amounts spent by the candidates on campaigning. "But the betting ended as it began—even money."

"In Ward 2 the organization leaders Patrick J. Kennedy, the Hon. Joseph K. Conry and their associates are trying to get out every vote they can for Donovan," *The Globe* reported—Kennedy boasting to one reporter that "Mr. Donovan will go out of the ward with a large majority," having already secured almost two thousand "pledges" from "loyal constituents."

In fact, to Kennedy's chagrin, Fitzgerald carried no fewer than twenty-one of the city's twenty-five wards. "John F. Fitzgerald won a great victory in the democratic primaries," *The Globe* reported the following day, "defeating Edward J. Donovan, the candidate of the organization leaders, for the democratic mayoralty nomination."

Fitzgerald's triumph—28,228 votes to Donovan's 24,301—was widely applauded in the press as a return to true democracy. "Mr. Fitzgerald will go into office free from the shackles of party machinery and unfettered by promises, which will give him a free hand to work for the city's best and highest interests," the Boston *Traveler* declared. Fitzgerald, who had spent the day getting out the Saturday edition of *The Republic,* the Catholic weekly paper he had bought, was elated. "I am going to do everything I can to make a busier Boston," he promised reporters, with his children's arms around his neck.

A Conflict of Wills

By nature John F. Fitzgerald was a forgiving man. Despite the sufferings wrought by Patrick Kennedy, one of Fitzgerald's first acts as mayor of Boston was to reappoint him as commissioner of wires. A skein of friendship was established, but when Fitzgerald's daughter fell in love with Kennedy's son, on a Democratic-party vacation in Old Orchard Beach, Maine, in the summer of 1906, the mayor became alarmed. "I suppose no father thinks any man is good enough for his daughter," Rose recalled sadly. "My father had extravagant notions of my beauty, grace, wit, and charm. As I entered young womanhood these delusions deepened."

Fitzgerald did not see himself as deluded. Rose was pretty, talented, and popular. Joseph Kennedy was by contrast big, brash, and insensitive—and the son of Fitzgerald's longstanding political rival. Mayor Fitzgerald therefore forbade Rose to accept the boy's invitation to the first dance of the season at the Boston Latin School, explaining that "he disapproved of a girl of sixteen going around to dances in strange places, and meeting people who might cause trouble."

Trouble would prove an understatement. Interdiction, however, worked merely as a bellows, not an extinguisher. The teenagers met in secret. Hearing of this, Fitzgerald blamed himself for having encouraged his daughter to be too independent and, after consulting the archbishop of Boston, forbade her to go from Dorchester High School to Wellesley Women's College—a Protestant university on which Rose had set her heart—saying she was still, at seventeen, too young and that such a move might upset his Catholic constituents. Instead, Fitzgerald made her attend the Sacred Heart Convent college on Commonwealth Avenue, where he and the nuns could watch over her.

When Rose *still* showed no signs of outgrowing her crush on young Joseph Kennedy, Fitzgerald took her, at age eighteen, to Europe, where he incarcerated her with her sister, Agnes, in a prisonlike nunnery in Blumenthal, Holland, for two excruciating years of Dutch discipline, hoping she would forget Joe Kennedy—who was now a freshman at Harvard—and "get religion" instead.

Rose got the latter, but refused to surrender the former. Behind her demure countenance she concealed an iron obstinacy, and she maintained throughout her Dutch ordeal a correspondence with the son of her father's archenemy. In vain Fitzgerald then sent her away, in 1910, to yet another Sacred Heart Convent, this time in Manhattanville, New York: It was a cumulatively wounding experience for Rose that was to leave psychological scars for the rest of her stoic life.

Rose later lamented, "My father was a great innovator in public life, but when it came to raising his daughters no one could have been more conservative. When you put 'Yankee ethic' and 'Irish Catholic ethic' together, the results are formidable. Which was sad. After all, you're only young once and young people should be able to get the most from those special years which last such a short time. But my father was adamant."

To Rose, Joe Kennedy appeared at this stage of her life almost godlike, "a serious young man," but with "a quick wit and a responsive sense of humor. He smiled and laughed easily and had a big, spontaneous, and infectious grin that made everybody in sight want to smile, too."

Spurred by the illicit nature of their romance, Rose saw in Joe Kennedy only the Galahad who would be strong enough to free her from the bonds of what she took to be her father's old-fashioned protectiveness. Her father remained, in her eyes, unreasonably unyielding. He still forbade "the Kennedy boy" entry to his house. When that did not prove effective, he declared he would take Rose to Palm Beach. Rose protested that she'd been invited to the junior prom at Harvard, by one of Joe Kennedy's roommates. "My father replied that he would hear of no such thing and I would be going to Florida," Rose recalled.

When Mayor Fitzgerald left America aboard the *Franconia* in the summer of 1911, he took not his wife but his daughter Rose with him, the liner escorted to the Boston Light by a large number of tugs and small craft, giving the most "wildly enthusiastic good-by which has ever signaled the departure of a Bostonian," the papers reported. He introduced Rose to England, Belgium, France, Austria, and Germany, traveling not only as mayor of Boston but as leader of the Boston Chamber of Commerce's delegation to Europe. He reveled in publicity, seeing himself as a supersalesman for his city, confidant of presidents and kings; but he also took care that Hugh Nawn, the eligible, Harvard-graduate son of his millionaire friend Harry Nawn, met and joined the party at Ostend.

As Rose later recalled, both her father and Harry Nawn hoped that the relationship might "blossom into romance and marriage." Fitzgerald had already paid for a huge coming-out party for Rose in January of that year, with a special marquee and more than four hundred guests. As the Boston trade party later steamed down central Europe's famous river, Rose Fitzgerald and Hugh Nawn waltzed to the strains of "The Blue Danube" before their admiring fathers: a match that would have allied wealth and beauty, and brought pride and satisfaction to their families.

It was not to be. Nor did Rose fall for any of the white-haired dignitaries they met on their travels, though she acted as the delegation's interpreter in French and German. On her dressing table she kept a framed photograph of the only beau she took seriously: Pat Kennedy's son, Joe. Nothing could shake her growing determination to become, one day, Mrs. Joseph P. Kennedy.

Mayor Fitzgerald then took Rose with a Boston Chamber of Commerce delegation to the newly opened Panama Canal; to Kansas and across continental America; to Washington to meet President Taft; to Baltimore to help nominate Woodrow Wilson as Democratic presidential candidate. Still Rose refused to give up on Joe Kennedy. To her credit, she had seen what her father hadn't—that although Joe's father was an East Boston liquor merchant, saloonkeeper, and behind-the-scenes politician, "the Kennedy boy" was destined to go places in the world.

The Fall of Fitzgerald

"I was never seriously interested in anyone else," Joe Kennedy later claimed—the accent on *seriously*. Arthur J. Goldsmith, a Harvard classmate, recalled that throughout his romance with Rose, Joe remained very much "a ladies' man"—with a penchant for chorus girls. In fact, the two of them "used to squire about Boston a pair of girls from the Pink Lady, and one day the four of them ran into Rose Fitzgerald, to whom Joe was paying court," Goldsmith later confided. "He talked himself out of that one."

Joe's self-assurance was certainly phenomenal. Running a tourist-bus business "on the side" at Harvard, he netted five thousand dollars—the salary of his father when a city commissioner. While Rose accompanied her father around Europe in the summer of 1911, Joe played professional baseball in the White Mountain League, living in a luxury hotel with the team's manager and profiting handsomely from sports and social news he got his classmate, John Conley, to ghost for him and which he then sent to *The Boston Globe*. "All I'm interested in is the money" was his motto.

Joe's entrepreneurial energy certainly seemed to cut him out for a successful career in business; indeed he immediately invested a portion of his profit from the tourist-bus operation in real estate speculation. But the *real* money, he was certain, lay in banking and investment.

Getting ahead in Brahmin New England, however, was not so easy for an ambitious Irish Catholic, even with a Harvard degree. The sign NO IRISH NEED APPLY had typified the prejudice of old Yankee families and still did. Though Joe had been permitted to go to Harvard, socially he'd been snubbed there. To his lasting chagrin he was blackballed by all the "final" clubs at Harvard—membership in which would have guaranteed subsequent acceptance by elite Boston society and a job in one of the great brokerage firms of the city.

Rose blamed Joe for ever entertaining the notion that he *would* get chosen. "It would have hurt him less, I believe, if he had accepted the social divisions at Harvard from the very start, just as I accepted them in Boston, as elementary facts of life not worth worrying about," she later commented.

For Joe Kennedy, however, such social divisions *were* worth worrying about. After leaving Harvard in 1912 and failing to get a position in any major Massachusetts financial institution, he was reduced to taking a job as a junior clerk in the Columbia Trust Company, the tiny Boston-Irish bank his father, with sixteen others, had helped set up on Meridien Street in East Boston in 1892. In twenty years its capital had risen by only seventy thousand dollars. Yet it was to prove an important if modest beginning for a would-be Boston-Irish banker, for Joe had no intention of being held down forever by the Yankees of New England, any more than he intended to let Mayor Fitzgerald stop him from marrying Rose.

Whatever stories circulated about Joe, Rose's will was indomitable. She'd made up her mind and was determined to stick by her choice, come what might. Her father's writ was still law in the Fitzgerald family, as it was in Boston. But despite the mayor's great popularity, his political fortunes remained shaky. He'd barely survived a Boston Finance Commission investigation into contract fixing and "backhanders" at the end of his first mayoralty. Now, in 1913, nearing the end of his second (this time, four-year) term, Fitzgerald found himself fighting a young Boston-Irish demagogue, Congressman James Michael Curley, a political maverick notorious for his smear tactics and determined to win the lucrative mayoralty. "The Roxbury Congressman has been ridiculing the ward chairmen from the stump," the *Boston Herald* soon reported. "This has embittered many of them."

What the Roxbury congressman had in store for Mayor Fitzgerald, however, was far worse than ridicule. Fitzgerald was well known for his popularity with women. He also had a deeply jealous and possessive wife. "It was not easy for a woman like Josie to live with a magnetic figure like John F.," one of his grandnieces recalled. "If only she had realized that he had enough love and feeling to encompass all the world with his left hand while he still had her in his right hand, she could have been happy. But she wanted him all to herself—and that was the one thing that he could never give her."

James Michael Curley's self-appointed task was to discover to whom the mayor did give himself. It didn't take him long. Through a Boston attorney who was still smarting at his failure to indict Fitzgerald in the finance-commission trial, Curley eventually found the weapon he needed: Elizabeth Ryan, a New York harlot known to all by her nickname, "Toodles." The Roxbury congressman then arranged for a black-bordered poison-pen letter to be sent to Josie, informing Mrs. Fitzgerald that her husband, the mayor, was having an adulterous affair with a hooker named Toodles—and that the information would be made public unless the mayor withdrew from the race.

At first Fitzgerald attempted to brazen things out. He was the pride of the Boston Irish, and according to the *Boston Herald* his third term was "as certain as anything in politics could be"—as well as "privately admitted by the shrewder politicians in the camps of all the mayoralty candidates."

In Curley's camp, however, there was no such admission. Against his brand of personal abuse and blackmail Honey Fitz had no recourse. He'd always depended on the domestic influence of women, who although still denied the vote, put pressure on their menfolk to vote for him. "I know the influence of the women was a great help," he once reflected.

> There were many instances where girls employed downtown as stenographers and typewriters would hear their employers talk of me derogatively after the manner of the Finance Commission, and these girls, although having no vote, would flush up and go home and argue with their brothers and fathers, with the result that in many cases they swung voters to me. In dozens of instances, they were so much wrought up that they even threatened to leave home unless their male relative didn't vote for the man he'd unfairly maligned. I recall coming down into the South End and going into a store near Dover Street, where I was fairly mobbed by the women. They surged about me, and I attribute no small part of my victory to their influence.

Now, however, Curley was intent on depriving Fitzgerald of his feminine support, slandering him as an adulterer. It was not long before a smutty ditty began circulating Boston:

> A whisky glass and Toodles' ass
> made a horse's ass out of
> Honey Fitz.

Considering that Curley himself had been sentenced to federal prison in 1904 for impersonation during a postal exam—and would be indicted several times more during his infamous political career—such tactics were ignoble. Curley's hide was as tough as a rhino's, however. Having sent his poison-pen letter to the mayor's wife and spread his scandalous rumors without avail, he raised the stakes. With the help of a university president he announced a forthcoming series of public lectures devoted to corruption in history, the first entitled "Graft in Ancient Times Versus Graft in Modern Times." The second lecture was to be called "Great Lovers in History: From Cleopatra to Toodles." A third—"Libertines in History from Henry the Eighth to the Present Day"—was to follow.

For Mrs. Fitzgerald this was too much. Her daughter Rose would be twenty-four next birthday. A dirty campaign, involving further "revelations" by Congressman Curley, might do irreparable harm to Rose's marriage prospects, as well as her younger sister's. And so on December 17, 1913, the mayor's assistant secretary, Edward E. Moore, announced to the press that the mayor would not, after all, be seeking reelection, quoting the mayor's statement that, "acting under the advice of my physician, who urged upon me the necessity for a prolonged rest in my present condition resulting from overwork, I withdraw my name from the mayoralty contest . . ."

Fitzgerald's colleagues affected to be stunned. The president of the Democratic City Committee declared, "The mayor had this fight won. Without lifting his hand he could have been re-elected. It was the easiest fight he ever was in. I had 100,000 campaign buttons all ready for him. . . . Then we had 60,000 envelopes all addressed, and we have been doing much systematic preliminary work. All I can say is that I am sorry. The city will lose the best mayor it has ever had."

Curley, of course, was overjoyed. "I am very much pleased to learn that his Honor has withdrawn from the mayoralty contest as this assures me of my election," he predicted, adding, "I regret exceedingly his illness, and trust that he will speedily be restored to health and strength."

For Honey Fitz it was in fact the end of an extraordinary and brilliant career in elective office, at the age of fifty—once again brought down by a fellow Irishman and Democrat.

Curley's spiteful tactics, however, would never be forgotten in the Fitzgerald family. Some four decades later it would be Curley's congressional seat that would be taken by Fitzgerald's grandson who, against all advice and entreaties, would refuse to sign Curley's petition for presidential clemency, leaving the ailing James Michael Curley to languish in a federal prison for corruption.

Betrothal and Marriage

Twelve days after Mayor Fitzgerald's withdrawal from the race there was a shock announcement in the newspaper: MAYOR'S DAUGHTER IS TO WED, SAYS RUMOR—REPORTED ENGAGEMENT OF MISS ROSE NOT CONFIRMED BY FITZGERALD FAMILY. Beneath the bold headline and a huge, quarter-page portrait photograph of Rose, there followed a confused story:

> The many friends of Mayor Fitzgerald are discussing the rumors of the engagement of his daughter, Miss Rose E. Fitzgerald, to the son of a well known businessman.
>
> Since the debut of Miss Fitzgerald, which occurred on January 2, 1911, Miss Fitzgerald has been a favorite in society. Her name has been linked with several and her admirers have been many, but so far

she has remained fancy free. Her present reported engagement is not confirmed by the family although it is reported that an announcement may be expected in January.

If Mayor Fitzgerald hoped thereby to chivvy his daughter into accepting an offer of marriage from Hugh Nawn, as Rose later hinted, his plan backfired. Rose remained intransigent, and the "expected" announcement did not materialize.

Woefully ignorant about sex, with a penchant for pretty challis blouses and long woollen skirts, Rose considered her determination to marry Joe to be romantic, not predatory. She perceived herself as musical and, having been made a member of the Boston Public Library's examining committee at the age of twenty, well informed. She was well traveled; she spoke French and German. Given the chance of marrying the man she loved, she was certain, she could bring her own femininity, education, and piety into the somewhat coarse and egocentric life of Pat Kennedy's boy.

Rose had waited almost seven years to marry Joe. Doubtless she would have waited another seven. But in the end there would be no need. As her father's political star, once so meteoric, began to fall, so that of her beau began at last to rise. Having served briefly as a clerk in his father's bank, Joe Kennedy had in 1912 obtained a post as a Massachusetts state bank examiner, enabling him to gain a unique insight into the workings of the very world from which, as a Boston Irish-Catholic, he was excluded. In this way, in December 1913, Joe had heard that the Columbia Trust Company was to be bought by the First Ward National Bank.

Immediately Joe swung into action, going straight to one of First Ward National's rivals and asking for a forty-five-thousand-dollar loan with which to spoil the takeover bid. By January 1914, having managed to line up 51 percent of the shares of the Columbia Trust, the twenty-five-year-old Joe Kennedy then single-handedly routed the attempted merger at the special meeting of the shareholders. As a result, the president of the Trust—a proponent of the merger—was forced to resign.

"Are you going to be treasurer?" one of Joe's friends had asked when agreeing to cover the twelve-hundred-dollar advance interest on the loan.

"Hell, no, I'm going to be president of the bank!" Kennedy retorted.

On Tuesday, January 20, 1914, Joseph P. Kennedy thus became the youngest bank president in Boston, if not the nation. Rose Fitzgerald was over the moon. Her father, however, was not—and the Fitzgerald home in Dorchester remained, as before, forbidden to "the Kennedy boy."

Disappointed, Rose countered by entering a secret engagement with Joe. Years later she could not recall whether Joe ever actually asked her to marry him. "It was less a matter of 'Will you marry me?' than of 'When we get married,' " she noted. "Everything is hazy: no dialogue, no details, not even the general scene."

In a life of shattered romantic illusions, Rose's selective memory would become as remarkable as her selective consciousness. Whether her father made a last effort to dissuade her from doomed matrimony we do not know, but sometime "during the late winter or early spring of 1914" (Rose could not recall exactly), Joe gave her a two-karat engagement ring, bought at a special discount from a Harvard classmate who'd entered his family's jewelry business.

The writing was on the wall. With Joseph Kennedy making an evident success of his new job at the Columbia Trust, the ex-mayor could not go on insisting Joe was a ne'er-do-well. His daughter was approaching her twenty-fourth birthday and might not receive such a good offer again. Finally Fitzgerald gave way, and on Saturday, June 13, 1914, the Honorable John F. Fitzgerald and Mrs. Fitzgerald officially announced "the betrothal of their eldest daughter Rose Elizabeth to Mr. Joseph P. Kennedy, Harvard '12, son of Mr. and Mrs. Patrick J. Kennedy of Winthrop."

Four months later, in a quiet ceremony in the private chapel of the archbishop on October 7, 1914, Rose and Joe were wedded, with a breakfast afterward for seventy-five guests—a far cry from the many hundreds who'd been invited to Rose's debut.

"After the return of the young couple from their honeymoon," Fitzgerald's newspaper, *The Republic,* announced, "they will take up their residence at their new home on Beal[s] Street, in Brookline, where they will receive on the second and fourth Tuesdays in January. The Bride, a great favorite with all, received many very beautiful gifts."

Married Life

Beals Street—named after the original speculator who bought the land— had been laid out during the streetcar-suburb boom of the 1890s. Over the ensuing two decades behind judiciously planted trees on either side of the street, a variety of brick and timber homes had risen, owned or rented by a variety of middle-class families: clerks, salesmen, engineers, a naval captain, an architect, an engraver, a distiller, a sculptor, a furniture maker, an insurance agent, a musician, and other professionals and their wives. Development had stopped with the depression of 1910, however, and Number 83, a modest two-and-a-half-story clapboard house with dormer windows, a hip roof, and a colonial-style front porch, had been the last one built on the street. Beyond it a succession of empty building plots then extended to the next avenue.

The average age of the residents of Beals Street was forty-five; Mr. and Mrs. Joseph P. Kennedy were only twenty-six and twenty-four and lucky to own their house at all, having borrowed two thousand dollars for the down payment and taken a Columbia Trust mortgage on the remaining forty-five hundred of the asking price.

While Mrs. Joseph Kennedy arranged the wedding gifts in her new home and received visitors, her husband took the trolley car on Beacon Street to his bank in East Boston. Joe had hefty loans to repay, on the purchases of both the bank and his house. Despite his age, he considered the institution his personal fief, his booming voice putting fear in the hearts of his staff, while his special telephone—its cupped mouthpiece defying eavesdroppers—added an aura of mystery to his young presidency. Clearly, he was a man in a hurry, and the doubling of the bank's business each year would soon give an indication of his ability. Already at Harvard he'd gotten a reputation for being a tough character, from whom it was unwise to ask for a preferential loan, since he would always require its strict and prompt repayment. He was the same now at the bank, whether dealing with strangers or old cronies of his father.

Whether Joe Kennedy was entirely honest was another matter, but he had abundant energy and a driving desire to succeed. He was willing to learn from his mistakes and to trust no one. Appearances meant nothing to him. After a few mistakes he trained himself to measure a man's caliber, and to trust that judgment—not what the man said or even his collateral.

His debts notwithstanding, Joe now went out and bought his own car. Rose later recalled:

> One of the great thrills of my life was the day my husband drove home in a brand-new, gleaming black Model T Ford. No Rolls has ever seemed so beautiful to me. Naturally, Joe was proud and excited about this surprise he had brought into our lives and was eager to take me out for a drive.
>
> There were road works near the house, however, and the lamps left by the workmen were too dim to be seen at speed. By the time I saw the lanterns and shouted a warning it was too late, and into the ditch we went.
>
> There was a terrible lurch and bounce; noises of metal grinding on pavement, motor racing, rocks and dirt flying, yells from Joe and from me; total confusion. But Joe went to full throttle, gripped the steering wheel while I gripped the side of the car with one hand and

his coattail with the other, and with another great bounce, seconds later, we were up and out and upright on the other side.

It was an episode that in many ways was to be symbolic of their lives. "They made tougher springs in those days," Rose commented wryly.

What Rose didn't say was that the glamour of marriage, after seven years of waiting, very quickly tarnished. No longer was Rose the sparkling eldest daughter in her father's lace-curtain Irish household. True, she and Joe had their own house, which "seemed to us just right, beautiful and comfortable, a dream realized," with "reproductions of the great masterpieces I had seen and especially admired during my travels in Europe"; an Ives and Pond grand piano given by two of Rose's uncles; a shamrock-crested tea set from Fitzgerald's English friend Sir Thomas Lipton; and "good, solid, serviceable" reproduction antique furniture "in the taste of the times," as well as a maid. The only thing the house lacked, most of the time, was a husband.

There was little time to reflect upon this, however, as Rose grew large with her first child. She had arranged that the birth should take place not in Brookline but in Hull, Nantasket, in a rented cottage close to Mr. and Mrs. Fitzgerald, who each summer leased a big Tudor mansion overlooking the sea. Rose gave birth to a ten-pound baby boy, whom they named Joseph Patrick Kennedy Jr., on July 28, 1915—exactly nine months and two weeks after the wedding.

"With the speed of a crack sprinter" Rose's father raced in from the beach when he heard the news, and telephoned the press. The ex-mayor's remarks on the birth his first grandchild were like those of an excited father. "He can yell all right," he announced, then quipped, "I'm sure he'd make a good man on the platform one day. Is he going into politics? Well of course he *is* going to be President of the United States; his mother and father have already decided that he is going to Harvard, where he will play on the football and baseball teams and incidentally take all the scholastic honors. Then he's going to be a captain of industry until it's time for him to be President for two or three terms. Further than that has not been decided. He may act as Mayor of Boston and governor of Massachusetts for a while on his way to the presidential chair."

Though Fitzgerald said this playfully, his prediction was not entirely made in jest, for he still gazed longingly at the seat of Washington power that Pat Kennedy had forced him to vacate in 1901. That winter he took Rose to Palm Beach with the baby, while his son-in-law remained in Boston. In the summer of 1916 Fitzgerald won the Democratic senatorial primary by more than sixty-five thousand votes—and threw down the gauntlet before the august and legendary figure of Senator Henry Cabot Lodge.

Fitzgerald Versus Lodge

I dwell 'neath the shades of Harvard
In the State of the Sacred Cod,
Where the Lowells speak only to Cabots
And the Cabots speak only to God.

Such, John F. Fitzgerald declared, was Lodge's bigoted approach to politics. Though Lodge had sat in the Senate for twenty years, he had never before had to submit to universal male suffrage, senators being elected until 1916 by the Massachusetts legislature, which had always been overwhelmingly Republican. For Lodge it was to be a rude awakening.

"The Case of the People Against Henry Cabot Lodge" became Fitzgerald's campaign slogan in Boston. From Faneuil Hall to West Boston industrial plants, the ex-congressman assailed the senator's record: "a record of twenty-four years in the Senate [which] does not show one single piece of constructive legislation tending to make the life of the average citizen more worth living." Lodge, Fitzgerald declared in charges blazoned each day across the front pages of the New England press, was a "brilliant but hard, cold and narrow aristocrat," a "constant opponent of every measure exclusively dealing with human rights and human betterment," including the Workmen's Compensation Act, the federal income tax, and direct elections. He had almost destroyed the Republican party by espousing William Taft four years before, and he *still* opposed immigration on racialist grounds, saying once that the Italians, Hungarians, Greeks, and Poles were "most alien to the great body of the people of the United States," and recommending they be "shut out like the Chinese."

Fitzgerald published a half-page advertisement, featuring a huge photograph of himself, in which he set out his own policies beneath the heading "What I Favor." These included public ownership of the coal mines, where "intolerable" and rigged coal prices were a scandal; a law to make the counterfeiting of capital stock a criminal offense as serious as the counterfeiting of money; noncontributory old-age pensions; insurance against accident, sickness, and unemployment; government subsidies to farmers—"the back-bone of the country"—as well as federal aid to schools and colleges to encourage more vocational training in America.

Fitzgerald then contrasted his own and Lodge's records in the national legislatures. From his first fight to get parks and playgrounds for the overcrowded tenement districts of Boston in 1891 to the bill taxing legacies and inheritances, Fitzgerald could point, he claimed, to more than twenty years of constructive social and economic effort, whereas Lodge's greatest claim to legislative fame was his passionate espousal of tariff measures "to make his intimate friends rich."

Fitzgerald's campaign—at first dismissed as an impossible task given the Republican sympathies of most rural Massachusetts voters—now began to bite. Even the manager of the famous Boston Red Sox baseball team wired from Maine to put on record his support for Fitzgerald: WISH YOU BEST OF LUCK. YOU ARE THE BEST ROOTER FOR BOSTON I HAVE EVER KNOWN.

On November 7, 1916, the nation balloted. Fitzgerald's performance in Boston outstripped that of every Democratic candidate, including President Wilson. With almost a quarter of a million votes cast in his favor, Fitzgerald even outpolled his fellow Democratic candidate for governor, beating Lodge hands down in Boston but failing to dis-Lodge rural Republican backers.

Fitzgerald had nevertheless knocked the first nail in Cabot Lodge's political coffin. "Another week and Mr. Lodge would have been defeated," he claimed in his concession speech on November 8, forecasting nevertheless "that with the proper work Massachusetts will land in the Democratic column for good."

Forty-six years later, it would—landed there by Fitzgerald's grandson. Meanwhile, like Fitzgerald's previous fights, the 1916 campaign against Cabot Lodge went down in the folklore of his family as a battle lost, but a war unfinished.

The Birth of John Fitzgerald Kennedy

While John F. Fitzgerald failed in his bid to oust Henry Cabot Lodge, Woodrow Wilson narrowly defeated his Republican opponent, Charles Evans Hughes.

Wilson had campaigned on the slogan "He kept us out of war." Though he subsequently tried to bring the two sides together in the Great War that was still raging in Europe, however, his "peace without annexation" proposals proved unacceptable as the basis of an armistice, and his pioneering call for a League of Nations fell foul of Henry Cabot Lodge (though it was adopted later by the European countries without American participation).

In the meantime, despairing of a negotiated settlement, the German government gave notice that from February 1, 1917, Germany would pursue a policy of unrestricted submarine warfare. Ignoring U.S. warnings, the German navy swiftly sank the American liner *Housatonic* in the Mediterranean. In the following three weeks some 134 unarmed ships of nonbelligerent states, including the U.S.A., were torpedoed. Overriding a Senate filibuster, President Wilson rushed an emergency bill through Congress to permit America's merchant ships to defend themselves.

It was too late, however.

On March 12 the United States steamer *Algonquin* was torpedoed and sunk. On March 18 both the *City of Memphis* and the *Vigilante* went down. Three days later Wilson asked for a special session of Congress to convene, and in a speech to the joint convocation of senators and representatives on Monday, April 2, 1917, the president made his historic address, noting what a "fearful thing" it was

> to lead this great peaceful people into war, the most terrible of all wars. But the right is more precious than the peace, and we shall fight for the things that we have always carried nearest to our hearts—for democracy . . . for the rights and liberties of small nations, for a universal dominion of right by such a concert of free peoples as shall bring peace and safety to all nations and make the world itself at last free. To such a task we can dedicate our lives and our fortunes, everything that we are and everything that we have, with the pride of those who know that the day has come when America is privileged to spend her blood and her might for the principles that gave her birth. . . . God helping her, she can do no other.

Six senators and fifty congressman objected; but with the approval of the rest, on April 6, 1917, Congress passed the declaration of war on Germany.

All over the nation recruiting stations began to open, and on May 18 the president set a date—Tuesday, June 5, 1917—as the day on which all American males between the ages of twenty-one and thirty must register for possible selection or draft into service with the United States armed forces.

Knowing that they would be ultimately drafted anyway, many joined up in advance. The financier J. P. Morgan announced early in May that his son Junius had enlisted. "Many other Wall Street men are reporting to the call of the colors," *The Boston Globe* reported, "and khaki has become a common sight in the financial district. It is estimated that about 3,000 employees of banks and brokerage houses have taken military training at Governor's Island." Word in Washington had it that the United

States would send an army to France forthwith, and that upward of a million men might be needed. Such an army would require, the Military Training Association stated, "real leadership among our new officers. The men responding to this first call [for volunteers] will be on the roll of honor in after years. They will have the feeling of pride that they did not wait for the second or third call."

In Boston Joe Kennedy, the youngest bank president in the United States, had no intention of answering the first, second, or third call. As the weeks went by, three fifths of all Harvard students joined up. Even Mayor James Michael Curley, a stouthearted believer in Ireland's right to independence, blessed Boston's first contingent of sixty-two volunteers to be accepted into the U.S. wartime army with the words: "You are going out not only to represent the most historic city in America but also the Commonwealth where first were sown the seeds of liberty. You are going to defend that liberty, as we in America see it, to the peoples of the world."

A vast camp was constructed at nearby Ayer to house the first thirty thousand recruits from Massachusetts, but Joe Kennedy, still in his twenties, refused to volunteer, though he knew he would have to register for the draft a few weeks later, on pain of imprisonment. The previous summer, following a bitter argument with some old Harvard friends about the plight of Europe, he had pointed to his sleeping son, Joe Jr., and remarked to his wife, "This is the only happiness that lasts," Rose recalled. "And then he walked away."

Walking away would become Joe Kennedy's speciality. Certainly his views about the war did not change. At the risk of alienating his friends and relatives, he remained a confirmed isolationist. As Rose later confided to Doris Kearns Goodwin, the family chronicler, "Joe believed he was right in not volunteering for the war, but, given the views of the circle he lived in, he could not feel good about his decision."

Soon, Rose related, Joe found himself to be "a stranger in his own circle of friends." War united all Americans, regardless of creed or immigrant origin. One by one Joe's friends and colleagues answered the president's call: the best man at his wedding, Joe Donovan; his Harvard friend Bob Potter, who was in line to become vice president of the National Shawmut Bank (the third largest in Boston); Bob Fisher, the football star with whom Joe had shared rooms at Harvard; even Joe Sheehan, his classmate and companion from the days of Boston Latin School. Meanwhile, ignoring the innuendos and even white feathers, Joe made his way each day to the little Columbia Trust bank on Meridien Street, hoping the war would go away and worrying only that his forthcoming and final attempt to gain a seat on the Board of Massachusetts Electrical Company would prove unsuccessful.

In Brookline Rose had other concerns, for once again she was pregnant. In addition to the cook and maid, a trained nurse had been engaged, for the birth was to take place at home on Beals Street. It was unseasonably cold—the temperature falling to the low forties at night. At eleven P.M. on May 28, 1917, there was a violent thunderstorm in the Boston area. Were the baby to arrive in the night, Rose had arranged, she would occupy the bed nearest the door and electric light; if during the day, the bed nearest the window, "because I did want Dr. Good and all concerned to be able to see exactly what was happening and what they were doing."

The next morning, May 29, 1917, the rain let up and although the sky remained overcast, the temperature rose a little. Rose's contractions began, and Dr. Frederick Good and his assistant arrived. Orders were given for kettles of hot water to be boiled as Rose "tried to sublimate my discomfort in expectation of the happiness I would have when I beheld my child."

Even fifty years later Rose could remember the exact fee charged by her physician—$125 for prenatal, natal, and postnatal care. She could remember Dr. Good's assistant's fee of $25 for administering ether, and that it was the same sum as the weekly wage she paid the nurse who attended the birth. Even the $1 per day she paid her maid she could recall. But though she chose the bed by the window, she herself had no wish to know what was going on. As she would later confess to her secretary, it was not until she was in her seventies that she learned the meaning of the word *fetus*.

This fetus was anxious to leave the womb, and at three P.M. on May 29, 1917, it emerged. Holding the baby up to the light from the window, Dr. Good announced that it was another boy.

Once again it was ex-Mayor Fitzgerald who made the announcement to the press, "wearing a pleased smile"—the more so when a few days later, Rose got Joe to agree that, since the first child had been named after a Kennedy, this second son should be named after a Fitzgerald—her beloved father.

Three weeks later, on June 19, 1917, at nearby St. Aidan's Roman Catholic Church, with one of Fitzgerald's sons in uniform standing as godfather, the infant was baptized, taking the names John Fitzgerald Kennedy.

This time, however, America being at war, the ex-mayor made no predictions.

PART
·2·
MAKING
MILLIONS

Joseph P. Kennedy, circa 1928 (John F. Kennedy Library).
Gloria Swanson (Archive Photos/American Stock)

No Romance

Although Joe Kennedy, Jr. remained a healthy child, little John Fitzgerald—or "Jack," as Rose's second son became known—had "trouble with his infant feeding," Rose related, and was often sick. Living in a lonely, middle-class, non-Irish suburb of Boston, surrounded by strangers a generation older than herself, Rose missed her old home.

Loneliness was one problem. Sex was another. The truth is, given Rose's long religious indoctrination and the confusion of her upbringing—part nun, part politician's pretty daughter—only the ministrations of a gentle and sensitive husband could have helped her to mature. Honey Fitz had foreseen this, and had known too that Joe Kennedy was neither gentle nor sensitive, a Boston-Irish boy who saw life simply as a jungle, ruled by survival of the fittest. Joe simply wasn't interested in nuances or subtleties—only the "bottom line." Thus when Rose withdrew into her brittle, frightened shell, shunning sex with him save as a necessary means of procreation, Joe at first protested. "Now, listen, Rosie. This idea of yours that there is no romance outside of procreation is simply wrong," he once said in front of their friends Marie and Vincent Greene. "It was not part of our contract at the altar; the priest never said that and the books don't argue that. And if you don't open your mind on this, I'm going to tell the priest on you."

But humiliating Rose in front of her friends or threatening ecclesiastical retribution was hardly the way to overcome Rose's Irish-Catholic inhibitions. Rose, who had wanted God, she recalled, "to flood" their whole life together, was bewildered, conceiving a lifelong distaste for the mention of sex or anything "dirty." "Whenever I begin to tell a joke," her friend from childhood later recorded, "she invariably says, 'Marie, is this going to be one of those dirty stories, because if so, I don't want to hear it.' And I'm not talking about filth, but just stories that are slightly off-color and wouldn't offend anyone. But they offend Rose."

Joe thus failed completely, and couched his disappointment in longer hours in the city, separating his life like his religion into two compartments: his duty on the one hand and his real life on the other—the latter made all the more profane by the deeper sterility of his marriage to Rose. At the Columbia Trust Joe spent more and more time—sixteen hours a day he once claimed (though he modified the figure when it was contested by an ex-bank employee who declared he must have been either "stupid or dumb," given the puny size of the company). According to his cronies, his philandering now increased, as he unashamedly enjoyed the company of chorus girls and demimondaines, as of old.

Throughout the years of courtship, Rose had done her best to understand and support Joe, loyally attending the college football games to which he and his Harvard friends were devoted, and in turn trying to introduce him to classical music rather than the Irish jigs, melodies, and popular tunes of the day with which he'd been brought up. But beyond that, she confessed in her memoirs, there was a void in the marriage, and the twin beds on the first floor of 83 Beals Street told much about the Kennedy marriage. "Joe's time was his own, as it had been and always would be. School and college had once taken much of it before, and now it was business that did so," she lamented. Left alone, she "continued as president of the Ace of Clubs," the social club she'd founded, devoted to the educational discussion of current affairs. As she once remarked, "One of the lessons of my life is that people have a better time at any interval of their lives if they stay with friends who have similar backgrounds, interests, and resources."

Without her friends Rose could not have survived the isolation into which Joe thrust her, in the gray clapboard house by the empty lot on Beals Street, Brookline, miles from her parents and, because Joe disliked entertaining, devoid even of the laughter, gaiety, and good company that had marked her upbringing on the occasions when her father was at home. Worse, however, was to come.

The Yellow Son-in-Law

On the same day his second son was born in Brookline, Joseph P. Kennedy had heard he'd been elected, on his third attempt, a trustee of the Massachusetts Electrical Company. When a friend asked why the appointment, largely honorary, was so important to him in the midst of a world crisis, he quipped, "Do you know a better way to meet people like the Saltonstalls?"

This was a strange reply to give at the very moment when the younger Saltonstalls were donning uniforms, not bow ties. Joe Kennedy, however, was unmoved. To delay or jeopardize a promising career in finance to serve his country in war was nonsensical to him, though he later took great pains to cover up this period of his life. To the journalist Joe Dinneen, who later wrote up his extraordinary career, Joe boasted that he had been engaged in war work since 1915. To others he said 1916. Even Rose Kennedy became involved in her husband's cover-up, claiming in her memoirs that Joe had begun "important war work" while her second child was still "on the way."

In fact Joe became all the more adamant in his refusal to enlist after the birth of his son Jack. By the time the infant was three months old, all Joe's classmates had joined up. America had been at war since early April 1917, but still Joe held out. On August 4, 1917, it was announced in Washington that draft resisters could be executed, and on the seventeenth, President Wilson proposed that even foreigners living in America should submit to the draft, but Joe merely clung more tightly to his job at the little Columbia Trust Company and his new seat on the board of the Massachusetts Electrical Company.

Both the Fitzgerald and the Kennedy families spent the summer of 1917 in Nantasket, where even on the beach Joe attempted to conceal his youth, wearing his formal starched collar, silk tie, and glasses while posing on the sands with the new baby, leaving his father-in-law, now aged fifty-four, to dash into the sea in a blue and white swimming costume, carrying his eldest grandson in his arms, anxious to teach the two-year-old to swim.

Joe Kennedy's lack of patriotism embarrassed the Fitzgeralds. Tom Fitzgerald, Rose's brother who'd stood godfather to Jack, had already become an infantry officer. America's first army ever to serve on the continent of Europe would soon be in action. Joe's job at the diminutive Columbia Trust Company could easily be handled by the older, experienced vice president, Mr. Wellington. Moreover, at a time when the sons of great financiers had volunteered for military service and a million more would soon be called up compulsorily, Joe's extreme youth as he sat with powerful, elderly businessmen on the board of the Massachusetts Electrical Company backfired. Why was he not eager to fight for his country like others—even his own brother-in-law?

August 1917, which would ordinarily have been a month of great family relaxation, thus became one of sourness, with Joseph Kennedy scowling at the camera, tormented by accusations, whisperings, and innuendos. Indeed his obstinate resistance, when the two families returned to Boston, threatened to become a public scandal. At last, however, late in September 1917, some six months after America's entry into the First World War, Rose's father spotted a solution for his "yellow" son-in-law.

As a congressman in Washington in the 1890s, John Fitzgerald had gotten to know Charles Schwab, the legendary rags-to-riches captain of the steel industry, and in 1914 Fitzgerald had been instrumental in getting Schwab's giant Bethlehem Steel Corporation of Pennsylvania to buy the ailing Fore River Shipyard at Quincy, a few miles south of Boston. The $4.8 million purchase of the Fore River Corporation, with easy access to skilled labor and the Atlantic Ocean, had paid off handsomely for

Schwab as the war broke out in Europe and Bethlehem Steel won orders for ten submarines for the Royal Navy. The subs were prefabricated at Fore River and sent to be reassembled in Canada.

Eighteen months later, at the behest of the energetic young assistant secretary of the Navy, Franklin D. Roosevelt, contracts were awarded to the Fore River Shipyard for a further nineteen vessels, including eight submarines and eight destroyers for the U.S. Navy. When America then declared war, tenders were immediately requested by the government to build even more destroyers and submarines. Schwab's price came in far below those of any rival, and orders were secured for no fewer than twenty-eight new destroyers and fifteen submarines, as well as one battleship.

Roosevelt's vast new naval order in the spring of 1917 was welcome news at the Fore River yard, but there was even more good news in store. As the months went by, the likelihood arose that the Fore River Shipyard would win orders for another thirty-five destroyers in the fall. This would necessitate the construction of a completely new shipyard at Squantum, next to the existing Fore River plant, to be financed by the government but run by the company, and given over entirely to the building of destroyers.

Given the enormity of such a crash program, Bethlehem Steel decided to rationalize its operations nationwide. The president of the Fore River Shipyard, Joseph Powell, was moved to Pennsylvania as vice president of the entire Bethlehem Steel Company's shipbuilding division, and Fore River's general manager went with him.

The new general manager of Fore River was to be Samuel Wakeman, hitherto general superintendant. A thirty-nine-year-old marine engineer, Wakeman had no knowledge of accounting and would therefore need an experienced administrative assistant. It was this position that the ex-mayor, in the fall of 1917, sought to obtain for his son-in-law.

On September 29, 1917, Joseph P. Kennedy presented himself at Young's Hotel in Boston to be interviewed by Bethlehem Steel's vice president, Mr. Powell, and the new Fore River general manager, Mr. Wakeman.

Impressed by the ambitious young banker from East Boston, Powell and Wakeman looked at other candidates and pondered the appointment. Finally, on October 16, 1917—eleven days after Josephus Daniels, secretary of the Navy, had given orders to proceed with the construction of the new destroyer works at Squantum, with ten slipways and four wet-docks—it was announced in the local newspaper, the Quincy *Patriot Ledger,* that "Joseph P. Kennedy, President of the Columbia Trust Company, Boston, has resigned his position as such and will come to the Fore River as assistant manager to Mr. Wakeman. Kennedy is son-in-law of ex-Mayor John H. [*sic*] Fitzgerald of Boston." As if to forestall raised eyebrows in the shipbuilding community, it added that "his duties will be confined to the office."

Causing a Major Strike

Joe Kennedy's arrival at Fore River soon caused the first major ship-building strike of World War I. While Mr. Wakeman conferred in Pennsylvania over the new destroyer orders, Kennedy took charge of the yard. The workers had previously made an agreement with Mr. Powell that they would be paid the same wage rates as in the Boston Navy Yard nearby, with the first wage increases to go into effect on October 15. To their astonishment, when the nine thousand men at the yard received their paychecks on October 27, there were no increases.

As the *Boston Herald* mistakenly reported on October 31, "Mr. Powell was transferred to another Bethlehem Steel plant and Joseph P. Kennedy, son-in-law of former Mayor Fitzgerald, was put in as head of the Fore River Company. The men charge that Mr. Kennedy denies knowledge of any agreement by his predecessor, President Powell, and in addition tells the workmen that even if there had been any agreement, the company was not bound by anything Mr. Powell may have done while President."

Within hours five thousand craftsmen, in the midst of a world war, were on strike. Kennedy threatened to sack the strikers, thus losing them their exemption from the draft, but his remarks were as ill-judged as they were ill-timed. Frantic telephone calls were made from Bethlehem's head-quarters in Pennsylvania. Charles Schwab, owner of Bethlehem Steel and head of the government's shipping board, had to travel posthaste to Boston to confer with leaders of the shipbuilding unions, while the assistant secretary of the Navy, Franklin Roosevelt, sent a personal telegram to one of the union organizers, begging him to convey to the men an urgent government appeal:

> There is probably no one plant in the Country whose continuous operation is more important to the success of this Country in the war, than that at Fore River. As a patriotic duty the Department urges both sides to sink all minor differences and to get together for the sake of the success of our Country in this war at once.

It was Franklin Roosevelt's personal intervention that ended the strike a week later. The men's new pay agreement, at Roosevelt's recommendation, was honored. Kennedy was dishonored, being demoted and as-

signed to the new Squantum yard project, where he would be out of the
way.

Humiliated by his brief and unsuccessful attempt at shipyard management, Joe Kennedy later covered up the story. Instead he circulated a
more self-aggrandizing version of his first brush with Roosevelt, maintaining he'd refused to deliver two battleships to the Argentine government "until all bills for the construction had been paid. Roosevelt's
attempts to arbitrate the matter got nowhere and finally, losing his patience, he told Kennedy that he was sending Navy tugboats to Fore River
at two o'clock the following afternoon to tow the ships away, which he
did." (Although this version would be repeated by subsequent biographers, it was moonshine—the saga of Bethlehem Steel's two battleships
for the Argentine navy, the *Rivadavia* and the *Moreno,* having taken place
two years *before* Kennedy appeared at Fore River.)

At twenty-nine, Joseph Kennedy had demonstrated his inability to
manage a large work force. By contrast, at thirty-three, Franklin Delano
Roosevelt had shown the makings of greatness: a Democratic administrator with world vision, a deep sense of America's best interests, and a
feeling of patrician responsibility toward ordinary working people. With
100,000 civilians working on naval contracts throughout the country, it
was Roosevelt's personality and managerial dexterity that permitted wartime output to soar and labor difficulties to be kept to a minimum in an
apprenticeship that would be sorely needed by his nation in the troubled
years ahead.

Far from impressing Roosevelt, Joseph Kennedy was lucky not to be
sacked, and he knew it. In an attempt to atone for his misjudgment, he
worked himself to near collapse preparing for the company's takeover of
the Squantum yard once constructed. Operating in a small office away
from the main management buildings, he was put in charge of the company stores. "I didn't know there was a Kennedy alive at the time," a
machinist at Fore River later recollected. "Certainly he had nothing to do
with shipbuilding. What the hell did he know about it? Nothing!"

However, another shipyard worker whose father and five brothers
worked at the yard later recalled that Kennedy had charge of the ware-
house, stores, and internal transportation. As far as he could remember,
"politics" was how Kennedy had gotten his job, but that he had made a
considerable success of it. "He was responsible for all materials that came
into the shipyard, in the main stores. That was where he had his office.
He held all the screws, bolts and rivets, inventoried. He set the business
up pretty good—he put organization into the thing, buying in all the
turbines, engines, reduction gears, piping and ship's furniture, storing it
after it came by railway. It was a well-run department and it helped the
yard to prosper."

Meanwhile, two months after he began work at Fore River, Joseph Kennedy was drafted, as he had feared would happen. He was placed by his local registration board in Class 1, liable to immediate call-up, but he fought the decision, and even got Joseph Powell, the vice president of Bethlehem Steel, to write personally from Pennsylvania to the local Boston board. When this did not work, the vice president was induced to cable to Washington on February 25, 1918, to protest, claiming there were "not over six men" in the entire yard whose importance could be compared with Kennedy's—a strange testimonial after his poor start in the yard only four months before.

One reason for Powell's testimonial was the nature of the company's accounting practices, to which Kennedy had become privy. (After the war there would be accusations of war profiteering and even a Senate committee examination of Fore River's accounts.) However dishonest the profits, though, production at the yard didn't suffer. In April 1918 the first five destroyer keels were laid at the completed Squantum site, and shipbuilding began in earnest. Fore River soon produced a four-funneled destroyer in record time, and eventually as many as two ships a day were being launched by the yard.

The laurels for this achievement went, of course, to the yard foremen and skilled workers who were able to train a novice labor force to work alongside them in an extraordinarily short amount of time. Using the experience gained in prefabricating submarines for the British navy, the yard took delivery of steel plates, engines, and component items from around the country, and the vessels were then put together using assembly-line methods similar to those the Ford Motor Company used in making its Model T.

Joseph Kennedy's task, however humble after his demotion, was a vital one—and the practices he developed at Fore River were to form the foundation stone of his later success in business. The yard's wartime contracts totaled over $100 million. The workmen might break all records in destroyer production, but it was Joseph Kennedy who drew up every contract and scrutinized every bill for parts and materials.

The young bank manager was becoming a shipbuilding executive of considerable promise. With his finger on the financial pulse of a company employing no fewer than twenty-six thousand men and women by 1918, he advised his father to buy shares in Bethlehem Steel, as he himself was doing. The war, once so threatening to the draft avoider, was turning out to be unexpectedly, one might almost say indecently, profitable. Not only was his basic salary handsome, but there were incentive bonuses too—as well as a contract, privately negotiated, to run the shipyard canteen. In addition the many formal ship launchings at the yard enabled him to meet visiting dignitaries as well as Bethlehem Steel's national board of directors. For a Boston-Irish publican's son, Joseph P. Kennedy was doing well.

The war, however, was entering its final stages. With the ending of hostilities on the Russian front and Ludendorff's vain attempt to break through the Anglo-French lines on the Western Front in the spring of 1918, the commitment to battle of vast numbers of American troops in the summer of 1918 finally turned the military tide in favor of the democracies. By the fall of 1918 the German armies were in retreat. Power in Germany passed from the kaiser to the government. Advised by senior military commanders that the war was lost, the Germans began to sue for peace, and on November 11, 1918, in anticipation of surrender terms to be agreed at a peace conference at Versailles, an armistice came into effect.

Work at Fore River continued regardless, as the shipyard workers slaved to finish U.S. government contracts before they could be canceled. By 1919 some seventy-one destroyers had been built in only twenty-seven months—more than at all other American yards combined.

Powell and Wakeman both urged Joe Kennedy to stay, promising promotion to the company's head office in Pennsylvania in due course. But Kennedy was restless. He was still only thirty years old. Helping to run a shipyard in a declining postwar industry, with huge numbers of employees being laid off, no longer appealed to him. The job had given him refuge from military service, a good income—and ulcers. If he wished to become a millionaire, he reasoned, it was time to move on.

Walking Out

The position Joe Kennedy took in 1919 in the offices of Hayden, Stone and Company on Boston's aptly named Milk Street kept him equally busy, as he sought to pick up the tricks of his new stockbroking trade. He later claimed he'd gotten the job when trying to interest old Galen Stone, chairman of the Atlantic Gulf and West Indies Steamship Line, in a shipbuilding contract with Fore River; racing to the railway station where he'd heard the broker was about to board a train to New York, he had booked the seat next to him, and while Stone had not been interested in a shipbuilding contract, he had been interested in Kennedy himself.

Joe Kennedy's memory would be as self-serving as his wife's would be selective; nonetheless it was a shrewd move. He'd made several healthy profits on investments during the war but had suffered a number of losses too. There must be a more reliable method of making or manipulating profitable investments, he reasoned, and his decision not to remain at Fore River or return to the Columbia Trust mirrored his decision to become a lowly bank examiner after Harvard in 1912. Working as a customer's man and taking a significant cut in salary, he set about mastering the secrets of insider trading, management pools, and selling short. Soon he was head of the stocks department and on his way to his first million—though not without paying a domestic price.

Whether it was word of Joe Kennedy's philandering that finally broke Rose Kennedy's spirit is uncertain. Doris Kearns Goodwin, the family chronicler who interviewed Rose and various friends later in Rose's long life, came to the conclusion that Joe's absence from home was the straw that snapped her stoic back. Joe had seldom come home before midnight while working at Fore River. "He was under such pressures that, except for Sundays, he came home just long enough to sleep," Rose recalled. It was not simply pressures, however, that kept Joe away from home. Nor did Rose intend to take her husband's behavior lying down.

In September 1918 Rose had given birth to her third child, a daughter, whom they named Rosemary. In the fall of 1919, she became pregnant for the fourth time in four years. Sick of Joe's philandering and his absences, she declared she'd had enough. Early in January 1920 Rose left her children and her husband and returned to her parents in Dorchester.

The separation lasted three weeks. But if Rose hoped her errant, perpetually absent husband would come crawling for forgiveness, she was to be disappointed. Joe did not come at all. It was thus left to her father, John F. Fitzgerald, to tell Rose her Irish-Catholic duty. He himself had won reelection to Congress in 1918 but had recently been forced to surrender the seat to his opponent, Peter Tague, after allegations of carpetbagging. He could not face another scandal in the family. Rose, he felt, had made her own bed and she must lie in it: "What is past is past. The old days are gone. . . . You've made your commitment, Rosie, and you must honor it now."

To her credit, Rose Kennedy did. She returned to Beals Street, her three children, and her husband. A few weeks later, on February 20, 1920, she gave birth to her fourth child, a second daughter, whom they christened Kathleen. Rose never again broke down or even complained. For good or ill, she would become the archetypal, stoic Irish-Catholic mother.

Scarlet Fever

No sooner had Rose returned to Beals Street than a new domestic crisis arose. Shortly after the new baby was born, Jack fell sick with scarlet fever.

Rose later confessed to "frantic terror"—on behalf not of Jack, but of his siblings. Brookline, however, had no hospital for contagious diseases. Once again it was Rose's father who came to the rescue, prevailing upon Dr. Place of the Boston City Hospital to take Jack there.

With Rose still in bed following the birth of Kathleen, it was left to Joe to visit his two-year-old son in the hospital. Jack was "a very, very sick little boy," often perilously close to death, Rose recalled. His "bad turns" were inevitable, the hospital nurse explained to Joe Kennedy, who wrote afterward to Dr. Place that he had "never experienced any very serious sickness in my family previous to Jack's, and I little realized what an effect such a happening could possibly have on me. During the darkest days I felt that nothing else mattered except his recovery." The priest was asked to say prayers, and Joe, distraught, offered half his worldly wealth to the church if the child's life was spared.

It was. For three months the three-year-old was then sent away to a sanatorium in Maine to convalesce. By the early summer of 1920, when finally he returned to Beals Street, Jack had so captured his nurse's heart that she begged to be allowed to stay on with him—a fun-loving and precociously humorous little boy who never complained.

The shock of his illness, meanwhile, had drawn Jack's parents temporarily closer, and shortly after Jack's return to Brookline, the Kennedys moved from the house on Beals Street to a more imposing residence at 51 Abbotsford Road, at the corner of Naples Road. It was a colonial-style mansion with two-story, curving bay windows, a wraparound porch, fourteen rooms, and a garage for the new Rolls-Royce. Built in 1897 and designed by the architects Greenleaf and Cobb, the eighteen-thousand-dollar house came with almost an acre of land and was registered in Rose Kennedy's name (a device that pleased Rose and enabled Joseph Kennedy to part with only thirty-five hundred dollars in his promised donation to the church).

For all her piety, Rose liked luxuries, and the new house was her suburban dream. She conceived a fifth child the week they moved in, the baby being delivered in the new house the following July—another daughter, whom they named Eunice, after Rose's youngest, consumptive sister.

"After Jack's illness, Joe was determined to keep up with every little thing the children were doing," Rose later claimed. "Every night we would spend hours together talking about the family and going over the children's activities. It made me feel that I had a partner in my enterprise."

"Enterprise" was a strange word to use—though a revealing metaphor for the Kennedy family after Rose's dutiful return in 1920. Joe might talk for hours with her "about the children," but he certainly refused, on principle, to discuss his business dealings—and with good reason. With others, too, he was tight-lipped. "The stock market game does not make for personal friendships. Every man has to be independent," a fellow speculator had once remarked. "You didn't ask him any questions unless you had a darned good reason," said another. "Joe confided in very, very few people."

The simple reason was the immorality of what Joe was doing. At Hayden, Stone Kennedy learned the technique that would, several years later, enable him to save the New York Yellow Cab Company and earn himself a further fortune. Known as stock pooling, it relied on a conspiracy between traders who artificially bidded up a stock and then dumped it once the market had been duped into raising the price.

Though Kennedy didn't confide to Rose what he was doing, Rose later confessed she felt "suddenly out of joint with the politics of the times and its dominant notes of cynicism, conservatism and indifference." However, she asked Joe no questions about the wealth that began to flood into the family in 1922, and Joe told no lies. Instead, Rose concentrated on managing the "enterprise" at 51 Abbotsford Road. As she later explained, she did little "diaper changing, but I had to be sure there were plenty of good-quality diapers on hand. . . . There were also the daily supply of bottles and nipples to be cleaned and sterilized. I didn't do much of it myself, but I had to make sure it was done properly, and on a schedule that wouldn't interfere with another vital schedule. If nursemaids were in the kitchen boiling bottles and nipples and preparing 'formulas' and pureeing vegetables when the cook needed the stove . . . there could be a kitchen crisis, sharp words and bruised feelings and, from a management point of view, a precipitous drop in morale and efficiency."

The Kennedy household was undergoing a metamorphosis. Sent back by her father to "carry out her commitment," Rose Kennedy was becoming a literal majordomo: a management executive rather than a mother, giving orders to the staff and regimenting the children. The self that had obstinately sought to move away from the suffocating possessiveness of her father had now petrified, humiliated both by him and by her husband. She became devout in the deeply committed manner of her mother, eschewing—as had her mother—the profession of her husband in order to concentrate on religion and the "proper" upbringing of her children. She began a card-index filing system to keep track of the children's medical histories and vital statistics (including their weight recorded bi-monthly); she took them for walks, and at a "daily inspection" she looked for signs of fraying garments, especially loose buttons. In an extra room she used as her "combination sewing room and office" she "spent many hours there seaming, sewing, mending and darning," as she herself recorded.

She was like Andersen's Ice Maiden, concealing her frozen heart beneath an exterior of courage and self-control. People marveled at the trim figure she maintained despite the unending childbearing. She tried to dress well, according to the fashion of the day—slim, neat, attractive. She kept up her presidency of the Ace of Clubs, as well as membership in other Catholic social circles. She went out all day to see her friends—taking care to be home by five in the evening lest "morale" of the staff dip at the end of the long day. Her relationship with Joe settled into a compact of convenience, relying on what she later recalled as a "synergistic" quality. "We were individuals with highly responsible roles in a partnership that yielded rewards which we shared."

This formalistic mumbo-jumbo was a depressing reflection of a love match that had gone wrong, that was now but a factory, producing and rearing middle-class Brookline children, with well-sterilized bottle-nipples and no loose buttons.

A Very Lively Elf

The wraparound veranda at Abbotsford Road was soon divided into territorial play areas, using folding gates to form sheep pens for the five Kennedy children. "That way they could be with each other and entertain one another for hours at a time," Rose later explained, "with a minimal risk that they would push one another down or stick one another with something sharp or perhaps pile heavy objects inside or on top of the baby carriage." Moreover, from the veranda the children had "the full panorama of neighborhood life to entertain them: cars passing by, people walking along (many of them acquaintances who waved), the letter carrier, the milkman with his wire basket loaded full as he came to our house and empty as he left, the policeman passing by on his patrol, the grocery boy, tradesmen, visitors, and friends of all degrees and kinds—everybody with a smile and cheerful greeting for the children."

Rose's vivid reminiscence was sadly revealing: the barricaded veranda somehow symbolic of a suburban family in quarantine, as in fact the Kennedys were, socially and even medically. The records at the nearby public elementary school (named after its posthumous patron, the seventeenth-century village constable Edward Devotion, whose clapboard house still stood on the site, dwarfed by the yellow-brick buildings) noted admission of the first Kennedy pupil, Joseph P. Kennedy, Jr., in the kindergarten class on October 11, 1920, age five—and his withdrawal a week later owing to a flu epidemic. Rose was taking no chances.

When the epidemic ended in November, Joe Jr. restarted school. According to his biographer, Hank Searls, who interviewed Joe Jr.'s teachers, the boy was husky and healthy, but unprepared by his mother for normal social life with children of his own age. Waving from the Abbotsford Road veranda to the postman or police officer had proved a poor substitute for the company of children other than his siblings. "Joe started badly," Searls wrote. "For weeks his attention wandered. He felt he was not doing as well as expected. He wanted help but though there were two teachers, Betsy Beau and Cornelia Fould, and a young assistant-in-training, there were sixty-two boys and girls in the class. . . . Drawing and painting defeated him. . . . He became nervous now and sometimes he cried in frustration."

This frustration was often taken out on his brother Jack. Though Rose Kennedy attempted to be home by five-thirty every evening "to help them with their schoolwork, doctor their colds, or to find out activities they had been interested in during the day," her emotional and physical absence— her "management" rather than maternal approach to child rearing—was bound to affect the psychology of her sons. She'd already run away from home once. Given the paucity of their mother's love, the two boys were thus bound to fight over it, and they did—at times like cats and dogs. "I suppose it was inevitable that they were rivals," Rose reflected. "Joe was much stronger than Jack, and if there was any physical encounter, Joe really whacked him."

In the new house Rose had a separate bedroom. Although she could not deny Joe his marital rights, even when he openly consorted with chorus girls and their like, she could deny him physical intimacy beyond her Catholic duty. "He was a real womanizer!" recalled Frederick Good, Jr., the son of Rose's obstetrician.

> Wherever you went, he had a girl with him; regularly, year in, year out, winter in, winter out. And Rose had to live with that. I have the highest respect for her, in retrospect, though I didn't at the time. I

don't think she saw as much of her children as, say, my mother did. But she had to put up with an awful lot! I respect her for that. She would find out if he was going east, and if he was, she took a trip west! And vice versa! They were not together too often. . . . Let's put it like that. She avoided him—which I think was a great thing to have done. At least she saved the marriage. And I don't know how many women today would put up with the shenanigans that went on with Father! With all due respect, I don't think he set a particularly good example. It has certainly unwound itself since, hasn't it?

Jack certainly resented his brother's role as primus inter pares in the absence of his parents. "The children had all kinds of governesses," Good recalled—and it was perhaps this infant rivalry for their mother's meager attention, as much as their father's later pressure on his children to fight to win in every endeavor, that chiseled Jack's psyche. He'd inherited his father's sandy hair, bluish eyes, and squarish face; but the jaw, with its wide mouth and prominent teeth, belonged also to his mother, as did his cooler temperament.

Joe Jr., by contrast, took after his father—aggressive, mercurial, quick to fly into a temper—and these characteristics became the bane of his younger brother's life. Asked later if he had enjoyed a happy childhood, Jack said yes—save for the fact that Joe was rather a "bully." "With their different temperaments, this brought flare-ups that included personal combat," Rose herself chronicled. "Joe Jr.'s temperament was different from Jack's in many ways, one of which was a better defined sense of neatness and order. . . . During the earlier years of their boyhood there were fights, few of which I saw but some of which I have been told were real battles. Joe Jr. was older, bigger, stronger, but Jack, frail though he was, could fight like fury when he wanted to."

On one occasion, on a summer holiday, Jack was caught putting on Joe Jr.'s new bathing costume by mistake (Rose had bought them a matching pair). "Joe Jr. was furious," Rose recalled.

> I quieted him and assured him that it would *never* happen again. Four days later, however, Jack made the same terrible mistake. . . . I was out at the time, so I didn't witness the scene, but I learned that Joe Jr. exploded and took off after his brother. Jack looked back over his shoulder momentarily and then sensibly took flight, across the lawn, through the marsh, and down the beach. He then ran along the old breakwater. Joe Jr. was gaining on him when, thank goodness, Eddie Moore [her father's erstwhile secretary and now factotum to her husband] arrived on the scene. He realized instantly that Jack had done something wrong and Joe Jr. was chasing him for

it, but this time the situation could be dangerous. He shouted: "Stop that! You two get yourselves back here. Right now!" They did, but it chilled me to think what could have happened if Eddie hadn't turned up at the right time. I daresay Jack thought about it too.

Jack also thought about why his mother was not there much of the time. Rose's announcement that she was departing on another six-week vacation with her sister, Agnes, earned the five-year-old's memorable rebuke: "Gee, *you're* a great mother to go away and leave your children all alone!"

When not engaged in fisticuffs with his older brother, Jack turned more and more to books. Though he'd survived his bout with scarlet fever, he remained frail, skinny, and subject to almost continual illnesses. According to Rose, it was his enforced incarceration that caused him to learn to read, with the aid of his governess. "The fact that he was so often sick in bed or convalescing in the house and needed entertainment," she reflected, "only encouraged what I think was already a strong natural bent."

The bent, however, was far from natural: a solitary escape from often unbearable domestic tension between his parents when home, as well as solace when they were not. Books certainly fueled a growing curiosity, however, about the world beyond his Brookline veranda. "Before he ever went to school," Joe Kennedy later recalled, Jack was asking schoollike questions. "I remember when he was a little bit of a shaver trying to find out where the Canary Islands were because he had read something about them in a Billy Whiskers book. Me, I had never heard of the Canary Islands at the time."

Rose had heard of the Canary Islands, but not the Sandwich Islands. "I confessed I didn't know but said I'd find out, as I did, and then showed him in the atlas," she later recalled. The Billy Whiskers book, however, Rose "wouldn't have allowed in the house except that my mother had given it to him. It seemed to me very, very poorly illustrated, with the pictures in brash flamboyant colors."

Brashness and flamboyance were anathema to the Ice Maiden of Abbotsford Road. Apart from hating the mention of sex, she recoiled from plays and novels that portrayed "poverty, dirt and sloth," as she put it. Her own taste in books remained as secondhand as the reproduction paintings with which she covered the walls of her home. For little Jack she permitted only volumes "from the P.T.A.- and library-approved lists." Like the films that would later be shown in the house, all had to be vetted, screened, and approved by others before the children were allowed to be exposed to them. As Rose explained her policy for the screening of movies, "Naturally, anything shown to our young audience was recommended or checked by someone in advance as being suitable for family viewing. If there was a slip-up and the plot became lurid," she went on, "the projector was switched off and the audience was sent out."

Psychologically Rose Fitzgerald Kennedy was showing signs of ominous prudery and rigidity of mind—characteristics that were bound to further upset children whom she never kissed or touched and rarely saw. When she was home, failures to conform to her idées fixes often ended in corporal punishment. At first she used a ruler, kept in her sewing desk, the better, she punned, to measure the punishment. As her eldest two became more mischievous, however, she began to use wooden coat hangers, "whacking" the children on the hand or buttocks. Coat hangers, she later explained, "were always within reach."

As one of her children later pointed out, there was nothing inherently wrong in such a punishment. Rose resorted to physical violence only as a last resort, and there is no evidence that she enjoyed "paddling" or beating her children. But because she was incapable of showing natural feelings of physical affection, these whacks with a wooden coat hanger or a metal-backed hairbrush were often the nearest thing to a warm embrace that the older boys ever received.

It was within this strange, rule-orientated stereotype of a family or "enterprise" that the multiplying children had, nevertheless, to find their niches. The oldest, Joe Jr., did so by performing the role his mother expected him to perform; he was neat, orderly, and responsible, even fatherly toward his younger siblings—though not toward Jack, his nonconformist rival. To Joe's indignation, Jack was often given "an extra portion of food, or perhaps some rich gravy left in the bottom of the pan," as Rose recalled, "because he needed it. He had a rather narrow face and his ears stuck out a little bit and his hair wouldn't stay put, and all that added, I suppose, to an elfin quality in his appearance. But he was a very active, very lively elf, full of energy when he wasn't ill and full of charm and imagination. And surprises—for he thought his own thoughts, did things his own way, and somehow just didn't fit any pattern. Now and then, fairly often in fact," Rose later confessed, "that distressed me, since I thought I knew what was best."

By September 1921, Rose thought it best that Jack enter Betsy Beau's kindergarten class at Edward Devotion School, though he was only four years old. Jack cannot have been well, however, for his surviving record card indicates that he attended school only ten weeks out of thirty-four.

Despite his abysmal health record, Jack was promoted in September 1922 to the first grade of Edward Devotion School. He was five years old, his chequered infancy over.

Weaving Daydreams

Like his grandfather, Honey Fitz, Jack was a natural wit. "He was a funny little boy, and he said things in such an original, vivid way," Rose recalled—even though she herself was often the target of his humor. At age five his response to her increasing religiosity was typical. "Jack did not much care about wishing for happy death, but thought he would like to wish for two dogs." His best friend, Charlie, had a dog whose name was Brandy, "because his father is a bootlegger," Jack told his mother, who felt Jack's sayings were so singular that she began to jot them down in her diary. "Daddy has a sweet tooth, hasn't he? I wonder which one it is?" There was, too, Jack's spontaneous comment when warning his mother his teacher was coming to his house to "tell on him" for idleness in class: "You know, I am getting on all right and if you study too much, you're liable to go crazy!"

Here, clearly, was a child whose humor distinguished him from the other children in his family—as did his attitude toward his clothes. While Rose recorded proudly in her diary her first couturier gown, bought for two hundred dollars (almost twice what she had paid Dr. Good for the delivery of her last baby), Jack seemed unconcerned about dress. His shirt never seemed to stay in his trousers, nor would his collar stay down. His behavior was equally lax. Of all her children, he was the worst about remembering to be prompt, Rose later recalled. If in the summer he failed to turn up at the assembly point on the beach at twelve forty-five, Rose would "drive off without him. . . . I had made it quite clear that tardiness meant starting in the middle of the meal, so he frequently had a meager lunch."

Rose's self-conscious, priggish discipline was evidently a trial to young Jack, however much he sought to ignore it by reading or refusal to abide by her rules. "I often had the feeling his mind was only half-occupied with the subject at hand, such as doing his arithmetic homework or picking up his clothes off the floor," Rose recalled, "and the rest of his thoughts were far away weaving daydreams."

What Rose could not see was that Jack was avoiding the same domestic nightmare that she was scuttling. Rose's reaction to her husband's infidelity had been to throw herself into her social activities and treat her progeny as a management exercise—a strategy that Jack was too perceptive not to recognize, even as a small boy. Though he never publicly criticized her, he would never wholly overcome his sense of abandonment and maternal deprivation, which would condemn him to a lifetime's fruitless romantic and sexual searching.

While his brothers and sisters later paid tribute to their mother's manic educational imperative with her children, Jack knew it was baloney. Her desire for neat, well-groomed, well-dressed, well-mannered, well-spoken, well-read, religiously observant, and clean-minded children was both comic and tragic, for it was clear to Jack that her copybook values and domestic rules were but a desperate form of self-preservation; a basically intelligent woman driven to stupidity. She wanted her children to become "effective people." She repeated her father's old arithmetical games and tried to pass along his interest in American and New England history. She railed against the children's bad grammar, insisting on the proper usage of *who* and *whom, I* and *me, shall* and *will, may* and *can.* Her zeal was extraordinary, but love, like a candle, had gone out of her life.

In 1923, at age six, Jack was promoted to second grade under Miss Bicknell. In 1924, at age seven, he went into third grade under Miss Manter, a year if not two ahead of most children his age. Rose, however, persisted in thinking Joe Jr. was the brighter of her two boys, until the results of a school intelligence test were sent to her. "I didn't think Jack's I.Q. was as high as his brother, because I used to work with them a good deal and somehow, Joe worked at things harder than Jack, because he would do things whether he was interested or not, [whereas] Jack was apt to concentrate on the things that he was interested in and not bother much about the others," Rose recalled. She protested to the school "because I thought the teacher was wrong and that Joe had a higher I.Q." The teacher, to Rose's surprise, confirmed the results of the tests, as well as Jack's unusually high score.

How much Rose really worked with her boys was questionable. Rosemary, only a year younger than Jack, was still proving a slow learner, with poor physical coordination; she was unable to hold a knife and fork at first, unable to keep her balance while skating, steer a sled in snow, or swim or row a boat in the summer. In her concern to get Rosemary to perform according to her increasingly stereotype expectations, Rose devoted more and more of her available time to Rosemary, only later asking herself what effect this might have had on Jack. "He was rather sickly," she acknowledged years after Jack's death, "and therefore needed attention: perhaps more than I gave him, in my worry and distraction about Rosemary. . . . The thought still bothers me a bit that he may have [felt neglected] when he was a little boy, and only realized later on why I spent so much time with Rosemary."

There is no evidence that Jack ever felt resentful of the time his mother spent with Rosemary. What he found difficult to accept was the unspoken tension between his mother and father, and Rose's absences.

Rose's "trips," however understandable in her own terms, came on top of a distressing lovelessness when she was home, reflected in an increasing *spiessbürgerlichkeit,* as button checking replaced basic motherliness. With five children to "manage," Rose now relentlessly modeled herself and her children on the image of a *Ladies Home Journal* family.

This social plagiarism would gradually make of Rose Kennedy a pathetic figure: a tiny, often ridiculed Boston-Irish Roman Catholic concealing her failed marriage behind a façade of proper manners, proper attire, proper talk, proper religious observance, proper reading, and proper film-viewing that was risible, were it not compensated for by the fact that the Kennedys, by 1924, had become millionaires.

Making Millions

Joseph P. Kennedy had made his first big killing in the winter of 1923. For an outlay of only $24,000—on credit—he'd used insider information given him by Galen Stone and had reaped a profit of more than half a million dollars—$675,000, in fact—on Pond Creek Coal Company shares. With this crooked windfall Joe had resigned his post at Hayden, Stone.

Joe was quite content to leave the company. The previous year he and Rose had been blackballed for membership at the Cohasset Country Club, and his chances of becoming a partner in the Hayden, Stone firm were equally "slim" owing to "his ethnic background," according to Doris Kearns Goodwin.

Joe was hurt, but not sorry to depart. The lesson he'd learned in his three years with Galen Stone was that he could hope to get rich quick only by dishonesty. At the firm of Hayden, Stone, fraudulent dealing could not be kept quiet for long.

Sitting in his own office, behind a door marked JOSEPH P. KENNEDY, BANKER, with only chosen henchmen such as Eddie Moore and E. B. Derr—an accountant he'd summoned from the Fore River Shipyard—Joe Kennedy now indulged in financial larceny on a vast and unseen scale, manipulating share prices with other hands in secret stock pools designed specifically to hoodwink investors. His growing expertise netted him a second fortune in the spring of 1924 when he left his pregnant wife and five children and moved to the Waldorf-Astoria Hotel in New York. There, with a fund of five million dollars, he did what he was best at: manipulating stock prices. Sitting in his hotel room for nine weeks with a specially installed ticker tape, he saved John Hertz's Yellow Cab Company, whose shares were being driven down by brokers working for the

competing Checker Cab Company; by arranging such unpredictable buying and selling across the country, he caused the raiders to finally lose
heart and pull out of the shares altogether.

In gratitude John Hertz gave Kennedy a secret cash sum as well as a
generous share of stock in his company, though he soon regretted this
when Kennedy promptly dumped the stock, leading to a fall in the
company's share price and Hertz's avowed promise that he would "punch
him on the nose the next time they met."

The Yellow Cab fight, however, confirmed Kennedy's growing reputation as a shrewd and ruthless market operator, but it did not make him
any new friends, nor did it endear him to his wife, who gave birth in the
meantime to yet another daughter, Pat, on May 6, 1924. "Daddy, Daddy,
Daddy! We've got another baby!" the older children shouted in unison
when finally Joe appeared at Boston's South Station in June. "My baby
Pat had been born and was almost a month old and I hadn't even seen
her," Kennedy later recalled. "They were smiling . . . but with a touch of
perplexity and sympathy, as if they might be thinking to themselves, what
that fellow there certainly doesn't need right now is *another* baby."

As Rose explained to the family chronicler, her husband had taken on
the Hertz fight because of his "desire for the freedom which money
provides, the freedom to come and go where he pleased, when he pleased
and how he pleased." Rose had already run away from him once. Joe
kept her now only by her religious sense of duty, his expensive gifts, and
the continual children he forced her to bear alone.

Yet for all her attempts to rear and regiment the children, from nipple
sterilization to book censorship, Rose Kennedy was forced by the summer of 1924 to admit that, in the more or less continual absence of her
husband, she had lost control. They often went wild when unsupervised—
as Jack's twenty-eight stitches proved, after Joe Jr. suggested they race
around the block on their bikes in opposite directions and collided. Joe
Jr. was seen on the roof of the neighbor's garage; Jack was always "in one
or another state of quixotic disgrace." When they were not warring, they
were swiftly becoming delinquent in her eyes: stealing from the local toy
store and even, to her chagrin, purloining people's empty milk bottles and
storing them in the cellar to resell. She therefore, she related, "decided to
take the boys out of the local school and enroll them in a nearby private
school," the junior department of the Noble and Greenough School,
where "there would be afterschool supervised play."

In fact, Rose was telescoping. Though Joe Jr. was initially transferred
to Noble and Greenough, Jack returned to Edward Devotion School,
according to its records, in September 1924.

Possibly Jack's mother had thought to keep Jack at Edward Devotion
to watch over his six-year-old sister, Rosemary, who had finished her first

year at kindergarten in June and would normally have entered Devotion's first grade in September. That summer, however, it had become clear that Rosemary's learning difficulties were more serious than Rose had been willing to admit. The school recommended that she be withdrawn, rather than face impossible classroom expectations, and be sent to a special institution. To her credit, after consulting the head of psychology at Harvard as well as a Catholic priest who specialized in the mentally retarded, Rose decided to keep Rosemary at home and to employ private tutors. Preoccupied with Rosemary's condition, though, she lost interest in Edward Devotion School. On October 22, 1924, therefore, after a month under Miss Manter in third grade, Jack was withdrawn and sent to follow his elder brother to the four-hundred-dollar-a-year Noble and Greenough Lower School, on Freeman Street in Brookline.

Jack was now seven, his brother nine. The principal of the school, Miss Myra Fiske, had already interviewed Jack in the spring, along with Joe Jr., and had written in a note to Mr. Wiggins, headmaster of Noble and Greenough (whose upper school was in Dedham), that she was "very glad that we decided to take this little John Kennedy. He is a fine chap." With his alert mind and easy wit, no doubt Jack was. Moreover, in Myra Fiske John Kennedy was to have a brilliant principal.

Socially, however, the transfer was important. Both Jack and his brother were now moving into a new world, peopled exclusively by Anglo-Saxons with names such as Barbour, Blake, Brewer, Bundy, Huntingdon, Hydes Langmaid, Mason, Sanborn, and Wright. "We were probably the first and only ones who were Catholic," Jack later reflected wistfully, "probably the only Irish Catholic family." Their grandfather John Fitzgerald—who had stood for the governorship of the entire state of Massachusetts two years before and had polled a staggering 400,000 votes (narrowly losing to the sitting Republican governor, Canning Fox)—had once claimed all that separated the Fitzgeralds and the Cabot Lodges was "the difference of a few ships." His grandchildren were now to discover that ethnic, religious, and racial prejudice went much deeper in the New World than a few ships.

Noble and Greenough

That she was sending her two boys into the very world of Yankees who'd kept her out of the Cohasset Country Club two years before and who would blackball her when she and Joe applied to Brookline's exclusive Country Club shortly afterward did not deter Rose Kennedy. Possibly she thought it might be easier for children than their parents. If so, she was mistaken.

Certainly the "afterschool supervised play" that Rose Kennedy fondly remembered in her dotage was a fiction. A contemporary of the Kennedy boys, Augustus Soule, recalled that at Noble and Greenough "the only man when we started out was the so-called athletic instructor. He was a veteran of World War I, who'd been both shocked and gassed. I'd never seen anyone like that. He was a complete nut and as a result, for the first years, there was no real athletic supervision. We just kind of ran loose in the afternoon."

As new boys, the two Kennedys were inevitably the object of derision and taunts. As Soule remembered,

> Almost everybody was a Protestant. There may have been a few Catholics, but no Jews at all. I think there was a sort of snobbery, which the children adopted. I think that in those days the upper crust Boston families, of which there were a great number sending their children to the school, were very down on the Irish. I mean those were the days of Mayor James Michael Curley—who was later imprisoned for corruption. The Irish were blamed, I think wrongly, for everything that went wrong with the Commonwealth of Massachusetts. To be an Irish Catholic was a real, real stigma—and when the other boys got mad at the Kennedys, they would resort to calling them Irish or Catholic.

As for Joseph P. Kennedy, Soule continued, "my father would have nothing to do with him. A lot of the parents wouldn't even speak to him because he was so disliked. The view was: Mr. Kennedy had made his money in ways that were known, in banking circles, to be unsavory; Mrs. Kennedy's father, Honey Fitzgerald, was a scallywag if ever there was one, and everybody put these two things together and they said, "This couple's up to no good.' "

Speaking sixty years later, Soule was embarrassed at the memory: "These were the attitudes of very narrow-minded people, but these were the sort who sent their sons to the school, Leverett Saltonstall amongst them! They would have nothing to do with the Kennedys at all, and I'm sure the boys, they must have had a hard time. Their sisters were never going to be invited to the debutante parties—the Kennedy daughters would never, never have been invited to them, because the feeling was so strong. . . . I'm embarrassed to tell you this, but it is the truth of the matter."

Joe Jr.'s reaction to such prejudice was very different from Jack's—as Soule recalled: "Joe, the older brother, was as different from Jack as day from night. He had all the bad Irish traits I can think of. He was very, very pugnacious, very irritable, very combative, and I can remember at recess—we had a very long recess—he would challenge older boys to fight."

Jack, by contrast, refused to brawl. Instead he would bet on his elder brother, using an unusual currency.

> In those days, marbles: that was the big thing. You always carried a little bag of marbles in your pants pocket. And I can remember going back to my father and saying, "I need some more marbles."
>
> "What happened to the ones you had?" he's ask.
>
> "Well, I lost them all in a bet."
>
> "With whom?"
>
> "I bet with Jack Kennedy."
>
> It's an indelible memory I have: Joe fighting and getting all bloody, and Jack going around, betting marbles very quietly. To my mind that illustrates how completely different the two brothers were!

If Rose Kennedy was initially ignorant of this hostile world her sons were facing, she gradually became aware of it. Her response, as with her husband's infidelity, was to avoid reality as much as possible. No child at the school ever remembered her appearing, whether to bring the children in the morning or to collect them in the afternoon. Nor did Rose attend, let alone help, at the many school social activities. Instead, the children were driven to and from school by car. "This big shiny car would arrive with Jack and Joe. . . . It was a very big black shiny car with a chauffeur with a cap. Rose, Mrs. Kennedy, never, never appeared," Soule remembered emphatically. Instead, her concern for her two boys was expressed in another way:

> An interesting thing that I remember very well indeed was the school uniform. The uniform all the boys had to wear was a red jersey and knickers—nobody wore long trousers in those days—and long stockings. And Rose Kennedy, Jack's mother, I guess felt that the sweater wasn't enough protection for him in the cold weather, so she knitted onto both her boys' sweaters a hood. And they were the only boys in the school who had this hood—which led to a lot of derision!

Rose Kennedy's attention to such matters was almost a fetish. She was adamant that her children would not go out improperly dressed or insufficiently buttoned up. As she later reminisced with pride, "I did want all to look brushed and neat at school, church, and in public. I bought them good clothes, and very often dressed them alike when they were children.

There would be identical sailor suits which were the fashion for Joe Jr. and Jack, and identical middy blouses and skirts for Rosemary, Kathleen, Eunice and Pat, in descending sizes.''

Unable to show physical warmth to her children, Rose was determined at least to sew for them. "Buttons, buttons, and more buttons. . . . In winter, whenever the young children were outside they were dressed in long leggings and I can't begin to calculate the hours the help and I spent buttoning and unbuttoning them. Also, no matter how strong the thread or how well sewn, it was forever pulling loose or wearing thin or breaking.''

Rose's attention to such minutia, while her husband fiddled the stock market and her children underwent their baptism in New England ethnic prejudice spoke volumes. Jack, modest and courteous in public, would never criticize her—but occasionally in his later life, with friends, he would let his mask slip and show something of the bitterness he felt about a mother who was often away, frequently at church, who never once held him in her arms yet later claimed credit for his precocious abilities, particularly his growing interest in history. "She would talk about history, too, but I wouldn't say she was *au courant,*" Jack later remarked. "No, I wouldn't say that the germ of my interest in history came from her. I have an enquiring mind, and I like history."

Jack's precocious intellect, nevertheless, had been noted by the alert Miss Fiske the first time she met him. Miss Fiske and her staff of women teachers soon put him through his paces. "It was a very friendly school," Augustus Soule recalled. "There were no men teaching at all: all women teachers, and they were very, very strict, and I dare say it's a lot like the English system as I picture it, very strong on multiplication tables, very strong on grammar, very drill, drill, all the time. . . . They were tough, and I don't think men would have been as tough as these women were."

Another of Jack's contemporaries, Holton Wood, recalled just how tough female discipline at Noble and Greenough could be:

> The English teacher was Miss Dow. She just caught this boy, Benny Hamilton was his name, his father was a dentist, when he was fooling. He didn't realize she was behind him and she just sort of cuffed him. She wasn't a great physical brute or anything; actually she was quite a small woman, stocky. . . . She cuffed him, from behind—his chin caught the desk and out he went like a light! There wasn't much fooling *after that!*

Miss Fiske's father had been a preacher. She'd studied Greek and Latin at Monson Academy and done a four-year postgraduate course in education at Westfield before starting to teach in 1896 and moving to the Noble and Greenough's primary department in 1904. "Miss Fiske was a very caring person, and she was very big on deportment, manners," Wood recalled.

> I can't remember whether she taught anything, but she did an extraordinary thing. She played the piano well and we'd have assembly in the morning and we learned to recite in unison, the whole school, things like Lincoln's Gettysburg Address, his second Inaugural Address, pieces from the Bible, notable pieces from English literature. . . . We learned them and we recited them. We sat there and we'd say a line and then we'd add another line and she'd get us going like that. I mean I can recite the Gettysburg Address like I'd just read it this morning, still, and the Second Inaugural.

Interviewed shortly before her death at age ninety-nine, Myra Fiske had lost none of her pedagogic enthusiasm. "The classes were small, and we knew each other so well," she related. "I loved the boys. Discipline was never a problem to me—it never worried me at all. How did I keep discipline? I simply feel the thing. I felt it so keenly that they, the children felt it! Love," she went on. "Doesn't that take care of a lot? And you know, they're twice as smart as you are!"

Jack Kennedy, with his piquant wit and his passion for history, became her special pet. One day, she recalled, he offered to get his father to loan his Rolls-Royce if she would take him, after school, to the nearby historic sites of Lexington and Concord. "I don't think Rose came," Miss Fiske remembered. "All the boys turned out to see the famous Rolls-Royce. And when it came it was a dilapidated old Ford! Jack never got over how the other boys hooted him—something had happened to the Rolls-Royce!"

For all the social and ethnic prejudice they suffered, however, both Joe Jr. and Jack liked the new school. On November 20, 1925, they acquired a new brother, christened Robert Francis Kennedy. However, a bigger shock was in store, for shortly after Christmas 1925, word went around that Mr. Wiggins, the headmaster, had sold off the junior-school site to a developer and would close down the Noble and Greenough lower school the following May, 1926.

Staying Put

"The trustees met on a Sunday," Miss Fiske remembered.

> There was a terrible snowstorm, and we all made our way as best as we could to the school building. Well, you know, Mr. Wiggins hadn't

announced he would sell. In order to keep the school going in Dedham, he had to put up another school building—and he couldn't afford it.

Dear Mr. Wiggins—we all admired him. But that did something to people, selling off the Lower School.

He came over with Mrs. Wiggins and everybody was there to protest—you never saw anything like it. Mr. Wiggins asked what was the trouble.

I said, "Mr. Wiggins, why didn't you notify anybody?"

He said, "They *were* notified."

I said, "In what way?"

And then I knew he was beginning to lose his mind, which he did later.

"Why, I told so-and-so—one of my good old families—to notify people . . . "

"Well," I said, "you can't notify a school that way—that you're closing it down!"

For all that Joseph Kennedy was persona non grata among the Yankee parents of Noble and Greenough Lower School, he was impressed by the stability and seriousness that Noble and Greenough had brought to his son's lives. With nine other parents, therefore, Kennedy helped form a committee to save the school, buying the site back from the developer for $110,000, starting a new school corporation, and appointing Miss Fiske as its principal.

At one-fifteen P.M. on January 28, 1926, at the Exchange Club, only a block away from Joseph Kennedy's office on Milk Street, seven members of the new committee of trustees met to incorporate the Dexter School, as it was to be called (named after the family that had originally built the house on Freeman Street): a corporation that was to be "devoted to educational purposes" and "never be operated for pecuniary profit." The school's avowed aim was "to teach the boy how to study, how to acquire the habit of the greatest possible effort in his work, how best to develop the habits of honesty, courage, perseverance, self-reliance and control— in short, how to express by his own earnest effort the ideals taught him in the school-room and on the field," as Miss Fiske proudly announced in her first school prospectus.

Joseph Kennedy's noble act, however, won him no friends. Though he blamed this on the same anti-Irish prejudice that kept him from golfing with the Boston Brahmins, much of it was simply dislike of Joseph Kennedy, a big, blunt, energetic man who knew what he wanted and would stop at nothing to get it. By a mixture of ruthlessness, fraudulence, and business acumen he'd begun to swell his fortune to figures that would in time astonish Hayden, Stone and be literally unimaginable to his fellow

Boston Irishmen. Manipulating share prices from his New York hotel room was indecently profitable, he declared at the time, telling his cronies, "We'd better get in before they pass a law against it!"

Thus arose the strangest of contradictions—Joseph Kennedy helping to save his sons' school, while pressing to move them and the Kennedy family from Brookline to New York. Ethnic prejudice irritated him, but he had a tough skin. What he wanted, above all, was to make more money while he legally could—and the unregulated stock market on Wall Street, not Boston, was the best place to do it.

Rose, however, disliked the idea. New York seemed like a foreign land to her. She felt secure in the gabled Brookline house on the corner of Naples and Abbotsford roads, even though her husband by then could have afforded a much more substantial home. Augustus Soule was surprised by this: "I can remember very, very well that the Kennedy chauffeur would drive the two boys in a great limousine to and from the house in Brookline—which was an anachronism because the old man, as we'd call him, could have afforded a very, very nice house, but why he didn't I don't know. . . . It's a mystery to me."

The mystery, however, was not difficult to fathom. To surrender a house that was her own, and in her own name, wasn't simple for Rose. To give up a home where her children were seemingly stable and where special teaching help was available for Rosemary was even harder. Rose was still president of the Ace of Clubs, despite her seven children. Notwithstanding the lonely travels with her sister, Agnes, she considered Boston, literally, her hometown, and she had no desire to abandon it—or her father, who was a very loving grandfather to her children.

Whatever insults other children might hurl at school, both Joe Jr. and Jack remained steadfastly loyal to the ex-mayor. Often he would take Joe Jr. and Jack with him when campaigning in his chauffeur-driven Locomobile, or on the swan boats in the Boston Public Garden, or to the State House where he'd once been senator. Grampa Fitzgerald's effervescent sense of fun, his natural wit, pride in his Irish heritage, and genuine love of learning were to his grandsons exemplary. (By contrast, when the boys were taken to visit P. J. Kennedy at his Winthrop home on Sunday afternoons, "he wouldn't let us cut up or even wink in his presence," Jack remembered.)

If Fitzgerald's name was anathema to proper Bostonians, his popularity among ordinary people never waned. Having lost the 1922 gubernatorial election, he entered, then withdrew from the 1925 campaign for a successor to Boston mayor James Michael Curley, leading one Boston newspaper to lament, "With John F. Fitzgerald sitting on the sidelines the mayoralty campaign will lack a certain thrill only he can provide. Lovers of the spectacular may regret that this most colorful personality will not be seen charging up and down the municipal gridirons, going through for gains, being thrown for losses, smearing his opponent or being smeared. The battle will not be quite the same with 'the doctor' out."

Rumor had it Fitzgerald was withdrawing after more anonymous phone calls to his wife regarding women. If so, age was proving no bar to his passionate nature. At his sixtieth birthday party in February 1923 Honey Fitz had clasped his two Kennedy grandsons and had told newspaper reporters his secret. "Mingle with the young people. Go through life good-natured and friendly. . . . You will derive the greatest happiness from making others happy." And he sang his signature tune, "Sweet Adeline," repeating it on the radio that night. "One of the most important missions in life," he declared on his sixty-second birthday, "is to make friends and keep them; show kindness at all times."

Rose thus clung to her adored father as much as her children did when he visited. The days of harmony, however, were almost over, as the career of Joseph P. Kennedy, early in 1926, took a dramatic new turn.

A Blow in the Stomach

In 1925 Joseph Kennedy had sailed to England to try and buy FBO (Film Booking Office), a film-production and distribution company with offices in London, New York, and Hollywood. His offer of one million dollars had been rejected as inadequate. Shortly after helping to rescue his sons' school in Brookline in February 1926, however, Kennedy received a phone call in New York, asking if he was still interested in FBO. Joe, on his way to yet another vacation in Palm Beach with a group of business cronies, responded immediately.

"Sorry, fellows, guess you'll have to go to Florida without me. I'm going to Boston tonight," Kennedy announced when he returned. "I've bought a moving picture company."

With the help of his father-in-law in Boston, Kennedy obtained the promise of financial assistance from a Massachusetts businessman, Louis Kirstein. Fitzgerald, excited at the prospect of going into films, also drew the son of a former mayor of Boston, Frederick Prince, into the project, as well as Boston's First National Bank and the National Shawmut— prompting the *Boston Post* to run a front-page headline: JOHN F. FITZ-GERALD IS LATEST MOVIE MAGNATE.

Once the financial package was successfully assembled, however, Joe Kennedy had no need of his father-in-law. Kennedy was not, he often made the distinction, a gambler: he was a speculator. In the early 1920s he had bought a chain of movie theaters in northern New England and his ever-growing receipts suggested there was big money to be made in film production. His purchase of FBO was, therefore, no random investment but a calculated effort to break into the production end of the market. Installing himself in the spring of 1926 in FBO's American headquarters in a Manhattan skyscraper, he imposed strict cost accounting and reduced the company's ruinous 18 percent loans by issuing more stock. He decided, moreover, that FBO should concentrate exclusively on philistine but popular family entertainment—an approach that denied the company the spectacular profits made by big-budget Hollywood studios but also avoided their disasters.

Certainly Kennedy's assistant, Eddie Moore, assumed they would settle in New York after the purchase of FBO. "We will soon prove to the industry that we are not looking for the easy money and once we do that we'll have the field all to ourselves and then you can sit in your New York office on your fat fanny and fight like a bastard," Moore wrote to him in the fall of 1926. Rose Kennedy, however, refused to budge. She "did not want to move each time Joe changed business enterprises," she said, "because I thought it was wrong to interrupt school, their friendships, and the routine of the family. . . . At best, changing schools is disquieting; moreover, since curriculums and textbooks are not standardized from one school and locality to another, a transferring student may find himself at a serious academic disadvantage. For that reason I stayed on in Brookline with the children a couple of years."

Joe Jr. and Jack thus remained at the newly renamed Dexter School under Miss Fiske, while Joseph Kennedy commuted between Boston and New York, as well as making frequent trips to California. Jack's classmate Whitney Wright, for instance, recalled being invited to Jack's tenth birthday party at Abbotsford Road on May 29, 1927, and his astonishment when he saw a screen and film projector set up in the living room, ready for the showing of a cowboy movie. Not only had Jack's father brought back the film from Hollywood, but he'd even bought cowboy outfits for the children. "Anyone old enough to remember Tom Mix can understand what a sensation those caused with the boys and among their friends," Rose related.

That summer, the family at last acquired a summer house at Hyannis Port, on the east coast of Cape Cod. Dexter School's second annual brochure went to press with the names of young Jack and Joe Kennedy both included, in Classes 5 and 6, respectively, for the fall term, slated to begin in September 1927. A further thirty children had been added to the school's enrollment, and more land purchased, bringing the site to "about four and half acres of well graded playing fields." Joseph Kennedy's name was still on the board of eleven trustees, and a new library—a gift in memory of William Lovell Putnam—had been installed on the third floor, containing "several hundred books, such as encyclopaedias, dictionaries, other books of reference, and the standard books of travel, poetry and fiction."

Jack Kennedy would never use them, however. When September came, his mother suddenly changed her mind. There had been another outbreak in Massachusetts of poliomyelitis—the same disease that had crippled Franklin Roosevelt in 1921. The Dexter School announced that it would not now reopen before October. Rose panicked, and in a moment of weakness she decided to leave Boston.

Traveling in a specially hired railway car, the family moved on September 26, 1927, to the furnished mansion their father had rented on the corner of 252nd Street and Independence Avenue in Riverdale, a leafy, still-rural suburb of New York overlooking the Hudson River. The following day Joe Jr. and Jack Kennedy started class at the exclusive, nonsectarian Riverdale Country Day School.

In her memoirs Rose Kennedy recorded that she consented to the move only when she was finally "certain" that Joe's shift to the movie business was "solidly successful and would be taking most of his time in the foreseeable future." She had chosen Riverdale, she claimed, because it matched her Brookline habitat, accepting the transfer from "our Boston suburb to a New York suburb, with the proviso that it be a place with excellent schools, preferably within walking distance of home. Walking to and from school," she believed, "is healthful exercise; it is fun in good weather and teaches perseverance when the weather is bad. It teaches punctuality and responsibility by making the child accountable for lagging and tardiness."

Such moralizing reminiscences give some idea of the extent to which Rose Kennedy—who never walked with her children or traveled with them by car to school—covered up her increasing loneliness and unhappiness, clothing them as always in her punctilious concern with rectitude and child discipline.

In fact the move to New York was one Rose would regret for the rest of her life. As she confessed later, it was like "a blow in the stomach," which in a way it was: Rose being pregnant for the eighth time. "For months I would wake up in our new house in New York and feel a terrible sense of loss," she told the family chronicler.

There was, however, another reason for Rose's unhappiness, beyond the move from Boston and the seemingly unending childbearing. Her husband's infidelities might have destroyed her schoolgirl innocence, but at least Joe could claim that he provided well for his family and that his extramarital affairs did not intrude into his family life. But having forced

Rose to leave the city of her roots and bring her seven children to New York, Joe Kennedy became passionately involved with a famed Hollywood siren.

Enter Gloria

Joe Kennedy met Gloria Swanson on November 11, 1927, in the Savoy Plaza Hotel on Fifth Avenue. One of the directors of First National Pictures, Robert Kane, had asked Kennedy to help put Gloria Swanson's faltering career (she had set up her own production company) back into financial order so that, in "proper hands," she could "become the artist again and stop trying to be a business woman producing her own pictures."

Ironically, Kennedy had only just attempted to stop her latest production, the film *Sadie Thompson,* based on Somerset Maugham's erotic story of the same name, by signing an open telegram of protest to the U.S. film censor, Will Hays. Swanson had ignored the telegram and had gone ahead with the film, but it had soared above budget, causing her to offer to sell her Malibu house to Robert Kane in order to raise money. Kane suggested she try to tap Kennedy for a loan and some much-needed advice. At a lunch at the Savoy Plaza Hotel on Fifth Avenue on November 11, 1927, she did—while haughtily reminding Kennedy of the telegram he too had signed, and telling him she'd never heard of his most successful FBO movie, *The Gorilla Hunt.* Kennedy, accustomed to servility on the part of people seeking loans, was bowled over.

Swanson's account, published a decade after Kennedy's death, is our best and most intimate portrait of the youthful banker, for Rose Kennedy could rarely bring herself to recognize, let alone to tell the truth about, her husband. What Swanson saw, immediately, was that Kennedy "didn't resemble any banker" she'd ever met. Not only did he have a heavy Boston accent, but his suit was too bulky, "and the knot of his tie was not pushed up tight. With his spectacles and prominent chin, he looked like any average working-class person's uncle."

The "uncle," however, soon set about impressing the star. He pretended he'd been to business school at Harvard, slicing his hands up and down to indicate parallel accounting columns in order to illustrate costs versus future receipts. "Nobody in Hollywood," he told Swanson, "knew how to make a balance sheet that gave a banker what he needed. The motion picture business was so young that nobody knew how to depreciate, to amortize, to capitalize—those very things, he said, that spelled success or failure in any other business. That was what fascinated him about motion pictures, he went on, that here was a giant industry but that nobody seemed to realize it."

Joseph Kennedy was well aware that his banking and accounting skills could help carve him a place in Hollywood history; in fact he would soon confide to Swanson that he wished to move his office there. But in the presence of the young movie idol who had starred with Rudolph Valentino, he revealed a greater ambition. As he confessed to Swanson, "he had wanted to produce an important picture for some time." By the time he returned to his office, in fact, he'd made up his mind he would take Swanson on as a challenge.

Taking Swanson out to dinner that evening, Kennedy put to her a proposition, namely, that he should become her secret business partner. He'd heard her next production was going to be a film called *Rock-a-bye,* but he wasn't interested in that. Instead, he suggested, she should close down her ailing production company and restart it with his own personnel—experienced accountants who would monitor every cent spent. Meanwhile, he told Swanson, he wanted her to team up with Erich von Stroheim, the greatest Hollywood director of the day.

"Mr. Kennedy kept repeating the word 'important,' " Swanson recalled. Admitting she was in dire need of "someone with business acumen" at that stage of her career, she felt certain "she had stumbled on the right business partner to straighten out my career."

But Swanson was wrong. In fact Kennedy was to wreck Swanson's marriage, ruin her career, and far from achieving something important, was to produce one of the biggest flops in Hollywood annals, a film fiasco so disastrous it was never completed.

Though Swanson waited more than half a century to tell her story, her portrait of Joseph Kennedy was not bitter. Despite being married to a genuine French marquis—and therefore being herself a marquise—she was attracted by the Boston bully's lack of social pretensions—"the fighting-Irish pride that came of having withstood oppression and endured prejudice." She admired his arriviste bravado, seeing him as a precociously successful banker, "healthy and rich . . . all due to brains and stamina." Above all, Swanson understood that Joseph Kennedy was at a crossroads in his life, as she was—indeed, as the motion picture industry was. Hollywood was coming of age; it was a billion-dollar industry, with worldwide exports and earnings, on the brink of technological breakthrough with the impending introduction of talkies, and in need of financial help. Kennedy had persuaded the Harvard Business School to invite the foremost producers and directors of Hollywood to participate in a seminar on the industry the previous spring—a shrewd move that put him in touch with legendary filmmaking figures of his day, from Cecil B. DeMille to Fox, Warner, Zukor, and Loew. And yet, as Swanson pointed out to him, what he proposed was the opposite of what he should be doing if he wanted to make money.

Kennedy's mind was made up, however. He followed Swanson back to Hollywood in December 1927, together with his "horsemen," as he called them—his aide, Eddie Moore, and his three accountants, Charley Sullivan, E. B. Derr, and Ted O'Leary—"gangsters in appearance," yet loyal to the Boston-Irish banker boss who had brought them thus far: "four working-class Irishmen who had risen by perseverance to responsible jobs under an Irish boss whom they admired greatly."

Within weeks Swanson was inveigled into giving power of attorney to Derr, enabling her to concentrate solely on "acting and other artistic concerns." Her production company was, at Kennedy's insistence, dissolved and restarted in Delaware in what Sullivan gaily said was a whirlwind formation so dubious "that if he didn't go to jail on this deal, he never would." Kennedy's impending merger of FBO with Pathé would enable him to remove Swanson's titled husband from the scene by offering him an appointment he couldn't refuse: the top job in Pathé's Paris office. Meanwhile, to put the final touches on the deal with Swanson, Kennedy begged her and her husband, the Marquis de la Falaise de Coudraye, to meet him in Florida late in December 1927. Having made arrangements to remove the marquis from the scene by sending him fishing off Palm Beach, and having pretended to go to his room to make "business calls," Kennedy then entered Swanson's suite at the Hotel Poinciana and raped her.

> He moved so quickly that his mouth was on mine before either of us could speak. With one hand he held the back of my head, with the other he stroked my body and pulled at my kimono. . . . He kept insisting in a drawn-out moan, "No longer, no longer. Now." He was like a roped horse, rough, arduous, racing to be free. After a hasty climax he lay beside me, stroking my hair. Apart from his guilty, passionate mutterings, he had still said nothing cogent. I had said nothing at all. Since his kiss on [greeting me at] the train, I had known this would happen. And I knew as we lay there, that it would go on.

One of Gloria Swanson's friends claimed that she had "put a spell on" Kennedy. In fact, Kennedy had snared Swanson in a business trap from which she could not wriggle free. He'd sacked everyone connected with her production company save her publicity man and had put his own stooges on her new board of directors. He'd pressured her into surrendering her distribution rights to both *Sadie Thompson* and her first production, *The Love of Sunya,* in order to pay off her debts. Her only assets were now her screen acting—and her sex. Both of these Kennedy controlled. "In two months Joseph Kennedy had taken over my entire life," she later admitted. Her husband was soon "in Joe's employ and I was literally owned by him. My whole life was in his hands."

Swanson claimed she "trusted him to make the most of it." If so, her trust was misplaced. Kennedy longed to be what he was not, longed to shrug off the reluctant Boston-Irish-Catholic baggage he had insisted on bringing to New York, sacrificing it all now for a new life as a movie mogul and consort of the beautiful young Gloria Swanson, with world-famous directors like Erich von Stroheim working for him.

Up to this point in his life, Joseph Kennedy had never made anything but prefabricated ships and money. For all his banking credentials and his Harvard lecture series on the movie industry, he lacked status in Hollywood. By now attaching himself to Swanson and employing von Stroheim, he hoped that they could supply it. "By rearranging his cards a bit, and by bluffing a bit, he had managed to win a hand," Swanson later summarized, "and now his ambition was to stay in the game and start winning pots."

This was to be the familiar pattern of Joseph Kennedy's life, a long series of enterprises into which he would throw himself, but which, for all the millions that he earned, always ended in flight or ignominy. His ruthless steel-blue eyes cut through the flannel surrounding most of his contemporaries, however exalted, and his business acumen was sound. "Take Boston," he told Swanson. "The Cabots and the Lodges wouldn't be caught dead at the pictures, or let their children go. And that's why their servants know more about what's going on in the world than they do. The working class gets smarter every day, thanks to radio and pictures. It's the snooty Back Bay bankers who are missing the boat."

The snooty Back Bay bankers did know better, however, than to fantasize that they could produce great movies. Kennedy personally requested Stroheim to develop a new story in which Swanson would star, and Stroheim quickly obliged—"as ready," Swanson wrote, "to make an important original film for someone who could pay for it as Mr. Kennedy was anxious to enter the temple of art in the company of an acknowledged genius."

How Joseph Kennedy, whose highest artistic judgment was reflected in his wife's reproduction art posters hanging in their living room, and whose films at FBO had been about cowboys, football players, and African gorillas, imagined that he could change overnight into a creative patron/producer of cinematic arts defies belief. "He was a classic example of that person in the arts with lots of brains and drive but little taste or talent," Swanson later remarked. But this was said with hindsight.

At the time, Kennedy seemed bewitched by the twenty-seven-year-old's huge, pale eyes, pointed nose, and flawless complexion. The irony of her Maugham film—the story of a priest who falls in love with a harlot he is trying to rescue from the street—was lost on the forty-year-old Boston Irishman as he bedded Gloria each night at his rented house on Rodeo Drive in Hollywood. "At the end of the evenings, after our intimate hours together, Joe would have one of his horsemen drive me home," Swanson fondly recalled.

The affair, in some respects, was similar to that in a French farce, complete with the arrival in Hollywood of one of the marquis's elderly aunts, accompanied by a young lover, who wished to be shown the sights of Los Angeles by her married niece. "I had two distinct existences," Swanson chronicled, "one with Henri [the marquis], and one on Rodeo Drive with Joseph Kennedy when Henri was abroad."

Likewise, Joe Kennedy had two existences. Embroiled with Gloria, he was again absent as his wife gave birth in February 1928—though he turned up afterward at Rose's hospital bedside in Boston "with three diamond bracelets, which he had taken on approval so I could have my choice," Rose recalled. "A girl friend of mine had dropped in to visit. I put all three bracelets on at once, the better to compare them—and to say the least it was a glittering sight. My friend's eyes opened wide, and she turned to Joe and gasped, 'What can you possibly think of to give her next if she has the ninth baby?' Joe glared at me, 'I'll give her a black eye,' he said gruffly, and broke down with laughter."

The joke, however, was on Rose. Unhappy in New York, she spent the final month of her pregnancy back in Boston, near to her parents and friends—abandoning her seven children to the care of Eddie Moore, her husband's whoremaster. After the baby—another girl, christened Jean—was born, Rose went to Paris—leading one of Jack's teachers at Riverdale to remark that "every time Mrs. Kennedy had a baby, she hired another nurse and took another trip abroad."

To a neighbor Rose herself later confided that she made her husband "pay" for his infidelity. "I made him give me everything I wanted. Clothes, jewels, everything," she remarked—oblivious of the cost to her children of her spite. "Jack told a friend he used to cry every time she packed her bags until he realized that his crying irritated her no end and only made her withdraw from him even more," the family chronicler recorded.

Meanwhile, as one of the "four horsemen," Moore circled Swanson in Hollywood like a moth, treating her every wish as his command, and as alive to Kennedy's business involvement in Gloria Productions as to his sexual incorporation. Years later Joe would openly brag to Jack and Jack's wife about his affair with Swanson, regaling them with intimate details of Swanson's body, particularly her genitalia, making fun of Swanson because, he claimed, she was sexually insatiable, having orgasms not once but "five times a night"; but at the time it was Joe Kennedy who could not get enough of Swanson. Soon all of Hollywood was in the know, despite Kennedy's attempts to keep quiet the affair—"a modified version of William Randolph Hearst and Marion Davies," Swanson dubbed it.

Once Stroheim had completed his script, Joseph Kennedy returned to New York to read it. There Stroheim had the script presented "on a silver platter" carried "by two black men clad as Nubian slaves in lion's skins." Kennedy was ecstatic about the story—a wildly improbable gothic romance set in Germany and East Africa, provisionally titled *The Swamp.*

Swamp was a better description of Kennedy's private life than of Stroheim's new film. Traveling back by train to his young mistress in California, the Boston-Irish banker proudly showed her the screenplay. He'd purchased his wife's stoic loyalty with a diamond wristband, Swanson's sexual favors with four horsemen, and now he had the promise of a blockbuster movie. " 'Oh, I tell you, Gloria,' he said with solemn pride, pressing my hand tightly, 'this is going to be a major, *major* motion picture.' " He was "like a college boy wanting to jump for joy but compelled to be serious by the matter at hand."

True to his caution as a banker, Kennedy had first shown the script to the film and drama editor of *Life* magazine, who'd told him it was "the best film story ever written." To cover his investment, moreover, Kennedy had hired two producers to keep the notoriously spendthrift Stroheim "on a tight leash." But in truth Joseph Kennedy was dabbling in waters too murky for a banker. Carried away by Swanson's glamour, compared with Rose's frigid, Boston-Irish-Catholic values, Joe Kennedy wanted to see his own name in lights. "He had to prove himself and to me," Swanson commented. "All he could think of was presenting me in something that was his. Something important."

The next important thing Kennedy proposed to give Gloria was a baby. According to Swanson, this was in the fall of 1928, after he had begged her to come to New York. She was, she later claimed, taken aback by the proposition, aware that it would wreck her public image as a screen idol as well as her career—but the notion indicated the extent to which Joseph Kennedy had taken leave of his senses. He wanted to take her out in the evenings unescorted, yet also insisted she come home with him to meet his wife and children who were having a Halloween party in Riverdale.

"There in that strange situation," Swanson later wrote, "was all of the man's complexity in a nutshell. While he was in control, he saw nothing as impossible or out of the question. I couldn't even argue with him, because it would have done no good."

Swanson's daughter by a previous husband was also called Gloria, and was celebrating her eighth birthday. A compromise was reached whereby Gloria's two children would attend the Halloween party, though Swanson would not. The ubiquitous Eddie Moore ferried the children to the Kennedy household where they had "a wonderful time." Little Gloria "could not get over the fact that one family could have eight children in it. She had taken a particular shine to a boy called Jack, she said, who was a few years older than she was."

Eleven-year-old Jack was more interested in little Gloria's father. Swanson was puzzled. "Really?" Swanson pressed her daughter. "Why?"

"Because I told him Tom Mix goes to his restaurant for lunch," little Gloria replied.

It was, as Swanson later reflected, an extraordinary situation, with Rose Kennedy and her children unaware of what was happening under their very noses. Jack even sent his father a postcard, begging him in a postscript to "say hi to Gloria." But whether even Gloria Swanson herself understood what was going on was debatable.

Napoleon Deserts His Josephine

In the summer of 1928 the New York *Journal* was dubbing Joseph P. Kennedy the "coming Napoleon of the movies," for having merged FBO and Pathé, he'd also become "special adviser" to First National Pictures at an extra salary of $150,000 and had demanded dictatorial power over production and distribution.

Neither the New York *Journal* nor Gloria Swanson, however, could read the mind of this strange Irish corporal. It was assumed, when his contract was made out in August 1928, that Kennedy would go on to merge FBO, Pathé, and First National Pictures, making it the giant of the movie industry. However, the president of First National Pictures balked, Kennedy's contract was revoked, and he had no option but to resign from First National. Any possible merger of the companies was scuttled. Kennedy immediately booked passage aboard the *Isle de France* with his fellow FBO director, John Murdock, "to confer at length about the future of their enterprises." On his return he merged FBO with RCA to create RKO, a holding company with assets of some $80 million. He not only pocketed $150,000 for arranging the deal but promptly sold his shares

in FBO, together with Guy Currier's, for $5 million. In December 1928, a
year after he began committing adultery with Swanson, he sold his shares
in the new RKO consortium—managed now by RCA—for a further $2
million profit. By Christmas he was at least $5 *million* richer, but on the
island of Elba in terms of movies. Apart from a nominal consultancy with
Pathé, he no longer held a title or even shares in the movie business. The
"coming Napoleon" of the movies had come—and gone.

Whether Gloria Swanson realized that Kennedy was scuttling the
world of movies at the time is unclear. Kennedy had promised to relieve
her of all business worries in return for her sexual favors, and she had
complied, certain that he was infatuated with her. But was he still? He'd
claimed he wanted to make his mark in Hollywood by producing an
"important" picture that would etch his name in celluloid with that of the
acknowledged genius, Erich von Stroheim. Yet before Stroheim had even
begun filming, Kennedy had abandoned his post like a cowardly general
before battle. Why? Was the lure of so many millions too much for him?
Did he have a presentiment of failure? Or did he sense that for all his
energy and business sense he was a born loner, incapable of the give and
take with colleagues and subordinates that is essential in the long-term
management of a large company, just as he had failed as a manager of
men at Fore River shipyard ten years before? Certainly he had had the
movie industry at his feet in August 1928, yet months later he was an
outsider again, and would have been glad to liquidate his interest in
Gloria Productions, Inc.—except that there was nobody to buy her
shares.

This indeed was the rub, for by January 1929 he had loaned Swanson
almost three quarters of a million dollars and was well on his way to one
of the biggest fiascos in Hollywood history—a sad epitaph to his dreams
of cinematic greatness as a producer.

As a silent film, Stroheim's epic was redundant even before it was shot.
Kennedy himself had said to Stroheim, "Von, the lousiest sound film will
be better than the best silent film." Retitling *The Swamp* as *Queen Kelly*
did no good. It soared above budget, and Swanson lost her nerve. Disgusted by the way Stroheim was shooting the film, she walked off the set,
and called Kennedy.

"Joseph, you'd better get out here fast. Our director is a madman," she
told him. "You and everybody else tried to stop me from making *Sadie
Thompson*. Well, believe me, *Sadie Thompson* was *Rebecca of Sunnybrook
Farm* compared with what *Queen Kelly* is turning into. It's ruined! And
awful! Now, are you coming out here and starting to make decisions or
aren't you?"

Kennedy, in Palm Beach, had to try and forge a truce, which he did by asking Stroheim to complete the silent movie while Ben Glazier, one of the producers, would direct a talking version.

Once he arrived in Hollywood, Gloria showed Kennedy the tens of thousands of feet of obsolete silent celluloid. Kennedy had had a special bungalow constructed for Swanson on the Hollywood lot, complete with private bedroom. There, an hour later, "he slumped into a deep chair. He turned away from me, struggling to control himself. He held his head in his hands, and little, high-pitched sounds escaped from his rigid body, like those of a wounded animal whimpering in a trap. He finally found his voice. It was quiet, controlled. 'I've never had a failure in my life,' were his first words."

Swanson, filming with Stroheim every day since November 1928, had known this would happen. Joe's wife, however, claimed that Stroheim had "altered the story in ways Joe would not have dreamed of"—and gave as an example the case where "from von Stroheim's fertile mind came a graphic scene of a convent girl being seduced."

That scene, however, was not an alteration. Unknown or ignored by Rose, it had existed since Stroheim first presented the script to Kennedy. At Kennedy's insistence, Stroheim had merely cut the number of scenes, not altered their content. Nor was it the alterations to the script that worried Swanson: it was the growing sense of decadence that was swamping the film, which, she was certain, would make it impossible for the film to get past Will Hays, the Hollywood censor.

It is hard, more than half a century later, to credit the hypocrisy, double standards, and anxieties of that era. Gloria, petite and still only twenty-nine, had been quite prepared to act a sixteen-year-old virgin, standing with a group of convent girls in an African meadow, curtseying when a German prince rides by. She'd been quite prepared to have her "panties drop down around my ankles" and to "struggle with my feet to step out of them," a scene which first draws the prince's attention. She'd been quite prepared, seeing the prince laugh at her discomfiture, to "wad the panties up and throw them at him." What she was not prepared to countenance was the prince's reaction. Under Stroheim's insistent direction, Walter Byron, the actor, had not only to catch the panties, but to "pass them in front of his face. The idea of putting such an act into a film was so unthinkable in 1928," Swanson primly recalled, "as to be unmentionable."

At that very time, however, in the UFA studios in Berlin, and under the direction of another German genius, Josef von Sternberg, another actress was dropping (literally, from her boudoir) *her* frilly panties onto the surprised face of a Prussian schoolteacher following errant schoolboys to the *Blue Angel* nightclub. Von Sternberg's musical, a talkie starring Marlene Dietrich, would become the sensation of the year in Paris, London, and New York. Stroheim's silent *Queen Kelly,* by contrast, was simply abandoned.

Though Joe Kennedy clutched at every straw in an attempt to rescue the film from disaster and recover his loans to Gloria Productions, Inc., it was too late. Gloria herself began to explore the possibility of ditching her production company with its mounting debts and accepting a contract with the Hollywood producer Jesse Lasky, her old boss.

Kennedy, however, was not a man to let himself be dumped, at least not without a fight. He had "a drastic showdown" with Swanson, insisting that "some sort of a finish must be made because there was too much money at stake and too much loss of prestige if the picture was not finished." Richard Boleslavsky, a Polish émigré, was thus employed to reedit and add sound to Stroheim's rough cut, and a trio of new people—Sam Wood, Delmar Daves, and Laura Crews—were engaged to prepare a talking version.

Meanwhile, to placate his wife, Joe had bought Rose a house in New York that spring—a big twelve-room colonial on Pondfield Road in Bronxville, next to Riverdale. To sweeten Swanson in Hollywood, he agreed to finance a new talkie, *The Trespasser,* and left California for Boston, having heard that his father was dying of cancer of the liver. However, in mid-May Kennedy returned to Hollywood, and it was on the studio set that he received the telegram announcing, on May 18, 1929, his father's death in the Deaconess Hospital, Boston.

Kennedy's feelings were black. He did not even return for the funeral—"a source of painful regret for the rest of his life," Rose later claimed—though he did write a letter to his thirteen-year-old son, Joe Jr., to thank him for taking his place: "I have heard such lovely reports about you at Grandpa's funeral," he penned on June 3. "I am more than proud to have you there as my representative. Help mother out and I'll be with you as soon as possible." However, when Gloria innocently offered the services of her nutritional expert on hearing that Joe's retarded daughter, Rosemary, was in the hospital, Kennedy became livid. "I had seen him angry with other people, but now, for the first time, he directed his anger against me. It was frightening. His blue eyes turned to ice and then to steel. . . . Poor Joe, I thought sadly. He was already, in my eyes, extremely complex. Did this mean I had seen the tip of the iceberg?"

She had. She'd correctly sensed Kennedy's longing to make a "major" motion picture, but she seems to have had little idea of the celerity with which Kennedy had now discharged his Napoleonic ambitions, nor of the torment the love affair had caused his conscience. Above all, however, she could not credit his fury over the money he'd loaned her company—a concern that had led him to leave his dying father rather than risk losing more. Though he'd encouraged Gloria to proceed with her new movie, he was so fearful it would be another catastrophe that he deliberately stayed away from the first reading, sending Eddie Moore in his stead.

This new picture, a comedy, was made in a month, and promised to recoup for Kennedy some of the expenditures made on *Queen Kelly,* if well promoted. Big premieres were arranged in New York, London, and Paris, and since he was financing the film, Kennedy insisted he and his wife accompany Swanson to Europe.

It was in this extraordinary way that Gloria Swanson, idol of the screen, arrived by plane in the summer of 1929 at Hyannis Port. "Miss Swanson and her party landed on the harbor near the breakwater not far from Kennedy's summer house, in a Sikorsky amphibious aircraft. Hyannis Port residents gaped from the beach as Miss Swanson—petite, chic, flawlessly coiffed and a member of the aristocracy since her marriage to the Marquis de la Falaise de Coudraye—deplaned," a local writer recorded.

For the Kennedy children it was a memorable occasion, with Gloria even leaving her autograph on the garage wall that served as a clubhouse for nine-year-old Kathleen Kennedy and her friends. But the situation for Gloria and Rose Kennedy was, to say the least, bizarre. Rose pretended to know nothing of the affair, which Swanson later considered incredible. "Was she a fool, I asked myself as I listened with disbelief, or a saint? Or just a better actress than I was?"

But who was fooling whom? Swanson assumed that Kennedy adored her. Perhaps, in his way, Kennedy had—the year before. But by the summer of 1929 his honeymoon with Swanson was long over, and his flattery concealed his determination to make enough money on the new film to offset his staggering losses on *Queen Kelly.* Although in her memoirs Rose Kennedy confused the year and the month and gave a third-hand account of the Stroheim "fiasco," her essential memory was correct: that her husband had invested a fortune in *Queen Kelly* and could hope to recoup his losses only by aggressive publicizing of *The Trespasser.*

To Swanson, meanwhile, Kennedy pretended he was only taking Rose and his sister along as a treat to his wife. "She's never been to Europe," he lied, "and I've promised her this trip. Please, Gloria, she wants to meet you," Kennedy soft-soaped the actress. "When his mind was made up, there was not a big enough lever in the world to move him," Swanson recalled. "I might argue all day, but I knew he would only out-argue me. . . . He said I was making him very happy. He said everything would be fine."

In truth, Rose had been to Europe many times, most recently for three weeks, on her own, the summer before. But Joe's promise to Gloria of "Europe, lots of people, lots of activity, lots of fuss" was fulfilled. Wherever they went, Gloria Swanson was a star, an idol. Crowds gathered and went wild at the sight of her. Rose Kennedy was short—five foot three—but Swanson was even shorter, and boasted a Cinderella shoe size: 2½.

For Rose, the trip to Paris became an education in acting. Swanson fought with her husband in private, but appeared hand-in-hand with him in public—at Joe Kennedy's insistence. In her memoirs Swanson blamed Kennedy for the final breakdown of her marriage, claiming that the marquis was mortified by Kennedy's "fervent attention." Swanson recorded:

> If Henri had ordered me then and there to leave pictures and live with him on the farm he owned in France, I would have obeyed him. But he didn't. He couldn't. Joe Kennedy had compromised us both with his promises of enduring security, which Henri wanted as much as I did. Never before had I ever trusted another person to the extent I had Joe. In addition, I was genuinely fond of him. The man fascinated me. I honestly didn't know what to do. . . . I prayed that Henri would have the patience and love to wait until I could simplify my life again. For the moment, however, our three lives were tied in a complicated knot, and there was no way I could untie it. I, too, had to wait and hope.

Far from waiting, it appears, Swanson opened a billet-doux from Constance Bennett, a younger Hollywood star, addressed to the marquis, and threatened to start divorce proceedings against her husband just before the Paris premiere.

The trip now turned into another French farce, with the marquis retreating to alternative chambers at the Ritz in Paris and Swanson refusing to be seen in public with him. Kennedy's suite became a conciliation bureau, with Rose and his sister, Margaret, "concerned and perplexed," as Rose recalled.

The farce, of course, was Swanson's hysteria at discovering her husband's infidelity while she herself was traveling with her lover—indeed not only with her lover, but with her lover's wife and sister.

Perhaps, Swanson was unconsciously engineering a showdown to get Kennedy to declare himself. Certainly it is she who, years later, proclaimed that Kennedy had sought permission from the Catholic church to leave his lawful wife and openly live with her, and that "after the London premiere, Joe was more enamored of me than ever. In addition to his great infatuation, he now saw me as the only person he trusted in pictures who could instruct him."

In fact Joe Kennedy was long ago finished with the movie business. The last thing he wanted was instruction. What he wanted was his money back—and out. Although subsequent writers mocked Rose Kennedy for her wilful ignorance or indifference to the affair, it was in fact Rose who was in the ascendant and who felt compassion for the deluded screen goddess. While reporters "mistakenly decided that something was going on between the two of them," Rose later confided, "I knew I never had a thing to worry about and I only felt sorry for poor little Gloria."

She had every reason. Though Swanson went on to take London and New York by storm—having at one point to be carried facedown over the heads of the crowds to reach the movie theater—she was washed up, both as Kennedy's mistress and as a screen idol. Her subsequent films were flops, and though her legend survived, her fall was sad.

Meanwhile Rose Kennedy, sensing her own triumph, hurried "back to our children in Bronxville," she recalled. Jack had done exceptionally well at school, winning transfer from Class 5B to 5A in the spring of 1928, excelling in Class 6A the following academic year (his bimonthly grades in history were 90, 90, 95, 90, 97, and 91), and even winning the Riverdale School Commencement Prize for Best Composition.

Rose, however, was not interested in Jack's compositions. A new chapter was beginning in her life. In Paris she'd sat "fascinated as the beautiful mannequins slinked and slithered the length of the ornate salon" where Lucien Lelong's latest dresses were shown to Swanson, whose clothes bills were legendary. "Of course, being with Gloria magnified the experience, for the vendeuses and management hovered around her, attentive to her every whim; and both the girls and the customers kept stealing glances at her. She was the great celebrity. I, by comparison, was a nobody. . . ."

To the consternation of her children, the nobody was determined now to become a somebody.

A Haunting Reminder

Triggered by competition with Gloria, Rose Kennedy now began to indulge an obsession with jewelry and *grande toilette* that would almost match that of Wallis Simpson, later the duchess of Windsor. With her special perfumes (the secret of which she would refuse to share even with her daughters), her Cartier jewelry, and haute couture wardrobe, Rose was determined to reassert herself. "My own special interest in clothes developed during this period," she later explained, "not just from this episode but from the general circumstances of which it was an especially vivid part.

"Obviously I couldn't compete [with Gloria Swanson] in natural beauty," Rose acknowledged, "but I could make the most of what I had by keeping my figure trim, my complexion good, my grooming perfect, and by always wearing clothes that were interesting and becoming."

But if Rose Kennedy thought that a Gloria Swanson–style wardrobe would make entry into New York social circles easier, she was to be cruelly disappointed. New York society continued to shun the Kennedys as "Irish micks," as one of Jack's friends candidly put it. "Rose Kennedy—such a lovely person," was one typical condescension, "but what a *dreadful* voice she has."

Catholic circles remained especially shocked by the Swanson "affair," no matter what Rose said to discount it. Moreover, whatever Rose might say in her memoirs, the emotional scars it left took decades to heal. The Fitzgerald family certainly saw Rose as the hapless victim of Joe's gigantic selfishness, and never forgave him. Years later came a haunting reminder. "We were at LaGuardia," an American Airlines stewardess recalled:

> I worked on the Boston–New York route. It must have been late in 1944 or early 1945. There was a throng of newspaper reporters—they'd heard there was a celebrity arriving from California, and they were still waiting for the West Coast plane, even though it had been delayed. It must have been one-thirty in the morning. As they brought forward the airplane steps, a limousine drew up, and this little old man got out. I asked a trooper who it was—and he explained it was John Fitzgerald, the former mayor of Boston.
>
> When Gloria Swanson came out of the plane with Joe Kennedy, the mayor went berserk—went straight up to him and started bawling him out, in front of everyone, calling him—and her—every name under the sun—"How dare you, you son-of-a-bitch, cavorting with that floozie while my daughter is at home . . . " I was in my early twenties and had no idea *what* it was all about—but it was certainly very embarrassing in front of the reporters.

Fitzgerald was by then in his dotage. The scene, however, was cruelly evocative of what had taken place so many years before, and of how much Rose's father still suffered on her account. On the surface, once Joe ended his relationship with Gloria in the fall of 1929, Rose won her husband back. However, she paid a heavy price: condemned for decades to ridicule and social exclusion in America that often left her lonely and depressed, entailing deeper piety on the one hand and on the other, even longer absences abroad, where she would seek out the latest couturier styles or diamond settings.

"Well, you know they had all kinds of governesses," the son of Rose's doctor recalled. "They had a nurse in their employ, all the time, and when they went to the Cape, the same thing. . . . I don't think that they had what I would call close friends. They had a lot of associates. But I don't think that the children as such had close friends. Whenever there was a party or a get-together, there were plenty of them there, but I don't think they were close to anybody but themselves."

Thanks to the Swanson scandal, the Kennedys found themselves even less accepted in polite society. Behind a smoke screen of good, well-buttoned Catholic upbringing, however, the Kennedy children had always lived in social quarantine, forced to rely on one another. Even this refuge was about to be whisked away from them, though—for in the wake of the Swanson affair, there would be a new cross for them to bear: boarding school.

PART
·3·
BOARDING SCHOOL

Jack Kennedy (center, front row) at Riverside Country Day School, New York, aged twelve (John F. Kennedy Library)

A Good and Right School

In the years to follow, many writers would dress up the tragedy of the Kennedy household, painting the family as a perfect showcase of American parenting. Article after article, book after book would describe the manner in which Joseph Kennedy instilled into his offspring the need to be well-informed, to compete, and to win, while Mrs. Kennedy was extolled (and extolled herself in her memoirs) for her concern with social grooming, religious observance, and good teeth.

Sadly, the fiction was self-serving—the truth too painful to address. Not only was the record of parental absenteeism shockingly high, but the business with Swanson and the general deterioration in the relationship between mother and father created an emotional wasteland, inciting a bitterness, even self-destructiveness, in them that would inevitably take its toll. "I was shuffled off to boarding school at the age of eight," one of them later chided her mother.

"Well, what was I to do?" Rose retorted. "Your father was always gone. . . . I had no time to spend with you children."

But her daughter, now a grown woman, was not placated. "That's why I'm still trying to get my head on straight," she cried.

To be sure, the fate of the Kennedys was little different from that of countless English families in which social standing was an obsession and emotional neglect of children the norm; perhaps the reason why the elder Kennedy children would get on so well later with their English counterparts, leading ultimately to a series of transatlantic amours and two tragic marriages.

In the meantime, during the "extraordinary circumstances" of 1929 as the Roaring Twenties came to an end, the question of boarding school had already arisen. Traditionally English children were sent away to boarding school as part of their "training for life." This system, extensively developed in the nineteenth century, had resulted in a patchwork of private schools, each with its own ethos, producing an elite of emotionally blocked but capable administrators for Queen Victoria's expanding empire, imitated in America by the establishment of schools such as Groton, Milton, and Andover.

Though not a fan of things British, Joseph Kennedy was anxious to see his children excel in life and to help them break out of the social confinement in which, despite his sudden wealth, he felt snared. Thus, in the spring of 1929, Joe had already written to Russ Ayres, a former Harvard student whom he'd coached in baseball, and who had subsequently become a history teacher at Choate School in Wallingford, Connecticut. In his letter Joe had asked about the possibility of transferring his eldest sons to Choate at some future date from their day school in Riverdale for a year or two, to give them a better chance of getting into Harvard.

Ayres passed on the letter to the assistant headmaster of Choate, Wardell St. John. St. John replied that the school did take three or four such boys each year, and that the Kennedys, if they "continue the good records that they are apparently making at present," would have a "pretty good" chance of being accepted. At the same time, however, he urged Kennedy to "consider the possibility of letting your sons have at least three years in the school from which they plan to enter college—four, we believe, would be better! More and more," he added, "we see the added advantage that comes to the boy who has a really adequate chance to grow into the spirit of the School and to make a real place for himself among his fellows."

Joe Kennedy, at his offices at Pathé Exchange, Inc., on West Forty-fifth Street, hastily replied that he was attracted by "the advantages you set forth. My only hesitancy about doing it is I realize that when the boys go away now to school, they are practically gone forever, because it is three years there and then four years at college, and you realize how little you see of them after that. I may be selfish in wanting to hold on for another year at least," he explained, shortly before setting off for another month with his mistress in California. "However I am talking the matter over with his mother," he wrote, "and will try to come to a decision and make out the applications as you suggest."

Wardell St. John could sense he'd hooked his fish, and now he played it. "I want to thank you for your good letter of April 20th in regard to Joe and Jack—and their going away to School. I like it because it expresses completely that spirit of hesitancy which is so truly natural to a Mother and Father who have made home a place of happiness for their boys," St. John wrote back innocently. "Our Headmaster has often said, quite truly, 'When a boy goes away from a really happy home to a good and right School, he is bound more closely to his home than ever before. If it were not so, I could not permit myself to be the Headmaster of a Boarding School.' " He urged Mr. Kennedy and his wife and the two boys to "visit us at any time convenient to you, and so come to know us and our School at first hand."

There was not time, for there followed Kennedy's trip to Boston, his return to California, and the death of his father. However, the months in Hollywood and the plan to spend three months in Europe convinced Joe Kennedy he was going to see very little of his sons even if they remained at Riverdale Country Day School. Rose, responsible for eight children, proved even less anxious than her husband to keep them at home in their teens. Despite her preference for a Roman Catholic boarding school, she therefore voiced no protest—indeed, according to Joe, she was most enthusiastic. Thus, in the turmoil that was Joe Kennedy's life in the summer of 1929—promoting Swanson's film *The Trespasser* while trying to extricate himself from his own, monumentally expensive marital trespass—the fateful decision was made to send Joe Jr. to Choate School that very September, with the understanding that Jack would follow in due course.

. The staff at Riverdale Country Day School were less than pleased. The headmaster, Frank Hackett, considered Joe Jr. "one of the very best of our boys," with a "scholastic aptitude high above the average—just the sort of boy you want," he remarked feelingly in a letter to Wardell St. John at Choate, "but by the same token he is just the sort who should stay with us."

Joe Jr.'s day school career, however, was coming to an end. His teacher had extolled him as a "manly, clean-minded boy . . . an excellent worker who ranks in the upper quartile of his class . . . has a sound appreciation of what constitutes fair play. I consider him a very desirable boy." But arriving alone in Wallingford in September 1929—his parents still in Europe with Gloria Swanson—Joe Jr. found himself at the bottom of the Choate School heap, and was soon at the bottom of his class. That his parents would never come to see him at the school he gradually learned to accept—"We shall keep hoping that you can be with Joe and us on Fathers' Day," his new headmaster wrote on October 31 to Joseph Kennedy, "though Joe and I understand how it is."

The situation was in fact critical, for on October 29, not long after the Kennedy's return from Europe, the Wall Street stock bubble burst, triggering a crash to which Kennedy and others had, by their manipulations and swindling, so ignobly contributed. Anticipating a crash, Kennedy had shrewdly moved most of his investments out of stocks, but coping with Black Monday as well as his current attempts to sell Pathé and dump Swanson, he simply had no time for Fathers' Day. Thus it was Rose Kennedy who wrote from her new home at 294 Pondfield Road, Bronxville, to thank the headmaster for Joe Jr.'s first report and to say how "very sorry indeed" she was to hear that Joe Jr. was "not up to what he should be in his studies. . . . I am going to write to Joe and urge him to do better work, and I am sure he will co-operate, as he has never been satisfied to have a low standing in his class. I have sent the various [school] notes on to his father, who is in California." Meanwhile, she also arranged for Rosemary, her eldest daughter, to be sent away to an institution.

Joe Jr., receiving his mother's admonition, was upset. Returning to Bronxville briefly in November, he was full of bull—or so Jack maintained in one of his earliest surviving letters to his father (who was still away with Swanson): "When Joe came home he was telling me how strong he was, and how tough. The first thing he did to show me how tough he was was to get sick so that he could not have any Thanksgiving dinner. Manly youth. He was then going to show me how to Indian wrestle. I then through [*sic*] him over on his neck." As Jack also reported to his father, Joe Jr. been caught "roughhousing" by a sixth-former and was summarily punished: "Did the sixth formers lick him! Oh man, he was all blisters, they almost paddled the life out of him. . . . What I wouldn't have given to be a sixth former! They must have some pretty strong fellows up there if blisters have anything to do with it."

Jack's own performance at Riverdale, however, was slipping. "Creditable, Jack, 75—now for Honors," his lenient and understanding headmaster, Frank Hackett, urged in his report card in February 1930. But by then it was too late. Jack's days at Riverdale Country Day School were coming to an end, as Joe Jr.'s had the year before. He too would be sent away to boarding school. But it would not be Choate.

Canterbury

The original application for Jack to enter Choate in 1931, in the fourth form, had been signed by Rose Kennedy in May 1929, while her husband was with Swanson in California. A school note to Wardell St. John in the spring of 1930, however, recorded a telephone call from Rose, asking about Jack joining Joe Jr. at Choate in the fall of 1930, and wondering "if there is any way Jack could take entrance examinations without coming here. Exams to be sent if proper supervision can be arranged. She says Jack is about two years back of Joe. She said she wanted me to understand Jack wasn't definitely entered for Choate next September," Wardell St. John noted, "they are trying to make up their minds but felt the boy should take exam. Joe has been in the third form this year. So I should think Jack should enter Second Form. Here are English and Arithmetic and Otis Test for Second Form if you wish to have them go."

Jack took the Choate entrance exam, under supervision, at Hyannis Port in June 1930. However, Rose Kennedy again changed her mind. The Choate headmaster's son (who later became headmaster himself) recalled that although the Kennedys were pleased that Joe Jr. was gradually settling in at Choate, Rose had always disliked the school because of its Protestant bias—the headmaster, George St. John, being an ordained Episcopalian minister. Taking advice from her chaplain, Rose suddenly decided, in the absence of her husband, to send Jack to a Catholic boarding school in Connecticut, farther inland than Choate: a place after Rose's now frozen heart, set on a bluff, cold hill, by the edge of the small New England township of New Milford, with a Roman Catholic priest as headmaster and Roman Catholic teachers. It had fewer than a hundred pupils on its rolls, and its bleak, separate houses were grouped around a huge stone church at its center. Its name, ironically, was Canterbury.

Without a uniform, Jack Kennedy, aged thirteen, thus signed in at Canterbury School on September 24, 1930. He was one of thirty-two new boys.

Whatever the deficiency of family life for the Kennedys in Bronxville, life at Canterbury School was worse. In Pondfield Road Jack had at least an occasional mother, even if she did not exude maternal warmth. His father, though absent much of the time, was at least an occasional father. Moreover, despite his tendency to ill health, Jack had at least found a comfortable identity among his siblings at Bronxville. Within the somewhat philistine, regimented Kennedy clan, he was the bookworm, "the intellectual," the family wit with a gift for singular expression; both a member of the family and yet looking in on it from outside; ironic, often precociously sardonic; deliberately unpunctual, careless in his dress, in trouble with the neighbors; above all, determined from an early age to be himself rather than conform to his mother's mold.

Now, suddenly, thanks to Rose's arbitration, Jack found himself consigned to an alien institution in the wooded foothills of Connecticut, surrounded not by his own brothers and sisters but by fathers, brothers, and sisters of a very different kind.

"It's a pretty good place but I was pretty homesick the first night," Jack admitted in a letter to a relative. The handwriting was bold, with significant spaces between words, and the *t*'s crossed high. His observations, whether about himself or school, were similarly bold and emphatic, revealing a pronounced sense of self. "The swimming pool is great even though the football team looks pretty bad," the new boy judged. "You have a whole lot of religion and the studies are pretty hard. The only time you can get out of here is to see the Harvard-Yale and the Army Yale [game]. This place is freezing at night and pretty cold in the daytime."

The lack of requisite clothes irked him. "Send me up a gray pair of pants like Joe's please," he wrote to his mother, "and I can wear them with my blue coat and new black shoes and then I will be able to get fitted for a gray suit next time in N.Y. They have my size in N.Y. Sac's [*sic*]. Please also send my gray knickers till others come."

Ignoring Jack's request, Rose sent him a school suit which he promptly returned, saying he "did not like the color," and that "it was pretty itchy looking material." "I felt pretty homesick but it's O.K. now," he wrote in another letter, adding that he would "be quite pius [*sic*] I guess when I get home," after having to attend chapel every morning and evening. The Canterbury inmates were from Catholic homes almost without exception, and though the monastic spirit of the school might appeal to his mother—who only once ever visited the institution to which she'd exiled him—it was something of a trial to Jack. "Things are going pretty well up here and I got a couple of 95's and 92's with a couple of 85's and 73's. Science is pretty hard but I got a ninety in it yesterday. We have religious talks on Tuesday and Catacism [*sic*] on Wednesday. A lot of things have been swiped," he reported. "My sweat shirt, $5.00, $1.50 worth of stamps, fountain pens, pillows and $35.00 with lots of other stuff."

Life on the hockey and football fields was similarly tough: "My nose my leg and other parts of my anatomy have been risked around so much that it is beginning to be funny. I am trying out for the school paper, The Tabard. Look in next Tuesday issue about the Midget game. Lots of love Jack."

With the onset of winter there was "lots of snow and coasting." Jack even bought his own toboggan—"Have jewed sled down to $3.00 and maybe down more," he boasted to his father in the anti-Semitic tone of the school. "Benziger [the sled's owner] is more than dumb. . . . Excuse hast [*sic*] but bell is going to ring."

Sledding proved as dangerous as football, however. Torpedoing downhill at forty miles per hour, one of his companions hit a stone wall at the bottom. Jack found the boy "lying on the ground holding his stomach. We lifted him up, he began to faint and so we put him on my sled and towed him ⅓ mi up a hill, and then a ¼ mile to school. He was all gray and as we carried him upstairs, he fainted. He went to the hospital a [*sic*] hour later and he was just a white grayish color. I think maybe he was operated on yesterday but I am not sure. He had internal injuries and I liked him a lot. That about all. Love to everybody, Love Jack."

Permeating all Jack's letters home was a restless momentum, perhaps inherited from his spry grandfather Fitzgerald, who was so vivid and individualistic. "Please send me the Literary Digest," he wrote to his father from what he increasingly thought of as a Catholic concentration camp, "because I did not know about the Market Slump until a long time after, or a paper," he added.

However ruthless Joseph Kennedy might be as a market operator, he was disturbed by Jack's homesickness. Unhappy with his wife's choice of boarding school, he had already begun corresponding with Wardell St. John about the possibility of Jack transferring to Choate after Christmas. Rose, however, refused to countenance the idea. She too had been homesick when first sent to the Blumenthal Convent of the Sacred Heart school in Holland, but she had persevered. She felt strongly that Jack should stick out his first year at Canterbury, and the staff at Choate reluctantly concurred. "When we didn't hear, we took it for granted Jack would be returning to Canterbury. . . .

"This is a better solution although we would have welcomed Jack here," Wardell St. John wrote on January 20, 1931. "In any case," he assured Mr. Kennedy, "Jack is on our definite list for next Fall."

Having made his lonely way back to Canterbury, meanwhile, Jack tried hard. English, in which he was required to read his favorite author, Sir Walter Scott, remained his best subject, earning him a 95 grade, followed by 93 in math, 80 in history, 78 in science, and 68 in Latin (he would never do well in languages).

Such efforts were doomed, however, and whether for psychosomatic or physiological reasons, his always-tenuous hold on health now deserted him. A missionary came to talk to the school about India—"one of the most interesting talks that I ever heard," the thirteen-year-old described—but "when he was saying the Confiteor I began to get sick, dizzy and weak. I just about fainted and everything began to get black so I went out and then I fell and Mr. Hume [the headmaster] caught me. I am O.K. now," he reassured his father, adding, typically, that his brother Joe was known to have "fainted twice in church so I guess I will live."

Would he, though? It was soon clear that Jack's medical problems were of a different magnitude from his elder brother's growing pains at Choate. Far from growing, Jack began to lose weight as well as his ability to concentrate. "I was weighed yesterday and I have lost one pound and have not grown at all," he wrote to his mother in the spring of 1931. "I guess the only thing wrong with me is that I am pretty tired."

A few months before, he'd boasted that "though I may not be able to remember material things such as tickets, gloves and so on I can remember things like *Ivanhoe* and the last time we had an exam on it I got ninety eight." The days of 98's were over, however. "He can do better than this," his headmaster reported after he got a 55 in Latin, which pulled his average down to 77. "In fact, his average should be well in the 80's," Dr. Hume complained. Jack's father had a stern word with him—causing a chastened Jack to write to his mother that he was "doing a little worrying about my studies because what he said about me starting of [sic] great and then going down sunk in. I will admit I did not work anymore than usual and I got pretty good marks."

Anxious about Jack's health and spirits, Mr. Kennedy arranged for him to go to Palm Beach at Easter. "I hope my marks go up because I guess that is the best way to say thanks for the trip," Jack assured his father on April 15. There was no chance to improve his academic performance, however, for no sooner had he returned to Canterbury than he collapsed again with abdominal pains. "A nurse and surgeon were flown down to attend him," one teacher recalled. The surgeon, Dr. Verdi, decided that an appendectomy was necessary, and the emergency operation was performed at Danbury Hospital nearby. Normally a routine operation, the surgery proved traumatic, and given the slowness of Jack's recovery, it was decided on May 2 not to send him back to Canterbury School that term but to let him convalesce at home and be tutored. Though Jack made up his work and passed the school examinations for the year, it was the end of his one and only stint at a Catholic school. "It was not one of his better years," Rose later conceded.

Once again Mr. Kennedy wrote to Choate, and again exam papers were sent to Hyannis Port. With an IQ measuring 119 on the Otis test and high scores in English and algebra, Jack had no difficulty in satisfying the Choate entrance requirements—except in Latin. Rose apologized and assured Wardell St. John that Jack would "work down here every day with an experienced teacher and I hope—and I will make sure that by the end of September—he will know his first year Latin."

Wardell St. John replied that he was "especially glad that it seems practical for Jack to concentrate on that Latin this summer. We shall gladly let Jack try another Examination in the fall on October 2nd, for we are just as anxious as he is in regard to his starting a straight Third Form schedule. I guess Jack will simply have to work on this job as one that just has to be done, even though there seems comparatively little at least in the elements of the subject to fire one's imagination. Perhaps there's a certain inspiration that comes from doing any job to the best of one's ability— though I agree with Jack that English and History are far more interesting in themselves. A good summer to Jack in spite of the Latin. We like to think, even, that some work during the summer is profitable simply from the standpoint of conquest."

Wardell St. John's letter typified the stuffy, worthy style of Choate School—a school with which Jack Kennedy was now to have a strange love-hate affair: the battleground of his adolescent ego.

Choate School

To slog away at Latin all summer in the Belmore Tutoring Studio was purgatory for Jack. Nevertheless his tutor, Bruce Belmore, was impressed by the fourteen-year-old and wrote to Wardell St. John to say that Jack was "a fine chap. He will be a credit to Choate."

Joe Jr. had meanwhile become not only a credit to Choate but the pride of his parents, who according to Rose were about to undergo a "golden interval" in their otherwise bumpy marital life. According to Swanson, Joe had merely switched his amorous tentacles to a new actress, Nancy Carroll; but the danger of a relationship that might break up the family had receded. "When Joe realized how close he had come to destroying his family," a friend later recalled, "he determined that from there on in, he would keep his encounters with women at a more casual level." The early summer of 1931 would be, however, the last time he slept with Rose: resulting in a ninth and final pregnancy. The child, born the following February when Rose was forty-one, turned out to be a boy, whom Jack recommended they christen George Washington Kennedy (since he was born on Washington's birthday), but who was instead given the names of Kennedy's trusted aide and confidant, Edward Moore.

Meanwhile, on Cape Cod in the summer of 1931, the family limelight shone on Joe Jr. as he proudly drove the family Rolls across the Hyannis airfield to greet Russell Boardman, whose plane *Cape Cod* had recently made the longest nonstop flight in history: fifty-five hundred miles in forty-nine hours. In front of thousands of spectators, at the head of six bands, a drum corps, and sixty floats, Joe Jr. drove the famed aviator and his copilot through the streets of Hyannis Port to a grand banquet, spawning in Joe Jr.'s breast the notion that he too would one day become a flying hero.

At sixteen, Joe Jr. had grown into a big, husky lad, quick-witted and determined to win his father's blessing. "Joe is established as one of the 'big boys' of the school on whom we are going to depend," the headmaster's wife confided to Mrs. Kennedy a few days after the fall term began. Jack, by contrast, had mislaid the notice telling him when to appear for his third attempt at the entrance exam, prompting his mother to cable the school from Cape Cod, where she was resting. At one-twenty P.M. on Friday, October 2, 1931, Jack signed in at Choate School and retook the Latin test, which he passed, thus permitting him to enter the third form.

"Everyone likes your boy," the headmaster's wife soon wrote to Mrs. Kennedy, "and he is rapidly making a real place for himself in the life of the school." Jack had come down "with the other new boys for ice cream, friendliness and singing around the piano," she assured Mrs. Kennedy. Her husband, George St. John, was equally solicitous about the new Kennedy's welfare, noting that "Jack sits at a nearby table in the Dining Hall where I look him in the eye three times a day, and he is fine."

Within weeks, however, the headmaster's tone had changed. Jack's square head seemed not to be fitting into the round Choate hole to which it had been assigned. As his housemaster, Earl Leinbach, reported, "Jack has a pleasing personality, and is warmly received by all the boys in the house, but rules bother him a bit."

This was an understatement. Jack had been billetted in the old timber-frame building known as School House with Godfrey Kauffmann, whose father owned the Washington *Star*. To Kauffmann, Jack's untidiness was as irritating as it had been to Jack's elder brother. Separated only by a dresser, their beds were too close for comfort—particularly as Kauffmann's stood by the window, while Jack's bordered the clothes closet, which rapidly deteriorated into a garbage heap. Kauffmann had brought his own antique oak desk, "double pedestal variety," as well as a Morris chair and appliquéd Egyptian wall hangings, which served as floor coverings. As he later recalled, "There was a small rug of sorts—or perhaps two, because I definitely remember after some major squabble we divided the room into two parts with his possessions on one side and mine on the other."

Jack's possessions, other than his favorite books, were minimal, from a family that had money but no genuine antiques. "Because of their explosive temperaments, Jack and Godfrey asked frequently to be separated," Leinbach related, and eventually, after a mammoth, two-day squabble, Leinbach had no option but to take the matter to higher authority—which, as Kauffmann later recalled, "rather abruptly resolved the disagreement."

Leinbach may have settled the dispute, but his trial with Jack Kennedy was just beginning. An ex-U.S. Intelligence officer in the Great War (hence his nickname, "Cap"), Leinbach taught mathematics, coached football, and was married to a beautiful blonde from South Carolina whom the boys all fancied. Leinbach had been captured by the Germans "behind the lines and doing intelligence work, I guess," the headmaster's son, Seymour St. John, later recalled, "and he was taken out to be shot. And in a way I've never quite understood, he disarmed his captors and got away, escaped. He was the kind of guy that would do that, if anybody would. 'Cappy' liked Jack, he was fond of kids, that was his 'basic.'"

This "basic" was to be of vital importance for a boy with considerable talent but little in the way of maternal love. The headmaster would later refer to Leinbach's "genius" in handling Jack, but undoubtedly the secret lay in Jack's respect for his housemaster's military courage and gratitude for his fondness. Leinbach reported a "gradual improvement" in the boy's behavior by the end of his first month, noting that "Jack found it irksome to settle down, is naturally active and impulsive, but he has responded and is now exceedingly cooperative. He is in all respects a fine citizen."

The accolade was premature, for Jack's performance in class left much to be desired. There was no history taught in the third form, and the dreaded Latin, under Mr. Warren, took up many hours of the curriculum as did French, neither of them subjects that "fired his imagination." Though Jack excelled in English, the headmaster was dissatisfied. "Jack's

results are not yet commensurate with the standard we set for him. . . .
His problem is still one of application," he wrote to Mr. Kennedy, who
replied that he had "read with a great deal of interest the master's comments on Jack's progress for the first month. I agree entirely. I feel that
Jack has a great deal of natural ability, but is careless in applying it.
Unless he receives pretty strict supervision, it might react against him as
time went on."

This was to be Joseph Kennedy's stance for Jack's next four, grueling
boarding-school years, reinforcing fourteen years of sanctimonious attempts by Rose Kennedy to discipline the boy. While Rose Kennedy
contented herself, from afar, in plying her children with trite warnings
about health, posture, teeth, eyesight, and diet, Joseph Kennedy's approach to parental guidance was even simpler: to urge his children to
compete and win. "Not once," acknowledged the family chronicler later,
"in more than two hundred letters did he put forward any ultimate moral
principles for his children to contemplate. On the contrary, he stressed to
his children the importance of winning at any cost and the pleasures of
coming in first."

But with Joe Jr. now performing a star role at Choate School, how was
Jack to come in first?

Black Sheep

It wasn't long before Jack fell sick at Choate, as at Canterbury. By
November 1932 he was in the school infirmary, and when he went home
for Thanksgiving, his father was disagreeably surprised. "Jack looks a
little thin," Mr. Kennedy complained in a letter to the Choate headmaster. "Maybe he still eats only the things he wants to eat," he added, a
remark which was soon followed by a torrent of missives from Rose
Kennedy to the headmaster's wife, insisting that Jack take regular doses
of cod-liver oil.

Back at school after Christmas, Jack was again ill, necessitating another sojourn in the infirmary. "Jack was looking most picturesque in a
lavender bathrobe, with lavender and green pajamas and seemed to be
settling in for a pleasant stay," Clara St. John reported to Mrs. Kennedy.
"I told Jack that Mr. St. John would give him a 'high A' when he
discovered that Jack had taken all his study books with him."

The stay, however, proved unpleasant. Mrs. Kennedy meanwhile discussed Jack's health with her nurse. "She and I remember that about
three years ago he had a condition similar to the one you describe," she

wrote back to Mrs. St. John. "He had had mumps and the doctor thought it was a cold which settled there. I am writing you this hoping it may help the doctor analyze the ailment."

It didn't, however. Nor did Kepler's malt, Rose's preferred solution. "Don't be discouraged with me for writing that Jack is still in the Infirmary," Clara St. John apologized to Mrs. Kennedy. "I have been wholly truthful with you, all along, and he is now no worse and we are in no way troubled about him, but he still has quite a cough and it doesn't seem worthwhile to let him go back to his room where he will have to go out to meals rain or shine (and it has been rain, pretty steadily!) and cannot be watched hour by hour."

Eventually Jack was released, though the doctor could arrive at no diagnosis. "I finally got out of the infirmary and the doctor said that I did not have the mumps," Jack wrote to a friend at Lawrenceville. Meanwhile, on Rose's behalf, Mrs. St. John instructed Jack's housemaster to give "Kepler's . . . until he is full of 'pep.' " Rose, however, had heard from Jack and was alarmed, writing immediately to complain to the school:

> Dear Mrs. St. John,
>   I understand from Jack's letter that he is much better, and he also said something about eating in the Tuck Shop in order to get "built up." I was a bit worried at that suggestion because the Tuck Shop usually means sweets to me, and Jack has no discretion; in fact he has never eaten enough vegetables to satisfy me.

Rose, unwell herself and in the final month of her last pregnancy while her husband cavorted yet again with cronies and other women in Florida, was subsuming a multitude of frustrations by such missives which, as St. John's son later recalled, "nearly drove my mother mad."

Jack was not the only object of Rose's nagging. Rose was also irritated by her twelve-year-old daughter Kathleen's growing popularity with boys. Vivacious and lively, Kathleen "was on the telephone with them for hours at a time and was being distracted from her schoolwork and other duties by boys inviting her to the Saturday-afternoon movies and so forth. My answer to the situation was to send her away to school," Rose herself admitted, insisting that Kathleen be sent to one of the very Sacred Heart convent schools at which she herself had been so unhappy, even when considerably older than Kathleen.

For Jack, meanwhile, the constant pressure to perform and to conform proved unbearable. More and more he sought sanctuary in the infirmary, however little consolation this brought from Bronxville. "I was often anxious about his physical health in those years; and so was his father,"

Rose later wrote of Jack. "Yet by that time, I suppose, both of us were accustomed to the idea that every now and then he would be laid up by some disease or accident. What concerned us as much, or more, was his lack of diligence in his studies; or, let us say, lack of 'fight' in trying to do well in those subjects that didn't happen to interest him." While Joe Jr. had "no trouble at all" operating in the "highly structured" system of Choate School, "Jack couldn't or wouldn't conform. He did pretty much what he wanted, rather than what the school wanted of him."

The result was another batch of disappointing school reports. "Jack's problem, with the exception of English, remains essentially the same," Mr. St. John wrote to Mr. Kennedy. "Emotionally, Jack wants to succeed and is quite distressed with the results. The fact remains, however, that Jack, at present, lacks the stability and the power of concentration to do a really effective job. But the ability is there in full measure—it is just a question of Jack's 'growing up.' "

St. John earnestly recorded how "Mr. Leinbach, Jack's House Master . . . is checking Jack carefully in his taking of medicine and also his tendency to carelessness. Though the same lack of responsibility characterizes his conduct in his house, Jack is gradually gaining a more mature point of view about it all. . . . Jack is so pleasantly optimistic and cheerful that he makes all of us want to help him. He challenges the best that's in us—and we're giving it, with full confidence in the outcome."

Though he went home for Easter, Jack fell sick yet again in April with another strange "swelling" on his neck, lying for a further week in the school infirmary, diagnosed this time as "non-infectious Parotitis"— mumps. His poor grades in French and Latin, however, alarmed St. John as workmen arrived to install Mr. Kennedy's promised talking-movie equipment (supplied at cost). "Is Jack studying any harder and any more steadily?" the headmaster asked in a guilty note to Cap Leinbach.

Jack's housemaster patiently replied that he had outlined for Jack "each step of his courses. I have required him to attend a conference every day in some failing subject. I have him repeat his French and Latin vocabularies to me every night. He is not allowed to leave his room during study period. I have worked with him in algebra. There is little left undone. The trouble is largely one of immaturity and inability to concentrate effectively. What makes the whole problem difficult is Jack's winning smile and charming personality. . . . It is an inescapable fact that his actions are *really* amusing and evoke real hilarity."

Jack's reputation for wit and clownishness was certainly being established. Plainly, he wanted to find an identity that would be his own, not his dutiful elder brother's, nor one that was in the image of his mother's *Ladies Home Journal* values. When his mother sent fresh oranges from Florida in an attempt to wean Jack from the Tuck Shop, he merely used them as ammunition with which to bomb passersby. A part of him yearned still to belong to the "orphanage" that was his Bronxville home, and he even wrote to beg that he be allowed to stand godfather to the lastborn, Edward, as his elder brother had been allowed to stand godfather to Jean. His letters were always filled with references to his younger siblings, for they at least looked up to him, and were privy with him to the family secret: the undeclared war between their parents, with its manic and repressive repercussions.

"We were really organized. It was an extraordinary thing the way she had us all—I guess the word is disciplined," Eunice later recalled of her mother. There was a downstairs bathroom in Bronxville, and after breakfast "we'd file in and out one by one. Then stand inspection for spots on our clothes and general neatness." Yet, when Joseph Kennedy was home, Rose became invisible. She "sort of let him take over." Not being a reader, Mr. Kennedy "disliked having the children indoors when he was at home," Eunice recalled. "So far as I can remember the first time in my life I ever stayed indoors was when I was in my thirties and had a baby and had to stay in. . . . And I thought, How odd, some people stay in and read all day." If Mr. Kennedy "discovered the children lounging around or relaxing," Kathleen's biographer was later told, "he would shoo them off their seats with the command 'Go *do* something!'"

He was "always rather harsh," Jack later confided. "I don't think his health was good, he was always living at a nervous pitch, he was speculating and all the rest. So he was always somewhat peremptory. . . . He was always emphasizing racing, that we always do well. . . . I make this point, that he set rather a stand for action."

Small wonder, then, that in such philistine surroundings Jack was considered by his siblings to be the odd one out. As Eunice put it, "Jack did the best on all the intellectual things and sort of monopolized them." He was also the family joker: witty, irresponsible, irreverent, careless, and tardy, refusing to conform like the other children to Rose's pathetic preoccupation with manners—manners that merely concealed the unhappiness of her marriage and her social exclusion.

School, though even worse than Rose in its mania for rules, at least provided Jack with plenty of targets for lampoon—and a larger audience than at home.

On one occasion Jack stole a life-size cardboard cutout of Mae West from the Wallingford cinema and slipped it into his bed to shock the cleaning woman the following morning. He was as late for chapel as for lessons. By the spring of 1932 matters came to a head, with poor reports and the likelihood that Jack would fail his end-of-year examinations. Rose was furious, as Mrs. St. John reported to Jack's director of studies, "I had an impassioned telephone message from Mrs. Kennedy, that things must be arranged so that Jack does not have to tutor this summer. She said that with nine children it was impossible for her to take on the additional burden."

"Mrs. Kennedy hopes awfully that Jack isn't going to study this summer, as it will be a great inconvenience to the family plans," Mrs. St. John simultaneously notified Jack's housemaster. "Will you have a talk with Jack emphasizing this?" Even the school secretary pressed Mr. Leinbach, urging him to "talk with Jack Kennedy, spurring him if possible to finish well this term so that he will not have to do any summer work. His mother telephoned Mrs. St. John particularly to ask that it be avoided if possible."

Jack's director of studies, however, was firm. "Jack Kennedy has a high IQ, and is one of the most undependable boys in the Third Form," he responded ominously. "I don't see how we can by any means guarantee he won't have to tutor this summer. We could relieve her of all worry if she would send him to the summer session."

As it turned out, further incarceration at Choate that summer became inevitable. Despite the efforts of his teachers, Jack failed both French and Latin in his end-of-year exams. The French teacher, Mr. Davis, was fond of Jack. In an allusion to his unkempt, bushy hair, he nicknamed Jack "Le Petit Chou" but could do nothing to inspire Jack's interest in the French language. "There is actually very little except physical violence that I haven't tried!" he lamented in a note to the headmaster. "His papers are chaotic, and he invariably forgets books, pencil or paper."

Cap Leinbach, in his report, was similarly despairing. "Impulsive actions characterize his every move, but very rarely are any of them malicious—just adolescent whims and fancies. This habit lends inconsistency to his scholastic drive with resultant mediocrity," Leinbach noted. "To fasten his mind upon an assigned task is his most difficult job, for he is bubbling over with a host of half-formed ideas of a different type.

"Whenever Jack wants a clean shirt or a suit," Leinbach went on, "it is necessary for him to pull every shirt or suit out of the drawer or closet, and then he 'does not have time' to put them back. His room is inspected night and morning every day, and I always find the floor cluttered up with articles of every description. When he sees me enter the room he will at once start to put everything in order. He does it willingly and often remarks, 'I never get away with anything in this place.' "

To Jack's father the headmaster admitted failure. "We have had a real job on our hands, one bigger than we could accomplish in one year. We have tried our hardest, but the amount of training and self-training which Jack has needed to become efficient have been too much for us. If Jack were my boy, I would send him to summer school from August 7th to September 15th. I think Jack needs to learn right now that work which is not done during the regular school year has to be made up in the summer."

Mr. Kennedy concurred. The assistant director of the summer school wrote directly to Jack on July 30, telling him to assemble with the other recalcitrants on August 7 "so as to make out their schedules and begin work promptly the next morning."

Jack's dream of a summer vacation on Cape Cod, sailing the new Wianno Star-class boat his father had bought (christened *One More* following the birth of "Teddy"), was shattered. "I am glad that you are coming," the assistant director added, "for I think you really need what the Summer School has to give."

What the summer school had to give, however, was not what Jack Kennedy wanted. Though he made sure he never failed his exams again, he was damned if he was going to change his ways.

Fostering a Gang Spirit

While Jack returned to Choate in August 1932 to make up for his idleness, Joe Jr. enjoyed the sun and sea at Hyannis Port. He even had a school friend to stay. This friend subsequently wrote to thank Mrs. Kennedy, and Rose was appalled by the letter. In her spindly hand she wrote instantly to complain to Mr. St. John:

> The fact has come to my attention that some of the boys at Choate do not seem to know how to write a letter correctly or how to address it. It seems to me it would be a very practical idea and a very useful one if a short period could be given demonstrating the different forms: if a boy wants to order a catalogue—if a boy wants to write to me after having visited Joe here at the house. I was astonished at the lack of familiarity with the usual forms.

The importance of forms was becoming more and more of an obsession with Rose. More troubling still was her assertion that "all nine children are well and happy, and Joe and Jack grow more helpful every year." In fact, she hadn't seen Jack since he departed for Choate on August 7, a month before. "Mr. Kennedy and I expect to go to Choate soon and are looking forward to seeing you," she wrote in closing—though she would never, in fact, visit the school in Jack's lifetime, and even missed Joe Jr.'s confirmation.

The ex–Hollywood czar had new reason to be absent, however. He had become involved in a fresh attempt at "production." This time the "star" was a politician, the very man who had had to sort out the mess at Fore River when Joe caused the 1917 shipbuilding strike: Governor Franklin D. Roosevelt, whose presidential aspirations Joe Kennedy chose now to espouse.

Later Kennedy boasted that he was "the only man with more than $12 in the bank who openly supported" Roosevelt. This was make-believe. Jesse Straus of Macy's, Edward Flynn, Colonel House, Judge Worth Bingham, William Woodin, and Herbert Lehman had all backed Roosevelt financially long before Kennedy appeared on the scene. However, Kennedy was certainly seized by the challenge of making Roosevelt president and already in May 1932 had left home to sell himself as a banking genius to the Democratic contender in Warm Springs, Georgia. From Warm Springs he went on to attend the Democratic Convention in Chicago in June, and once Roosevelt won the nomination, Kennedy was asked to board the "Roosevelt Special," Roosevelt's campaign train, for the first part of the candidate's journey through Missouri, Kansas, Utah, Montana, Washington, Oregon, and California.

To the *Boston Globe* reporter Joe Dinneen, Kennedy later boasted he'd "managed Roosevelt's tour of the country" as "the executive in command, assigning quarters to the staff on the special train and in hotels, arranging meetings with Democratic leaders in key cities, setting up press conferences." Dinneen reported that Kennedy "was quiet, efficient, the man to see before meeting the candidate, but otherwise unobtrusive in the background."

This, too, was moonshine. Roosevelt had his own hand-picked staff who made all arrangements on the trip, and Kennedy was only brought along in order to solicit funds from businessmen. When he managed to raise only $150,000, he felt compelled to raise the figure up to $200,000 out of his own pocket—though in typical fashion he gave the money not as a donation such as he was soliciting, but as a loan which he was entitled to—and later did—call in.

Forced, like all presidential hopefuls, to take strange bedfellows in his bid for the White House, Roosevelt tolerated Kennedy, but had no illusions about the Boston-Irish braggart. Kennedy, equally, had no illusions about what he was really up to. By nature an outsider, he was a shrewd insider when he wanted to be. Just as he'd used his eyes and ears to gain an inside view of banking, shipbuilding, share trading, and film production until the fiasco of *Queen Kelly,* so now he enjoyed the camaraderie of Roosevelt's campaign entourage while carefully observing the making of a U.S. president—lessons that one day he might put to his own use.

Meanwhile, as Jack's father sought to help make Roosevelt president,

Jack himself began his second year at Choate, this time in East Cottage under Mr. Eugene Musser.

To Jack's disappointment, Musser proved no challenge at all. "I want to come back to School House," Jack soon complained to Cap Leinbach. "Down where I am now, I can get away with anything and it's no fun!"

Fun—as it would be for the rest of his days—was fast becoming the leitmotiv of Jack's existence. His behavior at Choate became more and more outrageous. Musser was driven to complain of Jack's "tendency to foster a gang spirit." Disappointed, Mr. St. John noted, "All last year I worried about Jack Kennedy; but far less because he was under such a perfectly splendid housemaster as Mr. Leinbach, a genius in the way he dealt with Jack. Now, after all Mr. Kennedy has done for us [i.e., supplying the school's movie projector], Jack is in the East Cottage. He is an able boy with the cleverest turn of mind. I don't think Mr. Musser is at all the right man to handle him during this phase of his development. Can we place Jack with an older, experienced Master, one with a sense of humor and a rod of iron?"

The rod of iron, however, would have to wait. Before the headmaster could act, Jack once more fell ill.

Missing an Opportunity

Throughout most of January and February 1933 Jack was confined to Choate's infirmary with strange, "flu-like symptoms." He also suffered pain in his knee, which his mother in Bronxville had no hesitation in ascribing to the fact that "he has persisted in wearing cheap, rubber soled shoes during the last two or three years." "Jack's winter term sounded like a hospital report," the headmaster's son, Seymour, later recalled, "with correspondence flying back and forth between Rose Kennedy and Clara St. John. Again, eyes, ears, teeth, knees, arches, from the top of his head to the tip of his toes, Jack needed attention."

Even Jack's father joined the fray, complaining to him that "there is a charge of $10.80 for suit pressing for the month of March. It strikes me this is very high and while I want to keep you looking well, I think that if you spent a little more time picking up your clothes instead of leaving them on the floor, it wouldn't be necessary to have them pressed so often."

Joseph Kennedy was a disappointed man. After all the excitement surrounding Roosevelt's nomination, election, and inauguration, the new president had not offered Kennedy a job in his new administration. Kennedy, therefore, retreated to his specialty, the stock market. Within months he was implicated in the infamous Libby-Owens-Ford stock-jiggling scandal, a scam to confuse in the public mind two companies with the same name, which netted him a further fortune in the summer of 1933. "All through the campaign, his voice had been clear on the need to reform the speculative system in order to protect the ordinary man," the Kennedy family chronicler recorded sadly. "Yet now that he was being snubbed by Roosevelt, he was capable of ignoring everything he had said in order to act in his own self-interest," indifferent to "the effect of his profiteering on the continually declining market."

Meanwhile, unaware of his father's shenanigans, Jack slaved to avoid another summer of remedial classes. His results for the 1932–1933 academic year were in fact the best he would ever achieve at Choate: 81 in English, 71 in algebra, 73 in French, and 69 in Latin (a dreaded subject he was able to give up once he'd passed the college-board examination with a 75 for Latin and an honor grade of 82 in algebra).

Jack's teachers were pleased by this apparent progress. He'd written a "splendid final examination" in English, despite chronic misspellings such as "attemp, jelousy, comming and sieze." His algebra, too, was "an achievement for him in that it was neat, accurately (not one careless error) and intelligently done," Mr. Leinbach remarked. "I admire his whole-hearted tenacity when faced with an obstacle," Leinbach said, summarizing Jack's progress in mathematics. "He dogs my footsteps until he has obtained a comprehensive grasp of the difficulty. I look forward to steady improvement. . . . Jack has worked harder than ever before and richly deserves success."

The French teacher, however, complained that Jack "continually asks questions that have no bearing on the matter being discussed" in an attempt to get away from the rituals of French grammar. The school's overall view of Jack's progress was therefore guarded, especially in comparison with his elder brother's model performance, which ended that June in a blaze of glory when Joe Jr. won the coveted Harvard Trophy, awarded to the graduating student who best combines scholarship and sportsmanship.

"It must make you very proud, as it does us, that Joe should have won this award," St. John wrote to Mr. and Mrs. Kennedy, who once again had failed to attend Field Day. "I wish you could have been here on Saturday to see both your boys take part in the Crew races, and to see Joe march up the aisle for the Prize Day ceremonies, with a hundred and twenty other Sixth Formers. He is one of the fellows on whom we most completely depend, and it gives us a very tight feeling in the throat to think of his leaving us."

By contrast, some of the staff shuddered at the thought of Jack Kennedy rejoining them. Nor was Jack excited by the prospect of two more years of penal servitude at the school. "I'll see you next fall—which is a damn sight too near for comfort," he wrote to his classmate K. LeMoyne ("Lem") Billings at the end of June from Cape Cod.

Jack was barely sixteen but in spirit had already begun to outgrow the school. Joe Jr., as a reward for doing so well at Choate, was traveling to England where, on the advice of Supreme Court Justice Felix Frankfurter, he was to start a year's study at the London School of Economics under Professor Harold Laski. Jack's parents were sailing with Joe Jr. and were taking as their guests the president's son, James Roosevelt, and his wife. In a last bid to avoid reimprisonment, as he saw it, Jack begged to be allowed to accompany his parents on their trip to Europe. Rose, perhaps in guilt at the seventeen times she had traveled abroad without her children since the end of the Swanson affair, offered to call and ask Mr. St. John about taking Jack along.

"Said she wondered what we would think of Jack's being out of school for the first five weeks," Mr. Owen, the school secretary, noted on September 23. "It seems that the Kennedys are going to Europe with James Roosevelt and wife, of the President's family, to meet important people of Europe—Mussolini, etc. Mrs. Kennedy thinks it would be too bad to have Jack miss such an opportunity. Sailing in three or four days."

Rose's request put the school in an awkward situation. "It seems too bad that Jack should be away now when we have had such a time getting him started. I promised Mrs. Kennedy I would talk the matter over with various men who had taught Jack, and that I would call her next day at noon," Mr. Owen reported to the headmaster, who was away. Meanwhile he "telephoned Mrs. Kennedy Sunday noon. I tried to give her both sides of the story, and let her make her own decision. She wanted to get in touch with Mr. St. John or Mr. Steele, but I was fully aware she merely wanted them to say yes, when I conscientiously believe she ought to make that decision herself—or at least she and Mr. Kennedy ought to make it."

Jack, after all his efforts at self-improvement in the spring, was crestfallen when it was decided he would not be going, especially when he learned his father had written a plaintive letter to the headmaster, before embarking, in which he urged Mr. St. John to keep Jack's nose to the grindstone. "I feel that the fundamental thing to watch is the absolute necessity of keeping him employed in various enterprises. . . . He still has a tendency to be careless in details, and really is not very determined to be a success."

Mr. Kennedy's letter was to have serious repercussions, for St. John wrote back promptly to say Jack would now board in the school's West Wing under the notorious school disciplinarian, J. J. Maher. "There is no finer man on earth," St. John assured Mr. Kennedy. "Maher brought up all three of my sons, and all of our family are in his debt for life."

It was not a debt, however, that Jack intended to incur as he embarked on the next stage of what would prove grueling adolescence.

A Serious Illness

To many Choate students J. J. Maher was a god. "He was a highly disciplined fellow," St. John's son later recalled. "He lived in Bridgeport, came as a scholarship boy to Choate in the early 20s, was an excellent athlete, good at basketball, went on to Harvard, played on the Harvard team and then came back to Choate to teach. My family were very fond of him—he stayed with our family in the summers on Rhode Island as our family tutor. As I say, he was personally disciplined, and I liked him *very* much."

But Jack Kennedy despised Maher. He found his short temper, bullying nature, and nagging expectations similar to his father's. What Jack wanted was not exhortation but *affection*. Great teachers like Miss Fiske in Boston and Mr. Leinbach at Choate—even, in his good-natured but pompous way, Mr. St. John—provided that underlying love without which Jack could not perform. Mr. Maher did not. Seymour St. John recalled:

> I think Maher's only way, if people were going to fight him, was discipline, toughness. He disciplined himself, and by God he was going to discipline those who needed to be disciplined. And he knew that his floor, his corridor, so-called, had the reputation of being a very disciplined hall. The kids were on time, they were neat, and they knew that was the rule. They did their job.
>
> Jack Kennedy got tossed into that—and he wanted no part of it. He wasn't neat, he wasn't on time, he was a sloppy kid at that age. He didn't do his work effectively—he went through the motions, but he never really worked at it. . . . I think J. J. Maher got to the point where he did not like Jack Kennedy. I don't think he ever took it out on him, but it was not a happy relation.

It wasn't, and it became worse on Jack's father's return from Europe in November 1933. Mr. Kennedy had abandoned his plan to see Mussolini. Instead, having used Jimmy Roosevelt to open doors that would otherwise have been closed to him, Kennedy managed to obtain the exclusive United States distributorship for Haig & Haig, Gordon's Dry Gin, Pinchbottle, and other British liquors, in anticipation of the repeal of Prohibition. Pepped up by this scoop, Mr. Kennedy actually visited Choate. What he found, however, appalled him: an emaciated sixteen-year-old, sloppily dressed and cavorting with a gang of buddies without that earnest posture of self-discipline and determination that so marked his older brother for success in life.

"I can't tell you how unhappy I felt in seeing and talking with Jack. He seems to lack entirely a sense of responsibility," Mr. Kennedy complained in a letter from New York to the headmaster. "His happy-go-lucky manner with a degree of indifference does not portend well for his future development."

Mr. St. John, receiving Kennedy's complaint, was perplexed and not altogether in agreement:

> Jack and I talked together for a good while yesterday, and since you gave me permission, I let him read your letter. I hope very much that my conviction about Jack will not trouble you, and that you will sense that it is no hasty conviction. The fact of the matter is that I cannot feel seriously uneasy or worried about Jack. The longer I live and work with him, the more I talk with him, the more confidence I have in him. I would be willing to bet that within two years you will be as proud of Jack as you are of Joe.

St. John was firmly convinced that, behind the sloppy façade, Jack had "a clever, individualist mind. It is a harder mind to put into harness than Joe's, harder for Jack himself to put into harness. When he learns the right place for humor and learns to use his individual way of looking at things as an asset instead of a handicap, his natural gift of an individual outlook, and witty expression are going to help him. A more conventional mind and more plodding and mature point of view would help him a lot more right now; but we have to allow, my dear Mr. Kennedy, with boys like Jack, for a period of adjustment." Jack's "natural cleverness" was housed in an immature body, burdened with academic routines that were not easy for such a gifted child to knuckle down to. "In the work Jack is doing now, I don't think he is particularly brilliant at all. He has to work harder than we think for what he gets. English and history, to be sure, come easily to Jack. French, and especially geometry, on the other hand, come hard."

St. John was too good an educator, however, to believe that Jack's "problem" lay in his academic work. "I asked Jack if he had had a good chance to talk to you when you were here, and he said there really wasn't very much time. He said you had more time to talk with some of his masters than him and that when you talked with him, you were of course 'rather peeved.' "

Mr. Kennedy had been. It infuriated him to have a son whose ability was not being harnessed effectively. As he wrote to his son Joe Jr. in London, Jack's new history teacher had told him Jack "has one of the few great minds he has ever had in history, yet they all recognized the fact that he lacks any sense of responsibility and it will be too bad if with the brains he has he really doesn't go as far up the ladder as he should. If you can think of anything that you think will help him," Mr. Kennedy begged, "by all means do it."

Such a letter was hardly calculated to help the self-esteem of an eldest son engaged in an almost tragic endeavor to win his *own* place in his father's affections. Mr. Kennedy was, however, a frustrated, tormented man, oblivious to such niceties. Despite his entrepreneurial success in England, he had failed to realize his real ambition, namely to serve in Roosevelt's administration. A year had now passed since Roosevelt's triumphant election, and still no call had come from the White House. "I read and hear about you all of the time," he'd written in the spring to Roosevelt's secretary-cum-mistress, "and know that you must be terribly happy to think that things are going so well for your Boss and the country. I do miss seeing you and having a laugh, but maybe that will come one of these days."

As time marched on, Kennedy increasingly saw himself as the sole unrewarded architect of Roosevelt's victory—the first to finance Roosevelt and the one who brought William Randolph Hearst's deciding influence into Roosevelt's camp at the Chicago Convention of 1932. Even Rose Kennedy was aware of her husband's dissatisfaction. "Those months after the election seemed very long indeed," she later wrote, blaming everything on Roosevelt's chief-of-staff, Louis Howe, "a wizened, brilliant, vindictive little man" who'd "spent most of his life as Roosevelt's personal assistant and political secretary and who was utterly devoted and jealously resentful of anyone he thought might be a rival as chief confidant and lieutenant." In her wifely opinion Howe was simply envious of Joe's friendship with Roosevelt. "I can see why Howe was threatened by Joe, for while Joe too could be brusque and abrupt, he could be absolutely charming and his sense of humor perfectly coincided with President Roosevelt's."

In this view Rose was as deluded as her husband. Roosevelt in truth detested the jumped-up Boston Irish Catholic but was too well brought up to show his feelings. "Joe was keenly disappointed" by the president's decision not to appoint him secretary of the treasury, Rose described. "My father built his financial empire with a secretary and a telephone," Kennedy's daughter Eunice later recalled proudly. Yet neither she nor Rose could ever face the fact that Joseph Kennedy's close-fisted, secretive method of operating made him a brilliant speculator/swindler/entrepreneur but a hopeless long-term administrator, at least in a large organization.

At Choate, meanwhile, Jack's gathering contest with his new housemaster, having warmed up before Christmas 1933, had to be shelved. Once again, in January 1934, Jack fell ill—this time seriously so. Mrs. St. John wrote to tell Jack's mother how suddenly it had happened. "We are still puzzled as to the cause of Jack's trouble. He didn't look at all well when he came back after Christmas, but apparently had improved steadily since then—and it was a great shock to us to find him so sick when we ourselves returned from Florida Saturday afternoon."

What had begun for Jack as a routine confinement in the school infirmary turned into a nightmare. By February 4, when Mrs. St. John visited him, she told her husband that she had "never felt sorrier for any one than I did for him, when I dropped in on him yesterday in the Infirmary, and found him so miserable." She'd intended to go in again and read to him, but "then before there was a chance to get in that hour of reading, I hear you have gone down to New Haven 'for observation,' " she wrote in a rushed note to Jack. "I hope with all my heart that the Doctors will find out in the shortest possible order what is making the trouble, and will clear it out of the way even quicker than that."

This time, however, cheap-soled sneakers could not be blamed for Jack's illness. "Actually he came very close to dying," Jack's friend LeMoyne Billings later confided. Prayers were said in chapel, and rumors became rife. "It was diagnosed at one time as leukemia. Obviously it couldn't have been leukemia," Billings recalled. "It was some very serious blood condition."

Jack's sudden deterioration frightened not only the doctors but the whole staff of Choate School. The errant boy-knight, so sloppy and irresponsible, suddenly seemed a hero, and when a few days later Mr. St. John found himself preparing Jack's half-year report, he grew quite emotional, writing to Mr. Kennedy that "Jack is on the right track. The only thing he needs is just to be well, and he will make every man of us glad by his work as well as in his friendship and understanding. Jack is one of the best people that ever lived—one of the most able and interesting. I could go on about Jack!" In a P.S. he added, "*We pray Jack is better every hour.*" In a second postscript he summed up, "To see how sorry everybody is when Jack is ill, proves the kind of fellow he is."

"Jack's sense of humor hasn't left him for a minute, even when he felt most miserable," Mrs. St. John reported to Rose as the crisis began to abate. (Rose had remained at the family's new oceanside villa in Palm Beach, which her husband had purchased the summer before for $115,000.) "When he was complaining—not peevishly, but normally—of the hives, which covered him so completely on Sunday, Mr. Moore said to him:

'Well, you know, Jack, the Doctors are simply delighted to have the trouble come out to the surface instead of staying inside.' To which Jack instantly responded, 'Gee! The Doctors must be having a happy day today!' "

On Tuesday, February 6, 1934, Jack "had his first meal, after what must have seemed to him a terribly long time, and he said to me, 'It was just as well that they decided to give me breakfast; if they hadn't, I think the nurse would have come in pretty soon and looked in my bed and not been able to see me at all!' "

Although the doctors were puzzled, Jack was not. "If this had happened fifty years ago, they would just say, 'Well, the boy has had a case of hives, but now he's all over it," he told Clara St. John; whereas "now, they've got to take my blood count every little while and keep me here until that corresponds to what the Doctors think it ought to be."

"For the sake of all future times, I hope we find out what is the trouble with Jack," Mrs. St. John assured Mrs. Kennedy "but for the present . . . you may be sure that we are keeping in very constant touch with your boy, and that we are more sorry than we can say that you have had to endure these few days of real anxiety—multiplied a hundred-fold by your distance from Jack."

A Complete Individualist

If Rose Kennedy was anxious in Palm Beach, she had a strange way of showing it. She had ventured abroad seventeen times in four years, but could not manage the journey to Connecticut, where Jack lay in the hospital a further month. "I took his electric Victrola and records down to him this morning," Clara St. John recorded in February 1934, after visiting him in the hospital. Surrounded by books and records, Jack was not unhappy: he had been a nomad of the spirit ever since the family moved from Brookline to Bronxville and the latest villa in Palm Beach. Home had so often resembled a hotel; indeed, with absentee parents, changing staff, and children coming and going, there was little beyond books and records that was his. "They didn't have a real home with their own rooms where they had pictures on the walls or memorabilia on the shelves," Lem Billings explained, "but would rather come home from the holidays from their boarding schools and find whatever room was available." "Which room do I have this time?" Jack would ask his mother—if she was there.

Boarding-school dormitory, infirmary, hospital, town or holiday home: all were interchangeable, hardening Jack's emotional shell and giving his intellect a strangely independent strength. He had always "thought his own thoughts" and done "things his own way," in his mother's words. Increasingly, however, he expressed these independent thoughts as a means to defend his liberty in an adolescent world policed by blinkered men in authority: men like J. J. Maher.

Spared the nagging supervision of Mr. Maher, Jack was delighted when it was decided he should spend the remainder of the term convalescing in Palm Beach. From there he soon dispatched a charming letter to Clara St. John to "thank you for your numerous kindnesses to me when I was in the hospital. I'll never be able to repay them, so I'll have to be satisfied with just letting you know my appreciation."

On one level, Jack *was* appreciative. Yet there was trepidation, too, once he returned to Choate after Easter. "The weather has been awful up here, rain every day and I miss Palm Beach's sun very much," he wrote to his father. "Mr. Maher came back from his holidays looking blacker than ever."

With the help of a tutor in Palm Beach, Jack had kept up with his schoolwork in English, history, chemistry, and French. Yet his behavior, once he emerged from sick bay, dissatisfied Mr. Maher. "I think the main thing about Jack Maher," Seymour St. John acknowledged, "I don't think he was quite creatively imaginative enough to get Jack wanting to do what he wanted him to do. He tried, but at that time Jack needed, I think, a different kind of master—he needed a Leinbach more than he needed a Maher."

Maher certainly did not need a Kennedy. "Jack is such a complete individualist in theory and practice that the ordinary appeals of group spirit and social consciousness (even to the plea of not walking on the other fellow's feet) have no effect," he soon lamented in his housemaster's report. "To say that I understand Jack is more an expression of fond hope than a statement of fact." Though

> young in his ways, and sometimes childish in his actions, his head is old. At first his attitude was, You're a master or a sixth former and I am a lively young fellow with a nimble brain and a bag full of tricks. You will spoil my fun if I let you, so here I go; catch me if you can.
>
> When he discovered that no one was getting particularly excited about his silly game, or that he was playing the simpleton to his own amusement, the game lost its zest. And now for the first time I'm beginning to hope a little that Jack has learned to distinguish between liberty and license.

This was wishful thinking. Despite Jack's recent illness (speculatively diagnosed as "hepatitis") Jack had no intention of distinguishing between liberty and license. Lem Billings recalled,

> I've never known anyone in my life with such a wonderful humor—the ability to make one laugh and have a good time. He had a very sharp tongue when he wanted to use it. I think that people who knew him well liked him very much. I think others possibly didn't because he had a sharp tongue and could make fun of people. . . . Boys who are as full of fun and joie de vivre as he was, can't help but irritate teachers. He was not very popular with the faculty. We didn't take too seriously some of the rules which we felt were unimportant, such as getting to classes and meals on time, and keeping a neat room.

"Jack was always up to pranks and mischief," another pal, Hugh Wynne, remembered. "Witty, unpredictable—you never knew what he was going to do next. The masters certainly didn't—and that was a problem."

Those who knew Jack best, however, were surprised by how smart he was, behind the prankster façade, and how well read for a sixteen-year-old. "He read a great deal of history," Billings recalled. "As a matter of fact he read a great deal generally while he was at school. . . . He had a tremendous interest in history, and I think he carried this all the way through his life. But he was also very interested in what was then happening in the world. I don't remember any other boy subscribing to *The New York Times,* but Jack did—and he read it every day. He kept very much up on what was going on." Another contemporary agreed: "He conspicuously failed to open his schoolbooks, yet was the best informed boy of his year."

Reflecting on this, Jack's friend "Rip" Horton noted that when they listened to the popular radio program *Information Please,* "I'd know roughly 10 percent of the answers and Jack Kennedy would know a good 50 or 60 percent." When Horton asked how Jack managed to retain so many facts, he was surprised by Jack's answer: "I'll pick up an article, I'll read it, and then I'll force myself to lay down for about half an hour and go through the total article in my mind, bringing to memory as much as I possibly can and then analyzing the article, and then attacking it and tearing it down."

Thinking back forty years, Horton acknowledged that Jack's marks were "very mediocre" at Choate, but that this did not accurately reflect his native intellect. Jack possessed "an excellent mind," Horton emphasized. "It wasn't challenged in the type of work we were doing." "He read a great deal but not ostentatiously. He seemed to absorb on the basis of this retentive memory training that he worked on—he seemed to absorb what he read much better than the rest of us."

Harold Tinker, Jack's English teacher, felt the same way. "As we were leaving the class one day," Horton later recalled, "I remember Dr. Tinker called Jack aside. We'd all had to write essays or papers. He told Jack that when he went to college and graduated he ought to go into something like journalism because he had a very fluid, mature style for someone his age."

Joe Jr., by contrast, had no style. He was, as Russ Ayres had once put it, "better at facts than at imagination." However, he had impressed the Choate faculty, as he impressed his father, by his seriousness and determination to succeed. "I have great admiration for your capacity at all times to assume a job and then see it through," Joseph Kennedy had written at the start of Joe Jr.'s stint in London, and he relished the fine reports he began to receive from Harold Laski, Joe Jr.'s professor.

Had Laski known what fawning letters Joe Jr. was sending home about the Nazi regime in Germany, where he spent his Easter vacation, he might not have been so impressed with his student. At his Sunday-afternoon tea seminars, the famous left-wing political scientist had warned Joe Jr. about Nazi brutalities. But once in Hitler's new Reich, together with a companion chosen and paid for by Mr. Kennedy, Joe Jr. paid no further heed to Laski, applauding to his father the latest Nazi outrages. "The German people were scattered, despondent, and were divorced from hope," he wrote. "Hitler came in. He saw the need of a common enemy, someone of whom to make the goat. Someone, by whose riddance the Germans would feel they had cast out the cause of their predicament. It was excellent psychology, and it was too bad that it had to be done to the Jews. This dislike of the Jews, however, was well-founded," Joe Jr. assured his father, for the Jews were "the heads of all big business, in law, etc." The "brutality" used by the Nazis against the Jews was "necessary . . . to secure the whole-hearted support of the people, which was necessary to put through this present program. . . . It was a horrible thing but in every revolution you have to expect some bloodshed. Hitler is building a spirit in his men that could be envied in any country. . . . This spirit could very quickly be turned into a war spirit, but Hitler has things well under control. The only danger would be if something happened to Hitler and one of his crazy ministers came into power."

Joe Jr.'s anti-Semitism and juvenile admiration for Hitler—"I'm sure if I was a German . . . I would expend that slight effort which is required to raise my arm [in the Heil Hitler salute]"—was perhaps as much an attempt to impress his anti-Semitic father as to register his own thoughts. He was, after all, an innocent nineteen-year-old, a millionaire's son on his first extended trip overseas. However, he was also a boy who had, according to Professor Laski, "set his heart on a political career" and was determined to become "nothing less than the first Catholic President of the United States."

Unknown to both Joe Jr. and Professor Laski, this was an ambition that the Boston-Irish millionaire coveted for himself. His son's career could wait. On June 28, 1934, President Roosevelt finally rewarded Kennedy for his work in the 1932 election campaign. Countering all objections with the words "it takes a thief to catch a thief," he appointed Joseph P. Kennedy the first chairman of a new regulatory agency to tidy up the nation's stock market: the Securities and Exchange Commission, or SEC. To the consternation of all, the notorious stock-market swindler Joseph P. Kennedy would become stock-market reformer.

Hot Screw

While his elder brother brought his year at the London School of Economics to a close with a tour of the Soviet Union led by Professor Laski, Jack had looked forward to sailing and sunbathing on Cape Cod, especially as he'd invited his classmate K. LeMoyne Billings to join him. Billings came from a good, Protestant Pittsburg family, but his father had just died, leaving only a modest estate after the ravages of the Great Crash and the Depression. Lem would never forget his Hyannis Port induction: "I remember the first time that I ever stayed with Jack—we were staying at the Cape. I don't know what I did, but I remember something woke him up and he screamed, "God damn you, Billings, shut up." Well, I didn't know him so well then, and I was furious! I was even considering leaving. I felt I couldn't stay in the house with anybody who talked to me that way."

Billings's soreness soon wore off when he realized there was nothing personal in Jack's nocturnal expletive, but that behind the genial, fun-loving façade was a rather tense adolescent who "did not take to having people in the room that made noises, like snoring, which would wake him up. I was really fed up, but this was just his way, and then he went back to sleep and that was the end of it."

In fact, Jack still wasn't at all well. Scarcely had he settled down for the summer vacation when he once again became ill and had to be hospitalized. This time it was decided to send him to the famed Mayo Clinic in Rochester, Minnesota, for a battery of tests that would, it was hoped, finally determine what was the matter with him. When one of Joseph Kennedy's friends, Kay Halle, visited Jack in the hospital, she later claimed she'd found him "lying in bed, very pale, which highlighted the freckles across his nose. He was so surrounded by books I could hardly see him. I was very impressed, because at that point this very young child was reading *The World Crisis* by Winston Churchill."

This impression was common to all who visited the invalid. Surrounded by his history books, however, Jack was now undergoing his own crisis: a crisis of adolescence. "It looks now as if I am not going to get out of here till about 12 days," he soon scribbled to Billings from the Mayo. "I would say that Rochester is the Goddamnest hole I've ever seen. I wish I was back at school."

The thought that Billings would be enjoying life on the beach at Hyannis Port while he himself underwent weeks of medical torture infuriated Jack, even when he heard Billings had scalded himself in Mr. Kennedy's special shower, requiring three weeks of hospitalization. Billings's misfortune was his own fault; Jack's was not. From Rochester Jack now dispatched a series of wild, unhappy, and often obscene letters to his school friend. Sitting tearfully over Jack's school reports, the Choate headmaster might consider Jack "one of the best people that ever lived," but he had little idea of the emotional upheaval Jack was undergoing. To the problems of a talented but disoriented, directionless, and often unwell boy there was now added the business of sex. Indulgence in phallic and anal obscenities were, like masturbation, normal aspects of adolescence, especially in a boarding school. "I never yet saw a clever, witty boy who at some stage in his early development was not considered fresh," St. John had remarked the previous fall when defending Jack's behavior, yet even St. John could not foresee what trials were in store. In Rochester, missing his summer vacation and suffering more or less continual abdominal pain, Jack was put through a succession of humiliating tests and investigations that would have upset a mature adult, let alone a literally bare seventeen-year-old. "I am suffering terribly out here and I now have gut ache all the time," he complained to Billings. "I'm still eating peas and corn for my food and I had an enema given by a beautiful blonde. That, my sweet, is the height of cheap thrills."

His symptoms, as in February, defied easy diagnosis. "Talked to Dad last night. . . . For 20 mins he was trying to find out what was wrong with me and for 20 mins we were trying to hedge around the fact that we didn't know." Not even news of Billings's scalding could excite Jack's sympathy. "Tough about your burns but to get back to a much more interesting subject . . . my bowels have utterly ceased to be of service and so the only way that I am able to unload is for [someone] to blow me out from the top down or from the bottom up. Should get home a week from Sat. Burn this when you get finished and for God's sake don't leave it around because if you do I'll have all your letters wrapped up and sealed to be presented to your sister's un-born baby at the age of 21 so he can see what a dirty-minded shit his god-damn uncle was."

Two years before, Mrs. Kennedy had harped upon the need to teach the boys of Choate School how to write proper letters, properly addressed. Letters beginning "Dear Crap!" were hardly what she had in mind.

To some extent, this was the point: Jack's adolescent bawdiness aimed in part at his mother's sterile, convent-school values. Sending lurid descriptions of his medical ordeal to Billings at Hyannis Port gave Jack a distinct thrill. When he learned that several of his letters hadn't reached Billings, Jack wrote with mock anxiety, "I hope to hell that nobody read them because they would think I was a terribly unclean-cut guy. . . . God what a beating I'm taking. I've lost 8 lbs and still going down," he wrote on June 21. "I'm showing them a thing or two. Nobody able to figure out what's wrong with me. All they do is talk about what an interesting case. It'll be funny if there was nothing wrong with me. I'm commencing to stay awake nights on that. . . . Will be here probably a week more."

But a week later the doctors were no nearer to a solution and admitted him to nearby St. Mary's Hospital. "Just heard today that I may not get out from here till the 4th [July]. Shit!" he began. "I've had *18* enemas in 3 days!!! I'm clean as a whistle. They give me enemas till it comes out like drinking water which they all take a sip of," he informed his friend gratuitously, and described "the most harassing experience of my life" when, the previous day,

> they gave me *5* enemas until I was white as snow inside. Then they put me on a thing like a barber's chair. Instead of sitting in the chair I kneeled on something that resembles a foot rest with my head where the seat is. They (a blonde) took my pants down!! Then they tipped the chair over. Then surrounded by nurses the doctor first stuck his finger up my ass. I just blushed because you know how it is. He wiggled it suggestively and I rolled 'em in the aisles by saying 'you have a good motion'!! He then withdrew his finger. And then, the shmuck stuck an iron tube 12 inches long and 1 inch in diameter up my ass. They had a flashlight inside it and they looked around. Then they blew a lot of air in me to pump up my bowels. I was certainly feeling great as I know you would having a lot of strangers looking up my asshole. . . . I was a bit glad when they had their fill of that. My poor bedraggled rectum is looking at me very reproachfully these days.

For Jack it was a disturbing experience. His mind at school and now his body in Rochester were under siege. Fatherless and also overshadowed by a brilliant elder brother, Billings watched with fascination the way Jack handled his fate—and himself. On the surface Jack with all his charm reminded people of his grandfather Honey Fitz—ingratiatingly witty and self-deprecating. Moreover his bushy, tousled hair and gray-blue eyes set in a broad face, with its firm jaw, gave him an open, arresting quality. Inside, however, it was clear that Jack was pursued by demons.

"Surrounded by nurses," Jack underwent more and more tests. He became "the pet" of the hospital staff. Though his weight fell to 135 pounds, he was less interested in what was medically wrong with him than in the effect of endless enemas and a corn-and-peas diet on his vital organ—or, as he called it, his "implement." "My vitality is slowly being sapped," he lamented to Billings, having masturbated to orgasm only twice since he was admitted to hospital. "I'm just a shell of the former man and my penis looks as if it had been run through a wringer." One nurse had promised that Jack could give her "a workout" after lights-out, but probably because of his age decided against the enterprise, to Jack's chagrin. Most revealing of all, however, was an anecdote Jack related to Billings concerning a simple encounter in the cinema:

> Last night in the theater Ed and I were sitting in 2 seats when this guy and a girl sat down. He put his arm around her and that embarrassed me because you know how I am about that type of thing. However you've never smelt anything so vile as that girl. She stank.
>
> I motioned to Ed to move over. He moved and I moved.
>
> Well, the girl looked at me and then whispered something to the fellow. He took his arm down and stood up. I, nothing daunted, stared back. The girl grabbed his arm and he sat down. It was a lucky thing for him because he was only about 6'3" and I could have heaved him right into the aisle on his ass.

"I think I told you about our automobile accident in another letter so will omit that. That's all the news you blind creep [Billings suffered from notoriously bad eyesight]. Write!" he ordered his apostle.

Similar far-from-religious epistles were fired off at Billings every few days—insulting, provocative, mock-heroic, slightly bitter, with a touching mixture of juvenile bravado and adolescent pain. His continual stomachache and the medical tests made him testy and irritable, but the letters also betrayed a restless, searching self at variance with the "cleancut guy" he inhabited in public. He was obsessed by sex, and wanted to have it with the tantalizing blond nurses who manhandled him; yet his disgust at women who wore heavy perfume, as well as his embarrassment at normal public gestures of affection, spoke volumes. His mother's coldness and preoccupation with jewelry, clothes, and grooming gave him a lifelong aversion to such sexless artifice, as he buried his fractured psyche in a lifetime of fruitless womanizing, of continual, purgative sexual conquest that would relieve his libido yet never bring him contentment.

Except in sexual excitement he hated to be touched, hated the very idea of loving attachment to a woman involving lasting commitment or affection. To his Boswell, Lem Billings, he might strut and pose, spit and be distasteful, but Billings knew how much of it was sham, how much a fellow adolescent's cri de coeur. Born of ill-suited, unhappy parents, locked in an emotionally blocked, socially quarantined, and maniacally competitive family, there was no way out. His bilious, obscene letters from St. Mary's Hospital evinced a curiously symbolic quality as he railed against the white-frocked wardens of his medical imprisonment—"the dirtiest-minded bunch of females I've ever seen"—and his unnamed medical fate, which he summarized in the simple sentence, "I've got something wrong with my intestines—in other words I shit blood."

What was touching—and why Billings refused to "burn this letter" or any other of Jack's letters as instructed—was Jack's refusal to indulge in introspection or self-pity. The courage Mr. and Mrs. St. John had witnessed was real, leading Billings to marvel at Jack's humor in the face of such an ordeal, however barbed and even painful his wit. For beneath Jack's macho surface beat a loyal and sometimes disarmingly tender heart. "Weren't the crew races great! We certainly did have swell fun," Jack scribbled in an addendum—and worried about Billings going to a party without him.

"Still in this God-damned furnace and it looks like a week more," he wrote to Billings on June 30. "The nurses are very tantalizing and I'm really the pet of the hospital. All day they come in and let me tell you nurses are almost as dirty as you, you filthy minded shit. Pardon me Uncle Ike, Uncle Ben & Mrs. Billings," he added, lest the letter to Pittsburgh, where Billings had returned, was opened in error by someone else. "I only had 2 enemas today so I feel kind of full. They have found something wrong with me at last. I don't know what but it's probably something revolting like piles or a disease of my vital organ. What will I say when someone asks me what I got?"

But the doctors hadn't found what was wrong with him, despite all the tests. As Mr. Kennedy afterward explained to Jack's headmaster, "about the early part of the summer, we sent him to Mayo's and he remained out there about a month. They made a thorough investigation of his physical condition and came to the belief that they were unable to find out what had caused Jack's illness during the winter, and what was causing the continuation in a small degree of that condition. They finally sent him home and wrote me a letter in which they made very clear that if Jack showed the slightest tendency toward a relapse, he would have to be taken out of school for about a year and sent, possibly, down south. Of course this greatly concerns me and at the same time annoys Jack very much."

As if to confound the Mayo clinicians, however, Jack's stomach problems suddenly disappeared at home and he bounced back into indecent vitality, at least insofar as the bawdiness of his correspondence was concerned. "After your last letter which was as filthy a missive as I have ever laid hands upon," he scrawled in a letter to Billings in July, "I am writing a dirty letter to end dirty letters. You shit! That is the first of a long number of names which you will find imprinted throughout this letter." He gave Billings the lowdown on high life at Cape Cod. "Trox Box is coming down so that should be rosy. Mimi is back, as full of fun as ever, every 12 inches of her." He assumed he would return to Choate in September. "I guess I am coming back to that hole again this year as I'm getting disgustingly healthy and robust. Joe came back about 3 days ago and is a communist. Some shit, eh," he commented on his brother's return from the Soviet Union. Even his father's new job at the SEC was of scant interest compared with the sun-drenched sands of Cape Cod in late July—and Jack's discovery that girls liked him. "Ruth Zingly called up from Cleveland the girl next door to ask how my health was. I can't help it. It can't be my good looks because I'm not much handsomer than anybody else. It must be my personality," he boasted mockingly to Billings. "I am now sporting around the beaches in flesh-color silk bathing trunks acquiring that chocolate tan which is the rage this year at Newport and Hyannisport. Hot Screw."

Jack's new life as a playboy was beginning. It would bring him into direct confrontation with the school—indeed to the brink of expulsion—and try his father's notoriously tenuous patience to the limit. But perhaps that, too, was the point.

Dad's Idea of a Joke

Billings had seen, that summer, the strange relationship between Jack's parents: the way, when Mr. Kennedy was around, it was "his personality that dominated" while that of Rose shriveled. "When he was home she let him sort of take over." With his move to the SEC, however, Joseph Kennedy was rarely around, and Rose's attempts to keep order in his absence by laying down her own domestic rules merely aroused Jack's scorn. Jack's cousin, Joey Gargan, later described how Jack and his mother "were often in a way at cross purposes so far as household disciplines were concerned because he didn't fit into them too well."

Rose's obsessive desire to drill her children for a social world that would not accept her struck Jack as both loony and pathetic. "She certainly, almost constantly, supervised us," Rose's orphaned nephew recalled. "Appearance and conduct: 'Don't wear white socks with dress suit. Wear dark shoes with blue or gray suit, not brown shoes. Suit sleeves short enough so shirt cuff hangs below suit sleeve one inch. Don't say 'Hi' to people when addressing them.' " At the dinner table there were endless "instructions about good table manners in eating, and right forks and so forth and deportment, such as proper seating and 'ladies first'. . . . When a meal was over, the ladies and particularly Aunt Rose were to leave the dining room first. That was good manners. But very often Jack would forget. He would have been having an interesting conversation, or his mind was on something else, or someway he would unintentionally forget the order of departure. This happened so often that when a meal was over Aunt Rose would start quickly for the door. And then, quite clearly, it could be a race between her and Jack as to who was going to make it. And she would frequently mention this to Jack and he would say, 'Oh, yes, Mother, I'm sorry' . . . but a couple of days later it would happen again."

When not ridiculing his dotty mother (Rose even went around the house with notes pinned to her blouse), Jack ignored her, peopling the house at Cape Cod or Bronxville with pals from school such as Herb Merrick, Rip Horton, Smokey Wilde, and Hugh ("Bud") Wynne. "He had, it began to seem to me, innumerable friends," Rose later recalled, "for during vacations and special weekends when he came home he invariably had at least one, usually two, three, four or more school friends with him. We never knew whom to expect or how many. It became a joke in the family, a little shorthand expression that evoked a lot: 'Jack's surprises.' "

One of Jack's school friends, Paul Chase, later remembered what a model family Jack's at first appeared to him, with nine ebullient boys and girls vying for their place in the Kennedy sun. Over time, however, Chase came to see that, underneath, all was not well in the state of Denmark; that the storybook façade concealed an almost psychotic drama, with Mrs. Kennedy eclipsed by her ruthless, bullying husband and the tension of that unspoken interparental hostility pervading everything. The competitiveness Mr. Kennedy generated among his nine children was awesomely fascinating. When home, he behaved like a seal trainer at a zoo, tossing fishes from his bucket to the snouts of his charges and shouting a mixture of exhortations and imprecations as they dove to retrieve them. "Mr. K. really did preach that winning was everything," Chase recalled. "Several times," when sailing at Hyannis Port, "Jack asked me to crew for him when he could not find anyone else. Once we lost badly and caught a half-hour lecture from the 'old man' on our return to shore. He said he had watched the race and that he was disgusted with both of us. There was no sense, he claimed, in going into a race unless you did your damnedest to win, an endeavor at which we had failed miserably. He was really angry with us."

Rip Horton agreed. "He was just so competitive. We'd play Monopoly against him and he'd murder us. All three of us, Lem, Jack and I would gang up on him and he'd murder us. But that was to provoke [his] boys more than anything else." The same was true at table, where Mr. Kennedy would prompt his elder sons to discuss "current events, politics, international politics. I was fascinated because I loved politics," Horton recalled. "But if I asked Mr. Kennedy a question, believe me, he'd treat me like a piece of dirt, he'd ignore me"—an experience that would be common to all the friends Jack took home.

Incapable of retaining the loyalty even of paid subordinates for any length of time (all his "horsemen," save his whoremaster Eddie Moore, had abandoned him after the Swanson business), Joseph Kennedy could not resist the temptation to manipulate his own emotionally deprived children. Aware that a good animal handler must treat as well as trick, he proceeded to enmesh them in the same way he had once ensnared Gloria Swanson, pretending he'd set up million-dollar trusts in their various names to which they would each have access at age twenty-one. Moreover, the same inconsistency that made him such an unpredictable market operator characterized his parenting. He nagged Jack about his laundry bills, as Paul Chase recalled, yet "after a particularly fine dinner, the 'old man' told us all to look under our dessert plates. When we did so we found a fifty-dollar bill under each plate. Mr. Kennedy advised us that we were all going to Bradley's as his guests for an evening of gambling. Why we were allowed to gamble at our age is not entirely clear to me."

Perhaps most damaging of all was the sexual example Joseph Kennedy set for his children. On one occasion Jack returned home from school to find his bed covered by sex magazines, all open to display the female anatomy at its most immodest—an event which the Reverend Seymour St. John later recounted with a sigh of incomprehension. Did Mr. Kennedy thereby hope to make Jack an accomplice in his own sexual frustration at his wife's notorious prudery? "I think it's Dad's idea of a joke," Jack is said to have commented when he saw the array of pornography. Whatever the motive, it certainly added to Jack's own emotional confusion, as well as inciting in him a deliberately degrading, exploitive attitude toward women.

Jack's response, increasingly, was to seek refuge in his circle of friends. With his loyal gang of fellow pranksters at Choate he felt a sort of collective security in pursuing his nonconformist destiny—his sense that, with his brother now removed from the scene, "Choate was *his*," as Billings later put it.

If so, it was a very different Choate from the one in which his eldest brother had triumphed. "I still have your shaving brush, which I shall return when I get back my deer-Sucker coat you slimy fuck," Jack had written to Billings in late July 1934. "Have you laid Pussy yet? You bitch."

Now, in their final school year, Jack and Billings were to share a room in West Wing—but to their horror found it was cheek-by-jowl with that of Jack's nemesis, Mr. Maher. "We are up on Mr. Maher's corridor right next to him, and everything we say he lobs in and adds his comments," Jack lamented to his father. "We are practically rooming with him, which is more than we bargained for."

If this was Mr. Maher's way of keeping Jack Kennedy under strict surveillance and his nose to the grindstone, however, he was to be deeply disappointed. Billings vividly remembered the inevitable clash.

It was shortly after Jack returned to school from his summer vacation and we were dragging his trunk down the stairs to store it in the cellar. We were making a good deal of noise. Our housemaster, Mr. Maher, came out of his room. He reminded us this was during study period and the noise was a distraction for people who were trying to work. He ordered us to take the trunk back up and bring it down to storage the next morning instead.

So Jack and I got up at 6 A.M. We dragged the trunk out and down the stairs, bumping all the way down. Mr. Maher came tearing out of his room, in his bathrobe, wild-eyed, and demanded to know what we thought we were doing.

"But Mr. Maher," Jack said innocently, "you *told* us to take it down in the morning."

Jack was well aware how close he was sailing to the wind. But his brush with death, his undiagnosed stomach cramps, followed by rude good health gave him a devil-may-care zest that not even Choate's strictest disciplinarian, J. J. Maher, could tame. Swallowing his fury, Maher still felt he had the upper hand, reporting to the headmaster in October 1934 that Jack was "improving. Attitude poor at the outset; sloppy, seldom on time; but has shown a reversal of form and is really having an excellent try. Works best . . . if not hammered too hard or too often."

A few weeks later, however, the housemaster's tone had altered from one of hope to despair. "Matched only by his roommate, Billings, in sloppiness and continued lateness. All methods of coercion fail," Maher reported. "Jack's record is not as good as he ought to expect for himself," George St. John admitted when passing this on to Jack's father in Washington, where the new SEC chairman, vainly anticipating that his family would move in with him, had taken a lease on Marwood, a 125-acre estate by the Potomac with no fewer than thirty-three rooms. "He got off to a bad start, failed to correct habits of carelessness. It was an attitude not worthy of Jack," St. John remarked, but he was "almost too ready to forgive everything when I think of that serious illness he went through."

Jack, meanwhile, was also shown a copy of Maher's report, and his fall grades. "Was he scared of his father?" Billings later considered. "He was when he did something wrong," for "old man" Kennedy had "a sharp tongue and a sharp eye. Jack did not want to be exposed to either."

"Dear Dad: I thought I would write you right away," Jack thus apologized in extraordinarily neat handwriting on the first Sunday in December 1934. "LeMoyne and I have been talking about how poorly we have done this quarter, and we have definitely decided to stop any fooling around. I really do realize how important it is I get a good job done this year if I want to go to England," he acknowledged—knowing that his father wished him to follow in his brother's footsteps and study for a year under Professor Laski in London before going to college. "I really feel, now that I think it over, that I have been bluffing myself about how much real work I have been doing."

But Jack had no intention whatever of turning over a new leaf. "He really had no desire, at that time, to be respected or even to be popular," Billings recalled. "He was interested in having a lot of fun, he was interested in the studies that he liked, and he was bored to death with the studies he didn't. He was very, very interested in girls, he was interested in athletics. He certainly had a sense of humor. He would make fun of people if he felt like it, and I think for this reason a lot of boys didn't like him. He certainly wasn't at Choate the kind of boy whom you would say was one of the leaders of the school."

In this respect some observers saw Billings's complete subservience to Jack as pathetic, labeling him "Poor Lem," both for his poverty (he was given a school scholarship when his father died) and for his obsequiousness to Jack's whims. Yet in a world where Jack confronted an endless array of attempted intimidations from parents, doctors, and teachers, Billings's big heart and his willingness to go along with Jack's errant, adolescent protest were touchingly loyal. If a boy like Billings could follow him through the proverbial thick and thin and still *believe* in him, then life, *his* life, must be important, Jack reasoned—not in Choate terms, or his father's terms, but in his own terms.

The next crisis of Jack's school career was about to come. From the headmaster's point of view it would be a crisis of authority: his versus Jack's. In Mr. Kennedy's terms it would be a crisis of Jack's basic irresponsibility and lack of direction. But in the seventeen-year-old's terms, it was not a crisis at all, but a culmination. His shell of precocious wit and bookishness had protected him all the years of growing up. Nobody ever slapped him on the back, patronized him, or took liberties with him. Quick-witted and determined to come to his own conclusions about life, he was, from early childhood, his own master, and he was not going to surrender that sense of self now to ape his conformist elder brother or adapt to the conventional aspirations of an elite, largely Episcopalian school, any more than he had been willing to satisfy the expectations of his dysfunctional parents. He would therefore continue his bluff until he finally got what every adolescent craves: his father's love.

The Muckers Revolt

Despite her husband's move to Marwood, Rose Kennedy refused to follow him to Washington. Exhausted by his efforts at the SEC, Mr. Kennedy therefore arranged to spend the Christmas 1934 vacation with his family in Palm Beach. Jack's poor classwork and general disobedience, however, made it impossible for St. John to let Jack leave school early. "I quite understood your eagerness to have Jack start for Palm Beach as soon as possible," St. John explained to Mr. Kennedy, assuring him that the staff of the school "want to co-operate with you in every way that will work out best for Jack." Nonetheless, St. John didn't want Jack to "feel in any way that he had been cased out of a situation by extenuating circumstances." Though Jack was finally allowed to leave Choate on December 20, the young felon, much to his annoyance, was told to return to school "before the opening of the new term."

Mr. Kennedy was similarly disappointed by Jack's manner at Palm Beach. "I agree that he still lacks the proper attitude toward the consideration of his problems," he wrote to St. John. "I have always felt that he has a fine mind. He is quite kiddish about his activities and although I have noticed a tremendous improvement this year, I still feel that what he needs to be trained in most is the ability to get a job done."

The phrase was becoming ominous, as though Joseph Kennedy believed that in forcing Jack to do what he did not want to do, Jack's "problem" would disappear. Mr. Kennedy did at least accept some of the blame. "We have possibly contributed as much as anybody in spoiling him by having secretaries and maids following him to see that he does what he should do," he confessed, but the notion that Jack might be reacting against a lifetime of secretaries and maids instead of parents did not occur to him. Jack thus returned to Choate on January 7, 1935, "in lieu of the discipline" incurred in December.

Jack was neither converted nor intimidated. "With the winter term," Seymour St. John related, "J. J. Maher justifiably showed signs of getting to the end of his rope." "For a year and a half, I've tried everything from kissing to kicking Jack into just a few commonly decent points of view and habits of living in community life, and I'm afraid I must admit my own failure as well as his," Maher minuted the headmaster later in January. "Jack is prompt only under the club; neat virtually never. He has little sense of sportsmanship (not even the lower politic type of 'you scratch my back and I'll scratch yours'). Unfortunately, it must be all for Jack or he won't play." He lamented that Jack's "illness of last year and consequent physical condition prevent participation in athletics that can inculcate so necessary a quality."

This was the classic British private-school formula: physical exercise and cold showers. Indeed Maher actually admitted as much: "I had a great deal of fun out of our early morning 'shower team,' of which both [Lem and Jack] are regular members, but as soon as a situation changes from the general to the particular there is no question in anyone's mind as to how they will react." Maher recommended they be kept apart. "As I am convinced that they do not help each other by rooming together, and since I feel that they cannot regain a position of respect as reliable sixth formers among the boys on my corridor, I believe they should be separated and sent to younger houses to assume responsibilities with a fresh start and a different point of view." Clearly Maher—a repressed homosexual—was irritated by the two boys' intimacy.

Speaking on behalf of the Choate staff, Seymour St. John deplored Billings's servile participation in Jack's devilry:

> "Josh" Billings, LeMoyne's brother, was a very good friend of mine. Again, he was a first son, captain of the football team at Princeton, and he did everything right. And then LeMoyne came along, second son, he was a big handsome boy, did adequate work, but he had nothing really to hold on to, and when he found Jack Kennedy, he just thought this was it, this was for him. And he would do *anything* for Jack Kennedy. Anything Jack did, he would follow right along with, and be the stooge, and was inseparable from Jack those last two years, which were not good for Jack. Jack liked Billings, he liked very much having somebody at his beck and call and who'd always go along with his jokes, pranks or whatever. But there was never any LeMoyne saying: "I don't think that's a good idea." It was *always* a good idea if it was Jack's idea.

Jack's next idea, according to Rip Horton, was that Jack and Billings should lose their virginity to the same prostitute. Horton himself had already had a girl, he later confided. Now "it was time for Jack & Billings. They got in a cab and went to a whorehouse in Harlem. First they saw a dirty show and then they went off with the girls. It was about $3. Billings and Jack came back in a terrible panic because of VD. They went to a hospital and got all these medicines and creams and some sort of device you insert in the penis to clean it out. They woke up a doctor in the middle of the night to help them further."

The two boys had now become sexually and socially inseparable, their heterosexual initiation a rite of both passage and of solidarity. Back at Choate, to Billings's fawning applause, Jack now proceeded to perform his own version of Hamlet, playing out a self-absorbed yet swashbuckling identity that would amuse his companions and keep at bay his demons.

This inventiveness was not at all what Mr. St. John or Mr. Maher had in mind as responsible sixth-form behavior: particularly when it threatened the very ethos of a school George St. John had labored to build up over the past thirty years. Jack's increasing mockery began spreading to the rest of his clique—an antiauthoritarian disaffection among the very boys who, being sixth-formers, were expected to provide the rest of the school with a good example. Once again Maher gave way to despair, reporting to St. John that "neither Jack nor his roommate has accepted their duties as a Sixth Former. It is too late, I believe, for them to regain their lost position here, because from the outset they have demonstrated in their silly, giggling inseparable companionship that the good of the group takes second place to their convenience."

The "good of the group," however, was a matter of definition. For Maher, as for St. John, the group denoted the school establishment. For Jack it meant the friends he collected around himself. As his new girlfriend, Olive Cawley, recalled, Jack was "witty, clever, mischievous"—in that order. "He was always surrounded by excitement. In the group that traveled together, Jack called the shots: where they would go, what they would do. His friends were the satellites, especially LeMoyne."

Jack's refusal to obey Maher, and his patent bucking of the Choate ethos, perplexed St. John. "See Jack and LeMoyne and give them thunder," he wrote in a memo. "They need it. Can we separate them? Not feasible. Would a gland specialist help overcome this strange childishness?" he ruminated. In a letter to Jack's father, St. John now took up this idea: "Jack is the most childish, irresponsible sixth form boy in his house. If Jack were my son, I believe I should take him to a gland specialist."

Ironically, this would indeed turn out to be the root cause of Jack's medical problems—though impossible at the time to diagnose. However, the cause of Jack's "childishness" at school was not medical. It was simply a matter of growing up. In Jack's case this meant coming to terms with the oedipal loss of his mother while finding a new relationship with his demanding, bullying, yet distant father.

Alarmed, meanwhile, St. John lectured the school on the need to serve the ideals of Choate, referring to those pupils who did not share his Episcopalian school dream as "muckers" (a term of ethnic contempt for Irish laborers).

"The word cropped up in chapel talks to the assembled students that winter," the headmaster's son Seymour later recorded, "with thinly veiled references to a small cabal which included Kennedy. And then in a diabolically inspired moment, mocking authority, Jack and a dozen friends formed 'The Muckers Club.' "

Lem Billings, a cofounder of Jack's club, saw nothing diabolic in the genesis.

> We had a room that was very close to the dining hall. Between dinner and chapel there was a period of about twenty minutes during which time there was very little to do. We happened to have a pretty good Victrola and we found that every time we came to our room, we couldn't get into it ourselves. The Headmaster had constantly mentioned in chapel that the worst kind of boy he knew was what he referred to as a "mucker." He said that about 5 per cent of the boys of his school were "muckers." and that if he knew who they were he would expel them. Well, here is an example of a foolish but a normal boyish attitude—immediately we formed a club called the Muckers' Club.

"Why were we so devilish?" Rip Horton later reflected. "Maybe we didn't like to be structured. Each of those guys had a pretty damn good sense of humor. Jack had a very, very keen wit. We just liked to bug people, to see their reactions. None of us drank or smoked. . . . We were just nonorganization in some ways."

Membership was exclusive. "Only members of the Mucker's Club were allowed in our room after the dinner period," Billings recalled, for it was then that forthcoming pranks were discussed. Rip Horton, who considered himself the most "sophisticated" member (his grandfather had founded the great dairy company that ultimately became Kraft), was elected club secretary. His family had given him cards to various speakeasies during Prohibition, and his knowledge of New York nightclubs was, for a seventeen-year-old, prodigious. When Edward Bland joined the club and brought a "zanier" spirit to it, Jack was quick to compose a ditty.

Everybody's going Blambo,
No one wants, no one wants to go Hortino.
Last year it was Princess Sophy,
This year, Blambo's got us goofy. . . .

Envious of Maurice Shea, a fellow Mucker who had been specially favored by "Queenie," the popular and attractive wife of the assistant headmaster, Jack even composed another song, which carried the refrain:

Maury Shea, Maury Shea,
Drinking tea every day.
Maury Shea, what's your appeal?
Queenie, we want a new deal!

Jack's lyrics were soon on the lips of the whole campus. Jack was even asked to sing his tea song to Queenie herself. "We had to sing that thing to her," Horton later recalled. "We damn near died. Why we weren't thrown out of school, I'll never know."

The fun, however, was just beginning. Jack's instinct was not simply anarchic, but political. The Muckers Club grew steadily in size until it threatened, by virtue of its numbers, to supersede the official student council and become the opposition party within the school. "One evening in our senior year Jack called me as I walked down the hall toward my room. Out of the clear blue sky he said, 'You are a member of a club—the Muckers Club.' . . . I don't know whether there were 6 or 8 or 10, but do remember the main thesis was that we were such 'wheels' the Head could not kick us all out," one Mucker recalled.

Soon, after some defections (some students, such as Hugh Wynne, were understandably nervous about their scholarships or sponsors during the Depression), the Choate Muckers Club stabilized at thirteen members. It was decided to strike an emblem, in gold, that members could wear. "We had a little gold shovel made and on it we had the person's initial and also CMC which stood for Choate Muckers Club; and we proudly displayed those shovels," Horton remembered.

The emblems were expensive for those days. "About $12 as I remember," said another Mucker, Paul Chase, "and made by hand by a Wallingford jeweler." Proud of his insignia, Chase even boasted to his roommate of the latest Muckers prank. "I told him that we were going to bring in a pile of horse manure and have our pictures taken on the dance floor over Spring Festivities with our gold shovels! He apparently took me seriously and passed the word on to the head."

The headmaster, when he heard of this latest prank, was livid. Spring

Festivities was the main weekend dance of the school year. Many eligible girls were brought by eligible parents to meet eligible partners. At a time of grave national recession, when the school roll had fallen to its lowest figure since 1928, and when the very raison d'être of such an elite, expensive school amidst so much poverty in the nation was at issue, St. John took the matter deeply to heart.

In the notes he made at the time, St. John described the thirteen Muckers as "a colossally selfish, pleasure loving, unperceptive group—in general opposed to the hardworking, solid people in the school, whether masters or boys. The emblem of this group is a shovel. It was suggested among them that they have their pictures taken at Festivities, each pulling his girl on a shovel; and again that they have their pictures taken, standing beside a manure pile, to show that the shovels were used."

By the time he made these notes, however, St. John had acted. In the school dining hall that day St. John "read off the names" of the club members, "and it was interesting to hear the quiet undertone of appreciation that went up throughout the hall when I had finished the names on the list." All thirteen were told to assemble in his study. There he "told the whole group that I would expel one or all of them, I didn't care which if it came to that, if the spirit of our school was at stake. . . . I certainly read them the riot act, and at the same time tried to show them that I was for them, each and every one, in so far as each or any of them were four square and helpful to the school. The three of the whole lot who perhaps are the best candidates for expulsion are Ralph Horton, Jim Wilde and Jack Kennedy."

St. John's notes were made the following day. According to Maurice Shea, however, the boys *were* expelled. "I don't blame him. He thought that we were not quite the boys that he wanted to have the stamp of Choate on. So . . . we were all called into his study, and one by one as I remember, he talked to each one of us, told us our faults, and announced that there was a train somewhere between five and six o'clock and that was the train we should be on; that we were no longer students of his school."

Paul Chase also remembered being expelled. "At lunch the Head read off our thirteen names to the accompaniment of low whistles from the assembly. He demanded our presence in his study immediately after lunch. The Head ended a rather lengthy meeting with a statement that he deemed us unfit to continue at Choate, and we were thereupon dismissed from school." Rip Horton, too, confirmed that the boys were expelled: "At that stage of the game Mr. St. John dismissed each one of us from school—expelled us from school. . . . Our families were notified."

The thirteen wheels were crestfallen. However much they mocked, even hated school, expulsion was a stain that would affect their future careers.

Entrance to college—especially to the Ivy League institutions of Princeton, Yale, Harvard, Columbia, Dartmouth, and Penn—was predicated on the headmaster's report, with specific reference to school behavior (the so-called "Certificate of Honorable Dismissal"). Worse still was the shame of having to explain their expulsion to their parents.

Were the boys actually expelled? It seems that St. John, once his temper cooled, thought better of his decision, giving rise to all kinds of later rumors. "There must have been some kind of financial consideration," Horton reflected, assuming that Jack Kennedy's father had interceded on the boys' behalf, and had "thereafter donated 2 excellent projectors for the Saturday night movies."

The movie equipment, however, had been installed two years previously; moreover, St. John was not an easy man to be bought, as Maurice Shea later recalled. "I don't think Mr. Kennedy could have smoothed the water. In fact there is a story about one boy, not a Mucker, who was told he could not return. And at that time Choate had no swimming pool. And his mother came up and said if her son could return she would see that within the next year there would be a new building and that in the building would be the swimming pool that Choate needed. And the story went, the Head said, 'Choate needs a swimming pool, but it needs your son less.' "

All Shea could recall was that "somehow, between two o'clock and five o'clock," when the train was due to leave Wallingford with its contingent of expelled Muckers, Mr. St. John "relented or changed his mind and somehow we were given a second chance."

It is more likely that the Choate faculty interceded with the headmaster. Certainly LeMoyne Billings attributed the Muckers' reprieve to more considered counsels. "Actually all thirteen were rather outstanding boys in the school—all sixth formers. None of us had ever caused any *serious* trouble. Some of the Masters, who were more emotionally stable than Mr. St. John, reasoned with him to reconsider."

There was pressure also from outside. "Our parents spoke to the headmaster," Rip Horton remembered. As a result, after promising to disband the Muckers Club and to "more rigidly conform to the school administration and their regulations, we were taken back without ever actually having to leave school. We were punished by being kept over Easter vacation for three or four days and not allowed to go home with the rest of the students."

Doubtless this was so. In the case of the Irish arch-Mucker, however, Mr. St. John was unwilling to let the matter rest so lightly. St. John had already curtailed Jack's Christmas vacation; it had done no good. As he later put it, "At one time, it came to the point where I was saying to myself, 'Well, I have two things to do, one to run the school, another to run Jack Kennedy and his friends." St. John, therefore, cabled Mr. Kennedy.

Whether the headmaster realized he was the pawn in a psychological family drama is unlikely. According to an anonymous source (a member of St. John's staff), George St. John was prejudiced against Irish-Catholic "upstarts" such as the Kennedys, whose marital misbehavior and sudden wealth was subject to so much rumor. In telegraphing Mr. Kennedy, therefore, St. John may well have wished not only to further discipline Jack, but in a sense to discipline Jack's parents. Dispatching the wire both to Mr. Kennedy's office in New York and to the SEC in Washington, the headmaster asked, "Will you please make every possible effort to come to Choate Saturday or Sunday for a conference with Jack and us which we think a necessity."

Rose, meanwhile, was staying with her parents in Boston, and on behalf of her husband had blithely asked permission, in a telegram the previous Saturday, to "allow Jack to come to New York next Sat to see Father and Sister and spend night with them. Ask Jack to notify me at Hotel Bellevue Boston. Thank You." St. John was curt in his refusal: "Mr. Steele has shown me your telegram. I had just telegraphed Mr. Kennedy asking him to come to Choate on Sunday for a conference with Jack and us which I think a necessity. Very sincere regrets. George St. John."

Mrs. Kennedy remained silent. Mr. Kennedy cabled that he would arrive at the school at twelve-fifteen on Sunday, February 18, 1935. Jack, lamenting the cancellation of their planned weekend in New York, informed his sister Kathleen of events. Kathleen was impressed. Via Western Union telegraph, she lost no time in responding:

DEAR PUBLIC ENEMIES ONE AND TWO ALL OUR PRAYERS ARE UNITED WITH YOU AND THE OTHER ELEVEN MUCKS. WHEN THE OLD MEN ARRIVE SORRY WE WONT BE THERE FOR THE BURIAL.

This was, of course, intercepted by the Choate staff and immediately shown to Mr. St. John—further infuriating the already tormented headmaster.

"Mr. Kennedy and Jack and I sat together, in my study, and I rehearsed the chapter and verse of things that had happened," St. John recalled years later. "Well, we reduced Jack's conceit, if it was conceit, and childishness to considerable sorrow. And we said just what we thought, held nothing back, and Mr. Kennedy was supporting the school completely."

But was he? Even St. John recognized as time went by that a deeper change had taken place than he'd anticipated: that although the meeting was designed to chasten Jack, in fact it did the opposite, forcing Mr. Kennedy to see his son as he really was. "Psychologically I was enormously interested," St. John subsequently admitted. "I couldn't see how two boys from the same family could be so different." Nor could Mr. Kennedy, which essentially was the problem.

"Jack's father didn't hold back. In fact he spoke very, very strongly," St. John chronicled, adding that he would "always be grateful" to Mr. Kennedy for his support. Yet St. John was too acute an observer and too great an educator not to see beyond Mr. Kennedy's façade of righteous indignation. Mr. Kennedy, he added, had spoken "also with Irish wit. You know, in dealing with Jack, you needed a little wit as well as a little seriousness. Jack didn't like to be too serious; he had a delightful sense of humor always. His smile was, as a young boy, when he first came to school—well, in any school he would have got away with some things just on his smile. He was a very likeable person, very lovable."

Love was the issue. While Jack's mother sat in the Boston Bellevue Hotel with her own father, Jack's two fathers—his "headmaster-father" and his real father—sat with him at Choate. On the surface it was a meeting invoked to warn the chairman of the SEC and his son that, if there was any repetition of Jack's misbehavior or any further Mucker-like outrage, Jack would be expelled instanter, as Mr. Kennedy immediately warned his daughter Kathleen at her convent. "I know you want to do all you can for Jack," he wrote, "but I think I should tell you that one of the serious difficulties he found himself in was his characterization of public enemy and that group of his with the frightful name muckers. I really don't think there is anything smart about it and I hope it won't be the cause of having him expelled from the school. Therefore, I want to urge you to stop all this talk in letters and telegrams."

In truth, however, Mr. Kennedy *did* think Jack's Mucker gang was smart. That his wife had never appeared at Choate was due not only to her lack of maternal warmth, but to her timidity vis-à-vis the WASP aura such a school exuded. Joe Kennedy had kept away for similar reasons. Being carpeted now by his son's worthy, Republican headmaster was not to Joe Kennedy's liking. When the phone rang and St. John was unavoidably called away from the room, Mr. Kennedy could not help leaning over and whispering in Jack's ear, "My God, my son, you sure didn't inherit your father's directness or his reputation for using bad language. If that crazy Mucker's Club had been mine, you can be sure it wouldn't have started with an *M!*"

Capturing His Father's Heart

"Although the whole episode showed that Jack hadn't matured," Billings later acknowledged, "it showed some misdirected qualities of leadership in that we founded the club," a fact which Jack's father finally took on board. Mr. Kennedy himself had been a poor scholar at school, had had to repeat a year at Boston Latin, and though he'd won prizes for baseball and for captaining his school's drill squad, he'd been largely disliked, even feared—the college cad who then ran off with the winning ball when permitted to play in the traditional Harvard-Yale baseball match; the student blackballed by all the Harvard "final" clubs—as he was later by the Cohasset Country Club, the Country Club in Brookline and the Everglades in Palm Beach.

Even Rose Kennedy, for all her failure to be a real mother to Jack, recognized that the meeting at Choate in February 1935 after the "silly episode of the Muckers" was the "turning point in his life." "I'm sure he didn't like that confrontation with the headmaster and his father," she speculated from afar, "that three-cornered talk." Yet even she came to sense that "something certainly soaked in and deeply. There would be no way to measure the influence of this embarrassing necessity to talk things out—and to have a good talking-to, in open forum, from his father. . . . At any rate, his life took on a new momentum from then on."

The bleak journey that every adolescent must undergo in finding a personal identity and in testing the frontiers of parental affection had, at last, come to a head. As a mother, Rose had failed Jack; however, she was correct in sensing that the tête-à-tête between father and son produced a critical rapprochement. All at once Jack seemed to Joseph Kennedy very dear and very fragile, not only in regard to his physical health, but inasmuch as his very brilliance, mixed with his wild, untamed spirit, might lead to something far more worrying than the innocent Muckers Club. "I am afraid a boy with Jack's ideas, with too much time on his hands, could have a much more serious breakdown than a physical one," Mr. Kennedy confided to the chief physician at the Mayo Clinic, Dr. O'Leary.

Jack's friend Billings, too, felt it was an important moment in the relationship between father and son, though he put much of the blame on the headmaster. "What I'm really saying is that the Headmaster at that time was George St. John," Billings explained thirty years later. "As I think about him, he lacked the proper qualities to head up a boy's school. Although he had the ability to raise money and to favorably impress parents, he had absolutely no understanding of young boys in their most important, developing years. He took a very serious and dim view of the way Jack and I behaved. . . . Mr. Kennedy, wise as he was, saw that the Headmaster was making too much of little things. Although he wasn't at all pleased with Jack's immature behavior, he never had any interest in the school again after Jack graduated."

But Billings was overstating his point. However stuffy he was, St. John's heart was in the right place. At a critical moment in Jack's adolescence the headmaster had brought father and son together, forging a new, if uneasy, bond that was to last the rest of Jack's life. As he would capture so many other hearts, Jack had, finally, captured his father's.

The Psychologist's Report

"Has he been subject to discipline or censure of any sort during the present school year for deficiency in scholarship or for misconduct?"

Magnanimously, George St. John replied "No" on Jack's college-entrance applications in the spring of 1935, and penned a resounding "Yes" when asked to "vouch for the moral character of this applicant."

But would Jack pass the college-entrance examination in June? Was he to go to Princeton, where the majority of his friends—Rip Horton, Lem Billings, Bud Wynne, and others—would be going? "My desire to come to Princeton is prompted by a number of reasons," Jack entered on his application form in March 1935. "I feel that it can give me a better background and training than any other university, and can give me a true liberal education. Ever since I entered school I have had the ambition to enter Princeton, and I sincerely hope I can reach my goal. Then, too, I feel the environment of Princeton is second to none, and cannot but help having a good effect on me. To be a 'Princeton Man' is indeed an enviable designation."

Unknown to Princeton, Jack had given an almost identical explanation in his application to Harvard. If he favored Princeton, it was not because of its liberal education or beneficial environment, but simply because Rip, Lem, Bud, and many of his other WASP friends were planning to go there. Having spent two years free of the shadow of Joe Jr., who had matriculated at Harvard after his year in England, Jack did, however, have another reason.

Jack's "problem" with his elder brother went deeper than most people knew. Indeed there is a fascinating glimpse into Jack's psychology at age seventeen in the form of a report, undertaken shortly after the Muckers scandal by a Columbia University psychologist, Dr. Prescott Lecky, at Mr. St. John's recommendation. Dr. Lecky's analysis concluded that Jack was "undoubtedly a very able boy, but definitely in a trap psychologically speaking. He has established a reputation in the family for thoughtlessness, sloppiness and inefficiency, and he feels entirely at home in the role. Any criticism which he receives only serves to confirm the feeling that he has defined himself correctly; in fact the definition is the best possible defense that could be devised."

Lecky was intrigued. "How are you going to amount to anything if you have to be thoughtless and sloppy to be true to your role?" he asked Jack.

Jack appeared stumped. When Dr. Lecky "pointed out the great handicap he would be under in the business world he said, 'yes, that is true enough.' He thinks of himself as a self-reliant, intelligent and courageous boy, but he has never recognized the difficulty he will have in maintaining those definitions unless he sacrifices the defense device which he has built up through the years," and of which Jack was clearly proud. "He does not worry about his sloppiness, he says, and has never been neat in his life; but it is obvious that he must worry sooner or later, or give up the definitions which he values most."

How Jack had taken on the role of Mr. Sloppy in the first place Lecky sought to unravel. And why did Jack cling to the role so defensively? "A good deal of his trouble is due to comparison with an older brother," Lecky noted. "He remarked, 'My brother is the efficient one in the family, and I am the boy that doesn't get things done. If my brother were not so efficient, it would be easier for me to be efficient. He does it so much better than I do."

This struck Lecky as pretty smart. "Jack is apparently avoiding comparison and withdraws from the race, so to speak, in order to convince himself that he is not trying. He does not define himself as a left winger, and I have no doubt personally that he could be convinced fairly easily of the contradiction in his scheme and the necessity for revising his point of view."

But who was to do the convincing? Despite his reconciliation with his father, Jack was now almost persona non grata with the Choate staff. Certainly he refused to change his spots. He and Lem even wrote off in a vain effort to join the French Foreign Legion (the letter being intercepted by Mr. St. John, who promised to alter their diet and give them a sample of Foreign Legion cuisine if they really wished). Then, at the very Festivities Weekend that had originally given rise to the Muckers scandal, Jack couldn't resist the temptation to tweak the nose of the Choate establishment a little more.

"Each boy was allowed to ask a girl," Billings recalled. "Part of the entertainment was a show of some kind put on by the Dramatic

Club. . . . The show was always a musical by Gilbert and Sullivan. It was compulsory for the entire school to see the performance three or four times a year. . . . At this particular time, we had all seen the performance, and did not want to see it again." Instead, Jack and Lem decided to take their dates for a drink.

> A former roommate at Choate was Pete Caesar. He brought his car with him. It was just too much of a temptation for us to use it. Jack had Olive Cawley as a date and I, a girl from Pittsburgh named Pussy Brooks. This was a very scary experience for us. . . . Remember, this was our senior year, just about a month before graduation. During the performance of Gilbert and Sullivan, Pete Caesar drove us all to a roadhouse—where we may have ordered a beer—certainly nothing more serious because we didn't drink at that time. . . . We stayed away from Choate long enough for the end of the performance. We had hoped to return as everyone was going from the theater to the Dining Hall. Everyone was in evening clothes—in fact we were in "tails." Unfortunately, we were in an open car. As we approached the school, we discovered that another car was following us. These were the proctors, whose duty was to check on the activities of the boys. We knew if they caught us we would be in the most serious kind of trouble.
>
> Fortunately, it was a pitch dark night. Pete Caesar drove at top speed out into the country with the authorities in hot pursuit. Jack and myself couldn't have been more frightened. Knowing our past experience with the Headmaster, we knew this would really be enough to finish our careers at Choate. We'd have been thrown out, without any question.
>
> Remember, we were all in very formal evening clothes. The girls, of course, had very high-heel shoes. We drove into a farmyard, turned off the car lights and Jack, Olive and I all ran into the barn. Pussy stayed in the car pretending that she was kissing Pete Caesar.

Though the school proctors flashed their torches at the kissing couple, there was nothing they could do because, as Billings recalled,

> they had no authority over a graduate student. Nevertheless, they apparently were sure that there had been under-graduates in the car, although they couldn't identify us. . . . The school car stayed there. Pete Caesar's car stayed there. Finally, Pete Caesar drove off in the opposite direction from the school and away went the school car after him. At the barn we had no way of knowing whether the proctors had left someone behind or not.

You can imagine how harrowing this experience was. Finally, Pete Caesar came back and drove into the barnyard very fast; no other car was in sight. Olive rushed out and lay on the floor at Pussy's feet with a coat thrown over her. I dashed to the back—Pete opened the trunk and I jumped in. He closed me in. We didn't dare call for Jack—so we left him behind.

At that moment the school proctors' car reappeared and the chase resumed. Eventually Pete Caesar drove to the center of Wallingford and at top speed, careening around corners, lost his pursuer. "He delivered Olive and myself to the dance and we danced into the crowd despite the fact that Olive had lost one heel from her shoe and looked pretty messy. About half an hour later," Billings remembered, "Jack showed up," having walked the mile to the school.

It was a close shave, but fun. Bill Garnett, another contemporary, remembered that Jack "had extreme self-confidence—quiet, not cocky—and determination. Also he had a brilliant mind and had the ability to absorb quickly and remember all kinds of information and facts from 'the sublime to the ridiculous' "—the latter, as Jack's English teacher, Courtenay Hemenway, recalled, being expressed in his irrepressible wit. Even a quarter of a century later Hemenway could remember some of Jack's quips, as written for the year's yearbook, *The Brief:*

> Fathers Day. 300 odd fathers arrive.
> Yale Alumni drop in for meals on way to Smith prom.
> Sociable fellows.
> Gertrude Stein talks to those who understand. English masters in fog.
> Mr. Hemenway says his handicap in golf is his honesty.

Tradition also had it that, as part of the *Brief's* content, a poll should be conducted among the 112 graduating students to elect "the handsomest, the best dancer, and the wittiest, and so on," Rip Horton related. Jack was determined to cock a snook at the school establishment, and announced he would go for the title of "Most Likely to Succeed"—a complete travesty of his record at Choate.

This was to be Jack's first protopolitical campaign. The chairman of the student council, the body which had originally ratted on the Muckers' plan for scandalizing the school Festivities weekend, had been tipped to take the title, but Jack was undaunted. In a deft display of behind-the-scenes bargaining, votes were traded and Jack was able to snub the faculty and St. John. "Despite the opinion the Head might rightfully have had of us," ex-Mucker Paul Chase later recalled, "as a group we were quite popular among our peers, and had a certain amount of persuasive power among them." Tapping that power, Jack persuaded his fellow felons to become campaigners on his behalf. "We were very eager and willing. If we were successful with one person, we enlisted him to work on three others, and so on."

Some students resented Jack's winning ways, the fact that he did so little work yet managed to get away with passing grades; that in a school of Republican sons he was a publican's grandson; that his father was working for a president whose image, in Republican circles, was that of a dictatorial socialist waging war on big business in America. Such resentment could well have led to scapegoatism, certainly to ethnic prejudice. Yet Jack's clowning antics, his constant punishment at the hands of masters such as J. J. Maher, and the stoical way he coped with his medical trials eventually won over the majority of his classmates. "The result," Chase related, "was Jack's one-sided victory, astounding I am sure to many at the time. Funnily enough, it did not seem such an outstanding or undeserved result to me in 1935, because even at that time Jack, although only a mediocre student, had a tremendous charm and a lot of drive and ambition."

In fact Jack Kennedy won his title by a margin of thirty-seven votes over the nearest contender—the largest plurality of the graduating-class elections. Though rigged, the election reflected, as one of his teachers later recalled, Jack's extraordinary popularity among his peers rather than the expectations of the worthy staff. "Everybody knew him, most liked him, and all recognized his ability. The faculty would not have voted this way," Hemenway acknowledged, "which once more proves that the judgment of contemporaries is much more accurate than that of one's elders."

"The outstanding thing about Jack in school," Bob Lindsay recalled, "was his ability to win the friendship and admiration of everyone. He went at his work and play alike—energetically and enthusiastically. He was kind, friendly and forthright with everyone." Ed Meredith agreed. "Even in this formative period, his energy was extremely evident—as was his obvious attraction for the more desirable sub-debs inhabiting Palm Beach in those days!" Another boy summed up, "Jack always had qualities of leadership and would have reached the top no matter what school he attended."

Meanwhile, Jack's final year at Choate was coming to a close. He'd scraped his knee in April, and the wound had become infected, leading to further doubts about his immunogenic system when for weeks the laceration would not heal. Yet, with the end of his school days finally in sight, Jack began to pull out stops, taking even his classmates by surprise. The boy who regularly failed to open his classbooks finished the academic year with a 75 percent in English, 74 in physics, and 77 in English history.

And in the Harvard University entrance examinations, in June 1935, he was awarded an 85 percent in English and the same in History: honors grades. For a boy so often sick and who had been dramatically expelled from school only three months before, this—on top of his work as business manager in putting out the most financially successful Choate yearbook ever produced and being elected "Most Likely to Succeed" over the staff's favorite—was no mean achievement.

Courtenay Hemenway recalled later:

> He realized his high potential in History where he blossomed under the brilliant teaching and great knowledge of details of Russell Ayres. He appreciated Ayres' off-beat information and constitutional learning. In fact perhaps here began Jack's thorough and versatile understanding of government and politics. Jack also appreciated his experience with perhaps the best English Department in secondary schools: Douglas Shepardson, Harold Tinker, Dudley Fitts, Carey Briggs, Darrah Kelley, Allen Smart, and William Freeman, all of whom he had. He understood the reading even when he hadn't read it and always wrote fluently and incisively. . . . Stanley Pratt's Public Speaking course was his meat. . . . He was not so steady as his brother Joe, but there were flashes of brilliance.

As usual, J. J. Maher disagreed. In his final report, Maher concentrated on Jack's negative qualities, not his virtues:

> I'd like to take the responsibility for Jack's constant lack of neatness about his room and person, since he lived with me for two years. But in the matter of neatness, despite a genuine effort on Jack's part, I must confess to failure.
>
> I regard the matter of neatness or lack of it on Jack's part as quite symbolic—aside from the value it has in itself—for he is casual and disorderly in almost all of his organization projects. Jack studies at the last minute, keeps appointments late, has little sense of material value, and can seldom locate his possessions.

Maher was writing like a nagging old woman—an old queen in more ways than one. But he reluctantly acknowledged, that "Jack has lost some of the feeling that every master is an enemy who has to be outwitted at every turn."

Wardell St. John, the assistant headmaster, was more reflective in his final letter to Jack's parents. It was he who'd worked on Mr. Kennedy to transfer Jack from Canterbury, and despite the Muckers business, he was not without pride in his departing ward. "Jack," he predicted, "has it in him to be a great leader of men, and somehow I have the feeling that he is going to be just that."

Dragging his steamer trunk to the Rolls-Royce, Jack Kennedy, just turned eighteen, bade farewell in June 1935 to the "hole" that had been his prison, his adolescent battleground, the site of his growing up, for four years. It was time, at last, to go to college.

PART
·4·
FRESHMAN
YEARS

Jack Kennedy, Lem Billings, and Jack's dachsund Offie in The Hague, August 1937 (John F. Kennedy Library)

The Captain's Ball

On July 23, 1935, Jack heard he'd been accepted by Harvard. "Made it by God how about you?" he cabled Lem Billings. But once he learned that Billings had been accepted by Princeton, Jack hurled himself into the task of converting his father and transferring there.

Jack's father, however, had other ideas, having resigned as chairman of the SEC after only a year in office. He had lost, he claimed, at least $100,000 because in that position he was not permitted to play the stock market. Moreover, he disliked the direction in which Roosevelt's administration was heading, particularly in light of the latest Senate investigation of U.S. railroad companies. He'd accepted Roosevelt's commission, he explained, in order to help save the stock market as a capitalist institution in an age of socialism and frightening unemployment; but that did not mean he believed in state control, or bigger departments of Federal government.

In truth, Kennedy wanted a better job. Anxious lest he lose support he might need the following year when seeking reelection, Roosevelt had offered Kennedy alternative posts in the administration, such as the chairmanship of the committee overseeing his historic public-works program. Kennedy had declined them all. He wished to become secretary of the treasury, and despite his notoriety as a stock-market swindler, he could not understand why Roosevelt withheld the post from him, now that he had reformed the market.

Announcing to the press that he was "through with public life," Kennedy packed his bags for a vacation to Europe. Brushing aside Jack's protest, he not only insisted Jack accompany him, and spend a year under Professor Laski at the London School of Economics, but at his wife's behest he dragged his daughter Kathleen along too, to be confined in a strict Catholic convent school in France, as Honey Fitz had once incarcerated Rose at Blumenthal.

Jack was half excited, half mortified. "Send gray hat immediately," he wired Billings in Pittsburgh in September. "Sailing 1045 Wednesday morning."

The journey to England—Jack's first-ever abroad—didn't bode well. He soon wrote to Princeton from his cabin on the S.S. *Normandie*,

> Dear Lemmer,
> This is the fourth day out and it is getting pretty goddammed rough.
> Have had a pretty fair time so far, and have worked out 1 hr. a day

in the gym boxing. The food here is very pimp-laden and my face is causing much comment from the old man, and it is getting damned embarrassing. He really rang the bell when after helping myself to a dessert that was oozing with potential pimps he said my face was getting to look like yours."

Jack also claimed to have started a "budding friendship" with a "most unattractive" girl "with freckles and pimps . . . and we are comparing notes on your face." Putting Billings down, however, could not disguise Jack's boredom or envy of his pals back home as they began their Princeton careers. "There are not many young people aboard," he lamented, "except a French guy who is rather nice and a terrific girl." Nevertheless he had one "very strange experience," he confessed to Billings. "There is a fat Frenchie aboard who is a 'homo.' He has had me to his cabin more than once and is trying to bed me," he teased Billings. "Tonight is the Captain's Ball—don't be dirty, Kirk, I am not discussing his vital organs—and they give free champagne, as much as you want.

"How is everything going? I suppose you people are having quite a time. . . . Write me at the Claridge. My next letter on my foreign experience will be to Rip from London—remember me to him." Signing himself "Desiribles," he also asked Billings to "say hello to Wynne, Merrick, Blandbo and the boys," and in a final postscript remarked, "My French is driving these boys insane—*comme on ce va.*"

"Dear unattractive," Jack wrote a week after reaching London. "Got your exciting letter. Have had quite some time since I last wrote you," he scrawled, using the Hotel Claridge's smartest notepaper. "We were to get off at Plymouth at 3:00 Sunday night—we ran into a storm and we were blown to a place in France after staying up all night." Taking the ferry boat to Dover, they'd "found out the Channel was the roughest of the year. . . . We sat out and soon everyone began to yawk. I was on deck singing to one of the women in the party. I was singing 'The Man on the flying trapeze' and when I came to the part where you break into the chorus with O O O Ohhhh, etc, a woman behind me retched all over me with 'oh my God that's the finish'—you can imagine me covered from tip to toe with hot vomit."

There was more talk of pimples, Jack's refusal to believe that his friend's complexion had improved, and mockery of his sister Kathleen, who had a blemish on her chin.

However, buried amid the obsessive talk of pimples, vomit, sex, and other adolescent preoccupations was the stunning news that Jack might not, after all, attend the London School of Economics under Laski; that he was on the verge of returning to America and starting at Princeton.

The London School of Economics

In March that year Hitler had announced that he was reinstituting military conscription in defiance of the Versailles Treaty. German troops had brazenly marched through demilitarized Saarland (which had recently been returned to Germany from League of Nations control) and Italy had increased its mobilization, boasting a million men under arms. By July Britain—having already decided to triple its air force—agreed to abandon naval quotas. The European arms race became official. On September 30, tens of thousands of Italian troops moved to Africa, in preparation for Mussolini's invasion of Ethiopia. The outlook for peace seemed grimmer than Mr. Kennedy had expected. Jack, however, was ecstatic: "Am definitely coming to Princeton as London looks very tense and know Dad will let me so it ought to be very jolly. My complexion is still rather shady but is on the upward road."

Before his travel arrangements could be made, however, Jack fell sick again. Frantic cables were sent to Boston and to the Mayo for advice, Dr. William Murphy wiring back to Jack's father at Claridge's on October 10, 1935:

> DIAGNOSIS JACKS ILLNESS FEBRUARY 1934 AGRANULOCYTOSIS. ATYPICAL STRONGLY URGE INJECTION LIVER EXTRACT EVERY EIGHT HOURS UNTIL WELL IF DESIRED SUGGEST CONSULT LORD DAWSON OF PENN OR SIR THOMAS HORDER.

When he was hospitalized in London, Jack's condition first appeared grave, then miraculously took a turn for the better. "My health since my last letter has improved," he wrote in mid-October to Billings,

> and I am once more baffling the doctors. I am a "most amazing case." They are doing a number of strange things to me, not the least of which is to shove a tremendous needle up my "cheeks." Today was most embarrassing as one doctor came in just after I had woken up and was reclining with a semi [erection] on due to the cold weather. His plan was to stick his finger under my pickle and have me cough. His plan was quickly changed however when he drew back the covers and there was "J. J. Maher" quivering with life. As the nurses were 3 deep around the bed, I was rather non-plussed for a time.

Once again Jack adopted the mock-heroic, self-deflating, often cruelly witty style he'd made his own, determined to see his own life as a series of quixotic adventures. "We shall miss him in spite of all our grumbling," St. John had confessed when Jack left Choate, and it was not hard to see why.

Recovering meanwhile from his latest brush with the Reaper, Jack paradoxically decided to make a go of his LSE course. He was beginning to like London. "I have gotten a hell of a good roommate, an American about 25 who is really swell," he told Billings. "We are taking a house with a maid and it sounds very cozy. They say it is only a stone's throw from Buckingham Palace so I shall be shortly hurling stones at the king. There is a very good looking blonde whom Dad seems to know, about 24, who is a divorcee. She is studying here and comes to see me every day. She is going to St. Moritz with me at Christmas but I have not as yet laid her," he admitted. "The nurses here are very sexy and the night-nurse is continually trying to goose me so I have always to be on my guard."

The social scene in London challenged the precocious playboy in him, even though he affected to be unimpressed by the girls he met at the LSE. "The night before I got in here I attended the 'Fresher's Social.' It was the strangest affair I have ever seen. The place was lousy with Boogies who were holding in their arms pimply faced English school-girls. No one seemed to think anything of it. It would have made that old Baltimore blood of yours boil, however. I met quite a few Americans and some English, though, who weren't bad guys," the eighteen-year-old reported. "My most intimate pally became Hyman Purloff, a terrific yid. This would certainly be no place for you," he mocked Billings. Nevertheless he had, so he claimed, "met a cousin of yours in this hospital, Prince Surloff, who is supposed to be next Czar or some such shit. He ran at Oxford and knew 'Charlie' Stanwood. The Prince stated that old Charlie was certainly a Prince among men and I agreed heartily that he certainly was. I have met a number of Earls + Lords here and I am getting rather royal myself."

From the British aristocracy Jack proceeded to the nobility of Baltimore. "From your description and after talking it over with my nightnurse," Jack was now certain "you have sif. This will teach you a good lesson and will stop you from screwing every girl you meet. The nightnurse agreed that it would definitely cramp your style, at least she said 'until after he grows skin back on his penis after they scrape it off.' Evidently your hands will be full for the next 4 or 5 years taking care of your vital organ." He also warned Billings that "you will no doubt get kicked out of Princeton if you continue to try and hook the Nassau Bell Clapper" (the famous Princeton College bell, which Billings had declared he would silence). "If I were you I would worry more about my own clapper and the pimple on it than I would about the clapper on Nassau Hall."

In spite of the joshing tone in which he wrote to Billings, Jack remained a true friend, and Billings's current money troubles did not go unaddressed. "Your financial worries have also upset me, as Princeton would not be awfully jolly without your sif covered face," he wrote, offering to loan Billings "the $500.00 Steelegram now as it is still intact and I won't need it. You can pay me after you get out of college. You then would not have to borrow from that old Prick Uncle Ike. Let me know about this and wether [sic] you need it, because I won't be needing it. How is Olive? Let me know what she is doing and don't screw her. Dad says I can go home if I want to," he finally announced, getting to the point," but have decided to stay as figure it would be rather stupid to go home now."

Clearly, Jack had begun to enjoy himself, though he thought it possible he'd return for the Christmas vacation and told Billings to try and "get out of" any work he might be planning the following summer. "Remember me to the boys," he concluded, "and leave the chapel clapper + your own alone."

It was, however, the last letter Jack would write to Billings from London. The simple truth was, the London School of Economics didn't impress Jack as it had his brother. He had no wish to sit at Laski's feet—or anyone else's. What he wanted was fun, which was difficult when he wasn't feeling well. He therefore cabled Billings in Princeton to say he'd decided to return to the States after all.

Billings was overjoyed. "Nothing could possibly sound better so hurry home," he cabled back on October 17.

"They didn't seem to know what it was," Billings later recalled, referring to Jack's mystery illness in England. The LSE plan, at any rate, was permanently abandoned. "If he were going to be sick, he might as well be sick over here, so he left London and came home."

To Be a Princeton Man

"A chap by the name of John Fitzgerald Kennedy who graduated from the Choate School in June, is now re-applying for admission to Princeton," Dean Heermance wrote on October 22, 1935, to his opposite number at Harvard. "He has been on our list for some time but then I think transferred his allegiance to Harvard and finally decided to go to the University of London. He is returning from England this week and has asked for reconsideration from Princeton. Do you mind sending me the grades that he obtained on his Plan B examinations taken in June 1935."

Given his father's strong preference for Harvard, Jack's insistence on going to Princeton was, as his friend Hugh Wynne later reflected, "a considerable act of independence." True to his word, Mr. Kennedy—who had informed the American ambassador in London that he'd "found it necessary to send my boy home"—had told his New York office to contact Harvard. Thus, even before Dean Heermance wrote from Princeton, Harvard was sending Jack's results to New Jersey. "The Committee on Admissions do not give specific grades obtained by an admitted plan B candidate, but they do indicate where Honors (80–89) or Highest Honors (90–100) have been obtained. Mr. Kennedy, I am glad to tell you, received Honors in English and English History."

Jack was in. Anticipating this, he'd wired Billings, "Arriving Princeton Thursday [October 24] afternoon. Hope you can arrange rooming—Ken." All rooms on campus had, however, long since been assigned. Billings thus suggested that Jack share his and Rip Horton's two-man "suite" on the fifth floor of South Reunion Hall. Built in 1870, the dormitory building contained the cheapest freshman rooms at the college—"three dinky rooms, no bathroom, a single radiator, a cramped closet, no electrical outlets except a bulb suspended from the ceiling in each room," wrote a journalist shortly before its demolition in the 1960s.

Jack was perfectly happy with the scheme. Into Billings's narrow seven-and-a-half-by-twelve-foot bedroom the ex-Muckers squeezed another cot. The nearest bathroom was down one flight of stone stairs; the next nearest was in the basement. Their living room, however, felt more spacious—eleven by fourteen feet—with "a magnificent view" of next-door Nassau Hall, the original site of Princeton College, its ivy-covered walls capped by a white lantern-cum-belfry.

Mr. Kennedy, when he came to see Jack, was not amused. "I remember when Mr. Kennedy first came to visit us, he climbed those sixty-four steps, he thought there must be some other place his son could stay," Billings recalled. Rip Horton recalled the same: "Ambassador Kennedy pulled up there in a large Cadillac, chauffeur-driven, and we were up four flights. After he climbed two flights—he had on a very heavy coat of his for a football game that he had come to Princeton for—he was so fatigued that he stood out on the fire escape and threw it down to Dave the chauffeur."

Mr. Kennedy's anxiety was not confined to Jack's somewhat elevated dwelling. He'd insisted Jack return to the U.S. so that his son's health could be properly monitored, but although Jack never complained, his condition was alarming. As Bud Wynne recalled, Jack "kept turning yellow, a yellowish-brown tan, almost as if he'd been sunbathing." Mr. Kennedy thus took pains, on his visit, to speak with the university doctor,

Dr. Raycroft. As he wrote to Jack on November 11, two weeks after Jack's late start at Princeton, "We have decided to . . . see how you get along until Thanksgiving. Then if no real improvement has been made, you and I will discuss whether or not it is best for you to lay off a year and try and put yourself in condition. After all, the only consideration I have in the whole matter is your happiness, and I don't want you to lose a year of your college life (which ordinarily brings great pleasure to a boy) by wrestling with a bad physical condition and a jam in your studies. A year is important, but it isn't so important if it's going to leave a mark for the rest of your life."

To Ambassador Bingham in London, Kennedy meanwhile explained that "Jack is far from being a well boy and is giving me great concern, with the result that my time for the next six months will be devoted to trying to help him recover his health with little or no time for business and politics"—a bald exaggeration which obviated mention of the embarrassing fact that Roosevelt had still made Kennedy no new job offer.

Jack, meanwhile, refused to give in. He'd finally gotten to the university of his choice, and was united with his pals. "The three of us as freshmen stuck pretty much together," Rip Horton recalled. On weekends they would go into New York, an hour and a half away by train, in search of nocturnal amusement, and there was little attempt to study, even in the subjects in which Jack excelled. Jack's first results were therefore not very good. On a scale of 1–6, with 6 as the lowest grade, he obtained a 3 in "military science" (a two-year course with field-artillery instruction as its most demanding element), a 4 in history, a 5 in English, and a 7 in mathematics. "I didn't even know the scale went down to 7!" his friend Bud Wynne later marveled.

Six feet tall, weighing a mere 135 pounds, and unable to play any sports save light boxing, Jack was delighted to be with his old school cronies, but was otherwise less directed even than at Choate. On his application form in March, he'd given "banking" as the profession he expected to enter after graduation from college, but his freshman performance raised some question as to whether he would graduate at all. By late November the weather had turned miserable, and the little open fire in the South Reunion living room gave scant comfort.

Princeton, moreover, disappointed Jack. James Madison and Woodrow Wilson had attended the college; Einstein and Thomas Mann would later teach there. But its small campus in a tiny rural New Jersey town made it almost more insular than Choate, and certainly it was more oppressively Protestant. The campus reeked with Presbyterian chapels. The giant Presbyterian theological department, known as the Seminary and the target of Jack's ribald humor, had split off to one side of the university. Even the name of Jack's dormitory referred to the reunion of

Presbyterian schisms. Of the tiny Jewish quota of ten students, only two dared openly confess their religion, according to the secretary of the treasury's sons; and though Jack attended mass with his roommate Rip Horton off campus, there was no likelihood that, as a Boston-Irish Roman Catholic, he would ever be accepted by any of the socially desirable junior- or senior-year dining clubs, his friend Bud Wynne later admitted.

Princeton's provincialism was a comedown for Jack. Though later withdrawing the statement from his narrative of Jack's presidency at the personal request of Lem Billings, the historian Arthur Schlesinger was told by Jack's family that "Princeton had not greatly impressed him." This was undoubtedly true. "I think he was a little disenchanted with the country-club atmosphere of Princeton," Jack's best friend at Harvard would later recall. As Bud Wynne reflected, Jack had "wanted to come to Princeton as part of a rebellion against his father's distant wishes and expectations." Apart from his pals from Choate, however, Princeton itself appeared to have very little to offer Jack, and much that reminded him uncomfortably of boarding school.

Nor did Jack, normally so gregarious, make new friends at the college. "He stayed at Princeton about two months but he was sick the entire time he was there," Billings recalled. "He . . . he just wasn't well. He went to all of his classes, but just wasn't terribly well."

By early December the writing was on the wall. Together with his "roomies" Jack posed for a typical devil-may-care Christmas photograph, with lyrics based on Fred Astaire's latest hit, "Top Hat":

> We're puttin' on our top hat
> Tyin' up our white tie
> Brushin' off our tails
> In order to wish you
> A Merry Christmas.

Dressed only in long white winter underwear, Rip Horton was waving a top hat, Billings wrestling with a huge bow tie, and Jack brushing off one of the tails of his frock coat. Humorous and irreverent, it was meant to show how much fun the boys were having at Princeton. Before it could even be posted, however, Jack was taken sick and dispatched to the Peter Bent Brigham Hospital in Boston for observation by Dr. Murphy.

Rip and Lem were at first caustic in their concern. "Tell us what time to arrive for funeral," they cabled on December 10. "Guess what Mrs. Warren [the cleaning help] thinks you have. She wants to know where you've been fu--ing around. As a matter of fact everyone is wondering that."

The doctors in Boston, however, were no nearer a solution to the puzzle of Jack's ill health than was Mrs. Warren. They recommended getting a second opinion from a Richmond specialist, Dr. Warren T. Vaughan. Thus on December 12, 1935, Dr. Vaughan cabled Jack from Virginia to say he would "see you tomorrow morning" for a medical examination, and cautioning that "the study may require three or four days."

The university physician, Dr. Raycroft, was not disposed to wait. On December 13 he wrote to Dr. Gauss, dean of the college:

> You are probably familiar with the interesting case of John Fitzgerald Kennedy, [class of] '39. We have been in touch with his doctors ever since he came here and it now appears advisable for him to withdraw from the university for the purpose of having such examinations and treatment as his condition may require in the hope that he will improve sufficiently to return as a Freshman next fall. This arrangement for withdrawal should be dated December 12th.

It was the end of Jack's brave effort to stick things out. He would never return to the college, though. He'd been there six weeks—quite enough to cure him of wanting "to be a Princeton Man."

Leukemia

Jack's sudden departure from Princeton later gave rise to the rumor that he'd secretly gotten married and thus been forced to withdraw—an indiscretion then covered up by his powerful father, who managed to excise it from the court records. "Yes, he was married at Princeton," a classmate maintained. "Well, his father had that marriage annulled, but people who knew the Kennedys pretty much knew about it. It was such a short-lived thing, and then the annulment, and so he never mentioned anything about it." Yet another version had Jack marrying an English girl of low social standing, even a prostitute, and therefore being sent home from the London School of Economics when his father discovered what had happened.

Both stories were, however, intrinsically unlikely. It was Joseph Kennedy who was keeping the "terrific" twenty-four-year-old tart as his mistress in London, not Jack; moreover, Jack lasted only six weeks at Princeton, his career ended by genuine medical infirmity.

From Dr. Vaughan's clinic Jack made his way to Palm Beach. "Dear

Los Moine," the convalescent scribbled to apologize for not having been able to smuggle Billings aboard the overnight train to Florida, "Am writing this 'en-route' if you know what I mean, although I don't suppose you do. Did my best to wait. In fact stayed at Olive's till 7:45 phoning J.P. [his father]. I had made a temporary compartment reservation for the trip down for Friday night and after phoning Dad and arguing with him for 20 minutes I talked to Mother who said there was no need to get a compartment as it was 30.00 extra. Of course that immediately wrecked everything as I could not possibly have sneaked you down any other way. Did my best as Olive will testify and my best is 'as good as most and better than some,' to quote a favorite expression of our late Head-Master, Dr. St. John."

Apologies soon gave way to observant smut: "Just looked out the window in South Carolina and saw a little black boy taking a shit before the admiring gaze of 10 or twelve of his girl-friends. That's a line you might use." He hoped Billings would come down to Florida by bus; if not, that he'd drive down with Wynne and Merrick. (Billings didn't.)

Father and son were now both in limbo. Though Joseph Kennedy sent a crate of whiskey to the White House, he was given no new position by Roosevelt, and soon accepted a series of cost-cutting commissions for RCA, Paramount, and, in due course, William Randolph Hearst. The days of being paid half a million dollars for sorting out Pathé were over, however, and he made do with lesser emoluments—$150,000 from RCA and $50,000 from Paramount—still substantial sums when hundreds of thousands of Americans were dying of malnutrition and millions were still without work.

Jack's medical trial, meanwhile, recommenced after Christmas at the Peter Bent Brigham Hospital in Boston. Once again the intimate examination of his body was unsettling for an eighteen-year-old—"the most harrowing experience of all my storm-tossed career. They came in this morning with a gigantic rubber tube," he wrote to Billings in Princeton.

Old stuff I said, and rolled over thinking that it would [be] stuffed up my arse. Instead they grabbed me and shoved it up my *nose.* I didn't know whether they thought my face was my ass or what but anyway they shoved it up my nose and down into my stomach. They then poured alcohol down the tube, me meanwhile going crazy as I couldn't taste the stuff and you know what a good stiff drink does to me. They were doing this to test my acidosis. Soon I felt myself getting high. I had this thing up my nose for 2 hours and they just took it out (don't be dirty Kirk) and now I have a "head-on," and a "hard on" as when they had finished a beautiful nurse came in and rubbed my *whole* body.

Took a look at my chart and discovered I do not have sif as they gave me the Wasserman. I was just imagining the excitement that would have given!

Syphilis was not Jack's only concern. "My [white] blood count this morning was 3500. When I came it was 6000. At 1500 you die. They call me '2000 to go Kennedy.' . . . Tonight Dana Maher and I carry on and I'm expecting big things." In between hospital tests he'd been "learning the rumba at 50¢ an hour in a dirty little dance hall" in Boston. "Dana has been spreading a lot of stories that I am quote 'sloppy on the kissing' as I happened to kiss her on the cheek New Years Eve," Jack wrote, dismissing a current rumor. Ignoring the mysterious, even life-threatening nature of his malady, he boasted he was "the most popular guy at Dana Hall and simply took the place by storm."

"I don't know why you and Rip are so unpopular with girls," Jack jeered in another letter. "You're certainly not ugly looking exactly. I guess they're [sic] is just something about you that makes girls dislike you on sight. I was figuring it out this morning. . . . It certainly is too bad. I guess you are not just cut out to be a ladies man. Mr. Niehans even has a girl, and so has Ike England. Frankly, my son, I'm stumped. Well send me my belt you prick right away, Regards, Ken."

Jack's letters cascaded out of the Peter Bent Brigham Hospital, wild, witty, swaggering but never daunted—except when he thought he might be missing action elsewhere. "Received with your boring letter," he wrote on January 27, 1936, "one from Hankers Wankers, the debbies delight, who tells me that '*therre* [sic] are millions of beautiful young misses arriving in Palm Beach daily,' so am getting rather fed up with the meat up here, if you know what I mean."

Any hopes Jack had of hightailing it back to Florida to take advantage of the female influx was soon jolted by the medical staff, however. "They have not found out anything as yet," Jack reported, "except that I have *leukemia,* + agranulocytosis. Took a peak [sic] at my chart yesterday and could see that they were mentally measuring me for a coffin. Eat drink and make Olive, as tomorrow or next week we attend my funeral. I think the Rockefeller Institute may take my case."

Jack simply refused to take such a fatal diagnosis seriously. "Flash!" he appended to his letter. "Got the hottest neck ever out of Hansen Saturday night. She is pretty good so am looking forward to bigger and better ones. Also got a good one last night from J. so am doing you proud. Gave up Bunny Day, I must admit, as a failure," he confessed, though, after having previously boasted he would soon "climb" her "frame."

The weeks of tests, examinations, and consultations dragged on. Irritated but undaunted, Jack lived for weekends, when the hospital ran no tests and he could indulge his fondness for dances, girls, and action, and bask in his popularity. Making new "conquests"—whether sexual or simply charismatic—inspired him to produce his formidable charm. He flourished in adversity, and between the lines of his smutty, gossipy, deliberately profane letters, Billings had little difficulty in reading unspoken tenderness—a sort of vulnerability his friend hated to show, childlike and endearing, couched always in the humorous, epigrammatical style of a macho ladies man. Adoring Olive Cawley, Jack wanted Billings's help. "Am coming to you for advice on the Cawley situation—should I ask her after this deliberate slight? [Olive had failed to reply to Jack's last letter.] It's your roomie who is asking you and he's also asking you to leave my writing paper alone. That writing paper was a present from one of my feminine admirers, a woman who worships the very air I breathe," he described Billings's mother, "but who unfortunately has a son with bad breath."

The witticisms were all part of Jack's refusal to take himself, life, or death seriously; yet the way he wrote belied a certain intensity that was deeply serious. As Rip Horton recalled, Jack

> liked anything he did—if he didn't like it, he wouldn't do it. In those days even, he was a person of many interests. He liked sports, he liked rough-housing, he liked to be sloppy, he liked to play golf, he liked girls. But he would never stick to anything, he would never give himself over entirely to anything. He loved to come to New York and stay with me. We'd go out to these night clubs and I remember going to hear Helen Morgan sing. I remember Jack was there and Jack Sheinkle and Smokey Joe Wilde. . . . We were all fairly well to do. . . . That appealed to Jack—going out. He was a guy who *lived* very hard 24 hours a day.

"Here is something to think about also Lem," Jack warned at the end of January 1936 when asked to contribute to a new party Jack Sheinkle was organizing, for, as Olive Cawley pointed out, Jack considered himself the leader of his gang, however democratic the discussions. "There is something about this I don't follow."

> Is everyone chipping in $10.00 or what? I don't mind spending $10.00 in a party of Rip, you + Shink but I'm not going to chip in bucks for a lot of guys to come in and drink because that makes you a sucker no matter how you look at it. This is not a "share the wealth" program LeMoyne—I am perfectly willing to chip in with Shink as he has always been a gay sport but I want to find out how this is

being run. If the roads are snowy or something I shall probably have to fly which will cost me 25.00. Also am getting Smoke and going out Friday night so will have to put up plenty + also I don't want to waste $10.00 on a lot of guys whom you suddenly have taken a liking to so make up your mind to it as it will buy us a good bottle of champagne or a fuck. LeMoyne you've got to cut out this philanthropic stuff until you can back it up. I haven't had a god-damned thing to do with this party as yet and [am] not even going to drink so as you are the guiding spirit of it am writing to you. Have written Shink telling him I will chip in so please *don't* say anything to him about it, but I just wanted to give you my ideas. Now don't get excited about this and murmur "God if I were in his place, I wouldn't pull this." Don't forget you wouldn't even pay a buck bill which I asked you too [*sic*], so don't get feeling Christie. Enough of this however. I can bawl you out when I see you. I just wanted to give you the opportunity to think up some arguments as you are usually so much slower than I in a debate about what a worthless prick you are. Will have to be back here Monday but let's get the date Sunday night. We could go coasting on sleds till about ten and then go coasting on O. and W. Am really baffled Lemmer about wheather [*sic*] Von Elm screwed her or not. She had gotten quite a scare when I gave it to her so don't think she would try anything. However I couldn't feel any maidenhead and she is quite sexy. Frankly the old Cru-Magnon is baffled in spite of my "tall physique, handsome face and astonishingly large brain capacity." Flash. They are going to stick that tube up my ass again as they did at Mayo. All I can say it's bully of them. . . . Write immediately, Ken.

In a postscript he added, "Forget the bawling out. You're swell."

It was hard for Billings not to love Jack, or not to feel sorry about his hospital woes, though Jack wanted nothing as "boring" as pity, only a helping hand in his search for excitement. Yet for all his unremitting energy on the social front, Jack was nothing if not loyal to his friends. "Jack was a guy who if he had a friend, he'd never let him go," Rip Horton later reflected. "By that I mean, a friend could do no wrong. He was extremely loyal to his friends and some of them mistreated him."

Certainly, while Jack's attitude toward women was happy-go-lucky and emphatically noncommittal, he displayed a touching, almost fraternal loyalty to his chosen buddies. His spelling might be rushed and erratic, his syntax lax, and his subjects raunchy, but his letters conveyed an arresting vitality and a determination, as his mother had noted since he was a small child, to think his own thoughts and go his own way. Moreover, he wrote in a style compellingly his own: uninhibited, confi-

dent, sharp, and witty, the very antithesis of his father's style. It seemed
ironic that Joseph Kennedy, so blunt and forceful in his dealings with
people, should be incapable of writing a single sentence that reflected his
personality, whereas Jack, so superficial and breezy as an eighteen-year-
old, wrote with haunting asperity.

Meanwhile, in spite of his illness, impetuosity, and prankishness, Jack
remained very much in control and "called the shots." Though he'd left
Princeton under a medical cloud and without sign of academic ambition,
he was not all playboy. Beneath the surface, as Dr. Lecky, the Columbia
psychologist, had noted, he had ample confidence in his own ability, and
by extension, in the abilities of his chosen friends. When Billings failed his
midyear exams, Jack affected disdain. "Dear Out-on-your-Ass," he lectured Billings from the Peter Bent Brigham Hospital on February 13. "It
will serve you right to get kicked out, as you seem not to have been doing
any work, but have been spending all your time in Sandy's room."

Plainly, Jack expected better of his ex-roomie. Nor did he appear in the
least overshadowed by his brother's progress at Harvard. The two brothers, in fact, were beginning to draw closer, and on weekends Jack often
visited Joe Jr. in his rooms in Cambridge. Joe had brought an alligator
from Palm Beach, which, Jack reported to Billings, must be "languishing," since it "only succeeded in biting the end of my finger last night
instead of grabbing my whole arm as of yore." He'd also read in the paper
of Joe's latest love affair. "Did you see about Joe in Winchell's column—
Quote—'Boston Romance—J. P. Kennedy Jr., The Wall Streeter's lad,
and Helen Buck of the Boston Back-Bay bunch, are keeping warm':
fucking gold-fish is the way I would describe it," Jack sneered, anxious
to be off to the next dance on his agenda. "You and Ripper plan," he
ordered. "May fly but will let you know. My prick 'Lay More' has been
acting up lately, and I am eyeing it closely. . . . Flash—B.D. came to see
me today in the hospital and I laid her in the bath-tub. Get your work
done so we can go out Sunday night. . . . Don't forget to give your gold
jewelry to Mussolini."

With that, he signed off. The doctors, beyond misdiagnosing leukemia,
had drawn a blank. By the final week in February 1936, after almost two
months of hospital tests, Jack was back on the beaches of Florida, "already bronzed" and, after a hair rinse, manicure, and facial, "all set to
kill."

The Wild West

"I hope you are not planning a busy season," Joseph Kennedy remarked sarcastically to his son in Palm Beach.

Jack was, having invited a number of friends to stay. "The girls are few and far between," he lamented to Billings, "but speaking of between, I expect I shall get laid shortly."

In some ways Jack personified the philosophy that Tommy Dukes described in D. H. Lawrence's final novel, written as Lawrence battled against tuberculosis: "I believe in having a good heart, a chirpy penis, a lively intelligence, and the courage to say 'shit' in front of a lady. It would be wonderful to be intelligent: then one would be alive in all the parts mentioned and unmentionable. The penis rouses his head and says: How do you do?—to any really intelligent person. Renoir said he painted his pictures with his penis. . . . He did too, lovely pictures! I wish I did something with mine. God! When one can only talk!"

Jack, too, was having to content himself with talk much of the time, while his friends painted. Billings, at six feet two inches tall and weighing nearly two hundred pounds, was anxious to try for both football and rowing at Princeton that spring. "My suggestion to you," Jack advised from Palm Beach, "would be if you are going out for football seriously I would suggest your doing that this spring, or else go out for crew completely"—but not both. "Ever since J. J. Maher told you you were a natural, (a natural prick I would say), you think that you can be a three letter man, when we all know including the gang at Sevilla that you [are] definitely a 4 letterer."

When Jack heard a few days later that Billings had forfeited his scholarship at Princeton owing to his poor academic results, he was appalled. "It's too damn bad about losing your scholarship," he commiserated, "but here is my advice. You have been a damn fool—spending money you didn't have, taking week-ends you shouldn't have, and generally fooling around." Jack admitted he was himself partly to blame:

> It was a lot my fault but that doesn't do you any good. You have got to snap out of it, because you have made a flop of everything in the last two years, promising things you never kept in the slightest. From football on—you messed everything you came near. If you can't do small things you haven't a chance.
>
> Now it seems to me that the best thing for you to do is to stay in

Princeton the entire vacation and work. It's not a terrible thing as some guys do it and it's too damned bad if it is a terrible thing, you've got to do it. If you go on a vacation now you would be selling your birthright for a mess of potage, which is not meant to be funny. However, if you decide to go on a vacation you can come here as we have plenty of room. However, you have been a terrific ass, and unless you come around now, you haven't a chance. If you do good work now, maybe you can get the scholarship back.

Given that Jack had himself been expelled from school exactly one year before for fooling around, this must have seemed like the pot calling the kettle black, yet it was written with such genuine concern that Billings took the admonition deeply to heart. (Before long, in fact, Billings won back the scholarship.)

"Well, after losing sleep over your problems," Jack followed up his letter to Billings in mid-March, 1936, "the news just reached me that you were drunk in the Stork Club last Saturday night. How you can make merry—or Kay—while Rome burns is more than I can see." Meanwhile he had his own news to tell. "Flash—Had my handwriting read last night. Extraordinary mind + character—so it's your old roomie letting you know that you are the most worthless prick that he has ever run up against."

Despite his suntan, Jack's wasting physique did not impress his father. Mr. Kennedy mentioned it to Arthur Krock, Washington bureau chief of *The New York Times,* who happened to be staying in Palm Beach. At the time of Kennedy's appointment to the SEC, when many newspapers expressed outrage at the idea of a well-known stock fiddler being given such a senior post in the administration, Krock's steadfast support had earned what Joseph Kennedy promised would be his undying gratitude. To his bitter disappointment, Krock later realized he was simply being exploited. "I've often reflected since those days that probably he never liked me at all," Krock confessed, "but found me useful and thought he might be able to make use of me. . . . I happened to be in a position of value to him. I remember he called me once and said, 'I don't want to hear any nonsense from you. You look out the window Christmas morning and you'll see an automobile.' I said, 'I will see nothing of the kind. I'll have it towed away if it's there.' And that was the end of that. That was a pretty coarse kind of bribe. . . . That's the way his mind worked."

The bribes, in Krock's case, were thereafter kept more discreet. Meanwhile, however, Krock was intrigued by Jack. "The first time I met those boys was at Hyannis Port, at the family's summer place, because I used to go there occasionally, and then once or twice at the winter house in

Palm Beach. It was perfectly clear at that time that Mr. Kennedy thought of his son, Joe, as the political leader in the next generation," Krock recalled. "He was convinced it would be Joe. So much so, that I recall—it must have been about 1936—that Mr. Kennedy told me his younger son, his second son, that is, Jack, was a very frail boy and had various troubles and his other boy was strong and well, but he thought a good physical course . . . would be good for them. I talked to the boys about it several times in that period. That was the first time I really knew them at all well and I sent them out to a ranch called the 'Jay Six,' owned by a friend of mine named Jack Speiden, near Benson, Arizona."

Krock was telescoping; he only got to know Jack well in the years ahead, as will be seen. Moreover, his recollection that he sent both Joe Jr. and Jack to Arizona (a recollection repeated to Joe Jr.'s biographer, Hank Searls, as well as numerous other writers) was mistaken. In fact Joe Jr. remained at Harvard, not even going to Palm Beach that Easter.

Meanwhile, tired of Palm Beach, Jack flew to New York in mid-April, "bringing whatever parts of your 'wardrobe' (Ha Ha) that you left back with me," as he warned Billings, who'd preceded him by car. "Arrive in N.Y. about six. Will meet you at Plaza tea-dancing —Notify Olive to meet me there. All arrangements in your hands." He signed himself "Don John."

High life in New York did not last long, however. Billings had to return to Princeton, and by late April "Don John" was en route for Benson, Arizona, on Arthur Krock's recommendation, dropping a hasty, smutty note from Fort Worth to Billings, which he signed "At home on the range."

Not even Fort Worth prepared him for low life among the Herefords of the Jay Six Cattle Ranch, which came as an understandable shock to a Brookline-Bronxville boy whose farthest excursion at Palm Beach had been to the beach. "My latest disease is the lice which itch like hell and make me think that Arizona is a fucking uncomfortable [place]," he wrote to Billings, "so may be will be back soon for another goodly party." He also agreed to pay half the twenty-five-dollar fine they'd incurred for speeding. Someone had told Jack's father about the incident. "If I keep associating with you Billings," Jack joked, "I am going to be disinherited."

Joining Jack on the ranch, however, was Jack's Choate school friend Smokey Wilde, who was also suffering from ill health, and who was soon up to mischief with his ex-Mucker pal, as Jack related in his news reports to Billings. Jack's mother, significantly, never once featured in his letters—indeed she was now so completely out of touch with Jack's life and friendships that she later quoted in her memoirs a letter from Eunice saying that Jack "is having a wonderful time out West. Smokey is out there with him now." This, Rose primly explained, was a reference to "Jack's then-current dog, a shepherd of some sort"!

Meanwhile, by the end of the first week in May 1936, in a letter he entitled "Travels in a Mexican Whore-house with Your Roomie," Jack was describing to Billings his latest escapade. "Got a fuck and a suck in a Mexican hoar-housse for 65¢, so am feeling very fit and clean," he chronicled sarcastically. "Smoke and I set out yesterday, went over the border + arrived at a fucking Mexican town. Met a girl there who is really the best thing I have ever seen but does not speak English. Am writing her tonight to get a date with her because she wouldn't go out with me last time and it is really love at first sight. They have the best looking girls in those towns. Anyways Smoke + I ended up in this 2-bit hoar-house [*sic*] and they say that one guy in 5 years has gotten away *without* just the biggest juiciest load of claps—so Smoke is looking plenty pallid and even I occasionally think of it, so boys your roomie is carrying on in true 9 South style and is upholding the motto of 'always get your piece of arse in the most unhealthy place that can be found.' "

In a postscript marked for "Shink's" attention, Jack warned that no excuses would be accepted for nonappearance that summer in Hyannis Port. "It will be indeed a sore source with me if you are not present for the sunbaths + cocktail parties at tennis week at Kennedy acres as of last year," he wrote, and signed himself "your gonnereick roomie." He then added: "Next week my Hollywood adventures"—for his father, having accepted the consultancy with Paramount, had just cabled to invite Jack to Los Angeles to celebrate his nineteenth birthday. "So Smoke and I start off Friday to knock off a couple which ought to be very interesting."

Cheerfully anticipating a good "lay in L.A.," Don John nevertheless worried about his "Lay More." "Plunked myself down for an injection after reading of Irving Curtin's death from the same thing I have," he reported contritely to Billings. "While waiting for him read of 8,000 cases of sylf among the Baltimore boys so you had better keep away unless you want to make it 8,001—I don't know why it is that every time I have ever gotten my piece I have read some fucking article about all the people who get it."

Meanwhile, Jack related, the latest news in Benson, Arizona, was "that there are about 8,000 TB's recuperating in this place + this morning I woke with a hacking cough which Smoke assures me is TB in the more advanced stage. It will be the fucking last straw if I came down with TB in addition to a good load of claps on this health cure," he finished, and signed himself "the Arizonian."

In fact, apart from his fears of VD, Jack's health was dramatically improving. His boredom threshold, as he labored with Smokey Wilde to construct a new office building on the Jay Six Ranch remained low, however. "This thing of working," he wrote regarding Billings's latest plans for a summer job, "sounds good but you ought to try to work in college," he admonished, "as you will know the score better in 4 years, though the score of what is the question. It will probably be how many scores of time you have gotten your piece," he continued, unwilling to come on too heavy. "Be there for tennis week," he ordered, "as we can have a hell of a good time and your work can wait. That's being a good influence but to hell with all that. Be sure + try & make it as it will be my only bat of the summer + you will probably be working next September or at football camp."

Los Angeles proved every bit as exciting as he'd hoped it would be. "This Hollywood trip was the stuff," he wrote on his return "and will tell you all about it when I get back—Lost all the good that the ranch did & spent 150, so am feeling very grim. Smoke is leaving tomorrow so things will probably settle down. The way things look now will get back around June 24, Tuesday I think. You've got to be around + get Shink." He'd temporarily lost interest in Olive Cawley, who could, he claimed "take a ship for herself because I've met this extra in Hollywood that is the best looking thing I have ever seen. Will show you her picture when I get in." He also boasted how he'd played tennis with Constance Bennett, the film star who'd married Gloria Swanson's erstwhile husband. "I served four doubles in a row thereby clinching my social career out there," he quipped, and, having given Billings a "flash" news report that he was definitely "washed up" with Olive Cawley, now signed himself "The extra's delight or how I got my tail in Hollywood."

Meanwhile, Jack noted in his next letter to Billings, "if you could see what a thing of beauty my body has become with the open air, riding horses and Mexicans, you would stuff such adjectives as unattractive when you are speaking of my body right where they belong." His riding skills, however, were still far from perfect, he admitted when informing Billings of his latest "bad news": "It looks as though there will be no little rascals bearing the name LeMoyne Kennedy as yesterday I got kicked where I love which stretched me out for a few blissful minutes. I no longer have that free + easy stride and am consequently a bit worried," he claimed, the more so since "I have not heard from you for 3 weeks except for a couple of smutty post-cards. . . . Please communicate + let me know what you are planning to do + when you are planning to do it. . . . Have some plans that will get your dander up."

Plans, invariably, meant getting laid, or going out, or both. The flight home was fixed via Chicago, where he was going to stay with Rip Horton and Butch Schriber for a few days, as well as meeting Joe Jr., who was staying with Schriber's cousin Tom. But however eagerly Jack looked forward to seeing his old friends, the months of "recuperation" in Florida and Arizona had in reality ended his adolescent years. Life on the range had by no means cured him of his narcissistic ego, but it had given him a new determination to do something with his life.

"Fuck these women and lets get some others," Jack wrote in June to Billings, who'd reported the latest gossipy intrigue in their circle. He expected Billings to "handle" arrangements for a house party when he got back, but in a telling sentence he revealed his hand: "We can always change at the last minute so do what you want," he wrote. He then crossed out the "you" to read "we," and crossed it out again to read "I." He'd written to his father's secretary to book tickets "for Thursday night for 'Boy Meets Girl' " when he reached New York. "Maybe we could go & take in the Orpheum that night," he added. The schoolboy whom Horton had once found so "unsophisticated" in terms of restaurants and night life was coming of age. "Let me know air-mail if these plans fit with yours + they had better," he wrote imperiously to Billings.

Arizona, Mexico, Hollywood, and Los Angeles had brought the teenager not only better health but the distance every youth needs in shifting from an adolescent to an adult perspective. "Jack has rather superior mental ability," George St. John had written in his headmaster's remarks the year before, when Jack made out his applications for admission to college. However, St. John added, Jack lacked "deep interest in his studies or the mature viewpoint that demands of him his best-effort all the time. He can be relied upon to do enough to pass. We have been and are working our hardest to develop Jack's own self-interest, great enough in social life, to the point that will ensure him a record in college more worthy [of] his natural intelligence, likeableness and popularity."

Paradoxically, the months of convalescence away from school and college had developed Jack's "self-interest" more than any teaching could have done. "The Haile Selaisse [*sic*] was a riot," he commented on Mussolini's annexation of Ethiopia, giving Italy "at last her empire," as Mussolini boasted. "Am leaving here in a blaze of glory tomorrow," Jack wrote in his final missive from Arizona on June 19. He planned to arrive in New York on June 24 "in order to put all my eggs in some lucky girl's basket" at Jane Rovensky's house party. "Try + get your work done so we can go right up there," he scrawled, and signed off his sunburned self as "your nigger, Jack."

Bounding with self-confidence and in vigorous good health, Jack had had his fill both of the sunny South and the wild West. He was ready to go east—to Harvard.

The Summer of '36

The summer of 1936 Jack intended to spend sailing, beachcombing, playing tennis, and going to dances on Cape Cod, before entering Harvard. "Gentlemen," he addressed the Harvard Admissions Committee from Hyannis Port on July 6, 1936,

> I am writing you in regard to my entering Harvard this fall, in the class of 1940. I presented an application to enter Harvard. . . . last year to enter with the class of 1939 which was accepted. My plans changed, and I decided to go abroad to the London School of Economics for a year. At the end of a month, due to sickness, I was obliged to return to the United States. I then decided to go to Princeton, due to its proximity to New York, where the doctors who were treating my illness were located. I made up and passed four of my five courses by the second uniform examinations. . . .
>
> Again due to sickness, in the early part of December I left Princeton to go South, after spending more than two months in the Peter Bent Brigham hospital in Boston under the care of Dr. William P. Murphy. After my return from the South I went out to Arizona returning a week ago. After seeing my physician who said he thought it would be perfectly all right for me to attend college next year, I decided to present my application to Harvard. If there is any other information desired, I should be glad to communicate with you or go to Boston to discuss the matter.
>
> Very truly yours,
John F. Kennedy.

Except for the choice of Princeton, none of this was actually untrue. Just to be on the safe side, however, Jack sent a similar letter, omitting mention of Harvard, to Princeton. But within three days the dean of freshmen at Harvard replied, thanking Jack for his "entirely satisfactory" account of the "manner in which you have been occupied since you were admitted to Harvard." Term would begin in the last week of September. Once again, Jack was in—and breathing a sigh of relief, he returned to the joys of Nantucket Sound.

Jack's growing maturity was noted by a number of outsiders, though life among the Kennedys remained much the same. Rosemary, seventeen, Kathleen, sixteen, Eunice, fifteen, Pat, twelve, Bobby, ten, Jean, eight, and even Teddy, aged four, looked up to Jack not in the manner that they half-admired, half-feared their eldest, "responsible" brother Joe Jr., but as a gifted individualist who was considerate enough to bother with them—especially Rosemary. As Eunice later recalled, reflecting on the untrumpeted way Jack managed to make sure Rosemary was not left out at parties, "Jack would take her to a dance at the club, and would dance with her and kid with her and would make sure a few of his close pals cut in, so she felt popular. He'd bring her home at midnight. Then he'd go back to the dance."

Nevertheless, despite this "special grace," as one later admirer would call it, no one meeting Jack in the summer or fall of 1936 would have predicted a political future for the scrawny, wild, and gregarious under-graduate. As Bud Wynne recalled, much of the summer on Cape Cod was spent racing Jack's Wianno one-design. "His brother, Joe Jr., had a Star boat, keeled, while Jack had one of the family's two Wianno one-design-ers with a centerboard. His father was very competitive, and employed a Swede to look after the family's boats; whether at the father's orders or to please him, it was rumored that the Swede added illegal extra sail area." Together the boys raced in Joe's boat from Edgartown (on Mar-tha's Vineyard) to Nantucket and back to Hyannis.

Although he had visited the Kennedy's Bronxville house many times, Wynne had never seen Jack's mother; when he finally did meet Mrs. Kennedy at Hyannis, he mistook her at first for one of Jack's sisters, she was so petite. But as Cam Newberry—a classmate of Joe Jr.'s who be-came a friend of Jack's and took the earliest color movie of the family— recalled: "On those films of mine there's two or three very good shots of her. I thought of her then as a rather old woman, though she was still in her forties. She had no relationship with Joseph Kennedy at all. It didn't exist. And with her children? Well, she seemed to be sort of bemused by them. . . . You never knew quite where her thoughts were."

Jack's friends were impressed by the way the Kennedy children managed, increasingly, to create out of their parents' phony marital relationship a life pageant or play of their own. Not only did they encour-age and support their retarded sister Rosemary, but they did their best to be understanding and forgiving toward their "loony" mother, Kathleen having even invited her to travel with her in Europe in the spring of 1936—a trip that took the two of them to Russia and gave Rose a perspec-tive on Europe beyond its French couturiers and Catholic priests.

Kathleen—"Kick"—was very similar to Jack in her personality. Though far from beautiful, she had a small, lithe figure and an efferves-cent personality that enchanted men young and old. It is said that every friend Jack ever had was in love with Kathleen—as well they might have been, given her tantalizing mixture of virginal, Catholic prudery and bubbling, cosmopolitan energy. Like Joe Jr., she too would ultimately pay with her life for her parents' failed marriage and manic expectations; but in the meantime she made up for her mother's invertedness by being the opposite: fresh, open, intelligent, humorous, and popular—in fact adopting almost the same role Rose had undertaken before World War I, as a surrogate "wife" to her father.

Given the frigid, emotionally shriveled world that Rose now inhabited, Joseph Kennedy increasingly lived through these children—perhaps to prove to Rose that, in spite of her destroyed image of him, he could still win and control his children's loyalty and affection, while she, despite her obsession with buttons and grooming, could not.

Like Jack, Kathleen avoided the most potentially debilitating effects of this parental conflict by overlooking it—as she did her mother's advice. "Now Kathleen," Rose one day announced purposefully after summoning her into the house on a sunny afternoon at Hyannis Port, "I want you to learn how to arrange flowers." "Arrange flowers?" Kick asked. "Yes, it's very important that you know how to arrange flowers," Mrs. Kennedy repeated. "I want you to go out and pick flowers and arrange them." Kathleen cut the flowers the wrong lengths, then put the basket down somewhere and forgot about it. To Mrs. Kennedy's chagrin, the flowers soon died in the hot sun. "She had meant to do it correctly," her biographer recorded, "but like so many things Mrs. Kennedy tried to teach her, it just didn't seem very important at the time."

Kathleen's friends had the problem of avoiding Mr. Kennedy's frustrated sexual attentions. "Some of Kathleen's young friends became reluctant to watch movies in the Kennedy basement," Kathleen's biographer recorded after conducting lengthy interviews. "Mr. Kennedy would ask them to sit next to him and then proceed to pinch them during the feature"—a somewhat odious irony given Mrs. Kennedy's insistence that all films be checked for possible salaciousness before viewing. Mr. Kennedy even "kissed all female overnight guests on the lips—including girl friends of his sons," Kathleen's biographer recorded, and at his suite at the Waldorf in New York he outraged Kathleen's best friend, Charlotte McDonnell, by forcing her to join him in his bedroom in a trick to embarrass the U.S. film censor, Will Hays. Both Jack and Kick laughed off their father's pathetic prank; Charlotte, however, found it sick, and later claimed she "would have left home" had her father played the same hoax on one of her friends.

There was indeed something weird about a man who took New York harlots home to Hyannis Port when Rose was away, yet would retain private detectives to spy on his daughters. Yet for all his inconsistencies, Joseph Kennedy remained a powerful figure in his children's lives. In spite of all his criticisms he was proud of them, and determined that they should do well in life—the more so since his own life, after his brief tenure of office under Roosevelt, had come to a hiatus, which he now attempted to bridge by asking for Arthur Krock's help.

Krock's imprimatur in the *The New York Times* had been of crucial importance in overcoming the many objections to Joseph Kennedy's chairmanship of the SEC. Once again, in the summer of 1936, Krock came to the rescue with a brilliant proposal to win presidential favor, this time by producing a pro-Roosevelt campaign book in the run-up to the 1936 election. Since Kennedy could not formulate his own thoughts arrestingly on paper, he paid Krock to do so. Not only did Krock write the entire manifesto in a matter of days, but even more important, came up with the book's jazzy title, *I'm for Roosevelt*.

Aware that he would be accused of angling for high office by issuing such a fawningly pro-Roosevelt book, Kennedy got Krock to draft for him a humble disclaimer at the start, which read: "I have no political ambitions for myself or for my children and I put down these few thoughts about our President, conscious only of my concern as a father for the future of his family and my anxiety as a citizen that the facts about the President's philosophy be not lost in a fog of unworthy emotion."

This was so fallacious as to be ridiculous. Wealth had brought Kennedy, as his wife made clear, certain material and sexual freedoms that were important to him. He certainly wished to preserve that wealth under a new administration. But beyond this he simply wanted, as he had always wanted, power.

For the present, his children remained the only vehicles of this power drive, with Kennedy's eldest son, Joe Jr., the primary focus. Nevertheless he was pleased with the improvement in Jack's health—he weighed 150 pounds by the end of the summer—and when Jack wrote to Harvard requesting permission to take his four-year degree course in three, his father was taken aback. "If possible," he wrote quietly to the dean of freshmen, before departing for Europe for a month, "I should like very much to have one of your assistants confer with Jack to decide whether or not this three-year-idea is to be encouraged. Jack has a very brilliant mind for the things in which he is interested, but is careless and lacks application in those in which he is not interested. This is, of course, a bad fault, but it is a gesture that pleases me very much because it seems to be the beginning of an awakening ambition."

Jack, at nineteen, was certainly anxious not to be left behind by his peers. Toward his elder brother, however, he now showed a touching loyalty. As his Choate friend, Charles Wilson, later recalled, "when I visited him at Hyannis that summer, Jack took us out in the motor boat to watch a sailing race that included our classmate Herb Merrick, as well as Joe Kennedy Jr. When Herb started to pass Joe, Jack gunned our boat in front of Herb to slow him down."

The adolescent was becoming a man. As Jack would write later, after Joe Jr.'s almost suicidal death, "though a glance at Joe's record shows that he had great success, things did not come particularly easy for him." Joe Jr.'s achievements Jack ascribed not to talent but to willpower and "exceptional stamina. I do not think I can ever remember him to sit back in a chair and relax," Jack related. "Even when still, there was always a sense of motion forcibly restrained. . . . I suppose I knew Joe as well as anyone and yet, I sometimes wonder whether I ever really knew him. He had always a slight detachment from things around him—a wall of reserve which few people ever succeeded in penetrating. I do not mean by this that Joe was ponderous and heavy in his attitude. Far from it—I do not know anyone with whom I would rather have spent an evening or played golf or, in fact, done anything . . ."

But Jack was being kind. As Cam Newberry recalled, Joe *was* heavy, and few people enjoyed his company for long. "He was entirely different from Jack. He didn't have Jack's charm to begin with. Joe was a much more, was a more heavy-type person. Unfortunately more like his father, I think . . ." Or as another of Jack's friends at Harvard later put it, most people ended up disliking Joe Jr. "and found ample reason to confirm their feelings. He had a mean streak. He would kid people till they bled. He couldn't stop." "Joe was a great needler," another friend of Jack's confided. "You could never tell when he was saying something—he'd say it with a smile—you could never tell whether he meant it sarcastic, or if he was just saying the words."

Not only could Joe Jr. be spiteful, but he was a poor loser. Even his youngest brother, Teddy, later recalled how he was thrown into the ocean by Joe Jr. in a fit of pique, when they lost a sailing race. "On the way home from the pier he told me to be quiet about what had happened that afternoon," the twelve-year-old chronicled, protesting against Eunice's glorified picture of her brother as "wonderful and strong and calm." "One fa[u]lt Joe had was he got very easily mad in a race," Teddy pointed out. Moreover, far from being the Harvard student luminary of later myth, Joe Jr. failed, as his father had years before, to get chosen by any of the final clubs in the fall of 1935, and had had to settle for the Pi Eta. "It was better than nothing," one of Jack's roommates recorded, "but it created a bad feeling in him."

Jack, however, entering Harvard in September 1936, never spoke a derogatory word about his elder brother; in fact he forced one presidential-campaign biographer to alter his manuscript rather than allow himself to be quoted as considering Joe Jr. "a bully." His brother, Jack knew, had paid the ultimate price for his father's grandiose aspirations. The price he himself had paid was another matter.

Harvard Play-Boy

Jack's intention of completing his four-year degree in three years was soon abandoned. Thanks largely to his brother, he found he knew more students at Harvard than he did at Princeton, and, assigned a room in Harvard Yard, he was quick to meet more. On October 13, 1936, his academic adviser allowed him to drop Government 1 and French E, so that English, economics, history, and French F became the credit courses for his first year—two and a half of which he had to pass.

Jack's new friends saw in him little evidence of scholastic ambition. Denied the possibility of playing sports the previous year, Jack was determined now not to watch but to play. Once settled in Weld Hall—a freshman dormitory even older and uglier than South Reunion Hall at Princeton—he lined up with over a hundred fellow freshmen for the fall football tryouts by the Charles River.

"He was pathetic because he was so skinny," recalled Jimmy Rousmanière, who became one of Jack's closest Harvard friends. "I say pathetic because he was so light. You could certainly count his ribs!"

"Where size mattered, he was under quite a handicap," recalled another new friend, Torbert Macdonald. Earlier that summer, meeting Jack by chance on Cape Cod, Macdonald had been aware only of "an ungainly, rather non-prepossessing type of person in whom I did not have very much interest." However, Jack's keenness to try out for football among "a fairly substantial number of well-known athletes who had been captains of their preparatory schools" rather impressed Macdonald—particularly when Jack showed an unusual quickness of humor that picked up on Macdonald's somewhat snide puncturing of pretension. "We sort of looked at each other; I knew he was kidding, and he obviously knew I was kidding," Macdonald said, recalling a whopping fib they wove to the assembled freshman football freaks. "Our friendship grew from that moment."

Like Jack's friendship with Billings, this one would last until death.

Macdonald was also impressed by Jack's loyalty to his older brother. "Joe was physically more rugged and was sort of an outgoing type of personality, which at that time Jack was not. But there was no rivalry. . . . They got on very well and used to see each other practically daily." Moreover, when the brothers did disagree, Jack was perfectly capable of standing up for himself. Macdonald vividly remembered one occasion when he tried to intercede. "Mind your own business!" Jack snapped at Macdonald. "Keep out of it! I'm talking to Joe, not you!"

Joe Jr.'s tutor, Kenneth Galbraith, recorded that Joe was "slender and handsome, with a heavy shock of hair and a serious, slightly humorless manner. He was much interested in politics and public affairs," and "would invariably introduce his thoughts with the words 'Father says,' " whereas Jack "too was handsome but, unlike Joe, was gregarious, given to various amusements, much devoted to social life and affectionately and diversely to women. One did not cultivate such students."

Jack certainly did not cultivate such tutors. Restored to comparatively good health, he was determined to become immersed in college life, and volunteering to get his neck broken in American football was certainly one way of doing that. All his friends, without exception, gradually became aware of his talent for writing as well as his humor and assumed he would in due course become a journalist—"a James Reston," as Cam Newberry later reflected, referring to the celebrated *New York Times* columnist. What such friends could not easily see, since they were so close to the fun-loving nineteen-year-old, was that Jack's refusal to be a "mere" journalist reflected his inherent determination to be a derring-doer, not simply an observer. Just as he refused ever to feel sorry for himself when sick, so when well he demanded action, not delay; fun, not frustration; companionship, not lonely contemplation. In time this same urge would propel him, however ill or ill-adapted, into battle, and later still, into adversarial politics; but in the meantime Jack delighted those who played football with him by his wit and seemingly crazy ambition to play end for the freshman team. "Jack couldn't have weighed more than one fifty or one sixty," Macdonald remembered. "In those days you had to play both ways, and he was great on offense and could tackle very well on defense, but as far as blocking and that sort of thing, where size mattered, he was under quite a handicap. Guts is the word. He had plenty of guts."

"Am playing on the freshman squad," Jack wrote on September 29 to tell Billings the sensational news. "God knows for how long so will not be able to get down for awhile. Things are pretty fair up here & I think I shall like it. Schmucky boy is up here as is brother A. S. Lerner and Uncle Joe Quattrone and Cousin Alan Baldwin so we are having one hell of a fine time."

In this brief Indian summer of good health Jack saw himself as a man of action, reveling in the competitiveness and fun of football field and shower-room. As with the Muckers at Choate, this spirit of camaraderie could be enjoyed as raucous entertainment and also used to "buck the system"—thumbing one's nose at the serious and preening Harvard faculty. "Things going very well up here," he reported to Billings in mid-

October, "though I have been demoted to the 2nd team, although I may get up again. It's a pretty fair team although Exeter beat us 14–7 on two long runs. . . . I am not worth a hell of a lot but seem to be getting better—went down to the Cape with five guys from school—EM [Eddie Moore] got us some girls thru another guy—four of us had dates and one guy got fucked 3 times, another guy 3 times (the girl a virgin!) + myself twice—they were all on the football team + I think the coaches heard as they gave us all a hell of a bawling out."

This was precisely why Galbraith and other professors feared to tread among young men of Jack's ilk. "The guy who got the virgin just got a very sickening letter," Jack continued, "letting [him know] how much she loved him etc + as he didn't use a safer he is very worried. One guy is up at the doctor's seeing if he has a dose + I feel none too secure myself. We are going down next week for a return performance, I think."

For the moment Jack's health was fine. "Now weigh 160—10 lbs gain so am very healthy—Will put you up here—Should I get you date—Also get a date the day you play Dartmouth as we play Yale at New Haven + shall be in NY that night. . . . Regards to the Ripper & the boys—the name of the drug store where I buy my rubbers is Billings & Stower—Regards, Kennedorus."

A new Harvard coach, Dick Harlow, had been brought in. Like J. J. Maher, he saw Jack Kennedy as the cause of all mischief—and to Jack's chagrin, further demoted him. "This fucking football situation has now gotten out of hand," Jack was soon lamenting to Billings, "as the coaches found out about our little party + I am now known as 'Play-boy.' All the coaches except the head one are ineligible seniors + are getting quite out of hand so it now looks as if I will have to wank plenty to 'tame' it down, as they only give about 30 [of] their numerals and I have been shoved down to the 3rd team."

Fortunately, the Harvard-Yale game two weeks later marked the end of the football season, enabling Jack to "formally break training" that night and attend a party in New York with Billings, Merrick, Wynne, and Horton. According to Ed Sullivan, one of Jack's ex-girlfriends was pregnant. "The next thing they will [say is] Jack Kennedy is anticipating a bundle from heaven. Please keep all this under your skin and I wish now I had kept mine under my skin if you know what I mean. I would have less worries."

Nevertheless, he had to admit he was enjoying Harvard. "In answer to your question I really like Harvard pretty well, and was not long enough at Princeton to form an opinion [about the college]. Of course I miss all the lads, but it is much cheaper here," he joked, "if you know what I mean—Will you be in N.Y. around Thanksgiving as we should be getting our social career launched + I think Olive ought to know some good models. They work you much harder here than at Princeton. There are also plenty of shits!" He appended the latest anecdote he'd heard. "Mae West was walking down the street + bumped into Pres. Roosevelt. He said hello, who are you. She said Mae West—who are you? He said Franklin Roosevelt. She said, Well Franklin, if you can give me half the screwing you gave the people of the United States come up and see me sometime."

Writing only a few days before Roosevelt's triumphant reelection, Jack was doubtless voicing the blasé view of many Republican undergraduates of the time; but he was, too, being deliberately irreverent at a time when his father was being deliberately obsequious. Not only had Joseph Kennedy put out his *I'm for Roosevelt* book that summer, but on October 5 he had broadcast at his own expense a nationwide radio address urging Americans to vote the president back into the White House for another four years, and was that evening due to repeat the broadcast.

Football, girls, and irreverence were, perhaps, Jack's continuing marks of independence in a world his father sought so hard to dominate. Ironically, Joe Jr., after urging Jack not to go out for freshman football, suffered a serious knee injury, necessitating surgery. His father came to see him in the hospital and wrote to a friend to say that he would "never have any regrets if none of my boys get mixed up in inter-collegiate football . . . a bum nose or lame legs is not worth the coveted letter. . . . I have tried to impress these thoughts on the boys, but am somewhat doubtful as to my success."

Joe Jr. certainly still coveted the elusive letter *H*. Though he never missed a team practice in four years except because of injury, he tried in vain. For Jack, football was a passing fancy—fun while it lasted, but only as long as it did. "Strange how one's point of view changes," his father had written. "During undergraduate days making the team is of importance second to none other and we would never stop to reckon any price too great to pay for that honor." Belatedly, in late middle age, he'd come to realize it wasn't worth the candle. Jack, aged nineteen, had already passed through this phase, and though he would maintain a lifelong passion for the game, was quite unfazed by its honors system. The truth was, getting a chance to use his French letter was far more important to Jack Kennedy than getting his Harvard letter.

Renaissance Prince

Throughout his time at Harvard, Jack kept up his links with the "lads" at Princeton. "You are certainly a large-sized prick to keep my hat," he complained to Billings after the latest Boston party, "as I can't find my other one and consequently am hatless. Please send it as am sending yours—I don't know what the idea was walking off with it in the first place. Harvard has not made me grasping but you are getting a certain carefree communistic attitude + a share the wealth attitude that is rather worrying to we who are wealthy," he taunted. "Therefore I am going to crack down. Incidentally you are certainly wacking about your possessions as well as mine. . . . I haven't got a date as yet, so I don't know how I am going to get one, as Cawley has a date—wire me if anything occurs to you or if you can get me a date with Hartwell—Am going to take the train after the game—arriving in N.Y. around 8:oo. Will meet you where you want at what ever time you say. Let me know—started the last Freshman game," he scrawled from the bench, signing himself "Stout-hearted Kennedy, despoiler of women."

Jack's prowess on the romantic battlefield, though it earned him no credit with the Harvard faculty, certainly gave his work—when he bothered to do it—an individual charm, even insight. For French F he was, for instance, required to write a ten-page paper, half in French, half in English, on the life and times of the French ruler, Francis I.

The subject was a monarch after Jack's own heart, a Renaissance leader whose life span reflected Europe's transition from the medieval to the modern age. *"Un homme de talente extraordinaire il est la personification de cet age,"* Jack began, with numerous errors of spelling. A younger son of the Duke of Orleans, Francis began life with only a remote claim to the throne of France. As Jack noted, a series of fortuitous deaths altered his destiny. Aided by a devout mother whose principal passion, according to J. F. Kennedy, was to see her son crowned in succession to Louis XII—he made his tortuous journey to the throne.

It was this journey that fascinated Jack Kennedy, as well as Francis's legendary sex drive, which worried his king-making mother more than anything else, according to Jack. "Louis XII's first wife died barren," and "the ageing king, in a final effort to get an heir of his own flesh and blood, married Mary Tudor, an attractive young English princess." The "biggest problem now," Jack considered, was to keep Francis from having an affair with the young queen and thus defeating his own purpose—by obliging the aged king who was incapable of the job—giving him an heir. However, Francis restrained himself, the king died childless soon after the marriage and Mary departed for England. The king who now came to the throne as Francis the first was then in his twentieth year. Ambitious, spoiled, possessed of an unbounded vitality and a physique capable of tremendous physical activity, he was the pride and personification of his age. His lusty interest in life took many forms, the chase, war, and women.

Warming to this theme, Jack continued:

Women were one of the dominating interests in his life and he had many affairs. Unlike his contemporary across the channel, Henry VIII, he did not marry for reasons of the heart or the fulfillment of passion, but married for reasons of state and thus missed going down in the history books [as a lover]. Francis's marriages, definitely political, took up little of his time. He kept his first wife Claude, daughter of Louis XII, busy producing children, most of whom died while he continued his "amours guerreuses" with women like Le Foix. He knew women's place, however, and except for his mother and his sister, they never assumed a position of great influence, at least until his later life.

Clearly there was much of nineteen-year-old Jack Kennedy in this portrait. What intrigued him, apart from Francis's sexual bravado, was the way he had, at a young age, envisioned himself at the head of a powerful army sweeping through Italy, and how once crowned, he had surprised Europe by fulfilling his dream. The manner in which, as conqueror, Francis then studied the Italian Renaissance and inaugurated it back in France struck Jack Kennedy as significant, as did the Italians' impression of his "bold and masterful bearing: The Prince in him." By virtue of the Bologna Concordat with Pope Leo, Francis had made himself "undisputed and absolute" ruler of the most powerful country in Europe. "Hardly on the throne, he had reached in a short time the zenith of his fortunes," Jack wrote, though for all his patronage of the Renaissance in France, "Francis's grip on it was somewhat superficial, he was trying to pick the fruits without nourishing the roots."

It was this superficiality, Jack felt, that was to prove Francis's downfall as a statesman. "With the death of Ferdinand of Spain, Francis found a new rival," Jack chronicled, "the 'methodical machine' " of Charles V, who was "in direct contrast in personality to the swash-buckling Francis." Once Charles V became Holy Roman Emperor, Francis found himself ringed on all sides, leading to his disastrous defeat at Pavia. Though freed by the Treaty of Madrid,

> from now on Francis was pressed to retain intact his kingdom. He was ageing and the flaws in his character and appearance that had been passed off when he was young as just "youth" were now becoming apparent as moral weaknesses. . . . If his own body could not give him peace, then at least he could go seeking his distractions, living with his thousands of courtiers and living from one chateau to another. . . . And in this elegance, this sumptuousness, this mingling of the sexes, Francis himself [was] an Orleans to his fingertips. He was a worshipper of beauty. It might be a hollow, pompous beauty with something in it of the ostentation of Chambord, or it might be florid and ebullient like Fontainebleau. But it poured out [of] a temperament, a faculty of rising above the commonplace of existence and declaiming a conception of royalty, a conception of lordly magnificence and pride. Thus, racked by disease which violent living had irritated, Francis wasted away and finally died in 1547. . . .
>
> I have tried to give a picture of Francis's character and age. In studying his career it seems almost a pity that he could not have died at Pavia, as his career was an anticlimax [after that], although it had traces of glory. Francis was a man with an intense vitality for life: he was superficial but with some deep appreciations and as such was the perfect personification of the Renaissance. . . . On France he had written his signature in chateaux. He understood the technique of the architect, as patron and as connoisseur. We find the true spirit of the reign of Francis, at least the best part of it, in the Chateau of Chambord. It was a living monument of all that was great in his reign. His life was not futile. It served its purpose, that of jolting France out of Medievalism.

Professor Gregersen, the French instructor, was not impressed. Jack's French grammar was erratic, and his historical-biographical account was secondhand, relying largely on Francis Hackett's recent publication, *Francis the First*. Gregersen thus failed the essay with a D+.

Doubtless, as a freshman essay, this was all the teenager's account deserved. But as a mirror to Jack Kennedy at nineteen, this picture of a Renaissance prince—a man of action, superficial yet able to jolt medieval France into modernity—would become one of the most important documents of John F. Kennedy's early life. However little the Harvard freshman might foresee himself at the head of a mighty army or inaugurating a new renaissance in America, there can be little doubt that after reading the life and times of Francis I, Jack Kennedy had a new hero, whose birthplace and chateaux in France he was anxious to see for himself.

Stripped for Action

Compared with Cambridge, Palm Beach at Christmas 1936 was like a morgue. "Things are going pretty quietly down here," Jack reported to Billings, "as it is none too gay, as there are no girls. Been out only a couple of times on stray parties which is very boring." Moreover, the father of one of his girlfriends, Mr. Rovensky, had "got off to a bad start by calling Joe 'me in a de luxe [*sic*] edition,' " Jack recorded. Jack soon got his own back, however, when his brother asked Jane Rovensky "for a date and she gave him the merry laugh and 'why, of course not,' which won me a buck."

If Mr. Rovensky was derisive about Jack, Mr. Kennedy wasn't. "I am impressed with the almost complete turnaround you have made in yourself in the last year. You know I always felt that you had great possibilities and I think now you are starting to avail yourself of them. You are making a great hit with the older people," his father wrote soon after Jack's return to Harvard, brushing aside Rose's admonition about Jack frequenting the nightclubs of New York on his way. "Got a letter from J.P. purring on my shoulder," Jack wrote to Billings in February 1937. "He is really worshipping at my feet these days."

For Jack, the irony of his father's laudatory remarks lay in the fact that Jack was soon busier in bed than ever. He'd left Palm Beach on January 2 and by January 13 was writing to Billings from Boston to announce he'd made up for his quiet Christmas. "How would you like it if you had a dose + were a father at the same time! I can now get my tail as often and as free as I want which is a step in the right direction," he boasted.

Anxiety over gonorrhea and getting his girls pregnant clearly acted as no sexual deterrent. His first Harvard midyear exams were scheduled to take place over the following few weeks. By January 26 he had done two, with two to go. "Exam today so have to open my book & see what the fucking course is about," he scribbled to Billings in great haste. He'd signed up for boxing and swimming, and the furious pace of his life seemed to suit him. "Still out for boxing due to the coach labelling me "the most natural boxer in the freshman class," he bragged. Nor was this mere athletic bravado, as the Harvard backstroke champion found when Jack thrashed him in the hundred-yard swimming tryout.

For a boy whose ill health had recently caused him to miss a year of college, Jack was not only indecently active, but actively indecent. Moreover, he enjoyed his work. He studied, swam, and boxed with equal ferocity; on the weekends he flew to join his friends in New York, giving his letters to Billings a relentless anticipatory urgency. "Dear Le Moan Plenty," he scrawled after Billings complained how much time he was currently having to spend trying to get into one of the Princeton fraternity clubs, "I thought this club shit was going to be over by the end of this week so you can cut this hard-to-get stuff and report in N.Y. stripped for action on that hat-check girl."

"Jack Kennedy had no respect for women, no respect at all," his new Canadian friend at Harvard, Vic Francis, later reflected. "He *needed* to make conquests, for his own self-esteem—but he had no respect for women, and would not put on any airs or pretensions for them. For instance, there was one New York model he invited to come up for a weekend ball at Harvard. Jack booked a hotel for her in Cambridge, and asked me to meet her at South Station as he was delayed. I did so, but when I rang Joe to ask where the hell Jack was, he said, 'Oh no! Not again!' Joe had to take her to the ball. Jack never showed up the whole weekend!"

On another occasion, Vic Francis recalled, Jack was invited to go horseback riding with a debutante in New York. "He asked me to go along too—in fact he insisted, even though I was not a great rider and hadn't got the proper clothes. So we both went in a shirt and normal trousers. We arrived at the girl's apartment. She was properly dressed in riding boots, jodhpurs, etc. She immediately said, 'I'm not going with you two dressed like that!'

"'All right Vic, let's not waste any more time,' Jack said—and went straight down the stairs!"

In part, Francis considered, this behavior reflected Jack's determination not to allow himself to be cornered or outmaneuvered by "debby" girls who were, at heart, more interested in the eligible son of a millionaire than in plain Jack Kennedy. But in part it reflected Jack's indifference to women beyond the challenge of attracting and, if possible, bedding them. Unlike his mother—indeed in protest against his mother's Catholic prudery—he loved nudity and craved sex, Vic Francis said, recalling a get-together at Bronxville with Olive Cawley, whom Jack had invited over, as well as "some Princeton boys who brought a good-looking blonde with them, a hatcheck girl from the Stork nightclub. The boys took the girl inside, "presumably to bonk her," then reemerged. Olive Cawley affected outrage. She was there with another debutante. To put down the hatcheck girl, they asked where she worked, what she did, and pretended they too were hatcheck girls. Eventually they riled the blonde so much that she threw an ashtray at them. Olive and her friend fled, shouting for Jack, who reappeared. Vic Francis would never forget Jack's response. "Aw, Olive, you're such a goddamned *snob!*"

If Jack drove girls crazy by his casualness toward sex and society, he drove his friends frantic by his wild driving—especially once he acquired a new Ford convertible. Kenneth Galbraith later recalled Joe Jr.'s righteous indignation. Joe Jr. had set up a syndicate to bet on President Roosevelt's reelection and had asked his tutor to invest. "I encouraged the scheme but declined to invest," Galbraith related. "He went ahead . . . and made enough money to buy a new car. After the election we drove in it together to have dinner with some friends in Wellesley. He was in a dark mood. Jack, a day or so earlier, without consulting his father, had bought a new car on the installment plan. Why should his brother have a new car when he hadn't earned it?"

Lem Billings was one of Jack's first passengers.

> Jack drove pretty fast. We drove a lot around the Cape. You couldn't get arrested too many times without having trouble with your license. One night, we were riding along. I remember a cop was coming up behind us—another ticket would have cost Jack his license. While the car was still moving, we changed places, which is a very tough operation to do. If you ever try it, you'll find out how really tough it is. After we changed places, we suddenly realized that he had on a white coat and I had on a dark coat. There was much scrambling to get those coats changed. I don't know how we did it, but we got away with it and, of course, I got the ticket!

Vic Francis recalled similar escapades.

> I remember once when we were waiting for a bridge to rise, Jack started honking his horn. He was called to the side of the road by a cop for half an hour's talking to. "Why do you *always* get us into trouble, Jack?" I asked him. It was the same, another time, when we were attending the Yale-Harvard rowing races at New London. I met Jack there. At two in the morning we drove off. Jack had nowhere for his girl to stay, though she kept asking. Eventually he found a seedy joint, on the third floor. Then, when we drove off, we ran out of gas. We stopped at a gas station, unlit, in the dark. Jack started helping himself to gas. A window opened and the owner put his head out—with a shotgun! He threatened to blast Jack to bits. Jack shouted back to come out and serve him! "Jack, you always get me in these scrapes!" I complained.

Meanwhile there was the forthcoming summer to think about. "Do you know what Smoke wants to do about this summer or what you are going to do? Let me know *right away* as I've got to make up my mind *immediately,*" Jack wrote to Billings in March 1937. He was adding yet more sports to his athletic repertoire but did not wish this to inhibit his social life, and planned to attend the Princeton Ball. "In spite of the fact that I will be out for rugby and football I think I shall buzz down + look over Princeton on 19th, so line things up. . . . Get me a room way away from all others and especially from your girl as I don't want you coming in for a chat in the middle as usual and discussing how sore my cock is. I shall have the car + let me know if the prom is Friday or Saturday night + when I should get there. . . . The swimming is going pretty good—Am swimming in the medley relay team and so far have beaten my man every meet. . . . We go up to Dartmouth Friday. . . . Will have to close as the coach has just come by for me in his car."

By April 1937 Jack was writing from Weld 32 that he'd "never been so busy in my whole life," and excused his incoherent letter on the grounds that "these are the ramblings of a man who has been writing for 12 hrs right thru a night in order to finish a 6,000 word thesis due tomorrow morning but they are also the ramblings of a man who came second in the university championships in backstroke. Wire immediately," he ordered Billings, still concerned to finalize plans for the Princeton Ball.

Rambling or not, Jack seemed to thrive on hard work, hard play, and hard sex—at which, aged nineteen, he claimed he was still amateur only in the sense that he never needed to pay for his pleasures. His freshman swimming team, which he represented against Exeter, Dartmouth, and Yale, was not only undefeated that year, but was considered to be the greatest Harvard freshman swimming team ever assembled. At rugby he played against the Bermuda Naval Academy, the Army & Navy, and against Princeton, and in May he represented Harvard in freshman golf against Yale. He was also nominated, in May, to the 1937/38 student council, having already been elected chairman of the freshman Smoker Committee.

"Things are going pretty well up here," he scribbled to his father, "though am very busy. . . . Went last night to see the Gondoliers D'Oyly Carte production with Vin Fredley. It was much better than I thought it would be and I think that someone should tell the [Choate] Head that the school productions are certainly no way to get anyone to like Gilbert & Sullivan. Have been pretty busy on the Smoker. Went with Mr. Sternberg and we are going to get the show out from the Met. Also we may be able to get Gertrude Niesen who should be rather good. I thought I would get Grandpa to get Bill Cunningham + Clarence De Marc and I was wondering if you could get Neal O'Hara, or should I get Grandpa to try to do this too? It is going to take place two weeks from tomorrow."

Jack's freshman Smoker, or spring dance, proved the most successful in Harvard history, taking place on May 4 in Memorial Hall and boasting some forty entertainers, including two jazz orchestras, the Hollywood comedian Fuzzy Knight, and Gertrude Niesen, the legendary stage and screen actress.

It was small wonder that, on Jack's application to move to Winthrop House for his sophomore year, his interviewer noted that he and his projected roommate, Torbert Macdonald, were "two of most popular athletes. Think twice before rejecting a good boy." His freshman tutor thought Jack "well orientated, normal," and that, once the pace of student life slackened in his second year, "he will probably do better on the whole" in his studies.

Jack's chosen concentration was to be politics. "He is planning to do work in Government," his tutor recorded on his filing card. "He has already spent time abroad studying it. His father is in that work," he added—for once again, in the wake of Roosevelt's successful reelection, Joseph Kennedy had been given a job in government, this time as chairman of the U.S. Maritime Commission in Washington.

The Proper Purpose of Education

"The long skein of circumstances, beginning back in 1916 when FDR was Assistant Secretary of the Navy and Joe was manager of the Fore River shipyards, had made Joe the President's first and logical choice," Rose Kennedy later fantasized, conveniently forgetting Joe's disastrous strike at Fore River (and fudging the date).

The truth was, Joe's new job was not to Rose's liking. After years in the social wilderness, she felt she deserved a little limelight. She'd sought to improve her dress sense, to keep her figure trim, even to improve her "awful" voice by taking elocution lessons. Cardinal Pacelli, visiting the president in November 1936, had visited her home in Bronxville; her father had been named official Massachusetts elector in January 1937, entitling him to be known as "the Honorable" for the rest of his life. It was time, Rose felt, that Joe now be rewarded for all that he'd done for Roosevelt. "I felt that Joe deserved something better," she later admitted, "something really special."

What Rose had in mind was an ambassadorship. Aware that Joe didn't fit the conventional mold of a diplomat, she genuinely felt that, for the first time in their marriage, she could help him. "Mr. Kennedy was so lucky to have me for a wife," she boasted later to her secretary. "I had gone to college and was well educated, whereas the other girls from East Boston were just high school graduates. I had traveled abroad, met Sir Thomas Lipton, spoke French and German." In her memoirs she was equally revealing. "Joe spoke no foreign language and had no 'ear' or natural facility in languages. Thus the suitable possibilities were reduced to only one post. . . . When Joe came home for weekends, I would ask him, what has the President said? Couldn't you tell him what you want?" "Well I can't just walk in to the President of United States and say I want to be ambassador to England," Joe expostulated. But by putting pressure on "close friends in the Administration and with trusted and knowledgeable friends in the press, such as Arthur Krock," Rose candidly explained, the president was made fully aware of Kennedy's new wish.

At first Roosevelt scoffed at the very suggestion. "Through other means behind the scenes, however, eventually it was understood that if he did his usual excellent job at the Maritime Commission the next step beyond would be the ambassadorship," Rose recorded. Reorganizing America's shipping was thus to be a stepping stone to Prince's Gate: home of the U.S. ambassador to the Court of Saint James's.

Jack's Harvard grades, meanwhile—one B and three Cs—were undistinguished. Jack himself was unabashed. In an essay on Jean-Jacques Rousseau for his freshman history class, he had asserted that the "proper purpose of education" was not the parotting of other people's information, "but the formation of judgement [*sic*] and character." Shunned by the Galbraiths of Harvard, he continued to pursue his goal with unusual independence of mind and energy. However jejune his opinions at nineteen, they were *his* opinions, not Galbraith's. "We too readily accept what we read without subjecting it to our own personal criticism," Jack had applauded Rousseau. "I think he reaches his greatest truths in discussing property and education," Jack opined, explaining that it was impossible for a man like Rousseau to "fit in with the restricted life and beliefs of the French, affected and prejudiced as they were. . . . His whole life was a crusade against this superficiality and the sins of our civilization. His belief was: Nature is good, society is bad. . . . Everywhere the result of knowledge has been hypocrisy and affectation. . . . We thus see Rousseau's revolt against the strict dogmas of the religions of the eighteenth century," the young Boston Irish-Catholic sympathized. "Under Louis XIV conditions in France were quite bad. The court of Versailles was famous for its affectations. The upper classes spent much time in idleness and frivolities, while the lower classes were made to suffer. Things continued in much the same way under Louis XV. Rousseau's works appeared at a time when the people were in a desperate state of mind. The radical ideas suggested by Jean-Jacques favored the masses. No doubt these works contributed food for thought. They might be considered the seeds of the revolution that took place in 1789," Jack added, citing E. S. Bogardius's *History of Social Thought* to the effect that Rousseau's doctrine of life, liberty, and the pursuit of happiness had profoundly influenced Thomas Jefferson "as evidenced in the Declaration of Independence. Sovereignty," Jack quoted further, "rests not in a rule or monarch, but in the community of people—this was perhaps Rousseau's main contribution to social thought."

However naïvely, Jack Kennedy was finally beginning to grapple with political concepts that had shaped European and American democracy: a propitious time for the young student of government to see for himself the surviving monuments of Renaissance and Enlightenment history in Europe, and perhaps to witness what sort of new, twentieth-century revolutions were now being fomented in Spain, France, Italy, and Germany. Were the twentieth-century upper classes spending their time "in idleness and frivolities" at the expense of "the masses"? What *was* the attraction of men like Franco, Mussolini, and Hitler?

Jack had originally planned to spend the summer at Hyannis Port, "as I would like to race," he told Billings. However, "the family do not want me to do it because they think there may be a war soon and I should see Europe. . . . I wrote Smoke asking if he wanted to go to Europe. If he does not will definitely cancel the Europe [trip], if he does will have to talk it over with you."

Belatedly, Wilde informed Jack he wouldn't be able to go, but by then Jack's notion of a summer touring Europe in his convertible had taken root. Jack's father generously arranged with Billings's mother that he would pay Billings's fare, with Billings paying back half the amount from an inheritance due to him on graduation. Billings thus took Wilde's place. "We are planning our trip abroad," Jack wrote with some excitement to his father in Washington as the end of term approached. "Both Lem and I think that the best part of the trip would be getting into Spain either as Newspaper correspondents or as members of the Red Cross for about 3 weeks. If we can get in then it will affect our plans so hope you will be able to work it."

With this touching sign of faith in his father's ability to "fix" things, Jack's freshman year at Harvard came to a close, and together with his Princeton companion he set off on what promised to become the most educational experience of his life.

Inside Europe

The two boys boarded the S.S. *Washington* on July 1, 1937. Jack was taking three pajama tops and bottoms, seven handkerchiefs, sixteen pairs of socks, eight pairs of underwear, fourteen shirts, four pairs of pants, one bush shirt—and his car.

Mr. Kennedy had acted wisely. "We could have spent our time just fooling around, but we ended up having a really educational trip," Billings recorded without exaggeration. He himself had just finished a sophomore architecture course at Princeton, Jack had just completed courses in French and European history. It was thus a field trip for both boys, the first and last such trip in their lives. "I don't think either of us ever again toured museums and castles and chateaux and historical sights as we did that year," Billings remarked wistfully. "Gosh, we were both twenty."

Equipped by his sister Kathleen with a leather-bound diary bearing the title "My Trip Abroad" (and depicting an ocean liner resembling the *Titanic* sinking over the horizon), Jack began his chronicle of the voyage in typical fashion: "Very smooth crossing. Looked pretty dull the first couple of days but investigation disclosed some girls—chiefly Ann Reed. Had cock-tails with the Captain who knew Sir Thomas Lipton and thus grand-pa. The chief source of interest was General Hill and his rather mysterious daughter. He was a congressman, she might have been anything."

The two Ivy Leaguers stayed up to see Ireland—Jack Kennedy's first glimpse of his ancestral land. The next morning the S.S. *Washington* docked at Le Havre. Once the car had been unloaded, the students headed across the tidal flats to Mont-Saint-Michel, then turned eastward through the Normandy *bocage* to Rouen, where William the Conqueror had held court. "We proceeded to Beauvais," Jack recorded. "Stayed at a little inn where we ran into the first of our Fr. breaths."

The inn was La Cotelette. "It was necessary for me to operate on a very low budget," Billings later recalled. "I had to live very inexpensively and Jack Kennedy lived as cheaply, I suppose, as he had ever lived in his life. . . . It was no problem for Jack Kennedy to live as I did. He did it happily. He didn't mind it at all." Nor did Jack mind his friend's passion for cathedrals, "buildings which I had actually studied in college. I felt very much at home and I was very excited about it. He hadn't taken an architectural course, and yet, he was just as interested as I was."

For Billings, the monuments were architectural treasures; for Jack, markers of European history. "Up at 12:00," ran Jack's entry for July 8. "Wrote letters had lunch got our money and the medicine for Billings 'mal d'estomac' after much trouble—Then to Soissons—saw the Chemin des Dames—one of the great scenes of fighting during the war. Also saw the cathedral that had been bombed—Then to Reims where we looked at the cathedral and to the Hotel Majesty (1.00 for room for 2)—My French improving a bit + Billings breath getting French. Went to bed early—General feeling seems to be that there will not be another war."

French complacency was to be a feature of the trip, as the two students explored the gory testimonials to the "war to end all wars," a war in which Jack's father had refused to serve. "Went out to the French fort Pompernelle, scene of some of the war's worst fighting," Jack noted the next day. "Then had lunch and visited the Champagne caves of Pompernay—Created in the old chalk caves of the Gauls—Treated very well—then had a talk with the manager over a *fine* bottle of champagne. . . . The general impression also seems to be that there will *not* be a war in the near future and that France is much too well prepared for Germany. . . . From there we went to Chateau Thierry picking up two French officers on the way. Arrived in Paris around eight."

After an expensive first night in Paris the boys moved to a cheaper hostelry, the Hotel Montana, which faced the Gare du Nord and which charged a mere "eighty cents for both of us," Billings could later remember. "Have now acquired the habit of leaving the car around the block to keep the price from going up. Had the lights fixed and got another screwing," Jack noted in his diary. "These French will try to rob at every turn."

Jack was and would for the rest of his life be parsimonious, but his tightness with money was here to Billings's advantage, though it was too much to expect that Jack would rest content with cathedral gazing in a city such as Paris. "Went to Notre Dame then looked around Paris—That night went out to Moulin Rouge and Café of Artists and met some of the well-known French artists," Jack coyly chronicled, adding, "Billings wanted to come home early but didn't."

Sin bespoke religion—about which, strangely, the two boys had never spoken. "We never discussed religion in any way," Billings remarked of their school years. "I was a Protestant and he was a Catholic and it never came up." Yet throughout his childhood Jack had been conscious of the fact that as an American he was in a minority, a member of a faith that his WASP friends and their families considered to be idolatrous.

Now, for the first time in his life, Jack Kennedy found himself in a predominantly Roman-Catholic country, with a vivid history of Catholic martyrdom. However superficial his faith, he was certainly comforted by its traditions, and attended mass every Sunday, with his Episcopalian friend in tow, proudly worshiping in Catholic cathedrals whose architecture made the chapels of Canterbury, Choate, Princeton, and Harvard seem pallid by comparison. On Tuesday, July 13, for instance, on the eve of Bastille Day, he "got up early and went to Notre Dame to hear Cardinal Pacelli. Terrific mob but by tagging on to an official managed to get a good seat right next to the altar. A very impressive ceremony which lasted for 3 hours. Billings had to wait in the body of the church," he boasted. "There was a most fantastic crowd surrounding the entire cathedral," Billings recalled thirty years later. "Of course, the number of people who could go into the cathedral was very limited—I think it was by ticket only. Jack went up to the VIP entrance used by President LeBrun—in he went and I was stopped. How he did it, I don't know. I was right behind him. . . . Later Jack told me that he sat about five seats from the French president—Jack was always able to get into any place he wanted—I guess it was just gall."

If not gall, it was certainly gallic. After the ceremony in Notre Dame he and Billings lunched with the American ambassador's secretary, Carmel Offie. "Had lunch with C. Offie and then went out to Versailles which was very impressive. Found the stables and got a public bawling out." That night Jack invited his fellow *Washington* passenger, Ann Reed, to a performance by Maurice Chevalier "and was reminded greatly of the Old Howard." The following day, July 14, the boys "took a look at the crowds in the street." They met Bruce Lerner from Harvard "who now has a moustache" and lunched with some friends of Lem's from Princeton, "which was rather interesting though expensive. In the afternoon made flying visit thru the Louvre, which I had done once before. . . . Have picked up quite a bit although my knowledge is quite vague." They also met a Harvard colleague of Jack's, Alex de Pourtalis, whose family owned a house at St-Jean-de-Luz on the Riviera, and who invited Jack and Lem to stay with him while *en route* to Spain.

The festivities of Bastille Day had meanwhile set Jack thinking not only about France's great Revolution of 1789, but about the equally revolutionary currents threatening France itself a century and a half later. "Have decided to read Inside Europe by Gunther," he jotted on July 15.

Meanwhile the pace of their sightseeing in Paris intensified. "Got up early after much cursing and went over to Napoleon's tomb and thru the Palace of the Invalides which is very interesting. Then over to the exposition and went up the Eiffel Tower after finally persuading Billings that it had the makings of quite a long hike. In the afternoon went to the Concierge where Marie Antoinette was kept. Quite a contrast to Versailles," he added, and a further reminder of the mortality of great rulers, however sumptuous their palaces. He'd been told that the boat on which they were booked to return, the *President Harding,* was "terrible," so before leaving Paris they transferred their booking to the *Washington*. "This will necessitate me getting back 2 days late for football camp but it looks now as if I won't play," Jack accepted. They called in again at the American Embassy. There they were warned they would not be permitted to enter Spain, but nevertheless they started out for Chartres on their journey south. "Stopped at Versailles to see the Trianon and saw Marie Antoinette's idea of 'roughing it,' " Jack mocked. "Just got to Chartres— very impressive window and that night drove to Orleans arriving around 10.00."

Jack, especially, had been looking forward to this, the home territory of his Renaissance hero. "Went to Mass at cathedral," he recorded on July 18,

> and looked around a bit. Amazing what a small town it is. France is really quite a primitive nation. Went to the Chateau at Chambord which is quite a sight. A hunting lodge which held 2,000 people. The roof laid out like a village, built by Francis I. Billings, amidst many groanings, lost his pocket book but was able to recover it thru the assistance of a French girl. Picked up a couple of English fellows— one of whom went to Trinity College Cambridge—name of Ward. He said "to get on his scent" which at that point would not have been hard. He considered Roosevelt the best "dictator." Went for a swim in the Loire which has quite a current and then drove on. Looked at the Chateau at Blois and stopped in for the night at Amboise in order to look at that chateau. Remembering the dog at the American cemetery at Chateau Thierry decided not to go in the night. Went over to a fair. . . . Tree path at Blois impressive.

The next day they explored Blois. "Walls very high but beautiful inside. Saw Wall of the Conspirators where 1500 were hung and also the place where Charles XIII bumped his head and died. Finally thrown off the walls and continued to Chenonceau, built on the water, which is also very impressive. . . . Drove thru to Angouleme, thru Tours to Poitiers, both deserted towns, and spent the night for 10 francs each."

As they approached Spain, America seemed very far away. "Had our usual difficulty cashing our travellers checks. Europe is not nearly as tourist conscious as we expected," he recorded. "Very impressed by the little farms we have been driving thru. America does not realize how fortunate they are. These people are satisfied with very little and they have very little as it is really a very conservative country, at least outside Paris."

Staying with Count de Pourtalis in St-Jean-de-Luz the students were able to rest for a while. "Was out with French girl," Jack noted on July 22, but lamented that "their customs very strict, requiring a chaperone until 21 or so." The sight of Gary Cooper "speaking French as well as the Indians" in *The Plainsman* not only made up for this, however, but was "worth the price of admission." By July 24, though, the restless travelers were already tired of beaches and tennis, and they drove to Biarritz to secure tickets for the forthcoming bullfight, due to take place on the twenty-sixth.

As Billings recalled, Jack "was very anxious to get into Spain, but there was absolutely no way we could do this, since our passports were clearly marked 'Not Good for Travel Spain,' " owing to the Civil War. Jack nonetheless "spent a great deal of time talking to the refugees, making notes, and writing a good deal. . . . Those we met at St. Jean de Luz were probably the upper class refugees of the Franco group. So we heard some pretty blood-curdling tales of what the non-Francos were doing in Spain. At the time we were very much shocked, but I suppose that's because they were the only refugees we met. There were no refugees from the other side there at all."

In fact, Jack's mind remained remarkably open, professing himself to be "rather governmental after reading Gunther, even though St. Jean is rebel strong hold. England opposes Franco as they don't want Mediterranean a Fascist lake. Question of how much influence Germany and Hitler have, Russia's position. How far countries will go in having their side win? What type of government would Franco have? England and Germany?"

Leaving such questions in the air, Jack and Billings attended on July 25 high mass in the church "where Louis XIV married Marie-Therese—very beautiful," and after lunch "drove down to Spanish border with Wilson. . . . Saw the town of Irun, that had been bombed by the Rebels. Story of father starved, kept in prison without food for a week, brought a piece of meat, ate it—then saw his son's body without piece of meat, cut out of it. Turns me bit from Government. Government too divided also to make Spain unified ever. England changing a bit to Franco."

The stories of atrocities told by Spanish refugees seemed entirely believable, however, once Jack and Billings attended their first bullfight. "I think they were Spanish bullfighters but, since Spain was at war, the bullfight was held in the arena in Biarritz [France]. Both of us were pretty disgusted with the whole thing because we didn't like the cruelty of the sport," Billings remembered. "We felt the bull didn't have a prayer. Of course, maybe we didn't understand the finer points of the sport. I remember Jack's drawing my attention to a French woman and her child, a little boy, sitting beside us. When one of the horses was badly gored with his guts spilled out over the arena, and they led him out with his guts dragging out behind, the mother made a great issue out of it to make sure her child saw this very exciting episode. . . ."

"Very interesting," Jack recorded in his diary, "but very cruel, especially when the bull gored the horse. Believe all the atrocity stories now as these southerners, such as the French and the Spanish, are happiest at scenes of cruelty. They thought funniest sight was when horse ran out of the ring with his guts trailing."

Not even Hemingway would ever convince Jack that bullfighting was a noble pastime. Little by little, as the boys traveled through Europe, Jack was learning not only the political makeup of a Europe in transition, but who he himself was—and who he was not. That he himself would be shot in front of southerners of his own country, and be driven from the place of his assassination with his own brains trailing, to the applause of many who hated him, was something he could not foresee. "Of course, we didn't understand this temperament at all," recorded Billings, "and we were disgusted by it."

July was coming to an end, and the two Americans were anxious now to see to Mussolini's Italy. "After much excitement" they left the Pourtalises' and "headed for Marseilles" on July 27, 1937. "Stopped on our way to look at Lourdes," Jack noted, "the grotto where the Virgin appeared to St. Bernadette—and now the scene of thousands of sick people seeking cures. Very interesting, but things seemed to become reversed as Billings became quite ill after leaving," he observed with a touch of irony. "Decided to go to Toulouse for the night. Billings temp 103."

A Peek at Fascism

It was in August 1937 that the twenty-year-old Jack Kennedy took his first peek at European fascism, a movement which, in the months ahead, would give his father a brief moment of American glory before ending his political aspirations forever.

"Have continued reading Gunther," Jack recorded in his diary in Toulouse. "Not quite as positive now about Franco victory. Shows that you can be easily influenced by people around you if you know nothing and how easy it is for you to believe what you want to believe, as people of St. Jean do. The important thing in the question of victory is how far will Germany, Italy & Russia go in trying to secure victory for their side, how sincere the Non-intervention committee is—+ what the result will be."

The next day they left Toulouse and "stopped in at Carcassonne—an old medieval town in perfect condition—which is more than can be said for Billings," Jack quipped. "Very interesting. Arrived at Cannes around nine after a drive of 350 miles and stopped at a fairly expensive hotel 35 fr.—The service is 15% which is really robbery. Cannes seems to have much more life than Biarritz. Will stay here until the 'invalid' is well. A much different France here than the poor poverty stricken France through which we drove."

Looking back years later, the "invalid" reflected on the way Jack was "beginning to show more of an interest and more of a desire to think out the problems of the world and to record his ideas than he did two years before at Choate." Yet the remarkable thing to Billings was the way in which Jack remained Jack as he matured. "What I'm trying to say here," Billings said, struggling to articulate his perception, "is that there was a noticeable change in Jack Kennedy in the summer of 1937," yet one that did not change the leopard's spots. He was the same irrepressible, youthful, girl-obsessed millionaire's son from Bronxville, yet also a different Jack, for the intellect that he normally kept so well concealed was at last engaged. Harvard had begun to bite.

Meanwhile at Cannes, in the Palm Beach Casino, Jack "tried to do a bit of contacting with the American girls but to no avail," and they moved on to Monte Carlo where, although refused entry to the casino (on account of their age), they "managed to get in the Sporting Club. Broke even after giving them a scare," Jack noted in his diary, while in a letter to his father he related how he'd "played with my 5 fr. chips next to a woman who was playing $40.00 chips and she was quite upset by my winning $1.20 while she lost about $500.00." It was the "best-looking night club I've ever seen," the self-confessed playboy declared—and was relieved, after church the next day, to see "our first good-looking foreign girls" on the beach.

For all their attractiveness, however, the girls could not detain the travelers. "In the afternoon went over the border with a great deal of difficulty into Italy," Jack recorded. It was August 1, 1937, Jack Kennedy's first day on fascist soil.

At Harvard Jack had praised Rousseau's exhortation to subject what one read to one's "own personal criticism." On his travels Jack did just that. Writing later to his father, he complained about "the almost complete ignorance 95% of the people in the U.S. have about situation as a whole here. For example, most people in the U.S. are for Franco, and while I felt that perhaps it would be far better for Spain if Franco should win . . . yet at the beginning the government was in the right, morally speaking, as its program was similar to the New Deal. . . ." Even the Spanish government's confrontation with the church in Spain seemed justified to Jack. "Their attitude towards the Church *was* just a reaction to the strength of the Jesuits who had become much too powerful—the affiliation between church and state being much too close."

In assessing the validity of people's views, one had to be clear that their opinions reflected their pocketbooks, Jack reminded his father. "Peoples' financial status seem [*sic*] to form their political opinions, and even the newspapermen, at least the foreign ones, are all prejudiced, due to the peculiar position of the press as party instruments over here."

For a boy recently turned twenty, Jack was beginning to show powers of observation and judgment that were, as Billings recalled, far more advanced than that of the Choate or even the Princeton pupil. Though he was not personally drawn to fascism, Jack was surprised by the atmosphere of Italy once he crossed the border: "The Italian streets are much more full and lively than those of France, and the whole race seems more attractive. Fascism seems to treat them well," he noted, curious to see more. After "a bit of trouble over our hotel bill"—an occupational hazard for travelers in Italy—they motored down through Genoa to Milan, where they stayed in a hotel owned by a Fascist veteran of the Abyssinian campaign, "which he said was easy to conquer but uncomfortable. Very impressed by the intelligence of some of the children Bobby's age [his brother was now eleven] and by the fact that they all seem regimented. Pictures of Mussolini everywhere. How long can he last without money and is he liable to fight when he goes broke," Jack questioned in his diary. "If not—I don't see how there can be a war till 1945 or 50."

Billings was also impressed by Italy. "I must say, from what we'd read and thought about Italy before, Italy was cleaner and the people looked more prosperous than we had anticipated. . . . I had a feeling when I was in Italy that Mussolini had done a lot of good for Italy—and that there was much less poverty under the Mussolini regime and that the general public were not too unhappy. Of course, later on most Italians say they were unhappy, but at that time we felt Mussolini was doing a good job for the people. At least that's the way I felt."

Jack was torn. Both France and Italy, and even Spain, which they had not been allowed to visit, were countries of his own faith. Yet for all the fine beaches and attractive women, he still felt like an outsider, in language as well as political conviction. He could see the supposed benefits to Spain and Italy in having dictators who could forcibly unite the warring factions in their society, yet his own heart remained impervious to the patriotic chicanery of fascism. As the columnist Joe Alsop would later describe, there was something intrinsically English in the character of young Jack Kennedy, for all his enthusiasm over girls and determination to have fun: a love of unostentatious reading and a commitment to balanced, dispassionate judgment. "He was an extraordinary man," Alsop recalled years later, for once at a loss for the right words.

I still don't know what made him tick, quite. He was terrifically snobbish, you know; but not what people normally call snobbish. He was terribly old-fashioned, almost like, sort of English grandee kind of snobbishness. It was a kind of snobbery of style. . . . He liked people to be good looking and hated people who let themselves go. He was snobbish about courage, and he was snobbish about experience. He didn't want us to be ordinary and routine and kind of suburban, vegetable living. He wanted experience to be intense. Actually, I don't know how to put it quite. To my way of thinking he really wasn't like an American. He wasn't a foreigner, either, but the normal, successful American view of life was not really his view at all. . . . What I'm really talking about is a matter of style, of intellectual style, of viewpoint, of what you care most about, of what you like and dislike. It's very hard to pin down, but it's the best I can do after a long life of observing people, and I think it's not inaccurate.

It wasn't—the "style" already ingrained in the twenty-year-old American as he grappled with the great issues of his time: an alert, concerned, inquisitive young man anxious to make up his own mind, echoing neither rich Americans nor party-minded journalists, and never losing his sense of humor, which allowed him to keep life—his life and the lives of others—in perspective. Even the miracles of Lourdes and Catholic Italy he treated with polite irony. The cathedral in Milan, he noted in his diary on August 3, 1937, was beautiful. "A cardinal buried there with numerous jewels by Cellini etc. His skeleton carried thru the city in its glass coffin every 100 yrs. Last time in 1910, part of the glass broke and his skull turned black. Saw Last Supper of Leonardo da Vinci. Billings managed to take a picture of me in cemetery where forbidden but had the shutter wrong. Likewise I got him in the Cathedral but forgot to turn the picture so we have 2 more good ones for our collection." They had then driven on to Piacenza where Jack closed Gunther's book and came "to the decision that Fascism is the thing for Germany and Italy, Communism for Russia and democracy for America and England."

What form of government France should have, Jack didn't say. "Thought Gunther's book very interesting but he seems to be more than partial to socialism and communism and a bitter enemy of Fascism. What are the evils of Fascism as opposed to Communism?" he asked himself, a question that had to be shelved, for the next day they "had great difficulty escaping from" their hotel "due to Billings being accused of tearing Madame's towel, leaving one half on the writing table and the other in the toilet," an event which soon drew "a big crowd and much cursing in Italian." However, they finally managed an honorable exit and "picked up a German boy, Martin, on our way to Pisa. Rather interesting as he was anti-National Socialist and Hitler," Jack recorded—a view that rather dislocated Jack's new political subdivision of Europe. "He told us of many of the abuses they suffer . . . Told us how the Germans hated the Russians. Looks as if the next war would come from that direction especially as England and the rest of Europe seem to be drawing away from Russia. Went thru the tower of Pisa and the Baptistry which has an echo like an organ and then continued on our way to Rome, stopping at a little town about 150 kil." They'd picked up another German "voyager," Krause, who slept in the car while Jack and Billings slept in a hotel. "It's amazing with how little they can get along," Jack recorded. "Martin had some tomatoes and bread for supper the night before, costing a lira and a half. Decided to take a swim and it was almost our finish as it took more than two hours to get the car out of the sand and air back into the tires. Arrived in Rome around five-thirty . . . where I got a wire from Dad and heard that mother and Joe were on their way to Europe with Kick [Kathleen]. Dropped off Martin and Krause and then went and found a hotel. That night 'snuck' into the Colisseum [*sic*] and found it filled with people. Very impressive by moonlight."

It was August 5. Like children of the Enlightenment making the grand tour of Europe, they had finally reached the Eternal City.

Hitler's Germany

"Well, I think it was a bit difficult for Jack to buy a lot of the miracles which we were shown in Rome, for instance Veronica's veil or the steps down which St. Peter's head is supposed to have fallen," Billings later recalled. "I think these things were all very difficult for him to believe. He assured me that it wasn't necessary to believe this in order to be a good Catholic. During all my experiences with Jack Kennedy, he never really discussed religion much. I don't think he was a dedicated Catholic like his mother and his sisters, but he was a good Catholic. I cannot remember in my life when Jack Kennedy didn't go to Church on Sunday. . . . I never, never, never remember in my life Jack's missing his prayers at night on his knees. He always went to confession when he was supposed to. But I know he just wasn't as tied up with his religion as the girls in his family were."

This was a mercy, since Rose Kennedy's vengeful piety would have a crushing effect on her daughters, who could not pass off their mother's "obsession with trivia," her prudery, absenteeism, and stoic but hateful relationship with their father as did Jack. While Jack, like his father, expressed his contempt for such loveless chicanery in libertinism, his sisters were befuddled and confused—one of them, to the consternation of her husband, later guiltily crossing herself before submitting to normal marital sex.

Though Jack prayed, he certainly did not cross himself before or after sex. His icon might be Jesus, but his worldly savior was his own ironic sense of humor, allied to curiosity and youthful intelligence. "We did go to every museum of importance," Billings recalled, though "neither of us had had courses in painting or sculpture. . . . We went all through the Vatican and, although I don't think we understood too much about what we were seeing at that time, I remember neither of us were bored. Certainly Jack Kennedy was just as interested in it as I was. Actually this is true of our entire trip. We spent all our daytime hours as tourists, going to museums of every kind and seeing all the antiquities of Europe."

For Jack there were many dimensions to his journey. "Of course we had introductions to everybody in the Vatican," Billings recalled, "because Cardinal Pacelli was friendly with Mr. and Mrs. Kennedy. . . . Also, Count Galeazzi, the chief layman for the Catholic church, was a close friend of the Kennedys. So we had all the entrées to the Vatican that were necessary, and we were treated very well."

It was not quite as straightforward as Billings remembered, though. Nothing in Italy was straightforward, as Jack soon found out. "Up around nine," Jack noted in his diary. "but by the time I had my shoes 'painted' which took around 35 min it was over 11 before we got up to Galeazzi who wasn't in. Tried to see Cortesi, New York Times Correspondent. He wasn't in either, nor was Mr. Philipps, but was saved from complete failure by seeing Mr. Reed, Counselor for the Embassy. Very attractive fellow. Saw the St. Angelo Tomb of Hadrian, Pantheon, Colisseum [*sic*], Forum in the afternoon—have decided the Italians are the noisiest race in existence—they have to be [in] on everything—even if it is only Billings blowing his nose. Galeazzi called late and mumbled something about an audience."

The "audience" was to be with the pope.

"Went to Galeazzi early and met him," Jack recorded on August 7, "and learned we were going to have an audience. . . . Started out in Galeazzi's car and went to the Pope's summer palace. Had a private audience with Cardinal Pacelli first who asked after Mother and Dad. He is really a great man, although his English is rather poor. Afterwards had an audience with nearly 1,000 in the room which was painted." The Pope entered on a litter. "He looked very sick but made a long speech. After that we went to lunch and then to Tivoli to see the beautiful fountains which are amazing. The most unusual is the one that played music by means of the water rushing thru it. We then returned to Rome—and had dinner at Galeazzi's. He gave me quite a talk about the virtues of fascism and it really seemed to have its points especially the corporations system which seems quite an interesting step forward."

Like Jack's father, both Galeazzi and Pacelli would go down in history as pro-Fascists. Jack, meanwhile, was fascinated. Indeed the trip was turning out to be far more interesting than he'd ever imagined. After attending mass in St. Peter's the two boys drove down to Naples, where they "learned that the only way we could see Pompeii was to sneak in—which we did. Left for Vesuvius + picking up a couple of German soldiers on the way."

"We got to know them quite well, even though they spoke very little English," Billings later recalled of the hitchhikers. "They were with us for about a week and we gathered that their general attitude was pro-Hitler." Jack, having finished *Inside Europe,* was intrigued. "He was terribly inquisitive about everything in Europe at that time," Billings recalled. "While we were in France, Jack spent a great deal of time talking to the French as to how they felt about Germany, and whether there was going to be a war; and if so, could Germany invade France again"—questions he now directed at the young German soldiers as they traveled through Italy.

Taking an Italian guide, they drove up to the rim of Mount Vesuvius. "Amidst much cursing from the car we got to the top after great expense," Jack noted. "It was night by this time and Vesuvius which gave off minor eruptions every few minutes was very impressive. Got some pictures up there and then went down taking our guide with us who turned out to be the village smoothie. Had to run the autostrada as our ticket had been lost and it was quite exciting. Managed to get a room late at night; after much hand-holding with a very unattractive chamber maid managed to get a good room, tired but happy."

The more the boys were rooked, the more starry-eyed Count Galeazzi's enthusiasm for fascism seemed to them. In Capri they "went to the blue Grotto which is a cave under the water, the water having a beautiful blue color—although not beautiful and blue enough for 50 lira which we finally scraped together." Back in Rome Jack went to see "Mr. Cortesi, the N.Y. Times Man in Rome. He was very interesting and gave me some very good points," Jack recorded in his diary.

Seemed to feel that Non-intervention Committee was a safety valve but not much actual good as none of the countries would like to recall their armies [from Spain]—the Reds especially as most of their volunteers were from all corners of the world. It would be unlikely that Italy would bring out hers. Also said that there were few Germans in Spain. Also said that war seemed unlikely as if anyone had really wanted war there had been plenty of excuses for it. Also explained about Mussolini statement of war—which were just the latin way of saying what England was saying about Peace and rearmament. Said Fascism was not now unfair to the worker—in fact under it he got many advantages—Very much in favor of the Corporation system. He said chief danger of war was that someone would call Italy's or Germany's bluff—more Germany's as Italy had to digest Ethiopia. Spoke of Fascism being out and out socialism. Said Europe was too well prepared for war now—in contrast to 1914.

This was a further slant for Jack to digest. At the back of his diary he ruminated on the whole question of fascism. "Would Fascism be possible in a country with the economic distribution of wealth as the US? Could there be any permanence in an alliance of Germany and Italy—or are their interests too much in conflict?" Above all, what was the true nature of fascism? Was it, as Cortesi maintained, "out and out socialism"; or was it, as Pacelli felt, a sort of secular version of authoritarian Catholicism? Or, as Gunther maintained, "maybe the convulsive last agonies of the capitalist order, in which case Fascism will have been merely the prelude of Communism. Is that true?" Jack puzzled.

Here was considerable food for thought, especially when the two boys attended a "fantastic rally of Mussolini's in Rome." Billings later recalled, "I can remember it so well. He was such an unusual speaker. You know, he'd talk, then he'd jut his chin out."

If Jack was impressed, he did not record it in his diary. He did, however, chronicle his adventures with Italian women. "That night took out some dates that turned out quite well. Very beautiful girls although our not speaking Italian was a temporary damper. Billings knew some Italian parlor tricks that were worth remembering and we went to bed tired but happy!"

As always, there was a price to pay. The next morning they were shown through the Vatican museum and did not feel "so spry. Did it in about 1 hour. Went to lunch and were met by Billings's girl who needed car-fare. This went on quite a while and the Lemmer got a bit disgusted as well he might."

Arguing over money would be something Jack abhorred throughout his life, and it soured his opinion of Italians as a people—not realizing that for Italians, like Arab merchants in a Casbah, such negotiations were a joy, a form of entertainment as well as necessary social intercourse. Jack, however, was not amused, and by the time they had looked at some of the great churches of Rome and been told of "the steps that Christ used" and having "got thru the catacombs and heard about some more miracles" like those of "St. Luke and St. Peter's head," Jack had really had enough of Italian make-believe. The next morning, August 12, he and Billings left Rome "after much battling with the cross-eyed proprietor who turned out to be a terrific crook despite being 'an Italian and a gentleman,'" Jack mocked in his diary. "Left Rome amidst the usual cursing porters. Reached Florence late and stayed in our best hotel of the trip."

Florence "disappointed" Jack, although he was "quite impressed by Michelangelo's David," and in the afternoon they motored across the Dolomites, bound for Venice, where Jack complained of being at the mercy of mercenary Italians: "Once again we got our 25 lira room while the Germans got theirs for 8." But they'd been traveling pell-mell for five weeks since leaving Le Havre, and needed the rest that Venice afforded. On the beach at the Excelsior they "saw Barbara Hutton and Al Lerner, though not together. Ran into Joe and Elie Hoguet and had dinner with them that night. Very impressed by the Piazza at San Marco's which is really unbelievable. Getting a bit fed up with spaghetti also," he complained, and "found that the Hoguets were living much much cheaper than we. Put in our usual bad night with the mosquitoes as our net just seemed to lock them in."

Such grumbling belied Jack's pleasure at being in Venice with Americans he knew. After mass on Sunday they used Al Lerner's cabana on the Lido and wandered through the streets and piazzas to the American Bar, "and Billings finally had his picture taken with the pigeons." After dinner they "listened to the concert in the square" and "went out in a gondola which would have been quite romantic except that as usual Billings managed to make a gay threesome."

Later there would be those who saw in Billings a tragic character, clinging to Jack in his lifetime and going to pieces when Jack died. But as will be seen, this was no accidental or short-lived relationship. They had little in common except the fact that they were both second sons and had survived Choate together as well as a few awkward months at Princeton. Yet Jack clearly needed Billings and his loyal company "through thick and thin;" needed a companion he could mock for his bad breath, bad eyesight, bad luck, the bad impression he made on women, as well as his misfortune in being poor—but a friend who would accept all Jack's insults with equanimity and remain devoted. Later, when president, Jack would offer Billings any post he chose, including first director of the Peace Corps and first director of the American Tourist Bureau—offers Billings always refused, knowing that to accept would affect their strange yet enduring friendship.

Gondola days soon came to an end, when the weather changed and it began to rain. Once again Jack became restless. He'd had his fill of Italy and Italians and wanted to see Germany now. Setting off on August 16, he and Billings headed north with a female companion as well as their returning German soldiers. "Picked up a bundle of fun," Jack recorded, "to take with us in addition to Heinz and set out. Bad driving [conditions] and by the time we got to the Brenner Pass, it was pretty cold. The Austrian people impressed us very much as they were certainly different from the Italians. Stayed at a youth hostel in Innsbruck which caused "her Ladyship" much discomfiture. It was none too good as there were about 40 in a closet and it is considered a disgrace to take a bath."

The next day they were "up early, though not from choice. Her Ladyship stated that her night had been far from pleasant," Jack recorded, amused always by women's airs. "Started over the Alps to Germany after extracting money from Johann who was rather upset. Stopped at Garmisch where the Olympic games were held, then to Oberammagau [*sic*] where I saw the Christus—Anton Lang. Arrived in Munich around eight and went to the Hofbrau house which was very interesting."

Here Hitler had instigated his first, failed putsch. It was now a sort of Nazi drinking citadel. "Jack was absolutely overcome with interest in the Hitler movement," Billings recalled. In his diary, Jack recorded his initial impression. "Hitler seems popular here, as Mussolini was in Italy, although propaganda seems to be his strongest point."

"We got to know a black-shirt trooper in the Munich Hofbrau House," Billings recalled. "In those days they had floors based on your pocketbook. The cellar was for the poor and so on, all the way to the top floor, and there we met some of these black-shirt troopers. I remember one who spoke Oxford English. He had been educated in England. We drank beer with him and had a very friendly time. I remember, like every tourist, we wanted to take some of the big mugs when we left. Our German friend encouraged us and told us how to do it, which door to go out, and was generally helpful. However, when we got to the door he'd indicated, the waiters, who obviously knew about it, immediately came to us and took the mugs. We looked back. The German was laughing."

Jack was furious. He had had no patience with Italian "robbery" behind the high rhetoric of fascism. Being taken for a ride by a black-shirted Nazi on their first night in Munich "gave us a very bad impression," Billings related. "And we had many experiences like that in Germany. We didn't have the same impression in Italy. We had a terrible feeling about Germany and all the 'Heil Hitler' stuff. . . . They were extremely arrogant—the whole race was arrogant—the whole feeling of Germany was one of arrogance: the feeling that they were superior to us [Americans] and wanting to show it. Perhaps that's the inferiority complex coming out."

Joe Jr. had been swept up by the Nazi movement, approving its "scapegoating" of the Jews and lauding the "slight effort" of the Heil Hitler salute. Jack, by contrast, woke the next day in Munich "none too spry. Had a talk with the proprietor who is quite a Hitler fan. There is no doubt about it that these dictators are more popular in the country than outside due to their effective propaganda," he reflected sourly.

The Ivy Leaguers had come to see Europe, however, and were not easily put off by Nazi arrogance. "Went to the Deutsches Museum in the afternoon which is terribly interesting," Jack recorded, "as it outlines the different steps in mining and shows the development of aviation, etc. A great job and shows the German sense of detail," he acknowledged. "Went to see Swing High Swing Low for the 2nd time and enjoyed it more than the first. Probably because we haven't seen a picture lately." To their delight they then found a note on the car from Alex Pourtalis and another Harvard friend, Joe Garrety, with whom they spent the rest of the evening, ending in a "Munich night club which was a bit different."

It was clear, however, that if Hitler was popular in Germany, Americans were not, particularly the ilk of Kennedy and Billings, who'd spent years bucking the notion of regimentation and obedience to rules. Entertaining ladies in their rooms was *streng verboten*. "After the usual amount of cursing and being told we were not gentlemen we left the Pension Bristol," Jack recorded, and after saying good-bye to Pourtalis at the American Express office they set off for Nuremberg. "Stopped on the way and bought a dachshund of great beauty for $8.00 as a present for Olive," Jack recorded—a dog which, since it somewhat resembled the American ambassador's secretary in Paris, they called Offie. "Immediately got hayfever, etc, so it looks like the odds are about 8–1 towards Offie getting to America," Jack acknowledged sadly. Hitler was due to speak at the annual Nuremberg rally three days later, but the mood of the Germans they met was, as Billings later recalled, "insufferable. We just had awful experiences there. They were just so haughty and so sure of themselves. The German people were going through a very strange period then." In his diary Jack was more laconic. "Started out as usual except this time we had the added attraction of being spitten on."

Leaving Nuremberg to Hitler's fans, they now set off for England via Frankfurt and the Rhine, though having to stop in Würtemberg due to Jack's wheezing. "Jack discovered, for the first time in his life, that he was allergic to dogs," Billings explained. "The dachshund gave him asthma. It was a new malady to add to his already long medical history. From then on, until the day he died, he could never have a dog in the room with him."

Jack could not bring himself to part with his new pet, however. Indeed, for a boy so undemonstrative in terms of affection, his sudden infatuation with Offie was rather touching. Offie soon took pride of place in Jack's diary. "Offie is quite a problem," he admitted on August 20, "because when he's got to go—he *goes.*"

Sadly, Offie had to go in the larger sense, too, though Jack delayed the moment as long as possible, and even tried to buy Offie a mate before finally accepting defeat. "Started out for Cologne by way of Frankfurt," Jack recorded, "where we stopped to look for more dachshunds, Offie being so attractive. However, no luck, so continued on our way up the Rhine. Very beautiful as there are many castles all along the way. All the towns are very attractive, showing that the Nordic races certainly seem superior to the Latins. The Germans really are too good—it makes people gang against them for protection."

That the "German question" would, twenty-five years later, be the focus of his negotiations with the Soviet Union as U.S. president was of course something Jack could never have imagined. Not even his Sancho Panza could have predicted Jack's extraordinary career in politics, though he could see Jack growing all the time. "Jack Kennedy grew every single year of his life," Billings later recalled emphatically, "and this [journey in 1937] was part of his growth. If you'd gone to Europe with him in 1937 and then gone in 1939, you would have seen an entirely different man. The 1937 trip, during which he was so inquisitive and so interested in everything, was just an example. He insisted, for instance, that we pick up every German hitchhiker. This worked out very well, because a high percentage of them were students and could speak English. In that way we learned a great deal about Germany."

Jack was also learning more about the opposite sex. In Cologne the "bundle of fun" said good-bye to the unquiet Americans. "Got up in the worst day we've had yet and parted on good terms with the woman," Jack noted with surprise, "for about the first time. The [European] women seem to be the more honest, strange as it seems."

Grateful at least that his girlfriend had parted without recrimination or tears, Jack attended mass in the Cologne cathedral ("which is really the height of Gothic architecture, the most beautiful really of all we have seen") and then "headed for Utrecht on one of the new autostradas that are the finest roads in the world. Really unnecessary though, in Germany, as the traffic is small, but they would be great in the U.S. as the speed is unlimited. Looked around for some more dogs and then went across the border into Holland where everyone looks like Juliana + Bernhard. . . . Slipped in at Doorn and saw where the Kaiser lives, although his palace is entirely surrounded by barbed wire."

In Amsterdam they went to see Rembrandt's "Night Watch." Still determined to find a mate for Offie, Jack "had a test made to see if it was the Hunter who was giving me the hay fever. Decided it was."

The next day poor Offie was sold for five guilders, probably to end up, like Peter Rabbit's father, in a cooking pot, during the long nightmare of Nazi occupation. Meanwhile, from Antwerp Jack called his mother collect in Paris, "which however cost me 60 francs. I should learn more exact French," he recorded in his diary. But he was pleased to be on the final leg of the journey to England. He'd found the Hague "dull" after seeing the art treasures of France, Italy, and Germany, and the beach at Ostend was too cold for either sunbathing or swimming. Thus they raced on to Calais, "where we discovered we had missed the channel boat. Still had five minutes to get the mail boat but due to some misunderstanding with Billings over the passport missed it by ten seconds although Billings managed to get a good work-out which he badly needed."

It was clear that Jack resembled Offie in that once he needed to go, he went. Leaving Billings by the dockside at Boulogne, Jack took the mail boat, "as I wanted to see Joe & Kick before they left London. Billings stayed on with the car. Arrived in London with a Mr. Naylor who knew Grandpa, and went around to meet Kick. Joe & Sootie & Freddie Cosgrove who was with Kick. He gave me address to stay at."

London was home from home for Jack. The next day he went shopping v.ith Kathleen, having refused to accompany Joe Jr. in worshiping at the shrine of Harold Laski. Billings arrived with the car, and they went to see the private room Freddie Cosgrove had recommended at 17 Talbot Square, "which looked very good," according to Jack, who was fed up with hotel porters, concierges, and proprietors. In his diary, he'd marked himself as "Not [a] Gentleman!" at no fewer than ten of the twenty-six hotels, inns, pensions, youth hostels, and Salvation Army billets where they'd stayed. At Talbot Square he felt he'd be free of deprecating comments on his private life.

However, it was not to be. The following day, August 27, he accompanied Joe Jr. and Kathleen on the train to Southampton, where he met his mother, "helped myself to a liberal dose of chocolates and tomato juice," and dutifully admired his mother's latest wardrobe from Paris. "When I arrived back in London found myself with the hives," he noted in his diary. "Went home and was damn sick."

His yearlong period of good health was over.

A Shortage of Bathrooms

"It was very worrying because we didn't know anybody, and we didn't even have a clue what kind of a doctor to get," Billings recalled thirty years later. The rest of the family had gone home, "and this is when Jack got so terribly sick."

"Saturday, August 28, 1937: Still sick," Jack scrawled in his diary, "had very tough night. Billings got a 'neat' doctor who wondered if I had mixed my chocolate and tomato juice in a big glass. Finally convinced him I hadn't. Got another Dr."

"Somebody recommended a doctor, who wasn't very good," Billings remembered.

> We had a lot of trouble. I bring up sickness because Jack Kennedy all during his life had few days when he wasn't in pain or sick in some way. Jack never wanted us to talk about this, but now that Bobby has gone and Jack is gone, I think it really should be told. I seldom ever heard him complain. I knew his different maladies, and they were many. We used to joke about the fact that if ever I wrote his biography, I would call it "John F. Kennedy, A Medical History." At one time or another, he really did have almost every medical problem. Take any illness, Jack Kennedy had it. Many of them were very painful. He had a nervous stomach. I really don't know what was wrong with his stomach; I'm sure medical records show. But his stomach trouble was something he had all his life. It felt like a hard knot and gave him constant pain.

Meanwhile in London, as Billings recalled, Jack's illness was serious. "Jack broke out in the most terrible rash, and his face blew up, and we didn't know anybody and had an awful time getting a doctor."

Jack's diary, usually so full of incident, thoughts, and putdowns of his friend Billings, now withered to a few laconic lines. "Still with the hives," he recorded on Sunday, August 29. It was the first time he'd missed church since their journey began. A third doctor, a specialist, was summoned. "A new doctor for my hives + blood count is 4000." The next day a fourth doctor looked in. The crisis was passing, however, and there were fewer swellings. An old Mucker friend from Choate, Edward Bland, came by—prompting great rejoicing in the little boarding house off Hyde Park, as Billings recalled, for it was the day of the great Joe Louis-Jimmy

Farr world-heavyweight championship match "and there was tremendous excitement because we were rooting for Louis against the majority." "Blambo arrived in town—listened to Jimmy Farr fight Joe Louis + won 6 bob [shillings] from the Welch element," Jack recorded. "Met Blambo's girlfriend who was very entertaining."

Sport, friends, and the prospect of girls took Jack's mind off his ill health, and once his swellings abated, he paid no more attention to them than if he'd had diarrhea. By August 30 the hives were almost gone. "Felt okay so got up late in the afternoon and shopped a bit. Movie in the night." No sooner was Jack up and about, however, than he began to feel restless to see more of England. He therefore rang Sir Paul Latham, who knew his father, and the boys were invited down to Herstmonceux Castle in Sussex. "Terrific big castle with beautiful furnished rooms," Jack noted. "One room forty yards long—a bedroom. Had grouse for dinner and stayed up to about 3."

This was Jack's first real introduction to the gentlemanly life of the English upper classes—and he was soon smitten by it, as his sister Kathleen would be. Sir James Calder had meanwhile invited the boys to his estate in Scotland; tickets were booked on a sleeper on September 2, "but as the day wore on Herstmonceux got more and more appealing," Jack noted. "A wonderful place."

Sir James Calder also knew Jack's father, for it was he who had granted Joseph Kennedy the exclusive license to import Haig & Haig whiskey into America in the last months of Prohibition three years earlier. As owner of the Haig distillery "he was a terribly rich man," Billings recalled. "He had an enormous house in Kinrosshire—a gigantic house, as only houses in England can be. I think this was probably Jack's first experience with English-living."

No sooner had they arrived, after an "uncomfortable" night in a third-class railway compartment, than Sir James took them fishing. Jack's sense of humor had returned, and the new sport was grist to his ironic mill. "A rather difficult feat, casting that fly," Jack chronicled in his diary, "and Sir James caught most of them." After lunch they went rabbit shooting, also "without any success. Very good meals here," Jack added. There was no question of staying up late, however, as they'd done at Herstmonceux. "The bed hour is 10:00 and from then on it is quite perilous to move about as Sir James is very cautious on the electricity."

This was an understatement. True to his Scottish upbringing, Sir James brooked no waste. "It was a great shock to us," Billings recalled, "that, in this enormous house, which probably had twenty to thirty bedrooms, there was only one bathroom. We had a terribly difficult time with our old Scottish host. . . . The one bathroom was difficult to find because it was so far from our room. Sir James had the Scottish habit of turning off all the lights with a master switch at 10 o'clock at night. If you didn't get to the bathroom by that time you were in deep trouble. Jack and I had one hell of a time getting to the bathroom during our whole visit."

By day Sir James was a model host, however, and soon had the boys out grouse shooting. "Sir James had about 1,000 acres of heather. At the time of our visit," Billings recollected, "it was rather late in the grouse season. Sir James sent us out with his gamekeeper on a very rainy day. Neither Jack nor I were good shots. In fact, I don't think either of us had ever really used a shotgun before. I'm sure this was a new experience for the gamekeeper. Jack was determined that he would get more grouse than I did. We spent the entire, wet, rainy day tramping through the heather. I had a particularly hard time because of my glasses. I couldn't see anything," Billings admitted. "Jack did get two grouse. I was very upset but I did finally get one with my very last shell at the end."

This was unfortunate, both for the grouse and the American guests. "We were determined to bring the grouse back to the United States," Billings remembered, "even though we had another week in England. The gamekeeper hung our grouse in the kitchen icebox. When we left I'm sure they gave us grouse much older than ours. We carried them all the way to London. We stayed another week in London and we tried to keep them on ice. We turned them over to the ship's refrigerator on the way home. They had become old friends and we were anxious to eat them when we got home."

"As for the boat trip home," Billings recalled,

> the top professional wrestler of the world was aboard. He had beaten Jim Londos of South Africa. This man had some trouble finding anybody to wrestle with him. He had been wrestling one of the ship's cooks, but apparently he wasn't very satisfied. Jack became acquainted with this fellow. I had wrestled on the Choate Wrestling Team and I had also wrestled on the freshman team at Princeton. I guess I weighed about 175 pounds and wasn't in too bad shape. Unbeknown to me, Jack gave him a greatly exaggerated account of my wrestling career, and arranged to have me wrestle him. When I went to the gym the next day I had no choice but to wrestle him. From then on, I wrestled this guy every day and, thank God, the crossing wasn't very long. I couldn't move him! I mean, when we got in a wrestling position on the mat, I couldn't move him at all . . . he could do whatever he wanted with me. It was just not a wrestling match, the guy must have weighed 280 pounds. Nothing gave Jack more pleasure than those matches.

Jack's *schadenfreude* turned to simple *freude* once the ship docked in New York and they were met by Kathleen. "We carefully turned our grouse over to her for safe keeping while we went through customs—I remember they weren't looking too good. When we next saw Kathleen, she didn't have the grouse." To the consternation of the Scottish musketeers "she said the odor was more than she could stand and had thrown them off the dock." The boys were furious.

They had, however, enjoyed a memorable summer. It was the last voyage Jack Kennedy would make as an innocent abroad. His only "introductions" had been to Cardinal Pacelli and his father's whiskey-concession cronies in Britain, otherwise they'd been "on their own," living as cheaply as possible to fit Billings's budget. "Travel, in the younger sort, is a part of education," Francis Bacon had written three centuries before; "in the elder, a part of experience."

Returning to Harvard in September 1937, Jack chose as one of his courses The History of European Art. He'd learned much about Europe, and about himself too. His sense of fun might be Irish, but his deeper emotional coolness accorded with Anglo-Saxon society, as it did in his sister Kathleen's case. Increasingly Jack saw England as the political anchor of Europe, the guarantor of peace between arrogant Germans, complacent French, noisy Latins, and Communist Russians. "Isn't the chance of war less as Britain gets stronger?" he asked himself in his diary, with regard to belated British rearmament, "or is a country like Italy liable to go to war when economic discontent is rife? Wouldn't Mussolini go if there was a war—as in all likelihood Italy would be defeated in a major war?"

Such questions he hoped to ask his new professors as he entered his sophomore year at Harvard, the freshman playboy keen, at last, to become a serious student.

PART
·5·
THE AMBASSADOR'S SON

Jack Kennedy and his father, the U.S. ambassador to the Court of St. James's, at an embassy party, shortly before the outbreak of World War II, 1939 (Peter Hunter/Magnum)

The Rushing Season

Reorganized in the late 1920s, Harvard had sought to emulate the English collegiate system. Live-in sophomore students were now assigned to "houses," which offered resident tutors, libraries, common rooms, and dining facilities.

Shortly before leaving for Europe in the summer of 1937, Jack had been accepted by the master of his brother's residence, Winthrop House, comprising two contiguous buildings (Gore and Standish) overlooking Boston from the banks of the Charles River.

"Winthrop was known as a house that was less exclusive than some," recalled Jack's classmate Holton Wood, who'd attended Noble and Greenough and Dexter schools with him.

> Our housemaster, Dr. Ferry, was rather a shy man—his wife was the one that really wore the trousers—but a lovely man, a professor of chemistry; nice, quiet, and had an attractive daughter who was our age so that kind of caught our eye. Winthrop was more a sort of broader-gauged house, we felt—it had a lot of athletes in it, we always had good athletic teams, house teams in the intramural programs. . . . Right across the street was Lowell; in those days you thought of it more as the brighter kind of house, more academic types went there. Leverett was sort of nondescript, I guess. So was Kirkland. Adams was more like Elliot. Dunster was off sort of a little bit down the river and further away, so that, although it was a good house, people didn't like to be that far from the classroom buildings.

Had Jack been on any but good terms with his elder brother, he would scarcely have applied to Winthrop House. However, it was not only Joe Jr.'s presence that attracted him but the group of new friends he'd made in his freshman year: in particular Torbert Macdonald, Bill Coleman, and Jimmy Rousmanière.

Whereas at Princeton Jack had made no new friends, at Harvard he never stopped making them. Torbert Macdonald's father had been a football coach, and Macdonald himself would become a Harvard football star. Coleman was a hockey player and Rousmanière was a squash player. "The four of us applied to Winthrop House and there were no suites for four, so we ended with two twins alongside each other," Rousmanière recalled.

The mix of sports they went out for mirrored their mix of backgrounds and religions. While Macdonald and Kennedy were Catholics, Coleman and Rousmanière were Episcopalians. Coleman's father, in fact, was a Republican judge in Baltimore, though Coleman himself was the most liberal of the group. "He was a very idealistic man," Rousmanière reflected. "If he'd survived the war, I think he would have been probably something like, I won't say president of the Red Cross, but I think he would have gotten into some big charitable operation like that, and been a manager—because he was inclined that way, his social conscience was very great."

Rousmanière's father was also a Republican, a Boston lawyer who'd moved to New York but who'd served in the Massachusetts State Legislature in 1910, at the time when John Fitzgerald was mayor. "My father was a pretty staunch Republican," Rousmanière admitted. "Once, at Harvard, why, I had to get a train back to New York and I couldn't get a reservation on the train. So Honey Fitzgerald offered to go down to the train station with me, and he got me my reservation. I probably never discussed the Kennedys with my father that often, but I did make the mistake when I got back that day of saying, "Yeah, and Honey Fitzgerald got me the reservation on the train," and my father—who was a mild-mannered man—was very angry! He had enormous prejudice against Honey Fitz, who'd been indicted in 1909, and the only reason he beat the indictment was he adopted a defense, 'I can't remember'—which is what Ronald Reagan did in 1987!"

If Jack was popular, it was not because he was wealthy but because he was fun. "That's one thing that always stood out," Rousmanière later emphasized. "Anytime you were with Jack Kennedy you would laugh. He was a laugh a minute." Lem Billings agreed. "Jack was more fun than anyone I've ever known, and I think most people who knew him felt the same way about him."

Yet even Billings acknowledged there was something strange about Jack's ability to make so many friends when he was not, at heart, at all emotional. In the thirty-two years Billings knew him, he never once saw Jack Kennedy shed a tear. "He never was a bit emotional or anything like that, and he never showed any great affection for anybody. But if you needed him, he was sensitive enough to understand it and he'd spend whatever time was necessary in helping you."

"He would have done everything in his power to hide his emotions," Billings claimed on another occasion. "I certainly don't think he was cold in any way. He had a very warm personality. I think he cared a great deal about people and his feelings of loyalty were far above average—I'd even go further, I never knew anyone with stronger feelings of loyalty. I think that anytime that he really established in his own mind that a man was his friend, he never deserted him. This was true even when his loyalty was sorely tried. . . . I can think of two who had been his friends—yet they gave him many heartaches: I think that it was very difficult for him to ever conceive of any reason why they would turn against him."

To Jack loyalty meant far more than brilliance or profundity. In the opinion of Jimmy Rousmanière, neither Billings nor Macdonald ever really matured: "Torby Macdonald never grew up after senior year at Andover. Billings may have grown up a little bit until about second year of Princeton. . . . He was just a clown."

Billings himself was aware of this. "I think it is interesting," he later reflected, "because I, frankly, haven't had another friend whom I've known as long as Jack Kennedy. . . . There must have been something about him that kept people wanting him to be their friend through the years. Much more interesting," he speculated, "is why Jack wanted to keep all those friends, since his mind and interests did grow, let's face it, at a much faster clip than any of his contemporaries."

One reason was that in their various and collective ways Jack's contemporaries could help him. No sooner had the four musketeers settled into Winthrop House in October 1937 than the question of final clubs arose. Although elected to the Hasty Pudding Institute, Harvard's drama club which acted as a stepping stone to the final clubs, neither Joseph Kennedy nor Joe Jr. (contrary to the claims of Joe Jr.'s biographer, Hank Searls, and the family chronicler, Doris Kearns Goodwin) were ever invited to join one of the final clubs at Harvard. For a while it looked as if this would be Jack's fate, too, as Jimmy Rousmanière later remembered:

> There are eight final clubs at Harvard. Each of them elects ten to fifteen in a class, so there's only a hundred members accepted out of a class of a thousand.
>
> You're probably familiar with the rushing season. All of October of the sophomore year is sort of rushing season, and you get invited around every night for three weeks. They would invite perhaps a hundred people and finally find 15 that probably would like to join a particular club, and be acceptable—and I don't think that Jack Kennedy's name ever got on that 15 list! The power of the Boston alumni was still so great—and they didn't like Joe Kennedy or Honey Fitzgerald.

Holton Wood, who was accepted by the elite A.D. Club, was certain "that Jack Kennedy really never was considered for this club." Though Joseph Kennedy had left Boston a decade before, his reputation for stock-market swindling had stuck. "When it came time for approval of applications, none of the clubs would accept Jack Kennedy."

Donald Thurber, a contemporary, put the matter more bluntly.

Jack Kennedy was part of the Irish contingent, the Catholic contingent, and that set him apart somewhat. The class was, in those days,
just dominated by a WASP atmosphere. And Kennedy didn't fit into
that mold at all. Do I think Jack Kennedy ever suffered ethnic
prejudice? Well, yes, I think so—because he was such an obvious
Boston-Irish type. You could tell from the way he spoke—he had a
Boston accent as opposed to a Groton accent. And there were those
older, more puritanical Bostonians, many of whom were in the class
of 1940 at Harvard, who regarded the Kennedys as coarse, loud,
nouveaux riches upstarts. For those people, the Kennedys were just
irretrievably Boston Irish. . . . The Kennedys were known particularly by the Bostonians as a family on the make. For many of the
Brahmin families here, the Fitzgeralds were simply beyond the pale,
and the Kennedys also.

It was now that Jack's experience at school came to his rescue. Alone,
he was the victim of ethnic, social, and religious prejudice. United with
a group of peers, however, he stood at least a chance of surviving the
snobbery of the Harvard club alumni, and his friends willingly complied.
He had already achieved a measure of renown for his chairmanship of the
1937 Freshman Smoker. "It was considered to be a pretty fast program he
generated," Jimmy Rousmanière recalled.

The whole thousand classmates were there. It was one of the high
points of his college life even though it was early on. . . . It was a very
friendly and very meaningful event, the culminating social event of
the year—and he was head of the committee! No matter who you
were or what you did as a freshman, almost everybody went to the
Smoker. . . . There wasn't much student government at Harvard,
therefore to have some kind of notoriety in a class of a thousand you
had to function in athletics, or on the *Crimson* newspaper, or the
Lampoon—or on the Smoker. It was a leadership activity at Harvard. The Smoker was a big deal. . . . it was his first political success.
So by this time Jack Kennedy had made his mark.

"Coleman and I had started to room together," Rousmanière recalled,
"and I liked Coleman tremendously. And he said, 'It's wrong that Jack
Kennedy can't get in a club. Let's do something about it.' I mean, Jack
Kennedy was a very attractive guy, he was just as qualified or more
qualified to be a good club member as any of us."
    A pact was thus made: that none of the three-man group would accept
membership in a final club unless all three were accepted. At first Torbert
Macdonald, the fourth member of their Winthrop group, was to be

included; however as Rousmanière recorded, although "Macdonald certainly was a superior athlete in many ways," he drank "a little bit too much" and was "a pretty rough diamond," as even Jack, who roomed with him, acknowledged. Rousmanière was thus unwilling to link himself to Macdonald.

> Coleman and I said, "Well, we're gonna fight hard for Jack, but there's some problem with Torby." We liked him well enough, but we could see we would find it pretty hard to convince these club people. Coleman's father had never been in a club, my father had never been in a club, although they were Harvard people. So we said, well, we'll make a stand for Kennedy but we won't make a stand for Macdonald. And so Macdonald never did get in a club. . . . Mind you, Torby Macdonald really didn't need the clubs. He was a big athlete, a good football player, but also a good track athlete, a sprinter. So Kennedy wasn't worried about him; he said, "Well, if Torby can't get in, that's his problem, but I want to get in. I want to have some fun."

In targeting the Spee Club, the key was the graduate membership or alumni. Whereas at the other Harvard clubs "the Boston alumni were still thinking about Joe Kennedy and Honey Fitzgerald," Rousmanière explained, the Spee "was dominated by New Yorkers, and the Boston alumni system was not very great." Better still, the nomination or selection committee of the Spee was headed by Ralph Pope, a contemporary of Jack's elder brother.

"I had been on two or three different committees with Joe Jr. That's how I got to know the father, and Jack," Pope recalled.

> Joe was a very attractive fellow. He said all the right things when he wanted and he got along very well in our class at Harvard and was running certain things in the first and second year. He was a real politician from way back. There wasn't anything wrong with him, it was just that he was made that way. He had a group of fellows that he knew from school and around Boston and elsewhere as he traveled around. . . . The guys he had with him, the only one I could stand was [Ted] Reardon. The others were all nothing but so-so guys that would do whatever Joe wanted them to do. I can't say that I got along too well with him in those committees that I was on. I think some of the things that he was saying were somebody else's ideas that I didn't think too sensible.
>
> Jack never gave you that feeling. By the time you could say something, he had a question or a remark about it, which went right to

the heart. You never had to fool around or wonder, "What the hell does he mean?" There was no question about it. . . . I know when he came to our club in the fall of 1937, and it became known that I was the one that had talked to Rousmanière and Coleman about getting Kennedy, people said, "Why the hell did you pick Kennedy?"

Pope was ashamed of such prejudice "in a simple thing like a club at Harvard" and became determined to take Kennedy. "Just for that reason—that we needed somebody with some sense in the place. We were a bunch of lightweights."

"Ralph Pope did it," Rousmanière confirmed. "Ralph Pope came to us and said, 'O.K., if you guys want this three-man deal, we want it too. We'll take you all.' "

Jack had made it: the first Kennedy ever to break into the inner sanctum of Boston's WASP world.

The Spee Club

"Was it important to Jack Kennedy? You bet it was!" Rousmanière emphasized. "In those days, the Spee served three meals a day, five or six days a week—which was important because Jack had a diet problem. (We even installed an ice-cream making machine when his doctor altered his diet to try and fatten him up.) But above all, it gave him a base and a social standing which his brother never had. Jack and Joe were good friends, but I think that Jack always felt happy that he was able to do some things that Joe couldn't do. And the Spee Club was the means of doing that."

On the night of December 2, 1937, the eight newly selected members were inducted into the Spee Club through initiation ceremonies, or hazing, that remain secret to this day. Though the rites had become less orgiastic than when the club was first founded in the 1880s, they still involved the organs of the club's symbol, the bull, the humbling of the new members, and finally, their oath that for the rest of their lives they would do everything to aid one another.

In the spacious, well-appointed Georgian building on the corner of Mt. Auburn and Holyoke streets in Cambridge, with its graceful staircase, its Hogarth prints, paneled walls, Belgian tapestries, and high ceilings, Jack Kennedy was, at last, "home." Henceforth he would eat every breakfast at the Spee, and almost every lunch; from its quiet library he would write for the following three years on Spee Club notepaper to family and friends. For the rest of his life he maintained a gratitude, if not affection, toward the club and its members, for in the difficult journey he would make as second son of a despised and arrogant Boston-Irish millionaire and archetypal Catholic mother, it was his first personal triumph. "It was a status symbol for him," Rousmanière reflected: "that at last the Kennedys were good enough."

Not all students or faculty took Harvard's final clubs seriously. Kenneth Galbraith later considered that "Harvard undergraduates in the 1930s were also antiintellectual but not as single-minded as were those at Princeton. There were social clubs, but they had no great role. With one or two exceptions I've never known their names."

If this was so, Galbraith's social obtuseness was the matrix of his brilliance as an economist. For Jack Kennedy, certainly, the Spee Club had an immensely important role: a personal refuge, a sanctuary beyond the bounds of faculty supervision, parental pressure, or fraternal rivalry; a place he could share exclusively with his friends. "The Spee had a damn good membership in those days," recalled Holton Wood, a member of the rival A.D. "They had Blair Clark, he was the head of the *Crimson,* the college newspaper, and Cleveland Amory, also an editor of the *Crimson*—very nice, very bright—and many others."

As Rousmanière recalled, mealtimes at the Spee Club were opportunities not only for good fellowship, but for stimulating discussion—conversations conducted not as lowly students in Harvard houses run by preening faculty tutors, but as self-confident young men running their own affairs and accorded equal status with older members and alumni. It was in this quasi-English club society that Jack Kennedy reached his peak at Harvard, achieving an independence of which the "primes" of the faculty (as Ralph Pope called them) were ignorant but which was of seminal importance to Jack himself, burdened by his Boston-Irish background. Never again, as long as he lived, could anyone look down on Jack Kennedy.

Professors such as Carl Friedrich might later recall only a "bright young face which stood out in the class"; or, as William Langer loftily remembered, even less than that, since "the course which he took with me (European History) was a rather large lecture course in which there was little contact between the instructor and the students." But for Jack Kennedy, thanks to his acceptance by the Spee, his sophomore year became one of the most exciting of his life. Despite the faculty's often exaggerated self-importance, he enjoyed his courses and the required reading; moreover, he went all out for the college's second football squad, known as Junior Varsity. "I suppose none of you Princeton Pricks back a losing team," he proudly taunted his friend Lem Billings. "Where's that Princeton spirit you're always shooting off about? . . . That's the thing about you Princeton guys," he mocked.

Jack's own days as a football player were numbered, however. On the morning of October 30, 1937, "on a glorious, warm fall day," he had traveled to Trenton to play on the Harvard Junior Varsity team against Princeton. As Joe Jr. was also expected to play in the afternoon game for Harvard's first team, his father had motored from Bronxville to see the "fight."

Jack and his friend Holton Wood were Junior Varsity substitutes but were not called upon to play, as far as Wood could later recall. At the conclusion of the match, however, the Kennedy family chauffeur came racing across the field to say hello to Jack, and in the spirit of the morning's game threw a "half-baked tackle" at the unsuspecting boy, who was knocked to the ground. Though Jack struggled to his feet, it was obvious he was in great pain, and although he played for a few minutes in the subsequent Dartmouth game, it was clear that his back injury was serious. The coach, Dick Harlow, allowed him onto the field for a few moments in the all-important Yale game on November 19, thus entitling him forever to wear the coveted "minor *H*" on his jersey (his brother, however, remained on the bench and thus failed to get his major letter, to his own and his father's lasting chagrin), but it was for Jack's pluck rather than his performance. He had always coveted the position of end; now, ironically, it was his football career that had ended, thanks to the family chauffeur.

For Jack this was a disappointment, like his other illnesses. However, it was not something on which he proposed to dwell. Life at Harvard was too rich in companionship to take the demise of his football career seriously. Moreover, to cap his own triumph in gaining acceptance by the Spee Club, there was tentative news from home that, if true, would transform the social lives of the whole Kennedy family.

A Very Dangerous Man

"By December 1937 I had almost completed a report embodying my suggestions," the chairman of the Maritime Commission later told the ghostwriter of his proposed autobiography, James Landis, when "with mixed feelings . . . I received a message from the President that he would like me to take over the post of Secretary of Commerce. The opportunity thus presented would normally have been a challenging one," he admitted. However

> from the very start in my post as Chairman of the Securities and Exchange Commission, I had come into conflict with Henry Morgenthau, the Secretary of the Treasury. Our ideas and our approach differed sharply and during the years that passed, I made no secret of that difference in dealing with him or with others. . . .
>
> Almost the same differences in outlook lay between Secretary of Labor, Frances Perkins, and myself. . . . It seemed to me inevitable that further and more acute differences would occur were I to try and align the Administration's policy toward labor with what I believed should be its general policy toward business.
>
> These were the considerations I set before President Roosevelt early the next morning when he received me, at his bedside. To me, the potential disharmony that I would necessarily bring into his Cabinet seemed a sufficient ground for me to decline his offer and I told him flatly that that was my conclusion.
>
> It was then that he turned to me and offered me the Ambassadorship to the Court of St. James's, pointing out that due to illness, Ambassador Bingham had asked to be relieved of the post.

"The President's suggestion was a complete surprise," Kennedy claimed. "Diplomatic service had not suggested itself to me. To this day [1948] I do not know whether the offer initiated with the President himself or with one of his advisers. I asked for time to consider it. . . .

"The recital of these events may appear to be petty. But their importance lies in their personal nature, and the informal circumstances under which I was tendered and finally accepted the Ambassadorship to the Court of St. James [*sic*]."

This account, unfortunately, was a tissue of lies. In the public record of his life Kennedy simply could not bring himself to tell, or face, the truth. A few months before, in September 1937, *Fortune* magazine had carried a sympathetic biographical profile of Kennedy. As the family chronicler revealed half a century later, the widely disseminated article was a complete travesty of the journalist's original, highly critical article, which Kennedy managed to quash as "the brainchild of a psychopathic case." At the time, however, readers of *Fortune* knew nothing of such subversion, just as readers of *The New York Times* were unaware of the large sums of money lavished on Arthur Krock as public advocate for Joseph P. Kennedy.

Jack's Harvard football friend Charles Houghton certainly knew. As

Houghton later recalled, "The old man hired Arthur Krock for $25,000 to keep the Kennedy name in the papers. . . . It's the first time I ever heard about PR. This was back in 1937. $25,000 was a lot of money!" Jack himself told Houghton of the arrangement one day. As Houghton remarked, there was no attempt to keep it secret. "It just seemed to be common knowledge" in the Kennedy circle and "generally known at the time."

Another well-known American journalist, the columnist Drew Pearson, had lauded Kennedy's Maritime Commission exploits in the New York *Daily Mirror*—but was later revealed by the family chronicler to be, if not in Joseph's Kennedy's pay, at least in his debt, privately thanking Kennedy in 1937 for "your very lovely present. . . . It is most beautiful and I shall wear it with great relish and with many memories of a very swell friend."

What Kennedy could not bring himself to reveal to Landis was not only Krock's role in getting Roosevelt to make the offer, but the reaction of Roosevelt's advisers when they got wind of it. Smarting from continual press criticism after five years in office, Roosevelt had been wary of the increasingly active press artillery lined up behind Joseph Kennedy, and was undoubtedly anxious to get rid of a potential political thorn when, early in December 1937, he offered him, in principle, the appointment to England. However, "when it became known in the inner circle that the President intended to appoint Mr. Kennedy as ambassador to the Court of St. James [*sic*], there was great pressure from the inside, from the liberal inside, to prevent this from happening," Arthur Krock later confided. It was at this juncture that Roosevelt sent his son Jimmy to see whether the deed could be undone.

Though speaking from memory, Krock was telling the truth. "I heard that James Roosevelt, the President's son-secretary, had spent three hours with Mr. Kennedy, at his father's request, to urge him to take a place in the Cabinet—the portfolio of Commerce—instead of St. James [*sic*]," Krock noted in a secret memorandum at the time. After Jimmy Roosevelt's departure, "he [Kennedy] came back to me, clearly very indignant, very angry, and said, 'He tried to get me to take the secretaryship of Commerce and I knew it was only an attempt to shut me off from London, but London is where I want to go and it is the only place I intend to go and I told Jimmy so, and that's that.' " By leaking news of the impending appointment on December 9, 1937, Krock forced Roosevelt's hand—indeed, the president never really forgave Krock, subsequently claiming that his premature story had hastened the death of Ambassador Bingham, who was recuperating in a hospital in the United States. Meanwhile, on December 16, 1937, Krock wrote to tell the financier Bernard Baruch that Kennedy was under heavy pressure not to accept the ambassadorship, "but I am sure he will."

Krock was right. As Rose later revealed, Joe had been soliciting the ambassadorship via Arthur Krock and others for more than a year, and his reluctant acceptance of the chairmanship of the Maritime Commission had been laced with the guarantee of an ambassadorship, as a quid pro quo. Far from being surprised by Roosevelt's offer, as he pretended to Landis, Kennedy was delighted, and damned if he was going to allow it to slip from his grasp. Nor did he. From Shelby, Montana, he cabled Roosevelt on January 13, 1938,

> MY DEAR MR. PRESIDENT, MOORE AND I ARE ON OUR WAY HOME BY TRAIN. . . . JUST GOT NEWS OF MY CONFIRMATION. WILL THANK YOU WHEN I GET HOME. I WANT TO SAY NOW THAT I DON'T KNOW WHAT KIND OF DIPLOMAT I SHALL BE, PROBABLY ROTTEN, BUT I PROMISE TO GET DONE FOR YOU THOSE THINGS THAT YOU WANT DONE. ROSE AND I ARE DEEPLY GRATEFUL.

Rose, beleaguered in a social world that would not accept her ("When will the nice people of Boston accept Catholics?" she had asked one of Jack's friends at Harvard), was overjoyed. "Dear Mr. President," she penned in her neatest schoolgirl handwriting, "I do want to thank you for the wonderful appointment you have given to Joe. The children and I feel deeply honored, delighted and thrilled, and we want you to know that we do appreciate the fact that you have made possible this great rejoicing."

Kennedy's paid acolytes applauded the appointment in the press. Only one, the columnist Boake Carter, whose articles were published in both the New York *Daily Mirror* and *The Boston Globe,* warned Kennedy privately that it was a terrible mistake, pointing out that such a post, at such a time, "needs skill brought by years of training. And that, Joe, you simply don't possess. Do not think me unkind in saying that. On the contrary, I'm trying to save you some heartaches. . . . Joe, in so complicated a job, there is no place for amateurs. . . . If you don't realize that soon enough, you're going to be hurt as you were never hurt in your life."

Carter's prediction would come tragically true. But Kennedy, still smarting from a series of lampoons performed at the twenty-fifth reunion of his Harvard class in June 1937, paid no heed.

Roosevelt, at the time, never thought of the ambassadorial appointment as more than a brief reward for services rendered. To Henry Morgenthau, for instance, Roosevelt confided that he considered "Kennedy a very dangerous man and that he was going to send him to England as Ambassador with the distinct understanding that the appointment was only for six months and that furthermore by giving him this appointment any obligation that he had to Kennedy was paid for." To show how unseriously he took the short-term appointment, Roosevelt even asked

Kennedy to take down his pants in front of his staff in the Oval Office, and to hoots of laughter declared Joe to be definitely too bandy-legged to wear the traditional silk knee breeches of an ambassador to St. James's—a ribbing Joe took in good heart. He was, after all, making history: the first Irish-American ever to hold the office, and the first Roman Catholic.

Kennedy certainly had no illusions about the length of his tenure. As he told Harvey Klemmer, his aide at the Maritime Commission whom he'd asked to go with him to London as his publicist and speech writer: "Don't go buying a lot of luggage. We're only going to get the family in the *Social Register*. When that's done, we come back and go out to Hollywood to make some movies and some money."

But Joseph Kennedy's movie-making days were long since over. And the London embassy would be, for him if not for his children, an even greater fiasco than *Queen Kelly*.

A Moon to Joe's Sun

Meanwhile, Jack Kennedy, having made his minor *H* for football and gained acceptance to the Spee Club, stayed clear of the embassy imbroglio. Christmas was spent *en famille* at Palm Beach, but within days Jack was planning to fly up to New York, where he proposed to meet Billings and Horton at the Stork Club. "In those days that was the place to go," Billings later recalled, "and the Stork Club was very anxious to attract young people. They particularly encouraged young models and pretty girls to come there, and they made things easier for the boys who brought pretty girls. . . . There were presents for the girls and champagne. Of course we were always very careful never to have more than one drink each while we were there—we couldn't spend any more than that. Jack didn't mind spending on the same basis as I did. Jack wasn't much of a drinker, so it wasn't any hardship to take one drink. He liked to dance very much."

Jack planned to meet his latest date at the Stork Club on Sunday evening, January 2, 1938. "On Sunday nights they used to have a balloon game," Billings recalled. "Balloons would drop from the ceiling and you'd all grab them. Some of them contained hundred dollar bills and even one five hundred dollar bill, tickets for free meals at the Stork Club, bottles of champagne, etc."

In fact Jack took the train from Florida, having written to ask Charlotte McDonnell, Kathleen's friend, to accompany him to see *Lady in the*

Dark. He squired Frances Nalle, then moved on to a new girl, "and Nalle is in tears as Rip can tell you," he boasted to Billings. His brother had meanwhile given Jane Rovensky "quite a rush and is now in our class—I'm happy to say that gal needs a red hot poke although her old man gets the first helping," Jack remarked savagely, "as he accuses me of being 'a moon to Joe's sun'—the prick."

Jack's furious social and sexual energy certainly helped shield him from the dynastic ambitions of his father, currently resting upon Joe Jr., who was writing his final-year honors thesis on the Hands-Off Spain isolationist movement. Thereafter, Mr. Kennedy decreed, Joe Jr. was to go to the London embassy as his secretary (another idea stemming from the fertile brain of Felix Frankfurter).

In retrospect, what Joe Jr. needed was time and space to become his own man, not his father's secretary. At the time, however, even Roosevelt admired Kennedy's fierce paternal pride and his determination to watch over, spur on, guide, chide, and abide by his children, which Roosevelt saw as surprisingly unselfish in such a ruthlessly self-centered man.

What motivated Joseph Kennedy's overbearing paternal concern is difficult to say. By concentrating so hard on his children's progress, Joe was doubtless performing a penance for his failed relationship with Rose, but the down side of this was an array of unexamined feelings and expectations foisted upon his children, whose filial love and obedience could be made to compensate for the breakdown of their parents' marriage.

There were, too, darker areas of Joseph P. Kennedy's soul which no one could read. "He wouldn't be Mr. Kennedy if you really knew what his real purpose was in anything he ever did," Lem Billings later confided to one interviewer. What *was* Mr. Kennedy's ultimate goal in the upbringing of his children? "Aside from his work, his children were his only real interest," Billings recalled. "His social life was of little interest to him," while Mrs. Kennedy "had very little social life." The powerful energy that might otherwise have gone into forming extrafamilial relationships thus remained corralled, deliberately inciting an invertedness, a clannishness that superficially impressed outsiders, spawning articles and books with titles such as *The Remarkable Kennedys* and even a fawning eulogy, *The Kennedy Women,* by Nobel Prize winner Pearl S. Buck.

Yet these remarkable Kennedys, thanks to their parents, for the most part seemed unable to enjoy normal, healthy relationships with people in the outside world, let alone happy marriages. The children—especially the daughters—were under constant pressure from their mother to conform to her reproduction manners and religious preoccupations; from their father, simply to win. "We don't want any losers around here. In this family we want winners," was Joseph Kennedy's constant refrain. According to Billings, "he never liked a failure. He felt that his children, at least, should try and do everything they could to succeed. He was very disappointed if they didn't win. He made it very clear that he wanted to see them win at everything they did. If they didn't, they knew that he would be disappointed. He didn't like his children to be second best. Of course, the children were aware of this constant pressure. They knew that everything he did was because he loved them . . . so they automatically felt that they wanted to win and they wanted to do well for his sake. Of course, this developed into a real desire to win."

To win, for the Kennedy children, meant to gain their father's love; to lose, conversely, was to forfeit it—hardly a recipe for relaxed and self-confident children. Moreover, capitalizing on the close bonds formed among the children in their infant and early years when their parents were so often absent, Mr. Kennedy now encouraged his children as they grew up to count upon one another, not outsiders. Jack's friends were welcome at Hyannis Port, Bronxville, and Palm Beach but were not permitted to step across the strict family boundary Mr. Kennedy drew around himself and his children. In Florida Rip Horton recorded, "Mr. Kennedy was definitely the leader. He was at the head of the table and then there'd be Joe, Jack, then Ted Reardon, possibly Torby, Lem, myself. . . . I probably went down for three years. And Mr. Kennedy—all talk would be on current events, politics, international politics. Jack and Joe would ask questions and he would answer in great detail. But if I asked Mr. Kennedy a question, believe me, he'd treat me as a piece of dirt, he'd ignore me. He was interested in his family per se"—and no one else.

"Mr. Kennedy also built within the family a real loyalty to each other," Billings recorded. "This must have stemmed from his own great love and his feeling that together they could do better than alone. There's no question about it. It's very unusual the way the members of this family, all of them in their middle years, still have this very clan family feeling. . . . Mr. Kennedy always said that the family should stick together. He said the family would be happier as one unit than if they broke up into separate individual families."

Whether they were really happier would be debatable. But Mr. Kennedy's dynastic imperative was now reaching astronomical and psychologically disturbing proportions, since he had by will, fear, and the force of his bullying personality made himself the sun around whom the members of the Kennedy family revolved, held in orbit by his magnetism. Rose described it as "an almost physical emanation of energy and power and mental quickness and forthrightness."

This gravitational pull, while it offered great sibling intimacy as well as powerful encouragement, was hard to equate with spiritual growth or even independence. Shunned by American society, Mr. and Mrs.

Kennedy could offer no example to their children in making friends or normal socializing. Indeed at heart they hated, as Rose admitted, the idea of their children fragmenting into "separate individual families" as they grew up—an injunction that was to have grave ramifications for them all, including Jack.

"Jack Kennedy's father was a very important influence in his life," Billings later reflected.

> I don't think that those children were born with all the attributes that they later possessed—I think a great deal of their qualities were stimulated by Mr. Kennedy. Although I'm not a father, I know how difficult and what a tremendous responsibility it is to raise children properly; this is true particularly if you're as wealthy as Mr. Kennedy. It must be a temptation to spoil your children, to do too much for them. On the other hand strict parents who push their children too hard, who expect too much, often end up with antagonistic children who dislike their parents. Mr. Kennedy had as much love for his children as any man could have. They were his real interest in life. This must have made it even more difficult for him to be the kind of parent he was. Mr. Kennedy is not an unemotional man as some people might think—he is an extremely emotional one. I think it must have been very difficult for him to control himself as he did and not just overpower his children with love or push them so hard that they would be spoiled.

In Billings's retrospective view, Mr. Kennedy did not overdo his pressure. "He encouraged them and gave them ambition. I don't exactly know how he did this, but I watched him through the years encouraging and giving them confidence. If they did badly, he would let them know that he was disappointed and that he knew they could do better. He was able to think out how they should best be handled."

This handling, however, would have consequences that even Billings, for all his devotion to the Kennedys, could see was damaging, particularly in the case of Kathleen, for whom he felt a special affection. Moreover, Mr. Kennedy's discouragement of his sons from going into business— "he was absolutely determined that they would not follow in his footsteps as a businessman," Billings emphasized—kept his sons tied to his purse strings, like daughters waiting for their marital dowry.

Joe Jr.'s response was and would continue to be a determination to do his best to conform to his father's expectations. Kathleen's, as will be seen, would be to do everything she could to escape her mother's fanatical Catholicism, without being disloyal or sinful, and yet retain her father's affection.

For Jack, however, the challenge of handling his handler, of accepting the boons which a man of Joseph Kennedy's unusual caliber could bestow while avoiding the pitfalls of such a dependent relationship, would be perhaps the greatest test of his life—a test that now reached its climax as his father set sail in February 1938 to make history as America's worst ambassador to Britain: the arch-appeaser of the Nazis.

A Fucking Bunch of Fairies

Back at Harvard early in the new year of 1938, Jack threw himself into athletic, social, and academic life. "Just a note as in middle of exams," he scribbled to Billings on Spee Club stationery on January 21, enclosing "an especially brilliant piece of editorial writing"—a page from the latest *Choate News*.

For all his negative feelings about Choate, the shooting gallery of Jack's embittered psyche depended on targets such as Choate provided, and the school newspaper happily obliged. "For over a year the school has been watching the Paul Mellon Science Building grow gradually," began the main editorial column, under the heading "Endowed for the Service of Truth." "For over a year, the masters have been conjecturing, planning and preparing so that they might make the most advantageous use of the materials which would soon be put into their hands." "Can't you see Mehans 'conjecturing, planning and preparing'?" Jack asked Billings, underlining the paragraph. Another editorial, urging fifth-formers to recognize "the gravity" of their future responsibility as sixth-formers, also aroused Jack's mocking applause. "A smart bit of writing," he sneered in the margin at the author's affected analogy with car driving. "It is of prime importance," the author had asserted, that the class should shift into "a steady, smooth-sailing third year" by the time it took over from its predecessor—"a point that should be driven home early while the former is still in the shifting process. Then, something which is almost as important, there must be plenty of back-seat drivers in the car, planning, suggesting and considering new and shorter ways to go." "That's where we came in," Jack remarked.

Jack's prize, however, went to a letter, printed below the obligatory thank-you for the new science building, from a certain Paul Juliffe, which ran: "A book was recently written on the thesis that 'What America needs is more bum music'! I quote the author, who meant that two amateur musicians of uncertain technique are apt to get much more pleasure in playing together than they would be likely to do on their own. In this spirit I should consider it a privilege to furnish studio and a piano accompaniment of sorts to a Bach sonata or the Maiden's Prayer, whether rendered on the violin or the 'Frisco Whistle. Perhaps there are some of you readers who would be glad to join me in a little 'bum' music?'' "Especially sickening," Jack commented in the margin, adding, "What a fucking bunch of fairies go there."

Behind the derisive humor, however, there was gnawing pain. Once again Jack's delicate health was beginning to deteriorate. "Going to Mayo Feb. and then South," he scrawled on the back of his note to Billings, and reacted fiercely to Billings's long-distance diagnosis of either appendicitis or inflammation of his penis. "As regards my appendix— they have been [out] for only eight years and as for your rather unnatural interest in my becoming circumsized, J.J. has never been in better shape or doing better service," Jack boasted. "Would appreciate any of your gossip on Eileen Herrick who looks plenty good and sexy," he went on. "We swim Princeton up here [in March]—Are there any bets? My swimming is quite sad as I have sinus—Finish up around the 12th [February] and will see you then in NY." He added a P.S.: "Let me know about Herrick."

Jack's party-going, like his swimming, was soon curtailed, however. By the third week in February he was in the college infirmary, and though his roommate, Torby Macdonald, sneaked in steaks and extra food, Jack's weight plummeted. "Well, once more my athletic career has been blighted," he wrote disconsolately to Billings. "Have the grippe—been in the infirmary for 4 days now and it looks as though I shall be here another few days. The Yale meet is 2 weeks from Sat. so don't see how I can ever get back in shape again by then. It's a pain in the ass as it would have been a Major Letter as Harvard will whale the shit out of Yale and Princeton— may try and go South for a week in order to get healthy." To his mother, sojourning on her own in Palm Beach, he also lamented the cold that finished "my swimming career. . . . This is an awful pain as it means a whole season gone to waste. However, will endeavor—Otherwise healthy as I had a blood-count taken which is 7,000—Very good." Never dreaming he would one day bed the legendary ice-skating star, Jack also asked his mother if she'd seen "the Sonja Henie troupe—I'd like to be down there myself with that gal on the troupe. How did they look to you?" he teased, "The type you settle down with?"

As he feared, Jack failed to make the Harvard team, being beaten out by Richard Tregaskis. By the second week of March 1938 he was in the New England Baptist Hospital "trying to get rid of an intestinal infection I've had for the last two weeks. Was unable to get back in condition as I had this thing last week—so did not get my [Harvard] letter which is an awful pain in the ass. Did you call the house to tell them where you put

the car," he asked Billings, "as nobody knew and they called Boston, etc.
and finally located it at Casey's. My only comment was that 'Billings had
it last.' "

There was another problem too. The previous October Jack had come
in "rather unpleasant contact with a woman in a car who was such a shit
that I gave her a lot of shit. Consequently she wrote to the Registry of
Motor Vehicles saying I had leered at her after bumping her four or five
times, which story has some truth although I didn't know I was leering.
Anyways they got me in and are sore at me," he reported, with the result
that he'd now pretended he'd "loaned my car out that night to some
students" and had given Billings's name. "Tell him you come from
Florida if he asks for your license—also you're sorry and realize you
should not have done it, etc. . . . You write him a gracious letter and admit
it," Jack ordered.

It was not Jack's sole misdemeanor, either. At New Haven, forlornly
watching the Harvard swimming team perform without him, Jack had cut
his own throat "from ear to ear" with the two girls he'd invited—Frances
Nalle and Gillian Fox—"by leaving them Sat. night and then calling their
landlady an old son-of-a-bitch and telling her to kiss my arse while they
were listening. Fox said I was a big prick in as many words and Nalle's
big eyes just rolled and misted," with the result that he was back to Olive
Cawley as his date for the following Friday night—if he got out of the
hospital.

He didn't. Eventually he made his way to the house at Palm Beach,
which was empty. "Am going to rest and get healthy a couple of days and
will expect you around Sat. or Sunday," he wrote to Billings. Billings
remembered that he was "quite broke and I didn't have the dough to even
go down to Florida. Jack said I could bring down whoever I wanted, if
they would pay for the transportation. I asked two classmates, Sandy
Osborn and Eben Pyne. We drove down and stayed two weeks. This was
the first time he had ever met them.

"He was there alone. The caretaker had opened up the house and Jack
Kennedy was running the house, in effect," Billings related. However, far
from lying in bed or on the beach, as Billings expected, the invalid "was
taking a rumba lesson. The rumba was the big thing when we were young,
and he wanted to know how to do it."

Rumba lessons were followed by a rambunctious Easter. Billings recalled:

> Of course it was really fun for the guys to have a house down there
> completely to themselves. We were always trying to find some new
> action, and the word got out that a store known as the Oxford Meat

Market was giving a picnic down at the inlet for all the servants in Palm Beach.

Well, we went to the picnic, but without Sandy Osborn. Here we are, nobody's ever seen us before in our lives. We were obviously looking for pretty girls. Although there weren't too many, Jack did find one, a very pretty little Irish girl. He asked her if she'd like to go out with him, and she said didn't go out unless her friend went with her. Jack said that was easily arranged.

Billings would never forget her friend.

Her name was Rachel, and she weighed in the area of 250 to 275 lbs. She was about our age, but she was the fattest young girl I've ever seen. Rachel had chosen as her costume of the evening a sailor suit—sailor's pants, blouse, and hat etc.

It was incredible, and all of us immediately understood exactly what we had to do. We said that we all wanted to go out together but that unfortunately Eben and I had dates for the night we were talking about, but we did have a friend who would love to take Rachel out.

The innocent friend was Sandy Osborn. "By this time Jack had known Sandy for a week, and I knew him quite well. Sandy was in my class at Princeton; his prep school was Groton, and he has all the qualities of a New York dilettante: the Groton accent and the whole works—his family owns a great house on the upper part of the Hudson; in fact when he graduated from Princeton later, he was voted the snootiest of our class."

Jack was beside himself in anticipation.

We picked April 1st for the date. Rachel was more than interested and we could hardly wait until we told Sandy about his date. Jack was overjoyed at the prospect and spent a great deal of time selling Sandy on Rachel, explaining none of our dates were too good, but we did have a blind date for him and any of us would rather take the blind date than the ones we had . . . and we damned near died when we listened to him talking to her on the phone.

She had a nice, throaty voice and a sense of humor, like many fat girls do. Sandy was very excited about the whole thing. He thought he had the best date. He was so concerned that somebody else would try to get her that he signed a pact that anybody who left their girl during the entire evening would have to pay for the next evening, when we were going to take out some other girls and go to an expensive night club.

Well, we went to pick up the girl at the corner of such-and-such a street, and Sandy was so eager and excited; and suddenly the lights hit her standing on the corner. It was one of the funniest experiences I've ever had in my life!

It was also one of the funniest Jack ever had, the memory of it binding him to Osborn—who stoically remained with Rachel the entire evening, honoring his pledge—for the rest of his life. "They [Osborn and Pyne] became very close friends with Jack," Billings recalled. "I must say, during his later career he had no more loyal supporters in the world than those two guys."

Meanwhile, seemingly restored to good health and following a new diet of rich cream and dairy products dictated by Dr. Sara Jordan of the Lahey Clinic in Boston, Jack returned to Harvard in April 1938. He had plans to attend the annual Princeton dance along with Bill Coleman, and wanted Eileen Herrick's address from Billings "right away," as well as Billings's judgment whether "she will jump the hoop." (She wouldn't, and declined Jack's invitation.)

In truth, however, Jack wasn't better, though he refused to give in. For his tutor at Winthrop House he'd been reading a host of books on Hitler and Mussolini—*Dictatorship in the Modern World, Germany Enters the Third Reich, Mussolini's Italy, State and Revolution, Folklore and Capitalism, We or They, Essentials of Democracy*—and his tutor was mildly impressed. "Kennedy was ill part of the year," he subsequently noted on Jack's tutorial record, "and did no very large quota of tutorial work. Though his mind is still undisciplined, and will probably never be very original, he has ability, I think, and gives promise of development."

The Crab King

No such promising report could be written about Ambassador Kennedy's performance in London, meanwhile. Hardly had he settled into Prince's Gate than German pilots bombed Barcelona and Hitler annexed Austria. A few days before the invasion Kennedy had boastfully written Arthur Krock to "put down" in print his prediction that "the settlement of world affairs will be forced to an economic settlement rather than a practical one." It was a prophecy that already looked lame as Hitler triumphantly drove into Vienna on March 14, to the rumble of tanks and mechanized German army troops.

Jack's father was now to all intents and purposes America's number-one man in Europe, yet the significance of Hitler's move was lost on the Boston-Irish draft avoider, who steadfastly refused to see European affairs as impinging in any way upon America. Apart from a few Scottish distillers, Kennedy had known no one of any eminence or insight on his arrival, had no knowledge of international relations, nor had read any European history. Yet, just as he had fantasized that he could transform Hollywood with his principles of double-entry bookkeeping, so in London Joseph P. Kennedy made up his mind that the problems of Europe would be solved by better cash flow.

Even the drama of Hitler's invasion did not dent this view. "The march of events in Austria made my first few days here more exciting than they might otherwise have been," he wrote complacently to Krock on March 21, sending an identical letter to financier Bernard Baruch, "but I am still unable to see that the Central European developments affect our country or my job." Kennedy even dismissed the response of his own regular embassy staff as

> the semi-hysterical attitude which the professional diplomats here adopt whenever another [un]foreseen step occurs. . . . I have been to no great pains thus far in reporting to the State Department the various bits of information and gossip which have come my way, because they don't mean anything as far as we are concerned. The more I talk with people in the City, with diplomats, and with British Cabinet members, the more convinced I am in my own mind that the economic situation in Europe, and that includes Great Britain, is the key to the whole situation. All of the playing house they are doing on the political fronts is not putting people back to work and is not getting at the root of the situation. An unemployed man with a hungry family is the same fellow, whether the swastika or some other flag floats above his head.

The ex-King of England and his consort, the ex-Mrs. Simpson, believed the same. The duke of Windsor, as he now was, had actually visited Hitler the previous October in Obersalzburg, and, as he later candidly admitted, was completely "taken in" by the führer. However, the duke, at least, was shocked by reports of the Nazi pogroms in Vienna and elsewhere in Austria (during which his friend Rothschild was imprisoned), whereas Kennedy was concerned only by his conviction that the latest American recession would spread to England that year. Hitler's antics, he persisted in believing, were of no relevance to Americans.

Rose Kennedy was similarly blinkered. Later, in her memoirs, she pointed to this period as the high point of her life, with presentations at the royal court, diamond tiaras, and great balls at which she could launch her daughters into the sort of high society which, in America, avoided or cold-shouldered her. Now, as wife of the American ambassador to Britain, she found herself invited to Buckingham Palace and Windsor Castle, to Ascot and the Derby, while her husband was made an honorary member of elite British social and sporting institutions from the Athenaeum to the Royal Thames Yacht Club: an extraordinary turnabout after being blackballed in America from Massachusetts to Florida.

To some extent the Kennedys' myopia resulted from their knowledge that their stay in London would be short. For all the glamour, Kennedy continued to see his posting as but a brief interlude before returning to the stock market. "My private life is gone," he lamented to Krock in a handwritten postscript, and claimed he was through with government service when he returned to the States. "Don't bother about any future for me," he warned Krock, whose "persistent urging me to come here and your holding my hand during the uncertain days will always remain in my mind and heart—I'm in business *right* after this," he promised. "For God's sake start something or send me my carfare home," he begged Bernard Baruch a few weeks later, bored by the political drama in Europe and his ambassadorial status, which made stock-market speculation awkward, though not impossible.

As in the movie business in the 1920s, however, boredom soon gave way to delusions of grandeur. Where once it had been a femme fatale who turned Joe Kennedy's head, this time it was a father figure: Neville Chamberlain, the British prime minister.

Whereas Roosevelt had evinced "a certain coolness" toward Chamberlain, Kennedy confessed to being instantly impressed by the British prime minister: "a strong character; one that could easily dominate a situation," he reported to the State Department, possessing a "realistic, practical mind." This realistic mind, Kennedy reported, "has assumed the responsibility of trying to straighten out the Italian and German situation. . . . He is convinced concrete concessions must be made to Germany and is prepared to make them to avert war. He really doesn't expect America to do anything. . . ."

To Arthur Krock at *The New York Times* Kennedy reported the same. Chamberlain was, despite his seventy years, going all out for "rapprochement with Germany," he was a no-nonsense "tough guy and going to run the Cabinet."

"Chamberlain's speech last Thursday was a masterpiece," Kennedy soon afterward enthused to Krock. "I sat spellbound in the diplomatic gallery and heard it all. It impressed me as a combination of high morals and politics such as I have never witnessed. . . . All this means, as I size it up, that there will be no war if Chamberlain stays in power with strong public backing."

Kennedy, awed by Chamberlain's performance in the House of Commons, was infuriated to think the American stock market was more skeptical in regard to the situation in Europe. "I wish our fellows at home would attend to the worries they have on their own doorsteps and keep Europe out of their minds until they made some headway in their own country." Even if war were to break out in Europe, Kennedy failed to see why "it would affect the United States very adversely if it did." His gut feeling, however, was that there would be no war. Given strong trade agreements, as with Italy, he could see no reason for hostilities, particularly if Chamberlain remained prime minister.

Kennedy's letter to Krock on April 14, 1938, in which he lauded the Anglo-Italian agreement as "the high point in Mr. Chamberlain's foreign policy thus far," reflected the new American ambassador's shortsightedness. "There is a general feeling here that Mussolini realizes now that he will be more comfortable with Great Britain as a friend than he would be in relying exclusively on Hitler," Kennedy considered, and like his son Joe Jr., he chose to see Hitler's anti-Semitism and Anglophobia merely as a spur to German business productivity: "The Germans probably feel that they have to preserve some apparently bitter external enemies in order to whip up their own people to the necessary sacrifices, and England is cast in this role just now."

Some writers and historians have sought to justify Joseph Kennedy's attitude of appeasement toward Germany while he was ambassador to Britain on the grounds that he was merely reflecting American isolationism. Certainly his wife chose to defend his ambassadorship in this way: "As ambassador he was supposed to represent the viewpoint of the United States Government and the American people, and he could do so in perfect conscience."

Rose, however, had no concept of what the U.S. government's views were, let alone those of the American people. Her thoughts were concentrated upon English social life. Caught up in the social whirl of London as "wife-hostess consort," Rose now had the first important public function to fulfill since her youthful days as consort to her father, Mayor John Fitzgerald. "Rose, this is a helluva long way from East Boston," her husband remarked when they were staying as guests of the king and queen at Windsor Castle. Though Rose had never really known East Boston, "the pomp and circumstance and romantic storybook traditions" of Old England mesmerized her.

To Winston Churchill, Chamberlain's chief political rival, Kennedy meanwhile formed an instinctive aversion. "My first luncheon with Winston Churchill and his son, Randolph, deserves mention," Kennedy later told the would-be ghostwriter of his autobiography. "Churchill was scornful of the gains that might accrue to England through the Anglo-

Italian agreement" and warned Kennedy that appeasement wouldn't work, a conviction that had strengthened after Churchill's meeting with the German foreign minister, von Ribbentrop, who'd demanded Germany's old colonies back and insisted "England must close its eyes to the procedure in the East [i.e., Hitler's interest in Czechoslovakia and his obsession with *Lebensraum*]."

Churchill's warning, however, was ignored by Kennedy, who along with Chamberlain remained convinced that European economic revival and the expansion of world trade were the keys to the future. Chamberlain was making "the political offers necessary," Kennedy informed Roosevelt, assuring him the "time is going to come . . . for you to make a world-wide gesture and base it completely on an economic stand."

Kennedy, however, was not Roosevelt's sole informant in London. Indeed it infuriated the ambassador to discover that Roosevelt was corresponding with Harold Laski, a fact that drove Kennedy to express himself "on this score in vigorous language to James Roosevelt, suggesting that he call his father's attention to the unwisdom of such a procedure."

"As I look back, it was symbolic of much that was to come," Kennedy later reflected, his irritation further compounded when the State Department began to censor his speeches in Britain. His traditional Pilgrims' Society speech, in draft, declared that "it must be realized, once and for all . . . that the great majority of Americans oppose any alliance, agreement or understanding for joint action with any foreign country, even though the arrangement might be temporary and designed only for the prevention of war. . . . The United States, as things now stand, has no plans to seek or offer assistance in the event that war—and I mean of course a war of major scope—should break out in the world."

Deleting these remarks, secretary of state Cordell Hull informed Kennedy that "the President himself" had been involved in the decision, yet still Kennedy clung to his thesis that economic improvements, not alliances, were the key to peaceful coexistence. "Economic appeasement, in addition to its external aspect, means a higher standard of living for the workers of the world," Kennedy declared to his own and Chamberlain's satisfaction.

Kennedy's private letters home would sound tragically blinkered half a century later. "Of course," Rose later defended her husband, "no one knew then that Hitler was criminally insane and had no intention of living by humane standards except his own demented ones, and that his promises meant nothing to him."

But did Joe *wish* to know? "I am happy to report," he wrote to Krock a week after the U.S. government had recognized Hitler's conquest of Austria, that "the enlistment for the duration of whatever it was [i.e., his term of ambassadorship] bids fair to pass off pleasantly (if not profitably, to judge by the latest quotations from Broad & Wall)." He was, according to British Foreign Office officials, speculating "on the side" through nominees, and was thus able to use privileged information, as ambassador, to make a number of easy killings.

Meanwhile at Harvard Jack was far from coasting along, as later biographers maintained. He hated to waste a day. Told by his doctors that he ought to take time off, he made plans to take just three days' rest at Hyannis Port, then sped on to New York. He ran for the student council in May and finished fifth and "as they only take 3 messed up," he complained to Billings. "Would have liked to have made it so I could have had the pleasure of telling Steele [the Choate disciplinarian who had said Jack would never make good] to shove it," but by early June he was "in the middle of finals," having had to postpone his twenty-first birthday party on doctor's orders. "I would like to come to Bernardsville but due to my health I may have to go to the hospital for a couple of weeks—anyways if I don't I will go to the Cape and rest as I won't be able to have the party. . . . I will know in a couple of days. Why don't you come down there if I don't go to the hospital, for a week or so, as just Joe and Ted [Reardon, Joe Jr.'s roommate] will be the only ones in the house." Meanwhile he was hatching a plan to attend the annual university rowing regatta: "May go to the boat races. If so, going on Cummings' 200 ft. yacht and he has invited you so get a gal and meet me there—otherwise the Cape."

Not even the new ice-cream machine his friends had installed for him at the Spee Club could help stave off his mysterious loss of weight, however, and by June 15 he was once more "holding court up here at the New England Baptist Hospital. Got by all my courses," he reported proudly, "and may get Dean's list" (necessitating B-plus grades, or higher, in at least four courses). The term had ended on the thirteenth, and despite the "grippe," "intestinal flu," and weight loss, his morale was high. He liked Winthrop House, liked his roommate, liked his friends, had won his minor *H* letter for football, had swum for Harvard against Penn, Columbia, Dartmouth, and Princeton, had enjoyed his major in government, and had gained a deeper understanding of European history as well as current European politics and international relations. He'd been accepted by one of the eight exclusive final clubs, as well as the Hasty Pudding, had narrowly missed being elected to the student council for his junior year, and even had hopes, in a final spurt in May and early June, of making the dean's list.

Compared with Princeton, this was a different world, and when Billings boasted that they were awarding honorary degrees to generals at Princeton's commencement, Jack was quick to retort that "this stuff about you having generals is just that usual Princeton crap of copying Harvard where they were originated and have been going on for years. The sooner you realize just what Princeton is, a good, indeed darn good, prep school—the happier we at Harvard will be."

With its proximity to Boston and the many nearby women's colleges such as Radcliffe and Wellesley, as well as to the Cape, Harvard was ideally suited to Jack's temperament and frenetic energy. He wasn't due to leave the New England Baptist Hospital until June 21, but from his sickbed he was continually making new plans, the latest of which was participation in the Intercollegiate Yacht Regatta, due to be held at Osterville, near Hyannis, in the final week of June. The Wianno Yacht Club on Cape Cod had offered its members' boats for the annual event, and the temptation for Jack, who'd been sailing his family's own Wianno one-design with his brother for several years, was too great to miss.

Jack failed to get on the dean's list. Though his government professor, Payson Wild, gave him a straight B for the year, his remaining grades were all Cs. Undaunted, "the Crab King"—as he signed his letter to Billings—left the hospital, hit New York for a few days, stayed with Peter Grace (who was in love with and hoped to marry Jack's sister Kathleen), and then made his way with Jimmy Rousmanière and Loring Reed, another friend from Winthrop House, to the yachting championships at Osterville.

Ten colleges with twenty crews comprising more than sixty yachtsmen competed in the "finest and most hotly-contested intercollegiate yacht series yet held," the Harvard yearbook subsequently recorded. "The championship was in doubt until the very end of the series," with Harvard, Williams, MIT, and Dartmouth jockeying for the lead. Fortunately Bud Hutton, one of Jack's three-man crew, had long experience of gaff-rigged boats. Half a century later Hutton could recall adjusting "the peak halyard by easing it off wind, thereby moving the draft in the sail to the middle for better effect. Meanwhile Jack kept to the leeward of the entire fleet and always picked up many boats. We rolled up the points and no one could figure out how we went to leeward so fast."

Each college raced two boats, in separate divisions. Jack's performance in the sixth race put Harvard in front, but the final two races were vital to clinch the series. Joe Jr. captained one of Harvard's boats, and Jack skippered the other. Both came second in their respective divisions in the seventh race. In the eighth and final series Joe Jr. came in third, but any hopes other colleges entertained of snatching victory were dashed when Jack took second place, giving Harvard an overall seven-and-a-half-point victory in the regatta over its nearest rival, Dartmouth. All in all, it was a thrilling finish to Jack's sophomore year.

"Will Kennedy Run for President?"

For Jack's father, by contrast, the summer of 1938 was a calamity. "When it was announced that I was returning to the United States to see my son be graduated from my almer mater," Kennedy explained to his ghost-writer, "it was a good guess that at the same time Harvard would confer an honorary degree on me. Indeed, had I not known the contrary, I would have jumped to that conclusion myself for I could have thought that my varied and long services for the Government might have been suitably recognized in this manner."

Others did not see his services as long or distinguished—particularly in view of his inability to get on with fellow administrators such as Morgenthau, Ickes, and Perkins. When the list of honorary degrees was announced, therefore, Ambassador Kennedy's name was conspicuously missing. In Joseph Kennedy's eyes, however, it was yet another example of Harvard's prejudice against Boston Irish-Catholics and a replay of his humiliation when he failed to be elected to the Board of Overseers in 1936, (when his ranking at the bottom of the list was leaked to the press). The failure, as U.S. Ambassador to Britain, to be awarded an honorary degree "was a terrible blow to him," Rose revealed later. "After all those expectations had been built up, it was hard to accept that he wasn't really even in the running . . . suddenly he felt as if he were once again standing in front of the Porcellian Club [one of the Harvard final clubs], knowing he'd never be admitted."

Watching his two eldest sons sail to victory in the McMillan Cup series ought, in Rose's eyes, to have been enough to assuage any bitterness. After all, the ambassadorship to London was a social elevation *sans pareil.* But what Rose didn't realize, or chose later not to remember, was that the honorary Harvard degree wasn't merely "an honor he wanted for the entire family," as she later claimed, but the failure to receive it dealt a distinct and painful blow to Joe's latest ambition.

Just as Rose had no idea of her husband's financial dealings, so too she ignored what she did not wish to see in her husband's political aspirations at the time. Watching the businesslike Neville Chamberlain, Joseph Kennedy's fertile mind had conceived new hopes of supplanting Roosevelt, perhaps even in the next presidential election.

To fulfill such aspirations, Kennedy needed to nourish such an idea in the American press, and he lost no time. He wrote to Krock from England on May 24, 1938, that he'd ordered his staff "to make reservations for you and Martha" [Martha Blair, whom Krock married in 1939] to travel with him to England on June 29, at Kennedy's expense. Krock certainly had no illusions about Kennedy's motive. "Did Joe Kennedy Sr. want to be President of the United States? Yes he did! Very definitely," Krock later revealed. "He hoped to be nominated in 1940, without any question. . . . He was a very ambitious man. He felt he had a great deal to give. He was shrewd. He thought his services had so impressed the country, and there was money behind it for a gigantic propaganda machine and it might work. All he wanted to do was to beat Roosevelt in 1940."

Krock was not the only journalist to be enlisted in Kennedy's protopolitical campaign. "Will Kennedy Run for President?" was the title of a *Liberty* magazine article on May 21, 1938, a lead that was soon trumpeted by other newspapers across America. "Both the Democratic politicians and the country at large may demand a man who can make business and progressive reform pull together toward sound prosperity," the *Liberty* article pronounced.

In retrospect it seems incredible that Kennedy, who'd never achieved election to any political office in his entire life and whose shrewdness in business rested upon corrupt stock-pool practices, insider information, and knowing what to sell short, could have considered himself a possible Democratic nominee for the American presidency. When he submitted his recent London University speech on American isolation to the *Atlantic Monthly* for possible publication in tandem with Harvard's commencement ceremonies, for instance, threatening to "sell it to a newspaper" if they didn't accept it immediately, the editor noted, "That's where it belongs. It says nothing any village commencement speaker couldn't say."

Yet Kennedy obstinately believed he had a chance of becoming president, as he confessed to James Landis.

> During the last few weeks in public and in private considerable discussions had been taking place concerning the possibility of my being the Democratic nominee for President in 1940. It broke publicly in late May in an article by Ernest K. Lindley in *Liberty*. The idea was picked up by a number of newspapers including the Boston *Post* and *Sunday Advertiser*, the New York *Daily News*, the Washington *Herald-Times* [sic], and a host of papers of smaller-circulation too numerous to mention.
>
> No one can lightly turn away a serious suggestion from his friends that he is worthy of succeeding to the presidency of the United States. There were many reasons that militated against my candidacy

for that office, including my Catholic faith, but even these might be overcome.

The biggest obstacle, of course, was the incumbent president, as Kennedy was fully aware. "Mr. Roosevelt had made no announcement as to his attitude on a third term. I knew that many of his closest advisors were urging him to break with tradition and run for the third time in 1940. There was little doubt he had the matter under consideration." As Kennedy also knew, Roosevelt was not a king who liked potential usurpers. "Mr. Roosevelt also had a quality—a failing, some have called it—of resenting the suggestion that he was to be succeeded and cooling perceptibly towards a man who might be considered, by his friends, a worthy successor. For many years Mr. Roosevelt had been my chief; he still was. I wanted no such false issue to arise between us."

In New York, Kennedy insisted, rumors were rife. "The inevitable question of my candidacy for the presidency was put. My reply to that was as unequivocal as I thought I could make it. 'I enlisted,' I said, 'under President Roosevelt in 1932 to do whatever he wanted me to do. There are many problems at home and abroad and I am happy to be busy at one abroad just now. If I had my eye on another job it would be a complete breach of faith with President Roosevelt."

Roosevelt was not amused; nor was he taken in. He did not see in Joseph Kennedy "a worthy successor." What he did see was a man after his job. Through various confidential, FBI, and intelligence channels Roosevelt had over the past months been able to see and read all Kennedy's private letters to Baruch, Krock, Herbert Bayard Swope, Walter Lippmann, and others, letters which were not only gross breaches of ambassadorial discretion but gave Roosevelt an intimate idea of Kennedy's appeasement views and calculating ambitions.

Certainly Roosevelt, who remained unsure whether to try for a third term as president, was sensitive to aspiring successors in his own woodwork. Having interviewed Kennedy at the White House on June 21, 1938, ostensibly to hear from the horse's mouth what was going on in England, Roosevelt thus leaked his displeasure at Kennedy's presidential "boomlet," which was published the next day in *The Philadelphia Inquirer* and the *Chicago Tribune*. According to one reporter, "a chilling shadow of 1940" had fallen across Roosevelt's relations with Kennedy because of "positive evidence that Kennedy hoped to use the Court of St. James [*sic*] as a stepping stone to the White House in 1940."

"I think it would be a very helpful thing if agitation could be started to have me address the Senate and Foreign Relations Committee in Executive Session," was one passage Kennedy had written to Krock in

May 1938. "I feel that I certainly have the most interesting story that has come out of here for many years and I think it is bound to affect their judgement. . . . If you think this is worthwhile, you might start it in the works." This letter, in particular, had come to the president's attention, and had been shown by the White House to selected journalists.

As Kennedy recalled with venom, the *Chicago Tribune* "spoke of my general letter to my friends as a 'political' letter, replete with inside information, designed to egg my friends into initiating a campaign in my interest, and charged me with wanting to take a press agent back with me to London in order to keep my name before the American public."

By the time Kennedy read the *Chicago Tribune* piece, the damage was done. Smarting from Harvard's denying him an honorary degree, he'd refused to attend his eldest son's commencement—the supposed reason for his return to America—and had instead locked himself away at Hyannis Port with Jack, declining to take calls from newspaper reporters. He was thus embarassingly unaware of the *Tribune* article and its ripples throughout the American press when he attended a "pleasant dinner" with Roosevelt at the White House on June 24. When he learned of it the next day, he was beside himself with rage. "It was a true Irish anger that swept me," he told Landis. "The President and Secretary Hull were away and I could reach no one until Monday."

For Kennedy, after the blow to his amour propre at Harvard, it was another example of the murky, cutthroat world of Washington politics. "That Monday morning I saw Mr. Hull and offered to resign. He sought to calm me down and I recall him telling me that I should not be so disturbed because, as he said, 'He (the President) does those things. He treats me twenty times as badly."

Hull, too, was a contender for the 1940 presidency, but Kennedy wasn't mollified, insisting on a meeting with the president's aide, Stephen Early, who'd leaked the story. Several years earlier, Kennedy had tried to bribe Early by offering a large sum of money to supplement his government salary; Early had wisely declined. They now had "an angry interview," following which Kennedy asked to speak with the president himself, "with whom it was not my habit to mince words." This "brought a denial that he [the president] had had anything to do with it. In his way he assuaged my feelings and I left again for London, but deep within me I knew that something had happened."

Indeed, something had. Far from being rested, fêted, honored, and poised for the Democratic nomination in 1940, Kennedy was now returning to London chastened and in bad odor with the White House, by whom he was perceived as a man capable only of acting in his own interest.

At the boat, the press again assailed him. "This time they faced me with an article just published in the *Saturday Evening Post*. . . . It alleged among other things that as the owner of Somerset Distilling Company I had used him [James Roosevelt] to acquire certain preferential permits for the importation of whiskey in the days prior to the repeal of prohibition and in turn had given him my insurance business. It also said that he personally had been responsible for my appointment to the Court of St. James."

It was clear to Ambassador Kennedy as he walked up the gangplank of the ocean liner that he who lived by the press sword could equally die by it.

Appeasement at Munich

Traveling with their father to London in 1938—and witnessing the hostile press conference before they left—were Joe Jr., who was to serve as secretary to the ambassador, and Jack, who, the ambassador had earlier decreed, should accompany him for the rest of the summer vacation. ("I am also expecting Joe and Jack to come back with me," Kennedy had written to Krock, and had boasted to Bernard Baruch that he would be "sorry you're not on the boat with me coming back. Beautiful women and everything.")

Jack was not averse to the trip. The year before, he had traveled to Europe almost incognito; now he was sailing as an ambassador's son. Arthur Krock later recalled:

> The ship was very gay . . . and there was a beautiful actress aboard whom young Joe was fairly smitten with and that annoyed his father because he thought that the boy might be perhaps a little too impulsive and maybe this girl was making a play for a boy of his prominence, his wealth and so on—an attraction, I must add. Jack, also, was staying up pretty late at night, and he had a girl that I think his father didn't know too much about. . . . At any rate, he imposed a curfew on these two young men, and told them that they would have to be in their quarters with him in his suite at midnight. Well, the next midnight they arrived on time, and, by arrangement with me, I let them out by the back door of the suite, and I don't know whether the old man found out about it or not. At any rate the curfew was not maintained.

Rose Kennedy, meanwhile, had been too busy to return with her husband to America and had remained throughout the early summer in

London, playing host to her parents as well as supervising the dizzying
social life of her debutante daughter, Kathleen. In the brief period Joseph
Kennedy was expected to remain in Britain as ambassador, Rose was
determined that Kathleen and, if possible, Rosemary should be presented
at court. In his first act as ambassador, Rose's husband had abolished the
tradition of choosing American debutantes to be presented at the British
royal court. "No act of mine has ever had such public acclaim," he later
boasted, tongue in cheek. Nevertheless, Kennedy had reserved the right
to present his own daughters, those of his immediate staff, and a few
"American debutantes whose families had established residence in England as representatives of American enterprise" (a decision that
prompted George Bernard Shaw's immortal remark at a luncheon at
Lady Astor's, when asked whether he approved. "Certainly not," Shaw
replied. "We don't want the Court to have only *selected* riff-raff.").

Even in her seventies Rose later waxed lyrical about the Molyneux and
Lelong gowns she'd bought them, as well as the diamond-spangled tiara
her new friend, Lady Bessborough, had loaned her. The Oscar Wilde
scenario, however, had a tragic twist, both for Rosemary, who would be
lobotomized only three years later, and for Kathleen, whose sudden
elevation as the eligible daughter of the American ambassador opened
aristocratic doors that Rose had never dreamed would be unlocked.
When Peter Grace, son of the Catholic shipping magnate, arrived in
London in July to "claim" his prospective fiancée, for instance, Kathleen
was not even at the embassy, let alone Southampton, to greet him; rather
she was at the Sussex races, playing a rich field of even richer English
beaus, all of them Protestant.

How Rose Kennedy could imagine that Kathleen, after exposure to
such an array of suitors in a Protestant country, would dutifully settle for
a Roman Catholic defies ordinary understanding. In the meantime,
though, Rose busied herself overseeing arrangements for the annual July
Fourth ball at the embassy.

Kathleen certainly looked forward to the arrival of her elder brothers,
if not of Peter Grace. Before her court appearance on June 2 she'd written
to Lem Billings, wishing he could be there. "I so often think of you when
I meet a guy who thinks he is absolutely the tops and is just a big ham,"
she remarked of the English upper classes. "What laughs you and Jack
would get. Very few of them can take any kidding at all."

Kathleen was not disappointed. On his arrival in England, Jack was
an instant "hit." Joe Jr., however, was not. According to Kathleen's
biographer, who interviewed many of Kathleen's friends, Joe Jr.'s "manner seemed abrasive and his humor uncomfortably sharp-edged. He
lacked the finesse that enabled Jack and Kick to adapt readily to British

ways. . . . Some aristocratic young women were shocked by what occasionally surfaced as sexual aggressiveness and a violent temper."

This was all of a piece with Joe Jr.'s behavior at Harvard, indeed one of the reasons no final club would have him. Worse still, he was soon heard parroting the ambassador's views—a loudmouthed American isolationism that was found to be less than polite in a young guest receiving widespread British hospitality.

By contrast Jack was often mistaken for Kathleen's "younger" brother, so boyish and emaciated did he seem. William Douglas-Home, who was passionately in love with Kathleen that summer, met Jack at the Prince's Gate residence. "I was a friend of his sister Kick, and I got to know him when he was here on his vacation from Harvard. We used to play golf together," he related, recalling in particular their first visit to the Royal Wimbledon Golf Club, where they were astonished by the generosity of the club's assistant professional, who "gave us a dozen deluxe golf balls each in a box." Returning from their game later, the two young men saw "an ambulance waiting outside the club house to take the man away."

As Kathleen had predicted, Douglas-Home was instantly won over by Jack's ability to see the funny side of life—and the way the funny side of life seemed to reciprocate. "He was age 21, very young, and very interested in everything. I mean, not only politics, but the thing that struck you about him was that he was so vital about everything."

Joe Jr. seemed the more serious of the ambassador's sons, however, as Hugh Fraser later recorded. "Joe looked much more mature than Jack. I think Jack looked incredibly young for his age at 21. I think he was intellectual in a bright quick way, while Joe was much more serious and had . . . gravitas about him. He was the eldest boy in the family, and I think this weighed quite a lot with the Kennedys, who were sort of hierarchical." This was a view with which Douglas-Home concurred. "Joe was probably more serious than he was. Jack would never have a deep political discussion without jokes at the same time. He had a very highly developed sense of humor."

Forged in infancy and honed during his almost continual health problems, Jack's humor was his shield and his sword. He was determined to find fun and action wherever he went. Surprised at first by the way his somewhat plain-looking sister Kathleen had at eighteen become the belle of England, he admitted to her after a few disappointing dates with English girls that "she had no competition." According to her biographer, "One date of Jack's broke an evening-long silence only once—to describe the brook at the bottom of her father's garden."

"Kick's male friends marveled at Jack's easy conquests," Kathleen's

biographer described. "After he'd only been in London a few weeks, a
hush fell over the Ritz one lunchtime when Jack Kennedy arrived. On his
arm was a staggeringly beautiful woman, dressed in a gray two-piece
dress, a hat perched jauntily on one side of her head. Jack introduced her
around as Honeychild Wilder, the Cotton Queen of Louisiana, who had
just arrived in England to promote the cotton industry."

As Jack wooed his ladies, the European caldron was meanwhile coming to a boil. On May 28 Hitler had ordered his generals to fortify the
German "rear"—the Siegfried Line—while assembling some ninety-six
divisions for an invasion of Czechoslovakia to take place on October 1—*Fall Grün,* designed in Hitler's own words "to wipe Czechoslovakia off the map."

Joseph Kennedy's certainty that the recession would force the European nations to concentrate on common economic interests had already
begun to wobble. As Hitler put pressure on Czechoslovakia, Kennedy
now counseled military realism. In May he'd met Charles Lindbergh, the
legendary U.S. aviator, who was subsequently decorated by Hitler. Lindbergh had told Kennedy that the Nazi Luftwaffe was already so superior
to that of any foreign power that it was useless to attempt to stop
Germany by force, a message that Kennedy, who preferred figures to
arguments, was quick to circulate. Far from maintaining a diplomatic
distance from events, indeed, Kennedy now plunged into the controversy
over Czechoslovakia, supporting Chamberlain's isolationist stance and
helping defeat Churchill's call for a grand alliance. In fact, von Dirksen,
the German ambassador to Britain, began to report to the Reichskanzlei
that Joseph Kennedy was probably Germany's best friend in London.
Churchill, conversely, began to see in the American ambassador Britain's
greatest enemy.

Jack, meanwhile, maintained a twenty-one-year-old's neutral stance,
brushing off the ambassador's claims that he was an "idiot" when they
argued (according to Krock), and ribbing his father with his familiar
humor. With Parliament in recess, Rose had booked a villa for the family
at Eden Roc, near Cannes in the South of France, for two months—an
extraordinary act of hope given the gathering crisis over Czechoslovakia.
Kennedy joined her with his older boys "early in August" and, to the
chagrin of the English king and queen, was soon invited to dine with the
duke and duchess of Windsor.

Enjoying the "blue Mediterranean and the sun-drenched sands, the
casualness of people in a holiday mood, luncheons, teas, dinners and
golf," Kennedy recalled, he and his family sat out the growing Czech
crisis. But by the end of August the State Department in Washington lost
patience, and even Kennedy recognized that "the holidays were clearly

over." Taking Jack with him, he flew back to his post on the evening of August 29, 1938, giving Jack a ringside seat as Chamberlain and his Cabinet dithered and procrastinated. (Chamberlain, also, had been on holiday, and was heard to say to his colleagues at the end of one exhausting meeting, "This really isn't as much fun as shooting grouse.")

The presence of his entire family at Eden Roc had clearly had an emotional effect upon Kennedy. In the draft of a major speech he was scheduled to give in Scotland on August 31, the ambassador planned to ask his audience whether they knew of "any dispute or controversy existing in the world which is worth the life of your son, or of anyone else's son? Perhaps I am not well informed of the terrifically vital force underlying all the unrest in the world," he hoped to say, "but for the life of me I cannot see anything involved which could be remotely considered worth shedding blood for."

This draft statement, by the foremost U.S. representative in Europe at a time when Hitler was testing the resolve of the democracies, was, to say the least, unfortunate, and was immediately ordered to be expunged by the State Department which, to Kennedy's extreme annoyance, also informed Roosevelt.

Meanwhile Jack, having witnessed the excitement over his father's censored remarks, boarded the S.S. *Bremen* at Southampton and arrived back in New York on September 8, where he was met by not only Billings but a crowd of reporters anxious to know his father's assessment of the European situation. Saying there was no question of war or evacuation of American citizens, Jack tried to downplay the crisis, pointing out to the press that the rest of his family, including Joe Jr. and Kathleen, would be staying in Europe for the next year.

The Czechoslovakian crisis, however, was only warming up. Hitler had not mobilized ninety-six divisions and drawn up detailed invasion plans merely for amusement. He meant now to seize the Sudetenland by force or by force majeure. Chamberlain flew to Germany to plead for a peaceful solution, but it was only to get the British and the French off their guarantors' hook, as Hitler knew. So did Kennedy, having urgently invited Lindbergh and his wife from France to a special luncheon at the U.S. embassy in London to introduce them to a selection of English bigwigs and have Lindbergh give them the gist of his latest report on German air strength. "I was so impressed by his observations that I asked him immediately to dictate a brief summary of them. He did so and I put it on the wires," Kennedy later disclosed, "suggesting that it might be of interest not only to the State Department but also to the President and the War and Navy Departments. . . . Lindbergh during the next few days at my suggestion had a series of conferences with the top officials of the

British Air Force." Kennedy even made sure a copy went to Chamberlain, as the weary septuagenarian flew off for his second conference with Hitler at Bad Godesberg.

According to Lindbergh, German air strength now exceeded that of all other European powers combined; it could inflict sixty thousand casualties in a single day if it chose to attack British cities. War was not, therefore, in Lindbergh's view, an option: Britain and France must cede to Hitler's demands over Czechoslovakia for no better reason than that they too would be conquered by Hitler if they didn't: "Germany has such a preponderance of war planes that she can bomb any city in Europe with comparatively little resistance. England and France are far too weak in the air to protect themselves."

Kennedy's role in the political appeasement of the dictators was now reaching its odious climax. To King George VI, the American ambassador pointed to his daily trips to the Foreign Office and 10 Downing Street as signals to the Germans of U.S. moral support for Britain. But the truth was the very opposite: that Kennedy was applying daily pressure on Chamberlain, Foreign Secretary Halifax, and former Foreign Secretary Hoare to back off from war or even confrontation. While he circulated Lindbergh's prophecies of military doom, he ignored the latest British intelligence he was receiving about opposition to Hitler's threats from Hitler's own generals. Sir Robert Vansittart, permanent undersecretary at the Foreign Office, informed Kennedy that, according to impeccable sources at the most senior level in the German army, "the Reichswehr were opposed to action that could lead to war. They were fearful that Germany could not successfully wage a general war and they were convinced that the ensuing peace treaty would have as its sole design the permanent destruction of Germany as a potential disturber of the peace." Kennedy passed this prophetic report on to the State Department, but negated its impact by adding, "The situation in Nazi Germany was said by the British to have gone beyond their control." Meanwhile, when asked "what I thought the American reaction to a European war would be," Kennedy kept stressing to Chamberlain and Halifax that he had "not the slightest idea, except that we want to keep out of war," and begged Roosevelt to send a message advocating diplomacy rather than hostility.

Kennedy's faith in appeasement bolstered Chamberlain but not the more restive members of the British Cabinet. Chamberlain's no-nonsense approach had achieved nothing but shame. By forcing the recalcitrant Anthony Eden to resign from the Cabinet, Chamberlain had merely alienated Roosevelt. By pursuing his own British-Italian treaty and concessions to Hitler at the expense of Roosevelt's offer to chair an international conference, Chamberlain had then frittered away the chance of American involvement. Austria had been annexed by Germany earlier that year; Czechoslovakia was now on the brink of dismemberment.

By September 26, 1938, as the world waited to hear what Hitler would say at the *Sportpalast* in Berlin, Joseph Kennedy penned a quick note to Krock, who'd also returned to the States. "I have a few minutes before Hitler speaks. . . . I'm feeling very blue myself today because I am starting to think about sending Rose and the children back to America and stay here alone, for how long God only knows. Maybe never see them again," he wrote nervously, as the scale of the crisis dawned on him.

Rose was in Paris, shopping for dresses. "What a great man Chamberlain was," Rose recalled her husband saying at the time. After a subsequent parliamentary debate on the Czech sellout, Chamberlain actually thanked Kennedy directly. "He was kind enough to add that he had depended more on me than on anybody for judgment and support," Kennedy noted, boasting to Walter Winchell several months later that "Lindbergh's awesome respect for what Hitler could do from the air" had, thanks to him, been a decisive factor in the British prime minister's decision not to call Hitler's bluff.

As he had once contributed to the downfall of the New York stock market in the Great Crash of 1929, so now Kennedy was contributing to the downfall of the democracies in Europe. "We seem to be very near the bleak choice between War and Shame," Churchill had predicted to Lord Moyne on September 15. "My feeling is that we shall choose Shame, and then have War thrown in a little later." The first lord of the British admiralty, Duff Cooper, felt there was a third choice: "war with dishonour," when the leaders of the nation would be forced by public opinion to repent of their abandonment of the Czechs, and to face up, finally, to the fact that Hitler was not a man of peace.

Kennedy, however, refused to believe this, discounting Churchill in terms of his public support, even in terms of his parliamentary rhetoric, which he claimed in one letter to Krock was inferior to that of the most ordinary congressman. Listening to Chamberlain read out Hitler's consent to a four-power conference in Munich (which excluded Czechoslovakia), Kennedy was overwhelmed, and against all protocol in the House of Commons led from the Visitor's Gallery a burst of cheering for the prime minister, to the consternation of the speaker. "As we left the House of Commons," Kennedy later described, the tone of the crowds had improved. "They were cheering and laughing and waving at every passerby, crowding about the cars and even running beside them in their exuberance. I was happy, too. It was a smiling, grinning individual, I was told, who stepped into the Embassy that afternoon and said, 'Well, boys, the war is off.' "

That night, in his cable to the State Department, Kennedy was exultant. "A feeling is spreading all over London that this means that war will be averted. If it is, it is quite likely that, with these four men around a table and with President Roosevelt always willing to negotiate, it may be the beginning of a new world policy which may mean peace and prosperity once again."

Kennedy's role in appeasement and isolationism would ultimately shatter his career in government and in politics. It would also prove, together with his shady reputation in the stock market, a millstone for his children. For the moment, though, he felt himself to be on the "winning" side, despite growing concern in America when, at Munich, Britain and France agreed to the annexation of the Sudetenland under threat of war. Duff Cooper resigned in protest, deploring Chamberlain's openness to "the language of the mailed fist. What do those words [of the Munich Pact] mean? . . . Do they mean that he [Hitler] will get away with this, as he has got away with everything else, without fighting, by well-timed bluff, bluster and blackmail? . . . I have ruined, perhaps, my political career. But that is a little matter . . . I can still walk about the world with my head erect." Kennedy described Duff Cooper's resignation statement as "a most ordinary defense." Chamberlain admitted to the American ambassador he was "bitter about Duff-Cooper but was glad of the opportunity that the First Lord of the Admiralty had given him of accepting his resignation . . . [and] again shook hands with me and insisted that I must stay on the job because he believed I could do much for world peace."

Public euphoria over the Munich settlement soon gave way to criticism, however, and as a coconspirator Kennedy was not spared. "Within a few days after its announcement people in all quarters of the world, particularly in the United States, were to turn against it," Kennedy himself recalled. "Nor did I remain immune from a type of attack as slanderous as it was vicious. . . . Even my personal courage was put in issue. In some quarters of the American press, stories were widely circulated to the effect that during the crisis I was the most 'jittery' person in London, predicting that bombs would fall on the city before the end of that fateful day. I was accused of making strenuous attempts to whisk my children away to the safety of Ireland. Both accusations were false," he later claimed, forgetting the funk he'd been in when he wrote to Krock and others.

"I know what a wonderful job you have been doing," Arthur Krock meanwhile obsequiously wrote back on October 6, after the Munich settlement, "and I am highly indignant over the barrage of misrepresentation to which you have been subjected. That some of my [newspaper] friends are active in it disturbs me very much, and I have protested to two of them, as well as charging Alsop with getting a very inaccurate line of information."

But was it inaccurate? Kennedy rewarded Krock for his loyal words by offering to lend him his house in Palm Beach over Christmas. But even this nurturing of the Washington correspondent's goodwill could not protect Kennedy from public outrage once he gave his notorious Trafalgar Day speech to the Navy League.

Pretty Fucking Particular

For his junior year at Harvard, meanwhile, Jack had moved from the rooms he'd shared in Winthrop House with Torby Macdonald into larger quarters, this time a four-man suite with Macdonald and two other top football players, Ben Smith and Charlie Houghton, who was the same age as Joe Jr.

Houghton, in particular, was dismayed by Jack's untidiness. "Jack never hung up anything, he just dropped it. We had a colored guy named George Taylor who took care of all our stuff. He'd come in and pick up the clothes and press them. It was just a habit with Jack. He strewed things all over the suite."

"One time he was changing his clothes to go out," Torby Macdonald recalled, "heaving his things into a heap in the middle of the floor. I told him to watch the way he was throwing things around our room because it was getting to look like a rummage sale. 'Don't get sanctimonious,' Jack warned. 'Whose stuff do you think I'm throwing mine *on top of*?' "

Houghton was impressed by a razor sharpness behind Jack's careless manner. "Jack was a very stimulating person to live with. Very argumentative in a nice way. He questioned everything. I think the depth of his intellectual curiosity was shown in that he'd challenge anything you said. He had the best sense of humor of all the Kennedys."

Donald Thurber, who was also studying government, felt the same:

> He was a person who would ask questions of you, who would challenge your assumptions, not unpleasantly, but he'd say, "Why do you feel that way? What makes you think so?" And then he'd continue a line of questioning as long as it interested him—and then, having sucked the orange dry, he would go on to another piece of fruit. You got the impression that here was a mind that was learning from other people, and that longed to learn from other people—he would regard them as sources of information and knowledge to fill out his own. The questioning was never ruthless; he never just

shucked you off when he was through questioning you, but he wanted to know what you knew. . . .

I knew plenty of playboys. I could spot a playboy on the other side of the room. Jack didn't fit into that mold at all—he was someone who played hard when he played, but his motivation was a serious one—you got the idea that he'd already decided life was a pretty serious proposition, even though it wouldn't have to be, with lots of money and so on. But it was going to be a serious proposition.

A line from A. E. Housman strays across my mind: "The thoughts of others were light and fleeting, of lovers meeting or luck or fame; mine brought trouble, and I was readying when trouble came."

It wasn't exactly trouble that Jack Kennedy was looking for, but he was certainly readying himself. He was decidedly not a superficial person.

Certainly Jack intended to work a lot harder this year. As soon as the news of his father's appointment as ambassador to London had been announced the previous January, Jack had applied for permission to spend half his forthcoming junior year in England, a request which had been provisionally granted by the dean of the college, Chester Hanford, on the understanding that Jack take six courses for credit, instead of four, between October 1938 and January 1939, before being permitted to depart for London.

Jack's teachers and fellow students later expressed surprise at the change that came over him. According to Torbert Macdonald, Jack was not "in his early, first two years what then was called a grind, somebody who just worked for work's sake and tried to get great grades. . . . I don't think he really got interested in the intellectual side of academic life until perhaps his Junior year when war seemed to bring a lot of us, especially Jack, a realization that it wasn't all fun and games, and that life was about to get very real and earnest."

This was said, of course, in hindsight. It might equally be said that Jack, after the social swath he'd carved in England that summer, now felt that the best fun and games were to be had in London and was determined not to miss that chance by failing his courses. Whatever the truth, he threw himself into his studies with surprising zeal. As one of five hundred students he had been "down in the crowd below" when Professor Holcombe gave his introductory lectures on government the previous year. Holcombe had been "unaware of his presence in that course" and indeed made no effort to "meet the men unless they got into trouble. . . . They merely heard me, and looked at me. Most of them learned my name. I have met students in that course who didn't know what my name was, or who got it wrong; one man even called me Prof. Hokum, which naturally didn't make a very good impression on me."

Holcombe's views of the mass of 1930s Harvard undergraduates was not laudatory. "Of course Kennedy was a young man who had come to Harvard as well-heeled young men do, believing it to be an interesting introduction to life, more interested in life than in learning."

Jack's enrollment in Holcombe's third-year course was thus a puzzle to the Harvard pedant. "The next year he took a more advanced course that I used to give for Juniors and Seniors in the national government of the United States. How he got interested I cannot tell you. Whether something I said in lectures interested him, or whether it was something in the conduct of the discussion groups by my assistants—I had a dozen or more of them. . . . Perhaps there was talk at home, where there was a great deal of interest in politics and public affairs."

Holcombe, old, stuffy, and conceited, had

> taught his father a good many years before. I taught his older brother. I taught later on his two younger brothers, and the family were of course all interested in politics. But when Jack Kennedy was in college, politics wasn't a primary interest of his. His older brother, Joe Jr. was to be the politician of the family, and with reasonable amount of good fortune he would have been a great success in politics. Joe Jr. seemed to have everything that a politician needs. He had firmness of purpose, a happy manner with people; he had everything for success in politics. Evidently, at that time the family thought there could only be one real politician at a time, or in a generation, and Jack, I think, was more interested in history, from an academic point of view.
>
> He lived with a group of active young fellows, but of course, I didn't know them in their social relations. I only knew them in their class work, and in connection with their functioning as students.

There, Holcombe acknowledged, Jack was no wallflower. "He stood out among the group that he lived with. They all got by. But he of course did much more than get by." It was a "crowd that regarded a college education as much more than studying things. They were interested in life. But Jack was more interested in ideas than most men who have the means of doing whatever they wish to do when they're in college. He had a genuine interest in ideas, there's no question about that."

If Jack had no personal interest in entering politics, Holcombe related, he certainly had a surprising interest in studying the responsibilities, pressures, and performance of a typical politician.

I might tell you about the course in which I became well acquainted with him. . . . This upper class course of mine, Government 7, as it used to be in the old days, was a course in which I tried to teach the study of government as if it were a science, the way a natural science would be taught. . . .

I conducted the course by assigning to each student a congressman, preferably his own congressman, but in the case of those sections of the country where there were a good many students from the same district . . . I would assign them congressmen from other parts of the country. In the case of Jack Kennedy, since he came from Boston and there were a good many Boston boys in the class, and he being a Democrat, I figured that he'd learn more if he studied a Republican from some other part of the country. I assigned him an upstate New York congressman—he came from Potsdam, as a matter of fact—who was an influential representative of the electric power interests of upper New York. His name was Snell, Bertram Snell. He had no national reputation, but he was outstanding among upstate Republicans in New York and an influential member of the Republican leadership in the House in Washington.

The method of conducting the course was to assign a particular question each week. First week, how did your congressman vote? Well, that you can find out from the Congressional Record. It takes a little digging, but the facts are there. Second week, what did he have to say? Third week, what did he do in his committee, and so on: a series of specific questions that would carry through the term. The object was, in the first place, to get a line on the congressman's purpose in politics. Did he create the impression of trying to serve the public interest? Or some local or private interest? This particular congressman was interesting from that point of view.

Then came the problem of the congressman's method of work. Did he have much or little to say? Did he apparently try to accomplish his purposes in his committee work or otherwise, out of sight? Finally, there was the problem of the congressman's performance. Did he seem to accomplish his purposes? Did he get some private bills through? Did he influence the action of the House on important public measures? Was he an influential member?

The students would report their findings, and discuss their significance, so that there were three stages in the development of the main theme of the course, just as there are in a scientific experiment in a laboratory. First, the nature of the experiment: in this case, what can the citizen learn about his representative; secondly, the evidence, what do you find to be the facts; third, the inferences that you draw from what you see.

In a chemical laboratory you watch something happen in a test tube, that's really not difficult in many cases; but in studying the science of government, it's not so simple. The student gathers the evidence, and each draws his own conclusions about his particular congressman. If you have a fair sample of the whole Congress, you're going to get a group of findings which should throw a great deal of light on the nature of Congress, regarded as a political institution.

Holcombe's methodology appealed to Jack. "I used to tell my students that when they are discussing public affairs with others, the latter tend to offer their personal opinions." This, in Holcombe's view, was something a good student must guard against. "You don't simply contradict the man who holds a different opinion from yours. You ask him what's the basis of his opinion, what are the facts upon which his conclusions rest, what is the method by which he reached his conclusion? That's the effective way of dealing with a man who differs from you in some matter of opinion."

In Jack Kennedy, Holcombe found a surprisingly willing pupil. "In his academic work he was inclined to be by nature dispassionate and objective," Holcombe remembered. "He liked that method of study of politics, and was very much interested in that."

Holcombe's recollection would be important. Fusty, pompous, long-winded, and not given to praise, he was the first man at Harvard to recognize Jack Kennedy's keen intellectual interest in the political process, though it never occurred to Holcombe any more than it did to Jack that the student would be interested one day in becoming a congressman. "What he thought he might be, I'm not certain. Sometimes he gave the impression that he'd like to teach history in a college. Sometimes he gave the impression he'd like to run a newspaper; which it would have been, I don't know."

Another professor of government was the dean of the college himself. Like Holcombe, Chester Hanford also recognized Jack Kennedy's growing maturity of intellect, as well as the fact that his interest lay in national rather than local politics. "It was not until the fall of 1938 that I became acquainted with him personally," Dean Hanford later recalled. "At that time he enrolled in Government 9a, a course in American state government, conducted by me in Sever 23." It was a somewhat impersonal course which "at that time emphasized such subjects as state constitutional development, the position of the governor, the legislature, the state judiciary, problems of administrative organization, federal-state relations, plus a little about state politics." Hanford remembered Jack as "a rather thin, somewhat reserved but pleasant young man with an open counte-

nance which often wore an inquisitive look. He was regular in attendance
and took an active part in classroom discussion in which he made pertinent remarks. However, and much to my surprise, the grandson of
'Honey Fitz' showed little absorption in state politics, which were given
some attention in the course. John Kennedy was more interested in the
changing position of the American state, in federal-state relations and
state constitutional development."

Jack's eyes were on Washington and its relationship with the fifty
states. State and city politics he could not take too seriously, much as he
loved his grandfather. "Resistless defender of Boston's lot, / Alert in
giving the helpless care, / Loveable Chief, the first to bear, / Deserving
title, 'Boston's Greatest Mayor' " he and his brother Joe had written in
a poem to celebrate Honey Fitz's seventy-fifth birthday in February, but
Jack was amused rather than attracted by city-level operations. "Tonight
is a big night in Boston politics," he wrote to his parents in November,
"as the Honorable John F. Fitzgerald is making a speech in favor of his
good friend the Honorable James Michael [Curley]. Politics make strange
bedfellows. . . . Had my first exam this morning and I did allright with
three more coming up in the next two weeks."

If Jack impressed his professors by a greater interest in his academic
work, this did not mean he'd lost interest in women or socializing. His
first letters to Billings upon his return from England had been devoted to
the subject of parties and Harvard's superiority over Princeton at football. He scribbled in October,

> Dear Billings: Yours of the 19th received and horseshit noted. Nu-
> merous Harvard varsity men have been quoted as saying, "Four
> tough games in a row—Thank God we're playing Princeton." How-
> ever due to the records we shall bet $1.00 evenly. Will do what I can
> about lining up a bed—but it seems to me that you'r[e] pretty fucking
> particular. Speaking of fucking what do you think about going to the
> Cape that night. I have a date. . . . Anyways, try and get a girl but
> let me know what you're going to do so I can try and get her into
> Jenney's party—Also anyone else you're coming with. Try and get
> Horton up here as well as Penis Pyne & Osborne—Best, Ken

There followed a postscript exhorting Billings to "get a girl for Nov. 19
for the Harvard-Yale game as we're going to have a party in Bronxville."

Behind the relentless planning, Jack health still gave cause for concern.
A few days later Jack was confiding that he'd just written to decline Peggy
Sheldon's invitation because of a supposed cram on Saturday morning.
"The real reason," he explained to Billings, "is that I've been in rotten

shape since I've got back and seem to be back-sliding a bit so am not going out at all and think that it would finish me to go down to this. It makes me sort of sore as it sounds pretty good."

"Rotten shape" was no exaggeration. Jack's doctors insisted he go into the hospital for tests, but he refused. "Harvard may be lousy but the smart money says they will kick the shit out of Princeton, without any trouble," he boasted to Billings. It was a prediction that was duly fulfilled, as he proudly informed his parents. "Things have been going pretty well. Feeling much better," he lied. "Was in at Grandma's birthday last night—she looked better than I've ever seen her—she was out at the game Saturday for the Princeton-Harvard game which we won 26–7." Torby Macdonald "got three touchdowns and ran all over the field" while his other roommate, Ben Smith, had shamed the coach (who'd kept Joe Jr. on the bench throughout the Harvard-Yale game the previous year and thus deprived him of his letter) in a way that Jack knew would warm his father's vengeful heart. "Our good friend Dick Harlow only put [Ben Smith] against Dartmouth for 5 minutes and he scored a touchdown, which pleased us all, as it made Gentleman Dick look a little sick."

Determined to get to England, however, Jack glossed over not only the state of his health but the torrent of criticism that had cascaded upon his father in the American press following his Trafalgar Day speech. "It was the thought that if we wanted a world at peace we should seek for some *modus vivendi* between us and the dictator nations," Kennedy himself admitted, "that aroused the fury of a goodly portion of the American press. This simple thought was regarded as being at variance with the ideas expressed by President Roosevelt in his famous 'quarantine' speech. It was immediately seized upon as heralding a shift in American foreign policy. When the press broached this idea the State Department literally turned pale with fright. Through Mr. Hull and its public relations officer, it hastily repudiated its earlier approval of the speech."

Joseph Kennedy himself blamed "a number of Jewish publishers and writers. . . . The tactics of this group may some day be analyzed. Some of them in their zeal did not hesitate to resort to slander and falsehood to achieve their aims. I was naturally not the sole butt of their attack but I received my share of it," he complained, unable to see why his call for an accommodation with the Nazis, coming at the time it did, as well as its provenance, were bound to be construed as American, not Kennedy, policy.

From many quarters there were calls for Kennedy's diplomatic neck. The six months Roosevelt had intended to give Kennedy in London were long since up. Yet to bring Kennedy back to an America where his speeches could not be censored or repudiated seemed to Roosevelt a worse alternative than keeping him in London. Roosevelt thus contented himself by giving a radio speech implicitly condemning his ambassador's remarks, which Kennedy bitterly described as "a stab in the back."

Joe Jr., working for his father once again in London after a stint with Ambassador Bullitt in Paris, considered his father a realist, as did Rose. When Lady Asquith, widow of the First World War prime minister, stated that "the Munich business divided England into two camps as had the Dreyfus case," the American ambassador's wife put herself firmly in the Munichois camp. "For us there seemed to be no alternative," she wrote to a friend at the time. "Joe felt that another war would bring the end of civilization with chaos—economic ruin and Bolshevism—and the Czechs themselves no better off."

Joe Jr. felt the same way. "Germany is still busting, they are really a marvelous people," he wrote to an old school friend in America, "and its gonna be an awful tough job to keep them from getting what they want. Dad, as you know, got quite a lot of unfavorable comment in the U.S. press for his speech in trying to get along with the dictatorship. Makes me sore that all the rest of the people are trying to get everyone against the dictatorships," he commented. "If we are not ready to fight them, we might as well get along with them."

Many of Joseph Kennedy's erstwhile supporters, however, whom he had assiduously courted or bribed over the years, began to turn against him—especially Jewish Americans alarmed by the virulence of German anti-Semitism. Felix Frankfurter, the Supreme Court judge, complained bitterly to Roosevelt. "I wonder if Joe Kennedy understands the implications of public talk by an American ambassador. Such public approval of dictatorships, in part even, plays into their hands." Even Walter Lippmann turned against Kennedy in his syndicated column, while *The Washington Post* deplored the way America's official representative in London was dragging U.S. diplomacy into an appeasement stance. "For him to propose," the *New York Post* protested, "that the United States make a friend of the man who boasts that he is out to destroy democracy, religion and all of the other principles which free Americans hold dear . . . passes understanding."

Jack, seeing his father under attack, meanwhile loyally sought to draw attention away from the spate of criticism in America by recounting to his parents the play *Leave It to Me,* which had recently opened in New York and which featured references to the Kennedys. The protagonist, he explained, "has five daughters and is the wife of the Ambassador to Russia and says that if she had four more she would have had London." Nor was this all. "She is also making plans and figures that at the rate of one [a] year she won't give *that* for the Kennedys in 1943. In another part they give Victor Moore a big celebration at Red Square with Stalin, etc., and in the middle she says, 'I bet the Kennedy's [*sic*] are boiling.' It's pretty funny and jokes about us get by far the biggest laughs whatever that signifies."

What it signified was that the existence of a teeming Kennedy family drew some of the sting from the "Kennedy incident," as the Trafalgar Day appeasement speech became known. "The Navy Day speech," Jack wrote, "while it seemed to be unpopular with the Jews, etc. was considered to be very good by everyone who wasn't bitterly anti-Fascist, although it is true that everyone is deadly set against collective security," he added, unsure of the ramifications of a Western alliance against Hitler.

Without collective security, however, how could smaller European nations ever stand up to the armies of the dictators? This was the question posed by Jack's new tutor, assistant professor Bruce Hopper.

Whereas Jack's previous tutor, A. S. Daspit, had been modest and uninspiring, Professor Bruce Hopper was a showman. He believed in scholarly reading but his showmanship was, in a sense, a protest against the detached, clinical approach of his Harvard colleagues. He believed democracy was defined not only by principles but by the courage of people willing to stand up for them.

The American ambassador to Britain had declared in Aberdeen that no dispute in international relations was worth the lives of his children. Hopper profoundly disagreed. "Bruce Hopper was a fighting man," Jimmy Rousmanière recalled. "One of the great traditions when we were at college was Armistice Day, November 11, and Bruce Hopper would give a lecture. . . . On Armistice Day his room was crowded and Bruce Hopper would put on an old trenchcoat—he'd been in World War I—and would come in wearing this old trenchcoat, whether it was hot or cold, it was just a characterization. And he gave a eulogy on World War I. It was the same every year, it was almost a sermon. Certainly you knew where he stood on that—he was pro-military in every way. He pulled out every stop."

Hopper's influence on Jack, over the ensuing two years, was to be incalculable—a crucial counterweight to that of Jack's father, America's most prominent appeaser.

In the meantime, however, while Jack slaved to earn good grades and obtain leave of absence to go to London, his mind was only half occupied by his studies, for into his restless social life there has stepped a new and tantalizingly unattainable star: Frances Ann Cannon.

A Proposal of Marriage

Frances Ann was the first girl Jack had been smitten by since his relationship with Olive Cawley sputtered and coughed and finally came to an end. His roommate Charlie Houghton later recalled the impact that Frances Ann made on the juniors of Winthrop House. "Frances Ann Cannon was a very, very attractive and brilliant girl. . . . I don't know who found Ann first, whether I did or Jack did. I was in hot pursuit, I'll tell you. We both went out with her." According to one of Jack's other roommates, it was Houghton who "actually met her first. Then Jack met her and moved in. He seemed to like her. Frances Ann was quite a talented girl and she was athletic too. She played tennis and skied."

It was not Miss Cannon's tennis or skiing that drew Jack, however. One of her best friends, Connie Burwell, later considered her "one of the most beautiful people you've ever seen. And highly intelligent. . . . She must have been just about the same age as Jack. Frances Ann had always been interested all her life in writing and in political things . . . yes, Jack was really sold on her."

Jack had first mentioned Frances Ann to Billings in October 1938, when explaining his so-called "real reasons" for declining Peggy Sheldon's party invitation: namely, the state of his health. However, there was another reason: Miss Cannon. "My absence alone will probably ruin the party for her—if I'm any judge of women," Jack remarked of Peggy Sheldon, begging Billings to make sure he went in his lieu. "Have been down the Cape weekend and am going down Sat. night to try to drive up with [Francis] McAdoo [a mutual friend]. Frances Ann Cannon is here and is plenty good. She may come down this weekend."

Henceforth Frances Ann's name sprinkled every letter to Billings. He not only took her to the Harvard-Princeton football game in October and the Harvard-Yale game at New Haven in November, but he invited all his old pals to meet her.

Jack's sister Eunice later denied that there was anything serious behind the romance. "He used to take out Frances Ann Cannon," she acknowledged. "He brought her to the house several times in Bronxville. She was attractive. I liked her. I don't think he ever thought about marrying her. . . . I think at his age he wasn't interested in getting married. I don't think any of us were. We were all having a wonderful time. And my parents never encouraged us," she added. "My father was perfectly happy with us all around."

The latter was perfectly true, as Lem Billings observed. As a result "none of the Kennedy girls got married until they were thirty (with the exception of Kick who, of course, married in England). Boys often visited the girls at weekends—but they seldom came back twice. . . . I always felt sorry for them. . . . I couldn't imagine how I would have handled myself over a weekend as a guest of one of the Kennedy girls. Nobody was interested in the girls' dates," Billings recalled, a fact which was made abundantly clear by Mr. and Mrs. Kennedy to male suitors. "The whole thing must have been a very harrowing experience," Billings surmised.

Awed by her father and aware of so much parental discouragement—"I don't *ever* remember them saying, 'Don't you think he'd make a good husband?' "—it was simply impossible for Eunice to credit that Jack might be interested in matrimony. But Billings knew better. Exchanging confidences was "a common bond" between them. "He had never been secretive with me. We grew up as boys together and we shared secrets. . . . He always told me things and he never held anything back from me. Why were we close? Maybe it was because he could really tell me everything. Things that were certainly not for the family," he confided to one interviewer. "I knew more about his personal life than his family did."

Rip Horton was certainly bowled over by Cannon. "I can remember going out with Jack and Frances Ann in New York. She was a tremendously attractive girl," Horton recalled. "I thought she was the most attractive girl he ever went out with. Good-looking, good mind, good wit, provocative. A great girl. I can remember Jane and I double-dating with them. I can remember thinking, 'My God, why doesn't Jack marry this girl?'"

The truth was, Jack did wish to marry her, though to Charlie Houghton's disgust he dispensed with the usual conventions of courtship. "I really don't think he was a ladies' man," Houghton considered. "I don't think he'd spend any time to romance a girl. I think he was very shallow in his relationship with women. It wasn't a big part of his life. I don't think he cared. . . . I swear I don't think he ever made love to a girl, told her how wonderful she was, how sweet she was. I just don't think he ever did that. . . . I don't think he was sentimental. I don't think he was ever dependent on the companionship of a girl. He always felt they were a useful thing to have when you wanted them, but when you didn't want them, put them back."

Billings agreed, reflecting that Jack wanted women not as friends but only as evening companions—to screw, show off, then discard. But Frances Ann Cannon was different, as even Houghton subsequently acknowledged: "Later, I found out that Jack was more serious about Ann than I thought he was. She had a hell of a good mind."

Frances Ann was certainly "no bag," as Jack made clear to Billings. She'd already graduated from Sarah Lawrence in Bronxville, been presented at the British court in 1937, and had then taken a course in business administration at the Webber Business College in Boston. Above all, her parents were fabulously wealthy, belonging to the Cannon Mills family of North Carolina. She was, however, a Protestant, and this presented a problem.

Undaunted, Jack dated Frances Ann as often as he could. Far from distracting him from his studies, the romance actually seemed to spur him to higher achievement since, to be taken seriously as a suitor, he would have to prove to her parents that he was not just a Boston-Irish-Catholic boy on the make but a young man with a bright future.

In this respect, Jack's fortune was an attraction, but his father's reputation a liability. With war looming in Europe and his father's views becoming more and more controversial, old social prejudices were bound to surface, and they did. Franklin Roosevelt hadn't rested content with his "stab-in-the-back" radio repudiation of Kennedy's Trafalgar Day remarks. While the rest of the Kennedy family went skiing in Switzerland, Mr. Kennedy was recalled to Washington and "roasted" by the president. By then even Kennedy had recognized—as he admitted to reporters in New York—that in the wake of Munich "nothing has been accomplished in the way of appeasement," even though it was still "economic chaos" that he feared more than war. "My arrival in New York in December of 1938 had little of the gala aspects that characterized my homecoming six months earlier," Kennedy recalled. "I made it plain that Munich had as yet failed to bring the results that people had hoped it would bring."

Roosevelt, who talked for two hours with Kennedy at the White House, wanted to discuss "the plight of the Jews in the wake of the Nazi's *Kristallnacht.*" Even Kennedy later admitted "there was a trace of impatience in the President over Chamberlain's policy of watchfully waiting to see what Hitler would do. He thought that some rattling of the sabre would be more effective than continuing assurances of fair and reasonable dealing, and he said that he planned to do a little sabre-rattling himself."

The term having finished at Harvard, meanwhile, Jack came down to Washington and completed his study of Congressman Snell, while his father traveled down to Palm Beach. "He got so much interested that when the Christmas vacation came, he went down to Washington, met some of his father's friends, and got a clear picture of his congressman at work," Professor Holcombe recalled. "He did a very superior job of investigating, and his final report on his congressman was a masterpiece. Jack was genuinely interested in this phase of the political process. . . .

When he got interested in anything, he just threw himself into it with all the same energy and zeal that he threw into making the swimming team, or any other competitive activity. And at the end he had an opinion not only about an obscure Republican, but also about Congress as an institution which was much better grounded than the opinions that most people have about public institutions."

Joining his father in Palm Beach afterward, Jack found a cabal of journalists there. The ambassador, aware that Roosevelt was dissatisfied with his performance in London, had invited the columnists Walter Winchell, Boake Carter, and Arthur Krock to discuss the outlook with him—a move that prompted Henry Ehrlich, the Washington correspondent of the *Boston Herald,* to print another story stating that Kennedy was considering a future presidential campaign and that the Kennedy house in Florida had become "a virtual publicity bureau" for his nomination.

Roosevelt was furious at this second "Presidential boomlet" in six months to be sprung by the press on Kennedy's behalf. Although Kennedy had booked passage back to England with Jack on February 24, Roosevelt now insisted the ambassador leave immediately, feeling that Kennedy would be less dangerous abroad than plotting in Palm Beach. Kennedy thus sailed on board the *Queen Mary* on February 9.

Jack, meanwhile, returned to Harvard to complete his midyear exams. "It was John Kennedy's ability to answer his examination questions with clarity and style, combined with his skill in organizing his subject matter," that "particularly impressed" his professor of government, Dean Hanford, "especially with the long essays on the optional reading, since they were well organized and gave evidence of independent thinking, although I must admit the handwriting was at times difficult to decipher. He received a B in the course [Government 9A]," Hanford recalled, an honor grade which Jack also attained in each of his other five courses in history, government, and English composition—"no mean accomplishment for a student carrying 6 subjects," Hanford emphasized. "Jack's record during this term not only demonstrated his innate intellectual capacity, but gave promise of his understanding of challenging situations in his future career and his determination to meet them." As a result, Hanford had no hesitation in recommending to the administrative board that Jack's application for a half-year's leave of absence be granted.

By then, however, Jack was in the Mayo Clinic in Rochester to face another battery of medical tests. "I'll be godamned glad to get out of here as they are giving me a lot more shit than I'm used to," he wrote plaintively to Billings. "Shit is about all I'm getting in fact as they have put me on a diet of rice and potatoes 3 meals a day," he explained. "The nurses

are pretty good and was doing pretty well till they shoved that tube up
my arse, turned me upside down and they seemed to lose interest—after
they had gotten a squint down my big brown growler."

Nevertheless, the premature departure of his father was to be a godsend for Jack, since once he was discharged from the Mayo, he would be
master of not only Hyannis Port and Bronxville but also Palm Beach.
While his father set sail from New York, Jack thus flew down to Florida
to set up residence in the family villa. By Valentine's Day he was writing
to Billings that he'd "had Cannon down this weekend and had a damn
good time. Congrats on getting Dean's List—Also got it myself so that
ought to show 'em. Arriving up in N.Y. Wednesday night [22 February]
around 11 and sailing Friday noon. If you can get up let me know—try and
get a date as I will. Also ask Rip to try and get up sometime," he ordered.

Frances Ann Cannon was getting under Jack's skin, however. She'd
told him she was going to New Orleans for the Mardi Gras. With a small
suitcase Jack now set off in pursuit. Jack's Princeton friend, Robert
Walmsley, met him at the airport with Frances Ann. "She asked me if I
would take her out to the airport to meet Jack, which I did. Not many
people flew in those days," Walmsley later recalled. "I was the only guy
he knew around here. He didn't bring tails, which are obligatory down
here. I loaned him a pair of my brother's, who was five feet four and a
half inches tall and weighed one ninety." Jack, six inches taller but forty
pounds lighter, "cut quite a figure in those," Walmsley remembered with
amusement. "I don't remember one other thing about the visit, except the
general impression that Jack . . . was certainly chasing Frances Ann
hard."

"He was the first man who was in love with me. He proposed marriage
to me," Frances Ann told her friend Connie Burwell. "I had long talks
with Frances Ann about Jack," another friend, Jane Suydam, later related. "She said it was a great romance, but her father didn't want her to
marry a Catholic."

Such bigotry was somewhat of a blow to Jack, and to his friends. "I
don't think the fact she was a Protestant would have made much difference," Jack's Catholic friend Rip Horton reflected sadly. "Jack was a
deeply Christian person."

Since Jack was in any case scheduled to go to Europe for six months,
it was decided to postpone a decision. "I think Mama Cannon was trying
to bust up the Kennedy romance, as I recall," Connie Burwell related,
remembering how Mrs. Cannon "then took [Frances Ann] on a great
cruise around the world on the *Kungsholm.* She was gone four or five
months."

Jack, hiding his disappointment, flew back to New York, fetched a
trunkful of clothes and books from Bronxville, and on February 24, 1939,

boarded the liner that would take him to England. While Mrs. Cannon chaperoned her daughter around the world, he was determined to "show 'em" in London.

Duke John of Bronxville

The Atlantic crossing, Jack wrote the following week to Billings, was "plenty rough." Joe Jr., having written patronizingly to a friend that "Jack comes over in February, to begin his education," had meanwhile set off for Spain as an unofficial embassy observer, and Jack took over his duties as companion-secretary to his father. "Been having a great time. . . . Been working every day and going to dinners etc. with Dad," he related to Billings. "Met the king this morning at a Court Levee. It takes place in the morning and you wear tails. The king stands and you go up and bow. Met Queen Mary and was at tea with Princess Elizabeth with whom I made a great deal of time," he boasted. "Thursday night am going to Court in my new silk knee breeches, which are cut to my crotch tightly and in which I look mighty attractive."

Chinwagging with British kings, queens, and princesses was, however, the prelude to an even greater honor for a Roman Catholic. Pope Pius XI, whom Jack and Billings had seen on his litter in 1937, had died in February 1939, and had been succeeded by Cardinal Pacelli. Despite critical U.S. government negotiations to provide asylum for the Jews currently being persecuted in Germany, Austria, and the Sudentenland, Kennedy badgered the State Department until the president authorized him by telephone to leave his post in order to attend the new pope's coronation in Rome on March 12, 1939. In giving his imprimatur, however, Roosevelt added a bombshell: "After 1940 I am going to look at the performance instead of acting in the play." The race for the 1940 Democratic nomination was on.

"Friday I leave for Rome as J.P. has been appointed to represent Roosevelt at the Pope's coronation," Jack explained to Billings. "So far, it's been damn good and feel quite important as I go to work in my new cutaway. If you come over this summer, am contemplating driving to Greece and Constantinople so you can explain art to me. However we can see on that. Thanks for coming down to N.Y. Was sick from it all the way over on the boat," he mocked.

Mrs. Kennedy had meanwhile left her family again and was in Egypt, alone, when she received the news about the pope. From Cairo she flew directly to Rome. Her husband, accompanied by Jack, flew from Croydon to Paris for meetings with French ministers, while the rest of the children except for Joe Jr., still in Madrid, embarked by train with a governess and Eddie Moore. In Paris they chartered a whole wagon-lit on the Rome express, and in Rome they were greeted by the American ambassador and the becassocked boys of the North American College.

Ten Kennedys instead of one posed quite a problem, however, and a hilarious pantomime followed. Mussolini's son-in-law, Count Ciano, the foreign minister of Italy, entered the Basilica "immediately ahead of me," Joseph Kennedy later recalled. "As he marched through the church, he bowed and smiled to right and left, giving the Fascist salute. I put him down then and there as a 'swell-headed Muggo,'" Kennedy said, but omitted mention of the sequel, for when Ciano found his seat in the gallery of the official Missions occupied by ten Kennedys, he threatened "to leave the Basilica and desert the ceremony," as Cardinal Montini later recalled. Although the matter was resolved, Cardinal O'Connell of Boston (who'd married Joe and Rose in 1914) was heard to remark, "Oh, will Joe ever learn?"

Joseph Kennedy's recollections were strangely revealing. He himself wept floods of tears at the sumptuousness of this uniquely Catholic pageant and was outraged by Ciano's secular concerns. At a party given by the American ambassador to Rome, Kennedy was told that numerous "young attractive Italian girls had been invited to entertain Ciano, for otherwise he just would not come." Kennedy found "it was impossible to engage Count Ciano in any connected conversation. 'Most of his time,' I reported, 'he spent rushing girls into the corner for conversation and he could not talk seriously for five minutes for fear that the two or three girls, who are invited in order to get him to come, might get out of sight. Indeed, my judgment of Ciano was far from laudatory. As a result of my observations of Ciano,' I concluded my report, 'and the gossip that Mussolini now has a German sweetheart, I came away believing that we would accomplish much more by sending a dozen beautiful chorus girls to Rome than a fleet of airplanes and a flock of diplomats. If in spite of his tendencies Ciano becomes a great Secretary of State, then I have lost all judgment of men."

In the light of his own and his sons' "tendencies," this was an interesting cable. Meanwhile, Kennedy's years of assiduous courting of Roman Catholic dignitaries in America now paid off. Cardinal Pacelli had visited the Kennedys in their home in Bronxville. As the new pope, he not only invited them to a private audience ("The children were somewhat breathless," Joseph Kennedy later described, "for they arrived a little late and their arms were filled with countless packages of rosaries and holy things to be blessed by the Holy Father"), but he even offered Kennedy— according to Jack—the title of papal duke: an honor which, like the

Knight of the German Eagle awarded by the Nazis to Charles Lindbergh, would have made Roosevelt blanch, had he known.

Jack, however, took everything with a pinch of salt. "Just got back from Rome where we had a great time. Pacelli is now riding high, so it's good you bowed and grovelled like you did when you met him," he poked fun at Billings. "Teddy received his first communion from him, the first time that a Pope has ever done this in the last couple of hundred years. He gave Dad + I communion with Eunice at the same time at a private mass and all in all it was very impressive." He also informed Billings that "Galazzi [*sic*] was assigned to accompany Dad who represented U.S. at Coronation and asked for you + what's more remembered your name. They want to give Dad the title of Duke which will be hereditary and go to all of his family which will make me Duke John of Bronxville and perhaps if you suck around sufficiently I might knight you. However," Jack noted, "he's not going to accept it."

It was just as well, for Joseph Kennedy's appeasement policy, already controversial in America, looked decidedly passé as Hitler's forces moved to invade the rump of Czechoslovakia. "Despite the increased tension that was apparent in the European scene, I decided to stay in Rome for two more days," Kennedy later explained. "My son, Teddy, was to receive his First Communion from the Pope and I did not want to miss that occasion." Rose, however, had already departed for an appointment with her dressmaker in Paris. By the evening of March 15, 1939, Hitler was in Prague, and Kennedy was finally ordered to return to his proper post.

Rumor had it that at Christmas Roosevelt had again offered Kennedy the position of secretary of commerce but that Kennedy had declined, claiming his relationship with Chamberlain was too important to world peace. If so, Roosevelt was not impressed by Chamberlain's efforts in this direction. To Ambassador Bullitt, referring to the prime minister's speech in the House of Commons in which he refuted any British guarantee of Czechoslovakia's borders, Roosevelt had said on the telephone, "I have the evening papers in front of me with their headlines, 'Chamberlain washes his hands.' You know the last well-known man about whom that was said?"

As Chamberlain's stock began to sink, so did Kennedy's. Belatedly, the ambassador now began to see war as imminent. "Everyone thinks war inevitable before the year is out. I personally don't, though Dad does," Jack wrote to Billings in a postscript to his letter of March 23, 1939.

Dad was right, but Jack was enjoying life in London too much to care. "Having a great time. . . . Haven't done much work," he admitted, "but have been sporting around in my morning coat, my 'Anthony Eden' black Homburg and white gardenia smelling slightly like George Steele." He abjured Billings not to "say anything about" his father's papal title:

"*Be sure,* because I realize that this would be a great opening for that sense of humor." Meanwhile, he prepared to do a stint at the U.S. embassy in Paris. "Went to Paris with Dad + had lunch with La Belle Offlet [Carmel Offie]. Bullitt invited me to stay with him + the Offer but think I shall graciously decline," Jack wrote, not wanting to be tied socially as well as officially. "Going to the Grand National Friday and then flying to Paris Saturday with Dad + going to stay there for one month—then go to Poland, Russia, etc., then back to England." He still dreamed of summering in the Mediterranean with Billings. "That plan of sailing thru the Mediterranean along the Grecian coast over to Constantinople they say is the balls and if I could interest MacAdoo and if you came over would do it."

Billings, however, had no money. On graduation from Princeton he was intending to work for Coca-Cola, prompting a rushed but amusing letter from Jack at the U.S. embassy in Paris on April 6, 1939:

> Dear Kirk:
> Smacking this out on that old typewriter so it won't be making too much sense. Received your letter with that attractive clipping of us all [in Rome] and am pleased to relate that was a sash which was given to me by the Pope for being such a hell of a guy. Working hard these days and take it from the horses mouth that if you can possibly get out of working this summer I would—provided of course that it doesn't interfere with your getting a job as boy once you start you really have to stay with it. My idea of a poor way of spending the summer is scintillating with those roadside-stand boys who are selling that old Coke.

Since his last missive, Jack had received "an especially sickening letter from Choate wanting me to recommend a boy 'who will carry on the traditions of the present sixth.' " (This was an appeal from George St. John, which began with the unfortunate lines: "After Christmas or Thanksgiving dinner my Mother often said to us, 'I wish everybody had so good a dinner.' After a Fall or Winter Term, I often say to myself, 'I wish every boy had so good a school.' ") "So far," Jack commented, "I have not been able to think of a big enough prick but am giving it a lot of thought. Goin skiing for a week in Switzerland which should be damn good fun."

Fun was still Jack's leimotiv, and in his increasingly English way, this meant hard work, hard play, and hard socializing. "Was at lunch today with the Lindberghs and they are the most attractive couple I've ever seen," he remarked, oblivious to Lindbergh's pro-Fascist sympathies. Lindbergh himself, still convinced that Hitler wanted peace with France and Britain (on behalf of the Nazis he was helping negotiate a high-sounding but completely phony deal to sell German airplane engines to France), was not impressed by Jack Kennedy or anyone else at the gathering, writing in his diary that he had taken his wife Anne "to lunch at the American Embassy at 1:00. Probably forty people there, including some of society's greatest bores."

Jack, however, was charmed by Mrs. Lindbergh. "She takes a rotten picture and is really as pretty as hell and terribly nice," he reported. "Am living up at the Embassy and living like a king. Offie and I are now the greatest of pals and he really is a pretty good guy, though I suppose that it will make you a bit ill to hear it. Will only be in London a couple of days over the 4th [July] as Dad is giving a party for the King and Queen, which I am going to go back for and then I think I will leave for Poland, if things stay as they are now."

> Have not decided definitely what I'm going to do this summer but that Greece sounds good to me though naturally you had better not do anything that would interfere with your Coke job. Big Bull Bullitt is his usual genial self and has been as a matter of fact very nice to me. . . . The Pope didn't actually mention you by name but he gave me the impression he was thinking of you.
>
> Offie has just rung for me so I guess I have to get the old paper ready and go in and wipe his arse.

Living Like a King

Hitler had said to Chamberlain at Godesberg, "Remember, I have won more with words than with bayonets." "That may mean something one can hang on to, even if it is a straw," Chamberlain had confided to Ambassador Kennedy after Munich when excusing himself for not inviting Churchill, Duff Cooper, or Eden back into the Cabinet, afraid lest Hitler construe this as appeasing the warmongers in Britain. Now, too late, Chamberlain finally declared that Britain would guarantee Poland's frontiers against foreign invasion and began exploring the possibility of a military alliance to ring Germany. Even Chamberlain had lost real hope, however. In a meeting with Kennedy he had "opened a map to illustrate his policy of hemming in Germany. As I left," Kennedy recalled, "he folded it together and wryly commented, 'If this continues much longer, I will need a new map.'"

Chamberlain was not mistaken. On March 22 Hitler annexed the Lithuanian port of Memel and on April 5 gave orders for the conscription of all German youngsters from ten to eighteen. On April 8, 1939, Italy invaded Albania, and the British Mediterranean fleet sailed to prevent a possible invasion of Greece and Turkey. Jack's pet plan for a leisurely sailing holiday to Constantinople dissolved. He nevertheless decided to go ahead with his planned trip to Val D'Isère in France. From there he sent Billings a postcard saying simply, "Plenty of action here, both on and off the skis."

War in Europe was now approaching. Unwilling or afraid to sack Kennedy, President Roosevelt now bypassed him whenever possible. The ambassador was no longer permitted to make any speeches other than "talking about flowers, birds and trees," as he indignantly complained. "Criticism of me had begun to grow in the United States," he later admitted. "I knew, however, that the implications of Prague and Albania had struck deep into American thought and that the recoil from these actions would be an increased sympathy on the part of the American public for the cause of England and France. But I did not want war."

Gagged by Hull, Kennedy "grasped at every straw in the wind." He was like a "weather prophet," the historian William Kaufman wrote in his study of interwar American diplomats. "In the last dreary months before the war Kennedy's reports had something of a frantic inconsistency that one associates with accounts of mysterious natural phenomena."

By contrast, Ambassador Bullitt recognized belatedly that peace with honor, after Munich, "would depend, not on the kind of mediatory gestures that he had advocated before Munich, but on the organization of a strong front against Germany." Bullitt had previously been U.S. ambassador in Moscow, where he had formed a bitter dislike of Stalin and communism. A bon vivant, he loved France and things French, and once he saw that Hitler menaced France as much as or more than he threatened Russia, Bullitt bit the proverbial bullet; indeed Joseph Kennedy, who disliked Bullitt intensely, would one day accuse him of being directly responsible for the Second World War.

Jack, by contrast, enjoyed Bullitt's humor and company. "Bullitt has turned out to be a hell of a good guy," he confided to Billings. "Live like a king up there as Offie + I are the only ones there + about 30 lackies." Bullitt had "about 10 barrels of Munich beer in the cellar + is always trying, *unsuccessfully,* to pour Champagne down my gullett [*sic*]." Meanwhile Jack felt sorry for his father, whose resignation was being called for in the United States by Robert LaFollette, an ardent antiappeaser. "LaFollette is mad because he didn't have a dinner thrown for him [in London]," Jack commented. "The same day Goebbels attacked Dad for being a war monger against Germany so it made the LaFollette thing look a bit sick."

"Things have been humming since I got back from skiing," Jack reported to Billings. He didn't mean politically. He'd met in Paris "a girl who used to live with the Duke of Kent and who is as she says 'a member of the British Royal family by injections.' She has terrific diamond bracelets that he gave her and a big ruby that the Maharaja of Nepal gave her. I don't know what she thinks she is going to get out of me," he mused coyly, though clearly he hoped it would be further injections, if less royal. "Meanwhile very interesting as am seeing life."

This was an understatement. "On the serious side just listened to Hitler's speech which they consider bad, though it's too early to tell," he reported from the Rue d'Anjou, referring to Hitler's latest speech to the Reichstag in which he had demanded the "return" of the free city of Danzig (currently under Polish administration) to Germany. Anticipating such pressure, the Soviet foreign minister (or commisar) had proposed a six-nation peace front, comprising Britain, France, Russia, Poland, Rumania, and Turkey, that would create a defensive cordon around the Nazi Reich. In Parliament Churchill had begged Chamberlain to accept Russian overtures for such a military alliance, but Chamberlain was immutably opposed to an agreement with Russia and had scorned the idea of blocs in Europe.

"Things were looking better this last two weeks with the formation of the 'Peace Front,'" Jack reported to Billings; but now, with Chamberlain's rejection of the alliance and Hitler's new warnings over Danzig, the pot itself was beginning to melt. Jack wrote:

> The situation is so damn complicated that it is impossible to estimate the difficulties over there. For example: in trying to get Russia in the peace front, they have to be able to have her bring troops to help in case Germany attacks Poland or Rumania. However, Poland + Rumania have a defense alliance against Russia which they fear almost as much as Germany, as Russia has claims on both their territories and they feel that once Russian troops got in they couldn't get them out. The situation is even worse because due to the Siegfried line ⅓ of the German army can hold the whole French army—meanwhile Germany can march its other ⅔ into Rumania or Danzig. And what the hell can the English fleet do about it. So until they can iron out problems like these—they can't get started. However, the encouraging thing is that if Hitler was going to go, the time would have been a month ago, before Poland + England signed up. That he didn't shows a reluctance on his part, so I still think that it will

be O.K. The whole thing is damn interesting and if this letter wasn't
going on a German boat [the *Bremen*] and if they weren't opening
mail could tell you some interesting stuff.

That didn't stop him, however, from describing in a postscript the ciga-
rette case of the duke of Kent's mistress, "engraved with Snow White
lying down with spread legs, and the seven dwarfs' cocks in hands waiting
to screw her. Very charming."

While the Gestapo mail openers aboard the *Bremen* no doubt struggled
to decipher Jack Kennedy's handwriting, Jack himself departed for Danzig and the East. "Am now in Warsaw," he wrote to Billings in May 1939,

> where I've been the last week staying with Ambassador Biddle. It's
> been damn interesting and was up in Danzig for a couple of days.
> Danzig is completely nazified, much heiling of Hitler, etc. Talked
> with the Nazi heads and all the consuls up there. The situation there
> is very complicated but roughly here it is:
>   1st. The question of Danzig and the corridor are inseparable. They
> [Germans] feel that both must be returned. If this is done then
> Poland is cut off completely from the sea.
>   If they [the Poles] return just Danzig . . . they [the Germans] could
> thus control Polish trade, as by means of guns they could so domi-
> nate Gdynia (see map) that they could scare all the Jew merchants
> into shooting their trade thru Danzig. However, aside from the
> dollar + chits angle—which is only secondary—there is the question
> of principle. The Germans don't give a good god damn what hap-
> pens to Poland's trade—and they told me frankly that the best thing
> for Poland would be to come into a customs union with Germany.

The parallel with Napoleon was extraordinary.

> Poland is determined not to give up Danzig and you can take it as
> official that Poland will not give up Danzig and 2nd that she will not
> give Germany extra-territoriality rights in the corridor for the high-
> ways. She will offer compromises but never give it up. What Ger-
> many will do if she decides to go to war—will be to try to put Poland
> in the position of being aggressor—and then go to work. Poland has
> an army of 4,000,000 who are damn good—but poorly equipped. The
> roads are bad however and can be destroyed which will nullify
> Germany's mechanical advantage and it takes 1½ to twice as many
> men to attack as to defend but remember France can't help, due to
> the Siegfried line in the west and England's fleet will be of little

assistance, so Poland will be alone. But they are tough here and whether they get help or not they will fight over Danzig—as they regard it first as symbolic + 2nd as the keystone.

"The whole thing has many angles—but if Hitler can get out without losing face I should think he would," the twenty-two-year-old surmised (unaware that Hitler had long since been planning *Fall Weiss,* the battle for Poland) "as he has gotten so much now that he could sell his disarming at a good price. If however, Ribbentrop and the radicals win out, he will probably make a putsch in about 6 weeks by means of Danzig and it will be interesting to see how it works out."

An ink-blotched, hand-drawn map illustrated Jack's description. "The German fleet can blow up Gdynia while the Polish guns from Hell [the peninsula north of Danzig] will blow up Danzig. Troops will come in from Germany + East Prussia and cut Poland off from the sea. This is very rough," Jack apologized, "and its impossible to set down the whole thing on paper but you can get an idea of what it is. Would suggest your reading Buelle's 'Poland—Key to Europe.' Remember, however, the Poles are not Czechs + *they will fight.*"

Even at the brink of European catastrophe Jack's propensity for enjoying himself was not diminished. "Aside from the political side have been having a damn good time," he confided to Billings. "Mrs. Biddle gave a debut party for me last night and while the Polish gals are not so hot, it was pretty good fun. This is really damn interesting here. The people bow + scrape and the servants wear white wigs etc. All of the young people here own estates of around 100,000 acres with 10,000 or so peasants. If you get over here this summer we could go down to visit the Biddles who have rented one with around 12,000 on it who tip their hats with one hand + push forward their daughter with the other." To this rosy prospect he added, "Leave tomorrow for Russia. This last bit is very confidential but I have a divorced Roumanian Princess with whom—however on second thoughts will save this tid-bit till I see you."

The Coming of War

A skein of *liaisons dangereuses* wound through Jack Kennedy's helter-skelter grand tour of Europe on the eve of the debacle, his descriptions of royal mistresses, divorcées, landowners, princesses, and debutantes possessing an almost pre–French Revolution flavor, as he was well aware:

"Leningrad then Moscow, Kiev, Bucharest then I'm going to try + get to Turkey—then Vienna—Prague—Berlin + got to be home [London] by 22nd of June for Eunice's debut."

Despite his loyalty to his father, Jack had seen at first hand that the economic rationale of international relations had no relevance vis-à-vis Poland and Danzig. At Cliveden (Lord Astor's weekend house), Ambassador Kennedy had tearfully and proudly read out to a gathering of politicians, appeasers, and socialites his eldest son's letters from war-torn Spain. He offered to put his press secretary's children through college if he could edit and get Joe Jr.'s correspondence published, even pressing his ghostwriter, James Landis, to include long and asinine quotations from them in his never-to-be-published memoirs. But as Europe inched toward Hitler's *totalen Krieg,* there was no public appetite for Joe Jr.'s schoolboy reports from Spain, any more than there would later be a market for Ambassador Kennedy's self-serving whitewash of his performance as Chamberlain's confidant.

In the meantime, Jack sent his own reports from Russia, Rumania, Turkey, and the Middle East, letters which the American ambassador did not consider worth reading aloud in front of the Cliveden Set, yet which were, in spite of Jack's age and health, probably the best source of on-the-spot reporting which Kennedy received at the U.S. embassy in London, according to Professor James MacGregor Burns, who was shown the letters while compiling a campaign biography of Jack in 1959. (Sadly, most of the letters were later stolen or lost.)

Jack's letter from Jerusalem, as the British Parliament debated the future partition of Palestine in the early summer of 1939, did, however, survive in Jack's personal scrapbook. It is a remarkable document, which illustrates his growing maturity and balanced judgment.

"Dear Dad," he wrote. "I thought I would write you my impressions on Palestine while they were still fresh in my mind, though you undoubtedly, if I know the Jews, know the 'whole' story. It is worthwhile looking at in its entirety," Jack maintained, and briefly summarized Palestine's position as it had existed before the Great War, "inhabited by Moslem Arabs with a scattering of Christians. There were also a few thousand Jews, though at that time the Zionists' movement had not assumed great proportions." This stable situation had, however, been drastically altered by the First World War.

> During the war, the British Government, desiring both the assistance of the Jews and the Arabs, made separate promises to both, one in the MacMahon, the other in the Balfour declaration. . . . In considering the whole question now, it is useless to discuss which has the "fairer" claim. The important thing is to try to work out a solution

that will work, not try to present a solution based on these two vague, indefinite and conflicting promises. This is my objection to the White Paper.

The British government White Paper "theoretically presents a good solution," Jack opined, "but it just *won't* work."

One by one Jack listed the commissions and conferences that had taken place over past years, and the efforts toward partition under British rule. Behind the public statements of the Arab and Jewish groups, however, were "fundamental objections which, while they are not stated publicly, are nevertheless far more important. On the Jewish side, there is the desire for complete domination, with Jerusalem as the capital of their new land of milk and honey, with the right to colonize in Trans-Jordan. They feel that given sufficient opportunity they can cultivate the land and develop it as they have done in the Western portion."

This, however, was a claim which the Arabs bitterly resented, as they felt "that the Jews have had the benefit of capital, which had the Arabs possessed, equal miracles could have been performed by them." Jack himself allowed some truth to this—though in all honesty considered that "the economic set-up of Arabic agricultural progress with its absentee landlords and primitive methods of cultivation, could not under any circumstances probably have competed with the Jews"—a truth that belied much Arab "objection to the Jews. They realize their superiority and fear it." Moreover, with their religious and spiritual leader, the Grand Mufti, in exile, the Palestinian Arabs had no leader, condemning them to weakness of opposition compared with the Jews.

"I see no hope for the working out of the British policy as laid down by the White Paper," Jack concluded. Though it "sounds just and fair," the

important thing and the necessary thing is not a solution just and fair but a solution that will work:

As the British interest must and will be naturally safeguarded . . . it seems to me that the only thing to do will be to break the country up into two autonomous districts giving them both self-government to the extent that they do not interfere with each other and that British interest is safeguarded. Jerusalem, having the background that it has, should be an independent unit. Though this is a difficult solution yet, it is the only one that I think can work.

Whether such a partition of Palestine on these lines would have worked is conjectural. The approaching war in Europe certainly caused the British to be concerned about their "interest" in the region, however, and thus move cautiously, despite the many outrages and bombings. "There were 13 bombs set off my last evening there, all in the Jewish quarter and all set off by Jews," Jack informed his father. "Incidentally I have become more pro-British down there than I have been in my other visits to England as I think that the men on the spot are doing a good job. This roughly, in fact very roughly, is an outline of the situation. It will be interesting to see it develop and see what form the solution takes, as a definite solution has not been found yet. I thought Danzig was a tough problem, but I have never seen two groups more unwilling to try and work out a solution that has some hope of success than these two groups."

"Sympathy of the people on the spot seems to be with the Arabs," Jack reported. Partly this was because "the Jews have had, at least in some of their leaders, an unfortunately arrogant, uncompromising attitude," but it rested too on the fact that "after all, the country has been Arabic for the last few hundred years, and they naturally feel sympathetic. After all, Palestine was hardly Britain's to give away," given that Britain had assumed control only in 1916 while at war with the Turks, and the mandate from the League of Nations dated back only to 1922.

> The question is further complicated by the fact that both groups are split among themselves. There is the strongly orthodox Jewish group, unwilling to make any compromise, who wished to have a government expressing this attitude, there is the liberal Jewish element composed of the younger group who fear these reactionaries, and wish to establish a very liberal, almost communistic form of government, and there are the in-betweens who are willing to make a compromise. . . . As for the Arabs, while most of them are heartily sick of the whole business which is playing hell with their economic life, yet so strong is the hold of the Mufti by reason of his religious grip and because of the strength of the new nationalism, that it is going to be extremely difficult to effect a solution without bringing him back.

Even if the Mufti did return, however, the problem would not ease, since the British White Paper "calls for the Arab officials to be appointed by the British during the transition period," and the mufti would not be among them. Even an elected assembly, "given the general standard of the country," would "naturally be a farce." That is what makes the whole situation so impossible," Jack explained. "All three sides have such great interests all in a great measure conflicting, and all three sides having great means of putting on pressure. Poor Malcolm McDonald," he remarked, referring to the former prime minister who had sought to draw up the parliamentary report.

Meanwhile, the "theoretically just and fair solution" was "failing," Jack pointed out. Once having failed, the British should, Jack argued, "say that they have done the best they could under the circumstances and then arbitrarily force the partition plan to be accepted."

Ironically, this was what the British would attempt to do nine years later, although the effort would be thwarted by pressure from American Jews upon the American president, forcing him to "back off" from forced partition, and leading to decades of instability, terrorism, and hatred in the Middle East.

In the meantime, however, having stunned "staid Britons by wearing a lounge suit instead of a morning coat to the British high commissioner's party," held to celebrate King George VI's birthday on June 8, Jack scribbled to his father that he was "leaving now for Bucharest," returning via Beirut, Lebanon, Damascus, and Athens to London. There, however, he found an even more explosive situation.

"Had a great trip. The only way you can really know what is going to go on is to go to all the countries. I still don't think there will be a war this year," he reported to Billings, "based on the unwillingness of Italy + a number of other things—though August 20th to September 8th will be very tough + a lot of people expect a war then. Germany will try to break Danzig off gradually, making it difficult for Poland to say that at *this* point her independence is being threatened. However I don't think she will succeed."

Time would tell. Meanwhile, as ordinary Britons dug air-raid shelters in their back gardens, the last balls were given for the daughters of the English upper classes—and of the American ambassador. At her debut Eunice wore "a peach-colored dress from Paquin," Rose Kennedy proudly noted in her diary. "About half-past two they all started doing the Big Apple, a new dance, and everybody got very gay. I was quite surprised and even a little shocked. However, I was assured by some of the chaperones that the party was a huge success. . . . The Duke of Marlborough had asked if he might come, although the fathers don't usually come to the debut parties. He was one of the leaders of the Big Apple."

Jack, working in his cutaway for his father at the embassy by day and partying in his tuxedo by night, was in his element, especially when joined by his Harvard roommate, Torbert Macdonald, who came over as a sprinter with the American university athletics team. Macdonald was in love with Kathleen—indeed considered they were unofficially engaged at this point—and was desperately anxious to make a good impression.

Thus, when Jack, Kathleen, and the ambassador attended the athletics meet at White City in west London, Macdonald was understandably nervous. "Jack had pointed out that I'd won most everything I'd run against," Macdonald later described the fateful day.

> It's run on a dog track. . . . At Harvard you run two hundred and twenty just straightaway. At White City you start in staggered lanes. . . . I had the misfortune to pick the lane that was the furthest out. In other words I was ten yards ahead of everybody until you came off the curve. I'd never done it before; we'd never run around curves, and I felt myself far ahead and came off the curve and found myself about ten yards behind everybody. I tried very hard because I was showing off to "Kick" and the Ambassador and everybody. I made up quite a good deal of ground as I recall, but finished a close third. It was embarrassing to me to have that sort of thing after Jack had got the whole family out to see us run.

Jack was amused. "Torb ran third in the meet," he immediately reported to Billings, " + is looking a bit sheepish. Big Bill Buchel was over here + I took him to the debut of the Duke of Marlborough's daughter at Blenheim which is nearly as big as Versailles. It is really too bad you're not here as it's all darn good fun—never had a better time."

Indeed he hadn't. Not only was he a guest in the greatest homes of England—even 10 Downing Street, where he attended a reception on June 27, 1939—but he was also privileged to see and even help draft his father's ambassadorial correspondence, reports, and telegrams, as well as to meet the major political personalities of Britain on the eve of war.

For the most part Jack was discreet, an observer rather than a pontificator. English friends such as David Ormsby-Gore, son of Lord Harlech, were often unaware of Jack's fascination with international politics. "I mostly saw him at parties and in the family circle at home," Ormsby-Gore later recalled of that period, "having a good time. He was very thin, wiry-thin with, I don't know how to describe it, this energy exuding from him. I didn't see much of his serious side, and indeed, at that date—well, of course he was twenty-one and I was about the same age—probably neither one of us had a very serious side to be seen at that moment."

On reflection, though, even Ormsby-Gore acknowleged there must have been a more serious undertow to Jack than was evident in his party persona. "I didn't detect it," he later remarked, "although he must have been more interested than I thought, because of course he was preparing his thesis—it was a longer than normal thesis."

Unbeknown to his British hosts, Jack had indeed decided on the topic of his next-year Harvard thesis, in correspondence with his "arch-militarist" tutor, Professor Hopper. Hopper had recommended Jack read *History of Political Philosophy* while away, as well as Lippmann's *Good Society,* Maxey's *Political Philosophies,* and Coker's *Readings in Political Philosophy* and *Recent Political Thought,* but was impressed by Jack's letters recording the contemporary European scene. "Kennedy took six courses the first half," he noted on Jack's annual tutorial record sheet at Harvard, "and is following a course of reading I laid out for him while away in Europe this second half. I have been in correspondence with him regarding the gathering of thesis material and should very much like to have him next year."

Hopper had seen Jack's unique opportunity to investigate history in the making. How had Britain gotten itself in such a fix? Why had appeasement failed to halt the march of Hitler? Why was Britain so unprepared for war, having ended the Great War as the most powerful military and naval power in Europe? And what was the truth behind Neville Chamberlain's appeasement policy?

With his thesis more and more in mind, Jack now made a final trip to the Continent before war was declared. "We went from England to France, to Germany to Italy, and back to Paris," Torbert Macdonald later recalled. In Munich they met "Whizzer" White in the Hofbrauhaus. Jack had previously encountered White at a gathering of Rhodes scholars at the American Embassy in the spring. Standing six feet two inches tall, White had also been a professional football player as well as a scholar. "We got along very well, all three of us, so we decided to take a tour of the city," Macdonald recorded. "Whizzer had a car that some guy had loaned him, we got in it and we went by this monument to some beer hall hero, Worst Hessel [*sic*] or something, and we slowed down to take a look. They had a flame burning and they started to yell and at that time I didn't know who Worst Hessel was, frankly."

The students had been warned before leaving England not to provoke an "incident," according to Macdonald. "I recall very well indeed the Ambassador saying—calling us both in and saying—when we were in Germany, no matter what happened, not to cause any trouble and to bend over backwards to stay out of trouble. . . . He indicated that they [the Germans] were very tough and paid no attention to laws or rules, and, if anything happened, just to back away."

Heedless of the ambassador's warning, the American students stopped the car, unwisely, and the storm troopers got "rough." "We were yelling back and they started throwing bricks at the car. So we drove the car away for a while, and I turned to Jack and said, 'What in the hell is wrong with them, what's all this about? We weren't doing anything, I mean, we weren't agitating people or doing anything.' And Whizzer explained the car we were driving in had English plates on it—and they were so agitated

at the English people that they were throwing rocks at our car! And this
is the first time I ever heard Jack say it: he said, 'you know, how can we
avoid having a world war if this is the way these people feel?' "

At Harvard, Professor Holcombe had pressed his students to answer
the most fundamental of all political questions: Why do people obey? In
Munich in the summer of 1939, Jack recognized the primary reason: the
power of propaganda. "The German people are being whipped into a
fierce hatred of the British," he wrote to his father. As his German
drinking companions, one by one, were ordered to join their military
units, Whizzer White also became more certain there would be war. "The
south Germans are a friendly and attractive people," White remarked
later, "but there was never any doubt that they would fight for Germany
if a war came."

Returning to Paris in August 1939, Jack and Torby rented a car, intending to drive down to the South of France, where Jack's family was once
again staying in a rented villa. Macdonald recalled,

> We were wedged into the cramped front seat of a rickety jalopy we'd
> rented to drive to the Riviera for a party. The guy we'd rented from
> must've spotted us for a pair of green college kids, for the car was a
> real lemon, shaking and continually bucking to the right. Jack, who's
> not the world's most conservative driver, was at the wheel when the
> car gave an uncontrollable lurch and we slipped off the right shoul-
> der of the road, skidded on our top for 30 feet and ended upside-
> down with our baggage strewn all over the landscape. In the silence
> after the crash as we were literally standing on our heads in the
> overturned car, Jack looked sideways at me and said in a casual tone,
> "Well, pal, we didn't make it, did we?"

Eventually they did, however, and found to their delight Kathleen—
"exiled" from England at Rose Kennedy's insistence in order to stop her
from attending the coming-of-age party for Lord Hartington, the Protestant heir to the dukedom of Devonshire and Kick's latest beau. Rumors
of an engagement were rife.

Though Jack "immediately developed a terrific crush" on Kathleen's
best friend and houseguest, Sally Norton, his feelings were not reciprocated. Given Kathleen's fading interest in Macdonald, the two boys
decided to set off for a second helping of the Third Reich. "12th August:
Jack and Torb Macdonald leave for Germany," Rose penned in her
diary. "They would like to go to Prague, but we are told no one is allowed
to go there."

Undaunted, Jack wrote from Nazi-occupied Vienna to his father to tell
him he'd arrived "last night from Munich—where we stayed a day + saw

Tanhauser [*sic*]. Going over now to see if I get into Prague. Leaving for there or Berlin tonight. Torb is off to Budapest" (which Jack had already visited).

"No trains were running, no planes were flying, no frontier stations existed," a pompous U.S. Foreign Service officer later recalled. "Yet in the midst of this confusion we received a telegram from the Embassy in London, the sense of which was that our Ambassador there, Mr. Joseph Kennedy, had chosen this time to send one of his young sons on a fact-finding tour around Europe, and it was up to us to find a means of getting him across the border and through the German lines so that he could include in his itinerary a visit to Prague. . . . We were furious. Joe Kennedy was not exactly known as a friend of the career services, and many of us, from what we had heard about him, cordially reciprocated this lack of enthusiasm. His son had no official status and was, in our eyes, obviously an upstart and ignoramus."

Riding roughshod over State Department outrage, Jack interviewed as many people as he could in Prague and then made his way to Berlin. To Billings he wrote from the German capital on August 20, 1939, that he'd "left Cannes about a week ago and have been travelling thru Germany ever since. Ran into Butler and Lippit in Munich as well as Big Eddie Hobler—who is the same stupid-looking farmer he's always been," he remarked with his own brand of snobbery. "As I see he was the toast of 'our' class it makes me feel quite proud to be a class-mate. I suppose my picture appeared in that [Princeton class of '39] album with a big blank space and that everybody looking thru it probably said 'that just goes to show you how big Princeton is—I never saw that son-of-a-bitch before,'" he mocked. "I'm getting back the 13th on the Manhattan + I thought I would go up to the Cape for awhile or maybe go South to Charlotte [North Carolina, home of Frances Ann Cannon] etc. In which case I would drop in to see you. However, if you can + try to make the Cape . . . although I suppose those days are over," he stopped short, thinking of Billings's new life as a Coca-Cola employee.

Jack had bought a new German movie camera and projector "so we could spend a lot of time getting close-ups of you in color. Incidentally my face in color would be quite a sensation after one week of these German meals. . . . I still don't think there will be a war but it looks quite bad as the Germans have gone so far internally with their propoganda stories on Danzig + the Corridor that it is hard to see them backing down. England seems firm this time—but as that is not completely understood here [Berlin], the big danger here lies in the German counting on another Munich + thus finding themselves in a war when Chamberlain refuses to give in."

Despite the prim reaction of America's junior diplomats in Europe,

Jack Kennedy had witnessed a level of brinkmanship that would not be repeated until he himself became commander-in-chief of the most powerful armed forces in the world. In the meantime, from the Hotel Excelsior he went to his final briefing at the U.S. embassy in Berlin, where the chargé d'affaires, Alex Kirk, gave him a secret message for his father: namely, that there would be war within a week. Bearing the message, Jack made his way by train back to England. The next time he would see Berlin it would be in ruins: a devastated capital city symbolizing the price the Germans had paid for their arrogance in 1939.

PART
·6·
WHY ENGLAND SLEPT

John F. Kennedy as best-selling author, summer of 1940
(Archive Photos)

No More September Crises

Chamberlain clung to his hope that Hitler would back down, telling the American ambassador that if war was averted "we are witnessing the greatest and most expensive dress rehearsal for a show that will never be produced." To placate Hitler, he still refused to take Churchill into his Cabinet, telling Kennedy "he had no intention of doing so. Churchill was not nearly as good a man as people thought him to be, and if he had been in the Cabinet, England would have been at war long before this."

However, even Chamberlain realized how slim were the chances of avoiding war as Hitler, having signed a nonaggression pact with the Soviet Union, massed his troops on the Polish border. "I had never seen him more depressed or more downcast," Kennedy noted. Lord Halifax, the foreign secretary, maintained he was still "hopeful that some method of adjusting the differences would be found," but when Kennedy candidly suggested making more concessions to Hitler, Chamberlain was despondent. "I have done everything that I can think of, Joe," the prime minister confessed, "but it looks as if all my work has been of no avail."

"I can't fly again," Chamberlain explained. "That was good only once. It is no use for me to urge the Poles to make concessions, for that would be interpreted as weakness on our part. The thing that is frightful is the futility of it all. The Poles can't be saved. All the English can do is wage a war of revenge that will mean the entire destruction of Europe.' " To this Kennedy responded, "Can the Pope be of any use?"

Kennedy's other suggestion was a new Munich, with Roosevelt taking charge. To Hull he cabled that "some action of Poland in negotiating with the Reich which will render a further delay possible is the only hope. . . . In the event President Roosevelt has in mind any action for the preservation of peace, it appears to me the object of his efforts should be Beck in Poland and, to be effective, it must be done quickly. There is no other possibility, as I see it."

But would further concessions by the democracies help? At 10 Downing Street on August 25 Kennedy was shown Sir Nevile Henderson's latest report from Berlin, in which Hitler was quoted as saying "that it was useless for the British to bother about Poland since he and the Russians had agreed to cut it up."

"After I had read the dispatches [Sir Horace] Wilson, [head of the British civil service and treasury staff] asked me to step into the Cabinet Room. Chamberlain was sitting in the Prime Minister's chair dressed in a dinner jacket. Across from him sat Halifax in a business suit." Kennedy, in a lounge suit, made a fourth. Of these four high priests of appeasement, only Chamberlain had ever been elected, and he was now in his seventies. Their conversation was surreal. "In front of each of them were copies of the cables," Kennedy later described. "After Chamberlain had asked me to sit down, he turned to me and said: 'What do you think of it?' "

"If it weren't for Henderson's additional memorandum quoting Hitler as saying that Germany and Russia would divide Poland," Kennedy replied, "I might be convinced that Hitler wanted either to drive a wedge between the British and the Poles or else that he was really scared."

"We discussed the dispatches at length and the character of the answer that should be made," Kennedy later recalled.

> I outlined my own ideas. There could be no backing down now on Poland, I said. It would not only jeopardize the honor of Britain but it would destroy the [Conservative] party. To this they were all agreed. On the other hand, it was essential to get some reasonable settlement of the Polish question. "You must pass the hat before the corpse gets cold," I said.
>
> "What do you mean by that?" asked Chamberlain.
>
> "You have to make your solution more attractive to Germany than what she is trying now to get out of Poland. Do it this way," I went on. "Propose a general settlement that will bring Germany economic benefits more important than the territorial annexation of Danzig. Get the United States now to say what they would be willing to do in the cause of international peace and prosperity. After all, the United States will be the largest beneficiary of such a move. To put in a billion or two now will be worth it, for if it works we will get it back and more."

To imagine that Hitler could be swayed by greed or economic incentives, after the experience over the past sixteen months, did not say much for Kennedy's diplomatic or political insight; yet this same man was undoubtedly a financial genius of sorts, with what his financial adviser James Fayne once described as a "unique instinct for the right time to go ahead or back out." He was, too, an uncomfortable realist. As Roosevelt's legendary aide, Tommy Corcoran, once said, Kennedy

> analyzed the increments of power and he cut away the fuzzes on the edge. This was the realist in Kennedy—the cutting away until only the bare bones of a thing showed. He made people mad because he was telling the truth. He was speaking the real language of this age. Joe would say, what end is there? Only power. What delight is there

but to be part of great events; the sheer sense of control. There isn't any other end. "Power is the only end and if you don't like the code of the game, what is it then? Love of country? Let me see it in people who really command." How did the Tudors, Cecils, Brahmins rise? The source of power is money.

For Hitler, however, the source of power was not money. This left Kennedy as stumped as Chamberlain. "We talked for another half hour," Kennedy recalled of his meeting at 10 Downing Street, "and then I left. I put my hand on Chamberlain's shoulder and said, 'Don't worry too much, Neville. I still think God is working with you.'"

Thereafter Kennedy saw Chamberlain or Halifax several times a day. On one occasion, when Kennedy was driving the foreign secretary home from Downing Street, the crowd had to lift Kennedy's car, which he'd reversed onto the fender of Chamberlain's vehicle behind: a strangely symbolic reflection of the occlusion between appeasers. Even secret signals to and from Hitler were shown to Kennedy before other members of the Cabinet.

Shortly after Henderson's pessimistic dispatch from Berlin, Kennedy met Halifax again and was shown the text of Hitler's ultimatum to Warsaw, demanding a Polish emissary endowed with full powers to negotiate away Danzig. The British Cabinet's draft response was then handed to him, which Kennedy thought too unyielding: "There are two great difficulties with the present situation. The first is that the British, thinking they have Hitler on the run, will get too tough. The second is that the Poles, also believing Hitler to be on the run and thinking they have the French and the English all hooked up to help them, will get tough and make no concessions. The trouble with the draft, as I see it, is that it is not merely firm but tough. . . . I think the Cabinet should be firm but I think it should offer Hitler something to hang his hat on."

The under secretary of state, R. A. Butler, felt the same way.

"I agree. It's the Cabinet's draft but perhaps we could warm it up a bit. What do you suggest?" I pointed out a series of suggestions. Butler made them, and they were shortly thereafter cleared by the Cabinet. "You ought to see the P.M.," Butler said, "and give him your reactions. You are one of the few people that he not only likes and trusts, but who can influence him. . . . You know, I try to get across the same ideas you have expressed about 'jollying the Germans,' but every now and then the P.M. starts to remember how badly Hitler treated him, especially last March, and he gets very tough."

This was music to Kennedy's ears.

> "Like that remark he made yesterday in the Commons about Germany having to resort to ration cards, while England didn't need them," I said. "That was a dig at the Nazi economy. My son Joe," I said, "lunched with Miss Unity Mitford in Berlin the other day. She quoted Hitler as saying that he had great admiration for the British, but that he was heartbroken when Chamberlain went home and in one breath talked about 'peace in our time' and in the other about the necessity of arming for protection against Hitler."
>
> "I know," said Butler, "I was with the P.M. at the time. It was an off the text comment. The moment I heard it I knew it was a major mistake. . . . If only this Polish question can be settled so that we will have no more of these September crises! The Cabinet is ready now to deal on a broader front. They have already discussed the necessity for immediately taking up the question of colonies. That was a bitter pill for them, but it is about three-fourths of the way down their stomachs now. But I will see the P.M. now and get an appointment for you."

That the American ambassador should, without the backing of his own president and State Department, have continually sought to influence British appeasement policies toward Hitler at the highest level until the very last hour was a truth that would be sedulously concealed for decades to come. "At 6:30 I went to 10 Downing Street," Kennedy continued his unpublished "confession."

> Chamberlain was as cordial as ever. I repeated the suggestions I had made to Butler and Chamberlain agreed with them.
>
> "Why not put in some war regulations that will affect the whole people?" I said. "Give them a little taste of what is to come. They might not be so anxious for the Poles to refuse to negotiate and so start a war." Chamberlain thought that if he only could get the Poles and Germans really negotiating something could be done. He said he had told Henderson to brush Danzig away in Hitler's mind as a matter of real importance. The big thing was a European settlement. . . .
> "It could be done," said Chamberlain, "if I could only get the chance. I know, for I know these men now personally, and that is a great advantage. But first the Poles have to be reasonable. The unfortunate thing is that there is a great body of opinion in England, headed by men like Churchill and Eden, who are telling the Poles to give up nothing. . . . They are wrong. If they persist it will mean war."

As Kennedy later boasted, it was largely thanks to him that the British "belatedly but now almost hysterically" put pressure on the Poles, like they had on the Czechs the year before, to allow Britain to negotiate on their behalf with Hitler. The Poles, having seen what happened to Czechoslovakia as a result of Britain "negotiating on its behalf," procrastinated. "It was not until the evening of August 31 that finally a communication was made by the Poles to Ribbentrop. But even this communication did not comport with the British request and did not indicate that the Poles were agreeable to negotiating with the Germans," Kennedy recalled with disappointment. "That midnight of August 31 I talked with the President over the telephone. . . . We knew nothing of Hitler's determination to invade Poland," Kennedy later claimed. "Even the next morning we were unaware of what had happened."

If Kennedy did not know the exact timing of the German invasion, he had a shrewd idea, however—reinforced by a message that his son Jack had brought back from the American chargé d'affaires in Berlin; in fact Kennedy later admitted having put in a phone call to Ambassador Bullitt in Paris, who was certain Hitler would quit "if the British will only stand as firmly as the French." Kennedy had retorted, " 'Nuts!' I said. Hitler is not quitting. This is war."

And war it was. "I had hardly hung up the telephone when the news came. It came with a rush, like a torrent spewing from the wires— German troops had crossed the border; German planes were bombing Polish cities and killing civilians; the Germans were using poison gas. . . . Secretary Hull called me excitedly at noon. I could confirm little but the one fact. The German Army was on the march."

Declaring War

Even now, Kennedy felt, Britain could avoid war if it abrogated its guarantee to Poland. Shamefully, Chamberlain did in fact do everything in his power to wriggle out of the British commitment. Although on September 1 he sent a message to Berlin warning the German government that Britain would have to fulfill its obligations to Poland unless Hitler withdrew his forces, this was but a watered-down version of the British Cabinet's full-scale ultimatum that was, Kennedy recalled, deliberately "held up for the time being."

The next day, "Saturday, September 2, was a day of ominous waiting silence. There was no news from Berlin." Chamberlain's feeble statement in the House of Commons, which Kennedy witnessed from the Visitor's Gallery, incited the fury of the acting leader of the opposition, Arthur Greenwood, "who jumped to his feet," Kennedy remembered.

> He was literally sputtering with anger and excitement. The idea of a delay compromised England's honor; it aroused the suspicion of the French. "There shall be no more devices," he said, "for dragging out what has been dragged out too long." Sir Archibald Sinclair followed him, also breathing fire, fearful of "delay in the fulfillment of our honorable obligations to Poland". . . . The spirit elsewhere was the same. Young fliers were disgusted with Chamberlain for his apparent hesitation. I wrote that night in my notes: "These boys and all the rest of the country and these smart people in the United States of America who want England to fight will soon see what Chamberlain was trying to save them from."

Chamberlain's government was now in danger of falling. The Cabinet's ultimatum, ending at midnight on September 2, had never been sent by the foreign secretary, Lord Halifax. Only when Parliament threatened revolt that evening did Chamberlain finally give in, though not until after a futile attempt to set up a face-saving, five-power conference under Mussolini, designed to "authorize" Hitler's act, had failed. "The Italian proposal dropped. At two in the morning of September 3 I cabled Mr. Hull 'triple priority,' " Kennedy related. He had, he alerted the State Department, been "just informed" that the British Cabinet, after a meeting that went on past midnight, was finally about to dispatch an ultimatum "to the Reich Government within a few hours."

It had taken Chamberlain three days of dithering to dispatch it. Later that morning, on his way to the American Embassy in Grosvenor Square, Kennedy dropped his wife off at the Brompton Oratory ("where she told me later only a few men had assembled for mass although the chapel was packed with women") and had a small radio brought into his office. At eleven-fifteen the prime minister addressed the nation—indeed the world. Kennedy recalled:

> With the staff [I] listened to his short but significant speech. We were all terribly moved by the solemnity and tragedy of the occasion. The tears came to my eyes as I heard Chamberlain say that "all my long struggle to win peace has failed." I had participated very closely in that struggle myself and I also was seeing my hopes crash. As soon as Chamberlain stopped speaking, I picked up the receiver and asked for him. To my surprise he came on the line at once.
> "Neville," I said, "this is Joe. I have just listened to your broadcast

and it was terrifically moving. . . . It was really great, and I feel deeply our failure to save the world from war."

To which Chamberlain replied, "We did the best we could," he said, "but it looks as though we have failed. . . . Thank you, Joe. My best to you and my deep gratitude for your constant help—Good-bye, goodbye."

Chamberlain was due to address the House of Commons at noon. Jack, Kathleen, and Joe Jr. (who had also just returned from Germany), made their way to the House of Commons and joined their parents in the Strangers' Gallery to witness the formal declaration of war. "We rushed down to Parliament where Chamberlain was to speak," Ambassador Kennedy recalled.

> Another air-raid warning sent us down to a shelter in the House of Commons but that too was soon over. In the midst of Chamberlain's talk an attendant waved me out to answer an important telephone call—from the President, he said. He was not strictly accurate. It was "Missy" LeHand [Roosevelt's secretary] on the wire, telling me that the President would try to talk to me that afternoon, but that he wanted me to know now that he was thinking of me. She was crying with emotion and said that they all were thinking of me and that I should keep in touch with them.
>
> Greenwood was speaking when I returned. Sinclair and Churchill followed him.

Churchill, still speaking from the back benches as an ordinary M.P., evoked cheers from the House with his oratory. "This is no war," he maintained, "for domination or imperial aggrandisement or material gain; no war to shut any country out of its sunlight and means of progress. It is a war, viewed in its inherent quality, to establish on impregnable rocks, the rights of the individual, and it is a war to establish and revive the stature of man."

"But I felt no wish to cheer," Kennedy later confessed. "Chamberlain had mirrored my sensations better when he said, 'This is a sad day for all of us. . . . Everything that I have worked for, everything that I had hoped for, everything that I have believed in during my public life has crashed into ruins.' By then I had had enough and without waiting for other speakers, I made my way back through the silent crowds to the Embassy."

Jack's mother also later recalled Chamberlain's "heart-broken heart-breaking" speech, with its "tragic lines," as the high moment of the day. For Jack Kennedy, however, it was Winston Churchill's speech that remained indelibly engraved in his memory: a speech that caused all but Chamberlain's most faithful acolytes to recognize that the outcast Winston Churchill, not Chamberlain, would more likely become Britain's champion in the coming hardships.

"Outside, the storms of war may blow and the lands may be lashed with the fury of its gales," Churchill thundered, "but in our own hearts this Sunday morning there is peace. . . . our consciences are at rest." The prime minister's sadness at the onset of war was understandable, Churchill allowed, but there was another emotion, too, that could be felt at this hour, the sense of thankfulness that a new generation of Britons was "ready to prove itself not unworthy of the days of yore and not unworthy of those great men, the fathers of our land, who laid the foundations of our laws and shaped the greatness of our country. This is not a question of fighting for Danzig or fighting for Poland. We are fighting to save the whole world from the pestilence of Nazi tyranny and in defence of all that is most sacred to man."

Jack Kennedy, one of Churchill's most ardent readers in America, sat spellbound. But Rose Kennedy could not even recall the speech in her memoirs, recording only that as she and her children set off on foot to the ambassador's residence in Prince's Gate, "the air-raid siren began to howl, and we ran for refuge into the nearest shelter we could find."

Significantly, it was the basement of her couturier, Molyneux.

The Sinking Ship

Panic-stricken at the onset of war, Ambassador Kennedy booked berths aboard the first available American liner departing for New York (the S.S. *Washington,* sailing on September 9) for Rose and their nine children as well as the family nanny, Luella Hennessy, and Mr. and Mrs. Eddie Moore.

There were, however, an estimated fifteen thousand other U.S. citizens anxious to return to the States on the outbreak of European war. Sensitive to possible charges that the members of his own family were, like proverbial rats, deserting the sinking ship ahead of these other citizens, Kennedy agreed to stagger their departure. While Joe Jr. and Jack were put to work helping American nationals, the rest of the family waited their turn. Thus, when asked about himself and his brothers and sisters by a newspaper reporter, Jack replied, "Oh, we must get back to school, but we shan't go until all other American citizens have gone." (Diplomatically, he made no mention of his mother, the American ambassador's wife, returning to the United States.)

Meanwhile, "with the prospect of bombing now a reality, a sense of panic was in the air," Joe Kennedy recalled, describing the first evening of war. When President Roosevelt came on the line, Kennedy kept hysterically repeating, "It's the end of the world, the end of everything," the journalists Joe Alsop and Robert Kintner recorded. "As I told Hull by telephone and by cable," Kennedy admitted, "we still needed air raid protection at the Embassy. He seemed tired that evening, but we all were. I had hardly gone to bed before the telephone rang. It was two-thirty in the morning and the Foreign Office was on the line. The clipped accent of an unknown clerk spelled out a message that he said had just been received—'S.S. *Athenia,* Donaldson Line, torpedoed 200 miles off Malin Head, 1,400 passengers aboard, S.O.S. received, ship sinking fast.' "

In London the newly appointed first lord of the admiralty, Winston Churchill, announced that the *Athenia,* unarmed and carrying only passengers, had been sunk without warning by a German U-boat. Joseph Goebbels, the Nazi minister of propaganda, angrily interrupted a German news broadcast to denounce the "lying Lord," claiming there were no German submarines operating in the area, and damning "your impudent lies, Herr Churchill, your infernal lies."

It was Goebbels who was unashamedly lying. The British liner, bound from Liverpool to New York, had been sunk by one of no fewer than thirty-nine German submarines operating in the area. As Admiral Raeder later admitted at the Nuremberg trials, the U-30's captain, Kommandant Kemp, had in his excitement mistaken the *Athenia* for a British auxiliary cruiser.

Several hundred survivors were landed in Ireland, but the majority were brought by British destroyer to Scotland. Thus it was that on the evening of September 6, 1939, "Jack Kennedy was sent up to Glasgow to represent his father because the Embassy staff in London was so rushed with work that no regular member could be spared," the newspapers reported.

Jack's father felt it would be a routine matter, but as Jack soon found, the assignment was anything but that. It was the first torpedoing of a civilian liner in World War II. Over three hundred American passengers had been aboard, and more than a hundred people were killed or drowned, including twenty-eight U.S. citizens.

Though Jack Kennedy had now turned twenty-two, he still looked like a teenager, as the London *Telegraph* assumed he was in its report from Glasgow:

Mr. John Kennedy, the 18-year-old son of the United States Ambassador, faced a determined audience of fellow Americans who had survived the torpedoing of the British liner *Athenia* in the lounge of an hotel here this afternoon, and heard their polite but firm demands for some assurance of adequate protection when, next week, they sail for home in a specially chartered freighter now on its way from New York.

This schoolboy diplomat had been sent overnight to Glasgow to tell the *Athenia* survivors what their government is doing to alleviate their distress and get them home.

"I talked to my father this morning, and he has spoken to America since," he said. "He asked me to tell you that the Government has plenty of money for you all."

Ambassador Kennedy's financial reassurances were not what the survivors wanted, however. Huddled in blankets and secondhand clothes, the survivors were incensed by a mere "schoolboy" explaining that an American vessel would take them home and "that President Roosevelt had said there was no need for a convoy, as American ships would not be attacked." An American reporter cabled home to tell how "a storm of protest burst from the refugees. . . . Many Americans, still bearing bruises, burns and other traces of their ordeal on the *Athenia,* began to shout, 'You can't trust the German Navy! You can't trust the German Government!' Young Kennedy declared that American ships did not need a convoy because 'we are still neutral, and the neutrality law still holds. It is much better to be on an American boat now than on a British boat,' he said, 'even if it was accompanied by the whole fleet.' "

This, to survivors who had been through the trauma of enemy attack and shipwreck (as Jack himself would experience four years later), was like holding a red rag to a bull.

"I don't believe it," shouted a woman who had started the clamor. The rest of the survivors cheered and shouted: "That goes for us too." Mr. Kennedy again attempted to reason with the crowd, but was interrupted by grey-haired Thomas McCubbin of Montclair, N.J., who said: "A convoy is imperative. Ninety destroyers have just been commissioned by the United States Navy and surely they can spare us a few. Six billion dollars of United States Navy and they cannot do this for us!" Another survivor cried, "Two years ago the whole Pacific fleet was sent out for one women flyer [Amelia Earhart]." One college girl declared: "We defiantly refuse to go until we have a convoy. You have seen what they will do to us."

Young Kennedy was taken aback, but managed to shout above

the din. "You will be safe in a ship flying the American flag under international law; a neutral ship is safe."

The survivors, unimpressed by this assurance, continued to mutter, and Mr. Kennedy promised to inform his father of their demands. He caught the night express to London.

This was Jack's first-ever taste of a hostile American crowd. He did not lose his composure, the London *Evening News* reporter maintained. "Ambassador of mercy—19 year old Jack Kennedy, son of America's Ambassador, Joseph P. Kennedy, spent one of the busiest days of his young life today, going from hotels to hospitals in Glasgow, visiting the *Athenia's* American survivors. His boyish charm and natural kindliness persuaded those who he had come to comfort that America was indeed keeping a benevolent and watchful eye on them. I accompanied young Mr. Kennedy and Lord Provost Dollan. . . . Mr. Kennedy displayed a wisdom and sympathy of a man twice his age." Once back at the U.S. embassy in London Jack recommended:

1. That a convoy be sent with the boat that is going to take them back to America, because a) the natural shock of the people would make the trip to America alone unbearable, b) because of the feeling that they will have that the United States government exposed them to this unnecessarily.
2. That the boat when it arrives should be sent to Glasgow because a) it is the most convenient spot as most of the survivors are there, b) in appreciation of all Lord Provost Dollan in the city of Glasgow has done for them.
3. That the men in the destroyer who picked up the survivors be officially thanked by the United States government.
4. That the city of Glasgow be formally thanked by the government for all the work that they have done.

Though the city of Glasgow and the Royal Navy were thanked, Joseph Kennedy turned down his son's main recommendation. "Many of them demanded hysterically that they be returned under convoy by American naval vessels. This was impossible and unnecessary," the ambassador later recalled with indifference, conveniently forgetting his own hysteria. Jack was, however, put in charge of repatriating the survivors. The following week he wrote from London to the Harvard registrar that, since he was "now working in charge of the committee for the evacuation of the *Athenia* survivors, and due to the lack of transportation, it appears that I shall not be able to return back to America before the 29th of September." He hoped this wouldn't "endanger my standing."

It did not. Moreover, a last-minute seat was found aboard a Pan American clipper, the *Dixie,* flying from Foynes in Ireland, via Newfoundland, on September 20. Jack thus landed at New York on September 21, 1939, "the general favorite with all on the *Dixie,*" as *The Boston Globe* reported, "not because he was Ambassador Kennedy's son but because he was himself, bright and helpful and interesting."

Proposals of Peace and Marriage

The first person Jack met back at Harvard was his roommate, Torby Macdonald. Macdonald was now the captain of Harvard's football team, and for this, their senior year, he and Jack were to share a new suite in Winthrop House, F-14. "Handsome, tall, thin, and high-strung, with an ingrained habit of cocking his legs over the arms of his chair, Jack was having a hard time, after such an exciting seven months, in settling down to the humdrum life of a student. Radios, chairs, laundry and valises were scattered helter-skelter in the three-room suite at Winthrop House," a journalist described.

Having unpacked his clothes and registered for the first four classes of the year, however, Jack departed the next weekend to New York to see his family, now that they'd almost all returned from London—and to meet Frances Ann Cannon, who'd returned from her round-the-world trip with her mother.

Charlie Houghton, his roommate of the year before, met Jack in New York. Houghton had taken a job with Pittsburgh Plate Glass and was himself in "hot pursuit" of Miss Cannon. Houghton even had the advantage of being a Protestant. Both were invited to the Cannons' New York apartment on Sunday, October 1.

Jack had already talked to his sister Kick about his desire to marry Frances Ann, which had intensified during their separation. "Jack is taking out Frances Ann this weekend so we can all hardly wait," Kathleen wrote to her father. Even Mrs. Kennedy was aware of the romance, though whether she realized Jack was on the point of proposing to Frances Ann is debatable. When quoting some of Kathleen's letters in her memoirs forty years later as an example of her children's filial as well as spiritual piety, Rose noted of Frances Ann Cannon only that she was "an attractive girl in whom Jack seemed to be quite interested at that time, and evidently she was interested in him, too. At least Kick seemed to be implying that some 'announcement' was in the offing."

How such an announcement would have been received by Jack's

mother is a tantalizing speculation. Mercifully for Rose, however, the announcement never came. When Jack and his friend Houghton showed up at Miss Cannon's apartment, they were introduced to Frances Ann's new fiancé, John Hersey.

Houghton was astounded. "When she introduced me to Hersey—we thought he was a drip," Houghton recalled bitterly. Speechless, the two Harvard boys eventually made their exit. Years later, still smarting at his rejection, Jack would pretend to friends who enquired that it was he who had rejected Frances Ann. At the time, however, he was as crushed as Houghton was, and when he wrote to his father a week or so later, it was to admit that "Cannon and I have cooled a bit but am looking around sharply for a substitute." This "substitute" would be Kick's Catholic friend, Charlotte McDonnell.

In the meantime, on September 25, the university newspaper, the Harvard *Crimson,* had reported on its front page the merciless bombing of civilians in Warsaw by German planes—"a most dreadful bombardment killing more than 1,000 civilians in the last 24 hours and leaving half the city in ruins and flames." Two days later Warsaw surrendered, and Polish resistance to the four-week German invasion ended with an estimated 60,000 Polish soldiers slaughtered and a further 100,000 wounded.

Jack, who'd been in Warsaw and Danzig only weeks before, might have been expected to feel a sense of outrage or at least pity for Polish losses. However, the views of his defeatist father in the days surrounding the outbreak of war had been no less insidiously demoralizing upon Jack than on Chamberlain. "I can recall distinctly at one stage that Jack thought that the people whose motto then was 'America First' were correct," his friend Torbert Macdonald later confided, "and that we were just going to get, needlessly, entangled in what was basically a European war, or seemed to be at that time. He held these views for a while."

Jack's father was certainly convinced more than ever of the need to pursue peace proposals with Hitler. On September 12, while Jack was still in London and while the outcome of the battle in Poland was still undecided, Ambassador Kennedy had sent Roosevelt a personal plea, which he'd shown to Jack, beginning, "It appears to me that this situation may resolve itself to a point where the President may play the role of savior of the world." Roosevelt called it "the silliest message I have ever received." To Morgenthau the president confided, "Joe has been an appeaser and will always be an appeaser! If Germany and Italy made a good peace offer tomorrow, Joe would start working on the King and his friend, the Queen, and from there on down to get everybody to accept it. . . . He's just a pain in the neck to me." He instructed the State Department to rebuke the London ambassador. As Kennedy himself recalled, the reply came that very evening from Mr. Hull:

It is the wish of President Roosevelt that you be informed, for your strictly confidential information, and in order that you may thereby be guided, without this message being divulged to anyone, that, as long as the conditions which exist at present in Europe continue to exist, the Government of the United States sees no occasion nor opportunity for the American President to initiate any peace move. Any move for peace which the United States Government initiated that would make possible a survival or a consolidation of a regime of force and of aggression would not be supported by the American people.

Far from damping Ambassador Kennedy's attempts at appeasement, however, Hull's cable only inflamed them. Kennedy's realism allowed him to see through Ambassador Bullitt's overconfidence in France's military forces ("talking and acting like a damn fool"), but his own lack of moral fiber blinded him to the futility of trying to do a deal with Hitler.

Kennedy was not alone among millionaires; indeed, Max Beaverbrook, owner of the Daily *Express,* telephoned Kennedy " 'to get your President to see what plans can be worked out to save this catastrophe. All my papers, my money, and everything I have is yours to do with as you wish.' " By the end of September 1939, as Germany and Russia divided up their Polish spoils, Kennedy was moved to defy Hull and write yet again to Roosevelt to beg him to intercede with a peace plan. "A move for peace should somehow be made," he later recalled writing to express his abiding conviction. "England and France could not do it, but smart and bold diplomacy on the part of the President backed by American public opinion . . . might bring peace and still save face for the combatants. The only man in the world who could do this if he wished to do it, I still thought, was the President."

Kennedy evidently now thought of Roosevelt as an American Chamberlain. It was in this renewed plea that Kennedy made his notorious statement as United States ambassador to Britain that "I have yet to talk to any military or naval expert of any nationality who thinks that, with the present and prospective set-up of England and France on one side and Germany and Russia and their potential allies on the other, England has a Chinaman's chance. . . . England and France can't quit whether they would like to or not and I am convinced, because I live here, that England will go down fighting. Unfortunately, I am one who does not believe that is going to do the slightest bit of good in this case." He candidly described Britain as a country past its prime and with no substitute for its prime minister, Neville Chamberlain. "For all Halifax's mystical, Christian character and Churchill's prophecies in respect to Germany, I can't imagine them adequately leading the people out of the valley of the shadow of death." If Roosevelt didn't want "the world's greatest calamity to fall on our friends and subsequently on us," he begged the president to "curb our sentiments and sentimentality and look to our own vital interests. . . . These, to my mind, lie in the Western Hemisphere."

Roosevelt found his ambassador's sniveling, defeatist letter beneath contempt. "I never received a reply," Kennedy related mournfully.

Churchill, equally, would have nothing to do with such appeasement talk. But Churchill was not yet the prime minister, even though "talk of Churchill supplanting Chamberlain was much in the wind," Kennedy later admitted. When Kennedy tackled Halifax on the subject of Churchill succeeding Chamberlain, "Halifax took no comfort in that thought. Churchill's capacity for judgment disturbed him," Kennedy remembered.

> He told me that after a Cabinet meeting a few days before, when Churchill had told of the torpedoing of a Greek ship, talking about the wind shrieking and the high and fearful waves as if he were making a speech to ten thousand people instead of nine Cabinet members, Chamberlain had gently remarked to him [Halifax], "Winston has the art of a showman. I never could do that." Halifax went on, however, to remark that if nothing happened on the peace proposals, complaint about prosecution of the war was certain to increase and the demand for a new Prime Minister would be intensified. . . . We talked about the possible peace proposals and I told Halifax that I was anxious to lay the groundwork in the United States for genuine consideration of such terms as might be suggested. "It would be a calamity," I remarked, "if England felt she could accept them but would not because the United States would tell her that she could not." I was thinking to myself of the growing Jewish influence in the press and in Washington demanding the continuance of the war. . . .

To counteract such influence at home, the ambassador now began to mount his own appeasement campaign in America, sending letter after letter to his contacts at home, bad-mouthing Britain and urging Americans to seek a peace deal with Hitler before it was too late.

Sadly, the first "victim" in this campaign was to be Jack.

A Crimson Editorial

"I am enclosing an editorial I had written in the *Crimson*," Jack loyally reported to his father in October 1939. "The editorial chairman changed it a bit and didn't emphasize some of the things I wanted him to, but nevertheless, I think the idea was good, although we were the only ones to advocate it and though there were quite a few opponents to it."

There were—for the editorial was called, ominously, "Peace in Our Time." In it Jack argued a case even more craven than that of Lindbergh and Chamberlain at the time of the Munich agreement, appealing to fellow students to ignore the blood that had been shed in Poland and claiming that the "President is almost under an obligation to exert every office he possesses to bring about such a peace." Jack further claimed that Germany and England were "both painfully eager to end the fight after the first preliminary round. It would be the saddest event in all history if their peace hopes were frustrated merely because neither is in a position to make direct overtures. Obviously there must be a third power to bring them together, and just as obviously, the President of the United States is in the most logical position to act," he stated. "Mr. Roosevelt's first steps would have to be taken along secret diplomatic channels. He would have to ascertain in advance that there is some common ground for a settlement."

Jack's intentions were sincere. He had hoped Roosevelt would, through his father in London, attempt to secure peace at any price rather than a war in which Britain and France might be destroyed. However, Jack's editorial reflected also his father's defeatism: "There is every possibility—almost a probability—of English defeat," he predicted. "At the best, Britain can expect destruction of all her industrial concentrations and the loss of the tremendous store of invested wealth which she has been amassing ever since Drake brought home the Golden Hind. At the worst she can expect extreme political and economic humiliation. Peace is wisest by far," a "peace based on solid reality."

Jack Kennedy's "solid reality" was, however, no less dishonorable than his father's. "The restoration of the old Poland is an utter impossibility, come what may," Jack argued. "The war would be ended now not in the light of what should be done but in the light of what can be done." Unfortunately, as Jack acknowledged, this would entail "considerable concessions to Hitlerdom. It would mean a puppet Poland, and eventually it would mean a free economic hand for the Nazis in eastern Europe.

There would have to be a redistribution of colonies. But if Hitler could be made to disarm, the victory would be likewise great for the democracies. Hitlerism—gangsterism as a diplomatic weapon—would be gone, and Europe could once more breathe easy. The British and French Empires would be reasonably intact. And there would be peace for our time."

That Hitler would agree to disarm was a hope of almost incredible naïveté, particularly after Jack's travels in Germany. Fortunately for Jack, however, editorials in the *Crimson* were unsigned. It was, after a studiously apolitical career at Harvard, Jack's first major statement on Hitler and appeasement, and one he would soon wish he'd never made.

In a State of Ferment

Even before his *Crimson* article Jack had given "a one hour talk to the YWCA + WMCA which seemed to go very well—however I'm not going to give any more," he promised his father, citing Johnny Burns, a friend of his father who was a Massachusetts judge and who felt "it might lead to trouble. Everyone here is still ready to fight till the last Englishman," Jack added sarcastically, "but most people have a fatalist attitude about America getting in before it is over—which is quite dangerous."

Jack's isolationism reflected his father's. A British diplomat at the Foreign Office in London had already noted in his diary before Jack left London how the ambassador's son opposed Roosevelt's repeal of the U.S. Neutrality Act, on the basis that his father considered Britain too poor to pay for American goods. "Mr. Jack Kennedy, had interjected that even if the Neutrality Act were repealed it would not help us much as we had not got sufficient gold for large purchases in America," the diplomat noted. Writing to his father from Harvard in October 1939, Jack acknowledged that Roosevelt would probably succeed in repealing the Neutrality Act, but only by foul means: "Johnny Burns says he thinks the embargo [against helping any country involved in war, irrespective of who was the aggressor] will be off in a week or so—he figures that the fight [in Congress] petered out due to [Senator] Byrnes' cleverness in stealing away the opponent's thunder."

This was indeed the case, for only by claiming he would never allow America to become involved in the war in Europe could Roosevelt control the isolationist movement, currently burgeoning under men like Lindbergh and, potentially, Joseph P. Kennedy. With extraordinary dexterity, Roosevelt made clear that keeping the war away from American shores depended upon keeping the democracies in Europe going, and that a "cash-and-carry" program would not endanger American neutrality but would actually enhance it. (He also exerted much patronage pressure, from the White House and in Congress, writing to the governor-general of Canada that he was "almost literally walking on eggs.")

By late October, meanwhile, Jack won himself a place on the *Crimson*'s business board—though not the editorial board—and considered himself "quite a seer around here." "That year [in Europe] is really standing me in good stead," he boasted to his father—and even considered that perhaps his editorial in the *Crimson* was behind the recent *New York Times* call for a second, American-sponsored Munich: "Lippmann + Brown have written a couple of editorials half-suggesting peace so maybe an editorial in the *Crimson* may have been the leadoff," Jack congratulated himself.

If Ambassador Kennedy favored peace, however, he had a strange way of showing his faith in it. In London the Swedish ambassador was heard to say that, for all his noble words about peace and prosperity, Kennedy was involved in "funny" dealings on the stock exchange, dealings "capable of being interpreted as affording evidence of anti-British proclivities on his part, as well as, of course, of a desire to make money without being too scrupulous as to the methods employed!" a British diplomat noted. At the British Foreign Office Sir Alexander Cadogan had already written that Kennedy "sees everything from the angle of his own investments." David Scott wished he "could resist the feeling that Mr. Kennedy is thinking all the time about 1) his own financial position, 2) his political future." As an American journalist in London later summed up, "Joe Kennedy was operating the stock market seven ways till Wednesday," a fact confirmed when the British secret service bugged the American embassy's telephones and "discovered that Kennedy was making use of his 'inside information' in maneuvering his own personal investments," his biographer recorded.

In Boston Jack was equally unscrupulous and made no bones about it. He even brought his friend Lem Billings in on his investments, in conjunction with his father's old classmate, Arthur Goldsmith. "Big Arthur Goldsmith + I have been playing the market with pretty good success," Jack wrote to his father, "as we are sticking to aviation stocks. Have now gotten some of Jack Daly's company—Republic Aviation, formerly Leversley. Daly is Chairman of the board and talking big stuff so now I am now a stock holder—Have made a couple of hundred but am proceeding very cautiously."

Jack had last seen Daly, a Hyannis Port neighbor, during a weekend visit on October 21 with Bill Coleman, as he reported to Billings. His original investment with Billings "went to 25 + I sold on Goldie's recommendation + have bought Republic Aviation Co. at 5 on the curb which looks O.K. You make a $20 profit. If you decide you want to take your profit let me know."

Though he'd promised his father to go cautiously, Jack's impetuosity now carried him away as he piled everything he had into Republic Aviation. By the beginning of November, as Roosevelt's repeal of the Neutrality Act reached its conclusion, Jack was begging Billings to "send me the $100 from your stock as I am completely flat and will have to sell to raise some money."

Calling for peace and disarmament stood in somewhat naked contrast to such stock-market speculation in aviation shares. In advocating "peace for our time," Jack had excused his apparent deference to Hitler on the grounds that "to the United States, this solution is the happiest conceivable, regardless of our strong democratic sympathies. It would save us from a probable re-enactment—only on a more terrible scale—of the 1917 debacle. To the world as a whole, such a peace would be a boon from the gods. It would forestall a war which is beyond comprehension in its savage intensity, and which could well presage a return to barbarism"—a sentiment entirely overlooking the barbarity with which the Nazis were already behaving toward German and Austrian Jews, the Czechs, and the Poles.

Thus far, Jack's appeasement views reflected not only his father's but those of the majority of his fellow Harvard students. " 'Peace at any price' seems to be the theme of the numerous student pacifist organizations meeting over Armistice weekend," the *Crimson* reported on November 9, 1939, and the following day a Harvard Student Union poll echoed the result of the infamous Oxford Union debate three years before. Out of eighteen hundred students voting, ninety-five percent were "against immediate American entry" into the war; but "even if England and France were being defeated, 78 per cent of Harvard's undergraduates would oppose United States participation in the European war." A "very narrow margin" favored "an immediate peace conference" with Hitler. "Earlier in the day, 35 students at a Harvard Anti-War Committee peace rally in Sanders Theater followed David Todd in repeating the Oxford pledge, binding themselves 'not to support the United States in any war that it may undertake.' "

Such pacifism did not, however, go unchallenged at Harvard. "The whole campus was in a state of ferment," Donald Thurber recalled. "Movements came and went, swept over the college community. The atmosphere at Harvard in those days was electric. These movements were endlessly debated at Harvard, and I think that Jack Kennedy was very much influenced by the prevailing atmosphere."

Harvard's faculty certainly did not remain silent. Harvard's distinguished president, James B. Conant, was, from the start, outspokenly in favor of aid to Britain and France. "I believe that if these countries are defeated by a totalitarian power, the hope of free institutions as a basis of modern civilization will be jeopardized," he warned in an open letter to Alf Landon, the "leader of the opposition party." "To depart from our historic policy and by so doing handicap those who are fighting for ideals we share, seems to me inconsistent and unwise."

Jack's history and government professors were even more anxious to aid Britain and France. "The members of the Harvard faculty with whom Jack Kennedy was most closely in touch—those teaching his classes, and whom he was meeting in tutorials—they were to a man very interventionist, and not at all isolationist," Donald Thurber later emphasized, recalling that "it was a difficult matter, an extremely difficult matter to get, to find anybody of standing in the government department who would take the pro-Munich side."

Nor did Jack's professors confine their views to the classroom. In the pacifist columns of the *Crimson,* Professor Payson Wild was reported denouncing the outdated Neutrality Act on the grounds that only if Britain and France "hold their own we should be able to stay out of it." Professor Arthur Holcombe, in an address to the Harvard Student Union, claimed it was "impossible for the United States to be absolutely neutral in the war" and that America "would have to decide on which side to throw its influence." Professor Bruce Hopper voiced his concern about Japan's "dream of a new order in Asia," while Professor Elliott felt that "a truce at present would consolidate the Italian and German position in Europe," which "would be disastrous for this country." Like Hopper, Elliott also warned of the threat from Japan. "The greatest threat to the position of this country lies in possible action by the Japanese navy in the Pacific," he prophesied, "where it is essential that the United States maintain a balance of power in the Far East."

Hitherto, despite his father's prominence, Jack had studied government and international relations in a wholly theoretical environment, removed from the fog of political battle. Now, however, with war having broken out in Europe, Jack was intellectually and morally trapped. "He was genuinely interested in political problems and in international affairs," Payson Wild recalled. "His experience abroad—it was very stimulating, and it gave him a basis for knowledge he otherwise wouldn't have had. He could be very concrete and very specific about issues because he'd been there, he'd met people, and he knew firsthand what the issues were."

Jack, having been "indoctrinated" by his father and having issued his premature call for accommodation of Hitler, now belatedly began to listen carefully to his professors' views. The *Crimson* pulpit, like the YMCA/YWCA, was quietly abandoned. By November 4 Jack's name was already off the business board, and his questioning turned inward.

"Have been doing quite a bit of work as my courses are really interesting this year. . . . Am taking a course under Prof. Friedrich which is very interesting. I am still incognito but expect to go up and shake his palm and start discussing what a big impression he made on you when those papers start getting marked," he joked to his father.

It was Jack's sense of humor, in fact, that saved him from his brother's fate. He was not a doctrinaire political stalwart by heart, and his brief appearance in the *Crimson* was out of character. Looking back over Jack's life, Professor Holcombe later remarked that "the style of the man was formed while he was quite young. . . . He was never a crusader, as some men are. You can pick some crusaders out of a class, while they're still undergraduates; they have that commitment to act upon an idea, which to them is decisive of their behavior. That wasn't the challenge to which he [Jack] responded."

This matter of commitment would become a bone of contention in the years to come, as Jack's acolytes sought to package and present him as a liberal Democrat. Holcombe saw much deeper. "He wasn't interested in causes," Holcombe correctly described. Even Jack's party allegiance was "settled for him. He was born a Democrat. Otherwise, I don't think that he would have found much reason to prefer one party over the other."

It was this absence of "missionary" zeal which, in Professor Payson Wild's recollection, made it "preposterous to say that anybody had thoughts of his ever being President" while at Harvard. He lacked his brother's firmness of purpose and driving ambition. He was still unclear what he wished to do in life. His problem was not of talent, but of a superabundance, allied with a lack of direction, as at school. "Everybody knew that he was going to make a great success of whatever he turned his attention to," Professor Holcombe recalled.

For the moment, however, Jack concentrated on his courses, and on women. "I seem to be doing better with the girls so I guess you are doing your duty over there," he wisecracked in a letter to his father, whose prestigious London post still gave Jack a certain social cachet, and "so before resigning give my social career a bit of consideration. . . . Am taking Kick's friend Charlotte Macdonald [*sic*] out to the Princeton game which will be my first taste of a Catholic girl so will be interested to see how it goes."

Romance was not on Jack's mind, however, in his nocturnal dealings with the second sex. "Get something that likes lovin'," he ordered Billings when setting up a weekend's fun at the Cape, "preferably therefore not Kick this weekend." "I went to N.Y. last weekend for Thanksgiving," he reported in November "—and had quite a time. Met that model Georgia Carrol who is really something—also met some other good stuff."

Once again Jack was in his element, enjoying both "good stuff" as well as innocent debutantes who conferred at least social, if not sexual, favors. "Harvard as you probably know took quite a beating," he wrote after Yale overpowered Harvard in the annual intervarsity football match. "Torb played awfully well + finally made a touchdown—but Harvard was fumbling all over the field," an attribute he ascribed also to "Evil Eben [who] went to the Catholic dance where he figured prominently. He seemed to take quite a shine to Charlotte the Harlot Macdonald [*sic*]," he kidded. "I had her up this last weekend and she is really damn good fun."

Behind the fun, however, loomed the specter of war, though whether Jack would be well enough to participate, if America became involved, was another matter. His car accident in France had aggravated his already unstable back, requiring him to wear a special corset for the rest of his life. He also took a lot of medication. Ben Smith recalled how "we used to kid each other about our pills. Between the two of us, we had quite a collection." There were other therapies, too. "Took my first liver injection today," Jack wrote to his father in November, "and hope they work." He was frenetically busy "making up work" that he'd missed during his absence in England earlier in the year, and which "has to be finished before Thanksgiving. Have made up most of it, but it is hard work and get it very solidly and still do the daily work."

It was at this moment that Jack received a letter from his brother's friend Tom Schriber, who'd gone into the life insurance business. "I had insured Joe Jr.," Schriber later recalled, "and I was trying to get Jack to take out some insurance, saying the war is coming, better do it now, before they put a lot of restrictions up, in policies, etc., and I knew Jack had had this physical problem, this blood problem, but I still thought that we might be able to clear it up and get the coverage on him all right. So I got this letter from Jack, it isn't dated, but it would have to be about 1939, and it just says:

> Dear Shrive:
>
> Thanks for your letter. As I am now probably the best potential investment Northwestern [Mutual Insurance] has ever had, and as I am just money in the bank for you . . . , I will let your company be the lucky one, although all the other companies are fighting to get me.
>
> I'm in a bit of a quandary though, as on the one hand, if there is a war, I would just as soon be one of the last to go, due to my sensational health record at Choate. And yet, I would like to get insured in case I get killed. After I've consulted with Dr. Jordan, my doctor here, exactly what my status is as far as being a potential draft

dodger, and also as a prospective Northwestern gold mine, I will shoot the records at you. Hope to see you next time I'm in New York.

Best,
Jack K.

The Heritage of the Nineteenth Century

Jack's four courses in the fall of 1939—Principles of Politics, Elements of International Law, Comparative Politics (Bureaucracy, Constitutional Government and Dictatorship), and Modern Imperialism—were the most challenging of his whole career at Harvard. In consultation with his tutor, Bruce Hopper, Jack also finalized the subject for his honors thesis, to be written in lieu of one of his second half-year courses beginning in February. "I am taking as my thesis for honors England's Foreign Policy since 1931," Jack explained in advance to his father, "and will discuss the class influence in England."

Years later historians and writers would misread Jack's difficult handwriting and assume he'd intended to write about English foreign policy since 1731. Jack's interest, however, was clearly the 1930s, not the 1730s, and the best starting point for his investigation, he felt, would be Ramsay MacDonald's formation of a bipartisan national government in 1931. Though Rose Kennedy had only the remotest knowledge of Jack's Harvard courses, she had no hesitation in later ascribing Jack's choice of topic to his affinity for things British:

He had a Boston accent which is very much akin to the British, and then he responded to the British love of culture and literature and all that sort of thing . . . Most of the people in government circles and most of the people who had big houses and who entertained over there, were people whose families had been in government, and they had not only interest in government, in history and in politics, but they had had them for generations and so they were probably more cultured than the people were here, where most, or many, had started in very humble beginnings. And I think Jack responded to all that because he did like literature, and he did appreciate it, and then he was interested in government, and of course, he did enjoy seeing all the beautiful homes, because they were connected more or less with history. If you went away for the weekend, you'd see a house that

had been there for hundreds of years, like the Devonshires'. . . .
There were different souvenirs of the years they had spent in government, in those houses, and all those things Jack responded to, and
so he did enjoy himself [there] as did we all, I think; and then of
course it was more or less akin to Boston, because Boston is in a
great part British, the people there are of British-Irish heritage, much
more than they are in New York, for instance.

Rose's rambling reminiscence, recorded after Jack's death, contained
much that was true. Certainly no other student of government in Jack's
year undertook a thesis on a British topic. Subjects like "Electrical Utilities in Maine and Their Regulation" or "The Boston Registry of Motor
Vehicles" were more typical—even "East Chicago, Indiana, as a Problem
in Metropolitan Government." By contrast, Jack's choice of English
foreign policy did indeed demonstrate his fascination with Britain, from
its primitive plumbing to its social stratification, though he had no intention of writing anything controversial or extended. An average honors
thesis ran to sixty pages, twice the length of a term paper. Almost flip-
pantly, at the end of October 1939, he wrote to his father that he would
"get in touch with Jim Seymour [secretary to Ambassador Kennedy in
London] if I want him to send me stuff."

It was the quality of insight into contemporary history he then derived
from the courses of professors Elliott, Wild, Holcombe, Hopper, Friedrich, and Emerson, along with the prodding of his tutors, that prompted
Jack to think bigger. Of Dr. Payson Wild, Torbert Macdonald later
remarked, "I got to know and respect him very much, and so did Jack,
and I do know that he played a direct part in influencing Jack's intellectual ability, because he would needle Jack in my presence about why he
wasn't more interested in the same fashion that his brother Joe was. . . .
A very capable and a very good man, and very understanding of Jack's
nature. Even then, I felt that he was needling Jack on purpose, to sort of
light a fire under Jack, to get him going to where he would live up to his
intellectual capabilities."

Now the fire began to ignite. "He seemed to blossom once Joe was gone
and feel more secure himself and to be more confident as his grades
improved," Payson Wild recalled. "His grades had improved in his senior
year to a B+ average, and he was then eligible to write an honors thesis
. . . really for me as his tutor and for Bruce Hopper, who was associate
professor in international relations."

Jack's surviving case study in international law for Dr. Payson Wild in
October 1939 certainly showed his growing intellectual ability. "I've always had this feeling that he was a far deeper person than the public, or
many, give him credit for," Wild recorded later. "He genuinely was an

intellectual. . . . He was genuinely interested in political problems and international affairs."

From his journeys across Europe Jack brought to his studies an engaged curiosity about relations between nation states—why they act as they do and how such relations can legally be regulated, both in peacetime and in war. He had assured the American survivors of the *Athenia* that they would be safe under international law once aboard a neutral, U.S. vessel. Several hundred other survivors of the *Athenia,* however, had been plucked from the sea and had, Jack knew, been taken aboard the U.S. merchant ship *City of Flint.* Such neutrality had not, however, protected them; indeed their trials had proved far worse than those of the bedraggled survivors who landed at Glasgow, for the *City of Flint* was seized by the German battleship *Deutschland,* then taken by a German prize crew to Murmansk and finally to Norway before finally being released.

These and other recent cases gave Jack special insight into the real-life dramas behind the stately mask of international law. His case study for Professor Wild, examining whether it is a breach of neutrality if, in war, neutral pilots guide ships of belligerent nations through their waters, was argued with dexterity and precision. For his paper, covering also the problem of broadcasting and air flights, Wild gave Jack a B +, though he never imagined, as he corrected this and a second paper on the rights of submarines to attack neutral ships carrying munitions to an enemy power in a so-called war zone ("There is a question even whether the war zone is legal," Jack commented in his summary), that his pupil would one day be ordering a naval blockade off Cuba that would bring the United States and Russia to the brink of nuclear war.

It was Jack's performance in his international-law course that suggested to Wild that Jack might choose "to go to law school" after Harvard, just as also his later confidence in Jack Kennedy entering high office stemmed from the "conviction that he really did have ability to think deeply and in theoretical terms." For all his affection for Joe Jr., Dr. Wild felt that the older brother was, by comparison, "kind of slap dash. He would not put the time into the reading, and he was not as interested in discussing it as thoroughly as Jack."

Certainly once Jack's interest was aroused, his curiosity would not rest until, as his friend Rip Horton recalled, "he had completely absorbed and mastered" a subject. Jack's reams of notes in the fall of 1939 testify to his fascination with international law, both in its quirkiness (he noted with amusement, for instance, on December 12, that at international conferences, seating had traditionally been "alphabetically in French," thus leading to a change in terminology as the United States altered the name of its embassy to the "American Embassy. Thus we get to sit up near the front row") and in the importance of law in international politics. Do peace treaties have a binding status in international law? Does international law recognize treaties signed under duress, such as the Versailles Treaty? And if participating nations refuse to alter the terms of such treaties, how can nations seek redress other than by war—forcible redress which is then ratified by international law? "Once war begins it is legal and the treaties made at the end of that war (are) valid and legal," Jack noted, adding tartly, "You can't steal a horse, but if you steal it, it is legal."

Jack's study of fascism, communism, bureaucracy, and constitutional democracy under Professor Friedrich was equally challenging. Some of Friedrich's points were jejune, as indicated by Jack's course notes to the effect that "Soviet Russia wants no foreign land" only weeks before Stalin's unprovoked invasion of Finland on November 30, 1939, but, on the whole, the class enabled Jack to gain a perspective on current world political creeds that appealed to the paradox of his intellect: his engaged detachment.

Irony was the punctuating mark of Jack's curiosity. Stalin's "frequent speeches to inspire love for the fatherland" sat oddly beside the dictator's penalties for those who tried to leave this beloved fatherland, namely death and confiscation of property. "Representative government in Russia is now a mere caricature," Jack noted.

> Since Lenin's death, the government has, under Stalin, become a privileged bureaucracy—no longer the old organization of workers and peasants. Marx had no such idea as this for his Socialism. He held that under Socialism "the state as an instrument of compulsion" would "die away," and that this would begin as soon as the industries of a country should become socialized. Yet that happened in Russia over ten years ago; meanwhile, the state has become more powerful and intolerant than ever.
>
> Russia is no[t] Socialism now because it is as much a society of classes as any capitalistic country ever was. . . . The "Moscow Trial" sought to prove that Stalin's life was endangered by political henchmen of Trotsky. Every one of the defendants deprecated himself with amazing candor, said Trotsky was behind it, and glorified Stalin. Then all were taken out and shot. The explanation to this may be that Stalin had secretly promised pardons to the defendants if they would glorify him and deprecate Trotsky—and then went back on his bargain. At any rate, each of these defendants had been an ardent Bolshevik under the Lenin government; their extinction can mean nothing else but the winding up of the experiment of Russian Socialism.

Such observations led Jack, under Bruce Hopper's guidance, to a closer analysis of Russian communism as well as German and Italian fascism. Both Soviet and Fascist systems represented "an attack on *individualism* in the sense of personal dignity and freedom which is the heritage of the 19th century in the west," subordinating the "individual to the collectivity."

Though he would be an avid reader all his life, Jack's intensive courses in twentieth-century isms—capitalism, communism, fascism, imperialism, militarism, nationalism—were probably the most concentrated academic study he would ever undertake. Josephine Fulton, the wife of the Winthrop House janitor, later recalled how absorbed he became.

> I didn't know him in school—the only way I knew Jack is I'd be going up to the store and he'd be coming down the other side and he'd have his hands full of books. I never saw anybody with him, always his hands full of books, going, going, going, and I'd holler to him, "Where's your hat?" That was the thing: coming down the street, no hat on him, and snow. He never wore a hat. He was busy all the time. He never had time to talk to people. . . . The only time I saw Jack was when he'd come down to use the phone. Or a call'd come in for him. He didn't get many calls. One time he wanted to use the phone and I said, "Jack, where's your hat?"
>
> He had his overcoat on and everything. And he said, "Jo, I can't wear a hat. I have to keep my head clear!"
>
> In the spring, we'd be in bed, I could hear Jack coming in, we'd have our window open about that much, and he'd have his window wide open, and then you could hear him. His typewriter would go a mile a minute. Yeah, he typed himself. I'd say to my husband, "Jack's home. Listen to him." He used to come home at eleven o'clock, twelve o'clock at night. It would be all quiet around there and you'd hear his typewriter going a mile a minute.

From London Jack had returned a confirmed isolationist, like the majority of Harvard undergraduates. The achievement of his Harvard professors in the final months of 1939 was to bring Jack Kennedy's sometimes facile intelligence to look more deeply into the forces sweeping Europe and the world, as well as the sad history of the democracies when confronted by such isms. In a thirty-five-page paper on the League of Nations, tracing British liberal and conservative attitudes from 1919 to 1938, Jack was able to explore the difference between idealism and realism in British interwar politics, culminating in Britain's "failure to utter one word of disapproval" when Hitler annexed Austria, and in Chamberlain's fluttering piece of paper after Munich. Great Britain's policy of "localizing the danger spots has seemed to mean giving to Germany what twenty million people gave their lives to prevent in the four years following 1914," Jack remarked acidly. "It is undeniably a policy flowing from an isolationist source."

The time was now approaching for Jack to examine that source in depth.

To Run or Not to Run

British Conservatives, Jack concluded in his League of Nations paper, had failed to take seriously the menace of Hitler because they were "a propertied class which has never entertained any sympathy for [Russia] since it became Bolshevist. . . . Fear of an invasion of Communist ideas has prevented England from collaborating with Russia in international affairs," and had prompted the British upper classes—epitomized by Lord Lothian (who had since become the British ambassador to Washington)—to believe, incredibly, that "the sooner Germany completes its unification and the sooner her grievances are rectified, the sooner will Hitler collapse and Europe resettle."

"The British policy towards the League," Jack felt, had been "justified from the point of view of immediate national interests: the stabilization of the Commonwealth and 'peace in our time.' But from the point of view of the new international order [with] which England wholeheartedly professed to be in complete accord, the British League policy has been a denial of justice to weak states and a betrayal to the hopes" of those peoples, particularly the Czechs, who had glimpsed democracy in the interwar years.

Unquestionably Jack's sympathies were shifting away from those of his father, who arrived back in America on extended leave on December 7, 1939. Before leaving London, Kennedy had received a parting message from King George VI, with whom he'd lunched prior to the Russian attack on Finland. Lord Chatfield, Kennedy had noticed at the state opening of Parliament that morning, had

> carried the crown like a cigarette girl carries her tray and, when I commented on this later to the King, he said he thought it was not the real crown because it was too big. The Queen, however, assured him that it was, for it had to be "dug out," she said, at Windsor, where the jewels now were. . . . The King looked far from well. His face was thin and drawn and he stuttered more than ever. The main

course was hare. I tried a small piece and the Queen, noticing my hesitancy, said, "It's hare and, perhaps, you don't like it. After all, it's an acquired taste like your terrapin. Neither the King nor I could manage that [in America]. There was one dinner we had when that man who practically had his head on my shoulder all the time kept urging me to eat it. You know who I mean—the Speaker."

"Bankhead?" I asked.

"Yes," the King broke in, "Tallulah Bankhead's father, you know."

"I'm sorry, Madam, I don't like it," I said, speaking of the hare.

"What an honest man," she laughed. "Will you have some pheasant?"

The pheasant came with a purée of brussel sprouts and potato. I staggered through. We talked naturally of the war and of America.

When Kennedy argued against America sending troops, the Queen remarked, "That is what I thought you would say," and expressed her disappointment in Lindbergh's anti-British sayings. "I stood up for Lindbergh," Kennedy recalled. "He is honest, I said, and not pro-Nazi."

The king asked about Roosevelt, and whether the president would run for a third term. "I could give him no answer," Kennedy related. "There was little serious talk that afternoon but underneath the conversation there seemed to me a tone different than before. Both of their Majesties knew that England was fighting for her life and for her Empire and that their personal fate hung on the outcome."

This was a harsh comment. George VI had not sought the crown, nor had even been asked his opinion about succeeding his brother King Edward VIII. Were his primary concern the preservation of his crown, he could far more easily have clung to it by an accommodation with Hitler than by standing by his government and accepting the burden of war. For this very reason, in fact, King George dreaded the return of his elder brother, now demoted to duke of Windsor, with his nefarious American wife, both of whom had visited Hitler and were sympathetic to the Nazis. The next day, to reinforce in Kennedy's mind the commitment of the British monarchy, King George VI wrote to Kennedy to make certain the American ambassador was in no doubt that the British monarchy, as opposed to the duke of Windsor, stood four-square behind the British government and Parliament in prosecuting the war. "As I see it, the U.S.A., France and the British Empire are the three really free peoples in the world, and two of these great democracies are now fighting against all that we three countries hate and detest, Hitler and his Nazi regime and all that it stands for. . . . But what of the future? The British Empire's mind is made up. I leave it at that."

To this, Ambassador Kennedy had sent back the most cynical of replies: "The people of America, like the peoples of the British Empire, abhor war. They have watched, with sympathetic interest, the attempts of your Government to find a peaceful solution for the tragic situation which has now burst into open conflict. The people of America believe that we should remain at peace until and unless our vital interests are at stake, just as they feel the people of Britain took up arms only when their vital interests were menaced," he maintained, ignoring the tragic fate of Poland and Britain's belated guarantee. "It is inevitable that, with memories of the last war's disheartening fruit vividly in mind, the American people should be firm in their purpose to avoid entry into warfare in Europe."

The market bear, celebrated on Wall Street for selling short, was now selling out. Before leaving London, Kennedy visited Churchill at the Admiralty. "The future of the world is going to rest with England, the United States, Russia and Japan," were Churchill's prophetic words. As only Britain was at war among these nations, Kennedy snorted that Churchill might be right, "but that is not the line-up today." He then departed via Paris and Lisbon for the United States—and the question of whether to stand for nomination as United States president.

Kennedy was the first American ambassador to leave his post in Europe. The press mobbed him at Port Washington, not only to find out his assessment of the situation in Europe, but to discover his own political plans. Kennedy, however, needed to know Roosevelt's and those of other Democratic presidential contenders. Countering reporters' questions with half-hearted support for a third Roosevelt term, he then spent one day with his family at Bronxville—his first in a year—and rushed to Washington to see Roosevelt.

"My appointment with the President was at the unheard-of early hour of nine in the morning. I barely had time to clean up after a night on the train before I was ushered up to his bedroom. He was propped up in bed eating his breakfast and making his own coffee in a glass container. He looked terribly tired. . . . I went over my experiences and my observations and gave him a picture which he dubbed 'bearish.' I agreed but I said that was the picture as I saw it. . . . I then told him of my statement [to reporters] on the third term and he said, 'No, Joe, I can't do it, but we'll talk of that later.' "

Kennedy had gotten what he wanted. But if Roosevelt wouldn't run, who would? Kennedy immediately went to the State Department and sounded out Hull. "It struck me then that he was not wholly in sympathy with the group around Roosevelt. He brushed off my mention of his name as a candidate for the Presidency but in such a way that he impressed me with the fact that he was a candidate."

Later that day Kennedy returned to the White House to press Roosevelt further. " 'What about this third term,' I asked. 'You'll have to run.' 'Joe,' he replied, 'I can't. I'm tired. I can't take it. . . . I just won't go for a third term unless we are in war.' " Then, remembering to whom he was talking, the president quickly added, "Even then I'll never send an army over. We'll help them, but with supplies."

Kennedy asked the president about Hull's possible candidacy. Roosevelt dismissed him as a procrastinator.

"Well, if Hull won't do, whom have you got?" Kennedy asked.

"Lots of them," Roosevelt replied. "We've got a better group of young men than England has. There's Carmody who is doing a good job. There's McNutt who is a go-getter. . . . There's Harry Hopkins. He's gained sixteen pounds and he hasn't got cancer despite what the Mayo's said. There's Frank Murphy. . . . There's Bob Jackson. He's a fine fellow and very able." Roosevelt extolled Bill Douglas, then finally reached Kennedy. "There's yourself—"

This was the green light Kennedy was seeking. But if the president considered Kennedy a good potential Democratic candidate for the presidency, why had he "started his personal correspondence with Churchill," Kennedy asked, still sore at the way the president had taken to using secret naval codes that Kennedy could not break as well as sealed envelopes in the diplomatic pouch. His question elicited Roosevelt's immortal remark about Churchill: "I have always disliked him, since the time I went to England in 1918. He acted like a stinker at a dinner I attended, lording it all over us. Birkenhead finally made him stop and behave properly." But, Roosevelt added, "I'm giving him attention now because there is a strong possibility that he will become the Prime Minister and I want to get my hand in now. I'm perfectly willing to help the British all I can, but I won't let them play me for a sucker. All this can help when the time comes." These were, Kennedy realized, scarcely the words of a man who proposed to leave the White House the next year.

Kennedy was alarmed, knowing that Churchill would do everything in his power, if he became prime minister, to inveigle America into joining the Allies. Indeed Kennedy later claimed to have noted in his diary, on learning of the Roosevelt-Churchill private correspondence, that "I just don't trust him [Churchill]. He always impressed me that he was willing to blow up the American Embassy and say it was the Germans if it would get the United States in."

Kennedy didn't trust President Roosevelt either. Although Roosevelt's parting words were to "get the rest you came back for," Kennedy traveled instead straight to Boston, where he saw Joe Jr. and Jack, told them he might run for president if Roosevelt declined to do so, and, to Jack's discomfort, proceeded to give his first campaign speech.

Source Material

"The talk that I gave was extemporaneous," Kennedy later recalled of the address he gave in his old East Boston church, "and it re-emphasized the points I had made at the press conference when I landed. I pointed out that America's sporting instinct might well incline her to resent an unfair and immoral thing but that this was not America's war. There was no reason, economic, financial or social to justify the United States in going to war. 'As you love America,' I told the audience, 'don't let anything that comes out of any country in this world make you believe that you can make the situation one whit better by getting into the war. There's no place in the fight for us. It is going to be bad enough as it is.'"

These were strong words for an official representative of the American government to Britain, without first checking with the State Department. Kennedy, however, had become a law unto himself and was testing the political waters. Roosevelt "had said that I should return to London as quickly as possible after Christmas," Kennedy later admitted. To delay his return he therefore paid Dr. Lahey, his Boston doctor, to draw up and send to the president a report recommending "that at a minimum I should take two months of rest before going back to England."

Armed with Dr. Lahey's note, Kennedy traveled to Palm Beach where, as during the previous winter, he surrounded himself with conspirators, advisers, appeasers, cronies, and guests including Arthur Krock, Bill Douglas, Lord Lothian, and Sumner Welles. "Although I had made it clear to the press that I intended to support Mr. Roosevelt for a third term," Kennedy candidly admitted later, "the President's hesitation to declare himself on this issue kept the press's interest in other candidates in the ranks of the Democratic Party who might be presidential timber."

Jack, spending Christmas at Palm Beach with his family, was now reexposed to the defeatist prognostications of his father as well as his cabal of appeasers. At a time when Jack was about to undertake an in-depth study of British appeasement, however, the presence of the British ambassador, Lord Lothian, was a godsend, particularly when Lothian kindly offered to help Jack further if he cared to stop by at the British embassy on his way back to Harvard.

Lothian's house parties at Blickling Hall in Suffolk had matched Lady Astor's Cliveden Set for gossip, isolationist sentiment, and pro-German views in the 1930s, and he was at pains to paint a sympathetic picture of British appeasement policies when Jack in due course took him up on his offer. "It was our talk that day last January that started me out on the job," Jack would later write to thank Lothian, "and I am most appreciative of your kindness to me at that time."

Armed with Lothian's personal insights into the major figures of the 1930s in Britain, Jack threw himself into his project back at Harvard. He was determined to show just how the most powerful empire in the world, boasting the most powerful navy, had in the space of a mere generation become so enfeebled that its very survival was now threatened.

Though later writers would read into Jack's fourth-year thesis personal motives, even a family "plot" (masterminded by Joseph Kennedy) to excuse appeasement, the truth is that neither Jack's father nor his brother had anything to do with the thesis once it began. Even the Harvard faculty had little to contribute. A veritable battle was raging in the department over the position and appointment of assistant professors, and as Hopper recalled, Jack "took advantage of this extraordinary opportunity" to go his own way. Hopper was "used as first audience" each week at their tutorial meeting. "It was his *own* production," Professor Hopper later explained. "I didn't have much to do with the English, but asked for [full] documentation"—an expectation which could not be met from Harvard's Widener Library alone. Thus on January 11, 1940, Jack anxiously cabled to his father's press attaché in London, James Seymour:

SEND IMMEDIATELY PAMPHLETS, ETC, CONSERVATIVE, LABOR, LIBERAL, PACIFIST ORGANIZATIONS FOR APPEASEMENT THESIS DISCUSSING FACTORS INFLUENCING PRO CON 1932 TO 1939 STOP SUGGEST LASKEY [*sic*] AS REFERENCE ALREADY HAVE TIMES, MANCHESTER GUARDIAN, HANSARD THANKS, JACK KENNEDY.

Seymour, despite the London blackout and the world war in which Britain was engaged, swung into action. HURRYING MATERIAL WRITING, REGARDS, he wired back from the American embassy, and telegraphed instantly to Laski in Kensington to PLEASE TELEPHONE ME EARLIEST CONVENIENCE AMERICAN EMBASSY GOVERNOR 4111 REQUEST AMBASSADOR'S SON.

Individuals and organizations fell over themselves to comply, never questioning Jack's interest or slant, anxious only to be friendly to America's absent representative in London at a time when American help was vital to Britain's survival. By return on January 11 Seymour responded to Jack that "a word from your father had already sent me scratching to find you some source material, but your cable prevented my duplicating your other things—Hansard etc. I have promises from the Conservative, Labor and Liberal organizations . . . bearing on the subject. The Labor Organization told me also that the New York Public Library has a file of all their publications and that Arthur Greenwood has a book coming out

soon with a chapter or so devoted to the question of 'appeasement.' "
Seymour promised to send this in publisher's proof, pronto.

> I am checking with Chatham House and Oxford University Press.
> The latter has nothing on the subject among their recent pamphlets
> or books and Chatham House is to let me know. The latter's organi-
> zation has been evacuated to Oxford. Likewise London School of
> Economics has evacuated to Cambridge, but I reached Laski by wire
> and he . . . recommended a book by E. H. Carr on British Foreign
> Policy which he said covered the last ten years and would give you
> material as well as excellent references. The book—together with two
> others that may have something worthwhile—I've ordered and
> they'll be in my hands tomorrow. Also Laski said he would try to
> think of some other valuable sources and let me know within a few
> days. I shall follow him up. Also I have a couple of booksellers
> investigating for other publications on the subject and I am making
> a survey of articles and books listed at the British Museum Reading
> Room.

Seymour's services were to be invaluable, Laski's less so. No one had
ever compiled such a work investigating the origin and course of appeasement in Britain. Apart from his recommendation of Carr's forthcoming
book on foreign policy, Laski came up with only one further suggestion,
a week later, writing to Seymour that "on reflection, I think the two most
useful books Jack Kennedy could read for the statement of the 'anti-
appeasement case' are: Vigilantes. Inquest on Peace (Gollancz). Vigilantes. Road to War (Gollancz). They are admirably documented."

For most Britons, the advent of war was simply too shattering for them
to waste time investigating the peace it had replaced. For Americans,
however, the story of Britain's journey from isolationism to interventionism was of fearsome relevance, and in this respect it was the modest and
unassuming James Seymour who made it possible for Jack to transform
an ordinary fourth-year undergraduate honors paper into a work of
original and topical scholarship. Seymour had attended Harvard from
1913 to 1917 and was a devoted alumnus, working for the college as an
administrator, then editing Joseph Kennedy's *The Story of Films* and
working as a scriptwriter, director, and producer in Hollywood before
joining Ambassador Kennedy's staff in London.

A courageous, imperturbable, sensitive man, Seymour held the French
Croix de Guerre from World War I. He loved poetry, the theater, and the
arts, and would remain in London not only through the Blitz but for the
rest of his life. "We have had our share of cold and fog which has not
improved our lovely black-out," he wrote to Jack.

London is a different and almost incredibly beautiful place in these conditions. I get a rare kick out of walking the empty streets—moonlight especially makes it lovely. . . . The spirit of the people is marvelous—firm, serious and courageous, ready I feel to face any sacrifice or privation to achieve the one and only end they are willing to accept.

You probably know more about world affairs than I—but you may not know one thing, that your cheery presence is really greatly missed here. I mean it. Good luck to you—and here's hoping to hear from you before I see you. Ever, Jim.

A Very Foul Specimen

Meanwhile, Ambassador Kennedy's Boston speech had aroused a sort of shocked dismay in the British press. In diplomatic and social circles word had gotten around that he was predicting Britain would be "badly thrashed" by Hitler's armies, that he'd begged Roosevelt to reconsider a peace conference with Hitler, and that he was prepared to support a third term for Roosevelt only if the president kept America out of war. This prompted the Foreign Office's chief American adviser in London to minute that "Mr. Kennedy is a very foul specimen of double-crosser and defeatist. He thinks of nothing but lining his own pockets. I hope the war will at least see the elimination of his type. I suppose we will have to have him back, but once back he will be estimated at his true value."

Would Kennedy return to London, however? Everything hung on Roosevelt's intentions, and, to a lesser extent, the machinations of the postmaster general, James Farley. Kennedy later explained:

Farley in his ambition to become the Party's candidate had become a violent opponent of the third term and by generating opposition of this character was hoping to corral sufficient anti-Roosevelt sentiment to make impossible the President's renomination at the coming National Convention. . . . Consequently, Farley entered the Massachusetts primaries in early February to secure delegates pledged to him for the National Convention. Farley's entry into the Massachusetts race on February 10 precipitated an immediate and widespread public demand that I too should become a candidate. Due to the persistency of this demand, I announced early on the morning of

February 13th that I would make a statement on the subject that evening.

Kennedy's cousin, Joe Kane, had already filed nomination papers for Kennedy's candidacy in Massachusetts, but Kennedy was too shrewd to run without first knowing Roosevelt's plans. There thus followed another meeting with the president in Washington. To Kennedy's astonishment, Roosevelt brought up the Massachusetts situation himself. "Why don't you run in Massachusetts, Joe?" Roosevelt said. "You can easily win over Jim and he shouldn't have invaded your home state anyway."

The ambassador was caught between two stools. His cousin in Boston had told him he would never be forgiven by the Democratic party if he opposed Roosevelt—that any political aspirations he might have would be sundered (as would happen with Farley). Everything thus depended on Roosevelt, "but I could see that he had not resolved for himself the question as to whether he himself would run for a third term," Kennedy related.

Roosevelt's hesitation proved masterly. Like Hull and other potential presidential contenders, Kennedy remained wholly at the president's mercy. Meanwhile "Farley's efforts to force [the president] to resolve it and retire from the scene were clearly annoying him," Kennedy recalled, hence Roosevelt's suggestion that Kennedy scotch Farley's bid, with the added possibility of Kennedy being defeated while trying to do so. "I was rather surprised by his statement but I made no comment on it other than to tell him flatly that I had no intention of running." At the promised press conference that afternoon he reluctantly announced that, as things stood, he would not be a contender for the presidential nomination but would return to his post in London.

It was about time that he did. On February 24, 1940, the ambassador left New York on the *Manhatten,* bound for Genoa. Clare Boothe Luce was also on board, and it is said she and Kennedy became lovers. "Her gay conversation was a contrast to the greyness of sea and sky," Kennedy recalled. Impressed by his prognostications of certain Nazi victory in Europe, Clare began to put pressure on her husband, as publisher of *Life* and *Time* magazines, to clamor for Kennedy's official recall to America and possibly even convert him to the colors of the rising Republican candidate, Wendell Willkie.

Kennedy's moment of glory was fading fast, however. The contender manqué was leaving America more distrusted by the U.S. State Department than ever, having spent three months absent from his London post in the midst of a European war. Worse still, he was returning to an England in which, thanks to his widely quoted pronouncements in America, he was now deeply unwelcome. Harold Nicolson, Conservative MP, noted in his diary on February 29 that Vansittart, at the Foreign Office, was "very worried by the return of Joseph Kennedy, the American Ambassador. He says that Kennedy has been spreading it abroad in the U.S.A. that we shall certainly be beaten and he will use his influence here to press for a negotiated peace. In this he will have the assistance of the old appeasers." *The Spectator* subjected Kennedy to perhaps the most stinging attack ever inflicted upon a returning American ambassador. "He will be welcomed, of course, by the bankers and the isolationists, by the knights and the baronets. He will be welcomed by the shiver-sisters of Mayfair and by the wobble-boys of Whitehall. He will be welcomed by the Peace Pledge Union, the Christian Pacifists, the followers of Dr. Buchman, the friends of Herr von Ribbentrop, the Nürembergers, the Munichois, Lord Tavistock and the *disjecta membra* of former pro-Nazi organizations. . . . Few envoys, on returning to their post, can have received a welcome of such embarrassing variety."

Kennedy was well aware of likely British reactions to his outspokenness. On the train from Italy to Paris he met Sumner Welles, Roosevelt's latest fact-finding emissary to Europe. Kennedy urged Welles to consider not Hitler, but anyone who wished to stand up to Hitler, as a warmonger. Moreover, when he landed at Heston and faced British reporters he would retract none of the statements he'd made in America. "Those remarks, which I believe correctly summarized American thinking at that time, were not received graciously by the British press," he related. "In fact the press lashed out at me quite bitterly. Beverly Baxter, writing in the *Sunday Graphic* . . . bitterly criticized me for not telling the American public what I believed the British war aims to be. Others reiterated Baxter's criticism and it soon became evident that a coolness had developed towards me in those circles, official and otherwise, whose main use for America was to embroil her in war."

Even Nancy Astor, once so well disposed to Kennedy, now turned against him, and Neville Chamberlain looked at him with sad incomprehension when Kennedy announced that "if the Allies get a peace which they feel gives the right results in Poland and Czechoslovakia and also gives security to Europe, and if then Hitler sells his people the idea that he has done something great for them, why should you object? Based on these facts, I fail to see a good reason for continuing the war."

Kennedy's naïveté about these "facts"—particularly Hitler's current plans for a massive military attack upon the West—was extraordinary for a U.S. ambassador. As Nicolson predicted, his embassy office became the London watering hole of all those, however crackpot, who sought a rapprochement with Hitler, from Lord Tavistock to the duke of Buccleuch. When Sumner Welles arrived in England, Kennedy insisted on accompanying him to every interview and conference, and in a second meeting with Halifax and the prime minister, Kennedy thought he de-tected signs of wavering in Chamberlain's stated refusal to negotiate with the existing German government. "Chamberlain's 'yes' [to Welles's question] seemed to me to lack conviction so I broke in: 'I believe that the position of the British Government would be untenable if the world and its peoples believed that by these methods war could be averted and security be achieved and a peace brought about that was not merely temporary and precarious. If you took that position, why, I myself would like to lead the opposition to the Chamberlain Government.'"

Ironically, Kennedy had now become more of an appeaser than Chamberlain. However, the parade of "wobble-boys" whom Kennedy trotted out for Welles was brought to a salutary end by an audience with Winston Churchill at the Admiralty.

"We were shown into his office," Kennedy related,

> Churchill was sitting in a big chair in front of his fireplace reading the afternoon paper, smoking a cigar with a highball at his side. He offered us a drink but we declined. Churchill was not only positive but emphatic in his views. There could be no peace without the military destruction of Germany. More than this, after her defeat, Germany had to be disarmed. . . . "All this will cost us dear," he said, "but we will, of course, win the war and that is the only hope for civilization." He grew eloquent in talking of Germany and her misdeeds. He characterized the Nazi Government as a "monster born of hatred and of fear." Of England and the last war, he said: "The victor forgot, the vanquished plotted on." Only Welles and I were his audience, but his language, his emphasis, his gestures, were as if he were speaking to thousands. . . . I dropped Welles at the Dorchester, on the way homeward. We said little, for there was so little to say.

Churchill was only weeks away from greatness as prime minister; Kennedy, cold-shouldered and despised, only months away from the end to his public career.

King Charles's Head

James Seymour had meanwhile diligently listed for Jack Kennedy all recent British books covering the United Kingdom's foreign policy in the interwar years, including accounts by Carr, Hearnshaw, Mackintosh, Seton-Watson, Gathorne-Hardy, Francis, Churchill, Eden, and even

Chamberlain. What Jack really wanted, however, was material that gave the views of English isolationist, pacifist, and appeasement groups over the years, as reflections of the inner debate that had gone on in English minds and was now going on in America. He cabled to Seymour on January 30.

WIRE BY WESTERN UNION WHERE HERE COPIES LIBERAL LABOR MAGA-ZINE 32–38. IF NOT SEND IMMEDIATELY. IMPORTANT. CONSERVATIVE SPEAKERS HINTS SINCE 32. OTHER STUFF GOOD. THANKS. JACK KENNEDY.

The diplomatic pouch now bulged with magazines from the thirties, such as *Conservative Gleanings and Memoranda* and *Politics in Review,* all sent in the ambassador's name to Kennedy's private office in New York, from where they were then forwarded to Jack at Harvard. With his thesis due by the end of March he was now in a race against time. "On receipt of this letter will you please immediately telephone to the Mail Room of the State Department in Washington and tell them that six packages of printed matter have arrived in the pouch addressed to the Ambassador in your care. Will you ask that they be forwarded to you as quickly as possible," Seymour wrote by night courier to Paul Murphy at the Kennedy office in New York on February 8.

Still Jack's requests kept coming. On February 9 he cabled:

RUSH PACIFIST LITERATURE OXFORD CAMBRIDGE UNION REPORT, ETC., SPEAKERS HINTS ETC., ALL PARTIES BUSINESS TRADE REPORTS BEARING ON FOREIGN POLICY ANYTHING ELSE. REGARDS TONY [ROSSELYN] YOUR-SELF. KENNEDY.

"Dear Jack, your cables get tougher," Seymour wrote back stoically, having assembled a mass of Peace Pledge Union pamphlets and ordered Oxford and Cambridge Union debate records. He even got Chamberlain to autograph a copy of his *Struggle for Peace* (in the flyleaf of which Chamberlain penned the words, "The struggle goes on, though in another form. But this time we will not let peace elude us. N.C. Feb. 1940"). By February 27, 1940, a further twenty-two volumes of pacifist pamphlets and books had winged their way from London to Washington to New York to Harvard.

Despite the controversy raging over assistant professorships, Jack's history and government professors now become involved in Jack's project. As Professor Payson Wild recalled, "he would do some writing of chapters, and I would read them. I don't recall any great problems, just normal ones. Saying this again, 'Now don't take too long on this. This has to be done by April 1,' or something like that. He was pretty thorough on some things, as I recall. Both Bruce Hopper and I would have to say, 'Well, get along with it, Jack. Now you can't be absolutely definitive on every point!' "

Professor Holcombe himself had "little to do with it," he himself later acknowledged, but he was impressed by "how hard Jack worked, and by his active mind," which "developed as he went along. Once he put his mind on work, he showed imagination and initiative."

Bruce Hopper recalled how, after a "slow start," Jack had "blossomed as a junior" and "matured rapidly" thereafter, particularly after his return from London. The thesis was "Jack's own idea" and by no means reflected Hopper's views, for Hopper was an ardent anti-Nazi and interventionist. "I was *not* detached," Hopper recalled, and "disagreed with part of [the] thesis."

So did a number of Jack's friends, including Jimmy Rousmanière. The Spee Club, in fact, became a private debating chamber, with Blair Clark, editor of the *Crimson,* advocating American isolationism and Rousmanière arguing for intervention. "I was very politically motivated even then," Rousmanière recalled, "and so I guess we missed classes going over especially this interventionist business. . . . We discussed it at great length."

Although the discussions with his tutors and his Spee Club colleagues sharpened Jack's understanding of the issues and rhetoric—legal, political, economic, moral—surrounding American neutrality, they did not intrude upon Jack's thesis. Here he was his own master, assembling the untold story of previous debates across the Atlantic as they had exercised the minds and consciences of British politicians, religious leaders, writers, students, and voters through the thirties. Jack's deepening determination was to show how the indecision of the British Parliament in the 1930s was the result not of poor judgment by political leaders so much as the very problem America was currently experiencing: a pacifist carryover from the twenties, deeply embedded in the public consciousness. This had forced Britain's political leaders, as it was currently forcing American political leaders, to follow public opinion rather than to preempt it, if they valued their seats.

For militaristic moralists such as Hopper, this was equivocation, as it would be for the two professors to whom the thesis would be submitted for grading. But Jack was resolved to tell the historical truth as he saw it. Far from supporting his father's appeasement position, Jack hoped to explain its inevitability as a historian, with remarkable detachment for a twenty-two-year-old.

"We used to kid him about his thesis," Rousmanière later recalled. In the Spee Club "there was a library, where the portraits hang—Jack used to study there quite a lot. Jack always had a typist somewhere. I can't remember the mechanics now, but he would get his typed manuscripts delivered to the Spee Club. A steward would pick them up, and he'd be reading the manuscripts in the Spee—first his term papers, then his graduation thesis. 'How's your book coming, Jack?' we'd tease him, not really thinking it was gonna be a book. We only saw these manuscripts coming in the door from the typist wherever.''

"Did I know him at the time when he was writing his thesis? Yes. We all made fun of him!" recalled Cam Newberry, who like Joe Jr. had stayed on at Harvard Law School. "We used to tease him about it all the time," Newberry laughed, "because it was sort of his King Charles head that he was carrying around all the time: his famous thesis. We got so sick of hearing about it that I think he finally shut up."

For the first time in his life, Jack was consumed by a single project. Those who did not know him well, like those who became envious when the thesis achieved such extraordinary fame for an undergraduate, assumed retrospectively that it must have been written by someone else or with professional help. As Augustus Soule recalled, "There are those who will tell you that he never wrote a word of his own thesis, that it was all done by those people over in England when his father was then Ambassador to the Court of St. James's, and his thesis was written for him." Soule recalled that it was "more than a rumor," though whether the spreaders were "just jealous, I don't know, but that's the way it was. I know I wrote a thesis, and it took me a long, long, long time to do it. And I don't think Jack would have made the time to do that—Jack was not a fellow, in my estimation, who would have taken the immense amount of time."

Such rumors would multiply in the years ahead, in part reflecting the extreme dislike felt by most New Englanders of good social background for Ambassador Kennedy. "Harvard in those days was very, very snooty—extremely snooty," Soule acknowledged. "And very Who's Who. . . . I'd make a bet Jack was the only Catholic at that time to get into the Spee Club, or any final club—and the only person of Irish descent—and people really wondered, they said, now, how did he do this?"

The thesis, however, was very much Jack's own work, even down to the spelling. "I'll never forget," recalled Ted Reardon, Joe Jr.'s Harvard roommate, "when I was out of college I got a call from Jack and he was doing his thesis. . . . He called me and said, 'Ted, you're an English major, come on over willya, and look at my thesis.' So I went over and looked and made some grammatical changes—but I'll never forget saying, 'How the hell do you expect me to go over all this stuff? When are ya handing it in, tomorrow?' "

Jack finally titled his thesis "Appeasement at Munich (The Inevitable Result of the Slowness of Conversion of the British Democracy to

Change from a Disarmament Policy to a Rearmament Policy)." As Jack explained in a letter to his father, "it was only going to run about the average length 70 pages, but finally ran to 150." His father's only contribution had been a single cable. "Thanks a lot for your wire—worked it in," Jack loyally assured him, grateful for the tremendous exertions of his father's staff over the past few months. "I'll be interested to see what you think of it, as it represents more work than I've ever done in my life."

It was an astonishing effort for a mere undergraduate, with over fifty British and American volumes quoted, more than half of which had only been published in the past two years. Given that he'd only begun writing in January 1940 and was still receiving pamphlets and books from England in February and early March, it was amazing that Jack managed to complete its 147 pages by March 15. In his preface, Jack explained his revisionist intentions.

> Munich was regarded as decisive in the battle between Democracy and Fascism. For this reason many of the political facts and judgments upon which Munich was founded have been buried by a cloud of political emotionalism. In the debate that followed the agreement, especially in America, to be pro-Munich was to be pro-Hitler and pro-Fascist; to be anti-Munich was to be pro-Liberal and pro-Democracy.
>
> Though time and the declaration of the war in September have alleviated much of the earlier bitterness, the subject of Munich is still "dynamite." Upon no other topic, has the ordinary man, as well as the expert, such strong and intense opinions. Many of the documents and reports are still secret; until they are released it is impossible to give the complete story.

In the meantime Jack hoped to make calm, historical sense of Britain's agonizingly slow conversion from "centuries of isolation"—a switch that could only be termed "revolutionary" in terms of the change that took place in "fundamental beliefs held by most Englishmen." For this reason, he felt, it was unfair to lay the blame for Britain's unpreparedness on Munich or on Chamberlain's predecessor, Stanley Baldwin, since the "underlying factors" of a democracy of peace-loving people had made it difficult, if not impossible, for a deeply isolationist island-nation such as Britain to engage in an armaments race with a supposedly defeated central European state such as Germany.

By charting the history of British disarmament and pacifist pressures— backed by defense and munitions statistics on every other page—Jack's thesis recorded a profoundly symbolic story for Americans, almost two years before Pearl Harbor. Spelling, grammar, and syntax were often faulty; moreover, there was a certain jejune tone in the narrative that belied the undergraduate origins of the script ("This is mentioned," Jack wrote of one of Balfour's speeches, "as I want to bring home the fact, for example, in this group, Hitler's rearming would be little immediate cause for alarm—at least in the year 1934."). Nevertheless the relentless, meticulously researched exposition had an arresting quality for such an academic account, at once naïve and mature, that reflected its author's genuine curiosity and concern.

Nothing else Jack would write in his life would so speak the man. Throughout its long and painstaking narrative, "Appeasement at Munich" exhibited an unwillingness to make historical condemnations except on carefully examined evidence. This was a tribute to Jack's Harvard education in government. The constraints of democratic government in Britain were never forgotten or underestimated. Stanley Baldwin, for instance, did not necessarily believe in "peace and disarmament by international agreement" by the time of the October 1933 East Fulham By-Election (after Hitler's withdrawal from the League of Nations), but was compelled, Jack pointed out, to write to the conservative candidate in terms calculated to "appeal to the sentiments that were strongest among the people. . . . That he should have to write this letter in order to make sure of the election indicates that there is no doubt at all that the British nation, at this time, was completely and overwhelmingly pacifist, to an extent it is hard to understand now, when we *look back* on the cruciality of the year."

It was this unsparing political realism that characterized Jack's chronicle of British appeasement up to the time of the Munich agreement. However amateur the style, Jack's historical reconstruction reflected the honesty of its author, and his long quotation of Baldwin's famous 1936 self-incrimination in Parliament said much about Roosevelt and America in 1940: "Supposing I had gone to the country [in 1933] and said that Germany was rearming and that we must rearm, does anybody think that this pacific democracy would have rallied to that cry at that moment? I cannot think of anything that would have made the loss of the election from my point of view more certain."

"In analyzing the speech," Jack wrote,

> I am neither trying to attack or to defend [Baldwin], but merely trying to get at what he really meant. . . . From reading numbers of his speeches and comments on him by friends and critics alike, I think that there can be no doubt that Baldwin was a master political tactician. . . . What I think he was seeking to show—and he used the election [of 1933] as the best barometer of a modern democratic state's popular will—[was] the impossibility of having gotten support for

any rearmament in the country due to the overwhelmingly pacifist sentiment of the country during these years. And I think from my study he was right. I think his choice of words was extremely unfortunate and opened him up to enormous criticism, but I think it is very important that we try and get his real meaning. . . . I have gone into this at some lengths as it is a very crucial point in this thesis.

For almost a hundred pages Jack had diligently recorded, step by step, debate by debate in Parliament and the country, the course of an unwilling people toward rearmament in 1936. "This speech is responsible for much of the blame Baldwin got for Britain's failure to rearm and I think it is not only unfair to try to put all the blame on one man's shoulders but inaccurate. It is easy to pass the buck but this thesis is trying to prove that the slowness of the rearmament programme was not due to Baldwin as much as due to the slowness of the conversion of the British public in general. I believe Baldwin made mistakes," he acknowledged, "and I will try to point them out, but I feel the whole lesson to be learned from Britain's experience would be wasted if the British failure to rearm was passed off as merely one man's 'desire to win an election.' "

Even Jack's father subsequently missed this point, passing on to Jack the general opinion of those to whom he showed the thesis, namely, that Jack had "whitewashed" Baldwin and subsequently Chamberlain. But Jack's original purpose was to draw a lesson that went to the heart of democracy in an age of dictatorship. "When it requires a ton and one half of machinery and equipment to supply each soldier," Jack wrote, "and when it requires a period of years to build up an industrial system able to produce this armament, we see the disadvantage of democracy's position. She is forced to pay for everything out of our budget, and she is limited by the laws of capitalism—supply and demand. Therefore to sustain a huge defensive force over a long period of years will bring economic ruin, which will bring on totalitarianism. To neglect to do so will mean that she will be in a defenseless position. There doesn't seem to be an easy solution—and there isn't. It's a gloomy picture.

"I think the first thing to be done is to stop fooling ourselves," Jack finally moved on to the lessons of Britain's experience. Rather than boasting of the "glories" of American democracy in terms of its wealth, "we should realize the disadvantages in the international field." Democracy had become an endangered species, and withdrawal into isolationism was an unworthy response to tyranny abroad.

"Instead of claiming that our great national wealth and high standard of living are due to our democratic capitalist system, we should realize the great natural resources we have. Maybe they were the best form for developing the country, but that doesn't mean they don't have to be proved the best now. In other words, let us realize exactly what the advantages are it gives, and exactly what are its disadvantages. If you decide that the democratic form is the best, be prepared to make certain great sacrifices," he went on, using a phrase that would become the hallmark of his later political idealism.

> Try to see things as they are. Instead of looking at Munich as the result of one man's weakness or misjudgment, try to look at it as it really was, the penalty England had to pay for her year of grace. Instead of blaming the condition of British rearmament on Baldwin, try to realize the factors really responsible. On this basis then, be prepared to make the necessary sacrifices to save the system.
>
> England was fortunate in having the period after Munich; we are fortunate in having a broad ocean. But if the dictators win the present war, we are going to have to be prepared to make the same type of sacrifices that England made during the last year. We may be able to avoid totalitarianism due to our geographic position and great natural wealth, but let's be sure that we know where the credit lies and not expect a democracy to be flawless.
>
> It may be a great system of government to live in internally but its weaknesses are great. We wish to preserve it here. If we are to do so, we must look at situations much more realistically than we do now. Our foreign policy must take advantage of every opportunity so that we can use our natural advantages. We must keep from being placed on an equal keel with the dictator because then we will loose [*sic*]. We can't afford to misjudge situations as we misjudged Munich. We must use every effort to form accurate judgments—and even then our task is going to be a difficult one.

Though Jack's ending would be excised from the thesis when it was subsequently made into a book, it represented Jack's first avowal of political faith. The writing of his epic, cautionary English tale had forced him to examine his most basic assumptions about liberty and the real world. Through it, he had not only demonstrated his ability to examine in depth a salient theme of recent history, but he had arrived at his own personal conviction, perhaps the one creed to which he would hold his entire life: the defense of democracy as underdog.

A Tall Slim Figure

Before Jack could submit his thesis, however, a clean version had to be
typed—a process which gave rise to the biggest scandal of Jack's Harvard
career. "Kennedy said that he had tried an employment bureau on Holyoke or Dunster Street and the Darling Secretarial School. None of those
places had anything to offer, so he put an ad in the paper," Dr. Else, the
Winthrop House senior tutor, later reported to Dr. Ferry "Stenographer,
young, to furnish typewriter, assist on thesis," the advertisement read.
Left to "handle the whole thing" till Jack returned from Ben Smith's
wedding in Chicago, Torby Macdonald had unfortunately let the ad run
for ten days, by which time, Macdonald later recalled, there were "60
clamoring females outside our dormitory at 9:30 A.M."

Dr. Ferry was not amused. Jack was severely reprimanded and in turn
reproved his roommate with words Macdonald would never forget: "You
always were a ladies' man, Torby, but this time I think you carried things
a bit too far!"

Jack's final draft, nonetheless, made the deadline. Joe Jr. reported to
Prince's Gate that Jack "rushed madly around last week with his thesis
and finally with the aid of five stenographers the last day got it under the
wire. He seemed to have some good ideas so it ought to be very good."
Jack himself dashed off his own brief note: "Am finishing up a couple of
International Law papers—then will be finished and will be ready to get
down South."

Florida certainly more than made up for the stenographic faux pas and
provided two welcome weeks of relaxation. "The weather was about the
best I've ever seen," Jack informed his father in London. "An awful lot
of people were down—three girls to every man—so I did better than
usual."

Behind the boastfulness, however, Jack "still misses Cannon quite a
bit," Kathleen commented in her own report to Prince's Gate, and she
was not wrong. Having received an invitation to Frances Ann's wedding,
set for April 28, Jack had admitted to Billings, "I would like to go, but I
don't want to look like the tall slim figure who goes out and shoots
himself in the greenhouse half-way through the ceremony," adding sarcastically "that the only thing I will shoot is my lunch. . . . Am planning
to go to Baltimore Friday night and thought we might drive down Sat.
or if necessary I might dispense with Baltimore. I could fly down . . . then
we might be able to borrow a car. . . . I realize you may want to go to the

Hunt Ball and if you do, this is not life and death—so be sure and tell me what you would rather do."

To Jack's disappointment, Billings couldn't make it. The jilted lover had perforce to go to White Oaks alone, witnessing in the "palatial home" of the Cannons "one of Charlotte's prettiest, most charming, and admired members of society" being given away by her father to Jack's rival, John Hersey. Even taller and slimmer than Jack, Hersey had served as private secretary to the Nobel Prize–winning writer Sinclair Lewis and was already a feature writer for *Time* magazine, Jack wistfully noted.

The next day Jack returned to Harvard to learn how his thesis had fared and was soon told the disappointing news: that it had been given the lowest honor grade.

Cum Laude

There were three grades of distinction for a Harvard honors thesis: magna cum laude, summa cum laude, and cum laude. Professor Yeomans recommended magna cum laude, the middle grade, for a "laborious, interesting and intelligent discussion of a difficult question." Professor Friedrich, however, was less impressed: "Fundamental premise never analyzed. Much too long, wordy, repetitious. Bibliography showy, but spotty. Title should be: British armament policy up to Munich. Reasoning re: Munich inconclusive. . . . Many typographical errors. English diction defective," he marked on Jack's thesis report card, and reduced the grade to cum laude.

The thesis "seemed to represent a lot of work," Joe Jr. wrote to their father, "but did not prove anything."

Arthur Krock, fortunately for Jack, felt differently. Already on April 4, five days before Hitler's invasion of Denmark and Norway, he'd dropped a note to Ambassador Kennedy in London to say that he'd seen "Rose and most of the children at Palm Beach where I spent Easter at Stewart McDonald's house, and they were all fine. I read Jack's graduation thesis, and it is an excellent job, though I regret he has many doubts of the efficiency of democracy." The style, where Jack intruded with his own views, was somewhat artless and hastily phrased. "It was amateurish in many respects," Krock later recalled, "but not, certainly not, as much as most writings in that category are. And the result was that I told him I thought it would make a very welcome and very useful book, and I would, if he wanted me to, and his father wanted me to, I would attempt to get him a publisher."

The Harvard faculty, having awarded its lowest honors grade for the thesis, did not welcome the idea. Indeed even Bruce Hopper, who noted on Jack's tutorial record that Jack was "surprisingly able, when he gets down to work," was against publication—Jack later recalling that "Hopper was casual, didn't think he should do book," but that he, Jack, "didn't follow any of his advice."

Instead, Jack wrote to his father in London to apologize for not yet having sent him or Jim Seymour the promised copy of the thesis, but telling the ambassador that Arthur Krock had read it

> and feels that I should get it published. He thinks that a good name for it might be *Why England Slept* as sort of a contrast to Churchill's *While England Slept.* The conclusion I have now was done for college and can + should be changed, although I could keep some of the ideas. Krock felt it should be brought out in the spring—May or June—but that would depend on 1st: when you resigned + 2nd: If you thought it was worth it—3rd: If you stayed on thru the summer whether it could be published while you are in office. You can judge after you have seen it. As I get finished on May 10th with my divisionals, I thought I could work on rewriting it and making it somewhat more complete and maybe more interesting for the average reader— as it stands now it is not anywhere polished enough although the ideas etc. are O.K. I think.

Jack Daly, the Kennedys' Hyannis neighbor, had also read the thesis and "thought it should be done. Whatever I do, however will depend on what you think is the best thing," Jack assured his father. "Jim Seymour might be able to assist me in some way on the English if I went ahead. . . . Please let me know what you think about the thesis as soon as you can. Am sending it to an agent Krock gave me, and see what he thinks. The chief questions are," Jack recapitulated, "1. Whether it is worth publishing if polished up. 2. If it can be published while you're still in office."

Was it worth publishing? Krock certainly thought so. But Krock's motive—as was so often the case in his contradictory life—was double-edged. He had a journalist's nose for a good story, and he had a veritable genius for titles (it was Krock who later came up with the title *The Founding Father* for Richard Whalen's biography of Joseph Kennedy). Yet in submitting Jack's thesis to Gertrude Algase's small literary agency on Madison Avenue in New York, Krock undoubtedly had an ulterior motive. From the time he first met Joseph Kennedy in 1932, Krock had perceived in the brash Boston-Irish banker a man of destiny, a man indeed with presidential possibilities to rival those of Roosevelt, whom Krock disliked intensely.

How Arthur Krock, such an astute observer of the American political scene, should have so underestimated the patrician Roosevelt and so overestimated the Wall Street swindler, was perhaps typical of the poor judgment—as opposed to observation—of journalists. At any rate, Krock was quite candid in his subsequent note to Miss Algase when explaining why he had steered Jack Kennedy's thesis to her in the spring of 1940: "I had his father's future book production in mind when I sent the boy to you."

Certainly the story of Joseph Kennedy's ambassadorship looked a great deal more promising commercially than did his son's college thesis. Knowing Kennedy to be unhappy in England, Arthur Krock urged him to resign and return to America, where he could speak and write his mind. Jack, however, disagreed. "Krock seemed to think that you probably could get out in June without too much trouble. I don't quite agree with this," Jack remonstrated, "as it seems to be so much the style now to criticize Am[erican] diplomats due to election year—and it might undo the work of 7 years."

Nor did Jack agree with his father's negative attitude toward the children coming to England over the summer vacation. "I gathered from your last letter to Mother that you did not think it too advisable for us to come over the summer. I should like to come very much, if there is anything of interest going on," Jack protested. His sister Kathleen was also "very keen to go over and I wouldn't think the anti-American feeling would hurt her like it might us, due to her being a girl—especially as it would show that we hadn't merely left England when it got unpleasant."

The ambassador was abashed. "I note what you said about June and coming home," he replied to Krock. "I think I could be of more service if I were there [in the U.S.], even though I had no position with the Government, but I should hate to wind up six years of government service by getting out of a job and subjecting myself to criticism"—he paraphrased Jack's argument—"because, from what I gather, the American public believes ambassadors are supposed to perform some satisfactory service, even in times like this, and to walk out would convince them I was letting American interests down." He had not "changed one idea of mine in the last year," he assured Krock, however. "I always believed that if England stayed out of war it would be better for the United States and for that reason I was a great believer in appeasement." Now, however, he felt not Europe but "the United States looks like an interesting spot for the next six months," since the platform for appeasement had shifted to America. He still had, he maintained, the "greatest respect for your judgment of public psychology" and was "more than interested to know just how you feel I can get out. Of course, if the President really needed me and offered me some kind of job that I could fill, that would solve it."

Unfortunately for Kennedy, Roosevelt had no use for him in the U.S.A.—particularly in an election year. Exiled in London at Roosevelt's behest and on his son Jack's advice, Kennedy now gave the most wretched performance of his life. On his return to London in February he had in secret and without authorization from the State Department rented at his own expense a vast country mansion "as a place of retreat outside London in the event of heavy bombing. After a brief inspection of it I decided to take it over," he later revealed. "It was a large house of some seventy rooms situated just beyond Windsor about twenty-five miles out of the city." Here, for the rest of Joseph P. Kennedy's term as U.S. ambassador to Britain, he would run for cover nightly, leaving the staff of the embassy in London.

His failures of judgment were exacerbated by his personal cowardice and his extreme dislike of Churchill. By late April, for instance, the ambassador was cabling Hull and Rossevelt that "I have never, since I have been in this country, seen the undercurrent of discontent which exists at present. Mr. Churchill's sun has been caused to set very rapidly by the situation in Norway which some people are already characterizing as the second Gallipoli."

Far from setting on Churchill's career, however, the sun was setting on Joseph Kennedy's. The British public blamed not Churchill but those appeasers who had misjudged Hitler's ruthless military ambitions and caused Britain to fight with the leftovers of World War I. Nine months earlier, the crowds had cheered Chamberlain; now, as the Nazis proved victorious in southern Norway, the public turned on him. It was left to eighty-year-old David Lloyd George, prime minister of Great Britain during the previous world war, to give on May 8 the coup de grâce in the House of Commons, watched by Ambassador Kennedy from the same Strangers' Gallery from which he'd previously led the cheering after Chamberlain's return from Munich.

As prime minister, Neville Chamberlain had called for sacrifice, Lloyd George told the House. "The nation is prepared for every sacrifice so long as the Government show clearly what they are aiming at, and so long as the nation is confident that those who are leading it are doing their best. I say solemnly that the Prime Minister should give an example of sacrifice, because there is nothing which can contribute more to victory in this war than that he should sacrifice the seals of office."

This grave statement by a venerated political leader sounded Chamberlain's death knell. Though the government won the subsequent debate, Chamberlain "looked stunned and definitely beaten," Kennedy admitted.

The situation was fast deteriorating. Back at Grosvenor Square, Kennedy called President Roosevelt, who was worried not only by the spectacle that a weakened British government would present to the German propaganda machine, but by ominous reports of an ultimatum Hitler had given to the neutral Dutch government.

The next day the Labour opposition in Parliament called for the British government to resign. It was clear there would have to be a new national government, and "at six o'clock that evening there was a meeting at 10 Downing Street at which Chamberlain, Churchill, Halifax, Attlee and Greenwood were present," Kennedy related. "Chamberlain put two questions to the two leaders of the Labor [*sic*] party: One, whether they would join a government under Chamberlain as Prime Minister, and two, whether they would join a government under Churchill as Prime Minister. Attlee and Greenwood declined to give a definitive answer to either question until they should have consulted their colleagues but they indicated that the answer that would be given to the first question would be 'No' and to the second 'yes.' "

This was a bitter pill for Chamberlain, as he reported to Kennedy. He had made a disastrous error in calling for the support of his "friends" in the parliamentary debate, for wars could not be won by parliamentary friendship. Churchill implored Attlee and Greenwood to serve under Chamberlain, but they refused, declaring they would not serve in a Cabinet that even *contained* Chamberlain.

Deeply offended, Chamberlain refused to surrender the seals of prime-ministerial office. The crisis went unresolved until the next day, May 10, 1940, when Kennedy was awakened at six A.M. by a telephone call from Secretary Hull in Washington who informed him that Holland, Belgium, and Luxembourg had been attacked by German air and ground forces. The phony war was finally and irrevocably over. Western Europe was in flames.

Why England Slept

Ironically, Hitler's attack convinced Chamberlain he should remain prime minister rather than resign. Speaking to the newspaper magnate Lord Beaverbrook at noon, Kennedy "learned that Chamberlain had changed his mind in the light of Hitler's action and that he had written him [Beaverbrook] that he was determined to defer the reorganization of the Government until the present crisis should have passed."

How Chamberlain imagined he could command the support of Parlia-

ment without the backing of the Labour party in such a national crisis is
in retrospect incredible. Such delusions were short-lived, however. "A few
hours later," Kennedy related, "the picture had again changed. Chamberlain, I learned, had decided to resign. Labor was unalterably opposed
to joining a Government under him and he felt a National Government
was now essential. Churchill would consequently take his place and was
destined to see the King that evening to get his commission to form a new
government."

What Kennedy did not reveal was the extent of his own terror. Even
the American naval attaché later recalled how Kennedy was literally
"tearing his hair" at the news of Hitler's invasion of Holland. Maisky, the
Russian ambassador, also found Kennedy

> in a state of panic. Britain was absolutely powerless before Germany,
> he [Kennedy] considered. The war was hopelessly lost and the sooner
> she made peace with Hitler the better. He was absolutely amazed
> when I started to tell him that nothing was yet lost for Britain and
> that she had a very good chance of successfully resisting and repell-
> ing the German menace, provided of course that she stuck to her
> guns. As far as I had observed, the spirit of the mass of the people
> was unshaken . . . there was no call to paint the picture too black.
> When I had done, Kennedy exclaimed: "Why you are simply an
> optimist. . . . I haven't heard anything like it even from the British."
> And small wonder, for the British Kennedy associated with were the
> Cliveden brand and they had no faith either in themselves or in their
> country's future.

Chamberlain's belated resignation and Winston Churchill's takeover
as prime minister of Great Britain was, however, the only bright spot in
an otherwise bleak month for the democracies of Europe. First Norway
capitulated, then Holland, Luxembourg, and Belgium. Soon the whole of
northern France was cut off as German armored units, having smashed
their way through the Ardennes, raced toward the Channel coast.

At Harvard, meanwhile, Jack set up a student committee to raise funds
for the Red Cross to help refugees in Europe. The *Boston Herald* reported
on May 20; "Young Kennedy said yesterday, 'The desperate needs of
Europe's invaded population requires no more argument than the familiar facts reported in the daily papers. In making this appeal to Harvard
students, the committee knows that many of them are low on funds at the
end of the college year. I feel, however, that students can and should be
given an opportunity to contribute to the drive.' " To his father in London Jack proudly reported how he had "got up a Red Cross Drive at

Harvard during the last three weeks and raised $1700.00 which was five hundred over the quota that was set for us."

The ambassador, watching his worst fears being confirmed across the Channel, saw little hope for relief. Though his spirited daughter Kathleen assured him that "the British lose the battles but they win the wars," he refused to allow her or Jack to embark for London. "Mother told me you didn't think it best I came over which is probably right as it would be a short time and I guess I shall go to the Cape," Jack lamented. "Regarding my thesis . . . I should try and get it published as soon as possible, as I should get it out before 1) the issue becomes too dead. 2nd) before everyone goes away for the summer. I should like to get something in the conclusion about the best policy for America as learnt from a study of Britain's experience but of course I don't want to take sides too much," he remarked diplomatically. "Is 'Why England Slept' OK for a title—and will Churchill mind? What should I do about a publisher—keep Krock's agent or can you fix it?"

In fact Gertrude Algase had already begun the process of trying to get a publisher, having sent the original manuscript to Harper Brothers on May 20 with a covering note: "Arthur Krock read it, and praised it and referred him to me. I read the script and found that it was really a masterful handling of a subject, necessarily academically handled for its purpose. He had copies of the original thesis made and sent to several competent men in England . . . one of them Harold Nicholson [*sic*]. He and others praised and criticized the script, and each gave suggestions which Ambassador Kennedy is sending over for young Kennedy to incorporate into the revision. Harold Nicholson will write an introduction; Arthur Krock will give it a jacket blurb . . . because it really is deserving. The completed script will run about 50,000 words and will be completed by June 5th." To sweeten the bait, Algase also mentioned that "Jack's brother is going to write a book too, personal experiences when in Spain which entail some material never before released for publication." Above all, there was Jack's father's future memoirs. "I cannot make any promises about the Ambassador but . . . I do hope *he* will write his book someday!" Miss Algase remarked. She asked for an advance of only $250, payable on acceptance of Jack's final manuscript.

While Harper Brothers read the manuscript, Jack now went through his copy in the library of Arthur Krock's house in Georgetown and prepared to make revisions. "I can't say that I did more than polish it and amend it here and there because it was very, very definitely his own product," Krock later recalled. From the typed letter Jack received from his father (drafted by Jim Seymour), containing a digest of English criticisms of the manuscript, Jack corrected various errors and even lifted whole paragraphs. Nicolson and others had felt Jack was "putting the blame on the British public" too much in an effort to spare individuals such as Baldwin and Chamberlain. Reluctantly Jack concurred, and the compassionate conclusion of his original thesis was scrapped in order to incorporate a more urgent message to American readers—particularly once the British Expeditionary Force retreated to Dunkirk and, leaving its tanks, artillery transport, weapons, and allies behind, had to be evacuated.

Back in Cambridge, Jack could not wait for possible publication of his thesis. In the correspondence columns of the Harvard *Crimson* on June 9, despite his promise to his father, he now protested in print against those who still opposed rearmament in America:

> In an editorial on Friday, May 31, attacking [Harvard] President Conant's speech you stated that "there is no surer way to war, and a terribly destructive one, than to arm as we are doing." This point of view seems to overlook the very valuable lesson of England's experience during the last decade. In no other country was this idea that armaments are the prime cause of war more firmly held. Lord Grey's statement in 1914—"the enormous growth of armaments in Europe, the sense of insecurity and fear caused by them, it was these that made war inevitable"—was quoted again and again by the successful opponents of British rearmament. Senator Borah expressed the equivalent American opinion, in voting against the naval appropriations bill of 1938 when he said, "one nation putting out a program, another putting out a program to meet the program and soon there is war."
>
> If anyone should ask why Britain is so badly prepared for this war or why America's defenses were found to be in such shocking condition in the May investigations, this attitude toward armaments is a substantial answer. The failure to build up her armaments has not saved England from a war, and may cost her one.
>
> Are we in America to let that lesson go unlearned?

Coming from the same student who had written to urge "peace in our time" and international disarmament the previous October, this was evidence of an extraordinary transformation. By mid-June Jack had finished his revisions and had sent off the revised manuscript to Algase. It "was submitted about two days ago + I hear definitely about it tomorrow," he reported to his father from HyannisPort. "The theme is the explanation of why England was so badly prepared for the present war," he reminded his father, who still hadn't had time to read it. "I have made it about sixty pages longer, and have tried to make it more interesting and readable, as well as bringing it up-to-date. As soon as I hear, I will write you a letter. Leaving in a couple of days to go up and graduate. I don't know whether I had told you that I am all entered etc. for Yale next fall. Everyone fine. Rosie looks and acts 100% better. Love Jack."

A Fighting Foreword

The editors at Harper Brothers reported to Miss Algase on June 18 that they thought Jack's thesis "a careful and scholarly job and one of which he has every reason to be proud." Times, unfortunately, had moved on; there was a new book by Walter Millis, they claimed, that would take wind from Kennedy's sails. Most importantly, though,

> the disastrous turn of events in France has, we think, so shocked and shaken people in this country that, in our judgment, it would be practically impossible to get attention for any historical survey as this, even though the period covered is a very recent one. Events which preceded the outbreak of the war now seem to have occurred years ago, so rapidly has history moved since May 10th. Also, the collapse of France has made only one question seem important in people's minds, namely, what will England do now? And of course as a corollary to that, what will we do? In the face of this grave crisis, nothing else seems important. . . . Won't you please be good enough to show this letter to Mr. Kennedy, because we should like him to understand our reasons. Under the circumstances, there is nothing we can do except to cancel the contract. . . . The manuscript is being returned to you herewith.

It was a bitter blow for Jack, but he betrayed no emotion to his father. "Well, I just got through graduating," he wrote soon after receiving his Bachelor of Political Science degree cum laude on June 20. "Mother, Kick and Eunice were up and it was darn good fun. I have come down to New York on this book which is running into some snags, as Harpers felt that France's quick defeat has changed the interest, my stuff (what happened in the past) is not of such interest as what is going to happen in the future. However I am still working on it and will get someone to do it. I have changed it considerably, it is now about 210 pages where formerly it was only 150, and I have tried to make it more readable. . . . I am sending you a copy of the new edition as soon as I get some news on it." He also thanked his father for his generous graduation gift—a sum of money which would enable him to "remain solvent for a bit more," and assured his father he was still intending to go to law school. "I am still heading to Yale, as Judge Burns thinks it's good," even though "Bill Coleman's father did not want him to go to Yale—too radical—so he is heading for Virginia Law School."

Meanwhile Algase had wasted no time in resubmitting the manuscript to another publisher, Harcourt Brace, on June 20. "Jack Kennedy—Ambassador Kennedy's son—is a client of mine," Miss Algase explained to Mr. Harcourt. "Attached is a script that Ambassador Kennedy showed several outstanding people in England—Harold Nicholson [*sic*]—Harold Laski—etc. and each one felt that this was an historical contribution and deserved publication. I just suggested to young Kennedy that your house would be my first choice for the script," she lied, "and he told me that Harold Nicholson [*sic*] too, suggested this go to you. Arthur Krock read it—and feels it would be widely read for its factual content. He is willing to write a foreword for it, and I think perhaps Nicholson would if his official office does not keep him from doing so. A foreword from one; a blurb from the other, might be of import—don't you think?"

Unfortunately Mr. Harcourt didn't think so, any more than Harper Brothers had. Algase had promised that Jack—who "graduates from Harvard this week" and was "in constant touch with me"—would bring the story "up to date by another chapter, if you wish—in view of the French situation." Mr. Harcourt, however, thought "sales possibilities too dim. I'd vote No" (though he noted "the boy has written a much better than average thesis"). His chief editor concurred: "Book publishing not the medium at this time—things moving too fast."

Jack's friend Lem Billings later summed up the situation in late June 1940: "I remember Jack had some trouble finding a publisher. The established publishers were not interested."

Wisely, Gertrude Algase now made the decision to try a new, smaller publisher, and sent the manuscript to Wilfred Funk, who had established a small imprint in New York. Funk read the revised version and leaped at the chance of publishing it in book form, especially once Henry R. Luce agreed to read the book and possibly contribute a foreword.

Luce, the publisher of *Time* and *Life* magazines, later recalled how wary he'd been when "Ambassador Kennedy called me up by overseas telephone. . . . I said, 'Well, send me the manuscript and let me look at it.'"

When the manuscript, or rather the proofs, arrived, I was very impressed by it. I was impressed by the scholarly work, if you like, because this book was based on a comparative review of the proceedings in the Houses of Parliament for several years. At this time, of course, it was after Munich. . . . England, as they said, stood alone and the popular tendency was to put all the blame on the so-called appeasers, namely Mr. Chamberlain and the Tory appeasers, the Cliveden Set. This book showed that the blame would have to be shared quite generally by nearly all aspects of British opinion, including the Labor Party. The book made a particular analysis or used as one of its tests, the attitude on the appropriations for defense during the '30's. And while no great credit could be given to either party—if one must put it in party terms—there was certainly just as much lack of foresight on the part of Laborites as there was on the part of the Conservatives. . . .

What impressed me was, first, that he had done such a careful job of actually reviewing the facts, the facts such as attitudes and voting records, with regard to the crisis in Europe. And I was impressed by his careful scholarship, research, and also by his sense of personal involvement, responsibility, in the great crisis that was at that time in flames. And that's what made me very optimistic about the qualities of mind and of involvement in public affairs that was displayed in this book.

Luce's foreword, on the other hand, was hardly what Ambassador Kennedy had had in mind. Luce began it by extolling the book's young author: "I cannot recall a single man of my college generation who could have written such an *adult* book on such a vitally important subject during his Senior year at college." However, he then proceeded to rip into both Wendell Willkie, the Republican presidential candidate, and Franklin Roosevelt for beguiling the people of America into believing they would not be involved in war. "America will never be ready for any war," Luce wrote with passion, "not in one year nor in two nor in twenty— never until she makes up her mind that there is going to be a war. . . . Until that moment America will lose many wars—all the wars she does not fight and she will also lose the war she didn't believe she was going to fight. Or, if she doesn't actually lose it, she will win the last battle only at an appalling cost of blood and treasure—and with consequences to American civilization, which will make the horrible ravages of our War Between the States seem paltry by comparison." The sleeping giant, he warned, must awake, must countenance the prospect of war if it was ever to be successful in fighting it, and he quoted, from the book, Jack's simile between a boxer and the American people: "A boxer cannot work himself into proper psychological and physical condition for a fight that he seriously believes will never come off."

"The test of this campaign," Luce went on, "will be the simple test of honesty. It will be a test of leaders, but, far more importantly, it will be a test of democracy in its last bulwark. . . . Perhaps neither [Wendell Willkie nor Franklin Roosevelt] will be able to be honest with the American people in this campaign. We shall see. Ten billions for defense and not one word for courage? No—surely the democratic experiment will not perish from the earth so ignominiously as that."

Courage was indeed the issue behind democracy. Meanwhile, with the Battle of Britain spreading vapor trails across the English skies, Joseph Kennedy's prophecies of doom and destruction for England looked as if they might well be fulfilled, making him perhaps the most prominent isolationist of America. In his cables to the State Department, Kennedy certainly assumed Britain would be conquered. He'd refused to allow either Jack or Kathleen to come over. He was disturbed that the British, including the royal family, were not sending their children and their gold reserves to Canada (prompting the queen to remark, pointedly, that her children could not go without their mother, and their mother could not leave her husband, and her husband could not leave his country). When Kennedy visited the dying ex-prime minister in July, he candidly told Chamberlain "everyone in the USA thinks we shall be beaten before the end of the month"—scarcely a reassuring remark to an Englishman on his deathbed.

Kennedy's misjudgment of Britain's fate would ultimately put a torch to his public career. For the moment, however, he considered himself a realist and a prophet. It was therefore all the more puzzling to those around him when he made no objection to Luce's fighting foreword. As soon as the first copies arrived in England from New York, he began distributing them to every major figure in the land, from King George VI to Winston Churchill.

The spectacle was utterly extraordinary; here was "a self-centered, frightened rich man who thought only in terms of money," as the *New Stateman*'s editor called him, who had invested in many prime companies trading with the Nazis in the 1930s and had now liquidated all his shares in British companies during the Battle of Britain, openly lauding his son's exposé of British appeasement policies, with a battle-hymn foreword by Henry Luce.

Perhaps the ambassador hoped, at a moment when he had become persona non grata in British government circles, to curry some favor with Churchill and other British leaders who openly despised him. More likely, however, he was acting out of parental pride. As all but his most myopic sycophants and opponents would recognize, Joseph P. Kennedy was the strangest of swindlers, a man of extraordinary contradictions: insensitive and yet sometimes considerate, mean and yet sometimes generous, blinkered and yet sometimes broad-minded, vain and yet sometimes humble;

amoral and yet sometimes anxious to do good, a bullying and yet proud and loving parent.

Kennedy had still not read Jack's manuscript. Writing to Jack on August 2, 1940, the ambassador looked forward to reading the book version, predicting that, "if it reaches the problem as they now visualize it in England, the book will have quite a sale. . . . So, whether you make a cent out of it or not," he assured Jack, "it will do you an amazing amount of good, particularly if it is well received. You would be surprised how a book that really makes the grade with high-class people stands you in good stead for years to come. I remember that in the report you are asked to make after twenty-five years to the Committee at Harvard, one of the questions is 'What books have you written?' and there is no doubt you will have done yourself a great deal of good. Now that you've got the book off, get a good rest. You have the brains and everything it takes to go somewhere, so get yourself in good condition so you can really do things."

The letter was a strange tribute. Nor did Kennedy's feelings alter when, ten days later, he wrote to Rose to tell her he'd finally read the book. "I think it's a swell job. There is no question but that regardless of whether he makes any money out of it or not, he will have built himself a foundation for his reputation that will be of lasting value to him. Tell him I am taking the book today to Laski and I am going to have Laski give me some suggestions as to what people here might be helpful to get letters for Jack, and I am also looking up who would be likely to do the best job publishing it [in Britain]."

Like Jack's professors at Harvard, however, Laski was aghast at the idea.

A National Best-Seller

Laski's response typified the besetting sin of academia: envy. On August 20 he wrote to Ambassador Kennedy to protest against the idea of British publication. He even regretted that Kennedy had allowed Jack to publish the book in America. Although it would be easy "to repeat the eulogies Krock and Harry [*sic*] Luce have showered on your boy's work," he, Laski, wouldn't do so. "In fact, I choose the more difficult way of regretting deeply that you let him publish it. For while it is the book of a lad with brains, it is very immature, it has no real structure, and it dwells almost wholly on the surface of things. In a good university," he claimed, "half a hundred seniors do books like this as part of their normal work in their final year. But they don't publish them for the good reason that their importance lies solely in what they get out of doing them and not in what they have to say. I don't honestly think any publisher would have looked at that book of Jack's if he had not been your son, and if you had not been Ambassador. And those are not the right grounds for publication."

New York publishers had indeed looked at Jack's manuscript because of his father's position as ambassador. This had not stopped them, however, from turning the book down. Even Wilfred Funk was surprised by the public appetite for such a work. "The publisher anticipated a sale of three to five thousand copies and it looks as if his expectations will easily be met," Gertrude Algase reported to Krock in delight on July 12, for the book had "already had, since its announcement and ad in *Publishers Weekly,* an advance sale of over a thousand copies and a request from fifteen reviewers. Whether this is just a flurry because of the youngster's name and curiosity on the part of the book stores, we can't tell. It probably is," she wrote candidly, "and whether or not the book will renew its sale after the book shops have available copies I don't know." Nevertheless Miss Algase was impressed by Jack himself. "Jack Kennedy is one of the nicest youngsters I ever met," she told Krock, "unaffected, cordial and hard-working in his own right. I'd like to watch him grow up and go places."

Not even Miss Algase believed—any more than did Krock—that Jack Kennedy would grow up and go to the White House. In the meantime bookshop orders were soon followed by requests for magazine articles. The editor of *Current History* begged for a twenty-five-hundred-word essay and wished to meet Jack in New York. "Everyone agrees that you are a natural writer," Miss Algase's partner, Joel Satz, wrote him on July 16, "and with the book coming out soon, you should take advantage of the market and supply articles to the magazines. We would also like to talk to you about a radio interview with Lowell Thomas. . . . And if you agree, it should be done as soon after the book publication as possible. The reports from the trade are encouraging. Almost one thousand books have been sold . . . and the trade really hasn't been touched. We'll have a better estimate of what the book is likely to do when Frank Henry gets back from his sales trip next week. In the meantime our hopes are high . . . and I think the desire for a large audience [in his foreword Henry Luce had hoped a million people would read the work] for the book will be realized."

Why England Slept had gone on sale in American bookshops at the end of July 1940. Considering that Jack had only begun writing the original thesis in February, completing it in mid-March and rewriting and polishing it with Krock in early June, it was a tour de force. The family bookworm, perennially late for meals, careless in dress, unable to apply himself to any one task, almost expelled from school for irreverence and gang leadership, continually sick with undiagnosed blood disorders and several times seemingly at death's door, unable to cope at Princeton and initially dismissed as a playboy at Harvard, was on the point of becoming what everyone in their hearts knew he would become, yet somehow never imagined him becoming at such a young age: a runaway success.

On August 5, 1940, Jack was interviewed for the *Boston Herald*. "At his summer home he hastened to squelch reports that the book is any but his own 'brainchild.' He is pleased with its reception, 3,500 copies sold in two days, but irked by constant innuendo that he is his father's mouthpiece. 'I haven't seen my father in six months, nor are we of the same opinion concerning certain British statesmen,' " Jack defended himself, alluding primarily to Churchill.

> Young Mr. Kennedy had a purpose in writing this account. He wants the United States to wake up now. England slept until her enemy knocked at her very gates, he points out. But here, in this country, a great democracy is faced with the same problem that confronted England between 1920 and 1940. Young Kennedy pleads for immediate conscription to prepare the United States for defense. . . .
>
> A sequel to his book is now being prepared by Kennedy in an article to be published in the September issue of "Current History." It will probably be titled, "England Awakens" and is based on a factual study of the past two months.
>
> As Kennedy talked a letter arrived from the editor of the London Express. It offered an assignment for an article to be written by Kennedy on what part the United States should play in the current war.
>
> A rather modest youth, Kennedy's intelligence goes far beyond his years, for his book offers a capable diagnosis of the ills of a democracy facing international danger.

Offers and assignments poured into Jack's mailbox. "Jack's book has come out, he went to New York or someplace yesterday," Jack's sister Jean reported to their father. Jack had hoped to sail all summer at Cape Cod, but the book's publication now kept him too busy. "You surely are checking up an amazing number of unusually fine reviews, aren't you?" Miss Algase had written to him on August 1. "You must be gratified, as am I, when you read *The Times* and *Tribune* today. Men whose years and experience number far more than twice yours, seldom have such tribute paid them on their first book—or any!"

The reviews were indeed remarkable for a twenty-three-year-old. John Wheeler-Bennett, in the *New York Sun,* made clear that although Jack Kennedy had had "exceptional opportunities for the observance of his subject," he was not writing as "the son of the Ambassador of the United States to the Court of St. James's but with becoming modesty, as a young man of intelligence, forming his opinions for himself, sifting his evidence and finally evolving a political and psychological analysis of rare penetration, with an immensely appealing quality of freshness and breadth of understanding." Like Henry Luce, Wheeler-Bennett called for the young author to undertake now an examination of America's role in the collapse of world peace, from its failure both to ratify the Versailles Treaty and join the League of Nations to its current "somnolence."

Wheeler-Bennett's was not the only voice urging Jack to wield the power of his pen at this critical moment in history. It was as if Jack had touched the very nerve of democracy in an age of totalitarianism, and he was lionized not only in reviews but in private letters. President Roosevelt, addressing him as "My dear Jack," wrote to congratulate him, as did Mrs. Roberts, his former schoolteacher. "I have not had the pleasure of seeing you since you grew up," she wrote after hearing Jack on the radio. "I wish now to congratulate little 'Jackie' Kennedy of the Devotion School, Brookline. . . . I must confess I am very proud of your success. You are indeed a splendid example of American youth, and your success so early, I am sure, warms your mother and daddy's heart with pride. . . . I'm sure we can expect great things from you 'Jackie.'" Mrs. Pierrepont, wife of the financier, wrote to say how "thoroughly" they had enjoyed reading the book, and that Mr. Pierrepont "today has given me instructions to send it to at least half a dozen hard-bitten isolationists, whom he thinks will profit by the reading." Academics, politicians, lawyers, economists, and educators wrote to praise the work and press its author into the service of their professions. B. A. Brickley, a Boston lawyer, considered it "excellently written and shows both great study and a fine mind. It certainly augurs well for a successful legal career." The *Atlantic Monthly* used Jack to puff Mollie Panter-Downe's new book they were serializing. From Columbia University, a professor of economics wrote to "express my sincere admiration for the excellent and painstaking analysis of the real causes of democratic weakness in the face of fascist aggression . . . one of the major contributions to American political thinking." And from New York University, Geoffrey Brown, professor of history, wrote to offer his services in getting a bigger publisher, W. W. Norton, for Jack's next "project." Even Jack's old Choate headmaster,

George St. John, wrote a fulsome letter of praise of the book, extolling its "restrained, scholarly and convincing" character. "That could have been said of the book if it had been written ten or twenty years later in the light of History. Coming to the people of America *now,* it is the work of a patriot, a prophet, and a missionary. I join in the common gratitude which all Americans should feel for the record and the analysis of the causes of England's present plight. Your whole book drives home the needed lesson to America, and every responsible American must rise up and thank you."

By September, *Why England Slept* was listed by *Publisher's Weekly* as "a candidate for the national best seller's list," Jack's agent wrote, the book having already appeared on the *New York Times* and the Washington *Times-Herald* bestseller lists. "We're glad for you that the public has recognized the merit of your work," Joel Satz added. Miss Algase was prepared to follow up her expressed interest in Joe Jr.'s promised book on his experiences in Spain, and asked to meet him, remarking, however, "What will he do for publicity, now that you've stolen, quite innocently to be sure, the thunder?"

It was at this moment when, lionized, lauded, and sending out autographed copies of his bestselling book, Jack received in Hyannis Port perhaps the most important, cautionary advice of his young life. It was from his Harvard mentor, Bruce Hopper, and dated September 5, 1940.

Hopper began by thanking Jack for his letter and the inscribed copy of *Why England Slept.* "It is an excellent job, although not entirely a surprise to me," Hopper mocked gently.

> Henry Luce does you well in his introduction, although I believe he should have remarked that you did not intend to survey the planet. And certainly he should have noted the speed with which you turned out the copy after you were asked to convert your thesis material into a book.
>
> Now Jack, one private word. On page xxi Luce writes: "I hope Mr. Kennedy will now proceed to give us a book on the relation between American policy and the near collapse of civilized order throughout the world." My advice: lay off. That's a subject for an old sage, of the A. Laurence Lowell type, though younger.
>
> Secondly, don't do a book anyway. If you must write, limit the subject to article size for which you can do the research in reasonable time. Your book, after all, was the climax of four years' study, plus exceptional opportunities for observation during your eight months in Europe.
>
> Thirdly: Because of your years, you will be the object of all kinds of offers. Beware them all. Your job now is to complete your educa-

tion. (I don't remember that you had law in mind, but I do hope you will not be tempted into immediate allurements.) Of course, there are some of your readers who will assume that you got your material from your father. I know you got your material by yourself, and wrote your thesis by yourself. In the end it doesn't matter what anyone thinks.

What does matter is that you protect yourself from the pressure to lend your name to this or that cause. The public is fickle, and, in the end, ungrateful. And the public ruins its idols, yes?

I can't imagine you getting excited over public acclaim, so this word is really unnecessary. It is just that I know your mail box must be full of laudatory reviews, letters of appreciation, and offers (mayhaps even from Hollywood!). Take them all in perspective, as reward for a job well done, and then try to forget them.

If Mrs. So-and-So gurgles over your great achievement at dinner, just say: "Yes, lucky strike, wasn't it—probably couldn't do it again for a decade, what?" You know what I mean.

Meanwhile, my congratulations and best wishes always. If you are in Cambridge, the latch is always out. You have been launched, Jack, but you need machinery in the boat before you go to sea. Get the machinery, and you, with [your] mental quickness, will have a real ship for tough weather, right?

Cheers, mon brave.

PART
·7·
STANFORD
INTERLUDE

Jack Kennedy in Hollywood, fall of 1940 (John F. Kennedy Library)

Venereal Disease

Jack's friend Torby Macdonald spent the summer of 1940 playing professional football for the Eastern Shore League. Though he enjoyed the sex—"plenty of action along all fronts and even some backs"—he found life after Harvard a trial. "Wait till you get out & get to work boy, (if you ever do)," Macdonald warned his roommate. "We've or at least I've been living in a fool's paradise & the more I see of the Common Man & his brain & ideas, the more I think that Hitler has got a few good ideas. Let me know how long you're going to be around & I'll be up." He ended by asking Jack to keep him "posted about when your Honolulu junket gets under way."

Neither the Hawaiian "junket" (attending the wedding of Pete Dillingham) nor the Yale Law School plan came to pass, however, as Jack again fell ill. He was treated in Boston by Dr. Jordan of the Lahey Clinic but then had to be sent again to the Mayo Clinic for further tests. His former flame, Olive Cawley, wrote to say "how sorry I was to hear about it—I hope it's nothing serious, because I'm waiting for you to take me on a real binge in N.Y. on all that money I hear you've made on your book. Even if I didn't get my complimentary copy," she chided, "I finally managed the fee and bought myself the book. Jack, it was worth every cent. I didn't lay it down from the moment I started it. I've heard a lot of talk about it, all of it praise, and have been so proud to say I know you."

Whether Olive would have been so proud had she known what Jack was suffering from is questionable. Both the Lahey Clinic and the Mayo, being private institutions, would jealousy guard the secrets of Jack's medical life long after his death. Neither they nor Jack's family could expunge or even control the record, however.

Part of Jack's problem was his stomach. Another complaint, we know from recently released naval medical records, related to his spine. "August 1940 he pulled something in his back while serving at tennis. He was able to continue the match, but it recurred when he played again. He says that some times [sic] seemed to slip out in his back and after a while, if he sat in a special position, it would go in again. Gradually his back got stiffer and he had to stop all athletics. Even getting out of bed in the morning, if he sat in a certain position it made his left sacro-iliac region sore and would make him walk stiff-legged . . ."

This account was Jack's own, taken down by a naval doctor four years later. It deliberately obscured Jack's medical past: not only the physical breakdowns and pain Jack had suffered throughout his life, but the infection that had blighted the end of his Harvard career: venereal disease. This latest infection occurred "when he was in College in 1940," the Lahey Clinic's chief urologist later confided, adding that the urethritis cleared after "local urethral treatment and sulfonamides."

Sulfonamides could cure gonorrhea; however they proved ineffective against what became known as postgonoccal urethritis, a less severe but still painful disease usually contracted along with gonorrhea. Not even penicillin, once available, could cure this urethritis, which periodically caused excruciating pain on urination, inflammations of the genital area, and uncomfortable discharge that returned to haunt the patient—"recurrent episodes of frequency nocturia and discomfort in the region of the bladder and prostate," as the urologist noted on Jack's case history.

Now, informed by Carmel Offie that Jack "recently made a trip to Rochester," Ambassador Bullitt sent a note of encouragement, hoping "they told you there is absolutely nothing wrong with you. I am still convinced you are in perfect order."

But Jack wasn't. Spine, spleen, stomach, and seminal parts of his lower body hurt. The Mayo doctors were bewildered, but, as in 1935, concluded that a period of quiet convalescence, without the stress of full-time graduate law study at Yale, would be Jack's best hope of recovery.

"John F. Kennedy, 23, second oldest son of Ambassador to Great Britain, Joseph P. Kennedy, will not enter Yale Law School this fall as originally planned, he disclosed tonight," the *Boston Herald* recorded on September 10, 1940, when he returned from the Mayo. "Planning to remain at the family's summer home here for another fortnight, young Kennedy said he had no definite plans for the future. He expects to travel and will probably spend part of the winter in the West. . . . He plans to enter Yale Law School next fall."

To James Landis, an erstwhile colleague at the SEC and now head of the Harvard Law School, Ambassador Kennedy felt obliged to excuse Jack's choice of Yale. Jack had chosen New Haven "principally because he felt it would be better not to be constantly in direct competition with his brother, and I rather sympathize with him in that point of view." However, Jack had also "been having trouble for a number of years with his stomach and I now hear that the doctors advise him to take a year off. I hate to see him lose a year in these crucial times," the ambassador, who had become increasingly maudlin and depressed, lamented from London, "but, after all, his health is more important."

America's Most Bombed Ambassador

The truth was that the Battle of Britain and bombing of English air bases had unnerved Ambassador Kennedy. He'd rented the country mansion at St. Leonard's in a rush, and hadn't done the usual "background research" that marked his wisest investments. "I did not notice at the time that the house was only a few miles away from a group of factories and an airfield," he later confessed. Though his house was never hit, the nightly antiaircraft barrage disturbed his sleep. Moreover, after one particularly heavy raid, the tail of an incendiary bomb was found in the nearby park, fortuitously bearing Kennedy's initials: JPK. Within minutes he had reporters and a photographer around, prompting the picture caption, published worldwide, "America's Most Bombed Ambassador."

In England, however, Kennedy's nightly departure for the country, excused on the grounds of "my practice of avoiding formal dinners," but in fact so that "I could regularly get out of the city," aroused widespread contempt. Churchill declined to see, let alone consult him. Roosevelt did the same. So infuriated did Kennedy become that at one stage he complained personally to the British chancellor of the exchequer: "Finally I told him that I was sick and disgusted at coming down there and not being kept posted on current financial matters. I said it was apparently the policy of the present government to keep me from finding out as much as possible"—a complaint he also made to Henry Morgenthau, the U.S. treasury secretary, who bypassed him in negotiations with the British government. To Lord Halifax, the Foreign Secretary, Kennedy hurled the same accusation: "I told him what I thought of the complete lack of news during the last month even from him," Kennedy bitterly related; "that aside from the one Italian episode he had told me nothing and that if it were not that I did not want to walk out under the threat of bombing, I would rather resign than put up with such nonsense."

In order not to embarrass Roosevelt, Churchill had then consented to see Kennedy more frequently, thus treating the American ambassador to a series of intimate glimpses of greatness as the French collapsed, the Russians invaded the Baltic Republics as well as Rumania, and Britain, literally, "stood alone."

Sadly for Britain, Kennedy wasn't impressed, though he did at least jot down some of Churchill's more memorable sayings for posterity. To Kennedy's sarcastic remark that Churchill had "certainly picked a nice time to be Prime Minister," the longtime Conservative back-bencher responded with the memorable words: "They wouldn't have given me the Prime Ministership if there had been any meat left on the bone."

When handing Kennedy a letter for Roosevelt and describing his recent efforts to stiffen French morale, Churchill forecast "the French would not give up their fleet; they would turn pirates before that."

Churchill's oratory, his refusal to be bowed, and his gift for metaphor were an inspiration to the people of England and to many in America, but Kennedy foresaw only doom and destruction if Britain soldiered on, thus blinding himself to Churchill's stature and misleading Roosevelt as to Britain's chances of survival. He still worked assiduously on the "wobble-boys" of Whitehall, feeding on any sign of despondency to put forward his own proposals for appeasement. When the Foreign Secretary told him the French would probably "quit" but Britain would fight, adding that he was "much more optimistic about Germany's ability to invade than I am about our capability in holding out," Kennedy immediately demanded to know whether, "if the French attempt to make peace, would you want to be included in it?"

Halifax was uncertain and in his uncertainty had already asked the prime minister the very same question, as he told Kennedy: "I have said to Churchill, 'Well, assuming that the terms were on the basis of an indemnity and giving up the colonies and you were allowed to retain your freedom and independence, what then?" To this, the prime minister had delivered the chilling rebuke: "That is so unlikely that it is not worthy of consideration."

Kennedy, however, refused to believe that anyone would choose to fight rather than believe in a Hitler indemnity. "My own impression," he recalled his ignoble response, was "that should anything like that be offered it would be snapped up."

By whom, though? Had Lord Halifax become prime minister, Kennedy might have been right. Churchill, however, remained stalwart and majestic, and Roosevelt had risen to the occasion with a last-minute appeal to Reynaud, the French prime minister, not to give up: "I am personally particularly impressed by your declaration that France will continue to fight on behalf of Democracy even if it means slow withdrawal, even to North Africa and the Atlantic. It is most important to remember that the French and British Fleets continue mastery of the Atlantic and other oceans; also to remember that vital materials from the outside world are necessary to maintain all armies." In this respect "naval power in world affairs still carries the lessons of history, as Admiral Darlan knows."

Kennedy had delivered a copy of the message to Churchill at Admiralty House. "The Prime Minister was just sitting down to dinner with his wife and two daughters. . . . He was visibly excited. . . . He reread the cable himself three or four times, and said he would immediately convey to

Reynaud that his understanding of this message was that the United States would assume a responsibility if the French continued to fight. In other words, while the President did not say 'I am entering the war,' his message was a commitment first, because it promised all material aid and secondly, because it contained advice to France to continue fighting even if the French Government were driven right out of France." Even Kennedy felt "it was a commitment. . . . The Prime Minister ate quickly a very substantial meal composed of an entrée, followed by fish, jellied chicken and strawberries," Kennedy related. "While he ate he described to me the appalling conditions in France."

Not even Churchill's eloquence, backed by Roosevelt's "commitment," could make the French fight on, however. As Churchill predicted, they scuttled their fleet rather than see it in British hands and under Marshal Pétain and a Vichy government, settled down to their years of shame.

Kennedy's role, too, was shameful. When requested by Churchill to telephone Roosevelt to ask permission for the president's stirring message to be printed, Kennedy agreed to do so—but instead promptly returned to the embassy and cabled Roosevelt to urge him to retract his commitment. "Though I realize the tragedy of the present moment and how important it is for the success of these poor people that their morale should be bucked up, I nevertheless see in the message a great danger as a commitment at a later date," Kennedy signaled.

The "bear" who had become rich beyond dreams by selling short was selling short again, this time fantasizing in his message to Roosevelt that "if the English people thought there was a chance of peace on any decent terms an upheaval against the Government might come," an upheaval, Kennedy claimed, in which Churchill would be overthrown.

This was wishful thinking. Meanwhile, when asked by Halifax whether he thought Wendell Willkie "had a chance," Kennedy answered, "As it stands today, he very likely has"—a remark which, once it wended its way back to Kennedy's "boss," was considered disloyal. There followed a bitter confrontation over the telephone when Roosevelt scotched suggestions that Joe come home as the president's reelection manager. "I didn't want you to hear that you had been named and that your name has been turned down by me," Roosevelt explained. "You know how happy I would be to have you in charge," Roosevelt lied, and blamed the State Department which, he claimed, had vetoed the proposal. "The general impression is that it would do the cause of England a great deal of harm if you left there at this time."

Kennedy was not deceived. To Clare Luce he said, "The President telling me that the State Department wants to do something different from what he wishes is something new in my life." To Roosevelt, meanwhile, he protested, saying that he was "seriously considering going home; that, as far as I can see, I am not doing a damn thing here that amounts to anything and my services, if they are needed, could be used to much better advantage at home."

"I was damn fresh on the phone," Kennedy boasted to Eddie Moore afterward. "I think FDR rang me up because he was afraid I would walk out and he wanted to 'soft-soap' me." To his cousin Joe Kane, however, he later told "a fantastic story," which he vowed was true, about his last days as ambassador. As Kane recounted, "Seems that he and Neville Chamberlain hatched a plan; Kennedy was to go to Germany and make a proposition to Hitler; England would help restore German [colonial] possessions if Germany would stay on the Continent. They took the idea to King George, who had Roosevelt on the transatlantic telephone inside of minutes. First thing that Kennedy knew he was on the phone explaining it to Roosevelt, who said, 'I'm against it.' Kennedy said, 'I found out that Roosevelt was more for war than anybody in Europe.' Kennedy then said, 'I'm coming home.' Roosevelt replied, 'You stay there.' Kennedy answered, 'Goddamn you, no one is going to tell me what I'm going to do!' "

For the moment, however, Roosevelt could. Though the ambassador wrote to Eddie Moore that he'd threatened Roosevelt "that any one of these days I might say, 'The Hell with it. If this is the way you want to run the place, I will go home,' " he knew he could not resign against the wishes of the president without putting in jeopardy his reputation and public career. Thus he remained in London, exiled, silenced, and afraid.

When Roosevelt proposed the reinstitution of the draft and the training of the U.S. National Guard as part of his emergency measures in September 1940, Kennedy was scornful: "two critical acts of President Roosevelt bringing us a step closer to war," he later remarked. Meanwhile he had to acknowledge that "while people at home were becoming definitely alarmed as they felt the hot breath of a military regime on their necks, people in England had an interlude of cool calm," despite the Battle of Britain raging in the skies and the massing of German barges for a cross-Channel invasion. Churchill, he learned through Brendan Bracken, had found King George "shooting at a target with a rifle. His Majesty told the Prime Minister that if the Germans were coming, he was going to get 'his German.' Churchill told him that if he felt that way about it, he would supply him with a tommy gun so he could kill a lot of Germans. Churchill did, and thereafter the King practiced with a tommy."

Before long, however, Kennedy had proof he was being further bypassed by Roosevelt. "I learned not from the State Department but from British sources that Admiral Ghormley of our own Navy was com-

ing over to London with other military to 'observe' for the President,"
Kennedy recalled. Furious at such "circumventory tactics," he "cabled
my strong opposition to this back-room procedure, calling it a mistake in
policy."

Kennedy had no one to blame but himself. Despite the "cool calm" of
the British, he himself remained pessimistic and cold-shouldered. When
he took Roosevelt's message confirming the destroyer deal to Admiralty
House, he was refused entrance because Churchill was sleeping. "Imagine," the ambassador spluttered in retrospect, "this was the message
Churchill had been waiting for for weeks, and on which he said the fate
of Civilization might well depend, and he had to have his afternoon nap!"

Worse still, Churchill never seemed "to remember that I don't
drink"—an aversion to liquor that prompted Churchill to say, "My God!
You make me feel as if I should go round in sack cloth and ashes!" At
the subsequent celebratory "Destroyer Dinner" Kennedy was acutely
aware "I had been almost completely ignored in the destroyer-base
negotiations, being used merely to convey messages from the White
House to Downing Street." He was not even able to answer when the
prime minister, in sudden alarm, asked whether the American destroyers
had boilers, or would have to be towed across the Atlantic.

Once German bombing of British cities was stepped up in September,
however, Kennedy's cables and telephone calls to the State Department
became hysterical. He was convinced Americans would never agree to be
involved in such a war if they knew what it was like. "The Embassy, I
wrote home, was unsafe and 'when they drop these big bombs and every
five minutes for three or four hours and you see fires starting in a complete circle all around, Cape Cod seems like an awfully good place.' " To
Sumner Welles he complained that "no one in the State Department had
any idea of what we were going through and seemed to care less. Accordingly when President Roosevelt called me at 3 P.M. September 15 and said
perfunctorily that he hoped we were all right, I wasn't very cordial. For
ten days there had been continual bombing and at night the anti-aircraft
barrage made sleep impossible."

Kennedy's personal cowardice in leaving town every evening, while the
rest of his staff remained in London became embarrassing, and eventually
"a delegation of girls from the Embassy staff came to me and asked to get
them located where they could get some sleep," Kennedy later confided.
Arrangements were made to take a house at Sunnydale from Lord Derby,
with eighteen rooms for the staff—but the ambassador was, as he himself
put it, "determined to go home."

The Beast from the East

While Jack's father plotted to come home, Jack left home. Five years before, he'd recuperated on a farm in Arizona. This time, in September 1940, he also chose a "farm"—the nickname given to the erstwhile ranch of Governor Leland Stanford at Palo Alto, thirty miles south of San Francisco, nestling on the high ridge between the Pacific Ocean and San Francisco Bay, and since 1885 the home of Stanford University.

The Palo Alto climate was warm and dry; the university was coeducational, with almost two thousand female students enrolled; the buff, sandstone campus architecture by Olmsted and Coolidge, modeled on Romanesque and California-mission styles, was considered the most beautiful college design in America; half the students owned cars (some even airplanes); the college football stadium held over 89,000 spectators; and women were forbidden to walk on the quad unless wearing silk stockings.

This, and more, appealed to Jack. Betty Grable, in her starring role in *Campus Confessions* the year before, had enhanced Stanford's reputation for being "a predominantly rich man's college," as *Time* magazine wrote, boasting "one of the finest Pacific Coast golf courses, two lakes, a polo field as well as two great gymnasiums." Though one professor had protested to the university president of a "growing tendency to regard the University as a country club," it was precisely this aspect that now attracted the wandering New Englander.

On September 23, 1940, having bought a new car—a green Buick convertible—with the proceeds of *Why England Slept,* Jack decided to stay, and sent a quick note from the President Hotel, Palo Alto, to Dean Hanford at Harvard requesting a copy of his college record as he was "taking some pre-law work out here at Stanford."

What prelaw work Jack intended to do mystified his friends back east. Torbert Macdonald, who'd been accepted by the Harvard Law School, later thought that "Jack went to Stanford to enter into the School of Journalism." Lem Billings, however, explained vaguely that Stanford "was an enormous college and there were an awful lot of courses he could take that were ones he'd not had before and I think he probably was marking time, I really do."

Whatever the truth, Jack soon moved out of the President Hotel and took humbler lodgings in "The Cottage," behind Miss Gertrude Gardiner's house on Mayfield Road. It was there he received his first letter from Torbert Macdonald, who, if uncertain about what Jack was studying, assumed he was at least "firmly entrenched by now as the 'toast of the coast' & the 'Beast from the East.' " (He himself, he claimed, was "firmly entrenched as 'Torb the Grind, the horse's behind.' . . . Your book was 11th in Boston here last Sunday, but I suppose it's picked up along the West Coast," he mocked. "There has been a bit of favorable comment on it among the young intellegentsia [*sic*] here at school—& most of them figure you're gathering material for a new one.") "Has your health improved?" Torby asked Jack, and wished to know "how you're going in the wilds with that international flavor about you—are those co-eds yelling for more—or help? . . . Shoot me the dope boy and I'll keep you posted on all your Boston girls."

Given the multiplicity of women's sorority houses, Jack was spoiled for choice, but wary of spreading his venereal infection, he proceeded somewhat cautiously, writing to Billings on October 4, 1940, that he was "well, very well settled here. Have my own cottage on the campus + living very well. Have met a lot of people and they are all very friendly—quite a change from the East. Still can't get used to the Co-eds," he confessed, "but am taking them in my stride. Expect to cut one out of the herd + brand her shortly, but am taking it very slow as do not want to be known as the beast of the East," he quipped, quoting Macdonald.

One of the first girls to be "branded" by Jack's iron was Susan Imhoff, who was attending a junior college near San Francisco when she met him. "Jack was cute and smart and wise, but he was also stubborn," she remembered, "bossy and arrogant. He talked endlessly about his father, with whom he seemed unusually close. I know he had a bad back because even then he slept on a plywood bed board and couldn't drive for more than an hour without having to stop and stretch. Because of his back he preferred making love with the girl on top. He found it more stimulating to have the girl do all the work. I remember he didn't enjoy cuddling after making love, but he did like to talk and had a wonderful sense of humor—he loved to laugh."

Humor was, as always, Jack's saving grace. "He really is the funniest boy alive," his sister Kathleen had written to her father in May. "He had the Irish maid in fits the whole time. Every time he'd talk to her he'd put on a tremendous Irish brogue."

A lovely Pi Phi girl, Harriet Price, was next on Jack's agenda. "She was most attractive," Harriet's friend Jeanne Bouchard recalled. "She had wide-apart eyes and a rather broad face. She had a sexy figure and kind of slunk around when she walked. The boys were just crazy about her. It was natural that Jack should be attracted to her."

It was also understandable that "Flip," as she was affectionately known, should be attracted to Jack.

Jack Filor was a friend of mine. He'd been at Choate, and knew Jack—he brought him over to meet me practically the day he arrived at Stanford. Jack was not a drinker—there was a lot of drinking done at Stanford at that time, but he was not interested in drinking. He didn't smoke. And he was very attractive. I had a feeling—it wasn't a very hard feeling to have—that he was very interested in politics and government and probably wanted a career in that direction. I mean, it wasn't defined yet as to what, but he was fascinated with the news. He always turned it on in the car, on the radio. He was quite curious about it. . . . Everything is relative to the other young men I was seeing at the time. He seemed older and more sophisticated, really, and he was. And certainly more politically oriented. I remember once I turned off the radio when he was listening to the news and he got absolutely furious. He was very hot-tempered, at first. After, it flared down very quickly. But he was intrigued by what was going on in the world.

Another graduate remembered "what an utterly attractive couple Jack and Harriet" made. They went to Carmel together for the big Stanford football game and dance, to movies and restaurants. "He was sort of a minicelebrity," Flip recalled. "I was in love with him. I was wildly in love with him. I think Jack was in love with me. We talked about the possibility of marriage—a little bit, but not seriously."

It was far from clear whether Jack was looking for a marital partner. His mother had written after the Harvard commencement that "Jack seems a little depressed that he let his girl get away. He says she [Frances Ann Cannon] is the only one he really enjoyed going out with. And yet he admits that he did not want to get married." But Flip Price saw things a different way, at least in retrospect. "I don't think he was ready for marriage," she later reflected. "I also think that he was, almost calculating about his future . . . that everything was going to run the way he wanted it to run, and that included the right kind of marriage to the right person that would fit in with whatever he planned to be doing. I think that was always at the back of his mind. I don't think he was serious about anyone. I think he was as serious about me as about anyone else—we had a very good time together, usually just on our own—but no, he wasn't ready for marriage."

This was certainly the case at Stanford. Though he demanded complete loyalty from his male friends, the notion of lifelong loyalty to a woman was not something that fitted Jack's bruised, narcissistic psyche. "He was really bombing around that place," recalled one of his elder brother's friends, Tom Killefer; "I think he really had a much better time than he deserved to have." Flip Price recalled:

He would go down for weekends to Hollywood, where he had contacts thru his father, Joe Kennedy. He knew Robert Stack and all those people, and went out with girls down there. He told me about it. I didn't pay much attention.

He talked about his father's infidelities. He said his father went on these long trips, was gone so much of the time, and that he'd come back and give his mother some very lavish presents—a big Persian rug or some jewelry or something like that. Obviously Jack knew everything that was going on in the marriage.

I think his father was a tremendous influence, I don't think there's any question about that, but not all to the good! It seemed to me that his father's obvious rather low opinion of his wife and the way he treated her, that some of that rubbed off on Jack. He wasn't mean or anything about his mother, but I think that denigration, that came from the father, rubbed off on the son. And that's where all the womanizing and everything came from!

"I picked Stanford," Jack meanwhile explained in an interview with the *Stanford Daily,* "principally because of your ex-student body president and [graduate] student manager Tom Killefer. He was my brother's roommate at Harvard and he sneered so at the Florida climate when he was staying with us there that I had to find out if it really was the climate or just Killefer. So far he's right, but wait till I see that first cloud," he quipped.

Beyond the dry climate, it was the presence of so many women that attracted Jack to Stanford. He assured the *Stanford Daily* reporter, Jean Nowell, that at Harvard, "whenever they ask for undergraduate opinion on what would improve the school, about 80 percent of the suggestions are to make the school co-educational." He even attributed Stanford's undefeated football record to "the rooting section's spirit and thinks the women probably have something to do with it."

The Stanford ladies in their silk stockings were a joy—though Jack's mother frankly admitted to finding his choice of girlfriends dictated more by bust than by brains. "I don't think he'd be interested in anyone who was just a brain and no looks," Rose reflected later. "I think he'd rather looks than a brain at that point."

To the extent that Jack's mother was ever prepared to address the subject of Jack's sex appeal, she expressed surprise at his success. "He didn't have the sense of rhythm that Joe [Jr.] had," she remarked, comparing Jack's dancing with her eldest son's. "Joe was, I think in a way, better looking, but Jack had that sort of rugged face and then he photographed better than his older brother, which was quite interesting—he really always photographed well, so he was good looking, but I think, as

I said, Joe's features, his features if you look at them in a photograph, were perhaps more regular than Jack's."

Girls, Jack found increasingly, were not attracted by regularity. Jane Suydam, who'd met Jack at the New Orleans Mardi Gras when he was pursuing Frances Ann Cannon, found him "unbelievably handsome. He had this remarkable animal pull. The impact on me was overwhelming."

Miss Suydam was not alone. Jack's friend at Harvard, Jimmy Rousmanière, considered Jack an "odd mixture of serious scholar and fun-loving, girl-crazed fool." Jack's letters to his pals now bore this out to a T. "Do you ever remember a fat blond boy named Jim Filer [*sic*] at Choate?" he asked Lem Billings.

> Well he's out here—and is quite the man about the campus. He has quite a hero notion of me from Choate and from what I can gather most of the younger boys at school thought of me as sort of a god-like Casanova, if you know what I mean, and thought you were a big shit, as near as I can tell. Anyway Jim is launching me on the campus. I am glad I was nice to the younger fellows back at Choate as it only shows. The next time I see him I will go into more detail about why nobody at Choate liked you, although to tell the truth, he is rather vague about you—just thinks you're a shit. . . . Best, Jack.

Stanford Business School

"Have really settled down to a Health regime—in bed at 10:00 and taking a couple of courses at the business school," Jack meanwhile explained to Billings. He told Jean Nowell of the *Stanford Daily* that he planned "to go into some form of business law. So far," she ended her profile of Jack, "his schedule is a year in the business school here, and then a second grad year at Yale Law School."

Owing to his poor health, Jack did not, in the end, register as a full-time student for credit, but contented himself with enrolling to audit Professor Theodore Kreps's postgraduate Introduction to Business and Government class. Dr. Kreps was a well-known economist and adviser to the Roosevelt administration and had no great love or admiration for Joseph Kennedy, whom he had known in his SEC days; indeed, one of his students later recalled, "he frequently cited Joe Kennedy senior as one who 'got away with murder' in making his fortune, and these were the practices he wanted to eliminate in setting up the SEC. And then there was that classic remark which all of us at Biz School heard him make so often: 'The Irish potato famine of the 1840's was the greatest disaster that ever struck the U.S.' "

Whatever feelings Kreps might have harbored against Joseph Kennedy, however, he was genuinely delighted to accept Jack—a young honors graduate from his alma mater, Harvard, as well as a bestselling author in his own right—into his class.

If Kreps was pleased, however, his graduate students were not. Jack's casual attitude toward his business studies infuriated his colleagues. One graduate who boasted three congressmen and one senator in his family was scathing in his later recollections of "the young Boston Irishman" at Stanford:

> He seemed to have no interest in his courses per se except perhaps to explore the subject matter in a general way. He carried a very light load, and put in only very infrequent appearances. I don't believe I ever heard him refer to his father at all. . . . He was a very unobtrusive boy. That's the best word I can find for him; it's not that he was stand-offish, just that he kept to himself. The name itself meant nothing, so no one thought of him in connection either with large money or his father. And there are scads of Kennedys.
>
> At Dr. Kreps's home he once showed up in evening clothes, but wearing tennis shoes! I thought this odd, but then we started to argue about his book on England. Even though I had gone to school in Europe, and had a stepfather who was a Nazi MdR, later murdered by them, I told him I'd hesitate to write a book on Germany, whereas he, after only a few months in England, felt qualified to comment.
>
> He had no close friends from Stanford. I don't think anyone ever knew where he lived. What he really did with his time, no one could say. He just came and went at odd intervals, almost unnoticed. He never expressed any strong opinions . . . never mentioned girls or booze, kept to himself, polite, but no more, all in all apparently very unsure of himself, or just what he was doing.

"I have a vague recollection that Mr. Kennedy sat in the rear of the room," another student recalled, "and I cannot remember hearing his voice in this predominantly lecture class. I seem to recall that he was absent from time to time because Dean Jackson came to the classroom one morning to ask Mr. Kennedy to talk to his father on the telephone. The Dean was somewhat upset when no one knew where Mr. Kennedy might be."

Yet another classmate claimed later that "JFK did not participate in student affairs or campus activities to the best of my knowledge, and he did not attract attention as a person, despite his authorship of *Why England Slept*. This book was never a subject of discussion at Biz School; no one I knew had read it, even though the war had been going on [in Europe] for over a year. It may be that he considered his Stanford experience as just another lark, rather than as originally intended."

Such ignorant snobbery reminded Jack of Princeton. Fortunately, those who made the effort to get to know the "rather shy, reserved" young Boston Irishman were almost invariably won over, David Cuthbertson remembered. In the fifteen-minute seminar breaks, Cuthbertson "approached him to discuss various matters, in hopes of getting to know him better and seeing to it that he mingled and became acquainted with more of the graduate students. Once we took the initiative of talking to Jack and breaking the ice, so to speak, we found him to participate in our informal sessions on the lawn and oftentimes, after we got him going, we would be more than content to listen to him than try to participate ourselves. . . . While he only audited the course I had with him, he impressed me as being a brilliant student with seemingly an infallible memory capacity."

Harry Muheim, a contemporary, also dispelled the idea of Jack as a wallflower, vividly recalling how he was first introduced to Jack by Bruce Jessup, the Stanford student president. When Jessup complained about the impotence of student government, Jack "responded immediately to the problem," Muheim recalled, "explaining to Bruce that any government without power is naturally ineffective. He said that Bruce would have to find some genuine basis for power. . . . In a quiet way, Kennedy persisted on the point. He wasn't talking about overthrow [of the university administration]. 'Look at Roosevelt. He had made a kind of revolution within the framework of the United States Government, and a lot of people hadn't even noticed.' "

Such a remark, in Republican circles, was considered heresy. "Bruce replied that his father, an Altadena businessman, *had* noticed. Kennedy smiled and went on with some other illustrations not quite so close to home."

"Even when you didn't much care about the conversation, Jack Kennedy was compelling," Muheim related. "He was quick to explain, to ask, and to consider. His sentences flowed spontaneously. Gags were naturally interspersed with the straight material. Illustrations and examples were brought in without effort from several locations and several centuries. I had never before heard one of my contemporaries *allude* to so many things."

Part of the problem in understanding what Jack was doing at Stanford, Robert Murray admitted, was that "JFK never took the GSB [Graduate School of Business] seriously, and whatever time he devoted to study was spent over in the Political Science Department. This I never would have known were it not for the fact that the presidential campaign was going full blast—FDR vs. WW [Wendell Wilkie]—and Kreps was kidded a lot about failing to keep his protégé interested in the program."

This was indeed the rub. Professor Hopper had urged Jack to first "get the machinery" for his boat before setting out into the sea of life, but try as he might, Jack could summon no great interest in business studies, whereas the discussion of political ideas at a critical moment of world history still enthralled him. Fortunately or unfortunately, the senior professor in the political science department, by sheer chance, turned out to be Jack's neighbor on Mayfield Road, Tom Barclay. Forty years later, Barclay related how he'd gone to the 1940 Democratic Convention in Chicago, where Roosevelt was nominated for a third term, and later that summer when he came back to Stanford in September of 1940, "Miss Gardiner, who owned the apartment where I lived on Mayfield Avenue, told me she had rented 'The Cottage,' that was a little guest house out in the back. . . . She said she had a young man from the East and of course it turned out to be Jack Kennedy. I saw him every day, got to know him, and liked him very much. . . . He didn't take any work for credit but he attended classes; he attended some of my classes, especially the seminar course in A-1," Contemporary World Problems.

Though the subject matter of Barclay's course was more to Jack's liking, the political scale was weighted even more to the Republican side than in Harvard courses. Given that "the majority of the faculty regarded themselves as members of the Republican Party," and given that, by an estimated three-to-one majority, the students at Stanford backed Wendell Willkie, the Republican contender for the 1940 presidency, Jack was bound to attract opprobrium, even dislike among the snootier Stanford students. However, what distinguished Jack most from his contemporaries at Stanford, in Muheim's view, was something that few students, male or female, seemed able to grasp in the country-club atmosphere of "the farm" in the fall of 1940: namely, Jack's conviction that the United States of America would, sooner or later, have to fight. "Jack Kennedy's message for the remote westerners was that there was a war on, that it had been on for a year, and that we were going to get into it," Harry Muheim recalled. "I had heard the same thing . . . from President Roosevelt himself on the radio—but it was not until that night that I believed it."

Slam, Bam, Thank You, Ma'am

As a conspicuous member of Stanford's National Emergency Committee (set up to liaise with the Palo Alto Draft Board—"a very unpopular cause on campus," its chairman, William Turner, later admitted) Jack waited, along with seventeen million fellow Americans who had been compelled to register on October 16, 1940, for America's first-ever peacetime draft selection. Meanwhile, he made a new friend at Stanford: a tall, good-looking aesthete from Yale named Henry James.

"I was a stranger in a strange land," James recalled, "suffering from stomach ulcers and doing a postgraduate degree in English literature." James, like Jack, was a Catholic, but from a "good" family in New York. On his first meeting, he found Jack abrasive.

> One day after I'd been there about two months, I picked up the *Stanford Daily,* and there was an interview with Jack, and it said that Stanford has a man from Harvard who's written a best-seller. I thought: that's sorta interesting, because I knew Kick. She came down to see the McDonnells, and I'd go to dances with her, and she'd mentioned a bit about her brothers, but that's all.
>
> But since I was essentially lonely out there, I thought, I'll look up Jack. He'd be someone I'd like to see, and we'd have fun talking about being transplanted Ivy Leaguers.
>
> So I spent quite a bit of time trying to find out how I could meet him. I called people in the Business School. I finally tracked him down to a class. It was over, say, at eleven-twenty, and at eleven-fifteen I was standing outside in the hall, outside the classroom, which I had to guess at. But sure enough, down the hall comes Jack: even in those years surrounded by people who were talking to him— well, the interview had just come out and that made him a little notorious. And so I went up to him—stopped him in midflight, so to speak.
>
> "You're Jack Kennedy, aren't you?" I said. "I'm Henry James and I'm from New York and Yale and I, er, is there any chance we could get together sometime?"
>
> "Oh," he said, "I'm very busy. I've got an awful lot of things going on, and I've got to go—I'm afraid it's really not possible. But thanks for coming along anyway. Nice to see you. Good luck!"
>
> I said to myself, "Fuck you! Forget about him!"

James's second meeting with Jack was rather different. "I was at the Post Office getting my mail," he recalled, "and Jack came in to get his mail. He looked at me and said: 'Didn't I meet you somewhere?'

"I said, 'Yeah, I came up to you the other day, about a week ago.'

" 'What'd you say your name was?'

"We talked a little bit. I guess I said a few things which made him laugh, and he said some things which made me *really* laugh—about Stanford and so on. And so he said, 'Come and have lunch with me.' "

James explained that because of his ulcers he was obliged to sit at the special diet table. Jack was peremptory.

" 'I said, 'Come and have lunch with me!' "

"Well, I hadn't been ordered to do something like that in a long time. So I said 'Okay,' and we went to the cafeteria and sat at the counter. And I immediately fell under the spell of his charm."

Part of the charm was the very sharpness of Jack's intellect. "Whenever he met someone new, he'd quiz them—put them right on the griddle— 'Where are you from, where did you graduate, what did you study at Yale, how did you do, what are you doing here?' So he knew my whole life in five minutes! And I didn't know his, except what I'd read in the campus newspaper!"

They began to see a lot of each other. "We met regularly then. All the time. We went to all the football games together. I laughed for the first time since I left New York—in two months. Oh, he was so amusing. He was so much fun. He was so witty! He was—just lots of things!"

One of the things Jack was not was sentimental. When James unwisely shared a letter he'd received from his girlfriend back east, couched in high literary prose ("I can't tell you how devastated I am. . . . I walked past your house on 74th Street, and I wept so copiously I almost stumbled and fell'—things like that"), Jack remained unmoved. "I said, 'Jack isn't that beautiful!' 'Oh,' he said, 'it may be romantic to you, but it's shit to me!'

"It was a devastating blow, you know," James related. "But it was so devastating that I roared with laughter!"

Jack's attitude toward his Catholic religion, James recalled, was not very different.

> We talked about it a lot. He found great difficulty in believing most of the tenets of the Catholic faith. Church bored him! He hardly ever went. Religion didn't interest him. He was all for being au courant, very much up to date with the things that were going on at the time, but not eternal verities. He wasn't going to drop his religion. He liked the way it made him special, different in a Protestant world. But otherwise it didn't give him the things people need religion for. And

he wasn't going to wrestle with what far brighter, more capable, more feeling people did invest in—"I just don't have time for it."

For Jack, love of God was, like the love of a woman, a romantic conception for which he had little use. Despite the many women "throwing themselves at him," James observed,

> Jack was never in love. He liked women. He needed women, but he didn't want a commitment to a relationship.
>
> I remember my psychiatric counselor at Yale telling that the ideal marriage of two people occurs when the man says, "I want to devote myself to this one woman, who is going to be the mother of my children, the keeper of the feminine flame in this relationship, while I will in turn be conveying to her the masculine side of things." But Jack didn't want that at all from his women! He wanted—we used to laugh. His favorite phrase was "Slam, Bam, Thank You, Ma'am." That was the only thing that interested him about sex really—not the only thing, I wouldn't say that, that's an exaggeration, but that was the *principal* thing. I mean he admitted that to me! He told me that! He said, "I'm not interested—once I get a woman, I'm not interested in carrying on, for the most part. I like the conquest. That's the challenge. I like the contest between male and female—that's what I like. It's the chase I like—not the kill!"
>
> That was really his basic. That's why he wasn't a deep person in some ways. And that's why he wasn't an intellectual either—though he passed himself off as both of these things and got away with it. But he never got away with it with me! Because I knew him better. I didn't respect him any less for it. In fact I think I loved him more, because he wasn't perfect, he had these peccadilloes, these drawbacks.

Behind Jack's macho façade, James suspected there was a less masculine reality than Jack cared to allow, even to himself.

> I think Jack had far more of the feminine in him than he'd ever admit. He was not a real macho. He *pretended* to be. He worked hard at it. But his very frame as a light, thin person, his proneness to injury of all kinds, his back, his sicknesses, which he wouldn't ever talk about, you know—he was heartily *ashamed* of them, they were a mark of effeminacy, of weakness, which he wouldn't acknowledge. I think all that macho stuff was compensation—all that chasing after women—compensation for something that he hadn't got, which his

brother Joe had. Joe was truly macho, truly a man's man. Jack was not. Jack was a woman's man *and* a man's man. He wasn't as simple as Joe in that respect—he was a prism through which a lot of things would filter, and different lights would come out. He was very narcissistic, which is very characteristic of a gay person—incredibly so. If you know any homosexuals, you'll know how they are constantly looking in mirrors at themselves. Appearance is *very* important to them—and it was to Jack. I'd say, "Jack, it's *ridiculous* for you to go out in the sun like that! You just can't wait to get down to Florida to get your tan in the quickest time so you can come back and look so handsome at these parties you go to." And he'd say, "Well, Henry, it's not only that I want to look that way, but it makes me feel that way. It gives me confidence, it makes me feel healthy. It makes me feel strong, healthy, attractive."

Typical of this unashamed concern with his appearance was a letter which Jack wrote to his Spee Club comrade, Cam Newberry, who'd sent some photographs with a mocking note about Jack's complexion. "I was very much upset to receive your letter," Jack replied, affecting outrage, on October 28: the night before the draft selection was due to take place in Washington.

What I most feared would happen—has happened. Somehow, some-where there has been a leak—probably out of Washington—some Republican trying to dig up campaign material evidently—and you have learned that on my draft card in the complexion column the examiner placed a very large bold X opposite the word "ruddy."

Embittered—probably because you are catalogued in the records forever as "sallow"—in spite of almost strangling to death in the lobby due to wearing a shirt two sizes too small in the vain hope of choking yourself from sallow to fair, you are desperate—fright-ened—and are even turning on your old buddy—ruddy Jack.

You are heartbroken to learn that at the time of my examination, there was absolutely no pressure on my neck whatever. I was wearing my usual red turtle-neck sweater and rooter's cap—in which I attend all classes, meals and football rallies.

I suppose the added insult of having your registrar fill in on your card opposite the words "identifying features," the words "mottled forehead—should be bald within a year"—this has made you see Cuban yellow.

You may do something rash—you will undoubtedly buy the giant new Mega General Electric sun lamp—no 121—in a frantic effort to get back that rich lemon color with which I am told you glowed on returning from your desperate trip to Honolulu, where you hoped to regain the title taken from you in the winter of 1939 at Palm Beach.

You have no doubt heard of my hard work here, in preparation to defend my title this Christmas—rising at nine—a hearty breakfast of Brown mush—eggs well browned and black coffee—sun on the back from 10–11—from 11–12:30, sun on the chest with special emphasis on getting the correct angle on the face—then a short drive through the country with the top down. In the afternoons—busily at work in the lab—testing and checking carefully my pigment reaction to the various oils and creams—accepting no manufacturer's boast, but making sure for myself—all in preparation for the next day's work—occasionally I take a few minutes off for a helping of brownies. Happy evenings are spent reading Howard Springs' immortal classic My Son, My Son, with occasional breaks to hawk autographed copies of Why England Slept around the local sororities at a reduced price.

I thus expect that unless I become over-trained, I should be odds-on favorite to retain my title this Christmas. I imagine you will be there [in Florida]—in a frantic and pathetic effort to get a crack at the title. I suppose you will still be spoiling many otherwise pleasant meals by dropping bits of skin into the soup from your peeling forehead.

It would be a far better thing, Tiny Moe, if you would confine yourself to adjusting the lighting on your camera—and would admit that you have been outmaneuvered—or rather that you outmaneuvered yourself. You burned yourself out this summer on the beaches at Wakiki [sic] while I patiently and thoroughly laid a basis at the Cape, ignored your boasting cards and then when you returned to turn yellow with the leaves, like a bronze thunder-bolt, I struck for the West where I now sit awaiting my commission as a Captain in a negro regiment—the best in the West—the boast of the Coast.

This letter was, however, the last of Jack's facetious, narcissistic, college-kid productions. Not only would the matter of skin pigmentation become deeply serious with the onset of Jack's fatal adrenal disease, but in Washington the following day Henry Stimson, the secretary of war, "blindfolded with a strip of linen" and standing before a barrage of cameras, reached into a glass bowl at twelve-eighteen P.M. Eastern Standard Time and handed the first draft-lottery slips to President Roosevelt. The eighteenth blue capsule "bore the serial 2748. The holder of 2748 for the Palo Alto area was Jack Kennedy, son of Joseph P. Kennedy, U.S. Ambassador to the Court of St. James's, and student at the Stanford

Business School. Young Kennedy is the author of a recent best-seller on the conditions in England before the outbreak of World War II," the *Stanford Daily* reported the sensational news next day on its front page, beneath a smiling picture of Jack. John F. Kennedy, having postponed his studies at Yale Law School for reasons of ill health, had been drafted.

Blackmailing the U.S. President

"I swear to God Jack I thought I'd die of exhaustion from laughing," Torby Macdonald responded to the news. "I'd laugh going to bed & wake up at it, having dreamt of you in camp with Moe Sidelburg & Joe Louis as bunkmates." Each time he thought of Jack—Jack who was so sloppy in his appearance, so constantly ill, and so fundamentally antiestablishment—in uniform, he was reduced to paroxysms of hysteria. "Christ of all the guys in the world, boy you're fated. I now know why we were pincked & frustrated so many times—the finger's on you. It's a lucky thing you've got your stomach."

Likewise, Lem Billings immediately sent a teasing cable from the Coca-Cola Company in Connecticut:

> ORCHIDS TO 2748 OR THE PRESIDENT'S 18TH CHOICE. HAVE MAILED YOU ONE BALE OF KHAKI AND J PRESS SPECIFICATIONS SPECIAL DELIVERY. MY ADVICE IS TO KEEP OUT OF THE SUN BECAUSE AS FAR AS YOU'RE CONCERNED IT WILL BE FAR MORE STYLISH TO BE YELLOW.

Another friend, Rip Horton, recalled being in a movie house "just at the time the draft was put into effect. . . . [Jack's] picture was flashed on the screen and I remember getting quite a kick out of it, thinking of him being drafted into the service."

Jack himself was not amused by the enormous publicity surrounding his selection. "This draft has caused me a bit of concern," he confided to Billings. "They will never take me into the army—and yet if I don't, it will look quite bad."

"Get your pappy home here quick boy," Macdonald taunted, "before those bombs land on him instead of aside of him—we can't afford to lose the only protection left to two yellow guys in this draft business."

For the moment, as a registered student at Stanford, Jack could avoid the issue of call-up, since bone fide students were permitted to defer service until the end of the academic year. But beyond the ridiculousness of such a perennially sick and unmilitary student being one of the first

Americans to be drafted, however, was a much greater irony, as Rip Horton remembered: namely, "that his father was so opposed to our getting involved in any foreign commitments."

Jack's father was not merely opposed to such commitments, he was, behind his façade of blunt, no-nonsense Boston-Irish "realism," a coward. "I hear they're calling Dad 'America's most bombed ambassador' now," Jack had proudly remarked to the *Stanford Daily* reporter two weeks before. "That's a helluva title, isn't it?"

Alas, it was pure fiction. In fact, on September 27, 1940, Ambassador Kennedy had cabled to Cordell Hull, the secretary of state, his "complete lack of confidence in the entire conduct of this war," which he couldn't "impress on you strongly enough . . . because it would be a complete misapprehension to imagine for one minute that the British have anything to offer in the line of productive capacity in industry or leadership that could be of the slightest value to us." A few days later, while the Germans kept up an indiscriminate rain of terror on British cities, the ambassador made clear to the State Department that he wished to be rescued from the sinking ship. "I am very unhappy about the whole thing and of course there is always the alternative of resigning," he threatened Hull, if the State Department refused to recall him.

Roosevelt, however, would not hear of it. As the American correspondents Joe Alsop and Bob Kintner reported in their syndicated column, "The President regards Kennedy as likely to do less harm in London than in New York," for in Roosevelt's eyes, if Kennedy was allowed to return to the United States, "he will reduce large numbers of leaders of opinion to such a state of hopeless blue funk that our foreign policy will be half-immobilized by fear. In short, the President has repeatedly urged Kennedy to remain in London in order to keep him quiet."

Kennedy, however, had no intention of remaining quiet. If Roosevelt labeled him a defeatist, he would label Roosevelt as a warmonger. On October 10, 1940, Lord Halifax signaled top priority to the British ambassador in Washington to warn him that the American ambassador was now threatening to blackmail Roosevelt. "He told me that he had sent an article to the United States to appear on November 1st, if by any accident he was not able to get there, which would be of considerable importance appearing five days before the Presidential election. When I asked him what would be the main burden of his song, he gave me to understand it would be an indictment of President Roosevelt's administration. . . . He is plainly a very disappointed and rather embittered man."

Kennedy was not bluffing, as Arthur Krock later confided. Kennedy had not only drawn up "an indictment of President Roosevelt's administration," Krock confirmed, but had passed it to his right-hand man, Edward Moore, with orders that it be published in America from coast to coast unless Roosevelt permitted him to leave the bombing and come home immediately.

The British Foreign Office was as concerned as President Roosevelt was. "The article which Mr. Kennedy has written," the Foreign Office summarized in a secret memorandum, "is due to appear four days before the election in order to damage Mr. Roosevelt's cause." Indeed the Foreign Office understood from secret sources that "Mr. Kennedy has decided to ally himself with Mr. Roosevelt's opponent Mr. Willkie. . . . In view of Mr. Kennedy's role in London throughout the war, and of his long standing personal antagonism to the American Ambassador to France, Mr. Bullitt, his article, if it duly appears, will certainly be both sensational and influential."

In the circumstances, Roosevelt had no option but to give in. The next day, October 11, 1940, Cordell Hull authorized Kennedy's recall—though whether for consultation or for good "seems obscure," the Foreign Office's American expert, T. North Whitehead, noted.

"Churchill immediately assumed that my going home was for purposes of aiding the Roosevelt campaign," Kennedy recalled of his farewell visit to the prime minister. "I reminded him that I was having a row with Roosevelt because of the manner in which the White House ignored the Embassy and did business with the Prime Minister direct."

Contemptuous of Kennedy's sniveling concern with such niceties while Rome burned, Churchill left the room "for a parliamentary meeting." It was the last time the prime minister would ever exchange a word with Kennedy in his life, and the Labour members of his Cabinet, having also been alerted to Kennedy's blackmail, were similarly cold. "I found Mr. Attlee, even this early, the fall of 1940, contemplating what form of government labor [*sic*] would offer England after the war," Kennedy later recounted, amazed by the deputy prime minister's confidence that the Nazis would be beaten, and deriding Labour's ambitious welfare program as "some form of Democracy . . . saturated with National Socialism but stopping short of Totalitarianism."

This left only the former high priest of appeasement. Kennedy recalled:

On the eve of my departure I called on Neville Chamberlain, one of the most misunderstood and unappreciated men ever to occupy a commanding place in world affairs. And one of the bravest! My call was really at his death bed. He was to undergo an operation three days later, October 22. . . . He said with a smile that the failure at Narvik had made Churchill Prime Minister, although he, Churchill, was the author of the Norway campaign. People merely knew it was a failure and blamed the government; and Chamberlain headed the government, hence they blamed Chamberlain. "Leaders," he said, "have to wait until public opinion is formed and then try to be a little ahead. . . . To have put money into broad preparation for war and take it away from commercial business which was the life of England, the country would not have accepted."

Clasping my hand and deprecating his role in life saying, "I haven't had many successes in my life, but I've made real contributions, I think," Chamberlain said to me, "This is goodbye. I remember you always said you would stay after me. But we will never see each other again."

Chamberlain was right. On Tuesday, October 22, 1940, Kennedy departed from Southampton on the Pan Am flying boat to Lisbon, from where he would fly home via Bermuda.

The British were relieved to be rid of such a defeatist ambassador, but Roosevelt was understandably worried. The rift had become public with Alsop and Kintner's latest syndicated column, in which it was openly stated that the U.S. ambassador to Britain fully intended to embarrass Roosevelt by expressing "his opinions to every available American listener the instant he got through customs." When the flying boat landed at Lisbon, Kennedy was therefore given a message "specifically requesting me to come to the White House and to make no statements to newsmen. I was of course indignant," Kennedy related.

The weather, however, was inclement, and Kennedy's chances of being able to blackmail the president before the election on November 5, 1940, began to diminish while he cooled his heels for several days, first in Lisbon and then in Horta. There, Kennedy related, he again "received a confidential message from President Roosevelt urging Mrs. Kennedy and myself to come to Washington immediately after arrival at New York and to spend Saturday night at the White House."

Six days had passed and still Kennedy was en route. Early on Sunday, October 26, stranded at Bermuda, Kennedy received a *third* summons to stay with the president that very night. He managed to put through a direct call to the White House. According to a young congressman present in the Oval Office at the time—Lyndon Baines Johnson—Roosevelt took the telephone and greeted the caller with the words, "Ah, Joe. It is so good to hear your voice. Please come to the White House tonight for a little family dinner." Johnson watched awestruck while the president slowly drew a finger across his throat. "I'm *dying* to talk to you."

The Last Supper

Kennedy's plane reached New York at two-thirty P.M. on October 26, 1940. Roosevelt was taking no chances, and had instructed Max Truitt of the Maritime Commission to hand Kennedy "a personal letter from the President asking me to come to Washington at once"—his fourth such summons.

Certain that he possessed enough dynamite to imperil Roosevelt's reelection, Kennedy was now in a quandary. The press were waiting outside the VIP lounge. "After I had seen the children," he related, "we, Mrs. Kennedy and a few personal friends went into another room. We talked the situation over as to whether or not I would be for or against the President."

In this quasi-Shakespearean drama, Rose Kennedy counseled caution. Clare Luce, Kennedy's mistress, disagreed. She begged him to announce his resignation and vote for the Republican contender, Wendell Willkie, as he'd promised her he would.

Kennedy procrastinated. "I told them that I had many personal grievances, but questioned as to whether or not they were sufficient grounds on which to take a definite stand," he recalled his dilemma. Kept at arm's length in England, he'd been unable to cut a deal with Willkie; moreover, judging by the latest polls, it now looked doubtful that Willkie could win, even if Kennedy did switch allegiance.

"At any rate," Kennedy recounted, "Rose and I took the five o'clock plane to Washington." According to Arthur Krock, Rose begged her husband, aboard the plane to Washington, not to resign as ambassador. " 'The President sent you, a Roman Catholic, as Ambassador to London, which probably no other President would have done,' she said. 'He sent you as his representative to the Pope's coronation. You would write yourself down an ingrate in the view of many people if you resign now.' "

At Washington, Kennedy recalled, "we were met at the airport by the White House car" and taken straight to the president. The atmosphere in the Oval Office was tense. Kennedy had a letter from Chamberlain, the dying archappeaser and former prime minister. This he gave the president "and told him a little about the difficulties in England." Nothing, however, "was said about my relationship or anything on it," for Roosevelt had wisely invited two witnesses, Senator Jimmy Byrnes and his wife, to be present. Together with Missy Le Hand they all "went into dinner on the Upper Floor right off his Study where we had scrambled eggs and sausages, toast and rice for dessert." In Kennedy's view, this was scarcely a welcome fit for America's Most Bombed Ambassador.

It was not. In fact it was a dinner fit for a blackmailer. Halfway through the meal, Senator Byrnes, "acting as though a wonderful idea had just struck him," Kennedy related, "said he thought it would be a great idea if I would go on the radio Tuesday night on my own. He thought it absolutely essential that I go and most necessary for the success of the Roosevelt campaign. He constantly referred to the President on this matter and he agreed it was necessary. I didn't say Yes, Aye, or No."

Roosevelt, meanwhile, was using his considerable charm on Rose Kennedy. It had been the president's idea to insist she accompany her husband and stay in the White House that night—knowing this was an invitation the lace-curtain Boston-Irish-Catholic *materfamilias,* shorn of her ambassador's-consort status in London for more than a year, and living in her lonely social "exile" back in Bronxville, simply could not refuse. "He knew that one of the easiest ways to get around me was to tell me complimentary things about my father," Rose later recalled. "I knew what he was doing (later one of the Roosevelt boys told Jack it was true, and Jack told me). Nevertheless, even while I knew I was being charmed, the charm was difficult to resist."

According to Rose, the president specifically turned the conversation to her sons, flattering Mr. Kennedy with the silver-tongued words: "I stand in awe of your relationship with your children. For a man as busy as you are, it is a rare achievement. And I for one will do all I can to help you if your boys should ever run for political office."

Kennedy, meanwhile, was well aware of Roosevelt's strategy. "The President worked very hard on Rose, whom I suspect he had come down because of her great influence on me. He talked to her about her father. All through dinner, Byrnes kept selling me the idea, but I made no comment, because I wanted to talk alone with the President before making any decision.

"After going back to the Study, and it still looked as if they had no intention of leaving me alone with the President, I finally said, 'Since it doesn't seem possible for me to see the President alone, I guess I'll just have to say what I am going to say in front of everybody.'" At this, Kennedy subsequently told Krock, Roosevelt's "face turned white and Byrnes was aghast."

"In the first place, I am damn sore at the way I have been treated," Kennedy began. "I feel that it is entirely unreasonable and I don't think I rated it." To Byrnes's and Roosevelt's incredulity, Kennedy claimed he'd never said anything in private that he hadn't said to Roosevelt's face, nor had he said anything publicly "that ever caused you the slightest embarrassment." He asserted, moreover, that he'd loyally supported

Roosevelt's third term: "I wrote to you a letter from Cannes and told you what I was willing to do and in spite of all that, you have given me a bad deal. First, because [Colonel Bill] Donovan was sent to London without consulting me; secondly, your sending a general there and Britain's knowing about it before I did; thirdly, carrying on negotiations on destroyers and bases through Lothian and not through me; and fourthly, the State Department's never telling me about what was going on.

"I went on to say, 'All these things were conducive to harming my influence in England,' " forcing Kennedy in turn to threaten the British with the words: " 'If you don't let me know all about this, your country is going to find me most unfriendly toward the whole situation.' So I smashed my way through with no thanks to the American Government.' "

The president could have silenced Kennedy with three words: appeaser, defeatist, coward. He had, however, to keep Kennedy on his side for nine more days. "Roosevelt promptly denied everything," insisting he'd wanted to tell Kennedy about Donovan's mission and had asked the State Department "to clear those things up with me," Kennedy recalled. Kennedy was not mollified, telling Krock afterward that he didn't believe Roosevelt for one moment—"Somebody is lying very seriously, and I suspect the President." Meanwhile, he recalled, "I asked him how it was that Alsop had the content of one of my cables in his column. The President couldn't understand that. . . . He disclaimed any responsibility, and protested his friendship."

They were getting nowhere. The argument was demeaning. "Rose chimed in at this point and said it was difficult to get the right perspective on a situation that was 3,000 miles away." Kennedy glared at her. "So the discussion went on and on."

Whether a public split between Ambassador Kennedy and President Roosevelt would really have altered the outcome of the 1940 election is debatable. If so, the history of the world pivoted on a dinner of scrambled eggs. In truth, however, Kennedy was too much of a realist to think he could single-handedly outwit the president of the United States—particularly when Willkie's chances of election were perceived to be slim. He thus decided to play for time and turn his blackmail to further advantage, not only in escaping from the London Blitz, but in forcing Roosevelt to offer him an alternative post at home. "Finally I said that I had a great sense of responsibility and obligation and would make a speech, but wanted the situation cleared up between us before making such a decision. I said that I would write the speech without saying anything to anybody and say just what I felt."

Roosevelt and Byrnes instantly agreed, though when they suggested Kennedy travel back to New York the next day "on the same train with

the President and his party," as they had suggested to reporters in anticipation of the meeting, Kennedy refused. The days of the 1932 "Roosevelt
Special" were over. Leaving Rose to stay the night on her own at the
White House, Kennedy himself slipped away, telling newsmen that he
would give a press conference the next morning in New York.

Going to Pieces

Had Ambassador Joseph P. Kennedy traveled with Roosevelt, had he
thrown himself behind Roosevelt's campaign (as Churchill had pretended
to think was the case), and with the same energy and verve he'd shown
in 1932 and 1936, Roosevelt would almost certainly have been obliged to
give him some major alternative post in the administration. Indeed
Roosevelt actually kidded Rose after her husband's departure that she
was "not to let this fellow think he is going to get away from me and
loaf."

Instead Kennedy made one of the most disastrous judgments of his
public career. In declining to travel on the same train with the president,
he'd pointed out to Roosevelt "that if I did that, my attitude would be
perfectly plain to everyone and there would be no surprise; in fact," he
candidly admitted, "it would definitely leave an impression that I was not
likely to go against him."

Once spoken, this confession—that he was widely thought to have left
his post in London to plot against the president—was impossible to
withdraw. He'd forced his way home by blackmail, and like a miffed
child, he now slunk off into the night, reserving his position, leaving his
wife, and hoping Roosevelt would thereby be compelled to make him an
offer before the election.

Alternatively, had Joseph Kennedy but remained in England a further
fortnight and then tendered the traditional ambassador's resignation on
the advent of the presidential election, as Jack had recommended, he
could have returned to America a hero. Instead, determined not to be "a
dummy," as he put it to Roosevelt, he had become a sacrifical lamb—
enjoying one brief presidential supper before being thrown to the wolves.

Joseph Kennedy told different versions of this episode to different
people. To Jack, as also to Arthur Krock, he claimed Roosevelt had
promised to support him as presidential candidate in the 1944 Democratic
convention if he backed Roosevelt for a third term. To others, such as
Clare Luce, Kennedy claimed Roosevelt had promised to help his first-

born, if Joe Jr. were to put his name forward for governor of Massachusetts in 1942.

Whatever the truth, having canceled his promised press conference on the next Monday morning, and sitting in his New York office, Kennedy debated with himself and his aides the merits and disadvantages of switching presidential horses, while all the time hoping that Roosevelt would make him an offer that would get "the situation cleared up between us."

But Roosevelt didn't. Neither, to Kennedy's chagrin, did Willkie, though Republicans such as the Luces tried in vain to get through to Kennedy on the telephone to enlist his support for FDR's opponent. Finally, on the night of October 29, 1940, shortly after his own son had been selected for the draft, Kennedy spoke by CBS hookup to the nation, and to Roosevelt's intense relief, wholeheartedly endorsed him for a third term.

Those who'd heard Kennedy bad-mouthing Roosevelt over past months were astonished and assumed some sort of deal must have been struck between the two men. Roosevelt himself gratefully telegraphed to Kennedy's home: I HAVE JUST LISTENED TO A GREAT SPEECH. THANK YOU. F.D.R. The following night the president traveled from Boston's South Station to the Boston Garden, taking Honey Fitz and even Joe Jr. with him in the presidential limousine. Then, before a vast crowd, Roosevelt welcomed "back to the shores of America that Boston boy, beloved by all of Boston and a lot of other places, my Ambassador to the Court of St. James's, Joe Kennedy."

The smiles, however, were window dressing. In his radio broadcast Kennedy had refuted "the charge that the President of the United States is trying to involve this country in world war. Such a charge is *false*." At the Boston Garden, with six more days to go until the election, Roosevelt was obliged to keep his blackmailer sweet, reiterating his promise that "your boys are not going to be sent into any foreign wars!" But all wars, beyond civil wars, are foreign, and both Willkie and Roosevelt stated that America must fight if the country or its vital interests were attacked. "I personally told everyone that I thought Willkie might get us into war sooner than Roosevelt," Kennedy later admitted, "and the one thing I was dead set against was helping anybody who was apt to get us involved."

On November 5, 1940, President Roosevelt was triumphantly reelected. He became the first president ever to be returned to the White House for a third term, and by the huge margin of 449 electoral votes to 82. The following day Kennedy traveled to Washington to tender his formal resignation as ambassador to London. The secretary of state, Cordell

Hull, as well as assistant secretaries Sumner Welles and Breckinridge Long, received him. Far from being elated at Roosevelt's victory, Kennedy was in despair. "He sees England gone," Long noted that evening. "I think he is probably somewhat influenced by the situation he has been in. It could hardly be otherwise," Long added generously. "Bombs dropping around, industry paralyzed and communication lines being gradually disrupted must bring with them a sense of defeatism."

Defeatism was not an exaggeration, as Long explained. "Kennedy thinks that England is broke," he noted, recording Kennedy's hostility to the idea of giving England credits to buy U.S. goods. "He thinks we ought to be realists in our policy; that we ought to realize that the British Empire is gone; that the British Navy may be gone. Even with the British Navy afloat they have won only one victory and that at Montevideo. Every time they have gone in range of a shore battery or an air field or land they have been defeated. They have been unable to clear the seas of raiders. If Italy is successful in Greece and Germany goes on into Turkey, the British bases in the Mediterranean [Gibraltar, Malta, Alexandria, Haifa] will have to be abandoned, and they will be forced out of the Mediterranean, if they can get out."

It was small wonder T. North Whitehead minuted at the Foreign Office, some days later, that "it rather looks as though he [Kennedy] was thoroughly frightened when in London & has gone to pieces in consequence."

"He sees Hitler rampant on European soil, dominant over England," Long meanwhile quoted Kennedy's despondent scenario. "He sees a new philosophy, both political and economic, with the United States excluded from European markets and from Far Eastern markets and from South American markets, for he feels we are not able to absorb the products of South America except for gold. . . . Consequently he thinks that we ought to take some steps to implement a realistic policy and make some approach to Germany and Japan which would result in economic collaboration."

Though Joseph Kennedy would later go down in American history as an archisolationist, it was clear that his support of appeasement with the dictators came before his isolationism. "Kennedy told me Hitler had twice sent him a message asking him to go to Germany for a conference," Long revealed, invitations that Roosevelt had ordered Kennedy to refuse. "Hitler must have got the impression Kennedy had views which Hitler might use as an approach to us. As a matter of fact Kennedy thinks we ought to lay the basis for some cooperation," Long noted, though the extent of such appeasement "is undefined. His ideas as to what should be done are nebulous—but he is positive in the thought something should be done—some uncharted way found. . . . He does not believe in our present policy. He does not believe in the continuing of democracy. He thinks that we will have to assume a Fascist form of government here or something similar if we are to survive. . . . He thinks the English will soon be battered into a desire for some understanding with Germany and that Churchill will go and that Lloyd George [aged seventy-seven] will take his place. Furthermore, he thinks that the spirit and the morale of the world is broken," Long recorded, noting Kennedy's plan to fly to California to see his son Jack and to speak personally to three major American newspaper publishers: William Randolph Hearst, Robert McCormick, and Joseph Patterson. Long warned him of the dangers, particularly cautioning him against giving interviews "to the press or to talk in a way that would scare the American people or scare them [the newspaper proprietors]. . . . He agreed and said he would not do that."

Although he had finally come out on radio in support of Roosevelt's reelection, the Boston bully was determined to hold the threat of his forthcoming talks with Hearst, Patterson, and McCormick as a Damocletian sword over Roosevelt's head. Thus when he and the president met in the White House the next afternoon, on Roosevelt's victorious return to Washington, the atmosphere was cordial but still tense. As Kennedy subsequently told Arthur Krock, he "tendered his resignation to the President." The president, however, rejected it, saying "he couldn't accept it until he found someone to send in Kennedy's place," as Krock noted. "They discussed the situation of the British and the President agreed with Kennedy (1) that we must stay out of the war; (2) that if the Germans continue to batter the British ports [Southampton, Portsmouth, Liverpool, etc.] with present effectiveness the United States would be left in the position of being unable to help at all, and practically defenseless if the Axis struck in this hemisphere." In short, Kennedy warned the president of the United States, "whatever aid you extend to Britain, you must regard as a bet on a losing horse."

Horses, for some reason, were on Kennedy's brain. He'd taken a ride in Windsor Park, near St. Leonard's, every morning while in England. Still "sore" at his treatment by the State Department, he now issued in Washington perhaps the rudest warning ever made by an American citizen to the elected president, while urging Roosevelt to collaborate economically with the Nazis: "You will either go down as the greatest President in history, or the greatest horse's ass."

The Lyons Interview

In the event, it would be Joseph P. Kennedy who would go down in history as the greatest horse's ass, for on the afternoon of Friday, November 8, 1940, the *Boston Globe* reporter Louis Lyons—who had interviewed Kennedy in 1936 and had brought "both Kennedy and the Administration much favorable publicity"—arrived at the Ritz-Carlton in Boston for an interview Ambassador Kennedy had agreed to give him. In soliciting the talk, Lyons had requested Kennedy to speak "just as a traveler home from the wars, not political talk." The piece was to appear in *The Globe*'s Sunday edition.

But Kennedy was not interested in giving traveler's tales. He'd also agreed to see two other reporters staying in Boston for a Nieman Foundation for Journalism dinner, Ralph Coughlan and Charles Edmundson, who were anxious for "background information for future editorial guidance." When all three happened to meet outside Kennedy's suite, "Kennedy's secretary let the three in at the same time figuring, I suppose, that since they were all newspapermen it made no difference," the Nieman Foundation's director noted a few days later. The ambassador's remarks now defied belief in their indiscretion. "It was as though he were making a campaign speech," Lyons afterward recalled, "but not for Roosevelt."

This was exactly what Long had feared. He had specifically warned Kennedy, on behalf of the State Department, that "the American people needed education in foreign affairs and that to thrust it upon them too suddenly would be disastrous." Kennedy's promise not to give controversial interviews looked pretty lame as he "poured out to us his views about America and the war in a torrent that flowed with the free, full power and flood of the Mississippi River," Lyons wrote.

> He's started on a quiet but determined and fighting crusade to "keep us out." He's going to California to see one of America's influential publishers. He's already seen others and he means to see more, and let them have it straight and tough, as he sees it. He's talked to Congressmen and Senators and means to see more. "They've got to understand it," he says with passion. He's been amazed at how little—so it seems to him—the Congressmen who've visited with him so far do understand the war and America's relation to it. "I know more about the European situation than anybody else, and it's up to me to see that the country gets it," he says in explanation of the role

of carrying the torch that he has cut out for himself. . . . "I'm willing to spend all I've got left to keep us out of the war. There's no sense in our getting in. We'd just be holding the bag. I say we aren't going in. Only over my dead body. We couldn't send an army anywhere now. It would be senseless to go in. What would we be fighting for? . . . What does it mean to have labor men now at the center of [British] Government? It means national socialism is coming out of it. . . . Democracy is finished in England. It may be here. . . . I told the President in the White House last Sunday, 'Don't send me 50 admirals and generals. Send me a dozen real economists.' . . . Don't let anybody tell you you can get used to incessant bombing. There's nowhere in England they aren't getting it. . . . Their shipping losses are greater this time because they haven't so many destroyers and what they have, they have to divide, in the Mediterranean and for defending England, besides convoys. . . . Hitler has all the ports in Europe, you see. . . . People call me a pessimist. I say, 'What is there to be gay about? Democracy is all done.' . . . It is a practical question, how much [aid] to send. It is a question of how long England can hold out. If she collapses soon, then stop."

As Ralph Coughlan later remarked, "it was impossible for me to believe that an ambassador could be so stupid as to talk like that, if there was any danger that he would be quoted."

"Don't forget, Lindbergh's not so crazy either," Kennedy meanwhile warned the reporters, and when asked about America's most ardent isolationist senator, Burton K. Wheeler, Kennedy announced that "Wheeler and I are buddies. Why, I financed his campaign with LaFollette.' We must have gaped at that," Lyons wrote in his article, amazed that Kennedy, a possible Democratic contender for the presidency, would admit to having once financed a progressive Republican presidential candidate. To Ralph Coughlan, who asked whether America would refuse to trade with the Nazis if Hitler won the war, Kennedy retorted, "That's nonsensical." He even hinted that the queen of England would see to it that Britain did a deal with Hitler: "Now I tell you, when this thing is finally settled, and it comes to a question of saving what's left for England, it will be the Queen and not any of the politicians who will do it. She's got more brains than the Cabinet."

Not content with his remarks about the queen of England dealing with Hitler, Kennedy went on to the quasi-queen of America: Eleanor Roosevelt. "She's another wonderful woman. Jim will tell you," referring to Dean James M. Landis of the Harvard Law School, "that she bothered us more on our jobs in Washington to take care of the poor little nobodies who hadn't any influence than all the rest of the people down there together. She's always sending me a note to have some little Susie Glotz to tea at the embassy."

Neither Queen Elizabeth nor the First Lady were amused. Kennedy would later charge that the interview was "off the record" and that he'd been misquoted: KENNEDY DISAVOWS INTERVIEW ON WAR—Envoy Says He Talked 'Off the Record' in Boston—Story Gave Wrong Impression—INACCURACY IS CHARGED.

As Kennedy knew, however, the interview was all too accurate. Another *Globe* reporter, Joseph Dinneen, called Kennedy on Sunday morning to tell him the news of Neville Chamberlain's death, "and in the course of their conversation Kennedy asked what Lyons wrote because he had received some queries. . . . The whole article was read over the phone Sunday afternoon. Dinneen says Kennedy seemed so pleased with it that he (Dinneen) called Lyons to relay the good word." Kennedy was also heard to boast, "Well, the fat's in the fire, but I guess that's where I want it!"

In a letter to Arthur Krock two days later, on November 12, 1940, the head of the Nieman Foundation wrote that "there seems to be little question that what Louis reported was actually said and truly reflected Kennedy's view at the moment. Lyons admits that he may have made one or two minor misquotes in the course of this long article, but these he says were the result of Kennedy pouring it on so thick, and were probably understatements rather than overstatements. Lyons also says he realized the stuff was volatile and so backed into his story as gently as possible. He left out some of the strongest stuff by way of protecting K[ennedy]."

Kennedy's craving for attention—from the president and the American press—had now backfired. One by one every newspaper in the land repeated his most controversial remarks. The owner of the *St. Louis Post-Dispatch,* Joseph Pulitzer, wrote abjectly to Kennedy, regretting "that a reputable American newspaper man should have been charged by you with violating the confidence of an off-the-record interview, and of my disgust upon finding that that reporter, in his account of that interview, had quoted questions asked in confidence by Ralph Coughlan, editor of the editorial page of the Post-Dispatch." Pulitzer's disgust, however, did not stop the *Dispatch,* like every other newspaper in the United States, from carrying the story. Indeed when Ralph Coughlan phoned his paper, the *Post-Dispatch,* to ask if, given the exploding controversy, they wanted him to write his own summary of the interview, he was "told to forget it. They would use the A.P. summary," he later recalled.

Arthur Krock, recognizing the potential damage the interview would do, immediately sent Kennedy a letter of sympathy. "You seem to have got into trouble," he wrote loyally, "and so I shall make the move which a friend should make when a friend is in trouble. When everything was on the up and up, I could indulge my feeling that you took your time to get in touch with the only newspaper man in the United States who has steadfastly expressed a high regard for you in print. Now, however, I write to say that if there is anything I can do to dispel the ill-effect of that unfortunate interview I stand ready, as usual, to do it."

Krock was as good as his word. He sent letter after letter defending Kennedy to colleagues in the American press. Kennedy, however, was neither chastened nor grateful. The truth was that he was too contemptuous of mere journalists to think they could ruin him. In the past he'd always managed to use bribery or threats to intimidate editors and publishers when critical pieces were in the offing. When Henry Luce's *Fortune* magazine tried to run a story on Kennedy in 1937 mentioning his affair with Gloria Swanson, Kennedy threatened to mount a raid that would buy out Luce's *Time* magazine, and the story was squashed. Kennedy even managed to spike a gently critical piece by C. L. Sulzberger for the *Ladies' Home Journal* in 1938, to Sulzberger's amazement. "I showed him my manuscript and he was furious. He said that if I didn't change my piece he was going to have the company kill it. I sent it. Weeks later I got the galley proofs," Sulzberger later recalled. "It had been completely rewritten—in saccharin instead of ink."

Kennedy now tried to blackmail *The Globe* into a full retraction, ordering all Somerset Importers' whiskey advertising to be withdrawn from the newspaper. But, as even Krock pointed out, "whatever the facts about the off-the-record restrictions, the sentiments sound very much like yours." *The Globe* stood by its reporter, and this time the ink remained ink.

"There's been a big stink here about an interview some Lyons sneaked out on him after an 'off the record' chat," Torby Macdonald reported to Jack in California. Even Macdonald considered the ambassador's sentiments to be in keeping with what Jack had recently told him, however: "If you remember our conversation of 2 months ago at the Cape—parts of his speech rang with a familiar note."

In Washington news of the ambassador's Boston interview undid all the good that Joseph Kennedy's radio speech had done for the campaign. Thousands wrote to the White House, calling for the ambassador to be summarily dismissed. The reaction in the popular press was similarly one of outrage, both in America and England. Even *The Wall Street Journal* was shocked by Kennedy's "sensational" outburst:

Here is a government pledged to give every possible aid to England short of war. Here is a people overwhelmingly sympathetic to the English cause. Here is the Ambassador to France, Mr. Bullitt, appealing for moral as well as material support, painting a stirring picture of the heroic fight for freedom and democracy which the English are making.

And then comes back our Ambassador to Great Britain and gives an interview which by no stretch of the imagination could be construed as sympathetically helpful to the country he so recently left. . . . It is not surprising that the State Department was deeply disturbed by the Kennedy interview and greatly relieved by his repudiation. It obviously had to be repudiated. It is being pointed out that the Kennedy repudiation places more emphasis on having talked "off the record" than upon not having said the things reported. A more complete repudiation is hoped for in some Administration quarters. It is contended that, as things are now, the impression is general that these really were Mr. Kennedy's views and the repudiation came because the reaction was bad. . . . Whether Mr. Kennedy takes any further steps to correct the impression, one thing, it is agreed, has been made plain—to wit, that he has no intention of returning to his post in London. It is also held unlikely that he will accept any position at home in the Administration. It is anticipated that he will shortly resign and then, no longer ambassador, he can express his views with less embarrassment all round.

Food for Thought

Had America been at war, Kennedy's behavior as a senior U.S. ambassador would have amounted to treason; indeed President Roosevelt requested reports on Kennedy from both FBI and the Secret Service, which soon confirmed the "Pétain proposal": a plot involving Kennedy and the head of the Vichy government. The Foreign Office in London was informed that, "undeterred by Munich," Ambassador Kennedy "thought that it was possible to arrange a compromised peace between Germany and England and he was doing everything in his power to bring this about." According to the informant, "He had sent an emissary—Ben Smith, I think was the name, to see Pétain and Hitler and to try to find some formula for the reconstruction of Europe to which they would both set their names. Having secured this, he hoped that, with the help of two prominent persons in England—he did not mention their names but he said that they would be known to the British Government—to start an agitation in England in favour of a negotiated peace."

Joe Jr. saw the machinations of his father on behalf of appeasement as perfectly legal and commendable. At the Chicago convention earlier that summer, having won a seat on the official Massachusetts Democratic party delegation, Joe Jr. had been the sole member to vote against Roosevelt's renomination. Currently, at Harvard Law School, he was doing everything possible to mobilize support for a university anti-interventionist movement.

But for Jack in Stanford, the news of his father's scandalous interview came as a terrible embarrassment. Following his own shameful call for another Munich in the *Crimson* in the fall of 1939, he'd gradually cast off his father's shawl, writing a balanced and bestselling account of British appeasement during the 1930s, and was now not only a member of Stanford's University Emergency Committee and an unrepentant supporter of President Roosevelt, but a firm believer in America's eventual responsibility to fight for the ideals of democracy.

"Have become very fond of Stanford," Jack wrote to Lem Billings on November 13, the day before his father came out to see him. "The gals are quite attractive—and it's a very good life. Feeling much better the last two weeks," he confided, reporting proudly that *Why England Slept* had got "some good reviews" in England, where it had now also been published, "and they expect it to do about 60,000."

This figure was, like most publisher's estimates, way beyond reality. The British reviews, however, were extraordinary, especially in the light of Ambassador Kennedy's ill-concealed defeatism and cowardly departure. Letters of appreciation came from some of the most distinguished British politicians, writers, and thinkers of the day. Perhaps the most astonishing of all came from Captain Liddell Hart, the defense correspondent of the London *Times* and probably the most influential military writer in the world, who wrote Jack an extraordinary letter of congratulation.

"I would like to express my admiration for the outstanding way it combines insight with balanced judgement, in a way that nothing that has yet been written here approaches," Liddell Hart began. "It is all the more impressive by comparison with other recent books which I have read, by both English and American writers, who were apt to get led astray by superficial appearances."

Hart had become famous in the 1920s. Setting out novel theories of armored assault based on surprise, concentration, and an "expanding torrent" of tank-led troops, Liddell Hart's articles and books had become the blitzkrieg bibles of Panzer generals from Guderian to Rommel. Liddell Hart himself, however, had undergone a profound change of heart in the thirties "when the danger of another war became a looming contingency." He confided to Jack:

Unless one was content to go on spinning lecture-room theories—as the military colleges are inclined to do—one had to face the unpalatable fact that we [democracies] could never expect to start with the advantage of initial surprise which gave the offensive its best chance. That realisation, together with an acute appreciation of the way Germany was drawing ahead in the new offensive instruments, led me to concentrate increasingly on what might be done to improve our capacity for withstanding a surprise offensive by developing our defensive technique and means.

Unfortunately that aim was thwarted, partly by general complacency, partly by Governmental inertia—both of which factors you have most adequately brought out.

There was, however, a third reason, namely the wooly-headedness of British generals who'd relied on "preparation and training for the kind of theoretical offensive which we could not hope to carry out in practice, in face of superior forces." The Norway fiasco and the disastrous performance of the British Expeditionary Force, sallying blindly forth into Belgium under Lord Gort, had been the result. As a result, Liddell Hart pointed out, the situation was now akin to that of Britain during the Napoleonic wars:

Our fundamental purpose must be vitally different from that of our opponents'. While their natural object was expansion, through conquest, our proper object was not merely to defeat that purpose, but to take care that civilisation was not destroyed in the process of fighting to defend it. Since our [democratic] conditions deprived us of the possibility of gaining a quick victory by surprise, any conflict was bound to be a lengthy one.

Liddell Hart's eight-page letter would give Jack much food for thought in the ensuing months. In the meantime, however, in the wake of the press publicity surrounding his Boston interview, Ambassador Kennedy arrived in San Francisco, unrepentently bringing his message of Nazi doom to California, and anxious to see his second son in person for the first time since September 1939.

Taking Hollywood by Storm

Reporters crowded round the controversial ambassador as, with Jack by his side, he insisted his policy was only "to keep the United States out of war. If that is appeasement, make the most of it,' " Kennedy challenged them, adding, "I will work toward that end as long as I live."

Jack had driven to meet his father at the San Francisco airport, having vainly begged his friend Henry James to accompany him. Father and son then made their way to William Randolph Hearst's ranch at Wyntoon. En route the ambassador confided to Jack that he would never return to England, and that Roosevelt had agreed to accept his resignation as soon as a successor was found. In the meantime he asked if Jack could draft an outline for a major article on appeasement he could publish as soon as he was rid of the seals of ambassadorial office.

This request put Jack in an almost impossible position. "His father had taken a controversial position," Dr. Kreps recalled, "but Jack was making up his own mind. He had a good independent mind, and he was exploring the issue. He had questions." At the Kreps's Sunday evening parties Jack would "sit on the rug with his back up against the baby grand piano, eating a piece of Mrs. Kreps's speciality, lazy-day cake. From this position, he would discuss the question of America's entrance into the war," Kreps described. "The controversy perplexed and totally absorbed him—he was interested in this one thing only. Young Kennedy was in the middle of the problem since he had written that honors thesis at Harvard. He opposed his father. There was nothing personal and no family difference—just this difference of ideas.

"His father was not a pacifist," Kreps related. "Both believed in arming. It was not a question of arming, it was what we were arming *for*. Jack thought we would have to commit ourselves. He thought it might take years, but that it would come. I'd say he was a little more far-seeing than his father in this matter."

Lem Billings, however, disagreed with Kreps's assessment of Ambassador Kennedy. "It is my feeling," he later remarked, "and I'm sure I am right, that Jack absolutely disagreed with his father a hundred per cent!"

While the ambassador completed his round of meetings with newspaper publishers and Hollywood producers and returned to New York for Thanksgiving, Jack and his friend Henry James meanwhile made for Los Angeles. "As you may have heard," Jack afterward wrote to Billings, "went down to Hollywood and took it by storm. I have many glowing reports to tell you. . . . Ran into Spencer [Tracy] who I was very much at ease with," he bragged, "although he was a little flustered and self-conscious—however in my conversation with Clark Gable, there were several long silent periods. . . . Saw Lana Turner, in Hollywood—as she walked by me, I said in a loud voice 'Harry Dixon.' Her only response was to goose in a friendly way big, lovable, Jewish Tony Martin whom she was with. That's about the news—Regards, Jack."

Such hobnobbing with Hollywood stars said much about Jack, then as later. His narcissistic personality craved success—social, sexual, professional. Deprived of early maternal warmth, he wanted attention, adulation, affection. "Why not purchase a large *CHEAP* violin, and get in character?" his friend Bill Coleman humorously scrawled beneath a newspaper photograph that had been captioned, to Coleman's disgust, "JOHN F. KENNEDY: He sees both sides of question." "Boy!! What a whimsical pose!" He signed off with the injunction: "Get out in that sun, Moe—you *NEED* it!"

Behind the joshing, all Jack's friends were aware he possessed gifts that might enable him, backed by his powerful father, to achieve success in life. But where would these gifts lead him? Jack had never done more than hold a spear in the Gilbert and Sullivan chorus at school. Even as a bestselling author he knew that the sales figures for *Why England Slept,* however extraordinary for a fourth-year thesis hurriedly turned into a topical book, nowhere neared the figures he liked to hint at. (Eighty thousand copies was the figure Jack himself began to bruit at Christmas, and which then went into the history books; actual sales, according to the records of Wilfred Funk, Inc., were but a fraction of this—and a number of these were purchased by Jack's father, later to be found in the basement in Hyannis Port.)

Though he might strut and pose in Hollywood, Jack was not a star, and he knew it, as Henry James recalled.

> He was a celebrity—a minor celebrity, but a celebrity nonetheless. In Hollywood they all knew or knew of his father. And his father's position at the Court of St. James's of course didn't hurt. Now Jack traded on it like crazy, and made the best use of it, as also his instant fame as a bestselling writer. And so the result was, at parties he was lionized. I mean we'd walk into a party and the hostess would rush up to Jack. "Oh, Jack, da-a-rling! Lo-ovely to see you. Oh, Jack, how beautiful you look, oh, Jack! And your book's so exciting—a best-selling author—oh, my goodness, come over, you've *got* to meet so-and-so." It was the same when we went around the studio lots, the stars would come over and speak to him: "Oh, Jack, darling, I just loved your book. Isn't it wonderful, isn't it marvelous," and so on.

The Hollywood game was *fun* for him, but he would get tired of that sort of thing. He *put up* with these people, but he saw through them! It wasn't that important! He was fascinated by the stars and the glamour, sure—but not to take too much of his time. He wouldn't let it absorb his attention for too long. "I'm bored," he'd say, and we'd move on. We went to a couple of very fun parties, and met some very very glamorous and interesting people. But the world was going up in flames, after all; and Jack was more interested in *that*! And rightly so.

Once again, Jack's friend got a taste of Jack's cruel whip when, at a party in Los Angeles, James stepped beyond his role of Californian Sancho Panza. "Jack was a snob—a social snob," James observed. "This was an important streak in him. And one of the reasons why he liked me was because I came—he thought I came—from an old New York family. He knew that I had gone to deb parties and knew a whole range of attractive young people in New York society which he didn't know and couldn't get to know, because he was an Irish guy from Boston—he was a 'mick.'"

Thanks to his father's wealth and power, Jack could get to the front of the line outside the Stork Club or "21" in New York, but this did not usher him into society in the older sense of the word: Yankee society. "I mean, sure he had a good name and everything else, and people would pay him some attention. But the people that I knew, and had easy access to, were not the ones that would pay that much attention to his real achievements, his book, his intelligence, his charismatic charm, everything else—even his money. They didn't care about that! No, he didn't come from Top Drawer. He didn't belong to Piping Rock Club on Long Island—so why bother with him? 'He's not important.'"

This social prejudice irked Jack. "How could he help it?" James asked. "His family, his father had pulled up stakes from Boston and went to Bronxville because they would not be accepted—and Jack *felt* that! How could he help but feel that? I don't think Jack would ever *suffer* from it," James added, given Jack's refusal to be introspective, "but I think he would say, 'Goddamn those blue bloods! I'm going to be president of the United States or something, and then I'll say, Fuck them!' You know, he would say that. And he'd mean it. But I think a little bit of my attraction for him was that I had that aspect, d'you see? I moved easily among people amongst whom he didn't move easily. He was shy, you know."

Over the years Jack and his sister Kathleen had combated this anti-Irish, anti-Catholic prejudice by virtue of their charm, but the fight was by no means over, and friends such as Cam Newberry in Massachusetts or Henry James at Stanford were vital comrades in Jack's quest for social

acceptance and laurels—as long as they did not eclipse his smiling, orthodontically perfect sun. At the party of a prominent Stanford sorority
girl whose parents had a home in Los Angeles, James found himself
sitting beside his hostess.

> I said something. And she started laughing at what I said. And—it's
> only happened a handful of times in my whole life—after that there
> was no word I could utter, no sentence I could formulate that didn't
> get peals of laughter and appreciation and practically of applause.
> And Jack got really quite put out about it! He said to me afterwards,
> you know, "*James!* For Christ's sake! Don't you *ever* outshine me
> that way again! I don't like it!"
>
> He used to kid me about it when we were back at Stanford, with
> other people. He'd say, "You know, this guy here, he doesn't look
> anything but, boy! He really was a smasheroo hit down in L.A.!"

But Jack's period at Stanford University was in fact drawing to a close.
Torbert Macdonald had heard via Tom Killefer's sister "that you're a
'well known landmark on campus.' " In the wake of *Why England Slept,*
however, Jack had hoped to be a lot more than a landmark.

"The point is, he had this ambivalence towards people in Stanford,"
said Henry James, reflecting on why Jack did not stay for a whole year
as intended. "I don't think he particularly respected them, just as he
didn't respect women he'd got into bed with him. I don't mean he hated
them, because he'd go back to them. But it would be quite different. The
challenge was over—though the fun would still be there, the pleasures."

Jack's chief girlfriend, Flip Price, later professed to be puzzled as to
why Jack did not stay on at Stanford. Nevertheless, according to Henry
James, she was well aware what Jack wanted from her—and how little
Jack was willing to give for it. "Her role was as Jack's number-one girl
out there. She was the campus queen, she was considered to be very
beautiful," James related.

> And Jack was pursuing her very ardently. He wanted to get into bed
> with her. And she kept refusing him. I said to her, "Flip, you know
> Jack is very frustrated. . . . Jack is very attractive—he has women
> throwing themselves at him. How is it you keep your legs so tightly
> closed, so to speak"—because we'd talk like that a lot. And she said,
> "Henry, it's very simple. But you've got to swear on a stack of bibles
> that you'll never tell Jack.
>
> "I am a 'poor little girl from Little Rock'—I come from Phoenix.
> Here I am at Stanford. I belong to this good sorority, and the girls
> in this sorority all have more of a pedigree than I do, and they're all

brighter, and they're all everything. I have very good looks and I am sought after by men. But I have decided, if I want to get a good husband, I have got to go to that husband as a virgin. And unless Jack would propose marriage to me—which I would love dearly, because I would love to be his queen in real life—I ain't going to do anything with him. It's just not worthwhile my losing my virginity to a guy who's going back East in a short space of time, whom I may never see again. . . . So he will *never* get anywhere with me. I'll keep him guessing, I'll toy with him, but I won't go the whole way—not with Jack!"

Flip Price's adamant refusal to sleep with him marked the end of Jack's career "out west." He had no intention of marrying Flip. He was bored with his business studies. He missed his social life back east. His health—despite his boasting to Newberry—was still volatile. Above all, his father's folly worried him more than he let on. In a sense, Jack had gone west in order to avoid the difficulties of being east, sympathizing with Britain's plight, certain that America must prepare for war, but saddled with a prominent father who neither sympathized with England nor felt America should ever go to war.

Uncertain now about the future, Jack wrote to tell Billings he'd fly directly from Los Angeles on Monday, December 16, to New York to see a show (*Panama Hattie*) with him, then on to Boston the following evening and "see [Doctor] Jordan Thursday morning." Meanwhile he was "leaving here Sunday [December 8]," he scribbled on December 3, "to go to Meeting of Institute of World Affairs, Riverside, Cal beginning Sunday, for a week."

Before Jack could depart for the conference, however, there came a cable from his father, who was clearly irritated. The ambassador's final and public resignation, following further acrimonious meetings with Roosevelt and hostile comments in the press, was approaching. "When will outline on that appeasement article be ready?" his father demanded.

For Jack, the brief interlude of Stanford was over.

Ensign John F. Kennedy, intelligence officer, Washington, D.C., November 1941 (John F. Kennedy Library)

An Outline on Appeasement

Belatedly and at top speed, Jack dictated to a secretary on his last day in Stanford the outline on appeasement he'd promised his father. This *apologia pro vita patris,* as he noted in a covering letter to his father, "only shows an approach to the problem. . . . I don't present it in the form of a finished article," Jack apologized in advance, "as I first of all don't know what your view point is on some questions, and secondly I think the article should be well padded with stories of your experiences in England in order to give it authenticity and interest."

The draft began portentously:

> On November 6, the day after the election, I resigned from a post that I have held for nearly three years, that of the American Ambassador to the Court of St. James [*sic*]. In the statement which I gave when the resignation was made public I said that I would now devote my efforts to aiding the President to keep out of the war. And this I propose to do.
>
> For this reason I have decided to set down for the people of America what I really believe and feel about the great problems that face this country.

What were these convictions? And how could they be made palatable to the broad mass of the American people? Coyly, Jack backed into the crux of his father's beliefs:

> For my own part I have always felt that the art of diplomacy was far too shrouded in mystery. This tendency to treat diplomacy as a sort of Machiavellian poker game in which only experts could sit in on has been in a great measure responsible I think for the fatal inertia of the democracies during the last tragic years. How foolish it is to expect the people from whom the ultimate decisions must come to take the vigorous and forceful action necessary to match the dictators when they have been lulled into a false sense of security and complacency until the last hysterical moment.

Contrasted against such complacent leaders, the ambassador, Jack felt, should portray himself as a no-nonsense, common-sense Democrat trying to speak reason. "My views are not pleasant. I am gloomy and I have been gloomy since September, 1938. It may be unpleasant for American[s] to hear my views but let me note that Winston Churchill was considered distinctly unpleasant to have around during the years from 1935 to 1939. It was felt he was a gloom monger," Jack wrote, trying to attach his father to Churchill's coattails.

Comparison with Churchill could not prize the ambassador away from his identification with Chamberlain, however—and with Munich. "The manner in which the settlement of Munich was treated in this country demonstrated to me powerfully the danger that lack of adequate information could bring," Jack wrote, trying to turn the tables on his father's critics, but he was forced to add in parenthesis a note of advice: "Dad: You might work in here some of your own ideas of Munich and background of it. That is, what you thought; how you felt it would be serious danger to America if there was a war at that time; that America's own defenses were completely down as well as England's; that England might have been bombed into submission overnight due to her complete lack of defenses and America would have been in an exposed and dangerous position. You might put in here that it was worth any risk for America to have a Europe at peace and therefore you supported Chamberlain."

Unfortunately, this was only half the story, as Jack knew. The ambassador's friendship with Chamberlain, his unprecedented meddling in British Cabinet affairs, and his continuing efforts through Pétain to find an accommodation with Hitler stemmed not only from Kennedy's conviction that Britain and America were unready for war, but from his personal inability to see a valid economic reason or principle for ever going to war, just as when he avoided the draft in 1917.

Dimly Jack recognized this, and knew it could not be avoided in the outline. The charge had now been publicly laid, as Jack admitted on behalf of his father, "that I am a defeatist, that I am an appeaser. Joseph Alsop and Robert Kintner in their column said that I hold views unacceptable to 90% of the American people."

As Jack pointed out in parentheses, in order to explain to his father why he was tackling the Alsop-Kintner accusation so directly,

> it must be remembered continually that you wish to shake off the word "appeaser." It seems to me that if this label is tied to you it may nullify your immediate effectiveness, even though in the long run you may be proved correct. . . . No one—be they isolationist, pacifist, etc.—no one likes to be called an appeaser. . . . The word appeasement of course started at Munich; the background of it seems to be the idea of believing that you can obtain a satisfactory solution of the points in dispute by making concessions to the dictators. But you do not believe this—you predicate your views on other grounds. Where

I think Lindbergh has run afoul is in his declarations that we do not care what happens over there—that we can live at peace with a world controlled by the dictators—or at least that is the impression he has given.

It was also the impression Ambassador Kennedy had given. Where Kennedy differed from Lindbergh was in his abhorrence of war itself. "I would think that your best angle would be that of course you do not believe this [that the democracies could live at peace with the dictators], you with your background cannot stand the idea personally of dictatorships—you hate them—you have achieved the abundant life under a democratic capitalistic system—you wish to preserve it. But you believe that you can only preserve it by keeping out of Europe's wars etc. It's not that you hate dictatorship less [than interventionists do]—but that you love America more."

This was a neat phrase. Like all the points Jack confronted on behalf of his father, however, it opened another can of worms. For three years Ambassador Kennedy had held center stage as America's number-one diplomat in Europe; his speeches and his off-the-record briefings to journalists, not to speak of his indiscreet utterances and letters, had served to hoist him on a petard from which not even his loyal son Jack could now release him. "Of course it will have to be mentioned whether you feel that England can hold out and if so for how long," Jack admitted, recalling his father's defeatist prognostications when in California only weeks before. "You can avoid direct prophecy as you have before by stating that you cannot judge this unless you know Germany's strength. You can put in a boost by saying you know the bombing won't make them quit," he also suggested.

Yet, instinctively, Jack was aware that somehow his father had to cast off his reputation for despondency and defeatism if he truly wished to be included in the same category as Churchill:

In talking about the gloom charge—it might be well to mention that you don't enjoy being gloomy. It's much easier to talk about how pleasant things are. The only advantage of doing so is that you hope it may prove of some value to the country. You believe the optimists in England and France did their countries a profound disservice. It is not that you believe that come hell or high water everything is going to be bad.

I think you have to show some hope for the future or otherwise people will say—"Oh well—no matter what we do—he says we are doomed." Rather you think that by preparing for the worst [ie. the fall of England]—you may be able to meet it. You might bring it home by saying you have seen plenty of optimists cleaned out in the stock market before you went into the diplomatic service—and you have seen plenty of optimistic statesmen cleaned out since then.

The likely response to this, Jack realized, would be the charge that his father's very shenanigans on the stock market, as on the diplomatic front, had helped lead to their several downfalls. Even claiming to have been right all along would "have to be subtly expressed, as otherwise it will open you too wide to cracks from those wise-apple columnists that you are more interested in telling how right you've been than in helping the American people," Jack allowed. "In regard to Alsop and Kintner, you may not want to take direct issue with them as they have 365 days a year to strike back."

Ironically, Joe Alsop would in the years ahead become Jack's close Washington friend. It was in Alsop's beautiful, antique-filled George-town house that Jack would not only appear as a guest on the night of his inauguration as U.S. president, but would purposely commit adultery—as if, for all his avowed friendship, to get in a jab at the man who had helped destroy his father's public career.

In the meantime, on December 6, 1940, Jack completed his typed outline on appeasement and rushed it off to his father, who'd announced to reporters outside the White House that he would not be returning to London and the Blitz but instead, "after a short holiday," would be devoting his efforts "to what seems to me to be the greatest cause in the world today . . . to help the President keep the United States out of the war."

Aid to Britain

Leaving for Riverside, Los Angeles, Jack knew in his heart he'd failed to make a substantive case on behalf of his father. A friend of his had written "to have you carry a message to your old man . . . namely that there are a hell of a lot of us who are behind him in his stand on the war," and calling upon the ambassador "to organize a counter committee whose motto will be 'America First,' and whose purpose will be to keep this country out of war." Even Jack's friend Torby Macdonald praised, indeed glorified the ambassador's stand. Jack, however, was unsatisfied, feeling an ambivalence and discord that spilled into his relationship with Flip Price as he desperately tried to bed her before he left.

"Jack dear . . . I wanted to tell you that I hadn't 'cooled' in the way I feel," Flip later confessed in a farewell letter. "You are difficult at times and those last two nights were a good example—But you make up for that in a hundred other ways."

To the best of his ability Jack had tried to defend his father against the charges of appeasement and defeatism, but he recognized now that what needed to be defended even more than his father's reputation was democracy, and the only country left defending it at that moment was Britain.

On the United Airlines plane to Los Angeles he therefore took out his pen and, in "a supplementary note on the article," took issue with his father. "Dear Dad," he began gingerly,

It seems to me that our actual aid to Britain is pretty small, and that the defense program calling for more and more planes is falling behind. . . . We seem to be in the same psychological pattern that England was during the year from Sept. 1938 to Sept. 1939. As Munich awakened England—so the events of the month of May awakened us. But like England we are rearming in much the same leisurely fashion that England did—note the lack of genuine legislation empowering the defense commission.

Of course the reason we are so confident as a nation is that we know, especially after watching England hold out during the summer, that *we* cannot be *invaded.—We* are safe. We are failing to see that if England is forced to give in by summer due to our failure to give her adequate supplies, *we* will have *failed* to meet *our* emergency, as did England before us. As England failed from September 1938 to September 1939 to take advantage of her year of respite due to her feeling that there would be no war in 1939, we will have failed just as greatly.

Now as this affects your position. I realize that aid for Britain is part of it but in your message for America to stay out of the war— you should not do so *at the expense of having people minimize aid to Britain.* The danger of our not giving Britain enough aid, of not getting Congress and the country stirred up sufficiently to give England the aid she needs now—is to me just as great as the danger of our getting into war now—as it is much more likely.

If England is defeated America is going to be alone in a strained and hostile world. In a few years, she will have paid out enormous sums for defense yearly—to maintain armaments—she may be at war—she even may be on the verge of defeat or defeated—by a combination of totalitarian powers.

Then there will be a general turning of the people's opinions. They will say "Why were we so stupid not to have given Britain all possible aid. Why did we worry about money etc. *We should have put in more legislation.* We should have given it to them outright—after all—if we voted $13,000,000,000 for defense in 1940 at home we should have been ready to give England money—they were definitely another arm of our defense forces." (In discussing loans to Britain—it might be well to bring out that a dime does not leave the country—that it is spent here—as is W.P.A.—a simple point—but often not realized.)

Just as we now turn on those who got us into the last war, Hines Page etc. (which after all may have been the best thing when all the accounts are added up)—so in the future they may turn on those who failed to point out the great necessity of providing Britain in the crucial months of 1940–1941.

This was a dire and yet loyal warning, an extraordinary and moving admonition by a twenty-three-year-old son to his own father. "Of course, I do not mean that you should advocate war," Jack added, "but you might explain with some vigour your ideas on how vital it is for us to supply England. You might work in how hard it is for a democracy to get things done unless it is scared and how difficult it is to get scared when there is no immediate menace—We should see that our immediate menace is not invasion, but that England may fall—through lack of our support. Therefore you are gloomy in the hope that you can get the country stirred up—the situation is acute—America must get going." This brought him back to his father:

Of course no one wants war—the anti-war is the most popular *now*—But so it was with Chamberlain + the others—in the future as we look back—we may be shocked at our present lack of vigour.

The reason I [am] advocating the strength of this point is that while you do believe in aid for Britain, there is [your] popular fame (Time Magazine) that you are [an] appeaser + against aid—This you have to nip.

In some ways this would turn out to be the most crucial and influential letter of John F. Kennedy's early life. To the people of the United States, indeed the world, Ambassador Joseph P. Kennedy had become the embodiment of American isolationism. General Wood was currently begging the resigning ambassador to accept chairmanship of the burgeoning "America First" movement. Meanwhile, at Harvard Joe Jr. had at last formally established the Harvard Committee Against Military Intervention "for the purpose of making vocal the opinion of that overwhelming majority of Harvard students who want America to stay out of the wars in Europe and Asia," a movement dedicated, in the words of its manifesto, to the proposition that America could "create an impregnable hemisphere defense," with only "a calculable degree" of "industrial and financial aid to Britain" being permitted, "aid beyond this point" being "unwise."

For Jack to challenge his father's defeatist stance, as well as his brother's, was a measure of how far he'd come over the past year. As if to soften the blow, he pretended he was "just saying what you've been saying all along—but I feel you should say this part stronger," and he ended with the latest social news from the West Coast:

> Was an usher in Jack Moffet's wedding yesterday. It was good fun—everyone in San Francisco was there + I must say—you have more supporters there than I've ever seen in my life. *Everyone* was swooning with admiration—so I guess while some people read the columnists + pay attention to them, there are plenty that don't. Clarence Linder—the newspaper man who was up at Hearst—has been giving you a terrific build-up from what I understand also.

With this, his love, and the news that he was "on my way to the Round Table Conference," the young man signed off.

Lend-Lease

Aid to England was now the crucial debate in America, centering on the Lend-Lease Bill, which Roosevelt on December 17 announced he would forthwith send before Congress.

In the meantime the five-day Riverside conference drew academics and experts from throughout the West. The level of informed presentation and debate, at a critical moment in world history as Britain stood alone against the Axis powers, was quite remarkable. Professors came from the universities of Redlands, Southern California, Stanford, California Institute of Technology, Denver, Washington, California at Los Angeles, Mills College, Nevada, Oregon, and New Mexico. The tenor was unashamedly anti-Fascist and even interventionist: "Till that day [of victory of the lonely democracies over the "march of force"] the humanities should realize that their fate is bound up with the defense of the human spirit and be willing to make that 'costly sacrifice upon the altar of freedom,'" Professor Charles Martin declared in his opening address. Professor Douglas Miller, addressing the question "Can conflicting world economies be reconciled" in the session on War and the Future World Economy, cited a frighteningly complacent *Fortune* magazine poll which showed that some two thirds of American business executives held the view that America could adjust to dealing with victorious totalitarian states. Such tragic ignorance, Miller went on, took little or no cognizance of current Nazi trading contracts: contracts requiring the use of German ships, German insurance companies, German legal contracts, German inspectors, and even signature by American firms to a clause reading "This contract is made under National Socialist principles." "Every business deal is given political, military, social, cultural propaganda implications that we have never considered when starting to negotiate," Miller emphasized. Smaller countries like Sweden and Switzerland even had to submit names of company employees when pursuing business contracts with the Third Reich—a police-state mentality utterly inimical to most Americans.

Jack's job, apart from participating in the conference, was to act as "rapporteur," responsible for drafting summaries for publication of no less than four of the Institute's round-table discussions: War and the Future World Economy, Economic Hemisphere Co-operation, British Civilization, and Proposed Plans for Peace. In his round-table report on War and the Future World Economy, Jack emphasized that "one requisite for the restoration of multilateral trade is the achievement of collective security"—a necessity that would inevitably lead to "far-reaching political and military commitments by the United States" and a rethinking of America's post–World War I isolationist attitudes. In summarizing the round-table discussion on British Civilization, Jack also carefully noted Professor Linden Maher's remarks "on the unusual growth of power of the Labor party as contrasted to its weak position in the early thirties. This was considered significant in a consideration of the postwar political setup. . . . Some mention was also made of the postwar situation in regard to the Commonwealth. . . . Professor Mander felt that this [the state's obligation to provide security] contributed to the idea expressed before at the Institute that security can be obtained only by the states joining together in a world order. . . . It was again emphasized that the United States would have a most responsible part to play in the future, and that it could best do so by helping to promote freer international trade."

This need for collective security dominated all Jack's summaries, and culminated in the discussion of Proposed Plans for Peace. "The chairman [Dr. Eugene Harley of the University of Southern California] . . . emphasized the failure of the United States to join the League of Nations and characterized this as an ominous prelude to the events that were to begin with the incident at Mukden in 1931," Jack noted. "The chairman then called on Dr. Condliffe as a student of international economics to give his views on future world organization. Dr. Condliffe warned against the acceptance of the doctrine of regionalism in place of universalism and stated that all the discussion on Pan-Americanism might be interpreted as an escapist doctrine for the United States to evade its world responsibilities. He recalled the statement of Dr. Fairman that it would be a great moral victory if a new world order could be built on the foundations of the League. We must try something like the League, but the postwar organization must be adapted to new circumstances. . . . The United States must supply much of the energy and power. We need to increase the power of the Assembly, to develop it into some sort of constituent body of the world. . . . The afternoon session was concluded by Dr. Condliffe, who seemed to express the general sentiments of the group. . . . He stressed the importance of having generous negotiations when the time for peacemaking occurred. He warned, however, that before reconstruction of a world order was undertaken there must be a salvage of Europe. Railroads, the food problem, finances—all must be dealt with or otherwise communism would take over in Europe. Here the United States must be prepared to help."

These and other topics of discussion permitted Jack to rehearse views and ideas that went way beyond his father's shallow understanding of America's role in the world. Professor Charles Martin, who directed the conference, thought extremely highly of Jack, whose studies at Harvard had given him both familiarity and confidence in discussing and summarizing a bewildering array of current world problems. "He authored all the reports from the tables he served," Martin recalled, "and was interested in doing a good technical job. . . . I can remember his questioning many of the leaders of the Institute and taking an active part in the substance of the conference as well as its procedure."

Jack's energetic work, however, hadn't helped his health, which was clearly regressing. In New York he wrote charmingly to thank Clare Luce for inviting him to a dinner for her daughter on December 19. "I certainly enjoyed meeting you and Ann. Those 6 ft 4—220 pounders from Stanford will give her no trouble at all," he joked about Ann's plans to attend Stanford University the following year. His own plans he left obscure.

Dr. Sara Jordan was alarmed when she examined Jack at the Lahey Clinic in Boston the next day. He now weighed less than he did when he first went to California, prompting her to insist Jack should return to Boston after Christmas for further tests and observation at the New England Baptist Hospital. Moreover she did not recommend that he go back to college before the fall.

Jack thus spent Christmas 1940 in Florida, under a medical cloud. There was another cloud as well. Now that Joseph Kennedy had finally announced his resignation as ambassador, speculation had grown in the press and in governmental circles concerning his next move, particularly with regard to the Lend-Lease hearings, due to take place early in the new year. On December 29, 1940, President Roosevelt himself broadcasted to the American people to publicly denounce the appeasers in their midst. "The experience of the past two years has proven beyond doubt that no nation can appease the Nazis," the president declared, rounding on those "appeasers" who claimed "the Axis powers are going to win anyway, that all this bloodshed in the world can be saved, that the United States might just as well throw its influence into the scale of a dictated peace, and get the best out of it that we can. They call it a 'negotiated peace,' " the president went on.

"Nonsense! Is it a negotiated peace if a gang of outlaws surrounds your community and on threat of extermination makes you pay tribute to save your own skins? . . . For us, this is an emergency as serious as war itself."

For Joseph Kennedy, indicated in all but name, it was a presidential slap in the face, and the isolationists in Congress, as Jack had feared, were quick to ask him to testify before the Congressional Foreign Relations Committee against Roosevelt's new bill to aid Great Britain. In his defeatist and unbalanced mood, it was hoped, Ambassador Kennedy might join Lindbergh and help swing Congress to vote against the legislation.

Kennedy was in his element, aware that his support to either side could be crucial. To the president's son Franklin Roosevelt, Jr., who was a fellow passenger on the flight to Washington, the ambassador openly trumpeted his view that "Hitler would ride right over Europe and that we should pressure England into negotiating the best peace it could." Privately he'd written to Congressman Louis Ludlow to argue against more than token aid in a letter that Ludlow then read into the Congressional Record. Once in Washington, he was visited by former president Herbert Hoover, who "urged me to speak on the proposed Lend-Lease Bill and felt sure they could marshal enough Democratic votes in the House to kill it."

Roosevelt was incensed at this latest example of Kennedy's duplicity yet managed to make one final effort to charm Kennedy off his isolationist/appeaser perch. Dining with Kennedy at the White House on January 16, 1941, the president listened patiently while his guest again protested his supposed ill treatment. "I continued to complain of the way his 'hatchet men' were attacking me and stated my indignation," Kennedy related, as well as recalling his statement to Roosevelt that he proposed to make yet another "radio speech clarifying once and for all my position."

The two men faced each other. Roosevelt was aware that Kennedy was again attempting to blackmail him. As Kennedy later confided to James Landis, he pressed the president on what would happen if the Lend-Lease Bill was passed. "That's one of the difficulties the country worries about,"

Kennedy warned Roosevelt, "they are not sure you want to keep out of war."

The president's answer was unsatisfactory to Kennedy. "He said: 'I've said it 150 times at least. For the last seven years I have been going to get them into every war that has taken place in Europe and I haven't done it yet.' He added: 'I have no intentions of going to war.' I don't know whether it was due to my own suspicions, but it didn't sound as convincing as it did before when he said the same thing," Kennedy recounted.

Kennedy's own contradictions, however, were his greatest weakness. For all his stated complaints against the State Department, what most irked him was the president's continuing refusal to offer him an alternative job, while appointing other men, including Republicans, to prominent positions in the new coalition administration. "I told him it was too bad that all the big jobs had to go to men like Stimson, Patterson, Fox and Forrestal who had done nothing for his re-election," Kennedy recalled, "but he astounded me by saying he could find no good administrators among the Democrats who had worked for him."

Kennedy certainly still considered himself a good administrator, if a poor Democrat. Dangling before Kennedy the carrot of a post as special envoy to Ireland, where the thorny question of British military bases was being raised, Roosevelt sought Kennedy's assurance that he would not speak out against Lend-Lease. "He told me he would like to have a long talk with me about the Irish situation repeating that [Sumner] Welles insisted that I was the only one who could straighten it out."

Paraphrasing Jack's letters from California, the ambassador now gave his much-heralded NBC radio speech on January 18 and, to everyone's surprise, suddenly dropped his opposition to Lend-Lease. As he later put it, "in the circumstances and knowing full well that England couldn't survive without lend-lease, but wishing myself to give rather than make the silly gesture of lending something that could never be repaid, I heeded Secretary Hull's advice not to get tough in anything I had to say." Kennedy's subsequent appearance before the congressional committee on January 21, 1941, was thus a damp squib. The Lend-Lease Bill was reported out of the Senate committee by fifteen votes to eight and was passed by the Senate by a two-to-one majority.

For Jack Kennedy it was a triumph—perhaps, in its way, even more so than the publication of his book. His father, forever embittered by his fall from grace, however, declined to take any credit for his reversal of attitude over Lend-Lease. "For all practical purposes," he later remarked sardonically, "we were at war."

Irish Bases

If Ambassador Kennedy reluctantly gave way to Jack's argument over aid to Britain, Jack's brother did not. Instead, Joe Jr. hurried back to Harvard after Christmas to an "America First organizing lunch" to which he'd been invited, scheduled for December 30. Then at the Ford Hall Forum on January 6, 1941, against vehement protest, he spoke against sending supplies to Britain, even if this resulted in the defeat of England.

If the Nazis proved victorious, Joe Jr. declared, a barter trading system should be devised between America and Hitler to preserve the economic status quo. At a meeting of the Foreign Policy Association in Boston on January 26, 1941, Joe Jr. elaborated on this, declaring that the United States should not even send food convoys if this threatened to bring America into the conflict. This led to a vitriolic debate with Jack's former professor Arthur Holcombe.

Jack watched his eldest brother's performance in the self-appointed role as young isolationist with unease. "My elder brother Joe, he had a rather pugnacious personality," Jack wistfully commented later. Yet this same intemperate, pigheaded, handsome young man was Jack's brother, whom he could not bring himself to denounce any more than he could denounce his own father.

"Will be more than interested to hear anecdotes," Torby Macdonald meanwhile wrote to him, having heard that Jack was coming for further tests at the New England Baptist Hospital. "From here it sounds you've lost none of that golden touch of success of yours"—an ability which, he mocked, "inevitably leads to trouble & frustration."

If Jack could be tetchy and cruel in his remarks to Billings, Macdonald could be even crueller to Jack. Their Boston Irish-Catholic backgrounds bound them together, as did their passion for football and chasing skirts. However, in other respects they were vastly different. Macdonald was jealous and anti-Semitic. His humble circumstances as the son of a Boston-Irish football coach gave him a cynical, dissatisfied mien. At Harvard he'd considered himself just as handsome and intelligent as Jack, in vastly better health, and in a different league with regard to athletic ability. Jack's success in getting into the Spee Club, his genial ability to overcome anti-Irish Catholic prejudice, and the way he'd turned his fourth-year thesis into a bestselling book: all this had disconcerted the former Harvard football star, reversing their original relationship. "Let me know when & where you're arriving and will work on having those photographers, brass band & all due ceremony merited by your publishers," Macdonald promised sarcastically.

"I was glad to hear from you, and amazed that you were leaving Stanford so soon," Blair Clark, who was now working for the *St. Louis Post-Dispatch,* confessed. "I have had my physical exam for the draft, but haven't heard my classification yet. But I expect to be taken by Spring. What's happened to you in that line since you wrote me? I must say it's hard to start anything when you know it's going to be interrupted any time. Haven't you been tempted to marriage and exemption?"

Jack hadn't been. Instead, having successfully gotten his father to drop his opposition to the Lend-Lease Bill, he felt compelled to help him back into Roosevelt's good graces and, he hoped, a job. Thus, from his bed in the New England Baptist Hospital at the end of January 1941 the twenty-three-year-old author of *Why England Slept* now addressed the thorny question: "Should Ireland give naval and air bases to England?"

Quickly drafted for the *New York Journal-American,* Jack's article was published on February 2, 1941. "Is Ireland by her refusal to do so sleeping the same sleep that brought England to the brink of disaster?" he questioned. In his view the United States of America held the key, for Churchill's government dared not alienate American public opinion and nor did de Valera's—Britain because of its "growing dependence on the American arsenal," the Irish Free State because U.S. money would be decisive in helping "Ireland's long struggle" for independence and, currently, neutrality.

As in his thesis, the author took no sides. If Britain fell, Jack reminded readers, Irish independence would mean very little to the Germans; Ireland would "quickly follow in the tragic path of Norway, Holland, Belgium, Denmark, and other small countries who thought their neutrality would preserve their independence." Moreover, if Britain survived, Ireland "would stand a far better chance of living in peace and freedom in a world free from the menace of Hitler."

The Irish, however, saw the situation rather differently. "To give the British these bases [Cobh, Berehaven, and Lough Swilly] would mean the involvement of Ireland in a war for which they are completely unprepared," Jack stated. Nor, in Irish eyes, could Americans expect them to do so because, as the Irish bluntly put it, "the United States itself has refused to fight."

Although "racial ties and past bitterness should not influence our decision," Jack pointed out that the Irish dispute with England went deeper and had a far longer history than the "current German-British fight." In World War I the Irish had suffered "a greater percentage of killed and wounded than any other country" save France, and "for this great sacrifice, the Irish received nothing. Instead the Lloyd George Government, in which Winston Churchill was Minister for War, dispatched the Black and Tans who scourged Ireland for three years. Ireland has not forgotten this, and remembers further that in 1938 Mr. Churchill also led the group who opposed the return of the ports to Ireland. They do not feel they can depend on him to restore them once the war is over."

"It is hard to foretell the solution," Jack admitted. However, as he summed up, the bases themselves were of questionable value, since the British had "mined the Southern Channel and no shipping was going by that route," while Lough Swilly was duplicated by a British port twenty miles to the east, in Northern Ireland. Was it worth offending American public opinion for bases which would not prove decisive?

"Your article on Ireland got a rather less play than I anticipated," Torby Macdonald soon commented, "due to the element lacking which Hearst caters to in sensationalism. From what little facts I have on the matter and a dispassionate attitude, it seemed to me that you gave Ireland a little of the better of it, but perhaps that is due to fact that actually their view has the best reasons behind it."

As for Jack's disappointment that Torby hadn't acknowledged receipt of the specially inscribed copy of *Why England Slept* that Jack had recently sent, Macdonald claimed he "didn't know where the devil you were, N.Y., Palm Beach or Diggin in Hollywood. . . . Thank you very much for the book anyway Jack. I've taken your advice & I posted a piece of paper in over the inscription as I want people to think that it really was you that wrote the book and not, as gossip has it, written by a ghost writer & dictated by your father."

This brought Macdonald to the ambassador, with whom, for the next twenty years, Macdonald was to have a strangely filial as well as financially secretive relationship. In later years Macdonald liked to boast to his family that he and Jack's sister Kathleen were in love and that they would have married if it weren't for the intervention of Jack's father, who offered to give Torby a very senior position in his company. "He knew that was the quickest way to insult a proud man, and that killed off the romance *instantly*," Torby's wife loyally recalled him saying.

It was of course not so. On the contrary, Kathleen treated Torby with the same seductive coolness that she treated all her beaus. Meanwhile, unaware of Jack's part in the ambassador's NBC broadcast, Macdonald raved about Jack's father's radio address: "Tell your father that I thought his speech was wonderful—albeit a bit gloomy—God Jack why can't the rest of them realize what sort of a future we're going into—whether or not we do get in that war—your father seems to me to be the only guy (with the possible exception of that big stuffshirt Lindbergh) to see what is going on and not lose the woods for the trees. As a matter of fact I was going to write him a letter saying just how good I thought that speech was but thought it would be a little silly from his point of view, but if you get a chance and it doesn't sound too much like a pupil complimenting a master . . . you might tell him that's what a lot of people think." He added an even more alarming, Lindberghian postscript: "Have changed my mind about Communism v Fascism—*any* movement against those Jews will get not only my O.K. but actual support—from segregating them to killing them all at once or separately."

"When are you off to Stanford?" Macdonald closed. "Let me know if your back, health & charm are up to their usual high standard."

In fact Jack's stomach, spine, and unrequited lust for Flip Price still militated against a return to Stanford. Instead, after recuperating on doctor's orders in the Bahamas for several weeks in February 1941, Jack motored down from New York to Palm Beach. It was there that his father, impressed by Jack's help over the appeasement broadcast as well as Jack's recent article on Irish bases, asked if he would now help put together a record of his fateful years as U.S. ambassador to Britain.

Getting Restless

The ex-ambassador (Roosevelt having finally announced Kennedy's successor, John C. Winant) doubtless meant his proposal to Jack to be a compliment, an acknowledgment of Jack's growing authorial and speech-writing skills.

Jack, however, had no wish to become his father's scribe, and drew the line at this latest demand upon his fealty. He immediately shot off an urgent letter to John Hersey, Frances Ann Cannon's husband, asking for help. He had, as he explained, a person in mind for the undertaking: Connie Burwell, a friend of Frances Ann whom he'd met at the wedding, and "who impressed me very much, although I only talked with her for a short while. It seemed to me that this job might be of interest to her. It would take a year at least, probably two, and it would consist of correlating newspaper articles, Dad's daily notes and diary and actual events into a form somewhat similar, I imagine, to the three volumes of Walter Hines Page."

Connie Burwell later remembered discussing the book with Jack. "I expressed some reservations," she recalled. "His father had a reputation for being pro-German and I felt he ought to tell it like it was."

Furious that the president had still not offered him a job, the ex-ambassador made it plain to Miss Burwell, when she came to see him, that he indeed wished to tell it "as it was," wished in fact to take a massive swipe at President Roosevelt in the manuscript. Cabling his ex-press attaché Jim Seymour, Kennedy gave orders that all remaining copies of his 1936 campaign book *I'm for Roosevelt* be destroyed and the rest of his papers shipped back to America. "It was all set up," Connie Burwell recalled, "and the papers were en route over from England when they were sunk. I have a feeling the papers were later recovered, but that ended that and the book was never done."

Jack, meanwhile, was getting restless. He wrote to the Harvard records office requesting that a transcript of his undergraduate report be sent to Yale Law School, but for the moment he made no formal application to enter Yale the following September. It was during this limbo that Jack's father suggested he travel to South America with Rose and Eunice, who were leaving shortly by ship for Rio de Janeiro and then Buenos Aires, where they were to stay with the family of the Argentine ambassador to Vichy France, the Cárcanos.

"With arms wide open at docks all Cárcanos wait," the ambassador's son, Michael, telegraphed to Eunice on April 19, 1941. More interestingly, however, Michael had two beautiful sisters, Stella and Anna—nicknamed Baby and Chiquita—who would also be waiting.

Though it proved too late for Jack to get the necessary visas in time to travel with his sister and mother, Jack happily agreed to fly. In his report on hemispheric cooperation at the Riverside conference in December, he had noted the complexity of strategic and economic problems relating to the U.S. and South America. Should Mexico be included in the classification Latin America? How important was the Panama Canal? What difference would increasing air travel make, commercially and militarily? Could the United States absorb all of South American exports if trade with Europe collapsed? Could any individual South American state resist making trading agreements with Germany "merely because it does not like her ideology?" Was Argentina different from other Latin American countries in view of its nontropical climate and approaching industrialization? Was not Brazil the only country with heavy metals necessary "for building capital industries"?

Was "hemispheric solidarity" worth pursuing if the United States could not absorb South America's exports? Was South America "worth bothering about" at all? "The total volume of our trade is only about 7 percent of our entire trade," Jack reported. "With Argentina, our biggest customer, we do only about 1 percent of our business. If we got all their trade, at the most of it, it would be only about 7 percent of our national income."

There was the matter of military alliances. Would German penetration mean political penetration? "Hemispheric co-operation," Jack had reported Dean Victor Morris's argument, "should be military in its basis, to keep out the totalitarian regimes even if we have to take a large loss. He felt that the process would be so expensive, however, that it would be more economical to help England directly now."

How *did* the Latin American governments view the prospect of military alliances with the United States? How indeed did they view the United States? And what was their attitude toward Nazi Germany? Would any of them enter into a military alliance with Hitler?

As Jack had traveled to Central Europe and the Middle East in the spring and summer of 1939, so now, in the spring of 1941, he set off south to tour Latin America. On May 7, 1941, having flown from Miami, he began his investigation at Rio de Janeiro, sex center of the South American continent.

In Latin America

Despite reports of increasing Nazi atrocities against the Jews in Europe, Joe Jr. had meanwhile given an address at the Jewish temple of Ohabei Shalom in Brookline on April 29, 1941, in which he claimed it would be "perfectly feasible for the United States to exist as a nation, regardless of who wins the war," and stated that he was flatly opposed to U.S. convoys of Lend-Lease aid being sent to Britain, which he viewed as a "certain prelude to the sending of men and the inevitable dissolution of our social economic and political structure through war." By staying out of the conflict, Joe Jr. maintained, the U.S. could happily manage on its own. "He said military authorities considered invasion of this country impossible if we have strong South American bases," the Boston newspapers reported.

Jack, conducting his tour of the fleshpots and chancelleries of South America, did not agree. To Cam Newberry he sent a postcard of a very scantily clad Brazilian tart, on the back of which he scribbled, "Need I say more?" However, at a dinner at the American embassy in Rio de Janeiro several weeks later, the Brazilian foreign minister, when asked the attitude of his government to the present world crisis, ominously remarked that "it would be strongly influenced by which side won the victory abroad."

In Argentina, to which Jack flew on May 26, 1941, the mood was more decidedly pro-Nazi. Indeed it was clear that the United States was by no means as popular or its interests as secure in South America as people at home, particularly Jack's brother, assumed.

From Buenos Aires Jack was escorted to Francisco de Vittoria, the Cárcano family's vast and magnificent ranch. Señora Cárcano, her younger daughter, Chiquita, later recalled, was impressed by Jack. "There's a very interesting letter from my mother to my father, who was then ambassador in Vichy, where she mentions Jack Kennedy, because he came to our place in Córdoba in Argentina, and she's very revealing. she says: 'This young man is a very sort of rough American youth but he's very bright, he's very intelligent. He's always quoting the speeches of all the presidents! And one day he says *he's* going to be president—and I wouldn't be surprised if one day he isn't, because he's got a very inquisitive intelligence!'"

Certainly Jack was very inquisitive about Señora Cárcano's eldest daughter, Baby, with whom he began a passionate romance. Chiquita, meanwhile, was enchanted by Jack's humor. "He was a man who was very vibrant and very quick—snap, snap, snap. He was really a very colorful person, a very amazing person: one of the most amazing people I've ever met! What was so extraordinary about Jack when we met him at that stage: he seemed such a gangly young man—and always making jokes!"

The two girls, their brother, Michael, and the American visitor did much riding and hunting, as Chiquita recalled. "It was hilarious! At one point we were eagle hunting. Jack took careful aim—and nearly blew my head off! I have a lot of hair and I think he mistook it for the eagle!"

Jack's two weeks in Argentina would remain an indelible memory as well as the start of a lifetime infatuation on the part of Baby Cárcano, whose adoration of Jack never dimmed, despite Jack's cavalier treatment of her and his insistence, even though he was a fellow Catholic, that he didn't believe in "fidelity."

In the meantime, bidding farewell to the tearful beauty and her sister, as well as their brother and mother, the ex-ambassador's son flew to Montevideo, Uruguay, and from there to Santiago, Chile, on June 10, 1941. Four days later he boarded the S.S. *Santa Lucia,* bound from Valparaiso to New York.

Making his stately seaway home via Peru, Ecuador, Colombia, and the Panama Canal, Jack wrote ahead asking Billings to meet him. "Am on my way back—planning to arrive June 30th—Monday. I have a lot of packages, junk etc. and as I plan to stay in N.Y. a couple of days on some business, I'll need my car. So if you *happen* to go up to the Cape that week-end, bring my car back with you + I'll meet you in N.Y. You may not be able to get down but send me a message over to the Waldorf Towers. . . . Will give you the news."

Jack's news—apart from the fact that "he had a good time," as Billings remarked with a smile many years later, was completely overshadowed by the march of world events in his absence, however. On May 26, 1941, with the Japanese pressing to extend their power in the Far East, President Roosevelt had declared a full "state of emergency"; three weeks later, on June 21, had come the shattering announcement that Hitler's armies had invaded Russia.

But for Jack the most sensational news of all was personal. His isolationist, appeasement-minded elder brother, admirer of Hitler and cofounder of the Harvard Committee Against Military Intervention, had volunteered for military service, abandoning his Harvard law education and gaining instant acceptance in the United States Navy's aviation cadet program at Squantum, south of Boston.

Jack was flabbergasted, and determined not to let his turncoat brother steal all the military glory.

Joining the U.S. Navy

In her memoirs Rose Kennedy later described how, "on returning from his South American travels, soon after his twenty-fourth birthday," Jack "volunteered for the Officers' Candidate School of the Army. Because of the back injury he had suffered in Harvard football, he failed the physical exam. He tried the Navy and was rejected for the same reason. During the rest of that summer he did all sorts of calisthenics and corrective exercises. In September he applied again to the Navy."

Jack's induction into the U.S. Navy was by no means so straightforward. Nor did it involve calisthenics. Whether or not Jack was rejected by both the U.S. Army and the U.S. Navy on his return from Latin America is undocumented, but certainly, when Jack wrote to his friend Cam Newberry on July 8, he seemed all set to go to Yale Law School, as his badly typed letter from Hyannis Port showed:

> Dear Cam:
> Just returned from the America of the South to learn that the army has accepted you. My God, if that is true, no one, not even poor old broken down Zeke [John Coleman] and I are safe. . . .
> Am going to be working over at east Boston in a bank for the summer, and then go to Yale.
> I don't know about the army, my back was snapped several times during my trip South so I don't know as yet. This letter is beginning

to resemble the experts rhythm drill so I will save the stories of my triumphal tour of South America till you happen to be maneuvering around Barnstable.

This was followed on July 23 by an urgent telegram:

DEAR PRIVATE NEWBERRY AS THE COLUMBIA TRUST CO OF EAST BOSTON HAS HAD THE RATHER UNUSUAL GOOD FORTUNE OF ADDING ME TO THEIR STAFF FOR THE NEXT THREE WEEKS I WAS WONDERING WHETHER I MIGHT USE YOUR APARTMENT TO LAY MY HAT AND A FEW FRIENDS PENDING RENTAL WILL BRING MY OWN MATTRESS REGARDS MOE.

It was in fact while working at his father's old bank and preparing to enter Yale Law School that Jack decided to try a new route into the navy, one that had nothing to do with calisthenics but everything to do with Joseph Kennedy's former naval attaché in London. Reluctantly agreeing to help his eldest son to get into the Naval Academy Reserve class, Mr. Kennedy had earlier that year written to Captain Alan Kirk, who'd meanwhile been promoted to director of Naval Intelligence in Washington. Captain Kirk had conducted an inquiry into the sinking of the *Athenia* in 1939 and had been impressed by Jack's intellect. Thus, when the ex-ambassador wrote again in August 1941 to solicit help in getting Jack into the navy despite his poor health record, Kirk jumped at the opportunity to bring Jack to Washington. "I am having Jack see a medical friend of yours in Boston tomorrow for physical examination and then I hope he'll become associated with you in Naval Intelligence," the ex-ambassador wrote Captain Kirk from Hyannis Port.

Primed by the director of Naval Intelligence, the doctor gave Jack a perfunctory examination on August 5, 1941; in fact, the failure of the Naval Medical Board to investigate Jack's past medical history was inexcusable. To the formal question "History of illness or injury," the panel noted only: "Usual childhood diseases. T & A 1933. Appendectomy 1931. Has been restricted as regular diet to no fried foods or roughage. No ulcers." It was scarcely an honest or medically professional picture of Jack's calamitous case history of maladies and hospitalizations over the past twenty-four years.

Thus it was that John F. Kennedy, unable even to obtain life insurance given the severity of his health problems, was passed as fit by Boston's Naval Medical Board. Jack was euphoric. "It was no trouble to me to be helpful with such fine young men as yours," Kirk meanwhile wrote back on August 8, 1941, to his old "boss." "We are delighted Joe is getting along so well and I think it is fine he is in the Navy air game," he remarked, undisturbed that Joe Jr. had chosen flying rather than naval intelligence or even ship duty. "About Jack, I shall hope to hear that his plans are progressing favorably and I will see that he gets an interesting job."

The wheels of U.S. naval bureaucracy now began to grind in the North Station Industrial Building in Boston. Personal references, FBI and police records were checked. Jack Daly, the Kennedy's Cape Cod neighbor, commented that Jack "is the most intelligent boy in the Kennedy family, has a very active mind, re-acts quickly and is a damn good sailor. I have had occasion to race against him frequently and he handles his sails like an old veteran. He is an exceptional lad and I cannot recommend him too highly." Bart Brickley, a prominent Boston lawyer, considered Jack "one of the most outstanding youngsters I know. He did well at Harvard and was one of the most popular boys in his class. John has opinions of his own and this I consider one of his great assets. At no time have I ever heard anyone speak ill of him, and I would recommend him for anything, not because he is Joe Kennedy's son, but because I am satisfied that he is of the right material himself." Judge Johnny Burns knew Jack "very well. In many respects he is a very unusual youngster. He has good judgment, a keen intellect and a great reputation everywhere. Most boys with prominent parents get an inflated opinion of themselves, but John has never been that way. He is regular all the way through and shows definite signs of great character. I cannot recommend him too highly."

On August 28, 1941, Jack was interviewed by Lieutenant Commander J. A. Johnson and Lieutenant Carl Sternfelt in Boston, having filled out a questionnaire listing his brothers' and sisters' ages and occupations (Rosemary was given as a "student" and listed as living in Hyannis Port). "I am interested in coming into the Intelligence Service because I think I can exert my best efforts in it," Jack responded to Sternfelt's questioning. "Investigation has shown," Sternfelt subsequently reported, "that subject is an exceptionally brilliant student, has unusual qualities and a definite future in whatever he undertakes. Being son of a prominent father has not in the least affected subject. He is a clean, ambitious and likeable young American—anxious to make his own way in life. His loyalty is unquestioned, he is by nature and training very discreet, his judgment is sound, and he has the qualities essential for successful leadership. . . . At no time in investigation was there any trace or evidence of moral turpitude, gambling, drinking to excess or philandering," he noted in what would become famous last words.

At the Office of Naval Intelligence in Washington, Commander E. M. Major summarized Sternfelt's report and concluded on September 10 that "subject's education, ability, unusually wide acquaintance and background, together with his personal qualifications fit him for commission as Ensign, I-V(S). Subject appears qualified for service in OP-16F in the Office of Naval Intelligence." On September 15, 1941, the commandant of the First Naval District officially recommended Jack's appointment as "Ensign, I-V(S) USNR to fill a vacancy in the O.N.I. procurement quota under the cognizance of the Chief of Naval Operations of Intelligence Officers for Special Service."

Jack, with a sigh of relief, wrote from Hyannis Port to thank Sternfelt for "rushing through the application." Accepting the results of Jack's August medical examination without question, the Naval Bureau of Medicine and Surgery in Washington rubber-stamped his medical qualification, and on September 25, 1941, Jack Kennedy was commissioned as an ensign in the U.S. Naval Reserve, without needing to go through officer's school. He was, it appeared, in.

Captain Kirk, however, was on the way out. Six days after Jack received his commission, Kirk was summoned by the new under secretary of the Navy, James Forrestal, who said bluntly, "I think the Secretary is ready to see a change in Naval Intelligence—not that he doesn't think you've done a good job, but he thinks, you know, we ought to have some fresh blood."

Kirk had no regrets. "It had a very poor standing in the Navy Department," he later described Naval Intelligence in 1941, "not because of the caliber of the officers, but everybody sort of thought Naval Intelligence was striped pants, cookie-pushers, going to parties and so on."

Leaving the Office of Naval Intelligence immediately, Kirk assumed command of a squadron of destroyers escorting convoys to Iceland and weighed anchor. How the departure of his sponsor would affect Jack's nascent naval career remained to be seen.

Eastern Activity

Waiting "on inactive service" in Hyannis Port, Reserve Ensign John F. Kennedy for the time being heard nothing, and reverted to socializing. On October 9, 1941, he gave his latest, boastful "report on Eastern activity" to Cam Newberry.

> Went down to Dixon's wedding, he married a very pretty girl who looks just like him. Dixon looked well, but as I had been preparing for weeks for this occasion, I'm afraid as far as looking like a million dollars—I stole the show. Dixon said rather bitterly that I looked like a Hollywood actor, and little Moe—he didn't mean Mickey Rooney.
>
> From there I went back to N.Y. + drove by the [U.S. Midship-

man School training ship] S.S. *Prairie State* to see if I could find yard-bird [Bill] Coleman who has finally been caught—at Virginia Beach I believe the arrest was made. I didn't see him, but yelled Coleberg around there enough to make his name known.

From there I went up to Greenwich + saw your friend Pete Wick + bride—who is *well* along, but looking very nicely. Proceeded then to Boston to see Torb + Jonas, + heard Macdonald is going to be married December 19th to Polly Cotter—I was surprised too. I then drove back down here and as I couldn't get my top up I froze my balls off—and have been in bed ever since.

The summer has progressed very nicely. Zeke came for a day & stayed for a month. Macdonald came down to crew for me in a regatta—caught a quick load—and rolled gently over-board and had to be retrieved at a crucial point in the race. Kick has gone to Washington where she is now secy. of the editor of the Times-Herald—a very interesting fall both for her and the editor—who, I understand, dictates at a furious rate in the happy belief that Kick can take shorthand. I myself am off in the near future to join the Navy.

Jack had only a week more of civilian life to go. On October 17, 1941, the chief of the Bureau of Navigation heard from the chief of Naval Operations that "the services of Ensign Kennedy are required in the Foreign Intelligence Branch of the Division of Naval Intelligence"— subject to physical qualification. A week later, following a second perfunctory physical, a bill of good health was issued by the same Boston medical board that had passed Jack fit for service in the U.S. Navy, and on October 27, 1941, having found an apartment in Dorchester House on Sixteenth Street, NW, Ensign Jack Kennedy finally reported for active duty at the headquarters of the Office of Naval Intelligence, Washington, D.C.

Lobotomy

Donning his smart blue uniform, Jack soon sat down to work, collating latest reports and decrypts from foreign stations and rewriting them in clear English for the Office of Naval Intelligence's daily and weekly bulletins.

Officer status, Jack was aware, had been almost ridiculously simple to attain, a fact that Jack lost little time in rubbing into Seaman Second

Class Bill Coleman. "In addition to serving as toastmaster to that gathering of good fellows," Jack wrote of the forthcoming annual Spee Club dinner in Boston, "you will have a chance to personally ask me those questions concerning how I got into the Navy that I understand is seriously interfering with your sleep nights. Well, Coleman, the simplest answer is that there are officers and there are seamen second class, and it doesn't take much experience for a good Navy man to tell officer material when he sees it."

Coleman, however, could give as good as he got from Jack, and soon responded with disdain:

> Dear Admiral Mahan,
>   How you got that stripe is a source of mystery to the whole V-7 [reserve-officer training] class—yes, Kennedy, I've lost considerable sleep over it—and am troubled with nightmares depicting you getting out a tome on "Naval Tactics at Sea *and* Ashore," assigned to us as outside reading in Seamanship.
>   God man, next to Don Harvard . . . and Peter David Fielding Elser, the Bifocal Boast of the Brooklyn Navy Yard . . . you are considered the weakest link in the Atlantic Fleet Arm. And you might as well learn, Kennedy, that the stuff you used to pull on Black Jack along the Cape won't revolutionize maritime warfare (I might add that I've just discovered to my delight that there are no centerboards on merchant ships!) . . .

The friendly joshing turned a trifle irritable, however, when Coleman received a typed letter to Jack's father, mistakenly addressed to him. "Frankly, Kennedy, I don't get much of a kick reading the stuff you send your family. You are revealing yourself as 1941's nautical Don Quixote— no wonder they are worrying about the balance of sea power in the Pacific with guys like you doing the balancing—I won't trust you at the controls of my last year's electric train. . . . Just because you have a stripe or two on me is no reason to hand me second hand reading matter. Either write *me* or let's call it off. But at least I sense a little consideration in the fact that you 'type-write' to your Father, and spare him the countless hours of decripting those paleolithic scratches in which you delight. . . . I hope Papa Joe liked the letter you wrote me!"

Whether Joe Kennedy liked Jack's letter to Coleman is unrecorded. Washington had once been Joseph Kennedy's turf, with the vast mansion Marwood as his residence and imposing government offices as his headquarters. Now the ex-ambassador was persona non grata. He wrote gloomily to Krock that he didn't miss the inside track, but it wasn't true. The Bronxville house had been put up for sale, and with its disposal, the family nurse reflected later, there was "a loss of stability" in the whole family: "Mr. Kennedy began to withdraw more and more into himself. He was not as outgoing or as happy as he had been before, and the kids felt it."

This was an understatement. Kennedy was in fact now hatching ominous new plans on behalf of his various children—most especially Rosemary, his retarded eldest daughter, whose latest behavioral problems irked him. Smarting at Roosevelt's continued refusal to offer him a post in the bipartisan administration, he now made a decision about Rosemary that would reduce her to a human vegetable for the rest of her life and haunt the consciences of Rosemary's mother, brothers, and sisters for the rest of theirs. "Joe and I brought the most eminent medical specialists into consultation," Rose related "and the advice, finally, was that Rosemary should undergo a certain form of neurosurgery."

Years later Rose altered her version of the story, claiming Joe never actually consulted her in making the decision to operate. Rosemary's retardation had given rise to difficult behavior associated with delayed puberty. She became avid for sexual experience, Lem Billings recalled. "Her level of frustration grew so high that she became almost impossible to handle. Every day there would be fights where Rosemary would use her fists to hit and bruise people, long absences at night when she'd be out wandering the streets and violent verbal exchanges." Once the sweetest-natured of the Kennedys, she now became the most rebellious. "She was in a convent in Washington at the time, and many nights the school would call to say she was missing, only to find her out walking around the streets at two A.M.," Rose's niece recalled. "Can you imagine what it must have been like to know your daughter was walking the streets in the darkness of the night, the perfect prey for an unsuspecting male?"

"I was always worried that she would run away from home someday or that she would go off with someone who would flatter her or kidnap her," Rose said in defense of the decision to operate.

Some who witnessed Joseph P. Kennedy's own behavior at home, however, speculated as to whether he might have sexually abused Rosemary, thus explaining her delayed outbursts and Kennedy's guilty determination to quiet her. Others, such as Luella Hennessy, blamed the move away from a stable family home. Whatever the truth, and whether or not Rose was privy to the decision, Rosemary was taken from her Washington convent one day in the fall of 1941 and lobotomized.

The operation seemed an instant success. Rosemary never ran away again. Indeed she would never be able to go out again, at least among ordinary people. "The operation eliminated the violence and the convulsive seizures," Rose later confessed, "but it also had the effect of leaving Rosemary permanently incapacitated. She lost everything that had been gained during the years by her own gallant efforts and our loving efforts for her. She had no possibility of ever again being able to function in a viable way in the world at large." It was, Rose candidly admitted, "the first of the tragedies that were to befall us."

"My wife and I have given nine hostages to fortune. Our children and your children are more important than anything else in the world," Ambassador Kennedy had broadcast to the people of America the year before. Now he had given one of those nine hostages to misfortune, and sadly, more were to follow.

Dinner at Mrs. Patterson's

Notwithstanding Rosemary's tragic operation, Jack settled into the Washington world without difficulty. Kathleen, though she could take no shorthand, shared the same social energy and humor as Jack. She was also a good listener. Though she only began work on the *Times-Herald* in September 1941, she had by Jack's arrival late in October established a social network that was tailor-made for the former playboy. In the dim offices of the Navy Department, Ensign Kennedy was a nobody. In the dizzying social world of Washington, aided by Kathleen, Arthur Krock, and others, however, Jack was soon rubbing shoulders if not with the Almighty, then at least with the mighty. Inevitably, a few weeks after his arrival, Jack was invited to dinner at the home of Cissy Patterson—the legendary Washington hostess and owner of the *Times-Herald.* Like Anna Pavlovna Scherer's salon in St. Petersburg on the eve of war with Napoleon, evenings at Cissy Patterson's were a perfect reflection of the strange twilight world of Washington on the eve of Pearl Harbor.

So symbolic did Jack find the evening, in retrospect, that he afterward set down an account of it, thinking he might one day use it for an article or even a book. "Present at this dinner," Jack noted in his aide-mémoire, "were [under secretary of the Navy] James Forrestal, Senator [Burton K.] Wheeler, Herbert B. Swope, Bernard Baruch, John Foster, First Secretary British Embassy, Frank Waldrop and wives, etc."

No sooner had introductions been made than the fireworks began.

> Wheeler in shaking hands with Forrestal, immediately started an argument on the War. After about two minutes of talking he bet Forrestal one hundred dollars that the Republicans would win the Congressional election in 1942.
>
> At the dinner table the argument continued. Wheeler said that

there was not a real emergency here now—no one could possibly invade this country. With our strong air force we were invulnerable, no matter what happened to the British Fleet. He was very much against the Lend-Lease policy especially the grants to South America. He didn't trust them and he felt the Lend-Lease funds were just money down the drain.

Such isolationist sentiments were hardly novel to Jack's ears. Wheeler had actually stayed with the Kennedys in Palm Beach before the Lend-Lease hearings and had met Jack there. "He believed that the debt would go to one hundred and fifty billion and we would be unable to service it," Jack recorded, and noted the senator's "trip to Europe and through Russia at the end of the first war and . . . the economic hazards which he found there. He said when he was in Austria in 1922 'women sold their virtue for a piece of bread' and he said that experience convinced him that war could only bring misery to the U.S. (there is no doubt in my mind," Jack noted in parentheses, "that this trip of Wheeler's at that time is one of the great factor[s] explaining his position. Everytime I have heard him discuss the matter he has always brought up that argument)."

Wheeler was certain that "Forrestal was wrong politically"; that, while the general public might currently support Britain's lonely efforts against Hitler, as well as Russia's stand, such support was fickle and would in time return to isolationism. "After the first World War in 1920, Wheeler had been defeated by a tremendous majority—but on the wave of reaction against the war in 1922 he was elected by an even greater majority," Jack recorded. "Wheeler felt that this war would see a duplication of that experience. He felt that politically, while he might be at the weak end now, at the end of the war when the reaction set in he could write his own ticket."

Jack, entranced, hung on every word, listening to some of the great dissenting voices of his time, voices he would seek to re-create years later in his famous gallery of such characters, *Profiles in Courage*. Misguided or miscreant, these men had at least the courage of their convictions, something Jack, with his strong intellect yet enfeebled emotions and uncertain commitment, deeply admired, however much he might disagree. As his new friend Chuck Spalding (a Yale graduate who had gotten to know Jack through George Mead, a Cape Cod neighbor) recalled, Jack "never considered himself an intellectual . . . but he was always interested in intellectuals."

Here, in the dining room of a celebrated isolationist newspaper proprietor, there hung the same decadent, discordant air Jack had experienced at Lady Astor's house after Munich, while Britain dithered and debated on the brink of war. Now, however, it was the United States that dithered and debated. Whether America should fight was a subject that ignited the fears, prejudices, and hopes of the whole nation. Wheeler warned Forrestal that the interventionists were treading on dangerous ground, for they were inciting possible revolution and civil war and stirring up tides of bitterness that threatened to wreck American democracy. He warned that the charge they had leveled at him of being anti-Semitic was doing the Jews themselves more harm than it was him. "It made people stop and think there must be reasons for his being that way," Jack recorded. "He admitted he was a cold blooded Yankee and said while he was sorry for the Poles and the Czechs he believed that their misery should serve as a warning and not as an incentive for duplicating it."

This exposition, Jack noted, was delivered in a "quite good natured" way, "until Mrs. Swope inferred he had taken a cowardly position. He replied that it took plenty of "gutts [*sic*]" to buck the President of the United States and most of the Press"—the same defense Jack had heard his own father use when claiming that his treatment at the hands of the American press was worse than the sufferings of the inhabitants of London during the Blitz.

James Forrestal was a complete contrast to Wheeler. Like Jack's father, he also had been a Wall Street swindler, amassing a personal fortune in shady deals and dubious share trading. As Chuck Spalding later recalled, Jack "admired Forrestal tremendously, at the time. I think maybe because of Forrestal's approach—I didn't get to know Forrestal, but I get the feeling that he had a similar approach to things, a sensible approach, free from bigotry or isolated interest—that approach appealed to Jack a great deal. Outside of that, he [Jack] had then this great suspicion about everybody else's motives, especially the people who might be close to being zealous. The more excited they were, the more suspicious he became."

To Jack's surprise, Forrestal repudiated the label of "intervenient" [*sic*]. America, Forrestal considered, was already at war in all but name. "He said that the U.S. had entered the struggle when they gave aid to England as Germany would never let them wriggle out of the part they played in prolonging England's struggle. He gave a simile of a barroom fight," Jack chronicled. "If two men are fighting and one (England) is helped by a third, wouldn't the reaction of the man against whom help was given (Germany) be to turn on the third man who had given aid (the U.S.)? He asked me what I thought."

It was now that Jack, having listened to an isolationist and a fatalist, and having struggled with this issue for two long years, finally gave his own opinion—the climax of his education, his upbringing, his travels, and his strangely engaged yet dispassionate heart.

Becoming an Interventionist

I replied that I had been an isolationist due to the fact that I believed that the effort necessary by the U.S. to defeat Germany would be so great that in the end the U.S. would have lost what they were fighting for. I said that my belief has been changed somewhat by my trip to South America and Russia's long stand and I could see that if Russia continued to hold out—America's aid might become decisive and if the situation reached that point and if a quick victory could be achieved I would favor America going in.

Finally Jack had become an interventionist—four weeks before the attack on Pearl Harbor. He added, however, an important rider. "I felt that for people to take a die-hard position on the war was wrong," he explained. "Our policy must be flexible, fluid, it was to stay abreast of the changing conditions of the world."

Forrestal, moved by the twenty-four-year-old's honesty, "said that he also had been an isolationist. He had come to the conclusion, however, that America must be the dominant power of the 20th century." Burton Wheeler, the senator from Montana, "had built up Hitler in our mind as an invincible force, but," Forrestal claimed, Hitler "was tired, strained. We would have to fight him some day—it was best to take him on now, while we had allies. The job had to be done—Senator Wheeler was living in an idealistic world—a fool's paradise."

Next came the eminent journalist Herbert B. Swope, who "admitted being an interventionist—but denied being a funk-hole patriot as Wheeler had charged. He snorted at the opinion that there would not be any election in 1943 [*sic*] as the Patterson papers had charged. He denied that a revolution might come after the war—a proposal forwarded by Frank Waldrop—who mentioned the possibility of civil war over this issue."

James Forrestal backed up Swope's position. "Forrestal said that Civil War was out of the question," Jack noted, since the argument over "interventionist and isolationist had not split the country on a basis that would make revolution possible. (This is interesting," Jack noted in parentheses, "as it shows the academic way in which these men were looking at the possibilities of our getting into war. There was no suggestion that it would be done in the way it actually happened. They saw it rather as a political battle.)

"Swope continued that if there was even a suggestion that there should be no election in 1943 [*sic*] he, Swope, would be the first one to the barricades. He laughed off Wheeler's suggestion that Roosevelt might be impeached. He said his belief in the necessity of our getting in was based on moral grounds and he denied that he was one of those 'Wall Street Financeers' that Wheeler constantly was accusing of trying to get us into the war (Baruch injected here that Swope certainly wasn't a Wall Street Financeer," Jack could not resist recording in parentheses again, "but that he'd certainly like to be)."

It was now the turn of Arthur Krock. "Arthur Krock was claimed by both Swope and Wheeler as being on their side. As this was obviously impossible, Swope asked him to give his position. Krock said he would, but felt that it was of very little importance. To illustrate it he told the story of the bar tender calling up to the owner of the bar to ask whether Pat Murphy was good for a drink. 'Has he had it?' 'He has.' 'Then he's good for it.' Krock explained that this was the way he stood on the war. He said it did not make any difference whether or not we believed in it. We were actually in the war now. He laughed at Wheeler's suggestion that Roosevelt wanted to stay out of war." To the discomfort of Mr. Foster of the British embassy, Krock said he wanted "the Britishers present to know of the high plain upon which the repeal of the neutrality act has been conducted. He told of the Congressman who sold his vote for thirty million dollars worth of war contracts and of the Southern Democrat who sold his vote for a Judgeship."

To Jack's fascination, the wily Krock had thus managed to please both interventionists and isolationists, for "Wheeler agreed with this—and said that Kelly and the rest of the bosses had been called down by the White House at the last moment to Washington to put the heat on reluctant Congressmen. The need for this can be seen from the closeness of the vote, 212–200. Wheeler said if the Senate had voted its true convictions . . . the measure for repeal [of the Neutrality Act] wouldn't have gotten twenty votes.

"The discussion throughout the evening was conducted on a very good natured basis," Jack remarked, noting with satisfaction that "it seemed to approach very closely the English ideal of never permitting political opinions to interfere with personal relationships."

It was this final insight, on the eve of America's dramatic entry into World War II, that would provide Jack Kennedy with the key to the future, encouraging him to embark on one of the most extraordinary political voyages of the twentieth century.

PART

·9·

INGA
BINGA

Danish-born journalist Inga Arvad, 1941 (Ronald McCoy Collection)

Bores Cannot Be Saints

As in most families of abused children, the Kennedy siblings, as they grew older, became protective of their parents rather than accusatory. Thus the more the ex-ambassador had made a "horse's ass" of himself in 1940, the more, paradoxically, Jack had loved him: grateful for his paternal help in the past and compassionate now in his time of defeat.

For his mother, however, Jack had little compassion. "The mother and Jack didn't get on very well," Chiquita Cárcano candidly recalled, dashing the notion of Rose as a saintly mother with the unforgettable words: "Bores cannot be saints—and Rose Kennedy was a crashing bore! I mean, I am a Catholic, and I've got lots of Catholic friends. But she was *frightful!*"

Henry James reflected:

> I think Jack was wary of his mother because of her strong religion, which Jack felt he could never emulate. She was one of those fanatics who was "carrying the banners, flurrying in the breeze"—she went to mass every day of her life, I think. And Jack wasn't having that! . . . He talked to her all right, but he certainly wouldn't *ever* tell her anything about his personal actions, behavior or anything else. He kept her at arm's length because he was just ill at ease with her strong brand of Catholicism—and because, as I say, Jack had made it very clear to me when we had talks about religion that he found great difficulty in believing most of the tenets of the Catholic church.

By contrast, James related, Jack

> saw that his father was a political and public Catholic. Mr. Kennedy was not a Catholic in any of his practices. He committed adultery, flagrantly. He didn't obey the teaching of the church—unless it's the Irish concept, which is that everything is forgiven—you can commit any sin you want, by just going to confession: a very convenient way of getting out of paying for your indulgences!
>
> Jack was smart enough to see that his father was brazenly two-faced about it. And so, in Jack's case, if anything was to go, religion was to go—not the other. Jack's libertine ways were what he wanted to keep.

Before Rose Kennedy's reproving gaze Jack behaved as amorally as his father. After his death Rose painted a charming picture of Jack, recalling how she couldn't "think of anybody, I don't think in my life, that I've ever seen who was more attractive at a dinner table. . . . I don't know what it was, it was a sort of gaiety, and then it was a quick repartee, and then it was a knowledge of things that were going on, and was an interest in things that are fascinating for themselves, so that everybody was delighted to be with him, or hear him talk, and they knew that they could take part in the conversation, and at the same time be attracted and be interested in it. And enjoy it."

This, however, was said post mortem. When Jack was alive, there was little genuine communication between them—and much buried bitterness. "I enjoy your round robin letters," Jack wrote back sarcastically to his mother at the time of his dinner at Mrs. Patterson's. "I'm saving them to publish—that style of yours will net us millions. With all this talk about inflation and where is our money going—when I think of your potential earning power—with you dictating and Mrs. Walker [Rose's secretary] beating it out on that machine—it's enough to make a man get down on his knees and thank God for the Dorchester High Latin School which gave you that very sound grammatical basis which shines through every slightly mixed metaphor and each somewhat split infinitive."

"My health is excellent," he went on cruelly. "I look like hell, but my stomach is a thing of beauty, as are you, Ma—and you, unlike my stomach, will be a joy forever."

Not surprisingly, Rose did not quote this particular letter when assembling her children's dutiful missives for her memoirs. Jack's mockery of her prim, mission-school style could not, however, awaken a warm, loving, hugging tenderness that had never existed, and it was in the arms of a proverbial "older woman," on the eve of America's entry into the Second World War, that he was to find at age twenty-four the sort of love he craved.

Exuding Animal Magnetism

Inga Arvad resembled Jack's mother in certain ways. She was attractive, well-perfumed, well-groomed. Unlike Jack's mother, however, Inga liked sex.

Blond, blue-eyed, and Danish by birth, Inga Arvad could speak and write in four languages. Arthur Krock had "discovered" her in New York when she accosted him on Broadway after a meeting of the Pulitzer Prize board in June 1941 and asked him if he could help her find work on a newspaper in Washington. Inga had just completed a year-long course at the Columbia School of Journalism. "If she came, would I help her?" Krock remembered her question. "I was so stupefied by the beauty of this creature that I said I would."

Krock immediately recommended her to Cissy Patterson, who, Inga later recorded, "listened to what I had been doing in Europe as a journalist and immediately offered me a job writing a daily column for her paper."

Frank Waldrop, associate editor of the *Times-Herald,* recalled how intrigued he was by Arvad. "She couldn't write anything extended at all, she was not an analytical writer, but she had a good intuitive style of writing about people. Now we had a little feature at that time called, 'Did You Happen To See . . . ?' A great many people were coming to Washington at that time. I'd send her to talk to somebody and she'd come back and she had a neat little style of doing that interview column—that one little thing. And I didn't know a thing about her really, except she did the job, she was nice-looking, and she and Page [Huidekoper, a *Times-Herald* reporter] were all whooping it up in Georgetown together."

Whooping it up was the word. Page Huidekoper, who came from a Dutch-Virginian family, had previously worked at the U.S. embassy in London, where she'd met Joe Jr., Jack, and Kathleen. "I had been living in the house of some good friends of mine and I was looking for someone to live with me, so Arthur [Krock] asked me if I'd like to have Inga. I met her and she was very, very attractive. The house was in Georgetown. So she came to stay with me until she found a place of her own.

"She and Kathleen were great friends. Everything was done in groups. Whole households of boys would take out whole households of girls. Part of it was economics: a group of young bachelors would live together in an apartment and tend to go around together; the same was true of the girls. And there were so many parties to go to that everyone just traveled in groups. Indeed, you were almost looked at askance if you tried to get someone off by yourself."

It was in this innocent merry-go-round that, as Page recalled, "Kathleen introduced Inga to Jack."

Years later Inga recounted how it had happened. Kathleen was

> curled up like a kitten, her long tawny hair fell over her face as she read a letter, then she jumped up . . . her Irish-blue eyes flashed with excitement as she leaped onto the floor and began a whirling dance like some delightful dervish. "He's coming to Washington, I'm going to give a party at the F Street Club, you will just love him! . . ."
> "Who?" said I, being a few years older and not knowing what sort

of a creature could make Kick so happy. Was it one of her many admirers. "WHO?"

"Jack. He's in the Navy and is going to be stationed in Washington. Super, super."

He came. She hadn't exaggerated. He had the charm that makes birds come out of their trees. He looked like her twin, the same thick mop of hair, the same blue eyes, natural, engaging, ambitious, warm and when he walked into a room you knew he was there, not pushing, not domineering but exuding animal magnetism. . . .

His bestseller *Why England Slept* had been published and my boss, Cissy Patterson said: "Get an interview for your column with young Kennedy." I did.

Inga's page-two interview came out in the *Times-Herald* edition of November 27, 1941. It began disarmingly:

An old Scandinavian proverb says the apple doesn't fall far from the tree. No better American proof can be found than John F. Kennedy. If former Ambassador Joe Kennedy has a brilliant mind (not even his political enemies will deny the fact), charm galore, and a certain way of walking into the hearts of people with wooden shoes on, then son No. 2 has inherited more than his due. The 24 years of Jack's existence on our planet have proved that here is really a boy with a future.

Young Kennedy—don't call him that, he will resent it greatly— did more than boot the football about at Harvard. He was extremely popular. Graduated cum laude, was a class officer, sailed on the intercollegiate sailing team during his sophomore year, and most important, wrote a thesis.

Arthur Krock from the *New York Times* read it and suggested it be put in a book. Henry Luce of *Time, Fortune* and *Life,* must have thought the same because he wrote the foreword, and by putting in 12 hours a day, cooled off with as many showers, Jack polished it off during the summer and the much praised book, *Why England Slept,* was the result.

It sold like wildfire.

As Inga observed, "Jack hates only one subject—himself. He is the best listener I have come across between Haparanda and Yokohama. Elder men like to hear his views, which are sound and astonishingly objective for so young a man."

For a Dane who'd only reached the United States in February 1940, Inga's English was also astonishing, as was her understanding of Jack. To her fellow reporter John White, she was quite candid. "Jack's an interesting man because he's so singleminded and simple to deal with. He knows what he wants. He's not confused about motives and those things. I find that refreshing. I like it—and furthermore I like him. But I wouldn't trust him as a long-term companion, obviously. And he's very honest about that. He doesn't pretend that this is forever. So, he's got a lot to learn and I'll be happy to teach him."

Pearl Harbor

"We all built him up, he was devoid of conceit, but maybe a tiny hope was gleaming," Inga later reflected. "Most evenings he, Kick, Torby Macdonald, Chuck Spalding and a few others would have dinner, always the same menu: steak, peas, carrots and ice cream. Touch football—an incomprehensible game to a Dane, was played in Kick's living room, everything was discussed, mainly politics, but somehow it always got back to Jack. He was all of 24 and torn between a life of service to his country and teaching at some college. We planned halfheartedly and in some fun that some day he should be President. He laughed and said: 'If ever I decide to run for office, you can be my manager.' "

Thus, innocently and with modest fanfare in the Washington *Times-Herald,* began the greatest love of Jack's life.

In the complacent world of Washington military bureaucracy, meanwhile, laxity of security was endemic. On December 3, an officer in the U.S. Army War Plans Department telephoned Senator Burton K. Wheeler to ask if he would care to see the latest top-secret "Victory Program," which he'd just purloined from Colonel Wedemeyer's filing cabinet. Wheeler, unaware that the FBI was already tapping his phone, was nonetheless wary. "Aren't you afraid of delivering the most secret document in America to a Senator?" Wheeler asked before the officer handed the document over. The following day America's most secret plans for military engagement in Europe were in the hands not only of the German embassy, but of most of the American press.

The Washington *Times-Herald* was among the first to break the story. Cissy Patterson and Frank Waldrop, both of them rabid isolationists, hoped that publication of such information might frighten the American public. "A great war was drawing civilized society in Europe to its death," Waldrop later wrote in defense of his paper's stance. "In the United States, hate, fear, and malice split groups, close friends, and families."

Jack, having made up his mind over military intervention, meanwhile conscientiously carried out his duties at ONI. Most of his fellow officers in OP-16F were ex-journalists. As one of them recalled:

> There were six of us in the room—a plain room with metal desks. . . . Our job was to prepare three intelligence bulletins: a daily bulletin for the Secretary of the Navy and other top people, which was a summary of key developments; another daily bulletin—a four-page leaflet type thing—which was less sensitive and more widely circulated to shore stations and ships at sea; and a weekly four-page bulletin . . . We all had typewriters at our desks and spent most of the day writing, condensing, editing. . . . I remember Kennedy quite well. He was a man of high intelligence with a facile wit—a good writing hand. He also had a heavy social life. In those days he was still more or less in his playboy stage.

According to Rose Kennedy's latest round-robin, the family house in New York had finally been closed up early in December 1941, with Jack appropriating "the best of the Bronxville furniture." In the capital Jack was visited by his father, who "left for Washington Tuesday at midnight . . . and is to lunch at Jack's apartment," Rose informed her distant offspring. On Wednesday, December 3, having seen his father off on the plane back to New York, Jack wrote to Connecticut to tell Billings to bring his camp bed the following weekend. "I work on Saturday," he explained, "and probably will not be finished until 5:00. Kick however will be around. Just let us know your plans. I told Kick you probably wanted a date with her—bring your tux—we might go to Chevy Chase—Regards, Jack."

"During this period I spent a lot of time in Washington," Billings explained later. "I had bad eyes so I was not even able to be drafted." On the morning of Sunday, December 7, 1941, the two ex-Muckers went out "to find a touch football game," Billings distinctly recalled.

> Jack was a good touch football player. I was a bad touch football player. This was often a bone of contention. He wanted to play touch and softball, etc. all the time, while I didn't. This is an area where we really weren't congenial, although I usually gave in on it.
>
> I remember how I particularly disliked to play with people I didn't know. On the other hand, there is nothing he liked better on a Sunday than to find a touch game and ask if we could play. One team would pick me—and I wasn't half as good as he was. It didn't take them long to figure this out—I hated that! Anyway, on that particular Sunday we found a game near the Washington Monument. We'd

just finished the game and were driving back to his apartment. All of a sudden the news came over his car radio that the Japanese had attacked Pearl Harbor.

Billings was "terribly excited." Thick, billowing smoke rose above the Japanese embassy on Massachusetts Avenue as guilty diplomats burned their papers. Hundreds began to assemble outside the White House on Pennsylvania Avenue, waiting to know what would be the president's reaction.

The next day, December 8, 1941, Roosevelt addressed Congress. Briefly and tersely he referred to the Japanese assault the previous day—"a day that will live in infamy"—and in a firm, purposeful voice asked "that the Congress declare that since the unprovoked and dastardly attack by Japan on Sunday, December 7, a state of war has existed between the United States and the Japanese Empire. With confidence in our armed forces—with the unbounding determination of our people—we will gain the inevitable triumph—so help us God."

With only one dissenting voice Congress gave its overwhelming support to the president. Immediately the Office of Naval Intelligence moved into wartime gear. Instead of closing down at five P.M. every evening, a new round-the-clock system was instituted.

"This will gripe your arse but I can't come to the wedding," Jack informed Billings on December 9, referring to their friend Peter Gorman's forthcoming nuptials. "I'm not pulling a Coleman, but I'm on a new schedule—from 10:00 at night to 7 in the morning—it's a 7 day a week schedule." He still hoped to make their friend Eben Pyne's wedding, but "I will have a hell of a schedule—flying up after work, and then flying back for Sat. night. . . . Please convey my thanks and regrets to Pete's bride who was very kind to have us." So tired was he that he even forgot to sign the handwritten letter, adding an apologetic P.S.: "Isn't this a dull letter—but I'm not sleeping much nights."

"Saw Kick last night," Bill Coleman scribbled to Jack from New York. "She said you were on the night shift and tanned to a dusky hue! Keep it up and you'll be losing your eyes and sprouting feelers!"

The next day came news that Japanese troops had invaded Malaya, Hong Kong, and the Philippines at Luzon. On Thursday, December 11, in accordance with the Tripartite Act, Adolf Hitler announced that Nazi Germany would join Japan in hostilities aimed against the United States.

Finally and reluctantly, America was at world war.

Casualty of War

Poor Inga Arvad was to be one of the first casualties of Washington's war. If the atmosphere at the isolationist *Times-Herald* was already poisonous before Pearl Harbor, it became even more so afterward, Frank Waldrop recalled. Pearl Harbor supposedly ended divisive disagreements, but it didn't really. "The knives flashed as never before. It didn't take much, you know, to set the woods on fire," Waldrop related.

The first smoke came from Inga's ex-roommate, Page Huidekoper. Arvad later recalled, "A very good friend of mine, Kathleen Kennedy, who also worked on the same paper, told me that a girl in the office was telling people that I must be a spy or something, because in the 'morgue' she had seen a picture of me which was taken during the Olympic Games in Berlin and [I] was with Hitler in his box."

"Now I had never had my picture taken in Hitler's box. If I had, there would be nothing peculiar about it at all. Ambassadors were guests in that box, and it certainly did not mean that one sympathized with the German government. So that part of the story I didn't bother about. I did, however, bother about the girl's accusation that there must be something fishy about my relationship with the Nazis.

"I was vexed and mad as a hatter," Inga described in a malapropism that would have amused Jack, "so I went to Cissy Patterson and asked her what I should do. . . . I can still see Cissy Patterson sitting in her office disgusted with the rumors, wishing very much to help me, and seeing a wonderful story in the whole thing."

Cissy Patterson was famous for her courage and her obstinacy. Nevertheless the *Times-Herald* found itself in a delicate situation; as an isolationist newspaper that had just outraged the government by openly publishing secret U.S. military plans, it was now, in the backlash after Pearl Harbor, distinctly vulnerable to government retaliation. If Inga was innocent, as she maintained, it seemed advisable to preempt further allegations of espionage by going to the FBI and making a clean breast of the matter.

"Mrs. Patterson and I decided that I should go to the FBI with our chief editor and the girl who accused me," Inga related. "I thought that one could be completely cleared and practically receive a bill of health from the FBI if you were investigated and found innocent. That's where I made my first mistake."

Alerted by Mrs. Patterson, Waldrop summoned Miss Huidekoper,

Arvad's accuser. "I said, 'O.K., Get your coat.' She got her coat and I called Inga. She put on her coat, and I took the two young ladies by the arm and I walked them across to the Panama Railroad Office Building on Lafayette Square, up to the field office of the FBI."

"You should have seen the three of us marching down the street," Inga recounted, "and into the murky office of an FBI agent, who first listened to the accusations from the girl which I must admit I never heard as I was waiting outside. Then he called me in and asked a million questions.

"In my innocent belief in justice I asked this man if I could have a certificate from the FBI saying that I was all right providing they found nothing against me, which of course I knew they couldn't dig up even if they tried ever so hard as there *was nothing but silly rumor.* The little man looked up from his desk. One of these typical, little men who look like frightened mice, and that's the impression he gave: a little pink mouse caught in the act of stealing a gorgonzola cheese."

"*Mrs. Paul Fejos, alias Inga Arvad,*" the agent in charge titled the memorandum he sent to FBI director J. Edgar Hoover later that day.

On the afternoon of December 12, 1941, Mr. Frank Waldrop, editor of the Washington *Times Herald* called at this office with Miss. P. Huidekoper, a reporter of that paper, and Inga Arvad, columnist for the *Times Herald. . . .* Briefly, Miss Huidekoper several days ago stated to Miss Kathleen Kennedy, a reporter on the *Times Herald* and the daughter of former Ambassador Kennedy, that she would not be surprised if Inga Arvad was a spy for some foreign power. She remarked to Miss Kennedy that one of her friends had been going through some old Berlin newspapers and had noted a picture of Inga Arvad taken with Hitler at the Olympic games in Berlin. . . . Miss Kennedy, a very close friend of Inga Arvad, told her of Miss Huide-koper's statement.

Miss Arvad then contacted Mrs. Patterson and complained about such rumors. Mrs. Patterson was quite worried about this matter, stating to Miss Arvad that it might reflect unfavorably upon the *Times Herald,* an isolationist paper, if it became known that they had been employing a person suspected of being a spy; however, Mrs. Patterson professed to have complete faith in Miss Arvad and in-structed Mr. Waldrop to take both of the young women to the Federal Bureau of Investigation, so that a complete report might be made.

Page Huidekoper had meant nothing bad, Waldrop later considered. "I don't believe she believed anything except that it was Inga cutting her out," he reflected. "See, Jack was nothing but a nice kid, but an attractive young rich kid, and Page was a lady—a Virginia lady . . . . And here's Inga taking Jack out of control. Page and Inga had lived together. They were both setting their caps for Ensign Kennedy. . . . That's when it all began. How it started, I don't know. All these kids were helling around together."

Huidekoper herself was later ashamed at the very mention of the episode, or at least affected distanced outrage over the FBI investigation: "I think rumors like that were utterly unfounded. There were rumors about a lot of people in Washington. I don't think Inga was ever in any trouble of any sort."

Whatever Page Huidekoper really intended—whether, as Inga considered, she was acting as a "jealous female" or thought she was doing her patriotic duty as an American citizen and a Virginia lady—in the panic-stricken days after Pearl Harbor it quickly became clear that Miss Huidekoper had stirred up a veritable hornet's nest—one that would lead, however, not to Inga's expulsion, but to Jack's.

Inga Marie Arvad

Inga Marie Arvad was born on October 6, 1913, in Copenhagen. Her mother had studied in England to become a doctor, her father was the son of a Danish landowner. Marrying without parental consent, Inga's mother and father had eloped to South Africa, where Inga's father caught malaria, from which he died when Inga was four. For several years she went to school in England. At age eleven she trained as a dancer at the Royal Theatre in Copenhagen; she studied piano under Max Rytter, was crowned Beauty Queen of Denmark at age sixteen, competed in Paris for the Miss Europe title the next year, was offered a salaried role at the Folies-Bergere and at age seventeen eloped with an Egyptian diplomat, Kamal Abdel Nabi, divorcing him before she was twenty.

In one interview Inga blamed her mother for the adventurousness of her life. "She had great ambitions for me," Inga told a reporter, "always wanted me to 'be' something. First I must be a dancer, but while I was being trained at the Royal Theatre at Copenhagen, I fell ill. . . . It seemed then that I was musical, I might be a pianiste. . . . My mother spoilt me I suppose but she never pampered me. She tried to make me independent—but I don't want to be independent! I want someone who can buy my train tickets and get me a corner seat!"

In 1935, at age twenty-one, Inga had met such a man: Paul Fejos, a thirty-nine-year-old movie director who had studied to be a doctor during the Great War, served as a Hungarian cavalry officer and pilot, and then earned his medical degree. After the war he had entered the Hungarian theater, directed opera, films, and plays, was invited to Hollywood, and in 1929 became an American citizen. Becoming disenchanted with Hollywood's formula-style movies, Fejos had moved back to Europe to make films for MGM and it was there, according to an American newspaper cutting, paraphrased by the FBI, that Fejos met Inga. Fejos "wanted a very blonde girl. Her mother read about the American director in the papers and phoned Dr. Fejos to get a test for her daughter. The girl, then named Arvad, was not too keen on the idea but she got the test and the job and made the picture in the Norwegian fjords. According to Arvad six months of the movies were enough. The actress and director quarreled all the time. He went off to Madagascar; she became a Berlin correspondent."

This was the part of her life that would dog Inga Arvad to the end of her days. According to Frank Waldrop, there was a third man working for the FBI at the *Times-Herald*—the "friend" who, Page Huidekoper reported, had found the photograph of Arvad and Hitler. He had, Waldrop later reflected, no business going through old newspapers. "He was a fellow in the purchasing department, which is totally separated from editorial activities. How many sheets of toilet paper is in a roll and how much does a coir of copy paper weigh—you know, that sort of thing. And he was this agent, number three, as I learned after the war when I got the files. God damn it, see how clever they were! I give Hoover full credit. They planted this thing—this 'third man' planted it with Page Huidekoper to start an embarrassment, harassment, what have you."

If so, the FBI had chosen a colorful target, for Inga had met Himmler, Goering, and Goebbels, and had even gotten close to Hitler—a fact which, the day after Germany declared war against the U.S., made her immediately and understandably suspect. According to Arvad's statement to the FBI on December 12, 1941, "she began working for the largest newspaper in Copenhagen, known as the Berlingske Tidene," in April 1935. "She left the employ of this paper in January, 1936 [on her marriage to Fejos]. During that period she was in and out of Germany on frequent occasions, her assignments there being primarily to interview numerous prominent persons. She stated that she interviewed Hitler twice and also interviewed Goering and Goebbels."

It can be imagined with what wonder the lowly, Gorgonzola-eating FBI agent took down this statement. Inga had begun her voluntary confession by saying she had become "enraged" when "Miss Kennedy told her of the statements by Miss Huidekoper. . . . Arvad states that she detests the German people and their form of government and, if necessary, will bring suit against Miss Huidekoper to clear her name. She stated that Mr. Bernard Baruch had told her of an instance in the last World War in which some young newspaper woman had been falsely accused of being a spy and the Federal Bureau of Investigation had harassed her until her career was ruined. According to Arvad, this harassing consisted of tapping her telephone and burglarizing her residence. She stated she could not recall the name of the newspaper woman mentioned by Mr. Baruch."

Baruch's story, if slightly inaccurate (the FBI was only created after World War I, though its predecessor, the Bureau of Investigation, certainly indulged in wiretapping, larceny, and smear campaigns on a frightening scale, culminating in the Red Scare and mass deportations in 1919), was nevertheless uncannily prophetic. Not only would Arvad be harassed, bugged, and burglarized by the FBI over the ensuing years, but her career as a journalist would be destroyed. Meanwhile, however, her detestation of the German people and their Fascist government seemed to sit somewhat askew with her reported intimacy with Hitler and his cronies, despite her protestation that "her interviews with these individuals were not along political lines but were in the nature of human interest stories and included such matters as their viewpoint on marriage, what they ate for breakfast, etc."

She admitted covering the marriage of Goering for her Danish paper as well as attending the Olympic Games in Berlin in the summer of 1936, after she had supposedly ceased being a Danish newspaper correspondent. "One of her interviews of Hitler took place while the Olympic games were going on," Inga said as part of her statement. "Through the reason of her being a member of the foreign press, she was given a seat in Hitler's box at the Olympic games and he was present in the box on one occasion when she was there. She stated that it was possible that she was photographed in the box with Hitler; however, she states that she does not recall having been so photographed. She was definite in her statement that she did not pose for any photograph standing next to Hitler."

If Arvad was trying to minimize her involvement with top Nazis, she was making a mistake, since the FBI was bound to investigate further. After burglarizing her apartment as well as investigating other sources, the FBI gradually put together a disturbing picture of Arvad's Berlin past. "In Arvad's desk," a later report summarized,

> were located numerous articles which had been prepared by her. . . .
> Most of these articles concerned her contacts with high officials in
> the German Government. . . . The following are excerpts of articles
> which were written by her, one concerning Dr. Paul Joseph Goeb-
> bels, another concerning Emmy Sonneman and her husband, Her-
> mann Goering. This article set out the information that Arvad was

fortunate enough to obtain in an interview with Miss Sonneman prior to her marriage and that Miss Sonneman had been so impressed by the many, kind enthusiastic words of Arvad that she wired an invitation for Arvad to be a private guest at her wedding. She spoke of having attended this wedding and described the actual wedding and the dress of Adolf Hitler there. She stated that while in Berlin she stayed with her uncle, a Chief of Police in Berlin, and a former Admiral who used to be Aide-de-camp of the Old Kaiser, through whom she met Dr. Goebbels. Through Goebbels she arranged an interview with Hitler.

To have an uncle as police chief in Berlin was, in the aftermath of Hitler's declaration of war, something the FBI could not ignore, although it proved to be untrue (Admiral von Levetzow, though not Arvad's uncle, did grant her an interview, allowed her to visit the Berlin prison system, and introduced her to Heinrich Himmler, and his daughters befriended her). Meanwhile Hitler himself, who was said elsewhere to have described Inga as "a perfect example of Nordic beauty," summoned the twenty-two-year-old Danish reporter. Inga was buying dresses and at first seemed to have missed her unique opportunity. The FBI summarized:

> Dr. Goebbels called her and told her to go to the Reichskanzlei as soon as possible. Arvad stated that she was rushed into a long room, at one end of which Hitler was seated. She stated, concerning this, "I raised my arm and said, 'Heil Hitler.' He looked baffled, but I repeated it over again when I got no answer. Hitler was very obviously embarrassed. He offered me a chair and sat down on the edge of another himself. His first question was, 'What happened to Dr. Goebbels,' but as I did not carry the mefisto about in my pocket, I looked rather blank. Later, I was told that Hitler never received anyone alone and the person by whom one has been introduced always accompanies the guest."

"A million questions boiled in my head in utter confusion," Inga chronicled. "They fell over one another and not a single intelligent one crossed my mind. Hitler asked me about Germany; how did I like it, what mistakes I had found; what impressed me most; what suggestions had I gotten. Little by little we warmed up and sat comfortably back in our chairs. He became exceedingly human, very kind, very charming, and as if he had nothing more important in this world than to convince me that in National Socialism lay the salvation of the world. Naturally, he got into some rather long speeches now and then, which showed me that he was the world's greatest actor," Inga added. However, she commented naïvely, "he is not evil as he is depicted by the enemies of Germany. He is without doubt an idealist; he believes that he is doing the right thing for Germany and his interests do not go any further."

While Inga was won over by the führer, the führer was entranced by Inga. "I tried to get away a few times when it seemed that the interview had lasted long enough, but Hitler kept me back and a little later, Dr. Goebbels, who had attended an important conference, joined us. It was about two hours later when I left and Hitler said, 'I have enjoyed myself so much that I beg you to visit me every time you return to Berlin.' "

Inga did. She also became good friends with Goering and, through Goering's wife, with Rudolf Hess, "for whom she evidently had a great affection."

In due course, Inga would be asked, on her last visit to Berlin in 1940, to work for the German Propaganda Ministry when traveling to America, an offer she said she had declined, though the FBI claimed to have evidence from an International News Service in a 1936 clipping that "reflects that Hitler was struck with her perfect Nordic beauty and had made her Chief of Nazi propaganda in Denmark." That Hitler could sensibly make a twenty-two-year-old girl head of Nazi propaganda in a still-foreign country was something the FBI never questioned.

But even Inga's intimacy with Adolf Hitler and Nazi bigwigs such as Goering and Goebbels was overshadowed, in FBI eyes, by her current relationship with Axel Wenner-Gren, the legendary "Swedish Sphinx," who currently employed her husband, Paul Fejos.

Axel Wenner-Gren was one of the richest men in the world, founder and chief shareholder of Swedish Elektrolux and Bofors gun manufacturers. Inga and Fejos had first met him on his yacht while filming in Madagascar. It was a relationship that led Wenner-Gren to finance Fejos's subsequent film explorations in search of the lost Inca cities of southern Peru and to set up the Viking Fund, a philanthropic foundation in Delaware with headquarters in New York.

Such philanthropy, in the wake of world war, was now suspected by the American secret services to be a cover for enemy propaganda, and Wenner-Gren's Peruvian expeditions a mask for future German incursions into South America. In particular, Wenner-Gren's yacht, the *Southern Cross,* had attracted attention. The largest private luxury yacht in the world, bought from Howard Hughes, it sported not only sophisticated radio equipment but a battery of machine guns and rifles. American Naval Intelligence believed it was currently being used to refuel German U-boats.

Nor was this all. Establishing his own bank in the Bahamas, Wenner-Gren had made friends with the governor, the duke of Windsor (a Nazi sympathizer), and had become the duke's personal banker—a device that enabled the ex-king to circumvent strict British currency restrictions. By December 1941, the IRS had begun a multimillion-dollar lawsuit against Wenner-Gren, and he had been formally blacklisted by the U.S. government. He was living in Mexico, where, on top of other suspicions, he was said to have financed a possible coup d'état against the president.

Though Inga Arvad protested her complete innocence and demanded "a letter from the Federal Bureau of Investigation, stating that she was not a spy," it was impossible for the FBI to comply. As Inga recalled, the agent "shook his head and said, 'I'm terribly sorry, we couldn't give you such a diploma because if we did, you might become a spy the next day even if you weren't today. But if,' he continued, 'you are not arrested that will prove that you are all right.'

"I went home feeling as if I had all of the FBI trailing me. . . . I had a nervous devil-may-care attitude about the whole thing, but slowly fear seeped into me. After all, I had heard of innocent people spending years in jail, even going as far as the electric chair, and every man who looked at me twice or followed me for a block, I was convinced must be an FBI agent."

As things would turn out, Inga was not far wrong.

The Tap Dancer and the Nordic Beauty

Given the nature of his job at U.S. Naval Intelligence, Jack would have been well advised—and many times *was* advised—to leave Inga well alone, once she'd been denounced to the FBI.

Neither Jack nor Inga, however, were conventional people. In many ways Inga was the most intriguing woman Jack had ever met, and she would remain so. He'd toured Europe, Russia, the Middle East, and South America and had met ambassadors and diplomats. Yet his experience, so extraordinary for a twenty-four-year-old American, paled beside the exploits of twenty-eight-year-old Inga Arvad. She was well traveled, talented, stunningly beautiful, sophisticated, sexually experienced—and all woman.

Given his history of emotional abandonment by his mother, it was understandable that Jack should now find Inga a welcome contrast to the young debutantes, models, nurses, students, starlets, and harlots he'd pursued to date. Like Kathleen, Jack was going through a testing period as an adult only recently out of college. Indeed their respective posts at the *Times-Herald* and at the Office of Naval Intelligence were the first paid jobs either of them had ever held, and Jack remained bowled over by the Danish beauty.

"Her English wasn't perfect," Kathleen's beau, John White, later recalled of Inga. "It was better than perfect. 'I have gooey eyes for you' she'd say. Gooey eyes. . . . She was very smart—certainly smart enough to be a spy—but also extremely loving. What was it that enchanted Jack? Oh, sex. She was adorable, just adorable. She looked adorable and was. She was totally woman. She wasn't handsome, she was gorgeous. Luscious, luscious is the word. Like a lot of icing on the cake."

"We all sort of knew that he was really smitten with her beyond the ordinary," Waldrop recalled, as well as the inevitability that such a dangerous liaison would spur rumors in the gossip columns.

In order to help the lovers evade such rumors, Kathleen and White nobly acted as mock chaperones, beginning and ending the evenings with Jack and Inga. What happened in between was between the lines—or between the sheets, as White recalled, a somewhat frustrating arrangement for him, since he'd promised himself not to pressure Kathleen into overcoming her taboo against sex.

White later remembered of Kathleen:

> She was wavering about the Catholic religion. I was so charmed with the life in Washington. Six women to every man! It was a lovely time. And this girl, Kathleen, she was such a lively attractive little thing, that we got very fond of each other in the middle of fighting all the time. We fought about everything, but particularly about the Catholic religion. Being a lapsed Episcopalian, I didn't have any convictions to be bothered. We'd argue about all sorts of details that she didn't understand much better than I did. But when I realized how deep it was in her, then I thought even if I should seduce her, or somehow get around it, it wouldn't be a good thing. This thing is so deep, it would truly violate her. So then we settled very easily into a pleasant relationship. And then along came Jack . . . and then Inga: Inga Binga and Jackotobacco. . . .
>
> I was very fond of Kathleen and here comes her brother, who's sort of in the way, and I don't think he liked me any more than I liked him. Frankly I didn't like a thing about him. I knew he'd written a thing called *Why England Slept,* and I didn't bother to read it. I just was busy chasing women, and I didn't focus on him at all. It pretty soon became clear that he wasn't going to be hanging around Kathleen to my detriment. We used to have these double dates—it was sort of a game.
>
> So I didn't focus on him. One moment I remember, we were

talking about books and he said his favorite was *Pilgrim's Way* [the autobiography of the novelist John Buchan, Lord Tweedsmuir]. It was an astonishment. I suddenly thought, "What the hell is this— there's more to it than I thought. What is going on here that he likes a book as good as that," because I hadn't seen anything in him.

How had he appeared to me? A tap dancer: I thought he was a tap dancer. Very quick, very graceful, but he's tap dancing in an area that wasn't, didn't concern me. I didn't really give a damn about what he was up to. Did he really want to marry Inga? He didn't confide in me. I don't think he did. There she was, why would he marry her? She was an enthusiastic teacher and practitioner of the art of love. She liked to play about. And she played extremely well, it's like the old European tradition of the old mistress for the young boy.

Certainly French kings had been brought up that way, as had some great writers such as Balzac and Rousseau. They, however, had not fallen afoul of the bungling FBI.

Why the Washington Field Office of the FBI did not simply reinterview Inga, a compliant citizen, is incomprehensible. Instead, for the remainder of 1941 and the first few weeks of 1942, it resorted to surveillance, interception of mails, phone tapping, burglary, and information from janitors and postmen to piece together its own picture of Inga's past and present, guaranteeing a comic mishmash of distortion, paranoid speculation, and plain ignorance. Agent Hardison, setting up a watch on Inga's apartment at 1600 Sixteenth Street, #505, duly noted the arrival, the day after Inga's "confession," of Dr. Fejos, Inga's lawful husband, for the first time since his return from Peru. But the agent seemed to have no idea, once Dr. Fejos left on December 14, of the identity of the Nordic beauty's mysterious extramarital lover who then stayed each night in her room—a naval ensign who wore "a gray overcoat with raglan sleeves and gray tweed trousers. He does not wear a hat and has blonde curly hair which is always tousled . . . known only as Jack."

Similarly, Jack's tender telegram from New York on the evening of January 1, 1942, was successfully intercepted, but drew a pathetic blank at the FBI field office as to its origin:

THEY ARE NOT KEEPING THEM FLYING SO I WON'T BE THERE UNTIL 11:30 BY TRAIN. I WOULD ADVISE YOUR GOING TO BED, BUT IF YOU COME, BUY A THERMOS AND MAKE ME SOME SOUP. WHO WOULD TAKE CARE OF ME IF YOU DIDN'T?
LOVE, JACK.

Bamboozled, agent Hardison noted that all attempts by his office to break the code name "Jack" proved "entirely unproductive": a risible example of the FBI's detective skills.

Ironically, the rest of Washington knew exactly who Jack was but not the identity of his mysterious Scandinavian lover. What increasingly worried the Office of Naval Intelligence, for instance, was Washington gossip that Ensign Jack Kennedy, Ambassador Kennedy's son, was now so besotted by a married woman that he'd asked to marry her. At an interdepartmental intelligence conference on December 31, the assistant director of ONI, Captain Kingman, spoke to two senior FBI headquarters executives, Mr. Tamm and Mr. Ladd, "relative to Ambassador Kennedy's son, who is reported to be going to marry a woman who will divorce her present husband. . . . Captain Kingman stated that they find this boy is 'right here in our midst,' and he wanted to know more of the circumstances," an FBI official noted the next day.

It took Hoover only a few phone calls to establish what his own Washington Field Office couldn't. "After getting the facts, I called Captain Kingman and told him that the woman involved is Inga Arvad," the official added. "Captain Kingman stated that he will handle the matter properly."

Captain Kingman, however, had more pressing concerns in a burgeoning world war than a junior ensign's affair with a married woman. It was thus only on January 9, 1942, that the chief of Naval Operations submitted a request to the Bureau of Navigation that Jack be transferred out of Washington (citing Jack as "Joseph F. Kennedy," in a reflection of the confusion surrounding the case). The Bureau of Navigation, unaware of any urgency, took no immediate action.

But if the navy could afford to wait, there were others who couldn't.

Pa Kennedy No Like

Inga had already tried to intimate to her husband that she wanted a divorce.

As she later recorded in a reconstruction of their talk following his visit in December and return to New York, Fejos was "unsure" whether Inga was already "John's mistress. He is insanely jealous and is unable to keep a sneer from his tone of voice. He doesn't accuse her of infidelity, well knowing it would be the surest way of losing her at once. He does however ask her if she is in love with John, and being truthful, she admits it.

"It is obvious that he is very much in love with her and wants to keep her, come what may. She is undecided, she hates to hurt him, and feels a strong loyalty towards a man to whom she has been married for six years. The fascination which always overcame her when he was present still works magic, but she knows that she doesn't love him. It isn't only because she loves John, it is because she married him when she was nearly a child, a child full of admiration for a brilliant and famous man, who completely enveloped her in his adoration."

In truth Fejos was not only insanely jealous, but a most unpredictable man. The fact that Jack was twenty years his junior was devastating to his ego. "He begs her to give up her work in Washington, to come and live with him in New York. He promises to buy her a lovely home. He even sees to it that their walks include 57th and 59th streets, which are full of antique shops, knowing that she loves to decorate a house and longs to settle down again. When he realizes that he is unable to win her, he tries new tactics, frightening her with such remarks as 'It would ruin John's future, especially if he wants to go into politics, if it ever came out in a campaign that he was mixed up in a divorce scandal,'" an implied threat which left Inga "scared" and Fejos aware "that through John he can hurt her, and maybe bully her into returning to him."

Inga wisely decided to handle Fejos with kid gloves, writing to say that she was unsure what she wanted to do. Fejos, however, was not taken in. "I am a bit puzzled as to your intentions in the future," he wrote back on January 11, 1942.

> You, dearest, can be more cryptic than the prophets of the Old Testament. You write that if you would be eighteen, you would probably marry Jack. I suppose it means Jack Kennedy. Then you follow up with, "But I would, might probably, choose you instead." Now, my inconsistent child, what is all this about? Has anything gone wrong with yours or Jack's love? Or is this again your sweet charity feeling toward me? Anything but that please. You see, Darling, you have made me some very difficult days with those charity attempts, and honestly it is far more human if you don't do them. Slowly I will get used to it, that I am without you, and that you cannot be reached, had, [*sic*]—and things will heal, (I hope) and there would not be any use to try to be charitable and therefore unwillingly, but in the final result: Cruel.
>
> There is, however, one thing I want to tell you in connection with your Jack. Before you let yourself go into this thing any deeper, lock stock and barrel, have you thought that maybe the boy's father or family will not like the idea?

This was a timely warning, for Fejos had himself spoken to Jack's father in New York. As Inga's mother subsequently wrote to caution her, Fejos already "has a detective out after you who knows when Jack comes in your apartment and where he goes; he knows how many lights are burning and when the lights are turned off. He said that in two months you would be out of your job and the old Kennedy would not be sorry for you because he doesn't want his son to have anything to do with you. I hate to repeat all the terrible things he said about you. . . . As your mother I only beg you, little Inga, to live your life in accord with the finest and the best in yourself; do not lose your self-respect."

It was too late, however. On January 12, 1942, Walter Winchell's syndicated gossip column lobbed the grenade that would bring the scandal to a head: "One of Ex-Ambassador Kennedy's eligible sons is the target of a Washington gal columnist's affections. So much so she has consulted her barrister about divorcing her exploring groom. Pa Kennedy no like."

Inga would never forget the day. "When I walked into the office a friend of mine said, 'Did you read the item about yourself in Walter Winchell's column?' I said, 'No,' and grabbed the paper and read the paragraph. . . . My name wasn't mentioned, but at the time I was the only blond columnist in Washington with an explorer husband, and Washington is a very small rat hole when it comes to gossip. The paragraph was yanked out in the second edition in Washington because at the time the column was published in our own paper, but it went into hundreds of other papers all over the country and the repercussion was quick and furious."

This was no exaggeration. Jack, to Inga's chagrin, "was transferred in 24 hours. I have never been sure whether his father, who is extremely influential had something to do with it, or whether the 'G-2' [Intelligence] was afraid of a scandal and didn't want a navy officer implicated," she commented.

Fejos promptly sent his sarcastic congratulations. "Well here it is, your first break in the greatest institution of newspaper writing in the US. You made Winchell's column." In his diary, John White recorded Jack's outraged reaction at the publicity: "J. Kennedy in, evidently discussing story with Waldrop."

Everyone was mad at everyone else. Fejos saw himself as "the clown of the act, and all the laughs are on me. I have had enough in these last weeks." He was also appalled at the way Winchell had portrayed Inga. "If it would have been *you* who was the target of the affections of the gentleman, it would be better. But that HE should be the target—that is to say that you are the one who does the running after—that is pretty sour. That my proud, always dignified, ramrod wife gets this fifth rate slap across the face, that hurts. I feel like hell about it."

Mrs. Patterson, meanwhile, "was extremely mad at Winchell," Inga recounted. "Somehow she traced that Winchell had gotten his information about my seeing the navy officer from J. Edgar Hoover, who had told him about it. She, in fact, got so mad that she wrote an editorial on the front page saying something to the effect that it would be better if the FBI used their men for other things than being the informers to a key-hole peeper like Walter Winchell. . . . Of course, my name and the young navy officer's were not mentioned in the paper, but I assure you that everybody knew who it was, and it was deadly embarrassing for both of us. Besides, as Walter Winchell and J. Edgar Hoover were mentioned by name, I didn't add two friends but gained two enemies."

As Inga lamented, the damage could be checked but not undone. Several days later Lieutenant Horan informed the FBI that "it had come to ONI's attention that Ensign Kennedy had been 'playing around' with Inga Arvad and steps had been taken to put an end to this relationship. Lieutenant Horan stated that Kennedy would probably not be disenrolled but it was anticipated that he would be transferred out of Washington."

Horan was right. On January 13, 1942, the day after the appearance of Winchell's column, Jack had gotten his marching orders by telephone. The party was over; he would be forthwith transferred from Washington to a desk job at the navy base in Charleston. As Jack later confided to a reporter, "They shagged my ass down to South Carolina because I was going around with a Scandinavian blonde, and they thought she was a spy!"

Love Letters

Rear-Admiral Wilkinson, the director of Naval Intelligence, was unstinting in his assessment of Ensign Kennedy's ability. "This officer's services were eminently satisfactory in every respect," Wilkinson recorded on Jack's fitness report, giving him a 3.8 rating out of a possible 4.0. "His cheerful attention to duty materially aided the morale of his section."

In truth, however, Wilkinson had become "so upset over this situation that you might say he was really frantic," recalled Captain Hunter, Jack's ONI section chief; "he wanted to get Kennedy out as quickly as possible." Meanwhile the assistant director, Captain Kingman, "was very frightened at the time. Very upset over the whole situation. . . . It gives you some idea of the terror and the mood of the times. . . . The whole naval establishment was in a state of terror from the moment they heard of the attack on Pearl Harbor." In fact, Hunter recalled, the assistant director actually favored "cashiering" Kennedy.

As the FBI had not yet begun "technical" surveillance, however, there was insufficient evidence to hold a court-martial, particularly in view of the prominence of Kennedy's father, who might claim political foul play. Frank Waldrop later remembered how "Joseph Patrick Kennedy came boiling down here again, and I sat in on one of the head butting sessions with his children. . . . There are tottering elders around Washington yet who will tell you they know for a fact Inga Arvad was the love of John F. Kennedy's life. . . . Who am I to argue with them? I do know that in 1942, when he and his sister were struggling with their father, the word in the city room was that when Joe Kennedy burst out 'Dammit, Jack, she's *already* married,' the boy said he didn't care."

Inga reconstructed the scene rather differently. "She knows she ought to finish this romance before they both get in too deep," she described her own feelings. "If she asks him to go now, then maybe a lot of unhappiness will be avoided for all concerned. . . . Both want to shield the other. He asks her to get a divorce and marry him." Inga is "tempted, but she refuses." The next morning, Jack's father phones him. She described the ex-ambassador as "a typical slick politician, a good handshaker with a flashy smile but cold eyes, sly, intelligent and too sure of himself. He starts out the conversation amiably, and asks John about trivial matters, then he gets down to the item in the column. From years of habit, which John hasn't outgrown, he is scared of his father. 'Of course,' the old man says, 'you are not going to marry her, are you?' John wants to explain, but feels that it can't be done on the phone. He replies meekly, 'Honestly, Dad, I don't know, she is a great girl.' "

Inga's version, written three years after the events, had the ring of authenticity about it, however sentimental.

> The father, who knows better than to run her down, especially as it would be hard to find anything against her except that she is a married woman, says, "I understand. What about coming to see us? The children are going to be in Boston this week-end, and I know how you kids love to be together, besides we could talk the whole matter over." John, who isn't sure of getting a leave before he goes to his new assignment, tells his father so, and the old man smiles and says, "I guess I can pull a few strings for you."
>
> At the mentioning of "pulling a few strings" it strikes John that maybe his father had something to do with his quick transfer.

Whatever the truth of Joseph Kennedy's role, the mysterious tousle-headed "Ensign known only as Jack" definitely spent the nights of January 16, 17, and 18 with his paramour, according to agent Hardison who still maintained his FBI vigil outside Inga's apartment block. "It is the opinion of Agent Hardison that this man lives someplace in the immediate neighborhood and after spending the night with the subject, goes to his own apartment, changes to his uniform and then returns to her apartment for breakfast," the agent in charge recorded. However, when Hoover gave permission for surveillance to be extended to cover the ensign, Hardison drew another blank. "This surveillance was maintained from January 21, 1942, to January 28. . . . During this period no individual who fitted the description of this Naval Ensign left the apartment."

The reason was simple. Surrendering to his sister Kathleen his apartment ten blocks away at 2680 Sixteenth Street, Jack had indeed flown from Washington on Tuesday, January 19, 1942, to join his father in Florida before starting work in Charleston.

"Is the sun shining, the pool tempting and your family spoiling you?" Inga wrote the evening after his departure. "I do hope dearest Jack that you are having all the fun in the world. You should. Why? I don't know, except that you seem to be one of the very rare people born to sunshine and happiness. . . . When the plane took off, I said the same to myself as I did in church Sunday, 'Please keep him safe God.' He will, as you remarked before leaving."

The next day, however, Inga's tone became more lovesick. She recalled her father, who'd died when she was four, and her early childhood:

> My first spanking, because I deliberately threw mother's new fountainpen on the floor. . . . The first time anybody told me I was pretty. . . . When the Royal Theatre in Copenhagen declared that I probably would be a second Pavlova. . . . The first money I ever earned in Denmark ($10 a day) and the first check from the Times Herald $40. . . . All the people I have cared for, and all those I didn't love. My only cocktail party in Washington, in a noisy place, when I met a boy who was supposedly brilliant, who laughed the whole time. Dozens of dinners with the following menu—Soupe, Steak, mashed potatoes, green peas, carrots, and ice cream.
>
> January 19, 1942—the first time I missed anybody and felt lonely and as though I was the only inhabitant of Washington.
>
> Loving—knowing it, being helpless about it, and yet not feeling anything but complete happiness. At last realizing what makes Inga tick.

Though the Bureau's agents "lost" the suspect in their concern to remain discreet, their guess that Inga "probably" went to meet Jack in Charleston, South Carolina, the day of his arrival, on January 24, and then spent the weekend with him, was correct. "Leaving I saw a figure on the platform," Inga wrote to Jack immediately after she returned to Washington on January 26.

> The further the train pulled away, the less visible was the young handsome Boston Bean. . . . There was the good old feeling of stinging eyes and a nasty pull at the heartstrings, which always show up when too great a distance is put between us.
>
> I slept like a log. At midday we arrived to the Capital of the United States. To that same Union Station, where I went on January the first 1942 as happy as a bird, without a care, a fear or trouble in the world—just in love—remember?
>
> "Have you started making the baby yet," was a question asked me today. Guess by whom?

Jack could easily guess.

> The same person also said, "I know who gave you that four leaf clover. . . . "
>
> I am in bed. The two doctors swore I would not fail to be six feet under the ground otherwise, so I obeyed.
>
> I should tell you about my week-end. About my being late at the airport. The tiny streets of Charleston. Of the beautiful old iron gates. Of the drive to the Middleton gardens. Of my escort, who would rather have chewed one of his fingers off than pay $2 admission. . . . Of the big trees with the moss. Of how I pointed one out and never had the end of a thrilling story. . . . Of the old oak. The house. The ugly statue of a woman without anything that a woman should have. And—about the man.
>
> He is full of enthusiasm and expectations, eager to make his life a huge success. He wants the fame, the money—and what rarely goes with fame—happiness. He strives hard himself. More than any boy in the same cottonwool-position. He is a credit to the family and to his country. He is so big and strong, and when you talk to him or see him you always have the impression that his big white teeth are ready to bite off a huge chunk of life. There is determination in his green Irish eyes. He has two backbones: His own and his father's. Somehow he has hit the bulls-eye in every respect. "He can't fail," I have said to myself very often. I love him more than anything else or anybody in the world.

When Henry James had read Jack his girlfriend's lovelorn letter at Stanford, Jack had dismissed it as "shit." Now, however, the loving words were addressed to him.

Despite the nostalgic tone, Inga was determined not to be clinging. "It is funny. In reality, we are so well matched. Only because I have done some foolish things must I say to myself 'No.' At last I realize that it is true 'We pay for everything in life.'"

Jack, she was certain, was destined to do great things. "Plan your life as you want it," Inga exhorted. "Go up the steps of fame. But—pause now and then to make sure that you are accompanied by happiness. Stop and ask yourself 'Does it sing inside me today.' If that is gone, look around and don't take another step till you are certain life is as you will and want it. And wherever in the world I may be, drop in. I think I shall always know the right thing for you to do. Not because of brains. Not because of knowledge. But because there are things deeper and more genuine—love my dear."

Inga wrote in a later letter:

> Could I do what I wanted today, then I think I would go out West, buy a small place, purchase a lot of the best books, settle down, write what I felt like (but first learn a lot, lot more) and before I left, I would make sure I had your baby along with me. You say why mine? Well, not because I love you—I obviously must have a tiny weakness for you—but because you are the kind the world ought to swarm with. You have just sufficient meanness in you to get along and enough brains and goodness to give to the world and not only take. . . .
>
> I can't wait to see you on top of the world. That is a very good reason why war should stop, so that it may give you a chance to show the world and yourself that here is a man of the future. . . . Should I die before you reach to the top step of the golden ladder, then Jack dear,—if there is a life after death, as you believe in—be I in heaven or hell, that is the moment when I shall stretch a hand out and try to keep you balancing on that—the most precarious of all steps.

Something I Picked Up on the Road

A compassionate FBI director might have been disposed to see these as genuine love letters. J. Edgar Hoover, however, was and would remain for the rest of his life unmarried and of indeterminate sexuality. For him, the voyeurish insights into Inga's love affair simply offered an unexpected entrée into much more interesting zones of investigation. Indeed poor

Inga Arvad became, for as long as Hoover chose to toy with her, a legitimate excuse to spy upon a host of hitherto "off-limits" citizens, government personnel, and even military figures—men such as Hoover's erstwhile boss and nemesis, Colonel "Wild Bill" Donovan—all of whom Inga had interviewed for her column. Within days, in fact, Hoover was writing to the attorney general to report on his "current investigation of this woman as an espionage suspect," and noting that, as Inga might be "engaged in a most subtle type of espionage activities against the United States," a closer watch must be kept on her and her contacts. By January 29, 1942, the special agent in charge of the investigation was quoted as saying he believed that the case of Inga Arvad had "got more possibilities than anything I have seen in a long time"; indeed the premature claims of Hoover's acolytes soon threatened to derail the whole investigation, for on February 4, 1942, J. Edgar Hoover was asked by the director of the Alien Enemy Control Unit at the Department of Justice for a "report of all information you have in your files in respect of . . . Mrs. Inga Fejos, 1600—16th Street, NW, Washington, D.C. which I desire in considering whether a Presidential Warrant of apprehension should be issued."

Arresting Inga, however, would have abruptly ended Hoover's licensed snooping. Moreover, he still possessed no concrete evidence of any wrongdoing beyond making normal social contacts, approaching legitimate subjects for interview (including, to Hoover's embarrassment, his deputy and lifelong companion, Clyde Tolson, and his secretary, Helen Gandy), as well as a past file of scoop interviews in Germany and possible current adultery in Washington. Only twice had Inga seen her husband, the supposed henchman of blacklisted Axel Wenner-Gren, since his return from Peru, and according to her tapped telephone calls, she seemed intent on divorcing him. Even worse, the Washington Field Office, despite twenty-four-hour surveillance, had still failed to find the conclusive identity of Inga's mysterious ensign-lover, code-named "Jack." Indeed the only documentary material Hoover could produce in a court of law came from Walter Winchell's gossip column, and Inga's mother's letter about Fejos and "old Kennedy." As Hoover was well aware, these were hardly grounds for arresting a Washington journalist backed by the redoubtable Cissy Patterson as well as distinguished patrons such as Bernard Baruch. He therefore declined to recommend arrest. Instead he suggested the surveillance net be widened.

Inga, meanwhile, was anxious not only about Hoover's FBI surveillance ("everytime I heard the phone click, I was sure that it was the FBI," she recalled) but about Jack's father, knowing from Kathleen that the ex-ambassador was putting more pressure on Jack to quit the affair. Not having heard from Jack since the weekend, she wrote sadly on January 27 to protest her innocence.

Distrust is a very funny thing, isn't it? I knew when Kick got a letter today why you haven't written to me. There was a peculiar feeling at the realization, that the person I love most in the world is afraid of me. Not of me directly but of the actions I might take some day. I know who prompted you to believe or rather disbelieve in me, but still I dislike it. However I am not going to try and make you change—it would be without result anyway—because big Joe has a stronger hand than I.

Since you left Washington I have been restless, wondering what I want to do next, but having a distinct dislike of going out with anybody. When I do I am bored and want to get home to my solitary abode . . . Garbo-stuff.

"Inga returned with an infected throat," Kathleen simultaneously reported to Jack. "Torb and I want to know what you do to girls that cause T.B. or infected throats or cause them to marry someone else," she mocked her brother. "The doctor advised her to retire to bed but she refused and is now in the pink of condition."

Jack's friend Torbert Macdonald had recently turned up in Washington seeking a job that would bring him draft exemption. His marriage plans had fallen through, and he was distraught. He damned Roosevelt, the war, and law school. Increasingly he looked back to the golden years at Harvard when he was a football hero and the world lay at his feet. "It seems he is always in some sort of physical or mental dilemma," Jack's mother would subsequently write in one of her duplicated family letters—not without reason. Meanwhile Torby cast Jack as his fellow life-comedian, addressing him as "Laurel" and signing his letters "Hardy." The news of Jack's recent banishment to South Carolina had been music to his ears. "It does my heart good to see Laurel get himself screwed up—it gives me hope that I am not the only confusion maker in the country," he wrote to Jack gratefully. About Inga, he reported that though he'd seen her "for just a few minutes," he'd "had a long chat with her—on our only subject—and controlled my nausea long enough to do a good journeysman job—She either is crazy about you or is fooling a lot of people. 'How *was* he—*what* did *he* say etc etc. I lied as usual, Kennedy, even tho its like carrying coals to Newcastle."

Inga herself was generous and acute. Amazingly, she recommended to Macdonald working at the FBI as a safe wartime haven; Kathleen recorded how Inga "toted Torb around to see some guy yesterday who used to be in the F.B.I. but is now an independent lawyer." "The trouble is that Torb doesn't know what he actually wants to do in life," Inga remarked in her next letter to Jack. She also said that she liked "Torb an awful lot. He is a genuinely nice fellow. I would put my head on the block for that boy, he is O.K. in every respect, and very, very fond of you, as you know of course. Maybe you take it for granted, but it isn't in life, not as much as you think dear."

Jack's week-long silence was now broken by a furious letter which he called "Exhibit 3c in the case of INGA BINGA vs JPK Sr. What do you write that kind of stuff for, that I am afraid of 'your future actions' (very diplomatically put)?" he demanded. "My reason for not writing is that I've given you plenty of my writing to read and by God you won't read it," he complained, referring to the copy of his book which he'd given Inga when he left Washington and which she'd promised faithfully to read. "I don't know what you can talk about when you go out and the conversation turns to what England did in 1937, as I'm sure it does," he joked. "You will get letters now as I think it is cheaper to get sued than to telephone."

Soon, however, Jack relented. He telephoned to say he wanted to see Inga in Washington "next week . . . if I can get away,"—to which she responded by offering to fly to Charleston. "Will you?" asked Jack, disbelieving (his call was recorded by the FBI). "Of course it's better if you come here but there is no sense in you doing all the travelling, so I'll come up there next time."

Inga offered to meet him halfway, or indeed anywhere he wanted: "You can do anything you want, darling. If you want to go somewhere else, you're welcome."

Jack, however, insisted. "I'm coming to Washington. . . . If I can get away at 1 o'clock, I can get that plane, otherwise, if I have to work, I'll get away at 6 o'clock Saturday."

"Good God. Do you have to work Saturday?"

"Yes."

"When are you sailing?" Inga demanded, certain the navy was going to send Jack abroad.

"I don't know."

"Is that going to be soon?"

"No."

"I think it is."

"No."

"Are you sure?"

"I told you, I'll tell you."

Was Inga trying to follow Jack's movements for further espionage reasons, the FBI wondered. Or was she simply anxious lest her lover be transferred to the front, as any normal eavesdropper might conclude? The FBI could make neither head nor tail of the dialogue, except for the most obvious remarks, such as the climax to a lover's tiff about Jack's hopeless dress sense. To Torbert Macdonald Inga had said, "Why don't you tell

Jack about your tailor?" This, when retailed in Macdonald's sarcastic and taunting manner, infuriated the narcissistic ensign. "Did you say Macdonald was better dressed than I was?" Jack accused Inga. "Did you say I should go to his tailor?"

"That's a lie," Inga defended herself. Then she quipped, "I don't care what you wear, darling, I love you as you are. Darling, you look best without anything."

For the FBI, sex could only be associated with criminality or espionage. Such conversations were thus laboriously transcribed, pored over, analyzed for indications of spying. To the participants, however, sex was part of love—a kind of love Jack had never known before. Whatever Inga's ulterior motives, she tormented Jack with a depth of maternal, womanly affection he would never experience again in his starlet-studded life—an appreciative, forgiving, understanding, tantalizing, humorous, intuitive, feminine love that made every other relationship seem small and artificial. "Inga lets him walk all over her like linoleum," John White remarked to Kathleen. Yet from Inga Jack would receive the most haunting love letters of his life; to Inga he would confide hopes, ambitions, and fears he never told another mortal soul, and to her he exhibited a quality of strutting, boyish, witty candor no other man in Inga's career would ever match.

"How did you like my letter?" he asked when phoning Inga on January 30, having written in his missive that

> the name of the lady with whom I am now living is Middleton, the same name as the gardens so I will have a very close reminder of a very good day which was easily worth $4.00, but which would have been just as pleasant even if we hadn't gone into the gardens. That is not a lament for my departed dough, but is a compliment. I've returned from an interesting trip [a tour of nearby installations conducted by the intelligence officer he was replacing], about which I won't bore you with the details, as if you are a spy I shouldn't tell and if you're not you won't be interested. But I missed you.
>
> You know I really don't think they are sure of what they are fighting here but I suppose they are not alone in this. I guess we won't know until the bells start tolling. I hope they tolleth not for me. They had better not.

Enclosing a copy of "Dinner at Mrs. Patterson's," he signed off, "Love, Jack."

Inga was impressed. "Wonderful, wonderful. We put it in an extra edition with the [title] 'Why England Slept,' " Inga joked when Jack next called. "We all enjoyed it."

"I suppose Kick read it?"

"No, I read some of it aloud to her. Couldn't I? It was a family letter, darling. It is beautiful, I love it."

Several days later, Torbert Macdonald phoned Inga. He'd spent a few days in Charleston with Jack, reporting that "Big Jack is very good and looking well" and living in a private house "right up the street from the Fort Sumter Hotel. It's a brick house on Murray Boulevard about ten up from Sumter."

"Does he like it?"

"He is not crazy about the people whose house it is but I guess he likes it. He misses you, Inga." Together, Jack and Torby had been "to the President's Ball Friday night. I discovered a new Kennedy," Torby claimed, "it seems to me that he has a sort of different attitude towards girls now."

"Oh, you're just kidding," Inga responded, grateful though for the compliment. "You're just the sweetest thing in the world."

The latest news, however, was that Jack was virtually confined to barracks. "I don't think Jack will be able to get out of there for a time because he must get special permission from the Commander of the Yard in order to go 50 or 60 miles out of Charleston," Macdonald warned Inga.

"Isn't that amusing," remarked Inga, assuming that she, courtesy of the FBI, must be the cause.

"It isn't just Jack, it's a general rule. They are pretty strict about it," Torby protested.

"Does he say anything about going to sea?" Inga asked. "I can feel it in my bones that he is going to sea."

"If he does, it will surprise him," responded Macdonald, aware of Jack's miserable health record, and poked fun at Jack for his jealous outburst regarding their respective dress sense. "You don't know how funny that was. It has been the topic of conversation for 6 years," Torby laughed.

To which Inga added, "As a matter of fact you are the best dresser. He is a terrible dresser, nothing ever matches."

Whether Torby then called Charleston or not, Jack—who had been trying to reach Inga unsuccessfully the day before—telephoned at eleven P.M. to personally give Inga the news about his confinement to barracks. "Why don't you come here?" he suggested.

"I may," Inga answered coyly.

"Don't say you may," chided Jack. "I know I shouldn't ask you to come here twice in a row but I'll be up there as soon as I get permission."

"Isn't that sweet. I'll come maybe."

Such prevarication infuriated the sex-sick naval ensign. "I hate for you to come all this way just to see me," he apologized, prompting Inga to assure him, "Darling, I would go around the world 3 times just to see you." Flattered, Jack kidded her about "a big orgy" he heard she'd recently had in New York, and thus, unwittingly, elicited more than he'd bargained for.

"I'll tell you about it," began Inga. "I'll tell you about it for a whole weekend if you'd like to hear about it. My husband has his little spies out all over the place. . . . He told me all sorts of things about you, none of which were flattering." At Jack's insistence she reported that Dr. Fejos "knew every word you had said to your father about me. It made me look like shit, it amused me very much," said Inga bitterly.

"What does he mean by 'every word I said to my father about you'?" prompted Jack, unwisely.

"Somebody who knows your family very well and also knows my husband but I don't know who it is. The person has known you since you were a child and I think they live in New York. He said, 'Jack Kennedy shrugged his shoulders and said, "I wouldn't dream of marrying her; in fact I don't care two bits about her. She's just something I picked up on the road." '

"It's very amusing darling," Inga added, pretending not to be hurt. "Tell me, when are you going away?"

"I'm not leaving for quite a while yet," responded Jack, shaken. Whether or not he had spoken such words, they sounded very much in character. "What else did your husband say?" he prodded gingerly.

"Why, he said I could do what I wanted. He said he was sad to see me doing things like this. I'll tell you about it and I swear that he is not bothering us and that you needn't be afraid of him. He's not going to sue you [as corespondent] though he is aware what he could do by suing you."

"He would be a big guy if he doesn't sue me."

"He's a gentleman," Inga remarked pointedly. "I don't care what happens, he wouldn't do things like that. He's perfectly alright."

"I didn't intend to make you mad," Jack put in tamely.

"I'm not mad. Do you want me to come this weekend very much?"

"I would like for you to."

"I'll think it over and let you know. So long, my love."

"So long."

The call ended; the FBI recording apparatus clicked off. Whether as spy or merely as lover, Inga Arvad was playing the young ensign expertly. She had indicated she knew exactly how duplicitous he was in what he said to others—he didn't deny it, either—but also that she would overlook it. Maybe.

Engaged in Sexual Intercourse

In her latest newsletter to members of the family Rose naïvely reported that "Jack dashed off to Charleston last Saturday . . . and says his hours are regular and he seems to be fairly comfortably settled." A week later she claimed that Jack "seems to be quite interested in his work and is feeling very much better."

This was not how Lem Billings recalled matters. Billings was still frustrated by his inability to get into any branch of the military, despite the onset of war. "Jack understood and sympathized about my problem, but at the time, he was pretty much concerned about his own in that he wasn't happy at all in what he was doing. . . . He was very frustrated. . . . I mean it just seemed to him a waste of time. He wasn't happy at all. At the time there was nothing he could do about it. He was very frustrated and unhappy."

Jack's duties were still in Intelligence, but their nature—encoding and deciphering local signals—was mundane, and the naval base was in a backwater. "I don't know if you had heard that I've been transferred from Washington down to tired old Charleston," he lamented in a letter to Rip Horton. Thoughts of marriage preoccupied him. "My limited experience has shown a wife can bollix things up quicker than most people," he'd joked when congratulating Rip Horton's fianceé a few weeks before. But behind the skeptical façade he held to the fantasy of a non-Catholic union—marriage as elopement, as escape from the frigid, pious, antisexual morality of his mother and people like her. "The Irish are the *worst* form of Catholics—particularly the Irish-American sort," his friend Chiquita Cárcano once remarked in a conversation about Rose Kennedy. Rose's trite family circulars with their clichéd sentiments and references to bishops, priests, and the serving of mass simply infuriated Jack at a time when, far from being settled comfortably, he was deliberately continuing an affair with a married woman suspected of being an enemy spy.

Whatever contorted paths this affair with Inga took, and however tedious the exile to the "Siberia" of Charleston, Jack never let go of his determination to understand the forces shaping the larger world on which he hoped somehow to make his mark. Throughout his childhood and youth he'd eschewed introspection, indulging a ceaseless curiosity in history and current events, and this interest continued in Charleston with the same intensity as before. His account of the isolationist-interventionist debate at Mrs. Patterson's was soon followed, four days after he reached Charleston, by notes on a conversation he'd had in Palm Beach with Lord Halifax, formerly Chamberlain's foreign minister, who had now been sent by Churchill to Washington as British ambassador following the sudden death of Lord Lothian.

Halifax had been an archappeaser, Chamberlain's preferred choice as his successor. "I had a long talk with Lord Halifax, the British Ambassador, regarding Munich and its background," Jack jotted. "He affirmed the thesis that I have always maintained: that Munich should not have been the object of American criticism, but rather the condition of British armaments, which made it inevitable. . . . He said that if England had fought in 1938, she would have been licked immediately. As evidence he repeated the conversation that he had with Sir John Dill, chief of the British General Staff. He asked him whether he would rather have fought in 1938 or 1939. Dill thought for a moment and then said, 'I would rather have fought in 1940.' "

For Jack, such an insider's view of contemporary history was of absorbing interest. Mrs. Laski's later, highly trumpeted claim that Jack was ashamed of his Munich thesis, and that after the war he admitted to her he ought never to have published it as a book, was silly. Such diffidence stemmed from Jack's innate modesty and courteousness to the wife of a bigoted British academic. In truth the matter of English and American isolationism never ceased to absorb him. Far from resting satisfied with his thesis-cum-book, he was driven constantly to reexamine both the events and personalities of the recent past to better understand the present geopolitical calamity. Halifax's view of Chamberlain and especially of Churchill fascinated the twenty-four-year-old. "Halifax believed that Chamberlain was misled and defeated by his phrases as much as anything else—phrases which he did not really believe in—such as 'Peace in our time,' " Jack noted. "When he returned home from Munich, Halifax rode in from Heston with Chamberlain. Chamberlain remarked to him that all the wild celebration, all the roses in the streets would be over in two weeks."

This was a salutary insight into leadership during crisis. For the remainder of his life Jack would be measured by the causes he espoused; yet the truth was, for all his keen interest in great contemporary issues, he remained almost unnaturally detached and able to see both sides of a dispute. In this sense, his love of politics reflected his love life: an unwillingness to either surrender his obsession or surrender to it.

Neville Chamberlain's personality and, in particular, his venom toward Winston Churchill intrigued Jack. Halifax, sensing Jack's genuine fascination, had candidly recalled how, on that same journey back to Downing Street after returning from Munich, he'd recommended that

Chamberlain finally bring Churchill into the Cabinet. Chamberlain re-sisted the idea, not only because he feared Hitler wouldn't like such a move, but because he disliked Churchill. He promised "to mention it that night" to his private secretary, but it was clear he had no intention of acting upon the suggestion.

Personal dislike, even malice, was as much a part of history as rearma-ment statistics, Jack was forcefully reminded. "With Chamberlain there was no compromise," he noted of the man who had compromised the lives of millions of Czech citizens. "You were either in or out, and Chamberlain did not like Churchill."

What absorbed Jack, too, was Halifax's eyewitness story of Chamber-lain's resignation, following news of Hitler's invasion of the West on May 10, 1940, which Jack had previously only heard secondhand from his father. Now, from Lord Halifax's own mouth, he had the story of why Halifax was not now Britain's prime minister. Jack recorded:

> On the morning of Chamberlain's resignation Chamberlain told Halifax that he wanted to make him Prime Minister. Halifax said it would be too difficult—it would be similar to Asquith's experience— as in war time it would be practically a necessity for the Prime Minister to be able to appear on the floor of the House of Commons. Chamberlain called a meeting for David Margesson [chief whip], Halifax, Chamberlain and Churchill. Chamberlain spoke first and said he wished to make Halifax Prime Minister. Halifax repeated his arguments of the morning and Margesson also said he thought that it would be practically impossible for Halifax to be Prime Minister and at the same time be in the House of Lords. Churchill said he was interested to hear what Halifax had said because he was inclined to agree with him.

It was a neat way of making clear "he was the man for the job" without distressing Chamberlain or Halifax.

In answer to Jack's question, Halifax also discussed Baldwin's failure to begin rearmament in 1934, when he shunned higher defense appropria-tions in order to stave off electoral defeat. Halifax felt in retrospect that Baldwin should have accepted defeat in the interests of his country: "He should have chosen the former and England might have gotten rearma-ment a year sooner, as the General Staff and others could have explained the problems facing Britain to the Labour Government who probably would have seen the necessity for rearming."

Probably, but not necessarily. The tactics a politician has to employ to remain in power in a democracy versus the judgment of history was an issue that would exercise Jack's mind all his life. Roosevelt had gone to the polls promising that no American boys would be sent to war, but as Jack knew, it was a notion as transparent as "peace in our time." Leadership, in the inner sanctum of government and in times of national emergency, had very little to do with public platforms.

Halifax had even dismissed Jack's suggestion that an alliance with the Soviet Union in 1938 would have altered the course of history, maintaining that Russia was no more ready at that time to go to war with Hitler over Czechoslovakia than was Britain, particularly with Poland and Rumania refusing Stalin permission to cross their borders. Moreover, for the future, Halifax was skeptical about Britain's chances of holding Singapore, feeling that only if another fifty Hurricane fighters could be sent out would there be a chance of survival—a "terrible commentary, as this should have been done long ago," Jack noted, adding that Clare Boothe Luce (whom he'd seen on her recent visit to South Carolina) "said Churchill told John Gunther a week before the war that the Japs would cave in like the Italians. They were the wops of the Far East." Here was considerable food for reflection, and in the backwater of Charleston, with its former slave plantations and southern mentality, Jack did much reflecting.

He also did much lovemaking, once Inga rejoined him on Friday, February 6. Using the alias Barbara White, Inga checked in at the Fort Sumter Hotel, according to the FBI, who had ascertained her plans and alerted their Savannah field office. Ensign Kennedy had worked the remainder of the day, but at five thirty-five P.M. he had arrived in his 1940 black Buick convertible coupe, 1941 Florida license 6D951, and gone up to her room, where he remained until the next morning, except for a brief break for supper.

Both the FBI and Naval Security were now trailing the couple. The FBI agent, however, must have felt more like a divorce detective as he clocked the pair going in and out of Inga's bedroom. The lovers spent another eight hours together in the hotel room on Saturday, only leaving it for a midnight snack before going back to their love nest—or fest. "They were not observed to make any contacts during the entire time they were away from the hotel," the agent recorded with disappointment and he seemed somewhat surprised by their destination the next day, when the reputed spy and her victim/associate attended mass at the Catholic Cathedral on Board Street.

From bedroom to confession hardly seemed the typical movements of espionage agents. Even the couple's window-shopping at Schindler's Antique Shop on King Street seemed benign: "No contacts were made at this point, or while they were in church," the agent conscientiously noted. Though the couple spent Sunday afternoon at a private club a few miles outside Charleston, they were soon back in bed, until finally, in the early hours of Monday, February 9, Inga boarded the Atlantic Coast Line train for Washington, leaving Jack to sleep the rest of the night in her room.

Were these really to be taken seriously as the pernicious activities of a German spy and a compliant American naval officer? A listening device had been installed in the room by the Naval Security agent, but the only suspicious note sounded between the lovers was when Inga remonstrated with Jack for canceling a social visit to one of his superiors that weekend. "Mrs. Fejos stated that she thought Kennedy should have taken her out to see Lieutenant Commander Ravenell, inasmuch as if Kennedy had been in Washington and a socially prominent friend of hers had called up, she would have stated that Kennedy was in town and she would like to bring him by. It is pointed out that subject might have desired to meet Lieutenant Commander Ravenell in an effort to develop possible national defense information, as she appeared highly indignant over this," the agent noted.

This was verging on the paranoid. Inga's indignation was one of social outrage. Understandably, the former Danish beauty queen resented being treated as Jack's whore, whom he refused to introduce to his social equals or naval superiors.

What *was* the nature of their relationship, though? From the listening device it was clear that "Kennedy and Mrs. Fejos engaged in sexual intercourse on a number of occasions while she was occupying room 132 at the Fort Sumter Hotel," the agent summarized. Clearly this was adultery on Inga's part and a mortal sin on Jack's, but it hardly amounted to espionage. Moreover, it was equally plain that Mrs. Fejos was more interested in marriage than naval information. "The only information to Kennedy's official movements that was obtained from their conversation was the fact that he expected to go to Norfolk, Virginia within the next four or five days for a period of three weeks to study fire control. She did not press him further as to his future plans, or for any information concerning the movements of any vessels belonging to the United States Navy. As to her movements, she stated that she was going to return to Washington to go back to work and was seriously considering going to Reno to get a divorce from her present husband and marry Kennedy."

But would Jack Kennedy marry Inga? She was bright, feminine, sexually experienced, and motherly in a way Jack's own mother had never been. With his tormented psyche and recurrent, mysterious illnesses, his deteriorating back, and his uncertainty as to what exactly he wished to do in life, Inga's entrancing sexuality and physical affection overwhelmed him. Marriage, however, was another matter, as both of them knew.

In a memorandum to the FBI director, one of Hoover's underlings reported on February 6, the day Inga arrived in Charleston, that Jack's sister Kathleen had been heard discussing the possibility of Jack marrying

Inga and had "indicated that their father would be opposed to Jack's marriage to Arvad should she divorce Fejos since he is known to be a very strict adherent to his religion."

To anyone with the remotest knowledge of Joseph Kennedy, this was ridiculous. Inga, however, had every reason to want marriage. She was already twenty-eight. She had no money to her name other than that sent her by a suspected Nazi entrepreneur, Axel Wenner-Gren, and a monthly remittance promised by her more-or-less estranged husband, Dr. Fejos. She loved Jack, she claimed, and wanted children by him. Returning "home" to Washington, she felt more desolate than ever. "What is home?" she asked in a philosophical letter that evening.

> At our age—at mine at any rate—it probably should mean with a man and some children. Well, 1600-16th. Street is I would say anything but a home. It is an oblong ugly modern place, where I sleep, cook my quick breakfast, entertain very rarely and never put my heart into. What I really wanted to say is that No. 132 was more of a home, and as I said over the phone tonight, it was more difficult to say goodbye to you last night than two weeks ago. In that lies the danger. That is where the tears, grief and misery lies buried. Not only in loving which to me is the freest most exhilarating of all feelings, but in missing and being quite lost. I told you about it months ago and you looked very puzzled, maybe you don't even understand me now.

Jack did understand, but he was torn. On the one hand, he had every reason to be wary of Inga. She'd already been married twice, to an Egyptian and a Hungarian. A third marriage would free her from financial dependence upon her husband's employer, a blacklisted Nazi sympathizer, but it might also have untold repercussions on Jack's eventual career.

Against this was Jack's need for Inga. Because he was emotionally inhibited by his loveless infancy, Jack's previous amours had been—and would remain throughout the rest of his life—charades: games of vanity and conquest. But as Jack's friends and colleagues best knew, his relationship with Inga was much more than an amour, by any standard. From Jack's reluctant heart an extraordinary woman—part siren, part mother, part heroine—teased out the only admission of profound love Jack would ever make: enough, at any rate, to make Inga and at moments even Jack think that they could scorn the world, the difference in their ages and the FBI, and get spliced.

Good—and Damned Bad

Would Inga have made Jack unhappy had they married? "I always felt she had an enormous effect on him," recalled Kathleen's friend Betty Coxe, "and I never knew why or how or what went on between them. Well, I knew that he was going down to her apartment to sleep there while he was still in Washington, but she was different from the others. He liked, kind of Dallas cowgirl types—and this was a very different relationship! There was no question but that she had a hold on him. But I knew none of the details at the time. Inga wasn't somebody who talked to women! And of course, she was older, I was about twenty-one, the same age as Kathleen."

Kathleen, seeing Inga both at the newspaper and in the evenings, realized that Inga was a femme fatale who might well break Jack's heart, if he had one. The FBI and U.S. Naval Security also cast her as a femme fatale, but of the Mata Hari sort.

Meanwhile Jack was in understandable confusion. When he telephoned Inga in Washington after her visit to Charleston, it was to tell her he'd been "discovered" in her room after her departure and was being charged for it. "They were all out there this morning when I came traipsing down with a bag and radio under my arm. He [the clerk] yelled at me across the lobby. He said, 'Kennedy, are you taking care of this bill?' My name is mud down here."

When Inga, embarrassed, offered to pay for the room, Jack cut her short—"Don't you send it down or I'll send it back to you," he warned, adding that he'd heard the "hotel clerk at the Fort Sumter is an Investigator."

"For what?" Inga asked.

"The Navy."

"Oh really? . . . Wonderful!" Inga bubbled. "You'll soon be kicked out."

"There is more truth than poetry to that," Jack commented.

Jack was worried less by Naval Security or FBI surveillance than by ripples from the Winchell gossip column, however. *Life* magazine was now threatening to run a piece about them, according to a rumor he'd heard. "I'll try to get up this weekend," Jack promised Inga. "You didn't hear any more about *Life,* did you?" Inga hadn't, but was certain "they can't print anything about you."

Jack was not convinced. His sister was worried on his account. Inga defended herself to Jack: "I said [to Kathleen] I am not taking anything away from you, and she said that she was just thinking of the future and how unhappy I could make you and things like that. I said, 'Well, after all, if I make him happy now, don't you think that is something?' She says, 'Well, what are you going to do?' "

"What did you say?" asked Jack.

"I didn't say anything," Inga replied, which prompted Jack to lower his voice and declare, "I'm sorry you're not here."

What Jack didn't realize as he telephoned Inga at ten-twenty in the evening, was that a rival was in Inga's apartment, where both Naval Security and the FBI had now installed monitoring devices, as well as assigning agents to watch from the street. Inga had arrived back in Washington at eleven forty-five that morning, and twenty minutes later, shortly after midday, had spoken to an old Danish boyfriend in New York, Nils Blok. "He thinks he is coming to Washington," the translator of the FBI-taped conversation later summarized.

> She wants to know if he is coming down for something special, and he says he wants to visit her if he may. She says, "Yes, that would be cozy." She tells him she has been on a trip. When he asks where, she laughingly advises, "Far away." She wants to know if he has any particular desire to see her, and he says she knows he does. He advises he has time off from his job and she tries to persuade him to come down by plane. She appears to be anxious to see him for a while, then changes her mind. After a long conversation he decides he won't come down if he can't "go to bed with her." She refuses.

Inga's denial of sex, however, lasted less than half an hour. At twelve thirty-seven, according to the FBI, her lover called again from New York "and she decides she will see him. She is sort of put out," the translator chronicled, "because she can't tell him 'no' sometimes. She states, 'I don't want to sleep with a dozen men at one time.' It is decided that he will call her when he gets there."

Blok arrived at four-thirty P.M., staying closeted with Inga all evening and all night. Jack, a narcissistic Don Juan, had no idea he was being "two-timed," and was merely sore at the increasing evidence of being under surveillance. On February 11 he complained to Inga, according to the FBI phone tap, that "he had found out that the fellow in the next room had been copying all of his mail but he thinks he rescued most of it," but could say no more because his landlady was obviously listening in. The threat of the *Life* magazine story still hovered over them. All this, together with the current Washington controversy over Roosevelt's new appointments, conspired to irritate him beyond measure. "Don't you people in Washington have anything to talk about except a fan dancer and a movie actor being paid $1200 a year?" he wrote to Inga, referring to the current front-page headlines. "With everything in the world going down the drain and all that dough—and especially all that dough being spent—they just boil and stew over a stinking bit of New Dealism of which there have been other and better examples for the last ten years. I think that everything up there has gotten too complex for the average Congressman," he warned in a salutary blast. "Now they just can't wait until they can get hold of something they can understand and sink their teeth into like a fan dancer and then they just go to town. Nero had better move as he is getting plenty of company. The only thing that continues to measure up to expectations is you," he ended, switching to tenderness. "I hope you fully understand your responsibility."

Inga did, though sleeping with what felt like a dozen men at a time taxed her to the hilt. Meanwhile, to his friend Lem Billings Jack wrote on February 12 that

> this life I'm living down here is somewhat easier than was Washington. As a matter of fact you get a much better perspective on exactly what life in Washington is like when you are here. I wonder what's happening to this country. I never thought in my gloomiest day that there was any chance of our being defeated. But ignoring the military defeats we are suffering [in the Philippines], which seems to be what everyone else is doing, ignoring that and just looking at the furor caused by a dancer and a movie actor being appointed to Civilian Defense, which doesn't really mean a damn thing, to waste all that public indignation on that small event while all around us are examples of inefficiency that may lick us—Nero had better move over as there are a lot of fiddlers to join him.

This was Jack at his most acerbic. However besotted he might be by the prospect of sex with Inga, the twenty-four-year-old still read the newspapers with an avidity unmatched by most of his contemporaries. "As I read all that junk coming out of the Nation's Capital, all that confusion, Washington is beginning to look more and more like the Cuban Tea Room on a Saturday night with the Madame out," he mocked. "I suppose we will slide along taking an academic interest in Singapore and MacArthur, and getting excited over dancers and Melvyn Douglas and pensions until the bells really start to toll. It seems a rather strange commentary that it will take death in large quantities to wake us up, but I really don't think anything else ever will," he lamented.

This latter thought brought him to consider the larger war aims of America. "I don't think anyone really realizes that nothing stands between us and the defeat of our Christian crusade against Paganism except a lot of Chinks who never heard of God and a lot of Russians who have heard about him but don't want Him. I suppose we can't afford to be very choosy at a time like this," he remarked of the U.S. alliance with Stalinist Russia: an irony that prompted him to urge Billings—who had finally voluntarily joined the American Field Ambulance Corps and was slated to go to the Mediterranean—to "make friends with any brown or yellow man you happen to meet. In 'The Decline of the West' Mr. Spengler, after carefully studying the waves of civilization, prophesied that the next few centuries belonged to the Yellow Man. After the Japs get through uniting Asia it looks as though Mrs. Lindbergh's 'wave of the future' will certainly have a yellow look."

Such musings did not mean Billings was spared the usual lash of Jack's wit. Referring to the letter of recommendation his father had written on Billing's behalf to the U.S. Field Service, Jack now asked his friend to look at "paragraph 4 line 6 beginning 'To go on and add to this his peculiar qualities would be superfluous.' Now the particular word that interested me is 'peculiar.' What could he possibly be referring to? Your habit of picking your chin—your paranoic desire for a sunburn—or perhaps he means that rather 'peculiar' expression that comes over your face when you start inhaling your asthma medicine. All of these, of course, are peculiar and I'm just interested to know which particular ones he is talking about."

Such banter only made Billings more devoted to Jack, for Billings was the only male friend who could see Jack's bravado for what it was: the vexed, restless outpourings of a troubled, often sick young man in whose soul ambition played a constant duet with reckless sexual license. Self-doubt and self-pity were in Jack Kennedy turned inside out, with Billings the foil. In interview after interview Billings later made clear how "frustrated" Jack was in Charleston. "His job, as I remember, was still Navy Intelligence, but now he was working with defense factories, etc."—"he just wasn't interested in U.S.-based Intelligence at all, he hated it. He was the unhappiest man you ever knew in Charleston." "He was *very* unhappy there in Charleston. It was a boring, lousy, stinking job. . . . He was desperate to get out of Charleston. He wanted active duty."

Billings was not mistaken. On February 14, 1942, Jack wrote to Billings to describe the latest mapping of his crystal ball: "My plans are as usual varied and interesting as I have a number of irons in the fire. One is an assignment to Pearl Harbor—the other to a battleship—both of which will probably fall flat on their arse but both of which make interesting conversation—and make me a hell of fellow with these local gals."

This reference to the indigenous folk of Charleston brought Jack to the matter of southerners. Apart from Palm Beach society, Jack had really never been exposed to the rebel south. "Have I discussed Southerners with you?" he asked. "It's not so much that they say 'here' [hear] after every god damned remark—'now come and see us Kennedy, here'—but is the aboots and oots—and all the rest of the shit that convinces me we should have let the bootucks go."

Throughout his stay in Charleston, Jack's thoughts kept returning to Inga, and Inga's to him. In a love letter on Valentine's Day, 1942, Inga toyed with memories of the past, reflections on the present, and thoughts of Jack's future. She recalled her days in Siam, with its

> temples with their many colors, so gorgeous that the town looked like a huge rainbow when the sun glittered on the dragon-like roofs, winding and twisting themselves towards the sky, as if they wanted to pierce it and touch the throne of God. . . . There were many more Buddahs than Siamese. Most of them were made of gold, emeralds or other precious metals and stones. Many had a smile, which was very benevolent, or as if they would say "Why do you believe in me?" Women prayed to have their lovers returned of them, then they moved to another God and implored Him to make them prolific. Could faith have done it, both miracles would have been performed right there and then.
>
> The monks in their yellow garbs. Hollywood couldn't have chosen a better color for this perfect stage setting. They looked lean as it befits monks. Mornings at dawn they would get into their tiny boats, row up the streams and beg food. People who looked as if they had never had a meal in their lives would give what they had, and the monk would take it with a gesture as if he was doing them a great favor—and that, dear, is exactly what they themselves felt too. That is faith.
>
> Faith. You always say you have faith. Sometimes I wonder if you believe it yourself. To me it seems that the faith you are born with is an empty one. The one you acquire later in life, when God has risen the curtain and showed you life, showed you all its beauties and many of its miseries—well if you have faith then—that is worth something. That is built on a rock, which no new invention of Mr. Adolf can shatter.

This brought Inga to the point. "You are going away," she stated, knowing Jack had applied for foreign duty. "A thing I have known for months and I suppose most women would be proud and say 'Go and defend your country.' I say the same, but somehow the pride is not there, only a hope that God will keep His hand safely over you. And more important than returning with your young handsome body intact, to let you come back with the wishes both to be a White-House-Man and wanting the ranch—somewhere out West."

This reference to Jack's secret presidential ambitions was perfectly serious. Though Jack's casual friends might mock the idea of such an unkempt, happy-go-lucky fellow ever seriously imagining he could become president of the United States, Jack had known Inga would not expose him to ridicule. Nor did she, for she was quite convinced he had it in him to become president if he set his mind to it. Like Jack himself, she never lost her poise or her playful understanding of his failings. She wrote:

> You once said—as a matter of fact last Sunday—"To you I need not pretend—you know me too well." I do, not because I have put you on a pedestal—you don't belong there, nobody does—but because I know where you are weak, and that is what I like. A man or a woman who thinks and makes others believe that he has no weakness in him or her, well they are like diamonds cut with an unskilled hand.
>
> Maybe I am tolerant dear, because I know where the shoe hurts, as I have it on. I know where I failed and still do, but there is hope for that kind of human being, it is the contented ones, who never have time to stop, look see and pay attention, who are as lost as the wife of Lot. . . .
>
> Maybe your gravest mistake handsome, is that you admire brains more than heart, but then that is necessary to arrive. Heart never brought fame—except to Saints—nor money.
>
> Whatever happens, let us have lunch together the first day you are ashore, shall we? That of course provided you are not married, your wife maybe wouldn't understand. It is always hard to understand if you are very young and in love, and that is probably what she will be. But if not, if you are still free. . . .

Two days later Jack phoned to ask if Inga had received *his* letter and was a little stunned by her breathless "Hi" when he hadn't even had time to say who was calling. Inga, feline to the core, deftly extricated herself from her faux pas. Ten minutes before Jack's call, she'd been talking to Bernard Baruch, whom she nicknamed "the old goat" and whose friendship, in an alien society, was vital to her. ("Once," Frank Waldrop later recalled, "somebody with little enough sense asked her some impudent questions and she said, with total poise, that she had no fear as long as Mr. Baruch asked her for dinner.") "Are you living alone?" Baruch had asked her on the telephone. "Yes," she'd answered, "perfectly immoral and dreadful, don't you think? No, I am very, very quiet and don't do anything extraordinary at all," she'd remarked innocently—waiting for a call from her Danish lover.

Now, talking to Jack, Inga demonstrated the same extraordinary talent for thinking on her feet, completely besting Jack at his own forte. "She said she knew it was he," the FBI agent summarized in his report to J. Edgar Hoover, "and said 'I have no suitors, and I haven't got you either.'"

Like Jack, Inga knew that humor was the key to defusing awkward situations. "She said she was in the mood for kidding. Then kidded him about a letter she received from him; and said 'I am going to give out a book—love letters.' She then insisted the letter was wonderful—she didn't know he had such secret corners of the brain. . . . She asked when he expects to leave—as his father had said [something] over the phone to 'Kick,' and asked if it was Singapore. He said it had been for Pearl Harbor then somewhere else, but it had fallen through and he thought he would be stuck in Charleston for some time—remarking that all his plans seemed to fall through."

Was Ensign Kennedy now deliberately being kept at his post in Charleston in an attempt to snare Inga—and possibly Kennedy himself? Whatever the truth, Jack was certainly given continued access to naval codes and ciphers, as his colleague from Georgia, Ensign Fred Rosen, later remembered:

> I never quite understood, Kennedy being from the Boston area, why he was there. His job, when I arrived there, was on the Commandant's staff, breaking codes. In other words, when a batch of messages came in, in code, there were a group of five letters or whatever, and instead of breaking that out by hand there was a typewriter that did it for you, and he was sitting there, hunting and pecking on the typewriter putting those codes in, getting the English out of it. And that was his primary job.

If Jack's superiors were hoping to catch him colluding in espionage, however, they were disappointed. "She called him Honey, Darling, Honeysuckle, Honey Child Wilder, and said 'I love you,'" the FBI reported. Though they were watching her activities as an espionage suspect, they were witnessing a form of much deeper intelligence-gathering as well. Intuitively Inga knew that she must adopt the role of courtesan-confessor, promising Jack a love he had never received from his mother, even taunting him by withholding it, just as Rose had done in his childhood. Jack "asked when she is coming back to Charleston, and she said 'in 3 or 4 months,' " the FBI recorded, " 'or when you really want me very much to come!' He said that is now."

Teasing the lustful, lovesick ensign, Inga tantalized him by saying she would only come once she "sells her first story—writes her first book." Jack sarcastically told her "not to strain herself," but admitted that he liked her interview with Admiral Wiley, chairman of the Navy Board for Production Awards. To this Inga responded, according to the FBI, " 'I do the most terrible work—I don't know why.' When he said, 'you don't know what is good and what is bad,' she said, 'I know that you are good—and damned bad.' "

Such reference to the sinful side of his nature thrilled Jack's vanity and appealed to his honesty. Indeed no woman in his life would ever come close to Inga's mix of licentiousness and wit, talent for gossip, and adventurous ambition. She could turn a phrase or witticism as quick or quicker than Jack. To Baruch, a moment before, she'd said, "You played the leading role in the last war and I am playing it in this one apparently" (referring to her romance with the son of the ex-U.S. ambassador to Britain), according to the FBI. A moment later, she was indeed playing such a role to perfection, with no one, least of all Jack, knowing where it all might lead.

Sturm und Drang in Charleston

In the meantime Inga had met more of Jack's sisters—Jean, who was impossibly shy and thus "ain't no Kennedy," and Pat, who was "sweet, and will be beautiful, but giggled," so that she and Kick "felt like old spinsters," as she told Jack. They talked of Lem Billings's imminent departure for Egypt, then returned to Jack's future. "She wanted to know why the Singapore trip went down the drain, and if 'Big Joe' couldn't help him get it," the FBI summarized in its latest report. "He said when he learned about it it was all over, but he tried to call him (his father) tonight but he wasn't in. He applied for a transfer but fears he can't get it for six months. . . . He wants very much to see her."

Intellectually, sexually, and professionally frustrated, Jack was also experiencing mounting irritation at reports of the poor Allied effort against the militocracies of Germany and Japan. There was also the matter of his father, whose fall from presidential grace Jack had vowed somehow to avenge. On the night of the Japanese attack on Pearl Harbor, a full year after announcing his resignation as ambassador to Great

Britain, Joseph Kennedy had sent Roosevelt a loyal message of support: "Dear Mr. President: In this great crisis all Americans are with you. Name the battle post. I'm yours to command." The president, however, had no more use for Kennedy in war than in peace. As the weeks and then months went by, no word ever came from the White House—driving the ex-ambassador, in a fit of almost crazed pique, to send a telegram offering his services to Britain's Lord Beaverbrook. "He said he had already volunteered to work for this government but had received no assignment and so was eager to help England if she needed him," his wife explained to the children in her latest family letter.

Such an extraordinary cable from a disenchanted former member of the U.S. administration to a Cabinet minister in Britain (Beaverbrook had been made minister of War Production) spoke volumes. Clearly, the ex-ambassador's sanity had become unhitched by Roosevelt's continuing refusal to employ him—Kennedy still wilfully ignorant of the extent to which he was detested in both Washington and London. Clinging to his honorary title of "ambassador" despite his infamous performance in the role, he paced about in lonely exile in Palm Beach, as bored and frustrated as his son Jack in Charleston. To this was added a profound despondency.

While Kennedy's friends understood his mood, they became anxious lest he dishearten his children, particularly his normally sunny second son. "Jack," Clare Boothe Luce had chided the ex-ambassador on February 5,

> is a darlyn. He has everything a boy needs to be a great success in the world, and one of the things which gives me comfort is the thought that no set of circumstances can lick a boy like Jack . . . and surely there are lots of Jacks left in America, so we *will* be saved.
>
> He is vaguely unhappy about your pessimism. It alarms him ("so unlike Dad") and dispirits him, and I do think that you . . . and I have no right to add the burden of doubt to the other burdens that he, and a million like him, must carry from here out. After all, Jack and the other boys are the ultimate recipients of all the errors which we—and the men of our times have made. If Mr. FDR's foreign policy is to be implemented, it will be with the very bodies of these kids. And it's so tragically true that it's not theirs to reason why, they've just got orders to take . . . and we hadn't oughtta make them feel that orders are too mad, and too vain.

Having said this, Mrs. Luce penned for Kennedy not only a brilliant summary of the geopolitical situation confronting America, but, on the eve of her own trip to Britain and the Middle East as a war correspondent, a passionate rallying call to Americans to wake up and see that, if the Japanese were successful, America's place in the global economic sun was over. Whatever their qualms, Mrs. Luce felt, Americans must begin to *fight*.

Stung by Mrs. Luce's letter, "Ambassador" Kennedy had it copied and sent to Jack in Charleston, with a brief covering note. "Heavens knows, I don't want any pessimism of mine to have any effect on you," he apologized, "but I don't know *how* to tell you *what* I think unless I tell you *what* I think," he excused himself. He encouraged Jack to make the best of his transfer to Charleston, since it would not only be good experience "seeing different kinds of jobs," but would "also give you a firm conviction that there is plenty of room at the top for anybody in any line—most particularly in Government service."

Jack, touched by his father's words, carefully read Clare Boothe Luce's remarkable letter, which not only deeply impressed him, but coming at such an impressionable moment in his life, had an incalculable impact on him. Indeed it would not be fanciful to say that it marked a watershed in Jack's early career.

"The newspapers still go on printing headlines that say Victory, and a news-story that stinks of defeat," Jack immediately lifted one of Clare Boothe Luce's best lines when next writing to Rip Horton. He began to bombard his friends, from Coleman to Rousmanière, with similarly plagiarized themes and phrases. Moreover, he started to draft the sort of article he'd longed to write but never dared publish as long as his father was engaged in his self-appointed life's mission to "keep America out of war": an article that would breach the dam of his own thoughts and distill the insights he'd gained into isolationism and interventionism over the past three years.

"The situation that now faces the United States is grave," Jack began, "extremely so. The people of America must awake to the reality and extent of the war that we are fighting—or rather not fighting. We must realize that this war is not a debate over war potentials and possible production limits, but is a serious and long business that must be *fought*, and fought by troops. It is not a war that can be won by blue-prints of bombers that some day will cover the sky. This war must cease to be run as a political battle. Generals must take charge—must, if necessary, regiment the country to an extent that makes the Nazis look like starry-eyed individualists if we are ever to come out on top."

Six weeks before the fall of Bataan, and a full year before the American disaster at Kasserine, Jack's plagiarized call to arms in mid-February 1942 was a major step in his own politico-military journey. He who had hovered between isolationism and interventionism for almost three years, now, in the wake and often in the precise words of Clare Boothe Luce, who had become a congresswoman as well as a noted playwright, predicted defeat for America unless radical steps were taken.

That his own steps had been hesitant, that he had originally eschewed direct American involvement in the world war on his father's grounds that such involvement would destroy capitalist democracy as Americans knew it, did not impede his exhortation now to his fellow men to fight. Nor, for that matter, did his own contribution to the war effort, conducting a scandalous affair with a suspected enemy spy. "There are two menacing possibilities facing us," Jack warned, "possibilities which approach probabilities—and which if carried through may very well bring defeat to America."

The first was at that moment taking place—"a successful drive on Singapore and the Dutch East Indies by the Japanese which will be followed by a push through India, the possibilities of which seem to have been overlooked. This military drive," Jack predicted, "will be supplemented by a propaganda campaign which would present the Japanese in the guise of deliverers of the yellow man from white imperialism. This would have a powerful appeal," he admitted, claiming that "[t]here are more Indian Nationalists under British arrest in India than Hitler has in all the concentration camps in Europe."

"If this [Japanese] drive meets with success," Jack sketched the scenario, "the Indian Ocean would become a Jap lake, and the Japanese position would approach invulnerability. This drive would probably be coordinated with a German push through to the Persian Gulf via Turkey. This would serve in a triple capacity; coordinated with a German drive through the Ukraine, it would squeeze the Russians, it would stand as a dagger at the backs of the British who would be under pressure from Rommel in the West, and to the east would choke off any chance of the British reinforcing India."

Such a scenario led Jack, like Clare Boothe Luce, to lay out the likely consequences of German-Japanese success. "If these two drives succeed, and we should know by the end of May," Jack predicted, "if the Japs take Singapore, the East Indies and India, if the Germans succeed through Turkey, a Turkey which could put up little fight even if it were willing, the first phase of the war would be ended in defeat.

"The situation facing the Allies would then be a question of gloomy alternatives," Jack went on. "Churchill would be thrown out of office on the recoil of these double defeats and undoubtedly appeasement forces would be busy in Britain. The tremendous strength of the German-Japanese position would make Britain feel that providing she could be given suitable guarantees in regard to the empire, peace would be preferable.

"Beaverbrook might be the logical successor to Churchill, a strong man, a man who has the confidence of the people, and yet a man with appeasement background, a former leading isolationist, and a man who might see a greater chance for Britain in a peace—however difficult—than in a war sure to extend for years and one whose chances for success would appear slight."

Jack's speculative picture had an uncanny ring of truth. Beaverbrook was to Churchill as Jack's own father was to Roosevelt: a rich and powerful man whom the prime minister had to play with extraordinary dexterity lest he be supplanted by him. Certainly Jack's crystal-ball gazing came perilously close to reality in the case of Churchill, who within four months would be facing his first vote of no confidence in the House of Commons.

"It is assumed that Russia would have either made peace—or would have been rolled back to the Urals out of harm's way," Jack postulated, as he came to focus on his own country's fate—"either condition being possible, if not probable."

Jack brought his futuristic survey to its climax:

> It is now that America would be faced with its grave decision. It would here be faced with either *really* waging war or else accepting an uneasy peace. If it chooses war, it would literally mean millions killed and billions spent. It would mean long war, up-hill war, a war against fortresses—over great distances. To wage such a war successfully this country would inevitably go Fascist. Any remaining resemblance to our democracy as we now know it, would be purely coincidental.
>
> Roosevelt, keenly sensitive to public opinion would either retire, or if he refused, would be retired, to the background by a military clique—a rubber stamp. The public, discouraged by disaster, would turn upon him as in Britain the public turned on Baldwin. He who had lived by the Gallup Poll would die by it.

These were bold prognostications about a sitting American president, particularly at a moment when the author of such warnings was himself under Naval Security surveillance, with the president (who was being kept abreast of the Inga Arvad case by J. Edgar Hoover) as final arbiter on Jack's and Inga's possible arrests.

The American public, Jack contended, "might not be willing to make these sacrifices for victory. The fundamental isolationism of [the] American character, the feeling of invulnerability bred in their bones by centuries of security behind the broad expanse of the Atlantic and Pacific Oceans: this feeling, strengthened by the presence of a large army and navy, and air force, might cause it to prefer peace, however fitful."

This was certainly the view Jack's father had articulated at length the previous spring at Oglethorpe University in what his biographer called "perhaps the greatest speech Kennedy ever delivered." However, it was not the view Jack now adopted.

"This would be a fatal mistake," Jack pronounced. "We could stand up against Pan-Germanism in Europe—a movement which would probably fall apart under three years of peace—but a Pan-Asiatic movement led by militant Japan would be a different story. With the Japs in the driver's seats, the sleepy giant that is Asia would be stirred. The Japs would first make a deal with the Chinese. Above all the Chinese wish to get the Japs out of China, above all the Japs wish to get out. Hong Kong, a part of Burma, their territorial integrity, these would satisfy the Chinese. The Japanese themselves would have more than enough to keep them busy, developing Malaysia, the East Indies, the Philippines, and Australia. [Chiang] Kai-Chek [*sic*] would retire to the hills of Mongolia to wage a bitter and fruitless war. India, with the British out, would be welded into the gigantic economic and military block that Japan would form out of Asia, a machine which would eventually be turned against the United States. Russia, reeling from German blows in the West and faced with a drive into Siberia from the rear, would willingly join the movement. And then finally would come our day of reckoning—a day that might see Japanese invaders on our soil and thus bring to completion the prophecies of Homer Lee made in 1908 that some day the Japanese would defeat the United States in battle."

The jigsaw of Jack's politico-strategic thinking was at last coming together, but revealing a vastly different perspective from that of the Harvard youth who had once penned a *Crimson* editorial advocating appeasement with Hitler. Even his recent talk with Lord Halifax became grist for his mill as he continued, "Then would Winston Churchill's remark to John Gunther made a week before the outbreak of the Japanese war, 'The Japs will cave in—they are the wops of the East,' come back to plague him as did Neville Chamberlain's 'Peace in our Time.'

"These are some of the gloomy possibilities facing America," the young ensign concluded. "We are embarked on a war that will bring either certain defeat or such blood, such sweat, and such tears as no one in America from the White House to the man in the street has ever imagined."

In the later light of war in the Pacific, the Atlantic, the Mediterranean, North Africa, Italy, and Normandy, and in the bitter battles to reach Berlin, as well as in the decision to drop the atomic bomb on Japan, Jack would be seen not to have exaggerated. In America's favor, however, he remarked,

Our great asset is a willingness and a determination to fight through. Whether that spirit will stand through the kind of war we may have to embark on soon remains to be seen.

A realization of what we face will come, but the slower it comes, the more difficult becomes the task. We are fighting now for the vague principles of the Atlantic charter and the "Four Freedoms." When at long last we realize that what we are fighting for is self-preservation, when we see that we stand with our backs to the wall—fighting not a lofty crusade, but a long and bitter battle for survival—then and only then, far out on the horizon, will victory be in sight.

In retrospect, something of Jack Kennedy's political Sturm und Drang can be seen in this, his first would-be "platform" speech. Those who later assumed that Jack would have quietly served his isolationist, pro-Fascist, anti-Semitic elder brother in the same manner that he himself would later be served by his younger brothers can have had little idea either of Jack's own concealed presidential ambitions or of the restless political conscience that was at work in him even in 1942—and had been from his college days. Behind the mask of happy-go-lucky, skirt-chasing, directionless youth a complicated, precocious, and serious young man sought to come to terms with conflicting realities—domestic, romantic, and overtly political. What made him so attractive to men as well as to women was not simply the "elfin-like quality" his mother acknowledged in him as a child, but the evident tug-of-war concealed behind that genial façade. Sex and the battlefield both lured him. But so, too, did the political interplay of world forces on a global stage. While his elder brother merely parroted their father, Jack's political grappling was his own, and all the more moving because, symbolized in his struggle to confront the underlying issues facing Western democracy and his own country in the "fog of war," there was too the age-old struggle of a son seeking to emerge from his father's shadow.

Smoldering Ambition

While Jack was enduring his Charleston assignment, Billings, despite his poor eyesight, was getting ready to fight Rommel. "You know, I think it's an excellent idea you're going to Africa," Jack had written to him on February 12. "First, of course, because you would get more and more restless not being in uniform as things began to get going more and more—and secondly it will be a damned good experience for you to get away on your own without any buddies to go and see. When you lack that escapism you will find yourself much better equipped for the changing world, if you will excuse me sounding a bit like George St. John."

Two days later, however, Jack changed tack, ordering Lem to "try and get down here" after his brother Tremaine's wedding in Nashville and reverting to the smutty intimacy that had characterized his relationship with Billings since adolescence. He thought Billings a "glutton for punishment. . . . After you hear someone call you a fairy and discuss it for two solid hours," Jack admonished his friend, "and argue whether you did or did not go down on Worthington Johnson, you don't write a letter saying you think that fellow is a great guy—even if it's true [re Worthington Johnson] which it was." Jack also cautioned his friend against "any mention of your brother's loins or his seed" when proposing the toast at the wedding "as from experience that goes over just fair. You might mention the bride's though, as it will make her feel close to you."

Jack was doubly frustrated, and mention of the wedding and the bride's loins only reminded him of Inga. Should he marry her? Inga was certainly keen. When Jack asked her to come down to Charleston again over the weekend of February 21–22, Inga agreed.

Whether Jack's father was yet aware of Inga's promiscuous sex life is unclear. If not, Kathleen's visit to Palm Beach on February 14 certainly put him in the know. "Kathleen was sweet," Inga had written the week before. "I love her for admitting that what really gets her goat is that she is jealous of me. My God. What I give you—if I give you anything—and what I take—which is plenty—that is something she couldn't do for you anyway. But she is young and as yet intolerant," Inga allowed. "She is more afraid of the pain that I shall cause you in the future, than she is concerned with the happiness we may enjoy at present."

As Page Huidekoper had wreaked more havoc than she'd intended, so Kathleen's jealous reports to her father in Palm Beach were grist to Joseph Kennedy's mill. He'd already cautioned Jack against continuing the affair. Aware from Kathleen that Inga was visiting Jack in Charleston and that Jack was as besotted as ever, the ex-ambassador resolved to put an end to the business.

To Kathleen, informing on her brother was not disloyal. To her astonished boyfriend, John White, she revealed that her father regularly paid private detectives and informants to watch his children and particularly to "check out" their friends, an approach to parenting which, on top of Rosemary's catastrophic lobotomy, made Kathleen determined to go back to England.

Jack, meanwhile, was torn between heart and head, and sought refuge in silence. Inga had booked a seat on the seven o'clock Friday train, but when she heard nothing from Jack, and Kathleen seemed cagy about her Palm Beach trip, Inga was perplexed. When finally Jack called her on the night of February 19, she complained "she was the only person who did not know what Jack was going to do," as the FBI phone tapper paraphrased. Jack confessed he'd "talked to Big Joe the previous night and Big Joe had told him what he should do. Kennedy stated there were a lot of things he had to straighten out for her, but he couldn't do so over the phone."

Alarmed, Inga booked a flight to Charleston. Jack met the plane. Given the obvious surveillance at the Fort Sumter Hotel, he had arranged a room—this time under the name of Barbara Smith—at the Francis Marion Hotel—and it was there they spent the following three nights.

What Jack confessed to the priest at the Catholic cathedral on Sunday, February 22, the FBI could not know, since they had not thought to bug the confessional, or if they did, thought better of it. But almost every word exchanged between Inga and Jack in the hotel was monitored and subsequently scrutinized for clues by the various FBI agents charged with reporting on the case to Mr. Hoover. "A great deal of the conversation which passed between the subject and Kennedy in the hotel room was obtained," Special Agent Ruggles recorded with satisfaction on February 23. "It was learned," for instance, "that the subject was quite worried [about pregnancy] as a result of her two previous trips to Charleston, and she spoke of the possibility of getting her marriage annulled. It was noted that Kennedy had very little comment to make on the subject."

Apparently Jack had a good deal to say about the war, however. On February 15 General Percival surrendered the entire British garrison at Singapore without a fight, and worse disasters in Indonesia and the Philippines loomed. The conduct of the war vexed Jack deeply, inciting him to become more and more outspoken as he sought simultaneously to come to terms with his Scandinavian lover, his isolationist father, and his country's crisis.

A measure of Jack's increasing turmoil was provided by new tidbits picked up by the FBI on the evening Inga arrived at Charleston, as Jack—who had tried but failed to get through to his father in Palm Beach—raved in front of Inga about Allied mismanagement of the war. Inga and Jack

> became involved in quite a discussion in regard to the international situation, particular attention being paid to Winston Churchill's speech of last Sunday which [Inga] stated she heard. She described this speech as having "not one word of anything but defeatism." Kennedy agreed. During this conversation, Kennedy stated

"Churchill told John Gunther a while before this country got into the war that the Japs would fold up like the Italians." On another occasion, Kennedy stated that Churchill alone was responsible for getting this country into the war. Miss Arvad described the British soldiers as "No damn good." Kennedy stated that in his opinion the British Empire was through, that Churchill knew this, and it was the reason he tried to keep Britain out of the war [*sic*].

Such a hodgepodge of overheard and misquoted remarks scarcely did justice to Jack's difficult coming of age in terms of his father's isolationism. Yet the fragments of conversation noted by the FBI testified to Jack's frustration at having to sit out a historical world crisis in South Carolina, deciphering routine naval signals and teaching ARP (Air Raid Precautions) to munitions workers. "Upon another occasion, Kennedy stated that he was rather dissatisfied with his work in the Navy Yard and told Inga about being nicknamed 'Baby' by fellow employees."

Inga Arvad's complete absence of interest in this work at the Charleston Navy Yard ought to have cleared her of any suspicion of being a Nazi agent. Ironically, however, Jack's obsession with the conduct of the war and his seesawing views on isolationism, appeasement, and interventionism now led the FBI to a new subject—Joseph P. Kennedy. "Particular attention is called to records 8 and 9 which contain the telephone conversation between Kennedy to the home of Joseph P. Kennedy on the night of February 22, 1942," the FBI agent noted.

Since his widely reported speech at Oglethorpe the previous spring, the senior Kennedy had gone quiet, for reasons the FBI now overheard. "Later, on the same evening, Kennedy stated that his father's greatest mistake was not talking enough, that he stopped too quickly and was accused of being an appeaser. He stated that the reason his father stopped talking and didn't go on and present his side of the question fully was due to the fact that he believed it might hurt his two sons later in politics."

If this was so, it was one of the first documented references to the fact that Joe Kennedy had political designs for *both* his older sons, not only Joe Jr. The FBI also noted that "from their conversation on a number of occasions, it appeared that John Kennedy had prepared for his father at least one of the speeches his father had made, or was intending to make in answer to criticism for his alleged appeasement policies."

The ex-ambassador's master plan for Jack, however, was not one that would ever include Inga. Though they remained lovers, it soon became clear that Jack was *not* proposing to marry her. "On the same evening the subject and Kennedy had another discussion in regard to her worries over becoming pregnant. She accused Jack of 'Taking every pleasure of youth but not the responsibility.' "

Given Inga's own record the past week in Washington (where she'd once again gone to bed with Nils Blok), this was somewhat pious of her. Nevertheless, on her return to Washington Inga sent Jack another love letter, thanking him for his gift of two new hurricane lamps:

> I love them, they are perfectly beautiful, not that there is much of a place where they can show themselves to their true advantage, but nevertheless I feel deeply attached to them already and have sworn never to leave them. When some day, I shall be fleeing, maybe evacuating because the Japs are too near my heels to be comfortable, then I shall wrap them up in my bundle and carry them on my back. And why? Certainly not because Southern slaves with aching backs and welts on their hides from the master's last beatings obediently held them up to light the path of the belle returning from her first ball. But my dear, because I am slightly crazy about the person who gave them to me. A mink coat from F.D.R. would leave me cold and a violet from my sailor-boy throws me into raptures.
>
> Sometimes when I sit with you in your car, see your young eagerness on the golf course, or feel that you have some tenderness in you, then I would like to say "Darling, I am true, white, red and blue . . ." But it seems a bit odd certainly still more silly. Every time I see you I learn something new. As I told you yesterday I know you pretty well, and still I like you. You know Jack that is a hell of a compliment, because anyone as brainy and Irish-shrewd as you can't be quite like a white dove. But by Golly, you have a strong hand, one I like to shake, and it ain't bad looking into that steady left twinckling [*sic*] eye either. You will get there; as Clare says, "He has everything to make a success." Right she is, and I like her for discovering it so quickly. You have more than even your ancestors and yet you haven't lost the tough hide of the Irish potatoes.
>
> Put a match to the smoldering ambition and you will go like wild fire. It is all against the ranch out West, but it is the unequalled highway to the White House. And if you can find something you really believe in, then my dear you caught the biggest fish in the ocean. You can pull it aboard, but don't rush it, there is still time.

Inga herself knew the best odds stacked against her accompanying Jack on this journey. She distrusted Arthur Krock especially, "as I know he is a general agent for Palm Beach, and I hear from Kick that he has been entertaining Washington dinner parties about me—maybe you too," Inga warned Jack.

In his Charleston exile Jack was, mercifully, immune to the gossip his affair with Inga was still generating in the nation's capital. He was therefore shocked when Lem Billings wrote to tell him of "a rather interesting conversation with a slight acquaintance" of his mother. "She told Mother she'd heard I was a good friend of some of the Kennedys—Mother affirmed this & Mrs. Lord said then you must have heard about the big Romance that has been rocking Washington circles—that one of the Kennedy boys is madly in love with a very beautiful & ravishing Danish reporter—but that fortunately the gal has been married several times—so that it will be difficult for her to marry him."

Billings's letter coincided with even worse news. A member of the FBI called Joseph Kennedy to tell him that the ex-ambassador, too, was now also implicated in the FBI investigation, warning him that Inga's apartment was bugged and that every conversation she held in it as well as every phone call she made or received, was recorded by the FBI.

Jack, having spoken once again to his father, finally decided it was time to act. Though Inga cabled she would be working the weekend of February 28 and would only be able to come to Charleston the weekend after that (March 6), Jack felt the matter couldn't wait. Obtaining special permission to leave the Charleston area, he flew to Washington on the afternoon of February 28, spent a final night with Inga, and departed back to Charleston the following day.

Tipped off that Inga now knew of their monitoring devices, the FBI had already removed them from Inga's room for fear of being discovered. They were therefore unable to "listen to conversation which Arvad had with Kennedy while he was in her apartment," and thus had no record of what transpired. But the gist of Jack's whirlwind visit became clear the following day when Inga telephoned her husband in New York. As the FBI phone tappers listened, she told him "she was quitting her acquaintance with Jack Kennedy."

Torby Macdonald wrote from Boston, where he'd found a safe billet as an ensign in the Office of the Inspector of War Materials, asking Jack "how things are progressing with that sprightly spying Scandinavian?"

But things were not progressing. To all intents and purposes, the *grande affaire* that had rocked Washington was over.

Totally Dead Inside

Was the affair really over, though? Inga, unfazed, was soon arranging to see her Danish boyfriend in New York, but Jack, four years her junior and suffering increasing back pain, simply could not bear their separation. It was clear that he was attracted to Inga in a way he could not control. "Surprised to hear from me?" he asked when calling her on March 6, 1942.

"A little maybe," Inga answered coyly.

"It's about time," Jack grumbled.

"Kathleen says every day that you will call me," Inga remarked chidingly, putting Jack on the defensive.

"I've been in bed with a bad back," Jack apologized, and asked whether Inga had decided to go ahead and seek a divorce in Reno, Nevada.

There followed a sad litany, for Inga's apartment had been burglarized and she had lost seven hundred dollars in traveler's checks, two diamond rings, and a gold bracelet. She'd also canceled that day the flight reservation to Charleston that she'd made before the breakup.

"Why didn't you come?" Jack asked.

"What a question. Don't you remember that we talked it over on Sunday?"

"I know it."

"Oh, you don't think it's going to stay?"

"Life's too short."

"Oh, Kennedy!" Inga expostulated, and asked whether he was "not giving up what we promised last Sunday are you?"

"No," Jack responded, "not till the next time I see you. I'm not too good, am I?"

Inga, maternal and womanly, was touched by Jack's weakness. "I think you're perfect, dear. We'll probably meet again."

"You mean, next week?"

"I'm not coming. I don't know. I'm not trying to be stubborn. I'm only trying to help you. You know that, don't you?"

"I figured it out."

He asked what Inga was doing over the weekend. She explained. "Did you think I was coming to Charleston?" she added.

"I had big hopes."

This led to a discussion of divorce plans. Inga claimed she would go on with them, now that she was two weeks ahead with her work and "Sir Francis" [Frank Waldrop] was amenable.

"You don't have any doubts about going out [to Nevada]?" Jack asked.

She didn't, but she was worried about the stories circulating about her and about Axel Wenner-Gren. When Jack dismissed it all as "just a lot of ugly rumors" and talked of "all this gab going around," Inga suggested the rumors were designed "to scare you. That's what I think. Personally I think it is coming from Miami Beach"—that is, Jack's father.

Jack, unable to glide over this, admitted to Inga that "I talked to him

Sunday night and he spoke to me about it. He said he got the [FBI] report. He said he had just talked to [name deleted by FBI] and he said things aren't quite right up there [in Washington]. I said I didn't believe that. He said he was just telling me what he heard."

"What is it they say?" Inga prompted.

"I guess the thing isn't quite O.K. for some reason. You are mixed up in something."

"I wonder what it is?"

"It's probably me," Jack answered chivalrously, "but I don't know. Evidently you got something. You're not holding out on me, are you?"

"I'm quite sure of it."

"I don't know. It might have been something you said to [name deleted by FBI]," a remark, Jack postulated, which "could have then become the subject of general conversation."

"But what could the conversation be about except you and me? There's nothing illegal they can put their hands on. What's illegal about being in love?"

"But maybe there is some background on you. You can see that," Jack offered, thinking of Inga's associations with Hitler, Goering, and Goebbels, as well as her husband's work for Wenner-Gren in Peru.

"Yes, I can," Inga agreed. "Then it would be much better for me to get a divorce because the only thing they have on me is that my husband works for Wenner-Gren."

But would divorce solve that? Instinctively Jack thought Inga unwise to get divorced merely to dissociate herself from Wenner-Gren or her husband, who could "take care of himself. . . . I think your judgment in this case is not altogether good," he commented.

"I'll listen to your advice."

"I don't know. It's up to you whether you get [divorced]. I don't want to influence you in any way in getting it."

"That's childish. I'm still going to get it," Inga insisted, "and we decided not to see each other anymore, didn't we? So what do you have to do with it?"

Jack was unconvinced. "You think that's correct?" he asked, spurring Inga to bite back:

"No, it's not the wise thing and it's not the thing a Kennedy would do," she said sarcastically. "I'll do it because I want to do it . . . and I don't care if I even lose my job."

Meanwhile, Inga told Jack, she'd arranged to see the director of the FBI in an attempt to kill the rumors circulating about her.

"What are you going to say to him?" Jack asked.

"I'm going to say 'now look here Edgar J., I don't like everybody listening in on my phone!' You know that somebody is always listening in on this phone," Inga remarked—her very words being recorded as she spoke.

"How do you know?"

"Why on earth does it always cut? Don't you notice . . . ?"

"They must have little to do if they are listening to us. They must have had a pretty dull week," Jack joked.

"If they listen to us, then yes," Inga agreed. "I'm going to tell him that I would like to know a little bit about the whole thing myself because I hear nothing but a fantastic amount of rumors from everybody and I am after all, the chief actress in the play."

Jack was dubious as to whether Hoover would admit to ordering the FBI phone tap.

"Why shouldn't he?" Inga demanded naïvely. "I'll say it's spoiling my career—which it is."

Jack didn't agree.

"Do you think I am going to hush you up—to try to catch you?" Inga queried.

"Yes."

"Jack!"

"I was just kidding."

"You know how I think about worrying you and everything like that."

"Of course," Jack deferred. "But I was thinking you don't know about your job. Mrs. Patterson might wake up some morning and decide to cut that column out. There you would be—without a job and all these other things holding over."

But Inga remained adamant.

"I just wanted to be sure that this is what you want to do," Jack said, attempting to clarify the situation in his own mind. "From what you have said, I didn't have anything to do with you getting the divorce."

"You pushed the last stone under my foot," Inga declared, "but that doesn't hold you responsible for anything. Meeting you 2 ½ months ago was the chief thing that made up my mind. As far as I am concerned, you don't exist any more," she lied. "That's how I felt an hour ago. I still love you as much as always and always will. But you don't figure in my plans whatsoever."

There the matter was left. Though Jack pleaded from Charleston, where he was now virtually paralyzed with back pain, for Inga to "come down this week-end," Inga refused. In what she intended to be her final, valedictory love letter she wrote:

> My impulse is to throw everything overboard and get away. Not because I want you to make love to me and say charming things. Only because I wish more than anything to be with you when you are

sick. You know dear, everybody wants to be at your side, when you are feeling a 100% [*sic*] well. It is different when we are down for some reason or other. If I felt I could really be of help and do something, every hesitation would be pushed overboard and I would be down Saturday. But dear, there is a but. Probably it is wisest to stay here. There is one thing I don't want to do, and that is harm you. You belong so wholeheartedly to the Kennedy-clan, and I don't want you ever to get into an argument with your father on account of me. As I have told you a dozen times, if I were but 18 summers, I would fight like a tigress for her young, in order to get you and keep you. Today I am wiser, Nevertheless I may as well admit that since that famous Sunday evening I have been totally dead inside.

A human breast to me has always been a little like a cage, where a bird sits behind. Some birds sing cheerfully, some mourn, others are envious and nasty. Mine always sang. It did especially for a few months this winter. In fact it sang so loudly that I refused to listen to that other little sensible creature called reason. It took me the F.B.I., the U.S. Navy, nasty gossip, envy, hatred and big Joe, before the bird stopped. In the beginning I was just stunned darling. Then I slowly woke up. Hard to start and realize that you are a living corpse! . . .

Once I said, "If you ever need me Jack, call me." It still holds good. It wasn't said in a flippant mood. It was really written with heartblood, if that doesn't sound too drastic and repulsive. So, it stands. If ever I can ease you a pain, physical or mental, come to me, or I will go to you. It won't be a matter of petty pride. It won't be, "I can't go to you, but if you come to me, it's all right." Pride is fine. Too much spoils ones own and others' lives. Please don't ever let pride ruin a friendship which started, which I hope wasn't ruined because you had me too easily. If you feel anything beautiful in your life—I am not talking about me—then don't hesitate to say so, don't hesitate to make the little bird sing. It costs so little: a word, a smile, a slight touch of a hand. Those were the things meant, when some idealist said that "the beautiful things in life cost nothing." We shall realize all that in the near future, because life is going to be tough, and double hard for the people who have ideals, who have hopes, who have someone they really love; who understand humanity.

So writing, Inga made her way to Reno to seek her divorce while Jack attempted to get used to life without Inga.

Fighting for Dong Dang

Still unaware that the affair with Inga was over, Torby Macdonald wrote from Boston on March 9 to ask "how your plans with Inga are coming as I have more than an academic interest in that phase of your life—our troubles have funnily & coincidentally run in the same pattern," he maintained.

Torby's answer to romantic distress was that they should both put to sea "with me as your valet or in charge of diet & we can involve ourselves in some feminine troubles in the lower color scheme," he suggested.

> As a veteran habitué of the Balinese Room I figure a few days in Bali could get us in a lot of trouble (I hope). Seriously though I figure that we're rapidly joining the ranks of the young middle-aged & there's no sense helping old age creep up on us—let's get the hell out of jobs that were deemed for older men—and while I realize this war is no "Great Adventure" or a Harvard-Yale game, we might as well see what its like & not live the same sort of life we've lived in pre-troubled times—if we do we'll probably regret it later on.
>
> I figure that if we've lived through some of those Boston-N.Y. trips, Long Island Roads, Paris à Cannes, Kit Kat arguments etc., those German Japs haven't got our number, as we have a good many more friends (at least guys on the same side) than we ever had before; that food will be better than the Officer's Club at Charleston or the Thompsons Spa in Park Square [Boston]—& there undoubtedly will be a hell of a lot of laughs. Let's put the show on the sea.

Torby was not alone. One by one all Jack's friends from Hyannis Port were moving toward battle. George Mead had joined the marines and was shortly to go overseas on active duty. Chuck Spalding was training as a naval fighter pilot. Even Jack's brother, Joe Jr., was nearing the end of his training as a patrol pilot in Jacksonville.

Affecting disdain, Jack wrote to his Harvard buddy Jimmy Rousmanière, who was training under General George S. Patton, that "if I was getting up a list of unpleasant places to spend wars, somewhere near the top of the list would be sitting in a bumping, rattling, noisy tank with you sitting over me, kicking me, and bellowing into my ear which way you wanted me to go."

Charleston was nevertheless frustratingly quiet. Earlier, Inga had been heard by the FBI telling Kathleen she was "trying to get Jack to do book reviews for the paper, which he would be allowed to do, so he can keep his face and name alive in Washington, as Charleston and Norfolk are so dull," but the enforced ending of their romance had closed this avenue, and Jack decided not to pursue publication. "Inga seemed very sad, yesterday," Kathleen wrote Jack. "She says she isn't going to see you anymore. I haven't inquired into the story but I certainly would like to."

Denied the pleasures and anticipations of love, Jack devoted much of his time at Charleston to writing long letters in his office which were then beautifully typed by his clerk and often addressed to complete or relative strangers. In a long letter to the American-born Lady Astor, the doyenne of the Cliveden Set in England, for instance, he tackled the matter of isolationism in America head on, five days before the Allied surrender of 100,000 troops at Java and four weeks before the capitulation of American forces at Bataan:

> I imagine that you've been watching the manner with which your homeland has been getting on with the war with some impatience. Our criticism of England's mistakes has been great over the past decade, and like most ardent critics, we have been so busy with our criticisms that we have profited nothing. Rather, we seem to have studied them so carefully, they have interested us to such a degree, we have become so enthralled with them, that we have decided to carefully and painstakingly duplicate them in an American, and I fear, deluxe edition. This process can go on ad infinitum as England unfortunately seems to be able to think up new ones as fast as we appropriate her old ones. Our supply for the immediate future seems to be particularly well assured.
>
> I suppose you are wondering when we are going to realize that declaring war is only the beginning, and that wars are only won by fighting them. We're wondering that ourselves—a great American pastime is to try and figure out why we're not. And the ball is handed back and forth from labor to business to the farmers to the public and to the government. And so it goes around and around, and I suppose they are all right to a degree.
>
> Of course, one of the great troubles is that isolationism is by no means dead. It was supposed to have died a rather violent death December 7, but it didn't. It's merely recuperating for the second and major round, and it is aided in its convalescence by the disastrous news from the Far East.
>
> As an old and close "isolationist," I hate the new isolationism, which is nurtured upon fear and defeat, and which, I think, bears

little resemblance to the isolationist policy of pre-war days, at least as I understand it. If we pull out of this war now, we will be down the drain presently and permanently. Resistance to aggression through, we'll retire back to our none too secure fortress and await the inevitable day of disintegration and subsequent invasion. I doubt if this isolationist drive will succeed—I don't think you can stop a thing as big as this war in the middle. But this delaying action that the isolationists are fighting is exacting and will continue to exact a frightful toll from our war effort.

As a matter of truth, it isn't only these isolationists that are the great menace, it is really the great lack of comprehension of what exactly this war is about. I think that it is a fundamental truth of American policy that if you scratch the average American deep enough, you'll find an isolationist—I don't mean in the political sense, but rather in his whole ingrained psychology. He has to be sold this war idea (the Japs were the best salesmen), and the selling job hasn't been completed. He still looks at this war from a somewhat detached and academic point of view, as war for the vague principles of the Atlantic Charter and the Four Freedoms. As long as that's the spirit, and that's the argument, we'll go on expending small amounts of toil and sweat, and great amounts of money, in the confident belief that victory can be "appropriated." I am afraid that the criterion for success in this country has been money for so long—that we have been indoctrinated with the folk lore that money can buy anything—that certainly it can buy victory. We'll see that it can't, and then, maybe, we'll see that we are not fighting for Dong Dang, but for ourselves, and that while it doesn't matter a damn what happens to Dong Dang, it does matter and matters a great deal more than parity prices, 40-hour weeks, cost plus contracts, what happens to the U.S.A.—and then maybe we'll get down to the very disagreeable and very necessary job of fighting this war.

Jack's own enforced inactivity made such insight all the more aggravating to him. The inability of the Allied armies to match their German or Japanese counterparts disheartened him. Roosevelt seemed willing to commit only token numbers of troops to battle, and those merely "to give a boost to Churchill." Meanwhile the War Department seemed unwilling to bring MacArthur, currently embattled at Bataan, home to galvanize the military bureaucracy in Washington; "He seems to have planned his end a little better, although he is being licked too," Jack commented tartly.

To his sister he wrote even more gloomily. Lord Hartington, son and heir of the duke of Devonshire, was deeply in love with her still, but Jack now discouraged the romance, as she had discouraged his, though for different reasons.

> After reading the papers, I would advise strongly against any voyages to England marry any Englishman. For I have come to the reluctant conclusion that it has come time to write the obituary of the British Empire. Like all good things, it had to come to an end sometime, it was good while it lasted. You may not agree with this, but I imagine that the day before Rome fell, not many people would have believed that it could *ever* fall. . . . It was the same way with France. She's been a second rate power ever since Sedan in the 1870's but it wasn't until May 1940 that its fundamental weaknesses could be seen, stripped naked without the protection of the rosy glasses and the mist of its Napoleonic tradition. It's the same with England. Singapore was only the symptom, the cause goes back long before Chamberlain or Churchill. It goes back, I think, fundamentally, far beyond any special event. It goes back to a state of mind really, which is a phase of its organic growth. When a nation finally reaches the point that its primary aim is to preserve the status quo, it's approaching old age. When it reaches the point where it is willing to sacrifice part of its status quo to keep the rest, it's gone beyond being old, it's dying—and that is the state of mind England reached some time ago. . . . In a war like today's, tradition and a way of life and a great past history are merely excess baggage that impedes movement, and makes the way easy for the enemy. We've reached the same stage, ourselves. Of course, we are in a somewhat better position—we've got an old man's mentality, but unlike England, a young man's body, so we might pull through. . . . Now those aren't very happy thoughts, are they? But it's good practice for my typewriter, and they're probably not right. I wouldn't bet that they weren't, though.

Kathleen, in Washington, took Jack's frustrated crystal-ball gazing with a pinch of salt, but Lady Astor was alarmed by the undercurrent of Joseph P. Kennedy. "I loved getting your letter, but as you say, it was pretty gloomy, and you have no right, at your age, to be gloomy," she answered Jack. "You young people will have a wonderful chance to make a better world, but you have got to be very bold and very good to do it. You Jack, particularly. You have got to look at Europe and its consciousness, and see what's wrong with it. I need not tell you more; people have got to do their own thinking and lean on God, who is Spirit and Love, and not on men."

Jack's father, meanwhile, declined to alter his own morbid opinions, plying Jack with further predictions of disaster by telephone and by letter, and forwarding to him in Charleston every anti-Churchill, anti-Roosevelt, and anti-Hopkins cutting, confidence, or correspondence he received. He wrote, for example, to tell Jack a recent visitor from England had "stopped off to see me this week and he is definitely of the opinion that England's economic situation will force the people to crack, and that soon. The food situation, the cost of living, and no victories, he believes, will finally finish them off."

The British were far from being finished off, however, and Joe Kennedy's defeatist peddlings merely made him the more despised in America, and his children's lives the more difficult. To his daughter Kathleen on March 2, for instance, Kennedy complained "that with you popular opinions are frequently accepted as true opinions." However, he cautioned testily, "the majority are only occasionally well-informed. . . . So don't bum rides on other peoples opinions. It's lazy at best—and in some cases its much worse."

Kathleen refused to take her father seriously, never abandoning her belief that Britain in the end would prevail against the Nazis. Moreover, though she respected her father as a parent, she was constantly reminded by others of his reputation as a maverick. "A funny thing happened the other day," she reported from Washington to the whole family.

> A rather cultured gentleman called to give Mr. Waldrop an idea for a column. . . . I asked his name. He said that it didn't matter—it was just an old Irish name. I replied, "Tell me because I certainly have an Irish name."
>
> He said, "What is it?"
>
> "Kennedy," I answered.
>
> The voice continued, "I've liked every Kennedy I've ever known except Joe Kennedy."
>
> My ears perked up. "Why don't you like him, I hear he's quite a nice guy?"
>
> With a bite in his voice the answer came from the other end, "I know him; I went to college with him."
>
> That was his reason. I never did get his name. When I told Mr. Waldrop he said laughingly, "That will teach you not to be so curious."

Meanwhile Jack did his best to help his father. As he'd once written to persuade his father of the importance of the Lend-Lease Bill in helping Britain stand alone, so now he encouraged his father to change course and abandon his earlier isolationism, as Jack had done. "From what I've read and heard lately—the 'Cliveden Set of Washington' article—the Daily News and the Times Herald editorials—Roosevelt's speech—the battle between isolationism and interventionism is just beginning its second and major phase," he wrote on February 25, in an effort to make his father see that the new "fighting phase of this war" was distinct from anything that had gone on before. Even if "the country is somewhat undetermined exactly why we want the Phillipines [*sic*] or exactly why we really need Java if we have all those synthetic rubber plants that are going up like—mushrooms I believe is the word that is being used—aside from this suspicion," he pointed out that the president would be "aided by the fact that no one wants to quit when the going gets particularly tough. The fight for the fight's sake will keep us in as will no amount of Four Freedoms or Atlantic Charters. . . . When the tears and blood phase begins and the Bells really start to toll, then will come the great test. I imagine Roosevelt will swing it, he's got to swing it or he is presently and permanently down the drain."

Emboldened by Jack, Mr. Kennedy wrote to the president on March 4, pleading for a position. "I don't want to appear in the role of a man looking for a job for the sake of getting an appointment," Kennedy apologized, "but Joe and Jack are in the service and I feel that my experience in these critical times might be worth something in some position." Arthur Krock loyally orchestrated a newspaper call for Kennedy's return. Roosevelt dangled a carrot, and on March 12, 1942, Kennedy lunged, flying instantly to Washington. "Daddy arrived yesterday afternoon," Kathleen reported to Jack. "He is in quite a quandry about the job."

Kennedy's continuing state of national disgrace, however, was reflected in the mountains of mail the White House received once news leaked out that Roosevelt was thinking of offering Kennedy a post in his administration. Thus the job Roosevelt did offer was a humble one, advising on bottlenecks in the shipbuilding industry. After consulting various old colleagues such as James Landis, Kennedy regretfully declined.

For Jack this news came as a great disappointment. Once again, Jack's father had accepted his advice, but had followed it with poor judgment. Both Congress and the FDR administration were filled with former appeasers and isolationists who on the night of Pearl Harbor had altered their stance and rallied to the nation's colors. Had Kennedy once more joined the administration, even in a humble capacity, he might well have gradually earned his way back into presidential and popular favor in a long and grueling war. A maverick to the last, Kennedy chose, however— just as he had after returning from Britain in 1940 with his threats to blackmail the president—to hold out for something better. He got nothing.

In the circumstances, only his sons Joe Jr. and Jack could restore the family's honor.

The Simple, Touching Truth

While Jack urged his father to face up to the new realities of the war, he himself remained determined to understand its origins. He read every book and every editorial that appeared on the subject and was quick to take issue with the author or editor if he disagreed. Liddell Hart's long letter after reading *Why England Slept* still moved him, and the unending series of British defeats, from Norway to Singapore, bore out Hart's contentions. To one newspaper, which blamed Hart for his misguided theories of limited warfare—"symptomatic of a lamentable confusion of thought from which even the Democracies have not yet completely emerged"—Jack responded that the confusion lay in the mind of the misguided editor, not Liddell Hart or American Democrats. Hart had not argued that "defense is the best attack," as the newspaper claimed, but that a democracy is at a military disadvantage against a dictatorship, and must adjust its strategy accordingly. Initially the democracies would have to rely on their defenses, as they had during the Napoleonic wars, before raising and training forces to counterattack. Nor had Hart claimed sheer numbers of men would assure security of defense, Jack clarified, but that a ratio of at least one to three in tanks and aircraft was necessary. This ratio of equipment the Allies had not attained and still could not field. "If Hart and others had been followed, the French and British armies would have had far less man power, but they would have been completely mechanized and armored and might well have been capable of countering any German penetration in France," Jack argued. "The great trouble in England before the war was that the limited school of warfare was accepted only half-heartedly and it was accepted as meaning a limited effort rather than a limited, compact striking force. British desires for economy, complacency and inertia in high and low places—these caused a half-hearted acceptance of Hart's theory, which meant disaster."

Equally, those who blamed Munich without reference to its antecedents were treated to lengthy strictures from Charleston. On March 10 Jack wrote to the author of a new book, *Boom or Bust,* that Hitler had not, in Jack's view, succeeded solely on the back of domestic economic failure.

It was "the failure to solve the problem of mutual disarmament that doomed the Moderates," Jack considered, harking back to his Harvard paper on the League of Nations, as well as his honors thesis. "By the Allied failure to carry out the provisions of General Disarmament" Hitler had derived the ammunition he needed in speaking of "broken pledges. . . . In spite of later attempts to deny it, the Allies' obligation was clearly contractual, and the great aim of German policy in the 20's was to force the Allies to live up to this contract." By the time the British recognized the problem, it was too late. The 1932 Disarmament Conference was a failure and "that really doomed peace for our time. . . . I do not think it unreasonable to say the great crisis in diplomacy of the last decade was not reached at Manchuria, or in the Rhineland, or Spain, or Munich, which are popularly believed to be the great might-have-beens of the democracies. Rather, it came in the spring of 1932, when the German moderates led by Bruening [*sic*] came with their hats in their hands to ask not for an actual equality of armaments, but only that equality be conceded in principle, while ample safeguard would be granted the French to insure them practical superiority." If the French had only accepted this compromise, "it would have strengthened the German Moderates at home immeasurably. Bruening, with this great victory under his belt, a victory which would have raised the prestige of Germany through the world, and that of his own administration at home, might well have had the political ammunition to blow the rising forces of Nazism off the face of the earth."

French intransigence, in Jack's view, had sealed the German chancellor's fate. "It was too late now; Bruening had been thrown out on his return to Germany with his failure, and had been succeeded by von Papen and Schleicher. The German price was up. Nazism was on the march to complete power. The Germans, despairing of achieving equality through negotiation, decided to gain superiority through force. And so for want of an election [the French election of 1932, in which Tardieu played to a rightist gallery and was defeated] peace was lost; and Mr. Bruening teaches at Harvard, while Hitler rules Europe."

"I'm not defending appeasement," Jack added:

> It has been proved a failure both by our own experience and by Britain's. But what I am trying to show is that the popular version of appeasement and its causes is not completely the true one and that in our bitter attacks on it, we missed the fundamental truth that the Munich pact and other concessions were not so much a failure of British diplomacy to provide security as of British democracy to provide armaments. Chamberlain, and the other appeasers should have been attacked not for the appeasement policy as such, but for

their failure to take full advantage of the breathing spell that their policy granted them. We also may as well plead guilty to the same indictment, the prosecutor would need only point to the headlines to convict us. . . . We wasted bitter criticism on the symptom—and missed the cause. If we had not made the mistake of assuming that appeasement was purely a selfish policy drawn up by a group of Tories at Cliveden to save their own hides, our rearmament program might have started a year and a half sooner.

Firing off such historical salvos, however, was gallingly futile for a young naval ensign who, increasingly, wished to see action. He had completed the compulsory correspondence course he was taking in naval regulations and sea lore and in an effort to improve his physical fitness embarked on a course of back exercises. On March 11 he wrote to Billings that he'd "finished the Atlas courses and believe I'm well on my way to HEALTH, STRENGTH and PERSONAL POWER, whatever personal power is. I can see that with time I will be POWERFUL, GRACEFUL and MAGNETIC. The exercises are very enjoyable to do and most helpful. I only succeeded in throwing my back out on Exercise 1, lesson 4.

"Things are going nicely, and there is no real news. I haven't seen Inga, but I understand that she is heading for Reno. It would be certainly ironical if I should get married while you were visiting in Germany," he remarked, confirming that Billings was quite right "about owing me dough for your stay in Charleston. . . . The plane trip was 28.00 and the meals were about 4.00. You gave me 20.00. So you owe me 12.00. As I knew you would be bothered by it the entire time you were travelling I have deducted it from a [departure] present I'm giving you, as I can't wait 15 years. I need the money now. So consider it deducted." He added a postscript apologizing for the "shortness of the annals above, but the 4:30 bell just rang and my God, you can't expect me to write letters on my own time."

In truth, however, things were not going nicely. He missed Inga and by late March 1942 the pain in his spine was so intense and his stomach cramps so debilitating that he was granted ten days' unpaid leave to go and see his specialist doctors in Rochester and Boston.

Since Jack was traveling at his own expense, he flew first to Palm Beach to spend a weekend with his family, and to see his friend from his Stanford days, Henry James, whom he'd invited to stay. From the Kennedys' house on North Ocean Boulevard James dispatched a lovelorn postcard to Flip Price, saying he was "lonesome for the [Stanford] farm. Jack sends his best. In his Navy uniform he can't be surpassed."

Jack's naval uniform, however, didn't impress his father, who subjected Jack and James to such a "tongue-lashing" that the whole family cowered in their seats "apparently frightened to death," James later recalled.

"I didn't like him [Jack's father]," James recounted, "because he got very angry because we came in late for lunch. His father said, 'Jack, for God's sakes! Can't you even get on time to meals! How d'you expect to get anything done in your life if you can't even arrive on time?!' Jack said, 'Sorry Dad'—and blamed it on me, the bastard!'"

Henry James was appalled at the way the family deferred to such a despot. But for Jack and his brothers and sisters, this mealtime behavior was par for the course, knowing as they did that "the ambassador" was upset over something far deeper than the "grave sin" he accused them of committing; indeed, as Arthur Krock observed, they felt sorry for their father, seeing him so despised and rejected by Roosevelt.

Jack cannot have failed to be aware of this, and his lack of protest at being berated by his father belied not simply fear of an angry and disappointed man but compassion too. As later with the Communist witchhunter Joseph McCarthy, Jack simply couldn't bring himself to turn on a friend or relative when he was down, and the sight of his father being publicly humiliated by Roosevelt pained him deeply. At the end of his letter to Lady Astor he'd remarked, "I am afraid you might think that gloominess is hereditary," whereas in temperament Jack rightly felt himself to be very different from his father. The more his father was passed over, however, the more determined Jack became to somehow avenge his fall from grace. Winston Churchill's father, Randolph, had also once stood within reach of the prime ministerial crown, only to see it wrested from him by others and his own personal misfortune: syphilis. That experience had given Churchill an almost manic desire to succeed, first as an officer in the armed services, then as a politician.

In his own way Jack too wished to do right by his humiliated father. For years he'd rehearsed and reexamined the history of appeasement and isolationism, continuing to do so long after Pearl Harbor had made it redundant, determined to be as worthy of the father he loved as was his older brother, flying PBM Mariners.

Joseph Kennedy was not impressed. The sight of his scrawny, disabled second son still determined to put to sea was somehow pathetic—a further reason for his outburst at Palm Beach. Blinkered, ruthless, rich, and obsessed with power, Joseph Kennedy could not see the simple, touching truth: that Jack was doing this for him.

The Limping Monkey

"Henry, you know, there's this beautiful girl in Washington," Jack confided to Henry James at Palm Beach. "It was Kick who introduced us. I'm afraid she's dangerous. She certainly has connections with the Fascists in Europe, Germany especially. But as to being a spy, it's hard to believe she's doing that, because she's not only beautiful, but she's warm, she's affectionate, she's wonderful in bed. But you know, godammit Henry, I found out that son-of-a-bitch Hoover had put a microphone under the mattress!"

Henry James was horrified. "Jack!" he recalled saying. "This is more than just your aspirations! You could go to jail! You could go to jail for consorting with the enemy! I mean, she sounds like someone to stay away from! Jack, I hope you're not gonna continue *that* relationship!"

"He just looked at me," James remembered. "Wouldn't say anything— wouldn't say yes, wouldn't say no."

From Palm Beach, Jack flew to the Mayo Clinic in Minnesota, and from there to the Lahey Clinic in Boston to see Dr. Jordan. Both agreed that if Jack wished to go to sea, he would first have to have an operation on his spine.

"Dear Children: Since I stopped writing you regularly I am a little confused as to where to begin," Rose Kennedy wrote from Florida in her next newsletter to the children at their boarding schools. "Jack has had quite a history since I last wrote you. His back gave him considerable trouble at Charleston so he came down here to talk to his father about it. His little tummy was also kicking up, so he had a consultation with Dr. Lahey in Boston and it looks as though he would have to take care of them both for a while."

Lem Billings, having spoken to Kathleen in Washington, was disturbed. "She said you are having a lot of trouble with your back again & this time you may have to have an operation," he wrote to Jack, who had meanwhile returned to Charleston. "I hope like anything that this isn't true as it would mean that you would be out of the Navy for quite awhile—& I know what a big pain in the ass that would be. I can't imagine what started it up again—I hope it wasn't an overdose of Charlie Atlas exercises. You will remember that he doesn't guarantee anything unless his exercises are accompanied by a rigid schedule of good clean living," he reminded Jack, having previously noted that his own recent bout of infectious streptococcus was "as active in leaping as the crab with which you are so familiar." He ended by asking Jack to "let me know if this back stuff is true or whether it's sensationalism on Kick's part."

Unfortunately for Jack the "back stuff" was real. On his Charleston fitness report, Captain Pryor of the District Security Office gave him a 3.0 out of a possible 4.0 rating, remarking that Ensign Kennedy was "modest, quiet and unassuming in spite of much wealth. Earnest and studious. Interested in his work and does it well." Pryor added the ominous remark: "Has been greatly handicapped by trouble with his lower spine which will require long surgical attention."

To Billings Jack wrote on April 9, 1942, to record his latest plans. "I expect to be leaving here in about ten days for my operation. If you're still here why don't you come down—I thought I might go home for a couple of days, or at least as far as Jacksonville to see Joe. From there we could drive up to Washington as I am giving Kick my car. I'll let you know more definitely later." The same day he formally requested six months' leave in order to have the operation and the subsequent period of convalescence. The operation, he said, was "to be performed by the family surgeon at a private hospital for a condition which existed prior to entrance into the navy. The physician of the Sixth Naval District [Charleston] concurs that the operation is necessary."

Jack's immediate superior, Captain Pryor, recommended approval of the request. However, the commandant of the district did not, at least not without further investigation. Jack was therefore ordered "to report to the U.S. Naval Hospital, South Carolina, for determination of your physical condition."

There followed a veritable merry-go-round of hospitalizations and diagnoses. On admission to the Charleston Naval Hospital on April 13, 1942, it was noted that "during the past 6 months his attacks have been more severe. Recently he has been examined at the Lahey Clinic and the Mayo Clinic. They have advised fusion of the right sacro-iliac joint. . . . Impression: Dislocation, chronic, recurrent, sacro-iliac joint, right." The naval doctors disagreed, however, about the advisability of surgery as the best way to resolve such chronic dislocation. Only after a month of tests, examinations, and physical and pharmacological treatments in Charleston's naval hospital was Jack finally authorized to go to Boston, and then it was to the naval hospital at Chelsea, rather than the Lahey, though he traveled at his own expense.

Leaving Charleston in mid-May 1942, Jack finally reported at the Chelsea Hospital in Massachusetts on the eighteenth only to encounter further disagreement over the need for surgery. "He now feels that he is not getting ahead, and, as wants to get sea duty he came in here for a check-up. An outside doctor feels that pain in no way resembles a ruptured I-V disc, but is probably due to sacro-iliac strain from tight muscles, in his legs and abnormal posture consequent thereto," the medical officer at Chelsea reported to the Bureau of Medicine and Surgery in Washington.

Instead of having the back operation, Jack underwent a battery of new tests, X rays and anatomical examinations over the next month.

Inga, meanwhile, had written from Reno wondering "how you are getting on, how that back of yours is behaving, and what you think of life in general. It may be tough now and then, but you know how to hold the reins and steer your horses the right way. May you never be at a loss," she wished tenderly, "and let me know where and when you set sail. If you feel like hearing about the West then drop a line, and I shall try to entertain you. You do know that if you are sick, I will love to write to you, if you would like it, but let me know—that is all.

"So long," she ended, "some day we will have a steak, mashed potatoes, peas, carrots, and ice cream again. It won't ever be like the old days," she mourned, "but you have a great future, don't ever let anybody make you believe anything different."

Touched by her letter, Jack telephoned Inga from the Chelsea Hospital on May 24. She noted, "Last night there was a hard knock on my door. The janitor came in and said 'somebody wants a person called Inga-Binga. Is that your married name?' I looked puzzled, went to the phone and a very optimistic voice said 'Will you pay a collect call from John F. Kennedy in Chelsea Mass? Well! nobody ever knocked me with a hammer on the head, but compared to that news it would have been mild."

Jack had begged a "good long letter," and Inga complied, reflecting on Jack's imminent birthday.

25 years. I hear it weighs heavy on the shoulders. Responsibility and life is just starting. Happiness and pain. Hopes and failures. Love and hatred. And as I know you, you will have plenty of it. That golden goblet which contains the elixir of life will be drunk greedily by you. But you have so much brains that you will know when to sip and when to make it bottoms up. I hope you will be happy, and as I have said so many times before, that you will get all you want.

Now you are back in bed. That back of yours and all the other ailments your dad told me about, (you are grand at keeping secrets, but don't forget there are other Kennedys than you.) I can't see you tied to a bed, even with two steaks a day from the Ritz.

Plans? I love to hear that word, because you always have a hundred. The 99 you tell me, and the one you really hope will materialize you keep to yourself. Maybe wise. Maybe right. And I believe that a person ought to live, we can't monopolize each other, even if we are the best of friends. Even lovers shouldn't and too often do.

Be brave. I don't even mind to see you a Navy-hero. But duck when the Japanese or German bullets aim at that handsome chest or bright head. You are just too good—and I mean good—to be carried home.

Inga's own plans, once she obtained her divorce on June 3, were to clear herself of any suspicion of espionage. However, as Jack had feared, the divorce did not release her from J. Edgar Hoover's tentacles. Thanks to Axel Wenner-Gren's latest movements in the Bahamas and South America, the FBI suspected a new plot to prepare the way for a German invasion. One FBI informant claimed that "any attempted German invasion of South America would strike first at the Upper Amazon because an expeditionary force, once established there, would be very difficult to dislodge." Supplies for such a German invasion could, it was claimed, be brought by oceangoing ships up the "inland rivers from Bolivia through Peru and Brazil to Columbia. They can land supplies closer to the Panama Canal in a line of direct flight than any United States base in the Caribbean except Jamaica." The FBI was now convinced Fejos's expedition in Peru must be phony, and that Dr. Fejos must be a Nazi stooge. "His wife, who is divorcing him, is reported to be a former favorite of Hitler. At present she writes a column for the Washington Times-Herald under the name of Inga Arvad," Hoover reminded the president.

On May 4 Roosevelt replied that, "in view of the connection of Inga Arvad, who writes for the Washington Times-Herald, with the Wenner-Gren Expeditions' leader, and in view of certain other circumstances [including the affair with Ensign Jack Kennedy] which have been brought to my attention, I think it would be just as well to have her specially watched."

As Jack had predicted, divorce from Fejos—who was later found to be completely innocent of anything resembling un-American activity—had not brought Inga release from Hoover's nefarious tentacles. Once she returned to Washington, she was followed by FBI agents day and night, her telephone was tapped, her apartment broken into, and her mail intercepted. The FBI even overheard her saying that "she was very disgusted with the FBI business and how the FBI and the Navy handled Jack. She blamed it all on Washington bad luck and said the Navy moved him to Charleston because she and Jack were always together, though there was never anything wrong in what they did. She said she did not blame the FBI in the least because she thinks everyone should be investigated, and added that a lot of people pushed the FBI into investigating her. She said it was awful and that at cocktail parties, etc., it seemed as if each was looking at her and trying to decide if she was a spy or not."

Inga's lamentations, however, had not the least effect on Hoover's stony heart. Meanwhile in Boston, after a month of examinations and medical debates, the naval doctors charged with Jack's case concluded that Jack was indeed suffering muscular strain rather than a ruptured disc, and on June 24, 1942, he returned to duty in Charleston, South Carolina. Lem Billings, who'd heard the news from Kick, felt this to be a great mistake, regretting deeply "that you have decided to postpone your operation & take exercises instead. Of course I don't know a damn thing about the circumstances, but to me, it doesn't look like the best thing to do. As far as I can see you're merely putting off the inevitable, because you'll probably have to have the operation sometime anyway. You'll just fool around for a couple of years with exercises—being still unable to do anything you want for fear of throwing it out again."

Jack, however, agreed with the less drastic diagnosis of the Chelsea Hospital doctors. On his way back through Washington he'd begged for a seagoing appointment, as his father reported to Joe Jr.: "He has become disgusted with the desk jobs, and as an awful lot of the fellows that he knows are in active service, and particularly with you in fleet service, he feels that he ought to be trying to do something. I quite understand his position, but I know his stomach and his back are real deterrents—but we'll see what we can do."

Charleston, without the distraction of Inga, was more tedious than ever. "In this Navy as everyplace else it's not so much what you know as who you know," Jack had written to Billings in April; meanwhile, renting a small house on Sullivan's Island near the beach with some fellow officers, he waited impatiently while his request for sea duty was processed.

His mother's duplicated newsletters from Palm Beach, though written with the best of intentions, only served to irritate the lonesome ensign. "Thank you for your latest chapter on '9 Little Kennedys and how they grew,' Jack sneered. " 'Never in history have so many owed so much to such a one'—or is that quite correct? If you would look in that little book of yours under Churchill, Winston I imagine you can check it."

Inga had been both lover and mother to Jack. Reading his real mother's rambling, trite, prudish productions in which no observation was too trivial to mention yet no honest reflection ever broke the bounds of her Irish-Catholic mindset, Jack fumed. He craved Inga's company—yet knew in his heart of hearts the affair was over. In particular his mother's blinkered approach to religion acted on him like poison ivy. The navy had asked him to "conduct a Bible class here every other Sunday for about ½ hour," he informed his mother with a certain relish. "Would you say that is un-Catholic?" he asked, ridiculing her bigotry. "But don't good works come under our obligations to the Catholic church? We're not a completely ritualistic, formalistic, hierarchical structure in which the Word, the truth, must only come down from the very top—a structure that allows for no individual interpretation—or are we? However, don't worry about this, just send me Father Conway's Question Box as I would like to look through it."

Meanwhile, the end of Jack's Charleston torment was at hand. His fellow ensign at the Navy Yard, Fred Rosen, later recalled how "in the spring of 1942, the US Navy sent out a call to a couple of thousand officers in the same category as Kennedy and myself, who wanted to go to sea and yet had not been trained. There was a midshipmen's school being formed for them in Chicago, and we were asked to file applications."

Both Rosen's and Kennedy's first applications to Chicago were rejected by their superior officers, not because of unsuitability, Rosen made clear, but because replacements could not be found to take their places in Charleston. Fortunately for him and Jack, though, the demand for places at the Chicago midshipmen's school had proved so great that the navy decided to repeat the accelerated course, and sent out a second call.

Jack's superior officer was now of two minds. The U.S. Naval Reserve Educational Center on July 9 awarded Jack a "superior" 3.91 rating out of a possible 4.00 in a correspondence course in foreign intelligence. Yet it was equally clear to Captain Pryor that Jack's scandalous affair with a suspected enemy spy ruled out future promotion in Naval Intelligence. Captain Pryor thus changed his mind and, without insisting first on a replacement, approved Jack's second application.

Several weeks went by. When no response was received, the Charleston Naval Headquarters, at Jack's urging, cabled Washington. Finally, on July 22, 1942, a telegram arrived from the navy's personnel department addressed to the Commandant, Sixth Naval District:

ENS JOHN F. KENNEDY I V(S) USNR HEREBY DETACHED PROCEED CHICAGO
ILL REPORT TO NAVAL RESERVE MIDSHIPMENS SCHOOL ABBOTT HALL
NORTHWESTERN UNIVERSITY TEMPORARY DUTY UNDER INSTRUCTION.

Jack was overjoyed. On his way to Chicago he stopped off in Washington and, spurning his father's warning, saw Inga one last time. Inga was alarmed. As she explained in a telephone call to a friend (monitored, as always, by the FBI) "He went through town and just a few minutes ago he was here and then he is going on active sea duty. Only you know, his back—he looks like a limping monkey from behind. He can't walk at all. That's ridiculous, sending him off to sea duty."

Ridiculous or not, Jack's mind was made up. His days in naval intelligence were over. Concealing his bad back and tender stomach, the limping monkey now embarked upon the next, extraordinary phase of his career, this time as a warrior.

PART
·10·
ON THE WAY
TO WAR

Lt. (j.g.) John F. Kennedy (back row, left) graduating as one of John D. Bulkeley's "expendable" PT boat skippers, November 1942 (John F. Kennedy Library)

Sixty-Day Wonder

Northwestern University's Abbott Hall midshipman program had been designed to produce seagoing naval officers in three months. "Came back on the train with alot [*sic*] of little sailors who were being transferred from San Diego to Boston," Kathleen soon wrote to warn Jack. "One of them had been on the Oklahoma [at the Battle of Midway] and was hit by a piece of shrapnel. The way they talk about the ninety day wonders is unbelievable. They have absolutely no use for them at all and said they wouldn't salute unless they had to. Of course some of them are pretty good they said, but the idea of them learning how to be sea officers in 90 days just kills them."

What Kathleen didn't realize was that Jack, arriving at Abbott Hall on July 27 as an already-commissioned ensign, was taking an even more accelerated course in seamanship at Tower Hall which produced seagoing deck officers in just two months—"sixty-day wonders."

After months of relative idleness, the pace of instruction seemed unrelenting. "You are probably quite a bit leaner by now," Jack wrote to Lem Billings, who'd finally left New York for Egypt. "If you're not—I am. Am out at this sea school in Chicago—sleeping eight in a room—and B.O. can be exceedingly dismal," he complained. "This is certainly a different company I am working for now than before. The food is stinking—no fresh vegetables and the daily order of bologna is always pimento tinted. I'll go along with the Department a good distance in their drive for economy, but this concentrated drive to starve us to death will keep me off the editorial page just so long. However there is a good bunch here."

The good bunch did not include Torbert Macdonald. Torby had cabled to Charleston in July that "if going depends on me, hold off as unbelievable complication has hit me. Sorry isn't the word. Try to understand."

"Torb never got here due to that gal of his," Jack complained in his letter to Billings. "Zeke [John Coleman] was at Abbott Hall—but got kicked out of the Navy for high blood pressure three days ago after being in there for 7 weeks—he's trying to get in another branch of the service." Rip Horton had gotten married and was now "I understand in charge of colored troops. Incidentally," Jack joked, "there are some Princeton men stationed near here—they say they are doing very well under white officers." The chief and most disastrous news, however, concerned Inga.

"As you probably have not heard—Inga-Binga got married—and not to me," Jack mourned. "She evidently wanted to leave Washington and get to NY—so she married some guy she had known for years who loved her but whom she didn't love. I think it would have been much smarter for her to take the train as they have several a day from Wash to N.Y. Anyways she's gone—and that leaves the situation rather blank."

The shock of Inga's defection (Inga had resigned from the Washington *Times-Herald* at the end of July and had moved into an apartment in New York with Nils Blok, who'd begged her to marry him) was not made easier for Jack by the tough discipline of midshipman's school.

> You'll be interested in knowing that it bears a remarkable resemblance to Choate, and my record here is also exceedingly similar—being caught in bed one minute after reveille etc. and other serious offenses like that. Speaking of getting married, I imagine that you have heard that the work-horse of the New Deal Harry Hopkins, got married. I guess that he was referring to an entirely different idea when he told the Russian War Committee last May that he was going to open up a second and a third front this summer. I believe the third front may have been Miss Paulette Goddard. She stayed a weekend with him at Hyde Park—and got a commission as Major for her boy-friend Anatole Litvak. It must be quite a thrill for Harry to order contraceptives and heavy cruisers for the same week-end.

Closer to home, Jack's grandfather, Honey Fitz, now age seventy-nine, had decided to go into electoral combat once again, against the grandson of his archrival, Senator Henry Cabot Lodge. First, however, Fitzgerald had to win the Democratic primary. "He told me confidentially that he would win in a breeze and he does have a good chance," Jack thought. "It seems that his opponent—Casey by name—had a baby six months after he got married—and Mrs. Greene [Rose Kennedy's closest friend] and the Catholic women of Mass[achusetts] are busy giving him the black-ball for it."

Meanwhile Kathleen had been promoted by Frank Waldrop to write Inga's "Did You Happen to See . . . ?" column, and was "not doing too badly," Jack commented patronizingly. At a weekend house party at George Mead's house in Aiken, South Carolina, that spring, Jack had berated Kick for her fecklessness, but in his heart of hearts he knew Kathleen was neither feckless nor weak, but "playing the field" until she found Mr. Right. "She is still conducting that boys club down there [in Washington], but has found no one who can satisfy her very strict physical, mental and moral standards."

He noted that among civilians "the war fever rises slowly," but among the young men who would have to do the fighting against the Japanese there was more restraint. "George Mead has gone into the Pacific and we believe he may have gotten his big S. in the recent Solomon Islands engagement," he remarked, after scrutinizing reports of heavy American casualties in the landings on Guadalcanal. "Here," he evaluated North-western's war temperature, "it is subnormal. I haven't heard anyone say, 'I want to get a crack at those yellow bastards' since I last talked with 4F [medically unfit] Chic Farmer at El Morocco."

Finally getting to the point, Jack announced to his ex-Mucker friend that, with regard to his own future plans:

> I have applied for torpedo boat school under Lt. Bulkeley.
>
> The requirements are very strict physically—you have to be young, healthy and unmarried—and as I am young and unmarried, I'm trying to get in. If I last we get command of a torpedo boat—and are sent abroad—where I don't know.
>
> Everyone is away at schools and by winter's end will all be abroad in different directions. You are therefore not missing a damn thing, and are relatively the master of your own destiny—which I am definitely not—this goddamn place is worse than Choate—and Lt. J. makes Jack Maher look like a good guy—well, maybe not a good guy, but a better guy. But as F.D.R. always says, this thing is bigger than you or I—it's global—so I'll string along.

A Preference for PTs

Jack's decision to try and get into PT boats was news indeed, and stemmed from the remarkable publicity the handful of American torpedo boats in the Philippines had received in the United States after the Japanese invasion. Lieutenant John Bulkeley, in particular, had achieved undying glory by plucking General Douglas MacArthur from the fighting on Bataan in the Philippines in March and bringing the general back through 560 miles of Japanese-dominated waters to safety, a feat which, when written up in the American press, gave PT boats a glamour somewhat akin to that of Spitfires in the Battle of Britain, bravely battling against superior odds at a dark moment of the war. As a result the U.S. Navy had set up a new Motor Torpedo Boat Training School on the Atlantic seaboard at Melville, Rhode Island, with a two-month training program.

It was to Melville that Jack now wished to go, though he had no illusions about his life expectancy if accepted. A mutual friend, Francis McAdoo, was already there. "He got Bulkeley to take him even though married," Jack related to Billings. "I think personally he's crazy—he'll be away for years. So far in the war the fatalities in P.T.'s are ten men killed for every survivor—so I don't know why he leaves Cynth—but he must have good reasons for it."

The good reasons—as in the R.A.F. or the Long Range Desert Group of the British army—were comradeship, action, glory, and relative independence. With his ability to memorize and simplify complex data, Jack would undoubtedly have been better employed on a large warship or, as his Spee Club friend Ralph Pope reflected, in a naval headquarters. "Of course he should never have been allowed to serve in the [seagoing] Navy," Pope later admitted. "I found out later that he had kept his medical record quiet for all the years at Harvard, even at Choate— evidently nothing got out that he had a real back problem, a real serious one. But I never expected that he would ever want to go into PT boats."

Pope admired Jack's intelligence and powers of leadership, but failed to see that it was Jack's inability to tolerate discipline that dictated his desire to go into PT boats, discipline that inevitably brought back memories of Choate as well as his mother's mania for rules. Jack's entire life would be characterized by this fundamental dislike of authoritarianism, which he could barely conceal and at which he loved to thumb his nose. For these reasons a menial job at naval headquarters or in a minor role on a large warship was anathema to Jack. The rip-roaring "bucking broncos" or "devil boats," currently being churned out by the dozen in naval shipyards in New Orleans, New Jersey, and Miami, fitted Jack's bill perfectly. His performance at the Northwestern midshipman's school, in all areas from gunnery to navigation, was uniformly high. The only question that remained was whether Bulkeley would accept him.

Bulkeley's Fantasy

"Bulkeley had just returned, in about May, from the Philippines and he had had a terrible ordeal out there," recalled the Melville executive officer, Lieutenant Commander John Harllee. "He was assigned to temporary duty at Melville, but he was a national hero, who'd had a ticker-tape parade on Broadway and a best-seller, called *They Were Expendable,* written about him—it was written up in the *Reader's Digest.* So he was used to making bond-selling and recruiting talks at various patriotic rallies around the country."

Bulkeley had attracted so much publicity, in fact, that Roosevelt not only decorated him with the Congressional Medal at the White House, but treated him to a private audience in the evening. There, in seclusion, Bulkeley had not only extolled the virtues of PT boats to the president but had pleaded for two hundred of them to be rushed to the Pacific. With a sufficiency of PT boats, Bulkeley had promised the president, America could win the war against Japan.

Bulkeley subsequently repeated his juvenile fantasies to Jack Kennedy's class at Tower Hall in Chicago. "The PT boat is a great weapon. The enemy has not yet won a brush with one. Our little half squadron sank one Jap cruiser, one plane tender and one loaded transport, badly damaged another cruiser, set a tanker on fire and shot down four planes," he boasted, when in fact the only torpedo launched by Bulkeley's squadron that hit a Japanese cruiser failed to explode, while Japanese naval records would fail to indicate a single vessel even struck, let alone sunk by American PTs at this time.

To the inexperienced and innocent reserve officers and midshipmen at Northwestern University, Bulkeley nevertheless repeated the same absurd prediction he'd made to President Roosevelt: namely, that "500 PT boats would give the United States mastery over all the Pacific, and that a sufficient force could stop any kind of land invasion."

This was, in retrospect, a lunatic claim, as even Bulkeley's colleagues would later admit. Alvin Cluster, Jack's subsequent squadron commander, who knew Bulkeley well, recalled:

> He and I served on the *Saratoga* before we went to PT boats—he went about a month ahead of me. I liked John. It was only in later years that I realized that his zeal in promoting himself was outsize to the man himself.
>
> The big thing was MacArthur. If MacArthur had traveled out of the Philippines by any other method, you probably would never have heard of John Bulkeley. And that would have been a blessing.
>
> America desperately needed heroes after Pearl Harbor, and they would seize on any exploit or any battle to show how great we were. The only reason PT boats ever got the attention they did was that we had nothing else! They really didn't do a lot of damage. But Roosevelt had to point to somebody, and that's why Bulkeley and PT boats got all that attention. William White, who wrote *They Were Expendable,* seized on the exploits of Bulkeley's poor boats out there and expanded on them quite a bit. . . . John Bulkeley was really a joke to a lot of officers.

While Bulkeley fabricated the myth of PT boats across the United States, the war at sea against Japan was in fact already being won by American aircraft, warships, and above all, by submarines. PT boats were, militarily speaking, a deeply questionable employment of American time, resources, and magnificent personnel. Lieutenant Bulkeley, however, was as inspirational an orator as he was an inspirational warrior.

"Bulkeley arrived, I guess it was September at that point, and made this wonderful talk about the PT boats," Fred Rosen recalled. "He was actually recruiting for officers to volunteer for that service, because that was the only way you could get into it—the same as for submarines, and the same as flying."

Harllee, who accompanied Bulkeley to Chicago, later explained in all candor why they sought volunteers:

> The thing you really have to remember is that our torpedoes weren't much good. They went at twenty-eight knots and a lot of Japanese ships could make more than twenty-eight knots. So it was ridiculous to try and hit them with torpedoes unless you got very very close— *very* close. And it took an unusual type of person to go through the shot and shell that was required to get that near.
>
> Well, Bulkeley's doctrine was to get within five hundred yards of the enemy—this was before the days of radar, and we could only do that at night—you'd get blown out of the water at 10,000 yards in daytime. And it took a lotta nerve to get five hundred yards from a Japanese warship, even at night.
>
> You needed an unusual type of feller, and above all, you needed a volunteer, who was likely—that isn't always the case—but more likely than a person who's not a volunteer—to get in that close to the enemy, to that shot and shell.
>
> I made a preliminary talk at Northwestern. Then Bulkeley made his talk. Now he was a *very* effective public speaker. In the first place he was a national hero who'd been plastered all over the media at the time. In the second place he was a good and effective public speaker. So when he finished, most of them volunteered! I've forgotten the figure, but a *tremendous* number volunteered for PT boats.

Harllee was not exaggerating. Under the headline BULKELEY ASKS 50— 1,024 VOLUNTEER! the New York *Herald American* recorded on September 5 that

> Lieut. Commander John Duncan Bulkeley, of New York City, mosquito boat hero of the Philippines, was in Chicago today on one of his toughest assignments. He wanted 50 young men of surpassing courage to enter the dangerous service in which he distinguished himself, and when he issued his invitation at the Naval Officers School here, he practically was swept off his feet as 1,024 young

Ensigns, virtually every one in the battalion, stepped forth and asked for the job.

He then settled down with his staff to interview volunteers, trying by his own judgment to pick the 50 "fightingest," most aggressive, most eager men—which was not easy. His selections will train for torpedo boat commanders at the Navy's new mosquito boat school at Melville, R.I.

That a young lieutenant, temporarily promoted to lieutenant commander, could be given the pick of more than a thousand commissioned officers, all of them college graduates, was in retrospect incredible. Fortunately for the U.S. Navy, Bulkeley could choose only a small number.

What would be equally incredible, under the circumstances, was Bulkeley's consideration of Jack Kennedy. Not only was Jack no athlete, but he'd been in naval hospitals for almost two months already that year, with much medical opinion favoring a major operation on his back. Bulkeley later claimed he had "no idea Kennedy had any trouble with his back. And if I had known, it wouldn't probably have made a blind bit of difference, 'cos I had no idea what a dislocation of the spine was. I was looking for men who would fight!"

Harllee was even more emphatic, later characterizing as "a stinking lie" the suggestion that he had deliberately ignored medical evidence of Jack's incapacity: "Of course I knew later—all America knew. But I didn't know at the time he had any back trouble—nor did Bulkeley—and I didn't know it at the PT boat school at Melville! I don't think it showed up in the physical examination—most back trouble doesn't show up in a physical."

Harllee may have been correct about the routine physical examination, which, amazingly, was conducted without reference to Jack's medical file in Washington. But what Harllee *didn't* know was that Lieutenant Commander Bulkeley learned all about Jack Kennedy before making up his mind whether to accept him.

Lunch with Joe Kennedy

"It's true," Bulkeley revealed fifty years later. "Joe Kennedy approached me. I was pretty much of a public figure in those days. Joe Kennedy didn't need to go through anyone else to approach me—and he didn't. Contacted me himself—invited me to have lunch with him at the Plaza Hotel on Fifty-ninth Street, New York."

In Kennedy's special suite the no-nonsense naval officer was treated to the views of a no-nonsense businessman—and a father who took his role very seriously.

"Joe Kennedy had been fired as ambassador to England by his old friend Roosevelt," Bulkeley recalled,

> and he had a lot of bitter things to say about the president. Kennedy said that his son was a midshipman at Northwestern, and that he thought Jack had the potential to be the president of the United States. Joe said he wanted Jack to get into PT boats for the publicity and so forth, to get the veteran's vote after the war.
>
> Joe wanted to know if I had the clout to get Jack into PT boats, and I said that I did, and would interview his son the next time I was at Northwestern. If I thought Jack could measure up, I would recommend his acceptance, I told Joe.
>
> Mr. Kennedy seemed quite pleased and said he hoped Jack could be sent someplace that "wasn't too deadly," as he put it.

Though Bulkeley's memory may have suffered from the lapse of half a century, the gist of his account seems true to character for Joseph Kennedy. Even the FBI had already noted Kennedy's political aspirations for both his older sons; meanwhile Jack's letters to and from Inga made it quite clear that Jack himself harbored serious dreams of entering politics and even reaching the White House. Moreover, it was entirely in character that Joseph Kennedy should applaud his sons' military courage, while seeking to prevent them getting killed.

In some ways Bulkeley and Joseph Kennedy were opposites: the one a man of simple mind and legendary courage; the other a legendary appeaser, defeatist, and physical coward, of whom Walter Trohan, chief Washington correspondent of the *Chicago Tribune,* once said, "There ain't a gut in Joe's body. He'd cuss like a trooper when he got into a jam, but in a showdown he'd cut and run."

Bulkeley's stirring description of war in the Pacific was anathema to Kennedy, but he was wise enough to see that it would do Jack nothing but good in a later political career, just as Bulkeley was wise enough to see the advantages of having the Kennedy name attached to PT boats.

Harllee, voting for Jack's acceptance into the PT-boat school at Melville, was as enthusiastic as Bulkeley to take the ex-ambassador's son, for he too was reputed to be interested in getting "names" into the nascent PT-boat service. Meanwhile, as Harllee recalled later, it was "out of the question" to consider over a thousand applicants, so it was agreed that the program staff at Northwestern would first reduce the number to 240. Even then, Harllee admitted, it was really a bit ridiculous to interview that many people—but there was a war on and we didn't know any better.

It meant we only had a few minutes for each candidate. The school of course supplied us with a lot of information, and that helped keep the interviews fairly brief—we just had to make up our minds on a kind of empirical basis and decide who they were.

So that's the way it went. It was Bulkeley's talk and his publicity and whatnot. And furthermore, the people who were at Northwestern at that time—midshipmen and officers—were people who had volunteered—had rallied to the colors to use a cliché—very shortly after Pearl Harbor. They were patriotic people and top people who wanted to fight. The country was at war, and the ethos in those days was, "If the country's at war, I want to be up front."

And so these were some of the finest young men in America. It had taken some time to process them in the Navy and they had been sent to various schools—and they were pretty tired of schools! They wanted to get out into action! So they were very good candidates— excellent material from which to choose.

Bulkeley and Harllee spoke separately to each candidate, then compared notes. "He interviewed them and I interviewed them. We selected only those people we both agreed on," Harllee recollected.

Harllee was impressed by Jack's transparent belief in himself—the key to successful leadership—and by his genuine desire to get into PT boats. Not only did Jack have the requisite spirit and self-confidence to make a good PT-boat captain, in Harllee's view, but, like many Ivy League candidates, he had years of experience in small marine craft.

The later knowledge that Jack's father had worked behind the scenes to ensure his acceptance seemed entirely laudable to Harllee when comparing it with those families who sought to avoid their sons' call-up. "When you think of Dan Quayle, Vice President Quayle, and the stories about how his family kept him from going to Vietnam. . . . There's a lot of people in America who use political influence to keep *out* of combat, but Jack Kennedy used it to get *into* combat!" he remarked with feeling. Bulkeley had warned at Chicago: "Those of you who want to come back after the war and raise families need not apply; PT boat skippers are not coming back!"

Far from discouraging Jack, this had only increased his ardor. "His whole attitude about the war has changed," Rose chronicled in her latest family newsletter. "And he is quite ready to die for the U.S.A. in order to keep the Japanese and the Germans from becoming the dominant people on their respective continents, believing that sooner or later they would encroach upon ours. He also thinks it would be good for Joe's political career if he [Jack] died for the grand old flag, although I don't believe he feels that is absolutely necessary."

Meanwhile, the Chicago *Herald-American* reported on September 25, 1942:

> Fourteen hundred of an undisclosed total of naval officers taking technical training in seamanship, navigation and gunnery at Tower Hall will be graduated tomorrow, and 90 percent of them soon will be on active service.
>
> The young men are as truly a cross-section of American manhood as it is possible to gather. There are former lawyers, chemists, steel workers, salesmen, economists, professors and teachers; insurance executives, authors, newspapermen, merchant skippers, an orchestra leader, a son of an admiral and a son of an able seaman, bankers and booksellers, a member of the New York Assembly and a scion of the aristocratic Cabots. . . .
>
> Listen to these boys talk. It is the language of America—the hard-fisted, practical reply of free Americans to those who would enslave them; a breath of clean, invigorating, fresh air from the East, the West, the North and the South.

Pride of place among the fourteen hundred graduates was accorded to Jack Kennedy. "Listen," the report continued. "One says: 'I am John Fitzgerald Kennedy, 25. I come from Cape Cod, Mass. I have a brother, Joseph P. Kennedy Jr., who is an ensign. I have worked in the naval intelligence in the Navy Department in Washington and in the navy yard at Charleston, S.C. I am the author of a book: *Why England Slept*."

"It is action these boys want," the *Herald-American* declared. "Kennedy, son of the former U.S. ambassador to Great Britain, wants to get in the highly dangerous motor torpedo boat service as soon as possible. He may get his wish."

A Melville Rake

That Jack did get his wish was, of course, a medical scandal. Nevertheless his frustration was understandable. He was tired of desk jobs, and tired of the prospect of backwaters such as Charleston. He was also tired of schooling, as Harllee sensed that many of the candidates were. Aged twenty-five, Jack had attended six schools during his childhood and five colleges or universities. Yet to make it into PT boats, he again had to cover up his long history of back and stomach problems, as well as other, undiagnosed medical ailments dating back to his school days; a record of such continual physical breakdowns and hospitalizations that he'd often jokingly instructed his Boswell, Lem Billings, to title the biography he intended to write *Jack Kennedy: A Medical Story.*

The cover-up of Jack's medical record had, of course, started the summer before. But in that case his commission into the U.S. Navy had been as a specialist officer, inducted specifically for desk work in Naval Intelligence in Washington, where his health record was of little import. In concealing his medical history in September of 1942, however, Jack was embarking on deceit of a new kind: done deliberately to mislead his superiors into getting him assigned to a form of sea duty for which his health ruled him out: combat action in high-speed motor-torpedo boats, or "bucking broncos."

However little Jack thought about this matter, it was, biographically speaking, a key moment in his life. However noble his motive—to fight for his country—it would be significant: the start of a whole series of "necessary" deceits—medical, political, literary, and marital.

Of course, in a family where covering up was part and parcel of succeeding, there was nothing unusual in this. Rose Kennedy had for years covered up her disastrous marriage; Joseph Kennedy had managed to cover up a gamut of unethical behaviors from draft avoidance to stock-market swindling; together, they had even covered up the fateful decision to have their eldest daughter lobotomized, and had then sent Rosemary for the rest of her days to an isolated nursing convent in Wisconsin, never to be visited again or even mentioned again in Rose's newsletters to her children.

For Jack's mother the trick, as always, was not to know. "You cannot believe how well he [Jack] looks," she wrote to Joe Jr. on September 29, 1942, when Jack arrived at Hyannis Port with the exciting news that he'd been accepted by the Melville Motor Torpedo Boat Training School, "and how he has improved in his general attitude toward the ordinary conditions of life. . . . You can really see how his face has filled out. Instead of it being lean, it has now become fat."

Two days later, however, the ex-ambassador confided to his eldest son the truth. "Jack came home," he admitted, "and between you and me is having terrific trouble with his back. . . . I don't see how he can last a week in that tough grind of Torpedo Boats and what he wants to do of course, is to be operated on and then have me fix it so he can get back in that service when he gets better. This will require considerable manipulation and I have given up the idea of going to California with mother to see if I can be of any help to him."

Meanwhile, Jack began his training at Melville. Despite their vaunted speed (theoretically up to fifty-five knots) and shallow draught, the early PT (patrol torpedo) boats were in many ways an anachronism. Harking back to an age of wooden boats, they were constructed of plywood, were virtually unarmored, had execrable torpedoes, were without radar, and ran on highly inflammable aircraft-octane fuel. Modeled on British designs and dubbed by some writers "seagoing cavalry," the PTs were in many ways similar to steeds, not least the way they attracted rich and dashing rakes, as the old cavalry regiments had done.

Certainly Jack Kennedy soon qualified as a Melville rake. "I understand that you and Bunny Waters are twosoming it," Joe Jr. soon wrote to Jack, "and the bets are that there will be a threesome before long, and it won't be in bundling clothes but it will have a long beak and a shotgun, and he will answer to the name of Jolson, after he has given you a shot of lead up the ass."

Fred Rosen, Jack's friend from Charleston and Chicago, recalled how at Melville "Kennedy was the only one with a car. Every morning we'd begin by doing calisthenics, running and exercises. Then classes would begin at eight o'clock and would secure at three P.M. We used to play touch football every afternoon. Some of the officers would stay on the base if they wanted to study, and some of us would go to Newport—we weren't too far from town. And we'd all pile into Kennedy's car, oh, five or six of us in this convertible, and go to dinner. We'd have marvelous times in Newport. And on weekends we'd go down to New York; he and I would go down to New York almost every weekend."

After the boredom of Charleston and the grind at Chicago, Jack was back in his element. "It was quite an indoctrination!" Rosen remembered.

> Jack was familiar with New York social life is the way I'd put it. I wouldn't know which way to turn when I went down there at that time. I came from Dalton, Georgia. For goodness sake, it was the first time I was in the "21" Club in New York, was with Kennedy, and various other places we went to! Another fellow who went with us occasionally was Knox Aldridge—he was in the same hut with us at Melville, and he and I played on the same football team at the University of Georgia. We'd go down to New York and we had to catch a train at Grand Central sometime in the middle of the night to get back to base for our morning exercise around six A.M. That went on for two months!

The void that Inga had left in Jack's life was now filled by a series of chorus girls and models, in particular the Powers model Angela Greene. "I could tell you some stories about that! She was a wonderful person—

she became an actress and went to Hollywood after. We would go down every weekend and sometimes we would double-date. Angela would always get me a date with one of the Powers girls."

Charlotte McDonnell, Kathleen's friend and a Catholic, was another, more eligible playmate, though she would later deny that Jack ever actually proposed to her. "I went out with Jack lots of times," she recalled. "But he was never in love with me. He liked to think he was, when things were going bad and he didn't have anyone else, but he really wasn't. . . . He'd talk to Lem and he'd talk to Torby and he'd say, 'Hey, what would you think if I married Charlotte?' And they'd have a big pow-wow. But when it comes right down to the nitty gritty, did he ever ask me to marry him? No, he did not."

Part of the problem, for Jack, was that Miss McDonnell, like Flip Price, would not agree to sex before marriage, unlike Inga, Jack's Madame Butterfly. To Billings, meanwhile, Jack was his old imperious self. "No—that frantic looking figure riding that torpedo [the logo on the 'United States Mosquito Fleet' notepaper] above is not me—but it's the way I feel these days," he confided on November 19. "I'm just finishing a course up here at Motor Torpedo Boat School (PT.s). . . . Haven't heard a word from you—what the hell have you been doing? I was pleased to note that things picked up shortly after your arrival," he added, referring to Montgomery's triumphant victory over Rommel at Alamein.

"Things over here go on about the same. Zeke got bounced out of the navy due to high blood pressure and hasn't been able to get back yet though he still has hopes. Kick is still running that boys club down in Washington and doing that old column of Inga Arvad's."

This brought him back to Inga, who had at first refused to see or even write to him. "I know Nils will turn green and tear down the ceiling if I write to Jack," she'd explained in a letter to Kathleen, asking her to tell Jack that "afterall [*sic*] writing isn't so important, because the Navy marches by twice a day here, and I see their uniforms and only one face—a happy cheerful young one, who expects 100 percent from life and probably will get 99—that I pray for." Recently, however, Jack had heard from Kick that Inga "seems to be cooling towards her new husband so should be back in circulation again so maybe I'll grab her this time," though "speaking of that situation, as nothing new has been added—haven't seen anything that looks very different—so will probably end up with Charlotte."

"Ending up with Charlotte" was what Charlotte feared. Meanwhile the war was beginning to take its toll. "I suppose Kick wrote to you that George Mead had been killed—it happened out at Tulagi," Jack reported to Lem Billings. He did not dwell on the event. "Was down in N.Y. last week-end—Zeke was East for the Princeton-Yale game which Yale won—and we had a big evening—La Rue etc.—You were missed considerably. Drop me a line about your situation, Best, Jack."

In part, Jack's lack of sentiment reflected the hardened realism of a generation that would now reluctantly have to pay the supreme price for years of isolationist attitudes taken by their parents. But it also reflected Jack's earlier, devil-may-care approach to life, before he'd met Inga. From the "21" Club to El Morocco, and from the Bacardi Room in Providence to the Lobster Pot in Newport, he was determined to have a good time, enjoy fast company, and forget what he saw as Inga's betrayal.

Inga, however, saw the relationship rather differently. Reconstructing a typical scene at the climax of their affair, Inga later pictured herself and Jack spending a weekend together. "The atmosphere is one of understanding and great happiness. Their conversation is lively, sprinkled with good-natured gossip. We feel they are trying to avoid the main subject—their future, apart or together. He talks about his stay in Boston, and she feels through his enthusiastic account that his parents, sisters and brothers mean a great deal to him. He is attached to their way of life. She also knows, that if he marries her, he has to give it up, because his family disapproves wholeheartedly of divorces and wouldn't accept her. . . . She doesn't know whether John is mature enough to give up home, family and a big monthly allowance and live on the pay of a Lt., j.g."

This was, indeed, the dilemma. After twelve months' service as an ensign, having successfully completed his correspondence course in naval customs and lore, Jack had been promoted to lieutenant, junior grade. Yet, at an age when a twenty-five-year-old son might reasonably expect to be finding his feet in the world, Jack remained emotionally stunted. By nature he was open and affectionate, more like his beloved grandfather Honey Fitz than his Kennedy forbears. In a warm and sympathetic tribute to the ex-mayor of Boston, Inga Arvad had written in her 'Did You Happen to See . . . ?' column earlier that year that "Honey Fitz draws people to him. . . . In the Capitol the other day . . . when he had his lunch in the Senator's dining room, a dozen oysters on half shell, and oyster stew, everybody flocked around his table. . . . Like the stubborn Irishman he is, he sticks up for everything and everybody he believes in. He never brags. Never leaves anybody feeling small or miserable. Where he is, there is eternal sunshine."

This could scarcely have been said of Jack's father, who regularly left people feeling small and miserable, a trait that had grown worse the more the ex-ambassador was cold-shouldered and ignored. Thanks to his rift with Roosevelt, Kennedy now only rarely went to Washington. He had finally sold the family house in Bronxville. Apart from paid cronies, he had no friends. "I think the world outside his house was war for Mr. Kennedy," Jack's friend Chuck Spalding later surmised.

This war, however, was an increasing affliction to the ex-ambassador's children. After his years of absence during their childhood, he was now permanently at home, by turns hateful and loving, critical and helpful, gloomy and ambitious, deceitful and frank—a foul-mouthed, controlling, frightening evil eye his children could never escape.

Like his siblings Jack remained a victim of his father's bigoted, almost psychotic expectations, bound in the same powerful psychological vise that Inga, for all her beauty and womanly charms, had been unable to break.

Fred Rosen vividly recalled his incredulity when Jack showed him a letter he'd received from Hyannis Port. "Look at this, this is from my mother!' Jack said one day.

"Well, what is it, Jack?"

"Look at that, she's writing a letter!"

"I don't understand what you mean!"

"And he showed me," Rosen recounted. "In those days there were no Xerox machines—it was carbon paper, a *news*letter, to all of her children."

The letter ran:

Hyannis
October 9, 1942
Dear Children:

Dad came home from New York on Wednesday as it was our twenty-eighth anniversary. . . . Joe wrote to us this morning and it seems his latest concern is over a new moustache which he is raising . . . Bobby did not expect to get off for the holiday. . . . He will have to keep on his toes to get used to the new school. . . . We expected darling Teddy home over this weekend, but it seems the little angel got into a water fight in the lavatory . . . and got himself into trouble, so he was put on bounds for two weeks. . . . Kathleen wanted very much to get to Hot Springs this weekend. . . . I could not allow her to go down there without a chaperone . . . I do hope you will have a good time this weekend Pat. I do not blame you for being bored and I wish you knew a few exciting swains in Cambridge or New Haven. It is really not your fault that you do not. . . . I am sorry if you have to wear your old clothes, Jean. Your father and I are going to visit the Convent and I hope I shall have the pleasure of meeting Reverend Mother as I missed her last year. I also hope I shall hear words of praise for your application and industry. And please do not put on a lot of weight. It is so silly at school to eat that long bread roll, etc. . . .

Rosen remembered Jack going home only once, despite the proximity of Cape Cod; yet the emotional importance to Jack of belonging to a big family, despite the banality of his mother, the controlling authority of his father, and the secret tragedies such as Rosemary's lobotomy, was impossible to gainsay: still the one certain refuge in Jack Kennedy's tormented world.

Very Poor Training

Meanwhile, whether in El Morocco or the Quonset huts of Melville, Jack continued to cut his characteristic raffish, intelligent, witty, well-informed swath: the mixture of seriousness and callow, playboy lifestyle reflecting, as at Harvard, his always divided self. Yet, however self-confident and genial his manner, he secretly mourned the loss of Inga and hoped upon hope she'd repent of her mistake.

Sometimes Jack's shield would slip, and he would foist upon others the very ethnic prejudice he, as a boy, had himself experienced and which his father had transfused into Boston-Irish anti-Semitism. When Jack made an outrageous remark in his hut at Melville about the way the wily Jews were all "going into the Quartermaster Corps" to escape combat, his friend Fred Rosen, who was Jewish, bridled.

"They must be good at trigonometry, Jack," Rosen responded.

"Why?"

"Because the navy's navigators are drawn from the Quartermaster Corps."

"I guess I must have meant the Supply Corps, then," said Jack lamely.

Rosen, incensed, wouldn't let up, insisting that they take a survey of the religious backgrounds of all the volunteers at Melville, to see just how many Catholics there were compared with Jews. The argument became a cause célèbre in their hut, with Jack finally apologizing when Rosen proved the allegation to be untrue.

Rosen blamed Jack's father for Jack's unthinking anti-Semitism, and with good reason. Equally, he admired Jack the more for admitting his mistake. Indeed Melville marked, as Rosen later reflected, an important, perhaps crucial stage in Jack Kennedy's personal and political development. In the primitive Quonset huts, he was pitched in with officers from every state of the Union whether he liked it or not, thus forcibly enlarging his circle of friends and comrades.

Another PT-boat trainee, Sim Efland, later recalled how he'd first met Jack at Tower Hall, then shared a dormitory with him at Melville:

I was a southerner, and there wasn't too many southerners in there, you know. But I will say this: he was receptive to southerners, he was receptive to everybody. I did not consider him as a stuck-up individual, or superior in attitude.

Jack and I became very good friends, real close friends because he liked this tag football, which was pretty rough—I mean it wasn't just touch; our tag football was *rough:* you'd knock the hell out each other. Jack was a tall boy and he could jump, but he didn't know how to fake and feint. I'd coached for Tennessee. . . . I said, Jack, you gotta go down there and fake over this way and then that way, and I'll hit you. I played left half and would throw it to him. . . . We were very successful, our combination. We were on the same team, and we stayed close all his life—He'd visit with me in Carolina later.

Reflecting on what made their relationship different from other wartime friendships, Efland put it down to Jack's lack of pretension. "When I think of my association with Jack: he associated with people no matter who—and that was unusual. Here I was, a southerner, and all these other people from Harvard, Yale, and these other places would give me hell. Say, 'We can't understand what you're talking about, you don't talk like we do, you talk too slow,' or something.

"Now, Jack didn't do that. He respected people. He was also a good analyst, I felt, because he picked the boys we had on our football team. . . . I had a lot of respect for him."

While Joe Jr. failed to project himself as more than an ambitious, monied, Boston-Irish boy laboring under his father's grand designs, Jack somehow managed at Melville, as he had at Harvard, to win the hearts of his colleagues by his self-deprecating wit, reckless charm, and quiet courage. If Harllee did not know of Jack's back problem, Jack's fellow trainees did, and none gave him away. "One afternoon in Newport I had to drive all around town with him," Rosen recalled. "Finally we found a lumberyard to get him a piece of plywood that he could put underneath the mattress on the cot he slept on, because he had a bad back. Yes sir, he had problems with his back, way back then. But he'd go right on, I never heard a complaint out of him. I never heard him complain about anything, except he had to get this board to sleep on, which was common knowledge. . . . The boats were pretty shaking for someone who had a bad back—but I never heard him complain about it."

"Jumping Joe" Atkinson, a football star who followed Jack in the next batch of successful volunteers from Tower Hall to Melville, also recalled "the problem his back was giving him. He did have a back problem, and I used to tell him he was crazy—I said, 'You probably pulled strings to get this combat-zone job when people with connections would have done the opposite—but he wanted to fight in the war!'"

Whether the Melville Motor Torpedo Boat School was providing the right training to fight such a war, however, was a moot point.

"The first time I ever fired a torpedo was at the enemy!" Rosen later complained. "I never fired one at Melville! We *saw* one fired: there were twenty-five of us on the boat, and we saw Green, who was the torpedo officer at the base, fire one. That was the extent of our torpedo training at Melville—and torpedoes were our main weapon!"

Even more curious was the lack of night training when it was well known that PT boats were too vulnerable to enemy aircraft to operate *except* by night. "To my knowledge there were never any night torpedo runs against targets because the targets were too damn busy doing other things!" admitted Alvin Cluster, one of the officers responsible for designing the original course.

"This was a terrible mistake," Rosen reflected. Sim Efland agreed, saying, "We didn't have as much there as we should have." "The training was very poor," Cluster admitted. "A lot of the things we did at Melville were, in hindsight, ridiculous. Let's face it, the training that we gave at Melville was, in the light of the experience that they were to have almost throughout the war, relatively shallow. The main purpose was to teach you to handle boats, to be able to come alongside a pier, how to take care of your engines, torpedoes, radios—things like that."

Given Bulkeley's high-profile bragging and his attachment to the PT-boat school, the lack of appropriate training was scandalous. Bulkeley's boasting had sold the idea of a United States torpedo-boat navy, but not the substance. "It was unbelievable," Rosen recalled; "none of us had ever been to sea before, and here we're going out as either captains or execs of these boats!"

Meanwhile, as the eight-week course approached its end in late November 1942, the officers began to divide up into cliques and state their squadron preferences. "Jack had asked to go with us, a bunch of us from the South—we were going to get our boats in New Orleans, where they were being built; and while they were being built we were going there on precommissioning detail, a wonderful chance to learn how the boat works, and so forth," Rosen recalled—the "so forth" including New Orleans's well-known nightlife. "We could ask to go to the squadron of our choice. You weren't guaranteed to be taken, but you could ask for it. And he was going to go with us, to Squadron 14.

"Then all of a sudden one day he said, 'No, I'm not going to go.'"

PT 101

Rosen was dumbfounded. Lieutenant Harllee, it appeared, had interceded. As Harllee himself later recalled:

> I was Senior Instructor. . . . He [Kennedy] was a sincere and hardworking student and showed particular aptitude in boat handling. As a matter of fact, he was such an outstanding student that I selected him for assignment to the training squadron at Melville. . . .
>
> As soon as he was selected to remain in the training squadron as an instructor he saw me and insisted that he be sent overseas to one of the squadrons in combat. This was during the period of the war when PT boats were engaging very heavily in combat in the Solomons. . . . He felt there was no reason why he should be kept in the United States. . . . He was most insistent.

Jack was boiling with rage, certain that Harllee was keeping him at Melville not so much as an instructor but as a useful name. "He and I had some very hard words about this assignment, and I thought I had made another enemy for life, but I insisted that he remain with us," Harllee recalled.

Jack's disappointment was mitigated, however, by the fact that he'd finally managed to engineer a place for Torbert Macdonald at Melville. The Naval Material Inspector's Office in Boston was only too glad to see the back of Macdonald. As Jack's mother heard the story, Torb had been "in a dreadful mess again. It seems some woman, who signed herself 'A Conscientious Taxpayer,' complained that one Torbert Macdonald was using a Navy Station Wagon to call at a certain number on a certain street every day. The woman resented the fact that her tax money was put to such a use. The street and number turned out to be Polly Carter's [*sic*] house. . . . all very complicated."

"I got Torb in here yesterday so he will be reporting in a week or so," Jack meanwhile informed Billings on November 19, "and then I shall be around here instructing for a couple of months before leaving for someplace."

If Harllee thought that Jack was going to take his "shafting" (navy slang for unpleasant orders) without a struggle, however, he was very much mistaken. With the help of his grandfather, Jack quietly arranged an interview on November 29, 1942, with the all-powerful Massachusetts senator David I. Walsh, chairman of the Senate Naval Affairs Committee.

Walsh was impressed by Jack and his grasp of war strategy and international relations. "Frankly, I have not met a young man of his age in a long time who has impressed me more favorably," Walsh subsequently wrote to Honey Fitz. "He has a fine personality, energetic and outstanding qualities of leadership, and with all a becoming modesty."

"It was a distinct pleasure to see you on Sunday," the senator wrote to Jack, "and I am looking forward to keeping in contact with you, and will try to be helpful in the matter we talked about as I am returning to Washington today." He informed Jack that he was "sending under separate cover a book which I thought might interest you, entitled *New World Horizons.* I am sure the distances portrayed on the maps will be informative and will help you to follow the war more closely."

In the meantime, on December 3, 1942, Lieutenant (junior grade) John F. Kennedy began his new duties as a PT-boat instructor. On his latest fitness report, Lieutenant Commander Specht noted that "this officer only recently completed the course of instruction at the M.T.B. Squadron Training Center and is considered relatively inexperienced in PT-boat operations. He is however very conscientious, willing and dependable and will prove to be a highly capable officer with more experience. His personal and military characters are excellent."

Once he took command of one of the training squadron's seventy-eight-foot Higgins boats, *PT 101,* Jack's patience was sorely tried as a teacher. Ensign Paul Fay, recently arrived from the Abbott Hall training center, never forgot the day he failed to board *PT 101* for instruction and felt the lash of Jack's sarcastic irony, as Lem Billings had been doing since adolescence. Sending unintelligible semaphore signals to the effect that he wished to go out on another training boat, Fay had held up *PT 101,* carrying a full crew and fifteen students, for almost a quarter of an hour "so that I could make up my mind whether I wanted to go on his boat," Fay recalled. "Do you realize that if what you did was compounded by every single person in the United States going through training," Jack reprimanded Fay, "the war would be won by the Japs inside of three months?"

The episode revealed an even tougher, more determined officer than the "stringpole" whom Fay had first encountered during a touch-football game the day before. As Fay related, "the game was only underway for about half an hour when a seemingly young, bright-looking, skinny boy with a sweater turned inside out with an H sewed on the inside asked if he could get in the game. 'Get another man and you're in!' I replied. In about ten minutes this young fellow was back with another player—who looked like he had a lot more potential.

"Two plays hadn't been run before this skinny boy stopped the play with a claim that we were not adhering to the rules. I was piqued to think that after including him in the game he was taking issue with our interpretation; to my dismay, even over my vociferous contesting, his view prevailed."

Barney Ross, a big Princeton lacrosse player, later remembered the same game, and how young Jack looked:

> I mean, he seemed to me, the first time I saw him, I thought he was maybe 17 or 18 years old, and I thought he was a young enlisted man in the Navy. And he had a letter sweater with an *H* on his back, a red sweater with a black *H,* and I had just gotten out of Princeton that spring and down at Princeton we had the Hunt School, a prep school. I thought probably this young fellow was from the Hunt School.
>
> We were on the same team and we were huddling and he seemed to be running the team. That was okay with me. None of us were very old but—he seemed to be doing all right too. And the first chance I had, I said—to make conversation—Are you from the Hunt School, sort of introducing one another—and he said, No, I'm from Harvard. And I realized that I had a Harvard man on my hands!

As others would find, it was always a mistake to underestimate young Jack Kennedy. "We used to play there every afternoon for about a month," Ross related. "This was touch football—the kind where you can pass anywhere on the field, it's more like basketball. He was a good passer and he called all the plays."

Ensign Ross never dreamed for one moment that he would, within a year, be sharing Jack's rendezvous with destiny, any more than "Red" Fay imagined that he and Jack would become close friends. As much as he loved touch football, however, Jack was becoming more and more disenchanted with life as a Melville instructor, and his disenchantment was made worse by the pain in his back. "He suffered, even in PT-boat school," recalled Johnny Iles, another football star who'd come to Melville.

> I had the bunk next to him. Evidently they did it by alphabet and my name began with an *I* and his with a *K* and there weren't any *J*s. Torby was in there with us, in the other bed. He was a jock too, but he was a rather sophisticated jock.
>
> Jack had that plywood board. Also it was cold. I couldn't sleep 'cause of the cold weather. I woke him up one night and asked him to help me. "What do you Yankee boys do in this cold weather?" He

put newspapers under my mattress and from then on I was just like toast. He was always willing to help you. He was in pain, he was in a lot of pain, he slept on that damn plywood board all the time and I don't remember when he wasn't in pain.

I remember him throwing a book on my bed and saying, "John—get acquainted with this damn war—read my favorite book by my favorite author!" And he threw this book at me—his own book! I never read the book, though!

In addition to suffering the back pain, Jack was restless. He had not joined PT service to give lectures on navigation in a Quonset hut in Rhode Island. The work outside, aboard *PT 101,* was little better. Though the PT men did no night training, they put to sea in all weathers, and as Sim Efland recalled, "it was so cold that our wake would freeze on the fantail of the boat."

It was with great relief, therefore, that after five weeks as an instructor Jack received orders on January 8, 1943, to take four of the training squadron's boats on a thousand-mile journey to Jacksonville, Florida.

On the Way to War

"I was damn glad to get out of Melville," Jack wrote to Billings afterward. "That job of instructor you can have. That Newport was a different Newport than that which your family dominated in the years before 'jerry started his big stinks,' if I have quoted you correctly."

The only downside to leaving Melville, Jack acknowledged, was the disruption of his latest plan to go to war with Torby Macdonald.

I got them to take Macdonald in without him having gone to school beforehand for indoctrination. I was planning to tutor him, and then one day got my orders to go—which leaves Macdonald without a tutor, and the latest word I got was that he is having a hell of a time and he wishes he was back in the Park Square building [in Boston].

The setup had been perfect—I was going to go out with a squadron that Torb and Cy Taylor were going to be in, and Torb was going to be my executive officer [deputy]—and then I suddenly got the word. The only beauty of this is that I am the senior officer of the division and therefore have four boats, but I would rather have stayed up there and gone out with them, but that's war, as they say at Shepherd's [*sic,* the famous hotel in Cairo].

Though the five-day journey from the frigid waters of New England to the warmth of Florida held out the promise of winter sunshine, the voyage proved far from comfortable. "I got my orders yesterday and am on my way to war," he wrote to his brother Bobby from the boat. "For a guy who could never find Gardiner's Rock, Florida seems a hell of a distance. Am typing this as we bounce [typewriter keys wobble] along." Entering the Intracoastal Waterway at New York, the small flotilla was spared the high seas of the Atlantic, but on the third day, January 11, 1943, one of the boats went aground. While throwing a towline, Jack's boat itself ran aground, and the towline became fouled in *PT 101*'s propellers. Trusting to his swimming skills, Jack dived into the icy waters and untangled the rope, after which the four boats continued their journey south.

By the next day, however, when they docked in Morehead City, Jack became ill, with symptoms dangerously like those of his earlier bouts of sickness. Telephoning Torbert Macdonald at Melville, Jack asked what the weather was like. Macdonald said the water was freezing cold. "It's colder in North Carolina," Jack quipped from his sick bay.

Fortunately for Jack, his condition cleared within three days, the illness having been diagnosed as "gastro-enteritis, acute." ("While working in water freeing line from screws, had a chill and after turning in his own bunk became continually worse," Dr. Baumer recorded in a note that would be added in due course to Jack's mounting medical record at the Bureau of Medicine and Surgery in Washington.)

Meanwhile, on January 16, 1943, Jack rejoined his flotilla, which had proceeded through the protected waterway without him, at Jacksonville. Leaving the boats at the naval yard to be readied for war, he was given seven days leave and joined his family at Palm Beach.

"I'm now on my way to war, or so they tell us," he subsequently reported to Billings, "but we stopped off at Jacksonville for a little equipping. Went home last week and found Palm Beach never better. There are several changes in the situation as you knew it—the army has taken over the Breakers Hotel, but have installed some nurses who give the same excellent service that used to distinguish the Cuban Tea Room.

"Boogie Chase, who is 4F, was in Palm Beach with me, as he was taking a rest before starting his new job with a law firm. He's got a hell of a good one, and as he had just flunked his New York Bar, the manpower shortage must be acute. He says it's like going into J. Press to look over a suit—you can get in any law firm in the country. . . . You heard what happened to Zeke, how they flunked him out on account of his high blood pressure—well he got into the Coast Guard, and he just started his training. As a matter of fact," Jack pointed out admiringly, "you have seen more war than any of us as yet and I certainly think it was an excellent idea to go."

Jack didn't think it a good idea, however, for Billings to stay. "If you feel like coming back, I certainly would as you have done more than your share, and it's a well-known and well-acknowledged fact—so whatever you do you will have done a sufficiency."

Here, perhaps, was the key to Jack's attitude toward war. His father might well be nurturing a political master plan, as Jack's friend Chuck Spalding called it, for his eldest sons, involving a political future in which campaign medals could be won without action. Jack, however, had other ideas. Discussing grand strategy with men two or three times his age might challenge Jack's intellect, and teaching boat handling might keep him out of harm's way, but neither met the wayward urge to cut a figure—and to be seen to do so—that would bind him to his latest hero, Lord Byron, the roguish star of David Cecil's *The Young Melbourne.* His "reckless but handsome head," as Inga had once called it, now demanded action.

"Your friend Jock Pitney I saw the other day is reported missing," Jack reported to Billings, "and a class-mate of mine Dunc Curtiss, I think you may have met him, was killed on Christmas day." These were unfortunate casualties, but while they deterred Jack's father (who wrote to Father Sheehy, the Catholic chaplain at Joe Jr.'s base, that Jack's decision to go into PT boats "was causing his mother and me plenty of anxiety"), they didn't deter Jack. Not only did the battlefield offer a chance to raise high the Kennedy banner, but tempting fate was, in its way, a vital part of his narcissistic mystique.

According to Torbert Macdonald, competition with Joe Jr. played little part in Jack's yearning for such dangerous adventure. "It was a very normal, brotherly relationship. The amount of rivalry has been over-done." But was it? Johnny Iles disagreed. "The challenge of Joe [Jr.] being in naval aviation" was, Iles felt, a powerful stimulant. In Palm Beach the two naval officers posed together for a studio portrait in uniform for their mother, Ensign Joseph P. Kennedy, Jr., wearing the prized golden-wings emblem of a navy flyer, while beaming John F. Kennedy boasted the two gold stripes of a lieutenant on his sleeve.

A skein of friendly rivalry certainly ran through all Joe Jr.'s letters to Jack, even though he always signed himself "Your devoted brother." Joe Jr.'s courage, piloting huge, unwieldy American flying boats, was never in doubt, though the "yellow" ex-ambassador was certainly anxious that neither of his sons take too much battle heat. At Jacksonville Joe Jr. had ranked seventy-seventh out of eighty-eight graduating pilots. Despite unanimously negative reports of his "instructor potential," he also had been kept on as an instructor before being transferred to a safe backwater in South America, which looked suspiciously like his father's doing.

"Joe is in Puerto Rico preliminary to going out someplace," Jack subsequently wrote to Billings in North Africa, certain he could do as well if not better than his brother. Awaiting further orders in Florida, he displayed his usual mix of skepticism and eager anticipation. Rip Horton, he informed Billings, was currently in the Quartermaster Corps but was "contemplating going into Paratroopers—as he figured if my stomach could stand that, he could stand the other." Meanwhile, "Mac [Francis McAdoo] is in Guadalcanal which should be highly interesting." Kick, meanwhile, was still writing Inga's column, "which Inga told me the other day didn't quite pack the dynamite that hers did" (though not permitted to correspond with Inga, he had succeeded in speaking to her on the phone). Kick's roommate "Betty Cox is still free, white and 6 feet two—although both she and Kick are getting a little worried since Dinah Brand got engaged," he reported. Dinah's fiancé was thirty-four and "evidently one of those old bachelors that are set in their ways which is I believe to be our description when the war is over, as the marriage rate is extremely high. Inga incidentally is up in New York living with the old boy-friend of hers," Jack lamented. "Whether she is married or not is another story—but don't go into that with—" He began to write Kathleen's name, then crossed out the sentence.

"Well Lemmer, that is about all the news." He was not unhappy. "This job on these boats is really the great spot of the Navy, you are your own boss, and it's like sailing around as in the old days, though these motors take a bit of understanding as motors were never my strong point."

On January 22, 1943, Jack received orders to report to Squadron 14 in Norfolk, Virginia, when directed by the commander of Squadron 4 (Lieutenant Commander Specht) back in Melville. On January 27 Specht confirmed the orders, subject to direction by the superintendent of shipbuilding at Jacksonville. Finally, on February 11, Lieutenant John F. Kennedy was officially instructed to report to the assistant supervisor of shipbuilding at Jacksonville "for duty in connection with the fitting out of Motor Torpedo Boat Squadron 14," and it was there Jack learned the bitter truth: namely, that Squadron 14 would be sent to guard the Panama Canal.

A Change of Assignment

Squadron 14 to which Jack was now assigned had nothing to do with Fred Rosen's original Squadron 14 in Louisiana, which had lost all the boats it had been promised and had been renumbered Squadron 15, with orders to go out to the Mediterranean. Jack's newly formed Squadron 14, under

Lieutenant Commander Richard E. Johnson, would comprise a mere four boats, the same boats Jack had brought from Rhode Island.

After the business with Harllee over being held back in Melville as an instructor, this change of assignment looked suspiciously like Jack's father's doing. Meanwhile, to add insult to injury, Lieutenant Commander Harllee was given a dozen new boats to form Squadron 12, destined for service in the Southwest Pacific, and had decided to take Torbert Macdonald as one of the executive officers.

Jack, in Macdonald's eyes, had again been "shafted," and thus was leading given a new nickname, "Shafty." But the would-be warrior wasted no time. Guarding the Panama Canal was not at all what he'd had in mind as PT-boat service. Three days after the commissioning of Squadron 14, in a formal change-of-assignment request to the chief of the navy's Bureau of Personnel in Washington, Jack asked "that I be reassigned to a Motor Torpedo Squadron now operating in the South Pacific." Lieutenant Commander Johnson approved the request the same day, on February 20, 1943, but "only if relief is forwarded" to take Kennedy's place.

Unwilling to rely on naval bureaucracy or allow time for his father to interfere, Jack had already telephoned Washington and had spoken to Senator Walsh. The good impression he'd made the previous November now paid off. Even before Jack's formal application for transfer was processed, Walsh had set the wheels of the navy's personnel department humming. Though the orders took several days to reach Jacksonville, they were music to Jack's ears:

> You are hereby detached from duty in Motor Torpedo Boat Squadron Fourteen and from such other duty as may have been assigned you; will proceed via government or commercial air to the port in which the Commander Service Force, Pacific Subordinate Command may be and upon arrival report . . . for first available transportation including government or commercial air to the port in which Motor Torpedo Boat Squadron Two may be and upon arrival report to the commanding officer of that squadron for duty.

On February 22, 1943, Jack gleefully handed over the secret transmission codes for his four boats to his deputy, Ensign Sullivan, and the following day Lieutenant Commander Johnson endorsed Jack's orders to depart.

In a matter of days Jack would be fighting in the Southwest Pacific. Harllee's squadron would not get out for another six months. The shafter had been shafted, bearing out Jack's maxim that, in the U.S. Navy, it was not what you knew, but who you knew that mattered. The "limping monkey" was off to war at last.

PART
·11·
PT 109

Jack Kennedy (right) and his PT 109 *crew, Solomon Islands, southwest Pacific, in early July 1943, shortly before their traumatic sinking (John F. Kennedy Library)*

Steaming Toward Combat

On stationery headed "Mark Hopkins Hotel, Nob Hill, San Francisco" Jack wrote at the end of February 1943 to Billings's mother, asking her to forward to Lem in Africa what would "probably be my last letter to him for a good while." In the Harvard Alumni Bulletin for that month Jack claimed to have seen a picture of American Field Service personnel in the desert, and although they had "Lem listed as Somebody O'Malley Toole from Scranton, PA," Jack was positive "it was Kirk Patrick Billings from Baltimore. He looked very well. He is certainly doing his share—and more—and deserves a great deal of credit for doing so much more than he had to. I hope he gets back soon. Though the South Pacific is mighty large, I hope I shall run into Tremaine [Billings's elder brother] some place. Best always, Jack Kennedy."

The letter to Lem that Jack enclosed was uncensored. He was "finally" en route to combat, he told Billings, "and will be leaving in a day or so. . . . I am rather glad to get on my way—although I understand that this South Pacific is not a place where you lie on a white beach with a cool breeze, while those native girls who aren't out hunting for your daily supply of bananas are busy popping grapes into your mouth. It would seem to consist of heat and rain and dysentery + cold beans, all of which won't of course bother anyone with a good stomach." There were also "mosquitos and black marias with daggers. If it's as bad as they say it is, I imagine I'll be voting Republican in 44," he quipped. "By the way, I shouldn't be surprised to see Mac [McAdoo]—You probably have heard that Cynth is going to have a baby. If she can have one of those, I can stand the South Pacific. For awhile Torb and I and Cy Taylor were all in the same squadron but that bubble burst, so I am headed for another."

How long Jack expected to spend in the shark-infested Pacific was a moot point. "I may be back by fall as they keep revolving personnel around—and Inga Arvad's husband will still be here," he added sorrowfully. His sister Kathleen was planning on "going to England" with the Red Cross and "most everyone from here will be away," he wanted Billings to know in case he intended to return in the near future. Even Zeke Coleman was trying to get into the American Field Service, having been thrown out of the Coast Guard "last week—so you can see how tough they are," Jack remarked, referring to service medical requirements.

Jack's advice to Billings was to stay in Africa "thru the summer + fall if your assignment is any good—and maybe come back next winter," when Jack himself hoped to be home—"unless you are doing interesting work—or try to get sent to England or something."

As he set off for combat Jack made no mention in his letter of the possibility of death. Instead he called attention to the appearance, in a Baltimore paper, of a picture of LeMoyne Billings. "How did they happen to get a copy of the picture?" he asked. "Or did they just happen to find it in their morning mail from Cairo?"

With that and an injunction to "drop me a line" Jack was off. He reported at eleven A.M. aboard the U.S.S. *Rochambeau* in San Francisco on March 6, and at five o'clock that evening the troopship left from Pier 34, bound for the New Hebrides, northeast of Australia.

For Jack it was the beginning of the most dramatic episode of his life. Indeed it would be no exaggeration to say that the next few months in the Southwest Pacific would be the making of Jack Kennedy. Many thousands of miles away, across the Pacific, beyond the reach of his father, far from the disputations of appeasement, isolationism, and interventionism that had colored his early life, he would be on his own. At the age of twenty-five, moreover, he was at last steaming toward combat—the sort of action that had made his own heroes, from Winston Churchill to T. E. Lawrence.

Ironically, the talk on the officers' A deck as the ship passed Alcatraz and beneath the Golden Gate Bridge was of appeasement. A group of officers were arguing that if Neville Chamberlain had shown more backbone in 1938, at the time of the Munich conference, there would have been no Dunkirk or Pearl Harbor. Within minutes Jack was drawn into an argument with an officer in the next cabin, ensign J. A. Reed. Reed recalled:

> I was rooming with two other chaps, one from the state of Washington and the other was Paul Pennoyer, the grandson of J. P. Morgan, who had graduated from Harvard the year before and was going out as a torpedo pilot. Anyway a group gathered in the stateroom that we occupied, and in came this young man Jack Kennedy. I had heard his name—that was about all. But we got talking about Britain and appeasement. I was taking the position against Chamberlain and Kennedy listened to the argument, which was waxing very hot. He took the other side, and argued on behalf of Chamberlain. We argued for quite some time. . . . I did not know that he'd written the book *Why England Slept,* but I must say he made me look rather silly, but in the nicest sort of way.
>
> It was a trait of his: he could be critical of something, say an issue, but he wouldn't make it into a personal conflict, which was a won-

derful talent. As a consequence, he and I became fast friends. . . . He had a certain aura of shyness about him, which in itself was rather engaging. I must say that my first, initial reaction to him was a pure one—that is to say, I was attracted to him as an individual, having absolutely no knowledge who he was.

Reed soon became aware, however, as did another ensign. "We were all sitting around in my room one night when Rawley, who had also just graduated from Harvard, learned that Jack was Ambassador Joseph P. Kennedy's son. He told Jack that he'd heard his father speak on the radio and was so surprised that he didn't speak like the rest of the Irish trash from Boston. I think he meant it as a compliment! Jack just looked at him, but he told me afterwards he really had to control himself from punching that guy in the nose."

Here was the difference between Joe Jr. and Jack. Joe Jr.'s "famous patience" was, as Joe Jr. himself acknowledged, a euphemism for hot-headedness. He "lacked the ability to mix with those who were not of his background," Joe Jr.'s copilot in Puerto Rico, Norman Rudd, later remarked. He also seemed to abide by the New England Ivy League convention that you never speak to people unless introduced, another member of the squadron recalled, and you certainly do not nod at those to whom you have been, "the first time you meet them each day,"

Jack, by contrast, seemed to possess a quiet magnetism that drew people to him from wholly different social backgrounds, religions, educations, and states. Forty-five years later another young officer, Edgar Stephens from Missouri, recalled that "the ship was very basic—no frills about it. We were assigned seats to the mess table, and I was assigned a seat next to Jack. He impressed me then as a real quiet, very nice person . . . the type of person who knew how to state a point concisely, and a man who, having chosen a position, would stay by it."

Clearly, Jack was as captivating to men as to women, and to those his own age as well as older men such as Forrestal and Walsh. Whereas his elder brother was aloof and unconfiding, Jack managed to combine humility with intelligence. When he spoke about his father, it was not to boast or to seek kudos, but simply as a loving son awed by his father's personality and achievement. "I remember him talking about his family and father," Reed recalled. "He said to me, 'Jamey, you'd like my father. He thinks like this—he always goes *right* to the point.'"

Jack had certainly inherited some of his father's ability in this direction.

"We spent countless hours together, just talking," Reed recalled. "About books, life, history, girls. There was a kind of chemistry between us. We became the best of friends almost overnight." But forming new friendships was not Jack's first concern in traveling to the Southwest

Pacific. He had already toured Europe, crossed the Soviet Union, visited Palestine, and been to South America; he knew the Atlantic seaboard of the United States, from Massachusetts to Florida, better than most men of his age and station. He'd recuperated in Arizona and studied in California. But he'd never been to the Far East or crossed the international date line. The journey aboard the *Rochambeau* was, therefore, a journey to a new hemisphere for Jack, as well as a chance to review his feelings about the world he already knew.

Like Jack, Reed had sympathized with the prewar peace movement in America. "I was really persuaded that war was a terrible thing, and it was with great reluctance that I joined up in the navy. He was certainly not a warmonger, Jack Kennedy. Not at all. He was doing his duty like the rest of us, for a cause that he felt correct. Was he fearful? Did we discuss it? No, not that I recall. I know one thing we did, though. There were a lot of naval pilots on our troopship. He and I would sit and sort of look them over, and decide which ones just from their appearance were probable candidates to be killed. There was one young fighter pilot and both Jack and I decided he would be the first to go."

The Soft Underbelly

While the *Rochambeau* ferried its human cargo of officers and ratings to the New Hebrides, the whole direction of the war in the Pacific was taking a fresh turn. Though American marines and Australian infantry had finally succeeded in winning back the island of Guadalcanal, the American navy proved incapable of stopping the Japanese from evacuating much of their heroic garrison. Despite the courage of their crews, the much-vaunted PT boats proved particularly ineffective, owing to defective torpedoes, their wooden hulls, and their highly flammable gas tanks. Casualties in the PT units were high, without a single enemy transport vessel being disabled. Running steel-hulled destroyers down "The Slot"—the channel separating the northern and southern chains of the Solomon Islands—to Guadalcanal, the Japanese were able, in three nights, to evacuate almost twelve thousand troops with impunity. Even the patriotic American naval historian, Samuel Eliot Morison, was driven to express his admiration. "Never," he wrote, "in the history of naval warfare have there been such clever evacuations as those by the Japanese from Kiska and Guadalcanal."

It was as a replacement for casualties sustained in PT-boat Squadron 2, based in Tulagi, that Jack Kennedy was being sent out; but whether PT boats could serve an effective purpose in the area, given their recent performance, was questionable. Moreover, with the end of fighting on Guadalcanal in February 1943, the land struggle in the Southwest Pacific had now died down. Instead, the Allied commanders began fighting each other. Should the remaining Japanese garrisons on the Solomon Islands be allowed to "wither on the vine"? In fact, should the Allies concentrate their next offensive in the Southwest Pacific, or in the Central Pacific, closer to Japan?

The latter question had already been bitterly argued at Roosevelt's January 1943 conference with Churchill in Casablanca, where Admiral King, disliking Churchill's insistence on a "Defeat Germany first" strategy, had called Churchill a liar for promising to send British forces to help defeat Japan after the defeat of Germany without any real intention of so doing. Roosevelt, to cool tempers, declined Churchill's offer to write a special treaty on this issue. "The American people accept the word of a great English gentlemen," he had declared.

The ungentlemanly squabbles had resumed as soon as Admiral King returned to Washington. General Marshall wanted the entire Pacific theater to be under the command of an army general (Douglas MacArthur); Admiral King wanted it (or the Solomons end) to be under an admiral (Chester Nimitz). Irrespective of who was given overall command, the various Pacific chiefs also sent their headmen back to Washington to argue, this time over plans for minor offensive operations in the Far East, in the light of the Germany-first decision at Casablanca—plans that in turn provoked a major new controversy.

MacArthur's outrageous demand for more men and more planes was considered to be a bid for grandeur. Yet to fight the Japanese successfully, MacArthur had come to realize, he could not rely on the navy—and particularly not on Bulkeley's fantasy, the PT boats. U.S. planes, however, could only be furnished by the American air forces, whose frustrated generals wanted to unleash strategic bomber campaigns against Japan, not minor tactical operations in support of ground troops in the jungles of the Southwest Pacific.

MacArthur was thus opposed by the air force generals of his own army as much as by jealous admirals of the navy, and in the end the Joint Chiefs of Staff downgraded MacArthur's plans, agreeing only to a limited, two-pronged reduction of the smaller Japanese garrisons west and east of Rabaul (Japan's primary naval and military base in the Southwest Pacific), while Admiral Nimitz's Central Pacific strategy was approved.

The wrangles over strategy in the Pacific, ironically, mirrored those over the Second Front in Europe. In both cases, a tragically life-expensive compromise was reached, involving criminally costly landings and laborious land campaigns that sucked gigantic Allied efforts into areas of combat—Italy and the Solomon Islands—that were of no strategic value to the Allies, and allowed both the Germans and Japanese to demonstrate their formidable abilities of defense.

Far from stepping into the front line of the war, Jack Kennedy was thus entering a strategic and operational backwater by the time he arrived in Espíritu Santo, in the New Hebrides, on April 1, 1943. MacArthur's Southwest Pacific theater was destined to become, like the Allied campaign in Italy, simply theater: a grueling and divided sideshow, while the naval war in the Pacific would be concentrated on Admiral Chester Nimitz's Central Pacific force, boasting the largest naval fleet in history, comprising eleven aircraft carriers, six battleships, six cruisers, and a multitude of destroyers and smaller craft.

Fortunately for Jack, he had few illusions as he stepped off the *Rochambeau*'s gangplank at Espíritu Santo, though the sight of the misdirected American naval power crowded into the anchorage there was unforgettable. "I must say, as I look back on it, it was one of the most dramatic moments I have ever seen in my life," Reed recalled. "As we came in from the ocean into Espíritu Santo, there was a river a few hundred yards wide. It wound its way around so it finally opened into this harbor. And as we came in, fighter planes came down and flew over us, and as we came around the bend into this harbor, there was what was left of the American South Pacific Fleet. The *Saratoga* [carrier] was in there. Jack and I were standing looking at this thing, and I remember him saying, 'What a sight!' I mean, it really made the hair stand up on the back of your neck. It was so exciting."

Reed and Pennoyer were bound for Nouméa, in New Caledonia. Waving good-bye to them at Espíritu Santo, Jack disembarked into "one of those little boats they use as tenders," Reed remembered.

That evening, April 3, 1943, Jack boarded the transport landing ship, *LST 449*, which was to take him to Guadalcanal. The next morning at eleven A.M. the vessel weighed anchor and began its journey across the Coral Sea to Jack's destination, Tulagi.

Approaching the north coast of Guadalcanal at the end of its three-day voyage on April 7, 1943, however, the crew of *LST 449* suddenly saw a strange sight: a fleet of American transport ships and destroyers racing toward them. Having received no advance warning, they were in fact about to witness the largest Japanese air attack since the height of the battle of Guadalcanal: 170 aircraft from Rabaul reportedly making for Henderson Field and the Tulagi harbor. Within minutes the planes were overhead. One Japanese bomb lifted the entire stern of Jack's ship out of the water and broke the captain's neck.

Had the Japanese bomb hit the ship, loaded to the gunwales with fuel and high-explosive munitions for American squadrons operating in the

Russell Islands, the war, for Jack Kennedy, would undoubtedly have ended there and then, as it did for many of the men aboard the U.S. oil tanker *Kanawha*, which caught fire and sank, as well as the destroyer U.S.S. *Aaron Ward*, which was hit in the engine room and finally sank three miles from Florida Island.

This was not quite what Jack had expected of a war that was supposedly being won by America. "In regard to not liking the Jap way of fighting," Jack subsequently wrote to Lem Billings in Africa,

> to give you an idea what we are against—the day I arrived, they had a hell of an attack. As we were carrying fuel oil & bombs—and on a boat that was a tub—I thought we might withdraw + return at some later date, but the Captain evidently thought he was in command of the [U.S.S.] North Carolina as he sailed right in. Well, they dropped all around us—and sank a destroyer next to us but we were O.K. During a lull in the battle—a Jap parachuted into the water— we went to pick him up as he floated along—and got within about 20 yds. of him. He suddenly threw aside his life-jacket + pulled out a revolver and fired two shots at our bridge. I had been praising the Lord + passing the ammunition right alongside—but that slowed me a bit—the thought of him sitting in the water—battling an entire ship. We returned the fire with everything we had—the water boiled around him—but everyone was too surprised to shoot straight. Finally an old soldier standing next to me—picked up his rifle—fired once—and blew the top of his head off. He threw his arms up— plunged forward + sank—and we hauled our ass out of there. That was the start of a very interesting month—and it brought home very strongly how long it is going to take to finish the war.

The *LST 449* did in fact head back toward Espíritu Santo for some days in case of further Japanese air raids from Rabaul. Eventually the ship was ordered to turn about and finally reached Lunga Roads, Guadalcanal, on April 13, 1943, crossing north to Florida Island the next day. Disembarking, Jack then made his way by whaleboat across the channel separating Florida and Tulagi islands to Sesapi, or Calvertville, on Tulagi's west shore, home of PT-boat headquarters in the Southwest Pacific. At last, after eight months of training and travel, his PT-boat combat service was about to begin.

Home by Christmas

Johnny Iles and Joe Atkinson had preceded Jack to Tulagi, arriving "out there about the first part of April," as Iles recalled. "The war was pretty much over by then. Guadalcanal was secured. I told everybody about this fellow Kennedy, that he was a very dynamic person, I mean he had tremendous charisma. We were all in this big hut. It was just a big old native hut, kind of a bullpen, where we all slept. Our patrols were every other night. So we'd be resting around every afternoon just shooting the bull and I would tell them about this fellow Kennedy. They had a boat dock, and these metal aircraft plates, or matting, they used around the low areas of our base—and here I saw him coming up the 'runway'!"

Jack was relieved to see a friendly face so far from home. Reporting to the squadron commander, Al Harris, Jack was immediately assigned as temporary executive officer to Lieutenant George Wright, skipper of *PT 47,* a seventy-seven-foot Elco boat on which he went out on his first training patrols around Guadalcanal. "Squadron Two was in great flux," Harris recalled. "A lot of the skippers had done their time and were being rotated back to the States or elsewhere—and we had, really, a shortage of skippers."

The handful of tents and native huts were something of a shock to Jack after the Mark Hopkins Hotel. Moreover, Inga's failure to write him made the transition even more uncomfortable. "Dear Inga Binga," he began a six-page missive (which he had to send via Henry James lest Inga's Danish boyfriend open it), "It is becoming increasingly evident that since you have gone to work for the NANA [North American Newspaper Alliance] that you won't write a damned word unless you are paid and paid well. . . . This I refuse to do, and if an appeal for a report from you on the basis of our former friendly association leaves you cold, I will put it purely on the basis of a contribution to the war effort—and you can write it instead of knitting me a pair of socks."

In return Jack offered his latest impressions of the war.

> I would like to write you a letter giving in a terse sharp style an outline of the war situation first hand . . . in which I would use the words global war, total effort and a battle of logistics no less than eight times each. I refrain from this for two reasons, the first being I know you don't give a damn, and the second being that frankly I don't know a god-damned thing, as my copy of the Washington

Times Herald arrives two months late, due to logistical difficulties, and it is pretty hard to get the total picture of a global war unless you are sitting in New York or Washington, or even Casablanca.

I understand we are winning it, which is cheering, albeit hard to see, but I guess the view improves with distance. I know mine would. I wouldn't mind being back in the States picking up the daily paper, saying "Why don't those bastards out there do something?" It's one of the interesting things about this war that everyone in the States, with the exception of that gallant armed guard on the good ship U.S.S. Stork Club, commander—Lt. Commander Walter Winchell—want[s] to be out here killing Japs, while everyone out here wants to be back at the Stork Club. It seems to me that someone with enterprise could work out some sort of an exchange, but as I hear you saying, I asked for it honey and I'm getting it.

What Jack was getting, he admitted, was a far cry from the "picture that I had in the back of my greatly illusioned mind about spending the war sitting on some cool Pacific Beach with a warm Pacific maiden stroking me gently but firmly, while her sister was out hunting my daily supply of bananas." For one thing, the morale of the men was distinctly jaded after months of fighting in wooden boats that were temperamental, unable to reach their intended speed, armed with slow and ineffective torpedoes, which could not operate by day and for the most part lacked radar at night. Not long before, two of the squadron's boats, including the squadron commander's, had been sunk by Japanese destroyers, leaving the crews swimming in shark-infested waters until they were picked up the next day. What "the boys at the front" talked about was not the war, Jack pointed out, or even their corner of the war, but "first and foremost . . . exactly when they are going to get home. This is done with every conceivable contingency provided for, with no possibility of error and invariably is completely inaccurate."

"The second engrossing subject," he went on, "is a lurid discussion on how drunk they have been in their lives, and how drunk they are going to get," once home. "Mr. Rickenbacker was talking about other groups than those I've seen when he advocated bringing the boys back home from the front to increase production. They'd never even get down to the factory."

Meanwhile the shortage of skippers had at least guaranteed that Jack would be given his own boat. Accordingly, eleven days after arrival, on April 25, 1943, Jack assumed command of one of the squadron's only two eighty-foot Elco boats surviving from 1942: Bryant Larson's old *PT 109.*

Larson was a veteran of the savage engagements around Guadalcanal, and relieved to be going home. He felt sorry for the thin, gangly young

Bostonian. Though Larson was leaving behind his executive officer, Lennie Thom (who had been a student under Jack at Melville), the remainder of the *PT 109* crew was being transferred either to other boats or home; moreover, *PT 109*'s three huge, 1,350-horsepower aero-engines were now so unreliable that the boat had sometimes failed to move out of the harbor.

Jack Kennedy's new command was thus far from scintillating. Even Jack's background as the son of ex-ambassador Joseph Kennedy was considered by Larson a stigma—"a mark on his forehead. It was a handicap, I thought"—causing Jack to be the butt of much ribbing. "But he bore the handicap well," Larson later recalled.

"It's not bad here at all," Jack brought his friend Billings up to date. "I got a transfer from the Squadron I was in as it looked as though they were going to be stuck in Panama for the rest of the war—and am in a good squadron—have my own boat so am set from that angle."

To his parents Jack wrote in the same breezy vein. "As to conditions, they are not bad out here, though if this is the dry season," he added, "the wet season must be considerably damp. Rains every day four or five hours—solid rain—everything gets soaked and on my blue uniform a green mold had grown almost one quarter of an inch thick."

The blue uniform was, however, not required for combat. Like most of his companions, Jack simply wore a shirt, shoes, slacks, and a sheath knife in his belt. "We go out on patrol every other night," he explained, "and work on the boats in the day time," followed by sleep. "They get us up at 5:45 and the blackout begins at 6:30. The blackout is total as the huts we live in have no sides. They have just opened up an Officer's Club which consists of a tent," nicknamed the Royal Palm Club, where the "liquor served is an alcoholic concoction which is drawn out of the torpedo tubes, known as torp juice. Every night about 7:30 the tent bulges, about five men come crashing out, blow their lunch and stagger off to bed. This torp juice, which is the most expendable item on the island," he remarked (a sarcastic allusion to *They Were Expendable*), "makes the prohibition stuff look like Haig and Haig, but probably won't do anyone any permanent harm, as long as their eyes hold out."

That Jack had no intention of staying too long in the tropics he made abundantly clear to Billings. From Alamein in Egypt, Billings had marched with Montgomery's victorious Eighth Army to Tripoli and on to Tunisia, where more than a quarter of a million Axis troops would surrender to the Allied armies on May 12. But Billings's idea of then transferring to the British army's operations against the Japanese in the Southeast Asian theater was ill-received by the young *PT 109* commander. "Received your latest saga and was pleased to note that you are still in one piece," Jack wrote on May 6. "You have certainly had your share of thrills—and if I were you would return safely to the U.S. and join the

Quartermaster Corps + sit on your very fat ass for awhile. Burma sounds just fair, just fair. I'd go home + just take up the slack," he advised, but noted that he was "writing this bit of advice from the South Pacific—sitting in a native hut." Back in the States, the social picture was "about the same" as before: "Zeke + Kick in Palm Beach. Joe in Norfolk [having been transferred back from Puerto Rico]—Dad South and sore." In "regard to Kick becoming a Duchess" by marriage to her English beau, Lord Hartington, Jack was inclined to "doubt it—but it would be rather nice as I believe it would give me some title or other."

In this respect Jack was also mistaken, but there was no mistaking his desire to be back before long in the U.S.A. "I myself hope perhaps to get home by Christmas, as they have been good about relieving us—as the work is fairly tough out here. Re my gut and back," he confided, "it is still not hooray—but think it will hold out." In a postscript he suggested Billings call on a certain "Miss J. R. Doyle—345 E 57—Plaza 8-0587—for a cup of the tea that strengthens. I wish I could join you—but will this winter," he promised.

Brains in their Tails

The tangle with Japanese bombers on the day of his arrival and a recent visit to the Guadalcanal battlefields had soon awakened Jack to the reality of death. "Among the gloomier events," he wrote to Inga, "was a visit to George Mead's grave the other day. He is buried near the beach where they first landed. . . . his grave is in the front row. It's a very simple grave, over it is an aluminum plate, cut out of mess gear I think, and on it crudely carved: Lt. George Mead USMC. Died Aug. 20, 'A great leader of men—God Bless Him.' The whole thing was about the saddest experience I've ever had and enough to make you cry."

Would he too be a great leader of men? Would he survive close combat? "Just heard Aldie Howe was killed out here," Jack scrawled across the top of his letter to Billings. He still hoped Cy Taylor and Torby Macdonald would join him in the Solomons the following month. (They didn't: their squadron later supported U.S. landings further west, and Taylor subsequently lost his life off New Guinea.)

To his parents Jack meanwhile wrote again in good spirits. "Good bunch out here, so all in all it isn't too bad," he told them, and he tried to dispel any illusions they might have: "When I was speaking about the people who would just as soon be home, I didn't mean to use 'They'—I meant 'We.' " He was certain the United States would ultimately win the war, but deeply skeptical about MacArthur's strategy. "This island to island stuff isn't the answer," he had decided. "If they do that the motto out here 'The Golden Gate by 48' won't even come true."

To the men Jack met, MacArthur was far from the hero his father assumed he was from reading American newspapers. "I was interested in what you said about MacArthur's popularity," Jack noted. "Here he has none—is in fact, very, very unpopular. His nick-name is 'Dug-out-Doug,' which seems to date back to the first invasion of Guadalcanal. The Army was supposed to come in and relieve the Marines after the beachhead had been established. In ninety three days, no Army. Rightly or wrongly (probably wrongly) MacArthur is blamed. He is said to have refused to send the Army in—'He sat out in his dug-out in Australia,' (I am quoting all Navy and Marine personnel) and let the Marines take it."

In Jack's view, nevertheless, the marines had had no alternative but to go in when they did. "What actually happened seems to have been that the Navy's hand was forced, due to the speed with which the Japs were building Henderson Field," Jack explained. As he now recognized, air superiority was the decisive factor in modern war, and Henderson Air-field, on Guadalcanal, would have permitted the Japanese use of that decisive factor, both in covering their own naval and shipping movements as well as attacking American shipping. The U.S. forces "just moved in ready or not. The Marines took a terrific beating but gave it back. At the end the Japs wouldn't ever surrender till they had found out whether the Americans were Marines or the Army. If Marines they didn't surrender as the Marines weren't taking prisoners," he related candidly. "In regard to MacArthur, there is no doubt that as men start to come back, that 'Dug-out-Doug' will spread—and I think would probably kill him off."

Jack's political antennae were as sharp as ever, despite the seeming absence of political concern around him. "No one out here has the slightest interest in politics," he reported. "They just want to get home— morning, noon and night. They wouldn't give a damn whether they could vote or not and would probably vote for Roosevelt just because they knew his name."

Meanwhile, "Dad South and sore" had been an accurate, if terse, description of his father's mood. Like Lindbergh, the ex-ambassador was history, living in self-imposed exile in Palm Beach and, like his fellow appeaser, the duke of Windsor in the Bahamas, inviting journalists and itinerant dignitaries for free lunches at his favorite restaurants in the vain hope that they would show gratitude by agitating for his political restoration.

Jack's long letters from the South Pacific were thus a solace to his father. Not only were they written in the thoughtful and unsparing way the ex-ambassador liked—calling a spade a spade—but they evinced, too, a moving sensitivity toward a defeated man, as Jack criticized the conduct of a war he knew his father had never wanted and promised to "be back within a year." Then he added, "Brother, from then on it's going to take an act of Congress to move me."

It was hard for Joseph Kennedy not be impressed by such a display of intelligence, humor, and loyalty from a son at war. He felt proud of Jack—as well as he might, given his own conduct in World War I. Perhaps, mindful of this, Jack was reluctant to write in any sort of patriotic vein. If anything, he stressed the inefficiency with which America waged war. "As far as the length of the war, I don't see how it can stop in less than three years, but I'm sure we can lick them eventually. Our stuff is better, our pilots and planes are—everything considered—way ahead of theirs," he claimed (incorrectly, as he would soon find), "and our resources inexhaustible." The problem, as Jack saw it, was the bureaucratic attitude behind the U.S. effort. "A great hold-up seems to me to be the lackadaisical way they handle the unloading of ships. They sit in ports out here weeks at a time while they try to get enough Higgins boats to unload them. They ought to build their docks the first thing" (a problem that would be spectacularly solved a year later by constructing Mulberry harbors for the invasion of France). Meanwhile "they're losing ships, in effect, by what seems from the outside to be just inertia up high.

"Don't let anyone sell the idea that everyone out here is hustling with the old American energy," Jack warned his father. "They have brought back a lot of old Captains and Commanders from retirement and stuck them in as the heads of these ports and they give the impression of their brains being in their tails as Honey Fitz would say. The ship I arrived on—no one in the port had the slightest idea it was coming. It had hundreds of men and it sat in the harbor for two weeks while signals were being exchanged. The one man, though, who has everyone's confidence is [Admiral] Halsey, he rates at the very top." Jack would meet Halsey in person within days; MacArthur he would not meet until years later.

In the meantime Jack dismissed the notion of Joe Jr. joining him in the Pacific. "I know it is futile to say so," he wrote, "but if I were he I would take as much time about it as I could. He is coming out eventually and will be here for a sufficiency and he will want to be back the day after he arrives, if he runs true to the form of everyone else."

"I'm extremely glad I came—I wouldn't miss it for the world," he wrote to Inga, "but I will be extremely glad to get back. I won't be in a hurry to leave the old fireplace again, just long enough to get another log for it.

"What exactly is your situation?" he asked, anxious to know whether she'd finally married her Danish boyfriend or not.

Are you settling down permanently to a life of domesticity? Or do you remember a certain remark about dinner and breakfast when I got back? Just give me the straight dope on that will you, so I'll know if this whole thing is worth fighting for. You don't need to get too nervous. . . . It will be a few months but I'll be there with blood in my eye.

A number of my illusions have been shattered, but you're one I still have, although I don't believe illusion is exactly the word I mean. By an illusion I would mean the idea I had when I left the states that the South Seas was a good place to swim in. Now I find that if you swim there is a fungus that grows in your ears.

The upshot, he joked, was that "I shall return with athlete's foot and fungus growing out of my ears to a heroes [*sic*] welcome, demand a large pension which I won't get, invite you to a dinner and breakfast which I'm beginning to have my doubts about you coming to, and then retire to the old Sailors home in West Palm Beach with a lame back. . . .

"Well, honey," he signed off with love and gentle sarcasm, "I must go and get some of that delightful food, superbly prepared and cuisined, and served in pleasant and peaceful surroundings."

Life Among the Cannibals

It was the absence of girls as much as the presence of fungi on Florida Island that made Jack yearn to be back in Florida State, but as the weeks went by and he began to assemble his own, chosen crew, the camaraderie of combat began to make up for the lack of home cooking.

"We had a raid today but on the whole it's slacked up over the last weeks," he reported to his parents.

I guess it will be more or less routine for another while. Going out every other night for patrol. On good nights it's beautiful—the water is amazingly phosphorescent—flying fishes which shine like lights are zooming around and you usually get two or three porpoises who lodge right under the bow and no matter how fast the boat goes keep just about six inches ahead of the boat.

It's been good training. I have an entirely new crew and when the showdown comes I'd like to be confident they know the difference between firing a gun and winding their watch.

Even the difference between the food served to generals and that served up to the fighting men no longer irked him. To Inga he wrote:

> In regard to the food, it's lousy, but that was one of the things that didn't surprise me. . . . I have finally found out where those steaks are going that—and I quote—"the boys in the service are getting" end of quote. Have been ferrying quite a lot of generals around, as the word has gotten around evidently since MacArthur's escape that the place to be seen for swift and sure advancement if you're a general is in a PT boat. . . . Well, anyway, a general came aboard and my exec. and I managed to look as weak from hunger as we possibly could which required no great effort, so he finally broke down and invited us for a meal. We went, and they kept bringing in the steaks and the potatoes and the peas and the asparagus and the pie and the beer, all of which I disposed of in a style to which you had become accustomed. . . . Well, when we had finally finished he came out with the statement that he understood we got the same food, only he figured his was probably cooked a little better. . . . Having had a bottle of beer and therefore being scarcely in a condition to carry on an intelligible conversation, and remembering article no. 252 in Naval Regulations, that Generals are seldom wrong and Admirals never, and figuring that the problem of food distribution was a problem that was occupying better minds than the generals or mine, I merely conceded the putt and went on to the next hole.

Jack's increasing confidence as a skipper was reflected in the fitness report his squadron commander, Allen Harris, filled out in May. He marked Jack with a perfect rating, 4.0, in shiphandling, and a 3.9 in "ability to command." "This officer met all situations with proficiency and daring that make him a credit to the naval service," Harris noted in his final remarks.

Toward the end of May 1943, however, Lieutenant Commander Harris was transferred to another squadron. In his place came a mere twenty-four-year-old graduate of the Naval Academy at Annapolis, Alvin P. Cluster. Cluster was, if anything, less respectful of the U.S. Navy, the Solomons Islands strategy, and the effectiveness of PT boats than Jack Kennedy was. "The Japanese had outfought us completely," Cluster later recalled.

"Now, by the time Jack Kennedy got to the Solomons, things had changed. The Japanese had been pushed back, they'd been pushed off of Guadalcanal, they had been pushed off of the Russell Islands and we had air superiority during the day time, and we had superiority in destroyers and cruisers at night. We were learning how to fight at night. And things

were a heck of a lot better." Almost half a century later Cluster vividly
remembered his first brush with Jack Kennedy.

> My father was a Red Rock Republican and I had absolutely no
> respect for Roosevelt or any of his people. At night, if you weren't
> on patrol, you did nothing but sit around and talk because there was
> a blackout there to avoid the float planes that would come over. . . .
> I remember I was expounding—I always had a big mouth, and my
> father being a professional Republican politician in Missouri, I
> thought I was an expert on everything Roosevelt had done wrong.
> And one of my pet peeves was Roosevelt's tendency to appoint
> wealthy men to ambassadorships. So I was sounding off this particu-
> lar night, and really giving everybody the education that I thought
> they needed about what a terrible way it was to run a foreign policy
> when Lennie Thom, who was a wonderful, reasoned, balanced sort
> of person, tapped me on the knee and said, "Al, you know, Jack
> Kennedy's here, his father was our ambassador to Britain."
>
> I said, "Oh, God!" And for the rest of his life, Jack made fun of
> me for my Republican tendencies. . . . He and I fought like mad
> about politics all the time that I knew him!

Jack had meanwhile moved to his own Democratic quarters. "He
found this old thatched hut behind the reefer boxes, to the left of our big
hut, and he said, 'Johnny, let's you and me go clean it up and go live in
it,'" Johnny Iles recalled. "So we did. We went and cleaned that thing up.
It was a pretty big hut because later on people would come by and just
bunk in there with us. His Executive Officer, a boy named Leonard
Thom, came over and lived with us. And, I think, a boy named Gene
Foncannon. I know there was always a lot of company in there. He could
attract attention everywhere he went. We would sit around and drink
beer and he would write letters. He could really write some letters, very
interesting letters."

Given the primitive conditions, Jack's wit was much prized, as was his
attitude toward authority. "Just had an inspection by an Admiral," he
wrote in a letter to Inga.

> He must have weighed over three hundred, and came bursting
> through our hut like a bull coming out of chute three. A burst of
> speed when he got into the clear brought him against the machine
> shop. He harrumphed a couple of times, and then inquired, "And
> what do we have here?"
>
> "Well, General," was the answer, "this is our machine shop."

"Harrumph, and what do you keep in it, harrumph ah . . . MA-CHINERY?"

After it was gently but firmly explained to him that machinery was kept in the machine shop and he had written that down on the special pad he carried for such special bits of information which can only be found "if you get right up to the front and see for yourself" he harrumphed again, looked at a map, and wanted to know what we had *there*—there being a small bay some distance away. When we said nothing, he burst out with "well, by God, what we need is to build a dock." Well, someone said it was almost lunch and it couldn't be built before lunch. . . . After a moment of serious consideration and a hurried consultation with a staff of engineers he agreed and toddled off to stoke his furnace at the luncheon table. . . . That, Bingo, is total war at its totalest.

Meanwhile, though he was disappointed at the absence of Gauguin-like paramours to feed him grapes and bananas, Jack was intrigued by the diminutive Melanesian Islanders. "Have a lot of natives around, and am getting hold of some grass skirts, war clubs, etc.," Jack reported to his parents in May. "We had one in today who told us about the last man he ate. 'Him Jap him are good.' All they seem to want is a pipe and will give you canes, pineapples, anything, including a wife. . . . When the British were here they had them working for 17 cents a day but we treat them a heck of a lot better. 'English we no like' is their summating of the British Empire."

The Australians were not only mean, but did not, apparently, taste as good as their American allies. "We thought that had all ended," Johnny Iles later recalled, and recounted how they had taken a native boy into their hut. "He was a very agile native boy. He told us he was a cannibal. And we kidded him. He was a sharp boy and he could speak a little English."

It was through Lani, the native boy, that Jack learned a smattering of pidgin English, which would in time prove of life-and-death importance. But although the boy slept on the ground by Jack's side, it was Jack's deputy skipper whose "meat" Lani kept eyeing, for Lennie Thom was a blond giant of a man, six foot two, of Nordic descent and appearance, with the big limbs of a professional athlete (he had played professional football before entering the navy). As Iles recalled, the sight of Lennie Thom's flesh was almost too much for the little cannibal. "His mouth got to watering over Lennie Thom's forearms, he said the forearm was the best part to eat." Then one day the New Zealand authorities arrived and took the little cannibal away.

Threatened by sharks, cannibals, coral infections, and the dangers of torp juice, the men of Squadron 2 were nonetheless fortunate to be in a relative backwater insofar as the war in the Solomons was concerned.

Barney Ross, another hulking American, recalled arriving in Tulagi and his reintroduction to the skinny touch-football player with whom he'd played at Melville:

> Jack was sort of established already with what was left of the old guard at Tulagi, who looked at us newcomers with disdain, because they had been through the really rough days in the PT boats.
>
> Jack roomed with these guys. He was in with this group . . . he was holding his own with all kinds of guys, as I look back on it.
>
> The whole PT bunch was a bunch of individualists and a bunch of interesting guys—quite a few football players, even professional football players—big guys.
>
> Jack looked very thin. And these fellows would be like—Lennie Thom, he was about 210 pounds, and All Big 10 Tackle at Ohio State. Johnny Iles was a top notch football player from Louisiana. Jumping Joe Atkinson from Tennessee, as well as people like Byron White, who was quite an intellectual [later a Supreme Court justice] but also quite a football player. We were pretty long on football players in the PT's. . . .
>
> In the evenings we'd get together usually for a couple of drinks. It was a lot of good fellowship. They were the best bunch of guys I've ever met. Anywhere. The fellows in the PT boats.

It was with this "bunch of guys" that Jack Kennedy was now to meet his destiny.

Pilgrim's Way

"Jack was a good officer," his hut mate, Johnny Iles, declared.

> I thought he was a real good officer. His boat was shipshape and his crew was well organized, orderly. He was twenty-five, he was an old man, the rest of us were a bunch of kids. . . .
>
> He was jolly. He was a fellow who made you feel good to be with—and you would never have known about his personal, privileged life by visiting with him. He was always a genuine person. . . . We would swap letters, family letters that came in, and I would

censor his letters, and he mine. He was a prolific letter writer—and prolific in getting his ideas across. When the rest of us would be carrying on senseless conversation, he would be writing letters. God, those damn letters he used to write—to friends, to senators, Under Secretary Forrestal, Congresswoman [Clare Boothe] Luce: I was a good one to censor all that stuff because I was just a plain old yard dog that didn't take any of that too serious.

Serious or not, Iles became as certain as Lem Billings that Jack would one day amount to something.

It was written all over the sky that he was going to be something big. He just had that charisma. You could tell just by his nature, by the way people would stop by and visit with him, and the fact that he was writing to important people—he was writing to very powerful people. It was obvious that politics was in his blood. Maybe his dad was an inspiration. The Irish had to overcome a lot in Boston, and Jack would tell me about it. He told me about his dad, how he couldn't at first work for the banks, but then his grandfather, his grandfather was active in politics, got his dad a job. . . . His daddy was a financial genius at selling short. And while many sons of successful fathers don't have the same drive, Jack had it.

He loved to win. He loved competitive sports. I remember an old boy from Dallas, they'd play cribbage on my bed. Jack wanted to win—he would play to win, though he wasn't obnoxious about it. He was good-looking, had a fantastic smile, the tone of his voice, his sense of humor. . . . He loved sitting around talking with a bunch of guys, and he'd come out with these remarks—remarks like you'd never forget. One guy, I remember, appeared to be part Indian, and as he walked across the room Jack looked up at him, then looked back at us and said, "Half-Indian, half Harley-Davidson!"

Oh, yeah, he had politics in his blood. In fact I used to kid him—you see, Joe Atkinson—Joe's father I think was sheriff in Tennessee—and we used to kid Jack all the time. I'd say, after the war is over, Jack, I'm gonna work like hell and we're going to carry Louisiana for you.

There was talk of baseball and girls, and after the war how they'd just rest their weary limbs, "maybe setting up, going into South America. He said, 'John, you can live down there for two bits a day. The old man's got a lot of property down there, we'll just go down and do something'— nothing concrete, just dreaming out loud, and we'd elaborate on that."

Jack's shy, quiet manner contrasted with some of the brasher characters peopling PT boats. "He never tried to dominate the conversation," recalled James Reed, who had transferred to PT boats in Nouméa and followed Jack to Tulagi. "There was an aura about him that I've never seen duplicated in anybody else. He was an extraordinary fellow. First of all, he had such a broad interest. He was several steps ahead of all of us. He'd had the opportunity to be exposed to people in high places, he had first-hand experience of foreign affairs, plus the fact that he had such a marvelous sense of humor. He had a light touch, and a serious side." Though Reed did not see Jack in the mold of local politician, he nevertheless remembered writing to a friend in Massachusetts and telling him "all about Jack, and I said that I thought he would be president of the U.S. one day," not only because of Jack's inner drive and interest in political issues, but because of the remarkable way he appealed to people of every background.

"We also did a lot of reading out there," Reed said, and was as amazed as Kathleen Kennedy's boyfriend, John White, at the range and quality of Jack's taste. He had read almost every book on the American presidents. He had read every word that Winston Churchill had ever published. He'd read T. E. Lawrence and was a devotee of Lord David Cecil's racy account of Lord Byron and Lady Caroline Lamb in *The Young Melbourne.* Yet his "very favorite book of all time," Reed recalled, "was *Pilgrim's Way.* He recommended it very highly to me, but we didn't have it out there."

It was only later, reading the personal copy that Jack had sent him, that Reed came to understand its significance for the shy but ambitious young Boston-Irishman. Stiff and often precious, Buchan's autobiography was the story of a talented Scottish boy making his way in late Victorian and Edwardian England, culminating in a moving elegy to a generation swept away by World War I.

Stitched into Buchan's labored prose were tributes to lost friends that would be much quoted later by those seeking sentimental memorial stones to Jack Kennedy himself. For example, on the death of Raymond Asquith, the Liberal leader's son whom Buchan had met, admired, and become deeply attached to at Oxford, Buchan lamented, "For the chosen few, like Raymond, there is no disillusionment. They march on into life with a boyish grace, and their high noon keeps all the freshness of the morning."

Did Jack identify with Asquith? In Reed's eyes, the parallel with Asquith was certainly uncanny. Not only was Asquith one of the brightest men of his generation at Oxford, but "as a letter writer he was easily the best of us," Buchan had written. These letters, Buchan pointed out, "were dangerous things to leave lying about, for he had a most unbridled pen.

He could not write a sentence without making it characteristic and imparting into it some delicate ribaldry."

The same, Reed knew, could be said of Jack Kennedy. Moreover there were other parallels. Asquith's father, as Liberal prime minister, was very different from Joe Kennedy, but the problem of being the gifted son of a powerful man was the same. Asquith, too, had begun World War I as "a member of the Intelligence Staff," and bored and frustrated, he had insisted on transfer to a fighting unit a year later. In 1916 Asquith had thus been posted with his battalion to the Western Front, where in "the mingled bondage and freedom of active service" he'd at last found himself, reveling not only in the deadly seriousness of the challenge, but in "the same kind of light-hearted and high-spirited companionship in which he had delighted" at college.

This, too, could have accurately described Jack Kennedy in the spring of 1943. Raymond Asquith, however, met his death on the Western Front, in the disastrous Battle of the Somme in 1916. In the margin of his copy of *Pilgrim's Way,* Jack had marked this passage: "He loved his youth, and his youth has become eternal. Debonair and brilliant and brave, he is now part of that immortal England which knows not age or weariness or defeat."

Meanwhile, toward the end of May 1943 the lull in the South Pacific came to an end. On the thirtieth of the month Jack's squadron (actually parts of Squadrons 2 and 6, under Al Cluster's command) was ordered up to the Russell Islands to take over from PT boat squadrons moving forward to cover the next major assault in the Solomons: the disaster-ridden U.S. invasion of New Georgia.

All or Nothing at All

Ironically, MacArthur's campaign in the Solomons became a mirror to the very Mediterranean campaign it was intended to block. Admiral King, the U.S. naval chief of staff, fearing that Churchill's "soft underbelly" strategy in southern Europe would divert American forces from the Pacific, ordered MacArthur to hurry up his offensive—however costly and however unnecessary. Thus, to spite the British in the Mediterranean, there began "a step-by-step advance, largely determined by the radii of land-based aircraft" in the Solomons that would be as questionable as the step-by-step operations in Pantelleria, Sicily, and elsewhere in Italy—a "piece-meal" approach to planning that was, inevitably, reflected in piecemeal results.

As MacArthur's commanders concentrated on amphibious invasions, the Japanese turned over to the defensive. As Alvin Cluster recalled, this gave PT boats a new role, much more akin to their traditional one, namely, as coastal patrol vessels. "They started flooding that area down there with PT boats. There were more and more of them, and they were based not only in Guadalcanal, but in the Russell Islands and gradually everywhere else," for "the Japanese would still move troops around at night, they would reinforce, they would evacuate only at night because of our air power. And the PT boats offered a way to stop that flow of men and material at night."

Unfortunately, the seventy-seven-, seventy-eight-, and eighty-foot wooden launches carried wholly the wrong armament for this new scenario. German E-boats were metal-hulled and driven by powerful and reliable diesel engines, whereas the Allied torpedo boats used highly inflammable aviation fuel, had no armor plating, and had guns that were little better than rifles, nicknamed "fifty-calibers-at-fifty-paces." Against Japanese *Daihatsu*s, which were shallow-draught, steel-hulled, and gun-protected barges, the PTs found themselves more threatened than threatening. "The boats would leave around sunset and they would go to their stations," Cluster later described, "and the greatest hazard they faced were the Japanese float planes—seaplanes that would come out at night and would see the long V-shaped wake of the PT boats in the phosphorescent waters down there; a lot of times they wouldn't be able to see the boats in the dark, but they would see the tip of the V and they would just bomb that, because they knew there'd be a boat there—the propellers and everything would churn up this phosphorescence."

To his sister Kathleen, Jack wrote saying with what interest he'd read in *Life* magazine a piece by John Hersey about PT boats. "It didn't have the wild west stuff of 'They Were Expendable,' " he commented, but gave "a much truer picture. The glamour of PT's just isn't except to the outsider. It's just a matter of night after night patrols at low speed in rough water—two hours on—then sacking out and going on again for another two hours. Even with that however it's a hell of a lot better than any other job in the Navy. . . . As a matter of fact this job is somewhat like sailing, in that we spend most of our time trying to get the boat running faster"—not, however, to "beat Daly for the Kennedy cup" as at Hyannis in the old days. "It's the Kennedy tail this time," he related, as the PTs attempted to beat daylight and Japanese air patrols.

For Jack, however, it was not enough to beat the Japanese back to base. He must beat his fellow PT boats too, since the first boat home was the first boat to be refueled, and it was only after refueling that the crew, who slept on board, could get some sleep.

It was on one such dawn return to the Russell Islands that Jack almost smashed *PT 109* to bits. Having ridden the wake of another vessel until the final stretch home, he had pulled abreast and then played dare. As the two boats raced into harbor it became a question of which skipper would first throttle down. In the end Jack won, but when he then telegraphed down to the engineer to reverse the engines, all three Packard 1,350-horsepower motors died. As the author of *PT 109,* Bob Donovan, chronicled: "*PT 109* went streaking at the dock like an eighty-foot missile on the loose." The various dockworkers, when they recovered their wits, beheld "a single PT boat sliced into a corner of the dock, her skinny bronzed skipper standing in his motionless cockpit, ruefully surveying the scene. Some of his crew were motionless, too, having been knocked flat by the crash." One of the crew, Bucky Harris, recalled how thereafter "everybody used to run for the beach when they saw our boat coming. That's when they started calling him 'Crash' Kennedy."

Donovan recounted that Jack was saved from court-martial only by slipping away from the scene of the misdemeanor when attention was distracted by another boat slipping its moorings, but Barney Ross recalled a different ending. "Of course there's the famous incident where he was going a little too fast," Ross recollected, "and the reverse gear failed and he ploughed into the gas dock there on the Russell Islands, and how flustered the squadron commander was. Jack could see he was about to get chewed down and he said, 'Well, you can't stop that *PT 109!*' There were a lot of laughs."

There were indeed, as Jack's squadron commander later reflected. "I'm certain if you were to bring back some of the senior commanders out in the Pacific, they would say, PT boats were a laugh. The old hide-bound battleship navy had no use for PT boats at all. We were thrown loosely into that term the 'hooligan navy.' And in fact it persisted all during the war, and there were never any officers in PT boats who advanced to flag rank. It became something of a stigma, definitely—though many of us didn't realize it at the time."

Cluster certainly never claimed to be better than his "hooligans." One night he was riding, as squadron commander, aboard *PT 48,* skippered by David Levy, when it ran aground on a coral reef. With a line from *PT 109,* Jack pulled it off. This, however, was only the start of their troubles. "There was a heavy sea that night," Cluster recalled. "We took on water. We tried to lighten the boat by firing our torpedoes. The hole was above the waterline and we tried to keep the boat up on a step, like a hydroplane, but I misjudged and we smacked a couple and filled the boat again and we started yelling. As I remember, we radioed Jack; Jack was over the horizon and this was about dawn and he came tearing over."

Fearing that the boat would sink, Jack made for some U.S. destroyers nearby to borrow a bilge pump. When this didn't help, they decided to back the boat the rest of the way. Water ran low, as did rations; eventually they left the waterlogged vessel on Buruku Island for a repair crew to collect and all crowded onto Jack's boat.

"On the way back, I asked Jack if I could take the wheel," Cluster remembered, to his own embarrassment. "I had not been on an 80-footer. I got it going pretty good and was up on top of the waves. Then we misjudged and smacked another wave and a hot run started in the torpedo. Lennie Thom had read *They Were Expendable* [where a torpedo is stopped from arming itself by the novel use of toilet paper], so he crammed some toilet paper in the impeller on the exploder so it wouldn't go off in the water. The damn thing broke loose finally and pushed a depth charge right through the deck. . . . The crewman below had broken his nose when they went over to pick up the pump—it was very rough alongside. He'd been down in his bunk, but had got out when it got so rough, which is a good thing because the depth charge came whanging through, then went on its merry way."

Some four torpedoes on *PT 48*, a torpedo on *PT 109*, and a depth charge had all been expended. When Cluster reported this to Admiral Fort, the admiral exploded. "Jesus Christ! When I was captain of the [battleship] *South Dakota* I used to wonder how you PT people could fire so many torpedoes, and now I understand! You fired five and you haven't even seen the enemy!"

Those PT boaters who did see the enemy, however, fared little better, the highlight of the Solomons campaign being the moment when a flotilla of PT boats sank the U.S. invasion-force flagship, the U.S.S. *McCawley*. Commanding six PT boats, Lieutenant Commander Robert Kelly ordered Squadron 9 to attack, despite being warned by his own men that the target was a friendly vessel. One of the *McCawley*'s officers recalled being "in the Blanche Channel on the east side of Rendova," when all at once "we were surrounded by a squadron of American PT boats who immediately fired full salvos of torpedoes despite all efforts to give them recognition signals. This squadron was under the command of a Lt. Cmdr. Kelly. I later talked to an enlisted man who was aboard Kelly's boat. He said that they saw the recognition signals but that Kelly said it was a Jap trick and to let us have it."

"It was a typical minor PT screwup," Jack's friend in Squadron 2, Joe Atkinson, recalled. "Kelly blew up Admiral Turner's flagship and then they demoted him out of the flotilla command."

As a result, for the rest of the New Georgia invasion, all PT boats were ordered out of the landing area. Unsatisfied with having sunk Admiral Turner's flagship, however, Squadron 9 ran two more boats aground, on consecutive nights, and had to abandon and destroy them.

Running aground was considered par for the PT-boat course, as Jack's friend Sim Efland recalled. "Out there in the islands, the maps that we had were very old. Some of them were German. . . . Those maps were obsolete and they did not have all of the coral reefs that had developed in the Pacific. Hitting those coral reefs at night, we didn't have the equipment that we should have had; we'd have to spend a day diving down and taking those screws off and then beating them out."

The temperamental engines powering the PT boats, moreover, led to several fatal disasters involving American planes, as when *PT 166,* skippered by Charles Donohue, lingered on until daylight to help a fellow PT boat that was having engine trouble. "They were still out there in the morning," Barney Ross later related. "Some B-25s saw them, thought they were Japs and strafed them. So the next pass, the boats fired back and shot down one of the B-25s. Our boat was hit, burned and sunk by the American planes."

In the context of such a "hooligan" navy, Jack's run-in on the Russell Island dock was dismissed as small potatoes. The squadron's patrolling was restricted to reduce casualties from mistakes, and the only enemy Jack saw were the pilots of the Japanese seaplanes shadowing their wake.

Frustrated, Jack adopted the time-honored philosophy of war: loyalty to one's immediate comrades and profound skepticism about anything else, including religious faith. His mother's news that "all the nuns and priests along the Atlantic Coast are putting in a lot of praying time on my behalf is certainly comforting," he wrote home on June 24, having exchanged his boat's old Packard engines for a new, reconditioned trio at Tulagi and then resumed his every-other-nightly patrolling from the Russell Islands. "Kathleen reports that even a fortune-teller says that I'm coming back in one piece. I hope it won't be taken as a sign of lack of confidence in you all or the Church if I continue to duck."

Although fighting the war in the Pacific in some way assuaged it, Jack was still struggling in the battle he'd been fighting since childhood. He was aware that he possessed extraordinary talents: an intelligence superior to most of his colleagues'; a shy but genial personality; a beguiling, self-deprecating sense of humor; an unusual indolence in that what he chose to do he did conscientiously, competitively, and well. Yet, having turned twenty-six on May 29, 1943, the day before moving up to the Russell Islands, he still had no clear idea of how he would achieve his growing presidential ambition. In the margin of his copy of *Pilgrim's Way* he'd marked a series of arresting passages culminating in Buchan's description of T. E. Lawrence:

His character has been a quarry for the analysts, and I would not add to their number. It is simplest to say that he was a mixture of contradictories which never were—perhaps could never have been—harmonised. His qualities lacked integration. He had moods of vanity and moods of abasement; immense self-confidence and immense diffidence. He had a fastidious taste which was often faulty. The gentlest and most lovable of beings with his chivalry and considerateness, he could also be ruthless.

In his wooden Scottish style, eschewing psychology and preferring precious conceit to a modern *style engagé,* Buchan offered an understanding of Lawrence that came close to the heart of Jack's own fascination with Lawrence. "There was a fissure in him from the start," Buchan noted, "the dream and the business did not march together."

Did Jack's? None of Buchan's lamented heroes, significantly, had fulfilled their early promise, at least not in their own minds. None exactly matched Jack's personality or condition, but collectively they held up a mirror to Jack's underlying psyche, which few, if any, of his Pacific comrades recognized. The thought that he was behind in some race with time and with real or imagined rivals obsessed him. Those who later attributed this merely to his father's insistent expectations had only shallow insight into Jack's disordered ego, as did those who later bracketed his manic philandering with his father's sexual license. Like Buchan's gallery of gypsy souls, Jack's dilettantish, narcissistic, abundantly talented personality craved success, yet would never be content with it, always eyeing other pastures as greener, other figures as contenders. "Speaking of Johnny Hersey," Jack wrote to his sister after extolling Hersey's *Life* magazine article on PT boats, "I see his new book 'Into the Valley' is doing well. He's sitting on top of the hill at this point—a best seller—my girl, two kids—big man on *Time*—while I'm the one that's down in the God damned valley."

Waiting in the wings, in the old farmhouse on the Russell Islands that comprised his quarters, Jack played his favorite record, Frank Sinatra's "All or Nothing at All," on the faithful Victrola he always took with him:

> Hey, please don't bring your lips close to my cheek,
> Don't you smile or I'll be lost beyond recall.

Cribbage turned to poker. Once again, it looked as if Jack had missed the action. However, on July 15, 1943, two weeks after the invasion of New Georgia, *PT 109* was temporarily detached from Squadron 2 and ordered up to Rendova, where the PTs had their most advanced base, commanded by the bête noire of PT mariners, a man destined to become as hated by Jack as J. J. Maher had been: Thomas G. Warfield.

The Biggest Shit in the Pacific

Thomas G. Warfield had been a gunnery instructor at the naval academy until the attack on Pearl Harbor. He was a highly strung martinet, who refused to ride the PT boats, preferring to exercise command from the bunker that, after Commander Kelly's disgrace, he had had specially constructed on Lumbari, the small, island base for PTs next to Rendova, off the south coast of New Georgia. Using purloined high-frequency radio-communications equipment, he was determined to bring order to the chaos of PT boat operations in the Solomons.

This was certainly no easy task. The initial landings had succeeded, but the subsequent campaign proved a nightmare. From their bases on Bougainville and the Shortland Islands, the Japanese were again able to run a nightly flotilla of reinforcements, nicknamed the "Tokyo Express." Men and munitions were speedily unloaded off the shores of Kolombangara, a virtually impregnable island west of New Georgia, thus releasing in turn men and materiel to cross the narrow Kula Channel and defend Munda, the key tactical terrain on New Georgia.

Despite wave after wave of assault landings and hand-to-hand combat, the U.S. Forty-third Infantry Division and Ninth Marine Battalion failed to capture Munda. Several battalion commanders had to be relieved in the field, and hundreds of GIs fell victim to fear and exhaustion, so many that the regimental hospitals were flooded and a new illness, similar to shell shock in World War I, was recognized: "war neurosis." No less than *two and a half thousand* cases would be so diagnosed in the U.S. New Georgia assault forces alone. Near Munda Point, American soldiers knifed and threw grenades at one another in a sort of combat hysteria; by July 13, 1943, the corps commander, General Griswold, doubted whether the Forty-third Division would ever take Munda. Two days later Admiral Turner was dismissed, and the New Georgia invasion commander was relieved of his overall command. The American offensive was stalled.

Chaotic command, inappropriate training, poor leadership, poor medical backup, and a host of other reasons would later be given to explain the length and arduousness of this Allied campaign, which had been planned since January and was assumed would last but a matter of days.

It was this faltering campaign that Jack now came to support in *PT 109.*

Jack's assignment came as a bitter disappointment to his colleagues in Squadron 2. Joe Atkinson, for instance, had declined the chance to take his own *PT 110* to a new base on the north coast of New Guinea in order to remain with his colleagues and was chagrined when Jack's orders came through. Lieutenant Commander Warfield had, however, specifically requested an extra Elco boat at Rendova because of the far-flung patrols he was having to run. "The eighty-footers were more seaworthy and bigger boats—that's the reason Jack went up there," Joe Atkinson later explained.

For Jack, transfer to Rendova was to be nothing less than a nightmare. No longer would he be serving in his own squadron, with comrades he knew, under a young commander he liked and admired. Now he would be on special detachment to a squadron of strangers, under a commander he grew to detest.

Warfield's bunker-style rule, however, was as disastrous as Kelly's "Charge of the Light Brigade" style command, which had just ended. Two days after Jack Kennedy's arrival Warfield sent a "posse" of three PT boats, under a completely inexperienced lieutenant, to patrol the west coast of Kolombangara. Equipped with radar, the section leader disregarded a message from one of his boats, which reported having seen a green and white flare, indicating friendly forces in the area. Once again, the section leader ordered a night torpedo attack, causing an entire flotilla of U.S. destroyers to break off their artillery support of U.S. ground forces near Munda and to defend themselves with heavy shell fire while dodging the torpedoes.

Fortunately no hits were scored on either side, but several days later the incident took place in which *PT 166* was attacked by B-25s, one of which was downed in the melee. "I got confused," confessed the PT-boat gunner, "and thought it was a Jap plane with our insignia." Three of the B-25's crew drowned, while one member of *PT 166*'s crew was killed when the torpedo boat sank.

Instead of retraining his men and reexamining tactics, Warfield obstinately vested his trust in the powerful new radio aerial above his bunker and a belief in attack by numbers. John Meade, who had attended Melville PT-boat school with Jack and had reached Tulagi a few weeks after he had, considered Warfield to be "the biggest shit in the Pacific. He simply never learned the tactical lessons of the year before that PT boats were ineffective in groups larger than two. Because they were ordered by Warfield to keep strict radio silence save in emergency, the lead boat could not signal the trailing boats that he was about to move out. The second boat would react to the movements of the first boat, but at a delay. The delay was magnified with each boat. So, often, the fourth boat would get detached," Meade recalled. Since Warfield never rode the boats, he had no personal knowledge of the problems, an ignorance that would cost many lives.

For Jack it proved a trying time. He was captaining, as the sole boat from Squadron 2, the oldest surviving boat from the Guadalcanal campaign in support of an invasion of New Guinea that had gone seriously awry. Far from impeding the Japanese from resupplying their troops, however, the PT boats proved powerless to prevent Japanese barge traffic, were incapable of stopping the high-speed Japanese destroyers comprising the Tokyo Express, and were sitting targets for Japanese floatplanes.

Between July 19 and 31, Jack's *PT 109* would be mentioned five times in after-action reports, yet it never once saw a Japanese vessel. Despite advance warning that the Tokyo Express would be running on the night of July 19, for instance, Jack's patrol section was unable to find it. Japanese floatplanes caught the PT torpedo group, however, on their way out and again on the PTs' return, dropping a flare that illuminated the three boats and then selecting Jack's boat as the primary target. Although Jack resorted to high-speed zigzagging and smoke-laying, *PT 109* was straddled by two bombs, which exploded so close to his vessel that two members of his crew were wounded.

For one of Jack's crewmen, Andrew Kirksey, this near miss was too much. He became convinced that it was an omen. Though Jack debated whether to transfer Kirksey to shore work when next *PT 109* returned to Tulagi, there wasn't time. On July 21 Barney Ross's boat was sunk by B-25s, and on July 23 *PT 109* was ordered to patrol off the small island of Gizo, across the Blackett Strait from Kolombangara, where the Japanese were thought to be reinforcing their garrison. The following night *PT 109* was again out, and the section was again bombed, both on the passage out and on its return.

This time the Japanese seaplane struck lucky. One bomb actually hit *PT 105*, killing its executive officer, and, after midnight, scored narrow misses on *PT 109* and *PT 106*. As the boats wearily made their way back to Lumbari, they were again spotted. The war plane dumped a huge five-hundred-pound bomb, which fell so close behind *PT 161* that the boat was almost blasted out of the water. Clearly, the hunters had become the hunted. As Jack's father wrote to a golfing friend, "We had a letter from Jack the night before last, and evidently he's had a few close calls, a couple of his boys having been wounded and the ship shot up a number of times . . . he assures us that he is all right, except of course, there is a note that he's seen what he went out to see and he'll be glad to come home."

Home was very far away, however. On the night of July 27, *PT 109* and

four other boats (*157, 159, 162,* and *172*) made a five-man patrol right around
the island of Gizo, a hundred miles behind enemy lines, but once again
were spotted and chased by Japanese aircraft, though they managed to
avoid being bombed.

Two nights later *PT 109* was once more in Blackett Strait, west of
Kolombangara with a patrol group. Though *PT 109* was forced to return
to base because of a defective rudder, the others caught sight of a Japanese barge, which they attacked with gunfire, and even claimed to have
sunk.

If so, Jack reasoned, it was the use of PTs as *gunboats,* not torpedo-
attack vessels, that was the shape of things to come. Determined to show
some return for all the effort and danger to which he and his crew were
exposing themselves, Jack now made his own, unilateral decision to get
hold of a bigger gun. While PT *109*'s defective rudders were being fixed,
he therefore went over to the army base on Rendova. Finding a surplus
thirty-seven-millimeter antitank gun, he asked whether he might have it
and, returning to Lumbari, announced to his astonished crew that he
wished them to secure it to the forward deck.

This was no easy matter, and it also entailed removing the regulation
life raft. Though the crew managed to bolt the wheels of the cannon down
to the deck, the legs presented more of a problem, since they had to
absorb the gun's powerful recoil. In the end it was decided to tie them
temporarily to two huge lengths of coconut tree and lash these timbers to
the deck with rope, much as Nelson's cannons had been secured.

By the morning of August 1, 1943, the work was done. In addition to its
torpedos, *PT 109* could now claim to be a gunboat, of sorts.

However amateur in execution, this did at least show prescient thinking
on Jack's part. In the meantime however, fate decreed that PTs in the
southwest Solomons should fight one last torpedo battle against Japanese
warships—a final catastrophe in which *PT 109* would become the star
victim.

Mass Exodus

Compared with Tulagi and the Russell Islands, the Lumbari PT-boat
base was, like the island of Rendova next to it, a muddy swamp—a "lousy
place" composed of "tents with water-filled slit trenches just outside the
door," the communications officer later described.

The slit trenches had been dug because of Japanese air raids aimed at
Rendova, which climaxed the afternoon of August 1, 1943. "We'd been

playing poker that afternoon in a tent," Barney Ross recalled. "There was some sort of excitement outside the tent. We heard this air-raid siren and nobody paid much attention to it because we'd never had an air raid at that particular little island—we were sort of isolated from the main base [Rendova] there, and we didn't figure they would ever raid us.

"Sure enough, it became apparent there was something happening, and people started in the tent—the poker game sort of broke up, and if I recall correctly, Jack was part of the game. We had a fox hole dug right near the tent. I remember we all went. Jack was very slender and he could have got in the fox hole very nicely. I was one of the last to leave the tent, and ahead of me was this fat Lucinas from Detroit, who was about as wide as he was tall, and he got stuck in the hole, and I remember somebody sort of gave him a good kick and he sort of exploded into the fox hole where Jack Kennedy was."

This time, however, the Japanese air raid *was* aimed at Lumbari in a deliberate effort to disrupt the PTs before the forthcoming night's Tokyo Express to Kolombangara. Why Warfield—who had been specifically warned in advance by Admiral Wilkinson, his superior officer, about "Jap air out to get PTs"—did not advise his men or disperse his boats remains a mystery. Two PT boats were destroyed in the raid, and a number of men were killed or wounded.

Far from blaming himself, however, Warfield merely claimed that the air raid gave him a vital clue as to the route the Tokyo Express would take to Kolombangara that night. Commander Arleigh Burke had been ordered to take a force of U.S. destroyers *north* of Kolombangara, to intercept the Japanese convoy if it circled the northeast coast of the island before dropping off its crucial cargo of reinforcements. However, if the Japanese were so concerned about Lumbari-based PT boats, Warfield reasoned, it must mean the Express was going to come *south,* through the area where the Lumbari-based PTs normally operated: the Blackett Strait between Kolombangara and Gizo islands.

Once the aftereffects of the air raid had been assessed and two dislodged American torpedoes (which had raced in mad circles around the harbor) had finally beached themselves, Warfield summoned his skippers. He'd been ordered, he explained, to "operate the maximum number of PTs," and he intended to do just that. Without rehearsal or consideration of the likely confusion resulting from such a mass sortie, "all the boats that were available that night were to go out," Ross recalled, in the biggest PT operation in the Solomon Islands campaign so far.

Fifteen boats were found to be serviceable. To ensure that the Japanese did not get wind of such a large operation, the captains were ordered to maintain minimum long-range radio contact with Warfield's Lumbari bunker while observing strict silence among themselves, except in emer-

gency. Warfield then divided them into four groups, each group to operate completely independently of the others. The groups were directed to
follow the hit-and-run torpedo tactics that had proved utterly ineffective
throughout the previous nineteen months of the war: first firing their
torpedoes, then "getting the hell out" of the area to escape from both the
Japanese destroyers and one another.

Meanwhile, thanks to the Japanese air raid on the afternoon of August
1, there was no time to try out Jack Kennedy's makeshift cannon,
strapped to the bows of *PT 109,* though Jack did at the last minute acquire
an officer to take charge of the gun. "My boat had already been sunk by
our own planes," Barney Ross recalled,

> so Bill [Battle, skipper of *PT 166*] and I had no boat and we were sort
> of at loose ends on the beach. And with the beach having air raids
> and everything, I was down on the dock when Jack Kennedy and all
> the other boat skippers that were going out that night were running
> out to their boats to go out on patrol. The boats had come in from
> the anchorage, to pick them up after the intelligence briefing.
>
> So I was standing on the dock when Jack comes running down and
> the *109* started in to pick him up—they just nosed the bow in, and
> Kennedy jumped over, onto the boat, and I said, "Do you mind if
> I come along, Jack?" And he said, "No, come on—I'm short of men
> anyway"—because they'd lost a couple of guys the last time they'd
> been out on patrol, so he was short a couple of people. . . .
>
> And I remember, on the bow of the boat they had this contrap-
> tion, this old Army—well, I guess it wasn't too old, but was one of
> these Army single shot 37mm cannon with the wheels still on it, and
> the carpenters had been in the process of fastening this in some way
> to the decks so that it wouldn't roll around. So Jack said, "Do you
> know anything about these 37 mms?" I said, "No, I'm afraid I
> don't." He said, "Well I don't think any of us are too well informed
> on it either." So we both looked at it, and finally figured out how to
> operate it.

Ross, Jack decreed, was to be the gunner and forward lookout. "So we
proceeded then to go out, and it was, oh, just about getting dark—just
dusk, and this was the normal time for the PT boats to go out so they
would arrive on station just at darkness, so the Japanese couldn't spot us
from the shore as easily. I hadn't been in on the briefing, so I was
blissfully ignorant of what the purpose of this mass exodus of boats
was—which was to intercept these four [Japanese] destroyers."

Ross doubted whether the skippers were briefed on the exact route the
Tokyo Express would take. "They might come all the way to Vila [on the

south side of Kolombangara] or they might not," he recalled later. "They might come on the north side of Kolombangara or they might come on the south side. Our area was the south side."

A career officer, Lieutenant Hank Brantingham, was the first group's leader, replete with radar. As Ross recalled:

> Lieutenant Brantingham was in the lead boat, and I forget the fellows in the other boats, and Jack Kennedy was in the last boat.
>
> It was extremely difficult to keep station on the other boats for it was so dark—an extremely black night. People have often asked me, how could you get sunk in a PT boat by a destroyer? And I have to always say that it was as dark as if you were in a closet with the door shut—it was that kind of night—no moon, no stars.

What Ross neglected to say, as a close friend later revealed, was that he was night blind—unable to see at all in the dark, and therefore a worthless nighttime lookout, a fact of which Jack Kennedy was unaware.

Lieutenant Brantingham, meanwhile, was a PT-boat veteran, having served as executive officer to Bulkeley when they rescued MacArthur from the Philippines. More recently he'd been acting as temporary commander of Kelly's squadron operating out of Lever Harbor, on the north coast of New Georgia. "Kennedy's boat was not in my squadron," Brantingham later recalled, "but had been loaned to us for that night. I was assigned head of all the southwest coast of Kolombangara—maybe ⅓ of the way up. I had radar on my boat—you could call it primitive radar. There was a skipper of the boat, Lieutenant Pessolano—his boat [*PT 159*] was the flagship for my squadron."

Brantingham, like Warfield, was a firm believer in radio silence. "In our squadron we had a pretty firm commitment to radio silence, even to attacking without talking on the radio. When the leading boat saw something and attacked, the other boats were to follow right along without further ado and no further conversation."

This was to prove disastrous, for the Tokyo Express arrived in Blackett Strait a full hour early, thus eluding Arleigh Burke's ambushing force of destroyers that only arrived in the Slot north of Kolombangara half an hour after midnight.

Lieutenant Brantingham, not expecting the Express so early, first thought the pips appearing on his radar screen must be Japanese barges, "which we saw every night. As we got closer and they started shooting at us, it became obvious they weren't barges, they were the destroyers we were more or less expecting. We must have picked them up at a couple of miles because we ran towards them for some time, trying to intercept them. When I fired my torpedoes at them, it was less than a mile—less than two thousand yards. When the destroyer fired, we could see the shell splashes and knew it wasn't a small boat. We were too far off the beach to think they were shore batteries," Brantingham related, for the night was so black that the shore batteries "couldn't have seen anything to shoot at."

Given that the shore batteries could not see his PT boat, how Brantingham imagined that his own trailing team, in pitch dark and without radar or even the license to communicate by radio, would be able to first follow him and then sight the enemy defies explanation. Warfield's squadron policy had been allowed to override common sense, and the dismal story of PT-boat ineffectiveness in the Solomons was now dumbly repeated. Not only did Brantingham's torpedoes all fail to hit their target but his torpedo tubes caught fire, presenting a perfect target to the Japanese. "The destroyers were firing shells all around us," William Liebenow, the skipper of *PT 157*, recalled. "Brantingham's tube was on fire and it was like a beacon. I swung between him and the destroyer to lay a smoke screen so they couldn't see the fire and use it as a point of aim." Meanwhile, Liebenow himself had managed to fire two torpedoes—as ineffectively as Brantingham's. "Then we both got out of there, zigzagging and laying smoke."

According to Liebenow, the two PTs, having let the Japanese convoy go straight past them, didn't stop. "We zigzagged for ten or fifteen miles, I have no idea what direction we went. We were just going."

In fact they had allowed the entire Japanese convoy to pass them and had fled the wrong way, ending up in the Gizo Strait. Meanwhile no attempt at communication with the remaining two boats in their division was made by either Liebenow or Brantingham. By the time Liebenow finally came alongside Brantingham's flagship, behind Gizo Island, it was clear that they had lost all trace of Lieutenant Kennedy on *PT 109* and Lieutenant Lowrey on *PT 162*.

Instead of trying to raise them on the radio, Brantingham now made the fatal decision to go home, leaving Liebenow—who still had two torpedoes left—to return to Blackett Strait, but taking with him the only radar set in the division. Brantingham later blamed Warfield, claiming that Warfield "ordered all boats who had fired their torpedoes back to the base." But PT-boat skippers in other theaters of the war, such as Jack's friend Fred Rosen, considered it a gross dereliction of duty for a division leader's boat ever to leave the battle area without its fellow vessels. "It was unheard of in the Mediterranean," Rosen later declared, "like leaving your own family."

Sadly, it was not the only time it would happen that night.

A Screwed-up Action

On *PT 109* "things were going along fairly uneventfully until about I'd say around II o'clock," Ross recalled,

> when suddenly we were bathed in a searchlight. We were pretty close to the beach over on the Kolombangara side, and we found ourselves illuminated brightly by a searchlight. Some kind of heavy gun was firing at us, fairly close, and so Jack took what they call evasive action—the whole idea of PT boats is of course to surprise the enemy, and when they surprise you with a searchlight the idea is to get out of the path of the searchlight.
>
> We'd been just cruising with one engine as quietly as possible so we wouldn't be discovered, and so we gunned the motors and Jack zigzagged around and pretty soon the light went out.

Without word from Brantingham, who had disappeared into the night with the radar set, there was no way the crew of *PT 109* could be certain what had illuminated them. Ross related:

> Apparently from later reports [the light] was one of the Jap destroyers that was going along the beach. We were so close to the beach that it didn't occur to us, or to me at least—I didn't discuss it with Jack at the time—that this was a destroyer. We thought it was a shore battery, a searchlight on the beach. It didn't appear to be moving either—apparently this was one of the destroyers that either had stopped, was up against the beach, or was going very slowly down the beach. Later we learned that Brantingham, our lead boat, whom we'd lost station with, had fired torpedoes at this, for with his radar Brantingham had realized it was a ship and had fired torpedoes. At the same time we didn't know what the score was.

Another member of Jack's crew, Charles Harris, gave a similar but more vehement account. Because the Japanese destroyers arrived so early, "we had no idea there were ships out there that night. We didn't know the Express had gone down to Vila. We thought it was shore batteries firing. Our lead boat, the radar boat, picked something up but they didn't tell us anything about it. They took off after it and left us sitting there. We laid smoke once because the shells were landing pretty close. When we got back we were really going to look up that skipper and give him the business for leaving us high and dry like that. We were kind of mad. He had the eyes and we didn't."

Meanwhile, an almost identical fate befell the second of Warfield's four groups—PTs *171, 169, 172,* and *163.* The radar-equipped lead boat, *PT 171,* saw blips on its screen, vainly fired all its torpedoes, then made its way back to Rendova, leaving the other boats in its group spotlit by the destroyers and lucky not to be blown apart, especially *PT 163,* which could not start up its second and third engines for ten minutes—"the longest minutes you'll ever realize," skipper Phil Potter confessed later. "We were just lying there, sitting ducks. . . . The other two boats tried to follow Berndtson out of the strait, I think. We couldn't go because we had no engines. So we were left there, all alone."

Ironically, *PT 163,* stalled and alone in the pitch dark and showing no phosphorescent wake, was actually safer than the other two boats, PTs *169* and *172,* which lost visual contact with Berndtson's lead boat and tried to make their own way home. They were soon spotted by no fewer than four Japanese floatplanes, which dropped flares and bombs on them, fortunately without success.

Warfield's third group, sitting in Ferguson Passage, the gap through which the PT boats entered Blackett Strait, enacted the same story. The lead boat, equipped with radar, launched all its torpedoes against what it took to be two destroyers (the pips on the radar screen may well have been PT boats of the second group racing away from their encounter with the Express) and headed home, leaving its radarless colleagues in the dark. Revving up their engines, the other boats made their way toward Kolombangara, only to find themselves also attacked by Japanese float-planes, which had spotted their phosphorescent wakes. They also then went home.

The fourth group's experience, minutes after midnight, was even more chaotic. Its leader, Lieutenant Rome, was also equipped with radar. Recognizing the pips on his screen as warships, Rome fired off his four torpedoes and made off, pursued by not only destroyer shells but a Japanese floatplane. Like the other three division leaders, he failed to signal to the other two boats in his division what was happening. Thus, when Lieutenant Keresey, the skipper of *PT 105,* saw only gun flashes, he, like Kennedy, at first assumed that Japanese shore batteries were firing. "My first reaction was that these were shore guns," Keresey recalled.

> It was so dark, we were going in toward Kolombangara. . . . All I could see was a line of gunfire coming right down the coast.
> My division leader, I don't know if he ever fired his torpedoes or not, but all of a sudden I saw him turn around and slowly pass me

in the other direction. The other boat in the division turned around and followed him, but I hadn't got any command and I knew there was a target in there. . . . So I came up, we were not supposed to come up on the radio unless we absolutely had to, I came up on the radio, trying to call my division leader, and I said, "Where is the target?" because I knew it was up ahead of me somewhere. I didn't know where the hell this guy—the division leader—was going because he turned round and went the other direction. He was already astern of me about five hundred yards and I was kind of left in this pocket of islands and didn't know what was going on—just like Kennedy up the way. We both had similar experiences.

Right at that moment, by coincidence, a Jap plane dropped a bomb on him [the division leader]. Didn't hit him but dropped a bomb on him, about a half mile behind me. I knew they were bombs. Frankly, this division leader didn't have a hell of a lot of experience, but I knew a bomb when it went off as opposed to shell fire, because I'd been under both. These were definitely bombs—a couple of them.

And he came up on the radio and said something like, really reporting to the base, "I'm under fire from a Japanese destroyer and running."

So I came up on the radio and said, "Where is the destroyer?"

Then he realized that I hadn't followed, and he came up with my call sign, which was Oak Seven, and he said, "Get out of there, you're in a trap."

So I came up again and said, "Is the target behind me?"

And then the base [Warfield] came on, thinking, I guess, that I couldn't hear, with an order for me to get out of there, I was in a trap.

Back at the Lumbari base, Lieutenant Commander Warfield was more in the dark than his crews. "They were all excited," his communications officer later recalled. "They were sitting out there waiting for something to happen. It [the Tokyo Express] came through in a hurry and took them by surprise. And they were talking on the radio and I think Warfield said, 'What the hell is the matter with you fellows? Get in there and fight!'

"A lot of these skippers were pretty green, hell yes, we could hear them hollering—they were all excited and all hell broke loose and they fired their torpedoes, you'd think the damn war was starting all over again. Pandemonium broke out when that happened."

Warfield's imprecations on the airwaves were much resented. "He said a lot of things on the radio. . . . They said it was like he was directing a football team, you see, because he was back there and they were up forward. . . . A lot of the skippers out there that night later expressed resentment that Warfield was not with them, riding a boat. That he was sitting back at Lumbari, like a quarterback directing his team from the sideline."

"If you think these things are conducted with great skill and aplomb," the skipper of *PT 105* said later,

> forget it. I decided none of them knew what they were talking about.
>
> I didn't know why this guy [the division leader] had left. But I was convinced there was a destroyer ahead of me. I was approaching Kolombangara and it was very dark. One thing you've got to understand. Kolombangara was a big mountain. When a ship gets inboard of it and you're on the outside, you can't see them. Even something as big as a destroyer. Most people don't realize that, but you have to get a silhouette. But I was convinced they were in there because I'd seen this gunfire. It had stopped, but those destroyers must have been in there about 100 yards or so off the coast.
>
> Then, by God, my gunner's mate in my forward turret, seventeen years old, damned if he didn't spot this destroyer. I couldn't see it at first, then I did. . . . I let two tubes go off—I was hoping to get another shot at him—and I was taken under fire both by the destroyer and a Jap plane. Then I lost the destroyer entirely. I was getting this static from the Base to get out of there. So I turned around and went back to find my division leader.

All four leaders were now on their way back to Lumbari, taking with them the PT armada's only radar sets. Keresey, dissatisfied with his own performance, wheeled around and reapproached Kolombangara.

> I couldn't find him [the group leader], so I looked at the chart and figured the destroyers had gone into this narrow strait, which I think was actually [a continuation of] Blackett Strait, between Kolombangara and New Georgia. I knew that somewhere in there they had some kind of base, and that's where they'd be either unloading or taking on troops.
>
> I was closest to where they would have stopped. Kennedy must have been five miles up the line. He was in the beginning group when they first spotted them. I decided to sneak into that strait and see if I could spot one unloading. Then I'd have a real sitting duck.

Guarding against this very danger, the Japanese had sent seaplanes to circle the whole area. As Keresey recalled, "It seemed to me they had to have half the Jap air force out protecting these guys, they were intermittently bombing somebody, one of the boats. So I started to sneak in at very slow speed, about the same thing Kennedy was doing five miles up the line—though of course he was at that point out of it. He didn't realize it."

Soon Keresey's lookout spotted the shape of a vessel. "The gunner's mate—he had wonderful night vision—he spotted this guy sneaking out. After about thirty seconds I managed to get the glasses on him and sure enough, there was this destroyer. He couldn't have been going more than eight to ten knots. I got a good look at him and had no sooner figured what would be the right lead [for a torpedo attack] when he spotted me. I saw his wake boil up as he went up to full speed to get out of there."

Amidst flares and shells Keresey fired his remaining two torpedoes—to no avail. Then he, too, went home.

Abandoned by their leaders and enjoined to radio silence, the remaining PT boats had no real chance, in pitch dark, of ambushing the Japanese destroyers, Keresey reflected later. "Only the division leaders had radar, the rest of us had to depend on just regular vision. No one could alter the fact that the division leaders were the ones who fired, and left the rest of us out there with no radar." It was, he acknowledged gravely and with considerable understatement, a pretty "screwed-up action."

Sliced in Half

While the Tokyo Express unloaded its vital cargo of men and munitions at Vila, PTs *109* and *162* were left to themselves in Blackett Strait. "We didn't know what the score was, and so we resumed our patrolling back and forth with the other boat," Barney Ross later recalled.

No code name for the Express had been given, and though *PT 109*'s radioman, John Maguire, could hear something of the confused operations farther south, Warfield neglected to put out an intelligible update to the remaining skippers. As a result, neither Jack nor Lowrey knew what was going on, nor even for certain that the Express had passed them.

At two A.M. on Sunday, August 2, 1943, three hours after Jack's brush with the searchlight, PTs *109* and *162* were joined by a lost PT boat from the second group, Phil Potter's *PT 169*. Potter was certain, later, that the three skippers talked to one another over their VHF radios and concluded that the Express must have passed through their cordon but might well return the same way.

The Japanese were themselves unsure which route home to take. Three of the four Japanese destroyers—the *Hagikaze,* the *Arashe,* and the *Shigure*—had been converted into fast transport ships while the fourth, Captain Katsumori Yamashiro's Destroyer Division II flagship *Amagiri*, acted as an escort, watching for enemy vessels. When Yamashiro had first received signals from Rabaul that American destroyers would be waiting for them northeast of Kolombangara, in the Kula Gulf, there had been some discussion as to whether to cancel the operation. Owing to the vital need for reinforcements, "it was decided to carry on the action," Yamashiro later recorded: taking the southwestern route through Blackett Strait. "Thirty minutes before reaching the anchorage the force encountered a group of enemy motor-torpedo boats at the eastern end of Ferguson Passage. While these boats were being engaged and repulsed, the transports arrived at Vila, Kolombangara, at 2230 and began to unload."

For an hour and a half, Yamashiro related, while almost a thousand Japanese troops and much-needed arms and ammunition were put ashore, the "*Amagiri* patrolled at 21 knots in Blackett Strait, which is to the southwest of Kolombangara, between that island and Gizo Island, running north and south, on a track which described an east-west–oriented rectangle."

Finding no sign of American destroyers, despite the brush with PT boats that must have alerted the U.S. naval command, it was decided to go home the way they had come:

> During the unloading there was an enemy air raid in which four bombs were dropped but no damage was inflicted. Unloading was completed at 2400 hours and the Transport Unit departed the anchorage to return to base.
>
> *Amagiri* was on a westerly course, after about an hour and a half of patrolling, when we caught sight of the Transport Unit, its unloading completed, heading north and trailing whitish wakes along the southwest shore of Kolombangara. To avoid being left behind, *Amagiri* turned in the direction of the Transport Unit and increased speed to 30 knots. *Amagiri* was then to the west of and about 2,000 meters distant from the track of the Transport Unit.
>
> Five or six minutes later, precisely at 0200 hours, a black boat-like object was sighted at about 1,000 meters directly in front of our ship. For just an instant I thought it was one of our inter-island steamboats, and then I knew that it was an enemy torpedo boat. It did not change its heading in the slightest, but continued steadily to approach. The bow of the boat seemed to be pointing to starboard of *Amagiri* [i.e., due east]. In the event of a collision we would be damaged too, and if a torpedo should be detonated it would be much worse. Instantly, in an attempt to pass astern of the boat, I extended my left arm and shouted "Hard aport!" I cannot now recall whether my order was repeated by the ship's commanding officer or by the

navigation officer. *Amagiri* had just started to respond to the helm when the torpedo boat disappeared as though it had been swallowed up. In the same instant there was a dull thud with a flash of light, and in the next instant there was a smell of smoldering cotton. This was not occasioned by an exploding torpedo, but rather the igniting of fuel by the sparks which must have been caused by the tremendous impact of the ship against the light hull of the boat. The fire dissipated rapidly as it drifted off to starboard. Shortly thereafter (about eight seconds according to later calculations) the ship began to vibrate. This resulted from the ship's continuing turn to port, which threw a part of the torpedo boat into contact with the ship's starboard propeller.

Emergency measures were called for, but first of all, the order was given, "Hold steady on basic course!" There was minor damage to the bow of the ship which resulted in slight seepage from bow waves when the ship ran at high speed. We found there was more vibration in the ship at 24 knots than there was at 28 knots, so the latter speed was maintained. An urgent message was sent to headquarters reporting the incident and measures taken.

But did the *Amagiri* really try to pass astern of the PT boat, as Yamashiro later claimed? Or was the collision intentional, as the *Amagiri*'s skipper, Lieutenant Commander Hanami, later maintained? Captain Yamashiro subsequently called Hanami a barefaced liar. "I say definitely that it was a collision by chance," Yamashiro maintained, anxious to maintain good U.S.-Japanese relations, and "in no sense whatever a body blow intentional on the part of Mr. Hanami, the skipper, as he is publicizing. . . . All that suffices me being to see to it that Mr. Hanami's lie is brought to light and prevented from being composed into Mr. Kennedy's life history." In a highly publicized campaign, Yamashiro's version was later printed in Japanese newspapers under the headline HANAMI FABRICATED STORY, FORMER NAVY CAPTAIN SAYS. "Mr. Yamashiro considers Mr. Hanami guilty not only of distorting the facts but also of ignoring the existence of superior officers and even implying that these superior officers were actually under his (Hanami's) command."

Here was the rub, for Hanami, in his version of the incident, had never even mentioned the existence of a senior commander on board his destroyer. As the report of Yamashiro's account explained, "In the case of the *Amagiri* it was the lone ship forming the 11th Destroyer Fleet, so fleet commander Capt. Yamashiro was aboard as well as destroyer commander Lieutenant Commander Hanami. Naturally Capt. Yamashiro was giving orders from the bridge and Lieutenant Commander Hanami was acting according to these orders."

This was not how Hanami saw things. "Of course I was commanding on the bridge," he maintained adamantly.

It was August 2, 1943, that my destroyer was on her way to her base at 30 knots. That night it was cloudy and squally, so that our visibility was very poor. As we had confronted with U.S. PT boats on our way to Kolombangara, I ordered our men to take their offensive positions and keep watch especially.

At about 2.30 a.m. we discovered an enemy boat bearing at about 10 [degrees] right, 800–1,000 meters from us. In a moment I took it for PT boat and planned the heading straight for her, which we thought the best tactics. I ordered the helmsman, "Ten degrees turn! PT boat heading," and made our destroyer face to the PT, which was bearing as before (I think it did not discover our destroyer at that time). In an instant we crashed into her and cut her in two. She went past by and sank down near our stern, flaming up.

The sight of this collision—the fire started in, and the strange sound coming from the PT boat—is now deeply impressed in my mind. I, however, did not feel strong shock and did not find any crew of the wrecked boat in the water around.

In this connection we stopped our ship for a while and examined the extent of damages to the bow and screw, which was fortunately found to be bearable for high speed navigation. So we, in order to go out from the enemy's air-power before the sunrise, started for our base at about 26 knots, arriving there safely that day. . . . After the above collision, we had kept strict watch during stopping our ship and examining damages, but could neither find any crews of the wrecked P.T. nor other U.S. boats around us.

When Yamashiro disputed this version, Hanami reiterated his own. "I had come to the conclusion that it was too difficult to shoot and hit a target as small and fast as a torpedo boat, and that ramming was the best method of dealing with them. Such an opportunity had never arisen in my many previous encounters with torpedo boats, but this was a favorable situation for ramming and I decided to try it. Captain Yamashiro says that he had extended his left arm and ordered a hard turn to port in order to avoid a collision. At the time of this incident I was at the extreme starboard side of the bridge, leaning over the rail, straining to look forward, and I neither heard his order nor did I see his arm extended. . . . We headed towards it (without increasing speed) and, in a flash, sliced it in half!"

A Sorry Tale

If the Japanese officers vehemently disputed what had happened, so did the American PT-boat skippers. Some said they only learned on their return to Lumbari of the sinking; others claimed to have reported the sinking over the airwaves to Warfield. "I don't remember whether anyone radioed me that the *109* had collided with the destroyer or not," Warfield later maintained. "You've got to remember that there were a lot of things going on in those guys' minds, and they had a lot to do too."

Warfield, in his bunker, certainly had no idea of *PT 109*'s position—"I couldn't tell where he was"—and assumed Jack's crew was "kind of sleepy." He speculated that in the panic when the Japanese destroyer was sighted, "if he saw this thing coming at him, and got bugged a little bit and shoved his throttles forward, he'd have killed his engines, and I think that's what he did. I can't swear to that, but that's the only explanation that makes any sense. He shouldn't have been muffled. He knew the destroyers were coming out. . . . He may have been idling on all three [engines] or two, and shoved them up too fast and killed them."

From Warfield's perspective, there was no excuse for Jack not to have seen the destroyer. "We had a briefing every night. We had a map and we'd show them what was happening, where they were supposed to take up stations and where they were supposed to cover with their torpedo firing. We showed them exactly where the Express was coming and where they were going out again." In Warfield's view, the failure of his fifteen-strong PT-boat fleet was inexcusable, with *PT 109*'s failure to see and avoid a Japanese destroyer the least excusable part. "The stern wake [of the destroyer] would probably show up even worse than the bow wave. It was a pretty quiet night, and with the binoculars they should have seen it. That's pretty phosphorescent water, you know. They knew what time they [the destroyers] were coming down. I don't see how they could have avoided it."

Warfield clearly had no idea of conditions out at sea that night; indeed, as Lieutenant Potter later confided, Warfield had never trained his Squadron 10 crews in night patrolling before arriving in the Solomons, and thereafter never went out himself. Nevertheless Warfield was quick to accuse his crews of cowardice and later judged that Jack "wasn't a particularly good boat commander."

J. E. Gibson, who succeeded Warfield as commander of Squadron 10 and was not present at all during the fateful operation to stop the Express, was even more critical of Lieutenant Kennedy. "He lost the *109* through very poor organization of his crew," Gibson later declared.

> The person who sighted the destroyer that night was a passenger aboard the boat that night, not one of the regular crew. He'd been cruising with his engines muffled and so he couldn't speed up rapidly. Everything he did up until he was in the water was the wrong thing. Poor judgment. Every captain knew that the engines would spit and cough for maybe thirty seconds to a minute before you could get going, when you were running with your engines muffled. He was going over there that night to look for Japanese destroyers, and he got lost from the other three boats going over there. That was unheard-of. He could have continued down—he knew where the leader was going and he could have picked him up. . . . I was technical adviser to the picture "*PT 109*" [made in 1963] and when we got to that part the director said, "Well, Captain, why did he get lost?"
>
> Well, that shouldn't happen—he just wasn't watching. The helmsman couldn't have been watching and the lookouts couldn't have been watching. Then the director said,
>
> "Then what did he do?"
>
> Well, he cruised around muffled.
>
> The director said, "Why did he do that, out in the middle?"
>
> Well, I don't know why he did it. He could either have gone ahead, he knew the course and speed, there was a chance he would get tangled up directly with the destroyers, and one boat against several destroyers would have been pretty bad. Or he could have aborted and gone back to his own base. But he just stayed muffled out in the center there and there wasn't any reason for doing that really. Losing the *PT 109,* that was inexcusable, Nobody could understand that. Those who love Kennedy can't believe he made a stupid mistake like that. On the picture one of the team said, "We can't have him get lost out in the middle. You have to make up something to make it look good on the screen. You can't have Mr. President do anything stupid on the screen."

Gibson, however, was an ignoramus. For Kennedy, Lowrey, and Potter, the picture on the night of August 1, 1943, looked vastly different than that of a Hollywood set; it was a night of black confusion, with no attempt by the commanding officer in his bunker to control the battle other than by imprecations. Far from "staying out muffled in the center," Jack had grouped with PTs *162* and *169* to form a new division; they were the only boats in Squadron 10, in fact, to form a picket line across the

Express's escape route, even though they were deprived of radar. The remaining PT boats, south of Kolombangara, missed the Express's run home entirely, as did Arleigh Burke's six radar-equipped American destroyers, who departed for home at three A.M.

Far from committing a "stupid mistake," Kennedy, Lowrey, and Potter behaved with commendable courage and intelligence given the chaos, cowardice, and confusion elsewhere. Only radar-equipped boats would have been able to spot the Japanese destroyers in such dark conditions. Being without radar, Lieutenant Potter reiterated, "that's number one. We had to rely mainly on sight. It was a pitch black night. There was no moon and it was darker than hell and a couple of times a couple of float planes picked us up. They got tired of dogging us and left."

Because of the floatplanes, all three boats nosed along on one engine each, attempting to keep down their wakes, listen for enemy vessels, and keep station with one another. It was this latter imperative—keeping station a mile apart in pitch-dark conditions in an area of squall-lashed sea almost a third as wide as the English Channel, enjoined by their base commander to radio silence—that was the hardest part. The lookouts necessarily spent more time watching for one another than for the enemy. "It was extremely difficult to keep station on the other boats, for it was so dark," Ross distinctly recalled.

> At the time we didn't know what the score was, and so we resumed our patrolling back and forth, and with the other boat. And occasionally from time to time we would lose sight of the other boat, because we were trying to stay as far apart as possible so we would be able to cover as much of the strait as we could, and at the same time see one another. So occasionally we'd lose touch with one another. . . .
>
> In the early hours of the morning we were still patrolling, as slowly as possible, just back and forth. This strait was about eight miles wide; we'd go over to Kolombangara and back to Gizo, back and forth, back and forth. And trying to keep station with the other boat. And about one or two o'clock in the morning we had temporarily lost contact with the other boat and we were nosing along on one engine, when all of us more or less at the same time spotted this white water off the starboard bow.

Just how hard it was to sight or hear an enemy destroyer in such conditions was reflected by the fact that the *Amagiri* had patrolled for an hour and a half in the Blackett Strait during the unloading of its sister ships without being seen by or seeing any PTs. Thereafter all three Japanese transport destroyers had managed to leave Vila anchorage, pass

Ferguson Passage and through the three-boat PT cordon in Blackett Strait to "the Slot"—the sea highway between the two chains of Solomon Islands—without a single ship being observed. A mile and a half behind the transport destroyers, racing at thirty knots to catch up with them, came their single escort, the *Amagiri.* Potter, farthest away, was the first to see it.

"We were crossing back across Blackett Strait. It's hard to remember how far we'd gone or how long it had taken," Potter reflected, "but I'd say we originally formed up somewhere around one A.M. By the time we'd made that southward sweep and were going back again it was probably around two, two-thirty. The thing that amazes me to this day was we saw this destroyer's wake coming towards him and we radioed to Kennedy to look on his starboard bow, there was a wake coming directly toward him." Potter could not be certain in the darkness, but he recalled:

> It appeared to us to be a destroyer, and what else would you expect when you'd seen destroyers that night? It was black and in those waters out there, on a real dark night like that, any wake is very highly phosphorescent. Porpoises a lot of times if they were going at a good clip would come right at us and you'd think it was a torpedo coming at you. It's amazing, the phosphorescence, you can see it for great distances. . . .
>
> We could see this destroyer bow wake coming directly at Kennedy. It was closest to him and headed right to him and we were two miles behind him. We saw it and radioed to him. We tried to. We didn't get any response. No response. Nothing.

Lowrey, closer to both Potter and Kennedy, did not respond either, though his crew "also saw it because I think I recall them calling out to him after we had spotted it," Potter related. "But the thing that did amaze us was that we got no reply from either of those boats. We wondered how on the ball they were."

Three enemy destroyers had just passed them without being seen, their silhouettes lost against the black landmass of Kolombangara and the squally bleakness of the night. Why the *Amagiri,* at the tail end of the convoy, should suddenly have appeared so clearly is hard to say. By now, however, Kennedy's crew had finally seen the destroyer and were attempting to take action. From sighting to the collision was "ten or fifteen seconds," Potter later recalled—the same period Jack's crew calculated it took between seeing the destroyer and being hit. Helpless, Potter could only watch, distraught, as "the destroyer rammed the boat and it blew up. Just shot into flames. . . . You could see they went right through the boat.

There was an immediate explosion and you knew the gas tanks had exploded. It was high-octane aviation gas. . . . I was quite close to him. We could see men on deck and we could definitely make out the whole ship."

Potter didn't "recall what the heck Lowrey did," but after waiting for the destroyer to clear "the area where Lowrey was, I fired my two aft torpedoes." He claimed the Japanese destroyer was "firing at us by that time, so the only thing to do, seeing that was one destroyer and knowing there were a couple of more back there, we turned about, we made a port turn, and picked up speed and laid a smoke screen and headed south for Gizo. I never did see either boat again that night. I never remember what Lowrey did or how he got out that night."

Unknown to Potter, however, there was no reason to run away, since the *Amagiri* was the last part of the Express, which had now passed through their cordon and was "home free." Potter, meanwhile, raced behind Gizo Island, which he remembered circling before later returning to the area of the collision. He claimed he then saw a ship's wake, fired his remaining two torpedoes, "and saw them explode. We got credit for a possible hit on that one," he remembered, though what he could have hit is difficult in retrospect to imagine.

Potter claimed to have then spent half to three quarters of an hour patrolling in the area and watching out for signs of wreckage or life from *PT 109.* "We remembered seeing the fire after the explosion and we thought part of the hull might be burning if we'd gotten back to the area, which we did." The crew could see nothing in the blackness of Blackett Strait, however. "We didn't see another boat that night. I don't remember if we were on the radio to Warfield telling him what was going on. I definitely reported by radio that the *109* had been hit, for sure, after I fired the first two torpedoes and was laying smoke. No, there wasn't a general alarm from Warfield saying the *109* has been hit, go look for survivors. . . . After we fired our other two torpedoes, we headed for the base. I'd say we headed for the base around 3.30–4.00 a.m. We usually liked to get out of that area before daylight because the [U.S.] Army Air Force planes would take over in daylight. You usually feared them more, if you were in Japanese waters, than you did the Japanese."

Lieutenant Lowrey in *PT 162* also left the scene, having lost contact with *PT 169* and under the impression that *PT 109* had gone down with all hands, returning to base, apparently without bothering to search for survivors.

For the PT boats it had been a night of utter futility. Over thirty torpedoes had been fired without scoring a single hit. The four radar-equipped division leaders had all abandoned their comrades. The Tokyo

Express had brought sufficient supplies and men to Kolombangara to keep the battle for New Georgia going for another month and had escaped to Rabaul with impunity after sinking a PT boat.

"As soon as we had anchored at Rabaul," said Captain Yamashiro, "I went to flagship *Sendai,* accompanied by skipper Hanami, to report to my boss, Rear Admiral Ijuin, commander of Destroyer Squadron 3. On the quarterdeck the Admiral came forward to greet us and laughingly said to me, 'Captain, why didn't your radio report say that the torpedo boat had been crushed underfoot?' I can still picture that tall, wide-eyed man."

For the Japanese, as for the Americans, PT boats were a weapon of propaganda more than of war. By August 4 the Tokyo newspapers were ablaze with news of "Our Dauntless Destroyer Squadron in Vella Night Action." Beneath the headline ENEMY TORPEDO BOAT RUN THROUGH, the *Asahi Shimbun* proclaimed that "in the early morning darkness of 2 August these same ships engaged three enemy torpedo boats in Vella Gulf, west of Kolombangara Island. One destroyer ploughed through an enemy boat at high speed and, in a flash, sent it to the bottom of the sea. This is the first time in the Greater East Asia War that a destroyer has rammed an enemy boat in two. It serves as an example of the uniquely heroic feats of which our destroyers are capable."

For the United States Navy by contrast, it was a sorry tale of misfortune and incompetence. Not only had *PT 109* been sunk, but none of the accompanying PT boats had made the slightest attempt at rescue after the explosion. By the time one of the PT boats returned, an hour later, it could find no vestige of men or vessel. *PT 109,* with its skipper, John F. Kennedy, and its crew of ten officers and men, was simply washed off Warfield's slate, a symbol of the most screwed-up PT-boat action of World War II.

PART
·12·
SHIPWRECKED

Lt. John F. Kennedy, photographed shortly after his rescue,
August 1943 (John F. Kennedy Library)

Done For

Though he came from a different squadron, Jack was a popular skipper among the crews at Lumbari, and some of his colleagues did in fact press for a search party to go out to find him. Lieutenant Dick Keresey remembered that "the next morning, when it was found that he [Kennedy] had been lost, back at base I remember a group of us—we had no torpedoes so we were pretty light and could really travel fast—we wanted to go back and look for him. Although from the report we'd gotten, none of us thought—there was another boat captain who was within a couple of hundred yards, Lowrey. I remember this fellow saying, 'There's no chance. The boat went up in a ball of flame.' There was a whole discussion about it—must have been six A.M."

William Battle, another skipper, actually took on fuel for a search but was ordered to stop. "Bill Battle told me Warfield, who was commander of the base, would not permit anybody to go up there," Johnny Iles later recalled. "Battle was over there tanking up and he was told to get away, come on back and berth up, mind his own business. He told me this at the time."

Warfield wanted no more disasters. Al Cluster, Jack's Squadron 2 commander, recalled that he was still in the Russell Islands when he heard the news "that Kennedy's boat had been lost, that he had not come back from the patrol. Since I'd gotten out there in April, this was the first boat or men that I had lost. I think I hitched a ride up to Rendova on some other boat. I requested an air search." But even Cluster held out little hope in the light of what he had been told. "When the patrol commander came back, he said there had been a big explosion and fire, so it sounded like everybody was lost. The decision was made by the base commander, and I certainly don't fault him on it, that it would be hopeless."

Back in Tulagi, Johnny Iles was distraught. A fellow Roman Catholic, he and Jack had often argued about religion—indeed Jack had recently appeared to have lost his faith altogether, though he had promised he would talk to Father Sheehan, his father's chaplain, once he got back to the States. Now there would be no chance, prompting Iles to go and see Father McCarthy, the Catholic priest at Tulagi, to "say some masses for Jack and his crew," as Iles recalled.

"The night *PT 109* went out I was in the Florida Islands," Jim Reed remembered. "The next morning we heard that *PT 109* hadn't returned and they'd seen an explosion and a fire. I was very sad. I couldn't believe it. He had many friends there, almost everybody knew him. He was very well liked." Lennie Thom, too, was a popular figure. So was Barney Ross, with his big heart and reputation for getting into scrapes.

Barney's friend from Melville, Red Fay, simply refused to believe the report in Tulagi that "John F. Kennedy and his entire crew were lost. It was a stunning blow to everyone," Fay recalled.

> What crushed me most was the news that Barney, who had gone along for the ride, had perished with them. All the humor and laughter which made living in a remote war-ridden area many times a great ride suddenly vanished. I poured my sadness plus bitterness out in a letter to my sister Sally at Stanford. It seemed so totally unfair that someone who added so much to the pleasure of all those around him had to die.
>
> After the shock of the first report, more complete information started to pour in. *PT 109* was operating with *PT 169,* a boat from Squadron 10 whose captain was Lieutenant (junior grade) Philip Potter. In his report he claimed that a Japanese Destroyer ran down Lieutenant Kennedy's boat. It exploded, blowing apart itself and everybody on it so that there was no trace anywheres. Potter claimed he had gone back to the site of the explosion but found nothing.

Fay remembered being dissatisfied with this version. As he afterward noted in the first draft of his book, *The Pleasure of His Company:*

> To me that just didn't make sense. The more I dug into this episode, the more Potter's story disintegrated. Being down in Tulagi, several hundred miles from the site of the incident, the inconsistencies of the reports just magnified my suspicions that no concerted effort had been made to immediately go to the scene of the accident after its occurrence. My doubts were confirmed when I ran into Potter two or three days after the accident when he arrived down in Tulagi. He had just left the staff headquarters on the island just across the bay from Calvertville when we met in the street.
>
> "Phil," I inquired, "from all the reports and information that have been received down here the whole episode of the loss of *PT 109* has an aura of incredibility. Since you were on the other boat in the section, what is your account?"
>
> Potter then proceeded to recount the operation of the evening up until the explosion when the Jap Destroyer collided with Lieutenant Kennedy's boat. I cut in at this point.
>
> "Phil, it is from here on in that I lose contact with reality. It seems

almost incredible to me that an ocean, particularly an island waterway, can just swallow up all trace of people and material."

At this point Potter became somewhat irritated and countered,
"Listen, Fay, we went back and thoroughly searched the scene of the
accident and there wasn't a trace of anything."

Fay, distraught, accused Potter of lying. "Anger and loss prompted my
outburst," Fay related, "but my conclusion was further fortified by several members of Potter's boat who without pride admitted that no valid
effort was made to press the search. The same charge could be laid at
Commander Warfield's feet."

Accusing Potter could not bring back the dead, however. For good or
ill, *PT 109* was now a statistic—lost with all hands.

A World in Darkness

Miraculously, however, eleven of the thirteen members of *PT 109*'s crew
had survived. Although most subsequent reports claimed the Japanese
destroyer had cut *PT 109* in two, the description was misleading. As
Lieutenant Byron White's intelligence report later recorded, the two-
thousand-ton Japanese warship smashed into the torpedo boat's starboard side, "striking it forward of the forward starboard tube and
shearing off the starboard side of the boat aft, including the starboard
engine." The destroyer did not therefore cut *PT 109* in two so much as tear
a giant strip off its starboard side, killing two men in the process but
leaving the remainder largely unscathed—and still floating.

Given the force of the collision, it was amazing that anyone survived.
Lennie Thom, the executive officer, was lying down at the time of the
collision, as were three of the crew, who changed watch every two hours
to remain alert. Seeing the destroyer bearing straight at them, Harold
Marney, at the starboard gun, shouted, "Ship at two o'clock!" Bucky
Harris attempted to dive off the side of the boat but was catapulted into
the water by the impact of the collision. Down in the engine room Pat
McMahon was buoyed to the surface by his life jacket. Even the gigantic
fireball left the crew unharmed, since it was swept away from the wreckage by both the wind and the rush of air caused by the Japanese warship's
passage.

John Maguire, the radioman, had been standing to the skipper's right
in the "cockpit" or wheelhouse. He was a relatively old hand, having

joined *PT 109* at Tulagi when he heard that a new skipper was looking for a crew. "Guy named Kennedy," Maguire recalled. "There was a kid on the docks, just wearing khakis. I said, 'Where can we find Kennedy?' He said, 'I'm Kennedy.' I says to my friend, 'Geez, I don't know if I want to go out with this guy. He looks fifteen.' "

Of the collision Maguire recounted:

> We could see something out of the darkness. We're just cruising slow as we can. We're going six miles an hour. Kennedy says, "Sound general quarters!" Everybody was at their battle station anyway. I turned on keys to fire torpedoes. Kennedy signaled the engine room. To this day I don't know if McMahon signaled the engines. This ship's hauling ass at 30 knots. . . . They aimed directly at us to hit us. It crushed Marney. We never saw him again. Kirksey, we never saw again. We were carrying about 1,800 gallons of gasoline. McMahon obviously went down with the engine room. The life jacket brought him up. It was just an act of God. Kennedy got thrown against the wall of the cockpit. . . . The whole ocean was afire. I lift my helmet up. I hear voices. It was the Japanese running up and down the decks of their ship. They were on fire.

Maguire was certain the Japanese shelled the sinking remains of *PT 109*. "They fired two shots. They had these cannon. Kennedy said, 'Everybody in the water!' We all jumped into the sea. The fires were devastating. We swam not too far from the bow of the boat. Mauer [the quartermaster] couldn't swim. Half the Navy couldn't swim! Next thing you know, the whole world's in darkness. Japanese ship is gone. We swam back, got aboard the wreckage. Mauer got a blinker light we had. Kennedy stripped himself and swam out to Harris."

Harris had found himself alone in the water on the starboard side until Pat McMahon bobbed up beside him. "Then he started to yell," Harris recalled, "and I swam over to him and I pulled his helmet off his head because it was jammed. We started to yell and we heard voices. That's when Kennedy came out and he pulled Pop [McMahon] out and he told me to swim with them. I couldn't because I only had one leg and every-thing was so heavy. So he came out and held me up while I took my sweater and jacket off. Then I put my life jacket back on and swam back to the boat. That's when he gave me hell and that's when I told him to go to hell." "For a guy from Boston, you're certainly putting up a great show!" Jack taunted him. "He really did say that," Harris later con-firmed. "But I told him I couldn't swim because I only had one leg. Something hit me on the knee and it was all swollen and we thought it was broken."

Barney Ross also recalled the suddenness and impact of the collision. "I would say we spotted them at a distance of a quarter of a mile. First we thought it was a PT boat—that's what it seemed to be at first. Then we realized it was a destroyer, and then the skipper started turning towards the destroyer. Had we had enough room, enough time, it's a good chance we would have been able to sink him instead of the destroyer getting us, because at this point—up until this point I don't believe the Japanese had seen us."

But Ross was wrong, as he began to realize to his own dismay.

The destroyer saw us at I would say ten seconds before he hit us, and that was a sight I'll never forget. The mast keeling over at about a 45 degree angle towards us—this destroyer mast—and at this distance it would probably be maybe 100 feet. If he hadn't turned he would just have missed us, but by turning he caught us on the starboard bow at about a 20 angle to the longitudinal center of the boat. So he split the boat sort of longways—not across the boat. He hit the bow up there about five feet from my right, and it continued on back, completely obliterating the starboard turret where I believe a young fellow named Kirkscy was on watch, about two feet from the skipper's right.

Just before the moment of impact I grabbed onto this 37 mm army cannon and I was hanging on to that for dear life, and the boat of course lurched sharply to the right. It was like what I imagine it would be like to be hit by a train—it's about as close as I can think of it. We were fortunate the destroyer was very narrow and sharp, because only two of us were killed, I guess, or disappeared anyway. And the next thing I know, the boat is at about a 45–50 degree angle and everything seems to be lit up.

And I thought, my first fear was that the Japs had turned on their searchlight and were coming back for us. So I slid down— and I was also afraid that the gun would break loose and I would go to the bottom like a rock, so I disentangled myself from the gun and in doing so, slid into the water. That's the last I remember, for I guess—the next thing I remember is floating around in the darkness, not sure where I am, and finding myself with two of the other crew. . . .

The light I'd seen of course was the gasoline, which went up. This made a tremendous—not an explosion but a terrific roar that went up, I guess probably a hundred feet in the air. We had aboard probably at this time pretty close to 2,000 gallons of 100 octane gasoline.

And Maguire found the battle lantern and our little group of three

was floating out in the darkness in our life jackets—we must either
have been hit on the head by something or asphyxiated by the
gasoline. The wind was apparently taking the fire away from us, we
weren't burned, but as I remember we were in the gasoline, but the
wind was blowing the fire down away from the boat, which I guess
saved everybody.

So the next I remember, Lenny Thom, who was Jack's executive
officer, and Zinser and I were all practically together, and Lenny was
talking like he was out of his mind. He didn't know where he was and
he was trying to climb on top of me—thought I was a log or something—I remember Zinser and I were kind of slapping Lenny and
trying to get him to realize where he was. And so in short order we
were trying to get back on the boat, and I thought it was funny—the
boat was drifting, and the wind was sort of blowing it away from us.
So we were swimming toward the boat and it was floating away—
that was just a little nerve-wracking.

Zinser, an engineer, remembered:

It was so dark that night you couldn't hardly see a foot and a half
in front of your nose. . . . I'd just got off watch shortly before we got
hit. As I understand it, this destroyer had the island of Kolombangara for a background and that's what made it that much more
difficult for our lookout to spot it. He hollered down to Kennedy
"Ship at two o'clock" and Kennedy signaled down to the engine
room to make more speed, and at the same time he was going to turn
and that's when we got clipped.

When I went into the water I was unconscious for approximately
twenty minutes. When I came to, those of us in the water were
hollering to each other. The part of the PT boat that was still afloat
was pretty far away and they did have a lantern and they flashed it
at us every now and then so we could see where it was. So we got to
the boat and got aboard the part that stayed afloat—the bow. I'm
not sure who was out in the water with me. My arms and chest were
burned pretty severely. We lay on the front of the bow, right in front
of the cockpit. As far as I know, the section with the engines sunk
immediately. The bow was sticking up at a very steep angle. It
seemed to me the tide was taking us around in circles. Why the Japs
over on Kolombangara didn't come out and get us I'll never know
to this day. That was one of our biggest concerns.

Jack had hauled McMahon, badly burned, aboard, and by helping
Harris out of his heavy clothing and cajoling him to keep going, had

ensured that Harris got back to the boat too. Maguire had rescued Zinser, swimming out from the wreck with a line tied to his waist. "Please God, don't let me pass out," Zinser had screamed. "Bring the boat!"

"I said, Goddamn it, there is no boat!" recalled Maguire, who then pulled Zinser aboard. Finally, having recovered his senses, Lennie Thom rescued seaman Johnston, the last of the survivors, who had inhaled so much of the gasoline fumes that he was helpless and had to be tied down once he was hauled aboard lest he slide off the tilting deck.

"We all lay on the bow," Harris remembered. "We had a Very pistol, but we didn't shoot it off because we didn't know what had happened yet. We were in Japanese waters and we didn't want the Japanese coming out after us."

But no one came, neither Americans nor Japanese.

"We were waiting for the other PT boats to come back," Maguire later recalled with some bitterness. "Those sons of bitches ran away from us. We were left."

Leaving the Hulk

"As the dawn came up we found ourselves on the boat with the boat under water all way up to the bow," Ross related. "There was about 15 ft. of the boat, which was 80 feet long, still sticking out of the water at about a 45 degree angle, right side up. So we were hanging on to the boat, in the middle or toward the Gizo side of Blackett Strait. And we were quite exposed because over at Gizo there were, according to our intelligence, about 100 Japs at the Gizo anchorage, which was the old British government house for that area of the Solomons."

The situation was at once miraculous and daunting. On the far side of the strait there were an estimated ten thousand Japanese troops occupying Kolombangara Island. "We were expecting any minute to have the Jap launch come out and take us into custody, or whatever they would do to us," Ross recounted. "Our main concerns at that time were these guys that were in bad shape, and to try and decide among ourselves what we would do if the Japs came out."

Harris also recalled the discussion. "The next morning we were all talking about what to do," he related. "The Japs were all around us. Maguire, I think it was, went into the cockpit and got a machine gun and we had some 45s and 38s. We more or less took a vote as to what we would do if the Japs came. I think most of the guys agreed that we'd fight instead of giving up. A lot of the guys were married and they didn't go along with that too much, but they were a little bit overruled, you know."

In spite of his memories of the downed Japanese pilot reaching for his pistol and having his head blown off by a marine aboard the *LST 449* approaching Guadalcanal, Jack favored resisting capture. Ross remembered they "discussed whether we should continue to operate as a unit, a military unit, or whether we should give every man for himself. I think Jack was just trying to sound us out because we all wanted to remain as a military unit and so he sort of, I think, established, reestablished his authority at this stage of the game. He was testing us out to see what shape our morale was in.

"As I recall we were still in a state of shock from having been hit by the destroyer, but gradually emerging as the sun came up. We were not far from home but we were a lot closer to the enemy—I'd say Gizo anchorage was about a mile and a half away," Ross recounted. "And as the day went along we felt we might drift ashore on Gizo. We didn't know exactly what to do. We had to make a decision whether to stay with the boat and possibly drift ashore, or to leave the boat and strike out for some uninhabited island."

All morning they waited, hoping an American search plane might spot them even if no PT boat came to their rescue. Both sky and ocean remained empty, however, and by noon, Ross said, "it became apparent that the boat was not going to stay afloat through the night. At the rate we were drifting we didn't seem to be getting anywhere." Harris recalled their fear "that we'd drift to an island that was Japanese-held—that was the biggest concern," and remembered how "the boat started to settle and as it settled it slowly turned with the keel up and we couldn't stay on it then, it was too slippery. There was nothing to hold on to." Zinser was "almost positive the boat didn't turn turtle before we left it. We definitely knew the boat was going to sink."

Thus the decision was made to abandon ship. Ross recalled:

> Rather than have the boat sink on us in the middle of the night, we decided to strike out for land, and taking a large piece of wood that the carpenters had been in the process of fastening down the 37 mm gun with, we struck out for the smallest piece of land we could see that was in the opposite direction from the Gizo garrison.
>
> This would be in an easterly direction, toward our base at Rendova. It was, we estimated, three or four miles distant: a tiny little piece of land, like a *New Yorker* cartoon. At the distance from which we were looking at it, it looked like about 12 feet across, which was exactly what we wanted. Just some place that would be dry land and wouldn't have a hostile group of Japs staring at it.

"We had to leave the hulk," Harris agreed. "There was no way of staying on it. We picked out an island we thought would be least likely to have Japs on it and swam to that one.

"We had these two coconut logs to brace the legs of the 37 mm cannon. I'd say the logs were 8–9 feet long, about 10–12″ in diameter. I think we had just tied them down, I'm not sure. . . . When we swam to shore we used one coconut log. Pappy [McMahon] was so badly burned he couldn't hold on to the log, so when Kennedy said he'd tow him, we figured that was damn good because nobody else could do it. The rest of us had to help the others who couldn't swim."

It was to be an epic effort: Jack, with the straps of McMahon's life jacket like a bit between his teeth, swimming ahead of the others, tugging the badly burned McMahon behind him, and Thom alternately pushing and pulling the wooden log with four survivors clinging to each side, all acutely conscious of the danger of sharks beneath them, enemy soldiers on land, and Japanese aircraft above them. Though they took their pistols, the battle lantern, and a submachine gun, the gun was found to be too heavy, and they let it sink. When, after four hours, Jack finally reached the island, Bird Island, known as Plum Pudding Island by the white settlers, he collapsed on the sand. Eventually he and McMahon dragged themselves into the bushes and waved the others ashore when they too reached the island. They were, at last, on dry land.

Bird Island

"We didn't know what the name of the island was," Barney Ross later explained. "It was only, I'd say, about 100 feet across—circular in shape with bushes around the shoreline—I'd say about 25 trees, tall trees, not palm trees, some sort of leafy tree. And a reef extending out about 200 yards from the beach, quite sharp. Kennedy got there before we did, and he was waiting for us when we arrived—we were about 5 minutes behind him. We crawled up into the bushes and most of us were ready to call it a day. I don't remember anything for a couple of hours—I guess I fell asleep or something."

While Ross slept, others explored the island. "There were lots of coconut trees and bushes," Harris recalled. "We felt safe after we explored it and found there were no Japs on it—the Japs had been there because I found some, I still have blueprints I found on the island."

One of the men recollected that a Japanese barge passed by, causing them to scurry behind the bushes. But though they'd managed to destroy

PT 109's codebook and had brought small firearms and the battle lantern, "there was no water or food," Harris recalled. "Pop McMahon couldn't be moved." Harris's leg did not appear to be broken, but Johnston was clearly in poor condition. "He [Kennedy] had a situation where he didn't know how bad Johnston was," Ross recalled. "He sounded in terrible shape, he was coughing and retching, and he could see how bad McMahon was—very badly burned."

As the sun was going down, an Allied air patrol finally flew over, but too fast for Kennedy's crews to distinguish the markings before coming out from the bushes. "We didn't do anything to try to signal them," Maguire later lamented. "We should have, but we blew it." Jack therefore now made what appeared to be a foolhardy but brave decision: he would swim out into Ferguson Passage, hoping to flag down a PT vessel.

McMahon, the oldest crew member at age thirty-seven, thought it "foolish for Kennedy to go back in the water at night, swimming for help toward an island passage with a blinking lantern in one hand. In the first place it was a hell of a long way out to the passage. He'd go out there and float. Now in my mind," McMahon considered twenty-five years later, "if the boats had seen a light in the water, they'd have blown the light out of the water!"

Nobody attempted to stop the skipper, however. It was Jack's refusal to be defeated, even when they could see no sign of help or rescue coming, that would earn the admiration and devotion of his crew. "He had extraordinary energy," Zinser later remarked. "He just wouldn't give up. He just had to have something happening. That's what made him go out and try to flag down a PT boat. . . . None of us felt the base did enough to save us, but Kennedy done everything he possibly could."

"I think he felt that if he would just get out there . . . we were so near and yet so far," Ross explained. In the evening light they could see the peak of Rendova, some thirty-seven miles away. "Ferguson Passage was maybe a mile and a half away, and could be reached through shallow water and reefs with really not too much swimming. Of course he'd been in the water since two o'clock the previous morning, and all of us tried to persuade him not to do it, but he was determined. If he could just get over there in about an hour's time from now, these boats would be going by. And here would be a chance to get us all out of the soup right away."

According to Ross, Jack asked the others to hold the lantern by the reef, offshore. "He realized he was tired and he said, 'Now, if you boys will get out on the reef with the battle lantern'—which still worked—'and act as a landmark for me, I'll be able to see it, and I shouldn't be too long.' So that was the arrangement and off he went into the water." On another occasion Ross explained, "Any average person would have been content just to stay on the first island, but Kennedy figured there was a chance we could go out and intercept the [PT] boats. . . . He wasn't sure how far it was and he started in the dusk, it was getting dark. It was either courageous or foolish, I don't know what it was. So he took off and we never saw him again until the next noon. We looked for him during the night. We had the lantern out on the reef. But he was too tired and passed out or something and the tide carried him around in a circle."

When Jack did not return, the mood of the men sank. "We of course had figured he was gone. Our morale was fairly at the bottom at this point," Ross admitted. According to *PT 109*'s chronicler, Bob Donovan, the men were suffering from extreme thirst, their only resort being to lick the moisture off the leaves of the bushes after a rain shower—leaves coated with bird droppings, which inspired the men to nickname the island Bird Island. Certainly no one felt brave enough to look for Kennedy. In fact, by the time a figure stumbled over the reefs late in the morning, Maguire thought it was his missing buddy and shouted, "'Here's Kirksey!'"

The figure, now ominously yellowed, was Jack Kennedy. "Of course we were overjoyed," Ross recalled, "and pulled him in." His effort had, of course, been in vain, Warfield having refused to send any PT boats, though he knew almost the exact position where *PT 109* had sunk, and even that wreckage had been sighted. "Blackett St[rait]s approx between Vanga Vanga and group of islands SE of Gizo . . . Possibility of some survivors landing either Vangavanga or islands," headquarters at Guadalcanal had radioed in code to Reg Evans, the Australian coastwatcher stationed behind the enemy lines on Kolombangara, above the Japanese anchorage at Vila. Evans had signaled back, on the afternoon of August 2, that an "object" was "now drifting towards Nusatupi Is[land]."

Warfield's failure to send any PT boats into Blackett Strait or indeed anywhere near Kolombangara would be deeply resented in the days ahead. Meanwhile, smarting at the disastrous performance of his squadron on the night of August 1, Warfield dispatched a group of six boats, which avoided Ferguson Passage, then swung northward around the eastern side of Gizo Island to Vella Lavella, a large island northwest of Kolombangara. Two of the PTs turned back after being bombed by Japanese floatplanes, and the rest were easily repulsed by the steel-hulled Japanese barges. The performance was repeated the following evening, when the barges not only repelled five American PT boats but killed George Cookman, the skipper of *PT 107*, one of the four radar-equipped boats that had made off the night *PT 109* was sunk.

Whether or not Barney Ross simply lost faith in the prospect of rescue by PT boats, he certainly did not look forward to carrying out Jack's order that he take the lantern and revolver and repeat the same swimming sortie Jack had undertaken, on the night of August 3. Exhausted, Jack had collapsed on Bird Island at noon, but "before he went to sleep he said, 'Barney, you try it tonight'—which was great news for me," Ross recalled sarcastically. "This would be Tuesday night: my chance to go out into Ferguson Passage, which I wasn't exactly looking forward to."

Not only did Ross fail to carry out his mission enthusiastically, he spent only about twenty minutes in the water, having seen a group of sand sharks. Moreover, to Jack's added chagrin, he lost the battle lantern, becoming in Jack's eyes something of "a loser."

The men's hopes of early rescue began to dim. Some were patient, trusting in God. Most, however, felt sore at the navy, and, as Donovan recorded after interviewing the survivors, there was much cursing of Warfield and the other PT-boat crews for abandoning them. One man lost his nerve entirely and wished to surrender to the Japanese.

It was in this respect that Jack differed from the others. According to John Hersey, who interviewed Jack for *Life* magazine six months later, the first thought that flashed through Jack's mind when the *Amagiri* smashed into his floating firebomb was, "So this is how it feels to die!" His second, however, upon realizing he was still alive, was one of elation. Far more than even his closest friends recognized, there beat in his strangely unromantic heart an implacable desire to survive and win. It was this indomitable will that, in the ensuing days, would be the crew's only hope of survival as they waited, starving and thirsty, for a rescue patrol that never came.

The Coconut

"My trip out to Ferguson Passage proved to be of no avail," Ross admitted later. "So the next day we decided to move to an island that had coconut trees on it, because at this stage of the game we had nothing to drink and nothing to eat. So on Wednesday—we were sunk on Sunday night—we all paddled over about, oh, I'd say almost a mile to quite a bigger and quite a good-sized island to the west of us, which had coconut trees."

The crossing was exhausting and involved a rerun of the swim from the wreckage of *PT 109,* with Ensigns Thom and Ross and the crew holding on to the wooden plank while once again Jack towed the badly burned Pappy McMahon by his kapok strings until they reached the shore.

It was August 4, 1943. They were now, truly, shipwrecked on a desert island—known locally as Olasana Island—eating coconuts to stay alive. Ross recalled:

Harris, who was the most nimble of our group, shinneyed up the trees and got some green coconuts and threw them down and also some of the ones on the ground that weren't rotten, they were actually better than the ones up on the tree. . . . So we kept going, in other words. Jack never allowed us to sit around and mope. . . . Johnston had cleaned up—was in pretty good shape by now. So our main worry was McMahon. We all kept off the beach because we were afraid of being soloed—you could see for miles out there—silhouetted on the beach. So we all stayed in the bushes most of the time. Pappy lay in the water, and the salt water was apparently good for him. He kept moving his fingers so that he wouldn't lose the use of his hands. He instinctively did this. The doctor later told us that's what saved his hands.

Aware that the PT boats must now be using the southern route toward Vella Lavella, where he'd seen flashes of gunfire the night he swam into Ferguson Passage, Jack announced that he would explore some of the islands south of them, which overlooked this route. Taking Ross with him, Jack now swam across to an island named Naru or Cross Island. There, on Thursday, August 5, 1943, Jack and Barney "sneaked through the brush to the east side of the island and peered from the brush onto the beach," Lieutenant White, the Squadron 10 intelligence officer, chronicled in his report. "A small rectangular box with Japanese writing on the side was seen which was quickly and furtively pulled into the bush. Its contents proved to be 30–40 small bags of crackers and candy. A little farther up the beach, alongside a native lean-to, a one-man canoe and a barrel of water were found."

The water was better than pirates' treasure (although the canoe was broken in half). They then spotted two natives, near the wreck of a Japanese vessel that had caught on the reef a few hundred yards offshore, and attempted to get their attention. The natives, seeing them, took fright and "paddled swiftly off to the northwest."

Would the natives alert the Japanese? Without any way of ascertaining their loyalties, Jack was still determined, as he would be throughout the ordeal, to flag down a passing PT. Taking the broken canoe into Ferguson Passage as a float, he waited that evening until nine P.M., "but again no PTs appeared," Lieutenant White chronicled.

Swimming back to Naru Island in the dark, Jack found Ross asleep and was unable to wake him. "He had a higher metabolism than I did," Ross later explained. "I slept right through until morning. He was up and at 'em, you know, back to the other guys. I remember he was kidding me about being lazy and I wouldn't wake up."

Having failed to flag down any PT boats, Jack had resolved to take the water and Japanese candy they'd found to the rest of the crew on Olasana Island. This entailed another long swim, in darkness. "There was an iron-roofed coastwatcher's house there and Kennedy went over with an empty Japanese biscuit tin to collect the water from the tanks," one of the natives they had seen later explained. "He swam back, pulling the water on a broken canoe." The other native confirmed this. "He was taking water—he put it inside a tin, put the tin in a half-canoe (broken) and towed the whole thing swimming."

Arriving back on Olasana Island with his "cargo" of water and provisions shortly before midnight, Jack found, to his astonishment, two natives sitting with his crew—the very natives he and Ross had frightened off the reef around Naru Island. Named Biuku (Nebuchadnezar) and Eroni (Aaron), they were in fact coastwatching scouts, working for the Allies, and had been exploring the Japanese wreck for the coastwatcher when they were surprised by Kennedy and Ross, whom they were convinced were Japanese. After paddling swiftly back in the direction of their village base at Sepo, Biuku, tired after the precipitate dash from Naru Island, had persuaded Eroni to stop on Olasana Island, where there was an abundance of coconuts. "I was thirsty, so I told Aaron to leave me at the island so I could get a coconut," Biuku related.

> As I was going ashore, I saw a white man crawling out from the bushes near the shore. I said, "Aaron, a Japanese here," so we pushed the canoe out to get away. We were headed out when he stood up, waved and said, "Come!" I said, "Nomoa. Iu Japan. Iu Japan." (No! You're Japanese.) I think he understood me, because he said, "I'm an American, not Japanese." That time, I didn't really understand English except for a few words. He showed his arm and said, "Look at my skin. It's white. Japan skin red." So I gave him my reply—"No matter skin white or skin red—you Japan." He insisted that we come, but I still said no, we are afraid.

Biuku had reason to be, since he would have been executed summarily by the Japanese, whose movements on Gizo they had been monitoring over the past week (leading to repeated Allied bombing raids of the island). "They were very scared," Harris confirmed.

Eroni thought Thom must be a German. "We understood that Americans were smaller than this fellow. He had to be a German. But he said he was an American and showed us his medal [dog tag]," Eroni later recalled in Ranongga language for a Peace Corps volunteer. "Then we thought to ask him what sign the American planes had on them. Biuku asked and the man answered right—a white star. I said he was lying. Then the man asked if we knew John Kari, because he was helping them on Rendova."

Thom's mention of Kari, another native scout for the Allied coast-watching organization in the area, was crucial. The conversation had been held between Thom on the shore and the natives in their boat, ready to paddle away. Had they in fact paddled away, the story of the *PT 109* shipwreck might have had a very different ending, with the survivors not only failing to be rescued but possibly being bombed by their own forces. But Thom's mention of the native scout, who had once brought an American flier back to the PT-boat headquarters, clinched the matter. "Ia, mi save long John Kari—hem i stap long ples blong mi long Madou," exclaimed Biuku, who came from the same village as Kari.

"So then we felt good and forgot our worries," Biuku recorded in Roviana language. "We went ashore, and pulled up our canoe, and went to see the rest of the men. . . . We saw seven men standing up. Some of them cried and some came and shook hands. One man was badly burned, and for him they dug a small hole and covered him in leaves of the buni tree. But when he saw us, he stood up and shook our hands and cried."

"They gave us some canned food and started fires by rubbing some sticks," Bucky Harris later remembered. "We'd tried that too but we couldn't do it."

Biuku, however, recalled that the fire was started for a more characteristic reason.

"The first thing they asked for was cigarettes—they wanted to smoke. I used a very rough kind of pidgin with them, and they tried their best in broken English. I took out the tin of cigarettes and told Aaron to 'ino,' that is, to make fire from rubbing two sticks together. They were happy to smoke. We had some *kumara* [native food], but smoke was the big thing. While we were there, these fellows didn't really understand pidgin, but I managed to pick up that these were the men from *PT 109*. Then we told them that we met a Japanese on Naru. But they said that wasn't a Japanese, but our captain, Captain Kennedy.

"We stayed with them until night," Biuku went on. "Then two of them asked us to take them to Rendova, the PT-boat base at Rendova. They tied up life jackets around themselves and we left, me paddling. We got to the middle of Ferguson Passage, and the wind was really strong, so we turned back," he recalled. Eroni, however, remembered only one man, Ensign Thom, attempting the trip. "Their boss said for me to stay with the men while Biuku paddled him to Rendova. They left at five in the evening, but there was a big wind and they capsized. They turned back."

This was undoubtedly a mercy, since Lennie Thom clearly had little idea how difficult it would be to paddle forty miles across windswept water in his condition, with only one native to help and subject to Japanese strafing or interception. At any rate, when "Captain" Kennedy arrived at midnight there was much emotion, as Biuku recorded. "We laid down to sleep, but didn't realize that Kennedy was swimming back to us at Olasana from Naru. . . . When he arrived, he made a prearranged signal so they all knew he was there. They all said to him, 'We're saved! Two locals have found us!' When Kennedy saw us, he put the water [and candy] down and ran over and embraced us. He asked if it was us who came near the wreck the previous day. (It was easy to communicate with him because he knew pidgin.) We said yes, and he said why didn't we come when he waved. We answered that we thought he was Japanese."

Jack was still obsessed by the thought of flagging down a PT-boat patrol on its way home, and instead of sleeping he insisted upon returning to Naru "to look over the passage to check for any Allied ships" before dawn. "We suggested that we go paddle him over to that island," Biuku continued. "He agreed but said to make sure we covered him with coconut leaves.

"It was night. As we were paddling across, we heard the sound of a man swimming in the water nearby. We turned the canoe toward him, but he swam the other way. We figured that it must be Barney Ross, and he was afraid that we were the enemy. So Kennedy told me to say his (Kennedy's) name three times. So I said three times 'Captain Kennedy i stap inside kinu (canoe).' Then he wasn't afraid. We told him to get in canoe, but he wanted to stay on the outside and drag along the back. He was heavy and it wasn't until morning that we made to the point at Naru."

Once ashore, "we hid the canoe," Biuku recalled, and "they walked all around the island, looking for ships to take them back to Rendova."

There were none, however, though the native scouts "showed the two PT survivors where a two-man native canoe was hidden," Lieutenant White reported. With this, Jack decided to go out into Ferguson Passage once again that night. In the meantime, Biuku remembered, "he said, 'Biuku, I'm so sorry for my crew,'" and asked if Biuku and Eroni could "go ahead and paddle to Rendova. He asked what time we thought we could make it back. I said, 'Maybe tomorrow night.' So he said to go, by ourselves, first telling the others that we were leaving."

Would the authorities at Rendova believe the natives? "There's no paper," Jack had remarked to Biuku. "After a while, I guessed that he wanted to write a message, so I thought of this leaf we use for that," Biuku recorded. "In our language, it's called *poroporo*. Then I thought if we do get caught, even if we tore up the leaf, people could join the pieces back and read the message. So I told Aaron to climb up the coconut [tree]. First to drink, then I asked him to get a husk ready. Then I said to

Kennedy, 'We natives have lots of papers—you can write a message inside this husk of coconut.' So he scratched the message on with his pocket knife. He couldn't even rub it out with his hand. He looked at me and said, 'Jesus Christ, Biuku. How did you think of this?' He came over and took my head with both hands, twisting it slowly and studying it."

Eroni recalled the same. "Kennedy asked us, 'What can we use to write a message?' We said, 'Husk blong Coconut.' Kennedy said, 'O.K., let's try it.' So I climbed. Kennedy wrote the message and told us to [go] ahead with the message to Rendova, and to get on the PT boat they would send to pick up the crew."

As agreed, the two natives stopped at Olasana to tell the crew their mission. "What if the coconut falls into enemy hands?" the crew asked. "Kennedy had given me his pocketknife," Biuku related, "and I was to scratch off the message and throw it away and then just wait to die, I told them." To back up "Captain" Kennedy's message, Eroni recalled, "that bosun [Lennie Thom] wrote a small note too. We left Olasana at eight o'clock to Parara. The sea was rough."

On the husk of the green coconut they carried, Jack had carved the simple but immortal words: NAURO ISL NATIVE KNOWS POSIT HE CAN PILOT 11 ALIVE NEED SMALL BOAT KENNEDY.

On His Majesty's Service

Instead of paddling the long, exposed route to Rendova, the native scouts wisely crossed Ferguson Passage to Wana Wana Island, south of Kolombangara. There, on the evening of Friday, August 6, they chanced to meet one of coastwatcher Evans's English-speaking scouts, Benjamin Kevu. Kevu immediately sent word to Evans at his new lookout post on a small offshore island next to Wana Wana, while arranging for Biuku and Eroni to have another scout—the very John Kari whose name had convinced them the white men were really Americans—to help them paddle a larger canoe to Rendova, thirty nautical miles away.

On Naru Island, meanwhile, Jack Kennedy had no guarantee that the natives would get through, or if they did, how many days it would take. So yet again, on Friday evening, he insisted that he and Barney Ross try and flag down a passing PT boat, unaware that a new Tokyo Express was barreling down the Slot, and that Admiral Halsey had now given orders forbidding PTs to operate anywhere in the area.

Halsey was determined to meet the Express with destroyers. Guided by radar, the American destroyer group intercepted the Japanese not far from the position where the convoy had tangled with Jack's PT-boat division on August 1. This time, however, the Americans were successful, and at no loss to themselves they sank three of the four Japanese destroyers, together with nine hundred reinforcement troops and supplies bound for Kolombangara.

For the U.S. Navy it was a brilliant night action in confined, enemy-held waters. Not only did it persuade the Japanese high command that New Georgia could no longer be resupplied, but for the American high command it proved a final nail in the coffin of PT boats as torpedo vessels in the Pacific war.

In the meantime Barney Ross, eyeing the heavy surf off Naru, was not excited. "I said, 'Gee, I think we'll tip over, Jack, if we go out—it looks a little rough.' And he says, 'Oh, no, it'll be all right, we'll go out.' And we got out in the canoe and we lasted about five or ten minutes before we did tip over, and as we were being washed over the reef rather unceremoniously, he said, 'I guess this would be a fine time for you to say I told you so.'"

It was Jack's somewhat sardonic wit, in trying circumstances, that Ross found remarkable—an effortless ability to break tension with quips that would strike a humorous cord in everyone. Years later, at a special White House showing of the film *PT 109,* Jack would proudly but wryly introduce Barney. "The way he put it—it was the inflection in his voice, that made it funny: 'I'd like you to meet the lookout on *PT 109.*'" Even the fact that the film became a box-office hit was grist to Jack's skeptically humorous mill, Ross recalled. "One of the guys there was the skipper of the *108,* and Jack said, 'Next year we are going to make the *PT 108.* This was a big success, the *PT 109*—we'll have to make the *108.*'"

Jack might later joke, but the pounding he and Barney received on the reef, after two hours of swimming once high waves had swamped the canoe, almost did them in. John Hersey later described:

> It was too late to do anything . . . the wind and rain were carrying them toward the reef. When they were near the reef, a wave broke Kennedy's hold, ripped him away from the canoe, turned him head over heels and spun him in a violent rush. His ears roared and his eyes pinwheeled, and for the third time since the collision he thought he was dying. Somehow he was not thrown against the coral but floated into a kind of eddy. Suddenly he felt the reef under his feet. Steadying himself so that he would not be swept off it, he shouted, "Barney!" There was no reply. Kennedy thought of how he had insisted on going out in the canoe, and he screamed, "Barney!" This time Ross answered.

Jack was relieved, having almost caused his companion to drown by his insistence on going out. Ross, by contrast, blamed himself for his passivity. "I was always sort of a lead anchor around Jack Kennedy's neck," he related, feeling guilty and yet, in retrospect, grateful that he'd shared such an extraordinary experience with Jack Kennedy. "Even in those days, I always had kind of an unusual feeling toward him," Ross later confided. "He was always pretty cool, never got too tense, even on the island there. . . . I never felt that we had too much in common. We were from very different backgrounds, you might say; but nevertheless I always felt sort of close to the guy. Because we had sort of a special relationship. I always felt privileged that I was able to be the guy that had gone swimming with him, so to speak, on some of those islands. . . . I mean it was just he and I."

Like Billings, Ross would later idolize Jack, and the root of this veneration for both men was the sense of having undergone a critical period in Jack's life alongside him. Like Billings and Inga, Ross was well aware of Jack's weaknesses. He did not see Jack as a saint or even as a fearless warrior in the mold of many soldiers who seemed to value their own lives lightly. On the contrary, Ross knew just how highly Jack prized his own life and ambitions. "You know, Jack was not such a hero, as people make out," Barney once confided to James Reed and his wife. In Barney's affectionate retrospection, Jack's determination to get help during the dark days and nights after the sinking of *PT 109* was not so much fearless heroism as, at bottom, the fundamental human will to survive, the adamant refusal to give in to death.

Meanwhile, off Naru Island the wave that tore the two men from the swamped canoe had dashed Ross against the coral reef, lacerating his right arm and shoulder. Wading back to the Naru beach thereafter proved a nightmare—Ross's feet now so infected and sore that Jack had to lay the pieces of wood they had been using as makeshift paddles beneath Ross's feet until, finally, they got across the jagged coral to the sandy beach. There they fell down exhausted and slept.

Five days had now elapsed. The survivors had subsisted on leaf moisture, coconut milk, a cache of fresh water, some Japanese candy, and one tinned meal provided by the natives, which Ross had missed. As one of the *PT 109* crew, Gerard Zinser, later assessed, "Ross had a terrible coral infection in his foot or knee. It swelled up a lot. I think it would have been soon that we started dying off and I think Ross would have been the first to go."

But help was at hand. Soon after Jack and Ross awoke on the morning of Saturday, August 7, they saw a large canoe approaching. Out stepped no fewer than eight natives. Had Biuku and Eroni gotten through? With some trepidation Jack greeted them. It was then that their leader, Evans's chief scout Benjamin Kevu, said in perfect English, "I have a letter for you, sir," and handed over a written message from Evans.

On His Majesty's Service
To Senior Officer, Naru Is[land].
Friday ii p.m. Have just learnt of your presence on Naru Is + also that two natives have taken news to Rendova. I strongly advise you return immediately to here in this canoe + by the time you arrive here I will be in Radio communication with authorities at Rendova + we can finalise plans to collect balance of party
A. R. Evans, Lt
RANVR
P.S. Will warn aviation of your crossing Ferguson Passage.

Jack was overwhelmed. "You've got to hand it to the British," he twitted to Ross as he showed him the note.

They returned with the natives to Olasana Island to tell the others. The natives had brought food, water, and a stove, and the crew of *PT 109* now sat down to their first semblance of a proper meal in six days: rice, potatoes, boiled fish, yams, pawpaws, and C rations with roast-beef hash.

Once the meal was over, Jack set off with the natives in the big canoe to meet Lieutenant Evans, burrowing under palm fronds lest he be seen from the air. Halfway across, Japanese planes did in fact buzz the boat for identification, the last two only flying away when one of the natives stood up and waved.

When the eight-man canoe finally arrived at Evans's new camp on Komu Island at six P.M. on Saturday evening, Evans thought at first that the natives had failed to find the survivors. Then from beneath the green fronds in the canoe emerged a tall, lanky, smiling young white man who strode up the beach and, holding out his hand, said, "Hello, I'm Kennedy."

In retrospect the whole drama would seem surreal. They were still forty miles behind enemy lines. Jack's hair was matted, six days' growth of beard covered his wide jaw, he walked barefooted, and his feet and legs were blotched with coral wounds. Taking the proffered hand, Evans proposed that they go to his tent "and have a cup of tea."

Base Suspicions

Until Jack's arrival in the native canoe, Evans had had no real way of knowing whether Biuku and Eroni's story, which had been passed on to him by Kevu, was true. Nevertheless, as soon as he'd set up radio communication from his new base, Evans had at nine-twenty that morning sent a radio message to his headquarters that "eleven survivors PT boat" had been found on Cross or Naru Island and that he had already sent "food and letter advising senior come here without delay."

Evans's message was received with some skepticism when passed on to Warfield's Lumbari headquarters. Warfield suspected a Japanese trick and summoned Lieutenant Commander Cluster from his squadron base back in the Russell Islands. "The reason I went up there," Cluster later explained, "was because we were suspicious that the Japs were trying to pull something by sending the natives down." They had for a week assumed all hands aboard *PT 109* were lost. "We had to assume that the whole damn boat had exploded and sunk." Warfield's communications officer, Lieutenant Woods, even confided that they had frankly given up the search when a dispatch came from Admiral Halsey himself (possibly on orders from Washington, given the prominence of Jack Kennedy's father) to keep looking. Despite Halsey's order, however, no further sea or air searches had been conducted. Thus even when Evans reported further sightings of the wreck of a PT boat floating south of Gizo near the area where *PT 109* had gone down, Warfield had *still* declined to send a PT-boat patrol, so convinced was he that the crew had died. He simply requested that Allied fighter planes destroy the remains of the boat lest its codebooks be found by the Japanese.

Meanwhile, as Cluster made his way up to Lumbari from the Russell Islands, Biuku and Eroni landed at eleven-thirty A.M. on Roviana Island off New Georgia. Colonel George Hill, commanding the 192nd Field Artillery in support of the 43rd Infantry Division, recalled in a letter to Jack, many years later, how "on the morning in question, a native landed at Roviana, in spite of your instructions to go to Rendova, and contacted men of my Service Battery. . . . Capt. Robinson tried to understand the native with the [coconut] message. Robinson brought him to my command post a short distance on the island."

Hill and his senior staff officers, he remembered, had

studied a bit of pidgin English and were able to understand partially what the native was trying to explain: namely (1) Americans stranded on island behind the Japs. (2) One man with feet badly burned or injured and needs help. (3) That I as "Chief for Americans" could give him rescue boat immediately.

I judge this was about 11 a.m. I reported the incident to our Intelligence Section and then tried to remember where I had seen a Navy pool. I finally thought of Bau Island [Lumbari] back at Rendova. How could I make contact? I had regular intervals for ammo reports from Kokrana by radio so decided for a relay of your copra [coconut] message signed "Kennedy." The name at the time meant nothing to me except another joker needing help. I told them the Native Chief was at my command post and could be picked up at Roviana landing pier when a pick boat was available.

Biuku's loyalty was remarkable, as Colonel Hill remembered with amusement. "From this point on the Chief sat on the ground in my tent and just watched my every movement. Came noontime and I had a plate of food brought in which didn't interest him too much as he would keep saying, 'Boat where?—Man sick!' I had to stall by picking up my field phone from time to time and feign a conversation to someone about a boat. At one point the Chief started swinging his machete in my direction indicating I was not acting fast enough to save your party."

Biuku's own account confirmed this. "All the Americans in Roviana were Marines [soldiers] and they didn't know anything about any Captain Kennedy." He recalled his exasperation after paddling for over twenty-four hours: "We started to feel crazy not knowing what to do with the letter."

The rescue, however, was starting to take shape. "Fortunately about 2:00 P.M. I received word that your boat pool had received the message and a rescue party would pick up the Chief," Colonel Hill wrote. "Late that afternoon I had to cross to Division Artillery Headquarters on New Georgia when I spotted the Chief in the stern of one of your boats. He recognized me and I could see a happy smile on his face as he responded to my wave to him. At that time he still held the copra with your message in his hand."

Even when the natives finally arrived at PT-boat headquarters at six P.M., Biuku recalled that they were treated with suspicion. "We went to Lumbari, a place in Rendova. There was a Japanese man there to meet us—he was an interpreter for the Americans. We went inside a room with a big map. A man with lots of decorations on his uniform asked for our letter. I showed him the husk. 'Who wrote this?' he asked. 'Captain Kennedy,' I replied. 'Who showed him to do this with the coconut?' 'I did. He need something to write on but didn't have any paper.' He was surprised. But so was I when he gave me the same treatment as those other two and held my head, looking it over very closely."

Years later, on a doodling pad in the Oval Office, Jack Kennedy scrawled a little memoir about Biuku:

> I do not remember his name, I never knew it, but I'll always remember him. In August 1943 the PT boat I commanded had been rammed and cut in two while attacking a Japanese destroyer. A week later those of us who had survived—and some were badly burnt—were living on the thin edge of existence on a narrow reef drinking rain water—eating a few odd coconuts—freezing at night—and wondering how it all would end. About the 7th day we saw a native off the shore and small canoe. . . . He spoke no English. I carved out a message about our approximate position on a green coconut + shouted the name of our base Rendova—Rendova + pointed east. A day later a large war canoe arrived with a dozen natives who built a shelter + made a fire + gave us food. I rode with them some hours away to where a New Zealand Coastwatcher who was observing the Japanese activities on Kolombangara had his jungle camp. He told me that our friend had come by + told him our troubles and that the native had left the same night to row 50 miles to our home base.

It was the coconut message that did the trick, Cluster emphasized. "It wasn't till the coconut message came in that we realized there was a possibility that they were alive." There still had been no direct radio contact with Evans, so Cluster's idea of talking to Jack on the VHF radio "didn't work out," he related, "and then we saw the coconut that the native had brought in."

Less than an hour later Evans reported that Jack had arrived and was very much alive. Warfield's initial plan had been to send a rescue party straight to Olasana. "Three PT boats proceed tonight and will be at Gross Island about ten P.M. they will take rafts etc;" Warfield had signaled to Evans at 1:51 P.M.

Jack, when shown Warfield's signal, strenuously objected. Though the plan might have made sense as long as he was still en route in the native canoe, now that he'd arrived at Evans's camp he was nervous of entrusting the "bastard" Warfield with a tricky rescue operation. As the men's skipper, moreover, Jack felt it was his duty to bring his crew back himself, after their long ordeal. He therefore insisted that Warfield's party pick him up first. "Lieutenant Kennedy considers it advisable that he pilot PT boats tonight. He will await boats near Patparan Island," Evans radioed at six-fifty P.M. "PT boat to approach island from NW ten P.M. as close as possible. Boat to fire four shots as recognition. He will acknowledge with same and go alongside in canoe."

Warfield had no option but to accede, and later paid tribute to Jack's courage and leadership after the ramming: "I think in the situation he handled himself great. I think you have to give him a hell of a lot of credit for getting out there and swimming out almost every night, whether it was the most intelligent thing to do or not, you have to give him a hell of a lot of credit for doing that. He was trying to get some kind of action. . . . It's better than sitting there and starving to death. And if somebody is going to do it, why not the commander of the boat? I think you really have to give him a lot of credit for doing that. He really tried to take care of his boys—he deserves that, no question about it."

The Rescue Party

According to Biuku's account the rescue party was already under way when Warfield signaled that there was a change of plan. It was the tiny native's first trip aboard a PT vessel, and he stayed below. "The boats were really fast. I was afraid, but I was already inside," he recalled. "I don't know how far we went in this big sea. Then a wireless message came to the boat that we should go to Komu, another island, to the coast-watcher, Mr. Evans. We didn't believe it at first, but afterward I found out that Ben Kevu had taken Captain Kennedy to Komu on orders from Evans, to talk on the radio."

Six boats had set out, but because of impending U.S. naval operations around Vella Lavella, four of the PT boats had been assigned to patrol that area, while two were to split off: one to perform the rescue in the shallow, reef-ridden waters off Naru, the other to stand watch with radar lest Japanese vessels interfere.

Following the change of plan, these two boats now made their way through Ferguson Passage to Komu, arriving finally more than an hour late for the rendezvous off Patparan Island.

Berndsten's boat carried a regular crew, but Liebenow's *PT 157,* nicknamed "Aces and Spades," also carried a pharmacist mate, the three natives, Biuku, Eroni, and John Kari, two war correspondents (Leif Erikson of the AP and Frank Hewlett of the UP), the senior officer in charge of the mission, Hank Brantingham, and Al Cluster, Jack's squadron commander. Over the years others added their names to the party, leading Jack, during a later political campaign, to make his classic remark to Liebenow: "Lieb, if I get all the votes from the people who claim to have been on your boat that night of the pickup, I'll win easily!" "Then we heard Kennedy in the water, singing out to us," Eroni recalled. "He was floating near Petepara with some local people. They used a night telescope [radar] to find the canoe."

Al Cluster remembered with hilarity the moment when they finally made contact with Jack:

> We were supposed to go up to this little coral-enclosed lagoon on the *PT 157,* and the signal was supposed to be, I think it was four shots: bang, bang, bang, bang, just out of a revolver. And Kennedy was supposed to answer with four shots—we would then know that was him and go to where the shots had come from and pick him up.
>
> So we go up to the area that we're supposed to be in and we fire the four shots, bang, bang, bang, bang.
>
> Now we hear bang, bang, bang: three shots. And then kaplew and a splash!
>
> So we go over to where it was. Kennedy had had three rounds in this little snubnosed thirty-eight that he carried, which was aviation-issue, and he'd only had three shots there, but he had a Japanese rifle and was standing up in this little dugout canoe, and he fired the rifle—and it knocked him in the water! So he was soaking wet when we put a ladder over the side!

Jack, exhausted by the cumulative strain of the preceding week, was less than cordial, according to Lieutenant Berndsten, the skipper of the radar-equipped boat. "Where the hell have you been?" Jack shouted. "It was an unfortunate thing to say, I thought," Berndsten remarked. "I know it irked a lot of people on the two PTs. There was a war on. The guys were going out every night, getting killed and wounded. We were busy as hell. I had a patrol to lead that night and I was taking time from it. And then he hit us with that comment, like he was the only guy around."

But Jack was thinking of his men on Olasana Island. Berndsten's lateness typified in Jack's mind the general neglect of his crew, including the failure of the PT boats to look for survivors on the night of the sinking and to return to the area thereafter. When Liebenow shouted, "We've got some food for you," Jack could barely summon his characteristic humor. "Thanks, I've just had a coconut," he responded tartly.

Cluster, meanwhile, thought it funny, the more so when the natives—Biuku still hugging his coconut—greeted Jack.

> The little native, John Kari, who was with us, had been taught some English by British missionaries, and his British accent was like out

of the Court of St. James's, I mean it was that British! He was standing there on the deck, and Kennedy was crawling up the ladder. As he got on board, this little ninety-five-pound native in this dirty loincloth said in perfect English, "Good evening, Lieutenant Kennedy." If it had been a more relaxed thing, I think I would have laughed at that point!

It's a riot in retrospect. The little native got up on the bow of the boat, and we had Jack down below. Each boat had some medicinal whiskey, little bottles of brandy—about the same kind you get on airplanes today. We poured, I don't know whether it was one or two of these little bottles of brandy into Jack. He had had no food for six days, and needless to say it kind of lifted him to a new high.

According to Donovan's account, once they crossed Ferguson Passage, *PT 157* nosed along the reef that ran like an underwater necklace around the islands southeast of Gizo. "About midway between Leorava and Three Palm Islet Kennedy said there was an opening. When the crew questioned it, he insisted that he had that very afternoon come through an opening there. He scanned the dark off the port side, until he was sure he could see the contour of Olasana as he had fixed it in his mind. Others argued with him."

Liebenow, the skipper, later disputed this. "I never heard any arguments. JFK stood between me and the wheel, and the two natives. He pointed out the direction, the natives agreed, and we headed out. When we got close enough to worry about running aground, I stationed Welford West [quartermaster] in the bow of the boat and took directions from him. To me the only person on board who could countermand my orders was Hank Brantingham, who was my senior officer and in command of the mission. He didn't. Once we got up close to the island and put over our small dinghy, it took only a few minutes until the entire crew was aboard."

Al Cluster remembered those "few minutes":

We put this little eight-foot plywood boat over the stern. The little native got in the bow as I remember, Kennedy got in the stern, and Cluster manned the oars. That was my role in this whole rescue, was this strong back.

We start rowing in and I'm doing my best to oar as noiselessly as possible—I can see Japanese all around us, your imagination runs wild in a situation like that. There was dead silence.

So Kennedy figures he has to yell to Lennie. Now he's got a couple of shots of brandy in him. And he's yelling, "Lennie, where are you?"

I said, "Goddammit, keep your voice down, I don't want to alert the Japanese over on Gizo! Quiet!"

I'm trying to row quietly and he's yelling like an idiot. I remember I was about ready to hit him on the head with an oar if he didn't shut up. This brandy had really worked on him!

Barney Ross, who was waiting on the island, later recalled the other side of the coin—how the crew of *PT 109*, unaware of the rescue operation being mounted, was asleep when Jack returned. "As I remember it, most of us were pretty exhausted by this time. Although we'd set a watch all night long, apparently we were all asleep at the critical moment when Jack and the PT boat arrived off of our little haven in the bushes. They weren't particularly anxious to make too much noise because they were in the restricted waters and we would have been sitting ducks for any Japanese that might have been coming by in patrol boats." The backup boat, Berndsten's *PT 171*, however, had radar and could thus watch for enemy vessels. It was half past midnight, Ross recalled, when Jack's cries were finally heard. "They were hollering for us to wake—finally we woke up in time to be rescued. I will never forget, I felt sort of foolish—we were all asleep!"

"Pretty soon, though, we got an answer from Lennie: 'Here we are!' And then we started ferrying them back, one at a time," Cluster related. Once aboard, there was "much handshaking, backslapping and kidding going on," Liebenow remembered. "Of course the wounded were treated first, they were taken below to the pharmacist mate, but even they joined in the revelry. The pharmacist mate passed the torpedo juice and medicinal brandy, and pretty soon everybody was singing. The natives knew 'Jesus Loves Me,' so every song that was started ended up:

> Jesus loves me, this I know,
> For the Bible tells me so;
> Little ones to him belong,
> They are weak, but He is strong.
> Yes, Jesus loves me; yes, Jesus loves me."

Biuku and Eroni spent the journey below deck again, as Biuku recalled. "We went back to sea. . . . I got seasick. Then Aaron. We slept in the cabin until we returned to Rendova; only John [Kari] was still strong."

Erikson and Hewlett, the two war correspondents, passed among the survivors, taking down their stories. The men were full of admiration for Ensign Thom, who had kept up their morale. "As I recall, Kennedy went down below, probably to lie down, and we didn't talk to him much on the way home," Frank Hewlett remembered. "My main source was Lennie

Thom and Pappy McMahon. Lennie was a really striking guy. Big. He had a blond beard and looked like a Viking. He was very, very colorful."

"Ensign Thom used to tell us stories about the farm and college days and all his women and things he was going to do," Bucky Harris later recalled. "He kept everybody's spirits up. He was great. He had no worry in the world that way. He had no fear. Thom could rule anybody. You'd just look at him and do what he told you—he was that big. He was an awful nice man."

Their skipper, John Kennedy, the crew all "praised to high heaven," according to Frank Hewlett. "Kennedy was the hero," Harris declared. "He saved our lives. I owed him my life. If it wasn't for him I wouldn't be here—I really feel that. I venture to say there are very few men who would swim out in that ocean alone without knowing what was underneath you. Brother, I wouldn't do it. You could give me a million dollars and I wouldn't swim out there. That took a lot of guts. I thought he was great. Everybody on the crew thought he was top-notch."

At about seven A.M. on Sunday, August 8, 1943, *PT 157* docked at Lumbari, Rendova. "Kennedy's friends and the crew's friends came and some cried, they were so happy to see them," Eroni recalled. They gave everybody food. A ship came for us and one for the crew. We all stood up and shook hands all round. Kennedy said he wanted to get another ship and join the war again, and he said if he was alive, he would see us (Biuku and me) sometime later, in the Solomons. But if he died, he wouldn't see us. Kennedy gave us a medal, which I still have." This was an old gold coin which Clare Boothe Luce had given Jack the year before, when he passed out of midshipman's school, a "good-luck piece" which, as Jack subsequently wrote to Mrs. Luce, "did service above and beyond its routine duties during a rather busy period."

When Eroni married after the war, he named one of his children John Kennedy. Distressed at not knowing Biuku and Eroni's full names, Jack meanwhile put out an appeal to find them through the Australian administration, and when Biuku and Eroni were found, they were both invited to stay at the White House. At the last moment, however, when they were at the airport ready to fly to Washington, the plan fell through.

"Sometime after we came back, we heard that Kennedy died," Eroni related. "I was in the garden when the family heard the news on the radio. I came back inside the house and found the photo of him and I cried. I sat down with the picture and cried.

"The way they called us back after saying that we would go and see him, and now knowing that he was dead, my sadness was great. I knew I would never meet him. And his promise didn't come out. I wondered what he must have thought. I was sorry, and still am. I still think of Kennedy."

PART
·13·
GUNBOAT
SKIPPER

Jack Kennedy commands the first PT gunboat in the Solomons, fall of 1943 (John F. Kennedy Library)

A Legitimate American Hero

From Rendova the shipwrecked mariners were taken straight to the PT-boat headquarters at Tulagi, where all were checked for injuries and infections. Thereafter they were either kept in sick bay or, like McMahon, hospitalized at Blue Beach, on Florida Island.

"Admitted with abrasions, multiple," the medical officer noted on Jack's admission card. "Patient was on PT boat which was rammed and sunk by enemy destroyer. After being in water about 10 hours landed upon enemy occupied island without shoes, clothing or food. Stayed on island for five days before being rescued. At the present time he shows symptoms of fatigue and many deep abrasions and lacerations of the entire body, especially the feet." He prescribed "hot soaks and alcohol and glycerine dressings and bed rest. Multiple vitamin tablets and high caloric diet."

News of the PT wreck and rescue, meanwhile, began making its tortuous way back through naval censors and bureaucracy to Washington. Finally, on the evening of Thursday, August 19, the Navy Department in Washington passed Hewlett and Erikson's two on-the-spot news-agency accounts of Jack's rescue, and the story became headline news across America: SHOT FROM RUSTY JAP GUN GUIDES KENNEDY RESCUERS; KENNEDY'S SON SAVES 10 IN PACIFIC; KENNEDY'S SON IS HERO IN THE PACIFIC.

"Former Ambassador and Mrs. Kennedy today shouted in joy when informed of the exploit of their son," *The New York Times* recorded. "Mrs. Kennedy, first to hear the news by telephone at their summer home, expressed deep sorrow for the two crewmen who lost their lives. 'That's wonderful,' Mrs. Kennedy said when told her son was safe."

"Of course the news about Jack is the most exciting thing I've ever heard," Jack's sister Kathleen soon wrote ecstatically to her parents from her Red Cross posting in London. Overnight the gangly, "limping monkey" who should never have been in combat at all had single-handedly won back the Kennedy honor. As Jack would remark self-mockingly to a friend on his return to the United States, he had become a "legitimate American hero."

Back to Duty

"Crews of two other PT boats, patrolling close by, saw flaming high octane gasoline spread over the water," Leif Erikson noted in his AP dispatch. "They gave up 'Skipper' Kennedy and all his crew as lost that morning of Aug. 2." Frank Hewlett wrote, "The injured are in the hospital and Kennedy is now resting his weary body in his long vacant bunk which his mates never expected him to occupy again."

In the euphoria of the news that Jack was alive and was a hero, the question of why *PT 109* and its crew had been so readily abandoned went unaddressed. Al Cluster, however, was well aware of Jack's state of mind:

> I'll never forget this picture: he and I were sitting on a cot outside and the tears were streaming down his face and he said, "If only they'd come over to help me, maybe I might have been able to save those other two." He was very bitter that nobody had come to help.
>
> He was bitter, and that's the only word for it, bitter. And it was completely understandable. At least one of the other boats had seen the fire blazing up over there, so they knew something had happened, and yet they made no effort to go over there. He was very bitter about it.

Even Jack's humor took on a more savage edge, and though he gradually overcame his resentment, it would resurface at moments with surprising vehemence.

Johnny Iles vividly recalled seeing Jack when he emerged from the sick bay in Tulagi. "He was *really* skinny, and limping—from the coral cuts, I guess. I gave him a big hello. Then I happened to mention about the mass [said by the Catholic chaplain, Father McCarthy]. He was *furious*! He read the riot act to me. He said he wasn't ready to die just yet, and why the hell had I given up hope? I couldn't understand it."

Joe Kernell, a skipper from Squadron 5, also recalled seeing Jack at Tulagi. "He was in this hospital—not a real hospital, a tent affair, and wearing only skivvies . . . When I saw him in sick bay, I said, 'Jack, what went through your mind when you saw that destroyer coming and you thought you might be killed?' He looked real serious and asked, 'You really want to know? . . . I thought, my God, I owe Joe Kernell two hundred fifty dollars in bridge debts and I haven't paid him!' So, right there, he whipped out a check and paid me. Then, in that funny way of his, he made me feel terrible: that the only reason I'd come to the sick bay was to get my money!"

Jack was now more skeptical than ever about the glamour of PT boats and MacArthur's strategy, particularly when "Iron Mike" Moran, the new PT-boat chief in the Solomons, arrived. He was "a big harp if ever there was one," Jack remarked sarcastically in a letter to his parents.

> He's fresh out from six months in the States and full of smoke and vinegar and statements like: "It's a privilege to be here and we would be ashamed to be back in the States—and we'll stay here ten years if necessary"! That all went over like a lead balloon. However the doc told us yesterday that Iron Mike was complaining of head-aches and diarrhea—so we look for a different tune to be thrummed out on that harp of his before many months.
>
> When I read that we will fight the Japs for years if necessary and will sacrifice hundreds of thousands if we must, I always like to check from where [the writer] is talking—it's seldom out here. . . . It was a terrible thing, though, losing those two men. One had ridden with me as long as I had been out here. He had been somewhat shocked by a bomb that had landed near the boat about two weeks before. He never really got over it; he always seemed to have the feeling that something was going to happen to him.
>
> When a fellow gets the feeling that he's in for it, the only thing to do is to let him off the boat.

He explained how he'd intended to have Kirksey transferred to base work "the next time we came down the line. . . . He had a wife and three kids. The other fellow had just come aboard. He was only a kid himself. It certainly brought home how real the war is—and when I read the papers from home, how superficial is most of the talking and thinking about it!"

There was little time for such reflections, however. "We only had a small sick bay, not too many beds," recalled one of the medical officers, Dr. Joseph Wharton. "We got them out of there as soon as possible because we had a crew with infectious hepatitis. He stayed in the sick bay a very short time." "To duty very much improved," the medical officer noted on August 16—barely a week after the rescue.

Al Cluster recalled how, as squadron commander, he had wished to send Jack home. "Now there was—I don't know that it was an official tradition, but it was kind of an informal custom that if your boat was sunk, why, you'd get new assignments in the States." To Cluster's surprise, however, Jack emphatically turned down the idea. He was, as Cluster became aware, determined to get even with the Japanese.

The First Gunboat

"I think it was the guilt of losing his two crewmen, the guilt of losing his boat, and of not being able to sink a Japanese destroyer," Al Cluster later reflected. "I think all these things came together and he wanted to get back at them. I would say, if I tried to write a history of JFK's period in the Solomons, that Jack felt *very strongly* about losing those two men and his ship in the Solomons. He was *very, very bitter* that nobody had come to help him. And the second thing, *he wanted to pay the Japanese back.* I think he wanted to recover his own self-esteem—he wanted to get over this feeling of guilt which you would have if you were sitting there and had a destroyer cut you in two."

But how could Jack pay the Japanese back? Motor-torpedo boats had proved such a disaster in the Solomons that Commander Kelly had actually recommended the withdrawal of all PTs from the area. Kelly, however, had not counted on Iron Mike—or Thomas Warfield.

Meanwhile, with growing American air, destroyer, and submarine superiority in the Solomons, the Japanese had scaled down their destroyer operations and now relied almost entirely on coastal barges, moving by night. It was this traffic that offered the PT boats a final chance to prove themselves worthy of the vast effort that had been exerted in transporting them out to the Pacific, as well as the cost in men and materials to man, fuel, arm, and maintain them.

Even with the PT boats in this new, antibarge role, Commander Warfield was responsible for yet another disaster. This time he ordered out his entire flotilla in broad daylight. "I did all I could to prevent the attack being made," declared Lieutenant Evans, the coastwatcher who had helped save the lives of the survivors of *PT 109*, in his report. "Eight or nine P.T. boats entered Ferguson Passage shortly after dawn on 22nd August, steamed across to the Kolombangara coast and then followed the coast down to the Vohave and Ringi Coves. One or two P.T.'s entered the coves and met a very hot reception. Machine guns covered the entrance to both coves and a small coastal gun opened fire from Kukkuli Pt. The P.T. boats retired at high speed under a smoke screen. I was later informed that the U.S. casualties were 3 killed and 5 wounded. Had the Japs been good gunners they would have sunk half the boats. Apart from the absurdity of the attack," Evans judged, the "approach" was criminal: a head-on assault in broad daylight that gave the Japanese "half an hour" to prepare to repulse them. Even the official PT-boat historian was compelled to see the attack as "very nearly disastrous," while participating skippers called it Warfield's "suicide mission."

It had become clear that even attacking barges and protected anchorages was not a job for wooden launches armed with obsolete torpedoes. Yet with a further squadron arriving fresh from the States, there were now almost sixty torpedo boats and over six hundred PT crew personnel in the area, not to speak of base and maintenance staff. As the month of August 1943 came to an end, it seemed imperative to use the PT boats in some capacity.

Thus was born the official notion of converting PTs into gunboats, with Jack Kennedy, thirsting for revenge against the Japanese, to be the first gunboat skipper.

Filling the Gap

"About this time, we were trying to intercept all of this barge traffic that was going between these various Japanese-held islands," Cluster later explained.

> And the Japanese barges were not playing fair, they were shooting back. We would go running at high speed and pass these barges and they were too shallow to draw our torpedo fire, but we would shoot at them with our fifty-caliber machine guns. The Japanese even had a Class AI, I think it was called, gunboat, where they had a larger-caliber gun on it, that they were using to guard these barges. They were fantastic in the way they could move men and material around the northern Solomons in these barges at night, without anybody knowing they were there. We tried to use "black-cat" PBYs [night-patrol planes], but they weren't able to do too much. So it was my idea to get gunboats that would intercept this traffic.

Jack Kennedy had had the same notion.

> If you remember, he had a thirty-seven-millimeter army gun that he had tied to the bow of his boat, the *PT 109,* in case he ran into a barge. . . . Everybody wanted bigger guns. We even took a look at the seventy-five-millimeter guns that the B-25s had on their nose over on Guadalcanal; there were always a lot of them, there were always more planes around than could fly, so they were available. However, they proved too heavy, you couldn't mount them and everything.

Anyway, I took three of my PT boats—the *59,* the *60,* and *61*—and began the process of converting them into gunboats. I hadn't really started when the *PT 109* went down, but I was trying to. And Kennedy wanted one. He wanted to get back at the Japanese. He got the first gunboat.

Cluster assigned Jack the *59.* It took almost five weeks to strip the vessel of its torpedo tubes and depth charges and install new guns and armor plating. "I don't think I ever saw a guy work harder, longer hours," Cluster recalled. Heavy forty-millimeter guns were fitted fore and aft, as well as six fifty-caliber machine-gun nests—three on each side. Twin fifty-caliber machine guns were mounted behind the cockpit, and two thirty-caliber machine guns forward of the cockpit, on each quarter. The boat soon boasted so many muzzles, it bristled like a porcupine. Lennie Thom, Jack's former executive officer, was given command of a second gunboat to be converted, and Jack's friend Johnny Iles a third—the three boats to comprise, when ready, the first gunboat group in the Solomons.

Meanwhile, new crews had to be assembled. Five former members of Jack's *PT 109* crew—Mauer, Maguire, Drewitch, Kowal, and Drawdy— volunteered. Maguire recalled the moment he found Kennedy getting the new gunboat ready at Guadalcanal. "Mauer and I went down to the dock. Kennedy said, 'What are you doing here?' We said, 'What kind of a guy are you? You got a boat and didn't come get us?' Kennedy got choked up. The nearest I ever seen him come to crying."

Jack's new executive officer, "Dusty" Rhoads, later remarked that "what impressed me most about Jack then was that so many of the men that had been on *PT 109* had followed him to the *59.* It spoke well of him as a leader, I thought." Others, particularly Jack's young squadron commander, Al Cluster, felt the same. Commenting in a letter home to his mother about the *PT 109* story that had been front-page news across the United States, Cluster assured his parents the story was genuine. "Kennedy did a fine job," he explained on September 18, 1942.

He's in my squadron and is one of the finest officers I have. He did very commendable work in getting his crew out O.K. and we're all very proud of him. Somehow, when we heard of his boat going down, I could not believe that he was lost. He's just that type of fellow. You know that he can take care of himself and you can always depend on him.

His position and family never enter into any of our thoughts here. I've only known him about six months but I am proud to serve with him in my outfit. Whatever he does, he earns solely by his capabilities and not by the prestige of his name. People like that make me realize what an American is, something you find nowhere else in this world—men and women achieving ends in spite of their background. In fact, I'd say it would be just as hard for a boy like Jack to make good as it is for a kid from the slums. Both have disadvantages to overcome. No one out here has done a better job than Jack.

As proud as Cluster was of Jack, Jack was equally proud of his men. As he confided in a letter to his parents:

> On the bright side of an otherwise completely black time was the way that everyone stood up to it. Previous to that I had become some- what cynical about the American as a fighting man. I had seen too much bellyaching and laying off. But with the chips down—that all faded away. I can now believe—which I never would have before— the stories of Bataan and Wake. For an American it's got to be awfully easy or awfully tough. When it's in the middle, then there's trouble.

Meanwhile, as Gunboat Number One neared completion at Tulagi, its crew expanded still further. From his own erstwhile flagship, *PT 21,* which had broken its back and had had to be scrapped, Cluster assigned the skipper, Ensign I. J. Mitchell, and five more men to serve under Kennedy, the rest being made up from the squadron boat pool. Glen Christiansen, a first-class gunner's mate, was made the chief petty officer.

"One thing you have to understand about the *59* boat," Christiansen afterward related:

> It had so many guns on it that we literally had *two* crews: one that lived on the boat, and one that would come on the boat. We had sixteen men and three officers, whereas normally, a PT boat, a sev- enty-seven-foot Elco, would have eight men and two officers. Now, this boat was a seventy-seven-foot Elco, one hundred percent—I never rode a Higgins boat, so I know what I'm talking about. An eighty-foot boat, such as Mr. Kennedy's *PT 109,* had a twenty-foot beam at its widest, and they kept the width wider as the boat tapered towards the stern, which allowed more room in the engine room—it was a lot more comfortable boat. So we were now using a smaller boat with more men for the gunboat.
>
> I was part of the live-on crew. Mr. Kennedy lived on the boat, and so did the executive officer, Mr. Rhoads. . . . When the other eight men would get aboard and the third officer, then we'd head on out. . . .
>
> Mr. Mitchell, he was the gunnery officer as they called them, he

stayed aft in any kind of engagement and would stay in touch with
Mr. Kennedy on the bridge, you know, so that he could tell him what
was coming up from the stern of the boat. He was the sort of eyes
in the back of Mr. Kennedy's head.

Not all PT personnel approved the change of role from torpedo boat
to gunboat. Even Ensign Mitchell, having previously captained his own
PT boat, felt the new assignment to be a comedown. Christiansen had no
time for such a demonstrably outdated view. "Most of the torpedoes we
had were the Mark Eight, three-hundred-pound warhead, built probably
during or after World War I and most ineffective. Cost a lot of lives I'm
sure, of *our* people rather than the Japanese, because we didn't get explosions like we should have. Later on, of course, torpedoes came out that
carried a six-hundred-pound warhead and went much faster, but priority
went to the submarines and destroyers. We were the last to get them, we
were like a poor relation, sort of the ugly sisters."

What emerged from the refit of *PT 59* at Tulagi during September 1943
was certainly a vastly different vessel from its fellow PTs. "First of all, we
worked in Purvis Bay, alongside the *Oregon,* which was a repair ship, and
there we put the boat together," Christiansen recalled. "We worked as
late as we could work. It took the better part of a month . . . we worked
on into the night sometimes—we had to keep covered up of course
because of the blackout. The construction of the boat became pretty
heavy because we put armor plate on both sides of the gas tanks and
gunwale, all the guns were armored, all the fifty-calibers: there were
fourteen fifty-calibers and two forty-millimeters, so it was pretty heavily
armored."

Once Ensign Rhoads tested the protective plating, however, there was
consternation. "Shooting dead on," Rhoads vividly remembered, "we
riddled it like swiss cheese. It wasn't worth a damn." For all the extra
steel, which had taken so much effort first to prize from Halsey's supply
staff, then to mount, Gunboat Number One remained a wooden water
chariot.

Jack was unperturbed. "He was very determined," Christiansen recalled of his skipper's mood;

> and when we'd go out on patrol at night it was all business—there
> was no monkeying around, we had "a job to do and we're here to
> do it" was the tone.
>
> When I first met him I didn't really get to talk to him very much,
> but finally we started getting together more and more as the boat
> became finished. He was certainly a good naval officer—he had
> good, I thought extremely good, training and navigation and just

general seaworthy abilities. . . . He was always good to the men, he was just a nice man to be around, a genteel sort of person. There was nothing rough or nasty about him. (You'd find half were like that, half weren't. Now Commander Warfield—that SOB, I mean you couldn't find anything good to say about that son of a bitch, I swear! He was pitiful to work for, just a bad fellow all the way around. They even had fellows that pushed him off the dock, knocked him into the water a couple of times, they disliked him so much, they'd run like hell so he couldn't find out who they were. Things like that start happening when you're a bad officer.)

Christiansen had himself been sunk at Pearl Harbor, and half the new gunboat's crew had lost their boats through enemy action or running aground on the treacherous coral reefs, so there was no intrinsic shame attached to Kennedy or the ex-*PT 109* men. "We asked about things," Christiansen recalled his curiosity over the *PT 109* sinking.

They were told to cruise on one engine to conserve gas. And they just couldn't get those engines started in time. Fifteen seconds, hell, you couldn't have got *one* of them started in that short period of time. Starting those PT engines was never easy, they'd never start, bang, just like that. And they had to start them cold, they're not running, they're just dead. And with only one engine, you couldn't get any speed up. See, when you're dragging those two screws—so you're just idling along, you can't get up any speed at all. Until all three of them are running, you're kind of hurting. Well, the *PT 109* incident ended all that! It ended it. We never had to do that before [conserve gas] and I don't know that anybody ever did it after: I think that was a lesson the navy learned real quick—or the PT people learned.

"Haven't heard from you for a hell of a time," Jack wrote to Lem Billings in the Mediterranean on September 15, "but I presume you are O.K. What are your plans? When do you figure on getting back to the States? Bobby said you were staying another six months—so I figure you should be home by Dec. or January—which should be good as I ought to get back around then myself. It would certainly be nice to put in a month down at P.B. or in Canada skiing—as I'm getting god-damned tired of the boat. . . . We have been having a difficult time for the last two months—lost our boat about a month ago when a Jap can cut us in two + lost some of our boys. We had a bad time for a week on a Jap island—but finally got picked up—and have got another boat."

The brevity and understatement of Jack's account of the most traumatic experience in his life was extraordinary. Just as he had been when

the doctors had decided he had leukemia at the Mayo Clinic, so now, in
the aftermath of a shattering brush with death, he seemed more concerned with gossip and social prospects in his letters to Billings than with
raking over the ashes of *PT 109.* "Dad is putting on a show in N.Y.
[*Another Love Story*]—which unfortunately does not possess a large
chorus. I would certainly like to go back + tangle with a group of
choruses for about a week. As a matter of record—I haven't seen a
girl—black, brown or white—for seven months," though he assumed he
was "due for a breather in about 3 more."

Beyond tangling with chorus girls, however, there loomed ahead for
Jack the question of more serious entanglements. Bunny Waters had sent
him a photograph "with a very loving inscription," of which Jack was
particularly proud. "She was a good-looking blonde," Christiansen recalled. "She was an Amazon, as they called them—just shortly before
World War II started they had these Amazons and Bunny Waters was
one of them—tall, beautiful girl. They traveled in a group, and were
dancers or something. So Mr. Kennedy had her picture up inside one of
the lockers in his room. We'd go down there and peek at her—we didn't
have anybody else to look at!"

Bunny's apparent loyalty to Jack, however, had been somewhat tarnished by the news that she had "received a very large diamond bracelet
from Pal Al Johnson," as Jack reported to Billings. Meanwhile "Angela
Greene is playing the very promising part of a whore in a N.Y. show,"
prompting Jack to make the sarcastic remark that he didn't know
"whether she is able to keep her public + private life apart." As if to
excuse his tartness he added, "God, I've just remembered that Miss
Waters + Miss Greene came after you left—disregard the above item—
they merely filled the gap when Inga Arvad walked out of my life."

This was as close as Jack Kennedy would ever get to saying he was
heartbroken. It was also touchingly self-deceiving, since it was not Inga
who had first walked out, but Jack himself. "She's still in N.Y.—working
for the North America Newspaper Alliance + living with the same
husband," he complained, having heard this from Henry James. With
Frances Ann Cannon having had a second baby, "it looks as though I'll
have to start with a totally green team when I get back to the States.
Maybe I'll end it all and marry Charlotte [McDonnell]."

The memory of Inga, however, continued to haunt him. He had still
not heard from her since his long letter to her in the spring. Now he
penned a part-angry, part-jocular love letter:

> Inga Binga:
>   What the hell is the story? I write you a six-page letter—trash I
> admit—but not as bad as that last story of yours in which you tied

up Joe Stalin, Wendell Willkie + Cupid into a sort of Blessed Trinity—but anyway—that six pager cost me a good deal of sweat and toil—plus a little blood when I cut myself trying to fix the type-writer—and what do I get—nothing—not even a rejection slip. What's the idea—Has your "husband" come between us?

According to Henry James who is a very nosy Parker—I told him to send the letter to you, not deliver it—he says you are extremely attractive—but he also said that your heart belongs to Daddy [in postscript Jack explained he meant "Nils—not JP"].

Well, I suppose the war brought us together—that and Miss K.—and it's doing an excellent job of separating us—lately, it appears permanently. However, I'll be back—and we can discuss then over the break-fast table how you shattered my morale out here.

Incidentally—that picture I had of you that Kick took—which was really good—has met a watery grave. Please send me another—will you.

As ever
Young Kennedy
What does *that* remind you of?

A Hell of a Letter

Jack's letter crossed a loving note from Inga in the mail.

Inga had read with wonder of his *PT 109* sinking and rescue. She'd also received, at last, Jack's long letter from the Solomons, delivered in person and belatedly by Henry James. She hadn't married Nils Blok after all. She even taunted Jack by saying she found James tall, handsome, and of good family. But the most exciting news concerned her journalistic career: namely, that despite the machinations of Mr. J. Edgar Hoover, she'd been chosen to stand in for Sheilah Graham of the *Los Angeles Times,* whose Hollywood gossip column was syndicated in newspapers across America, and who was taking a leave of absence. This would entail moving, without Blok, to California.

"Dearest Inga Binga," Jack wrote back immediately on the squadron signals typewriter (which only printed in block capitals) on September 26, 1943:

Rec'd your letter at long last today, and while I'm still fed [*sic*] as hell that you didn't answer before, this will keep me for awhile. You still have the knack of making me feel one hundred per cent better after talking with you or hearing from you. You know, I wrote you about a week ago, and sent it to you care of Henry James as he never sent me your address. It was unfortunately written when I was a little under—so disregard it. I've got a new boat and am up the line again. We had a small celebration after we had some luck, we got the alcohol out of the torpedoes, but anyways I think that an indignant, incoherent letter to you was the result.

The war goes slowly here, slower than you can ever imagine from reading the papers at home. The only way you can get the proper perspective on its progress is to put away the headlines for a month and watch us move on the map. It's deathly slow. The Japs have dug deep, and with the possible exception of a couple of Marine divisions are the greatest jungle fighters in the world. Their willingness to die for a place like Munda gives them a tremendous advantage over us. We, in aggregate, just don't have the willingness. Of course, at times, an individual will rise up to it, but in total, no . . . Munda or any of those spots are just God damned hot stinking corners of small islands in a group of islands in a part of the ocean we all hope never to see again . . .

We are at a great disadvantage—the Russians could see their country invaded, the Chinese the same. The British were bombed, but we are fighting on some islands belonging to the Lever Company, a British concern making soap. . . . I suppose if we were stockholders we would perhaps be doing better, but to see that by dying at Munda you are helping to insure peace in our time takes a larger imagination than most men possess. . . .

The Japs have this advantage: because of their feeling about Hirohito, they merely wish to kill. An American's energies are divided; he wants to kill but he also is trying desperately to prevent himself from being killed.

In the air or on the sea we don't have the same situation, and we have moved fast, but what it all adds up to is that in this type of warfare, where control of the air and the sea are not the same decisive factors that they are in Europe, we will move slowly, until the day comes when we can simply smother them by weight.

This war here is a dirty business. It's very easy to talk about the war and beating the Japs if it takes years and a million men, but anyone who talks like that should consider well his words. We get so used to talking about billions of dollars, and millions of soldiers, that thousands of casualties sound like drops in the bucket. But if those thousands want to live as much as the ten that I saw, the people deciding the whys and wherefores had better make mighty sure that all this effort is headed for some definite goal, and that when we reach that goal we may say it was worth it, for if it isn't, the whole thing will turn to ashes, and we will face great trouble in the years to come after the war. . . .

I received a letter today from the wife of my engineer, who was so badly burnt that his face and hands and arms were just flesh, and he was that way for six days. He couldn't swim, and I was able to help him, and his wife thanked me, and in her letter she said, "I suppose to you it was just part of your job, but Mr. McMahon was part of my life and if he had died I don't think I would have wanted to go on living." . . .

There are so many McMahons that don't come through. There was a boy on my boat, only twenty-four, had three kids, one night two bombs straddled our boat, and two of the men were hit, one standing right next to him. He never got over it. He hardly ever spoke after that. He told me one night he thought he was going to be killed. I wanted to put him ashore to work, he wouldn't go. I wish I had . . . He was in the forward gun turret where the destroyer hit us. . . .

I don't know what this all adds up to, nothing I guess, but you said that you figured I'd go to Texas, and write my experiences—I wouldn't go near a book like that. This thing is so stupid, that while it has a sickening fascination for some of us, myself included, I want to leave it far behind me when I go . . .

Inga Binga, I'll be glad to see [you] again. I'm tired now, we are riding every night, and the sleeping is tough in the daytime, but I've been told that they are sending some of us home to form a new squadron in a couple of months. I've had a great time here, every-thing considered, but I'll be just as glad to get away from it for awhile. I used to have the feeling that no matter what happened I'd get through . . .

It's a funny thing that as long as you have that feeling, you seem to get through. I've lost that feeling lately, but as a matter of fact I don't feel badly about it. If anything happens to me I have this knowledge that if I had lived to be a hundred, I could only have improved the quantity of my life, not the quality. This sounds gloomy as hell . . . I'll cut it . . . You are the only person I'd say it to anyway. As a matter of fact knowing you has been the brightest point in an extremely bright twenty-six years . . .

Now that I look back, it has been a hell of a letter. It isn't what I was going to say at all . . . I think it's great about your job, this should really be a great chance for you, and you really ought to be just right for the job. By the way, Henry James may be a good fellow and all that, but I'd never see you marry him on his best day and your worst. When I get relieved, I'll come down to L.A. if you are going to be there. Write me when you can.

                         Much love
                         Jack

Missing the Marriage Boat

The good news from Inga was followed by bad news from Miss McDonnell. "I understand Charlotte is getting married," Jack scribbled to Billings on October 8 from Tulagi, where he was still carrying out trials aboard *Gunboat Number One*. "That frankly came as quite a surprise as I've been corresponding very frequently and nothing was ever said. In fact she never has told me about it. It's certainly amazing how all these girls are so strong for me—and then marry someone else. I'm back where I started—I don't know anybody again."

At first Jack could not believe his ill luck, on top of the *PT 109* experience, but the news was soon confirmed. "As you can well imagine the news of the day, week + month is that Miss McDonnell and Capt. Harris are about to be as one," he reported to Billings on October 30. "Although I have long realized that God ordained that one from the beginning of time—as it united two prominent Catholic families, both from New York—it came as a bit of a blow to yours truly. It looks as though I've missed the [marriage] boat again. I sometimes wonder whether I'm ever going to make the trip—when I do it will probably be by tramp steamer. I suppose I am now entitled to wear a gold star as a man who has lost his girl in the war."

Weeks later Jack realized that he had probably contributed to the tragedy, "Charlotte receiving my letter addressed to Dearest Darlyne," he explained to Billings, which "leads to the obvious conclusion that Darling Darlyne got one addressed to Dearest Charlotte"—thus explaining why "I have heard from neither for 3 months. Darlyne is not, incidentally—although I hate to prick any bubble of yours + Charlotte's—a 'West Coast Queen' but a poor but honest working girl at Finchleys in P[alm] B[each]."

Jack had now been jilted both by his lover and his fall-back fiancée, though at least Inga wrote to him "occasionally." "As you may have heard," he told Billings, "she is writing a Hollywood column," though a further mishap in the mails resulted in Inga receiving in Hollywood "a publicity hand-out from Bunny Waters' press agent about the torrid romance between Lt. Kennedy + Miss Waters. That fickle finger of fate was certainly working over-time as was the long arm of coincidence."

Meanwhile, the pace in the New Georgia campaign had quickened at the end of September, as the Japanese successfully evacuated their twelve-thousand-man garrison from Kolombangara—a feat rivaling the German evacuation of Sicily several months earlier.

Humiliated by this Japanese success, there was much recrimination in U.S. naval headquarters, with PT boats the natural whipping boy. Why were the Japanese being allowed to move and remove their island garrisons so easily? What were the PTs doing to stop it? Overnight Al Cluster's three-gunboat flotilla became the envy of other squadrons, which still had not converted from torpedo boats. "I wanted to take those three boats and go up and sink Japanese barges," Cluster later lamented. "However, when I got these boats done, there were some senior officers out there that thought, boy, I would like to have those boats too! And so Kelly of Squadron 9 grabbed one of them, and somebody else grabbed another one—and I never was able to take my gunboats out and operate them as a single unit!"

As a result Jack ceased to operate with Lennie Thom and Johnny Iles and was instead ordered up on October 18 to Lumba Lumba, the new forward PT base on Vella Lavella, to help interdict Japanese barge traffic during Allied landings on Choiseul and Bougainville. "Am now Capt of a motor gun boat with which we fight small armed Jap auxiliaries + armed barges—which they are using in great numbers. It's extremely interesting—all of the crew are volunteers—and I think we can do some good," Jack explained to Billings in a letter on October 30. There was just one problem: "If one of those Jap incendiaries ever hit our gas tanks some night, though, the only thing torrid about Miss Waters + Mr. Kennedy will be Lt. Kennedy. I'm not planning to let that happen though—I've given the Japs one good crack at me and that's par for the course."

To Pat Monroe, a fellow skipper in Squadron 23, Jack meanwhile described the general situation of PTs in the Solomons in his best no-nonsense American prose. "The nerve center, Sesapi [on Tulagi] is fucked up beyond all recognition . . . Com[mander] Cal[vert] is being replaced by Specht, who hasn't arrived as far as I hear. Westy [Westholm] is screaming to go home + Marion G. Pettit has a candle in his window—and asks in a cracked + broken voice every new ensign if he is his relief—and so far the reply is negative." He could even joke now about the *PT 109* affair, thanking Monroe for his "good wishes on our rescue. We were extremely lucky. After today it won't happen again. Working out of another base + went in to see the doc about some coral infections I got. He asked me how I got them. I said swimming—he then burst loose with: 'Kennedy—

you know swimming is forbidden in this area—stay out of the god-damned water.' So now it's an official order—so no more strain.''

He was, or seemed to be, the same old Jack—except to Al Cluster, who knew how desperately Jack was itching to get back at the Japanese and avenge the deaths of his two men. "I think up to that time, all of us probably looked on the Japanese somewhat impersonally,'' Cluster recalled. "They were somebody 'over there'; they would move at night; you didn't know them personally or anything—you were just doing what you were supposed to do in warfare, but it wasn't a personal involvement like Kennedy experienced after his boat was sunk.'' Once back in combat, however, Jack began to realize that retaliation, even in command of the navy's first converted gunboat in the Pacific, was tantalizingly difficult.

The new gunboat carried radar, a crew of nineteen, and no fewer than sixteen guns, yet it was frustratingly hard to locate the Japanese barges, even when patrolling all night behind enemy lines in Japanese-controlled waters. Japanese planes constantly shadowed the boat and on October 26 almost hit it, the bomb exploding only 150 yards away.

As with the near-miss foreshadowing the sinking of *PT 109*, *Gunboat Number One* had already received an omen. On October 7, the day *PT 59*'s refit was finally complete, one of the *109*'s surviving crew was killed aboard another boat. "They picked up some Jap prisoners and he went forward to the part of the boat to give one of them a drink of water—as they had been floating around all night,'' Jack wrote to his family. "He reached out his canteen—the Jap sprang forward—grabbed a tommy gun he held in the other hand—and in spite of the fact that he had four slugs poured into him, shot the boy. It is tough to go through what he went through and then get it that way—but you just can't fool around with these babies.''

To his father Jack promised to take no unnecessary risks. "Don't worry at all about me—I've learned to duck—and have learned the wisdom of the old naval doctrine of keeping your bowels open, your mouth shut—and never volunteering.'' But this was written to amuse and placate the cowardly ex-ambassador in Hyannis Port. To the crew of *Gunboat Number One* it seemed as if, on the contrary, Jack was spoiling for a fight, and on the night of November 2, 1943, he finally got one.

Growing Up

Gunboat Number One had just returned from an all-night patrol and was tanking up when ordered to move out and help evacuate a unit of marines trapped on the island of Choiseul. Landed as part of a diversionary raid, the marines had become lost in the swampy jungle and surrounded by Japanese troops. Eventually they were rescued from the Warrior River, under fire, by three American landing craft, one of which sank after hitting a coral reef. The survivors scrambled aboard the other landing craft, while ten were taken aboard Jack's *Gunboat Number One,* including the marines' doctor and three badly wounded men. One of them, a corporal, died in Jack's bunk. By three A.M. the gunboat, which had set out with only a third of its tanks filled, ran out of fuel and had to be laboriously towed by the other two PTs in the patrol in broad daylight, prompting Jack to radio for air cover. A flight of four Australian P-40s was dispatched. All were shot down.

By nightfall Jack's gunboat was off again on another mission to withdraw the remaining marines from Voza, and they were out again the night of November 5, when they took Warfield's intelligence officer, "Whizzer" White, along. White asked to take a turn at firing one of the machine guns and quickly regretted it when he injured his hand on a malfunctioning gun bolt. It was clear that operating a gunboat was not a task for the incompetent.

"I remember riding on his boat a couple of times," White recorded later. "As a result of these encounters I began to get a strong feeling about what kind of fellow he was. He proved himself to be very intelligent in the way he ran his boat, as well as cool and courageous under fire."

Jack's crew, however, became increasingly anxious lest their skipper become *too* courageous. On the night of November 5 Jack had refused to head home after their fruitless patrol south of Choiseul Bay, and at five-thirty A.M., in the dawn light, he and his crew had finally found and destroyed three Japanese barges they found beached on Moli Island. The following night *Gunboat Number One* was out again, and again two nights later, on November 8. Three nights after that, *Gunboat Number One* caught two barges emerging from the Warrior River, but they scuttled back to harbor. Finally on November 13, the gunboat successfully shelled Sipasa and Guppy islands at the mouth of Choiseul Bay.

"The [Warrior] river had high bluffs on each side of it, that the Japanese had guns on," Christiansen recalled. "We happened one night to fire at them and we hit one of their guns. They made one bad mistake, they fired at us and we picked up their flash and of course from then on we just fired automatic weapons into them. I think we put them out of commission because they never fired back! And the next day 'Tokyo Rose' said that there was a light cruiser off Choiseul firing at their shore installations!"

Emboldened by their success, Jack now proposed a daylight raid right up the Warrior River. Christiansen, as chief petty officer, was consulted. To him the idea of a daylight attack, however bold, seemed "harebrained."

> We were standing on the stern of the boat and he was talking about his plan—"What would you think of this?"—and I said, "Jesus Christ, Mr. Kennedy," I said, "there's no way," I said. "We don't know what's up there."
>
> We didn't even know if we could turn around—we didn't have any intelligence. And we had had one incident where a boat had gone up a river looking for a scrap with somebody and they had a thirty-seven-millimeter on the bow. I think they lost all but four people in a daylight attack, and I don't think any Japanese were taken out, so it was a total failure—the blood was running off the stern of the boat, it was so bad. They just slaughtered them.
>
> I mean if you're going to fight a war, you want the odds to be at least fifty-fifty. If you're going to make some heavy damage, fine, but the odds have got to be at least even. . . .
>
> It just happened to be that Mr. Cluster was there on Vella Lavella at the time, and I said to Mr. Cluster, "I hope he doesn't go through with this, because we're going to get slaughtered up there!"

Christiansen was not alone in his misgivings. "I saw him after he'd made several patrols," Cluster, who was reconnoitering a future PT base on Bougainville, recalled. "I've forgotten the name of the guy—it wasn't Christiansen, it wasn't King, but there was another man that was on his boat that came to me and said, 'My God, this guy's going to get us all killed! He's going in and shooting up shore installations and things like that!'"

"Mr. Cluster finally made the decision [not to carry out the attack]," Christiansen related, adding however that the whole crew shared their skipper's sheer frustration.

> We had a hell of a boat. We wanted to put it into action. We had this great boat that was operating beautifully and had radar and all the latest gear on it, and we were looking for a scrap, a bad one.

It was. . . . We weren't really getting them [the Japanese]. You know, we'd go up there and we'd shoot it out with them a little bit, and this and that, but we weren't really hitting them at all, and we were really ready for it.

That's the way I felt. I would have loved to have had a fight—not [with] a battleship, but I think we could have taken on an escort vessel or something. Because we were good shots, we had good crew members on the guns that were excellent. And we were aching for a fight, but it just didn't hit and that's frustrating.

Though Cluster forbade the daylight mission, he did not think Jack was concerned with winning medals or glory; rather he saw in Jack's fighting spirit a turning point in the young Boston man's life.

I think probably there was a serious side to Kennedy that started evolving at that time that had not existed before. We were kind of a happy-go-lucky bunch down there in the Solomons—"knights of the sea" and all that crap, going out and attacking these large ships and all that kind of stuff with all that glamour: whereas in reality it had become a dirty, minor war in which you just had to do the best you could.

If I were a psychologist, I would say that there was probably in JFK at that time a change of seriousness. His evacuation of the wounded marines off Choiseul, when they made their diversionary raid over there, when one of the marines died on his bunk. . . . These are all sobering things that happened to him: that made him—I hate to use the term "grow up," but I would say that it made him grow up emotionally at that time.

The millionaire's son, buttoned and valeted all his life, was finally becoming a man. A Catholic priest at Buna, New Guinea, wrote home that Jack Kennedy was a "fine, upstanding lad, guts, brains, courage to give away, generous, worshipped by his lads."

Jack's days as a gunboat captain were numbered, however. The war was leapfrogging west, beyond Choiseul and Bougainville, which were masked and only partly seized in order to provide airfields for MacArthur's real weapon: his strategic air force. Moreover Jack's health, always precarious, began to deteriorate, with both his stomach problems and his back trouble worsening. "I think he was in pain most of the time—I don't know how he put up with it really," Christiansen remarked later.

I don't know how much he slept. I can't say whether he slept good at night or got rested up enough during the day, because it was hot, nasty weather, jungle-type weather, so you were never comfortable sleeping unless you got drunk and fell asleep. Mr. Kennedy, he didn't drink. He got a ration of whiskey and he'd always bring it down and give it to us. He never did have malaria that I know of, but his back. . . . He didn't look too well, but none of us did. Everybody had dysentery and was gaunt and thin. I don't care how well-shaven and groomed you were, you still looked like death warmed over because it was just part of the life-style. And the food particularly—if you were living on the boats, it wasn't very good. It was edible, but just. And then being on the patrols—God, we'd go out sometimes in the evening before dusk and start out and wouldn't get home until well after the sun was up. And then it was clean the guns and get the boat cleaned—you had to do all that. Maybe some nights you got several hours' sleep, a couple of nights we didn't get any because the planes were bombing the island, and with one thing and another there was just no sleep for about seventy-two hours. You began to look pretty fierce.

"If I were you I wouldn't reproach myself too much for picking the wrong horse in May," Jack had solaced his friend Monroe. "It begins to be more + more apparent that a little of this goes a fairly long way—and lately our helpings have been extremely generous." It was certainly not in character for Jack to show pain or ill health, Christiansen recalled. "If he was sick, he certainly didn't reflect it to us. He wouldn't want you to know he wasn't feeling well. I knew there were times we'd go out and he wouldn't joke around or anything and that could have been an indication that he wasn't feeling well. But he was always very civil, you know. Even in the heat of an exchange—why, of course he would get, his voice would go up and he'd be screaming at somebody to shoot over that way or something like that, but that's normal. That's when the adrenaline is really pumping. That's not abnormal at all. He was trying to get his boat to its top efficiency."

The more the campaign moved west towards Rabaul, the more Vella Lavella became a backwater, and the more Jack's vendetta against the Japanese lost its fire. Given the cramped quarters of the boat, meanwhile, there was much ribbing among the crew. "I remember most of the crew slept nude," Ensign Rhoads recalled, "and ----'s penis was not too long and the crew gave him an unmerciful riding for that!" There were moments of hilarity too, such as the time "we got a couple of replacements," Rhoads remembered. "We didn't use the boat heads [toilets], by choice, because they operated imperfectly and were difficult to repair. So we used to hook an arm over the 40mm at the stern and let fly. These new kids got aboard and noticed that none of us used the heads if we could help it. So one night we were going out on patrol. Jack was at the wheel and I was on the radar, and I looked up and saw Jack holding out his hand as if checking for rain and looking up at the sky. One of the new kids had decided to go to the john, but he went up to the bow and with the boat making about 25 knots the spray was intense!"

Camaraderie was one of the few facets of war that made it bearable. "It was miserable. Steamy hot, high humidity," Christiansen described. "As the war progressed up the Solomons, we were getting extended further, which meant supplies were difficult to come by and we went without food for instance at Vella Lavella for like three weeks. They sunk one of our small ships bringing our supplies up there, and by the time they got the supplies through it was three weeks later. So we were living on dill pickles and cheese."

One night Ted Berlin's *PT 167* slipped into the Lambu Lambu cove, where Jack's gunboat was. The executive officer, Paul Fay, recalled:

> The *PT 59* was an old seventy-seven-foot Elco. Lieutenant (junior grade) John F. Kennedy was the skipper. Until that time I never appreciated the difference three feet in length, a foot or so in width, and change in basic design could make in the habitability of a small boat. With a crew of about twelve enlisted men and officers on board [plus a further eight men and third officer ashore] the *59* resembled a boater-home tenement district. Blankets and mattresses lay all over the forward decks. Laundry was hanging from lines stretched between the radar mast and the radio antennas, so there was a vague atmosphere of a Chinese laundry. Now and then you would hear a slightly irritated New England-accented voice exclaim in some such manner as "For Christ's sake, Jenson, will you take your dirty laundry off the food," or, "What in hell kind of hash is making that God awful smell!" Whoever made up the complement to man and maintain the ordnance and propulsion plant had forgotten they also had to live on board. As a result, for the week or so that we were at Lambu Lambu, Jack would have his breakfast and lunch on our palatial eighty-footer.

Fay was fascinated by a certain wild bravado lurking beneath Jack's genteel New England façade, and he marveled at Jack's love of challenge. Once when returning from a patrol in the early hours of morning, Jack lifted his gunboat's planing bow clear over the stern of Berlin's *PT 167*. "Jeez—if one of our engines had cut out!" Fay recalled years later with a shake of his head.

Even the pleasure of camaraderie began to pall, however, as Jack's health got worse. His back and stomach were giving him constant pain.

When summoned to take a routine medical examination for promotion to full lieutenant on October 20 (he had at last been formally transferred from special Naval Intelligence to deck-officer status on October 1, pending medical examination), Jack scoffed at the doctor's report. "What a farce!" he wrote to Billings, who had finally returned to the United States and was now trying for a commission in the U.S. Navy. "I looked as bad as I could look, which is ne plus ultra, wheezed badly, peed on his hand when he checked me for a rupture to show I had no control, all to no avail. I passed with flying colors, ready "for active duty ashore or at sea" anywhere, and by anywhere they mean no place else but here. They'd give you twenty-twenty with no strain," he assured Billings. "Everyone is in such lousy shape here that the only way they can tell if he is fit to fight is to see if he can breathe. That's about the only grounds on which I can pass these days."

What irked Jack most was the sight of other men going home. On November 15 Christiansen, King, and a third crew member from *Gunboat Number One* were posted back to the States; many of Jack's officer friends, too, were departing or had been reassigned. "Long John Iles rides now in Farrow's squadron and as you probably have heard a good many have hit stateside," he'd written to Pat Monroe, "among them Prep Sydney Rabakoff who gave a new and very interesting interpretation to 'red right—return' [the navigational rule for boats entering harbor]—and went on the right of the buoy. This put him well up on a rock in Purvis— and Prep Sydney was routed to the Post-waste Nouméa—where he stroked his way home. Searles got Louie ["Louie Lopez," nickname for Joe Kernell], Jake Carney + Snow[ball] out without Calvert or Moran knowing it—merely sent for orders— + Rosie Ryan left a couple of days ago."

Meanwhile Jack had also heard from Torbert Macdonald, as he informed Billings, that their mutual friend Francis McAdoo had become "a nervous wreck" and "ought to be getting home soon"—a prospect that now appeared to Jack to be getting remoter rather than closer in his own case.

"Is it true that back there you can't walk down the street without women tearing your trousers off?" he'd asked Billings on October 8. "Confirm or deny."

Billings had denied it, but Jack was unconvinced. "That the pleasure of being home goes a little sour after a month or so, I can well believe, but a remark like that one, here, sits about as well as that last can of fried spam I just ate." Moreover, "it looks as though I won't be getting that old sour feeling for a quite a while," he remarked with resignation on November 19, for "by a process of elimination I am now executive officer [senior seagoing lieutenant under Cluster] of my squadron, ain't it won-derful—now I don't know when I'll *ever* get back."

To his seventeen-year-old brother, Robert, who'd joined the Naval Reserve in Boston while in his final months at Milton Academy, Jack wrote,

> The folks sent me a clipping of you taking the oath. The sight of you up there, just as a boy, was really moving, particularly as a close examination showed that you had my checked London coat on. I'd like to know what the hell I'm doing out here, while you go stroking around in my drape coat, but I suppose that what we are out here for—or so they tell us—is so that our sisters and younger brothers will be safe and secure. Frankly I don't see it quite that way—at least if you're going to be safe and secure, that's fine with me, but not in my coat, brother, not in my coat. . . . I understand that you are going to be there till Feb. 1, which is very nice because it is on the playing fields of Milton and Groton, and maybe Choate, that the seeds will be sown that in later years, and on other fields, will cause you to turn in to sick bay with a bad back or a football knee. Well, black Robert, give those Grotties hell and keep in contact with your old broken-down brother.

Broken-down was no exaggeration. As Christiansen recalled, the doc-tors often had little choice but to pass good officers as fit, whatever their actual health. "They were short of good officers to begin with, and even when new officers would arrive, they'd have to ride on a boat for weeks or months before they'd really get the hang of things." So Jack had thus remained skipper of *Gunboat Number One* at Vella Lavella. On Novem-ber 18, however, following a final patrol around Redman Island, Jack had "a recurrence of abdominal symptoms," as the Lahey Clinic later re-corded. This time the breakdown in his health was welcome. The doctor at the rat-infested Lambu Lambu PT base ordered Jack off the boat. From the Buloa airstrip on the south side of Vella Lavella he was flown to Tulagi. He was back where he'd started.

Going Home

The "dirty business" of war against the Japanese still had many months to run, but Jack Kennedy's part was over. After X rays had been made and a careful examination undertaken at Tulagi, "a definite ulcer crater was found," which, with increasing stomach pains, "would indicate an early duodenal ulcer," the Tulagi medical officer made his diagnosis on November 23, 1943.

Al Cluster later blamed himself for not recommending Jack for the Silver Star for his work as skipper of *Gunboat Number One,* in view of the medals that other commanders seemed to "scatter like confetti" in their squadrons, often for utterly phony feats of PT-boat glory. At the time, however, Cluster had been convinced that Jack would receive the Silver Star he'd already recommended for Jack's sterling leadership following the sinking of *PT 109.* "His subsequent action in keeping the crew together and saving them and getting them back, I thought was exemplary," Cluster said, and on Jack's fitness report in December 1943 he assigned Jack a perfect 4.0 for his overall performance and leadership as commanding officer of *PT 59,* remarking that "this officer has demonstrated a cool effectiveness under fire and exhibited good judgment and determination in entirely strange conditions. His cheerful attitude and initiative qualify him to be the exec. officer of a PT Squadron."

Among his fellow PT officers, Jack was now an almost legendary figure. He impressed people neither through bravado nor chumminess, but by a confident friendliness and courage. "My most vivid memory of Jack is seeing him walking up and down the veranda of the Liugatu plantation house carrying a sacroiliac belt, looking for someone who had a needle and thread," recalled a PT-boat intelligence officer, Nick Wells, who had ridden several times on *PT 109.* He found Jack "a blue and gold sewing kit with gold embroidered anchors, a going-away gift from my children. I can still see the skillful sweep JFK had with a needle and thread, a sight perhaps even his mother never saw! I was there [in the Solomons] three weeks before I realized he was the ambassador's son. That seems hard to believe, but to me he was just a guy named Jack Kennedy from Boston."

The sacroiliac belt was necessary for Jack's increasingly painful back. Torby Macdonald, writing to Jack on December 7 from Squadron 12, assumed the back problem alone would suffice to get Jack "out of the boats." Jim Reed recalled, "His back was troubling him, he wasn't well.

But I tell you this about Jack—he never complained. He always had a terrific humor—a really acute sense of humor. He was very self-deprecating. He claimed to me once that he'd never had an unhappy day in his life. Now, whether or not he'd had an unhappy childhood, he had come to fall back on his inner resources. He loved to read. He was curious—he had a natural curiosity about anything. And ability."

To Jack's huge disappointment, however, this ability did not extend to poker, which he discovered after Red Fay's *PT 167* had been caught in an air raid by Japanese torpedo bombers. One torpedo had gone straight through the bow of Fay's boat. "We came down to Tulagi to be repaired, and he [Jack] was still there," Fay recalled. "He was trying to get his health back up and that's when I spent a lot of time, every single day practically, with him."

Though Fay was younger, the two had much in common. Both came from large Irish-Catholic families, with many siblings and a powerful father at their head. Brash, fun-loving, and uninhibited, Fay's warm-hearted bonhomie attracted Jack. "We'd meet up every night in his quarters," Fay remembered.

> I tried to get him to play poker. He just couldn't play poker. He was the world's worst poker player—they just skinned his hide! He just didn't get a sense for it—and the Texans were in there just dying to get him because they were all such damn good poker players!
>
> But then we gave up the poker, and in the evening, before we'd go to the officer's club, we would drop into his tent and he'd have us reading during the day. We'd pick up a *Time* magazine or *Life* or *Saturday Evening Post* or *Collier's* or whatever was available, and read it on any subject—and then we'd discuss the particular subjects in the different magazines. . . . He made us all very conscious of the fact that we'd better do some reading, we'd better be concerned about why the hell we're out here, or else what's the purpose of having the conflict, if you're going to come out here and fight and let the people that got us here get us back into it again. . . . He made us all very aware of our obligation as citizens of the United States to do something, to be involved in the process. . . . We felt the United States was now numero uno, that we had taken that role, and the United States was the leader of the free world—that the British and the French and the Allies really weren't going to make it without us. Yet side by side with this seriousness he had a great sense of humor— that laugh of his: the laugh was so contagious that it made everybody laugh. You'd tell a story or a joke and then that laugh would come out, he just had everybody laughing.

What was perhaps most remarkable was Jack's ability to relate to different people from different backgrounds without in any way distorting or being untrue to his own character. Yet it was this very absence of phoniness that, in the eyes of many around him, precluded him from a possible political career. For some, such as Warfield's signals officer, Lieutenant Woods, Jack was simply not bullish, forceful, or opiniated enough. "I didn't think he had any more chance of being president of the United States than the man on the moon," Woods later remarked. Even Al Cluster, whose father was a Republican politician, ridiculed the notion.

> If people asked me later, when did I first think Kennedy would ever be president, my answer was a loud laugh! You must remember, during the six or eight months that I saw him down in the Solomons, his brother had not been killed. You've got to remember that Kennedy—he wasn't an introvert, but he was a writer. We would often talk about what we were going to do after the war. Of course, I was regular navy, so I did not have any ambitions outside the navy at that time. But Kennedy, I think, wanted to be a writer—that was the thing that came across to all of us who knew him at that time.
>
> There was never any talk about him going into politics. At that time he thought if anybody went into politics, it would be his older brother Joe. And that was it.

Only to Inga Arvad and a handful of friends had Jack ever vouchsafed his growing ambition, which he kept largely to himself in the company of his comrades. Yet, as Fay remarked in retrospect, the talk at Tulagi was dominated by politics—and women. "We would argue about politics all the time," Cluster also recalled. "There wasn't a lot to talk about there except girls and politics. And JFK was as normal in talking about girls [as others], and the only time he really talked about them was at night when you couldn't do anything else."

All were aware after talking to Jack that his father was a major influence on his life. "Most of the talk about his family was about his father," Reed remembered. "Jack was very embarrassed by the fact that his father had not served in World War I; the things Mr. Kennedy had said when he was ambassador must also have spurred Jack on to a lot of things. He always had that sense of leadership: quietly assertive. Not at all flamboyant. And that magical quality that everybody liked him."

With Reed, Jack could talk about books; with Fay he could exchange lighthearted banter; with Johnny Iles he could confide his thoughts about religion; with Joe Atkinson, Al Webb, Ed McLaughlin, John Meade, and others he could discuss a range of topics from Broadway to boating. "He was interested, vitally concerned, with problems of all kinds," Reed recalled, "and he brought to it not only a great deal of knowledge but a great aura of humility about him. He always made the listener feel that he, the listener, knew a great deal more about the subject than he really did. He brought out, he elicited the best from the person with whom he was holding a conversation." Even the PT-boat medical officer, Dr. Wharton, was impressed by Jack. "I talked to him every day. Jack initiated the conversation; he had such vast knowledge. It was fascinating."

Since his arrival in the Solomons in April 1943, Jack had certainly learned a great deal about war—about fear, courage, camaraderie, and the futility that characterized so much of human conflict. "Most of the PT boys were a wonderful group of guys. My best friends today are still from that group. But I don't think we made a hell of a contribution to the war," Reed confided. "The PTs really didn't do a hell of a lot, to be honest. Maybe in rather confined waters they could play a role, but in the broader ocean they couldn't do a hell of a lot. We used to blow up—some of the boats blew up some barges, but that's about all."

Nevertheless Jack had done his best. It was time to go home, once he could get medical authority to do so. "Am told it's a bit of a job," Torby Macdonald acknowledged in his letter, though he still offered "a couple of more addresses for you if you want them, one very tasty indeed: an airline hostess in N.Y.C."

Dr. Wharton, having ordered new X rays of Jack's back, now added "chronic disc disease of the lower back" to Jack's sorry litany of medical ailments. In retrospect it seems a miracle that Jack had managed to survive the rigors of PT-boat action—let alone the sinking of *PT 109*—as long as he had, and it was Wharton who finally put in a recommendation that Jack be transferred to the United States. When this recommendation became bogged down in the red tape of the Southwest Pacific Command headquarters, Al Cluster cut the Gordian knot, as he did for so many of his "boys."

> I guess his back was giving him a problem at that time. I'm really a bit hazy about him going back. I think somebody may have gotten ahold of me—I was still up north on the Bougainville situation—and said, the doctor recommends that Kennedy go back. . . .
>
> I was sending guys back to the States with no authority. And I mean that seriously. The PT boats—their role had to all intents and purposes been taken over by surface ships and aircraft and things like that. We would get a dispatch from the States to send say two torpedomen and one pharmacist's mate and one gunner's mate back

to Melville, because they would need them for additional training or maybe the staffing of new squadrons. So I would select somebody with those ratings and send them back. . . .

All of a sudden it became obvious to this yeoman and me that nobody ever checked up on that. In other words, if you got a dispatch, you could send one man back—or twenty. So I made a list of all the enlisted men who had been out of the States as long or longer than I had. And I started going down this list. And I was just gleeful that we were beating the system by getting rid of all these people. . . .

Nobody ever checked. I mean it was a very loose organization. So it may have been during this time of gleeful orders that this yeoman and I were formulating—Jack's back was getting worse and worse—it may have been that we used something like that to send Jack back.

Hobbling around Tulagi with the support of a cane and weighing barely 145 pounds, Jack duly heard the good news on Wednesday, December 15, 1943. "In accordance with a dispatch dated 14 December 1943 from Commander South Pacific, which cannot be quoted herein, you will consider yourself detached from duty in Motor Torpedo Boat Squadron Two. . . . You will proceed via first available air transportation, Priority Four, to the United States," Cluster ordered. After taking thirty days' leave in the United States, Jack was thereafter to report to the commandant at Melville. There was no mention of medical ailment.

"Would we have been in the soup [if anyone had found out]?" Cluster wondered. "The 'Commander South Pacific' thing we used to quote all the time. If you had a merchant ship that was tied up in Tulagi, and a guy came aboard with an order like that, why, you wouldn't pick up a phone and call Halsey and say, is this order valid?"

Jack certainly did not question Cluster's solution. "Am heading back stateside in a week or so—and should get to Cal[ifornia] around the middle of January," he wrote to Billings, who'd announced that after a series of medical rejections he'd finally been accepted in the navy's Service Corps. "Was extremely glad to hear that you had gotten into the S.C.— It's a good organization," Jack commented, "and has some damn good guys in it. You will, in addition, have the opportunity of studying at Harvard—which ought to make a big difference in your life," he pointed out, tongue in cheek. He was going to contact Billings from California on his arrival. "I hope you are free—and that you can head to Palm Beach for a short term of indoctrination. I should be able to put you well ahead of the other ensigns when you all start in school together."

Palm Beach was Jack's immediate objective, though there was some unfinished business he wished to attend to first in L.A. On December 21 his orders were officially drawn up and signed by the base officer, D. Agnew, on behalf of Lieutenant Commander Cluster, and Jack set off for Espíritu Santo, where he was told to board a fast escort carrier, the U.S.S. *Breton,* for the passage home. Fortunately, he found the vessel still moored in the Segond Channel on the morning of December 23, having delayed its departure. Later that afternoon the carrier set sail for Tutuila Island, Samoa, to pick up another forty-nine planes and more personnel for the journey back to San Francisco. On Christmas Day, 1943, they passed Good Hope Island, and on December 26 they docked briefly in the Pago Pago harbor. By evening they were once again at sea, and twelve days later they made out the unmistakable outline of the Golden Gate Bridge on the horizon.

Shortly after midday, on January 7, 1944, the U.S.S. *Breton* arrived at South Pier, Naval Air Station Alameda, in San Francisco Bay, and Jack was free to disembark.

He had done extraordinarily well. To his father he had promised that "after this present fighting is over will be glad to get home. When I do get out of here you'll find that you have a new permanent fixture around that Florida pool. I'll just move from it to get into my sack."

But the first sack he intended to get into was Inga's.

PART

·14·

THE HOME
FRONT

Home from war, Jack Kennedy relaxes with PT buddies Red Fay and Lennie Thom at the Kennedy house in Hyannis Port, fall of 1944. Teddy Kennedy is kneeling in front. (John F. Kennedy Library)

None of That Hero Stuff

Once back on American soil, Jack wasted no time. "I regret that I did not get a chance to look over the establishment of the Fay Construction Company," Jack apologized later to Red Fay, "but due to what is known in train circles as an 'extremely close connection,' I had time for only a short pilgrimage up Nob Hill on my knees to light a candle—and then I executed Tare 90° + headed Southward where I spent my next days in a Mexican Bordello in Lower California."

Clearly Jack's wit was still fit for action. However, his southerly destination was not a Mexican bordello, but Inga's house in Beverly Hills, where she had settled while writing what had been Sheilah Graham's column. She'd left Nils Blok for good (she had never in fact married him) and was now a journalist of some eminence, as well as a spectacular beauty.

It was a moment Jack had looked forward to with lonely longing, yet it was not the great love reunion Jack had fantasized. "Jack just looked like hell," Inga told her son years later. "He was so thin. He came to Hollywood and stayed several days. . . . He was just drawn and out of it." About the *PT 109* incident, in private, he was self-disparaging. "He said it was a question of whether they were going to give him a medal or throw him out. . . . The romance was over. He'd been out there in the war and she'd been back here doing her thing. There just wasn't a hell of a lot to talk about. . . . Her life was fine, she was having a good time. She could see that Jack was in no condition to make decisions about anything. He was just worn out."

In Inga's own words, nearer the time, Jack arrived with his "health wrecked," and deeply "embittered." As Jack's angel of maternal mercy, Inga tended to blame this on the series of misfortunes that had befallen them in Washington at the hands of J. Edgar Hoover, Joseph P. Kennedy, and her jealous husband.: "The boy was sent overseas, which probably never would have happened otherwise. He became a big hero, and saved several lives at the expense of his own health which will never be regained."

Jack was certainly bitter—but it was not Hoover he blamed so much as the bitter reality of war, and the loss of many illusions. Paramount among the latter was the illusion of Inga, whose once-maternal hold no longer held. "I wonder sometimes," mused Kathleen's friend, Betty Coxe, years later; "men have to get rid of their mothers somehow, grow past them. . . . There are so many cases of men who have these sort of liaisons at a certain point in their life before they marry, with these women who are kind of maternal, and they go through it—they work out their mother business with these women, or a particular woman. That seems to me in many ways what Inga was for Jack."

Certainly the old magic was gone. Not only was Jack worn out and jaded by combat, but Inga too had grown older. Besides, she had another iron in the fire, a brilliant young Jewish naval doctor, William Cahan, who was currently working on the film *Winged Victory* in Hollywood. Previously, Inga had kept her two competing lovers, Nils and Jack, well apart. Now, however, she decided to introduce Jack and Cahan to each other. "Inga arranged for us to meet at her apartment," Cahan later recounted. "He and I talked Harvard, football, show business, etc. After a while, however, it became clear that one or the other would have to leave. To my great relief, he did."

Jack was in no condition to fight for Inga. Nevertheless, put out or played out, the change in Jack's character was not lost on Inga the journalist. As a young desk ensign in Washington he had first intrigued her by his precocious judgment on international relations, his dreams of one day getting to the White House, his "animal magnetism," and his self-deprecating sense of humor. These qualities were unchanged, but onto his boyish, reckless, genial personality had been seared a firsthand experience of war that would probably never be erased, and which Inga was too good an observer to miss.

On January 11, 1943, Jack's picture appeared on *The Boston Globe*'s front page, larger even than Churchill's and Eisenhower's; beneath it was an exclusive interview by Inga Arvad, headlined TELLS STORY OF PT EPIC: KENNEDY LAUDS MEN, DISDAINS HERO STUFF. Describing the *PT 109* incident, Inga wrote, " 'How it felt?' Lt. Kennedy looked up as he said, 'I can best compare it to the onrushing trains in the old-time movies. They seemed to come right over you. Well, the feeling was the same, only the destroyer didn't come over us, it went right through us.' "

True to his promise to his men, Jack had telephoned their families. The wife of Pappy McMahon, the burned *PT 109* engineer, lived in the Los Angeles area and had insisted on meeting Jack. She had come over to Inga's apartment, and Inga, moved by what the woman said, described her in her interview. She wrote of how she'd "talked to Mrs. McMahon this afternoon, and with tears in her eyes and a shaky voice she said, 'When my husband wrote home, he told me that Lt. Kennedy was wonderful, that he saved the lives of all the men and everybody at the base admired him greatly."

This, Inga felt, was an eloquent testimonial to Jack's qualities as a leader of men, though Jack rejected the epithet of hero. "None of that hero stuff about me," he told Inga. "The real heroes are not the men who return, but those who stay out there, like plenty of them do—two of my men included."

"Please, please send me the article you did on Jack," Kathleen would write to Inga a few weeks later. "I was so pleased by your letter as it was the first one I had had with a report on Jack's arrival home. Goodness I wish I had been there. I hope he doesn't go back for a very long time."

Jack, however, had no intention of *ever* going back.

Grand Illusions

Meanwhile, in a small item of news from Los Angeles, *The Boston Globe* on January 11 recorded Jack's departure "by plane here last night for Palm Beach, Fla., to spend two weeks of his 30-day leave with his parents at their winter home."

In fact Jack flew from Los Angeles to the Mayo Clinic in Minnesota. On the plane he penned a quick letter of condolence to Clare Boothe Luce, whose daughter, he'd just heard, had been killed in an auto accident at Stanford. "I can't tell you how shocked I was to hear about Ann," he scribbled. "I thought that I had become hardened to losing people I like, but when I heard the news today, I couldn't have been sadder. She was a wonderful girl—so completely unspoiled, and thoughtful—and so very fond of you—I can't believe it."

Ann's death was to be a portent. In Rochester, meanwhile, Jack was met by his father, and together they discussed Jack's health with the doctors. The ex-ambassador then flew on to Boston to visit "three of his children who are attending schools in this area," *The Globe* reported on January 14. "The former diplomat told newsmen that his son John, a naval lieutenant, whose heroic action in the South Pacific when his PT boat was cut in two was carried in dispatches last August, is now on his way to visit his mother at the Kennedy winter home at Palm Beach, Florida. He said that the youthful naval officer was quite thin, having lost weight as the result of his service in that theater of action. John is expected to visit Boston within the next week or 10 days."

In Palm Beach Jack's mother did not even go to greet him at the airport, but asked Jack's friend Chuck Spalding if he would do so. Spalding was in the final stages of naval air training, having published one of the most successful books of 1943, *Love at First Flight*—in part, he later avowed, inspired by Jack's success three years before with *Why England Slept*. Jack "looked very thin," he recalled, noting the effect of front-line combat on his friend. "There was this place in Palm Beach where everybody went, a supper club and night club. It was right opposite the Paramount Theater. It had a roof that pulled back, it was great. Immediately after he got off the plane, that's where he wanted to go.

"It was a great shock, having got back from this thing he'd been through, and going to this place where he used to dance all the time, and seeing everybody and trying to fit in. The difference between the tensions of being at war and the pleasures of Palm Beach. It was kind of a tough night, even for him—and he could usually make those kinds of transfers easily."

Young, charming, eligible, and talented, Jack had been an integral part of the Palm Beach scene. "He could make my mother smile, in spite of herself, in a way no one else ever could," Spalding later remembered wistfully. " 'Would you believe it, Mrs. Spalding, I couldn't make it with the hatcheck girl!' he would sigh, shaking his head. How my mother, who despised the Kennedys, laughed at that!"

Palm Beach was still the same, but was Jack Kennedy? "I'll never forget Jack," Spalding recalled, "sitting at our table, watching the 'home front.' All he felt was cynicism—everybody dancing, the lights, the women. . . . It was the only time I ever saw him reacting like a real soldier. It was the rapidity of his move from the Pacific to Palm Beach, the juxtaposition."

But it was more than that. Jack's homecoming marked the end of his grand illusions. His romance with Inga was finally over, and so, for him, was the war.

Like Lazarus from the Dead

Jack had sworn he would not leave the poolside once he was home, but in truth he'd had enough swimming to last a lifetime. In Miami, where he sought solace at a variety of nightclubs, he watched new PT boats "piling up. . . . They are turning them out faster than they can get them out there," Jack wrote to Red Fay, still in the Pacific. "I was extremely glad to hear that the relief situation was finally getting worked out + that you + Ted [Berlin] had good prospects for getting out this spring." He worried, too, about his brother Joe, who'd been posted to England as an antisubmarine-patrol pilot.

Jack's father, meanwhile, worried about Jack. "We found him in reasonable good shape when he returned, but the doctors at Mayo's don't entirely agree with me on this diagnosis," the ex-ambassador wrote to Al

Cluster. "Jack is insistent that he wants to get going again, so he left here Saturday to go and see his brothers and sisters and then report for duty."

Jack, however, had no desire to report for duty or to go near his brothers and sisters. Instead he flew on February 5 from Palm Beach to New York, where he made a new conquest, a pretty, ex-Powers model, Flo Pritchett, who was fashion editor of the New York *Journal-American* and had recently divorced her rich, Catholic husband. Together with John Hersey and his wife, Frances Ann Cannon, they went to the theater *à quatre,* and over drinks afterward in the Stork Club Jack talked a little of his escapade on the desert island.

Hersey, as a writer and war correspondent, was immediately interested.

"Yes, he told me about it, enough to cause me to ask him right away whether I could write about it," Hersey later recalled. "What appealed to me about the Kennedy story was the night in the water, his account of floating in the current, being brought back to the same point from which he'd drifted off. It was the same kind of theme that has fascinated me always about human survival. . . . It was really that aspect of it that interested me, rather than his heroics. The aspect of fate that threw him into a current and brought him back again. And that sort of dreamlike quality. His account of it is very strange. A nightmarish thing altogether."

Jack said he'd think about the idea. The next day he called his father, who was delighted, having tried in vain to interest *Reader's Digest* in an article on Jack the previous August, as soon as the AP and UP dispatches from the Solomons were published.

An article in *Life* magazine, with its millions of readers, would be a coup indeed. Jack thus agreed to it, insisting, however, that Hersey speak first to those of the crew who were now back in the States at the Melville PT-boat base, to get their version of the story. He himself, he explained, would be unable to speak to Hersey for a week or so, since he'd promised to attend his grandfather's eighty-first birthday celebration.

John F. Fitzgerald had lost none of his vigor, or his belief in Boston. Before his birthday luncheon at the Parker House Hotel on February 11 he spoke with reporters about his concerns, excoriating the failure of Bostonians to put "ventured capital in new enterprises."

"Look," Fitzgerald said. "When I went in as mayor, they were just shifting from the horse and carriage to the automobile. I went to the town of Merrimac, where they made carriages, and talked about building automobile bodies there. What happened? The industry went to Detroit. And who led the industry? The Fisher Brothers. And where did the Fisher Brothers learn their trade? Right at the foot of Beacon Hill. Why did they have to go west? Because there was no ventured capital in Boston."

Pointing to a *Herald* editorial, Honey Fitz pounded home his point:

It says here that 90 percent of all the airplane engines made in New England last year were made in Connecticut. Why? Because here in Massachusetts we haven't trained help. Sure, we have the brains, because the men who supervised all that work in Connecticut were graduates of Massachusetts Institute of Technology. . . . Why am I forever talking about what's wrong with Boston? Simply because no one else will talk about it. No one seems concerned about our declining valuations. We don't own a single shipping line and we don't own a single trunk line railroad, and nobody seems to care. You can't give away a waterfront property, and nobody seems to care. The Boston atmosphere is a white collar atmosphere instead of trade, as it used to be.

As for the Boston Port Authority, of which he was a member, "we have no authority, whenever we propose anything they refer it to some committee to study. . . . You can talk all you want, but this development of brain and brain alone is the curse of the state. See who's at the door someone.' "

At the door was another Boston stalwart, Clem Norton of the Boston Schools Committee, who announced that Jack Kennedy, John Fitzgerald's grandson, his plane delayed by snow, would nevertheless be at the mayor's luncheon. "He's the boy they thought was lost in the South Pacific. He came back, just like Lazarus from the dead. Lazarus is the most dramatic episode in the Bible," Fitzgerald prattled on proudly. And when Jack finally turned up, Fitzgerald was beside himself. "I haven't seen this boy for more than a year, and he's been through hell since that time." Fitzgerald wept, embracing Jack. Beneath a photograph of the ex-mayor and his grandson, *The Boston Globe* caption read: "Lieut. Kennedy was mentioned in dispatches from the South Pacific last summer for heroic action as his PT boat was cut amidship by a Jap destroyer."

Jack Kennedy's attendance at the luncheon, along with three hundred guests, was a preview for an even bigger event the following day, a Lincoln's Birthday War Bond Rally, at which Governor Saltonstall and Mayor Tobin were to preside, and at which Lieutenant John F. Kennedy was to be the main speaker. "Come and buy YOUR bonds," newspaper advertisements ran, "and hear Lieut. John Fitzgerald Kennedy—son of a former Ambassador to Great Britain, grandson of a former Mayor of Boston—of whom James Morgan of The Boston Globe said, 'his resourcefulness after his PT boat was rammed and sunk by a Japanese destroyer is one of the great stories of heroism in this war.' "

Overnight Jack Kennedy had become, in his way, the new John D. Bulkeley. Those expecting a Bulkeley-type speech were disappointed, however. It was the first major public address Jack Kennedy ever gave, delivered before an audience of a thousand. "I've read accounts of action since I came back. And things seem to be going fast. Then I look at a map and think how long it took us to get from Guadalcanal to Bougainville, and I realize it's going to be a long war," *The Boston Globe* quoted him, beneath a huge headline that ran: LONG PACIFIC WAR SEEN BY LT. JOHN F KENNEDY.

This was not quite what the organizers had in mind for their hero, though they could hardly complain when the rally raised a staggering half million dollars in war-bond purchases. Joe Kane, his father's cousin, had been watching the evolving political scene in Massachusetts on the ex-ambassador's behalf for almost a year and was impressed by Jack's performance at the war-bond rally. "There is something original about your young daredevil," Kane wrote in a confidential report on electoral possibilities for both Joe Jr. and Jack. "He spoke with perfect ease and fluency, but quietly, deliberately and with complete self-control, always on the happiest terms with his audience. He was the master, not the servant of his oratorical power. He received an ovation and endeared himself to all by his modesty and gentlemanly manner."

Jack, however, was disappointed by his performance the following day, when he gave another speech. "Spent the week up in Boston where I gave an exhibition of talking where I should have been listening," he berated himself in a letter to Red Fay. "I topped it off by speaking to a group of children who had written essays on religious toleration. The Mayor called for a few words + up I stepped. I told them about the natives saving us being all Christians + in talking about a Jew I told them about [a survivor from the *PT 109* crew] + how he had been killed giving a Jap some water. Well that was O.K., but some bastard got it wrong + had it a Jewish *Rabbi* who was killed. Well, that was big stuff—'New Jap Atrocity' on the front page—the Navy gets pigged and I slink into this hospital—never, I say again, never will I open my mouth."

These were famous last words for the would-be president. Far from reporting fit for duty at Melville, meanwhile, Jack had asked to delay reporting for duty at Melville until March 1—"such delay to count as leave"—in order to undergo further tests and examination at the New England Baptist Hospital. There the Lahey's doctors conferred over X rays of his stomach and his deteriorating spine, and decided the major surgery recommended the previous year while he was stationed in South Carolina would have to be performed if he was ever to walk normally again.

Slow and Deep in the South

"I'm in the hospital for another couple of weeks on my back + then down to report at Melville + then in a month or so later I'm afraid I'm going to have an operation on it," Jack confided to Red Fay on February 21, 1944.

The level of wishful thinking in America, meanwhile, both amused and distressed him. "Everyone very optimistic and it's very true that 'hell hath no fury like a civilian,' and when I read the papers I think the war will be over tomorrow—but I know it won't. You don't have any chance to tell any war stories as everyone is too busy telling you one. . . . The bull some guys are handing out here is unbelievable. The favorite question they ask you is, 'How many destroyers did you get?' If you didn't get at least five, which they think makes you an ace and is par for the course, there is no sense coming home."

The more bull he heard, the more Jack warmed to Hersey's interest in a story not of killing, but of human survival. Hersey had visited Jack in the hospital. "I don't remember how long I was with him," Hersey recalled, "but it was certainly a long time for him at that point. I would think all afternoon and part of the evening too. . . . He drew me a map of the area particularly to illustrate the night he got off the reef and was in the water all night long and was carried out by the current. And also to illustrate the actual collision that took place. . . . I was then interested in using novelistic techniques in journalism. I went back to New York and wrote the piece fairly soon after that."

By the first week of March 1944 Hersey had completed and submitted the story to *Life*. Jack's orders, in the meantime, were again altered. Pending the proposed operation on his back, he was directed on March 8 to report to the Submarine Chaser Training Center in Miami, where the winter climate was less formidable.

It was there that Jack read the first draft of Hersey's survival story. "Needless to say you did a great job with the story—even I was left wondering how it all would end," Jack congratulated him. But he was not entirely happy with Hersey's account. "As you say, everyone sees the same thing differently but I have listed below a few points that I believe might be changed."

Among them was Hersey's failure to do proper justice to the executive officer on *PT 109*, Lennie Thom: "I understand, of course, that in an article of this length—in order to keep the story's continuity and to prevent over-flow with detail—you have to limit the story to a few central themes. But Thom did a splendid job—did so much to hold the group in a disciplined body that I think you might credit him more." It was, Jack pointed out, Thom who'd "pulled Johnston in" after the ramming and Thom who'd "organized and directed that group's swimming—a difficult job with burned and exhausted men." On the island, "again it was Lenny Thom who saw the group of nine through." Moreover it was also Thom who had first tried to get help himself; "natives paddled away with Thom to go to Rendova for aid. Rough water forced them back."

On the matter of naval security Jack felt Hersey had "handled the coast-watcher extremely neatly but I imagine that you will have to have it cleared by the Navy—as they are so rabid on this subject." He also felt Barney Ross should be given credit for having "towed in another burned crewman—Zinser—engineer."

Jack's chief criticism, however, concerned one of the crew, subsequently killed, who'd lost his nerve during the long ordeal:

> I realize, of course, that his fate is ironic and dramatic and that his lack of guts is an integral part of war—and one that probably is not mentioned enough. I feel, however, that our group was too small, that his fate is so well-known both to the men in the boats and to his family and friends that the finger would be put too definitely on his memory—and after all he *was* in my crew. To see whether or not I was being oversensitive on this I asked two officers to read the story—and they both, independently of me, brought up the matter.... If you feel that you would like to discuss this thing with me, just send me a wire where I can reach you and I will call you. I believe however you will agree with me on this—that it should be omitted.

Hersey did omit the mention. Meanwhile, as to "conditions here, may I say that I am playing it slow and deep—with no strain or pain. Once you get your feet upon the desk in the morning the heavy work of the day is done. Miami has really girded up its loins for war—no mean feat considering the general state of loins in this particular part of the sunny South." As the Allies prepared the greatest amphibious assault of the war in Europe, the people of Florida "all wait anxiously for D-day, and you can find the beaches crowded every day with people—all looking seaward and towards the invasion coast," he mocked.

Jack himself did little work at the PT base, being seen more often chasing models than enemy submarines. "Girls were almost an obsession with him," one of his fellow officers recalled. "We liked them too, but we didn't make a career of it the way he did!" "There is no sense handing out any bull-shit — though it's *nice* to be home," he wrote to Red Fay, "and

I surely hope to see you boys soon back here, or back here soon, (which is better English? Ever since I went to Stanford I've had trouble with my English.)"

Lem Billings, meanwhile, had graduated from his course at Babson College and wanted naval combat duty before the war ended. Jack, however, was thoroughly disenchanted with heroics, and though he gave the name of a friend in the Bureau of Naval Personnel—his old Harvard roommate Charlie Houghton—who could help Billings, his own efforts mostly focused on getting the last of his erstwhile crew back from the Solomons. Commenting to Billings on some bad photographs Eunice had taken—"you and Teddy mugging furiously and me—though looking well—covered by a dull blur"—he remarked that "everything Eunice touches seems to turn into sugar hyporitentare—shit to you, you red-assed Ensign. Excuse me a minute, the Baron is telling a good one. (25 min. later). (Boy, that sure was a good one). Understand that you have been consorting with enlisted personnel + have been going to the Cape with Bobby," he ribbed, though he affected indifference whether it was Lem Billings or his younger brother Bobby who borrowed his car. "While I'm sure that I will be shafted one way or another, it's O.K. because that just happens to be the kind of guy I am."

In truth the news from England continued to worry him, especially the mounting numbers of aircraft in Joe Jr.'s unit shot down or involved in flying accidents. "Heard from Joe a while back—they have had heavy casualties in his squadron—I hope to hell he gets through O.K." He even asked Billings to help dissuade Bobby from following in Joe Jr.'s footsteps. "I really think that Bobby shouldn't go into aviation," he wrote. "I don't see where it is any more fun than P.T.s or D.D's [destroyers] or any other small ship—particularly as Bobby has spent so much of his life on small boats. I'm going to write him to that effect + I wish you would advise the same thing. It would be just his luck to get hit when old worn out bastards like you + me get through with nothing more than a completely shattered constitution."

Despite this shattered constitution, however, "things have been active in P.B.," he reported, "with my life getting more and more complicated." Eunice had finished her studies at Stanford; now, "completely equipped with a brand new set of gay deceivers (extra large)," she was "having quite a whirl and can usually be counted on to bring around some male monstrosity." He also described the latest antics of his father's crony from Boston, Joseph Timilty. The ex-Boston police commissioner had been staying in Palm Beach "as a guest of the Kennedy family," Timilty himself recalled, since November 1943. "I was Joseph Kennedy's closest friend," Timilty boasted. "I traveled everywhere with him. My room was next to Jack's in Palm Beach and I'd go in and sit with him. He used to read a lot in the tub. He was a great reader."

The great reader, however, was not overly impressed by Timilty. "Timilty left when the rest of the family did," Jack reported to Billings on May 3. "Pappy was in a rather grim humor the last few days so consequently Timilty spent the greater portion of his time cowering in his room to emerge only for meals + once to drop and break Dad's glasses— the sound of tinkling glass causing him to shriek and run giggling to his room."

For Jack, the sight of the ex-police commissioner quaking before his tyrant father was one of almost surreal amusement, as were some of the other Ocean Boulevard vignettes. "Bertram the Butler also wended his merry way after stealing several of Dad's shirts or so the fine finger of suspicion points," he wrote to Billings. "He walked out with great dignity and many spots on his coat and around his fly and with his dentures snapping and crackling while Timid Denise padded after him, carrying 14 bags—believed to contain 8 bottles of Kinglederan + Haig + Haig and most of my 15 best shirts in her hot little hands."

For all his amused observations, however, there was the more serious matter of Jack's health, which was becoming increasingly frail. He'd never once suffered from malaria in the Solomons yet was still prone to the same bouts of fever—when his skin would turn a yellowy brown— such as he had suffered since his schooldays. Timilty recalled vividly going "to the hospital with him on three different occasions when you wouldn't give 2¢ for him. . . . These were days in Palm Beach when we'd go to St. Mary's Hospital . . . after he came back from the Solomons. He'd go into a fever and he'd be shaking with cold and his face would be yellow. We all thought he might die. We'd call the ambulance and I'd go with him. They'd all be in the living room when we went out to the ambulance. But in three or four days he'd snap out of it."

No diagnosis could be offered. For the moment Jack simply awaited his medical recall to Boston, and it was while on "limited duty" in Miami that he heard, first, that Hersey's article had been rejected by *Life* magazine, then, that his sister Kathleen was going to get married—to a Protestant.

Kathleen's Marriage

The problem had been debated over many months. Kathleen wrote, for instance, on February 6, 1944, to tell Inga that she'd decided to "marry an Englishman and if it wasn't for this religious difficulty I'd be married to him now. Yes, it's the same one as before. He's standing for Parliament at the moment so there's lots of excitement about whether he'll get in."

In the event, Billy Cavendish, the Lord Hartington and heir to the duke of Devonshire, had been trounced in the by-election and had returned to his battalion of the Coldstream Guards to prepare for the D-day landings in Normandy. Casualties were expected to be heavy. Though Kathleen was not deeply in love with Billy, she was fond of him, and was touched by how deeply enamored of her he was. It seemed to her a cruelty to deprive him of the happiness marriage promised when in a matter of weeks he might be dead. Denied the right to be married in church, since neither wished to surrender the faith into which each had been born, they had thus made arrangements for the wedding to be conducted at the Chelsea Registry Office on May 6.

For Jack the news of his sister's impending marriage was a blessed relief after the months of rumor and counterrumor. But to Rose Kennedy the decision to go ahead with the marriage was the greatest tragedy in the family since Rosemary's lobotomy.

At the nadir of her own marriage in 1920, Rose had consented to return to her husband only out of duty, sent back by the same brilliant but old-fashioned Catholic father who'd forbidden her to attend college or even date Joseph Kennedy in the first place. Unable to discipline or deny her spouse, having to bear him a further six children as well as endure the shame of his openly flaunted mistresses, Rose had paid a heavy price for her dutifulness. She was determined her children should bear their share, too; the domestic rules and trivial regulations she'd subsequently imposed on them being an exquisite and protracted form of revenge.

For Rose the "defection" of her daughter threatened to puncture this carefully contrived public façade of the Kennedy family. As she later explained, she was "horrified" by Kathleen's plan because "I thought it would have such mighty repercussions in that every little young girl would say if Kathleen Kennedy can, why can't I? . . . . Everyone pointed to our family with pride as well-behaved, level-headed and deeply religious." Then she added: "What a blow to the family prestige."

On the surface Rose opposed Kathleen's engagement solely on religious grounds, since marriage between a Catholic and a Protestant was not permitted by her faith unless by special Vatican dispensation. To those around Rose, however, it was clear that her religious scruples masked deeper, less benign motives. "All the Kennedys were blocked, totally blocked emotionally," remarked Kathleen's friend Betty Coxe. "Knowing the old man and Mrs. Kennedy, spending so much time in the house, I can readily see the limitations. Mrs. Kennedy, for all her kids, was not a mother. . . . And the old man—having his mistresses at the house for lunch and supper! I couldn't understand it! It was unheard of!"

Nevertheless Rose Kennedy had by now become, in Betty Coxe's view, a "driving, dominating force" in her neurotic determination to make the Kennedy family stick at least publicly to the tenets of their Catholic faith, despite the seamy reality. Having learned to paper over the gaping fissures in her marriage and present to the world a phony semblance of good Catholicism, she simply could see no reason why her daughters, if not her sons, should not also do so. "Heartbroken. Feel you have been wrongly influenced—sending Arch[bishop] Spellman's friend to talk to you. Anything done for Our Lord will be rewarded hundred fold," she cabled Kathleen.

Kathleen, however, was determined to have her way, with or without her mother's blessing. She was twenty-four. Choosing a Catholic husband had not brought her mother happiness, though unhappiness, she accepted, could certainly be seen as part of God's great design. Having weighed the alternatives and having consulted her chaplain, she nevertheless decided to go ahead.

News of Kathleen's engagement finally hit the Boston papers on Thursday, May 4, together with a report that the wedding would take place two days later in London. Rose, playing for time, simply denied the announcement. "Members of the Kennedy family here," the *Boston Herald* reported "said last night that although Miss Kennedy and Lord Hartington have had a 'very fine friendship' dating back to when her father was ambassador to Great Britain, they did not know of plans for a marriage."

Honey Fitz, however, felt it better to roll with the punch. "I was afraid I would be accused of boasting about getting royalty into the family," he jokingly explained his reluctance to discuss details of the marriage, but he admitted "this thing has been in the works for some time. The former mayor did not know whether the British nobleman, a member of one of the leading Protestant families of history, would embrace the Catholic faith. He intimated that the ceremony would be a Catholic one, saying that even apart from her family training in that faith his granddaughter was by choice a staunch Catholic. 'When non-Catholic young people were week-end guests at the Kennedy home,' he said, 'Kathleen would take them all to mass every Sunday morning. The proud grandfather added: 'She's all quality, and that boy must have quality to have won her.' "

No such loving words came from Kathleen's mother, however. Instead, at the suggestion of Joseph Kennedy's fellow isolationist, Joseph Patterson, owner of the New York *Daily News,* Rose entered the New England Baptist Hospital for a phony "check-up" by the Lahey's Sara Jordan. In this way Rose would be spared the agony of being interviewed by the press. As *The Boston Globe* reported the next day, Rose Kennedy was "under medical care at the New England Baptist Hospital—condition good."

The Depths of Righteous Catholic Wrath

On the day of the nuptials, Rose left the hospital. "Appearing wan from two weeks hospitalization," *The Globe* reported (in fact Rose had been in the hospital for three days), "Mrs. Joseph P. Kennedy, wife of the former Ambassador to the Court of St. James's and mother of Kathleen Kennedy, who wed a British nobleman today, left Boston by air today to join her husband in New York." The bride's mother was accompanied, the report stated, by ex-police commissioner Joseph Timilty, the "beard" used by Mr. Kennedy to mask his public trysts with starlets and harlots. "I'm sorry, but I don't feel physically well enough to grant an interview now," Mrs. Kennedy told news reporters at the airport. 'I'm sorry it has to be this way,' " she apologized as Timilty shooed away the reporters. Hospitalization had not, however, stopped Rose from indulging her by-now obsessive concern with clothes. Indeed she was better dressed (though wearing black, as if in mourning) for her flight from Boston to New York than Kathleen was for her wedding in wartime London. "The former Rose Fitzgerald was clad in a black wool dressmaker's suit, a tricorn beret with black nose veil, black strap pumps and black gloves," *The Globe* described. "She wore a jeweled gold lapel pin with earrings to match and carried a silver fox stole on her arm."

Poor Kathleen was not even informed of her mother's hospitalization, and assumed innocently, when she eventually heard of it on her brief honeymoon, that she herself was the cause. She wrote to say how "very worried" she was "about a newspaper report here that you were very ill. They made out that it was because of my marriage." Without direct word from her mother, Kathleen had no way of knowing if this was so, and could "only hope and pray that things will not be too difficult for you and the rest of the family with the McDonnells etc."

That Kathleen should have had to worry about a nonexistent medical complaint and Rose's standing in New York Catholic circles spoke volumes. Meanwhile "the marriage of the Boston girl and British nobleman," *The Boston Globe*'s reporter wired from London, "is now providing a choice morsel of gossip for the dowagers, matrons and debutantes of Mayfair, as well as the crusty and tweedy set of the British squierarchy." Prime among these was, shamefully, Evelyn Waugh, England's greatest living comic novelist, who'd been virtually cashiered by the Royal Marines for rank snobbery. After his first wife cuckolded him, Waugh had converted to Catholicism and then managed to get an annulment of his own marriage, after which he'd married again. Oblivious to his own bigotry, the convert now condemned Kathleen's "heathen friends" who were, he considered, responsible for the marriage, adding the bêtise: "It is second front nerves that has driven her to this grave sin and I am sorry for the girl."

Those who themselves reveled in the self-denials of Catholicism felt cheated by Kathleen's refusal to submit to Catholic rules. Jealousy, too, was rife. "Envious must be the concern of match-making mothers of the British aristocracy over the turn of events, for the personable and wealthy Hartington took first rank as a matrimonial prospect," *The Globe*'s reporter in London shrewdly commented. Thus, while Rose Kennedy worried about what the McDonnells would think, the ladies of England writhed in anguish at the prospect of an Irish-American commoner one day becoming the duchess of Devonshire, and by tradition mistress of robes to the queen, an honor that went back to the time of Henry VIII. She would "take first place in the Queen's personal entourage. . . . As the Duchess of Devonshire, the Boston-born girl will also be on the standing list of His Majesty's box party within the royal enclosure at Ascot. Again, she will always be included in the royal party at Cowes when that function is resumed," *The Globe* pointed out with glee. Moreover Kathleen would be, one day, mistress of Chatsworth House and Hardwick Hall in Derbyshire, Bolton Abbey in Yorkshire, Compton Place at Eastbourne, a huge hunting estate in Scotland, the finest stables and kennels in Britain, as well as the fabulous Lismore Castle on the Blackwater River in Ireland.

Jack was impressed neither by his mother's antics nor by the handwringing of certain of his friends. Cant of any sort Jack despised, just as he knew from Kathleen herself that she was not deeply enamored of Lord Hartington. Nevertheless, for a squat, somewhat heavy-legged, far-from-beautiful Boston-Irish granddaughter of a saloonkeeper to have captured the heart of Britain's most eligible heir was, as his grandfather pointed out, a tremendous tribute to Kathleen's gifts and personality. As the only Kennedy ever to have won admission to a Harvard final club, Jack now doffed his cap to a sister who had gone one better, gaining entry into the

most exclusive club in Europe: the English aristocracy. To Lem Billings
he wrote a tart note on May 19, 1944: "Your plaintive howl in not being
let in on Kathleen's nuptials reached me this morning. It was certainly
evident that you weren't irked so much by her getting married as by her
failure to inform you. You might as well take it in your stride and as sister
Eunice from the depth of her righteous Catholic wrath so truly said: 'It's
a horrible thing—but it will be nice visiting her after the war, so we might
as well face it.' At family dinners at the Cape, when you don't pass
Hartington the muffins, we'll know how you feel."

A week later, on May 27, 1944, having been told that the doctors were
ready to begin surgery, Jack asked formal permission to proceed from
Miami to the naval hospital in Chelsea, Massachusetts, where "an operation is to be performed." The Chelsea hospital had been selected because,
his application explained, "this officer's family lives in Boston, Massachusetts," and "during the period of recuperation, which will be several
months, he wishes to be near them."

In truth, the Chelsea Naval Hospital had been chosen so that a specialist from the Lahey Clinic—who had misdiagnosed Jack's problem—
could perform the surgery. Captain Harrison, Jack's commanding officer
at the shakedown unit, approved, and generously marked Jack with a 3.5
out of 4.0 as an instructor and stores officer on his fitness report. "Lt.
Kennedy is a pleasant, quiet young officer," he entered under "Remarks." "He is very intelligent and has cooperated well. He has performed his duties of instruction in a thorough and conscientious
manner."

As a million Allied troops finally embarked for the long-awaited invasion of Normandy, Jack Kennedy made his way to New England for the
next great trial in his own life—this time upon the operating table.

A Classic Story

Once again Jack's journey to Boston took him first to New York. There,
yet again in a nightclub, he met John Hersey ("Those were the times!"
Hersey chuckled at the memory). Hersey had news for Jack. Though *Life*
magazine had rejected his *PT 109* story, he had succeeded in selling it to
The New Yorker.

Jack was "slightly disappointed," as Hersey recalled. Jack's father,
however, was "dismayed." *The New Yorker* had only a "limited highbrow
audience." Having failed to interest *Reader's Digest* in the story the year

before, Joseph Kennedy now "proposed to the *Reader's Digest* that they publish a condensation of the piece," Hersey recalled.

In retrospect Hersey could only marvel at Joseph Kennedy's gall—and admire his bulldozing determination. The publisher of *The New Yorker*, Harold Ross, refused at first to countenance the idea, Hersey related, since the *Reader's Digest*, when it bought a book or story for condensation, usually reserved the right to reprint it in perpetuity. Early in June Joseph Kennedy, however, managed to persuade Paul Palmer, the publisher of *Reader's Digest*, to drop this stipulation and purchase a single, one-time condensation right. Hersey himself even consented to give his author's fee for the *Reader's Digest* condensation to the widow of one of the two men drowned in the *PT 109* disaster, Mrs. Andrew Kirksey. In this way, both literature and charity would be served—alongside Joseph Kennedy's almost manic determination to exploit his son's heroism.

This latter imperative was perhaps the more odious aspect of the ex-ambassador's driving paternalism. Hersey's story had been written not to extol heroism, but to explore the nature of human endurance in adversity. *The New Yorker* entitled Hersey's story "Survival." Of Jack's ordeal in Ferguson Passage Hersey had written:

> He stopped trying to swim. He seemed to stop caring. His body drifted through the wet hours, and he was very cold. His mind was a jumble. A few hours before he had wanted desperately to get to the base at Rendova. Now he only wanted to get back to the little island he had left that night, but he didn't try to get there; he just wanted to. His mind seemed to float away from his body. Darkness and time took place of a mind in his skull. For a long time he slept, or was crazy, or floated in a chill trance.

This was writing of a very high order, but it was not what Joseph Kennedy was primarily interested in. When Jack entered the Chelsea Naval Hospital on June 11, five days after the Allied invasion of France, there was a battery of photographers on hand to record the award of the Navy and Marine Corps Medal—which the ex-ambassador had harried Forrestal to announce, and which had been sent to Miami too late to be awarded in Florida—to Lieutenant John F. Kennedy. As time went by, the caption on the picture would change. Instead of a chief doctor awarding the medal in Boston, the name would be changed to Admiral Nimitz, and place of the award to the South Pacific. Moreover, the ex-ambassador would ignore the contract between *The New Yorker* and *Reader's Digest* and again and again reprint the condensation, without permission or even further monies to Mrs. Kirksey—for in his grotesque but brilliant way, in the midst of total war he had understood what others hadn't: namely, the crucial importance of such an article in reversing his own reputation for cowardice, as well as the incalculable advantage that the timely advertising of his son's performance might bring to his career. Even Jack's widow was later sucked into and overwhelmed by such "marketing," telling Hersey in a moment of high emotion "what your story of *Survival* meant to President Kennedy. It shaped what people thought about him—Now I read it to John. . . . He is so little—where do I start—I am so glad to have that to start with—It teaches him things that he can understand—Thank you."

But if it was John Hersey who'd shaped what people thought about Jack Kennedy, it was Joseph P. Kennedy who, single-handedly, had ensured that millions, not a mere handful, got their thoughts shaped.

A Grim Time

Jack, meanwhile, braced himself for surgery on his spine. To Hersey he penned a quick letter of thanks for the way he'd agreed to donate his *Reader's Digest* royalties to Mrs. Kirksey: "As I have said before, I think it's really good of you to turn this over—and all of the crew are tremendously pleased. I resume the Battle of the Baptist sometime tomorrow—but it was nice being away for awhile. Enjoyed our night in New York—no need to tell you that I missed my train also." The next day, June 22, 1944, after a series of preoperative biopsies and X rays, he reentered the New England Baptist Hospital, by special arrangement with the Chelsea Naval Hospital.

The Lahey Clinic's Dr. James L. Poppen performed the operation. As Poppen afterward wrote to Captain Conklin at the Chelsea Hospital after the complete failure of his surgery:

> On June twenty-third I did a unilateral exploration of the fourth and fifth lumbar spaces. The fourth space was completely normal. However, the nerve in the fifth interspace was reddened and underlying this the disk interspace material was abnormally soft and the posterior longitudinal ligament was firmly adherent to the nerve root. There, however, was very little protusion of the ruptured cartilage. A thorough removal of the degenerative portion of the cartilage was carried out. The microscopic report showed fibrocartilage with degeneration. . . . The patient did well following the operation for a period of two weeks. Upon having the patient get up and about,

however, severe muscle spasms in the low back took place. These necessitated fairly large doses of narcotics to keep him comfortable.

This was an understatement. When Torbert Macdonald returned from the South Pacific, he found Jack "lying in bed all strapped up as part of the treatment to mend his back. . . . His skin had turned yellow. His weight had dropped from 160 to about 125 pounds. When I came into his room, he raised a bony wrist and gave me a shaky wave. I asked him how he felt. He tried to lift his head. I had to lean over to hear him. 'I feel great,' he said. 'Great?' I echoed. 'Well,' he smiled, 'great considering the shape I'm in.' "

Lennie Thom and his new bride, Kate, also visited him, and were shocked by his appearance. "That was my first meeting with Jack," Kate Thom recalled. "He had private nurses. We didn't realize he was as sick as he was. He was just lying there in bed. He looked awfully frail and sick. He was awfully delighted to see the guys. I do remember that the nurse came in very soon after we went in and said we'd have to leave and he didn't say, oh, no, or anything like that. You could tell he was visibly tired."

From his yellowy brown complexion, Thom's wife surmised, as did Macdonald, that Jack was suffering from malaria as well as the aftereffects of his back operation, and indeed Jack's medical records indicated that "he had an attack of Malaria, Benign, Tertian," during his hospitalization. The slow recovery and increasing stomach pains gave Dr. Sara Jordan, the Lahey's gastroenterology expert, cause for special concern, "As you know, it is now his twentieth post-operative day, following operation for a ruptured intervertebral disc," she wrote to Captain Conklin at the Chelsea Naval Hospital on July 14. "Both before and since operation, he has had exceedingly severe abdominal pain, intermittently at first but now almost constant, and at the present time relieved only by codeine. We carried out an X-ray study before the operation, which again showed extreme spasm and irritability of the duodenum, without a definite ulcer crater, but with a lipping of the base of the cap which was suggestive of a duodenal ulcer scar. There was also again rather marked spasm of the colon, and on Tuesday of this week we again X-rayed the colon with the same visualization of spastic colitis which had been constantly present, but which seemed accentuated at this observation."

By August 1, when he still had not improved, she again wrote Captain Conklin at Chelsea Naval Hospital, that "Lt. Kennedy has continued to have low abdominal distress rather constantly . . . . The pain has been quite severe at times. We have used the antispasmodic medicines such as pavatrine, trasentin, as well as a mixture of belladonna, phenobarbital and elixir of pepsin, and while I think there may be some improvement in his condition, I feel that he is still far from completely relieved of symptoms referable to the spastic colitis. He has had very few symptoms during his stay in the hospital which I think could be attributable to the duodenal ulcer or duodenitis."

Jack was understandably disappointed. "In regard to the fascinating subject of my operation," he wrote to a girlfriend in Miami, "I should naturally like to go on for several pages . . . but will confine myself to saying that I think the doc should have read just one more book before picking up the saw." Meanwhile he sent a note of congratulation to his squadron commander, Al Cluster, on his recent marriage, and gave an update on his own, bachelor condition. "I am putting in my eighth week at the hospital where things are fairly grim," he described. "Have an advanced case of bedsores and a slight touch of scurvy . . . . Should be leaving here in a few days for the Old Sailors Home, where I go before a survey board, probably to be issued a rocking chair + a sunny place on the lawn, with the thanks of a grateful Republic ringing in my ears."

His imminent discharge was not unwelcome. The happy-go-lucky camaraderie of his early PT-boat days was, he recognized, over.

> They say it's murderous down at Melville, with the knives and shivs [utensils] flying. They say that if an officer happens to make a remark like "this place is horse-shit" or "I wouldn't mind getting out of here," that his name rank and serial number with his fleet preference (this so they can send him the other way) are on Walsh's [the Melville commandant] desk in an hour, initialed by every officer who heard him make it. If he was in his rack when he said it, he leaves that afternoon, if not, the next morning. [Bill] Rome [the *PT 174* officer who had been conspicuous by his alacrity in getting home on the night of the *PT 109* sinking] seems to be Gauleiter and Comm[ander] Rons [PT boat squadrons] Gestapo down there.

As he told Cluster, he himself would be "leaving here for the Naval Hosp. and then will probably be sent home to the Cape for awhile," where he hoped Cluster, despite being an arch-Republican, would visit him. "It would be a broadening experience for you to meet some Democrats."

That Jack could still joke said much for his stamina. Dr. Poppen, apologizing to Captain Conklin, recorded that he had operated on "over five hundred ruptured intravertebral discs," and only nine were surgical failures. "They have all subsided in a few days or few weeks. I am indeed sorry that this had to happen with Lieutenant Kennedy. . . . At the present time the neurological examination still shows considerable tenderness. . . . The patient has definite pain in the standing position. . . . It is my impression that, in view of the postoperative course of Lieutenant Kennedy, it will be at least six months before he can return to active duty."

But had neurosurgery been the correct answer to Jack's problem? The naval neurosurgeon, Dr. Heintzelman, was intrigued by the question. "An interesting complication of disc surgery where the surgeon at the Lahey Clinic may well have failed to get to the bottom of the situation," he noted on August 4.

> Only an air spinogram was done (which gave him a very severe headache) and the pathology seen at operation was not evidently a clear cut disc. He also had a normal C.S.F. protein. The post-op. muscle pains which he had were apparently very severe (we have had one such case here—Lt. Taylor, but he has been back on active duty for over a year).
>
> He now (a week out of Baptist hospital) is obviously incapacitated by pain in low back & down L[eft] leg. *Impression:* This is a high strung individual (peptic ulcer) who has been through much combat strain. He may have recurrent disc [pain owing to] an incomplete removal, but better bet is that there is some other cause for his neuritis.

There was. Pain alone had never kept Jack down for long, however, and it did not do so now. Joe Kane, the ex-ambassador's cousin, later related how he and Mr. Kennedy "went to see Jack at the Naval Hospital in Chelsea, and they learned that Joe's car, driven by Jack, had been stolen. The Ambassador was about to turn the state upside down, but Jack persuaded him to let nature take its course. 'Don't worry. When whoever took it learns that it belongs to a Vet, he'll return it.' When the Ambassador was out of the room, Jack admitted what had happened," Kane went on. "Seems he sneaked out of the hospital with the nurse the night before and left the car with the keys in it. When they left their rendezvous, it was gone."

The theft, when reported in *The Boston Globe* ("Lt. Kennedy's Auto Stolen in Back Bay . . . automobile was stolen from in front of 14 Newbury St., while he was at the roof garden of the Ritz-Carlton"), soon had the speaker of the state House of Representatives calling for "combat-leave stickers for servicemen. . . . Lt. Kennedy only typifies hundreds of Massachusetts men who in the next year will be returning for short leaves or furloughs after hard and heroic service in combat. . . . Even an automobile thief, you'd think, would want to give a fighting man on leave a break.' " The interesting question of what a desperately sick lieutenant was doing out of the hospital that night was, fortunately for Jack, completely ignored.

Jack, meanwhile, was no longer a fighting man, and unperturbed by the matter of his father's car. What concerned him much more was the failure of his brother Joe Jr. to return home after completing his latest tour of duty in England.

Noble Frère

Back in May 1944, Joe Jr. had been interviewed for *The Boston Globe* beneath the headline KENNEDY'S SON CHAFES AT HUNTING U-BOATS. *The Globe*'s war correspondent, touring American air bases in England, had been amazed at Joe Jr.'s apparent inability to recognize his own gallantry in going out, day after day, to search for German U-boats in the Bay of Biscay, off the Nazi-occupied French coast. "Really good planes," Joe Jr. had remarked of the navy Liberators, "only I'll still take carrier duty with a fighter. Things happen [there]. You don't fly 1,700 hours and see nothing. You don't make 29 trips, 10 to 12 hours each, and see nothing. Yeah, I've made 29. The next one is my 30th. You know what happens after you've made your 30th? You go out on your 31st."

Joe Jr. was not joking. He turned down his right to the return to the U.S. and persuaded his crew to volunteer with him for a further ten missions. Meanwhile, Jack, cavorting with his nurse in Boston, was also alarmed to hear from ex-police commissioner Timilty the truth about Joe Jr.'s farewell dinner at Hyannis Port the previous September, before he left for England. As it was Joseph Kennedy, Sr.'s birthday also, Judge Jimmy Burns had raised a toast to "Ambassador Joe Kennedy, the father of our hero, our *own* hero." To Joe Jr.'s chagrin, however, the hero toasted was not himself, on the eve of his departure, but "Lieutenant John F. Kennedy of the United States Navy." Later that evening, in the bedroom Timilty shared with Joe Jr., the ex-police commissioner had found Joe Jr. lying on his cot "clenching and unclenching his fists" and, as he sobbed himself to sleep, murmuring, "By God, *I'll* show them!"

Whether or not Timilty was exaggerating Joe Jr.'s response to the toast—indeed whether or not he really understood the psychological drama unfolding within the Kennedy family—Jack certainly had a shrewd idea of the truth. Even Rose later remarked that "in their long brotherly, friendly rivalry, I expect this was the first time Jack had won such an 'advantage' by such a clear margin. And I daresay it cheered Jack and must have rankled Joe Jr." When Jack heard in the hospital toward the end of July that Joe had completed the ten extra missions he'd volunteered to fly but had elected to stay on even longer, he was filled with anxiety. From the Chelsea Naval Hospital he wrote urging his brother to return. To this Joe Jr. replied in his usual crabbed style on August 10:

> Your letters are always a great source of enjoyment to your noble frere, and my tardiness in writing is not attributable in any way to an attempt at discouragement of such a fine pen relationship, but rather to several pressing matters, which at this time have dwindled greatly. For the last ten days I have been stuck out in the country, far beyond striking distance of any town. Every day, I think will be my last one here, and still we go on. I am really fed up, but the work is quite interesting. The nature of it is secret, and you know how secret things are in the Navy.

This was all Joe would say of his impending mission. With regard to Jack, however, he expressed concern over recent reports suggesting Jack had crossed the strict territorial sex-lines which they had long ago agreed to observe. "My informants have disclosed that you have got the better of C——," he wrote. "I understood that we had an unwritten agreement ever sent [since] the affaire Cawley, that we would not meddle. How about it?"

Having issued his warning, Joe Jr. moved on to the recent publication of Hersey's *PT 109* story. "I read the piece in the New Yorker, and thought it was excellent. The whole squadron got to read it, and were much impressed by your intestinal fortitude." But then he added tartly, "What I really want to know, is where the hell were you when the destroyer hove into sight, and exactly what were your moves, and where the hell was your radar? I also think McMahon must be awful sick of talking about you," he wrote, referring to the battery of newspaper cuttings his parents had proudly, but perhaps unwisely, just sent. "Has he been visiting at the Cape?"

On the subject of his own love life, Joe Jr. explained he'd been "having a rather pleasant time over here, until the last ten days. I was all set to go to Virginia Gilliat's (Lady Sykes) for my leave, and had arranged for another beauty to be present, and gave it up for this job. I'm probably a damn fool. I have expected to get up there any day, but at this point, I don't know whether I'll ever make it . . . Tell the family not to get excited about my staying over here. I am not repeat not contemplating marriage nor intending to risk my fine neck (covered in the back with a few fine silky black hairs) in any crazy venture."

But Joe Jr. was deceiving his brother. His venture, code-named *Anvil,* was crazy in every respect. It was canceled the next day, but only because of fog. The following day, August 12, 1944, it was rescheduled, and by six o'clock in the evening boxes containing almost ten tons of high-explosive TNT had been crammed into the fuselage of his converted Liberator, which was to take off into the wind, followed by two Ventura "mother" planes. Using the latest, secret televisual topographical monitors, the Venturas were to begin radio-control guidance of the bomber and, once Joe Jr. and his copilot had bailed out, steer the "flying bomb" through heavy German flak all the way to its target near Calais in France, flanked by two air-force B-17s and protected by a covering flight of sixteen P-51 Mustang fighters.

Twice before takeoff Joe Jr. had been warned that the electronic circuitry was potentially faulty; twice he refused to take any heed of the warnings. He'd been sworn to complete secrecy and had been kept incarcerated at Fersfield Aerodrome from the moment of selection but had managed to make nightly telephone calls to his girlfriend, Pat Wilson, from a phone in the village. On the morning of August 12, aware the mission was now definitely "on," he left a final message at his sister's flat in London, asking her to tell Pat that he'd be a day late in joining her in Yorkshire. "I'm about to go into my act," he explained, adding, "If I don't come back, tell my dad—despite our differences [over Kathleen's wedding]—that I love him very much."

There was no mention of his mother. Joe Jr.'s final message of love to his father was, however, gruesomely revealing: at age twenty-nine he was still struggling to impress and be worthy of the ex-ambassador. According to Angela Laycock, the wife of the commanding officer of Britain's Commandos, Joe Jr. had one evening "confided to her that he was sure it was his brother Jack who would ultimately be President." Mrs. Laycock "had the feeling Joe was in awe of Jack's intelligence and believed that his own was no match for it, particularly since his younger brother's recent triumphs."

Joe Jr.'s last letter to Jack certainly bridled with envy and competitiveness. He complained that Rose's round-robin and "most of the letters from home are filled with bulletins about the progress of your back and stomach." Even the mention of Jack's lifesaving medal irked the Liberator pilot. "To get anything out of the Navy is deserving of a campaign medal in itself," he complained. "It looks like I shall return home with the European campaign medal if I'm lucky."

In fact, Joe Jr. had been assured of the navy's highest honor, the Navy Cross, if the *Anvil* mission succeeded. According to colleagues in his squadron as well as friends of Kathleen, Joe Jr. had begun to gamble wildly on anything that moved. Poor Pat Wilson was convinced he'd volunteered to stay on only to be near her, and she subsequently wrote an anguished letter asking Joe Jr.'s parents to "forgive me, even if you blame me for loving him so much that he wanted to stay here and took this job. He would have taken some job anyhow and the only way I could have made him go back to America would have been to say I didn't love him which he would not have believed."

Joe Jr. had, in reality, already sent the bulk of his kit to Southampton for shipment home. To Jack, moreover, Joe Jr. confided that he had not the slightest intention of remaining in England beyond the summer. "I should be home around the first of Sept and should be good for about a month's leave. Perhaps you too will be available at that time, and will be able to fix your old brother up with something good," he suggested, but with rapidly graying hair, he needed Jack to help him "get something that really wants a tired old aviator."

Joe Jr. embarked on his mission with commendable courage. Shortly before six P.M. he took off from Fersfield Aerodrome. His aircraft had been in the air only twenty minutes and Joe had just switched over to remote radio guidance when there were two mighty explosions. President Roosevelt's son Elliott, flying a special Mosquito photoreconnaissance fighter, was taking pictures of Joe Jr.'s Liberator when suddenly it disintegrated, almost blowing Roosevelt's plane onto its back. Though bits of wreckage were scattered across a mile-wide area of New Delight Woods, near Blythburgh, Suffolk, and some fifty-nine houses were damaged by the blast, no particle of Joe Jr.'s body or that of his loyal copilot was ever found.

A Futile Death

Joe Jr.'s heroic and supreme self-sacrifice later proved to have been totally unnecessary. Allied military intelligence had made a grievous error over the target, Mimoyecques. Blitzed by Allied conventional bombers all spring, work had finally been suspended on the deep bunker being built there to house one of Hitler's latest secret weapons, a projected V-3 battery of high-pressure pump guns. Not only was the site incomplete and already abandoned when Joe Jr. volunteered for his fatal mission, but the V-3 gun itself had proved so defective in trials that there were no such weapons to install, even had the site been completed. The final irony of the mission was that, in the wake of the Allied breakout in Normandy, the empty site at Mimoyecques would be overrun by Canadian troops barely two weeks after Joe Jr.'s tragic midair detonation.

The telegram announcing Joe Jr.'s death was delivered to Hyannis Port on Sunday, August 13, 1944. Joseph Kennedy had retired to his room for an afternoon nap. "There's a big storm coming up . . . my Joe might be flying through that storm. If anything ever happened to one of my boys, I'd die," he'd once said to Clem Norton before the war. The new secretary of the Navy, James Forrestal, knew Joe's feelings all too well; he had therefore given instructions that the news be broken to Kennedy by two priests.

The ex-ambassador was shattered. EX-ENVOY KENNEDY, CRUSHED BY SON'S DEATH, REMAINS IN SECLUSION, *The Boston Globe* reported on August 14. " 'What can I say?' the father said tonight. 'We received word yesterday. All my younger children are here, and young John (Lt. John F. Kennedy, the PT boat hero) came down from Chelsea Naval Hospital, but had to go right back.'

"From the time the family received the Navy telegram," the newspaper went on, "the ex-Ambassador has kept to his room. His grief is deep. He hasn't learned yet details of how the oldest of his nine children—the first son—died."

Rose later described Jack's reaction to the news of his brother's death. "Joe went out on the porch and told the children. They were stunned. He said they must be brave: that's what their brother would want from them. He urged them to go ahead with their plans to race that day and most of them obediently did so. But Jack could not. Instead, for a long time he walked on the beach in front of our house."

On August 15, as "countless messages of sympathy from national leaders were arriving" and "as the nation shared his grief in the loss of his oldest son," the ex-ambassador himself leaked news that Joe Jr. "had volunteered for a secret flying mission, had completed some 50 combat missions and had twice refused leave home under the rotation plan after completing his first 30 missions."

Inevitably, newspapers contacted Kennedy family friends for their reactions. "As early as 1939, young Joe had a premonition of death in war, according to [Boston] school committeeman Clement Norton," *The Globe* reported. "Norton and Kennedy met in England, and again at the Democratic convention a year later, and on both occasions, Kennedy predicted that he would be killed while flying in the war he was certain would come. 'But don't you dare tell Dad,' he warned."

On August 16, 1944, Kathleen arrived from England, having been granted priority air travel. "It was a quiet reunion, with the family bowed in grief. . . . The girl had seen her brother a short time before he left on his fatal flight," the *Boston Herald* chronicled. "He was the only member of the family in England at the time of her marriage, and he witnessed the ceremony. Now the Lady Hartington, Miss Kennedy arrived at La Guardia Field, N.Y. in an Army transport plane early this afternoon and transferred immediately to a plane for Boston. Lt. John Kennedy, PT boat hero of the South Pacific, now recuperating from injuries at the Chelsea Naval Hospital, met his sister at the Logan airport and accompanied her to Hyannis."

The Boston Globe was more descriptive. "Kathleen Kennedy, last of her family to see Lt. Joe Kennedy Jr. before he died at his Navy plane controls on Saturday, arrived here from London by plane yesterday to join her family—her first visit since her marriage in May to Lord Hartington. . . . She ran up the ramp alone, to be greeted by her brother, Lt. John F. Kennedy, holder of the Navy and Marine Corps Medal for heroism aboard a PT boat in the Southwest Pacific. 'Hello, Kat!' called John. In a robin's egg blue American Red Cross Summer uniform, the Marchioness of Hartington and prospective Duchess of Devonshire smiled wearily for an instant. Then she ran into John's arms and wept. After a moment, she squared her jaw, faced the crowd and walked resolutely up the ramp, arm in arm with her brother."

For years the ex-ambassador had bribed a veritable corps of Washington, New York, and Boston newspapermen with lavish gifts to write up the Kennedys; now he was forced to live with the result, as the press and thus public gloated at his family's grief. Since the spring the ex-ambassador had been sending Roosevelt signals that, with the end of war in sight and having served his penance, he desperately wanted a job in the administration, particularly the secretary of treasury post after Morgenthau's heart attack. He'd given a major speech on postwar American trade in Boston in May, which *The Globe* described in a front-page report headlined MARITIME DAY SPEECH FIRST BY EX-ENVOY IN 3 YEARS. "Although a crowd of more than 1,000 . . . jammed the ballroom of the Copley Plaza" to hear his speech, and although Roosevelt remained unresponsive, there was a growing feeling that, with the 1944 presidential election approaching, the ex-ambassador might again become a political force to be reckoned with.

Now, crushed by the news of his eldest son's death, the ex-ambassador withdrew into silence, the spectacle of his grief, for the surviving children, being almost worse than their own. In a family where feelings were unmentionable and constant activity/endeavor the order of the day, there was only one place of solace: the little clapboard Hyannis church of St. Francis Xavier. It was there that Jack and Kathleen went the evening Kathleen arrived. According to Kathleen's biographer, Kathleen was "appalled" by Jack's appearance. "He couldn't have weighed more than a hundred and twenty-five pounds. His cheek and jaw bones jutted out prominently, and his skin had a terrible yellow cast to it. . . . The operation on his back had been a failure."

On August 17, the day after Kathleen's arrival, Jack underwent rectal surgery by Dr. Hensen at the Chelsea Naval Hospital. By August 22 "back pain and leg pain is less," his doctor noted, and he could "walk with less discomfort." Ominously, however, "the abdominal symptoms continue."

Despairing of a solution and "believing that subsistence at home would be of benefit in a general sense," Dr. Heintzelman recommended that Jack go home.

Home, however, in the aftermath of Joe Jr.'s death, was even worse than the hospital.

Bordering on Madness

Jack was now the eldest Kennedy son. However, in the wake of Joe Jr.'s death it was a far-from-comfortable position, as he found over Labor Day weekend two weeks later.

He'd invited his two fellow officers from *PT 109*, Lennie Thom and Barney Ross, as well as lieutenants Red Fay and Jim Reed, to stay with him at Hyannis Port.

Lieutenants Thom and Reed were accompanied by their wives. As Mrs. Reed later recalled, "We were organized from the moment we arrived. The Kennedys organized everybody. I hated playing tennis, so Eunice invited me to play golf. The next day we played touch football, which was hideous. But we *had* to play and it was relentless. At the dinner table at night, Mr. Kennedy went around the table checking on what you'd done that day. . . . The whole weekend we were always competing with somebody over something."

Mrs. Thom painted the same picture. Her pregnancy entitled her to no special privileges. "I remember Eunice was in a sailing race and didn't have a crew. I'd never been in a boat in my life and I was made her crew. They were in everything to win, not just to participate. . . . We won the race."

Kathleen later explained the family approach to grief. "I am a Kennedy. I have a very strong feeling that makes a big difference about how to take things. I saw Daddy and Mother about Joe and I know that we've all got the ability to not be got down," she wrote in her contorted English.

Yet Kathleen knew it was not quite so simple. The ex-ambassador's grief hung over the younger Kennedys like a black cloud. He had given orders, for instance, that only a single cocktail be served before dinner. When Bobby found Jack and his four fellow lieutenants, like D'Artagnan and his friends, sneaking scotch from the kitchen, the priggish eighteen-year-old threatened to tell his father. "But Kathleen handled him," Mrs. Thom recalled of the "scrawny little guy in a white sailor suit," who was currently taking a midshipman's course at Harvard. However, when the PT brigade began to sing and clap hands outside on the lawn, "Mr. Kennedy leaned out the window and bawled, 'Jack, don't you and your friends have any respect for your dead brother?' " In the ensuing silence Bobby emerged from the house whispering, "Dad's awfully mad!" The incident effectively put an end to the evening, and the next day the ex-ambassador "froze" Lieutenant Ross when he tried to apologize. He even insisted Jack never have anything more to do with "that clown."

Mixed with Joe Kennedy's understandable grief was another, less noble emotion, as Arthur Krock later confided. The shock of Joe Jr.'s death was "one of the most severe . . . that I've ever seen registered on a human being," he remembered, but he also added that guilt and shame contributed to the ex-ambassador's distress. As Krock confided, "Joe Jr. when he volunteered on this final mission which was beyond his duty, beyond everything, was seeking to prove by its very danger that the Kennedys were not yellow. That's what killed that boy. That's why he died. And his father realized it. He never admitted it, but he realized it."

Certainly Krock realized it. He'd known Joe Kennedy Sr. intimately since 1932 and had no illusions about the millionaire's limitless ambitions. "He wanted to be President of the United States. Very definitely. He was a *very* ambitious man. He felt he had a great deal to give. He was shrewd. He had an iron grip on his children." Now, at the peak of his powers, the ex-ambassador had seen the war wash away his entire life's work. In the space of four short years he'd lost all hope of himself becoming president, his eldest daughter had been reduced to a human vegetable, and now his eldest son was dead in combat. At one point the ex-ambassador threatened in a letter to "go mad" unless he found some way of channeling his grief and his energies after Joe Jr.'s death. "You know how much I had tied my whole life up to his," he confessed to another friend in September, "and what great things I saw in the future for him. Now it's all over." To yet another crony he wrote that "all my plans for my own future were all tied up with young Joe and that has gone smash." More bad news, however, was to come. On September 17 a hurricane hit Cape Cod. Two days later, while Kathleen shopped on Fifth Avenue in New York for silk stockings and gifts to take back to England with her, a cable arrived from the War Office in England.

As We Remember Joe

It was her sister Eunice who finally found Kathleen in Bonwit's, but for all her pluck as a racing-boat skipper, she was unable to tell Kathleen the terrible news, saying only that their father had an important message for her at his suite in the Waldorf-Astoria.

The telegram that Kathleen's father handed to her was very simple. It regretted to inform Lady Hartington that her husband, Captain, Lord Hartington, had been killed on active service.

"So ends the story of Billy and Kick. . . . Life is so cruel. I am on my way to England," Kathleen noted sanguinely in her diary as she flew back to attend the family memorial service at Chatsworth, the 150-room Derbyshire mansion with gardens landscaped by Capability Brown that would one day have been hers, had Billy lived. Now Billy's brother, by British law, would inherit the title and family estates. "Writing is impossible."

Jack was concerned for his sister, knowing the sacrifices Kathleen had made to enact her dream of social glory and go against the objections of her mother. "I thought so much before we got married about what it would be like, living in England away from home and living with all the difficulties. Then I made up my mind and nothing could budge me." Now she was desolate, a widow in a foreign country. "Try and write her a cheery letter, as she is extremely broken up," Jack exhorted Billings.

In due course Kathleen, helped by the Cavendish family rather than her own, would come to terms with the death of her young husband, and elected to stay on with the Red Cross in war-torn London—indeed live there for the rest of her brief life—rather than return to her mother's sanctimonious hypocrisies in America.

For Jack, however, there was no refuge. "Am still in that god damned hospital," he wrote to Billings in October. "Have had two ops. and Handsome Hensen who is now in charge of my case, wants to get cutting again. He is the stupidest son of a bitch that ever drew breath. He said that you 'were a pretty nervous patient' [when Billings had been incarcerated at the hospital with scarlet fever]. There is one guy that is nervouser than you," Jack assured his friend, "—and that's the little Lt. He's a mad man with a knife.

"Cappy Leinbach was down for a weekend," Jack went on. "I took him racing with me. What an afternoon I gave him! I just got a letter from him apologizing for losing the race, so that will give you a rough idea how

I put the fear of God in him. He was full of bull-shit but I handed it back in several large helpings, and the upshot of it is that I am invited to speak to the 'assembled school.' I am debating in my mind whether or not to expose Steele in Chapel, or wait till all of us are gathered for shredded wheat in the master's room. Let me know your new assignment," he asked. "I hope the hell it is Supply Officer first wave Manila, or have you ever thought of just getting a sword and committing hari kiri?"

In fact Jack had taken pains, at Billings's request, to get him alternative sea duty, but "you neglected to give me any address that I could reach you. . . . In regard to Inga's address I sent it right away, but all I ever heard was that you were not at the address you gave. You stupid bastard."

Meanwhile, convalescing at the Chelsea Naval Hospital, Jack had received many messages of condolence on the death of his brother. One was an extraordinary letter from an old Harvard classmate, Michael Grace, who'd transferred from Harvard to Notre Dame and was currently serving in an infantry-training center in Texas. When Grace had lost his mother and sister he had been comforted by the Kennedys; now, as he wrote, he wished to repay that kindness by telling Jack what he saw as the true meaning of Joe's death.

At Harvard, Grace reminded Jack, it was Joe who'd "set the pace," serving as an example Jack had had to match. For instance, Grace reminded Jack how, "hearing Joe speak against the Townsend Plan you and I, impressed, took public speaking for better or for worse." In sport, too, Joe had paved Jack's way; "You tagged along and I barely kept out of the Waterboy class."

Yet, for all Joe's endeavor and determination, it had been obvious to Grace that Jack was the biblical Joseph of the family. "I would always say that Joe will carry on the Kennedy fame, but Jack is the heart behind the name."

Now, however, things were different. Not only was Joe dead, but the name of John F. Kennedy had, in Grace's words, "become a sort of household symbol for heroism, humor, and faith for a lot of people you will never know.

"Today you, from Reader's Digest to some doughfooted doughboy I may inveigle into benediction, you are the Kennedy fame," Grace asserted, "but it becomes all too plain that Joe was the heart behind your name. He set the pace and blazed the trail, took a beating on his Varsity letter so that you and Torbie would know the guys, making Harvard life worthwhile."

What this all added up to, Grace maintained, was a divine pattern. "In all you have seen," he was certain, "you know the meaning and purpose

of these changes—God's all powerful Will. . . . Joe has left behind to you
a great responsibility—for when God calls one of us away from a job, it
is so another can do it alone."

Grace's letter—magnanimous and sincere—came at the very moment
when Jack needed encouragement and personal advice. Reading and
rereading this letter, which he would keep to the end of his days, Jack
mulled over Grace's thoughtful and religiously inspired words. Whether
or not God was behind the "changes," Grace's references to Joe Jr. now
stirred Jack to action. Joe Jr. had been incapable of writing articulately
or arrestingly; he was snide, bullying, short-tempered, standoffish, aggressive with girls, insincere in his affairs and slavishly anxious to do his
father's bidding, the apple of his father's eye, heir presumptive of the
Kennedy clan, the young man supposedly destined for greatness on
America's political stage. Yet he'd known, in his heart of hearts, that he
wasn't up to it. His succession of misjudgments, from his early admiration of Hitler to his obstinate vote against Roosevelt's third nomination
in the 1940 convention, as well as his cofounding of the Harvard Committee against Military Intervention, gave but scant evidence of potential
future distinction as a Democratic politician. Nevertheless, for all his
manifest failings, he had *tried.* Before embarking on his own political
journey, therefore, Jack recognized he must first find an appropriate,
symbolic way of paying tribute to his brother's finer qualities—of inter-
ring the bad while giving thanks for the good.

Thus arose Jack's decision to gather together material for a memorial
book, honoring his brother Joe as a sibling, friend, and standard-bearer.
Taking up pen and paper, Jack now wrote to Joe's old teachers and
professors, his roommates, his valet, his companions at school and college, even his chaplain, commanding officer, and last mistress, soliciting
reminiscences he vowed to publish privately as an act of fraternal homage
thus to free himself forever from his brother's shadow and his rivalry: *As
We Remember Joe.*

Medical Discharge

As Jack sought to bury his brother with love, his father seemed still
consumed by hate. Roosevelt's note of sympathy on the news of Joe Jr.'s
heroic death merely added insult to Kennedy's grief and grievance. In his
heart Kennedy remained bitterly opposed to the war, and the triumph of
the Allied landings in Normandy and the great American breakout in the

Loire only made his defeatist prognostications of the past five years more humiliating. Now, under Roosevelt's wartime leadership, America was moving inexorably toward victory against the Axis powers, but without Joseph P. Kennedy.

To spite Roosevelt, therefore, Kennedy now threatened to give a radio speech that would be broadcast across the nation, attacking Roosevelt's policies and endorsing the Republican candidate, Thomas Dewey.

Alerted to this, Roosevelt was yet again forced to invite Kennedy to the White House, on October 26, 1944, for an interview that Roosevelt afterward said left him with "a bad taste" in his mouth. Kennedy, in his own subsequent account, took the offensive and flayed Roosevelt's choice of administrators and aides, claiming that the president was "surrounded with Jews and Communists" and urging Roosevelt to sack them all, from Harry Hopkins to Sam Rosenman. "They will write you down in history, if you don't get rid of them, as incompetent," Kennedy warned, "and they will open the way for the Communist line." He warned that not he, Joseph P. Kennedy, but this "crowd" of Jews and Communists would lose Roosevelt the election.

Though Roosevelt managed to dissuade Kennedy from openly supporting Dewey, he did not offer Kennedy a job. Nor did he assuage Kennedy's bitterness. "Harry, what are you doing campaigning for that crippled son of a bitch that killed my son Joe?" the ex-ambassador snarled at Roosevelt's new vice-presidential running mate, Harry Truman, when he met him in Boston early in November 1944.

Truman was stunned by Kennedy's rancor, and never forgot it. Meanwhile Kennedy refused to attend Roosevelt's and Truman's appearance before fifty thousand Bostonians at Fenway Park. To Walter Trohan of the *Chicago Tribune* Kennedy blamed Roosevelt for having gotten America into the war, claiming he would have contemplated suicide if he thought that he himself had had "any part in causing the war to be fought."

Trohan, by contrast, considered Kennedy a man "yearning to be President," yet a despicable coward without "a gut in his body." The ex-ambassador's record of defeatism even aroused the sarcasm of his widowed daughter, Kathleen, who wrote to Jack on October 31 to say that she'd "just read in the paper this morning that Archie [Cardinal] Spellman brought back a tremendously high decoration to Daddy. What was that for? His children's war record?"

Jack's stomach problems, in the meantime, had not improved. On November 6, 1944, the diagnosis of hernia, intravertebral disc, was finally abandoned. Despite endless laboratory testing, for the time being no better diagnosis could be made, and by November 13 Dr. Heintzelman considered "the lack of improvement in the abdominal pain and the failure to gain weight is now evidently going to take an indefinite amount of time to correct. The patient is unfit for service."

Two weeks later, on November 25, 1944, Jack was officially told that his problems, after two operations, were unlikely to be cured by further hospitalization and that he would shortly be discharged from the navy. "This patient's abdominal symptoms have persisted and he has failed to gain in strength or weight," Dr. Heintzelman recorded. "Because the pain is consistently present in the left lower quadrant, any active duodenal ulcer is excluded and a diagnosis of Colitis, Chronic established. The background of his present physical status is an exhausting combat experience in the South Pacific. Recovery in his case is dependent on a long period of rest in a secluded outdoor environment. It is the opinion of the Board of Medical Survey that this officer is unfit for service and it is recommended that he be brought before a Retiring Board."

"Sometime in the next month I am going to be paying full price at the local Loews," Jack joked in a note from the Chelsea Naval Hospital to Red Fay. "I will no longer be getting the forty per-cent off for servicemen—for the simple reason that I'm going to be in mufti. This I learned yesterday, as they have given up on fixing me up O.K. From here I'm going to go home for Christmas, and then to Arizona for about a year, and try to get back in shape again."

Jack hadn't reckoned on naval bureaucracy, however. Although his father pleaded via the Lahey Clinic that his son be allowed to convalesce at home, the Bureau of Medicine & Surgery in Washington demurred. "From a review of the enclosure it is noted that the subject officer is recommended for appearance before a Naval Retiring Board because of colitis, chronic, which disability, according to the Board's opinion, was incurred in the line of duty," Captain Adams commented on Captain Heintzelman's report. "In this connection a review of the records on file shows that the medical examiners who examined this officer on 5 Aug. 1941 to determine his physical fitness for appointment in the U.S. Naval Reserve recorded the information that he 'has been restricted as regular diet to no fried foods or roughage.' This seems clearly to indicate that the subject officer suffered from some type of gastro-intestinal disease prior to his appointment in the U.S. Naval Reserve."

Warming to his suspicions, Captain Adams added a second accusation: that the Board of Medical Survey's opinion that Jack's condition was related to his exhausting combat experience "would appear to be not supported by the past history as set forth above and in view of the recommendation on the enclosure, such a statement should be supported by circumstantial information if it is to be included in such a report."

Furious, Jack was now forced to remain in Boston until still further tests, examinations, and reports had been made. Captain Heintzelman, clearly irked by Washington's procrastination in the case of a sick and wasting war hero, pointed out to the Bureau that Jack's abdominal sensitivity prior to entry into the navy related to his duodenum and "was not associated with lower abdominal cramps nor lower bowel disturbance" as the patient was now suffering. He concluded with words intended to shame Captain Adams: "While on PT duty in the South Pacific, the patient's boat was rammed and sunk by a Jap DD at Vela Gulf, Aug. 1, 1943. He spent over 50 hours in the water and went without food or drinking water for one week. Following this experience his present abdominal symptoms began."

The case now dragged on. Jack's original request that the matter be dealt with by correspondence rather than personal attendance at the Retiring Board was turned down. Only after Jack called his old roommate Charles Houghton was the matter expedited. At last, on December 26, he was ordered by telephone to appear in person before the Retiring Board in Room 100 of the Corcoran Annex of the Navy Department in Washington at nine A.M. the next morning. There, on December 27, 1944, Jack faced yet another battery of medics, this time five retired medical officers, from Rear Admiral Dorsey to Commander Curley.

Admiral Dorsey, once he met Jack and read the voluminous medical files on his case, was clearly ashamed of the navy's attempt to question and delay his discharge. After conducting a brief medical examination, the admiral and his panel unanimously recommended not only that Jack be discharged on account of incapacity sustained on active service, but that it be recorded that his incapacity was incurred "subsequent to October 20, 1943, the effective date of commencement of service in the grade of Lieutenant."

Having been congratulated for his devotion to duty, Lieutenant Kennedy was ordered home and told that, assuming the findings of the Retiring Board were confirmed, he would legally be released from active duty on March 1, 1945.

After three and a half extraordinary years of naval service, Jack was free, and that evening he flew down to Palm Beach to join his family for the remainder of the Christmas vacation.

A Collision of Dreams

Jack had promised his friend Red Fay that at Palm Beach "the facilities are ample for even a guy who throws his weight around like you. Pappy is going down with Commissar Timilty the 29th November. . . . At the

Kennedys' on Christmas, the wassail flows like molasses, but the Chow is excellent."

Fay was not disappointed. "Florida from one end to the other was enjoying a boom in gambling, nightclubs and cabarets. The horses were running at Hialeah and the dogs at Gulfstream. The men in uniform were being catered to, but mostly as a form of absolution for the gambling, nightclub underworld operations.

"Good scotch or bonded bourbon was almost unheard of. At least that was what I thought until Jack said, 'Dad and Commiss are going to the races at Hialeah' (at that time Joseph Kennedy owned one of the largest individual holdings in the track); they wanted us all to meet at the Park Avenue Restaurant in Miami Beach after, for dinner."

At six o'clock Fay appeared at the restaurant, in uniform. "Almost immediately in walked Big Joe with the Commiss, Eunice, Jean, and some other lady—not Mrs. Kennedy—whose name I never got. Suddenly we were surrounded by a profusion of waiters, the owner, and well-wishers. We were conveyed to a special alcove, which overlooked the common man."

For Fay, son of a sewer and heavy-construction contractor in San Francisco, it was an eye-opening glimpse into the world of big money as well as the fawning obeisances paid to millionaires such as Jack's father. Mr. Roosevelt might ignore Mr. Kennedy, but the restaurant staffs of Miami did not. Mr. Kennedy offered genuine Pinch Bottle whiskey or Old Forester bonded bourbon. "Liking bourbon, I replied, 'Mr. Kennedy, that Old Forester looks good to me.' Suddenly I felt Jack's penetrating eyes boring into me, and looked his way to receive a look of mild horror. Leaning across the table, he whispered just so his dad could hear, 'My God, do I have to tell you everything? When Dad is around we all drink Pinch Bottle. He owns it.' "

Mr. Kennedy soon took a liking to Fay, for he warmed to the brash Californian's fun-loving, loyal style: a young man with a sparkle in his big blue eyes, and cheerful company for his sick son.

Here indeed was the irony: the ex-ambassador's now-oldest son attempting to solace and amuse his half-demented, grieving father; while the father did everything possible to entertain and stimulate his physically broken son.

Jack had hoped his memorial volume to the memory of Joe Jr. would be a peace offering to his grieving father. However, as Fay recalled, the book was nowhere near ready for printing at Christmas 1945. Invited to spend a day at the Kennedy home, Fay had quickly put together an array of little gifts for the various members of the family, which elicited Rose Kennedy's pleasure but Jack's mock disdain: "Here I am spending five thousand dollars, working my head off to give something that really means something to my dad and mother, and what happens? You come down here with ten dollars' worth of drugstore supplies, the tail of somebody's silver fox wrap [found in the back of a taxi], and you're the star of the day. What am I, an inconsiderate, selfish adult who doesn't love his family? Thanks, Pal."

But as Jack quickly became aware, his father wanted no Christmas trinkets nor even a memorial book. His tears for Joe Jr. had been shed. What he wanted now was a sign from Jack that he was ready to consider a career in politics. "I can feel Pappy's eyes on the back of my neck," Fay vividly remembered Jack saying at the time. As Jack himself confided, "it was like being drafted. My father wanted his eldest son in politics. 'Wanted' isn't the right word. He demanded it. You know my father."

The risks were immeasurable. Not only was Jack's father a frightening figure in the Kennedy family, before whom his wife, children, and visitors alike trembled, but he had an even worse reputation in public. Was it really possible to find a "working relationship" with such a man? No one, whether as Joseph Kennedy's superior or subordinate, had long survived the ordeal, all eventually becoming either enemies or lackeys.

Yet to take up the challenge was, for Jack, like volunteering for PT boats. Politics promised action, competition, power, leadership, and status. It was also the logical conclusion to a boyhood and youth dominated by the political legend of his grandfather John F. Fitzgerald, congressman and mayor. It promised, too, a chance to build upon the high offices held by his father in Roosevelt's first and second administrations—and to avenge the ex-ambassador's fall from political grace. Above all it promised, in the distant future, to achieve that which his father had failed, and his brother, in all honesty, would never have been able to achieve: election to the White House.

"A lot of stories have been written and said about Joe Jr.," Lem Billings later reflected. "I think a lot of people say that if Joe hadn't died, that Jack might never have gone into politics. I don't believe this. Nothing could have kept Jack out of politics: I think this is what he had in him, and it just would have come out, no matter what. . . . Somewhere along the line, he would have been in politics."

Billings was not romanticizing. Jack had already studied the science of politics, in its domestic and international context, for six long years at college, from 1935 to 1941. Although the war had interrupted his career, it had also added maturity and depth to Jack's understanding of men and of world problems. Leaving the navy, he was returning to his erstwhile ambition, in shattered health but without an older brother to contend with. The road, at last, was clear to become a "White-House man" and drink, as Inga put it, the "elixir" of life as he aimed to go to the very top.

There was only one problem: the role Jack's father would play in this drama. Perhaps only Inga, with her maternal intuition, could have foreseen the collision of dreams that took place in Florida at the end of 1944, as with honeyed words the ex-ambassador sought to enslave the son; the son to remove the venom from his father's fang and find his own path.

The ex-ambassador was one step ahead of his sick son. Anticipating a positive response to the idea that Jack should take on the mantle of his fallen brother, Joe Kennedy had, prior to Jack's arrival, already taken the first secret steps on Jack's behalf. Late in December 1944 his cousin Joe Kane had alerted him to an ironic and unexpected possibility. Kane's gloating eyes and sharp ears had been quick to catch rumors of financial problems affecting Congressman James Michael Curley, the very Boston-Irish demagogue who in 1913 had put an end to Honey Fitz's career as mayor of Boston. Curley, as the incumbent of Massachusetts's Eleventh Congressional District in Boston, was still in financial difficulties after a fraud conviction had forced him to pay back forty-two thousand dollars from a 1938 illegal "back-hander." Now a second, federal indictment for fraud was hanging over him and due to come to court.

Kennedy moved swiftly. Using ex-police commissioner Timilty as his emissary, he secretly sent Curley twelve thousand dollars in cash to pay off his longstanding debt, with the promise of significant campaign money and help if Curley would vacate his seat in Congress and try for the mayoralty of Boston in the 1945 election. "Curley knew that he was in trouble with the feds over the mail fraud rap," Joe Kane later confessed to the scheme. "The ambassador paid him to get out of the congressional seat, and Curley figured he might need the money."

How much Jack's father told Jack of these shenanigans when he reached Palm Beach may never be known. However, in the days after Christmas 1944, a bargain was struck between father and son. To his friend Lem Billings, out in the Pacific and approaching Iwo Jima, Jack soon afterward confided his political plan: "As I may have told you . . . I am returning to Law School at Harvard (not John[s] Hopkins) in the Fall—and then if something good turns up while I am there I will run for it. *I have my eye on something pretty good now if it comes through.*"

No names were mentioned. Almost to a man, Jack's other friends would have ridiculed the suggestion of a tough political career for the sickly, scrawny, medically discharged PT-boat commander: unaware of the sorcerous yet touching compact between Jack Kennedy and his father that would, in the years ahead, have vast and unforgettable consequences both for Jack and the people of America as, shortly after New Year's Day, 1945, Jack made his way to Castle Hot Springs in Arizona to fatten himself up for his chosen career.

Jack Kennedy tours the ruins of Berlin during the Potsdam Conference, July 1945, as reporter and personal guest of Secretary of the Navy James V. Forrestal (right) (National Archives/Seeley Mudd Library, Princeton University)

Scratching a Beggar's Ass

Though the Second World War still had months to run, it was clear that the old order was passing, with Roosevelt now visibly failing in health after winning his fourth successive presidential election. The burden of government was falling increasingly on his staff, and Jack's father had antagonized too many of them to hope he would ever be restored to the president's good graces. Harry Truman, the new vice president, had told Kennedy in Boston that "if you say another word about Roosevelt, I'm going to throw you out of that window." Though Kennedy's paid rooters, from Krock to Boake Carter, kept up an insistent campaign to have him employed by the U.S. government, the ex-ambassador was and would continue to be turned down for every possible post in the United States government, including head of the federal lending agencies in early 1945, then the Reconstruction Finance Corporation, and finally membership in the Export-Import Bank.

It was clear that although money could still buy Kennedy the support of paid cronies, it could no longer, as in the 1930s, buy him a position in government. As Jack wrote candidly in his letter to Lem Billings from Castle Hot Springs, "The South was the same as ever with Joe Timilty more horrified of Dad than ever."

Now that their compact over Curley's congressional seat had been made, however, Jack could afford to relax, and at the Castle Hot Springs Hotel in Arizona, early in 1945, he attempted to do just that, while putting the finishing touches to his memorial tribute to his brother. "I have gathered together some essays and some pictures etc. and am having it put in book form and it should be finished in about a month," he wrote to Dr. Tinker at Choate on February 9. "It's not much, but as you knew Joe well, I have been planning to send you a copy.

"Joe's death was naturally a great shock. He had developed his capabilities to an extraordinary degree since leaving Choate, and I always felt that he could have reached whatever goal his ambition set." Anticipating possible objections to such a bald assertion, Jack explained that it was "naturally difficult, in fact impossible, for a younger brother to look at an older brother with any degree of objectivity, but I think he had a great contribution to make.

"As for myself," Jack continued, "the doctors told me to come out here for about a year—and so I don't plan to return till the Fall." The war, he commented, "makes less sense to me now than it ever made and that was little enough—and I should really like—as my life's goal—in some way and at some time to do something to help prevent another."

These were pious sentiments, penned for a revered (and revering) schoolmaster. In the meantime, Jack expressed himself more baldly to his friends. The food was "just fair," considering the expense. "You can have all you want for thirty bucks a day," but "if I stay here very long, I'm going to end up my life scratching a beggar's ass," he told Red Fay. Even his exploits on *PT 109,* so graphically rendered by John Hersey, gave him little kudos among the septuagenarians and octogenarians of the spa. "I'm sorry I haven't come through with a report on how the Irishman is doing," he apologized. "Frankly, Red, it's a bit slow. Either they haven't read the August issue of the Reader's Digest or something, for everytime [*sic*] I introduce Kula Gulf into the circle (in itself no mean feat), the conversation just seems to pick itself up and walk into a corner and die. In all fairness to myself I've got to admit it's a tough audience, former Presidents of the local Kiwanis who have put in their three score and ten and are half way around again. When you fire a fast one at them—that's high and just hitting the corner of the plate, they make no attempt to go for it, for they just *know* that they have one that is going to knock you out of that easy chair. I don't mean it in a derogatory sense. . . . it's just that Castle Hot Springs is where self-panickers come to die."

Jack was hardly a self-panicker. Equally, his father could hardly wait for Jack to get himself into physical shape for the coming battle. "Red," Jack confided to Fay, "when the war is over and you are out there in sunny California giving them a solid five and a half inches for a six inch pavement, I'll be back here with Dad trying to parlay a lost PT boat and a bad back into a political advantage. I tell you, Dad is ready right now and can't understand why his fine son Jack isn't ready."

A Wild Horseback Rider

One of Jack's immediate tasks was to take stock of Curley's congressional district. Writing to his grandfather's personal secretary at the Boston Port Authority, he asked for subscriptions to *The Boston Post* and the *Boston Herald* to be started immediately and requested information about Boston's business outlook. "I have sent quite a little material about the Port, also all I could get on Boston Finance and Real Estate," Honey Fitz's secretary wrote back promptly on receipt of Jack's letter on February 7, 1945. "There seems to be very little on the past history of the airport but I expect to have postwar plans in a day or two and will send them at that time," she promised. "I am sending, under separate cover, five envelopes of material. If you read them all you will certainly have to burn the midnight oil."

Burning the midnight oil in Castle Hot Springs, Jack acquired a new friend, thirteen years older than himself but also of Irish extraction and a self-made millionaire to boot: Patrick J. Lannan of Chicago, Illinois. Among the largely elderly crowd at Castle Hot Springs, the two became inseparable and soon moved to their own self-contained cottage nearby. Reflecting on their friendship, Lannan later remarked that Jack

> knew that I was a self-made man and maybe he was interested in that, the fact that I got rolling early; and maybe he could see some elements of his father in me, I don't know.
>
> I think he wanted to do something. The war was over for him, all the stimulation in the war effort was behind him. He had survived, he knew that a hell of a lot of people hadn't survived on a world-wide basis and he was lucky. He had survived, and what was he going to do?
>
> There was only one thing he was sure of when I first met him: he knew what he *didn't* want to do. He knew that very clearly, he said it to me so strongly that I knew he would never veer from it, and that was, he was not going to go into business. His father had made enough money. There was no point in going into business to make more money, so he was going to try to dedicate himself to public service.
>
> He was a perfect gentleman, up to that time. Every time he referred to politics it would be to public service, and I'd kid him about it. "You mean politics like your grandfather, don't you Jack?"

Whether it was politics or public service to which Jack aspired, there was the small matter of his health to be resolved. "I do remember that Jack was not the healthiest guy in the world in Arizona," Lannan commented.

> I think he was putting on a brave front all the time. I remember him complaining about the back, I think he was wearing some kind of belt then. I think he just pushed himself—he didn't like people asking how is your health, because he just didn't want to talk about it. He would complain about his stomach, too. I thought at that time it might be psychological—I think he was really troubled by what he was going to do. . . .
>
> He was completely and absolutely concerned about his future, and he had positively and absolutely made up his mind to devote it to

public service—as he called politics—and he was already then talking about what guy he would run against. Yes, he was that specific.

Lannan, who'd founded his own firm of investment brokers and had financial interests both in industry and publishing, counseled Jack that labor and union problems would be the key postwar issue on the domestic front. No sooner had Jack relayed this prediction to his father in Palm Beach than "a whole crateful of books on labor and labor law arrived," Lannan recalled. "Jack sat up to one or two in the morning reading those books until he'd finished the whole crate. He earned my respect for that."

Jack's father also earned Lannan's respect. "What impressed me in those days: the telephone would ring every night at 5 o'clock. Now I know what it is to have a father-son, father-daughter relationship. But I just don't know many fathers who I have ever run into that call their sons like that. At five o'clock—like you'd set your clock, and the phone would ring. 'How are you? What did you do today? How are things going? Is there anything I can do for you?' "

Lannan recalled that the ex-ambassador sent not only books but food.

> At that time Jack was having considerable difficulty with his stomach. I got him occasionally to have as much as half a glass of red wine with his dinner. I think it sort of helped him when he was having trouble with his digestion—he was very uptight at that time, he looked jaundiced—yellow as saffron and as thin as a rake—and complaining about his inability to properly digest his food, I remember. And I remember his father shipping us a whole boxful of steaks and chops, and turning them over to the chef. We really didn't have anything to do for weeks but sit down and talk in that cottage, because we never received anybody in that cottage, and we didn't join anybody. We'd have a fire in the fireplace and talk.

Like Jack's father, Lannan prided himself on being a good judge of character. Naturally he'd heard of the Kennedys. "They were a prominent family in America because of the reams of publicity the family got when Joe was ambassador with nine kids and so on. They were in every Sunday supplement for years, so you had to be rather a stupid person by 1945 not to have heard of the Kennedy family. Joe Kennedy was prominently mentioned as a possible presidential nominee of the Democratic party when he got in a quarrel with Roosevelt—there were all sorts of people in the country that were Democrats that didn't like Roosevelt and they were talking about Joe Kennedy for president."

Jack, by contrast, gave Lannan no hint of being presidential timber. "Certainly when I met Jack in 1945, never in my wildest imagination was there an idea that he would become a future president of the United States! At the end of the war he seemed like really an extremely normal fellow. A thoroughly amusing guy. . . . a very simple, pragmatic sort of yes-and-no fellow. I never sensed in Jack a morose, complicated thinker."

Jack's reckless bravado surprised the Chicago businessman. Each day the two would go horse riding together. "It was up in the mountains, a wonderful place to ride. He was a wild horseback rider. God, I remember how he would charge down a mountainside, taking terrific chances—he loved speed, you know. He was a very daring fellow! I don't think he was all that good a horseman either, but he just loved to ride the hell out of those horses—we were always racing one another. He was very competitive that way—but competitive in a very nice way."

For all his simplicity and pragmatism, however, there were emotions in Jack that ran deeper than Lannan at first assumed. "One time we were having dinner in Arizona together, and Jack was kidding about his father, who'd gone up to Hyannis—'Daddy's tearing the house apart apparently, up in Hyannisport, they're going to do a lot of work,' something like that. And I said something in response that maybe had a little edge of criticism about his father. And Jesus, he pulled me right up by my suspenders at that table! . . . There was a very good, solid relationship there."

Lannan had yet to meet Joseph Kennedy. In the meantime Jack and Lannan lamented the paucity of women at Castle Hot Springs. "It got pretty dull for both of us," Lannan conceded. "We decided we had to get out of there and have a vacation." The two cowboys therefore abandoned Castle Hot Springs and traveled to Phoenix to try out the bedsprings of the Biltmore Hotel, and it was there that Jack received the news that Harvard friend Bill Coleman, who had visited with Jack in Palm Beach while stationed in Melbourne, Florida, had been killed in a flying accident.

"The news about Bill Coleman was a shock to me all right for he had been down to the house with his wife over New Year's," Jack wrote sadly to Billings. "He was keen as hell on flying, and I was more sure than I had ever been that he would do extremely well later."

Jack was certainly chastened, and became uncomfortable in the Biltmore Hotel, despite its Frank Lloyd Wright distinction. "It was an expensive place and we shared a room together, we didn't even have a sitting room," Lannan recalled. Worse still, the Biltmore was dressy. "And of course Kennedy was wearing his old fatigue pants from the navy, his fatigue shoes, which he would not lace all the way up—I would say by the social standards and the standards of dress that they have at the Biltmore—jacket-and-tie—he was so irreverent that they were relieved when we left. I could just sense these people looking at him!"

"Went down to Phoenix the other day," Jack afterward boasted to

Billings, "and stayed at the Arizona Biltmore which is terrific—designed by Frank Lloyd Wright—in modern Chinese—which would have really interested you. Anyways there was some pumping which interested me and I did take V.L. [for] a ride in my car—she looks a bit like Pissy Brooks in her younger days if you can believe it—absolutely no make-up—she looks as though she came out at the Sewickly Country Club in 1940—but she does get off a few more god damns than perhaps they are accustomed to out there. I don't mean by all this that I pumped her," he cautioned Billings, "or that if you should ever see her you should get a big hello—you would get the usual blank stare you get under similar circumstances."

At the Camelback Inn, to which Jack and Lannan moved, there was a much less formal atmosphere, as well as more interesting people. "James Stewart was there," Lannan recounted, "just mustered out of the service, big, tall, and rangy, and all the girls loved him, always such a hell of a nice fellow; the head financial brains of *Time* magazine, Hillman; and John Hersey and his wife, Frances Ann. It was a very interesting end-of-the-war grouping." Jack "sort of came to life when there were women around. Of course Jack liked girls and girls liked him—I mean, God, I was astounded how every time any of them would see him—" Lannan's voice trailed off as he marveled at Jack's seemingly magnetic pull.

Invigorated by the social scene at the Camelback Inn, Jack then returned to Castle Hot Springs. Whether his health was really improving was a moot question. "I've been out here for about a month," he wrote to Billings, "but the back has been so bad that I am going to Mayo's . . . about the first of April unless it gets a little better." Arizona was "nice—you would really like it—natural hot pools right in the rocks—good riding"; but in truth, his restless mind was bored, and at such times he often dredged up his abiding "Choate problem."

> I think I wrote and told you in several letters about Cappy Lieback and my chewing out his ass—since then the Head has been to the house in PB—and told Dad that he hoped that I didn't hold my trouble at Choate against them—so the boys are really eating humble shit. I got a letter from Tinker a couple of weeks ago that I am saving for you as it will make you very ill. I'm still planning to go up there and make a speech and give the faculty hell indirectly and JJ Maher directly. I'm going to wait till he comes back from fighting the war which he is doing out in Tennessee. I have gathered together all my reports from Choate and when you read what that son-of-a-bitch wrote—it makes me sore as hell.
>
> The only laugh I ever got out of that guy was the night he backed you up against the fireplace for making faces at him and shook the

hell out of you while you trembled and tearfully apologized. Well, we all have our bad days.

Such festering wounds to Jack's psyche—like his sense of abandonment after the *PT 109* ramming—would never go away. Despite his joshing, however, Jack admired Billings for the way he was "now seeing a bit of the war" off the coast of Iwo Jima. "Iwo is getting a terrific play lately—it must be tough as hell. What do think of the marines?" he asked. "You are the only person in the world about who has seen both the marines and the [British] eighth army in action—you could write a good article comparing them I think."

About his own war exploits Jack remained touchingly diffident. "What you said about the break I got when Hersey did the article is extremely true I guess," he acknowledged, but "it was such an accident that it rather makes me wonder if most success is merely a great deal of fortuitous accidents. I imagine I would agree with you that it was lucky the whole thing happened if the two fellows had not been killed which rather spoils the whole thing for me."

By contrast, Jack was pleased that his brother Joe Jr. had at least been awarded the Navy Cross, posthumously; "He was recommended for the Congressional Medal but they changed it to the Cross," Jack explained. His memorial book, meanwhile, was "going slower than I had hoped, but it should be out in another month or so and I think will be pretty good. The piece I wrote for it is the best writing I ever did—and Kick wrote an excellent piece and so did Teddy—the gay illiterate. I also have done a piece called 'On Post-War Peace' which I sent to Life and Reader's Digest who I don't think can use it but if they don't stall around too long I think I can get it in the Atlantic Monthly—perhaps."

Jack's caution was well warranted. In the meantime Kick wrote from the Nurses Club of the American Red Cross in London to say, "You sound like you are getting a good rest but somehow I can't see you staying there for long. Am sure you'll get the wanderlust and other kinds of lust before the passing of many moons."

Kathleen's prediction proved correct. Barely a month had passed before Jack was writing to tell his friend Billings he was "heading out of here to Palm Springs, where I expect to tangle tonsils with Inga Binga among others. She has gone to work for MGM. With that sensational bit of news I will close."

Tangling Tonsils with Inga

Life in Hollywood, after the arid wastes of Arizona, was intoxicating.
Lannan had gotten to know the actor Walter Huston before the war and
now arranged for Jack to meet him. Huston was working on a movie with
Sam Spiegel, and soon Jack was caught in a dizzying social round. "The
period we were in Hollywood," Lannan recalled, "anywhere that Jack
went, I went and anywhere I went, he went. I think he sort of came to life
when he got to Los Angeles. People were always trying to invite you to
parties." At Spiegel's there were "four or five attractive girls—one really
pouring on the charm." There was also Sonja Henie, the famous ice
skater—married to Dan Thompson, still in the U.S. Navy in the
Pacific—who soon succumbed to Jack's charm. Through Spalding, Jack
also met and dined with Gary Cooper, the legendary actor, who'd bought
the movie rights to Spalding's bestselling book, *Love at First Flight.*

Jack, as Spalding remembered with amusement, was genuinely puzzled
by the notion of success without brains, and was horrified by Cooper's
lack of conversation. "Gee, Charlie, I don't know how you're going to
make it," Jack remarked to Spalding. "That's about a three-word dinner
we had. Nobody said anything, and if they did, Gary said zero!"

Inga Arvad had sized up Jack pretty well when telling him in Charleston about his "gravest mistake"—namely, "that you admire brains more
than heart, but then that is necessary to arrive." Jack was still determined
to arrive; indeed in Spalding's eyes Jack's very ill health gave him an
exaggerated desire to live and to have fun. "That heightened feeling—
'How many days have I got left?'—that's what gave him this impatience.
You know, 'if it isn't all that good here, let's go someplace else!' "

The three musketeers spent a comic evening with Olivia de Havilland,
into whose closet Jack mistakenly walked instead of exiting the front
door, resulting in Jack being buried beneath a cascade of her shoes and
tennis rackets. Jack saw Angela Greene again, his beautiful nurse from
the Chelsea Naval Hospital, Ensign Anne McGillicuddy—and, of course,
Inga.

Spalding was as impressed with Inga as Jack had been:

> She was blond and well-dressed, always with bright colors and look-
> ing great. But the thing about her, her conversation was miles and
> miles ahead of anybody. I mean, it was really great! There was
> something adventurous about her which I'm sure appealed to him—

she'd *done* so much, been *involved* in so much. She was almost—you know, she was a fictional character almost, walking around. Nobody else that I knew was at all like that.

She was somebody that, of all the people that I *ever* saw him with I'd say she was the most compatible. . . . I thought she was *terrific!* Interesting. Amusing. And sexy in a European way—not smolderingly quiet, just sexy because she felt good about herself. She *liked* being with Jack, he amused her. I think she was trying to enjoy the time with him as much as he was with her.

The relationship, however, was for old time's sake. Inga's boyfriend, Bill Cahan, was overseas, but she corresponded frequently with him and at great length. Meanwhile at MGM, where she was now employed as a screenwriter, she was still being watched by the FBI. There seemed no way in which her old intimacy with Jack could be reestablished without inviting the same difficulties they had encountered in Washington three years before, and Inga wisely refused to try, particularly with Jack having made up his mind to run for a congressional seat.

So Jack made do with other women. "Sorry to learn that your dissipation finally caught up with you and that you landed in bed for a week's visit with the flu," remarked Lannan in a letter to Jack from Chicago on April II. "Are you sure it wasn't just plain collapse? The news about Miss Kunts was amusing. Have a good time and try hard to join me for the trip to Mayo's. It is a pretty gruesome ordeal going through that place alone, whereas if we go together we will perhaps have a good many laughs."

The next day, however, there was shattering news. Roosevelt was at Warm Springs, Georgia, with his erstwhile mistress, sitting for his portrait in "The Little White House" and working on his keynote address to the impending San Francisco conference to establish the United Nations organization when, a few minutes past one P.M. his trembling hand went to his forehead, and muttering "I've got a terrific headache," he groaned and fell forward, his head collapsing on the desk. Despite massive and continuous injections of papaverine and amyl nitrate, caffeine sodium benzoate, and finally Adrenalin directly into the heart muscle, the president was dead within hours.

Lannan, looking back, felt that Jack "was patterning himself more after Roosevelt than his father," and others agreed. Certainly there were surprising parallels: Roosevelt the son of a millionaire, born into a politicized family dominated by his famous cousin, Teddy (who had become the youngest president in American history in 1901); Roosevelt the graduate of Harvard; and above all, Roosevelt who was for much of his life crippled by polio and, in his later presidential years, suffered from heart disease and other ailments. Once, when asked whether his polio had affected his mental powers, his wife, Eleanor, said, "Any person who has gone through great [medical] suffering is bound to have a greater sympathy and understanding of the problems of mankind."

If so, Jack showed little enthusiasm for seeing such problems firsthand. Far from being interested in taking a closer look at his potential congressional district, he left it to his now-invigorated father to size up and, where necessary, soften up the political scene in Massachusetts on his behalf. At the New England Mutual Hall on April 15, the notoriously tightfisted ex-ambassador suddenly gave "a surprise gift of $10,000" to the Guild of St. Appolonia, the "professional organization of Catholic dentists of Greater Boston." He also lunched with the governor of Massachusetts, Maurice Tobin, and called upon "Boston employers, employees and legislators to work together to make great and important the city's sea and air ports," *The Boston Globe* reported on its front page, beneath a photograph of Joseph Kennedy and the governor, and the massive headline N.E. 'NO GRAVEYARD,' SAYS KENNEDY AT PORT MEETING.

Kennedy recalled how the transatlantic speed record for ships had only improved by twenty-four hours in the thirty-eight years between 1907 and 1945, then begged his audience to face up to the lesson: "Don't you see that that means that so far as fast passenger and fast freight is concerned, the Merchant Marine is all through?" He continued:

> Here is Boston's big opportunity for Boston young men, for only young men are trained in the new industries of the future, air transport, electronics, radar, etc. Out of every war some new industry is born. You will say radar and electronics will come out of this war—and I agree with you. But the everyday field that will utilize radar and electronics more than any other, I would guess, is the air transportation field. You know usually we hear about a new revolutionary invention and then complacently sit back to await its impact. The old story of "seven years from test tube to market" was a pretty safe one to follow, although penicillin smashed that theory. But here is a new industry which doesn't have to be developed. It is an actual daily operation, clothed in the secrecy of war, moving military material and personnel with a precision and accuracy not equalled in any civilian activity. . . . So fundamental a change has not come into our lives to affect our standards and methods of living since the automobile.

Joseph Kennedy's speech was a tour de force, followed on April 29 by news that governor Tobin had recommended Kennedy "to head an industrial study of the state with a view to formation of a State Department of Commerce": a study that would give Kennedy a unique overview and insight into the current economic condition of the state and its future.

All this was fine, except for the fact that the prospective candidate, in Joseph Kennedy's paternal view, was again wasting his time and endangering his health in the fleshpots of Hollywood. Thus, no sooner had Jack arrived at the Mayo Clinic with Pat Lannan to see Dr. O'Leary about the advisability of yet another operation on his back than he received an important message. The executive editor of the Chicago *Herald-American,* Louis Ruppel, was urgently trying to contact him. "Visited with his father Saturday [April 21]," Ruppel's cable to Dr. O'Leary ran. "Anxious to find out if young Jack will cover an assignment."

Ruppel's assignment came as a complete shock. The proposal was that Jack should travel to San Francisco immediately to cover the forthcoming official birth of the United Nations "from the point of view of the ordinary G.I." For the broken-down warrior it was the chance of a lifetime. Packing his travel bag, Jack accepted the job and on April 25, 1945, set off to cover the greatest gathering of world politicians and diplomats to come together since the Versailles Peace Conference in 1919.

All the Way

Some of Jack's friends were amazed to hear that he was a reporter in San Francisco. "I haven't heard from you for so long I thought you'd killed yourself in L.A.," Torby Macdonald wrote to him, "and was relieved to find you a G.I. at San Fran. . . . I wrote 2 or 3 times to that ranch with requests to forward but no word—I've imagined everything from marriage to hari-kari at Inga's shinto shrine."

Lem Billings was plainly disbelieving. "You certainly are a rotten correspondent," he wrote from the Pacific. "Bobby tells me you are now writing up the San Francisco conference for some Chicago papers—why they are trusting you with so important a job I do not know, it must be rather an unimportant paper. Before they get too involved with Conferences anyway, they should be damned sure they have the Japs on the way to being licked." He complained about the "unhealthy" optimism in the United States. "The Japs do not seem to have the slightest intention of quitting—and apparently plan to carry this war on to the bitter end."

Such pessimism also led Billings to mock Jack's failure with Inga. "Haven't you found any girl that will have you, Kennedy? It seems to me you're destined to never fall in love with anyone unless she's married or a divorcée. You know you're no spring chicken any longer, 28 in a couple of weeks—& as I recall, when I last saw you your hair line was receding conspicuously. You're getting to be less of a bargain every year—& since they closed Hialeah I don't imagine you have much dough—So what the hell have you?—Take it from me you'd better cut out being so particular—You're on the road down."

In fact Jack was on the road up, despite Billings's mockery and the poor response to his article on disarmament. "I find this rather jejune," the submissions editor of the *Atlantic Monthly* had noted to an editorial colleague, "an oversimplification of a very complicated subject. Some profounder thinking is needed here and conclusions not based on clichés. Don't believe this is our dish in its present form." *Life* magazine had been wholly unresponsive to an article on disarmament in the wake of the massive German counteroffensive in the Ardennes, and *Reader's Digest* was similarly unreceptive, despite the ex-ambassador's urging. "Jack felt so strongly about the question of rearmament that I suggested he put his feelings on paper," Kennedy had explained to Paul Palmer, the editor. Palmer had thought the article "intelligently reasoned and well-written" but "not definite and exact enough for The Reader's Digest—we do not use the exhortative and editorial type of article very often. I wish I could give you a different answer on it, but I can't."

After dining with the ex-ambassador, however, the editor of the *Atlantic Monthly* had reconsidered. Times had changed. With the imminent birth of the United Nations as a force for peace in the world, Jack's article suddenly seemed rather topical. "I have been talking with your father about the possibility of your revising your article on rearmament," Mr. Weeks had written to Jack on April 17. "It seems to me that in the issues [of the magazine] approaching, it will be more appropriate than ever for a veteran like yourself to press home this argument that has been pretty well lost sight of in our efforts to get some kind of machinery in operation at San Francisco."

The news that Jack would be a correspondent in San Francisco, however, altered everything. Weeks rushed off another letter to Jack, saying, "Your Dad told me there was a possibility of your attending the Conference." The disarmament article was shelved as Weeks attempted to sign Jack up to write his San Francisco conference "impressions—impressions which I honestly believe it would be in the public interest for you to share with other service men."

By the time Weeks's second letter reached Jack at the Palace Hotel in San Francisco, however, he was in full swing. Indeed it would be no exaggeration to say that it was in San Francisco in the spring of 1945 that Jack's political career actively began. Certainly it was now, at last, that he openly declared to friends such as Spalding his intention to run for political office. "Charlie, I've made up my mind—I'm going into politics," he announced to a startled Spalding one day in San Francisco—and was himself startled by Spalding's enthusiastic response.

"Geez, Jack, that's terrific! You can go *all the way!*"

"Really?" Jack countered.

"*All the way!*" Spalding repeated.

For Jack, the support and backing of his father was one thing; the support of his close friends another. That Chuck Spalding hadn't mocked him but had applauded his announcement was to be something the narcissistic, reckless, still girl-crazed Boston-Irish boy would never forget. It would also be the basis for Jack's "brain trust" of close friends the following year: not because such friends had the remotest political experience or insight, but because they would be a vital counterbalance to his overcontrolling, in some ways dementedly ambitious father.

Spalding's enthusiastic espousal of Jack's newly declared political career was, moreover, spontaneous and clearly genuine. "It was a very beautiful relationship between Jack and Chuck," Pat Lannan would later confide. "I think it was the most beautiful relationship of all the relationships Jack ever had." Over the years, most of Jack's intimate friends would profit by their friendship in one way or another, receiving government posts or ambassadorships. "I'm sure Jack would have done anything in the world for Chuck," Lannan remarked, "except that Chuck didn't want anything. A guy like Kennedy was very lucky to have people like that around him."

In Spalding's view, Jack's declaration finally removed the debris of all that had stood in his path:

> In the long run, he'd have had to go into politics, to help his brother. Now his brother's death really cleared the way. I didn't like his brother, he was, in my opinion, not a lovable figure—he was overbearing. Some of Joe Jr.'s friends, like his Californian friend Tom Killefer, thought he was a god; I thought he was all over himself. Totally without humor, totally different from Jack. And without him, the path was clear for Jack.
>
> Jack hadn't got Joe's priceless asset, his good health. Jack's health was awful. But by guts and determination he'd kept up with Joe. When Joe got accepted into the navy air program, Jack had got himself accepted. It wouldn't have been in character for Jack to have missed the war—he wasn't the kind of guy that would have wanted to live and have to show you a medical piece of paper. He'd much rather get around the medical piece of paper and get into the war—which he did. Basically he must have thought how idiotic it was, given his health. But on the other hand he must have had in the back

of his mind, if Joe can do it, so can I—I'm sure he never said so, but he must have felt he was Joe's match by this time.

With Joe Jr. out of the game, it suddenly seemed utterly logical to Spalding that Jack should take his place.

> Jack didn't really have any alternatives. The old man had repeated and repeated that the great thing was public service. Joe's death cleared the way. Jack had been having a tough time going from day to day, in terms of his health. It made him restless, impatient—it gave him this quality, this impatience that he passed on to others, which made everybody around him feel quicker. And by April 1945 he'd finished his book about his dead brother. There'd been no body to bury, no grave. Now, with Jack's book, there was at least a memorial—a really beautiful, thoughtful, loving memorial. He laid his brother to rest, literally. And the rest was academic—he didn't have any time to think about it. "Joe's gone; the old man's got the dream."

As Spalding put it, Jack was not "the blueprint the old man would have taken to be president of the United States—'I mean, if you're gonna have to have a kid who's going to have to take over for Joe, why do we have to have one that's sick!' When he says sick, he means that he isn't strong enough: 'He can't do it, he's just too fragile!'—that's the way he talked about Jack. '*Why don't you get yourself a live one?*' was the old man's question to Jack's girlfriend one night as we were going out to dinner in Palm Beach. Now that was meant to be funny—but that's the most terrible thing to say! Inspired, I suppose, by bitterness that young Joe wasn't around to take up the mantle."

After his long, grieving incarceration, however, the ex-ambassador had swallowed his bitterness and was a hundred percent behind Jack; indeed of this period in her husband's odious life, Rose Kennedy would later remark that Jack "was still pretty unsure at that time whether politics was the right thing for him to do, but his father had enough enthusiasm for the two of them."

Spalding disagreed about Jack's uncertainty, though he did not quarrel with Rose's comment about the ex-ambassador. To Spalding and his new wife, Betty Coxe, who honeymooned with him in San Francisco (and who had herself known the Kennedys, through Kick, since 1936), Rose Kennedy was a cold, unmotherly, and distant woman whose main contribution to Jack's character was his strangely split psyche, leaving him emotionally crippled in his relations with women; a young man who disliked people embracing him, who showered compulsively—often five times a day—and yet perpetually craved the most symbolic and intimate of all touching: sexual union.

As Spalding later reflected, Jack

> hated physical touching—people taking physical liberties with him—which I assume must go back to his mother and the fact that she was so cold, so distant from the whole thing.
>
> Touch! Mrs. Kennedy—she just didn't have the time, you rarely saw her. Maybe the other Kennedy kids would say the same thing. She never touched me, either. I never saw her with her arms up, outstretched. I never saw her in any easy, sophisticated position—by sophisticated I mean a woman who knew that her son needs some fondling and so she rumples his hair or something like that. That is not Mrs. Kennedy. I doubt if she ever rumpled the kid's hair in his whole life. . . . It just didn't exist: the business of letting your son know you're close, that she's there. She wasn't. She was with eight other kids and one of them retarded, and that husband—she just had problems enough herself if she was going to stay afloat.

Whereaver the blame lay, Jack's lifelong need not simply to flirt with women but compulsively to lie with them—obsessively, maniacally, to the point of sexual addiction—would owe much to his twin obsessions: sexual revenge against his mother and, quite simply, the need for a quality of physical touching denied him from infancy.

"What *is* touch?" Spalding reflected. "It must come from some deeper maternal security—arms, warmth, kisses, hugs. . . . Maybe sex is the closest prize there is, that holds the whole thing together. I mean if you have sex with anybody you care about at all, you feel you've been touched, it seems to me, if there's anything successful."

Jack's dramatic career as a Don Juan, so fitfully started in his student years, was now about to take off in tandem with his political career. The two did not seem, at the time, inconsistent to Spalding, since both were characterized by Jack's impatience: indeed in some respects it might be said that Jack would make as poor a lover as he did a traditional politician: in both he was unwilling take trouble, flatter, swoon, or deepen his understanding.

In the meantime, to become a politician, he had to be elected, and while waiting for James Michael Curley to move over, Jack now had a unique opportunity to observe international politics at its very highest level. Though he'd conscientiously read the literature his grandfather and his father had sent him, he was in truth unexcited by labor relations and the local economic outlook for Massachusetts. What inspired his curiosity was the dynamics of the larger postwar world: and it was on the stage of

San Francisco in April and May 1945 that Jack was treated to a ringside view of the new world order taking shape, an experience that would color his thinking, his perceptions, and his political ambitions for the rest of his days.

The San Francisco Conference

Whereas the League of Nations had been castrated at birth by America's decision not to join, the boot was now on the other foot. America was the sponsor of the United Nations, and it was another major power, the Soviet Union, that was dragging its heels and threatening to boycott the proceedings. Chip Bohlen, a special assistant to the U.S. secretary of state, recorded in his notes how President Truman was adamant in his intent "to go on with the plans for San Francisco and if the Russians did not wish to join us they could go to hell."

In the end Stalin sent two ruthless lackeys, Molotov and Gromyko, to represent him. Meanwhile President Truman, although appointing ex-senator Jimmy Byrnes to take over the State Department after the conference, kept Edward Stettinius, Roosevelt's ineffectual secretary of state, as America's senior representative. As James Reston, *The New York Time*'s correspondent at the conference, wrote privately to his bureau chief, Arthur Krock, in Washington, Stettinius was hopeless. "I don't believe he [Stettinius] has been able to overcome his lack of knowledge or experience in the foreign field. I do not believe he has acquired the admiration or in some cases even the respect of his own unofficial family or of the men at his own level who lead the other delegations." Not only was Stettinius "overwhelmed by the rudeness and directness of Molotov," and let meetings with the Russians get out of hand "with the result that both he and the United States were embarrassed," as Reston confided, but even in small meetings with Anthony Eden, the British government's chief delegate, Stettinius could not hold his own. "Even in a small man-to-man meeting such as this, the Secretary did not feel qualified to express the American policy without constantly taking out a small card on which was written only a couple of sentences and referring to this every time he undertook to discuss the question."

Nevertheless, it had been Stettinius's original idea to hold the conference in San Francisco. Remembering the demise of American participation in the League of Nations at the hands of Henry Cabot Lodge and other Republican senators in 1920, the State Department had recommended, moreover, that the San Francisco team be a bipartisan one—two senators and two congressmen from both parties, as well as a prominent Republican from the Midwest and a woman, collectively representing the United States. It was this team—particularly the Minnesota ex-governor Harold Stassen—that became openly contemptuous of its own secretary of state's performance.

Jack Kennedy, by contrast, was immensely sure of himself now—indeed he was in his element. "I saw much of him in the off-hours devoted to social activities," Arthur Krock later recalled.

> But I shall always regret that I was not one of those in his bedroom at the Palace Hotel one evening, where according to a friend . . . Jack, dressed for a black-tie evening, with the exception of his pumps and evening coat, was lying on the bed, propped up by three pillows, a highball in one hand and the telephone receiver in the other. To the operator he said, "I want to speak to the Managing Editor of the Chicago *Herald American.*" (After a long pause:) "Not in? Well, put someone on to take a message." Another pause. "Good. Will you see that the boss gets this message as soon as you can reach him? Thank you. Here's the message: 'Kennedy will not be filing tonight.' "
>
> I think it was this same evening I saw him cutting in on Anthony Eden, who was dancing with the beautiful lady who became the Viscountess Harcourt—and getting promptly cut in on again by Eden himself.

Red Fay, who had managed to get posted to San Francisco from Florida to help Jack "give the serviceman's view," remembered Jack meeting on equal social terms not only Eden, but Chip Bohlen and Averell Harriman, the U.S. ambassador to Moscow. "We had dinner together—Bohlen, Anthony, Jack, and I, and we went up to Jack's suite after dinner, and were deep in conversation. The next thing, Averell Harriman's got a girl out on an enclosed balcony. It was kind of dark out there and Jack was hardly listening to what Bohlen and the rest of them were talking about. He was more concerned about the girl that he had brought up there that Harriman had taken out on the veranda!"

According to Fay, Jack was not worried about Harriman as a romantic rival—"Jack just thought that Harriman didn't have enough charm"—but *was* worried by Harriman's superior status. As the grandson of a Boston-Irish barkeeper, the matter of social status had always spurred Jack. In Los Angeles, Chuck Spalding recalled, Jack had been nonplussed by the way Olivia de Havilland declined his dinner invitation, yet was found dining later with the writer and artist Ludwig Bemelmans. "I just can't understand it! Just look at that guy! I know he's talented, I know he's got great ability, but *really*!" he had remarked in disgust. Then he asked anxiously, "Do you think it was my walking into the closet? Do you think that's what really did it?"

At San Francisco Jack now learned a new lesson: namely, that while women in New England might be interested in a man's ethnic standing, and while women in Hollywood might be attracted by artistic genius, women on the coterie of politics were drawn to political power. However dashing a figure he might cut in his evening clothes, he was in San Francisco a mere journalist-observer. The spotlight was on the players, reinforcing Jack's determination to become one of them.

Whether Jack was aware he was "cutting in" on a future prime minister of Great Britain is unknown, but the truth was, at San Francisco, he was consorting and cavorting with political figures with whom, at a later date, he would become very much involved. Chip Bohlen had been the primary liaison man between the State Department and the White House, as well as American interpreter in the Russian language at Yalta; he would one day become Jack's primary adviser on the Soviet Union. Averell Harriman, too, would become a key figure in Jack's administration, as roving ambassador, a sort of Harry Hopkins. There were many others too, the most important of whom, in terms of Jack's career, was Bohlen's colleague and special assistant to the secretary of state: Adlai E. Stevenson.

Stevenson, a warmhearted liberal of limitless talent and prolific vocabulary, would become the guru and conscience of the Democratic party in the 1950s, as well as its presidential contender during its years in the Republican wilderness. Meanwhile at San Francisco it was Stevenson who, at the prompting of Arthur Krock, set up Operation *Titanic,* a quasi-official daily news leak to ensure that—given the inability of the U.S. bipartisan delegation to agree to a daily communiqué—American newsmen would get the emerging United Nations story from their own rather than from British and even Soviet delegations. "It was all a little ridiculous," Stevenson later recalled, "me interpreting developments play by play in a secret room at the Fairmount Hotel, whose number was known to not less than 50–75 U.S. correspondents."

By this method, however, Jack became well acquainted with not only Stevenson's virtues as a sub-rosa spokesman, but his vices too, for Stevenson's strengths were also his weaknesses. Stevenson reveled in flattery and adulation, and was a better servant than master. He'd been assistant to the secretary of the Navy, Frank Knox, for three years from 1941 to 1944, until Knox suffered a heart attack and died. Knox's successor, James Forrestal, disliked Stevenson, whom he considered "too diffuse" to be made assistant secretary of the Navy. Stevenson was dismissed, and although he was too brilliant a civil servant not to be quickly reemployed by the administration, Forrestal's label had stuck.

If his character lacked resolution, Stevenson did not lack heart or intelligence. His summary of the proceedings of the San Francisco conference to the American Bar Association in Chicago would become the most masterful of its kind; lauding the conference's success, in the midst of a world war, in establishing a lasting U.N. charter, protocol, and framework for international discussion and settlement of problems among nations. What it did *not* do was accurately reflect the darkness that had fallen upon prospects for the postwar world.

Stevenson's problem was that he was too close to the daily business of the conference to see clearly what was happening. From Eden, Harriman, and Bohlen—all of whom had attended Stalin's Yalta summit—Jack Kennedy obtained a remarkably intimate picture of the Soviet menace that would bedevil international relations for the rest of his lifetime. Shortly after Yalta, Joseph Goebbels had written a perceptive article, quoted in the London *Times,* containing a most pregnant phrase: "If the Germans lay down their arms, the whole of eastern and south-eastern Europe, together with the Reich, would come under Russian occupation. Behind an iron curtain," wrote the master of mass butchery, "mass butchering of people would begin, and all that would remain would be a crude automaton, a dull fermenting mass of millions of proletarian and despairing slave animals knowing nothing of the outside world."

Goebbels's warning was prophetic. Soon after, on May 12, 1945, Churchill sent Truman his famous telegram, cribbing the Nazi minister of propaganda's remark—"An iron curtain is drawn down upon their front," Churchill warned the president about Russian behavior in eastern Europe. "We do not know what is going on behind."

At San Francisco, Anthony Eden, Averell Harriman, and Chip Bohlen meanwhile saw exactly what was going on, and while sentimentally pro-Russian journalists such as Walter Lippmann were "outraged" by Harriman's warning about Soviet intentions and walked out of his specially convened briefing of correspondents, Jack Kennedy remained sanguine.

Another Versailles

Beneath his picture, byline, and bio ("a PT-boat hero of the South Pacific and son of former Ambassador, Joseph P. Kennedy"), Jack Kennedy's first *Herald American* dispatch opened on April 28, 1945, with a timely warning:

There is an impression that this is the conference to end wars and introduce peace on earth and good-will towards nations—excluding of course, Germany and Japan.

Well, it's not going to do that.

The best that can be hoped for is some changes in the voting procedure of the security council as set up at Dumbarton Oaks and that the Russians can be persuaded to make some compromises on their stiff-necked attitude toward the Polish question. If we can gain those two points, we shall be doing well. And the old hands out here know this.

There is only one delegation that can make big news at the conference and that's the Soviet and they don't talk—never to the press and seldom to each other.

Vyacheslav Molotov deviated from the party line of strict silence for a few minutes at a press conference Thursday but he was singularly uninformative.

It was all handled so smoothly and smilingly though that no one realized until they read transcripts of the conference afterwards how uninformative an uninformative Russian can be.

Molotov's apparent readiness to pick a fight over the comparatively small question of who was to be permanent chairman of the Security Conference—job ordinarily given to the foreign minister of the host nation—was the tip-off that the Russians are going to make a fight on all of the little issues in the hope they can write their own terms on the big ones.

The average GI in the street, and the streets of San Francisco are crowded with them, doesn't seem to have a very clear-cut conception of what this meeting is about. But one bemedaled marine sergeant gave the general reaction when he said: "I don't know much about what's going on—but if they just fix it so that we don't have to fight any more—they can count me in."

Me, too, sarge.

It was the underlying note of realism running through Jack's piece that marked the twenty-seven-year-old as a journalist of uncommon sense. Day after day he wrote not what the public wanted to hear, but used what the public hoped to hear as the litmus test of his own maturing perception, and his pieces were soon widely used in Hearst's other newspapers, from the New York *Journal American* to the Philadelphia *Examiner*. He even quoted on April 30 an aphorism he'd heard from Anthony Eden:

Winston Churchill once said that Russian policy was an enigma wrapped in a mystery.

I'd like to report to Mr. Churchill that the Russians haven't changed.

From the moment that Mr. Molotov hit San Francisco the Russian policy has mystified even the most experienced of the delegates. The most current explanation now given is that the Russians have an "Oriental" mind and therefore of necessity cannot be understood.

Unfortunately that cannot be accepted as the complete explanation as there are several other delegations here that can lay claim to being even more Oriental than the Russians—notably the Chinese— who have followed perfectly understandable patterns.

Let's look at the Russian demands so far. At the opening executive session they battled over the routine question of who was to be chairman—a job which ordinarily would have gone without question to Stettinius. They won that fight.

The next day, even though Molotov had won a very important point by gaining acceptance of the Ukrainian and White Russian delegations, he also requested that a delegation from the Lublin [Polish Communist] government as it is now constituted be seated.

Now he must have known that he was headed for certain defeat on this demand for he had admitted at his press conference the previous day that no changes had been made in the Lublin government along the lines agreed upon at Yalta.

Why then did he attempt to seat the delegation?

Jack's question went to the heart of what would become the postwar Soviet terror in Eastern Europe. Bohlen years later described how astonished the Belgian foreign minister was "that the Soviet Foreign Minister at that stage of world history should introduce into the middle of the formative conference probably the most delicate—'brûlante' was his term—question on the international scene, particularly after the concession to the Soviet Union on White Russia and the Ukraine." Senator Vandenberg, the senior Republican on the American delegation, was equally astonished by the Russian move—the more so when Jan Masaryk, representing the government of Czechoslovakia, "read a statement" supporting Molotov's Polish proposal.

"This was *serious*," Vandenberg noted afterward.

If any such action had been taken it would have wrecked *any* chance of American approval of the work of the Conference. . . . I was sitting directly behind Stettinius. I told him *this* move *must* be *killed* at once and in the open. I sketched out a quick, brief statement and handed it to Stettinius reading as follows: "I remind the Conference that we have just honored our Yalta agreement in behalf of Russia.

I also remind the Conference that there are other Yalta obligations which equally require allegiance. One of them calls for a new and representative Polish Provisional Government. Until this happens, this Conference cannot, in good conscience, recognize the Lublin Government. It would be an exhibition of bad faith." To Stettinius's credit *he never hesitated an instant.* He took the floor and read exactly what I had written—and with great emphasis. Molotov showed surprise. Eden promptly seconded Stettinius.

Bohlen recalled that later that day he saw Jan Masaryk "drinking a whiskey and soda" at the bar of the Fairmount Hotel. "Bohlen," Masaryk asked, "What can one do with these Russians? Out of the clear blue sky I got a note from Molotov saying Czechoslovakia must vote for the Soviet proposition in regard to Poland, or else forfeit the friendship of the Soviet government. . . . You can be on your knees and that is not enough for the Russians."

Masaryk, as foreign minister of Czechoslovakia, would later be murdered—or driven to "suicide"—for refusing to go on kowtowing to Moscow. Those idealists who were predisposed to see the Soviets as the martyrs of Europe, however, accepted Molotov's insistence on bringing Poland into the initial U.N. as perfectly understandable, particularly in view of South American pressure to accept Argentina, which had done nothing to halt or hinder German aggression and had only declared war on Germany a few days before the opening of the conference.

Jack Kennedy's lack of sentimentality, as well as his contacts with Eden, Harriman, Bohlen, Krock, and others, permitted him to view the proceedings with unrelenting clarity. "There are three possible explanations for the Russian attitude in addition to that one about their Oriental mind," he summarized on April 30.

> The first is that while Stettinius and Eden have full freedom of action—Molotov undoubtedly has to get the word from the Kremlin.
>
> Secondly, Molotov probably comes to this conference with a series of proposals worked out before and with Oriental singlemindedness—there they now have me saying it—they are trying to bull them through without much regard to existing conditions.
>
> Lastly and most important there is the heritage of 25 years of distrust between Russia and the rest of the world that cannot be overcome completely for a good many years. . . . This week at San Francisco will be the decisive one in Russian-American affairs. It will be the real test of whether the Russians and the Americans can get along. So far, they seem to be doing better on the Elbe.

This was no less than the truth. American officers and troops in Germany respected their Soviet counterparts; Stalin feared them. Behind the brave march of the Soviet armies, rigid Communist-party control was imposed, decorated officers such as Solzhenitsyn were summarily arrested, and over the ensuing years millions were "eliminated" in camps and gulags. Even Gromyko, the most loyal of Stalin's henchmen at San Francisco, would later confess that "beside his [Stalin's] mass of crimes, the worst evils of Russia's past autocrats and their henchmen pale into insignificance. The snake of Stalinism slowly stifled its victims, using the most cunning ploys and attacking with equal lack of mercy the worthy Representatives of the Bolshevik Old Guard and the ordinary Soviet citizens, workers, peasants, intellectuals, communists and non-party people—No wonder those who survived are still angry." At the time of the San Francisco conference, however, Gromyko was an unmitigated Stalinist lackey. "Poor Gromyko can't spit without permission from Moscow," Stevenson wrote to his wife.

Jack's foreboding grew stronger each day, though he maintained a tone of engaging familiarity and wit that went well with the smiling, honest countenance in the accompanying newspaper photograph. "This conference from a distance may have appeared so far like an international football game with Molotov carrying the ball while Stettinius, Eden, and the delegates tried to tackle him all over the field," he began his dispatch of May 1, 1945. "Well, that part's over—at least temporarily—and they are scheduled tomorrow to get at the real work of the conference."

Three days later, however, he was reporting that although the "stormy sessions of the first week have done much to clear the air," the resultant picture was a frightening one, showing "the tremendous differences between the viewpoints of Russia on the one hand and the U.S. and Great Britain on the other. The extent of these differences has come as a shock to many people who had been lulled into a feeling that all was well by the reports of complete agreement that came out of the conferences at Teheran and Yalta. There, any signs of dissension were carefully concealed on the theory they would give aid and comfort to the enemy. That time is over," Jack warned. The United Nations organization would, Jack predicted, be "merely a skeleton. Its powers will be limited. It will reflect the fact that there are deep disagreements among its members. . . . It is unfortunate that more cannot be accomplished here. It is unfortunate that unity for war against a common aggressor is far easier to obtain than unity for peace. We are commencing to realize how difficult and long the road is ahead. San Francisco is only the beginning."

Jack was the first to recognize that his proposed article on postwar disarmament was now redundant. The editor of the *Atlantic Monthly* had written that, despite the priority of first "subduing Germany and Japan" and the "feeding and refinancing of a hungry and broken world . . . disarmament as an objective has never really been out of our thoughts." Where he and his staff had originally dismissed Jack's article on disarmament as a topic of only preconference concern, Weeks now felt that "if you will speak out this summer as I should like you to do in the *Atlantic,* you will still be far in the van," for, he predicted, the "desirability of freeing ourselves from the slavery and suspicion of armament will spread throughout the country." Moreover, "remembering your service record and reading the idealism which shows here between the lines," Weeks remarked of Jack's draft, "people will respect your words."

Jack's idealism remained the same, but his experience at San Francisco had changed his tune. Idealistically he might deplore the continuation of vast military budgets in the postwar world, but realism dictated that unilateral American disarmament, in the face of Soviet intransigence, would quickly lead to another Munich. Each Hearst dispatch mentioned that he was the author of the bestselling *Why England Slept.* Five years had now passed since the book's publication. The democracies of the West, having awakened too late to the menace of Germany and Japan, must henceforth stay awake.

"I have delayed answering," Jack finally replied to the *Atlantic Monthly*'s editor, "as I wanted to see for myself whether there was any possibility that a world security organization strong enough to permit comprehensive world disarmament would come out of San Francisco. Frankly, and though the Conference is only in its first week, it appears as though there will not be. The Russians have demonstrated that they believe that a country's voice in the conference should be heard only in direct ratio to its military power—and it hardly seems feasible to advocate disarmament under that condition. Furthermore they have demonstrated a suspicion and lack of faith in Britain and the United States which, while understandable in the light of recent history, nevertheless indicates that in the next few years it will be prudent to be strong. I am naturally disappointed in this," he lamented to Mr. Weeks, "as I haven't changed my views that disarmament is an essential part of any lasting peace."

In another disheartening dispatch from San Francisco, Jack coined a new adage: "Diplomacy might be said to be the art of who gets what and how as applied to international affairs." On May 7, Victory in Europe Day, he finally felt compelled to articulate the servicemen's view of the conference.

It is natural that they should be most concerned for its result, because any man who has risked his life for his country and seen his friends killed around him must inevitably wonder why this has happened to him and most important, what good will it all do. In their concern, and as a result of their interest, and because they wish above all else to spare their children and their brothers from going through the same hard times, it is perhaps natural that they would be disappointed with what they have seen in San Francisco. I suppose that this is inevitable. Youth is a time for direct action and simplification. To come from battlefields where sacrifice is the order of the day—to come from there to here—it is not surprising that they should question the worth of their sacrifice and feel somewhat betrayed.

The same thing, Jack pointed out, had happened after World War I, and viewing the internecine squabbling, he came to the doleful conclusion that for all the loss of life and noble aspirations, "the world organization that will come out of San Francisco will be the product of the same passions and selfishness that produced the treaty of Versailles."

An Iron Curtain

Behind the procedural, technical, and linguistic squabbles, as well as the disputes over trusteeships and arguments over transcripts, the underlying question at San Francisco was what the Russians really wanted. "There is growing discouragement among people concerning our chances of winning any lasting peace from this war. There is talk of fighting the Russians in the next ten or fifteen years. We have indeed gone a long way since those hopeful days early in the war," Jack summarized on May 18. "What these disagreements have demonstrated clearly is that there is a fundamental distrust between Great Britain and the United States on the one hand, and Russia on the other. It is this distrust—which is becoming deeper—that is causing grave concern and considerable discouragement.

"Where then, is the hope? Will there not be years of distrust and suspicion finally exploding in the awful climax of war?"

On May 19 Jack warned that

unless the Big Three can get along, all the legal devices and provisions of the world charter being drawn up in San Francisco will be useless. . . . Our preoccupation with the war, and our desire to remain on good terms with our Red allies, have prevented us from taking a strong stand against Russian infiltration through Europe. . . . Up until now Russia, because of her territorial proximity, has played a lone hand in the small countries of Eastern Europe, and has pushed her advantage hard. She has moved so fast and has hit us so often "where we ain't" that she has formed those countries into a strong Soviet bloc. In Poland, Rumania, Austria, Bulgaria, Estonia, Latvia, and Lithuania she has met us with a fait accomplis [*sic*]. . . . She has ignored continually military commissions of Americans and British that have succeeded in penetrating into any of the countries she has occupied. She has continually neglected to answer our notes.

She has done all of these things, it has been argued, because she wants peace and security, and must make safe her western defenses.

This was an argument with which Jack had sympathy but no truck. "This argument may be sincere—but it does not justify her apparent decision to get that peace and security on her own terms," he pointed out. "Her tactics in Poland illustrate her technique. A year ago the big question was whether Russia would succeed in her claim to all Polish territory east of the Curzon line. That question was settled in Russia's favor a short time ago with scarcely a ripple. Today we are worrying . . . whether the Russians will allow Americans in Berlin. . . . Those who favor a showdown with the Russians feel this is the time for an accounting. Unless some agreement is reached," he remarked presciently, "our relations with Russia will rapidly worsen. The political battle will go on in Europe and will be continued in Asia at the end of the war with Japan."

It was clear to any astute observer that John F. Kennedy was far more involved in the ramifications of the conference that he was reporting "from a GI viewpoint" than the average GI—or indeed the average journalist. Though Arthur Krock and others were impressed by Jack's journalistic aptitude and thus supposed he might now choose the pen after the sword, Jack's closer confidants could see the outlines of a committed politician emerging from the chrysalis. "Although at that time Jack shammed indifference to his friends to the whole idea of a political career, there was an underlying determination to get started on what he considered a very serious obligation," Red Fay described Jack's earlier diffidence. Now, at last, he was starting.

"Jack was out there reporting for the Hearst papers and we saw him every day for about six weeks," Betty Spalding recalled, for Jack had managed to get Chuck and Betty a room at the Palace Hotel. "We'd just have dinner with him, really. He was doing his work and he would get us into some of the meetings. There was a lot of talk about Cord Meyer, who was a young political hopeful at that time—an aide to Senator Stassen. He was married to Mary Pinchot at that time, so Cord and Mary, Chuck and I, and Jack and his girlfriend would spend time together."

Mary Meyer would reappear in Jack's life years later, shortly before his—and her own—death. In the meantime, in San Francisco, Chuck Spalding was fascinated by the difference between Meyer and Jack, both of whom had lost brothers in the war. "Cord Meyer did come back from the war with the loss of an eye and the loss of a brother in a similar respect to Jack and was so affected by it," Spalding considered. "But Kennedy was never affected like that. He was never pushed off this hard, sensible center of his being. . . . I think he was beginning to get a kind of picture of himself. And he had gotten behind him something, in a brilliant way, something that he didn't care much about, that was the military. He couldn't have done it any better. So that was out of the way. I think he enjoyed writing a great deal, and I think the picture of a public figure interested and capable in this area added to the dim outline of a successful politician."

Neither Chuck nor Betty Spalding believed that Jack intended to pursue journalism other than as a subsidiary string to his political bow. "I didn't think of Jack as a serious newspaperman," Betty recalled. "I thought of him as a very bright fellow and very rich and looking around for something he really wanted to do." Chuck, however, having seen Jack with John Hersey and a number of writers over the years, was aware of the inherent importance of writing to Jack's self-image. He reflected perceptively:

> So many of his friends were writers and he was interested so much in what was being written that he was incorporating that into his make-up. Either wittingly or unwittingly, he began to write as a politician. Even though it was a thesis, he had been to England and he had seen firsthand why England slept. That was the form that all his writing took, a kind of reportage. There wasn't any necessity to worry about his development as an artist the way maybe Thomas Wolfe or Scott Fitzgerald or Hemingway would. He wasn't concerned with that problem. He never got to it because he never wrote in that vein. . . . He just automatically thought of writing in terms of current events and that didn't require any attention to those other problems. He wasn't by nature given to that kind of prolonged introspection.

Through all of this, Jack's poor health continued to plague him. "He had the bad back at the time, he was wearing the brace . . . he didn't look really robust," Betty Spalding recalled. "He was kind of recovering. He wasn't his usual joyful self—he was funny as usual, but he spent a lot of time in bed. We used to go in and talk to him in the morning before he got out of bed. He was his usual wry kind of humorous self, but not full of energy, not jumping around."

On May 24, 1945, Jack learned that Congressman James Michael Curley had taken out nomination papers to stand in the forthcoming November election for the mayoralty of Boston. "Last night he delivered his opening campaign speech over the radio, reviewing his municipal admin- istration and outlining his plans for Boston," one Boston paper re- corded—failing of course to reveal or comment on the strange fact that Curley's campaign was in part being financed by Joseph P. Kennedy and assisted by Kennedy's crony, ex-police commissioner Joe Timilty.

Jack, however, still had no plans for Boston. His eyes were on Europe now, and with the same strange fatefulness that had seen Jack traveling in Europe on the outbreak of war in 1939, involved in naval intelligence in Washington at the time of Pearl Harbor, fighting in the Solomon Islands after Guadalcanal, and reporting in San Francisco on the birth of the United Nations, he now received a summons from Hearst Newspa- pers' head office to fly to England.

Following Churchill Around

Churchill, against the advice of many advisers, had decided to hold a general election before the subjugation of Japan. "The British Labor Party is out for blood," Jack warned in his final San Francisco dispatch. "They are going all the way: Public ownership of the Bank of England, Government control of rents and prices, gradual Government ownership of mines, transportation, planned farming—the works. . . . While every- one knows Churchill's strengths, they are not sure that he can buck the recent strong surge to the left."

This was prescient reporting. "Everyone evidently thinks you're doing a simply fine job out there," Jack's brother Bobby wrote from Cape Cod, "except Mother who was a little upset that you still mixed 'who' + 'whom' up. Get on to yourself."

Amused by Bobby's wry humor, Jack now visited his father in Hyannis Port, en route to England. *As We Remember Joe* had finally come off the press in a privately printed edition of 360 copies, each packed in a special maroon box.

Two hundred fifty copies were sent to relatives, service colleagues, teachers, friends, and girlfriends. All were enchanted. "Your book 'As we remember Joe' is one of the loveliest memorials to a devoted brother, by a devoted brother, I have ever read," Mrs. Louise MacColl wrote from Wianno, Cape Cod, recalling the sailing-club dances in the 1930s when "I saw you and Joe come into the Ball Room—look around at the group there—go and 'cut-in' on your sisters, before dancing with any of the other girls." The headmaster of Choate School, George St. John, congratulated Jack on a "real tribute, a tribute with breadth of appeal, showing the many facets of Joe's personality." Even Lem Billings was surprised at the level of affection the book conveyed. "When two brothers are growing up and they are two years apart you aren't aware of a great love between them, but Jack's editing of Joe's memorial book was a real work of love."

No amount of memorials, however, could bring Joe Jr. back, as Jack's father fully realized. If he was never able to finish reading the book, as he once confided, it was not simply because he could not bear to "read about that boy without it affecting me more than I ever thought anything could affect me in this life," but because he'd now made his compact with Jack and could think only of that. To Kathleen, for example, the ex-ambassador claimed he was seriously considering asking Truman for a job—not for himself, but for Jack. "If he's going to give me a job, I'd rather have him give it to Jack and maybe make him minister to some country or Assistant Secretary of State or Assistant Secretary of the Navy," he wrote, touchingly oblivious to the unlikeliness of the president appointing a twenty-eight-year-old to such senior positions. Meanwhile he arranged for Jack to give a short address in Boston on the subject of the San Francisco conference. "Lt. John F. Kennedy, son of Joseph P. Kennedy, former Ambassador to England, was introduced in the Massachusetts House yesterday," *The Boston Globe* reported on June 12, "and expressed disappointment about the progress of the San Francisco conference. He added, however, that it was 'the best we can get, and deserves the support we can give.' "

Joseph Kennedy was delighted; indeed, according to the family chronicler, his "heart swelled with a pride that he had not thought he could ever feel again."

Joseph Kennedy, however, was not the only one with his eye on Jack's future. James Forrestal, secretary of the Navy, was now considering the reorganization of the Navy Department in Washington. In his diary Forrestal quoted a passage from a letter sent by Admiral Halsey to the chairman of the Congressional Committee on Postwar Military Policy: "We need men who understand the causes of war and conflict, who understand the fundamentals of our aims and ideals, who understand the interrelation of international policies. . . . We must find and train such men—outstanding civilians who have served their country under arms. . . . If we *don't* find and train and employ such men in the service of the United States, we will lose our shirts as we have in the past—and then what avails the sacrifice of life, blood and treasure that we have made?"

In Forrestal's eyes, Jack Kennedy was just such a young man, and meeting Jack in Washington, he "offered him a responsible position in the Navy department," once Jack returned from Europe. "If it's open when he returns the latter part of July, I'm sure he would like to take it," the ex-ambassador wrote to a naval acquaintance, Vice-Admiral Wilson.

A "responsible" post in the Navy Department, however, held limited appeal for Jack. Not only was he reluctant to become a bureaucrat, but his real interest was international relations and politics, not naval strategy or administration. Leaving Forrestal in Washington, Jack flew straight to England to begin covering the British election. It was in the English capital that his Arizona companion, Pat Lannan, finally caught up with him.

"Count me in on the English deal, kid," Lannan had written excitedly to Jack on May 31, having secured a European radio-reporting assignment. "We arrived within a few days of each other," he later recounted. "I knew the head of the London bureau of the *Chicago Tribune* and he got us into the Grosvenor House hotel, because it wasn't easy to get accommodations in London at that time." Their first visitor, Lannan remembered, was Jack's sister. Kathleen had already warned Jack by letter of "the terrific swing to the left" in Britain and had assured him she had "a few girls lined up for you here," including Baby Cárcano, who was "still keen on you."

To Lannan, Kathleen seemed to be an anglicized female version of Jack.

> She was a very industrious, animated young woman, and very by that time sort of English, or British, oriented. I felt that she had really melded herself into the city of London and England, as though it were her adopted home—that was my very distinct impression. . . . Whereas I felt that Jack was an outsider, he was an American visiting there, as I was an American visiting there—but I never felt that way about Kick.

The British election campaign was already in full swing. Without wasting any time, Kathleen launched the two horsemen in her car, an Austin 7—"a little, small, G-D thing," Lannan described. "When the two of us got in it we were filled. I remember it ran like hell—the windshield wipers didn't work and a lot of things like that, but we were grateful to have it because in following Churchill around, he was delivering speeches at racetracks, dog tracks and what have you, and usually they were very difficult places to get to."

Would Churchill win? Many thought the aging prime minister should have stood down in this, his finest hour, allowing Eden as a younger leader to take the Conservative helm. Eden, however, had a duodenal ulcer and on doctor's orders rested for the whole of June while Churchill, against doctor's orders, took the brunt of campaigning. Jack was enthralled. "We went for the sheer fun and joy of hearing the man stand this crowd off," Lannan recalled. "They'd boo him and he'd just stand up there and take his time."

Lannan was convinced Churchill would lose, while Jack "damn well thought he was going to win." Lannan recalled:

> Everything I heard, everywhere I went, everything told me something else. I suppose having had to be an analyst all my life, my analysis was the tide was running against Churchill. The English didn't want to make those sacrifices. They figured they had made them, and he was preaching the other thing and they were just booing the hell out of him. In fact I've never heard a politician in America booed like he was.
>
> I couldn't believe my eyes because, believe me, I was the greatest admirer of Churchill. I thought this was such a sensational human being.

Reluctantly, Jack eventually was forced to agree with Lannan's prognosis. "Britishers will go to the polls on July 5th in the first general election in almost ten years and there is a definite possibility that Prime Minister Winston Churchill and his Conservative party may be defeated," Jack acknowledged in his dispatch on June 23, 1945.

> This may come as a surprise to most Americans, who feel Churchill is as indomitable at the polls as he was in war. However Churchill is fighting a tide that is surging through Europe, washing away monarchies and conservative governments everywhere, and that tide flows powerfully in England.
>
> England is moving towards some form of socialism—if not in this election, then surely at the next. What will be the significance for America if Churchill is defeated by the Labor party? Who are its members and what are its policies?

The Labour party was "composed of a hodgepodge of leftwing doctrinaires, trade unionists and simple men with high ideals," Jack answered his own question. What the Labour party stood for, he made clear, was out-and-out socialism: "There is no genuflection to private enterprise that even our most liberal politicians in America feel they must make. Capitalism must go and private enterprise must go. Why are so many people in England willing at the end of a long and savage war to accept the further controls that Socialism will entail?" Jack asked, and again supplied his own answer: namely, the indelible stigma of Tory appeasement before the war and the "treatment of the depression during the 30's. The Conservative government, instead of indulging in a broad program of public spending as we did, tightened the country's belt and advanced its budget with consequent hardship for the people and political unpopularity for themselves."

Before leaving San Francisco, Jack had considered the Conservative party's postwar program as "somewhat similar in philosophy to our New Deal." In England, however, he found a different story. The Conservative-party program was disastrously short of constructive economic or social ideas. In fact Churchill's New Deal amounted to the "firm belief that Socialism cannot work in England." Whether the incoming socialist tide would reach Downing Street at this election or its sequel, only time would tell. "But what one can be sure of," Jack continued, "is that England will carry through in the next few years some economic changes that many people in America and England feel cannot be made without an important limitation on democratic government. By watching England, we still have much to learn."

Jack was certainly speaking for himself. His own area of interest had always been international relations. He had never evinced the remotest interest in domestic issues such as poverty, health programs, conditions in the mines, or a more equitable distribution of wealth. Britain, however, had been under arms since 1939 and its entire population had been involved in the war, its civilians blitzed at home as much as its troops were in battle. There was no easy way back to the complacencies of the prewar class structure, as Kathleen's husband Billy Hartington had found when vainly standing for Parliament in his family's traditional constituency shortly before his death. Churchill's harping on Britain's past, stressing the future only in terms of outdated and unquestioned imperial obligations, thus did little justice to the intense social and political debate going on in England.

Helping Jack to understand this were a group of English friends and acquaintances, the number of which astonished Lannan.

> They were friends that he knew dating back to the years he had lived there with his family. These were friendships that had been established before the war—there was a renewal of these friendships. I'd say that over the period of time we were there, if I had to ask the maid the number of visitors we had, it would have run up to about 24, 25. Oftentimes in this little sitting room which wasn't very large there could be seven or eight of us at one time, and they would all have been his friends. . . . I think Jack was very seriously excited about the election, about what was going to happen in Europe, what sort of Europe was going to emerge from the war. Our talks were

always around—well, I was always speaking about the horrible economic problems, how the hell they were going to ever get Germany going again. I was always approaching politics from economics, and he was always approaching politics from I don't know what the hell standpoint at that time. I don't suppose his ideas were that well formulated then, you know.

Lannan was right. Although Jack was full of curiosity, his immaturity stemmed from his filial dependency, as it would for the virtual remainder of his life. By raising his children to be deliberately ignorant of business or money concerns, Joseph Kennedy had done them a terrible disservice, preserving his own parental hold over them, but weakening their ability to understand or relate to ordinary people.

Alastair Forbes, a distant but penniless English cousin of Franklin Roosevelt, was keenly aware of Jack's ignorance of everyday reality for most people. He'd first met Jack through Kathleen. "We were very great friends and I loved her, and she brought Jack closely into my life at the end of the war," Forbes recalled. "I was then running for Parliament as a Liberal. Jack came up to listen to speeches. That was the first time we really seriously began talking about politics together. What struck me then was that he was more intellectual than any other member of the family. He read more, but nevertheless I don't believe to the day of his death he was what is normally described as an intellectual. He had a fantastically good instinct, once his attention was aroused in a problem, for getting the gist of it and coming to a mature judgment about it."

Such disinterest made Forbes think of Churchill. "He had a detachment which reminded me very much of Winston Churchill in the sense that his life had been protected by money. Money was a great insulator. If you don't sort of make your bed and get your own breakfast and have a certain amount of conversation with people who are doing all sorts of ordinary, simple jobs, it does rob you a great deal of empathy. I mean, whole areas in which empathy should naturally play a part are closed to you."

There were other similarities between young Kennedy and Churchill, not the least of which was Jack's reportorial quest, which demonstrated something of the same animation that had driven the young Winston Churchill in earlier years as a newspaper correspondent, after his combat experience on the North-West Frontier, in the Sudan, and in the Boer War, before he stood for Parliament.

Witnessing Churchill's uphill struggle in the summer of 1945, at the very apogee of his political career, however, taught Jack an important lesson. What had been almost unimaginable while in America—that Churchill and his Conservative government should fall at the general election—had become all too understandable once he witnessed war-torn, bankrupt Britain and, at last, the plight of ordinary people.

Several other friends were standing for Parliament. "The first time I really got to know Jack was after the war," Hugh Fraser recollected. "It was when he came over as a journalist and he came and watched my election in Stafford and Stone. He came up for two days. . . . It was my first shot at politics, and I must have been pretty peculiar. Certainly Jack thought I was very peculiar! He was always a great questioner. He always asked an enormous number of questions. He was very interested in things. For every one question I asked him he asked two, at least. 'Why?' He always wanted to know why things were and how things worked, the root cause of things. . . . He had an inquisitive mind."

Barbara Ward also recalled Jack's visit. "Kathleen was an acquaintance of mine and she said, 'My young brother Jack just wants to see something of the electoral campaign. Please, can you do anything about it?' Well, as it happened, that night I was going to talk to Herbert Morrison in Lambeth, so it was arranged Jack should pick me up, and I think Helen Miller came along with us. We all crowded into a tiny little Austin 7, and out we went to Lambeth."

Jack, Miss Ward recalled, was absolutely "fascinated by the political process. He asked every sort of question of what were the pressures, what was Mr. Morrison's significance in the London scene, and you could see already that this young lieutenant was political to his fingertips. So my chief memory is of a very young man, still hardly with the eggshell off his back, he seemed so young, but with an extraordinarily, I would say, well-informed interest in the political situation he was seeing."

Radical Solutions

Within the somewhat callow makeup of a Boston-Irish millionaire's son, a genuine and belated curiosity about social issues now started to form, encouraged by his English friends. "He wasn't predicting; he was just asking questions," Barbara Ward remembered.

"He was really picking my mind," Pat Lannan recalled. To Lannan's surprise, however, "none" of Joseph P. Kennedy's evil reputation as ex-ambassador to Britain nor his right-wing views "at that time rubbed off on Jack." To Lannan the relationship between father and son seemed to be remarkably positive. No transatlantic telephone calls had been permissable during the European war for civilians or even journalists.

For five days following Bell Telephone's announcement that the wartime telephone blackout was over Jack tried to get through to Boston. Finally on June 29 he reached his father at Hyannis Port, with a Hearst staff member in Boston listening in on the call. As the *Boston Post* reported:

The elder Kennedy was called from his bed [at two A.M.] to talk to his son. There were the usual "hellos," and then John burst out happily, "Who is this—Dad? I know it is. Gee, it's swell to talk to you. I received word that I was going to get through to you when I got back from my election tour, and I could hardly wait."

"How are you, son, and how are you getting along?"

"Fine, just fine."

"How are the people in England adjusting themselves?"

"They are pretty tired now—a letdown after victory—but they are beginning to smile again and get back on their feet. I've been doing a lot of writing and travelling in covering the campaign over here. I wrote a story last Sunday. Did you see it?"

"Yes, son, I did and it was great."

"I'll have one next Sunday, and expect good ones every Sunday for the next five weeks. There is a lot of interest in the election. Most people think that Churchill is going to win, but a lot of the campaign has swung to the left. There's a lot of Socialism over here. They think the Tories will win, but will lose a lot of seats to the Labor party.

If the Conservatives did, in fact, win, "it will be on account of Churchill's personal popularity," Jack felt. Meanwhile, after the election he proposed to go "to Ireland and then to Germany" in July, and would keep in touch by wire.

Jack's father was almost speechless with emotion. Mrs. Kennedy had not been heard; in fact she had not been awakened. "There is not much more we can say except we all send our love to you and Kickie. We'll watch for your stories. We are all pulling for you," the ex-ambassador assured his son.

"Thanks a lot, Dad," Jack responded. "When I was with Kick over the weekend she said if she wasn't here when we talked to give you her love. Tell all my friends I'm coming home in August."

American interest in the British election campaign was far weaker, however, than Jack supposed. His next piece from London went unpublished. Meanwhile, on July 5 the British public went to the polls. Churchill had announced the previous day that "we are going to win. I feel it in my bones that you are going to send me back to power with a great majority. The eyes of the world will be on us tomorrow. If we go down, then all the ninepins of Europe will go down with us. France and Belgium will go forward, not to decent Labour or Socialism, but to a vile form of Communism."

Because of the need to count the votes of British troops serving abroad, the results of the general election were not to be announced until three weeks later, on July 26. In the meantime "the tumult and shouting of the election campaign have died," Jack informed his readers. "This election has been bitterly fought, and, although the Conservatives should win, the voting will be close.

"Most Americans must find it hard to understand why as famous a figure as Winston Churchill, upholding the popular cause of free enterprise, should have been obliged to fight so vigorous a campaign." Jack went on to explain, in the starkest of terms, Britain's economic plight. "In all her history, England has never faced such a critical period. . . . She has an external debt of five billion pounds sterling (approximately $200,000,-000,000). Her export trade, on which she depends for life, has been severely cut by the demands of war. She faces a housing shortage of 4,000,000 homes. She must import enough food and goods to support 25,000,000. Her machinery is old. Her important textile industry has only five per cent of its looms mechanized against 95 per cent of America's textile industry." Meanwhile the Labour party, as the opposition party, "have been free to promise everything to everyone, which they have. The farmer, agricultural worker, shopkeeper, small business man and worker have all been promised happier days. Although the Conservatives should win this time, it will only be a question of time before Labor gets an opportunity to form the government. That will be Labor's great crisis," he warned prophetically.

In the meantime Jack was hatching his own crisis, preceded by a sudden fever. His father had cabled excitedly that he'd talked by phone with George Brennan at the State Department in Washington "who is leaving for Ireland on fifteenth July. He is most enthusiastic about your visit there and has cabled Devalera [*sic*]. Think it most important as do important people here that you go and cover the situation minutely. All papers and magazines will be vitally interested I know. Expect to be able to wire you in few days about trip to Germany and time of it," he added, referring to the possibility of Secretary Forrestal taking Jack to Potsdam for the Allies' summit with Stalin.

At the time Jack's sickness was thought to be just a reaction to recent vaccinations, as George Bilainkin, a diplomatic correspondent, noted in his diary. "To Grosvenor House to see Jack Kennedy who has had several injections against likely troubles on the continent, and is suffering from fever," he recorded on July 10. "His friend, Patrick Lannan, who looks fifty because of grey hair but is forty, has brought along imposing machinery for recording. Jack's sister, Kathleen, beautiful young widow of Marquess of Hartington, was sitting on foot of Jack's bed. With her was Capt. W. Douglas-Home, who caused stir in British Press some months ago, because he was court-martialled for refusing to carry out senior officer's command on battlefield." The group was then joined by Hugh Fraser, who repeated his Staffordshire speech "to imaginary audience" for Lannan to record. "Sick Jack, Lannan and I provided necessary noises 'off' to add realism to 'meeting,' necessitating frequent shouts of 'Vote Labour!' "

It was typical of Jack that despite his fever he would still participate. Moreover, his "probing" questions, as Barbara Ward called them, were thoughtful in a way that even the imperturbable Bilainkin found unsettling. "Jack asked whether Britain had been unwise, in light of subsequent events, in recognizing Marshal Tito instead of continuing support of General Michailovich," Bilainkin entered in his diary. "I said this was begging question, which was far wider than Yugoslavia, Greece, or Poland. Jack pleaded that Russia was behaving exactly as Nazi Germany had done by refusing any form of independence to Baltic republics. I said argument scarcely held water." Bilainkin claimed that only Lithuania had ever been free prior to 1917 and could not therefore complain. "That concluded the Baltic," he noted with relief. Unfazed, Jack "said democracies were surely wrong in consenting to support system of government in Rumania, Poland and Yugoslavia which permitted only one party," which forced Bilainkin to defend himself by quoting the example of Franco. "This was too much, and we turned to 'ultimate truths,' " Bilainkin recorded. "Jack said it was perhaps unjust to have laws of inheritance of property operating as now," though he "could not help feeling that much encouragement would have been destroyed if, for instance, his father had known all through that he could not make enough money to leave to his sons and daughters."

It was clear, as Fraser later reflected, that "looking back on it, I think he was a much more serious character than he gave on. The impression he probably wanted to give was one of a lightness of touch, which he never lost even in the most serious matters, which was very engaging. . . . He was always probing. And the thing that impressed you when you got in a serious conversation was he was prepared to take a very radical view about things, starting off from a fairly conservative premise to end up with a pretty radical solution."

Jack's radicalism was not confined to politics. His attitude toward the teachings of his church was less than obedient, and his approach to Catholic sexual mores blatantly liberal. He squired his dead brother's mistress, Pat Wilson, around London and took up with Kay Stammers, a famous British tennis star, to whom he was introduced in a nightclub.

Kick had once written to Jack that she couldn't "really understand why

I like Englishmen so much as they treat one in quite an offhand manner and aren't really as nice to their women as Americans, but I suppose it's just that sort of treatment that women really like. That's your technique isn't it?"

Kay Stammers certainly felt so. "I was in a nightclub in London," she recalled, "and Jack came in with Pat Wilson, who knew everybody in London. I found Jack terribly attractive. Wonderful sense of humor. . . . British men treat women differently from the way American men do. American men idolize women, but to an Englishman, his clubs and sports are likely to come before his women. . . . Jack had much more of an Englishman's attitude toward women. He really didn't give a damn. He liked to have them around and he liked to enjoy himself but he was quite unreliable. He did as he pleased. I think he was probably spoiled by women. I think he could snap his fingers and they'd come running. And of course, he was terribly attractive and rich and unmarried—a terrific catch really."

Hugh Fraser later excused Jack's inconstancy. "I think he liked a good time, he liked girls. Very healthy attitude to life," Fraser commented. But was it? Just as there was no political issue apart from the multiparty diversity of democracy in which Jack deeply believed, so his love life demonstrated no other principle than multiwoman diversity. "Jack, were you ever in love?" Chiquita Cárcano once asked him, toward the end of his life. Jack looked out of the window of the car in which they were traveling. "No," he said in a matter-of-fact tone. Then he smiled, as he turned back to face her, "though often *very* interested!"

This inability to give himself wholly, whether to women or to causes, would be both Jack's strength and his weakness, condemning him to a peripatetic existence in which, for many people, he was not taken seriously either as politician or as lover. Nevertheless his intelligence, his sense of humor, his refusal to be bowed by illness, his slightly detached but engaging curiosity, as well as a certain shy reserve, proved to be a tantalizing concoction in a young, rich, and handsome American.

"Did I love him?" Kay Stammers asked years later. "I thought he was divine."

A Visit to Ireland

Leaving Miss Stammers, Jack traveled to Ireland, as his father had encouraged him to do. It was a trip calculated both to interest Jack's future Boston-Irish constituency and to permit him finally to see firsthand the island from which his immigrant forefathers had come.

At issue in the summer of 1945 was southern Ireland's international political status. President De Valera had declared in the Irish Dail, "We are a Republic." But if so, how could the country at the same time be a member of the British Commonwealth, owing allegiance to the British crown? In the debate that followed a week later, Jack cabled to Hearst Newspapers, De Valera's elaboration of his remark left the situation "as misty as this island on an early winter's morning." Handily quoting Sheridan, Jack accepted that " 'A quarrel is a very pretty quarrel as it stands. We should only spoil it by trying to explain it.' " Nevertheless, he felt it incumbent upon himself to make at least the attempt.

Describing the division between the twenty-six counties of the South and the six of the North, Jack reported that "De Valera is determined to end this partition, as it is called, and to that cause he has dedicated his life. In this cause, all Irishmen of the south are united."

Irishmen of the North, however, were equally determined not to become subjects of a southern, Catholic republic. Moreover Britain, whatever the rights or wrongs of the division of Ireland, had a grave strategic interest in the matter. Without Northern Ireland it could not have stood alone against Hitler in the darkest years of the war. "Militarily, England will never consent to see a completely neutral and weakly armed power on her vulnerable western flank," Jack acknowledged, pointing out that "only if England has a guarantee that this and other bases are put at her disposal, in case of war, will she consent to give up her great base of Ulster, which served her so well in this war." Were this to be done, the union of all Ireland might, in time, be achieved. "By cooperating and the building of mutual trust, the partition can be broken and all Ireland united. So argue Dillon and a substantial section of the Irish populace."

De Valera, however, did *not* see things this way, as Jack explained.

> Ranged against this group is the powerful Fianna Fail Party, led by the brilliant, austere figure of De Valera, born in New York, the son of a Spanish father and an Irish mother.
>
> De Valera is fighting politically the same relentless battle they fought in the field during the uprising of 1916, in the war of independence and later in the civil war.
>
> He feels that everything Ireland has ever gained has been given grudgingly and at the end of a long and bitter struggle.
>
> Always it has been too little and too late.
>
> He is surrounded by men of the same background in his government. . . . Many were in the abortive uprising of 1916. All fought in

the war of independence against the Black and Tans and later in the civil war of 1922.

All have been in both English and Irish prisons, and many have wounds that still ache when the cold rains come in from the west.

They have not forgotten, nor have they forgiven. The only settlement they will accept is a free and independent Ireland, free to go where it will be the master of its own destiny. . . .

In the north Sir Basil Brooke, head of the government of Ulster, listened to the debate and roared down to the gentlemen in Dublin that "not an inch" will he give up of the six counties.

And in the south, De Valera hurled back the challenge that from his present position he will retreat "not an inch."

At this weekend, the problem of partition seems very far from being solved.

Jack's dispatch, though scarcely Churchillian, showed his knack of simplifying a complex problem without being unfair to either side or minimizing the obstacles to resolution.

Jack's father had urged him to cover the Irish situation "minutely." In the event, however, there wasn't time, for Forrestal was as good as his word, cabling to Jack's father "that we will pick him up in Paris." The next stop was to be Berlin, and the summit conference between Stalin, Truman, and Churchill that would decide the carve-up of Europe, and the final subjugation of the Japanese.

For Jack to be invited to Potsdam with the secretary of the Navy was a privilege indeed. Before Jack could get to Paris, however, there was even more extraordinary news. Churchill had been defeated at the British general election and would not return to Potsdam.

Back to Berlin

Of Clement Attlee, the new British prime minister, Churchill was reported to have said, when objecting to his becoming a member of his club, "I think not. He is an admirable character, but not a man with whom it is agreeable to dine."

Even Attlee's Labour colleagues felt the same way. But behind Attlee's modest manner, as in Truman's case, there was a no-nonsense, serious, and far from weak-minded politician. Even Dean Acheson, later Truman's secretary of state, remarked on the similarity between the two leaders, saying that Truman "recognized Attlee as somebody like himself, a man with his feet on the ground, who spoke in simple, direct terms, and as briefly as possible, and whose thinking about politics was inspired not by admiration of heroes but by identification with 'the common man.' "

The sheer magnitude of Labour's landslide victory, however, was as much a shock to Jack Kennedy as it was to the English people. "England has been hit by some blockbusters in the last five years," Jack immediately cabled to America, "but none of them ever shook her like the election results. As the Labor Party majority piled up, even the most optimistic Laborites were stunned by the extent of their victory . . . Prof. Laski himself told me he had only anticipated a Labor majority of 50 seats." Instead, Labour had gained a landslide 150-seat majority.

Jack himself gave two main reasons for Churchill's defeat. There was the "general feeling that after 10 years of conservative government it was 'time for a change,' " and the fact that "living conditions in England have always been difficult for the working man. Long ago, Disraeli wrote of two nations in England, rich and poor, and in the last five years things have been particularly difficult." It was a lesson worth pondering by the would-be congressman as he made his way across the Channel to meet Forrestal's plane.

From Paris, Forrestal's plane took off for Germany, with Jack bearing the U.S. diplomatic pouch from Dublin. Forrestal, meanwhile, was avid for Jack's assessment of Churchill's fall. Even Kathleen's beau, William Douglas-Home, deferred to Jack's insight. "What about the election? Your initial offerings to Mr. Hearst were right," he congratulated Jack. "Even I, with my deep loathing for the Conservative Party, did not contemplate a swing like that. Now, of course, that they lie grovelling, I want to lift them up again. . . . Will it last five years? I think not. I think they'll slip and split over Russia, when young Ernie [Bevin, the new British foreign minister] finds that Chamberlain was not quite such a bloody fool as superficial people like to think. The policy of unconditional surrender—vis à vis Japan—is not the policy of Arthur Henderson, whom Attlee quoted on election day. So still we need a Fox and a Disraeli."

Douglas-Home berated himself for not having taken on the now former prime minister in his Woodford constituency, and he forecast that "as I have repeatedly told you, Tory, Lib and Right Wing Labour will unite." In the meantime, he was going back to his first love, writing. "I've written one hell of a play, Kennedy. It's got everything. It's even got two women in it, now," he boasted. "It's a stupendous, breath-taking, magnificent, epochmaking two hours of concentrated boredom on sex, and love and death and drink."

It was clear that Douglas-Home (whose brother Alec had been private secretary to Chamberlain and would one day become prime minister), was as much at sea in politics as in the army, where he had been court-martialed for refusing an order to shell innocent civilians. He would, however, remain a lifelong friend of Jack's, who loved to discuss his plots, scripts, and plays. Some years later, vacationing in France for two weeks with Jack, Douglas-Home recalled how "Jack used to talk about politics there a lot. And I used to talk about plays. And he always used to say, "Let's get it straight. What are we talking about now, my politics or your plays?"

For Douglas-Home, born into an aristocratic Scottish family, there was nothing strange about Jack choosing political rather than literary theater. "I mean you always read that the father said Joe Jr. is going to be President. But whether that's so I don't know. Jack was right in the political world from the start, if only from the fact that his father was Ambassador. I mean, he met all the English politicians of that time."

Douglas-Home certainly respected Jack's political sagacity. "Write to me, if you have time, placing your views on the political future of this country concisely and effectively before me," he urged in his letter, "for my education and my future action."

Forrestal—older, distinguished, and responsible for the vast American fleet now closing in on Japan—was equally won over by Jack's political insight. Both men had an abiding interest in international relations and a keen concern with postwar political developments. In Paris, Forrestal had been told by the U.S. ambassador that "unless France got some coal or fuel from the U.S. for the coming winter, there would inevitably be Communism and possibly anarchy in France." The next evening, after dining with Truman in Babelsberg, Forrestal noted in his diary that "the President referred to the British elections and expressed surprise that no one seemed to have any idea in advance what the outcome might be. In our country the Republicans have no leader capable of crystallizing opinion behind him and certainly cannot steal the liberal lead from the Democrats. The time is not yet ripe for the conservative reaction which can presumably be expected to set in."

For Jack himself this was good news—if Truman was right. More immediately, Forrestal's group touring Berlin the next day was swelled by Averell Harriman and then Chip Bohlen, both of whom were now deeply disturbed by Soviet intentions in Europe.

The "stories of destruction" of Berlin, Forrestal noted, were "not overdone." With Jack at his side in a pin-striped suit but refusing to wear a hat, Forrestal surveyed the "skeleton of pre-war Berlin. Very little of it untouched by bombing. All government buildings, hotels, Unter den Linden, the Reichstag, museum, Imperial Theatre—all, if not leveled, at least so damaged that leveling will be necessary. A tour through the

Reichs Chancellery conducted by a Russian captain from the Caucasus and a Russian-speaking American first lieutenant . . . I asked if he ever had political conversations with the Russian captain. He said no, that there had been a few incidents where Americans began explaining what our democratic, republican system was, but after Russians in the higher echelon discovered it, such conversations ceased."

For Jack the ruins of Berlin were especially moving. Only a week before the outbreak of the war he had stayed in Berlin's Excelsior Hotel and had written to Billings that he still didn't "think there will be a war but it looks quite bad as the Germans have gone so far internally with their propaganda stories on Danzig + the corridor that it is hard to see them backing down." Now, as he stood in the rubble of that same city, listening to stories about Russian soldiers shooting German women who would not give up their jewelry or their virtue, he wondered about the future. Harriman, in particular, was "gloomy about the influx of Russia into Europe. . . . He said the greatest crime of Hitler was that his actions had resulted in opening the gates of Eastern Europe to Asia."

They met America's most senior State Department experts, John McCloy, Bob Murphy, Joe Davies, and Will Clayton. They saw Hitler's bunker. Then on July 30 General Eisenhower, supreme commander of the Allied forces in Western Europe, attended Forrestal's breakfast with President Truman, at which there was much discussion of the postwar armed services, including the thorny subject of a single Department of Defense, which Truman favored.

Three present and future American presidents were now in Potsdam: Harry Truman, the sitting president, Dwight D. Eisenhower, who would succeed him, and Jack Kennedy, who would succeed Eisenhower. Eisenhower later claimed that at Potsdam Truman invited him to join the Democratic party and run for president in 1948, in which case Truman would step down and serve, if Eisenhower wished, as vice president (Eisenhower would subsequently repeat this story to Jack when he was a junior congressman).

Whatever the truth, history was being made at many different levels. Astonishingly, Forrestal was not part of the official U.S. delegation to Potsdam, even though he was the political chief of the world's most powerful navy at the climax of the Second World War. Forrestal's counterpart, the secretary of war, Henry Stimson, even the chief of U.S. Naval Staff under Forrestal, Admiral Leahy, and the army chief of staff, General Marshall, had accompanied Truman to Potsdam, and to Forrestal it seemed churlish that he'd not been invited to participate at a moment when the defeat of Japan—and the need to bring the Soviet Union into that process—was a major feature of the talks.

In fact Truman was not concerned about Japan, for as he told Stalin on July 24, "We have perfected a very powerful explosive which we are going to use against the Japanese and we think it will end the war." Told of this, Forrestal was calmed. Stimson had in fact already gone home to take charge of final preparations to use the atomic bomb if the Japanese rejected the final Allied ultimatum calling for unconditional surrender. On July 28 Truman authorized the bomb to be dropped "after about 3 August"—that is, after he had left the conference with Stalin.

Satisfied that there was nothing further he could do, Forrestal left the politicians and flew off at ten-thirty A.M. on July 30, taking Jack and his party for a tour of German ports and cities. Wherever they went, the question of Russian intentions dominated the conversation. Passing a three-mile convoy of equipment belonging to a U.S. armored division outside Berlin, Forrestal learned that "the Russians were much impressed by it," which reminded him of Stalin's remark when Churchill talked of what he hoped would be the helpful postwar influence of the pope: "Stalin snorted and said, 'How many divisions has the Pope got?' "

The group visited the ruins of Bremen and Bremerhaven, followed by Frogge, where the Germans had built a submarine-assembly line similar to that at the Fore River Shipyard during World War I, capable of producing a new submarine every twenty-four days. It was a reminder of how nearly the Germans had won the war in the Atlantic. "We were impressed in Bremen and the surrounding countryside by the generally healthy, well-kept, and distinctly helpful attitude of the Germans. They were in sharp contrast with the appearance and spirit of the Germans around Berlin," Forrestal noted. "Fields well tilled, crops growing, and many cattle in the fields en route from Bremen to Bremerhaven." By contrast the Russians were known to be removing everything they could from their own sector prior to an agreement on reparations. "I wonder if the Russians' objective is not to reduce the German standard of living so that it compares more nearly with their own and keep it at that level," Forrestal commented sagely in his diary. If so, he reasoned, the Allies should do the opposite in their sectors by building on the German virtues of orderliness and professionalism.

The secretary's party then flew to the headquarters of the German navy in Kiel and from there, on August 1, 1945, to Frankfurt, where they again met General Eisenhower, the Supreme Allied Commander. Seymour St. John, son of Jack's Choate headmaster and a naval staff officer, recalled his surprise upon seeing Jack. "The plane doors opened, and out came Forrestal. Then, to my amazement, Jack Kennedy. Ike was meeting Forrestal, so Jack met Ike."

For the would-be congressman it was proving an auspicious trip, on top of his visits to England, Ireland, and Paris, though, because of his status as personal guest of Secretary Forrestal, he could not use his tour of Germany for Hearst Newspapers. Having seen Eisenhower's Supreme Headquarters at the I. G. Farben complex and having toured the remains of Frankfurt, Jack then set off with the secretary of the Navy for the last leg of the German trip, flying to Salzburg and then motoring to Hitler's mountain retreat at Berchtesgaden. On August 2, 1945, they were shown Hitler's aerie, the "Eagle's Nest," to which, Eisenhower had mistakenly believed, Hitler would withdraw for a "last-ditch" stand.

Eisenhower's error, and his "political" decision to halt both Montgomery and Patton in their tracks rather than allow them to take Berlin and Prague in April, had cost the Allies dearly at San Francisco and Potsdam, as even he himself had begun to realize. To both Forrestal and Jack, Eisenhower confided that at Potsdam he belatedly begged Truman "not to assume that he had to give anything away" to get the Russians into the war with Japan. "In Eisenhower's opinion" there was no question but that Japan was already thoroughly beaten," Forrestal noted, while Jack, in a private memorandum which he later gave to Arthur Krock, recorded Eisenhower stating "that he asked Truman at Potsdam not to beg Russians to come into war."

It was plain that in showing weakness toward the Russians, the Allies were *not* improving the chances for postwar peace. Even Ernest Bevin, Labour's new Foreign Secretary, admitted to Forrestal at Potsdam that "he was quite familiar with tactics of the Communists because he had had to deal with them in his own labor unions in England."

For the twenty-eight-year-old former naval lieutenant, there was here an extraordinary amount to think about. In a matter of weeks he'd come into contact with virtually all the major players on the international scene, including Truman, Eisenhower, Molotov, Harriman, Gromyko, Eden, Churchill, Attlee, Bevin, and De Valera, as well as an array of supporting cast from Adlai Stevenson and Chip Bohlen to Herbert Morrison and Harold Laski.

In the meantime, from Hitler's mountain aerie Forrestal's party made its stately way back to Salzburg and then to London, and it was there, after returning to the Grosvenor House hotel, that Jack fell mysteriously ill.

Relapse

"He was sick, he was really sick," Patrick Lannan recalled.

> Oh, my God, he scared the hell out of me, you know. I must admit I'd never seen anybody go through the throes of fever before—you know, when I saw the bedclothes wringing wet and this guy burning

up, I said, Oh my God, what the hell is this? I don't know why, but I was convinced it was a recurrence of malaria. In fact he told me that, and of course the doctors came in, the Navy doctors, and he was really sicker than a dog. It went on for several days. It kept going on, and then it finally came to pass. . . .

I remember Forrestal was so tender with Jack. He was beautiful with him when he was sick. He did beautiful things. That endeared me to him, you know. He was really worried about Jack. He was with him two or three times. Jack was really sick, he was a very uncomplaining kind of a fellow, he was not a phony.

For two days, in fact, Jack was hospitalized at the U.S. Naval Dispensary in London. "Patient flew in from Germany yesterday where he has been eating Army rations and drinking Army certified water," noted Commander Weddell, the senior naval doctor. "Had a similar episode in 1942, from which he recovered in 3 or 4 days. No other member of his party is ill. Was well until yesterday afternoon when he had a chill, became nauseated, vomited several times, had vague abdominal discomfort. . . . Slept fitfully during the night due to some nausea and recurring abdominal discomfort." Under "past history," Commander Weddell added, "Malaria in 1944. Lumbar injury in fall '43 (PT boat rammed), operated on for ruptured lumbar disc in June '44; only partially successful as he still has low back pain on walking. Has hay fever at odd periods and is sensitive to dog dander. Was retired in April '45, because of back disability."

As mysteriously as it had begun, however, the fever, nausea, and stomach pain disappeared. It was diagnosed, as in Morehead City, as "Gastro-Enteritis, Acute." The larger question of Jack's susceptibility to such fevers went unaddressed. On August 6, the day the United States dropped the atomic bomb on Hiroshima, Jack was well enough to fly back to America aboard Forrestal's plane. From Hyannis Port, a week later, he sent Forrestal a thank-you gift, along with a belated, handwritten letter of gratitude:

Dear Mr. Secretary,

I am sorry that I did not get the opportunity at the airport to say goodbye—and thank you.

I appreciate more than I can [say] your taking me—and your consideration on the trip itself.

It was a great opportunity: and I'll always remember it as about as interesting a two weeks as I have ever had. Again my thanks.

Sincerely
Jack Kennedy

A Hat in the Ring

Basking in the relief and triumph of the sudden end to the war with Japan, James Forrestal wrote back from Washington to thank Jack for the box of "very fine cigars. I don't know whether that makes me a venal public servant but I've already smoked half of them, so I guess I'm convicted.

"What are your plans? Do you want any work here—if so why don't you come down and see what there is in hand? I can put you up."

Lem Billings, still aboard the U.S.S. *Cecil*, found Jack's intimacy with Forrestal sickening. "I hope my pessimism in regard to the length of the war did not in any way jeopardize your fine friendship with the Sec of the Navy," he soon wrote from Tokyo Harbor. "Possibly you passed it on to him or in one of your eloquent speeches at those dinners, as the thoughts of those men in the thick of things overseas. Actually I was not the only one over here who was damned surprised the Nips folded up so soon. Certainly those Kamikaze kids at Okinawa gave us no indication that they were ready to throw in the rag." He even kidded Jack for having visited their old school in the spring. "Why? There are no Massachusetts votes near there," he pointed out, though he assured his friend that "since you told me your hat is in the ring in Massachusetts—I've been pushing your stock ahead with the Mass. constituents aboard ship."

Meanwhile, once at home, Jack learned the extent to which his father's campaign to put him in Congress was already under way. All July his grandfather and his father had been making speeches and giving press conferences on the postwar future of the state. Undoubtedly their biggest coup to date had been the naming at Fore River of the navy's newest and largest (2,200-ton) destroyer, the U.S.S. *Joseph P. Kennedy, Jr.,* with the whole Kennedy family invited to attend the launching on July 26. Invitations to the much-publicized event had gone to hundreds of dignitaries, from the new secretary of state James Byrnes to the diplomat Robert Murphy, as well as dozens of prominent newspaper owners and journalists. Jack's sister Jean had performed the christening, attended by "maids of honor," with photographers in abundance. Even *The New York Times* covered the event, its reporter noting tears welling "in the eyes of Kennedy, who stood at rigid attention while the 'Star-Spangled Banner' sounded across the yard where workmen on other warships paused to watch the big destroyer slip into the water."

Kennedy was also relaunching himself in business, having made the surprising announcement, on July 21, that for the sum of $26 million he had purchased the world's second-largest building, the Chicago Merchandise Mart. In the months ahead Kennedy would not only be featured in *Time* and *Life* magazines, but would begin donating huge sums of money to Boston-based charities.

Some five years after his fall from presidential grace in 1940, Joseph Kennedy was now well on the road to rehabilitation, inspiring some journalists to question whether he was not once again angling for a government appointment, this time under Truman.

Jack, however, had no illusions. The question was only whether his father could get James Michael Curley made mayor of Boston in spite of the federal fraud rap. Within weeks a columnist in New York leaked a story that Jack Kennedy "May Run If Curley Is Elected Mayor." Jack quickly denied the rumor, but the writing was on the wall.

In truth Jack was now more than ever convinced that politics was his vocation. His friends Hugh Fraser, Michael Astor, Andrew Cavendish, Tom Edgarton, William Douglas-Home, and Alastair Forbes had all stood for Parliament in England. "It will look like a club," Kathleen had warned, "but of course none of them really expect to get elected." By contrast, Jack *did* expect to be elected, with his father's backing, though he knew the price he would have to pay for such support.

Ironically, it was Pat Lannan, who had so admired Joe Sr.'s support of his son, who became the first casualty of Jack's political ascent, as orchestrated by Joseph Kennedy. As he later related of his visit to Hyannis Port, after returning from Paris, he would

> never forget the first time I met the grandfather and I took a walk, with young Bobby and Teddy behind, down the beach. I think it was about 5 o'clock, with Fitz talking about a mile a minute to Jack, you know, crowding him with information, crowding it into him—just hammering it into this guy's skull, you know. Jack had heard this all his life and of course loved the grandfather, and the grandfather doted on him. That was a beautiful relationship. The man had a strong Irish personality—he was filled with pride and exuberance: It was a nice picture, you know.
>
> But I'll never forget the father, not as long as I live!
>
> I guess I made a terrific faux pas. We were all sitting down, and Joe came down with the goddamnest outfit on, your eyes would come right out of their sockets: it was kind of a red silk coat and shawl collar on and silk pants—the strangest getup. We finally sat down for dinner and Joe got on into a big argument about the British

Parliament, and at that time he had turned very anti-English. God, he went on and on about the British Parliament.

I took the position just directly opposite to the old man, and I could hear every fork and knife at the table suspended in midair, because you know, this was something you didn't do!

I wasn't impressed by the father, because at that time I was rolling pretty well myself and he was just another guy that had made good in America. He didn't awe me a bit. So I took him on. . . .

I didn't realize until I left Hyannis Port what had happened, and then it finally crashed in on me in a plane somewhere and I realized there must have been a great discussion afterwards: "Who the hell is this guy Lannan you've picked up with?" I can just imagine, because you just didn't do that! While I was there, these guys were coming up from Washington and elsewhere, presenting deals to Joe about Liberty ships, etc., and they were geneflecting when they saw the guy!

Though Lannan remained the loyalest of friends for the rest of Jack's life, the days of shared vacations were over. Henceforth Lannan would be persona non grata with the ex-ambassador, and was never invited back to Hyannis Port or to Palm Beach. Only the obsequious, the useful, and the unremonstrative would be permitted in the family compound. As a result, Jack's "home-going" friendships largely deteriorated, as will be seen, to be replaced by a motley gallery of second-raters, court-jesters, and hangers-on: men who would amuse or comfort, even pimp for the young hopeful, but never, never contradict the ex-ambassador. Financially and intellectually independent souls such as Patrick Lannan—men who might have challenged Jack's ideas and broadened his horizons, or simply questioned the nature of the Faustian bargain he had struck with his father—were, from now on, strictly taboo.

The Old Bullshit with a New Twist

Crisscrossing Massachusetts from Boston to Greenfield, from Brockton to Lowell, from New Bedford to Fall River, Joseph P. Kennedy traveled some thirteen hundred miles in September 1945 as chairman of the Governor's Committee on Commerce, determined to wrest maximum publicity for the family from his whirlwind gatherings of Massachusetts businessmen and legislators. By September 16 *The Boston Globe* was reporting— beneath the headline KENNEDY LEADS CAMPAIGN AT DIZZY PACE—that the ex-ambassador had already made twenty-six speeches "on the same subject in eight days," not to mention radio interviews and broadcasts. According to *The Globe*:

> The state Senators and Representatives who have gone with him since the motorcade left the archway of the State House last Sunday and who have in their own experience been on many a political barn-storming tour, are frankly amazed at Mr. Kennedy's apparent inexhaustible energy. . . . He gets up at 6 o'clock or before, takes a walk and then breakfast. Then he rounds up the other members of his party and goes to a public hearing on the proposed department [which] may involve an auto ride of 25 to 40 miles.
>
> There he delivers a speech, conducts a question period, and then, sometime after 11, makes a quick trip to a radio station to make a transcription of a talk on the same subject, which the station will use during the evening.
>
> Then he goes back to a luncheon meeting arranged by the local Chamber of Commerce. Another question period. Then he gets into his convertible coupé and off to another city, which may be 50 to 60 miles distant.
>
> And in midafternoon there is another hearing, then another radio transcription. And at 7 or 7:30 in the evening there is a public hearing and more questions and answers. At about 10 he either goes to a hotel room or to bed or he motors to Boston or his summer home in Hyannisport for the night. The next day the schedule resumes. During the first five days he delivered more than 120,000 words—about the equivalent of two average-sized books. And added to all this, he talked for hours to a representative of a national news magazine, as well as posing for hundreds of pictures for a photographer from a national picture-news magazine.

All the energy and publicity, however, was bound to come to grief. Joseph Kennedy's message—that Massachusetts had enjoyed a wartime economic boom but that bad times were ahead unless the state was prepared to promote itself better—became more strident, his warnings more unequivocal, his manner more arrogant. By September 17 the Republican lieutenant governor, Robert Bradford, could bear it no longer. BRADFORD AND KENNEDY SWAP VERBAL BLOWS, *The Globe* headlined a report. "Lt-Gov. Robert F. Bradford today charged Joseph P. Kennedy with asserting in his tour of the state that 'Boston is moribund, Massachusetts dead and that there are no opportunities here for young men seeking a bright business future,' and compared Kennedy to Jeremiah. . . . The Lieutenant Governor said: 'Jeremiah wailed louder and longer than any men in history. In fact his very name is a by-word for lamentations. Such utterances on the part of the chairman of a commission seeking to build up the economic future of our Commonwealth can only encourage an atmosphere of doubt and a philosophy of foreboding, which is completely belied by our history."

Though Chairman Kennedy defended himself in New Bedford by saying "there is too much emphasis on past achievements rather than looking forward," he began to sound very much like the Joseph P. Kennedy of old, predicting the fall of Britain in 1940. *Time* and *Life* both carried features on Kennedy and predicted an important government post for him, but the damage was done. By September 18 the *Boston Herald* was publishing a major piece on the dispute, headlined BRADFORD SAYS KENNEDY IS SELLING STATE SHORT.

For the rest of the month the ex-ambassador refused to take heed of Bradford, slamming Massachusetts complacency and Bay State bankers while ignoring the fact that Bradford might run for governor at the next election and might win, thus ruining chances of success for his own fifteen-man commission. When Kennedy presented his first report to the State House on September 28, it was not only contradicted by one of his own team but roundly condemned at the House hearing by Worcester attorney Edward Ryan, who said that "in his opinion Kennedy's efforts would be received with greater sincerity if he 'voted in Massachusetts rather than Florida, and if he had invested $20,000,000 in Boston rather than in Chicago.' "

Kennedy's vigor and enthusiasm had all been for nought, and it was his own fault. By contrast, Jack gave only one major speech in September, and it was an outstanding success. "JACK" KENNEDY SHINES IN DEBUT AS SPEAKER the *Herald* headlined a report of his address to the American Legion on September 11. Distilling his Hearst articles from Ireland and London, Jack had added material on his experience of visiting war-torn Germany and titled the talk "England, Ireland and Germany: Victor, Neutral and Vanquished."

"Any doubt that this is fast becoming a young man's world was dispelled at the Hotel Statler yesterday when 28-year-old John Fitzgerald 'Jack' Kennedy held the attention and then won the applause of several hundred persons, many nearly twice his age," Arthur Stratton reported.

JACK KENNEDY, NAVY HERO, SEES IRISH TEST FOR BRITISH read *The Boston Globe* headline of its account.

> John F. "Jack" Kennedy, son of the former Ambassador to England, hero of a PT boat sinking in the Pacific and under hospital treatment as a result of it for months, discussed England, Ireland, Germany and American foreign policy before the members of the

Crosscup-Pishon Post, American Legion, in the Statler Hotel. Young Kennedy saw the emergence of the Labor party in England as the outstanding political event of the year and said that millions of Americans pouring through England and millions of dollars worth of American goods were partly responsible for it. The workers of England, he said, were impressed for the first time by the American as an individual, by the kind of life he lived at home in America and by the country itself as an industrial giant. English workers wanted to be like American workers and the Labor party held out a promise like that to them.

This was scarcely what Jack had said, but it reflected the essence of his speaking style: namely, his ability to make his audience feel comfortable about themselves before reading out any homilies on what they must do. The speech, broadcast on radio that evening, elicited a veritable cascade of appreciative letters. He had described, modestly and informatively, his European journey, lauding the American occupation troops in Germany as men "as fine as any I ever saw. I watched an inspection by General Eisenhower of several thousand troops in Frankfurt. They were rugged looking and their discipline was perfect, but it remained for a Marine Major with whom I was standing to give the final accolade. 'Why,' he said with astonishment, 'They look like Marines.' "

"I have spoken today of three countries," Jack reminded them:

England, Ireland and Germany. All these countries are different and all face different problems. But from each one, and indeed from every country that I visited in Europe, I came away with one great impression—the greatness of my own country, America. Unless he has been abroad since the war ended, no American can possibly realize what a tremendous place America occupies in the world today. In England, for example, before the war, an American was just a tourist and America the land where the tourist came from. When I was in Russia in 1939, Americans were viewed with darkest suspicion and considerable dislike.

But now a change has come about. All of our millions of young men who swarmed over Europe, all the millions and millions of tons of equipment that were poured by us into the war has made Europeans realize that here, indeed, is the great productive giant of the world.

During this war we fought on two fronts, and at the same time shipped 41 billion dollars' worth of lend-lease equipment abroad for the use of other countries. No other country in the world could have ever duplicated the tremendous job. We occupy a great position in the world today. We must measure up to our responsibility.

But we must not forget that we have here in our own country a problem just as great as that of any other country in the world. And that is the problem of keeping our great productive machinery going at full capacity. We must do this if we are going to provide jobs for all those young men who are coming home. This is the first and most important task we face. We will be in a far better position to help solve the world's problems if we have first solved our own.

Though his voice was "somewhat scratchy and tensely high-pitched," as a Cape Cod journalist later described when Jack gave the same speech to the Hyannis Rotary Club, "an appealing, waif-like quality showed through, and above all a winning sincerity impressed his audience more than did the frequently high-flown language of his speech. . . . The general feeling in the meeting room that day was that Jack Kennedy 'was going places.' "

"I'm sending you my speech—which went over pretty well," Jack reported to Pat Lannan on September 23. "It's the old bull-shit with a new twist." Then, in thanking Lannan for his collection of recent articles on Britain and Europe in the *Journal of Commerce,* the twenty-eight-year-old could not resist the temptation to tweak the forty-one-year-old Chicago businessman's nose. "They were damn good," Jack congratulated Lannan. "I guess reading my stuff improved your style."

On the Road to Active Participation

Although "his suit of grey cheviot hung slackly from his wide, but frail-seeming shoulders and gave him the look," a Rotarian recalled, "of a little boy dressed up in his father's clothes," Jack did not speak or act like his father. His talks for the charity in October 1945 were not assertive or threatening like the ex-ambassador's, but personal, humble, informative, and infused with a questioning sincerity that evoked not hostility but goodwill.

"I want you to know that it was a great joy and comfort to have you with us during the past few weeks," the chairman of the Greater Boston United War Fund campaign wrote to Jack on October 19. "I think you may suspect that everybody around here likes you. Your contribution in work, deed, thought, and action are tremendous. I hope we have started you on the road to active participation in Greater Boston affairs. We need young men like you and I am happy that I have exposed you to a great many citizens and the reaction has been excellent—now keep it up."

Fred Good, son of the family obstetrician who had brought Jack into the world, likewise wrote on October 22 to say he'd

> never been involved in politics and don't pretend to know a great deal about them, but as one who stands on the sidelines I have my own definite views as to the type of men who should aspire to public office. Frankly, and I don't believe I am telling you anything as you are a keen observer, the caliber of men (and I mean Democrats) who have been running the state in recent years is a reflection on the intelligence of the voters of Massachusetts. Motivated by selfish interests and lacking in the qualifications of their office they have squandered the tax payer's money for the sole purpose of building up patronage and perpetuating their lofty existence. They have not had the best interests of the state at heart.
>
> I read your denial of the statement in a New York paper that you were seeking a public office in Cambridge. . . . However, why don't you give serious consideration to running for Congress in Curley's district when he is elected Mayor of Boston next month? There is little doubt that he will be elected and that will leave a vacancy in that Congressional district which will have to be filled. A clean-cut, sincere, intelligent and honest candidate with your background and following is a natural and believe me when I say Massachusetts needs men of your type. Maybe my idea is not original and you have already given serious thought to public life—if so you can rely on me to personally carry your case to the voters.

Such letters, which came after every talk Jack gave in the fall of 1945, were an important counterweight to the more depressing side of politicking in Massachusetts. It was as though, unwittingly, Jack conveyed in his shy but engaging manner an idealism that transcended the mundane but human concerns of his fellow people—an idealism that people wanted to hear. Moreover, as his navy friend Jim Reed, who was now studying for a law degree at Harvard, recalled, "Jack Kennedy always had what I thought was the common touch, despite his wealth and background. He had an ability to communicate with people of all levels."

Reed's wife, Jewel, felt the same way, while making it clear that Jack's touch was far from common.

> Jack could talk to the man downstairs, as well as the man of affairs—he had the ability to make conversation with anybody. I

thought he was an extremely mesmerizing person. I could see why Jim was totally bedazzled, from the time he started writing to me from the Pacific about Jack. Jack was an extremely sophisticated person. I couldn't help but think of those lines from E. A. Robinson's poem, "Richard Cory":

> He was a gentleman from sole to crown,
> Clean favored, and imperially slim. . . .
> And he was always human when he talked;
> But still he fluttered pulses when he said,
> "Good-morning," and he glittered when he walked.

As Jewel remembered with a blush, "I was perhaps a little awed, because I had the feeling that this man was—I felt I was kind of a brown wren, and he had been mingling with birds of paradise!"

Jack mingled with less exalted birds too. One night he invited Jewel's husband to an after-theater party. "I thought, 'How nice!' " Jewel recalled. "But Jim said, 'You're not invited.' I said, 'Hey!' In my middle-class mind, a man was never invited unless along with his wife. I said, 'I don't think that's a good idea.' I guess Jim conveyed that to Jack. As he was going out of the door, Jack was kinda cute. He said, 'Sorry about that, Jewel!'

"Some wealthy woman had invited Jack to a party, and he was going to bring Jim—and meet showgirls! I thought, you know, his concept of what marriage is about is *not* what middle-class America has!"

In Jewel Reed's view, the culprit was Jack's father, who'd "sold his sons on his marital practices—practices which were diametrically opposite mine, but Jim's too. Jim was frankly shocked," she recalled of her husband's first response to the ex-ambassador's open philandering. "But he was so bedazzled by Jack that he passed that off."

"I think Jack looked on women in a different way than I do," Jim Reed later acknowledged. "I think he thought they were there for a purpose. . . . I think he had the feeling it was a war between the sexes. A man would always conquer a woman. And she was there to be conquered. Sort of a game. It was hard for him to wrap around a woman the American concept of furniture and motherhood and all that type of thing. I'm sure it must have flowed from his father's attitude toward women."

Jack's casualness about women struck Reed as very British. "I think this is an English attitude towards women—they look upon women entirely differently. Maybe it was a confirmatory thing—seeing his father's attitude and then seeing these people he admired—the English—having the same attitude about women. He always had pretty women with him," Reed said, but as ornaments and trophies, not as people. As Jewel Reed recalled of Jack's favorite nurse, Anne McGillicuddy, "she was *gorgeous*! He brought her to our apartment once. And he said, 'Jim, I want to talk with you'—and left me sitting with this perfectly beautiful, but perfect stranger!"

For all his philandering, Jack's determination to use his time and talents to their fullest impressed Jewel Reed. "When he wanted to accomplish something, he did!" She remembered how, one evening, Jack arrived late at their apartment and announced he'd just finished a four-day, one-to-one evaluation of his aptitudes at the Johnson O'Connor Human Engineering Foundation in Boston. "He wanted to find out what his aptitudes were, to make sure he was taking the right step. . . . He conveyed such enthusiasm. . . . He said for example he'd had the mistaken idea along with a lot of other people that people in data processing had to be good at numbers, whereas in reality you had to be good at logic, analytical ability. 'Here, let me show you what the test was today,' he said. 'Where's a piece of paper?' I was going to bed, I was in curlers! Now there happened to be a shirt cardboard; he picked it up, wrote six letters, flashed it, then wrote six more. 'Now read them back to me,' he instructed. . ."

Whatever Jack did, he did with a mixture of fun, intentness, and brazenness. At a dinner party Jim and Jewel gave for him he openly chewed caramels plucked from his pocket during the meal. On another occasion he leaped out of his car and said he wanted to be godfather to their first child—despite the Reeds being Protestants. He even invested two thousand dollars in a deal Reed was cutting with a friend, Fred Wilson, to buy the *Narragansett Times* on Rhode Island, but showed no interest whatever in the newspaper itself.

As his friends were aware, Jack was now marking time. He did not have much longer to wait, however. Nor did the people of Boston. With money from Joseph P. Kennedy to finance his campaign and with Kennedy's crony, ex-police commissioner Timilty, to guide and protect him, James Michael Curley encountered little opposition in his bid for the mayoralty. On November 4 the *Boston Herald* recorded the "despair that overwhelms many of Boston's citizens at the prospect of getting a good mayor out of Tuesday's election. The chances that the city will emerge with even a presentable mayor are negligible." Curley was summed up in one devastating sentence:

> Three times mayor, once Governor and four times elected to the National House of which he is now a member, he is a candidate for the seventh time: a professional politician whose only visible means of support has been his salary from public office; under a federal indictment in Washington on a charge of using the mails to defraud;

in 12 years as mayor he loaded $50,000,000 on the city's debt and in two years as Governor he increased the Commonwealth's debt by $20,000,000; is 71 years old, not in rugged health, he offers no new program for the city.

The following day the newspaper pointedly noted how, "all in all, this has been the most fruitful campaign Curley has ever conducted. There is plenty of money around, and from the start, the wealthy contributors have been standing in line."

The wealthiest had been Joseph P. Kennedy. On November 6, as expected, James Michael Curley, ancient rival of John F. Fitzgerald, was elected mayor of Boston by Fitzgerald's son-in-law's money and by 110,920 votes, almost as many as were received by his five rivals combined. As his biographer later noted in *The Purple Shamrock,* "they voted him back into office for a fourth term as mayor in spite of the fact that as the campaign progressed and election day came closer it had been made perfectly clear from Washington that Curley would go on trial charged with using the mails to defraud."

Jack, watching Curley's performance, was filled with relief at the seemingly effortless success of his father's stratagem. Proper Bostonians, however, were disgusted and ashamed. "The kind of administration Mr. Curley will give is anybody's guess," the *Herald* commented in its leading editorial the next day. "His record in his last term as Mayor and his first and last as Governor was of such a kind that Bostonians who are proud of their city and eager to have it advance can simply groan and hope for the best."

As Jack knew, the people of Boston had his father to thank for such an unmitigated crook being foisted upon their city, despite the probability of facing a jail sentence. Nevertheless, the Faustian bargain had been made, and Curley, at least, had stuck to his part in it. There was only one consolation. For all his political inexperience, after the opening of his eyes to the Soviet menace at San Francisco and on his trip to Europe, Jack was certain that as a congressman in the U.S. House of Representatives he could do better than James Michael Curley. He could scarcely do worse.

PART
·16·
ELECTION TO CONGRESS

John F. Kennedy seeks to recapture his grandfather Honey Fitz's congressional seat in Boston, 1946 (John F. Kennedy Library)

Congressman—Or Lieutenant Governor?

"The first thing he did," recalled one of Jack's earliest helpers in his campaign, "was to get one of Dowd's staff pregnant." (John Dowd had been hired by Jack's father as a publicity agent and was giving secretarial help to Jack.) "I went in one day—I was taking a law degree after leaving the navy—and I found him humping this girl on one of the desks in his office. I said, 'Sorry,' and left! Later, the girl told my wife she had missed her period, then learned she was expecting. I told Jack.

" 'Oh, shit!' was all he said! He didn't care a damn about the girl—it was just the inconvenience that bothered him! In that sense he was a pretty selfish guy."

This was scarcely the best way to begin a congressional campaign. But was it to be a congressional campaign? Jack certainly thought so, as did Charles Bartlett, who met Jack in a Palm Beach nightclub that Christmas. Bartlett had spent the war in Naval Intelligence, monitoring Japanese signals in the Pacific—the very job Jack might have had if the Inga scandal hadn't intervened. As Bartlett recalled, Jack's mind was wholly made up. "Sometimes you read that he was a reluctant figure being dragooned into politics by his father. I really didn't get that impression at all. I gathered that it was a wholesome, full-blown wish on his part . . . Some of the Palm Beach figures would come and pat him on the back and say, 'Jack, I'm so glad you're running for Congress.' I remember his saying, 'In only a year or so they'll be saying I'm the worst son of a bitch that ever lived!' "

If Jack's mind was fully made up over running for Congress, his father's, strangely, was not. The governor of Massachusetts, Maurice Tobin, was looking for a Democratic running mate for the next election and paid a special visit to Joseph Kennedy in New York to propose that Jack run for lieutenant governor.

The ex-ambassador was intrigued by the idea. In Boston Jack's grandfather, John Fitzgerald, was not. For sentimental reasons Fitzgerald favored Jack running for Congress, and on this his judgment never wavered. It was Honey Fitz, in fact, who assembled Jack's first political "team," beginning with Billy Sutton and Patsy Mulkern, the latter a character straight out of Damon Runyon: "small, wiry, always wearing a hat. Talked a mile a minute, swore like a sailor," a fellow Boston stalwart described him. "He talked politics twelve months a year. The night before Christmas, Christmas Day, Rose Bowl game, he'd have no other interest."

Mulkern himself recalled the moment he and Sutton met Jack at Walton's Lunch Bar on School Street, soon after New Year's Day, 1946.

> He was with his grandfather, Honey Fitz. Then he sat down, and we started a campaign.
>
> He wanted me to do the street work, me and Billy Sutton. Take him through the congressional district because we knew it better than anybody else in Boston. I took him through Roxbury, the South End, parts of the North End . . . East Boston, Charlestown, West End, Somerville, Brighton and Cambridge.
>
> We had a hell of a job with him.
>
> First day I met him he had sneakers on. I said, "For the love of Christ, take the sneakers off, Jack. You think you're going to play golf?"

The next problem was the accusation that was likely to arise that Jack was a carpetbagger. Mulkern recounted: "I said, 'Here we have a candidate, a millionaire, and we ain't got an address for him.' So John F., I think, spoke up and said, 'What about upstairs?' . . . So we got him a two-room apartment he had upstairs [at the Bellevue Hotel]—and that was the address that went in the book."

The choice of Billy Sutton to be Jack's political secretary was a wise one. Though still in uniform after three years in the army, Sutton had previously served as political secretary to two members of the Massachusetts State House of Representatives—John Cotter and John Higgins— and came from Charlestown where, thanks to a job reading meters for the gas company, he knew everybody. Jack Kennedy "reminded me of Charles Lindbergh," Sutton candidly recalled of their first meeting in the Bellevue Hotel. "I thought: a hundred and fifty pounds of pure cash."

Inimical to Honey Fitz, but also anxious to get in on Jack's congressional act was Joseph Kennedy's cousin, Joe Kane. Jack's mother considered Joe Kane "a rough diamond." Like Mulkern, Kane always wore a hat, his with the brim turned down in the manner of Edward G. Robinson. "He smoked a cigar and wore a vest," another pol described him. "He was cute, smart, clever and cunning . . . a very colorful fellow, a sort of mystery man. He was about five foot nine, white hair, ruddy complexion, rather large nose and some false teeth that used to get in the way of his being able to talk as fast as he thought. He was an old-school politician, familiar with every facet of the trade."

"In a state where money as well as public office is handed down from generation to generation," Kane had told the ex-ambassador two years before, "your Jack is worth a king's ransom." In Kane's view Jack should present himself unabashedly as the scion of a noble Boston-Irish family: as rich, distinguished, and certainly as heroic as the Cabots, Lowells, Lodges, and Saltonstalls. "Brother, would they [the voters] puff and go for that line," Kane had predicted.

As Jack began to get his electoral feet wet, however, his father's got increasingly cold. The Eleventh Congressional District was a safe seat for whichever candidate won the Democratic nomination that summer. But *would* Jack win the party ticket? Life could be more vicious and backstabbing among competing Boston-Irish Democrats than against opposing Republicans, as Joseph P. Kennedy well knew from his own father's experience. (P. J. Kennedy had been defeated by a fellow Democrat at the height of his political power in 1908, when standing for nomination as Boston street commissioner, an event that had left a black memory in the family. One of Joseph Kennedy's friends later remarked that it was his father's defeat in the 1908 nomination contest that had turned Joseph Kennedy against any thoughts of a career in elective politics. His father had given "all he had twelve months a year for twenty-five years to the people of Boston, and yet in six short weeks a totally unknown candidate could come out of nowhere and defeat him.")

The six wards of the Eleventh Congressional District were predominantly blue-collar areas, with only a handful of well-to-do streets. Even a decade later it was described as "probably one of the most have-not, heterogeneous districts in the country," comprising 328,000 voters of thirty-seven different nationalities. By far the largest ethnic vote remained Irish, followed by Italians "and, of course, Yankees," but including "Boston's Chinatown and a Syrian section." For almost six weeks, Jack had tramped around the district with Billy Sutton, Patsy Mulkern, Joe Kane, and as many converts as he could make. He had set up the rudiments of a political organization, the hub of which was his dingy, two-room suite just across the street from the State House in the Bellevue Hotel—"home of more rigged rumors than any hotel lobby outside of Washington," as it was once later described. The rumor that now began to circulate was that Jack was abandoning his bid to be a congressman and was going for the lieutenant-governorship.

Having bribed Curley to move out of this safe Democratic congressional seat, Joe Kennedy had indeed become fearful. Given the enmity he himself had engendered in his failed bid to establish a Massachusetts Commerce Department (which had been duly turned down by the state legislature), the ex-ambassador now doubted whether his still-sickly son could withstand the accusations of being a millionaire carpetbagger in such a "tough" area. Better, he reasoned, for Jack to tie himself to the coattails of the popular Democratic governor, Maurice Tobin, and run as lieutenant governor, a post for which—he was assured by Tobin—there would be no competition in the Democratic party, and which would provide a perfect springboard for future political advancement.

This time the rumor wasn't rigged. As Joe Kane later recalled, the word that Jack was giving up on his congressional campaign grew out of a message from the governor, brought by Frank Morrissey. "He was a spy," Kane later remarked. "When I caught him in the Kennedy camp, I said, 'What are you doing here?' Morrissey said, 'I'm here to help Jack.' 'You're here to get him to run for lieutenant-governor, aren't you?' I accused him; 'Tobin sent you.' Morrissey said, 'You're right.' "

Tip O'Neill, the state representative who would eventually inherit the Eleventh Congressional seat, later blamed the hiatus on Paul Dever, the governor's original choice for running mate. Dever was a popular attorney who had only narrowly lost the election for governor of Massachusetts in 1940, but who had no wish to run in the 1946 election, preferring to help his friend Mike Neville, former minority floor leader of the state House of Representatives, to contest Curley's congressional seat. "So Dever went to work on the ambassador, trying to convince him that Jack should let Neville have the 11th Congressional District and go on the ticket with Tobin," recalled O'Neill (who, like Dever, was also backing Mike Neville for Congress).

As Joe Timilty later confided, the ex-ambassador was attracted by the idea, not only because he had become more and more fearful for Jack's chances in a bruising congressional primary fight, but because the lieutenant governorship was the very post he had always had in mind for Joe Jr.

Ed McLaughlin, a PT-boat comrade who had helped Jack set up a VFW post named in memory of Joe Jr., and whose wife, Cis, had begun doing secretarial work for Jack in the evenings, related Jack's response to the emissary:

> It was Washington's Birthday, February 22, 1946. We were going out to dinner with Jack, so we came into the hotel to meet him. When I got there he was taking one of his habitual baths, for his back. He was in his tub, he's in there soaking up, and there's a fellow there named Frank Morrissey, whom I'd never met before, but he was then the Deputy Commissioner of Corrections under Tobin, the Democratic Governor. Tobin was running for reelection and was in difficult political trouble because of meat rationing and prices and everything, and he was getting hurt on issues that had nothing to do with state government, but was the times. And they were looking to buttress Tobin with a strong candidate for Lieutenant Governor and buttressing the ticket. That was the discussion in the bathroom.

Jack got out of the bath and got dressed and we all got in the car and drove down to the Ritz Carlton Hotel for dinner.

Morrissey left.

Cis and I and Jack went upstairs in the Ritz for dinner. We sat down and Jack said, "Well, what do you think about it, McLaughlin?"

I looked at him. You know, to me, at that time, Lieutenant Governor, a statewide office: that was a big job!

I said, "You know it's bad enough, we have enough gall running you for Congress, let alone running you for lieutenant governor. And in addition," I said, "you know they only want you to buttress the ticket because you're—"

Jack, however, halted McLaughlin mid-sentence.

"I'm not going to do it," he assured McLaughlin.

Ice in the Veins

Convincing the ex-ambassador that he should not run for lieutenant governor proved considerably more difficult for Jack than convincing McLaughlin. As Jack's paymaster, it was ex-Ambassador Kennedy who called the shots.

Meanwhile both Kane and McLaughlin had seen the emerging irony: that the Democratic party was now in trouble and, at the state level, was pleading for Kennedy's financial help.

Weeks went by without a decision. Finally Kane exploded.

"Give the kid a break!" he began a special memorandum addressed to the ex-ambassador in March 1946: "A Tobin-Kennedy victory, with a chance of [Senator] Walsh dying, Tobin taking the Senate seat and Jack moving up [to governor], is a big lure and a gamble that fascinates you . . . Has it ever occurred to you Tobin might be licked and Jack win?"

This was a chastening thought. In such an event, as a Democratic lieutenant governor serving a Republican governor, Jack "would be exposed to Republican party and press attacks where he is most vulnerable without any public record," Kane warned. Any hopes of moving up into the governorship would then evaporate. "On the other hand," Kane explained, "Jack, seeking a seat in Congress in a district where the Republican party and press cannot hurt him and where his political strength is greatest, would only have to overcome the opposition of his opponents."

This led Kane to a further consideration. "As outstanding Congressman with national and international reputation he would be in demand as public speaker," Kane predicted, while "as lieutenant governor he would be simply a silenced political priest."

In all Jack's early years as a politician, no one would better sum up Jack's potential. Whether Kane—who was soon discarded by his cousin—truly foresaw the extent to which Jack would become America's "political priest" is uncertain, for he was acutely aware of Jack's shortcomings. "He quits in a fight," Kane remarked candidly. For Kane's taste, Jack was too soft, too much like his grandfather Honey Fitz. Kane had helped oust Honey Fitz as congressman in 1919 on behalf of Peter Tague, and there was no love lost between the two men. As for Jack, he "too readily accepts the ideas of others instead of forming his own, and he isn't as discriminating as he should be in what ideas he takes. Jack's weak to me, and he isn't creative. He'll take any piece of stuff that you pass to him. The fellow always wanted to know what you know—but he wouldn't tell you what he knows, which is nothing," Kane considered, echoing Pat Lannan's experience the year before. "He'll ask you, 'What do you think of so and so?' And you ask, 'What do you think?' and he'll say, 'I asked you.' So you'd tell him and then ask him, 'Now what do you think?' But he wouldn't have an opinion."

This, of course, was said in hindsight and with some bitterness, once he'd been dropped from the ex-ambassador's team. What Kane nevertheless perceived in 1946, as he had done in 1944, was that the shy, somewhat scholarly Harvard graduate might make a new kind of Democrat in town, a sort of aristocrat of the masses, at once engagingly modest yet quick of mind, well-read, and self-confident. In thirty-two years only a single lieutenant governor had ever made governor, he reminded Jack's father. "At the moment the boys helping Jack only to see him win," he pointed out, "are for Congress," whereas those "greedy boys who want to cash in, are for lieutenant governor."

But the ex-ambassador, who'd spent a lifetime surrounded by spongers, sycophants, and servants, was still incapable of crediting the possibility that people might help Jack without pecuniary motive. As he wrote back to Kane, he would "still rather see Jack as lieutenant governor," but he did understand the force of Kane's arguments about the possibility of Tobin being defeated and dragging Jack down with him. "Therefore, since he would have an easier chance to win in Congress, I believe I am inclining more towards that idea," he admitted on March 11, though he obstinately refused to give his final approval. When he summoned Dave Powers (another local veteran and ex-street enumerator) and heard of the work being planned for a Democratic-party registration drive in Charlestown, his eyes lit up. "Can this be done statewide?" he asked.

Powers considered it impossible. "Why?" Kennedy demanded. "Because the primary date has been moved up to June 18 instead of September," Powers explained, "and while we can organize a registration drive for the returning vets of Boston wards 1, 2, 3, and 22 [Brighton], Cambridge, and Somerville, it would be impossible to do the same in the 351 communities of Massachusetts in such a short time."

This was a powerful point. Although the actual election traditionally took place in November, the party primaries had been advanced so as to allow the subsequent election ballots (listing the winning two-party nominees and any independent challengers) to be distributed in good time to military personnel overseas.

Meanwhile, Jack showed no impatience. Indeed his self-confidence mounted almost to arrogance in the eyes of some of his helpers. Fred Good, Jr., for instance, recalled how "underneath the surface he was *very* positive. He had complete control of himself. He knew *exactly* what he wanted to do—and out he went and did it!"

As a volunteer, Good arranged a whole series of speaking engagements. He recalled:

> He didn't know his way around Boston so well, in spite of the fact that he was a Bostonian. I'd go to the Rotary or to the Lions Club, or some contact I might have who was in another chamber of commerce, and line up luncheon engagements for him. You know, you try to "win friends and influence people." Jack didn't seem to do that. He would make a speech—he had two or three canned speeches—at a luncheon. When he finished he would sit down and then when the luncheon was over, he would look my way and sort of nod his head as if to say, "Let's get out of here quick!"
>
> He wasn't a mingler. He didn't mingle in the crowd and go up to people and say, "I'm Jack Kennedy." Nobody knew him. He was totally unknown, except as a Kennedy. He was known strictly as Joe Kennedy's son—younger son, I might add!
>
> At the luncheons he'd introduce himself. He would talk about his family, very briefly. Never dwelt too much on his father, but say, "I'm one of nine children," that sort of thing. Then he'd get into what he wanted to accomplish and what he felt should be done for his district—which was a strange district for him to represent. It was a blue-collar district: the other side of Beacon Hill, Somerville, Charlestown—all heavily Irish, which didn't hurt him any! Bit of Cambridge. . . . But it wasn't the kind of district you would have expected him to represent, is what I'm saying. It was Curley's old district.
>
> I've often thought how unpolitical he was—shy and rather retir-

ing, but highly intelligent, calculating, prepared to do the necessary, but no more than that! If he could do a little less and get away with it, he would do that too! He never had to worry about money.

I think of the typical politician as a backslapper—"terribly glad to see you, I forget your name, now tell it to me, I'll never forget it again" sort of thing—but Jack wasn't like that. What always impressed me was how unpolitical Jack was. I saw him a couple of times a week for three or four months. I lived around the corner, at the beginning of Commonwealth Avenue. One day my wife and I went out for a walk with the baby in the carriage, and passed the Ritz-Carlton. And standing in the doorway was Jack and a relative of his. The relative came up and greeted me and greeted Genevieve, my wife, and asked about the baby. . . . And all the time Jack stood there.

I was so damned mad, to think of all the work I was doing for him! It just shows how unpolitical he was. He stood in the doorway. He never came out, never said hello to my wife. The baby—forget it! I've thought about it all the days of my life, because the average politician would have seized on the opportunity to make a good impression. Not Jack. Sometimes I used to feel that ice water rolled in his veins.

Quite frankly, I don't know if he was shy or a snob. All I'm getting at is that he was very unpolitical for a man who was going to run for Congress.

Candidate for Congress

Jack still had until April 1946 to declare his candidacy. Meanwhile, to counterbalance the pressure from his father, he cast around among his friends for help.

Torbert Macdonald was living in Cambridge while working toward his law degree. He'd married the film star Phyllis Brooks, and Jack had consented to become godfather to their first child, born in January 1946. "Jack didn't like Phyllis," Cis McLaughlin recalled candidly. "And Torby didn't like Phyllis—I mean they were having their problems. Jack sided with Torby—that's the kind of guy Jack was. Torby was his friend and the girl was no good. I never knew her that well, I mean she was a big star. But when she married Torby, she had felt that she had come down a bit. . . . I can remember Jack making comments to me like 'She's a bitch!' That's the way he talked. . . . I suppose that he wanted the guys to stay with him, and that caused tension at home—the wives not wanting to give him so much time."

It was indeed a problem Jack would have all his life. Torby Macdonald later recalled how Jack "broke the news" of his impending political career:

> One day he came over to my apartment, sat down, and started asking me what did I think of his running for Congress from that area. . . . It was sort of a novel idea to me. I had always thought of congressmen in those days as being old, sort of fatherly people, and Jack didn't fit the concept!
>
> I thought about it, and then said, "Well, I don't know, Jack. If you want to do it, I'm sure you'd probably get elected." Anyway, we kicked it around for a while. I went out in the area where my wife shopped and I asked questions: Did they know him? And could he get elected?—that sort of thing. Then I reported back to him.
>
> What I did report, as I'm sure many other people did, is that if he worked very hard and got himself better known, he would have a very good chance to do it.

Red Fay was also inducted. "When he asked me to come East to campaign for him, I came," Fay later recalled—"even though I was a Republican!" He continued:

> When I walked into the Bellevue Hotel in Boston, all ready to go to work for Jack, I happened to meet him as he was coming down in the elevator. He was with two or three other people, on his way to some campaign meeting.
>
> "Red," he said, "it's good to see you. I'm going to a couple of meetings. Why don't you go up to the room, and I'll see you when we get back." He handed me the key to the room and off he went.
>
> And that was it.
>
> I thought, "God, is this the sort of reception I get, after coming three thousand miles?" I was ready to catch the next plane back to California.

One look at the confusion in Jack's suite, however, convinced Fay he should at least "straighten out the mess" before going home. "The desk drawers were filled with unpaid bills, unanswered invitations, letters that hadn't even been opened. I made a list of all the bills, wrote out the checks to pay them, addressed the envelopes, stamped them, and made a list of all the speaking invitations."

Jack, sensing Fay's irritation on his return, affected to be stunned. "God, no wonder there has been no organization around here. Nobody around here was big enough to recognize the candidate's real problems and do something to correct them. Red, you're staying right here to get this campaign running on a businesslike basis!" he ordered. As Fay himself recorded, "Flattery will get you everywhere, at least with me. All my irritation vanished. I was suddenly right in the middle of John Kennedy's first political venture."

On April 10, 1946, Jack "authorized the circulation of papers in his behalf for the Democratic nomination in the 11th Congressional District now represented by Mayor James Michael Curley," one newspaper reported. Nevertheless, Jack was reported "Still Undecided on Running for Seat in Congress," according to *The Globe*. "Denying reports he had announced his candidacy," the newspaper went on, "John F. Kennedy, 29, son of Joseph P. Kennedy, former Ambassador to Great Britain, last night said that while he had given the matter consideration he has not made up his mind."

Soon every journal in Massachusetts was speculating on whether Jack would in fact decide to go for the lieutenant governorship. In the Norwood *Messenger* Bill Griffin remarked that "it is no secret that he gazes longingly at the post of Lieutenant Governor, and has been holding off to see what former Atty-Gen. Paul A. Dever will do. But Daddy Kennedy promised to discuss matters with Son John. . . . There'll be all sorts of conferences, and telephone calls, and personal interviews, and whatnot and then the average person, like you and me, will find out what it is all about. Right now," Griffin warned on April 13, "a lot of politicians are trying to get on the Kennedy gravy train, no matter what he runs for."

The *Boston Herald* didn't agree, saying that Dever was in fact Tobin's second choice, but that père Kennedy was worried by the fact that two other candidates had circulated papers for the congressional seat under the name of John F. Kennedy, and might thus confuse the voters—a foretaste of a dirty-tricks campaign. "It is not certain whether these Kennedys have been promoted into the contest by one or some of his prospective rivals or whether the idea dawned simultaneously on both. It is typical Boston Democratic politics," the *Herald* concluded.

Once again Joseph Kennedy's preference veered toward lieutenant governorship, and he was saved from a disastrous misjudgment only by a secret poll he himself had commissioned. Major John I. Fitzgerald, another Pacific veteran and campaign volunteer (who had himself coveted the congressional seat) remembered the result: "This was the poll they had that indicated the Democrats were in trouble—it was done by someone with a doctorate degree from somewhere, for Joe Kennedy."

With the poll's findings before him, the ex-ambassador finally saw the light. The long months of vacillation were at last over. During the week-end of April 20 at the Kennedy house at Hyannis Port, the irrevocable decision was made, and on Monday, April 22, 1946, the *Cape Cod Times* announced Jack's candidacy for Congress, as Jack drove to Boston to draw up his formal announcement to the press and radio as well as file his papers.

John Galvin—who, coincidentally, had also been sunk in the Solomon Islands, at Vella Lavella—had first become a gifted fundraiser and PR executive for the Red Cross on leaving the U.S. Navy, and then had been given a job at the Dowd advertising and PR agency. Galvin vividly recalled being summoned by Mr. Dowd.

"Dowd asked me one day would I be around this afternoon. I said, 'What have you got in mind?' He said, 'A young guy named Jack Kennedy is coming in. He's either going to announce for Congress or lieutenant governor, and I'd like you to hang around and write the announcement.'"

Red Fay remembered how difficult it had been to get Jack to write the speech. Thanks to his father's ambivalence about the lieutenant gover-norship, Jack had been forced for many vital weeks to remain silent about the precise office he intended to seek, suggesting to the public a certain indecisiveness. At long last, the decision having been made, the fight was on—but there was no speech.

"It was incredible. Here he was, with all these guys on his father's payroll!" Fay related. "So somehow, I sat him down, and we cobbled something together, and we took it down to the station."

In fact they took it to the Dowd agency. "Jack came in—late as usual," Galvin recalled. "It was very late in the afternoon. He had part of a speech with him that had to go on the Yankee Network, WNAC, at seven-fifteen that night. He had to make an announcement about it on the radio. So there were two things to do: one, write a release; the other, the speech for radio."

In order to meet the deadline, Galvin telephoned Mark Dalton, an old college friend in Cambridge who had done much speech writing and speaking at Boston College High and Boston College, "to come in and try to doctor up the speech while I finished up on this [press release]." Dalton was delighted to help:

> I said I'd be glad to, I'd be right over. So I took a cab over to the Dowd agency, and that was the first meeting I had in my life with John Kennedy.
>
> I was as thin as I could be at that time—but he was even thinner! He was actually a skeleton, and with him was John Galvin and also Red Fay. . . . The speech was almost in complete shape at that time.

I went over it and they asked my reaction to it, and I told them I thought it was a fine speech. Very few changes were made in the speech. We went up in a cab to the radio station. John Galvin, Red Fay, John Kennedy, and myself.

"Up in the station, we went into the newsroom and we used the typewriters there to finish this thing off," Galvin related. Clutching the final version, Dalton recalled, "John Kennedy went on [the air] with his speech that night. No one introduced him. He went on alone."

"Voters of the Eleventh Congressional District," Jack began.

The people of the United States and the world stand at the crossroads. What we do now will shape the history of civilization for many years to come. We have a weary world trying to bind up the wounds of a fierce struggle. That is dire enough. What is infinitely far worse is that we have a world which has unleashed the terrible powers of atomic energy. We have a world capable of destroying itself.

The days which lie ahead are most difficult ones.

Above all, day and night, with every ounce of ingenuity and industry we possess, we must work for peace. We must not have another war.

The hopes of those who expected a rehash of his father's and his brother's prewar appeasement/isolationism sentiments, however, were soon dashed.

It is no answer to the problem to say that we shall not go to war again, no matter what the cost, and leave it at that.

If another Hitler were to appear on the world scene, if totalitarianism were to threaten once again to engulf the world, then we would face the same situation which we faced so recently and the only course would be war. We must see to it that such a situation is never allowed to be created again.

To accomplish that task calls for abilities of a high order. It calls for intelligence, for forthrightness in speech and for action.

During the course of this campaign I will give you forthrightness in speech and when I go to Congress I will give you action.

This is no time for double-talk and pleasing generalities.

I want the people of this District to know where I stand. I would rather not go to Congress than go there under false colors. Win or lose this campaign, when it is finished the people of this district will know my position on the most important issues of the campaign.

There followed his espousal of the Patman and Wagner-Taft-Ellender housing bills, of continued price controls, and of a national health system that would give "every man, woman and child" in the United States "adequate medical care." "We in the United States have the resources to see that every person receives such care. It is a national crime that we have been too slow in accomplishing this objective." Nevertheless he did not want "the government enslaving the medical profession," as in Britain.

"I stand for free enterprise. I stand for democratic government in a capitalist economy. I oppose communism, fascism, nazism and social-ism. . . . I believe that American democracy can accomplish the goal of a healthy nation without adopting any communistic, fascistic, totalitarian system." He stood for "the essential rights of labor" including the rights to a living wage, to organize, to pursue collective bargaining, and to strike. And, finally, he stood for "a strong United Nations—a much stronger one than the one we have now." The United States, he felt, should never have given Russia the power of veto in the Security Council. Equally,

> We should never have adopted the policy that the United States will take for itself bases in the Pacific which we consider essential to our national defense. How can we oppose Russia's claims before the United Nations when we ourselves are taking land?
>
> I say, put the Pacific bases under a United Nations trusteeship. . . . If we disclaim any claims to territory, then we can stand forth as the leader of the conscience of the world. China and France will stand by us. The Labor government of Britain will stand by us. The small nations of the world will stand by us. Then we can appear before the United Nations and make our stand clear to Russia that we will not permit Russia to spread its totalitarianism throughout the world. It will be Russia against the conscience and power of the world and Russia will be forced to yield.
>
> Only by forthright action now can we avoid war. I will give you that action as your Congressman.

This was the formal beginning of John F. Kennedy's political career. In the wake of James Michael Curley's trial, conviction, and sentencing to eighteen months in jail for fraud in January, Jack's high rhetoric was welcomed by the media. KEEP AN EYE ON HIM, the *Boston Herald* urged its readers in a banner headline. The article stated:

> Mr. Kennedy will not be twenty-nine years old until next month and in the probable event of his nomination and election in the Eleventh district, he will go to Washington as one of the youngest, if not the

youngest, member. Mr. Kennedy graduated from Harvard in 1940 with honors and made a brilliant record as a PT boat commander in the South Pacific. Since his return home he has been much in evidence as a speaker at gatherings of veterans or as spokesman for veterans at general meetings. He has performed on such a generally high level on all such occasions that there are many in the Boston area who hold him to be the real "white hope" of Boston Democracy. . . . Certainly there is a ring of statesmanship in Mr. Kennedy's statement that "the temper of the times imposes an obligation upon every thinking citizen to work diligently in peace, as we served tirelessly in war." That matches well with Henry Cabot Lodge's remark of the day before that it is "the binding duty of all who have special training in our kind of government to offer their services in peace."

Jack had forgotten one small thing, however. While the Boston newspapers dutifully carried reports of his candidacy for Congress and his "call to arms" in the service of peace, *The Boston Globe* ran a big headline in its early afternoon edition on April 23: KENNEDY PAPERS FOR CONGRESS NOT IN AS TIME NEARS. "The deadline for filing nomination papers for the state primary election expires at 5 P.M. today. At an early hour this afternoon the election commissioners had not received any papers from John F. Kennedy for the Democratic nomination for Congress in the 11th district, the seat to be vacated by Mayor James M. Curley."

At five P.M. the commissioners closed up. Had Kennedy changed his mind yet again? Or had he simply forgotten to file?

Irish Excitement

John I. Fitzgerald remembered the situation well, some forty-five years later. "You have to get the nomination papers from the State House, get your signatures, take them to the town or the city to get them certified," he explained. Once verified,

> they give them back to you and you're supposed to then take them to the secretary of state's office, to say that you qualify to go on the ballot. Now, Jack's suite in the Bellevue was only two rooms—a living room and a bedroom, I think. He had a three- or four-drawer steel file cabinet, and the papers were up there.
>
> I was worried why they hadn't been filed, but he said to me one day, "Oh, it's all been taken care of. We've had them photostatted."

So I assumed these were photostatic copies, and that he'd already turned in the originals, so I gave no second thought at the time that they hadn't been filed.

Fortunately, the Bellevue was just across the street from the State House. "A series of frantic phone calls was made," Red Fay later recalled, for "the office where the papers had to be filed had been closed since five P.M."

In the end money and influence prevailed. "Very quietly, the candidate and some loyal retainers went down, opened up the proper office and filed the papers. Another couple of hours, and all the thousands of hours of work by the candidate and his supporters would have been completely wasted," Fay related.

The "work," meanwhile, was absorbing. "He enjoyed learning about people," John I. Fitzgerald recalled. "His eyes were opened to a lot of things, and during the campaign he got interested in housing—particularly after we took him to the CharlesBank homes—a private housing-development company, owned by a firm of book publishers over in Cambridge and built for the working man. His meeting with different longshoremen gave him a sense of labor, of the importance of the right to strike—and that's one of the reasons for his later minority report on the Taft-Hartley Bill."

Soon, in fact, Fitzgerald began to see in Jack a future mayor of Boston, in the footsteps of his grandfather. However, it was equally clear that the style of Jack's campaigning represented a complete break with tradition.

"I would say that it was rather a unique campaign," Peter Cloherty, one of Jack's campaign secretaries, later commented, "inasmuch as there were a great many young people who I don't think ever had been interested in politics before. . . . I think of all the campaigns I've been involved in—and I've been at this since I was fifteen, which goes on thirty years—that I've never seen a campaign like it as far as having an overabundant supply of workers. People were very, very anxious [to help] and very, very interested, and there was a glamour to Jack as a candidate, and there was an abundance of workers at all times, both at 18 Tremont Street and at the Bellevue, and in all of the district headquarters that were opened up."

Jack's opponents made the fatal mistake of underestimating him in comparison with his predecessor, said Cloherty. "A lot of them thought that particular district, that was so strong in its support of his predecessor, James Michael Curley—who was a real old-time politician in every sense of the word . . . that there just didn't seem to be a correlation between this young novice going into battle, that it took an old pro like Curley to mastermind and win. . . . But I don't think the campaign was on very long before they had a very different view of the approach to it, because the thing went into high gear, and it moved—as most of his succeeding campaigns did—at a very fast pace!"

Lem Billings, who had left the navy and been accepted into Harvard Business School, decided to go to Boston in the few weeks before school was scheduled to begin and see how Jack was getting along. "Of course, I was very interested," he later recorded. "It was exciting to me to have him running for Congress which, at the time, seemed a very high office indeed."

Billings's testimony is valuable, because despite his somewhat slavish devotion to Jack, he was an intelligent and perceptive observer of his friend—a true Boswell. "Jack had tough local competition," Billings remembered.

> He had never lived there in his life. Talk about carpetbaggers! Jack hadn't lived in Boston since he was *nine.* He was living in the Belle-vue Hotel, just down the hall from his grandfather, Honey Fitz, who was darned interested in having him run . . . he was thrilled to have his grandson enter Boston politics.
>
> Mayor Fitzgerald never lost his intense enjoyment of life. He was probably in his very late seventies when Jack ran for Congress. He was so excited about his grandson coming up there and going into politics in his own home area that he was beside himself. . . . They were absolutely crazy about each other. Jack was undoubtedly the old man's favorite. He was a very attractive old man, full of the Irish blarney, full of mischief, and full of life. So much of Jack's love of life and his inquisitiveness about life and his interest in everything comes from his maternal grandfather. He was a man who was never still for one moment. His humor was something that Jack loved so much; he adored his grandfather's sense of humor.
>
> It wasn't that his stories were so good, because we heard the same ones over and over again. Certainly Jack had heard them many, many times. But each time the Mayor told a story, he'd tell it in a different way and he'd laugh and enjoy it so much himself that everybody else had to enjoy it and, I must say, nobody enjoyed it more than Jack. He always took every opportunity to ask his grand-father to tell some story that he'd heard at least ten or twelve times.

Honey Fitz's love of people was certainly in complete contrast to Joseph P. Kennedy's disdain. In the opinion of John I. Fitzgerald (who was not related to Honey Fitz), "Jack was closer to being a Fitzgerald than whatever I saw of him being like Mr. Kennedy. He had more of John F. Fitzgerald's personality." But if Honey Fitz's "love of politics had some influence on Jack's coming into the congressional fight"—as Billings felt it did—it also caused problems. Honey Fitz "probably wanted to be involved more than Jack allowed him to be," Billings observed. "He brought out all his old buddies, all sort of over-the-hill Irishmen, who were living in the past. They wanted to go back to the old kind of politics. In Jack they thought they saw an opportunity to do this. Their eyes were filled with Irish excitement for the new battle."

For Jack, Honey Fitz's excitement threatened to be de trop, especially when "Grampa" seemed to forget who was the candidate. As Billings recalled:

> Jack had to discourage his grandfather's desire to run the campaign. He enjoyed his grandfather's exuberance and he did let him take part, but he had to hold him back. . . . He really wanted to do it on his own.
>
> He certainly didn't have any choice about his grandfather's friends. These old people were all over his living room—I remember when I first got there, his entire living room was filled with old Irish politicians smoking up a storm.
>
> He was concerned, but he had to feel his way and he wasn't going to insult anybody. . . . He listened and made up his own mind as to what he was going to do. He certainly didn't turn away anybody who wanted to help him, young or old, whoever they were.

In this sense Jack's 1946 congressional primary, with its multitude of helpers, would become the archetype for all his political campaigns. There remained, however, the question of whether, if elected, Jack's health would stand up to the job of congressman. Looking at his sickly pallor and frail physique at Palm Beach at Christmas, his sister Eunice had asked, "Daddy, do you really think Jack can be a congressman?" The ex-ambassador, who later remarked of Eunice that if she'd "been born with balls she would have been a hell of a politician," dismissed her question with a snort. "You must remember," he explained cynically, "it's not what you are that counts, but what people *think* you are."

Drifting Over to Money

Money was not a problem for Jack's campaign. "We're going to sell Jack like soap flakes," the ex-ambassador was heard to boast, though he would later lament that "with the money I spent, I could have elected my chauffeur."

At a conservative estimate, a quarter of a million dollars was expended on the congressional election; others considered the amount to have been at least double that figure. Billboards, newspaper advertisements, radio broadcasts and newsreel and national-magazine publicity were purchased in perhaps the most extravagant Democratic primary campaign ever witnessed in the state. Moreover, although Rose Kennedy later considered that her husband "was as invisible as he could be," the ex-ambassador was quite clearly "the boss," attended by his adjunct, Eddie Moore, and his henchman, ex-police commissioner Joe Timilty.

"I was very much involved in the 1946 campaign," Timilty later confessed. "I was carrying out the instructions of Joe. Joe was the mastermind of everything. . . . I reported to Joe all the time."

While Timilty "arranged for Jack to meet various so-called leaders" and recruited more campaign staff, Eddie Moore paid them. Dave Powers, who after meeting Jack had switched loyalties from John F. Cotter, the local Charlestown candidate for the congressional election, recalled how funds for the campaign were disbursed. "It was the strangest experience," he related. "I would meet Moore at the campaign's headquarters at 18 Tremont Street and he would then lead me into the men's room, where, putting a dime into the slot, he would take me into a closed toilet. There, with no one able to watch us, he would hand me the cash, saying, 'You can never be too careful in politics about handing over money.' "

In the aftermath of war and with the specter of unemployment ahead, Jack was frankly considered a "rainbow in the sky, a pot of gold," another Timilty recruit, James Kelley, remembered. Word soon spread, in fact, that the ex-ambassador was even buying out campaigners for rival candidates and bribing the rival candidates themselves.

Ranged against Jack were ten contenders: John Cotter, Joseph Russo, Catherine Falvey, Joseph Lee, Francis X. Rooney, Michael DeLuca, Robert B. DiFruscio, a second Joseph Russo, and Mike Neville. Chief among these rivals was Neville, the former state representative of Cambridge, who, to his credit, refused all blandishments. Neville's son Robert later stated that "money had to be a big factor. They came in with half a million: it was unbelievable. They made all kinds of offers to him, but he was a proud man. The offers were rejected. He just felt that he'd made a commitment and he was going to stay in it."

He explained, "In those days you could run a campaign for twenty-five thousand dollars." To raise this amount of money Neville took out a mortgage on their house. "He went to the grave paying off the mortgage," Robert recalled sadly of his father, for the flood of Kennedy money turned likely victory into a rout.

"Neville had the decided edge," his aide Daniel O'Brien later insisted, "and he had the support of friends that he had made in all of his years in the State House as a representative, a leader of the Democratic forces. Mike had made friends throughout the whole district."

Even Jack felt guilty in this respect, and later confided to John Galvin, his chief publicity aide, that Neville was "the better man for the district and deserved to win." At the time, however, Jack looked the other way while, from his Ritz-Carlton suite, the ex-ambassador dictated all expenditures in the campaign, including all bribes.

To Daniel O'Brien it was pitiful to watch as the "very men that [Neville] had supported all his life drifted over to money. They drifted over because they were bought," he remarked bitterly. And where they refused to be bought, they were simply steamrollered by the ex-ambassador's control of media advertising and publicity. As Neville himself once put it, "The Kennedy strategy was 'Buy them out or blast them out!' "

Fred Good, working for Jack, acknowledged, "There was a feeling it was being bought to a certain extent. He didn't go out and buy votes or anything like that, but anything that was needed was paid for. There was never any campaigning for money. Money was never discussed, never thought of. Money was—it was just assumed that money was there. Signs, billboards, radio time, newspaper interviews—Joe Kennedy could have anything he wanted. So I suppose you could say it was bought in that respect."

As always, Joe Kennedy's self-appointed task was succinct: to buy Jack an "image." Once Kane came up with a stirring campaign slogan—"The New Generation Offers a Leader"—the ex-ambassador bought every billboard and poster site in Boston to display it, which also deprived opponents of sites. The veteran aspect, too, was done to death. Jack had not only formed his own VFW post in January, but was a member of the Cross-Pishon post of the American Legion and in a special deal organized by the ex-ambassador had even been made president of the forthcoming national VFW convention, which was expected to attract more than twenty thousand veterans and to which Eisenhower, MacArthur, Marshall, King, Halsey, and many hundreds of distinguished warriors had been invited. Not content with this, Joseph Kennedy had made a special arrangement with the publisher of *Reader's Digest* to illegally reprint no fewer than 100,000 copies of John Hersey's *PT 109* article and then distribute them to every voter in the Eleventh Congressional District. "Christ! We had *millions* of them!" John Galvin later recalled in embarrassment.

Jack, the victim of his father's zeal, was often embarrassed. "No one was ever unaware of [Jack] Kennedy's war record and injury, it was played up all the time," Neville later complained. John Galvin recalled in particular the occasion when the art director at the Dowd agency designed a billboard for the ex-ambassador with a huge picture of Jack in naval uniform, his medals prominently displayed. "Of course it was shown to the candidate, and he turned it down. Jack disliked—totally opposed—putting his wartime ribbons on a billboard. . . . They were very colorful—I mean he had the Navy and Marine Corps Medal, the Pacific Theater Medal, and the World War II Medal, and of course he had the Purple Heart. But Kennedy did not like ostentation. He never did in his life. He always wanted to get all the credit that he was due, but he felt that everybody in the United States had those medals. He didn't need that. And I don't ever think that billboard got up."

Jack understood, however, how much he had to go along with his father. Galvin recounted that "Kennedy used to say, when I'd talk over ideas with him, 'John, I know you're right about this—but Dad's putting up the money and we have to let him win a couple.' " The challenge was not to avoid his father's expectations, but to exceed them, while all the time avoiding the pitfalls.

According to Billy Sutton, "He met city workers, he met letter carriers, cabbies, waitresses, and dock workers. He ate spaghetti with the Italians and Chinese food with the Chinese. He was probably the first of the pols around here to go into the firehouses, police stations, post offices, and saloons and poolrooms as well as the homes, and it was probably the first Jack ever knew that the gas stove and the toilet could be in the same room."

Lem Billings saw how difficult it was for Jack to overcome his natural reserve with people he did not know:

> We can all remember when we had to do whatever job we had to do in the early years, whether we were salesmen or whether we were lawyers. Everything's hard. I think it was hard for Jack Kennedy. For instance one of his first acts was to call on all the city councilmen in Cambridge. I called on these men with him.
>
> They were extremely hostile and really rude to him. They treated him like a young kid who had absolutely no business going into politics. He was wonderful with them and treated them with great tact. He didn't gain their backing, but I was proud of the way he handled himself and how intelligently he talked to them and how small and petty they appeared in comparison. Out of the entire city council in Cambridge, he had only one councilman who was with him. That was Joe De Gulielmo. . . . Jack Kennedy never forgot people like Joe Gulielmo, who were his supporters in the early days when it really counted.

Billings had only intended to stay a week and "just sort of be an observer—go around where he went and listen to him make his talks and generally just enjoy the excitement of the whole thing." Instead, he was asked to help run the Cambridge headquarters.

> We encouraged volunteers to come in. We had mailings going out all the time. We were constantly going over the voting lists to find where the Democrats were. We had four or five telephones going all the time, with volunteer girls calling up and getting out the vote and encouraging people to vote for Jack Kennedy. We had people calling on every democratic house. We were as well-organized as an organized group could be. We used to stay until three and four in the morning . . . even the young people who were going to school would stay that late. We'd send all of the girls home in taxis to make sure that they'd get home all right. . . .
>
> I went back to the Bellevue every night about three in the morning. I'd come back and there Jack would be with the greatest cross section of people you've ever seen, jammed into his living room and bedroom, all smoking cigars and sitting around talking—most of them were no help at all. When we went to bed, even at three or four in the morning, there'd be people sitting and smoking cigars on my bed as well as the candidate's. I don't know how we ever got any sleep. When we'd wake in the morning, we'd find people *still* sitting around the room smoking cigars.

As for Jack's health, Billings didn't notice that it affected his rigorous schedule.

> I don't remember his health problems during the entire congressional campaign. . . . He may have been in pain, like he was so much of the time, but if he was, his mind was on other things and he never discussed it. It never crossed my mind whether he was sick during that period, whether he had a bad back, whether he had malaria or this or that or the other thing. He was thin, as pictures will show, but he certainly was working as close to twenty-four hours a day as a man can work. He never let up—many *healthy* men could not have kept up that pace!

Even Jack's father was astonished. "I would have given odds of five thousand to one that this thing we were seeing could ever have happened. I never thought he had it in him," the ex-ambassador recalled saying to a companion when one day in East Boston he saw Jack introducing himself to a group of longshoremen.

In his myopic determination to buy the very town he'd left because "there was no economic opportunity," Joseph Kennedy had overlooked his son's priceless forté, his personality. To the bluff, ruthless, swindling millionaire, personality meant being bluff, ruthless, and swindling. That his own second son—shy, witty, fun-loving, a bookworm who impressed bookish people—that this ne'er-do-well with his constant, unexplained medical crises and bad back, could first outshine his healthy elder brother in the grim trial of war and now win votes that were not bought: this was something the Boston braggart simply could not credit. He had assumed the election *had* to be bought. "Everything Jack's father got," Joe Kane explained, "he bought and paid for. And politics is like war. It takes three things to win. The first is money and the second is money and the third is money."

Neither Joe Kane nor Joe Kennedy, however, had ever been close to war. Jack had. Thus arose the saddest of contradictions: Jack's father seeking to buy the election while Jack tried to win it on his own merits. The ex-ambassador "spent a staggering sum in the congressional race of 1946," Kane later concluded, "but Jack could have gone to Congress like everyone else for ten cents."

Only Millionaires Need Apply

"The father's position and father himself were always in the background of everybody's minds," Mike Neville later said of Jack's congressional campaign, "and that money was unbeatable." O'Brien agreed: "The Kennedys pulled no punches in the fight. We didn't have the resources to even begin to compete with them, between the *Reader's Digest, Liberty Magazine, Look, Life,* and the various other sources of information. . . . We couldn't touch those things, and it wasn't very long before we knew that our battle was a lost cause."

But was it? Joseph Kennedy's campaign for a state department of commerce, despite vast efforts at publicity, had backfired, ending with complete rejection by the state legislature, and now, in the spring of 1946, Jack found resentment against his father growing into a vicious backlash that threatened if not to torpedo his candidacy, at least to poison it to the point where he would withdraw.

"Congress seat for sale—No experience necessary—Applicant must live in New York or Florida—Only millionaires need apply" was a typical example of countercampaigning by other contestants for the post. "Jawn Kennedy of Florida" was another. When *Look,* a national picture magazine, published an illustrated, multipage profile of Jack's campaign, one

Boston newspaper columnist felt compelled to protest. Under the name "Dante O'Shaughnessy," the columnist, Albert West, wrote, "Now I've seen everything! I could hardly believe my eyes but there it was. Look Magazine for this week contains an article by a super high-priced publicity man about Jawn Kennedy's campaign for Congress. And so help me, it proves every point I've tried to make about the youngster being oh, so British."

O'Shaughnessy bridled at *Look*'s description of Jack's prospective district: "Edging the waterfront and brimming the slums, it is populated overwhelmingly by Irish and Italian Americans." He was brought to apoplexy by *Look*'s account of Jack visiting his proposed parish with his black manservant: "the indispensable George Taylor, Jack's Negro valet and chauffeur, whose calling card distinguishes him as a gentleman's gentleman."

> Whoops, my dear, a valet! This is the gospel truth! Buy the magazine and see for yourself. They even have a picture of the valet and Jawn looking over "the slums" as he calls them. That's the way they do it in Merrie England you know. Lord Whatsit decides to help out the slums so he stands for Parliament in some benighted area far removed from his castle. One must help out the slums you know. . . .
>
> In my opinion, Kennedy's candidacy is the nerviest thing ever pulled in local politics.
>
> He moves in and establishes a phony residence in a hotel and solely on the strength of his family connections announces that he is undecided whether to become lieutenant governor or a congressman. He exploits every connection meanwhile and moves in on groups better left out of the dirty mess of politics.
>
> And you know what I mean. It is positively shameless! . . .
>
> A classic exhibition of the new rich. What is the history of this distinguished family? Joe Kennedy masses a fortune, and if you haven't heard the story about Fore River you had better look it up. Look Magazine didn't touch upon that. He then moves out of the State. He ducked to Florida where there isn't any income tax and wasn't seen again in these parts until he joined in a scheme to create a Department of Commerce in the Commonwealth, then he came back and travelled all over the state telling us we were gone to the bow wows and that commerce and industry was dead on its feet here and that Massachusetts could never come back industrially or commercially. To prove his point he bought up a city block building in Chicago for a staggering sum. He knocked the State everywhere he went, at our expense, and gave us the worst publicity we have had since the Sacco-Vanzetti trial. . . . Great stuff.

Then he hopped a plane and beat it. . . . This left Joe's son John F. Kennedy. What has he, himself, to offer? What has he, himself, ever done to merit your vote? Nevertheless he moves in, valet and all, and demands that because of his family you send him to Congress. If you can beat that for bold, brazen gall, I'll quit and campaign for deah Jawn, and fly the British Union Jack from my flagpole.

Not even Jack's voluntary helpers were spared the lash of O'Shaughnessy's invective. *Look* had carried a photograph of Jack sitting "with his amateur brain trust of a dozen ex-Navy men he knew at Harvard and in the Pacific," as the picture caption ran.

The Look article tells about Jawn's campaign too, and discloses that the campaign is being run by "braintrusters" who are some of the boys from deah old Harvard. One of them, according to the article, flew in from California to manage things properly, another is from Ohio and another from Baltimore.

The nearest to the district comes from Malden, but then he's a Republican. The simple question boils down to this: Is the Congressional seat in the Eleventh Congressional District for sale?

Apparently, Jawn F. Kennedy thinks it is. If you think so too, run in and get your hair cut at either the Bellevue, where you may see the out of state brain trust, or at the Kimball Building. Many of the boys have already. How about it, Billy, you got yours? Don't be greedy, Daddy has plenty more!

Weeping in Disgust

"Because of his pre–Pearl Harbor position as a non-interventionist, which opponents twisted to label him an 'isolationist' (which he was not)," Rose later primly maintained, her husband "had become a controversial public figure and he didn't want any of this to rub off on Jack's candidacy. . . . Therefore, Joe was as invisible as he could be, while knowing exactly what was going on, and why, and where, and how, and with hard-headed analytical judgments and prescriptions to offer when needed."

Invisible to Rose, the ex-ambassador was plain for others to see. Jack's mistake had been to allow his father to take the commanding role in the running of the campaign, and it was now too late to stop the inevitable whiplash.

Kathleen's young husband had stood for election in England in the spring of 1944 and had experienced the same problem, being resoundingly defeated by his Common Wealth–party opponent, Charlie White, in what was considered a safe family seat. It was an experience so bruising that when the duke of Devonshire, Hartington's father, afterward said, "I don't know what the people want," Hartington just said, "I do, they just don't want the Cavendishes." Kathleen had written home that "his father pulled a few fast ones which made everyone rather mad. In short, Billy had everything against him. His own personal charm was the only thing he had in his favor."

In Boston Jack had charm. He also had brains, wit, and precociously good judgment. But attacks such as O'Shaughnessy's reflected an increasingly bitter tone as the primary campaign reached its climax in June which led W. E. Mullins to headline his column in the *Boston Herald* KENNEDY IS PRESENT FAVORITE IN THE 11TH DISTRICT, COMMON TARGET OF HIS GENUINE ADVERSARIES. "This one taste of Boston politics is likely to cure this youngster of any future ambitions," Mullins wrote. "They have hit him with everything within reach. . . . His chief offense, however, seems to be his capacity to finance his own campaign in a somewhat lavish manner."

W. E. Mullins was not the only one to assume that, once bitten, Jack would fight twice shy of electoral politics and devote himself to less bloody pursuits. John I. Fitzgerald felt so too. "I would say if he ever was defeated he would never have tried to make a comeback. He would have gone off into something else, definitely." Dave Powers saw it the same way. "I always said that if he lost the first one, there wouldn't have been any more. You know, politics are not that easy."

Men like Fitzgerald and Powers, brought up in the hurly-burly of Boston politics, accepted the rough nature of the game as a given but could see that it was foreign to Jack's nature. Moreover, though Jack himself had a tough shell that was as hard for rival politicians to crack as for women who sought an emotional commitment from him, his loyalty to his family and close friends meant that he could easily be hurt by an unfeeling attack upon them. Hostility to his father, in particular, he found, seemed to know no bounds. The ex-ambassador's wealth tainted everything he tried to do. Even the loyalty of Jack's staff became dubious, tinged by the suspicion that, at heart, it was based on his father's money. As Patsy Mulkern openly stated to Jack, "Every guy in here tells ya der wit ya. Well, I'll tell ya da troot. I don't know if I'd be wit ya if ya wasn't a millionaire."

Matters came to a head when one day Clem Norton found Jack in his room at the Bellevue actually "weeping in disgust at what he had gotten himself into."

Norton, as a close friend of Honey Fitz, had known Jack since he was an infant, and had great respect for Jack's intellect. Unlike Kane, Norton saw Jack's avid interest in other people's views and ideas as a strength, not weakness. "I never met a man that picked your mind like he did," Norton later remarked. "Now, whether you like it or not, that's education, that's curiosity, that's the basis of all knowledge. I never heard Jack Kennedy ask me a silly question. It was always on the target, something contemporaneous, and something of value—the import of it, going right to the basis of important subjects, picking everyone's mind that he thought might have a suggestion."

Before the 1942 election of James Michael Curley, Norton pointed out, the Eleventh Congressional District had been represented by Thomas Eliot, a Harvard graduate and scion of the famous Eliot family. Jack had just as much to offer the nation and the people of Boston, Norton assured him, and in comparison with Curley, nothing of which he need be ashamed.

At Norton's suggestion, Jack decided to go to the source of the problem: Joseph Lee, the opponent on whose behalf O'Shaughnessy was making his vitriolic attacks.

Norton knew Lee well, for they were both serving on the Boston Schools Committee. Lee was by birth a Cabot, and counted in his family Lodges and Storrows. To this patrician Brahmin, Jack now made a personal plea.

The ex-ambassador, Lee later revealed to an interviewer, had already preceded him—in vain: "Joseph Kennedy went to Lee asking why there was such a fight between him and his son and asked Lee if there was not some position in government he would like to have. Lee felt he could not at that time withdraw."

It was now Jack's turn. "At some point," Lee's interviewer recorded, Jack Kennedy "went to him with tears in his eyes, and asked if he would not call off [O'Shaughnessy's] articles. He asked why bring in his family, why not just fight against each other."

Lee, looking at the emaciated, attractive, intelligent youth, was won over. He knew he himself had no chance of winning the primary, for he had already stood against Curley in the mayoral election without success and had only a patchy following in the congressional district. "Then Lee did something he has regretted ever since. He called up [O'Shaughnessy] and asked him to lay off this young man."

Jack's charm had paid off.

A Secret Weapon

Meanwhile, the *Boston Post* had published the results of a new poll pointing

> to John F. Kennedy, the former PT boat commander, as the winner
> of the spectacular race in the 11th Congressional district. . . . The
> results of the straw ballot taken under the supervision of [a] Harvard
> educator, who has made a speciality of this kind of work, coincides
> fairly well with the opinions of the political experts, though the poll
> shows Kennedy winning by a wider margin than the political observ-
> ers anticipate. Kennedy's strength seems to be so well balanced that
> he could win this fight without carrying a single ward or section. One
> of the surprising features of Kennedy's strength as shown by the poll
> is that he is as popular with the old voters as he is with the young
> groups, though his supporters are mostly comparatively young ex-
> servicemen and women who constantly astonish the political leaders
> by the energy with which they rush around, making the campaign
> almost a crusade.

The ex-ambassador refused to believe the poll. He paid a further huge
sum for a team from the New York *Daily News* to come to Boston and
conduct its own straw poll. To Joseph Kennedy's amazement, this
showed Jack not only in the lead, but leading all other contenders combined by a margin of two to one.

Lem Billings, meanwhile, needed no straw poll to tell him what was
happening. He'd been watching his friend from the age of fourteen, and
saw him as something of a genie in a bottle, waiting to be opened:

> It was exciting to me to find that he had a natural ability to speak
> well in public—I really hadn't realized this. You see, I never really
> thought about him as a public speaker or as somebody who could
> influence people by what he said.
>
> It was inspiring to hear him make a speech in front of complete
> strangers who were usually people who were thinking "Here's a
> young, rich kid, let's hear what he has to say." It was really one of
> the great experiences of my relationship with Jack.
>
> Through the years, in the advertising business, I've had to do a lot
> of selling. If you have a good product and you are able to expose that

product properly, then you can be successful. That's really the whole secret of marketing.

In Jack Kennedy we found we had a good product and a product that, if properly exposed, would convert voters to his side. This was so encouraging because, after a very short time, we found all we had to do was expose him.

This was the crux of the matter. Where Jack's father thought his job was to sell a product by remote control, bribery, and lavish advertising, Lem Billings was finding that the electorate, once they met or heard him speak, felt as Billings did: that the candidate possessed qualities of intellect and personality that raised him head and shoulders over any contender.

To Billings, who had watched for years as another Kennedy was being groomed for this race, indeed for a more exalted political office, the comparison with Joe Jr. was perhaps the most telling way of proving that Jack was not merely "Jawn the pawn" of a rich and ruthless father. Joe Jr., after all, had been the apple of this father's eye, possessing the very same advantages as Jack, and with better health. He had studied in Europe, visited Germany and the Soviet Union, gotten into war-torn Spain, worked hard at Harvard, won a commission in the navy's elite flying corps. Out of all this Joe Jr. had gotten only one juvenile letter from Spain published in the *Atlantic Monthly* and had the dubious distinction of having helped set up Harvard's isolationist movement.

By contrast, Jack, despite almost being expelled from school and suffering recurrent physical breakdowns, had evinced the happy knack of being at the right place at the right time, even turning misfortune to his advantage. Whereas Joe Jr. had failed to get his Harvard *H;* failed to make the dean's list; failed to get into any of the Harvard final clubs; had backed Hitler, appeasement, and Roosevelt's opponent, and had also failed to win glory in combat save in a courageous but unnecessary death, Jack's career had resembled that of an innocent golddigger who strikes it rich. His college thesis had become a bestselling book; his affair with a suspected enemy spy had led him from a tedious job in Naval Intelligence into PT boats in the Pacific; his shipwreck had become a classic story of survival; his coverage of the San Francisco conference and the British general election had expanded his reputation as a perspicacious international observer.

Despite his joyous recognition that his friend could address a crowd effectively, Billings was well aware that Jack lacked not only the robust health his elder brother had enjoyed, however, but his elder brother's speaking skills. As Joseph Healey, one of Jack's speechwriters in the congressional-primary campaign, later remarked, "He was not an effective speaker in those days. . . . We had to spend a great deal of time polishing something into a speech that we thought was fairly worthwhile and then, frankly, in our opinion he would not do it justice."

Healey had gone to Harvard with Jack's brother, and could not help comparing the two. Jack spoke too fast, rushing his words and failing to pause. "I just don't think he [Jack] was as forceful in those days as he was subsequently. I think that he just had not had a great deal of experience. I think that basically he was somewhat, in those days at least, on the shy side. That's a strange thing to say about somebody who has political ambitions, but I think it's true. I think he reluctantly met people. . . . I think, in this respect, he was greatly different from his brother Joe, who was outgoing by nature and, I think, an absolutely born political figure during all the time that I had known him. Joe, too, was a much more effective speaker during the period when I knew him, when he was interested in Massachusetts politics and a delegate to the Democratic National Convention in 1940."

Fortunately, Jack's speeches and his oratorical ability were not the only things that counted in 1946. Even more important was something no political diehard had taken into account, something Jack had inherited from his grandfather Honey Fitz: his appeal to women.

"Women compose the majority of voters now," Jack had proclaimed in a speech to the League of Catholic Women the previous November. "Women not only have political power, but they have financial power. Women control 50 percent of the wealth of this state, they spend about 85 percent of the money spent, and they inherit 75 percent."

For this very reason John Droney feared that the favorite Somerville candidate for the congressional nomination, Catherine Falvey, might attract the women's vote. "We thought there was a little danger in that, because she was a woman. We didn't know how the women would react. 'They may go for her.' "

Recently demobilized as a Women's Army Corps major, Catherine Falvey was described by the press as an "attractive, well-mannered young woman." Countering Jack's generational-leader slogan, she issued a clever slogan of her own: "Major versus Minor." But for all her verve, the major was no match, in the eyes of women voters, for the broad grin and gray-blue eyes of the "Miami candidate," as his detractors called Jack. Though Jack's opponents urged him to "go home to Florida," his audiences turned up in ever-increasing numbers to hear and, above all, to watch him. As John I. Fitzgerald later summed up, "I think it was the start of the modern campaign. Let's put it that way."

Women were not the only ones mesmerized. One of Jack's early volunteer helpers in Brighton, Tom Broderick, recalled frankly, "He hesitated a little. I mean, as a matter of fact, my first impression in listening to him was that I was more interested in watching him than I was in listening to what he said." Impressed, Broderick went up to introduce himself to Jack at the end of the meeting and was soon working for Jack's campaign. "I was so enthused with the fellow that I said, 'Gee, would it be possible [for you] to come out and meet some people?' And he said, 'Great! When do we go?' "

Thus began the informal "house parties" that would become a feature of all Jack's campaigns. Broderick telephoned his sister in Brighton from the Bellevue and in short shrift "we had, oh, fifteen or twenty people out there. . . . Jack just sat down, he put his big long legs out, and he just talked. He was glad to meet everybody, nothing political, just that he was so glad to be able to sit down. He felt as though he was amongst friends. Well, I mean everybody there wanted to marry him then!"

In the kitchen Jack talked politics to Broderick's father; in the living room he "wowed" the ladies. Soon Jack's sisters Eunice and Jean were involved, helping plan the parties and ferry him from one to another, while Jack's brother Bobby, just demobilized from the navy, became responsible for a small corner of the Cambridge ward. Jack's sisters now looked upon their brother with the same idolatrous adoration harbored by Jack's growing contingent of female fans. When Broderick told Eunice that she looked like broad-mouthed Jack (which, given her sex, was unfortunate), Eunice beamed, but Jean was furious. "Who do I look like?" Jean demanded. "And we said 'Bobby.' She had a very bitter fight about that, she didn't want to look like Bobby, she wanted to look like Jack."

Bobby struck Lem Billings as being "very, very young."

> Probably twenty, and he was just out of the service. . . . He came in after we had already gotten started and after I actually had been established in the Cambridge headquarters. I remember Bobby showing up and he was still in his sailor suit. He was just a seaman.
>
> He wanted to do something, and it's funny that Bobby showed his aggressive strong nature even then. . . . He came and started working with me in Cambridge. He didn't want to work under me in Cambridge. Very shortly he wanted to go out on his own and there were eleven districts in Cambridge. He took over three. He went down there and that was completely his area. He wasn't married then, but there was a young girl named Ethel Skakel, who was a roommate of his sister Jean. Ethel and Jean and Pat Skakel, Ethel's sister, who was also sort of a sweetheart of Bobby's at the time, all were down there helping him in his little headquarters. As I recall, it was the poorest part of Cambridge. I'll never forget it—Bobby wouldn't let me near the place.

Bobby Kennedy had his own, strange journey to make, from awe of his conservative father and his charismatic brother to a final, traumatic Pauline conversion. In the meantime, however, he too was overwhelmed by his brother's charm, wit, energy—and ease with women. "John F. Kennedy spoke before the students of the East Boston High School and the girls rushed around shouting 'Sinatra!' " one newspaper recorded. Another noted that "one of young Jack Kennedy's most devoted followers, now that he has filed for Congress, is Lucy Cochran, Boston's handsomest postdeb, who more than once has attended meetings just to hear him speak." Another ran a vast headline: 1500 WOMEN JAM RALLY FOR KENNEDY.

This was Jack's secret weapon: the aspect that made all the glad-handing worthwhile. At house parties or on the platform Jack was, increasingly, a star, and he knew it and relished it. "He really thrived on it," Red Fay recalled.

> He loved it because, God, when you get that response—when people honestly love you, it's very flattering to go out there. God, they just melted! He had that, you know, sense of humor: the way he'd kind of be hesitant, but he'd go out there and his opening remarks would be always right to the point and he'd put the place into gales of laughter. We'd go to the junior colleges, girls' colleges, and he'd come in there like Frank Sinatra in the early days. They would scream and holler and touch him—absolutely, in 1946. I mean, these girls were just crazy about him. . . .
>
> Were they old enough to vote? I doubt it. He wanted them to go home and tell their mothers and fathers: vote for the candidate.

Even Jack's father was staggered by the reports, and by the amount of unpaid voluntary work being done by so many people. Dave Powers was there when the ex-ambassador "dropped over to Charlestown one night."

> Oh, it was my biggest night; I had a headquarters on Main Street, and I had borrowed chairs from an undertaker, those folding chairs. So I must have about fifty or sixty people working in there. . . .
>
> A limo drove up. It's Joe Timilty driving, and it's Ambassador Kennedy, and he went into the headquarters, and you never saw anyone so pleased! On one side they were stuffing envelopes and addressing them, working from voting lists. And he was so impressed, he said, "Do you mind if I say a word?"
>
> He stood on one of those folding chairs. And God, I was nervous, I'm thinking, Christ, if that chair goes. . . . And he's thanking everyone, he almost had tears in his eyes, he was overwhelmed. "You

know, you people made my day—to think that you ladies would come out of your homes, down to the headquarters to help my son is so gratifying!"

The hard work was paying off. By mid-June everything pointed to a landslide Kennedy victory, barring last-minute accidents. This was certainly what Billy Sutton most feared.

> During the hectic days of his first congressional campaign in 1946, Jack attended every breakfast, luncheon, and dinner possible, and joined as many clubs and organizations as would admit him.
>
> One night, Bob Morey [Jack's chauffeur], Jack, and I were driving to Chicopee for a communion breakfast that was being held at the Holy Name Parish the next morning. Morey was driving and we had planned to stay overnight at the rectory.
>
> As usual we were late, not getting on the road until after 11 P.M. Bob didn't like being blamed for any tardiness, so he reluctantly gave in to Jack's back-seat prodding to drive faster.
>
> I regretted ever having stepped into the car and was sure we were headed for some kind of trouble when Jack turned to me and said, "Billy, if we get into an accident you'll have to remain conscious so that you can give our names, but more important than that, don't forget to tell the reporters that I was in a state of grace."

Wit like this made much of the drudgery worthwhile for Jack's campaign workers.

On the eve of the primary, Monday, June 17, 1946, Jack meanwhile marched with 150 fellow members of the Joseph P. Kennedy, Jr. VFW post in the annual Bunker Hill parade through Charlestown. In less than twenty-four hours polling would take place. "The reviewing stand was opposite my home," recalled Robert Lee, a Massachusetts state senator who'd been helping Jack's campaign. Lee had been struck by how frail Jack looked when he'd first met him the previous autumn. "My first impression was that he was a very sick boy." By mid-June Jack was physically done in, unable to move without his back brace, unable to continue without at least five sitz baths a day, or without back rubs by a local boxing trainer, "Cooky" McFarland. "He had a bad back," Patsy Mulkern remembered, shaking his head, "That guy had a bad back." Despite the blistering heat, however, Jack not only insisted on marching in the parade but refused to wear his hat. Robert Lee saw what happened next. "It was a very, very hot day, and Jack was exhausted, and collapsed at the very end. He was brought to my home. . . . I called his father and I was instructed to wait until a doctor came, and after several hours they moved him from my residence. . . . He turned very yellow and blue. He appeared to me as a man who probably had a heart attack."

The incident, however, was hushed up as the registered voters of Massachusetts prepared to cast their ballots in the first congressional primary since the war and, in the Eleventh Congressional District, to choose a successor to the fraudulent crook James Michael Curley.

The Newest Bombshell

As the polls predicted, Jack won the primary by a landslide, receiving 19,426 votes against 10,875 for his nearest rival, Mike Neville.

"At Cambridge more than 200 workers waited until 1:30 to cheer his arrival," the Boston *Traveler* reported. Certainly Lem Billings would never forget the climax:

> Remember, we were all amateurs, and all very young. There weren't any old people at all. Everybody was either a young veteran or a young girl. In the case of Cambridge, we had taxis and volunteers to take voters to the polls. We had people who'd lived in each district all their lives stationed at the polls. We tried to get as many volunteers with cars as we could, but we also had to hire an awful lot of taxis and these were all sent to addresses of Democrats who hadn't voted. Consequently we had I don't know how many phones in headquarters to find out why people weren't voting and if they needed rides, etc.
>
> I remember one experience at the end of the evening, before votes were even counted. All the taxi drivers came into headquarters to get paid. I had a certain amount of money there. Headquarters was jammed packed. We had rather a big headquarters; somebody had given us an old office.
>
> Suddenly all the lights went out and there was a tremendous drive towards the little office where I was with the money.
>
> It was only through the efforts of some of our great volunteers that we were kept from being robbed. . . .
>
> Later, when we knew that Jack had won, it was terribly exciting because, of course, he came round to every headquarters. It was so much more a personal thing—not just to me, who knew Jack well, but for every single person who had worked hard for this victory. I'll never forget when he came into headquarters. It was incredible because he knew exactly how to show his appreciation to those who

had worked so hard for him. Of course, he was building loyalties which he kept until the day he died.

Undoubtedly this was the case—and justly lauded by the press as news of Jack's victory was splashed across the region's newspapers: YOUNG KENNEDY ASSURED OF SEAT; KENNEDY NOMINATED FOR CURLEY'S SEAT; KENNEDY GOING TO CONGRESS; KENNEDY, PT BOAT HERO, WINS SEAT IN CONGRESS.

As once Fitzgerald had trounced the sitting congressman Joseph O'Neil and the system of Boston ward bossism, using young volunteers and a direct appeal to the voters, so fifty-two years later his grandson had reintroduced a fresh, vigorous young campaigning style—and triumphed. "Thus the slender blonde nominee is headed towards the seat in Congress once held by his grandfather, the colorful John F. Fitzgerald," the Boston *Herald American* concluded its account the next day.

"John has been living at the Hotel Bellevue, where his grandfather makes his home, and the one-time Boston mayor followed his grandson's campaign with great relish," the Boston *Traveler* reported. " 'Grandfather took over last night,' Kennedy said, with the wide, white grin that is one of his best campaign assets. The newest bombshell in Massachusetts politics neither drinks nor smokes and has no steady girlfriend."

The *Herald American* reported Honey Fitz's proud and uncharacteristically brief statement: "Of course I am a happy man tonight. John F. Kennedy has brains, industry, and above all, character. He will make a great representative of the 11th Congressional District." In response to numerous demands, the paper recorded, " 'John F.' sang his favorite 'Sweet Adeline' in a voice that shook with emotion."

Mike Neville, conceding defeat, asked sadly, "How d'you beat a million dollars?" The Boston *Traveler,* however, allowing for the sense of injustice, commented that

the money aspect has been exaggerated by the politicians. If any of the other candidates had spent twice as much as the Kennedy campaign cost, Kennedy would still have won. . . . Kennedy as a candidate had attributes which his opponents did not have and could not buy—a well-known name and family background and connections. He also had personality and a superior war record.

In addition, the new congressman had one asset which has been ignored by almost everyone, although it should be of the utmost concern to the older politicians. Kennedy was the only candidate with an effective personal machine and it was built overnight and it was based on voters under the age of 35. The key positions in his organization were held by young men, generally fellow veterans, who were full of enthusiasm and "idealism." Most of the workers who crowded into his seven headquarters nightly for two months, addressing envelopes and making telephone calls, also were youthful. They may have been amateurs, but they did the tiresome tasks which bring in votes, and they were worth more than all the ward "pols" in the district combined.

Although this assessment was true, it skated over the ex-ambassador's role in the campaign, a role which had cost Jack the votes of many liberals, such as the historian Arthur Schlesinger, Jr., who obstinately refused to promise Jack support. "He was the only guy who turned me down," recalled Jack's Harvard classmate and Cambridge supporter, Tony Gallucio, "He said Jack's father never did anything creative, he was only interested in making money, and this sort of stuff, so Arthur wasn't going to help Jack Kennedy."

At the victory celebrations, the Boston newspapers noted, the ex-ambassador "remained in the background, giving his son the spotlight." Those familiar with Jack's campaign, however, were not deceived. Not only had the ex-ambassador bankrolled the candidate, but he'd watched carefully how every dollar was spent. No one had been taken onto the paid staff without first being vetted and cleared by him. No day had passed without Jack consulting him. Even Mark Dalton who had reluctantly accepted the designation of campaign manager, later gave credit to the "old man."

> He was one of the ablest men I ever met and he was deeply interested in that congressional campaign, and if there were an essential campaign manager, I would say that it was Mr. Kennedy. I think, for history, that that should be clear. . . . Mr. Kennedy called me many, many times, to know exactly what was happening. He was very, very interested, and he would talk at great length and wanted to know about every facet of the campaign—as a matter of fact, that was one of my problems. He'd keep you on the phone for an hour and a half, two hours. . . . He was very, very interested in what was going on, although he did not project himself into the picture publicly.

This was a remarkable tribute considering that Mark Dalton would, in Jack's next major campaign in Massachusetts, come into direct confrontation with the arrogant, rabidly antiunion and anti-Semitic Boston Irishman, effectively ending his own remarkable contribution to Jack's career and embittering him against the Kennedys for the rest of his life.

Jack's youth, especially in contrast to Curley's age, was also a crucial factor. Apart from a few seasoned helpers, "the rest of us were fairly

young," Dalton recalled, "and I think a good deal of it happened naturally. There was a tremendous ferment after the war. The whole feeling
of taking over—that it's a new era. The young veteran wanted to *do*
something, and he was naturally attracted to John Kennedy. The older
fellows through loyalty would remain with the older candidates; and the
younger fellows didn't know the older people and wanted to go with a
new young fellow. And it was exciting. There is no question about that."

In Jack Kennedy Dalton recognized a symbol of the "new era." According to Dave Powers, "in 1946 if you didn't have the word *veteran*
beside your name, you were in trouble—you couldn't get elected dog-
catcher." But seeing Jack close up, Dalton also recognized, as did John
I. Fitzgerald, Fred Good, and other intimates, that the fact that Jack was
so unlike the conventional stereotype of an American politician was
ultimately to his advantage.

To Dalton "he did not seem—this is true—to be built for politics."
Apart from being "extremely drawn and thin," Dalton recalled,

> he was not affable and easygoing, and certainly he was not a speaker,
> [though] he later developed into a fair speaker.
>
> He was an excellent debater but not an excellent orator. I have not
> seen this distinction made by anybody else.
>
> He was not a great orator in the sense of a Patrick Henry or a
> Daniel Webster, one who could arouse your emotions. I don't think
> I ever heard him give an emotional address even then or later.

For those saturated with the emotional charlatanism and personal
invective of James Michael Curley, this was a blessed relief, as the newspapers noted. JOHN KENNEDY'S HIGHLY SUCCESSFUL CAMPAIGN / EXAMPLE
OF RESTRAINT LEARNED FROM LODGE, the *Boston Herald* headlined its
retrospective on June 21, 1946, and reminded readers how Henry Cabot
Lodge, Jr. had fought Curley for the Senate in 1936. "Throughout a long
and acrimonious campaign, he was subjected to ridicule and abuse. His
grandfather was dragged into it. He was scornfully referred to as 'Little
Boy Blue.' A book he once wrote was distorted," the *Herald* recalled. "In
the face of great temptation to reply in kind, he pursued his original
course. . . . Not once did he mention his opponent's name. He won easily.
In a subsequent campaign, he pursued the same course, and again won."

Jack's victory was now compared to Lodge's resounding defeat of
Curley ten years before.

> Multiply by ten the abuse and vilification Lodge was buried under in
> 1936, and you have an idea what was poured on Kennedy in his recent
> trial. The charge that he was using his wealth to purchase the seat

was minor in contrast to the scurrilous methods employed in dragging innocent members of his family into the fight. . . .

He [Kennedy] was dazed by the bitterness and the extent of the assaults that came at him from every side, but he remained outwardly calm, and at no time did he mention the name of a single opponent. On occasion, when he was assailed from the same platform, he undertook to reply, but never was ill-tempered about it. As in Lodge's case, it paid dividends.

Kennedy has the finest opportunity of any Democrat in his generation to make a reputation for himself in public life. He will take office without any obligation to a single professional politician. . . . He showed that an attractive candidate does not need the professionals.

The newspaper noted that even Curley himself had remained "neutral" during the campaign, refusing to endorse any of the candidates for his seat. "Thus Kennedy has no obligation to the man he will succeed in Washington."

The *Boston Post* went further. Jack Kennedy's "nomination is tantamount to election," it noted. "He brings to Congress talents that will be useful to the nation. He has a broad understanding of international affairs and has been a world traveler. With a keen mind and maturity beyond his years, he has a fine grasp of domestic problems."

Meanwhile, as Jack left the Bellevue Hotel for a "two-week vacation at the Kennedy estate in Hyannisport," no one considered the candidate's feelings about politics after his baptismal campaign. What had it all meant, and what had he learned?

Jack had campaigned, as he himself put it, as "a fighting conservative." "The candidate's political stance was almost ultraconservative," his secretary, Billy Sutton, later admitted. "Personality, religion, and background proved to be the big factors in the district's voting booths."

John I. Fitzgerald later recalled that, "most of the fellows in the legislature thought Jack was a carpetbagger. Jack himself was shy. I would say he was reluctant to give in to the nitty gritty of local politics. I mean he didn't want to be involved in getting contracts for getting mail out at Christmastime. He wasn't interested in patronage—he wanted a political or public life that didn't involve patronage—and that made him different from other politicians. He wanted politics, but he didn't want to be involved with what goes with it. He didn't want the 'You do this for me and I'll do that for you.' "

Jack's heart was clearly not in old-fashioned politicking nor in the daily play of power and influence. "I do think that people are taking politics more seriously than before. They no longer consider a campaign just a political game," he told the *Sunday Advertiser*. "Most people who voted for me did so because of the things they hoped I could do. . . . In the next six months I intend to learn as much as I can about the needs of the district and try and think out remedies."

The needs of the district, however, came second in Jack's restless mind to the problems of the world. Aboard the aircraft taking him to Hyannis, Jack sat next to George Lanigan, a lawyer who had supported Mike Neville. Years later Lanigan recalled the journey and their conversation:

> He asked, "What's the major problem with the district?"
> I said, "Welfare."
> "What about communism?"
> "What about communism?" I'll never forget him saying that—while I'm thinking about putting guys to work and raising their welfare allowances and unemployment benefits!

Some Elements of the American Character

Among the many congratulations Jack received on his nomination was a letter from Pat Lannan, who claimed to have "followed many magazine and newspaper articles about your campaign and have decided you have become the most frequently photographed man in America. You know that I wish you luck in everything you tackle and furthermore, I am sure that you will always make your own luck."

Jack's sister Kathleen, who'd now bought herself a house in Smith Square, near the Houses of Parliament in London, wrote "just to tell you how terrifically pleased I am for you. Everyone says you were so good in the election and the outcome must have been a great source of satisfaction. It's nice to know you are as appreciated in the 11th Congressional District as you are among your brothers and sisters. Gee, aren't you lucky?

"The folks here think you are madly pro-British so don't start destroying that illusion until I get my house fixed. The painter might just not like your attitude!"

For two months Jack had been trying to project himself before his prospective constituency, yet had remained wary lest he provide his opponents with ammunition against him. Now, in the aftermath of his primary victory, he could afford to be more philosophical. On July 4, 1946, he "delivered before the City Government and Citizens of Boston in Faneuil

Hall, on the one hundred and seventieth anniversary of the Declaration of Independence of these United States," the annual Boston Independence Day oration, entitled "Some Elements of the American Character."

As Lanigan had found, Jack's mind was locked on world issues rather than local or even national matters. John F. Fitzgerald had given the oration exactly half a century before, in the same hall. Now, standing before his white-haired grandfather, gaunt and sallow-skinned so that his ears stood out, giving him the same "elfin" quality his mother attributed to him in childhood, the newly nominated Democratic candidate for the Eleventh Congressional District analyzed the American character and lauded the virtues that had made the nation successful in peace and in war, but that would now have to contend with perils unknown and inconceivable to the founding fathers.

Though unremarked in the Boston press and never later published, "Some Elements of the American Character" went to the heart of Jack Kennedy's strange mix of idealism and realism. He began by discussing religious morality, which in America had led to the abolition of slavery and on foreign battlefields to the recent defeat of racism as practiced by Germany and Japan, but which was now challenged "at home in the cynical philosophy of many of our intellectuals, abroad in the doctrine of collectivism, which sets up the twin pillars of atheism and materialism as the official philosophical establishment of the State." He referred to the "idealistic elements" in the American character, abhorring the view of cynics that American history could be reduced to "an economic interpretation" alone. He pointed out that the soldiers both of the North and the South had fought for principles in the Civil War, whether the right of secession or the preservation of the Union, as had the American troops in both world wars. "It is now in the postwar world that this idealism—this devotion to principle—this belief in the natural law—this deep religious conviction that this is truly God's country and we are truly God's people—will meet its greatest trial.

"Our American idealism finds itself faced by the old-world doctrine of power politics. It is meeting with successive rebuffs, and all this may result in a new and even more bitter disillusionment, in another ignominious retreat from our world destiny. But, if we remain faithful to the American tradition, our idealism will be a steadfast thing, a constant flame, a torch held aloft for the guidance of other nations. It will take great faith."

Sketching both the "patriotic" and the "individualistic elements" of the American character, Jack brought his Independence Day oration to a close with an expression of his most fundamental political philosophy, which would remain with him, despite many upsets and challenges, in the years ahead.

Conceived in Grecian thought, strengthened by Christian morality, and stamped indelibly into American political philosophy, the right of the individual against the State is the keystone of our Constitution. Each man is free. He is *free* in *thought*. He is *free* in *expression*. He is *free* in *worship*. To us, who have been reared in the American tradition, these rights have become a part of our very being. They have become so much a part of our being that most of us are prone to feel that they are rights universally recognized and universally exercised. But the sad fact is that this is not true. They were dearly won for us only a few short centuries ago and they were dearly preserved for us in the days just past. And there are large sections of the world today where these rights are denied as a matter of philosophy and as a matter of government.

We cannot assume that the struggle is ended. It is neverending. . . .

May God grant that, at some distant date, on this day, and on this platform, the orator may be able to say that these are still the great qualities of the American character and that they have prevailed.

Listening to Jack's speech, his grandfather's heart burst with pride. Others wondered at the difference between the father, Joseph Kennedy, and his son, the shy, unemotional, scholarly, and sickly looking youth, who could so move his audience by his idealism.

"John F. Kennedy will be a member of Congress at 29," commented one of the Boston papers. "Could be he'll yet outshine his dynamic and famous dad."

The Hunt for Sex

Joseph Kennedy later expressed surprise at how well Jack got on with Joe Kane, his cousin: "I thought Jack wouldn't last five minutes with him." What the ex-ambassador failed to see was the extent to which Jack warmed to Kane's picture of the politician as a maverick: "In politics you have no friends, only co-conspirators. You conspire to grab the diamonds and everybody runs, see?"

Jack saw, and having grabbed the Democratic-party diamonds in June 1946, he now ran to Hollywood. Traveling first to New York, he visited Inga Arvad, but found her currently being courted by the elderly John Gunther, whose books on European politics Jack had so admired before the war. Then there was the pretty, brown-eyed, dark-haired Flo Pritchett. But of "eligible" women there was no more sign than in Boston. "They were all divorcées," Cis McLaughlin noted. "They were all safe, he knew he couldn't marry any of them."

In New England class and education counted. In New York, wealth was the lingua franca. But in Hollywood, Jack recognized, it was sex and image—the one feeding the other. It was this that lured the now-official Democratic candidate for Congress.

On previous trips to Los Angeles Jack had tried to get his foot in the Hollywood door: in 1936 as the playboy son of the U.S. ambassador on leave from Princeton; in 1940 as the Stanford student and bestselling author of *Why England Slept;* in 1945 as a medically discharged naval war hero, going to parties and prominent restaurants. Now, flushed with his first political success, he made his way straight onto the film sets, bent on "knocking a name," as he put it to his friend Chuck Spalding.

The beautiful Gene Tierney, on the set of *Dragonwyck,* remembered how, when directed to turn toward the camera, "I turned and found myself staring into the most perfect blue eyes I had ever seen on a man. . . . He smiled at me. My reaction was right out of a ladies' romance novel. Literally, my heart skipped. . . . A coy thought flashed through my mind: I was glad I had worn a lavender gown for my scene that day. Lavender was my best color."

Though later gilded, Tierney's portrait of the twenty-nine-year-old Jack Kennedy had certain similarities to Gloria Swanson's portrait of the thirty-nine-year-old banker and film producer Joseph Kennedy. But whereas Joseph Kennedy had brazenly used his money and power as a studio producer to force his way into Swanson's affections, Jack's style of seduction was very different. "Jack was tall and thin," Tierney related. "He had the kind of bantering, unforced Irish charm that women so often find fatal. He asked questions about my work, the kind that revealed how well he already knew the subject." Where Joe Kennedy had exploded when Swanson dared talk of Rosemary, his retarded daughter, Jack was sympathetic and frank. "I was separated from my husband [Oleg Cassini] and though I had not yet filed for divorce, both believed our marriage to be ended. I was nearing the decision to place Daria, our retarded child, in an institution. Jack understood. He told me about his sister Rosemary, who had been born retarded, and how his family had loved and protected her. The subject was awkward for him. The Kennedys did not survive by dwelling on their imperfections. 'Gene,' he said, after a silence had passed between us, 'in any large family you can always find something wrong with somebody.' "

Gene Tierney became so enamored of Jack that, she later claimed, she even spurned the advances of Tyrone Power. Whatever he might whisper to her on the dance floor, however, Jack was in love neither with Tierney nor with any of the married women, divorcées, ice skaters, and starlets whom he dated.

Soon Jack was quoted in the papers as the constant companion of Peggy Cummins, an aspiring British actress. "News from the Hollywood love front," Sheilah Graham breathlessly noted in her gossip column on August 15, 1946; "Peggy Cummins and Jack Kennedy are a surprise two-some around town during the congressman-for-Boston's visit here. Jack, as you know, is the son of Joseph P. Kennedy, former ambassador to Great Britain."

Such constancy on Jack's part was, however, highly doubtful. Like his onetime interest in the Stanford campus queen, Flip Price, Jack's pursuit of Cummins was remorseless only as long as he believed she might go to bed with him. "She was a nice girl—an English girl—better educated than most starlet types," Betty Spalding recalled, as well as Jack's disappointment when Peggy refused to surrender her virtue.

"It wasn't a serious thing," Betty emphasized:

> She was just a girl to date. . . . Jack was quite thin and sickly at that time and he got out of Boston, deliberately, because he didn't want to be sucked into paying off a lot of election debts and be bound by it. So he ducked out there for his jollies and sun and rest. . . . He was marvelous company. . . . We went to the movies a lot. . . . His clothes were always horrible. . . . His manners were really terrible. He didn't have any manners, in the sense of letting women go through the door first or opening doors for them or standing up when older women came into the room. He was nice to people, but heedless of people, heedless about his clothes, and heedless about money. He never had any money with him. And he was very tight with his money too. He was parsimonious. Just a funny habit he had. . . . I have no idea why this was.

One reason was that though Jack was hunting for sex, he was equally fearful that women might be hunting for his money. By not having any on his person, he was consciously or unconsciously testing the genuineness of their affection for him. His carelessness was doubtless similarly inspired, and certainly effective in a shallow yet haunting way. "Jack told me how he was going to conquer the world. He was so sure of himself, but there was also this wonderful little boy quality about him," Gene Tierney recalled. "I am not sure I can explain the nature of Jack's charm, but he took life as it came. He never worried about making an impression. . . . Gifts and flowers were not his style. He gave you his time, his interest."

How little Gene would be able to count on this interest would become clear to her in the years ahead, just as it had become clear to Inga, and even to Jack's loyal male friends. For instance, Red Fay, at his home in Woodside, near San Francisco, waited for Jack to make his promised trip to meet his parents and friends, following his stay in Hollywood. A grand welcoming party was laid on, complete with a humorous banner announcing KENNEDY FOR PRESIDENT across the drive.

To Fay's indignation, Jack announced by telephone he was too busy to come to San Francisco and would stay in Hollywood. Fay insisted. "I picked him up at the airport. He was bragging about screwing Sonja Henie," Fay recalled. "I remember he didn't have any money. I loaned him twenty dollars—a lot of money to me in those days—and I had to write him a couple of letters to get it back. I was really irritated."

Having reluctantly made the journey to Woodside, Jack made no attempt to ingratiate himself with Fay's family and deeply offended Fay. "Jack didn't make too many friends with my father or mother or myself," particularly when he abandoned the party halfway through with an old PT buddy "and went to the movies!" It seemed a very cavalier way for Jack to behave toward a friend who himself had traveled thousands of miles and spent a number of weeks helping "the candidate" in Boston.

Such arrogance and lack of consideration seemed at odds with the wholly genuine, unstuck-up PT-boat captain. Was Jack changing, his friends wondered, now that he'd passed the first hurdle in becoming a politician? Or was this the dross floating on a young man who knew at last his destiny?

Coming of Age

Perhaps Henry James, who'd seen Jack in New York and Hyannis Port as he limbered up to go into politics, best described the metamorphosis in Jack's character: "You can say that I knew him at the very peak of his humanity," he later reflected of their friendship at Stanford in the fall of 1940: "charming, intelligent, self-searching—and of that I'm everlastingly proud."

However self-searching Jack might once have been, the politician had been born, and the result, James observed, even though Jack so little resembled a typical politician, was inevitably unsavory. "I didn't see the whole evolution of the process," James said, "but I did see certain signs, which made it very clear to me that I was losing him as a person and that perhaps the only way I could ever see him again was as a former friend, unimportant probably, for I wasn't going to be his toady like Lem Billings—I put more value on myself than that. . . . I envied people like Billings for their continuing close relationship to Jack, but I didn't respect them for it."

What saddened Henry James was Jack's gradual abandonment of honesty, egality, and fraternity among friends as he donned his political mantle, like Prince Hal who, on coming of age, surrenders the boyhood friendships that have been his lifeline to truth. Even friends who *wanted* Jack to go into politics, to become a force for good on the national and international political stage, would be hurt by Jack's behavior.

Following Red Fay's party, Jack went back to Boston, where there were certain vital meetings he had to attend. "He was going to be the chairman or commandant of the National Encampment of the Veterans of Foreign Wars for that year," Peter Cloherty explained. "It was going to be held in Boston. He liked to see the letters he sent out—didn't [just] sign a form. So we'd mail out packages of letters to the [West] Coast. He was vacationing around Los Angeles and Hollywood. I don't think there was any particular girl out there—anyplace he went there would be a bevy. We used to say that you could see the dollar signs in the [eyes of the] mothers of most of those girls! He had some very attractive girls he went out with in New York. But there wasn't any one girl in particular. He must have been having a good time, though, because when he finally got back from the Coast, there in his luggage were all the letters we'd sent out to him! He had not taken the time to sign them and send them out. We had to do them all over again because they were all messy!"

It was this messy aspect of Jack's character that worried Jack's more thoughtful political collaborators. Since the evenings they'd spent discussing world affairs in the native huts of Tulagi, Red Fay and Jim Reed were convinced Jack Kennedy had it within him to achieve the very highest office. So did a number of the volunteer helpers who'd crowded the various headquarters of his congressional primary campaign. He had the brains, the courage, a shy charisma, good looks, idealism, money. . . . Yet, as always, there was something missing—a certain depth or seriousness of purpose—that seemed to wary observers to be as indicative of his politics as of his amours. Both were, in a way, all too easy. The chase was the challenge, with voters as with women. Once the voters or the women were won, there was a certain vacuousness on Jack's part, a failure to turn conquest into anything very meaningful or profound.

Inga Arvad had once confided to Arthur Krock that Jack was a poor lover—a boy, not a man, intent upon ejaculation and not a woman's pleasure. As Jack's friend Lem Billings remarked, Jack never changed: "He knew he was using women to prove his masculinity, and sometimes it depressed him. I think he wanted to believe in love and faithfulness and

all that but what he'd seen at home didn't give him much hope. So he sort
of bumped along."

Humped along might have been a better description. In politics it was
no different, according to Tony Gallucio, who later became Jack's secretary in Boston. Of the 1946 primary Gallucio later remarked, "Kennedy
didn't have a political issue. If you had to analyze the Kennedys in depth,
they were master political technicians. They knew how to get elected.
They had no philosophy. The instincts were there."

Peter Cloherty thought the times were perfect for Jack. "It was more
a day of having the candidate meet the people and shake hands with them
than now. Not so much issues. So there wasn't any grand strategy, it was
more trying to touch all the bases, get him into every district, get him out
on the street as much as possible, meeting people and shaking hands."
Robert Lee, the state senator in whose house Jack had collapsed, said the
same. "The speeches were very short and brief and he always believed in
mixing with the crowd and shaking their hands. But always moving . . ."
John Droney saw it that way too. "We kept moving, never allowing the
crowd to ask him too many questions. We didn't want him to talk
campaign issues."

As Tony Gallucio observed, Jack's personality perfectly matched the
"young amateurish mood" of the time. "His political base was the young
people who had no political affiliations. . . . He wasn't forceful. He was
a lousy speaker when he started, he was pathetic. . . . The only thing, he
was quick. . . . He was relaxed up there. . . . His big asset was that he was
so relaxed and smiling and informal."

Jack had consented to a political career for a variety of reasons, most
of all to prove to himself, his family, and his friends that he could do it:
that he could make that journey to the top of the mountain that had
eluded his father and grandfather. For the first time in the history of the
Fitzgeralds and the Kennedys since 1918, a Kennedy had won an election.
Yet in the deeper sense of political mission, Jack was still very unclear
how he would achieve his cherished dream or what his agenda should be.
"Did I ask him about his long-term plans? Yes," Jack's voluntary helper
Fred Good recalled. "He said, 'Well, I will serve in Congress and we'll
sort of see which way the wind is blowing,' or words to that effect; 'I
certainly don't intend to remain in Congress all my life. I would like to
represent my state as Senator. . . .'

"He definitely was *very* ambitious. And between the two of us, I don't
think he wanted to waste any time as congressman. He felt he could do
nothing of any national importance there, and I think that's what he had
at the back of his mind all along."

Jack had still to be elected congressman, however. In the meantime, he shielded his emotions, as he always had, behind a shell of tart, bewitching humor. "I have been hoping that you would be dropping East before now and if you do I hope you will give me a call at the Hotel Bellevue," he wrote to thank Pat Lannan for his congratulations on his success in the primaries. "Grandpa Fitzgerald asks every day if I have seen you as he wants to know what has happened to that window glass," he went on, referring to the fall in American Window Glass's share price. "As a matter of fact I want to know. Is it time to buy or sell, or too late to do either? You can see Pat that your patrons' accounts need some attention, so I hope you will keep in touch with me. I sent that scotch about two months ago and I imagine by this time you have not got any. I will be glad to help you out again."

Lannan replied that "if you ever did send me any Scotch, it must have been by way of China, The Cape, Europe, New York and Chicago. *Believe me, I did not receive it."* Lannan was more worried by growing signs of a big swing toward the Republican party, however, "I hear rumors of a very strong GOP wind. . . . I cannot say I am surprised but no matter how hard that wind blows, I hope with everything that's in me it does not affect your District and that you bring your campaign to a successful conclusion. I expect a special invitation to join you your first day in Congress and *I mean just that."*

Always There

Going to stay at Cape Cod later that year, Gene Tierney described how "Jack met me at the station, wearing patched blue jeans. I thought he looked like Tom Sawyer." He looked at her with the same wistful smile with which he faced the many hundreds of audiences that had gathered and still gathered to hear him.

In a very real sense Jack was now making himself up as a politician as he went along, his shirt hanging out, his unsigned letters lying in his suitcase. And in the interval between fierce electoral contest and the reality of forthcoming congressional office, it was his father, as always, who for all his misjudgments and odium brought stability and nuts-and-bolts, back-room professionalism to Jack's burgeoning career. All through the primary campaign he'd ensured that Jack's paid staff serve Jack, yet answer to him. "The father was a great help in the campaign," John Droney recalled, "because we were as green as grass. Even though he stayed out of it, he wasn't out of it. He was very much in it. Anytime I ever had a problem, I'd call him and he'd help us. . . . He took a very active part in it." Peter Cloherty felt the same way. Though Jack made "a very happy candidate, the father was the most serious of all. He'd come into town and put up at the Ritz and send for different people individually to get reports from them. He compared them. He compared the stories of what each one had to say about the progress of the campaign. . . . He was strictly business. . . . You'd go up to his suite at the Ritz. Generally there'd be somebody with him—a secretary or somebody. . . . He would ask you three or four very pointed questions about how this one was doing and how that one was doing. He was all business. Not severe, but he didn't spend a lot of time on amenities. And then you were just dismissed, that's all."

"He tried not to be visible to the general public," recalled John I. Fitzgerald of the ex-ambassador's role, "but he was always there. If there was a big rally at Symphony Hall, he was near the rear exit door, where he could see everything but nobody would ever think of going out that way." He was also completely indifferent to what people thought of him, sneering once to Dave Powers that "more people die of jealousy than cancer."

Odious or not, the ex-ambassador's determination to second-guess every move and watch over the spending of every cent had paid off, demoralizing opponents and ensuring that Jack's carelessness and the shenanigans of old-time rival candidates would not harm his progress. When a priest in a North End pulpit claimed that Jack was not a churchgoer, retribution was swift: Joseph Kennedy instantly called the cardinal. "The great success of the Kennedys was that he [Joseph P. Kennedy] operated on one side of the street with guys that Jack didn't like," John Galvin reflected; "The Ambassador—as he liked us to refer to him— would operate with McCormack, leader of the Massachusetts team in Congress, and Paul Dever. And he would operate with Bill Mullins and the old political writers and everything else at the Ritz. And Jack wouldn't be speaking to half these guys!"

While the ex-ambassador's constant vigilance threatened at times to demoralize the candidate, it was at least a manifestation of unfailing parental commitment. Others might sniff and scoff at such a controlling, overbearing, and ambitious father, but at least the ex-ambassador *cared* enough to act. A quarter of his holdings in the Chicago Mart, for example, he now gave over to a charitable foundation in the name of his dead son, Joseph P. Kennedy, Jr., and on August 12, 1946, in front of flashing cameras and a multitude of journalists, Jack, as president of the new foundation, handed over a check for $600,000 to Cardinal Cushing to help the children of the poor in Boston.

The ex-ambassador's own politics might be raw and cynical, but his energy and growing faith in Jack knew no bounds, and it contrasted

sharply with the apathy, war weariness, and blinkered concerns of many
New Englanders. "It was the part he played. He was always there," Dave
Powers recorded. "It was great to know that you had someone like that
in your corner."

Returning from Hollywood, Jack's speeches more and more took on a
moral tone, conveyed in a strangely persistent appeal to others to commit
themselves to deeds, not talk. At a meeting of young Democrats in
Pennsylvania on August 21, discussing "the stake of the veterans in the
national elections," Jack scorned the malaise, as he saw it, of political
indifference:

> There are some people in this country, and there are veterans among
> them, who feel this coming election is of little importance. Perhaps
> the fatigue of post-war America explains this indifference.
>
> Perhaps it is explained by the fact that politicians are regarded in
> this year of our Lord as a necessary evil, and there is even some
> question about their necessity. Whatever the reason, to me, this lack
> of interest, this apathy, is dangerous and may be disastrous.
>
> Remember the words of Rousseau: "As soon as any man says of
> the affairs of state 'What does it matter to me?' the state may be given
> up as lost." Today many men—and women—are saying, "What
> does it matter to me?"
>
> It should matter a lot, and especially should it matter to the
> veterans. The veterans now comprise about 43 percent of the men in
> this country. A large percentage—too large to permit ourselves to
> feel that we are a privileged minority; too large to feel that we have
> only rights, not duties—too large to see clearly that it was not for
> others that we fought, but for ourselves. Too large indeed, to be
> indifferent to the future of our country.
>
> I think most veterans recognize that this is true. They recognize
> that their work has only begun. And they understand also that the
> next year will be decisive years in the country that they worked so
> hard to preserve.
>
> On the decisions of the next congress rests our future. . . .
>
> This, then, leads us to the question: Which political party can best
> meet the critical problems we face?
>
> There are some people in this country, and there are veterans
> among them, who feel that party designations have become unim-
> portant. They point to conservative Democrats and progressive
> Republicans. But parties are not made by single men. The philoso-
> phies of political parties are hammered out over long periods—in
> good times and in bad—in war and in peace. And anyone who views
> objectively the political parties of this nation cannot but come to the

conclusion that, from the days of Andrew Jackson on to the present days, the Democratic party has always fought the people's fight, has always been the party that supported progressive legislation.

That is why I believe the Democratic party is the party that most veterans will support. . . . They recognize that the Democratic party is best for the country and only if the country as a whole prospers will the various groups within the country prosper. For prosperity is not divisible.

While most veterans are grateful for what our political parties have done for them in the past, they are more concerned with what our political parties offer them to help meet the future. . . . The Democratic party stands for full employment and high production. It stands for an extension of social security, to give full protection to the unemployed and aged. It stands for a minimum wage, not only for humane reasons but because it recognizes that, only by strengthening of consumer purchasing power can prosperity in this country be maintained. . . . It stands for regional development and projects, such as TVA [Tennessee Valley Authority]. It stands for effective price control to protect wage earners and consumers until production in this country approaches demand. It stands today as it has stood in the past, for the enactment of progressive legislation that will be of aid to the people, that will preserve our system of private enterprise and strengthen the fabric of our society. And most important, in my opinion, the Democratic party recognizes that our present prosperity is precarious and to protect it the government must be prepared to use its strength and its resources in fighting economic stagnation wherever it threatens.

This is the program of the Democratic party. This is the political philosophy that is at stake in the election this fall.

As Jack's friend Pat Lannan noted, this was very much more the example of FDR that Jack was embracing than of ex-ambassador Kennedy. Yet, if this philosophy had little to do with Joseph Kennedy's narrow views, it did owe its semipriestly idealism and call to commitment at least in part to the unrelenting commitment of his ignoble father. In Hollywood Jack might strut and pose, determined to crack the code of its mystique and glamour, a proverbial playboy to his fingertips. Returning to the challenging winds of New England, however, he returned to the onerous but bracing expectations of his fearsome father, behind whom, like a vaudeville chorus, stood Jack's brothers and sisters—Bobby, Pat, Eunice, Jean, and Teddy, chanting to the same tuneless but insistent melody: "Do, do, do! Win, win, win!"

On September 2, 1946, before Admiral Chester Nimitz, Governor

Tobin, Mayor Curley, and twenty thousand veterans assembled for the 1946 national encampment, Jack repeated his call to political awareness and action. At Choate School on September 27, 1946, Jack harped on the same theme. He chided the faculty for teaching Plato and Aristotle but being indifferent to the machinery of mid-twentieth-century politics that distinguished democracy from collectivism:

> I believe that in the future, if Choate is really to survive, the men who teach at Choate must instill in its students an active interest in our politics and in the National life around us.
>
> I remember when I announced my candidacy, I was slapped on the back by a great many lawyers, bankers, and stockbrokers who wished me well and said they were glad to see young fellows going into politics. But that was the last I ever saw of them.
>
> They helped neither me nor my opponents. . . .
>
> The figures show it. In Brookline, a very well-to-do community, only twenty percent of the people voted in the primary; in New York in a recent congressional election only ten percent. They called themselves independents, they voted only in a presidential election, which meant in fact that they were too lazy to vote in a primary. And they are the people who have the greatest stake in our society. They are the ones who criticize the most and who have and will have, in the future, much to lose; but they take little or no interest in our political life. And many of them are graduates of schools like this. . . .
>
> We must recognize that if we do not take an interest in our political life we can easily lose at home what so many young men so bloodily won abroad. . . . It is the greatest challenge of our times.

To those listening to the erstwhile enfant terrible of Choate, the arch-Mucker of 1935, the transformation must have seemed incredible, perhaps even somewhat suspicious, given that Jack himself had never voted in a local primary election in his life until his own candidacy that year. Meanwhile, for all his evil genius, it was the swindling, sacked ambassador Joseph P. Kennedy who, by his bullying, relentless, even caustic expectations, kept Jack harnessed to the challenge, a challenge that would shortly move to a national stage. "You would have been as proud as we of Jack, (you couldn't have been any prouder!)" Jack's old headmaster wrote to the ex-ambassador. "It must have been quite an ordeal for him to make a four-minute speech in a program which included all the leading educators of the East; but of all the talks that were given, I think I heard more honest praise of Jack's than of any other. He spoke simply and convincingly and inspiringly: leaving an ineffaceable impression on the hearts and minds of all who heard him—and saw him!

"These are exciting days for you all, with the election so close at hand: but there seems to be no question in anyone's mind of Jack's success—or of his worthiness to fill an all-important place in our country's service."

Cri de Coeur

More and more it looked as if Jack's exhortations to the public were an appeal to share with him his own forthcoming journey: a journey born of both his own dreams and his father's vicarious ambition, yet one Jack seemed to hope, by sharing with others, he could enact upon a larger stage than his father's tyrannous compounds at Hyannis Port or Palm Beach. The New Frontier was thus already a territory, if unnamed, in Jack's mind—an area of untainted idealism, spawned in duty, even psychological oppression, yet promising freedom.

In the whole of Jack's political vocabulary at this time freedom was, interestingly, the only word that aroused real and powerful feelings in him, a fact vividly demonstrated when ex-vice president Henry Wallace was dismissed as secretary of commerce by President Truman.

Wallace's pro-Soviet views outraged the president. They also outraged Jack Kennedy, who turned a routine electoral radio speech in Boston in October into a passionate plea for courage and clear-sightedness in handling the Soviet Union. "The time has come when we must speak plainly on the great issue facing the world today. The issue is Soviet Russia," Jack began his broadcast, and went on to explain how, at a meeting of Young Democrats of New York which he'd addressed "a few nights ago," he'd finished his talk by asking if there were any questions.

> Immediately, one of the men present asked me how I felt about Soviet Russia. I told the group that I felt that Soviet Russia today, is run by a small clique of ruthless, powerful and selfish men, who have established a government which denies the Russian people personal freedom and economic security. I told them that Soviet Russia today is a slave state of the worst sort. I told them that Soviet Russia is embarked upon a program of world aggression. I told them that the freedom-loving countries of the world must stop Soviet Russia now, or be destroyed. I told them that the iron curtain policy and complete suppression of news with respect to Russia, has left the world with a totally false impression of what is going on inside Soviet Russia today. I told them that the people in the United States have been far too gullible with respect to the publicity being disseminated

throughout the world by the clever and brilliant Moscow Propagandists.

I knew that my remarks would alienate the entire group which I was addressing. And I did alienate them.

"If I wished to be expedient, I could have gained their votes," Jack maintained, but he had declined to do so. "Many people will tell you that the Russian experiment is a good one, since the Russians are achieving economic security at a not too great cost in loss of personal freedom."

Jack, however, had been to Russia. Moreover he knew the foremost experts on the Soviet Union, from Averell Harriman to Chip Bohlen. "The truth is," Jack stated unequivocally, "that the Russian people have neither economic security nor personal freedom. Here is the evidence"— and he listed everything from the lack of the right to strike in the Soviet Union ("punishable by death") to the "deportation for five years to the remote regions of Siberia, of all dependents of a man who escapes military service by deserting abroad, even though the dependents do not know about his desertion. Russia is the only country in the civilized or uncivilized world which punishes a man who has committed no crime. Food consumption per head, far from rising during the period of Soviet rule, has actually fallen," and now stood 30 percent *below* that found for the *worst fed* 10 percent of the British population. "Is that economic security?" Jack asked. "If it is, I hope and pray that we never have Soviet economic security in the United States!"

He referred to the "Russian concentration camps" in Siberia; he listed the countries "grabbed since 1917" from the north and east of Russia, from Finnish Carelia to the Baltic States, eastern Poland, and islands of Japan; he noted the countries "under Soviet domination" from "Poland to Manchuria," and those areas where Russia was currently "waging a relentless struggle to gain control," including Greece and Turkey. "Mr. Wallace believes it natural that Russia should be suspicious of America and England in these post-war days and that her efforts to control the countries surrounding her are merely to build buffers against invasion from the East and West. Mr. Wallace believes that only by speaking softly, of not carrying the big stick, at least not waving it . . . can we ease Russia's suspicion, and work out a peaceful solution."

Jack firmly disagreed with Wallace, and supported secretary of state James Byrnes's "get tough with Russia" policy. "Dante," quoted Jack, "once said 'the hottest places in hell are reserved for those who in a period of moral crisis maintain their neutrality.' This crisis is both moral and physical. The years ahead will be difficult and strained, the sacrifices great, but it is only by supporting with all our hearts the course we believe to be right, can we prove that that course is not only right but that it has strength and vigor."

The radio talk was converted, on October 21, 1946, into a speech to the League of Professional and Business Women in Lynn, Massachusetts, and was given at a number of further meetings before Election Day, November 5, 1946, as well as thereafter.

To some, it seemed no more than the growing tenor of the times. To others, such as his political secretary, Billy Sutton, it was a mark of Jack's "ultraconservative political stance." Yet to those who knew Jack's normally detached and balanced approach to historical and political issues, this passionate denunciation of the Soviet system suggested something deeper; as though the issue touched upon a raw and personal nerve; as though, in its threat to "freedom," the Soviet menace touched an area of Jack's own psyche where he was most sensitive.

Certainly the word *freedom* was not one that had appeared in Jack's father's eight-page article, entitled "The U.S. and the World," in *Life* magazine earlier that year, However good the ex-ambassador's scriptwriters—the *Life* article was in fact ghosted by Robert Coughlan, a brilliant New York journalist—the ex-ambassador was incapable of concealing the purely selfish nature of his own interest in world affairs. In the ex-ambassador's vocabulary, America had no business "minding other people's business on a global scale." He found American foreign policy a mishmash of "good intentions, lofty ideals and high-hopes," of "worldwide meddling under the guise of benign interest." "In other words," he stated, "our present policy is based on a concept that is demonstrably unworkable and perilous" and he proposed instead the same appeasement policies that had characterized his approach to Hitler and the Nazis: "a realistic policy to take its place," one that concentrated "all its efforts in preventing another war."

Jack, by contrast, felt his father's assessment of Russia to be clinical and flawed. Whereas his father saw Russia as a nation with "the most direct-acting and effective government in the field of world affairs," Jack saw it—as he'd found at San Francisco—almost paralyzed by bureaucratic fear. Whereas his father, who had never been to Russia, saw it as possessing a "great and growing productive capacity . . . aggressive, confident and ruthless," Jack—who had actually visited the country— saw it as economically backward, masking its deficiencies by stealing what was left of East German industrial machinery, using forced German labor, and concealing its lack of genuine self-confidence by propaganda and uniforms, behind which lay a reality of Siberian concentration camps and a complete disregard for human dignity.

Although later writers assumed Jack Kennedy's anticommunism to be an offshoot of his father's right-wing sentiments, they were profoundly mistaken. Indeed, it might be said that Jack's peculiar sensitivity to the issue of communism in the fall of 1946 was a *rejection* of his father's views, in the wake of his triumphant primary.

As a carpetbagging, out-of-state millionaire's son, Jack felt that in order to win that contest he had had to accept his father's financial and organizational help while avoiding his father's disastrous misjudgments and habit of antagonizing people. This legerdemain, however, was not without cost. Nor was it easy. Preserving his own individuality and dignity in the shadow of such a controlling, irascible, threatening, demanding, and often demeaning father was paradoxically more difficult now than ever. His shielding brother was dead, and his widowed sister was living in self-imposed exile in Britain while his father intruded deeper into Jack's adult life than he ever had before. Not only did the ex-ambassador still flirt with and make passes at Jack's girlfriends as he had to his daughters' girlfriends, but as Cis McLaughlin recalled, he constantly tried to bribe or bully these girls into sleeping with him when they stayed at Hyannis Port or Palm Beach. "He had the reputation of being a bounder, and he really *was* a bounder!" Mrs. McLaughlin remarked, recalling how the ex-ambassador had invited her out in New York and had suggested she join him in his private apartment in Miami and have sex with him. " 'You are a good-looking girl and what are you wasting your time for?' he said. 'I pay my butler more than your husband will ever make for a living, you know you can do better.' This is the ilk of the guy—not at all nice! All the stories that I've heard, like Gloria Swanson—it has to be true, from my experience."

Inga Arvad certainly later concluded—according to her son—that "the Kennedy family was weird. The family was just an extension of the old man's schizophrenic condition. . . . She thought old Joe was awfully hard—a really mean man. He could be very charming when she and Jack were with him, but if she left the room, he'd come down on Jack about her and if Jack left the room, he'd try and hop in the sack with her. . . . She thought it was a totally amoral situation, that there was something incestuous about the whole family."

Why Jack accepted such tyranny, just as his mother Rose and the rest of the family had, Inga could never later understand. Reflecting on Jack and Kathleen, "she couldn't understand how two people who were that bright could stand for all that bullshit," Inga's son related.

In the end, Kathleen hadn't, and had determined she would spend the rest of her life in England. Without Kathleen, and with his sister Rosemary lobotomized, his elder brother killed, and his own election "bought," Jack's sensitivity to the concept of freedom—threatened by overbearing and brilliantly deceitful Russian Communists—was meanwhile sharpened to an extraordinary degree. He took his new speech to every gathering he addressed. "Kennedy Favors Stronger U.S. Foreign Policy," *The Boston Globe* reported about his address to the Boston Boot and Shoe Club. "Soviet Russia was criticized as a 'slave state run by a small clique of ruthless, powerful and selfish men.' " This and other of Jack's remarks were soon splashed across newspapers throughout New England. The people of Russia were "literally chained to the Hammer and Sickle," Jack declared, without the right to strike or even to travel. A Soviet citizen "cannot enter the industrial areas without special permission from the government. He cannot leave his home for more than twenty-four hours without reporting the fact to the police.

"The most serious matter of all inside Soviet Russia," Jack emphasized, "is the Siberian Labor Camp. On this matter there is a total black-out of news. It is here that the iron curtain covers, most effectively, Soviet Russia's greatest crime. Soviet officials will not deny the fact that the number of Russians in Siberian Labor Camps runs to eighteen to twenty million persons. What is going on in these camps?" Jack demanded.

The astute observer might well have asked the same question with regard to Jack's own life—at least with regard to his father. Was Jack not chained to the ex-ambassador's Hammer and Sickle? Was he not a prisoner of Hyannis Port and Palm Beach, requiring a permit to travel? Did his father not watch and control his movements, employ private detectives, pay the men working for Jack and insist upon constant communication? Moreover, was there not a complete blackout of news of his father's true behavior, from assaulting women guests to lobotomizing his daughter and running his son's political campaign? Kennedy and Stalin even shared the same first name.

It would be fanciful to suggest that young Jack Kennedy's political philosophy was rooted in his servility at home. Yet to ignore the parallel would be to miss the key to Jack's political heart. As a millionaire's son, privileged by private education and having seen war only in Naval Intelligence and the tragicomedy PT boat errors, Jack's experience of American life was sheltered and removed. Save for his brief, traumatic experience in the Solomons—an experience he never wished to repeat—he had never known hardship or the oppression of poverty nor even the need to earn a living. Nevertheless he *had* experienced oppression of another kind, in the tyrannical, Stalinesque figure of a father he both loved and resented.

"He was running because it was required," Billings later decided, "but he was also running because he thought he might be able someday, somehow, to locate *himself* in the middle of this complex mix of duty, expectation, and all the rest of it."

Concern with veterans' housing, social welfare, price controls—these were issues that Jack had a duty, as a veteran and as the likely political representative of a predominantly poor, urban American community, to champion. However, these issues did not in all honesty engage Jack's heart; indeed, there was considerable skepticism as to whether Jack *had* a political heart. "At a Liberal Union–sponsored conference of student progressives Saturday morning in Emerson Hall," the Harvard *Crimson* reported in October 1946, "a young lady delegate in the audience stood up to ask the speaker, former Congressman Tom Eliot, whether he thought John Kennedy, 11th District Democratic candidate in the current Massachusetts elections, would make the kind of progressive representative we're working for. Eliot replied, 'I spoke with Jack for about three hours the other afternoon on many of the issues facing this country—and I don't really think I'm qualified to answer your question.' "

The *Crimson,* interviewing Jack, had the same response:

> Product of a wealthy family notable in the nation's public life—his Grandfather "Honey Fitz" Fitzgerald, was Mayor of Boston, and his father was Roosevelt's ambassador to England—he has breathed the air of politics since childhood and is now engaged in selling himself as a regular guy to the plain people of Boston's poorer districts. "If you must tag me," he asks, "let's make it 'Massachusetts Democrat.' I'm not doctrinaire. I'll vote 'em the way I see 'em." . . . Kennedy seems to feel honestly that he is not hedging, nor playing politics by refusing to offer a positive specific platform. He feigns an ignorance of much in the affairs of government, and tells you to look at his record in two years to see what he stands for.

The *Crimson* did point out Jack's vehement stand against Soviet communism. "While working in the Paris Embassy in the summer of 1939," the *Crimson* recorded, "he succeeded in touring Russia and will tell you that it wouldn't be a very nice place to live. He views Russian expansionist policies as a real threat to this country, supports the halting of Communist influence no matter what the cost. 'Russia is the main threat, the only power militarily strong enough to constitute a threat to peace,' he asserts."

Until the final, predeath opening of his eyes to the threat arising *within* American society over civil rights, this was and would remain the first and only fundamental plank in Jack's political philosophy—a conviction so deep that it would surprise and indeed alarm most of Jack's liberal supporters in his later years, as it did the liberals who'd questioned him in 1946. In truth, however, there was no conundrum: the candidate of 1960 the same anti-Soviet as the congressional nominee of 1946, detached in the strangely disembodied way in which he approached all political issues save this, the one moral crusade that stirred his soul: the defense of freedom.

Congressman-Elect

On November 5, 1946, the people of Massachusetts, as throughout America, went to the midterm election polls. Maurice Tobin, the governor of Massachusetts, was overthrown, and his running mate for lieutenant governor, Paul Dever, also went down, as did the Democratic senator David I. Walsh, whose seat in Washington was taken by Republican Henry Cabot Lodge, Jr., for the statutory six-year term.

Against this avalanche of Republican successes, Jack Kennedy's triumphant victory over Lester Bowen in the Eleventh Congressional District of Massachusetts—by 69,093 votes to 26,007—not only demonstrated the near-disastrous political judgment of the ex-ambassador, but vindicated Jack's quiet insistence on running for Congress rather than for lieutenant governor.

"Congratulations! Am glad you survived the Republican 'tidal wave' because even the famous and somewhat notorious Kelly Machine took a terrific 'shellacking' here in Chicago," Pat Lannan wrote. "Remember, I am looking for big things from you."

Jack, according to those who were with him, was subdued. In its October headline the Harvard *Crimson* had referred to Jack as "Joe Kennedy's Boy." But was he really Joe Kennedy's boy? Was he not a very different son than Joe Jr. who Joe Dinneen in the *Boston Globe* once described as a "big, square-shouldered athlete with tousled bronze hair . . . greeting his father aboard the Queen Mary in a suite crowded with newspapermen—a good-natured, grinning son with smiling eyes that were always determined, looking at his idol—his father"?

Though he feared and admired his father, Jack did not idolize him—and felt more and more compassionate feelings for his dead brother, who *had* idolized the despised ex-ambassador, and had paid the supreme price both to bring honor to the family and be worthy of him. On Armistice Day, November 11, 1946, Jack addressed the American Legion post in Charlestown. "He was going along fine, giving a good speech until he came to 'No greater love has a man than he who gives up his life for his brother,' " a local supporter, Mary McNeely, recounted many years later. "Then he broke down and was unable to finish the speech."

The breakdown reflected not only Jack's unusual loss of composure at the memory of his brother's death, but the frailty of his own health. As events the following summer would prove, his condition was even worse than he himself realized, beset by a fatal illness that had already, unbeknownst to him and to the multitude of private and naval doctors who had attended him, destroyed the major portion of the gland producing adrenal hormone, without which his immune system was so weakened that he could be carried off by a common cold.

Meanwhile, over the course of the summer and fall, Jack had done much thinking about the larger domain of American postwar politics. "The traditional parties with their traditional viewpoints are held together by abnormal and precarious prosperity," he had warned in a speech to the Massachusetts Democratic Junior League. "When that prosperity breaks, which I believe it will, the alignments may change. . . . Strong sectional policy may find the party divided along conservative and liberal lines instead of as now containing elements of both. But that is for the future," Jack had cut himself short, contenting himself with a quotation from John W. Davis, who in a 1929 speech at Princeton had addressed would-be politicians:

> Do not expect to find a party that has always been right, or wise or even consistent. . . . Independent judgment and opinion is a glorious thing, on no account to be surrendered by any man: but when one seeks companionship on a large scale, he must be content to join with those who agree with him in most things and not hope to find a company that will agree with him in all things.

"All the things the Democratic Party has done I cannot approve," Jack had stated, "but most things done by the Democratic Party have made us stronger at home and abroad. This has been the great contribution of the Democratic Party and I am proud to be found among its members."

On November 26, 1946, the *Boston Post* published a photograph of Jack Kennedy before the great rotunda of the Capitol, looking through the houses-for-rent advertisements in a Washington newspaper. The caption read, "New Congressman Goes to Work—As House-hunter, not Lawmaker."

Tom Sawyer had finally reached the capital. But almost as soon as he had arrived he was off again, to spend Thanksgiving at Hyannis Port. James Kelley recalled how he had accompanied Jack in the plane of the secretary of the Navy, who had offered Jack a lift: "I remember that all the way up to Newport, Forrestal was talking to us about the threat posed by Communism—Soviet Russia. In Eastern Europe, Berlin, China. It was like an obsession with him."

If so, it was an obsession Jack shared with Forrestal: a single, emotive, challenging issue that would color Jack's entire political career and take him one day to the White House as the West's most committed anti-Soviet freedom fighter, willing to risk even nuclear war rather than submit to the dictates of "a small clique of ruthless, powerful and selfish men" running a "slave state."

In the meantime, Phyllis Brooks Macdonald would never forget Thanksgiving 1946 in Hyannis Port:

> By this time I had a little son, who I guess is eight or nine months old, and Jack calls us and starts to talk and invites us down to Hyannis for Thanksgiving.
>
> I said to myself, "Oh, God this is so wonderful, I'm going to go down there and be taken care of and there'll be people to cook for me and I can just relax." I was worn out, my first baby, my husband's college hours and all that sort of stuff.
>
> So we went down to Hyannis, I can't remember how I got there—somebody must have driven us, we didn't have a car at that time.
>
> We arrived in Hyannis and I noticed immediately there were no servants in evidence. I picked my own room for the baby and myself. I can't remember who was there . . . a fellow I think from Ohio who had roomed at one time with both Jack and Torb. . . . Anyway, I can't remember who was there. George Taylor was there, though—Jack's black valet and man-of-all-whatever. So I got settled, and was walking around with little Torby in my arms; the guys are sitting around, talking, and Jack says, "George, will you show Phyllis where the kitchen is?"
>
> It's getting clearer and clearer why I am invited!
>
> The stove was restaurant size, really! George had never cooked on this stove and it took an hour and a half to figure what buttons to press—it was a monstrosity. . . . So we spent a good part of the first afternoon figuring out how to run this monster!
>
> Then George said, "Well, I guess the farmer has dropped some chickens off."
>
> That's the way that vacation went! Nobody was there. Not even a caretaker that I saw. Just George and myself and these men! It was unbelievable.

She could not even relax on the drive back to Cambridge.

> On our way home George was driving.
>
> I don't know if it was Jack's car or the family car, he had this sort of Buick, small, like a roadster, there were seats in the back and it was open. I'm sitting in the back seat with Torbert. Jack and George are in the front.

Now, George Taylor was just one of the worst drivers! So I leaned over. I tapped Jack on the shoulder. I said, "Jack, you stop this car this minute! You stop George driving and you can leave me here on the sidewalk and I will thumb—I've got the life of my little child here to consider!"

Jack was—well, he agreed, told George to stop: "O.K., George, pull over."

Jack started to drive. But for Phyllis, this was still worse. In her view they were all heading straight for eternity. Not prepared to meet her maker so soon, Phyllis tapped Jack on the shoulder.

I said, "Jack! Stop the car, you pull over! Let Torbert drive."

"Sorry," he said, and he did. Torbert drove the rest of the way home. . . .

I haven't any other recollection of that Thanksgiving: I didn't think about anything but trying to get through that whole damned weekend in one piece, and with my baby! Forget politics—absolutely!

For Jack, however, there was no forgetting politics. "You have my best wishes for success in the tough job with which you have been entrusted," Herbert Bayard Swope had written to congratulate him the day after his election to Congress. "My crystal ball reveals you as the centre of a fascinating drama—one that carries you far and high. I hope I'm a true prophet."

Swope was, though how close Jack would come in the course of the drama to medical, sexual, marital, and political disaster, and what price he would pay for fulfillment of his dream, the crystal ball did not divulge. In the meantime he'd survived the Grim Reaper's many thrusts, both on and off the battlefield, had found a strange but effective modus vivendi with his father and, to Honey Fitz's ineffable joy, had won back the family seat in Congress surrendered at the behest of P. J. Kennedy some forty-six years before.

But above all, Jack had, by his performance as a student, his ability as a writer, his courage in war, and his honorable conduct in electoral combat, single-handedly reinvented the Kennedys. By his self-deprecating wit, his love of history, curiosity about others, and reckless spirit of adventure, Jack Kennedy had escaped his father's and his elder brother's narrow, selfish Boston-Irish bigotry and found a pluralist, idealistic, and yet internationally committed liberalism, a liberal spirit that would, one day, define a whole generation of Americans.

He had not, however, found true love—or if he had, he had not been able to hold on to it. That search would go on for the rest of his days.

With bags of talent but little in the way of possessions, the boy from Boston thus made his lonely way back again to the capital; his extraordinary early life over, his even more extraordinary political career about to begin.

Author's Note and Acknowledgments

The genesis of this book goes back to the summer of 1963. At the suggestion of my father* and thanks to the kindness of Kay Graham, the *Washington Post* trained me as an American reporter.

I was nineteen years old, and had just completed my freshman year at Cambridge University. I met Bobby Kennedy, covered a civil rights demonstration, played tennis with senators, argued about politics with congressmen, and lived with that most erudite of Americans, James Russell Wiggins, editor of the *Washington Post,* and his wife, Mabel. Though I turned my back on journalism and became in the end a biographer and historian, the excitement and buzz of the U.S. capital at the height of the Kennedy administration has never left me.

It was Russ Wiggins who, twenty years later, while I was researching my biography of Field Marshal Montgomery, asked if I had thought of my next biographical subject. I said that I had: John Fitzgerald Kennedy.

Russ was surprised. Library bookshelves groaned under the weight of Kennedy books, he protested. I agreed, but maintained no one had ever written a *complete* life, in the English tradition.

The next morning, having searched his literally voluminous library in Maine, Russ became enthusiastic. "You get down to it!" he ordered (ever the editor).

I couldn't. My biography of Monty became a three-volume affair, followed by a BBC television documentary, *Monty—in Love and War,* broadcast on the centenary of Monty's birth in November 1987. It was thus only in 1988 that I could begin work on JFK, moving to America with my wife and two of my children and setting up camp in JFK's birthplace, Boston.

As official biographer of Lord Montgomery I had enjoyed unique access to all Monty's private papers, as well as the trust and cooperation of the field marshal's relatives, military colleagues, and friends.

As unofficial biographer of JFK I have had a very different reception; indeed, when I first began my research I was warned at the JFK Presidential Library I might as well pack my bags and go home. The Kennedy family, I was politely informed, were deaf to the entreaties of potential biographers, and there was no public interest, it appeared, in a complete life of the president such as I envisaged.

*Sir Denis Hamilton, editor of the London *Sunday Times* 1961–1967 and editor in chief of the London *Times* and *Sunday Times* 1967–1981, as well as chairman of Reuters 1979–1985.

Persisting, I got down to work and, over the ensuing four years, found the whole climate of Kennedy studies and public interest in the life of JFK altering. As more and more revelations about his private life surfaced and as public attention refocused on the assassination of the president, the need for a serious, balanced, and scholarly biography grew more imperative. I can only hope that this first volume, despite its length, will not disappoint those who have awaited its long gestation. I have recorded JFK's formative years as conscientiously as I could, and I would like to express my gratitude to those who made the project possible.

First, I am deeply grateful to those members and former members of the Kennedy family who, despite natural reservations, helped me with what was sometimes a discomfiting task. President Kennedy's widow, Mrs. Onassis, was from the start of my undertaking gracious in her support and goodwill. Senator Edward Kennedy and his sister Mrs. Eunice Shriver were, at various times, warmly encouraging. However, my greatest debt as biographer is to JFK's closest friend, the late K. LeMoyne Billings. Despite severe eye disability, "Lem" Billings volunteered to serve in World War II in the American Field Ambulance Corps, participating in the decisive Allied victory at Alamein under the generalship of Bernard Montgomery, the subject of my previous biography. Access to Mr. Billings's collection of many hundreds of letters from JFK, as well as his own letters to JFK, and his eight-hundred-page oral history at the JFK Library, permitted me a unique insight into the growing pains—and ambitions—of the future president, and I am most grateful to those who made this possible.

Outside the Kennedy family, I owe an immense debt to President Kennedy's closest surviving personal friends: Chuck Spalding, Red Fay, Jim Reed, Henry James, and Bill Walton, all of whom freely gave their time, their memories, and their intimate insights. Without their trust, their goodwill, and their cooperation I could not have told this story, and I thank them from the bottom of my heart.

Writers do not always speak unto fellow writers. In undertaking this biography, I called upon many distinguished authors and historians who toiled in the fields of JFK studies before me. I would like to thank especially Professor Arthur M. Schlesinger, Jr., for his generous welcome and stalwart support throughout the undertaking; Professor McGeorge Bundy, Professor Burke Marshall, Professor John Kenneth Galbraith, and Professor James McGregor Burns for their unstinting encouragement, advice, and contributions; and also Professor Sir Michael Howard, who, with Arthur Schlesinger, encouraged my project in its earliest days and "sponsored" my soft landing in American academia. Theodore Sorenson, Pierre Salinger, Richard Goodwin, William Manchester, Milton Gwirtzman, Ben Bradlee, Robert Donovan, Richard Whalen, Herbert

Parmet, Doris Kearns Goodwin, Michael Beschloss, David Koskoff, David Horowitz, J. H. Cutler, Robert Coughlan, Ralph Martin, Thomas C. Reeves, and David Heymann have all given help, perceptions, and in many cases access to their research papers, and I am most grateful to them. Most especially among fellow authors, however, I'd like to single out Joan and Clay Blair, who opened to me their unique oral history collection and research papers, collected for their pioneering book *The Search for JFK.*

Although I originally came to the United States intending to stay for only a year, I was soon the recipient of a scholarship and visiting professorship at the University of Massachusetts at Boston. As the John F. Kennedy Scholar and Visiting Fellow in the John W. McCormack Institute of Public Affairs within the university, it has been my privilege both to teach and to learn. To the chancellor of the university, Sherrey Penney, and to Dr. Edmund Beard, the founding director of the McCormack Institute—the university's political, social, and economic think tank for matters concerning New England—my lasting gratitude, as also to my colleagues Ray Torto (acting director), Murray Frank, Ian Menzies, Dick Hogarty, Joe Slavet, Lou DiNatale, Barry Bluestone, Al Cardarelli, Tom Ferguson, Padraig O'Malley, Sandy Matava, Marcy Murningham and the institute's dedicated staff—Pat Pugsley, Kathleen Foley, Pat Mullen, Madeleine Pidgeon, Kathy Rowan, Megan Early, Mary-Beth McGee, and Ruth Finn. Paul Paquin and Ray Sawyer of the University of Massachusetts Computing Services deserve special mention for their technical guidance and help. To my colleagues in Graduate Studies—Dean Fuad; the former assistant dean, Robert Carter; and historians Clive Foss, Paul Bookbinder, Malcolm Smuts, and Jim O'Toole—my appreciation and thanks, as to my long-suffering students, many of whom have gone on to write their masters theses on JFK-related topics.

An especial boon in living, teaching, and researching in Boston has been the proximity of the John F. Kennedy Presidential Library. To the former director of the JFK Library, Professor Dan Fenn, I shall always be grateful for advice and unremitting encouragement. To Charles Daly, the present director, I also owe a great deal. Although a federal employee—since the library is a branch of the National Archives in Washington—Mr. Daly also wears the hat of ex-officio director of the JFK Library Foundation, a private body working within the library and wholly dominated by the Kennedy family. The JFK Library houses at considerable public expense the still secret, largely undeeded papers of Kennedy family members. Mr. Daly, like his predecessor, walks a veritable tightrope—anxious to fulfill the scholarly functions and public goals of the existing library, yet always under pressure not to upset the members of a wealthy and politically active family who might withdraw their papers without deeding them. We have often disagreed about this, incurring mutual wrath; but the outcome of my research in the "open" documents has been, I hope, a work of lasting value not only to those interested in knowing who was the real JFK, but also to those who want to understand the intricate human and historical factors that went into the making of a modern politician.

At the helm of the JFK Library archives stands the dedicated figure of the chief archivist, William Johnson. A thorn to those who still covet family favor more than the truth, he has been a tower of strength to me, my research assistant, my students, and to hundreds of other researchers over the past four years, and I thank him for his wise counsel, his professional expertise, and his abiding belief in furthering good scholarship. To his archival staff I would also like to extend my thanks—especially to Megan Desnoyers, Suzanne Forbes, Ron Whealan, Susan D'Entrement, Maura Porter, June Payne, Mary Bulloch, Lisa Middents, Michael Desmond—as well as to the library's historian, Sheldon Stern, his library colleagues John Stewart and Frank Rigg, and audio-visual archivists Jim Cedrone and Jim Hill.

In addition to the private papers of John F. Kennedy and all presidential records pertaining to the White House from 1961 to 1963 (where not withheld from public access), the JFK Library boasts an extensive collection of papers freely donated by colleagues and officials who served with or under JFK. It also houses some fifteen hundred specially commissioned interviews, the majority of which are finally being made available to the public (I am especially grateful to those who permitted special access to still-closed or undeeded interviews). Recorded in the 1960s in an era when it was considered lèse-majesté to criticize a recently slain president, these "oral histories" have the great advantage of nearness to events, but, to a historian and biographer, the disadvantage of infuriating bashfulness and reticence (usually in understandable deference to the president's widow and surviving family). Wherever possible I therefore tried to conduct fresh interviews with surviving JFK friends and historical witnesses and, while allowing for the passage of time and the dimming of memory, these enabled me to round out and balance the vast JFK Library oral history program. I would therefore like to thank the following for their great kindness in talking to me: the late Joe Alsop, William Anderson, the Hon. Mrs A. I. Astor, Joe Atkinson, George Ball, Charles Bartlett, Toni Bradley, Henry Brandon, Vice Admiral John Bulkeley, Vincent Celeste, Paul Chase, Glen Christiansen, Blair Clark, Al Cluster, William Coleman, Jr., Margaret Coit, Helen Cotter, the late Paul Corbin, the Duchess of Devonshire, William Douglas-Home, Sim Efland, John I. Fitzgerald, Benji Fraser, Alastair Forbes, Barry Goldman, Harriet Price Fullerton, Josephine Fulton, Vic Francis, John Galvin, Ruth Galvin,

Frederick Good, Jr., Michael Grace, Kay Graham, Rear Admiral John Harllee, John Hersey, Johnny Iles, Dr. James Lamphier, Dr. Timothy Lamphier, George Lanigan, George Leary, Francis McAdoo, Dr. Ronald McCoy, Laurie Macdonald, Phyllis Brooks Macdonald, Torbert Macdonald, Jr., John Meade, Ed McLaughlin, Robert S. McNamara, Billy Morrissey, Robert Neville, the late Camman Newberry, the late Lawrence O'Brien, Bob Pierpoint, Ralph Pope, Dave Powers, Ted Reardon, Jewel Reed, Martha Reed, Chalmers Roberts, James Rousmanière, the Rev. Seymour St. John, Gene Schoor, Senator George Smathers, Betty Coxe Spalding, Augustus Soule, William Sutton, Dr. George Thorn, Donald Thurber, Anne Truitt, Frank Waldrop, Al Webb, Nick Wells, Mrs. Nancy Wilder, John B. White, Holton Wood, Whitney Wright, and Hugh Wynne. Congressman Chester B. Atkins was especially helpful during my research trips to Washington; Professor Douglas Brinkley, Verne Newton, Mrs. "Fitzy" Goodman and William vanden Heuvel at Hyde Park; Dr. David Baker and Emmet Chisum and Claudia Stewart at the American Heritage Center in Laramie, Wyoming; Kasi McMurray at the Lannan Foundation in Los Angeles; Lee Sylvester at the Choate Rosemary School; Larry Leamer in Washington and Los Angeles; Len Bushkoff in Boston; John Newberry in Beverley Farms for especial kindness over photographs; and my friend Lt. Colonel Carlo D'Este on Cape Cod.

Beyond the JFK Library in Boston, I had access to a number of collections in archives throughout the United States, and I would, as a practicing historian, like to record my indebtedness to the following institutions and their invariably courteous staffs: American Heritage Center, University of Wyoming; Atlantic Monthly archives; Bancroft Library, University of California at Berkeley; Boston Public Library; Boston University archives; Brown University archives; Canterbury School archives; Choate School archives; College of the Holy Cross Archives; Columbia University archives; Courtenay Library, Harvard Medical School; Dexter School archives; FDR Library; HarperCollins archives; Edward Devotion School archives; FBI records; Gerald Ford Presidential Library; Harvard University archives; Hearst Newspapers archives; Healey Library, University of Massachusetts at Boston; House of Lords Library archives; Indiana University archives; Lannan Foundation, Los Angeles; The Library of Congress; Massachusetts State archives; National Archives, Washington, D.C.; National Archives, Military Reference Branch, Washington, D.C.; National Archives, Northeast Regional Branch, Waltham; Naval Historical Center, Washington Navy Yard, Washington, D.C.; Naval War College, Rhode Island; Newton Free Library; Princeton University archives, Seeley G. Mudd Library; Providence College archives; Public Record Office at

Kew; Rhode Island state archives; Riverdale Country Day School; Royal Archives at Windsor; Spee Club Library; Stanford University archives; Yale University archives; and Widener Library, Harvard University.

Thanks to generous advance royalties from my publishers in Britain and the United States, as well as a two-year research fellowship from the Leverhulme Trust, I enjoyed for the first time the services of a full-time research assistant, Stephen Corsaro, a graduate of Northeastern University recommended by Professor Ray Robinson. Stephen's diligence, perseverance, and dogged curiosity led to many untangled knots in JFK's complicated life thread. He also brought a Boston Italian-Irish Catholic perspective that has oftentimes rescued the English author from unwitting error, and to him I owe more than I can say. My British agent, Bruce Hunter (David Higham Associates), nursed this project from seed a decade ago, for which I shall always be indebted, as I am to my New York agent, Claire Smith (Harold Ober Associates). Mark Booth, my original commissioning editor at Hutchinsons in London, remained firmly committed to the project throughout its vicissitudes and thus enters for me the publisher's hall of fame—as does my late father's former colleague Harold Evans, who rescued American publication (and the author's peace of mind) at a critical moment in New York. However, it is to that legendary editor at Random House, Robert D. Loomis, that I and the reader owe whatever stylistic merit this once dangerously sprawling narrative now possesses—for it was he who recognized the strengths of this saga of youth and early manhood, and by identifying the weaknesses in the manuscript, with the aid of his young colleague Jennifer Ash, refused to be satisfied with less than the author's best.

Lastly, but not leastly, let me thank in print the companion who transcribed my illegible scrawl into Word Perfect and shared my nomadic life as an English biographer on American shores: my wife, Outi. Without her and my irrepressible kids, I simply couldn't have done it.

NIGEL HAMILTON

Notes on Sources

Abbreviations

AKP Arthur Krock Papers, Seeley Mudd Manuscript Library, Princeton University, Princeton, N.J.

AMA Atlantic Monthly Archives, Boston.

AMSD Arthur M. Schlesinger, Jr. Diary, by kind courtesy of Professor Schlesinger.

APCP Alvin P. Cluster Papers, by kind courtesy of Alvin P. Cluster.

AWRH *John Fitzgerald Kennedy—As We Remember Him* (N.Y.: Rand McNally, 1965).

BA *Boston American.*

BBP Bernard Baruch Papers, Seeley Mudd Library, Princeton University, Princeton, N.J.

BG *Boston Globe.*

BH *Boston Herald.*

BHCL Boston Herald Cuttings Library, by kind courtesy of Pat Purcell, publisher, the *Boston Herald.*

BT Boston *Traveler.*

CBSI CBS Interviews, Audio-Visual Archives, JFKL, by kind permission Columbia Broadcasting System/Macmillian Publishers.

CNP Camman Newberry Papers, by kind courtesy of John Newberry.

CSA Choate School Archives, Wallingford, Conn.

DEK David E. Koskoff, *Joseph P. Kennedy* (Englewood Cliffs, N.J.: Prentice-Hall, 1974).

DEKP David E. Koskoff Papers, by kind permission of David E. Koskoff.

DKG Doris Kearns Goodwin, *The Fitzgeralds and the Kennedys* (N.Y.: Simon & Schuster, 1987).

DSA Dexter School Archives.

FBI Federal Bureau of Investigation.

FDRL Franklin D. Roosevelt Presidential Library, Hyde Park, N.Y.

GS Gloria Swanson, *Swanson on Swanson* (N.Y.: Random House, 1980).

HS Hank Searls, *The Lost Prince: Young Joe, The Forgotten Kennedy* (N.Y.: New American Library, 1969).

JBKO Jacqueline Bouvier Kennedy Onassis.

JCB Joan and Clay Blair, *The Search for JFK* (N.Y.: Berkley/Putnam, 1976).

JCBP Joan and Clay Blair Papers, University of Wyoming Archives, Laramie, Wy., by kind permission of Joan and Clay Blair.

JFK John Fitzgerald Kennedy.

JFKL John F. Kennedy Presidential Library, Boston.

JFKLOH Oral history conducted for the John F. Kennedy Presidential Library, Boston.

JFKPP JFK Personal papers, John F. Kennedy Presidential Library, Boston.

JFKPrePres JFK Pre-Presidential Papers, John F. Kennedy Presidential Library, Boston.

JFKPOF Presidential Office Files, John F. Kennedy Presidential Library, Boston.

JFP James Forrestal Papers, Seeley Mudd Manuscript Library, Princeton University Archives, Princeton, N.J.

JHC John Henry Cutler, *Honey Fitz* (Indianapolis: Bobbs-Merrill, 1962).

JHP John Hersey Papers, by kind courtesy of John Hersey.

JMB James MacGregor Burns, *John Kennedy, a Political Profile* (N.Y.: Harcourt Brace, 1960).

JMBP James MacGregor Burns Papers, by kind permission of Professor Burns.

JML James M. Landis, draft manuscript for the unpublished "diplomatic memoirs" of former Ambassador Joseph P. Kennedy, Library of Congress, Washington, D.C., and JFKL, by kind permission of the daughter of Dean Landis, Anne McLaughlin.

JPK Joseph P. Kennedy, Sr.

JPK Jr. Joseph P. Kennedy, Jr.

JPLP J. Patrick Lannan Papers, Lannan Foundation, Los Angeles, Calif.

JSP James Seymour Papers, John F. Kennedy Presidential Library, Boston.

KK Kathleen Kennedy.

KLB Kirk LeMoyne Billings.

KLBP K. LeMoyne Billings Papers, John F. Kennedy Presidential Library, Boston.

LMT Lynne McTaggart, *Kathleen Kennedy* (N.Y.: Dial Press, 1983).

MB Michael Beschloss, *Kennedy and Roosevelt* (N.Y.: Norton, 1980).

NYT *New York Times.*

PBF Paul B. Fay, *The Pleasure of His Company* (N.Y.: Harper & Row, 1966).

PBFP Paul B. Fay Papers, Dept. of Special Collections, Stanford University Library, Stanford, Calif., by kind permission of Paul B. Fay, Jr.

 PPP Paul Palmer Papers, Sterling Library, Yale University, New Haven, Conn.

  PT Patrol Torpedo Boat (also known as MTB or Motor Torpedo Boat).

 PUL Princeton University Libraries/Seeley Mudd Manuscript Library, Princeton, N.J.

 RFK Rose Elizabeth Fitzgerald Kennedy.

 RJW Richard J. Whalen, *The Founding Father* (N.Y.: New American Library, 1964).

RJWP Richard J. Whalen Papers, JFKL, by kind permission of Richard Whalen.

RKRC Rose Kennedy with Robert Coughlan, *Times to Remember* (N.Y.: Doubleday, 1974), by kind permission of Doubleday Publishers.

RMEPP Ralph Martin and Ed Plaut Papers, Boston University Archives, by kind permission of Ralph Martin.

 RMP Ron McCoy Papers, by kind permission of Dr. Ronald McCoy.

RCDSA Riverdale Country Day School Archives, Riverdale, N.Y.

  SU Stanford University Archives, Stanford, Calif.

 YJK Gene Schoor, *Young John Kennedy* (N.Y.: McFadden-Bartell, 1963).

  WM William Manchester, *Death of a President* (N.Y.: Harper, 1967).

Prologue: The Birth of Camelot

xix "At nine-thirty": The rotunda was to have been closed to the public at 8:30 after 21 hours of public lying in state, but owing to the 12,000 people still waiting to pay their last respects (108,000 had already done so), an extension was granted until 9:00, according to Melville Bell Grosvenor, "The Last Full Measure," *National Geographic*, March 1964. However, the official "After Action Report on President John F. Kennedy's Funeral" prepared for the commanding general of the Military District of Washington, D.C., by Lt. Col. Paul C. Miller, chief of Ceremonies and Special Events, records that "the public was allowed to file past the casket beginning at 241400 Nov. 63 and ending 260930 Nov. 63 [i.e., 19½ hours]." Copy in Box 23, U.S. Military District of Washington Papers, Gerald Ford Library.

xix "We're all going": WM, p. 491.

xix "Her brother": ibid.

xix "Irish 'mafia'": ibid. The Irish mafia had history on their side, for only two American presidents had ever been buried outside their native state: Taft, in Arlington Cemetery, and Wilson, in the National Cathedral, Washington. Philip Bigler, *In Honored Glory* (Arlington, Va: Vandamere, 1986), p. 89.

xix "Even the new": WM, p. 490. Cardinal Cushing, when questioned by Senator Edward Kennedy, advised against the Kennedy family plot in Brookline's Holyhood Cemetery (where JFK's children, an unnamed stillborn daughter and a son, Patrick Bouvier Kennedy, who died when a day old, were interred), claiming it would create too many traffic problems—a strange concern for a priest. Instead, according to WM, Cushing proposed a tomb in the center of Boston Common: WM, p. 372. Cushing denied this—at least could not later recall making such a suggestion. "It seemed to me that it was just not practical to have a national shrine here. We faced the problem of bringing the body back to Massachusetts. The body would have been unburied another night, and then the family would have to endure another ceremony here"—again a strange concern on the part of a distinguished priest accustomed to the long rituals of the Catholic church: John H. Fenton, *Salt of the Earth: An Informal Portrait of Richard, Cardinal Cushing* (N.Y.: Coward-McCann, 1965), p. 203. Once Cushing switched his preference from Boston to Washington, however, Eunice Kennedy Shriver caved in. "Anyone who was a Cardinal, she was a total patsy for." William Walton, interview of June 12, 1991.

xix "The secretary for defense": WM, p. 491.

xix "president's widow": "We had to do a bit of selling to Eunice who wanted to take him to Brookline. Jackie was absolutely firm about Washington. Jackie was never in favor of Brookline. There was no debate. . . . Jack, in a way, didn't have a hometown as Lincoln had

Springfield. There wasn't a relation to one place. They lived in Bronxville and around. I asked one of them which was their hometown, and they couldn't say. Anyway there was no debate. Jackie was determined it was going to be Washington. 'Bury him here.' *Nobody contradicted her.* Anyone who says so is lying through his teeth, frankly. . . . Bobby asked me and McNamara to go to the [Arlington] cemetery. It hadn't been totally decided, 'but if it's fair, describe the site.' . . . We looked at two or three sites and it was perfectly obvious to me, it should be on the axis from the Capitol right through the Lincoln Memorial. . . . It was a marvelous site to convince Jackie. And she was entirely for it. No debate after it. And this is honest to God the truth." Walton interview.

xx "Eternal Flame": WM, p. 550. The local gas company constructed a propane gas torch until a more permanent system could be installed.

xx " 'You can't beat' ": Anonymous interviewee (close personal friend of JBKO), 1990.

xx "not permitted to attend": According to JPK's nurse, "He looked at me after the sound of the plane had disappeared into the night. . . . I knew then that regardless of the personal cost, he should have been going with his family, and had he been consulted as to his wishes, I know what his decision would have been." Rita Dallas and Jeanina Ratcliffe, *The Kennedy Case* (N.Y.: Putnam, 1975), p. 248.

xx " 'We have told him' ": AMSD.

xx " 'a nobody' ": "I said, once, to Jackie, 'Don't you think Jack has inherited a lot from his mother?' Jackie cut me short. 'Are you kidding? That woman is a *nitwit*, a *nobody*!": Anonymous interviewee (close personal friend of JBKO), 1990. "It was only natural that at times Rose and Jackie acted like North and South Korea, with periods of warfare and periods of uneasy truce. Lucianne Cummings, one of President Kennedy's speech writers, told me: 'Rose was only an occasional visitor at the White House, and then, more often than not, when Jackie was away": Fred Sparks, "Mother of the Clan," New York *Daily News*, July 23, 1970. JFK was no less dismissive. "My mother is a nothing," he said tartly to a friend of his brother Bobby, in a discussion about the family. See Peter Collier and David Horowitz, *The Kennedys* (N.Y.: Summit Books, 1984), p. 174.

xx "Jackie had been impressed": "From the hospital a telephone call was made to the Kennedys' friend, Mr. William Walton. Mrs. Kennedy remembered a book in the White House library; in it were drawings and photographs made when Lincoln's body lay in state in the East Room. Could Mr. Walton find the book and prepare the East Room in the same way?": Grosvenor, *Last Full Measure*. Walton was not only a personal friend of the president and First Lady, but one of the most courageous of American war correspondents in World War II, having parachuted into Normandy with the 82nd Airborne Division on D day. JFK appointed him to head the Fine Arts Commission and subsequently referred to him as "the Czar of Lafayette Square." He had first collapsed at the news of the president's assassination, but had been summoned back to the White House by the national security adviser, McGeorge Bundy. "He said, 'Look, I know how shattered you are, but there's something you have to do. You've got to come down and run the White House. I will run the country. I'm very serious, there's nobody else [Lyndon Johnson, the new president, was in transit from Dallas, together with Jackie and their respective entourages] to do these two things. We have to do it. A car's coming to get you and it will be there any minute.' " Walton interview. "I look at these men, these famous men who knew Kennedy intimately. I am distressed that I keep noticing Schlesinger's crooked bow tie that proves he tied it himself, his baggy suit, the striped shirt. He looks just like an active historian. And the brilliant McGeorge Bundy (born on Monday, christened on Tuesday, Harvard on Wednesday, etc.). McGeorge Bundy, crisp and nasal. Sleek in an Italian suit with slash pockets, no belt, no cuffs, pointy black shoes and cheap plastic glasses. He has to go soon. He is the White House civilian who must make sure no wrong military word gets out to those Polaris submarines with the nuclear weapons pointing up. . . . Walton, natty and urbane, is quietly giving instructions to a furniture upholsterer who is up a 20-foot ladder, hanging black window curtains. Walton belongs at a Palm Beach garden party. Not in the White House on this blustery November night. Blue blazer, striped tie, flannel pants, and polished loafers. Absolutely cool. Talking with him as we go from the East Room back to Dungan's [special assistant to the president] office, I am amazed at Walton's poise. I know he is very close to the President, and especially to Mrs. Kennedy. It strikes me again that these people for whom Kennedy had such high respect are acting just as he would have wished them to. They have an almost superhuman ability to remain in complete control . . . emotions sheathed . . . fine and gentle humor . . . restraint." From David Pearson (auxiliary White House press officer), "The Night They Brought Kennedy Home," *Miami Herald,* Nov. 22, 1967. "I got a message through from Jackie, at around four o'clock, saying: 'Make it as much like Lincoln's funeral as possible.' And I asked the Library of Congress to quickly send me prints of how the White House looked [for Lincoln's funeral]. Within half an hour I had a whole stack of illustrations. I see the sort of contrivance, the catafalque that Lincoln's coffin lay upon, and I think: 'We want something like that.' We found the original one out somewhere around [actually a replica, used for the 1958 ceremonies for the Unknown Soldier and taken from storage at Arlington Cemetery, according to B.C. Mossman and M.W. Stark, *The Last Salute: Civil and*

Military Funerals 1921–1969 (Washington, D.C.: Department of the Army, 1971), p. 189].": Walton interview. Richard Goodwin (presidential adviser on Latin America, secretary-general of the Peace Corps Secretariat, as well as designee special consultant to the president on the arts), however, remembered the replica being located at Fort Myers. See R.N. Goodwin, *Remembering America* (Boston: Little, Brown, 1988) p. 228.

xx " 'Jackie had sent' ": AMSD.

xx "the naval doctors at Bethesda": Commander Humes, the chief pathologist, later admitted to the House Select Committee on Assassinations that "he wasn't really supposed to do a full autopsy. He was just supposed to find the bullet. . . . Humes couldn't explain exactly how he knew. Somehow he absorbed it from the FBI and the Secret Service. . . . It was apparent that the body had been brought to Bethesda against the coroner's objections, to accommodate the wishes of the family. Humes understood, he told us, that the Kennedys were not interested in having an autopsy done. . . . He was not in a position to press the issue. The room was chaotic. Generals, admirals and cabinet members milled around, shocked. Humes, a mere commander, seemingly had no command of his own autopsy room. He was there to please his superiors. . . . It took Humes about two hours to do the autopsy. . . . The autopsy should reasonably have taken the better part of a day. . . . Humes explained that he was in a hurry, that the family was waiting for the body. . . . He was deeply concerned about the Kennedy family's feelings. . . . He burned his notes." Michael M. Baden, M.D., *Unnatural Death* (N.Y.: Random House, 1989), pp. 11–14.

xx "the late president's venereal": Commander James Humes had "worked on the autopsy report from Saturday afternoon until about 3:00 P.M. Sunday. . . . It is not clear what facts he used from his original notes," Dr. Baden—distinguished forensic pathologist and chairman of the medical panel advising the 1977 House Select Committee on Assassinations—later wrote. "The result was an autopsy report filled with errors, sins of omission and commission. . . . The weights and measures of body organs made no sense. . . . Other organs—the pancreas, the prostate—were not described at all. . . . The family didn't want any mention of any diseases that might be present, he said": ibid., pp. 14–16. Examination and description of the president's prostate threatened to cause especial scandal, given the sexual pathology known to White House physicians Dr. Janet Travell and Rear Admiral George G. Burkley. Despite Dr. Travell's insistance, after the assassination, that JFK's medical records belonged "to the country," they have remained for a quarter of a century sealed (and until 1992 concealed) in the JFK Presidential Library. However, JFK's venereal diseases had already become so disturbing in the 1950s that an outside specialist, Dr. William P. Herbst, was approached by the Lahey Clinic for help, and his records have recently been released. According to the Lahey Clinic, JFK had first contracted probable gonorrhea in 1940. However, in 1950 his "non-specific urethritis," as the Lahey Clinic's urinary specialist coyly explained to Dr Herbst, started to become a real problem. JFK was suffering "intermittent slight burning on urination and on examination at that time I found only a mild, chronic, non-specific prostatitis. Studies of the urine for acid-fast bacilli were all negative. He was treated by periodic massage [of the penis and prostate], sitz baths and a sulfonamide mixture [compounds of the sulfonomide series were considered, in the 1940s, "of great value in any type of gonoccocal infections": *A Textbook of Medicine,* ed. Russell L. Cecil, Philadelphia: W.B. Saunders 1943, p. 171] "and later, gantrasin, and various antibiotics [gantrasin was a more assimilable derivative of the sulfonamide group; penicillin, by the 1950s, had become "the drug of choice for the treatment of gonoccocal infections. In gonoccocal *urethritis* a single intramuscular injection of 600,000 units of procaine penicillin will cure over 95 per cent of cases": ibid., 1955 edition, p. 188]. Since he was travelling about a good deal, his treatment was somewhat sporadic. . . . In the winter of 1951 and '52, however, he began having recurrent symptoms. . . . In May of 1952, I cysto-scoped him under anaesthesia. . . . In August of 1952, because of recurrent symptoms, he was again hospitalized, partly to give him a little rest since he had been campaigning very vigorously, and partly to restudy his problem. . . . Since that time he has continued to have varying degrees of urinary distress . . . the only abnormality recently has been that of a few remaining pus cells in the prostatic secretion but mostly always less than ten per high power field." Admitting failure, the Lahey Clinic "suggested [to JFK] that perhaps we were a little too close to his problems and that a consultation with a urologist outside the Clinic would be of help." Thus began Dr. Herbst's ten-year treatment of JFK's recurrent symptoms of venereal disease, postgonoccocal and non-specific urethritis—burning urine, prostate pain, secretion of pus, anxiety about the effect on his fertility before becoming engaged in June 1953 to Jacqueline Bouvier, and persistent "acute prostatitis," mostly treated with massive doses of penicillin, antibiotics, erythromycin, and tetracycline. Shortly after JFK became president, Dr. Herbst noted that "as a matter of record Senator Kennedy called by telephone from Hyannis, San Francisco and other places to get advice concerning his prostatitic discomfort and dysuria." Even as president, with his own personal physicians, JFK continued to rely on Dr. Herbst's professional help. For instance, on April 17, 1961, the very day of the Bay of Pigs invasion, Dr. Herbst noted that "Dr. Travell called. Gave 600,000 Pen[icillin] today. Just came in and asked for shot." Dr. Herbst proudly felt, in retrospect, that JFK had "experienced a profound psychochemical influence for the better in a spectacular way," as a result of his ministrations: William P. Herbst, Clinical Notes, 1950–1963, Medical File, MS-83-38, JFKL.

xx "and Addison's": Addison's disease was a fatal illness, first identified by Dr. Thomas Addison in 1855, that involved the inexorable deterioration of the adrenal glands, without whose hormonal output the human body is unable to combat medical stress. "It was a well-kept secret [that JFK had Addison's], and the family wanted it to remain one. . . . Civilians, such as the medical people at Parkland Hospital, couldn't be controlled, but the military could be trusted. . . . Addison's disease is not mentioned in the autopsy report, nor are the adrenal glands." Baden, *Unnatural Death,* p. 15. Even in 1977 Commander Hume refused to explain to the House Select Committee why he'd ignored JFK's adrenal glands in the autopsy, saying, "I'd prefer not to discuss it. . . . I'd only comment that I have strong personal reasons and certain other obligations." David S. Lifton, *Best Evidence* (N.Y.: Macmillan, 1980), p. 529. Colonel Finck, assisting Commander Humes in the autopsy, blamed an unnamed army general for forbidding him to examine the president's neck or the site of the adrenal cortex, whereas Commander Humes implied it was Admiral Burkley, "physician to the President's family," who was responsible for the abbreviated and bungled examination. Ibid. Dr. George Thorn, who developed the first successful treatment of Addisonian patients in the 1930s by injecting a hormonal substitute derived from dogs, and later perfected the use of cortisone, was incensed by the cover-up employed during JFK's lifetime and the deliberate failure to report on the late president's adrenal glands during the autopsy at the Walter Reed Hospital in Bethesda. "It was *tragic* that no endocrinological examination was made!" Interview of July 14, 1989. The cover-up, he was certain, was as deliberate in death as it had been in JFK's lifetime (admitting only a "slight adrenal insufficiency"). Dr. Thorn's disappointment with the political necessity for such a cover-up (a cover-up that continued for almost three decades following JFK's death) rested upon his own tremendous achievement in transforming Addison's from a fatal into a non-fatal illness—a fact proved by the survival of JFK's sister Eunice after medication (though she suffered a much milder version of Addison's). The full story of JFK's Addisonian crisis and survival will be given in Volume II of this biography. However, the incontrovertible, documentary proof that JFK *did* have Addison's disease is contained in the medical files of the Lahey Clinic, whose staff themselves revealed in writing to Dr. William Herbst in March 1953: "Senator Kennedy has been a patient of the Lahey Clinic at intervals since 1936, and has had quite a variety of conditions. The most serious of these has been Addison's disease which was first discovered and treatment instituted in October of 1947. When he was in Boston last week, his medical condition was checked by Dr. Elmer Bartels who has been following his Addison's disease since it was first discovered. He felt that he was getting along satisfactorily and plans to implant further pellets of DOCA on April 10th.

He is taking cortisone daily": Herbst Clinical Notes.

xx "black crepe": "That evening, Professor James Robertson, the executive director of the United States Civil War Centennial Commission, was contacted by the White House and asked to complete the required research on the Lincoln burial. Robertson called David Mearns, the Director of the Library of Congress, and arranged to meet him an hour later at the government repository. . . . Armed only with flashlights, Robertson and Mearns descended into the stack areas rummaging through the library's extensive holdings for pertinent copies of *Frank Leslie's Illustrated* and *Harper's Weekly* which depicted the 1865 Lincoln funeral in graphic detail. Once they located the copies, Robertson took the material to the White House and carpenters used the century-old drawings to transform the East Room with mourning crepe." Bigler, *Honored Glory,* p. 91. Neither time nor 1960s taste would permit a perfect reproduction, however. Pearson recalled Walton saying, " 'If they're going to get here about two-thirty [A.M.], I really doubt that we can match the Lincoln scene by then.' . . . Now, and contrary to later press versions, Walton, Goodwin and Shriver decide not to recreate the Lincoln decor exactly. It is felt that heavy black curtains over all the chandeliers would make the room too morose and too dark.": Pearson, "The Night They Brought Kennedy Home."

xxi "And television": The lying-in-state and funeral ceremonies were watched by 175 million people in the U.S.A. alone, it is reckoned, at a network production cost of $35 million: Grosvenor, "Last Full Measure," and John B. Mayo, Jr., *The President Is Dead: The Story of John F. Kennedy's Assassination As Covered By Radio and TV* (N.Y.: Exposition, 1967).

xxi "her new Greek friend": WM, p. 555.

xxi " 'absolutely appalling' ": WM, p. 541. The line "and so she took the ring from her finger and placed it in his hand" was apparently repeated by Senator Mansfield not once but five excruciating times: Associated Press, *The Torch Is Passed* (N.Y.: A.P., 1963), p. 79.

xxi " '. . . stumbled after her.' ": WM, p. 542.

xxi "it was her duty": All contemporary observers and commentators were aware of this aspect—e.g., Dr. Calvin Plimpton, president of Amherst College (which awarded JFK his last honorary degree in October 1963), who remarked during the Amherst memorial service: "On this, the longest weekend, there was another figure, another star. She had a role to play for which there was no time to rehearse. . . . Her preparation was all literary and artistic. She redecorates the White House and brings music to it. She is lovely. She rides, she water skis. . . . We see her riding with the coffin, sitting in a vigil, and then going to the Capitol with Caroline and John-John. Again yesterday she decided what her role was and she played it. She saw her duty and she lived up to it." Quoted in Grosvenor, "Last Full Measure."

"He loved history, and the imagery of its pomp was woven tightly into his sense of it. It was a widow's wish that those three days be swept with majesty." Pat Saltonstall, "Protocol Went into Action Minutes After Action," Washington *Sunday Star,* Dec. 8, 1963. "God, I wish we were a monarchy and the kid was taking over and that woman was the regent," a veteran reporter was heard to say. See J.H. Cutler, *Cardinal Cushing of Boston* (N.Y.: Hawthorn, 1970), p. 245. Cardinal Cushing felt likewise, extolling Jackie at Christmastime 1963 in Miami as "the most extraordinary woman I have ever met. I wish I could say to the young girls of the future that I think instead of looking to motion picture actresses for ideals, they should look to Jacqueline." Quoted in Cutler, *Cardinal Cushing,* p. 246. Perhaps the Associated Press best summed up newspaper reaction of the time in *The Torch Is Passed:* "Alone with her grief in a 17th floor suite of the hospital, Jacqueline Kennedy thought about the future. Her husband had lived in a world of heroes. History meant people to him, not events. . . . She determined that his death would be remembered as a hero's death; his funeral a hero's funeral; his grave, a hero's grave. There and then this remarkable woman, a heroine transfixed with tragedy but gallantly carrying on, worked out in amazing detail the plans for the extraordinary funeral that would bring a rare sense of majesty to her countrymen." A.P., *Torch Is Passed,* p. 31.

xxii " 'Versailles after the king' ": WM, p. 546.

xxii "Jackie remained 'in her parlor' ": AMSD.

xxii "Shriver, composed and pale,": "Shriver is, without question the dominant figure here," David Pearson considered in his 1967 account, "yet when a national magazine is later to publish a detailed account of his life, there will be not even a hint of what should go down as one of the most superb contributions of his career. The plain truth is that he is more creative than the professionals tonight, more creative than the protocol experts, the clergy, the military, and more creative than Andy Hatcher, Lloyd Wright or me with the press." Pearson, "The Night They Brought Kennedy Home."

xxii " 'too waxen' ": AMSD; quoted in Arthur M. Schlesinger, Jr., *Robert Kennedy and His Times* (N.Y.: Houghton Mifflin, 1978), p. 610.

xxii " 'seal the casket . . . wax effigy' ": The decision not to leave the casket open to public view has been attributed to different people in different texts. Gawler's morticians, in their three-hour cosmetic race against time, later admitted that "we did not know whether the body would be viewed or not. . . . There were about thirty-five people, led by General Wehle [Commanding General, Military District of Washington], breathing down our necks. We were worrying about skull leakage, which could be disastrous." A fragment of JFK's skull, found on Elm Street, Dallas, and flown to Washington by federal agents, had also to be—literally—incorporated. When the prepared body was brought to the White House and the casket placed in the East Room (cleared of the grand piano), there followed a dispute similar to that concerning the burial site. Jackie wished the casket closed; the Irish "mafia"—particularly the president's assistants Kenny O'Donnell and Larry O'Brien, who had engineered the "theft" of the corpse from Dallas—wished it open. Robert McNamara, the secretary of defense who had favored Arlington as a national burial shrine, also recommended an open casket, lest the public feel there was something to hide, even that there was no body in the casket at all. Jackie, having stated her preference, asked her brother-in-law to decide. Bobby Kennedy then asked each of JFK's colleagues and close friends to peep inside the casket and report their opinions. "It is really not like him," was Chuck Spalding's verdict—JFK's face resembling "the rubber masks stores sell as novelties." "It's a wax dummy," William Walton concluded. Even Jackie referred to it as "something you would see at Madame Tussaud's." WM, pp. 442–43. Walton's was evidently the decisive opinion, though he later claimed that the element of privacy played a major part in his recommendation to Bobby. "I came back and I said, 'Close the casket at once.' Bobby was in total tears. I was too. I said it because I was convinced my friend [JFK] did not want the world looking at him. I knew it totally"—a strange assertion to make about such a lifelong narcissist, yet one which reflected the other, private side of JFK, a man who disliked being touched: Walton interview.

xxii   " 'Harlem or Coney Island' ": WM, p. 553.
xxii   " 'Do one thing' ": ibid.
xxii   " 'Susan Mary Alsop' ": AMSD, also quoted in WM, p. 490.
xxii   "As she followed on foot": WM, p. 580.
xxii   " 'Jacqueline Kennedy walked' ": Grosvenor, "Last Full Measure."
xxii   " 'majesty' ": Jean Campbell in London *Evening Standard.*
xxii   " 'child of [King] Arthur' ": Garry Wills, *The Kennedy Imprisonment* (Boston: Little, Brown, 1982), p. 107. For a summary of the Kennedy family's attempt to suppress Manchester's book see Thomas Brown, *JFK: History of an*

Image (Bloomington, Ind.: Indiana University Press, 1988), pp. 7–8. For the negative effects of the attempts at censorship on the political fortunes of Robert Kennedy see Lawrence Van Gelder, *The Untold Story: Why the Kennedys Lost the Book Battle* (N.Y.: Award Books, pp. 88–92); see also Gore Vidal's essay "The Holy Trinity": "Not since Mary Todd Lincoln has a President's widow been so fiercely engaged with legend if not history." *Esquire,* April 1967.

xxiii   " 'was displaced by cars' ": WM, p. 591.
xxiii   " 'whim of iron' ": McGeorge Bundy to author, 1988.
xxiii   "lace veil": Ironically, Jackie decided against her own wardrobe of veils, preferring one that hung lower down, below her bosom; she was therefore reduced to borrowing one from Rose Kennedy, her mother-in-law, who had brought two—purchased in readiness for the death of her paralyzed husband, Joseph P. Kennedy. "I wanted to ask your opinion," Rose had said to Rita Dallas, her husband's nurse in Hyannis Port. "You're a widow, so you might know which veil I should take to the funeral. . . . I'm wearing the same dress I've had in the closet in case Mr. Kennedy died. How ironic it is that I'll be wearing it to Jack's funeral. We never know, do we, Mrs. Dallas?" Dallas and Ratcliffe, *Kennedy Case,* p. 246.
xxiii   " 'even the famous salute' ": "She played the role of First Lady to the hilt, and used the children as part of the family image of the president. . . . Occasionally she was theatrical, sure. The gesture of John-John saluting was Mrs. Kennedy's doing. Caroline kissing her father's casket in the Rotunda of the Capitol, that was her prompting. But those were gestures that we needed, and it really helped us in our grief." George Tames [Washington photographer for *The New York Times*], Oral History interview, Jan. 20, 1988, Senate Historical Office, Washington, D.C.
xxiii   " 'I had never understood' ": Quoted in WM, p. 555.
xxiii   " 'This was her' ": Letitia Baldrige, JFKLOH.
xxiv   " 'It was like the fall' ": WM, p. 504.

Part 1: Boston Beginnings

3   " 'Old Ironsides' ": Nickname for U.S.S. *Constitution,* still on display at the Old Navy Yard, Boston.
3   "Boston a relative backwater": For the history of Boston's rise and fall between 1630 and 1900 see, inter alia, Thomas. H. O'Connor, *Bibles, Brahmins and Bosses* (Boston: Trustees of the Public Library of the City of Boston, 1984); Cleveland Amory, *The Proper Bostonians* (N.Y.: E.P. Dutton, 1947); Stephen Thernstrom, *The Other Bostonians, Poverty and Progress in the American Metropolis* (Cambridge, Mass.: Harvard University Press, 1973); Oscar Handlin, *Boston's Immigrants, 1790–1880* (Cambridge, Mass.: Harvard University Press, 1959); and Barbara M. Sol-

omon, *Ancestors and Immigrants* (Chicago: University of Chicago Press, 1956).
4   " 'The young man' ": *BG,* Sept. 24, 1894.
6   " 'I had been . . . life insurance business' ": *Boston Sunday Post,* series beginning Dec. 28, 1913.
6   " 'Keaney was of the old' ": ibid.
6   " 'There was a combination' ": ibid.
6   " 'I was going' ": ibid.
7   " 'Strategy Board' ": JHC, p. 61.
7   " 'I had no show' ": *Boston Sunday Post,* series beginning Dec. 28, 1913.
8   " 'They say I' ": *BG,* Sept. 21, 1894.
8   " 'the prevailing opinion' ": *Boston Sunday Globe,* Sept. 23, 1894.
9   " 'My record' ": *BG,* Sept. 20, 1896.

9   " 'torchlight procession' ": ibid., Sept. 21, 1894.
9   " 'eclipsed all previous ones' ": ibid., Sept. 22, 1894.
11 " 'The only topic' ": ibid., Sept. 23, 1894.
11 " 'wasn't large enough' ": ibid., Sept. 22, 1894.
12 "Fitzgerald duly elected": Fitzgerald received 11,459 votes to Jesse M. Gove's 9,545: Harvey Rachlin, *The Kennedys, A Chronological History, 1823–Present,* (N.Y.: World Almanac, 1986), p. 21.
12 "fared as a congressman": Fitzgerald was not only the sole Democrat from Massachusetts, representing Wards 1, 2, 3, 6, 7, 8, 12, 16, 17, 18, some of 19 in the city of Boston and the town of Winthrop, but the sole Catholic in the House of Representatives. He soon became a hero to New England immigrants as the man who persuaded President Cleveland to veto the Immigration Literacy Bill; he fulfilled his promise that he would get the Charlestown Navy Yard in Boston reopened after a quarter of a century, with its corresponding impact on jobs and suppliers in East Boston; he led the fight to save the historic warship the U.S.S. *Constitution,* built in Boston but rotting in Portsmouth, N.H., for posterity; he helped pass a $6 million appropriation in Congress for Boston Harbor; he visited the American "fever camps" during the Spanish-American War, and prevailed upon President McKinley to see that the Massachusetts Militia received proper food and housing. JHC, pp. 63–67.
12 " 'As my father' ": RKRC, p. 21.
12 "a bitter, five-day battle": Fitzgerald, far from meekly stepping down, as Rose assumed, made a secret deal with "the Mahatma" of South Boston, Martin Lomasney, who had originally ensured his election as a state senator. Lomasney agreed that at the forthcoming Democratic-party caucus he would withhold the votes of his Ward 8 delegates from Joe Conry, Kennedy's choice for the nomination, thus leading to stalemate—and Fitzgerald's renomination as compromise party candidate. The congressional caucus, beginning on Oct. 12, 1900, turned out to be the most dramatic in Boston history. "That congressional convention was stacked something like the Presidential one we had in Madison Square Garden in 1924," Lomasney described years later. True to his bargain, Lomasney refused to give his Ward 8 delegates' votes to Conry, Pat Kennedy's contender. "We started balloting on the 12th October, and we had to file a certificate of nomination by 5 o'clock on the 16th. We went more than 40 ballots, with several adjournments, without practically any change in the vote, and we finally met on the last day for filing with no break in sight." By then *The Globe* was convinced Fitzgerald would win the nomination. The delegates had been convening for five days with only a six-hour recess. THE GLOBE LATEST it headlined its evening edition on Oct. 16: "Nomination in Ninth Almost in Fitzgerald's Grasp. NEEDS 2 VOTES. On Reassembling, Delegates May Flock to the Congressman. . . . At 2:30 this afternoon it was said that Congressman John F. Fitzgerald had within two votes of enough to nominate him in

the Ninth democratic congressional convention. Wards 1, 6, 3 and 13 are claimed for him, and if he can get the other two delegates necessary his name will be sprung in the convention this afternoon." Kennedy and his fellow "consuls," however, refused to switch to the incumbent congressman, and when the rumor started that Fitzgerald was involved in a plot with Lomasney, Fitzgerald's support cracked: "The word had got around that Fitz was in some kind of deal with me, so there wasn't a chance of starting a stampede for him," Lomasney recalled. Finally, on the fifty-fifth ballot, Kennedy's nominee won a majority. "There was just 20 minutes to get the certificate up to the State House, but Conry saw to that, and in November he was elected." Thomas Carens, "Martin Lomasney," *BH,* Dec. 8 and 15, 1925.
12 " 'This fight will' ": *BG,* Nov. 8, 1905.
13 " 'Nobody in Boston' ": JHC, p. 89.
14 " 'You remember' ": *BG,* Nov. 14, 1905.
15 " 'Conservative estimates' ": *BG,* Nov. 16, 1905.
15 " 'In Ward 2' ": ibid.
15 " 'Mr. Fitzgerald will go' ": *BT,* Nov. 17, 1905.
15 " 'I am going to' ": *BG,* Nov. 17, 1905. In a record turnout on Dec. 12, 1905, Fitzgerald became the youngest mayor of Boston ever elected, beating the Republican contender, Louis Frothingham, by 44,171 votes to 36,028. "He is a bundle of dynamos that never seem to run down," one newspaper recorded—responsible for a bureaucracy spending a million dollars a week, and eighty-five aldermen and councilmen "in my office every day trying to get jobs for somebody," as Fitzgerald put it. JHC, p. 98. Despite trade-offs with his supporters, Fitzgerald saw himself as not only the head of a great business corporation, but the conscience of the city. He was always the first man at a bad fire or accident. When news came in of the San Francisco earthquake, he was the first mayor in America to send relief. He fought hard for the first city pension scheme for employees over the age of sixty-two, and also to get a hospital for consumptives (sadly, his own second daughter, Agnes, would die of the disease). According to a contemporary account, he made three *thousand* speeches, attended twelve hundred dinners, two hundred picnics, and fifteen hundred dances. He only needed five or six hours of sleep a night. To help boost the fortunes of the city he staged a week-long Boston Fair, boasting Houdini, trade shows, parades, athletics competitions, baseball matches, yacht races, concerts, banquets, and historical tours of Boston. Ibid.
15 "a forgiving man": JHC, pp. 91–92.
15 " 'I suppose no father' ": RKRC, p. 62.
16 " 'he disapproved' ": ibid., p. 57.
16 " 'My father was' ": ibid., p. 27.
16 " 'a serious young man' ": ibid., p. 57.
17 " 'My father replied' ": ibid., p. 60.
17 " 'blossom into' ": ibid., pp. 55–56.
18 " 'I was never seriously' ": Joe McCarthy, *The Remarkable Kennedys* (N.Y.: Popular Library, 1960), p. 33.
18 " 'used to squire' ": Arthur Goldsmith interview, RJWP.

18 " 'All I'm interested in' ": RJW, p. 29.

18 " 'It would have hurt' ": DKG, p. 214.

18 "Massachusetts financial institution": Before World War I, banking and investment were closed shops, reserved for Yankees. According to Russell Ayres, who attended Harvard as a freshman in Joe Kennedy's senior year, "Joe Sr. tried to get into the investment house of Lee & Higginson in Boston when he got out of Harvard. Apparently L & H wasn't hiring Irish Catholics at the time and he didn't get the job. Bishop O'Connell heard about this and promptly withdrew all the church money from L & H." JMBP. John F. Fitzgerald was similarly outraged. To his campaign biographer, James MacGregor Burns, JFK later confided what his grandfather, Honey Fitz, told him: "Fitz was upset by no Catholics being on boards of trustees of a bank. He enquired, was told this was true, but two or three tellers were Catholics. 'And I suppose the charwoman too,' he said, turned on his heel and left": JMBP.

19 " 'The Roxbury Congressman' ": *BH*, Dec. 18, 1913. Standing six feet tall, blessed with a golden baritone voice, Curley showed a vindictiveness toward opponents that became legendary; few men would ever stand against him in an election. Precisely because he was so unashamedly bigoted and corrupt, many Boston-Irish voters saw him as their most effective champion and provider; outside the Boston Irish, however, he was despised "as a cunning, contriving, cold-blooded charlatan, wholly unreliable and unscrupulous": JHC, pp. 183–84.

19 " 'It was not easy' ": DKG, p. 90.

19 " 'as certain as' ": *BH*, Dec. 18, 1913.

20 " 'I know the influence' ": *Boston Sunday Globe*, series beginning Dec. 28, 1913.

20 " 'A whisky glass' ": *Irish America Magazine*, Oct. 1989.

20 "With the help": DKG, p. 251.

21 " 'acting under' ": *BH*, Dec. 18, 1913.

21 " 'The mayor had this fight' ": ibid.

21 " 'I am very much' ": ibid.

21 " 'Mayor's Daughter' ": *BH*, Dec. 29, 1913.

22 "as Rose later hinted": Robert Coughlan interview of Oct. 1990.

22 " 'Are you going' ": RJW, p. 39.

22 " 'It was less a matter' ": RKRC, p. 67.

23 " 'during the later winter' ": ibid.

22 " 'the betrothal of' ": *The Republic*, June 13, 1914.

23 " 'a far cry' ": "I was married at the cardinal's house. We just had a small wedding": Recorded interview with Nan Rickey for sound accompaniment in the John F. Kennedy National Historic Site at 83 Beals Street, MS-78-32, JFKL.

23 " 'After the return' ": *The Republic*, Oct. 10, 1914.

23 "Beals Street": Tax records, street directories, and descriptions of historic houses, Local History Room collection, Brookline Public Library, Brookline, Mass.

24 "the doubling of the bank's business": Deposits increased from $580,654 to $1,055,759, loans from $516,112 to $822,109: DKG, p. 258.

24 "was entirely honest": For example, JPK was not above accepting favors in lieu of interest: See RJW, p. 43.

24 " 'One of the great thrills' ": RKRC, pp. 72–73 and Rickey interview.

25 " 'seemed to us' ": RKRC, p. 72. See also Rickey interview.

25 " 'With the speed' ": *Boston Post*, July 26, 1915.

26 " 'I dwell 'neath": *BG*, Oct. 20, 1916. By contrast, Fitzgerald saw himself as nobly humble. His counterverse ran: "I dwell in the homes of Massachusetts/The abode of Democracy/Where the Lord speaks to Jones/In the very same tones/He uses with Johnson and me." Ibid.

25 " 'The Case of the People' ": *BG*, Nov. 2, 1916.

25 " 'a record of twenty-four' ": ibid. Nov. 5, 1916.

26 " 'What I Favor' ": ibid.

26 " 'Wish you best' ": ibid. Nov. 8, 1916.

27 "Fitzgerald's performance": "Although his hopes of winning a seat in the United States Senate were shattered, Ex-Mayor John F. Fitzgerald yesterday polled the biggest vote of any candidate on the ticket in Boston. . . . Fitzgerald's vote in Boston was 56,751, Wilson's 56,089": ibid., Nov. 9, 1916. Lodge polled only 35,546. However, the total Massachusetts voting tallies came to: Lodge 267,439, Fitzgerald 234,440: ibid., Nov. 9, 1916.

27 " 'Another week' ": ibid.

27 " 'He kept us out' ": Robert Leckie, *The Wars of America* (N.Y.: Harper & Row, 1968), p. 626.

28 " 'fearful thing' ": *NYT*, April 3, 1917.

28 "Many other Wall Street": *BG*, May 1, 1917.

29 " 'real leadership' ": ibid. May 2, 1917.

28 " 'This is the only' ": DKG, p. 272.

29 " 'Joe believed' ": ibid., p. 275.

29 " 'a stranger in his own' ": ibid.

30 " 'because I did want' ": RKRC, p. 78.

30 " 'tried to sublimate' ": ibid.

30 "the word *fetus*": Barbara Gibson with Caroline Latham, *Life with Rose Kennedy* (N.Y.: Warner Books, 1986), p. 177.

30 " 'wearing a pleased' ": *Boston Post*, May 29, 1917.

Part 2: Making Millions

33 " 'trouble with his infant feeding' ": RFK, CBSI.

33 " 'Now listen, Rosie' ": DKG, p. 392.

33 " 'Whenever I begin' ": Gail Cameron, *Rose* (N.Y.: Putnam, 1971), p. 56.

34 " 'Joe's time' ": RKRC, p. 73.

34 " 'Do you know' ": RJW, p. 44.

34 "Joe Dinneen": Joseph P. Dinneen, *The Kennedy Family* (Little, Brown, 1959), p. 18.

35 " 'on the way' ": RKRC, p. 80.

35 "scowling at the camera": RJW, p. 42, and Harvey Rachlin, *The Kennedys, A Chronological History, 1823–Present* (N.Y.: World Almanac, 1986), p. 34.

35 "Fore River Shipyard": See Anthony F. Sarcone and Lawrence S. Rines, *A History of Shipbuilding at Fore River* (Quincy, Mass.: Quincy School Department, 1975). (Further monographs and information are available at the Quincy Historical Association.)

36　"Squantum": The area "taking in the land formerly used as the Harvard Aviation field" covered seventy acres, cost $15 million to build, had ten covered building ways, and six wet slips. Ibid., p. 18.

37　"Joe Kennedy's arrival": The author is indebted to David Palmer, whose research work and draft, Brandeis University Ph.D. dissertation, *Organizing the Shipyards, Unionization at the New York, Federal Ship and Fore River, 1898–1945,* 1989 (to be published in book form by Cornell University Press), were invaluable.

37　"five thousand craftsmen": *BT,* Oct. 31, 1917. "Practically all the skilled trades were called out, and ordered to remain out until the company promised, in writing signed by responsible agents of the company, an agreement to pay navy yards rates." Ibid.

37　" 'There is probably' ": Palmer, *Organizing the Shipyards.*

38　" 'until all bills' ": Joe McCarthy, *The Remarkable Kennedys* (N.Y.: Popular Library, 1960), p. 35.

38　" 'I didn't know' ": Arthur Boyson interview of Oct. 4, 1988.

38　" 'He was responsible' ": Irving Coughlan interview of Oct. 4, 1988.

39　"Joseph Kennedy was drafted": DKG, p. 280.

39　" 'not over six men' ": Joseph Powell to Myer Bloomfield, Feb. 25, 1918, as quoted in DKG, p. 281.

39　"Senate committee": Senate Hearing, U.S. Congress Senate Special Committee Investigation, The Munitions Industry Hearings (10 volumes), 74th Congress, 1st Session (Washington, D.C.: Government Printing Office, 1935). See also John E. Wiltz, *In Search of Peace: The Senate Munitions Inquiry 1934–1936,* (Baton Rouge, La.: Louisiana State University Press, 1963), and also Stephen and John Raushenbush, *War Madness* (Washington D.C.: National Home Library Foundation, 1937).

39　"in record time": The four-funneled destroyer *Reid* was completed in forty-five days: Sarcome and Rines, *Shipbuilding at Fore River,* p. 18.

40　"seventy-one destroyers": ibid.

40　"refuge from military service": " 'He always knew,' Rose later said, that 'but for the grace of God and the powers of Washington, he too might have been among the hundreds of Harvard men killed in the war.' " DKG, p. 283.

41　"The family chronicler": see DKG, pp. 303–7.

41　" 'He was under' ": RKRC, p. 80.

41　"won reelection to Congress": Fitzgerald beat the incumbent congressman of the Tenth Congressional District by only 50 votes in the primary. Tague then stood as an Independent in the election, and again lost to Fitzgerald, by 229 votes, but refused to accept the result. Fitzgerald subsequently likened Tague's protest to Congress in March 1919 to an "opera bouffe show" that was too hypocritical to take seriously (Tague contesting the names of voters who had previously voted for him). Fitzgerald refused to testify before the congressional subcommittee and in October, in a surprise judgment, was unseated. "I am not disturbed over the result in the House today," he responded. "I would rather walk the streets of Boston a beggar than to gain office through the betrayal of those who had been my friends. Mr. Tague never would have been known in Washington were it not for the votes of men who today were disenfranchised on his charges. . . . His conduct is despicable." JHC, p. 229.

41　" 'What is past' ": DKG, p. 307.

42　" 'frantic terror' ": ibid. p. 309.

42　" 'a very, very sick' ": RKRC, p. 85.

42　" 'never experienced' ": JPK to Dr. Place, July 2, 1920, as quoted in DKG, p. 310.

42　"Eighteen-thousand-dollar house": Local History Room, Brookline, Mass. The house had three baths and four fireplaces. Most doors were flanked with Ionic columns. The reception rooms were large and imposing, with an open stairway leading up to the second and third floors. All rooms had dark wooden wall paneling—even the garage, which had a room and bath for the chauffeur. An intercom system covered the entire house. 1959 notes made for James MacGregor Burns, JMBP.

43　" 'After Jack's illness' ": DKG, p. 313.

43　" 'The stock market game' ": RJW, p. 65.

43　" 'You didn't ask him' ": ibid.

43　" 'suddenly out of joint' ": DKG, p. 315.

43　"diaper changing": RKRC, p. 81.

44　" 'daily inspection' ": ibid. p. 82.

44　" 'spent many hours' ": ibid.

44　" 'morale' of the staff": Recorded interview with Nan Rickey for sound accompaniment in the John F. Kennedy National Historic Site at 83 Beals Street, MS-78-32, JFKL.

44　" 'synergistic' quality": RKRC, p. 79.

44　" 'That way they could' ": ibid. p. 83. In her interview with Nan Rickey, Rose recalled that "as the children got older, sometimes we used to divide them in the piazza, so they would see each other but still not be able to push one another down or stick a toy in one another's eye, and then I could watch them very easily from the window." Rickey interview.

45　"The records": Courtesy of Edward Devotion Elementary School, Brookline, Mass.

45　"public elementary school": "People asked me why he didn't go to a parochial school, but there was no parochial school in our neighborhood . . . and so he went to the Brookline elementary school." RFK, CBSI.

45　" 'Joe started badly' ": HS, p. 39.

45　" 'to help them' ": RFK, CBSI.

45　" 'I suppose it was' ": RKRC, p. 119.

45　" 'Joe was much stronger' ": RFK, CBSI.

45　"separate bedrooms": When the Kennedy children visited other houses, they would be astonished to learn that some parents slept in the same room. "Kathleen and Eunice came up," recalled Rose's Brookline friend Marie Greene, "and they were very interested in the fact that I did not have a bedroom to myself, that I slept in the room with my husband, you know; they thought that was very odd." Cameron, *Rose,* p. 93.

45　" 'He was a real' ": Frederick L. Good, Jr., interview of Dec. 2, 1991.

46 "rather a 'bully' ": JFK interview, JMBP. "I always had the problem of my older brother who was a couple of years older, who was physically larger. . . . He was rather heavy on me on occasions. Physically we used to have some fights which, of course, he always won. . . . It was a problem in my youth—boyhood. I think it is a problem to all second brothers—second sons." Ibid.

46 " 'With their different' ": RKRC, pp. 119–20.

46 " 'Joe Jr.'s temperament' ": ibid.

46 " 'Joe Jr. was furious' ": ibid. p. 120.

47 " 'Gee, *you're* a great' ": ibid. p. 93.

47 " 'The fact that he' ": ibid. p. 110.

47 " 'Before he ever' ": McCarthy, *The Remarkable Kennedys* (N.Y.: Popular Library, 1960), pp. 19–20.

47 " 'I confessed' ": RKRC, p. 111.

47 " 'wouldn't have allowed' ": ibid.

47 " 'poverty, dirt and sloth' ": DKG, p. 206.

47 " 'from the P.T.A.' ": RKRC, p. 110. Rose later listed the books she did allow Jack, which included *Arabian Nights*, Stevenson's *A Child's Garden of Verses*, *Kidnapped*, and *Treasure Island*, A.M. Hadfield's *King Arthur and the Round Table*, Kipling's *Kim* and *The Jungle Book*, Stowe's *Uncle Tom's Cabin*, Barrie's *Peter Pan*, Sewell's *Black Beauty*, James Fenimore Cooper's *Wing and Wing*, Bunyan's *Pilgrim's Progress*, and *Wonder Tales from East and West*. RKRC, p. 112.

47 " 'Naturally, anything shown' ": RKRC, p. 117.

48 "never kissed or touched": Interviews with, inter alia, Charles Spalding, Paul Fay, Jr., Elizabeth Coxe Spalding, Hugh Wynne, Alastair Forbes.

48 "she used a ruler": ibid., pp. 132–33. Also Rickey interview.

48 " 'whacking' ": Edward M. Kennedy, quoted in RKRC, p. 133. Almost every later interview with RFK featured corporal punishment. See also ch. 3, "Growing Up Disciplined: Life with Mother" in Nancy Gager Clinch, *The Kennedy Neurosis* (N.Y.: Grosset & Dunlap, 1973), pp. 45–70.

48 " 'were always within' ": RKRC, p. 133.

48 "As one of her": Edward M. Kennedy, quoted in RKRC, p. 134.

48 " 'an extra portion' ": RKRC, p. 94.

49 " 'He was a funny' ": ibid.

49 " 'He said he did not' ": ibid. p. 93.

49 " 'because his father' ": ibid.

49 " 'Daddy has a' ": ibid. p. 97.

49 " 'You know, I am' ": ibid.

49 "Rose recorded proudly": ibid. p. 90.

49 " 'drive off without him' ": ibid. p. 102. "He had that very nonchalant air about some things, when he was growing up. . . . I remember telling my daughter-in-law that, when he was married, I said, 'don't be discouraged, don't be disheartened if Jack forgets to bring home your hat from the milliner, or some cosmetics from Elizabeth Arden, because those things just don't sort of enter into his mind." RFK, CBSI.

49 " 'I often had' ": RKRC, p. 111.

50 " 'effective people' ": ibid. p. 107.

50 "proper usage": ibid. p. 113.

50 " 'I didn't think Jack's I.Q.' ": RFK, CBSI.

50 " 'He was rather sickly' ": RKRC, p. 153.

51 "crooked windfall": DKG, p. 328.

51 "equally 'slim' ": ibid. pp. 325–29.

51 "financial larceny": JPK never denied his stockmarket shenanigans (viz. DKG, p. 507). His family and sycophants did. As a result, all JPK's private papers remain sealed in the JFK Library.

52 " 'punch him on the nose' ": RJW, p. 68.

52 " 'Daddy, Daddy' ": RKRC, p. 75.

52 " 'desire for the freedom' ": DKG, p. 331.

52 "twenty-eight stitches": HS, p. 40. "Of course, Joe was so much stronger than Jack, and if there was any physical encounter, Joe really whacked him, considerably. So when they were young, everybody was trying to protect Jack, more or less, from Joe." RFK, CBSI. A 1929 summer governess, Gertrude H. Frazer, recalled how "the two boys were quite different in many ways. The older one felt his importance and was quite a tease. As a rule they were compatible, as much so as two brothers—twelve and fourteen—could be. They usually sailed their boat together with great joy, but I well remember one occasion when they really had quite a spat. I had taken the girls to the wharf where the boat was tied up to watch them take off for a sail. We found the boys on the pier arguing. Before long, fists were flying, and soon the older boy lost his balance and fell overboard. His brother jumped in right after him. I never did find out which boy won the fight." Gertrude H. Frazer, "The Governess' [sic] Tale," *Cape Cod Life* magazine, Feb.–March 1990.

52 " 'in one or another state' ": RKRC, p. 97.

52 " 'decided to take the boys' ": ibid.

53 " 'very glad that we' ": Richard T. Flood, *The Story of Noble and Greenough School 1886–1966* (Dedham, Mass.: Noble and Greenough School, 1966), p. 79.

53 " 'We were probably' ": Told by JFK to James McGregor Burns, JMBP.

53 " 'difference of a few ships' ": JHC, p. 64.

54 " 'the only man' ": Augustus Soule interview of Dec. 28, 1988.

54 " 'Almost everybody was a Protestant' ": ibid.

55 " 'This big shiny car' ": ibid.

55 " 'I did want all' ": RKRC, p. 119.

56 " 'Buttons, buttons' ": ibid. p. 82.

55 "let his mask slip": Charles Spalding interview of Aug. 29, 1990.

55 " 'She would talk' ": JHC, p. 243.

56 " 'It was a very friendly' ": Soule interview.

56 " 'The English teacher was' ": Holton Wood, interview of Jan. 9, 1989.

57 " 'The classes were small,' " Myra Fiske Oral History for Dexter School, DSA, courtesy of William Phinney, headmaster, Dexter School, Brookline, Mass.

57 " 'The trustees' ": ibid.

58 "At one-fifteen P.M.": Copy of Agreement of Association, DSA. In addition to the building, the grounds were purchased for a further $58,-000. Ibid.

58 " 'to teach the boy' ": *Dexter School 1926–1927*, brochure, DSA.

59 " 'We'd better get in' ": RJW, p. 66.

58 " 'I can remember' ": Soule interview.

59 " 'With John F. Fitzgerald' ": JHC, p. 241.

60 " 'the doctor' ": Fitzgerald had been awarded an honorary degree by Notre Dame University in 1916; together with his abandoned Harvard Medical School training, this led to the popular press nickname.

60 " 'Mingle with the young' ": JHC, p. 241.

60 " 'One of the most important' ": ibid.

60 " 'Sorry, fellows' ": DKG, p. 343, citing Terry Ramsaye, "Intimate Visits to the Homes of Famous Film Magnates," *Photoplay*, Sep. 27, 1927, p. 125.

60 "JOHN F. FITZGERALD IS": JHC, p. 245.

61 " 'We will soon prove' ": Edward Moore to JPK, Oct. 8, 1926, as quoted in DKG, p. 345.

61 " 'did not want to move' ": Quoted in JHC, p. 245.

61 " 'At best' ": RKRC, p. 166.

61 "Jack's tenth birthday": Whitney Wright interview of Dec. 29, 1988.

61 " 'Anyone old enough' ": RKRC, pp. 116–17. Thomas Mix (1880–1940), became the silent screen's most successful cowboy star. In 1928 he left Fox studios to join Joe Kennedy's Film Booking Office (FBO) studios.

61 "a summer house at Hyannis Port": After being blackballed by Cohasset's country club, Joseph Kennedy had looked farther afield for a summer house. Marchant Cottage had been built in 1904 as a small seafront property, just south of Hyannis Port's harbor, and was first rented by the Kennedys in 1926. The following year the cottage was purchased by Joseph Kennedy for about $25,000. L. Frank Pine, who had designed the original house in 1903, was retained to double its size to fourteen rooms, nine baths, and, in 1928, a basement movie theater. Leo Damore, *The Cape Cod Years of John Fitzgerald Kennedy* (Englewood Cliffs, N.J.: Prentice-Hall, 1967), p. 19.

61 " 'about four and a half acres' ": *Dexter School 1927–1928.*

62 "Riverdale Country Day School": To James MacGregor Burns, JFK noted that "at Riverdale School there wasn't any such [discriminatory] impression" as in Brookline, since Riverdale had "a rather polyglot group in a sense—there were Protestants, Catholics, and Jews." JMBP.

62 "she was finally 'certain' ": RKRC, p. 166.

62 " 'our Boston suburb' ": ibid.

62 " 'Walking to and from' ": ibid.

62 "punctilious concern": "A tough, constant, minute disciplinarian with a fetish for neatness and order and decorum": Lem Billings's description of RFK, quoted in DKG, p. 353.

62 " 'For months I would' ": ibid., p. 367.

63 " 'proper hands' ": Robert Kane to JPK, Nov. 7, 1927, as quoted in DKG, p. 382.

63 " 'didn't resemble any' ": GS, p. 327.

63 "pretended he'd been": JPK never in fact attended the Harvard Business School. However in March 1927 he had organized a lecture series there, inviting thirteen distinguished Hollywood personalities, including Harry Warner, Marcus Loew, Adolph Zukor, Jesse Lasky, Cecil B. De-Mille, and Will Hays, the Hollywood censor, to speak on the film industry. Axel Madsen, *Gloria and Joe* (N.Y.: Arbor House/Morrow, 1988) p. 134. A book incorporating the lectures, *The Story of Films,* was compiled by James Seymour (a Harvard administrator who joined FBO thereafter to work for JPK), and published in the fall of 1927 by A.W. Shaw of New York, carrying JPK's name as editor. James Seymour entry, "The 25th Annual Report of the Class of 1917," Harvard University Archives, Cambridge, Mass.

63 " 'Nobody in Hollywood' ": GS, p. 328.

64 " 'he had wanted' ": ibid. p. 339.

64 " 'Mr. Kennedy kept' ": ibid.

64 " 'someone with business' ": ibid. p. 340.

64 " 'the fighting-Irish pride' ": ibid. p. 353.

65 "his 'horsemen' ": ibid. p. 342.

65 " 'gangsters in appearance' ": ibid.

65 " 'acting and other' ": ibid. p. 343.

65 " 'that if he didn't' ": ibid. p. 349.

65 " 'He moved so quickly' ": ibid. pp. 356–67.

65 "surrendering her distribution rights": To lighten her debts, JPK persuaded Gloria Swanson, against her better judgment, to sell her rights to her Maugham film, *Sadie Thompson,* to Joe Schenck, to whom she owed money. This proved a disastrous mistake, as *Sadie Thompson* quickly became Gloria's biggest hit. Madsen, *Gloria and Joe,* pp. 174 and 195.

66 " 'In two months' ": GS, p. 357.

66 " 'in Joe's employ' ": ibid. p. 389.

66 " 'trusted him to' ": ibid. p. 357.

66 " 'By rearranging his cards' ": ibid. p. 337.

66 " 'Take Boston' ": ibid. p. 339.

66 " 'as ready to' ": ibid. p. 346.

66 " 'He was a classic' ": ibid. p. 397.

67 " 'At the end of' ": ibid. p. 359.

67 " 'I had two' ": ibid. p. 358.

67 " 'with three diamond' ": RKRC, p. 76.

67 "every time Mrs. Kennedy": Cameron, *Rose,* p. 112.

67 " 'pay' for his infidelity": Ralph G. Martin, *A Hero for Our Time* (N.Y.: Macmillan, 1983), p. 34.

67 "Jack told a friend": DKG, p. 353.

68 " 'five times a night' ": William Walton interview of June 12, 1991. "The Ambassador enjoyed talking about his female conquests. For hours he would tell Jackie about Gloria Swanson, Marion Davies and countless others past and present." KLB, quoted in C. David Heymann, *A Woman Named Jackie* (N.Y.: Lyle Stuart, 1989), p. 142.

68 " 'a modified version' ": GS, p. 383.

68 " 'on a silver platter' ": Thomas Curtis, *Von Stroheim* (N.Y.: Farrar Straus, 1971), p. 246. Stroheim was a Viennese Jew from the ghetto, a milliner's son; the title "von" was a fake: Madsen, *Gloria and Joe,* p. 160.

68 " 'Oh, I tell you' ": GS, p. 359.

68 " 'like a college boy' ": ibid. p. 358.

68 " 'the best film story' ": ibid.

68 " 'on a tight leash' ": ibid.

68 " 'He had to prove' ": ibid. p. 392.

68 " 'was a baby' ": ibid., p. 366. See also Madsen, *Gloria and Joe,* p. 209.

68 " 'There in that strange' ": GS, p. 367.

69 " 'a wonderful time' ": ibid. pp. 367–68.

69 " 'to his restaurant' ": Herbert Somborn, Gloria Swanson's second husband, first blackmailed her into an expensive divorce by threatening to publicly cite her adultery with fourteen men, then with the proceeds started the Brown Derby restaurant in Hollywood: GS, pp. 187 and 294.

69 " 'say hi to Gloria' ": Gene Schoor Papers.

69 " 'coming Napoleon' ": RJW, p. 98.

69 " 'to confer at length' ": ibid.

70 " 'Von, the lousiest' ": Peter Noble, *Hollywood Scapegoat* (N.Y.: Arno, 1972), p. 79.

70 " 'Joseph, you'd better' ": GS, p. 373.

71 " 'he slumped' ": ibid.

71 " 'altered the story' ": RKRC, p. 190.

71 " 'panties drop' ": GS, p. 370. According to the director of photography, Paul Ivano, JPK watched the rushes with Gloria Swanson and Stroheim the following day, JPK approving the scene with the words, "All right, I guess we'll get away with it." Madsen, *Gloria and Joe*; p. 218.

72 " 'drastic showdown' ": JPK letter of March 13, 1929, to Henri, the Marquis de Falaise de Coudraye, quoted in DKG, p. 409. Nothing came of Kennedy's machinations, save a 1931 Viola Lawrence cut of the Stroheim footage with two new happy-ending scenes and a musical score, shown in a handful of European cinemas. It proved a disaster, and was not shown in the U.S. until 1950 at the Museum of Modern Art. This was followed, a quarter of a century later, in 1985, by a restored ninety-six minute version, complete with stills and outtakes, in New York and Los Angeles. Madsen, *Gloria and Joe*, pp. 227–28, 232, 249, and 297.

72 "twelve-room colonial": Rachlin, *The Kennedys*, p. 57. According to Gail Cameron, Rose Kennedy's biographer, it was found for Joe Kennedy by Eddie Moore and acquired for $250,000—"a huge Georgian mansion with red-brick walls and large white columns in front; it was at 294 Pondfield Road, in the Republican stronghold of Bronxville, had twenty rooms and extra dwellings for the gardener and chauffeur, a winding approach, and a beautiful arched doorway. . . . It was the most elegant house Rose had ever lived in—far more distinguished than the Fitzgerald mansion on Welles Avenue in Dorchester, which she had left only fifteen years ear-

lier to marry an intense, ambitious young man and move into an undistinguished frame house in Brookline": Cameron, *Rose*, p. 116–17.

72 "his father's death": P.J. Kennedy died, aged seventy-one, on May 18, 1929, of "carcinoma of the liver," according to his death certificate: JFKL.

72 " 'I have heard' ": JPK to Joe Jr., June 3, 1929, as quoted in DKG, p. 412.

72 " 'I had seen him' ": GS, p. 380.

73 " 'Miss Swanson' ": Damore, *Cape Cod Years,* p. 21. According to some more farfetched accounts, JPK took Gloria sailing in the family sailboat, *Rose Elizabeth,* and anchored offshore, but the couple were disturbed in their lovemaking by young JFK, who had stowed away below deck and subsequently tried to swim ashore in confusion, only to be hauled back by his father—triggering JFK's compulsive adolescent and adult philandering: "The incident was hushed up with Kennedy money and Kennedy influence. The story seeped out through the neighbors' children. . . . What happened out on Nantucket Sound that August afternoon in 1929, however, would remain as an explanation of traumatic beginnings and randy proclivities, of the family's inner story." Madsen, *Gloria and Joe*, p. 241.

73 " 'Was she a fool' ": GS, p. 387.

73 "the Stroheim fiasco": RKRC, p. 190.

73 " 'She's never been' ": GS, pp. 385–86.

73 " 'Europe, lots of people' ": ibid.

74 " 'fervent attentions' ": ibid. p. 389.

74 " 'concerned and perplexed' ": RKRC, p. 189.

74 " 'after the London premiere' ": GS, p. 390.

75 " 'mistakenly decided' ": DKG, p. 416.

75 " 'back to our children' ": RKRC, p. 190.

75 "done exceptionally well": RCDSA.

75 "she'd sat 'fascinated as' ": RKRC, p. 187.

75 " 'My own special' ": ibid.

76 " 'Irish micks' ": Henry James interview of Aug. 23, 1991.

76 " 'Rose Kennedy—' ": Peter Collier and David Horowitz, *The Kennedys: An American Drama* (N.Y.: Summit Books, 1984), p. 49.

76 " 'I worked on' ": Edna Bauckman, interview of June 1991.

76 " 'Well, you know' ": Good, Jr., interview.

Part 3: Boarding School

81 " 'I was shuffled' ": Barbara Gibson, with Caroline Latham, *Life with Rose Kennedy* (N.Y., Warner Books, 1986), pp. 40–41.

82 " 'continue the good' ": Wardell St. John to JPK, April 17, 1929, CSA. What this spirit was Wardell St. John did not say, but mentioned the enhanced status that came with so many years of incarceration, since it was "to such boys that the School votes, by and large, its positions of responsibility, and I think you will agree that the more responsibility of such extra-curricular nature a boy may have before he enters college, the better are his chances of making good afterward. It's the old question of adjustment and the amount of time it takes a boy to grow into the life of the School in such a way that

he may contribute most to it, and so get most out of it—the two things go together." Ibid.

82 " 'the advantages you' ": JPK to W. St. John, April 20, 1929, CSA.

82 " 'I want to thank you' ": W. St. John to JPK, April 22, 1929, CSA.

83 "was most enthusiastic": "When I spoke to Mrs. Kennedy originally about writing to you, she said she had always felt that it would be difficult for me to have a boy whom I cared for more than I did Russ Ayres, so the association of my boys with you at Choate would bring me the greatest pleasure." JPK to Russ Ayres, May 1, 1929, CSA. Though Kennedy promised to "make it my business to get up there and spend some

time" at Choate, there is no record that he or
Rose ever did.

83 " 'one of the very best' ": Frank Hackett to W.
St. John, July 31, 1929, CSA.

83 " 'manly, clean-minded' ": Mrs. Guiney to
George St. John, May 27, 1929, CSA.

83 " 'We shall keep hoping' ": G. St. John to JPK,
Oct. 31, 1929, CSA.

83 " 'very sorry indeed' ": RFK to G. St. John,
Dec. 11, 1929, CSA.

84 " 'When Joe came' ": JFK to JPK, Dec. 9 (1929),
JFKPP, Box 1.

84 "sixth former": In the British public (actually
private)-school system, final-year pupils were
traditionally given disciplinary privileges over
younger boys, especially with regard to corporal
punishment—a system formally and informally
adopted at many American private schools.

84 " 'Creditable, Jack' ": Upper School Scholarship Report, Feb. 25, 1930, JFKPP, Box 1.

84 "The original application": Choate admission
application, May 1, 1929, CSA.

84 " 'if there is any way' ": J. Cushman to W. St.
John, June 10, 1930, CSA.

84 "disliked the school": "I don't know all the reasons why, but his mother was restive about Joe
being at a non-Catholic school. She was a little
nervous about that—and I think she rather
pushed for Jack to go to a Catholic school."
Seymour St. John, interview of April 11, 1989.
Rose later claimed she was "advised that he
[JFK] should first have a year away, at some
other boarding school, so he could mature and
become accustomed to boarding-school life. . . .
I wanted each of them to have at least a while in
a Catholic school, so it was decided he would go
to the Canterbury School." RKRC, p. 174. JFK
himself recalled, "[My mother] was terribly religious, and [my father's] not so religious. All my
sisters went to religious schools . . . so that they
were all terribly religious." Asked if he wanted
to go to boarding school, JFK responded, "No,
it was just a sort of normal thing. . . . I think it
improved [Joe Jr.] a good deal, which my family
felt. But they just sent me there." JMBP.

85 "Its name, ironically": Canterbury, in the English county of Kent, is the traditional see of the
archbishop of Canterbury, primate of the Protestant Church of England.

85 "thus signed in": *The Tabard* (weekly school
newspaper), Canterbury School Archives. There
were ninety-two pupils recorded in 1930, from as
far as Tennessee, Santo Domingo, Utah, Indiana, Illinois, Philadelphia, and Detroit. Fourteen teachers were employed, four of whom
taught sports. "There was daily chapel held in
the evening. Canterbury's Chaplain was the
Roman Catholic priest assigned to the parish of
New Milford. The basic curriculum included
language, history, math, English and science;
though as an 8th grader, Kennedy would probably not have had a science course." Cathy Bolster, Canterbury School archivist, to author,
Dec. 8, 1988. Writing to JFK's biographer in 1959,
one of the masters described Canterbury as "a
school for Catholic boys run by Catholic lay-
men." Letter of Oct. 29, 1959, JMBP.

85 " 'the intellectual' ": RKRC, p. 126.

85 "in trouble with the neighbors": Dr. James
Lamphier, interview of May 1, 1991.

85 " 'It's a pretty good place' ": JFK to Jack Fitzgerald, Mon., n.d., JFKPP, Box 4B.

85 " 'Send me up a' ": JFK to RFK, n.d. (1930),
JFKPP, Box 1. Letters to RFK were always ad-
dressed "Dear Mother," those to JPK, "Dear
Dad."

85 " 'did not like the color' ": JFK to RFK, n.d.
(1930), JFKPP, Box 1.

85 " 'I felt pretty homesick' ": JFK to RFK, n.d.
(1930), as quoted in JMB, p. 24.

86 " 'Things are going' ": JFK to RFK, n.d. (1930–
31), JFKPP, Box 4B.

86 " 'lots of snow' ": JFK to RFK, n.d. (1930–31),
JFKPP, Box 4B.

86 " 'lying on the ground' ": JFK to RFK, n.d.
(1930–31), JFKPP, Box 1.

86 " 'Please send me' ": YJK, p. 37.

87 " 'When we didn't hear' ": W. St. John to JPK,
Jan. 20, 1931, CSA.

87 "earning him a 95 grade": Canterbury School,
Record of Nov. 1 to Dec. 6, 1930, JFKPP,
Box 4B.

87 "68 in Latin": "If it were not for Latin I would
probably lead the lower school but I am flunking
that by ten points." JFK to RFK in letter, n.d.,
JMBP.

87 " 'one of the most' ": JFK to JPK, n.d. (1930–31),
JFKPP, Box 1.

87 " 'I was weighed' ": JFK to RFK, n.d. (1930–31),
JFKPP, Box 1.

87 " 'though I may not' ": JFK to RFK, n.d. (1930–
31), JFKPP, Box 1.

87 " 'He can do better' ": Canterbury School, Record of Nov. 1 to Dec. 6, 1930.

87 " 'doing a little worrying' ": JFK to RFK, n.d.
(1930–31), JFKPP, Box 1.

87 " 'I hope my marks go up' ": JFK to JPK, April
15, 1931, JMBP. JPK had taken to renting a house
on Clarke Avenue in Palm Beach, next to the
Harold Sweatts, from the late 1920s. John Ney,
Palm Beach (Boston: Little, Brown, 1966), p. 18.

87 " 'A nurse and surgeon' ": Notes from an interview with Mr. Brodie, an English teacher at
Canterbury School, JMBP.

88 "The surgeon, Dr. Verdi": JCB, p. 23.

88 "convalesce at home and be tutored": RKRC,
p. 174. See also Canterbury School attendance
records, Canterbury School Archives.
"Kennedy was probably very homesick during
his time at Canterbury. . . . In May, he left
school with appendicitis and did not return":
Bolster to author.

88 "Jack made up his work": "He must have completed his exams elsewhere, as he was given
credit for the year." Bolster to author.

88 " 'It was not one of' ": RKRC, p. 174.

88 "Once again Mr. Kennedy wrote": Mabel Ma-
lone to W. St. John, on behalf of JPK, May 14,
1931, CSA.

88 "high scores": 83 percent in math, 75 percent in
English, 57 percent in Latin: JFK Scholastic Record, 1931–32, CSA.

88 " 'work down here' ": RFK to W. St. John, July
3, 1931, CSA.

88 "'especially glad that'": W. St. John to RFK, July 8, 1931, CSA.

88 "'a fine chap'": Bruce Belmore to Choate School, July 11, 1931, CSA.

89 "'golden interval'": RKRC, p. 192.

89 "According to Swanson": GS, p. 408.

89 "'When Joe realized'": DKG, p. 425.

89 "the last time he slept": "According to Marie Greene, Rose remained firm in her beliefs and years later, after her last child was born, she simply said, 'No more sex.'" DKG, p. 392. "I knew a girl who was his [JPK's] mistress for years. She was a showgirl. Joe bought her an apartment at Beekman Place in New York. . . . She told me Rose didn't care how many women Joe kept as long as she had her family. The only time Rose had sexual relations with her husband was for the purpose of reproduction. She was that devout a Catholic. Once she had her family she was no longer interested. So the fact that he had women on the side didn't mean anything to her." Doris Lilly, *New York Post* journalist, quoted in David Heymann, *A Woman Named Jackie* (N.Y., Lyle Stuart, 1989), pp. 140–41.

89 "George Washington Kennedy": DKG, p. 426.

89 "Joe Jr. as he proudly drove": Leo Damore, *The Cape Cod Years of John Fitzgerald Kennedy* (Englewood Cliffs, N.J.: Prentice-Hall, 1967), p. 33.

89 "'Joe is established'": Clara St. John to RFK, Oct. 7, 1931, CSA.

89 "Jack, by contrast, had mislaid": RFK to Choate, Sept. 30, 1931, CSA.

89 "At one-twenty P.M.": Choate School Register, Oct. 2, 1931, CSA.

89 "'Everyone likes your boy'": Clara St. John to RFK, Oct. 7, 1931, CSA.

89 "'Jack sits at'": G. St. John to JPK, Oct. 20, 1931, CSA.

89 "'Jack has a pleasing'": Quoted in Seymour St. John, "JFK: 50th Reunion of 1000 Days at School," June 1985, CSA.

90 "'double pedestal variety'": Godfrey W. Kauffmann to Earl Leinbach, March 4, 1966, CSA.

90 "'Because of their explosive'": S. St. John, "JFK: 50th Reunion."

90 "'rather abruptly'": Kauffmann to Leinbach.

90 "'behind the lines'": S. St. John interview.

90 "'gradual improvement'": S. St. John, "JFK: 50th Reunion."

90 "'Jack's results are not'": ibid.

91 "'read with a great deal'": ibid.

91 "'Not once'": DKG, p. 351.

91 "'Jack looks a little thin'": JPK to G. St. John, Dec. 3, 1931, CSA.

91 "'Jack was looking'": C. St. John to RFK, Jan. 18, 1932, CSA.

91 "'She and I remember'": RFK to C. St. John, n.d. (1932), CSA.

92 "'Don't be discouraged'": C. St. John to RFK, Jan. 23, 1932, CSA.

92 "'I finally got out'": JFK to Jeffrey Roche, at Lawrenceville School, n.d., signed "Smuttily yours, Jack Kennedy," sold at auction Jan. 14, 1965, kindly furnished to author by Barry Goldman.

92 "'Kepler's . . . until he'": C. St. John to Earl Leinbach, Jan. 25, 1932, CSA.

92 "Dear Mrs. St. John": RFK to C. St. John, as quoted in RKRC, p. 175.

92 "Rose, unwell herself": DKG, p. 389.

92 "'nearly drove my'": S. St. John interview.

92 "'was on the telephone'": RKRC, p. 167.

92 "'I was often anxious'": ibid. p. 176.

93 "'Jack's problem, with'": G. St. John to JPK, Feb. 17, 1932, CSA.

93 "'non-infectious Parotitis'": Infirmary note, April 23–28, CSA.

93 "'Is Jack studying'": S. St. John, "JFK: 50th Reunion." Paradoxically, JFK's measured IQ increased four points, to 123, at this time. Ibid.

93 "'each step of his'": ibid.

93 "When his mother sent": KLB interviews, JCB and JFKLOH.

94 "be allowed to stand godfather": JFK to RFK, Feb. 1932, JFKPP, Box 1.

94 "'We were really organized'": RKRC, p. 135.

94 "'Sort of let him take over'": ibid., p. 148.

94 "'So far as I can remember'": ibid., p. 149.

94 "'discovered the children'": LMT, p. 12.

94 "'always rather harsh'": JFK interview, JMBP.

94 "'Jack did the best'": RKRC, p. 126.

94 "Jack stole a life-size": James H. Williamson to S. St. John, April 9, 1961, CSA.

94 "'I had an impassioned'": S. St. John, "JFK: 50th Reunion."

95 "'Mrs. Kennedy hopes'": C. St. John to Leinbach, May 3, 1932, CSA.

95 "'Will you have a talk with Jack'": Note for Mr. St. John, May 3, 1932, CSA.

95 "'Jack Kennedy has a high IQ'": S. St. John, "JFK: 50th Reunion."

95 "Jack failed both French": ibid.

95 "'Le Petit Chou'": William C. Hardy to S. St. John, April 10, 1961, CSA.

95 "'There is actually'": S. St. John, "JFK: 50th Reunion."

95 "'Impulsive actions'": ibid.

95 "'We have had a'": ibid.

96 "'so as to make out'": Choate School to JFK, July 30, 1932, CSA.

96 "'I am glad'": ibid.

96 "'The fact has come'": RFK to G. St. John, Sept. 6, 1932, CSA.

96 "'all nine children'": ibid.

96 "Joe Jr.'s confirmation": HS, p. 47.

97 "the 'only man with'": JHC, p. 264.

97 "Jesse Straus of Macy's": RJW, p. 119.

97 "'managed Roosevelt's tour'": Joseph Dinneen, *The Kennedy Family* (Boston: Little, Brown, 1959), pp. 41–42.

97 "he felt compelled": DEK, pp. 47–49.

98 "'I want to come back'": Courtenay Hememway memo, CSA.

98 "'tendency to foster'": S. St. John, "JFK: 50th Reunion."

98 "'All last year'": ibid.

98 "'flu-like symptoms'": ibid.

98 "'he has persisted'": RFK to C. St. John, March 9, 1933, CSA.

98 "'Jack's winter term'": S. St. John, "JFK: 50th Reunion."

98 "'there is a charge'": JPK to JFK, April 12, 1932, as quoted in DKG, p. 462.

99 "'All through the campaign'": DKG, p. 440.

99 "His results for the 1932–1933": "Principal's Report on Applicant," April 30, 1935, JFKPP, Box 2; and S. St. John, "JFK: 50th Reunion."

99 " 'splendid final examination' ": S. St. John, "JFK: 50th Reunion."

99 " 'an achievement for him' ": ibid.

99 " 'continually asks questions' ": ibid.

99 " 'It must make you' ": G. St. John to JPK, June 2, 1933, CSA.

100 " 'I'll see you' ": JFK to KLB, June 23, 1933, KLBP.

100 "perhaps in guilt at the seventeen times": Nancy Gager Clinch, *The Kennedy Neurosis* (N.Y.: Grosset & Dunlap, 1973), p. 77. "Is Mother still in Bermuda?" was one typical query from Jack. JFK to JPK, n.d. (1931), JFKPP, Box 4B.

100 " 'Said she wondered' ": George Owen minute, Sept. 26, 1933, CSA.

100 " 'It seems too bad' ": ibid.

100 " 'telephoned Mrs. Kennedy' ": ibid.

100 " 'I feel that the' ": JPK to G. St. John, Sept. 25, 1933, CSA.

100 " 'There is no finer man' ": S. St. John, "JFK: 50th Reunion."

101 " 'He was a highly' ": S. St. John interview.

101 " 'I think Maher's' ": ibid.

101 "Mr. Kennedy had abandoned": DEK, pp. 51–53. James Roosevelt's part in the liquor deals became shrouded in rumor and suspicion. See RJW, p. 136, RJWP, and DEK, pp. 51–53.

102 " 'I can't tell you' ": JPK to G. St. John, Nov. 21, 1933, CSA.

102 " 'Jack and I talked' ": G. St. John to JPK, Nov. 27, 1933, CSA.

103 " 'has one of the few great' ": JPK to JPK, Jr., Nov. 21, 1933, as quoted in DKG, p. 463.

103 " 'I read and hear' ": JPK to Missy Le Hand, Dec. 23, 1933, as quoted in DKG, p. 438.

103 " 'Those months after' ": DKG, p. 438.

103 " 'a wizened, brilliant' ": RKRC, p. 196.

103 " 'I can see why' ": DKG, p. 438.

103 " 'Joe was keenly' ": RKRC, p. 197.

103 " 'My father built' ": Peter Collier and David Horowitz, *The Kennedys: An American Drama.* (N.Y.: Summit Books, 1984), p. 50.

104 " 'We are still puzzled' ": C. St. John to RFK, Feb. 6, 1934, CSA.

104 " 'never felt sorrier' ": C. St. John to JFK, Feb. 5, 1934, CSA.

104 " 'then before there was a chance' ": ibid.

104 " 'Actually he came' ": KLB interviews.

104 " 'Jack is on the right' ": G. St. John to JPK, Feb. 8, 1934, CSA.

104 " 'Jack's sense of humor hasn't' ": C. St. John to RFK, Feb. 6, 1934, CSA.

104 "oceanside villa": Harvey Rachlin, *The Kennedys, A Chronological History, 1823–Present* (N.Y.: World Almanac, 1986) p. 61. The seven-bedroom, American-Spanish Mizner hacienda at 1095 N. Ocean Blvd. had been built in 1923 for the retail magnate Rodman Wanamaker. It had four hundred feet of shore and two acres of grounds. Ney, *Palm Beach*, p. 13.

104 " 'When he was complaining' ": C. St. John to RFK, Feb. 6, 1934, CSA.

105 " 'had his first meal' ": ibid.

105 " 'If this had happened' ": ibid.

105 " 'For the sake of' ": ibid.

105 " 'I took his electric' ": ibid.

105 " 'They didn't have' ": KLB interviews.

106 "all were interchangeable": When interviewed by his presidential-campaign biographer, James MacGregor Burns, JFK had only the vaguest recollections of his childhood habitats: "First I lived on Beals Street in Brookline, I would say I can't remember that. Then we moved to the corner of Naples and Abbotsford Road where I guess I spent some years. . . . Then we moved to Riverdale, New York. . . . Then I went to Choate School. I have no recollections of Beal [sic] Street. I'm conscious of time passing, but not, at least at first thought, of any overpowering incident which had any lasting impression or influence." JFK interview, JMBP.

107 " 'thought his own thoughts' ": RKRC, p. 94.

107 " 'thank you for your' ": JFK to Mr. and Mrs. St. John, March 4, 1934, CSA.

107 " 'The weather has been awful' ": JFK to JPK, n.d., JFKL, courtesy of Milton Gwirtzman/Senator Edward Kennedy. In the spring and fall of 1989 the author gave a series of public lectures entitled "JFK: The Education of a President" at the Massachusetts State Archives, under the sponsorship of the Public Affairs Division of the Secretary of State and the John W. McCormack Institute of Public Affairs. The lectures were subsequently published in the *New England Journal of Public Policy,* Vol. 6, No. 2, Fall/Winter 1990, and the author received many encouraging letters, including a charming one from Mr. Milton Gwirtzman, a well-known Washington lawyer and former Kennedy political aide. Ironically, in response to later criticism from Senator Kennedy that the account of the relationship between JFK and RFK was unduly harsh, Mr. Gwirtzman was ordered by the Kennedy family to put pressure on the author to amend his portrait. Despite the clandestine and vaguely threatening nature of his request (Mr. Gwirtzman flew to Boston and met the author in the foyer of the Emerson Majestic Theater at the end of an opera performance with a specially annotated copy of *New England Journal*), the author declined to alter his account unless he was given fresh evidence by the senator that would merit a more charitable interpretation—in particular JFK's remaining letters to his parents, sealed in the still-secret papers of Joseph P. Kennedy and Rose Kennedy, housed at public expense at the John F. Kennedy Presidential Library. Senator Kennedy duly authorized Mr. Gwirtzman to fly to Boston again and monitor these crucial letters with a view to making them available. However, when Mr. Gwirtzman reported that the sealed letters did not in any way contradict the author's account, indeed only fortified it, permission for special access was denied. A few innocuous letters were, however, kindly made available, for which the author is most grateful. They are hereafter referred to as "JPK/RFK Letters."

106 " 'I think the main' ": Seymour St. John interview of April 8, 1989.

106 " 'Jack is such a complete' ": S. St. John, "JFK: 50th Reunion."

107 "(speculatively diagnosed as 'hepatitis')": ibid.

107 " 'I've never known' ": KLB interviews.

107 " 'Jack was always' ": Hugh Wynne interview of Jan. 18, 1990.

107 " 'He read a great deal' ": KLB interviews.

107 " 'He conspicuously failed' ": S. St. John, "JFK: 50th Reunion."

107 " 'I'd know roughly' ": Ralph Horton, JFKLOH.

107 " 'an excellent mind' ": Ralph Horton interview, JCBP and JCB, p. 35.

107 " 'It wasn't challenged' ": ibid.

107 " 'He read a great deal' ": Ralph Horton, JFKLOH.

108 " 'As we were leaving' ": Ralph Horton interview, JCBP, and JCB, p. 35.

108 " 'better at facts than' ": Quoted by G. St. John in letter to JPK, June 27, 1933, CSA.

108 " 'I have great admiration' ": JPK to JPK, Jr., Nov. 21, 1933, as quoted in DKG, p. 470.

108 " 'The German people' ": JPK, Jr. to JPK, April 23, 1934, as quoted in DKG, p. 471.

108 " 'I'm sure if' ": ibid.

109 " 'set his heart' ": John F. Kennedy, ed., *As We Remember Joe* (Cambridge, Mass.: University Press, 1945), p. 43.

109 " 'I remember the first' ": KLB interviews.

110 " 'lying in bed' ": Kay Halle, JFKLOH.

110 " 'It looks now' ": JFK to KLB, June 19, 1934, KLBP.

110 "Billings had scalded": ibid. See also David Michaelis, *The Best of Friends* (N.Y.: William Morrow & Co., 1983), pp. 142–3.

110 " 'I never yet saw' ": G. St. John to JPK, Nov. 27, 1933, CSA.

110 " 'I am suffering' ": JFK to KLB, June 19, 1934, KLBP.

111 " 'I hope to hell' ": ibid.

111 " 'God what a beating' ": JFK to KLB, June 21, 1934, KLBP.

111 " 'Just heard today' ": JFK to KLB, June 27, 1934, KLBP.

112 " 'My vitality is slowly' ": ibid.

112 " 'Last night in' ": JFK to KLB, June 21, 1934, KLBP.

113 " 'the dirtiest-minded bunch' ": JFK to KLB, June 30, 1934, KLBP.

113 " 'I've got something' ": JFK to KLB, June 27, 1934, KLBP.

113 " 'Weren't the crew races' ": ibid.

113 " 'Still in this God-damned' ": JFK to KLB, June 30, 1934, KLBP.

113 " 'about the early' ": JPK to G. St. John, Sept. 15, 1934, CSA.

114 " 'After your last letter' ": JFK to KLB, July 25, 1934, KLBP.

114 " 'Ruth Zingly called' ": ibid.

114 " 'his personality that dominated' ": KLB interviews.

114 " 'were often in a way' ": RKRC, p. 129.

115 " 'He had, it began' ": ibid. p. 178.

115 "Paul Chase, later remembered": Paul Chase interview of Sept. 11, 1989.

115 " 'Mr. K. really did' ": S. St. John, "JFK: 50th Reunion."

116 " 'He was just so' ": JCB, p. 34; and Ralph Horton interview, JCBP.

116 " 'after a particularly' ": S. St. John, "JFK: 50th Reunion."

116 " 'I think it's Dad's' ": S. St. John interview, April 8, 1989.

117 " 'Choate was *his*' ": KLB interviews.

117 " 'I still have' ": JFK to KLB, July 25, 1934, KLBP.

117 " 'We are up on' ": JFK to JPK, n.d., Sun. (1934), JFKPP, Box 4B.

117 " 'It was shortly after' ": KLB interviews.

117 " 'improving. Attitude poor' ": S. St. John, "JFK: 50th Reunion."

117 " 'Matched only by' ": ibid.

117 " 'Jack's record is not' ": ibid.

118 " 'Was he scared' ": KLB interviews.

118 " 'Dear Dad: I thought' ": JFK to JPK, n.d., Sun. (rec. Dec. 4, 1934), JFKPP, Box 1.

118 " 'He really had no desire' ": KLB interviews.

118 " 'Poor Lem' ": Olive Cawley, quoted in S. St. John, "JFK: 50th Reunion."

119 "Rose Kennedy refused to follow": RKRC, p. 200.

119 " 'I quite understood' ": G. St. John to JPK, Jan. 9, 1935, CSA.

119 " 'I agree that he still' ": S. St. John, "JFK: 50th Reunion."

119 " 'We have possibly contributed' ": JPK to George Steele, assistant headmaster, Jan. 5, 1935, quoted in DKG, p. 463.

120 " 'In lieu of discipline' ": G. St. John to JPK, Dec. 19, 1934, CSA.

120 " 'With the winter term' ": S. St. John "JFK: 50th Reunion."

120 " 'For a year and a half' ": ibid.

120 " 'I had a great deal' ": ibid.

120 " 'Josh' Billings, LeMoyne's brother": S. St. John interview, April 8, 1989.

121 " 'it was time for Jack' ": Notes on interview with Ralph Horton, JCBP. According to Henry James, as a result of this revelation (subsequently published in 1976 in JCB, p. 34), Lem Billings never again spoke to Horton.

121 " 'neither Jack nor' ": S. St. John, "JFK: 50th Reunion."

121 "his new girlfriend, Olive Cawley": Olive Cawley, who later married Tom Watson, first met JFK when invited to a Choate School dance by Smokey Wilde. Wilde suddenly became ill. "As she got off the train in Wallingford she was met by a tousled boy in khakis and sneakers who started off in his Bostonian twang with 'I am Jack Kennedy and I have to take care of you for the weekend,' and followed it up with 'But I'm in love with Ruth Moffett, so don't fall in love with me' "—which, she later confessed, "I promptly did." Ibid.

121 " 'witty, clever, mischievious' ": ibid.

121 " 'See Jack and LeMoyne' ": ibid.

121 " 'Jack is the most' ": ibid.

122 " 'The word cropped up' ": ibid.

122 " 'We had a room' ": KLB interviews.

122 " 'Why were we so' ": Horton, JFKLOH.

122 " 'Only members of' ": KLB interviews.

122 " 'sophisticated' member": JCB, p. 33.
123 " 'Everybody's going Blambo' ": Horton interview, JCBP.
123 " 'Maury Shea, Maury Shea' ": JCB, p. 35.
123 " 'We had to sing' ": ibid. pp. 35–36.
123 " 'One evening in our' ": S. St. John, "JFK: 50th Reunion."
123 "(some students, such as Hugh Wynne"): Wynne interview.
123 " 'We had a little' ": Horton, JFKLOH.
123 " 'About $12' ": S. St. John, "JFK: 50th Reunion."
124 " 'a colosally selfish' ": ibid.
124 " 'I don't blame him' ": Maurice Shea, JFKLOH.
124 " 'At lunch the Head' ": Paul Chase interview.
124 " 'At that stage' ": Horton, interview, JCBP.
125 " 'There must have been . . .' ": JCB, p. 37.
125 " 'I don't think Mr. Kennedy' ": Shea, JFKLOH.
125 " 'Actually, all thirteen' ": KLB interviews.
125 " 'Our parents spoke' ": Horton, JFKLOH.
125 " 'At one time' ": AWRH, p. 17.
126 "George St. John was prejudiced": Anonymous interview with Choate master.
126 " 'Will you please' ": G. St. John to JPK, Feb. 11, 1935, CSA.
126 " 'allow Jack to come' ": RFK to G. St. John, Feb. 9, 1935, CSA. The weekend before, Mr. Kennedy had traveled to see Kathleen at Noroton, her convent school in Connecticut, and his intention, as he wrote to Jack on Feb. 6, 1934, was to take Kathleen, Jack, and Billings out for an evening's entertainment in New York if they could get permission to leave Choate: "She is coming up on the 16th and I told her if you and LeMoyne or another of your gang can get off, I will blow you all to a party." DKG, p. 486.
126 " 'Mr. Steele has shown' ": G. St. John to RFK, Feb. 11, 1935, CSA.
126 "cabled that he would arrive": JPK to G. St. John, Feb. 16, 1935, CSA.
126 "Kathleen was impressed": "She really thinks you are a great fellow," JPK had written to JFK after seeing Kathleen at Noroton. "She has a love and devotion to you that you should be very proud to have deserved. . . . She thinks you are quite the grandest fellow that ever lived and your letters furnish her most of her laughs in the Convent," JPK to JFK, Feb. 6, 1935, as quoted in DKG, p. 486.
126 "DEAR PUBLIC ENEMIES" KK to JFK, Feb. 1935, as quoted in Michaelis, *Best of Friends*, p. 138.
126 " 'Mr. Kennedy and Jack' ": AWRH, p. 17.
127 " 'Psychologically I was' ": ibid.

127 " 'I know you want to' ": JPK to KK, Feb. 20, 1935, as quoted in DKG, p. 488.
127 " 'My God, my son' ": DKG, p. 488.
128 " 'Although the whole' ": KLB interviews.
128 " 'silly episode of' ": RKRC, p. 183.
128 " 'I am afraid' ": JPK to Dr. Paul O'Leary, Feb. 18, 1935, as quoted in DKG, pp. 488–89.
128 " 'What I'm really saying' ": KLB interviews.
129 " 'Has he been' ": Principal's Report on Applicant, April 30, 1935, JFKPP, Bx. 2. Copies of all JFK's Harvard records were donated to Harvard University to the JFK Library, and are quoted by kind permission of Harley Holden, chief archivist, Harvard University, on behalf of the trustees of the university.
129 " 'My desire to come' ": JFK file, Princeton University Records, PUL.
129 "an almost identical explanation": Harvard Application for Admission, April 23, 1935, JFKPP, Box 2.
130 " 'undoubtedly a very' ": S. St. John, "JFK: 50th Reunion."
130 "He and Lem even wrote": Gene Schoor, interview of Nov. 19, 1990.
130 " 'Each boy was allowed' ": KLB interviews.
132 " 'had extreme self-confidence' ": Bill Garnett to S. St. John, April 24, 1961, CSA.
132 "Father's Day": Courtenay Hemenway memo, CSA.
132 " 'the handsomest, the best' ": Horton, JFKLOH. Horton was known by his fellow Muckers as "The Ripper"; Jack, appropriately, as "Jack the Zipper."
132 " 'Despite the opinion' ": Paul Chase, quoted in S. St. John, "JFK: 50th Reunion."
133 " 'We were very eager' ": ibid.
133 " 'The result' ": ibid.
133 " 'Everybody knew him' ": Hemenway memo.
133 " 'The outstanding thing' ": Robert Lindsay to S. St. John, May 2, 1961, CSA.
133 " 'Even in this' ": Ed Meredith to S. St. John, April 6, 1961, CSA.
133 " 'Jack always had' ": Pierre Sichel to Earl Leinbach, April 10, 1961, CSA.
133 "scraped his knee": Secretary to Mrs. St. John, Choate, to RFK, April 10–30, 1935, CSA.
133 "finished the academic year": Harvard College Record Card, JFKPP, Box 2.
134 " 'He realized his' ": Hemenway memo.
134 " 'I'd like to take' ": "Report on John F. Kennedy for the 4th Quarter," JFKPP, Box 4B.
134 " 'Jack has lost' ": S. St. John, "JFK 50th Reunion."
134 " 'Jack,' he predicted, 'has' ": ibid.

Part 4: Freshman Years

139 " 'Made it by God' ": JFK to KLB, July 23, 1935, KLBP.
139 "and transferring there": In pencil, on Jack's original application to Princeton in the spring, Leslie Laughlin, the assistant to the director of admissions/dean of freshmen, had noted: "Son of the Chairman of SEC. Plenty of ability but immature and does not work very hard. Will probably study Economics and French in University of London for one year before entering Princeton. Attractive personality": April 9, JFK file, Princeton University Records, PUL. No further correspondence took place. However, in July 1935 JFK contacted Laughlin on the Cape,

where Laughlin had a house, to say he was not going to Europe and would like to come to Princeton, if his Harvard exam results could be recognized as valid for Princeton. Laughlin agreed to ask the Princeton dean of freshmen, Radcliffe Heermance, and was as good as his word. "I mentioned to you the case of Jack Kennedy, a candidate for both Harvard and Princeton whose papers went to Harvard. He wants to transfer to Princeton and asked whether we would take him if he is accepted by Harvard. . . . Will you write to me what procedure he should follow if he gets a notice of admission from Harvard?" Handwritten letter, n.d., JFK file, Princeton University Records. Heermance replied on July 27 that JFK "should immediately request someone in the admissions office to forward his certificate to Princeton and also his grades on the Scholastic Aptitude Test": JFK file, Princeton University Records.

139   "resigned as chairman": RJW, p. 174.

139   "at least $100,000": ibid.

139   "offered Kennedy alternative posts": DEK, p. 70. According to David Koskoff, Kennedy accepted the Works Program post, but then declined it, saying he could not work with Harold Ickes, Roosevelt's secretary of the interior. Ibid.

139   " 'through with public life' ": *NYT*, Sept. 21, 1935.

139   "insisted Jack accompany": The decision must finally have been made at the end of August 1935. "I wish to receive permission to enter Harvard in the fall of 1936 instead of this year as planned," JFK wrote from Hyannis Port on Aug. 30 to the Harvard dean's office. "I have been accepted as a freshman from the Choate School, Wallingford, Conn. My father has decided that a year abroad, studying at the London School of Economics, a branch of the University of London, would be beneficial to me and to my college career": JFKPP, Box 2. Since he had still not formally requested admission to Princeton, he did not write a similar letter to the Princeton authorities, though he may have told Leslie Laughlin informally.

139   " 'Send gray hat immediately' ": JFK to KLB, David Michaelis, *Best of Friends* (N.Y.: William Morrow & Co., 1983), p. 146.

139   " 'Dear Lemmer' ": JFK to KLB, Sept. 29, 1935, KLBP. The *Normandie* had broken the transatlantic speed record in June 1935, averaging just under thirty knots. It carried a crew of 1,250 and 1,070 passengers. "Jack is the same," RFK soon complained to the rest of her children, in what would become her preferred method of communication, namely a round-robin letter. "He was terribly late for dinner last night because he cut himself with your father's razor." Marguerite Higgins in "Rose Fitzgerald Kennedy," *McCall's* magazine, May 1961.

140   " 'Dear unattractive' ": JFK to KLB, Oct. 9, 1935, KLBP.

141   " 'Am definitely coming' ": ibid.

141   "DIAGNOSIS JACK'S ILLNESS": Dr. William Murphy to JPK, Oct. 10, 1935, JFKPP, Box 4B.

141   " 'My health since' ": JFK to KLB, n.d. (Oct. 1935), KLBP.

142   " 'We shall miss him' ": Seymour St. John, "JFK: 50th Reunion of 1000 Days at School," June 1985, CSA.

142   " 'I have gotten' ": JFK to KLB, n.d. (Oct. 1935), KLBP.

143   " 'Your financial worries' ": ibid.

143   " 'Nothing could possibly' ": KLB to JFK, Oct. 17, 1935, JFKPP, Box 4B.

143   " 'They didn't seem . . .' ": KLB interviews, JCB and JFKLOH.

143   " 'A chap' ": R. Heermance to A. Macdonald, Oct. 22, 1935, JFKPP, Box 2; and JFK file, Princeton University Records.

144   " 'a considerable act' ": Hugh Wynne interview of Jan. 18, 1990.

144   " 'found it necessary' ": JPK to R. Bingham, Oct. 21, 1935, as quoted in DKG, p. 490.

144   " 'The Committee on Admissions' ": A. Macdonald to Dean C. Gauss, Oct. 21, 1935, JFKPP, Box 2.

144   " 'Arriving Princeton Thursday' ": JFK to KLB, Oct. 21, 1935, KLBP.

144   " 'three dinky rooms, no bathroom' ": Jacqueline Pellaton article in *The Evening Times*, Trenton, N.J., June 11, 1965. Cutting in JFK file, Princeton University Records.

144   " 'I remember when' ": KLB interviews.

144   " 'Mr. Kennedy pulled up' ": Ralph Horton, JFKLOH.

144   " 'kept turning yellow' ": Wynne interview.

145   " 'We have decided' ": JPK to JFK, Nov. 11, 1935, as quoted in RKRC, p. 202.

145   " 'Jack is far from' ": JPK to R. Bingham, Nov. 12, 1935, as quoted in DKG, p. 490.

145   " 'The three of us' ": Horton, JFKLOH.

145   "On a scale of 1–6": JFK file, Princeton University Records.

145   " 'I didn't even know' ": Wynne interview.

145   " 'banking' ": JFK file, Princeton University Records.

145   "its small campus": The Princeton University Catalogue for 1935 listed a total of 2,295 undergraduate students, of which 552 were freshmen: PUL.

146   "only two dared openly": Wynne interview.

146   " 'Princeton had not greatly' ": JFK file, Princeton University Records.

146   " 'I think he was' ": Torbert Macdonald, JFKLOH.

146   " 'wanted to come to Princeton' ": Wynne interview.

146   " 'He stayed at Princeton' ": KLB interviews.

146   " 'We're puttin' on' ": President's Stills Collection, JFKL.

146   " 'Tell us what time' ": KLB to JFK, Dec. 10, 1935, JFKPP, Box 4B.

147   " 'see you tomorrow' ": Dr. W.T. Vaughan to JFK, Dec. 12, 1935, JFKPP, Box 4B.

147   " 'You are probably' ": Dr. Raycroft to Dr. Gauss, Dec. 13, 1935, JFK file, Princeton University Records.

147   " 'Yes, he was married' ": Dr. Timothy Lamphier interview of May 1, 1991.

147   " 'Dear Los Moine' ": JFK to KLB, Dec. 14, 1935, KLBP.

148 "lesser emoluments": DEK, pp. 78–80.
148 " 'the most harrowing' ": JFK to KLB, n.d. (Jan. 1936), KLBP.
148 " 'I don't know why' ": JFK to KLB, n.d., (Jan., 1936), KLBP.
148 " 'Received with your boring' ": JFK to KLB, Jan. 27, 1936, KLBP.
148 " 'They have not' ": ibid.
148 " 'Flash!' ": ibid.
148 " 'climb' her 'frame' ": JFK to KLB, n.d. (Jan. 1936), KLBP.
150 " 'Am coming to you' ": JFK to KLB, n.d. (Jan. 1936), KLBP.
150 " 'liked anything he did' ": KLB interviews.
150 " 'Here is something' ": JFK to KLB, Jan. 27, 1936, KLBP.
151 " 'Jack was a guy' ": Horton, JFKLOH.
152 " 'called the shots' ": S. St. John, "JFK: 50th Reunion."
152 " 'Dear Out-on-your-ass' ": JFK to KLB, Feb. 13, 1936, KLBP.
152 " 'languishing' ": JFK to KLB, n.d. (Jan. 1936), KLBP.
152 " 'Did you see' ": JFK to KLB, Feb. 13, 1936, KLBP.
152 " 'already bronzed' ": JFK to KLB, Feb. 28, 1936, KLBP.
153 " 'I hope you are not' ": Quoted in JFK to KLB, Feb. 28, 1936, KLBP.
153 " 'The girls are few' ": ibid.
153 " 'I believe in having' ": D.H. Lawrence, *Lady Chatterley's Lover* (Cutchogue, N.Y.: Buccaneer), pp. 37–38.
153 " 'My suggestion to you' ": JFK to KLB, Feb. 28, 1936.
153 " 'It's too damn bad' ": JFK to KLB, March 3, 1936, KLBP.
154 " 'Well, after losing sleep' ": JFK to KLB, March 18, 1936, KLBP.
154 " 'I've often reflected' ": JCB, p. 17.
154 " 'The first time I met' ": Arthur Krock interview, JCBP.
155 " 'bringing whatever parts' ": JFK to KLB, April 13, 1936, KLBP.
155 " 'At home on' ": JFK to KLB, n.d. (April 1936), KLBP.
155 " 'My latest disease' ": JFK to KLB, April 29, 1936, KLBP.
156 " 'is having a wonderful' ": RKRC, p. 210.
156 " 'Travels in a Mexican' ": JFK to KLB, May 9, 1936, KLBP.
156 " 'Next week my Hollywood' ": ibid.
156 " 'Plunked myself down' ": JFK to KLB, May 15, 1936, KLBP.
157 " 'This thing of working' ": ibid.
157 " 'This Hollywood trip' ": JFK to KLB, May 25, 1936, KLBP.
157 " 'if you could see' ": JFK to KLB, n.d. (May 1936), KLBP.
158 " 'Fuck these women' ": JFK to KLB, June 1, 1936, KLBP.
158 " 'Jack has rather' ": General Estimate, Principal's Report on Applicant, March 1935, JFK file, Princeton University Records. In an extra submission regarding "any mental qualities or emotional characteristics, the knowledge of which would enable us the better to understand

him," St. John had entered: "Part of Jack's lack of intellectual drive is doubtless due to a severe illness suffered in the winter of his Fifth Form year. Though he has recovered, his vitality has been below par, he has not been allowed to enter into any vigorous athletics, and has not, probably, been able to work under full pressure. There is no reason to suppose, however, that Jack will not come up to par soon." Ibid.
158 " 'The Haile Selaisse [*sic*]' ": JFK to KLB, June 1, 1936, KLBP.
158 " 'Am leaving here' ": JFK to KLB, June 19, 1936, KLBP.
159 " 'Gentlemen,' ": JFK to Harvard Admissions Committee, July 6, 1936, JFKPP, Box. 2.
159 " 'entirely satisfactory' account": Harvard Admissions Committee to JFK, July 9, 1936, JFKPP, Box. 2. Princeton responded also on the same day: "Your application for readmission as a member of the class of '40 has been accepted. . . . If for any reason you cannot accept readmission next fall, will you please be good enough to let me know at once?" Leslie I. Laughlin to JFK, JFK file, Princeton University Records.
160 " 'Jack would take her' ": RKRC, p. 155.
160 " 'His brother, Joe Jr.' ": Wynne interview.
160 " 'On those films' ": Camman Newberry interview of June 7, 1989.
161 " 'Now Kathleen' ": LMT, p. 16. See also Gail Cameron, *Rose* (N.Y.: Putnam, 1971), p. 101.
161 " 'Some of Kathleen's' ": LMT, p. 18.
161 "join him in his bedroom": JCB, p. 73.
161 " 'would have left home' ": LMT, p. 19.
162 " 'Krock came to the rescue' ": Krock interview, JCB, p. 43. See also DKG, p. 495, quoting JPK's letter to Krock of June 24, 1936, in which JPK offered Krock five thousand dollars to write the book. Krock noted in his files that he declined the payment, and in his interview with Joan and Clay Blair he referred to other "coarse bribes" such as the offer of a limousine as a Christmas present. Most Kennedy family intimates, however, were aware that Krock received a substantial annual retainer from JPK. Viz Benjamin Smith interview, JCBP.
162 "Not only did Krock": Krock interview, JCBP.
162 " 'I have no political' ": Joseph P. Kennedy with Arthur Krock, *I'm for Roosevelt* (N.Y.: Reynal and Hitchcock, 1936), p. 3.
162 "as his wife made clear": DKG, p. 331.
162 " 'I should like very much' ": JPK to Delmar Creighton, Aug. 28, 1936, JFKPP, Box 2.
163 " 'when I visited' ": Charles Wilson, quoted in Seymour St. John, "JFK: 50th Reunion."
163 " 'though a glance at' ": John F. Kennedy, *As We Remember Joe* (Cambridge, Mass.: University Press, 1945), pp. 3–4.
163 " 'He was entirely' ": Newberry interview.
163 " 'and found ample reason' ": James Rousmanière interview of April 6, 1989.
163 " 'Joe was a great' ": Torbert Macdonald interview, CBSI.
163 " 'On the way home' ": JFK, *As We Remember Joe*, p. 59.
163 " 'It was better' ": James Rousmanière inter-

view with Herbert Parmet, Herbert Parmet Papers.

163 " 'a bully' ": JFK interview, JMBP.

164 "On October 13, 1936, his academic": Committee on the Choice of Electives, Oct. 13, 1936, JFKPP, Box 2.

164 "in Weld Hall": JFK was assigned Room 32. Ibid.

164 " 'He was pathetic . . .' ": Rousmanière interview. 1989.

164 " 'Where size mattered' ": AWRH, p. 22.

164 " 'an ungainly' ": Macdonald, JFKLOH.

164 " 'Joe was physically' ": ibid.

165 " 'Mind your own' ": YJK, p. 88.

165 " 'slender and handsome' ": John Kenneth Galbraith, *A Life in Our Times* (N.Y.: Ballantine, 1982), p. 53.

165 " 'would invariably introduce' ": DKG, p. 479.

165 " 'too was handsome' ": Galbraith, *A Life in Our Times*, p. 53.

165 " 'a James Reston' ": Newberry interview.

165 " 'Jack couldn't have weighed' ": AWRH, p. 22.

165 " 'Am playing on' ": JFK to KLB, Sept. 29, 1936, KLBP.

165 " 'buck the system' ": DKG, p. 486.

165 " 'Things going very well' ": JFK to KLB, Oct. 16, 1936, KLBP.

166 " 'This fucking football' ": JFK to KLB, Oct. 21, 1936, KLBP.

166 " 'formally break training' ": JFK to KLB, n.d. (Oct. 1936), KLBP.

166 " 'The next thing' ": JFK to KLB, Oct. 21, 1936.

167 "Ironically, Joe Jr.": DKG, p. 480.

167 " 'never have any regrets' ": JPK to J. Reilly, Oct. 7, 1936, as quoted in DKG, p. 480.

167 "still coveted the elusive letter *H*:" Augustus Soule had observed the two Kennedys while at Noble and Greenough School. Entering the Class of '40, in Sept. 1936, he once again noted the difference between them: "I can remember very well that Joe, Jack's older brother, had pretensions of being a big football player, but again, he had the worst temper. And one of the things that you cannot do if you play a contact sport, you cannot lose your temper. And the coach kept saying, 'Joe,' he said, 'you're never going to make it if you can't control that awful temper of yours.' Joe would swear and stamp. . . . In football, you simply have to take the rough with the smooth. He couldn't. And he never got his letter for that reason. Not only is it unsportsmanlike, but you incur a large penalty and you hurt your team by behaving like that.": Augustus Soule interview of Dec. 28, 1988.

167 " 'Strange how one's views' ": JPK to J. Reilly, Oct. 7, 1936, as quoted in DKG, p. 480.

168 "kept up his links with the 'lads' ": Beyond social contact, JFK attempted one post-Mucker commercial arrangement, entitled "The University Distribution Agency," a three-college football-program distribution company, together with Billings at Princeton and Paul Chase at Yale, largely in order to help boost Billings's precarious finances. "Can distribute samples at football games—that is at the entrances as long as *I am not on university property*," JFK explained the parameters of his participation. "I will gladly continue in the organization—helping where I can, advising when necessary and paying your god-dam fucking bills." JFK to KLB, n.d. (Sept. 1936), KLBP. However, such participation came to an abrupt end on Sept. 29, 1936, when he was ordered by his college to desist. "It is tough luck but that is all there is to it. . . . I'm sending you the [headed] paper and you had better cross out my name or I shall get the hell bounced out of here." JFK to KLB, KLBP.

168 " 'You are certainly' ": JFK to KLB, Nov. 9, 1936, KLBP.

168 " '*Un homme de talente*' ": "Francis the First," JFKPP, Box 1.

171 " 'Things are going pretty' ": JFK to KLB, Dec. 29, 1936, KLBP.

171 " 'I am impressed' ": JPK to JFK, Feb. 15, 1937, as quoted in RKRC, p. 214.

171 " 'Got a letter from J.P.' ": JFK to KLB, n.d. (postmarked Feb.), KLBP.

171 " 'How would you like' ": JFK to KLB, Jan. 13, 1937, KLBP.

171 " 'Exam today' ": JFK to KLB, Jan. 27, 1937, KLBP.

171 " 'Still out for boxing' ": JFK to KLB, Jan. 20, 1937, KLBP.

172 " 'Dear Le Moan Plenty' ": JFK to KLB, n.d. (postmarked Feb. 1937), KLBP.

172 " 'Jack Kennedy had no' ": Vic Francis interview of April 8, 1989.

172 " 'some Princeton boys' ": ibid.

173 " 'I encouraged the scheme' ": Galbraith, *Life in Our Times*, p. 54.

173 " 'Jack drove' ": KLB interviews.

173 " 'I remember once' ": Francis interview.

174 " 'Do you know what' ": JFK to KLB, n.d. (postmarked Feb. 1937), KLBP.

174 " 'In spite of the fact' ": JFK to KLB, March 3, 1937, KLBP.

174 " 'never been so busy' ": JFK to KLB, April 20, 1937, KLBP.

174 "His freshman swimming team": The team, in which JFK swam backstroke, trounced Brown, Exeter, Andover, Dartmouth, Huntingdon, and Yale. Interestingly, JFK's weight was given as 164 pounds—probably the most he weighed until the 1950s: The 1940 Harvard Freshman Red Book, Activities file, 1936–37, JFKPP, Box 2.

174 " 'Things are going pretty' ": JFK to JPK, n.d. (April 1937), JPK/RFK Letters.

175 "Jack's freshman Smoker": The program featured the Dancing Rhythmettes, Mady and Cord in "Comedy Moment," Trado Twins in "Just Fun," Fuzzy Knight, Chilton and Thomas, the Six Lucky Boys tumbling act, Frankie Frisch and the Saint Lewis Cardinals, Dizzy Dean, Ramona and her piano, Neal O'Hara of the *Boston Traveler*, and Gertrude Niesen, as well as Phil Layne and his Swing Band: 1940 Harvard Freshman Red Book.

175 " 'two of most popular' ": John Winthrop House Application, May 1, 1937, JFKPP, Box 2.

175 " 'well orientated, normal' ": Freshman Advisor's Report, March 19, 1937, Box 2.

175 " 'The long skein' ": RKRC, p. 211.
175 " 'I felt that Joe deserved' ": ibid.
176 " 'Mr. Kennedy was so lucky' ": Barbara Gibson with Caroline Latham, *Life with Rose Kennedy* (N.Y.: Warner Books, 1986), p. 157.
176 " 'Joe spoke no' ": RKRC, p. 212.
176 "Jack's Harvard grades": Academic Records, 1936–37, JFKPP, Box 2.
176 " 'proper purpose of' ": "Jean Jacques Rousseau," JFKPP, Box 1.
177 " 'as I would like to race' ": JFK to KLB, Jan. 13, 1937, KLBP.
177 " 'We are planning' ": JFK to JPK, n.d., JPK/RFK Letters.
178 "boarded the S.S. *Washington*": Diary, European Trip, July 1–Sept. 3, 1937, JFKPP, Box 1 (hereafter referred to as DET).
178 " 'We could have spent' ": KLB interviews.
178 "French and European history": French F had included "Introduction to France" under Professor Morize, while History I had included "European History from the Fall of the Roman Empire to the Present Time" under Professor Merriman. Abstract of Harvard courses 1936–1940, prepared in 1961, JFKPP, Box 2.
178 " 'Very smooth crossing' ": DET, entry of July 1–7, 1937.
178 " 'We proceeded to Beauvais' ": ibid.
178 " 'It was necessary' ": KLB interviews, JCB and JFKLOH.
179 " 'Up at 12:00' ": DET, July 8, 1937.
179 " 'Went out to' ": ibid. July 9, 1937.
179 " 'eighty cents for' ": KLB interviews.
179 " 'Have now acquired' ": DET, July 10, 1937.
179 " 'Went to Notre Dame' ": ibid.
179 " 'We never discussed' ": KLB interviews.
180 " 'got up early' ": DET, July 13, 1937.
180 " 'There was a most fantastic' ": KLB interviews.
180 " 'Had lunch with' ": DET, July 13, 1937.
180 " 'Have decided to read' ": ibid., July 15, 1937.
180 " 'Got up early' ": ibid., July 16, 1937.
180 " 'terrible' ": ibid., July 17, 1937.
181 " 'Walls very high' ": ibid., July 19, 1937.
181 " 'Had our usual difficulty' ": ibid., July 20, 1937.
182 " 'was very anxious' ": KLB interviews.
182 " 'rather governmental' ": DET, July 24, 1937.
182 " 'I think they were' ": KLB interviews.
183 " 'Very interesting' ": DET, July 26, 1937.
183 " 'Of course, we didn't' ": KLB interviews.
183 " 'After much excitement' ": DET, July 27, 1937.
183 " 'Have continued reading Gunther' ": ibid., July 28, 1937.
184 " 'beginning to show' ": KLB interviews.
184 " 'tried to do a bit' ": DET, July 30, 1937.
184 " 'played with my 5 fr.' ": JMB, p. 32.
184 " 'best-looking nightclub' ": DET, July 31, 1937.
184 " 'the almost complete' ": JMB, p. 32.

185 " 'The Italian streets' ": DET, Aug. 1, 1937.
185 " 'I must say' ": KLB interviews.
185 " 'He was an extraordinary' ": Joseph Alsop, JFKLOH.
186 " 'A cardinal buried' ": DET, Aug. 3, 1937.
187 " 'Well, I think it was' ": KLB interviews.
188 " 'We did go' ": ibid.
188 " 'Up around nine' ": DET, Aug. 6, 1937.
189 " 'learned that the only way' ": ibid., Aug. 8, 1937.
189 " 'We got to know them' ": KLB interviews.
189 " 'Amidst much cursing' ": DET, Aug. 8, 1937.
189 "went to the blue Grotto": ibid., Aug. 9, 1937.
190 " 'fantastic rally of Mussolini's' ": KLB interviews.
190 " 'That night took out' ": DET, Aug. 10–11, 1937.
190 " 'the steps that Christ' ": KLB interviews.
191 " 'after much battling' ": DET, Aug. 12, 1937.
191 "a tragic character": Viz. Seymour St. John interview of April 8, 1989.
191 "offer Billings any post": KLB interviews.
192 " 'Picked up a bundle' ": DET, Aug. 16, 1937.
192 " 'Jack was absolutely' ": KLB interviews.
192 " 'Hitler seems popular here' ": DET, Aug. 17, 1937.
192 " 'We got to know a black-shirt' ": KLB interviews.
192 " 'gave us a very bad impression' ": ibid.
193 " 'none too spry' ": DET, Aug. 18, 1937.
193 " 'Went to the Deutsches' ": ibid.
193 " 'After the usual amount' ": ibid, Aug. 19, 1937.
193 " 'insufferable. We just had awful' ": KLB interviews.
193 " 'Started out as usual' ": DET, Aug. 20, 1937.
193 " 'Jack discovered, for the first' ": KLB interviews.
194 " 'Offie is quite' ": DET, Aug. 20, 1937.
194 " 'started out for Cologne' ": ibid., Aug. 21, 1937.
194 " 'Jack Kennedy grew' ": KLB interviews.
194 " 'Got up in the worst' ": DET, Aug. 22, 1937.
194 " 'which is really the height' ": ibid.
195 " 'which looked very good' ": ibid., Aug. 26, 1937.
196 " 'It was very worrying' ": KLB interviews.
196 " 'Saturday, August 28' ": DET, Aug. 28, 1937.
196 " 'Somebody recommended' ": KLB interviews.
196 " 'Still with the hives' ": DET, Aug. 29, 1937.
197 " 'and there was tremendous' ": KLB interviews.
197 " 'Blambo arrived in town' ": DET, Aug. 29, 1937.
197 " 'Terrific big castle' ": ibid., Sept. 1, 1937.
197 " 'he was a terribly rich' ": KLB interviews.
197 "an 'uncomfortable' night": DET, Sept. 2, 1937.
197 " 'It was a great' ": KLB interviews.
198 " 'As for the boat trip' ": ibid.
199 " 'Isn't the chance' ": DET, Sept. 3, 1937.

Part 5: The Ambassador's Son

203 " 'Winthrop was known' ": Holton Wood interview of Jan. 9, 1989.
203 " 'The four of us' ": James Rousmanière interview of April 6, 1989.
204 " 'My father' ": ibid.
204 " 'Jack was more fun' ": KLB interviews, JCB and JFKLOH.
204 " 'He would have done' ": ibid.
205 " 'Torby Macdonald never' ": Rousmanière interview.

205 " 'I think it is interesting' ": KLB interviews.
205 "contrary to the claims": DKG, p. 477; and HS, p. 92.
205 " 'There are eight' ": Rousmanière interview.
205 " 'that Jack Kennedy' ": Wood interview.
205 " 'When it came time' ": Rousmanière interview.
206 " 'Jack Kennedy was part of' ": Donald Thurber interview of June 7, 1990.
206 " 'It was considered' ": Rousmanière interview.
207 " 'Macdonald certainly was' ": ibid.
207 " 'the Boston alumni' ": ibid.
207 " 'I had been on two or three' ": Ralph Pope interview of January 24, 1989.
208 " 'Ralph Pope did it' ": Rousmanière interview.
208 " 'Was it important' ": ibid.
208 " 'It was a status' ": ibid.
209 " 'Harvard undergraduates' ": John Kenneth Galbraith, *A Life in Our Times* (N.Y.: Ballantine, 1982), p. 52.
209 " 'The Spee had a damn good' ": Wood interview. See also Ch. 12, "The Harvard College Clubs," in Alexander W. Williams, *A Social History of the Greater Boston Clubs* (Barre, Mass.: Barre Publishers, 1970), pp. 87–102. First established as the Harvard chapter of the Zeta Psi Fraternity, the club was closed in 1857 and again in 1869 during the crackdown against secret societies. It was formally defraternized as the Zeta Psi Club in 1892, and acted as a feeder to final clubs such as the Porcellian and A.D. In 1900 the Spee became a final club in its own right, with rooms at 44 Church St. In 1904 a brick property at 15 Holyoke St. was erected, to be traded in 1932 for the old Institute of 1770 on the corner of Mt. Auburn and Holyoke sts., which was enlarged to create the current 76 Mt. Auburn St. club building. See "Club History" in *Spee Club Annual Record,* privately published by the Spee Club, 1968, pp. 3–5. See also Cleveland Amory, *The Proper Bostonians* (N.Y.: E.P. Dutton, 1947).
209 " 'bright young face' ": Carl Friedrich to C. Shipton, Aug. 3, 1964, JFKPP, Box 2.
209 " 'the course which he took' ": William Langer to C. Shipton, July 19, 1964, JFKPP, Box 2.
209 " 'I suppose none of' ": JFK to KLB, Nov. 12, 1937, KLBP.
210 " 'on a glorious, warm' ": Wood interview.
210 " 'By December 1937' ": JML, Ch. 1, p. 4.
211 " 'the brainchild of' ": JPK to Rita Davenport, May 28, 1937, as cited in DKG, p. 502.
212 " 'The old man hired' ": Charles Houghton interview, JCBP. Roosevelt was not unaware of Krock's private patron. In a letter to JPK, shortly before the outbreak of war in Europe, Roosevelt warned: "Krock . . . is, after all, only a social parasite whose surface support can be won by entertaining and flattery, but in his heart is a cynic who has never felt warm affection for anybody—man or woman": Letter of July 22, 1939, Presidential Safe Files Subject File, Box 155, FDRL.
212 " 'your very lovely present' ": Drew Pearson to JPK, Jan. 13, 1937, as cited in DKG, p. 500.
212 " 'when it became' ": Arthur Krock, JFKLOH.

212 " 'I heard that' ": Krock memo, Dec. 23, 1937, AKP.
212 " 'he [Kennedy] came back to me' ": Krock, JFKLOH.
212 "had hastened the death": MB, p. 155, and Arthur Krock, *Memoirs: Sixty Years on the Firing Line* (N.Y.: Funk & Wagnalls, 1968), p. 333.
217 " 'but I am sure' ": Arthur Krock to Bernard Baruch, Dec. 16, 1937, BBP.
213 "As Rose later revealed": RKRC, pp. 211–12.
213 "MY DEAR MR. PRESIDENT, MOORE AND I": Presidential Safe Files Diplomatic Files, Box 37, FDRL.
213 " 'When will the nice' ": Peter Collier and David Horowitz, *The Kennedys: An American Drama* (N.Y.: Summit, 1984), p. 464.
213 " 'Dear Mr. President' ": RFK to FDR, n.d., (1937), Pres. Personal File, Box 207, FDRL.
213 " 'needs skill brought by' ": Boake Carter to JPK, Dec. 28, 1937, as cited in DKG, pp. 510–11.
213 "lampoons performed": "Instead of the grin and wisecrack his classmates expected, Kennedy's cheeks flushed crimson and he sat down unsmiling. This was the last class reunion he attended." RJW, p. 197.
213 " 'Kennedy a very dangerous' ": Henry Morgenthau Diary, entry of Dec. 8, 1937, as quoted in DEK, pp. 116–17.
213 "Roosevelt even asked": James Roosevelt, *My Parents—A Differing View* (Chicago: Playboy Press, 1976), pp. 208–10.
214 " 'Don't go buying' ": Collier and Horowitz, *The Kennedys,* p. 82.
214 " 'In those days' ": KLB interviews.
214 " 'On Sunday nights' ": ibid.
215 " 'and Nalle is in tears' ": JFK to KLB, n.d. (Jan. 1938), KLBP.
215 " 'He wouldn't be Mr. Kennedy' ": KLB interviews.
215 " 'We don't want any' ": RKRC, p. 143, inter alia.
216 " 'he never liked' ": KLB interviews.
216 " 'Mr. Kennedy was definitely' ": Ralph Horton interview, JCBP.
216 " 'Mr. Kennedy also built' ": KLB interviews.
216 " 'an almost physical' ": RKRC, p. 139.
217 " 'Jack Kennedy's father' ": KLB interviews.
217 " 'He encouraged them' ": ibid.
217 " 'he was absolutely determined' ": ibid.
218 " 'Just a note' ": JFK to KLB, Jan. 21, 1938, KLBP.
218 " 'For over a year' ": *Choate News,* Jan. 1938.
218 " 'A book was recently' ": ibid.
219 " 'Going to Mayo' ": JFK to KLB, Jan. 21, 1938, KLBP.
219 " 'As regards' ": JFK to KLB, Feb. 1, 1938, KLBP.
219 " 'Well, once more' ": JFK to KLB, Feb. 24, 1938, KLBP.
219 " 'my swimming career' ": JFK to RFK, n.d., JFKPP, Box 4B.
219 " 'trying to get rid of' ": JFK to KLB, March 15, 1938, KLBP.
220 " 'rather unpleasant contact' ": JFK to KLB, Feb. 10, 1938, KLBP.
220 " 'from ear to ear' ": JFK to KLB, March 15, 1938, KLBP.

220 " 'Am going to rest and get' ": JFK to KLB, March 19, 1938, KLBP.

220 " 'quite broke' ": KLB interviews.

222 "address from Billings 'right away' ": JFK to KLB, April 15, 1938, KLBP.

222 "declined Jack's invitation": JFK to KLB, April 29, 1938, KLBP.

222 " 'Kennedy was ill' ": Tutorial Record, 1937–38, JFKPP, Box 2.

222 "Krock to 'put down' ": JPK to Arthur Krock, March 8, 1938, AKP.

223 " 'The march of events' ": JPK to Krock, March 21, 1938, AKP.

223 " 'taken in' by the führer": The duke of Windsor, *N.Y. Daily News,* Dec. 13, 1966. See Charles Higham, *The Duchess of Windsor: The Secret Life* (N.Y.: McGraw-Hill 1988), pp. 224–43.

223 "Later, in her memoirs": RKRC, pp. 217–29. To Doris Kearns Goodwin, RFK later described her one-and-a-half-year embassy stint as "by far the happiest years of my life." DKG, p. 539.

224 "made an honorary member of elite British": DKG, p. 524.

224 " 'My private life' ": JPK to Krock, March 21, 1938, AKP.

224 " 'persistent urging' ": JPK to Krock, March 8, 1938, AKP.

224 " 'I'm in business' ": JPK to Krock, March 21, 1938, AKP.

224 " 'For God's sake' ": JPK to Bernard Baruch, March 28, 1938, BBP.

224 " 'a certain coolness' ": JML, Ch. 1, p. 10. According to JPK, Roosevelt felt Chamberlain was intent on removing from his own British Cabinet anyone who was anti-Hitler. Roosevelt, JPK noted, was particularly "disturbed by [Foreign Secretary] Eden's resignation as 'a further omen of the growing power of the dictators' ": JML, Ch. 3.

224 " 'a strong character' ": JML, Ch. 2, p. 4.

224 " 'tough guy and going to run' ": JPK to Krock, March 8, 1938, AKP.

224 " 'Chamberlain's speech' ": JPK to Krock, March 28, 1938, AKP.

225 " 'I wish our fellows' ": ibid.

225 " 'the high point' ": JPK to Krock, April 14, 1938, AKP.

225 " 'The Germans probably' ": ibid.

225 " 'As ambassador he' ": RKRC, p. 241.

225 " 'Rose, this is' ": ibid., p. 221.

225 " 'the pomp and circumstance' ": ibid., p. 229.

225 " 'My first luncheon' ": JML, Ch. 2, p. 8.

226 " 'the political offers necessary' ": ibid., Ch. 3, p. 7.

226 " 'on this score in vigorous' ": ibid., Ch. 2, p. 7.

226 " 'once and for all' ": ibid., Ch. 3, p. 9.

226 " 'the President himself' ": ibid., p. 8.

226 " 'Economic appeasement' ": ibid., p. 12.

226 " 'Of course' Rose later defended": RKRC, p. 242.

226 " 'I am happy' ": JPK to Krock, April 14, 1938, AKP. An identical letter was sent to Baruch, BBP.

227 "and 'as they only take 3' ": JFK to KLB, May 24, 1938, KLBP.

227 " 'in the middle of' ": JFK to KLB, June 1, 1938, KLBP.

227 " 'May go to the boat races' ": JFK to KLB, June 2, 1938, KLBP.

227 " 'holding court up here' ": JFK to KLB, June 15, 1938, KLBP.

227 " 'this stuff about you' ": ibid.

228 " 'the Crab King' ": ibid.

228 " 'finest and most hotly' ": Leonard M. Fowle, "Harvard's Crimson Waves Over Intercollegiates," *Harvard Crimson Yearbook,* 1938.

228 " 'the peak halyard' ": "Hutton Recollects," 1989 recollections of Edward ("Bud") Hutton, "taken from his notes in recent days, 51 years after the event," kindly furnished to author by Loring Reed, Jr.

229 " 'When it was announced' ": JML, Ch. 9, p. 4.

229 "bottom of the list": "Kennedy ran for the board of overseers in the mid-1930's and polled the smallest vote in a field of five candidates. The defeat rankled Joe badly. . . . Lowell [a member of Harvard Board of Overseers] says Kennedy 'hates Harvard' and has openly admitted his hatred in a letter to classmate Oscar Haussermann." Ralph Lowell interview with William Gill, RJWP. Haussermann himself remarked that "as for the board of overseers defeat, what hurt Joe was having his puny vote published": Oscar Haussermann interview, RJWP.

229 " 'was a terrible blow' ": DKG, pp. 534–35. "The honorary degree he wanted was refused by the degree committee, headed by Charles Francis Adams, which took a wait-and-see attitude." Haussermann interview, RJWP.

229 " 'an honor he wanted' ": DKG, p. 532.

229 " 'to make reservations' ": JPK to Krock, May 24, 1938, AKP.

230 " 'Did Joe Kennedy' ": Krock interview, JCBP.

230 " 'sell it to a newspaper' ": Memorandum on "Thoughts on War and Peace—Joseph P. Kennedy," for Mr. Weeks (editor) by "m.b.," dated June 14, 1938, AMA.

230 " 'That's where it belongs' ": ibid.

230 " 'During the last' ": JML, Ch. 9, p. 3.

231 "Through various confidential": According to Walter Trohan, Arthur Krock himself "bound up Kennedy's 'Private and Confidential' messages and sent them to Roosevelt." MB, p. 168. According to Charles Higham, JPK was being carefully watched by the MI5, the British domestic counterintelligence service. Charles Higham, *American Swastika* (N.Y.: Doubleday, 1985), p. 26. Certainly, when Early spoke to reporters about JPK's machinations, he was able to quote verbatim from supposedly private correspondence between the U.S. ambassador to Britain and American citizens. MB, p. 171.

231 " 'a chilling shadow' ": *Chicago Tribune,* June 23, 1938.

231 " 'I think it would' ": JPK to Krock, May 24, 1938, AKP.

232 " 'spoke of my general' ": JML, Ch. 9, p. 7.

232 " 'pleasant dinner' ": ibid., p. 8.

232 " 'It was a true' ": ibid.

232 " 'That Monday morning' ": ibid.

232 "tried to bribe Early": DKG, p. 536.

232 " 'an angry interview' ": JML, Ch. 9, p. 9.

232 " 'This time they' ": ibid.

233 " 'I am also expecting' ": JPK to Krock, May 24, 1938, AKP.

233 " 'sorry you're not' ": JPK to Baruch, May 31, 1938, BBP.

233 " 'The ship was' ": Krock, JFKLOH. See also Krock, *Memoirs*, p. 341.

234 " 'No act of mine' ": JML, Ch. 5, p. 3. See also RKRC, p. 226.

234 "waxed lyrical about the Molyneux": RKRC, p. 227.

234 "When Peter Grace": LMT, pp. 44–45.

234 " 'I so often think' ": KK to KLB, June 2, 1938, quoted in David Michaelis, *The Best of Friends* (N.Y.: William Morrow & Co., 1983), p. 160.

234 " 'manner seemed abrasive' ": LMT, p. 42.

235 " 'I was a friend of his sister' ": William Douglas-Home, JFKLOH.

235 " 'Joe looked much more mature' ": Hugh Fraser, JFKLOH.

235 " 'Joe was probably more serious' ": Douglas-Home, JFKLOH.

235 " 'she had no competition' ": LMT, p. 42.

236 " 'to wipe Czechoslovakia' ": William Manchester, *The Last Lion, Winston Spencer Churchill: Alone, 1932–1940* (Boston: Little, Brown, 1988), p. 323.

236 "Lindbergh had told Kennedy": Charles Lindbergh, *The Wartime Journals of Charles Lindbergh* (N.Y.: Harcourt Brace Jovanovich, 1970), pp. 72–73.

236 "Germany's best friend": MB, pp. 164–65; DEK, pp. 136–37, 143, 220–21, 279, 282; Manchester, *The Last Lion*, p. 439.

236 "an 'idiot' when they argued": Krock, JFKLOH.

236 " 'early in August' ": JML, Ch. 11, p. 12.

236 " 'blue Mediterranean' ": ibid., Ch. 12, p. 1.

236 " 'the holidays were clearly over' ": ibid., Ch. 12, p. 16.

237 " 'This really isn't as much fun' ": ibid., Ch. 13, p. 12.

237 " 'any dispute' ": ibid., Ch. 13, pp. 5–6.

237 "Jack tried to downplay": unidentified news clip, Sept. 8, 1938, BHCL.

237 "urgently invited Lindbergh": Lindbergh, *Wartime Journals*, p. 72.

237 " 'I was so impressed' ": JML, Ch. 15, p. 3.

238 "he even made sure a copy": "While he was [later in 1938] in Palm Beach, Kennedy made the news section of *Life* again with another item that must have annoyed Roosevelt no end. A caption under a picture of the ambassador smiling in the Florida sun mentioned that he had divulged to Walter Winchell that during the Munich crisis he had persuaded Colonel Charles A. Lindbergh to give the famous Lindbergh estimate of the impressive strength of German air power to Chamberlain. It was intimated that Lindbergh's awesome respect for what Hitler could do from the air may have been a factor in Chamberlain's appeasement move": Joe McCarthy, *The Remarkable Kennedys* (N.Y.: Popular Library, 1960), p. 62.

238 "According to Lindbergh": JML, Ch. 15, pp. 3–5.

238 " 'the Reichswehr were opposed' ": ibid., Ch. 13, p. 3.

238 " 'The situation in Nazi' ": ibid., p. 3.

238 " 'what I thought the American' ": ibid., p. 12.

239 " 'I have a few minutes' ": JPK to Krock, Sept. 26, 1938, AKP.

239 " 'What a great man' ": DKG, p. 562.

239 " 'He was kind enough' ": JML, Ch. 17, pp. 2–3.

239 " 'Lindbergh's awesome respect' ": McCarthy, *Remarkable Kennedys*, p. 63.

239 " 'We seem to be' ": Quoted in Manchester, *The Last Lion*, p. 336.

239 " 'war with dishonour' ": ibid., pp. 346–47.

239 " 'As we left' ": JML, Ch. 16, p. 16.

240 " 'A feeling is spreading' ": JPK to Cordell Hull, Sept. 28, 1938, Foreign Relations of the United States (F.R.U.S.), 1938, pp. 692–93; and JML, Ch. 16, p. 16.

240 " 'a most ordinary' ": JML, Ch. 17, p. 1.

240 " 'bitter about Duff-Cooper' ": ibid., Ch. 17, p. 3.

240 " 'Within a few days' ": ibid., pp. 3–4.

240 " 'I know what' ": Krock to JPK, Oct. 6, 1938, AKP.

241 " 'Jack never hung up' ": Houghton interview, JCBP.

241 " 'One time he' ": Gerald Walker and Donald A. Allan, "Jack Kennedy at Harvard," *Coronet*, May 1961.

241 " 'Jack was a very' ": Houghton interview, JCBP.

241 " 'He was a person' ": Thurber interview.

242 " 'in his early, first two' ": Torbert Macdonald interview, CBSI.

242 " 'down in the crowd' ": Arthur Holcombe interview, CBSI.

243 " 'Of course Kennedy was' ": ibid.

243 " 'The next year he took' ": ibid.

243 " 'taught his father a good many' ": ibid.

244 " 'I might tell you' ": ibid.

245 " 'In his academic work' ": ibid.

245 " 'What he thought he might' ": ibid.

245 " 'It was not until' ": A. Chester Hanford, JFKLOH.

246 " 'Resistless defender of Boston's' ": Harvey Rachlin, *The Kennedys, A Chronological History, 1823–Present* (N.Y.: World Almanac, 1986), p. 70.

246 " 'Tonight is a big' ": JFK to parents, n.d. (1938), JFKPP, Box 1.

246 " 'Dear Billings' ": JFK to KLB, Oct. 20, 1938, KLBP.

246 " 'The real reason' ": JFK to KLB, n.d. (Oct. 1938), KLBP.

247 " 'Harvard may be lousy' ": ibid.

247 " 'Things have been' ": JFK to parents, n.d. (1938), JFKPP, Box 1.

247 " 'It was the thought' ": JML, Ch. 18, pp. 3–4.

247 " 'a number of Jewish publishers' ": ibid., Ch. 18, p. 4.

248 " 'a stab in the back' ": RJW, pp. 250–51.

248 " 'the Munich business' ": RFK to Marie Greene, Dec. 6, 1938, MS-88-91, JFKL.

248 " 'Germany is still' ": JPK, Jr. to Thomas Schriber, Nov. 5, 1938, cited in Thomas Schriber, CBSI.

248 " 'I wonder if' ": Felix Frankfurter to FDR, Oct. 27, 1938, *Roosevelt and Frankfurter: Their Correspondence, 1928–45* (Boston: Little, Brown, 1967), p. 464.

248 "Even Walter Lippman": *N.Y. Herald Tribune,* Oct. 22, 1938.

248 "*The Washington Post* deplored": *Washington Post,* Oct. 21, 1938.

248 " 'For him to propose' ": *N.Y. Post,* Oct. 21, 1938.

248 " 'has five daughters' ": JFK to parents, n.d. (1938), JFKPP, Box 1.

249 " 'The Navy Day speech' ": ibid.

249 "Professor Bruce Hopper was": Rousmanière interview. Hopper, a Harvard graduate, Class of '18, had served as pilot and flight leader, 96th Squadron, in World War I: Harvard Class of 1918, Fiftieth Anniversary Report, Harvard University Archives.

250 " 'Frances Ann Cannon was a very' ": Houghton interview, JCBP. See also JCB, p. 69.

250 " 'actually met her first' ": Benjamin Smith interview, JCBP.

250 " 'one of the most beautiful' ": Connie Burwell White interview, JCBP.

250 " 'My absence alone' ": JFK to KLB, n.d. (Oct. 1938), KLBP.

250 " 'He used to take' ": Eunice Kennedy Shriver interview, JCBP.

251 " 'none of the Kennedy' ": KLB interviews.

251 " 'I don't *ever* remember' ": E. K. Shriver interview.

251 " 'a common bond' ": KLB interviews.

251 " 'I can remember going' ": Horton interview, JCBP. See also JCB, p. 68.

251 " 'I really don't think' ": Houghton interview, JCBP.

251 "Billings agreed": Billings, watching Jack's conquests, watching Jack's *need* to make conquests from an early age, addressed the matter straightforwardly when asked. "Whenever he was at home, there was always a girl around. Usually it was a different girl each time. Almost without exception, every girl he showed any interest in became very fond of him. I think the reason for this was that he was not only attractive but also had tremendous interest in girls. They really liked him and he was very, very successful. This was important to him because he wanted to be successful in this area. He really enjoyed girls." When asked what sort of girls Jack tended to be attracted by, whether for instance he liked "athletic" girls (such as Jack's sisters and sisters-in-law turned out to be), Billings recalled that "they were usually very feminine and beautiful girls, whom he would date at night. He was not, in the least, interested in their athletic abilities as he was primarily interested in dating them at night and didn't want them particularly as friends or pals." This was an important distinction. For Jack, good-looking girls were challenges to his prodigious narcissism, targets of his strong libido, as well as stylistic decoration. Jack's pals were men; women, for him, were denizens from a foreign tribe, to be hunted in the dark hours and whenever possible branded. Moreover, as Billings related, Jack might constantly question the outside world, but he was not given to self-examination, and hated moodiness, sulking, or self-pity in others, male or female. Born into a family with parents who largely despised each other, he had early on created his own, alternative world, one in which he tirelessly sought affirmation, attention, affection, and admiration. Depression, moodiness, or self-absorption in others threatened his narcissistic drive, and he would not tolerate it, alternating his female partners, as Billings recorded, in an endless quest that precluded self-questioning. "He liked a new face and he liked to change around," Billings observed. "He had the ability of enjoying life. Was he moody? He certainly wasn't. He wasn't moody in any way and he couldn't bear anyone around who was moody. The one thing Jack Kennedy could not abide, was anybody who was moody": KLB interviews.

251 " 'Later, I found out' ": Houghton interview, JCBP.

252 " 'nothing has been' ": *NYT,* Dec. 16, 1938.

252 " 'My arrival in' ": JML, Ch. 21, p. 1.

252 " 'the plight of' ": ibid.

252 " 'there was a trace of' ": ibid. p. 2.

252 " 'He got so much interested' ": Holcombe interview, CBSI.

253 " 'a virtual publicity bureau' ": *BH,* March 26, 1939.

253 " 'It was John Kennedy's' ": Hanford, JFKLOH.

253 " 'I'll be godamned' ": JFK to KLB, Feb. 5, 1939, KLBP.

254 " 'had Cannon down' ": JFK to KLB, Feb. 14, 1939, KLBP.

254 "set off in pursuit": "Leaving for Mardi Gras and will be flying up from New Orleans Wednesday [to N.Y.]": JFK to KLB, n.d. (Feb. 1938), KLBP.

254 " 'She asked me if' ": JCB, p. 69.

254 " 'He was the first' ": C.B. White interview, JCBP.

254 " 'I had long' ": JCB, p. 68.

254 " 'I don't think the fact' ": Horton interview, JCBP. See also JCB, p. 68.

254 " 'I think Mama Cannon' ": C.B. White interview, JCBP. See also JCB, p. 108.

255 " 'plenty rough' ": JFK to KLB, n.d. (March 1939), KLBP.

255 " 'Jack comes over' ": HS, p. 125.

255 " 'Been having a great' ": JFK to KLB, n.d. (March 1939), KLBP.

255 " 'After 1940' ": JML, Ch. 22, p. 8.

255 " 'Friday I leave' ": JFK to KLB, n.d. (March 1939), KLBP.

255 "Mrs. Kennedy had meanwhile": RKRC, p. 243.

256 " 'immediately ahead of' ": JML, Ch. 23, p. 5.

256 " 'to leave the Basilica' ": Pope Paul VI, JFKLOH.

256 " 'Oh, will Joe' ": William Phillips Diary, March 10, 1939, as cited in DEK, p. 190.

256 " 'young attractive Italian' ": JML, Ch. 23, p. 9.

256 " 'The children were' ": ibid., Ch. 23, p. 7.

257 " 'Just got back' ": JFK to KLB, March 23, 1939, KLBP.

257 " 'Despite the increased' ": JML, Ch. 23, p. 10.

257 "Rose, however, had already departed": ibid.

257 " 'I have the evening' ": ibid., Ch. 24, p. 1.

257 " 'Everyone thinks war' ": JFK to KLB, March 23, 1939, KLBP.

257 " 'Having a great time' ": ibid.

258 " 'Dear Kirk: Smacking' ": JFK to KLB, April 6, 1939, KLBP.

258 " 'After Christmas' ": George St. John to JFK, March 24, 1939, KLBP.

258 " 'Was at lunch' ": JFK to KLB, April 6, 1939, KLBP.

259 " 'to lunch at the American' ": Lindbergh, *Wartime Journals,* p. 174. Hitler had personally awarded Germany's highest decoration for foreigners, the Service Cross of the German Eagle with star, to Lindbergh on Oct. 18, 1938, three weeks after the Munich agreement, for having "deserved well of the Reich": Manchester, *The Last Lion,* p. 317.

259 " 'She takes a rotten' ": JFK to KLB, April 6, 1939, KLBP.

259 " 'Have not decided' ": ibid.

259 " 'Remember, I have' ": JML, Ch. 25, p. 9.

259 " 'opened a map' ": ibid., Ch. 26, p. 6.

260 " 'Plenty of action' ": JFK to KLB, n.d. (April 1939), KLBP.

260 " 'talking about flowers' ": JML, Ch. 26, p. 11. Roosevelt was worried about Kennedy's propensity not only for appeasement rhetoric, but for back-room dealings. According to *American Swastika,* Kennedy told James D. Mooney, head of General Motors (and also recipient of a Hitler decoration, the Order of Merit of the Golden Eagle), on May 3, 1939, that he would be willing to attend a meeting with Emil Puhl of the Reichsbank in Paris to discuss an American gold loan to Hitler, subject to Roosevelt's permission. Roosevelt forbade the meeting. Disregarding the presidential embargo, Mooney then flew to London on Hitler's behalf with Helmuth Wohlthat, a Nazi economist, to meet Kennedy on May 9, 1939, at the Berkeley Hotel. "According to Mooney's report, Kennedy and the Nazi economist agreed on everything." However, agents of MI5, British counterintelligence, were watching carefully. Once informed, Roosevelt quashed the Kennedy-Mooney plan, and forbade further meetings: Higham, *American Swastika,* pp. 26–27.

260 " 'Criticism of me' ": JML, Ch. 26, p. 10.

260 " 'grasped at every' ": William Kaufman, "Two American Ambassadors," in *The Diplomats,* eds. Craig and Gilbert (Princeton, N.J.: Princeton University Press, 1953), p. 667.

260 " 'would depend, not on' ": ibid., p. 671.

260 "of being directly responsible": Walter Millis, ed., *Forrestal Diaries,* (N.Y.: Viking Press, 1951), pp. 121–22.

260 " 'Bullitt has turned out' ": JFK to KLB, April 28, 1939, KLBP.

261 " 'Things were looking' ": ibid.

262 " 'Am now in Warsaw' ": JFK to KLB, n.d. (May 1939), KLBP.

263 " 'Danzig and the corridor are inseparable' ": ibid. Clearly, in view of the next sentence, JFK meant "inseparable," although the original ALS reads "not inseparable" (the word *not* being the last word on p. 1, and *inseparable* the first word on p. 2).

264 " 'Leningrad then Moscow' ": JFK to KLB, n.d. (May 1939), KLBP.

264 "Ambassador Kennedy had tearfully . . . read": DKG, p. 577. Ironically, it was on June 14, 1939, a week before Eunice's debut, that Churchill was stung "into a magnificent oration," as Harold Nicolson recorded in his diary. "Winston is horrified by Lippmann saying that the American Ambassador Joe Kennedy had informed him that war was inevitable and that we should be licked. Winston is stirred by this defeatism. . . . He sits hunched there, waving his whisky-and-soda to mark his periods, stubbing his cigar with the other hand: 'It may be true, it may well be true . . . that this country will at the outset of this coming and to my mind almost inevitable war be exposed to dire peril and fierce ordeals. . . . Yet these trials and disasters, I ask you to believe, Mr. Lippmann, will but serve to steel the resolution of the British people and to enhance our will for victory. No, the [American] Ambassador should not have spoken so. Yet supposing—as I do not for one moment suppose—that Mr. Kennedy were correct in his tragic utterance, then I for one would willingly lay down my life in combat, rather than, in fear of defeat, surrender to the menaces of those sinister men": *Harold Nicolson: Diaries and Letters, Vol. I,* Nigel Nicolson, ed. (N.Y.: Atheneum, 1966), p. 403.

264 "market for Ambassador Kennedy's self-serving": "I should like to make this comment," wrote Arthur Krock to JPK on July 6, 1948, having read JPK's draft memoirs. "I found them heavy going. Little that is new is included. . . . I think a single chapter is all that should be given to the events that began with the Austrian crisis [i.e., the start of JPK's ambassadorship] and wound up with the ultimatum to Poland. . . . I know you want me to be frank, and this is my opinion." AKP.

264 "letters were later stolen or lost": Chief archivist, JFKL, to author, 1991, after extensive search of JFKL holdings, including undeeded JPK/JFK Papers. Doris Kearns Goodwin also could not find the letters when given access to the RFK/JPK Papers while compiling *The Fitzgeralds and the Kennedys.* It seems likely these historic letters were originally deposited with JFK's Private Papers in the JFKL, but were removed by a member of the Kennedy family (possibly during the writing of Rose Kennedy's memoirs *Times to Remember*) and never returned.

264 " 'Dear Dad' ": JFK to JPK, n.d. (1939), JFK POF, Box 135.

265 "British government White Paper": Issued on May 17, 1939, the White Paper recommended independence for Palestine, with the Jewish population limited to one-third of the total, and Jewish immigration after 1944 being al-

lowed only by Arab consent. The plan was debated in Parliament and approved by a majority of eighty-nine, although Churchill criticized it as "another Munich," a "mortal blow" to the Zionists who had been settling in Palestine since the 1920s and had been promised, in the Balfour Declaration of Nov. 1917, an eventual homeland in the area. Manchester, *The Last Lion*, pp. 399–400.

266 " 'There were 13 bombs' ": JFK to JPK, n.d. (1939), POF, Box 135.

267 " 'staid Britons by wearing' ": *BH*, June 9, 1939. JFK also stunned his mother and staid Boston Irish-Catholics in her circle by saying, when he came home, "I saw the rock where our Lord ascended into Heaven in a cloud, and [in] the same area, I saw the place where Mohammed was carried up to Heaven on a white horse, and Mohammed has a big following and Christ has a big following, and why do you think we should believe Christ any more than Mohammed?' He gave this question to one of the priests, who was quite flabbergasted: thinking or daring to ask such a question. And the priest told his father he should have instruction immediately, or else he would turn into a very [bad?] atheist if he didn't get some of [his] problems straightened out." RFK, CBSI.

267 " 'leaving now for Bucharest' ": JFK to JPK, n.d. (1939), POF, Box 135.

267 " 'Had a great trip' ": JFK to KLB, July 17, 1939, KLBP.

267 " 'a peach-colored dress' ": RKRC, pp. 249–50.

268 " 'Jack had pointed out' ": Torbert Macdonald, JFKLOH.

268 " 'Torb ran third' ": JFK to KLB, July 17, 1939, KLBP.

268 " 'I mostly saw him' ": David Ormsby-Gore, Lord Harlech, CBSI. See also AWRH, p. 24.

269 "Hopper had recommended": Tutorial Record, 1938–39, JFKPP, Box 2.

269 " 'Kennedy took six' ": ibid.

269 " 'We went from' ": Macdonald interview, CBSI. See also AWRH, p. 28.

269 " 'I recall very well' ": Macdonald, JFKLOH.

269 " 'We were yelling back' ": Macdonald interview, CBSI. See also AWRH, p. 28.

270 " 'The German people' ": JFK to JPK, n.d. (1939), YJK, p. 110.

270 " 'The south Germans' ": Quoted in Alfred Wright, "A Modest All-America[n] Who Sits on the Highest Bench," *Sports Illustrated*, Dec. 10, 1962. (Associate Supreme Court Justice Byron White has declined all requests by serious historians for interviews relating to JFK).

270 " 'We were wedged' ": Walker and Allen, "Jack Kennedy at Harvard." See also Torbert Macdonald interview, JCBP; and JCB, p. 65.

270 " 'exiled' from England": See LMT, pp. 64–65. Marlene Dietrich recalled in her memoirs how she and her daughter got to know the Kennedys at Antibes, Jack swimming with Dietrich's daughter by day and in the evening dancing with Marlene. "What a summer! . . . I loved all the Kennedy children, and this love has never ceased": Marlene Dietrich, *Marlene* (N.Y.: Grove Press, 1987), p. 182. Marlene's good opinion was grist to JFK's vanity mill. Following JFK's return to America, Lem Billings wrote to Kathleen about a wedding reception at which "brother John was right in his element as he found Dotty Burns and Missy Greer there—all anxious to hear about how Marlene Dietrich thinks he's one of the most fascinating and attractive young men she's ever met.": Michaelis, *Best of Friends*, p. 152.

270 " 'immediately developed' ": LMT, p. 64.

270 " '12th August' ": RKRC, p. 251. On Aug. 9, 1939, JPK had written privately to President Roosevelt from Cannes: "The chief thing I have noticed in the South of France, on the part of the caddies, waiters and residents, is a very strong anti-semitic feeling. Beyond that, and a general sense of wary waiting for almost anything to happen, I can contribute nothing to an understanding of the international state of affairs": Presidential Safe Files Diplomatic Files, FDRL.

270 " 'last night from Munich' ": JFK to JPK, n.d. (1939), JFKPP, Box 4B.

271 " 'No trains were running' ": George F. Kennan, *Memoirs, 1925–50* (Boston: Little, Brown, 1967), p. 91.

271 " 'left Cannes about a week' ": JFK to KLB, Aug. 20, 1939, KLBP.

272 "from the Hotel Excelsior": ibid.; see also McCarthy, *Remarkable Kennedys*, p. 63.

Part 6: Why England Slept

275 " 'we are witnessing' ": JML, Ch. 31, pp. 9–10.

275 " 'he had no intention' ": ibid.

275 " 'I had never' ": ibid., Ch. 33, p. 2.

275 " 'Can the Pope' ": ibid. The British ambassador in Berlin, Sir Nevile Henderson, was as much an appeaser as Ambassador Kennedy, and also considered that Vatican involvement, perhaps even "a neutral frontier patrolled by Catholic priests," might help. Unknown to Henderson or Kennedy, however, the pope had already advised the Poles to surrender Danzig: William Manchester, *The Last Lion, Winston Spencer Churchill: Alone, 1932–1940* (Boston: Little, Brown, 1988), p. 515.

275 " 'some action of Poland' ": JML, Ch. 33, p. 3.

See also JPK to Cordell Hull, Foreign Relations of the United States (F.R.U.S.), 1939, vol. I, pp. 355–56.

275 " 'that it was useless' ": JML, Ch. 33, p. 7. See also JPK to Cordell Hull, F.R.U.S., 1939, vol. I, pp. 369–70. On Aug. 25, 1939, the British government had signed a formal Treaty of Mutual Assistance, encoding its earlier guarantee of Polish territorial boundaries against aggression.

275 " 'After I had read' ": JML, Ch. 33, p. 7.

275 " 'unique instinct' ": James Fayne interview, DEKP.

276 " 'analyzed the increments' ": Tommy Corcoran interview, RJWP.

277 " 'We talked for another' ": JML, Ch. 33, p. 8.

277 " 'There are two' ": ibid., p. 12.

277 " 'I agree. It's the' ": ibid.

278 " 'At 6:30 I went' ": ibid., p. 14.

279 " 'belatedly but now almost' ": ibid., p. 15.

279 " 'It was not until the evening' ": ibid.

279 " 'if the British will only' ": ibid., pp. 16–17.

279 " 'held up for the time' ": ibid. According to Leslie Hore Belisha, the minister of war, a "unanimous decision was taken that ultimatum [that Germany should withdraw its invading forces from Polish territory, on pain of war with Britain, as Poland's treaty-bound ally] should end at midnight." Halifax and Chamberlain appeared to accept this, yet according to William Manchester, Halifax "broke his word to his colleagues and did nothing—did, in one instance, worse than nothing: he told Ciano that Britain saw her role as that of a 'mediator' and, flatly contradicting the cabinet, repeated the line that HMG's warning 'was *not* an ultimatum' ": Manchester, *The Last Lion,* p. 525.

279 " 'Saturday, September 2' ": JML, Ch. 33, p. 18.

280 " 'The Italian proposal' ": ibid., p. 19.

280 " 'where she told me' ": ibid., Ch. 34, p. 1.

280 " 'With the staff' ": ibid.

281 " 'We rushed down' ": ibid.

281 " 'This is no war' ": Quoted in Martin Gilbert, *Winston S. Churchill,* Vol. 5: *The Prophet of Truth, 1922–1939,* 1977, p. 1112. Misquoted in JML, Ch. 34, p. 3.

281 " 'But I felt no wish' ": JML, Ch. 34, p. 3.

281 " 'heart-broken, heartbreaking' ": RKRC, p. 252.

282 " 'Outside, the storms' ": Quoted in Manchester, *The Last Lion,* pp. 538–39.

282 " 'the air-raid siren' ": RKRC, p. 252.

282 "booked berths aboard the first": Handwritten notes by James Seymour, JPK's secretary, JSP, Box 1, JFKL.

282 " 'Oh, we must' ": *London Daily Telegraph & Morning Post,* Sept. 8, 1939.

283 " 'with the prospect of bombing' ": JML, Ch. 34, p. 3.

283 " 'It's the end' ": Joseph Alsop and Robert Kintner, *American White Paper* (N.Y.: Simon and Shuster, 1940), p. 68.

283 " 'As I told Hull' ": JML, Ch. 34, p. 4.

283 " 'your infernal lies' ": Manchester, *The Last Lion,* p. 548. The German Minister in Ireland called on the American Minister, John Cudahy, on Sept. 5, 1939, with a statement from his government denying "that German naval forces took any part in the sinking of the ship. There were no German naval forces at all in the mentioned area. Furthermore, German naval forces had got strict order to proceed in accordance with the rules of International Law and of the agreements signed by Germany." Captain Alan Kirk, the U.S. naval attaché in London, had flown to Ireland, however. After first being imprisoned by mistake, he interviewed British and American survivors, whose eyewitness descriptions left no doubt that the passenger ship had been sunk by a submarine (Memorandum for the Ambassador by Cmdr. N.R. Hitchcock, as-

sistant naval attaché, Sept. 6, 1939). Moreover, Cudahy himself had interviewed the captain of the *Athenia* and many of the crew. "The Minister agreed from my account that the evidence was convincing of a submarine attack, but stated the submarine could not have been a German one since there were no naval forces in the area," Cudahy recorded in his report to the secretary of state in Washington, even though another merchant ship, the *Bosnia,* was also "torpedoed by a submarine off the Aran Islands" that night. Letter of Sept. 6, 1939, contained in records of the U.S. embassy in London, Class 300, Vol. 8, "The Athenia Affair," on microfilm at the JFKL, Box 1, JFKPP.

283 "thirty-nine German submarines": Manchester, *The Last Lion,* p. 548.

283 " 'Jack Kennedy was sent' ": BG, Sept. 26, 1939.

284 " 'Mr. John Kennedy, the 18-year-old' ": *London Daily Telegraph & Morning Post,* Sept. 8, 1939.

284 " 'that President Roosevelt had said' ": ibid.

284 " 'a storm of protest' ": *Buffalo Evening News,* Sept. 8, 1939.

285 " 'Ambassador of mercy—19 year old' ": *London Evening News,* Sept. 7, 1939.

285 " '1. That a convoy' ": "The Athenia Affair," Box 1, JFKPP. JFK's many letters to American survivors, courteous and concerned, are in interesting contrast to the sometimes abrasive responses of older embassy staff. When JFK proved too compassionate, for instance, he was upbraided by JPK's publicist, Harvey Klemmer. Survivors had no cause for complaint at the prospect of free gangway cots or a 200 percent increase in fares (with no reimbursement from Donaldson Lines), Klemmer told JFK to point out to survivors on Sept. 16, 1939. "These people wanted a battleship first. On a battleship they would not even have cots. They would have to sleep in hammocks, if indeed they could get hammocks. . . . The people on the ORIZABA are really getting a break." Ibid.

285 " 'Many of them demanded' ": JML, Ch. 34, p. 5.

285 " 'now working in charge' ": JFK to the Harvard Bureau of Registration, Sept. 13, 1939, JFKPP, Box 2.

286 " 'the general favorite' ": BG, Sept. 21, 1939.

286 " 'Handsome, tall, thin . . .' ": ibid., Sept. 26, 1939.

286 " 'hot pursuit' ": JCB, p. 69.

286 " 'Jack is taking out' ": RKRC, p. 256.

286 " 'an attractive girl' ": ibid.

287 " 'When she introduced' ": Charles Houghton interview, JCBP.

287 "that it was he who had rejected": William Walton interview of June 12, 1991.

287 " 'Cannon and I' ": JFK to JPK, n.d. (1939), JFKPP, Box 4B.

287 " 'I can recall' ": Torbert Macdonald, JFKLOH.

287 " 'It appears to me' ": JML, Ch. 34, p. 14. See also F.R.U.S., 1939, Vol. I, p. 423.

287 " 'the silliest message' ": James A. Farley, *Jim Farley's Story—The Roosevelt Years* (N.Y.: McGraw-Hill, 1948), pp. 198–99.

287 " 'Joe has been' ": John Martin Blum, *From the Morgenthau Diaries, Vol. 2: Years of Urgency* (Boston: Houghton Mifflin, 1965), p. 102.

287 "the reply came": JML, Ch. 34, p. 14.

288 " 'talking and acting' ": ibid., Ch. 35, p. 8.

288 " 'to get your President' ": ibid., p. 7.

288 " 'A move for peace' ": ibid., p. 15.

288 " 'I have yet' ": ibid., p. 19.

288 " 'For all Halifax's' ": ibid., p. 20.

289 " 'I never received' ": ibid., p. 22.

289 " 'talk of Churchill' ": ibid., Ch. 36, pp. 6–7.

290 " 'I am enclosing' ": JFK to JPK, n.d. (1939), JFKPP, Box 4B.

290 " 'President is almost' ": Harvard *Crimson*, Oct. 9, 1939. The editor, Blair Clark, has confirmed to the author that this was indeed the editorial to which JFK was referring.

290 " 'There is every possibility of' ": ibid.

290 " 'The restoration of the old Poland' ": ibid.

291 " 'a one hour talk' ": JFK to JPK, n.d. (1939), JFKPP, Box 1.

291 " 'Mr. Jack Kennedy, had' ": Gage minute, Sept. 20, 1939, FO 371/22827, as cited in DEK, p. 210.

291 " 'Johnny Burns says' ": JFK to JPK, n.d. (1939), JFKPP, Box 1.

292 " 'almost literally walking' ": James MacGregor Burns, *Roosevelt—The Lion and the Fox* (N.Y.: Harcourt Brace, 1956), p. 396.

292 " 'quite a seer around' ": JFK to JPK, n.d. (1939), JFKPP, Box 1.

292 " 'capable of being interpreted' ": Perowne minute, Sept. 27, 1939, FO 371/22827, as cited in DEK, p. 217.

292 " 'sees everything from' ": Entry of Sept. 9, 1939, David Dilks, ed., *The Diaries of Sir David Cadogan, 1938–45* (London: Cassell, 1971), p. 215, as cited in DEK, p. 542.

292 " 'could resist the feeling' ": Scott minute, Sept. 30, 1939, FO 371/22827, as cited in DEK, p. 217.

292 " 'Joe Kennedy was operating' ": DEK, p. 217.

292 " 'discovered that Kennedy' ": ibid., p. 216.

292 " 'Big Arthur Goldsmith' ": JFK to JPK, n.d. (1939), JFKPP, Box 1.

292 " 'went to 25' ": JFK to KLB, Oct. 23, 1939, KLBP.

293 " 'send me the $100' ": JFK to KLB, Nov. 1, 1939, KLBP.

293 " 'to the United States' ": Harvard *Crimson*, Oct. 9, 1939.

293 " 'against immediate American entry' ": ibid., Nov. 11, 1939.

293 " 'The whole campus' ": Donald Thurber interview of June 7, 1990.

294 " 'I believe that' ": James B. Conant to Alf Landon, Harvard *Crimson*, Oct. 4, 1939. (Landon had opposed Roosevelt in the 1936 presidential election.)

294 " 'The members of the Harvard' ": Thurber interview.

294 " 'hold their own' ": Harvard *Crimson*, Sept. 26, 1939.

294 " 'impossible for the' ": ibid., Sept. 28, 1939.

294 " 'dream of a new' ": ibid., Oct. 3, 1939.

294 " 'a truce at present' ": ibid., Oct. 13, 1939.

294 " 'He was genuinely' ": Payson Wild, JFKLOH.

295 " 'Have been doing' ": JFK to JPK, n.d. (1939), JFKPP, Box 1.

295 " 'the style of the man' ": Arthur Holcombe interview, CBSI.

295 " 'He wasn't interested' ": ibid.

295 " 'preposterous to say' ": Wild, JFKLOH.

295 " 'Everybody knew' ": Holcombe interview.

295 " 'I seem to be' ": JFK to JPK, n.d. (1939), JFKPP, Box 1.

295 " 'Get something that' ": JFK to KLB, Oct. 23, 1939, KLBP.

295 " 'I went to N.Y.' ": JFK to KLB, Dec. 7, 1939, KLBP.

296 " 'Harvard as you probably know' ": ibid.

296 " 'we used to' ": Benjamin Smith interview, JCBP.

296 " 'Took my first' ": JFK to JPK, n.d. (1939), JFKPP, Box 4B.

296 " 'I had insured' ": Thomas Schriber interview, CBSI.

296 " 'Dear Shrive' ": JFK to Thomas Schriber, n.d., as cited in AWRH, p. 37.

297 "Jack's four courses": Academic Records—1939, JFKPP, Box 2.

297 " 'I am taking' ": JFK to JPK, n.d. (1939), JFKPP, Box 1.

297 "English foreign policy since 1731": Herbert Parmet, *Jack, The Struggles of John F. Kennedy* (N.Y.: Dial Press, 1980), p. 67; and DKG, p. 604, inter alia.

297 " 'He had a Boston' ": RFK interview, CBSI.

298 " 'Electrical Utilities in Maine' ": Honors Thesis in Government, 1939–40, JFKPP, Box 2.

298 " 'get in touch with' ": JFK to JPK, n.d. (1939), JFKPP, Box 1.

298 " 'I got to know' ": Torbert Macdonald interview, CBSI.

298 " 'He seemed to blossom' ": Wild, JFKLOH.

298 " 'I've always had' ": ibid.

299 " 'There is a question' ": Government 4, Case 99—11/15/39, JFKPP, Box 4.

299 " 'to go to law' ": Wild, JFKLOH.

299 " 'he had completely' ": Ralph Horton, JFKLOH.

299 " 'alphabetically in French' ": JFK Course Notes, JFKPP, Box 4.

300 " 'Soviet Russia wants' ": "International Relations," JFKPP, Box 4.

300 " 'frequent speeches to' ": ibid.

301 " 'an attack on' ": ibid.

301 " 'I didn't know him' ": Josephine Fulton interview of Jan. 10, 1989.

301 " 'failure to utter' ": "League of Nations," JFKPP, Box 4.

302 " 'a propertied class' ": ibid.

302 " 'carried the crown' ": JML, Ch. 37, p. 15.

303 " 'As I see it' ": John Wheeler Bennett, *King George VI* (N.Y.: Macmillan, 1958), p. 419.

304 " 'The people of America' ": Draft, n.d., JSP, Box 1, JFKL.

304 " 'The future of' ": JML, Ch. 37, pp. 21–22.

304 " 'My appointment with' ": ibid., Ch. 38, p. 4.

304 " 'It struck me' ": ibid., pp. 6–10.

305 "using secret naval codes": According to David Irving, the American Gray code was regularly

broken by British intelligence; thus, although Halifax officially requested Churchill to desist—possibly to placate Kennedy—the prime minister, Neville Chamberlain, was kept well informed of the communication: David Irving, *Churchill's War* (N.Y.: Avon Books, 1991), p. 195.

305 " 'I just don't trust' ": JML, Ch. 36, p. 3.

305 " 'to get the rest' ": ibid., Ch. 38, p. 10.

306 " 'The talk that I gave' ": ibid. In an interview afterward with a *BH* reporter, Kennedy added, "There is no justification, economically, socially, financially, politically, for the United States entering this war." John O'Connor, *BH,* Dec. 11, 1939.

306 " 'had said that I' ": JML, Ch. 38, p. 12. See also MB, p. 201.

306 " 'Although I had' ": ibid., Ch. 39, p. 8.

307 " 'It was our talk' ": JFK to Lord Lothian, Aug. 12, 1940, Lothian Papers, Foreign Office notes, DEKP.

307 " 'took advantage' ": Bruce Hopper interview, JMBP.

307 "SEND IMMEDIATELY": JFK to James Seymour, Jan. 11, 1940, Box 1, JSP.

307 "HURRYING MATERIAL": Seymour to JFK, Jan. 11, 1940, Box 1, JSP.

307 "PLEASE TELEPHONE ME": Seymour to Harold Laski, Jan. 11, 1940, JSP.

307 " 'a word from your father' ": Seymour to JPK, Box 1, JSP.

308 " 'on reflection' ": Laski to Seymour, Jan. 12, 1940, Box 1, JSP.

308 " 'We have had' ": Seymour to JFK, Jan. 11, 1940, Box 1, JSP.

309 " 'badly thrashed' ": Gage minute, Sept. 20, 1939.

309 " 'Mr. Kennedy is a' ": Vansittart note, Jan. 22, 1940, FO 371/24251. See also DEK, p. 239.

309 " 'Farley in his ambition' ": JML, Ch. 39, p. 9.

310 "filed nomination papers' ": MB, p. 202.

310 " 'Why don't you run' ": JML, Ch. 39, p. 10.

310 " 'Her gay conversation' ": ibid., Ch. 40, p. 1. "How shocked Harry [Henry Luce] would have been she felt, if she had told him that his old acquaintance, Joe Kennedy, had had an affair with Clare. 'Oh, no question they did,' she said.' " Lady Jean Campbell, quoted in Ralph G. Martin, *Henry and Clare: An Intimate Portrait of the Luces* (N.Y.: G.P. Putnam's Sons, 1991), p. 342. JPK also openly boasted to his son JFK about the affair: William Walton interview, JCBP, and interview with author, June 12, 1990.

311 " 'very worried by' ": Nigel Nicolson, ed., *The Diaries & Letters of Harold Nicolson, The War Years, 1939–45, Vol. II.* (N.Y.: Atheneum, 1967), p. 60.

311 " 'He will be welcomed' ": *Spectator,* March 8, 1940.

311 " 'Those remarks' ": JML, Ch. 40, p. 6.

311 " 'if the Allies' ": ibid., p. 29.

312 " 'Chamberlain's 'yes' seemed' ": ibid., p. 39.

312 " 'We were shown' ": ibid., p. 32.

313 "WIRE BY WESTERN UNION": JFK to Seymour, Jan. 30, 1940, Box 1, JSP.

313 " 'On receipt of' ": Seymour to Paul Murphy, Feb. 8, 1940, Box 1, JSP.

313 "RUSH PACIFIST LITERATURE": JFK to Seymour, Feb. 9, 1940, Box 1, JSP.

313 " 'Dear Jack, your cables' ": Seymour to JFK, Feb. 12, 1940, Box 1, JSP.

313 " 'The struggle goes' ": Handwritten annotation on E.M. Watson letter to Seymour, Feb. 9, 1940 ("I think I should mention, for your private information, that Mr. Chamberlain has received many similar requests, with which he has found it impossible to comply. He has, however, made an exception in this particular case"). Ibid.

313 "a further twenty-two volumes": Murphy to Seymour, Feb. 27, 1940, Box 1, JSP.

313 "controversy raging over assistant professorships": In the late fall of 1939 the Harvard faculty mounted a virtual revolt over the failure of the university to promote assistant professors to full professorial status, even after twenty years of teaching. This led to reduced tutorial and extra-classroom help: Hopper interview, JMBP.

313 " 'he would do some' ": Wild, JFKLOH.

314 " 'little to do with' ": Holcombe interview, CBSI.

314 " 'slow start' ": Hopper interview, JMBP.

314 " 'I was very politically' ": James Rousmanière, interview of April 6, 1989.

314 " 'We used to kid' ": ibid.

315 " 'Did I know him' ": Camman Newberry, interview of June 7, 1989.

315 " 'There are those' ": Augustus Soule, interview of Dec. 28, 1988.

315 " 'I'll never forget' ": Ted Reardon, interview of May 23, 1989.

315 " 'Appeasement at Munich' ": "Appeasement at Munich (The Inevitable Result of the Slowness of Conversion of the British Democracy from a Disarmament to a Rearmament Policy)," title page, Box 26, JFKPP.

316 " 'it was only' ": JFK to JPK, n.d. (1940), JFKPP, Box 4B.

316 "In his preface": "Appeasement at Munich," Preface, p. 1.

316 " 'centuries of isolation' ": ibid., Ch. 1, p. 1.

317 " 'This is mentioned' ": ibid., Ch. 4, p. 46.

317 " 'peace and disarmament' ": ibid., Ch. 3, p. 43.

317 " 'appeal to the sentiments' ": ibid., p. 44.

317 " 'Supposing I had gone' ": ibid., Ch. 6, p. 97.

317 " 'In analyzing the speech' ": ibid., p. 98.

318 " 'whitewashed' ": JMB, p. 43.

318 " 'When it requires' ": "Appeasement at Munich," Conclusion, p. 146.

320 " 'Kennedy said' ": Memo: Feb. 9, 1940, Dr. Else, JFKPP, Box 2.

320 " 'Stenographer, young,' ": ibid.

320 " '60 clamoring females' ": Gerald Walker and Donald A. Allan, "Jack Kennedy at Harvard," *Coronet,* May 1961.

320 " 'rushed madly around' ": HS, p. 156.

320 " 'Am finishing up' ": JFK to JPK, n.d. (1940), JFKPP, Box 4B.

320 " 'The weather' ": JFK to JPK, n.d., (1940), JFKPP, Box 4B.

320 " 'still misses Cannon' ": RKRC, p. 263.

320 " 'I would like to go' ": JFK to KLB, April 16, 1940, KLBP.

321 " 'one of Charlotte's' ": Unidentified newspaper cutting, JCBP.

321 " 'laborious, interesting' ": H. Yeomans, Report on Thesis for Distinction, JFKPP, Box 2.

321 " 'Fundamental premise' ": C. Friedrich, Report on Thesis for Distinction, JFKPP, Box 2.

321 " 'seemed to represent' ": HS, p. 156.

321 " 'Rose and most of' ": Arthur Krock to JPK, April 4, 1940, AKP.

321 " 'It was amateurish' ": Arthur Krock, JFKLOH.

322 " 'surprisingly able, when' ": Tutorial Record—1939–40, JFKPP, Box 2.

322 " 'Hopper was casual' ": Hopper interview, JMBP.

322 " 'and feels that I' ": JFK to JPK, n.d. (1940), JFKPP, Box 1.

322 " 'thought it should be' ": ibid.

323 " 'I had his father's' ": Krock to Gertrude Algase, April 17, 1940, AKP.

323 " 'Krock seemed to think' ": JFK to JPK, n.d. (1940), JFKPP, Box 1.

323 " 'I note what you said' ": JPK to Krock, April 22, 1940, AKP.

324 " 'as a place of retreat' ": JML, Ch. 41, p. 4. "Mr. Horace Dodge of Detroit had available a country place known as St. Leonard's. . . . The grounds were enormous and included a nine-hole golf course. The house required a staff of some twenty-five persons to run it." Ibid.

324 " 'I have never' ": JML, Ch. 43, p. 2.

324 " 'The nation is' ": *Hansard,* May 8, 1940.

324 " 'looked stunned' ": JML, Ch. 43, p. 8.

325 " 'at six o'clock' ": ibid., p. 10.

325 "Churchill implored Attlee": ibid., p. 11.

325 " 'learned that Chamberlain' ": ibid., p. 12.

326 " 'tearing his hair' ": "The Reminiscences of Alan G. Kirk," Columbia University Oral History Collection, Columbia University.

326 " 'in a state of panic' ": DEK, pp. 254–55.

326 " 'got up a Red Cross' ": JFK to JPK, n.d. (1940), JFKPP, Box 4B.

327 " 'the British lose' ": KK to JPK, May 21, 1940, as quoted in DKG, p. 607.

327 " 'Mother told me' ": JFK to JPK, n.d. (1940), JFKPP, Box 4B.

327 " 'Arthur Krock read it' ": Algase to Mr. E.C. Aswell, Harper & Brothers, May 20, 1940, HarperCollins Archives.

327 "Krock's house in Georgetown": Arthur Krock, *Memoirs: Sixty Years on the Firing Line* (N.Y.: Funk & Wagnalls, 1968), p. 343.

327 " 'I can't say' ": Krock, JFKLOH. Once the book proved successful, a number of other journalists vied with Krock for credit in having made a readable narrative out of a student thesis. Blair Clark, isolationist editor of the *Crimson,* for example, recalled being asked to help make revisions, after meeting Jack in the Harvard Widener Library. "I spent three or four sweltering afternoons with the manuscript. I might have written a few paragraphs that were original, but mostly I rewrote and edited. Frankly, I was surprised he found a publisher for it": Quoted in C. David Heymann, *A*

Woman Named Jackie (N.Y.: Lyle Stuart, 1989), pp. 173–74. Harvey Klemmer, JPK's embassy publicist, claimed to have "worked two weeks on it, night and day, delivered it at four o'clock in the morning on the day that Eddie Moore was to go to New York and take it to the publisher. When I got it, it was a mishmash, ungrammatical. He had sentences without subjects and verbs. It was a very sloppy job, mostly magazine and newspaper clippings stuck together. I edited it, and put in a little peroration at the end." Peter Collier and David Horowitz, *The Kennedys: An American Drama* (N.Y.: Summit Books, 1984), pp. 477–78.

328 " 'putting the blame' ": JPK to JFK, May 20, 1940, JFKPOF, Box 129.

328 " 'was submitted about two' ": JFK to JPK, n.d. (May 1940), JFKPP, Box 4A.

329 " 'a careful and scholarly' ": Aswell to Algase, June 18, 1940, HarperCollins Archives.

329 " 'Well, I just' ": JFK to JPK, n.d. (1940), JFKPP, Box 4B.

330 " 'Jack Kennedy—Ambassador' ": Algase to Mr. Alfred Harcourt, June 20, 1940, JFKPrePres, Box 73.

330 " 'sales possibilities too' ": Handwritten annotation dated June 21, 1940, on Algase to Harcourt.

330 " 'Book publishing not' ": Handwritten annotation dated June 24, 1940, on Algase to Harcourt.

330 " 'I remember Jack' ": KLB interviews, JCB and JFKLOH.

330 " 'Ambassador Kennedy called' ": Henry Luce, JFKLOH.

331 " 'I cannot recall' ": John F. Kennedy, *Why England Slept* (N.Y.: Wilfred Funk, 1940), Foreword, p. xiv.

332 " 'everyone in the USA' ": Iain Macleod, *Neville Chamberlain* (London: Frederick Muller, 1961), p. 279.

332 " 'a self-centered, frightened' ": Kingsley Martin, *Editor: 'New Statesman' Years, 1931–1945* (Chicago: Henry Regnery, 1970), p. 313.

332 "trading with the Nazis": See DKG, pp. 572–73, Charles Higham, *Trading with the Enemy: An Expose of the Nazi-American Money Plot, 1933–1948* (N.Y.: Delacorte Press, 1983), pp. 168–70.

333 " 'if it reaches' ": JPK to JFK, Aug. 2, 1940, as quoted in RKRC, pp. 261–62; and DKG, pp. 606–607.

333 " 'I think it's a swell job' ": JPK to RFK, Aug. 13, 1940, as quoted in RKRC, p. 271.

333 "easy 'to repeat the eulogies' ": Harold Laski to JPK, Aug. 20, 1940, as quoted in Max Freedman, *Roosevelt and Frankfurter, Their Correspondence, 1928–45* (Boston: Little, Brown Co., 1967), p. 590.

334 " 'The publisher anticipated' ": Algase to Krock, July 12, 1940, AKP.

334 "editor of *Current History* begged": Joel Satz to JFK, July 16, 1940, JFKPrePres, Box 73.

334 " 'Everyone agrees' ": ibid.

335 " 'Jack's book' ": Jean Kennedy to JPK, July 29, 1940, as quoted in RKRC, p. 268.

335 " 'You surely are' ": Algase to JFK, Aug. 1, 1940, JFKPrePres, Box 73.

336 " 'exceptional opportunities' ": *N. Y. Sun,* Aug. 2, 1940.

336 " 'My dear Jack' ": FDR to JFK, Aug. 27, 1940, JFKPrePres, Box 74.

336 " 'I have not had' ": Lillian Roberts to JFK, n.d. (1940), JFKPrePres, Box 74.

336 "how 'thoroughly' they had": N. Pierrepont to JFK, Aug. 15, 1940, JFKPrePres, Box 74.

336 " 'excellently written' ": B.A. Brickley to JFK, Sept. 30, 1940, JFKPrePres, Box 73.

336 " 'express my sincere' ": A.F. Sturmthal to JFK, Nov. 17, 1940, JFKPrePres, Box 74.

336 "Geoffrey Brown": Geoffrey Brown to JFK, Aug. 27, 1940, JFKPrePres, Box 73.

337 " 'restrained, scholarly' ": G. St. John to JFK, Sept. 6, 1940, JFKPrePres, Box 74.

337 " 'a candidate for' ": Algase to JFK, Sept. 7, 1940, JFKPrePres, Box 73.

337 " 'It is an excellent' ": Bruce Hopper to JFK, Sept. 5, 1940, JFKPrePres, Box 73.

Part 7: Stanford Interlude

341 " 'plenty of action' ": Torbert Macdonald to JFK, n.d., JFKPP, Box 4B.

341 " 'how sorry I was' ": Olive Field Cawley to JFK, n.d. (1940), JFKPP, Box 4A.

341 " 'August 1940' ": Naval Medical Records, Medical Record, Dec. 15, 1944, p. 2, JFKPP, Box 11A. " 'the late president's venereal,' " see earlier source note to p. xx on pp. 808ff.

342 " 'when he was in College' ": Dr. Vernon Dick to Dr. William Herbst, March 20, 1953, MS 83-38, JFKL.

342 " 'recently made a trip' ": William Bullitt to JFK, Aug. 26, 1940, JFKPrePres, Box 73.

342 " 'principally because he' ": JPK to James Landis, Aug. 6, 1940, James Landis Papers, Library of Congress.

343 " 'I did not notice' ": JML, Ch. 41, p. 5.

343 "Kennedy's nightly departure": JPK's embassy publicist, Harvey Klemmer, recalled how "once the Blitz started, he went to the country almost every night. He kept saying he had nine kids to look after, this big family he was responsible for. He took off every night before it got dark": Peter Collier and David Horowitz, *The Kennedys, An American Drama* (N.Y.: Summit Books, 1984), p. 107.

343 " 'my practice of avoiding' ": JML, Ch. 41, p. 5.

343 " 'Finally I told him' ": ibid., Ch. 46, p. 9.

343 " 'I told him what I thought' ": ibid., p. 10.

343 "not to embarrass Roosevelt": ibid., Ch. 49, p. 8.

343 " 'certainly picked' ": ibid., Ch. 46, p. 6.

344 " 'the French would not' ": ibid., p. 14.

344 "probably 'quit' ": ibid., p. 16.

344 " 'I am personally' ": ibid., p. 18.

344 " 'The Prime Minister was' ": ibid., p. 19.

345 " 'Though I realize' ": ibid., p. 25. In a telephone conversation with JPK, Roosevelt said, according to JPK: "Joe, I see a great opportunity for an economic tie-up here with South America and with other countries not involved in this struggle that would make it, with the assistance of the French fleet, most difficult for the Germans ultimately to win the war": ibid., p. 22. Just as Churchill was prepared to continue the fight against Germany from Canada, if a German invasion of Britain proved successful in the early stages of the world war, so Roosevelt expected the French to fight on from their colonial and naval bases.

345 " 'if the English people' ": ibid., p. 29.

345 " 'had a chance' ": ibid., Ch. 47, p. 3.

345 " 'I didn't want you' ": ibid., Ch. 48, p. 2.

345 " 'the President telling me' ": ibid., p. 3.

346 " 'I was damn fresh' ": ibid., p. 6.

346 " 'a fantastic story' ": Joe Kane interview, RMEPP.

346 " 'that any one of these' ": JML, Ch. 48, p. 5.

346 " 'two critical acts' ": ibid., p. 6.

346 " 'I learned not' ": ibid., p. 7.

347 " 'Imagine,' the ambassador": ibid., p. 11.

347 " 'to remember that I don't' ": ibid., p. 18.

347 " 'I had been almost completely' ": ibid., Ch. 49, p. 1.

347 "American destroyers had boilers": ibid., pp. 2–3.

347 " 'The Embassy, I wrote' ": ibid., p. 6.

347 " 'no one in the State Department' ": ibid.

347 " 'a delegation of girls' ": ibid.

347 " 'determined to go home' ": ibid., p. 8.

348 "The Palo Alto climate": See Margo Davis and Roxanne Nilan, *The Stanford Album* (Stanford, Calif.: Stanford University Press, 1989).

348 " 'a predominately rich' ": ibid., p. 221.

348 " 'growing tendency' ": ibid.

348 " 'taking some pre-law' ": JFK to A. Chester Hanford, Sept. 23, 1940, JFKPP, Box 2.

348 " 'Jack went to Stanford' ": Torbert Macdonald interview, CBSI.

348 " 'was an enormous' ": KLB interviews, JCB and JFKLOH.

349 " 'firmly entrenched' ": Macdonald to JFK, n.d. (1940), JFKPP, Box 4B.

349 " 'well, very well settled' ": JFK to KLB, Oct. 4, 1940, KLBP.

349 " 'Jack was cute' ": C. David Heyman, *A Woman Named Jackie* (N.Y.: Lyle Stuart, 1989), p. 149.

349 " 'He really is' ": RKRC, p. 263.

349 " 'She was most attractive' ": JCB, p. 97.

350 " 'Jack Filor was a friend' ": Harriet Price Fullerton interview of April 9, 1992.

350 " 'what an utterly attractive' ": Henry James interview of Aug. 23, 1991.

350 " 'He was sort of' ": JCB, p. 98.

350 " 'Jack seems a little' ": "Rose Fitzgerald Kennedy," *McCalls,* May 1961.

350 " 'I don't think he was ready' " H.P. Fullerton interview.

350 " 'He was really bombing' ": Tom Killefer interview, JCBP and JCB, p. 92.

351 " 'He would go down for weekends' ": H.P. Fullerton interview.

351 " 'I picked Stanford' ": Jean Nowell, "Author Kennedy Follows Killefer Recommendation," *Stanford Daily,* Oct. 16, 1940.

351 " 'whenever they ask' ": ibid.

351 " 'I don't think' ": RFK interview, CBSI.
352 " 'unbelievably handsome' ": JCB, p. 68.
352 " 'odd mixture of' ": James Rousmanière interview of April 6, 1989.
352 " 'Do you ever remember' ": JFK to KLB, Oct. 4, 1940, KLBP.
352 " 'Have really settled' ": ibid.
352 " 'he frequently cited' ": letter to Douglas C. Hall, July 25, 1965, Douglas Hall Papers, M213 (papers generated for an article, "JFK's Stay at the Farm" by Douglas Hall, published in the *Stanford Daily*, April 2, 1965), Department of Special Collections, Stanford University Library.
353 " 'the young Boston Irishman' ": letter to Douglas C. Hall, April 12, 1965, Douglas Hall Papers.
353 " 'I have a vague' ": Prof. Walter S. Palmer, Jr., to Hall, March 29, 1965, Douglas Hall Papers.
353 " 'JFK did not participate' ": letter to Douglas C. Hall, July 25, 1965, Douglas Hall Papers.
354 " 'rather shy, reserved' ": David G. Cuthbertson to Hall, March 23, 1965, Douglas Hall Papers.
354 " 'approached him to discuss' ": ibid.
354 " 'responded immediately to' ": Harry Muheim, "Rich, Young, and Happy," *Esquire*, Aug. 1966. Bruce Jessup later claimed that, "as I heard the story at the time," JFK "came out here to study under an international political scientist named Graham Stuart. Stuart was the intellectual draw. . . . Of course he created a hell of a stir, his dad the ambassador and we didn't have too many of those at that time. There were only about three or four thousand [students] there and he was the talk of the place before he got there. And then when he got there and was so personally attractive and such a good egg. . . . He had this big Buick convertible and was never pushy or fussy. It was really a very great treat for the student body just to have him there, and he seemed to enjoy it. He was having not a hell of a good time but a goddamn good time. He wasn't raising Cain. The important thing was how attractive he was and how impressed everybody around the campus was." Bruce Jessup interview, JCBP.
354 " 'JFK never took' ": letter to Douglas C. Hall, July 25, 1965, Douglas Hall Papers.
355 " 'Miss Gardiner, who owned' ": Thomas Swain Barclay Oral History, Department of Special Collections, Stanford University Library.
355 " 'majority of the faculty' ": Thomas Barclay interview, JCBP; and JCB, p. 100.
355 " 'Jack Kennedy's message' ": Muheim, "Rich, Young, and Happy."
356 " 'a very unpopular' ": JCB, p. 101.
356 " 'I was a stranger' ": James interview.
358 " 'throwing themselves at' ": ibid.
359 " 'I was very much' ": JFK to Camman Newberry, Oct. 28, 1940, Camman Newberry Papers.
360 " 'blindfolded' ": *Stanford Daily,* Oct. 30, 1940.
360 " 'bore the serial' ": ibid.
361 " 'I swear to God' ": Macdonald to JFK, n.d. (1940), JFKPP, Box 4B.

361 "ORCHIDS TO 2748": KLB to JFK, Oct. 30, 1940, JFKPP, Box 4B.
361 " 'just at the time' ": JCB, p. 102.
361 " 'This draft has' ": JFK to KLB, Nov. 14, 1940, KLBP.
361 " 'Get your pappy' ": Macdonald to JFK, n.d. (Nov. 1940), JFKPP, Box 4B.
362 " 'that his father was so opposed' ": JCB, p. 102.
362 " 'I hear they're calling' ": *Stanford Daily,* Oct. 16, 1940.
362 " 'complete lack of confidence' ": JML, Ch. 49, p. 10.
362 " 'I am very unhappy' ": MB, p. 211.
362 " 'The President regards' ": *BG,* Oct. 7, 1940.
362 " 'He told me' ": Halifax to Lothian, Oct. 10, 1940, FO 371/24251, Public Record Office, Kew, England. See also DEK, p. 271.
362 " 'an indictment' ": Arthur Krock, JFKLOH.
363 " 'The article which' ": Secret Foreign Office memorandum "on the Retirement of Mr. Joseph Kennedy from the Embassy of the United States in London, Oct. 18, 1940," FO 371/24251, Public Record Office, Kew, England.
363 " 'seems obscure' ": T. North Whitehead minute, Oct. 19, 1940, FO 371/24251, Public Record Office, Kew, England.
363 " 'Churchill immediately assumed' ": JML, Ch. 50, p. 8.
363 "Labour members of his Cabinet": Whitehall had already given orders that no financial information of any importance was to be divulged to the American ambassador, explaining that "if Mr. Kennedy is permitted to have access, before leaving this country, to the fullest details of our financial position and expectations in the United States, he might make damaging use of them, both against Mr. Roosevelt and, indirectly of course, against us." The British ambassador in Washington, Lord Lothian, was similarly "warned of this possibility which is only in line with many other indications which we have had throughout the last year of Mr. Kennedy's ultimate intentions." Secret FO memorandum. According to the editor of *The New York Times*, C.L. Sulzberger, the British Secret Service "had been tapping Kennedy's wires and found out he was anti-British and also that he was certain they were going to lose the war." They therefore "consulted Winston Churchill and other Cabinet members on what to do": C.L. Sulzberger, *The Last of the Giants* (N.Y.: The Macmillan Co., 1970), p. 630.
363 " 'I found Mr. Attlee' ": JML, Ch. 50, p. 9.
363 " 'On the eve' ": ibid.
364 " 'his opinions to every' ": *BG,* Oct. 7, 1940.
364 " 'specifically requesting me' ": JML, Ch. 51, p. 1.
364 " 'received a confidential' ": ibid., p. 2.
364 " 'Ah, Joe it is so' ": Krock, *Memoirs: Sixty Years on the Firing Line* (N.Y.: Funk & Wagnalls, 1968), p. 399.
365 " 'a personal letter' ": JML, Ch. 51, p. 3.
365 " 'After I had seen' ": ibid.
365 "begged him to announce": Ralph G. Martin, *Henry and Clare: An Intimate Portrait of the*

Luces (N.Y.: G.P. Putnam's Sons, 1991), p. 204. JPK had boasted before Lord Beaverbrook in London that he could "put twenty-five million votes behind Wendell Willkie to throw Roosevelt out." MB, p. 16.

365 " 'I told them' ": JML, Ch. 51, p. 3.
365 "According to Arthur Krock": Krock, *Memoirs,* p. 335.
365 " 'we were met' ": JML, Ch. 51, p. 3.
366 " 'acting as though' ": ibid.
366 " 'He knew that one' ": RKRC, p. 275.
366 " 'I stand in awe' ": DKG, p. 612.
366 " 'The President worked' ": JML, Ch. 51, p. 4.
366 " 'face turned white' ": Krock, *Memoirs,* p. 336.
366 " 'In the first place' ": JML, Ch. 51, p. 4.
367 "Donovan was sent": Donovan's two-week mission for the president, during which he never spoke to JPK, was to weigh up Britain's chances of military survival. The British ambassador, Lord Lothian, reported to London on Donovan's return to Washington in August 1940 that Donovan had "found the Administration in a mood of extreme depression to which, he remarked sourly, Mr. Kennedy had himself largely contributed." Nicholas Bethell, "Joseph Kennedy: The Embarrassing Ambassador," *London Sunday Times,* June 20, 1965.
367 " 'Roosevelt promptly denied' ": JML, Ch. 51 p. 4.
367 " 'Somebody is lying' ": ibid., p. 5.
367 " 'I asked him how' ": ibid.
367 " 'Rose chimed in' ": ibid.
367 " 'Finally I said' ": ibid, p. 6.
367 " 'on the same train' ": ibid.
368 " 'not to let this fellow' ": ibid., Ch. 52, p. 3.
368 " 'that if I did' ": ibid., Ch. 51, p. 6.
368 " 'a dummy' ": MB, p. 211.
368 "Roosevelt had promised to support": *Saturday Evening Post,* Aug. 13, 1960. See also MB, p. 218.
368 "To others, such as Clare Luce": MB, p. 221. See also Martin, *Henry and Clare,* p. 204.
369 " 'the situation cleared' ": JML, Ch. 51, p. 6.
369 "I HAVE JUST LISTENED": Krock, *Memoirs,* p. 336.
369 " 'back to the shores' ": *NYT,* Nov. 1, 1940.
369 " 'the charge that' ": ibid., Oct. 30, 1940.
369 " 'your boys are not' ": ibid., Nov. 1, 1940.
369 " 'I personally told' ": JML, Ch. 52, p. 1.
370 " 'He sees England' ": Entry of Nov. 10, 1940, Breckinridge Long Diary, Breckinridge Long Papers, Library of Congress, typescript p. 256. See also Fred Israel, *The War Diary of Breckinridge Long: Selections from the Years 1941-44* (Lincoln, Neb.: University of Nebraska Press, 1966).
370 " 'it rather looks' ": T. N. Whitehead minute, Nov. 15, 1940, FO 371/24251, Public Record Office, Kew, England.
370 " 'He sees Hitler' ": Long Diary, p. 258.
371 " 'tendered his resignation' ": Krock, *Memoirs,* p. 336.
371 " 'They discussed the situation' ": Krock memo, Dec. 1, 1940, AKP.
371 " 'whatever aid you' ": Hoover memo, Nov. 22, 1944, Herbert Hoover Papers, as cited in MB, p. 228.

371 " 'You will either' ": Krock, *Memoirs,* p. 336.
372 " 'both Kennedy and' ": John Crider to Arthur Krock, Nov. 12, 1940, AKP.
372 " 'just as a traveler' ": Louis Lyons to JPK, Nov. 7, 1940, as quoted in DKG, p. 614.
372 " 'background information' ": Crider to Krock.
372 " 'It was as though' ": Louis Lyons, *Newspaper Story—100 Years of the Boston Globe* (Cambridge, Mass.: Belknap & Harvard, 1971), p. 291.
372 " 'the American people' ": Long Diary, p. 148.
372 " 'poured out' ": *BG,* Nov. 10, 1940.
373 " 'it was impossible' ": Ralph Coughlan to Richard Whalen, April 21, 1965, RWP.
373 " 'Don't forget, Lindbergh's' ": *BG,* Nov. 10, 1940.
373 " 'She's another wonderful woman' ": ibid.
374 "KENNEDY DISAVOWS INTERVIEW": From selection of unidentified newspaper clippings, Nov. 12, 1940, BHCL.
374 " 'and in the course' ": Crider to Krock.
374 " 'Well, the fat's' ": *Boston Evening Transcript,* Nov. 13, 1940.
374 " 'there seems to be' ": Crider to Krock.
374 " 'that a reputable' ": Joseph Pulitzer to JPK, Nov. 15, 1940, copy in AKP.
374 " 'told to forget it' ": Coughlan to Whalen.
374 " 'You seem to have' ": Krock to JPK, Nov. 12, 1940, AKP.
375 "Henry Luce's *Fortune* magazine": Martin, *Henry and Clare,* p. 194.
375 " 'I showed him' ": Sulzberger, *Last of the Giants,* pp. 630–31.
375 "Kennedy now tried to blackmail": RJW, p. 344; and MB, p. 224.
375 " 'whatever the facts' ": Krock to JPK, Nov. 12, 1940.
375 " 'There's been a big' ": Macdonald to JFK, n.d. (Nov. 1940), JFKPP, Box 4B. Macdonald felt that, since "Joe [Jr.] campaigned around here for 'our leader' and spoke very well on the radio the couple of times I heard him," and Honey Fitz had resembled a case of champagne bottles "popping off at a great rate over all the [radio] stations all the time," Ambassador Kennedy was at perfect liberty to speak his mind: ibid.
375 " 'Here is a government' ": *Wall Street Journal,* Nov. 14, 1940.
376 " 'undeterred by Munich' ": U.K. High Commissioner, NZ, to Sir Eric Machtig, Feb. 4, 1941, FO 371/255, Public Record Office, Kew, England. See also Charles Higham, *American Swastika* (N.Y.: Doubleday, 1985), p. 157.
377 " 'Have become very fond' ": JFK to KLB, Nov. 13, 1940, KLBP.
377 " 'I would like to express' ": B.H. Lidell Hart to JFK, Oct. 24, 1940, JFKPrePres, Box 73.
377 " 'when the danger' ": ibid.
378 "would give Jack much": "I can't begin to tell you how much it interested me, and how much I appreciate your taking the time to write to me in such detail," Jack responded. "I really feel it is the greatest compliment on the book that I could have received. I want to apologize for getting the 'motto' wrong," he added, having mistranscribed the quotation from Liddell Hart

that he'd appropriated as the motto of *Why England Slept:* "I do not criticize persons, but only a state of affairs. It is they, however, who will have to answer for defensiveness at the bar of history." Liddell Hart had actually written, "deficiencies at the bar of history."

"I remember how it happened," Jack explained. "It was just the day before the manuscript was to go to the publishers. I had been looking through some of my notes in a desperate effort to get a good motto and I suddenly came upon two sentences in pencil, somewhat smudged as they had been made way back in February. I said, 'Why didn't I notice them before. It hits it right on the nose.' I realize now that the reason that I didn't notice it before was that 'deficiencies' did not get blurred into 'defensiveness' until the heat of summer. Nevertheless, deficiencies or defensiveness, it expresses perfectly what I hoped the book would express and I hope you will forgive my error—it is really a great sentence": JFK to Lidell Hart, Dec. 6, 1940, JFKPrePres, Box 73.

378 "message of Nazi doom": At his conference in Hollywood, Kennedy threw "the fear of God into many of our producers and executives," Douglas Fairbanks, Jr., complained in a letter to the president, "by telling them that the Jews were on the spot and they should stop making anti-Nazi pictures or using the film medium to promote or show sympathy to the cause of the democracies versus the dictators," and categorically asserting that "this country can reconcile itself to whomsoever wins the war and adjust our trade and lives accordingly": Douglas Fairbanks, Jr., to FDR, Nov. 19, 1940, Mellet Correspondence, FDRL.

379 " 'to keep the United States' ": *Stanford Daily,* Nov. 15, 1940; and *BH,* Nov. 14, 1940.

379 " 'His father had taken' ": Dr. Theodore Kreps, quoted in Douglas Hall, "Kennedy," six-page transcript, Douglas Hall Papers.

379 " 'It is my feeling' ": KLB interviews.

379 " 'As you may' ": JFK to KLB, Nov. 14, 1940, KLBP.

380 " 'Why not purchase' ": William Coleman to JFK, n.d. (1940), JFKPP, Box 4A.

380 "actual sales": "In answer to your letter dated November 24, 1959, the records available indicate that the total sales of your publication 'Why England Slept' were approximately 12,000 copies." William Boulet, president, Wilfred Funk, Inc., to JFK, "Why England Slept" file, JFKPOF, Personal Secretaries Files, Box 129.

380 " 'He was a celebrity' ": James interview.

381 " 'How could he help' ": ibid.

382 " 'I said something' ": ibid.

382 " 'that you're a "well" ' ": Macdonald to JFK, n.d. (1940), JFKPP, Box 4B.

382 " 'The point is' ": James interview.

382 "professed to be puzzled": "Why did he leave Stanford? You know, I can't answer that! I really don't know. I think he was through with auditing his courses, and what he wanted to accomplish there, he'd done. . . . I was very sorry to see him go and we had a real sad parting of the ways. . . . But he was leaving for good. He gave me his radio. He let me have his car for as long as I wanted it (he asked me to arrange to have it shipped home for him). But we made no plans to see each other again. I saw him off on the plane when he left": H.P. Fullerton interview.

382 " 'Her role was' ": James interview.

383 " 'see [Doctor] Jordan' ": JFK to KLB, Dec. 3, 1940, KLBP.

383 " 'When will outline' ": JPK to JFK, Dec. 5, 1940, JFKPP, Box 4A.

Part 8: Joining the U.S. Navy

387 " 'only shows an approach' ": JFK to JPK, Dec. 5, 1940, JFKPP, Box 4A.

387 " 'On November 6' ": ibid.

388 " 'that I am a defeatist' ": ibid.

390 " 'have to be subtly' ": ibid.

390 " 'after a short holiday' ": *London Times,* Dec. 2, 1940.

390 " 'to have you carry' ": letter to JFK, Dec. 9, 1940, JFKPP, Box 4B.

390 " 'Jack dear, I wanted' ": Harriet Price to JFK, n.d. (Dec. 1940), JFKPP, Box 4B.

391 " 'a supplementary note' ": JFK to JPK, n.d. (Dec. 1940), JFKPP, Box 4A.

392 "Hines Page": Walter Hines Page had been U.S. ambassador to Britain, 1913 to 1918, and was later excoriated by American isolationists for his pro-British attitudes.

392 " 'for the purpose of' ": Original press release on organization of the committee, Dec. 15, 1940, HUD/36, Harvard University Archives. An official Harvard Committee Against Military Intervention letter was sent the following day, inviting Joseph P. Kennedy, Sr., "to Harvard

and address us as part of your campaign 'to help the President keep the United States out of the war.' " Ibid.

393 " 'just saying' ": JFK to JPK, n.d. (Dec. 1940).

394 " 'Every business deal is' ": *War and Society,* Proceedings of the Institute of World Affairs, Eighteenth Session, the Mission Inn, California, December 8 to 13, 1940, Volume XVIII, Rufus B. von Kleinsmid and Charles E. Martin, coeditors, Published for the Institute of World Affairs by The University of Southern California, Los Angeles, California, 1941, pp. 59–63.

394 " 'one requisite for the restoration' ": ibid., p. 68.

394 " 'on the unusual growth of' ": ibid., p. 231.

394 " 'The chairman' ": ibid., pp. 291–294.

395 " 'He authored' ": JCB, p. 104.

395 " 'I certainly enjoyed' ": JFK to Clare Luce, Dec. 19, 1940, Clare Boothe Luce Papers, Library of Congress, Washington, D.C.

396 " 'The experience of' ": FDR "Fireside Chat on National Security," Dec. 29, 1940, Samuel

Rosenman, ed., *The Public Papers of Franklin D. Roosevelt, 1940: War—and Aid to the Democracies* (N.Y.: Macmillan, 1941), p. 633.

396 " 'Hitler would ride' ": MB, p. 235.

396 "a letter that Ludlow": ibid., p. 232.

396 " 'urged me to speak' ": JML, Ch. 52, p. 7.

396 " 'I continued to complain' ": ibid.

396 " 'That's one of the difficulties' ": ibid.

397 " 'I told him it was too bad' ": ibid., p. 8.

397 " 'He told me he would like' ": ibid.

397 " 'in the circumstances' ": ibid., p. 10.

397 " 'For all practical purposes' ": ibid.

398 " 'America First organizing' ": telegram to JPK, Jr., Dec. 25, 1940, JFKPP, Box 4B.

398 "a meeting of the Foreign Policy": unidentified news clip, BHCL.

398 " 'My elder brother' ": JFK interview, JMBP.

398 " 'Will be more than interested' ": Torbert Macdonald to JFK, n.d., (1940), JFKPP, Box 4B.

398 " 'Let me know' ": ibid.

399 " 'I was glad' ": Blair Clark to JFK, Jan. 11, 1941, JFKPP, Box 4A.

400 " 'Your article on' ": Macdonald to JFK, n.d. (Feb. 1941), JFKPP, Box 4B.

400 " 'He knew that was' ": Phyllis Brooks Macdonald interview of June 2, 1991.

400 " 'Tell your father' ": Macdonald to JFK, n.d. (1941), JFKPP, Box 4B.

401 " 'who impressed me' ": JFK to John Hersey, Feb. 22, 1941, JFKPrePres, Box 73.

401 " 'I expressed some' ": JCB, p. 109.

402 "Kennedy gave orders": JPK to James Seymour, Feb. 13, 1941, JSP.

402 " 'It was all set up' ": JCB, p. 109.

402 " 'With arms wide' ": M. Cárcano to Eunice Kennedy, April 19, 1941, JFKPP, Box 4B.

402 " 'merely because it' ": JFK, Round Table Summary, Economic Hemispheric Co-operation, Kleinsmid and Martin, *War and Society*, p. 165.

402 " 'for building capital industries' ": ibid., p. 166.

402 " 'hemispheric solidarity' ": ibid., p. 167.

402 " 'The total volume of our' ": ibid.

403 "On May 7, 1941": JFK passport file, JFKPP, Box 6.

403 " 'perfectly feasible for' ": *BG*, April 30, 1941.

403 " 'Need I say more?' ": JFK to Camman Newberry, n.d. (1941), CNP.

403 " 'it would be strongly' ": RKRC, p. 279. To Col. Edwin Sibert, the U.S. military attaché in Rio de Janeiro, JFK later sent a thank-you note for his special briefing on South American defense postures, enclosing a copy of his book: letter, n.d. (May 1941), sold at auction Dec. 11, 1964. Arthur Krock had meanwhile given JFK several letters of introduction to contacts "for John to take to South America" and had recommended JFK "look up John Payson in New York. John will give him the best possible introductions to the government in Colombia": Arthur Krock to JPK, April 24, 1941, AKP, Box 31.

404 " 'There's a very interesting' ": The Hon. Mrs. A.I. Astor interview of Jan. 14, 1991. The letter is preserved in the Cárcano family archives at Córdoba.

404 " 'He was a man' ": ibid.

404 " 'Am on my way' ": JFK to KLB, n.d. (June, 1941), KLBP.

404 " 'he had a good' ": KLB interviews, JCB and JFKLOH.

405 "volunteered for the Officers' ": "I think, in that Jack is not doing anything, and with your stand on the war, that people will wonder what the devil I am doing back at school with everyone else working for national defense." JPK, Jr. to JPK, quoted (no month or source given) in Arthur Schlesinger, Jr., *Robert Kennedy and His Times* (Boston: Houghton Mifflin, 1978), p. 40. Although the papers of JPK, Jr. are still sealed at the JFKL, a letter from Capt. Alan Kirk, the director of Naval Intelligence, to Captain C.W. Carr, director of the Naval Hospital, Chelsea, Mass., is on file at the Naval Historical Center. Dated March 24, 1941, the letter requests preferential treatment in passing JPK, Jr. into the Naval Academy Reserve class. The letter refers to "the second son of Mr. J. P. Kennedy, our late Ambassador to England," and has thus been thought to refer to JFK, although the letter clearly states that "the boy is at the Harvard Law School" and has a handwritten attachment, "Harvard 1938, magna cum laude, Law School, J.P.K., Jr., USNA—Mar, 3 mns [months] & sea duty": Alan G. Kirk Mss., Operational Archives, Naval Historical Center, Washington Navy Yard, Washington, D.C.

405 "on his return from": RKRC, p. 284.

405 " 'Dear Cam: Just returned' ": JFK to Newberry, July 8, 1941, CNP.

406 "DEAR PRIVATE NEWBERRY": JFK to Newberry, July 23, 1941, CNP.

406 " 'I am having Jack' ": JPK to Alan G. Kirk, Aug. 1941, as quoted in JCB, p. 113.

406 " 'Usual childhood diseases' ": Report of physical examination, Aug. 5, 1941, Naval Records files, JFKPP, Box 11A.

406 " 'It was no trouble' ": Alan G. Kirk to JPK, Aug. 8, 1941, as quoted in JCB, p. 114.

407 " 'is the most intelligent' ": Office of Naval Intelligence, Investigation Report, Sept. 10, 1941, MS-88-105, JFKL.

407 " 'one of the most' ": ibid.

407 " 'very well' ": ibid.

407 "On August 28, 1941": JFK to Lt. Sternfelt, Aug. 28, 1941, JFK Vertical File, Box 2, JFKL.

407 " 'I am interested' ": Naval Intelligence, Investigation Report.

407 " 'subject's education' ": ibid.

408 " 'rushing through the' ": JFK to Lt. Sternfelt, Sept. 22, 1941, JFK Vertical File, Box 2.

408 " 'I think the Secretary' ": "The Reminiscencs of Alan G. Kirk," Columbia University Oral History Collection.

408 " 'It had a very' ": ibid.

408 " 'report on Eastern' ": JFK to Newberry, Oct. 9, 1941, CNP.

409 " 'the services of Ensign' ": Chief of Naval Operations to the chief of the Bureau of Navigation, Oct. 17, 1941, JFKPP, Box 11A.

410 " 'In addition to serving' ": JFK to William Coleman, n.d., CNP (Coleman forwarded the letter to Newberry, writing across the top: "Quite a gem!").

410 " 'Dear Admiral Mahan' ": William Coleman to JFK, n.d., Wed., (1941), JFKPP, Box 4A.

410 " 'Frankly, Kennedy,' ": William Coleman to JFK, n.d., Tues. (1941), JFKPP, Box 4A.

410 "wrote gloomily to Krock": JPK to Krock, Oct. 10, 1941, AKP.

411 " 'a loss of stability' ": DKG, p. 637.

411 " 'Joe and I brought' ": RKRC, p. 286.

411 "Rose altered her version": DKG, pp. 640–44.

411 " 'Her level of frustration' ": ibid., p. 640.

411 " 'She was in a convent' ": ibid.

411 " 'I was always worried' ": ibid.

411 "sexually abused Rosemary": Anonymous interview (close female friend of JFK).

411 " 'The operation eliminated' ": RKRC, p. 286.

412 " 'My wife and I' ": *NYT*, Oct. 30, 1940.

412 " 'Present at this dinner' ": "Dinner at Mrs. Patterson's—About November 10, 1941," Speech and Book Material, Nov. 11, 1941–Jan. 23, 1942, JFKPrePres, Box 11.

413 " 'never considered himself' ": Charles Spalding interview of Aug. 29, 1990.

414 "Wheeler warned Forrestal": "Dinner at Mrs. Patterson's."

414 " 'It made people stop' ": ibid.

414 "claiming that his treatment": JPK to Max Beaverbrook, Nov. 13, 1940, as quoted in DEK, p. 301.

414 "had been a Wall Street swindler": Forrestal, beginning as a bond salesman, had become an early partner in 1923 in the firm of Dillon, Read & Co: "a collection of new men, ambitious arrivistes led by a buccaneer of exceptional ability who was determined to push his firm into the very front ranks of wall street." Townsend Hoopes and Douglas Brinkley, *Driven Patriot, The Life and Times of James Forrestal* (N.Y: Knopf, 1992), p. 55. After the Wall Street crash, the company was exposed by the Senate Subcommittee on the Stock Exchange Investigation for having fraudulently and secretly deprived stockholders of their rightful shares, as well as for making astronomical "killings" in fees, at the expense of smaller merchant houses: Ibid., pp. 95–101. Forrestal himself was arraigned for deliberate tax avoidance using Canadian companies: ibid., pp. 73 and 101–5.

414 " 'admired Forrestal tremendously' ": Charles Spalding, JFKLOH.

414 " 'He said that the U.S.' ": "Dinner at Mrs. Patterson's."

415 " 'I replied' ": ibid.

Part 9: Inga Binga

419 " 'The mother and Jack' ": The Hon. Mrs. A.I. Astor interview. Jan. 14, 1991.

419 " 'I think Jack was wary' ": Henry James interview of Aug. 23, 1991

420 " 'think of anybody' ": RFK interview, CBSI.

420 " 'I enjoy your' ": JFK to RFK, Nov. 1941, as quoted in DKG, p. 631.

421 " 'If she came' ": Arthur Krock interview, JCBP.

421 " 'listened to what' ": Inga Arvad, "Consequences" (sequel to "Truth"), memoir, n.d. (1945), RMP.

421 " 'She couldn't write' ": Frank Waldrop interview of May 15, 1989.

421 " 'I had been living' ": Paige Huidekoper interview, JCBP.

421 " 'curled up' ": "Kennedy 1941–42," Arvad memoir. RMP.

423 " 'Jack's an interesting' ": John White interview of Oct. 11, 1988.

423 " 'We all built him' ": Arvad, "Kennedy 1941–42," Arvad Memoir. "Sundays the Kennedy kids would get on the phone, all bright and gay, all reporting their news. . . . Even among the kids there was an admiration society seldom seen in any family. I remember when Robert visited his brother and sister in Washington. He must have been about 14 or 15. Jack was so proud of him and he said, 'this is the brightest of all the kids, he is going to be a lawyer.' It was an embarrassed blushing youngster, but with a determined look." Ibid.

423 " 'Aren't you afraid' ": Burton K. Wheeler, *Yankee from the West* (N.Y.: Octagon Books,

1977), p. 32. Hitler, in his fateful speech of Dec. 11, 1941, referred to the Victory Program document as one of his reasons for declaring war on the United States. See Ch. 11, "The Theft of the Victory Program," in Charles Higham, *American Swastika*, (N.Y.: Doubleday, 1985) pp. 134–48.

423 "hands not only of the German embassy": Hans Thomsen, the chargé d'affaires at the embassy, cabled Ribbentrop on Dec. 4, 1941, that publication in "leading isolationist newspaper, the Washington Times-Herald, of the secret report of the American High Command . . . is causing a sensation here." Ibid., p. 144.

423 " 'A great war' ": Frank Waldrop, "JFK and the Nazi Spy," *Washingtonian*, April 1975.

424 " 'There were six' ": JCB, p. 120.

424 " 'the best of the Bronxville' ": RFK to children, Dec. 5, 1941, JFKPP, Box 4A.

424 " 'I work on Saturday' ": JFK to KLB, Dec. 3, 1941, KLBP.

424 " 'During this period' ": KLB interviews, JCB and JFKLOH.

425 " 'a day that will live' ": Franklin D. Roosevelt, *The Public Papers and Addresses of Franklin D. Roosevelt: The Call to Battle Stations*, ed. Samuel Rosenman (N.Y.: Macmillan, 1942), pp. 514–16.

425 " 'This will gripe' ": JFK to KLB, Dec. 12, 1941, KLBP.

425 " 'Saw Kick last night' ": William Coleman to JFK, n.d. (1941), JFKPP, Box 4A.

426 " 'The knives flashed' ": Waldrop, "JFK and Nazi Spy."

426 " 'A very good friend' ": Arvad, "Consequences."

426 " 'Mrs. Patterson and I' ": ibid.

427 " 'I said 'O.K.' ' ": Waldrop interview.

427 " 'You should have seen' ": Arvad, "Consequences."

427 " 'Mrs. Paul Fejos, alias' ": "Memorandum for the Director, Re: Mrs. Paul Fejos, nee Inga Arvad," Dec. 12, 1941, Hoover Confidential Files: JFK, FBI Records.

427 " 'I don't believe' ": Waldrop interview.

428 " 'I think rumors' ": Huidekoper interview.

428 " 'jealous female' ": Arvad, "Kennedy 1941–42."

428 "Inga Marie Arvad": "Mrs. Paul Fejos, nee Inga Arvad, WAS," file no. 100-3816, April 8, 1942, Hoover Confidential Files: JFK.

428 " 'She had great' ": ibid.

429 " 'wanted a very blonde' ": ibid.

429 " 'He was a fellow' ": Waldrop interview.

429 " 'she began working' ": "Memorandum Re: Mrs. Paul Fejos," Dec. 12, 1941, Hoover Confidential Files: JFK.

429 "with what wonder": Inga had been repeatedly denounced (by women, interestingly) to senior officials in the FBI, however, since her arrival in the U.S. in 1940. See Hoover Confidential Files: Inga Arvad, Nov. 16, 1940 (to J. Edgar Hoover), and Nov. 14, 1941 (to L.B. Nichols), and from Nichols to Clyde Tolson—"I was confidentially advised today that Arvid [sic] was Hitler's publicity agent in Norway [sic]. . . . According to my source of information she was picked up by Mrs. Patterson and has either thoroughly hoodwinked Frank Waldrop or else Waldrop is acting under orders." Hoover Confidential Files: Arvad, FBI Records.

429 "she had become ' "enraged' ": "Memorandum Re: Mrs. Paul Fejos," Dec. 12, 1941, Hoover Confidential Files: JFK.

430 "the FBI was only": See Curt Gentry, *J. Edgar Hoover, The Man and the Secrets* (N.Y.: Norton, 1991), pp. 70–84.

430 " 'her interviews with' ": "Memorandum Re: Mrs. Paul Fejos," Hoover Confidential Files: JFK.

430 " 'One of her interviews' ": ibid.

430 " 'In Arvad's desk' ": "Mrs. Paul Fejos, WAS," Hoover Confidential Files: JFK.

431 "Admiral von Levetzov": Inga Arvad, "1935: Von Levetzov," Arvad memoir, n.d., (1945), RMP.

431 " 'Dr. Goebbels called her' ": "Mrs. Paul Fejos, WAS," Hoover Confidential Files: JFK.

432 " 'for whom she evidently . . .' ": ibid.

432 " 'reflects that Hitler' ": The actual caption/credit ran: "International News Photo: *Gets Nazi Job*. Copenhagen, Denmark . . . Meet *Miss Inga Arvad*, Danish Beauty, who so captivated Chancellor Adolf Hitler during a visit to Berlin that he made her Chief of Nazi Publicity in Denmark. Miss Arvad had a colorful career as a dancer, Movie Actress and newspaper woman before Herr Hitler honored her for her 'perfect Nordic beauty' ": "Mrs. Paul Fejos, nee Inga Arvad, Internal Security," file no. 100-3816, Jan. 6, 1942, Hoover Confidential

Files: Inga Arvad, FBI Records. As Inga later lamented when Louella Parsons, a fellow journalist in Los Angeles, resurrected the same photo and caption in 1945 to destroy Inga's romance with Robert Boothby, the Scottish M.P. and protégé of Winston Churchill, she could have sued, but didn't. "My experience as a newspaper woman had taught me that the old Danish saying that 'the more you stir in dirt, the more it smells,' is true. . . . On the other hand if one lets it ride and die down, something else would happen someday: I'll get married, or I'll die, or I'll have a baby, and again some irresponsible reporter will dig in the 'morgue,' find the *same* picture with the *same* caption, and see a good story in it. . . . To sum it all up, what has actually happened? *I interviewed Hitler. At the time it was a journalistic feat which was greatly envied and much appreciated by the paper I worked for.* For years it lay dormant. There was no trouble about it. In fact, on occasions I was praised for it. Then suddenly during a war hysteria, coupled with jealousy of a co-reporter, what had been a halo fell down and became a noose." Arvad "Consequences."

432 "Axel Wenner-Gren": See Ch. 14, "The Swedish Sphinx" in Higham, *American Swastika,* pp. 165–73. A more sympathetic view of Wenner-Gren was taken by John W. Dodds in *The Several Lives of Paul Fejos* (N.Y.: The Wenner-Gren Foundation, 1973), pp. 78–81.

432 "the Viking Fund": Wenner-Gren established the Viking Fund in Feb. 1941 with an endowment of $2.5 million—"the proceeds of the business transaction which the [U.S.] government was challenging. . . . Paul [Fejos] lived in a kind of love-hate relationship with the man who used him time and again, but whom Paul bent toward benevolent purposes which Wenner-Gren would never otherwise have dreamed of. Like many men of power, he [Wenner-Gren] was seduced into philanthropy." Ibid., pp. 78 and 80.

432 "the *Southern Cross*": Ironically, the *Southern Cross*, "headed for New York and Nassau with a giant cargo of gold, supplied by Goering for the use of Nazi agents overseas," had found itself on the same course as the S.S. *Athenia,* and had picked up three hundred survivors, which it transferred to the ill-fated *City of Flint*: Higham, *American Swastika,* p. 166.

433 "circumvent strict British": ibid., p. 167. The duke's most recent biographer, Philip Ziegler, considers him a weak, rather pathetic, and easily misguided individual, and portrays Wenner-Gren as, in retrospect, equally harmless: Philip Ziegler, *King Edward VIII* (N.Y.: Alfred Knopf, 1991). This was not, however, the view of British and American intelligence, nor of the FBI, at the time. Higham, *American Swastika,* pp. 157–64 and 168–70.

433 "a possible coup d'état": ibid., p. 169.

433 " 'a letter from' ": Arvad, "Consequences."

434 " 'Her English wasn't' ": John White interview, JCBP; and JCB, p. 134.

434 " 'We all sort of' ": Waldrop interview.

434 " 'She was wavering' ": White interview, Oct. 11, 1988.

435 " 'a gray overcoat' ": "Mrs. Paul Fejos," file no. 100-3816, Jan. 22, 1942, Hoover Confidential Files: Arvad.

435 "THEY ARE NOT KEEPING": JFK to Inga Arvad, Jan. 1, 1942, as quoted in "Mrs. Paul Fejos," Jan. 6, 1942, Hoover Confidential Files: Arvad.

436 " 'relative to Ambassador Kennedy's' ": "Memorandum for Mr. Ladd," Jan. 1, 1942, Hoover Confidential Files: Arvad.

436 "on January 9, 1942,": The chief of Naval Operations to the chief of the Bureau of Navigation, Jan. 9, 1942, JFKPP, Box 11A.

436 " 'unsure' ": Inga Arvad, "The Story," treatment, n.d. (c. 1945/6), RMP.

437 "a most unpredictable man": "A little under six feet in height, he was well-proportioned, lithe and graceful. He had sharp blue eyes and a long upper lip which could twist at the corners into a kind of elfin smile, or could turn grim when he wanted to be grim. . . . All his life he walked out on careers, and women . . . it was not always clear what orbit his mood would take him into": Dodds, *Lives of Paul Fejos*, pp. 52–53.

437 " 'He begs her' ": Arvad, "The Story."

437 " 'I am a bit puzzled' ": Paul Fejos to Arvad, Jan. 11, 1942, file no. 100-3816, Hoover Confidential Files: JFK. Original letter in RMP.

438 " 'has a detective' ": Olga Arvad to Inga Arvad, Jan. 17, 1942, as quoted in "Fejos, nee Arvad" file, Hoover Confidential Files: Arvad. Original letter in RMP.

438 " 'When I walked into' ": Arvad, "Consequences."

438 " 'was transferred' ": ibid.

438 " 'Well here it is' ": Fejos to Arvad, Jan. 12, 1942, RMP.

438 " 'J. Kennedy in,' ": Diary of John White, quoted in DKG, p. 633. White's entry for Jan. 13, 1942, ran: "No sooner in office than become embroiled in the great case of the Ambassador's Son and the Beautiful Blonde Spy." LMT, p. 108.

438 " 'the clown' ": Fejos to Arvad, Jan. 12, 1942, RMP.

439 " 'was extremely mad' ": Arvad, "Consequences."

439 " 'it had come' ": "Memorandum for Mr. Ladd, Re: Mrs. Paul Fejos, alias Inga Arvad," Jan. 17, 1942, Hoover Confidential Files: Arvad.

439 " 'They shagged my' ": Robert Donovan, JFKLOH.

439 " 'This officer's services' ": Report on the Fitness of Officers, Oct. 27, 1941–Jan. 19, 1942, JFKPP, Box 11A.

439 " 'so upset over' ": S.A.D. Hunter interview, JCBP; and JCB, p. 136.

440 " 'Joseph Patrick Kennedy' ": Waldrop, "JFK and Nazi Spy."

440 " 'She knows' ": Arvad, "The Story."

440 " 'The father, who knows' ": ibid.

441 " 'It is the opinion' ": "Memorandum for Mr. Ladd, Re: Mrs. Paul Fejos," Jan. 21, 1942, Hoover Confidential Files: Arvad.

441 " 'This surveillance' ": "Mrs. Paul Fejos," Jan. 2, 1942, Hoover Confidential Files: Arvad.

441 " 'Is the sun' ": Arvad to JFK, Jan. 19, 1942, JFKPP, Box 4A.

441 " 'My first spanking' ": Arvad to JFK, Jan. 20, 1942, JFKPP, Box 4A.

442 " 'Leaving I saw' ": Arvad to JFK, Jan. 26, 1942, JFKPP, Box 4A.

442 " 'Guess by whom?' ": Inga was referring to KK.

443 " 'It is funny' ": Arvad to JFK, Jan. 26, 1942, JFKPP, Box 4A.

443 " 'Could I do' ": Arvad to JFK, n.d., Wed. (1942), JFKPP, Box 4A.

444 "Colonel 'Wild Bill' Donovan": Hoover's almost pathological jealousy and hatred of Donovan is well chronicled in Gentry, *Hoover*, pp. 74, 152, and 391. See also Anthony Cave Brown, *The Last Hero: Wild Bill Donovan* (N.Y.: Times Books, 1982).

444 " 'current investigation' ": J. Edgar Hoover to the Attorney General, Jan. 21, 1942, Hoover Confidential Files: JFK.

444 " 'got more possibilities' ": "Memorandum for Mr. Kramer, Re: Inga Arvad," Jan. 29, 1942, Hoover Confidential Files: JFK.

444 " 'report of all' ": Edward J. Ennis to Hoover, Feb. 4, 1942, Hoover Confidential Files: Arvad.

444 " 'everytime I heard' ": Arvad, "Consequences."

445 " 'Distrust is a very' ": Arvad to JFK, Jan. 27, 1942, JFKPP, Box 4A.

445 " 'Inga returned with' ": KK to JFK, Jan. 28, 1942, JFKPP, Box 4A.

445 " 'It seems he is' ": RFK to children, Oct. 9, 1942, JFKPP, Box 4A.

445 " 'It does my heart' ": Torbert Macdonald to JFK, n.d. (1942), JFKPP, Box 4B.

445 " 'toted Torb around' ": KK to JFK, Jan. 28, 1942.

445 " 'The trouble is' ": Arvad to JFK, Jan. 27, 1942.

446 " 'Exhibit c' ": JFK to Arvad, n.d. (1941), "Mrs Paul Fejos, WAS," April 8, 1942 Hoover Confidential Files: JFK.

446 " 'next week' ": "ARV Summary," Jan. 30–31, 1942, Hoover Confidential Files: Arvad.

446 " 'Why don't you tell' ": "ARV Summary," Feb. 3, 1942.

447 " 'Did you say' ": "ARV Summary," Jan. 30–31.

447 " 'Inga lets him' ": Quoted in Arvad letter to JFK, Dec. [sic; should be Feb.] 4, 1942, JFKPP, Box 4A.

447 " 'How did you like' ": "ARV Summary," Jan. 30–31, 1942.

447 " 'the name of the lady' ": JFK to Arvad, n.d. (1941), "Mrs. Fejos, WAS," April 8, 1942, Hoover Confidential Files: JFK.

447 " 'Wonderful, wonderful' ": "ARV Summary," Jan. 30–31, 1942.

448 " 'Big Jack is very' ": "ARV Summary," Feb. 3, 1942.

448 " 'Why don't you' ": ibid.

450 " 'Jack dashed off' ": RFK to children, Feb. 2, 1942, JFKPP, Box 4A.

450 " 'seems to be' ": RFK to children, Feb. 10, 1942, JFKPP, Box 4A.

450 " 'Jack understood' ": KLB interviews.

450 " 'I don't know if' ": JFK to Ralph Horton, n.d. (1942), JFKPP, Box 4B.

450 " 'My limited experience' ": JFK to Jane Mohan, Jan. 11, 1942, as quoted in JCB, pp. 126–27.

450 " 'The Irish' ": Astor interview.

451 " 'I had a long' ": "Talk with Lord Halifax," speech and book material, Oct. 1941–Jan. 1942, JFKPrePres, Box 11.

451 "Mrs. Laski's later,": Freda Laski, JFKLOH. See also Herbert Parmet, *Jack, The Struggles of John F. Kennedy* (N.Y.: Dial Press, 1980), p. 75, inter alia.

451 " 'Halifax believed' ": "Talk with Lord Halifax."

452 " 'He promised' ": ibid.

452 " 'On the morning of' ": ibid.

453 " 'terrible commentary' ": ibid.

453 "Friday, February 6": The day Inga arrived, the Charleston *News and Courier* noted, under the headline ON DUTY HERE and a full-length photograph of JFK in uniform, JFK's own arrival "for duty at the navy yard here. A graduate of Harvard in the class of 1940, Ensign Kennedy is the author of 'Why England Slept.' "

453 "the alias Barbara White": "Mrs. Paul Fejos, alias Inga Arvad, Barbara White," file no. 100-3816, Feb. 9, 1942, Hoover Confidential Files: Arvad.

453 " 'They were not observed' ": ibid.

453 " 'No contacts' ": ibid.

454 " 'Mrs. Fejos stated' ": ibid.

454 " 'Kennedy and Mrs. Fejos' ": ibid.

455 " 'indicated that their father' ": D.M. Ladd, "Memorandum for the Director," Feb. 6, 1942, Hoover Confidential Files: JFK.

455 " 'What is home?' ": Arvad to JFK, n.d., Mon. (Feb. 9, 1942), JFKPP, Box 4A.

456 " 'I always felt' ": Betty Coxe Spalding interview of Dec. 19, 1990. (The Dallas Cowboys football team boasts a famous, physically well-endowed group of female cheerleaders).

456 " 'They were all' ": "ARV Summary," Feb. 10, 1942.

457 " 'He thinks he is coming' ": "ARV Translations," Feb. 9, 1942, Hoover Confidential Files: JFK.

457 " 'he had found out' ": "ARV Summary," Feb. 12, 1942.

457 " 'Don't you people' ": JFK to Arvad, n.d. (Feb. 1942), as quoted in "Mrs. Paul Fejos, WAS," April 8, 1942, Hoover Confidential Files: JFK.

458 " 'This life I'm living' ": JFK to KLB, Feb. 12, 1942, KLBP.

458 " 'As I read' ": ibid.

459 " 'paragraph 4 line 6' ": ibid.

459 " 'how frustrated' Jack was": KLB interview, CBSI.

459 " 'It was a boring, stinking' ": JCB, p. 148.

459 " 'My plans are' ": JFK to KLB, Feb. 14, 1942, KLBP.

460 " 'Have I discussed' ": ibid.

460 " 'temples' ": Arvad to JFK, Feb. 14, 1942, JFKPP, Box 4A.

461 " 'You once said' ": Arvad to JFK, n.d., Wed. (1942), JFKPP, Box 4A.

461 " 'Whatever happens' ": Arvad to JFK, Feb. 14, 1942, JFKPP, Box 4A.

461 " 'Once,' Frank Waldrop later": Waldrop, "JFK and Nazi Spy."

461 " 'Are you living' ": "ARV Summary," Feb. 17, 1942.

462 " 'She said she' ": ibid.

462 " 'I never quite understood' ": Fred Rosen interview of Nov. 1, 1990.

462 " 'She called him' ": "ARV Summary," Feb. 17, 1942.

463 " 'You played the leading' ": ibid.

463 " 'ain't no Kennedy' ": ibid.

463 " 'She wanted to know' ": ibid.

464 " 'Dear Mr. President' ": JPK to FDR, Dec. 7, 1941, in Elliott Roosevelt, ed., *FDR, His Personal Letters: VOL II* (N.Y.: Duell, Sloan and Pearce, 1950), p. 1290.

464 " 'He said he had' ": RFK to children, Feb. 10, 1942, JFKPP, Box 4A.

464 " 'Jack is a darlyn' ": Clare Boothe Luce to JPK, Feb. 5, 1942, JFKPP, Box 4A.

465 " 'Heavens knows' ": JPK to JFK, Feb. 9, 1942, JFKPP, Box 4A.

465 " 'The newspapers still' ": JFK to Ralph Horton, n.d., JFKPP, Box 4B.

465 " 'The situation that now' ": Draft manuscript dated Feb. 14, 1942, "Speech and Book Material," N.Y. Office, 1937–43, JFKPrePres, Box 11.

466 " 'There are two' ": ibid.

467 " 'It is assumed' ": ibid.

467 "(who was being kept": Hoover to Gen. Edwin Watson for FDR, April 20, 1942, and Gen. Edwin Watson to FDR, May 4, 1942, Justice Dept., FBI Reports, Box OF 10b-15, FDRL.

467 " 'might not be' ": "Speech and Book Material." "What really would have brought it home would have been if the Japs had grabbed off the Dutch East Indies a week ago," JFK wrote to his father, " + we would have have had our Munich—there would have been much gnashing of teeth in the Waldorf Towers, etc." JFK to JPK, n.d. (penciled 'Spring 1940?'), noted in JMB "material for inserts" file, JMBP.

468 " 'perhaps the greatest' ": DEK, p. 311.

468 " 'This would be a fatal' ": "Speech and Book Material."

468 " 'Then would Winston Churchill's' ": ibid.

469 " 'You know, I think it's' ": JFK to KLB, Feb. 12, 1942, KLBP.

470 " 'try and get' ": JFK to KLB, Feb. 14, 1942, KLBP.

470 "weekend of February 21–22": "ARV Summary," Feb. 19, 1942.

470 " 'Kathleen was sweet' ": Arvad to JFK, n.d., Mon. (1942), JFKPP, Box 4A.

470 " 'her father regularly paid": White interview.

471 " 'she was the only' ": "ARV Summary," Feb. 19, 1942.

471 " 'A great deal' ": J.R. Ruggles to Director, FBI, Feb. 23, 9142, file # 100-1181, Hoover Confidential Files: Arvad.

471 " 'became involved' ": ibid.

472 " 'Upon another occasion' ": ibid.

472 " 'On the same evening' ": ibid.

473 " 'I love them' ": Arvad to JFK, Feb. 23, 1942, JFKPP, Box 4A.

473 " 'as I know he is' ": Arvad to JFK, n.d., Tues., (1942), JFKPP, Box 4A.

474 " 'a rather interesting conversation' ": KLB to JFK, n.d., Mon., (1942), JFKPP, Box 4A.

474 "the ex-ambassador, too": JPK had been mentioned many times during the FBI investigation, always as a third party. By late February, however, telephone calls direct to his house were being recorded: "Particular attention is called to records 8 and 9 which contain the telephone conversation between Kennedy to [*sic*] the home of Joseph P. Kennedy on the night of February 22, 1942." Agent Ruggles to Hoover, Feb. 23, 1942, Hoover Confidential Files: JFK. For JPK's reaction, see Gentry, *Hoover*, p. 469. (In her "Story" treatment, Arvad certainly suspected JPK of involvement in JFK's January exile from Washington, writing: "It strikes John that maybe his father had something to do with his quick transfer.")

474 "Jack, having spoken": S.K. McKee to Director, FBI, Feb. 24, 1942, and "ARV Summary," Feb. 25, 1942.

474 " 'listen to conversation' ": "Memorandum for Mr. E.A. Tamm, Re: Inga Arvad," March 2, 1942, Hoover Confidential Files: JFK.

474 " 'she was quitting' ": ibid. The special agent in charge of the case, notifying Hoover, wrote that "it is believed Jack Kennedy had broken off relations with Inga Arvad, giving the reason that some friend of his, probably the Naval Intelligence, had told Kennedy the Naval authorities were watching him and apparently had a microphone in her room": McKee to Director, March 5, 1942, file no. 100-3816, Hoover Confidential Files: JFK.

474 " 'how things are' ": Macdonald to JFK, March 3, (1942), JFKPP, Box 4B.

475 " 'Surprised to hear' ": "ARV Summary," March 7, 1942.

475 "apartment had been burglarized": ibid. Some of the items were recovered from a chief petty officer of the U.S. Coast Guard, who had resided in the same building as Inga. He claimed he had bought them for fifty dollars from a third party. No attempt, however, was made to locate the original thief, raising some question about the FBI's involvement. "Memorandum for Mr. Tolson," from L.B. Nichols, Dec. 10, 1943, and subsequent files nos. 87-332, Hoover Confidential Files: Arvad.

475 " 'Why didn't you come?' ": "ARV Summary," March 7, 1942.

477 " 'come down this week-end' ": ibid.

477 " 'My impulse is' ": Arvad to JFK, March 11, 1942, JFKPP, Box 4A.

479 " 'how your plans' ": Macdonald to JFK, March 9 1942, JFKPP, Box 4B.

479 " 'with me as your valet' ": ibid.

479 " 'if I was getting' ": JFK to James Rousmanière, n.d. (1942), JFKPP, Box 4A.

480 " 'trying to get' ": "ARV Summary," Feb. 25, 1942.

480 " 'Inga seemed very sad' ": KK to JFK, n.d. (1942), JFKPP, Box 4A.

480 " 'I imagine that' ": JFK to Lady Astor, March 3, 1942, JFKPrePres, Box 73.

481 " 'to give a boost' ": ibid.

482 " 'After reading the papers' ": JFK to KK, March 10, 1942, JFKPP, Box 4A.

482 " 'I loved getting' ": Astor to JFK, April 17, 1942, JFKPP, Box 4A.

483 " 'stopped off to see me' ": JPK to JFK, March 14, 1942, JFKPP, Box 4A.

483 " 'that with you' ": JPK to KK, n.d. (1942), JFKPP, Box 4A.

483 " 'A funny thing happened' ": KK to parents, March 20, 1942, JFKPP, Box 4A.

483 " 'From what I've read' ": JFK to JPK, Feb. 25, 1942, JFKPP, Box 4A.

484 " 'I don't want to appear' ": JPK to FDR, March 4, 1942, President's Personal File, Box 207, FDRL.

484 "Arthur Krock loyally orchestrated": MB, p. 247.

484 " 'Daddy arrived yesterday' ": KK to JFK, n.d., Tues. (1942), JFKPP, Box 4A.

484 "mountains of mail": See OF 3061-3074, Box 2, FDRL. "There are plenty of capable men in this country besides this Kennedy" was a typical remark in these letters. "He has done enough damage while he was in England and belongs to the native fascist or appeasement group." H. Klein, ibid. "Such an appointment would have serious effect on the morale and faith of both the British and American people who have followed Kennedy's record, and want this war run by people we can trust." Frank and Isabel Stewart, ibid. "As our ambassador to England he was a complete flop. One mistake is conceivable but to repeat it, is deplorable." Celia Cohen, ibid. In the newspaper *PM*, the editor, Ralph Ingersoll, blasted the proposed appointment of Kennedy to be "Shipping Czar" with a damning "Open Letter to the Friends of the President," recalling what Ingersoll had heard and seen in London: "So Joseph Kennedy is tough is he? . . . I was in London when Joe Kennedy was there and the bombs were falling and they had a different definition of the word *tough*. It did not include Kennedy's anxiety to get out of town when the bombs fell. Joe Kennedy was scared from the beginning of the blitz until he quit and went home, and everyone knew it. . . . Kennedy's personal brand of loyalty was to turn on his chief and always to end his insincere public flattery with personal attacks on Roosevelt. He did the same thing with the British. . . . The man you are recommending is personally disloyal to the President and has been spreading the most fantastic tales ever since he lost his nerve in England. The man you are recommending is is an expert—in what? In gambling on the Stock Exchange? . . . In loud mouthed defeatism?" *PM*, April 12, 1942.

484 "regretfully declined": MB, p. 245. "Naturally, I am very unhappy that I have not had a

chance to do anything, but I've made every effort that I could," he lied to Lord Beaverbrook. JPK letter of Aug. 12, 1942, Beaverbrook Papers, House of Lords Library Archives. The next effort Kennedy made was to ensure that Roosevelt's choice for the Democratic nomination for senator from Massachusetts was defeated by the Republican, Henry Cabot Lodge, Jr.: MB, pp. 248–49; and DEK, p. 320.

485 " 'symptomatic' ": draft typescript letter with handwritten JFK annotations, n.d. (1942), JFK to JPK Correspondence file, JFKPP, Box 4A.

486 " 'the failure to solve' ": JFK to Blair Moody, March 10, 1942, JFKPrePres, Box 74.

487 " 'finished the Atlas courses' ": JFK to KLB, March 11, 1942, KLBP.

487 "was granted ten days' leave": Ensign John F. Kennedy to Capt. F.D. Pryor, n.d. (1942), JFKPP, Box 11.

487 " 'lonesome for the [Stanford] farm' ": Henry James to Harriet Price, n.d. (1942), JCBP.

487 " 'tongue-lashing' ": JCB, p. 149.

488 " 'I didn't like him' ": James interview.

488 "as Arthur Krock observed": Krock interview, JCBP.

488 " 'I am afraid' ": JFK to Lady Astor, March 3, 1942, JFKPrePres, Box 73.

489 " 'Henry, you know' ": James interview.

489 "Jack flew to the Mayo": Medical Record, Lt. John Fitzgerald Kennedy, Dec. 15, 1944, JFKPP, Box 11A.

489 " 'Dear Children: Since I' ": RFK to children, March 27, 1942, JFKPP, Box 4A.

489 " 'She said you are' ": KLB to JFK, n.d., Thurs. (1942), JFKPP, Box 4A.

489 " 'as active in leaping' ": KLB to JFK, March 14, 1942, JFKPP, Box 4A.

490 " 'let me know' ": KLB to JFK, n.d., Thurs. (1942).

490 " 'modest, quiet' ": Report on the Fitness of Officers, n.d., 1942.

490 " 'I expect to be' ": JFK to KLB, April 9, 1942, KLBP.

490 " 'to be performed' ": Ens. John F. Kennedy to the chief of the Bureau of Navigation, April 9, 1942, JFKPP, Box 11.

490 " 'to report to the U.S.' ": The Commandant, Sixth Naval District, to Ensign John F. Kennedy, April 11, 1942, JFKPP, Box 11.

490 " 'during the past 6' ": Medical Record, Lt. John Fitzgerald Kennedy.

490 " 'He now feels' ": Clinical Record, Ensign John F. Kennedy, May 21, 1942.

491 " 'how you are getting' ": Arvad to JFK, April 23, 1942, JFKPP, Box 4A.

491 " 'Last night' ": Arvad to JFK, May 25, 1942, JFKPP, Box 4A.

491 "a 'good long letter' ": ibid.

492 " 'Be brave' ": Arvad to JFK, May 23, 1942, JFKPP, Box 4A.

492 " 'any attempted German' ": "Memorandum re Iquitos and the Axel Wenner-Gren Expeditions" sent by Hoover to Gen. Watson, secretary to the president, "as of possible interest to the President and to you," April 27, 1942, FDR Official File, OF 10b-15, FDRL.

492 " 'His wife,' ": ibid.

492 " 'in view of the connection' ": FDR to Hoover, May 4, 1942, FDR Official File, OF 10b-15, FDRL.

492 " 'she was very disgusted' ": "Mrs. Paul Fejos, was. [sic], Weekly summary from June 23 to June 28, inclusive, 1942," July 1, 1942, Hoover Confidential Files: Arvad, FBI Records.

493 " 'that you have decided' ": KLB to JFK, n.d., Fri. (1942), JFKPP, Box 4A.

493 " 'He has become disgusted' ": JPK to JPK, Jr., June 20, 1942, as quoted in DKG, p. 634.

493 " 'In this Navy' ": JFK to KLB, April 9, 1942, KLBP.

493 " 'Thank you for' ": JFK to RFK, n.d. (1942), as quoted in DKG, p. 635.

493 " 'conduct a Bible class' ": ibid.

494 " 'in the spring of 1942' ": Rosen interview.

494 "on July 9 awarded Jack": Officer in charge to Ens. John F. Kennedy, July 9, 1942, JFKPP, Box 11A.

494 "ENS JOHN F KENNEDY": The Commandant, Sixth Naval District, to Ens. John F. Kennedy, July 22, 1942, JFKPP, Box 11.

494 " 'He went through town' ": "ARV Summary," July 24, 1942. JFK asked to come to Inga's apartment, but she refused. Ibid.

Part 10: On The Way To War

497 " 'Came back on' ": KK to JFK, n.d., Wed., (late July 1942), JFKPP, Box 4A. KK was hoping to get transferred to London as a war correspondent, but the prospects seemed poor. "The London trip is off. I have been to see quite alot [sic] of folk in the State Dept. and this government has an agreement with London about the number of correspondents they will send abroad. Also your visa has to be okayed by the Embassy which [thanks to JPK's reputation in Britain] I don't think the British will be too happy to do." Ibid.

497 " 'You are probably' ": JFK to KLB, n.d. (July 1942), KLBP.

497 " 'if going depends on' ": Torbert Macdonald to JFK, June 26, (1942), JFKPP, Box 4B.

497 " 'Torb never got here' ": JFK to KLB, n.d. (July 1942), KLBP.

498 " 'You'll be interested' ": ibid.

498 " 'He told me confidentially' ": ibid. JPK, smarting from Roosevelt's unwillingness to give him a war appointment commensurate with his rank, had immediately embroiled himself in the Massachusetts senatorial primary campaign, determined that Roosevelt's choice for the Democratic nomination be defeated. He therefore sponsored his father-in-law to run against Joseph Casey, though backed off when Roosevelt personally asked him to desist, and the cost of victory—about $200,000—in advertizing seemed unlikely, in the end, to be enough to beat Henry Cabot Lodge, Jr., in the runoff.

Having split the Democratic party, Kennedy is believed to have backed Cabot Lodge, Jr., the Republican, rather than see Roosevelt's nominee take the seat: MB, pp. 248–49; and DEK, p. 320.

498　"'not doing too'": JFK to KLB, n.d. (July 1942), KLBP.

498　"'the war fever'": ibid.

499　"'I have applied'": ibid.

499　"'He got Bulkeley'": ibid.

500　"'Of course he never'": Ralph Pope interview of Jan. 24, 1989.

500　"'Bulkeley had just returned'": Adm. John Harllee interview of Sept. 23, 1990.

500　"Congressional Medal": Aug. 4, 1942: See William B. Breuer, *Sea Wolf* (Novato, Calif.: Presidio, 1989), pp. 102–3.

501　"'The PT boat is'": *N.Y. Journal American*, Sept. 5, 1942.

501　"the only torpedo launched": Robert J. Bulkeley, *At Close Quarters: PT Boats in the United States Navy* (Washington, D.C.: U.S. Government Printing Office, 1962), p. 24.

501　"'500 PT boats'": *N.Y. Journal American*, Sept. 5, 1942.

501　"'He and I served'": Alvin Cluster interview of Nov. 8, 1990.

502　"'Bulkeley arrived, I guess'": Fred Rosen interview of Nov. 1, 1990.

502　"'The thing you really'": Harllee interview.

503　"'no idea Kennedy had'": Adm. John Bulkeley interview of Sept. 23, 1990.

503　"'a stinking lie'": Harllee interview.

503　"'It's true'": Bulkeley interview.

504　"'Joe Kennedy had been'": Quoted in Breuer, *Sea Wolf*, p. 108.

504　"'There ain't a gut'": Walter Trohan interview, RJWP.

504　"'out of the question'": Harllee interview.

505　"'When you think of'": ibid.

505　"'Those of you'": *Chicago Tribune*, Sept. 5, 1942.

505　"'His whole attitude'": RFK to children, Oct. 9, 1942, JFKPP, Box 4A.

507　"'Jack Kennedy: A Medical Story'": KLB interviews.

507　"'You cannot believe'": RFK to JPK, Jr., Sept. 29, 1942, as quoted in DKG, p. 647.

507　"'Jack came home'": JPK to JPK, Jr., Oct. 1, 1942, as quoted in DKG, p. 646.

508　"an anachronism": "Looking back at the evolution of PT boats and the integral administrative work, any comprehensive survey shows missteps, false tacks, and incongruities.... The program was undertaken blindly": "An Administrative History of PT's in World War II," prepared on Feb. 15, 1946, by the Office of Naval History, but quickly censored and in the end never published: Microfilm copy (catalogued as "The Unpublished History of PT Boats in WWII"), Operational Archives, Naval Historical Center, Washington Navy Yard, Washington, D.C.

508　"Modeled on British designs": ibid., pp. 19–39. The story of Henry Sutphen and Irwin Chase's visit to England in February 1939 to buy, privately, a British MTB, and the manner in

which American torpedo-boat fantasies grew not from tactical naval needs (the General Board of the U.S. Navy feeling that guns, listening gear, and depth charges would be more important for coastal defense), but from pressure from civilian entrepreneurs, was one of the many reasons why the highly critical "Administrative History of PT's" could never be published. In its 1942 sales booklet, *Elco: The Inside Story of Motor Torpedo Boats,* the Elco company proudly pointed to Lt. John Bulkeley's feats of courage and supposed torpedo triumphs, and quoted Governor Charles Edison, at the launching of *PT 103,* "who spoke too of the great debt of gratitude which this country owes to daring officers like Lieutenant Bulkeley. . . . He paid special tribute to Henry R. Sutphen, executive vice-president of the Electric Boat Company, whose enterprise and ingenuity have been largely responsible for the success of the torpedo boat program. . . . 'We would not have the PT boats today if he had not had the confidence in their future; if he had not, at his own expense, gone to England to buy the first one; and if he had not dared to risk $750,000 on the Bayonne plant that builds them.'" *Elco: The Inside Story of Motor Torpedo Boats,* p. 19. Over 300 Elco PT boats were eventually built. Bryan Cooper, *PT Boats* (N.Y.: Ballantine, 1970), p. 42. (In Britain, MTBs formed part of the U.K.'s Coastal Forces, dubbed "costly farces" by the regular navy. Ibid.)

508　"'I understand that you'": JPK, Jr. to JFK, Tues., n.d., JFKPP, Box 4A.

508　"'Kennedy was the only'": Rosen interview.

508　"'I went out with'": JCB, p. 73. According to Charlotte McDonnell's college roommate, Ann Kelley, Charlotte's father so hated JPK that he would not allow Charlotte to bring JFK into their house: "No child of that man is entering my home!": Peter Collier and David Horowitz, *The Kennedys: An American Drama* (N.Y., Summit Books, 1984), p. 92.

509　"'No—that frantic looking'": JFK to KLB, Nov. 19, 1942, KLBP.

509　"'I know Nils'": Inga Arvad to KK, n.d. (1942), JFKPP Box 4A.

509　"'seems to be cooling'": JFK to KLB, Nov. 19, 1942, KLBP.

509　"'I suppose Kick'": ibid.

510　"'The atmosphere'": Inga Arvad, "The Story," treatment, n.d. (c. 1945/46), RMP.

510　"'Honey Fitz draws'": Copy in "Mrs. Paul Fejos, nee Inga Arvad," file no. 100-3816, March 4, 1942, Hoover Confidential Files: JFK, FBI Records. According to a telephone call monitored by the FBI on Feb. 18, 1942, Inga had lunch with Honey Fitz that day. "He told her that Jack is tops of the Kennedy family. . . . She said that Paige Heidekoper [*sic*] told her that Honey Fitts [*sic*] had been offered a job [by the White House] four months ago just to tease his [Jack's] father—that Jimmy Roosevelt had told her [Paige]. Arvad said that Paige Heidekoper always had information from the White House back door." "ARV Summary," Feb. 19, 1942,

Hoover Confidential Files: Inga Arvad, FBI Records.

510   " 'I think the world' ": Charles Spalding interview of Aug. 29, 1990.

511   " 'Look at this' ": Rosen interview.

511   " 'Dear Children' ": RFK to children, Oct. 9, 1942, JFKPP, Box 4A.

512   " 'going into the Quartermaster' ": Rosen interview.

513   " 'I was a southerner' ": Sim Efland interview of Nov. 6, 1990.

513   " 'One afternoon' ": Rosen interview.

513   " 'the problem his back' ": Joe Atkinson interview of Nov. 28, 1990.

514   " 'The first time' ": Rosen interview.

514   " 'To my knowledge' ": Cluster interview.

514   " 'This was a terrible' ": Rosen interview.

514   " 'The training was' ": Cluster interview. See also "History of PT's" pp. 122–154. The Melville center had begun operating on March 16, 1942. "Normally, the Training Center was equipped to handle 860 enlisted students and ninety student officers. . . . The staff comprised forty-six officers and 187 enlisted men. . . . Physically the base was comprised of 286 buildings: thirteen structures devoted to office space, thirty-four classrooms, forty-two maintenance buildings and 197 living quarter huts. . . . By 27 March 1942. . . . ten boats of Motor Torpedo Boat Squadron Four had reported to the Training Center to provide basic operational training for personnel under instruction. . . . The Training Center . . . tried desperately to make each man a jack-of-all-trades. The result was inevitable: the caliber of men turned out was lowered by inefficient training. . . . MTBSTC cannot be held entirely responsible for the poor training that evidenced itself in MTB personnel . . . for the basic training of students was generally poor. Melville was then confronted not only with its own task of training men to become efficient PT boat operators, but it was also necessary to give them grounding in subjects which should have been assimilated in boot camp." Ibid., pp. 126–27. (By Feb. 1, 1943, the Melville Training Center numbered 119 officers under instruction and 569 enlisted men. Melville War Diary, National Archives RG no. 181, Records of the U.S.N. Districts and Shore Establishments, 1st Naval District, MTB Squadrons Training Center, Melville, R.I., Military Reference Branch, National Archives, North East Regional Office, Waltham, Mass. The MTB Center was disestablished in 1946, having given training to almost 2,000 officers and 12,500 enlisted personnel. Unpublished PT history, chapter entitled "Kennedy," p. 87, furnished to author by Naval War College, Naval Historical Collection, Newport, R.I.)

514   " 'It was unbelievable' ": Rosen interview. "In a gunnery subdepartment, Torpedo Fire Control, problems did arise. This was the problem of instructing officers in the proper methods and procedures of accurate torpedo firing." "Administrative History of PT's" p. 136. The size of the Melville classes in torpedo firing, moreover, numbered "seldom less than thirty

and running as high as seventy. Because of the lack of individual instruction in such large classes . . . instruction suffered." Ibid., p. 137.

514   " 'Jack had asked' ": Rosen interview.

515   " 'I was Senior Instructor' ": Rear-Admiral John Harllee, JFKLOH.

515   " 'in a dreadful mess' ": RFK to children, Oct. 9, 1942, JFKPP, Box 4A.

515   " 'I got Torb' ": JFK to KLB, Nov. 19, 1942, KLBP.

516   " 'Frankly, I have not' ": Sen. David I. Walsh to John F. Fitzgerald, Dec. 21, 1942, as quoted in DKG, p. 648.

516   " 'It was a distinct' ": Walsh to JFK, Nov. 9, 1942, David I. Walsh Papers, Holy Cross College.

516   " 'this officer only recently' ": Report on Fitness of Officers, March 1, 1943, JFKPP, Box 11A.

516   " 'so that I could' ": AWRH, p. 39.

516   " 'the game was only underway' ": Paul Fay interview of June 11, 1989; draft ms. in PBFP and AWRH, p. 39.

517   " 'I mean, he seemed' ": Barney Ross interview, CBSI.

517   " 'He suffered' ": John Iles interview of Nov. 28, 1990.

517   " 'in all weathers' ": The author of the U.S. Navy's "Administrative History of PT's" concluded that Melville was an inappropriate location for initial training: "New England winters are not kind, and sub-zero in PT boats are not pleasant and many times not practical. The lack of of underway training of personnel attending Melville during the winter months could not be replaced by classroom work, and the consequent effect was a lack of proficiency in boat handling upon the part of personnel reporting to the operating squadrons. . . . The only solution to this problem is a move to a more favorable climate. . . . The success of the activity at Miami suggests that a PT school could have been set up more efficiently in Florida. Weather caused the cancellation of at least thirty per cent of scheduled underway operations at Melville": "Administrative History of PT's," p. 142. "Climatic and sea conditions were the determining cause of Melville's failure as a shakedown base. The rough winter weather made operating almost impossible. The crews were more concerned about hanging on and keeping warm than they were about learning their duties." Ibid., p. 164.

518   " 'it was so cold' ": Efland interview.

518   "on January 8, 1943": The Commander, Motor Torpedo Boat Squadron 4, to Lt. (jg) John F. Kennedy, Jan. 8, 1943, JFKPP, Box 11.

518   " 'I was damn glad' ": JFK to KLB, Jan. 30, 1943, KLBP.

519   " 'I got my orders yesterday' ": JFK to Robert F. Kennedy, Jan. 10, 1943, as quoted in Arthur Schlesinger, Jr., *Robert Kennedy and His Times* (Boston: Houghton Mifflin, 1978), p. 51.

519   "Entering the Intracoastal Waterway": Medical Record, Lt. John Fitzgerald Kennedy, JFKPP, Box 11A.

519   " 'It's colder in North Carolina' ": Torbert Macdonald interview, JCBP.

519   " 'gastro-enteritis, acute' ": Medical Record, Dec. 15, 1944, Lt. John Fitzgerald Kennedy.

519   " 'While working in' ": "Report on Civilian, Medical, and Hospital Treatment of the Personnel of the Navy and Marine Corps," form dated Jan. 14, 1943, JFKPP, Box 11A.

519   " 'I'm now on my way' ": JFK to KLB, Jan. 30, 1943, KLBP.

520   " 'Your friend Jock' ": ibid.

520   " 'was causing his mother' ": JPK to M. Sheehy, Oct. 28, 1942, as quoted in DKG, p. 647.

520   " 'It was a very normal' ": Macdonald, JFKLOH.

520   " 'The challenge of Joe' ": Iles interview.

520   "Despite unanimously": HS, pp. 187–88.

520   " 'Joe is in Puerto Rico' ": JFK to KLB, Jan. 30, 1943, KLBP.

521   " 'for duty in connection' ": Supervisor of Shipbuilding, U.S.N. to Lt. (jg) John F. Kennedy, Feb. 11, 1943, JFKPP, Box 11.

522   " 'shafted' ": Macdonald, JCBP.

522   " 'that I be reassigned' ": Lt. (jg) John F. Kennedy to the Chief of Bureau of Personnel, Feb. 20, 1943, JFKPP, Box 11.

522   " 'You are hereby' ": Chief of Naval Personnel to Lt. (jg) John F. Kennedy, Feb. 19, 1943, JFKPP, Box 11.

Part 11: *PT 109*

526   " 'probably be my last' ": JFK to Mrs. Billings, n.d. (Feb. 1943), KLBP.

526   " 'finally' en route": JFK to KLB, n.d. (Feb. 1943), KLBP.

526   "He reported at eleven A.M.": Naval Orders, Naval Records file, JFKPP, Box 11.

526   " 'I was rooming with' ": James Reed interview of Oct. 7, 1990.

526   " 'grandson of J. P. Morgan' ": "Came out with a fellow called Pennoyer—whose grandfather is J. P. Morgan. In addition to having a fine set of cigars with JPM on the band—which would undoubtedly have pleased brother Joe—but which seemed to me inferior to my Robert Burns—he had lived a good bit of his life out at Wall Hall," Jack wrote tongue-in-cheek to his parents. They had even shared the same butler: "Evidently the whole Morgan family has lived in some awe of Butler Bengley and he was extremely interested in Bengley's reaction to the nine Kennedys." JFK to parents, May 10, 1943, JFKPP, Box 5.

527   " 'We were all sitting' ": James Reed interview, JCBP; and JCB, p. 173.

527   " 'famous patience' ": HS, p. 190.

527   " 'lacked the ability' ": ibid., p. 193.

527   " 'the first time' ": ibid.

527   " 'the ship was' ": "Edgar Stephens Remembers JFK He Knew in Navy," *Albany Gazette* (New Albany, Mo.), Nov. 23 and 25, 1988, JFKPOF, Box 132.

527   " 'I remember him talking' ": Reed interview, JCBP; and JCB, p. 173.

527   " 'We spent countless' ": Reed interview, JCBP.

528   " 'I was really persuaded' ": Reed interview, Oct. 7, 1990.

528   "PT boats proved particularly ineffective": "The Japanese had outfought us completely. They had better torpedoes, they had better night tactics. The American navy was inexperienced. We didn't, at the start, have much down there. It was very loosely organized, and Nimitz had sent the PT boats down there because he had nothing else. It was really desperate times; there were many times when the high command, I think, even back in Washington, wondered whether they would have to evacuate the marines off of Guadalcanal. It was almost a Dunkirk situation, it was touch and go all the

time. Now, the PT boats came in and they really didn't do an awful lot of damage to the Japanese. They sank a submarine, they sank a destroyer, but they were more of a threat really, because they did not do a lot of damage. The people that were manning those PT boats to a great extent were inexperienced. Many of them were what they called ninety-day wonders—there were a few professional longtime officers, but most of them were pretty green kids. The navy never did have that much respect for PT boats; the navy tolerated PT boats as they tolerated John Bulkeley. Guys like Bulkeley and Rickover are thorns in the side of the navy. They are not in the same cast of naval officers like the Halseys and the Nimitzes and people like that. They are a very odd bunch—as most of us in PT boats were. PT boats had a lot of color. Young guys that would want to go out, be brave in battle and everything after Pearl Harbor, wanted to get into the air force. But that took some doing. You had to have quite a bit of training, and there were a lot of people standing in line for it. Many of the people in PT boats were unable to get into flight training, so they chose PTs second, because they were exciting and glamorous. They had a lot of write-ups in newspapers and magazines. And then after MacArthur was taken out of the Philippines on Bulkeley's boat, that gave them even more glamour. And it was an exciting thing because all the young officers of JFK's rank in those days knew if they went on board ship they would be relatively insignificant, as an ensign or a junior lieutenant, they would be a minor cog in the whole thing. So it was an exciting thing to go to PT boats. It was a way to have your own destiny in your own hands: you were captain of your own ship, even though it was relatively small": Alvin P. Cluster interview of Nov. 8, 1990.

528   " 'Never,' he wrote, 'in the history' ": Samuel Eliot Morison, *History of United States Naval Operations in World War II, Vol. V: The Struggle for Guadalcanal, August 1942–February 1943* (Boston: Little, Brown, 1949), pp. 370–71.

529   "Admiral King, disliking Churchill's": See Ch. 11: "Cartwheel," Ronald Specter, *Eagle Against the Sun* (N.Y.: Vintage, 1985).

529   " 'The American people' ": ibid., p. 222.

529 "The ungentlemanly squables": ibid., p. 225.
530 "arrived in Espíritu Santo": Naval Orders, JFKPP, Box 11.
530 " 'I must say' ": Reed interview, Oct. 7, 1990.
530 " 'one of those little' ": ibid.
530 "Approaching the north coast": JCB, p. 175.
531 *"Kanawha"*: Confidential Report by the Commanding Officer, U.S.S. *Kanawha*, April 12, 1943, forwarded to JFK by Stanley C. Myers, Nov. 20, 1961, JFKPOF, Box 132.
531 " 'In regard to not' ": JFK to KLB, May 6, 1943, KLBP.
531 "finally reached Lunga Roads": JCB, p. 176.
532 " 'out there about' ": John Iles interview of Nov. 28, 1990.
532 " 'Squadron Two was' ": JCB, p. 177.
532 " 'Dear Inga Binga' ": JFK to Inga Arvad, n.d. (spring 1943), RMP.
533 "on April 25, 1943, Jack assumed command": JCB, p. 181.
533 "Bryant Larson's old *PT 109*": Built in Bayonne, N.J., the Elco Company's *PT 109* was delivered to the navy on July 10, 1942, sent to the Panama Defense Force, and then shipped out to the Solomons after the invasion of Guadalcanal, becoming Squadron Two's flagship in Oct. 1942, and commencing patrol duty in Nov. 1942: the start of three exhausting months of combat as American naval forces attempted to stop the Japanese from reinforcing and finally evacuating their troops from Guadalcanal. Later in February *PT 109* helped screen the invasion of the Russell Islands and on April 7, 1943, shot down an enemy bomber attacking Tulagi harbor: "History of U.S.S. PT-109," seven-page stenciled monograph compiled by the Navy Department, Office of the Chief of Naval Operations, Division of Naval History (OP 09B9), Ships' Histories Section, Jan. 5, 1961: JFKPOF, Box 132. Under "Combatant features," the ship's history noted: "Motor Torpedo Boats, contrary to some beliefs, did not go seventy miles-per-hour nor did they launch torpedoes at high speed. PT 109 was a plywood boat measuring 80 feet in length and had a maximum beam of 20 feet. Her maximum draft was six feet and she was powered by three 12-cylinder Packard engines, each of which developed 1,350 horse power. She could carry as many as four 21-inch torpedoes and originally mounted four .50 caliber machine guns in twin turrets. One 20-mm was mounted on the fantail and small arms included tommyguns, springfield rifles and riot shotguns. She could communicate with a blinker tube having an eight-inch searchlight, and by voice radio which had a range of 75 miles. Her maximum speed for a range of 358 miles was 35 knots. A full-load patrol speed of nine knots would be usual in covering a 600-mile range. Under ideal conditions, and after torpedoes have been fired, a maximum speed of approximately 46-knots is possible. Her usual complement was three officers and nine men." Ibid.
534 " 'a mark on his' ": JCB, pp. 178–79.
534 " 'It's not bad here' ": JFK to KLB, May 6, 1943, KLBP.

534 " 'As to conditions' ": JPK to parents, April 1943, as quoted in DKG, p. 648.
534 " 'Received your latest' ": JFK to KLB.
535 " 'Among the gloomier' ": JFK to Arvad, n.d., RMP.
535 " 'Just heard Aldie' ": JFK to KLB.
535 " 'Good bunch out here' ": JFK to parents, May 14, 1943, JFKPP, Box 5.
536 " 'I was interested' ": ibid.
536 " 'What actually happened' ": ibid.
536 " 'No one out here' ": ibid.
536 "his father's mood": "I am still in the leper colony. . . . I am so disgusted at sitting on my fanny at Cape Cod and Palm Beach when I really believe I can do something in this war effort." JPK to Frank Kent, March 2, 1943, Frank Kent Papers, Maryland Historical Society, Baltimore (misdated in DKG, p. 636). In his diary, Felix Frankfurter noted on May 12, 1943, that Kennedy was consumed with hate of Hopkins and himself "whom he, in his foolish and ignorant way, blames for his exclusion from participation in the conduct of the war. I don't suppose it ever enters the head of a Joe Kennedy that one who was so hostile to the war effort as he was all over the lot, and so outspoken in his foulmouthed hostility to the President himself, barred his own way to a responsible share in the conduct of the war." Felix Frankfurter Diary, Felix Frankfurter Papers, Library of Congress.
537 " 'be back within' ": JFK to parents, May 14, 1943, JFKPP, Box 5.
537 " 'As far as the length' ": ibid.
537 " 'I know it is futile' ": ibid.
537 " 'I'm extremely glad' ": JFK to Arvad, n.d., RMP.
538 " 'We had a raid' ": JFK to parents, May 14, 1943.
539 " 'In regard to the food' ": JFK to Arvad, n.d., RMP.
539 "He marked Jack": Report on the Fitness of Officers, May 29, 1943, JFKPP, Box 11A.
539 " 'The Japanese had outfought' ": Cluster interview, Nov. 8, 1990.
540 " 'My father was a Red Rock' ": Alvin Cluster interview, JCBP.
540 " 'He found this' ": John Iles interview, JCBP.
540 " 'Just had an inspection' ": JFK to Arvad, n.d., RMP.
541 " 'Have a lot of natives' ": JFK to parents, May 14, 1943.
541 " 'When the British' ": A mimeographed history and guide to the Solomons, *The Solomon Islands Today*, by Ens. George Spiegel, USNR, had been published by the Lunga Press, U.S. Naval Base, Lunga, Guadalcanal, in April 1943, and JFK obtained one of the first copies. On p. 4 it was stated that the antagonism of natives toward white men stemmed from the "rapid depopulation that followed the coming of white explorers, traders, missionaries and settlers" who brought "white diseases of small pox, measles, dysentery, influenza, and tuberculosis. A further cause of this reaction was the 19th century practice known as 'black birding' of enslaving these people to work on Aus-

tralian sugar plantations and in the Fiji copra industry." MS-92-54, JFKL.

541 " 'We thought that had' ": Iles interview, JCBP. "Head hunting and cannibalism were common throughout the Solomons until a recent date and are said to exist still in parts of Malaita and Bougainville. Until lately the more peaceful and civilized natives of Guadalcanal were often terrorized by excursions of these fierce man eating tribes from Save Island." Spiegel, *Solomon Islands Today*, p. 4. "Me ate padre," Lani told Iles. Robert J. Donovan, *PT 109: John F. Kennedy in World War II* (N.Y.: McGraw-Hill, 1961), p. 49.

541 " 'His mouth got to watering' ": Iles interview, JCBP.

542 " 'Jack was sort of' ": Barney Ross interview, CBSI.

542 " 'Jack was a good officer' ": John Iles interview, Nov. 28, 1990.

543 " 'It was written' ": ibid.

544 " 'He never tried' ": Reed interview, Oct. 7, 1990.

544 " 'very favorite book' ": ibid.

544 " 'For the chosen few' ": John Buchan, *Pilgrim's Way* (Boston: Houghton Mifflin, 1940), p. 50.

544 " 'as a letter writer' ": ibid., p. 51.

545 " 'a member of' ": ibid., p. 59.

545 " 'He loved his youth' ": ibid., p. 60, from JFK's own original copy of *Pilgrim's Way*, by kind courtesy of James A. Reed.

545 "ordered MacArthur to hurry": "King pointed out that in the past two months the Pacific had been inactive except for conferences and exchanges of telegrams. . . . In his opinion, the inactivity should be ended as soon as possible with the inauguration of offensive operations in the Solomons-Woodlark area." Maurice Matloff, *Strategic Planning for Coalition Warfare, 1943–1944* (Washington, D.C.: Office of the Chief of Military History, Dept. of the Army, 1959), p. 98.

545 " 'a step-by-step advance' ": ibid., p. 99.

546 " 'They started flooding' ": Cluster interview, Nov. 8, 1990.

546 " 'The boats would leave' ": ibid.

546 " 'It didn't have the wild' ": JFK to KK, June 3, 1943, as quoted in DKG, p. 650.

547 "*PT 109* went streaking": Donovan, *PT 109*, p. 68.

547 " 'everybody used to run' ": Charles Harris interview, JCBP.

547 " 'Of course there's the famous' ": Ross interview, CBSI.

547 " 'I'm certain if you' ": Cluster interview, Nov. 8, 1990. See also JCB, p. 198.

547 " 'There was a heavy sea' ": Cluster interview, JCBP; and JCB, p. 198.

548 " 'On the way back' ": ibid.

548 " 'Jesus Christ!' ": Cluster interview, JCBP.

548 " 'in the Blanche Channel' ": Mitchell Britt to Henry Hall Wilson, White House, April 3, 1961, with P.S.: "Several hits were scored on McCawley, which sank like a stone. The re-

mainder of the force escaped [from the PT boats] to the South at flank speed." JFKPOF, Box 132.

548 " 'It was a typical' ": Joe Atkinson interview of Nov. 28, 1990.

549 " 'Out there in the islands' ": Sim Efland interview of Nov. 6, 1990.

549 " 'They were still out' ": Barney Ross interview, JCBP.

549 " 'all the nuns' ": JFK to RFK, June 24, 1943, as quoted in DKG, p. 651.

550 " 'His character' ": Buchan, *Pilgrim's Way*, p. 212. Marked on JFK's personal copy, given to James Reed and kindly loaned to the author.

550 " 'There was a fissure' ": ibid., p. 213.

550 " 'Speaking of Johnny Hersey' ": JFK to KK, June 3, 1943, as quoted in DKG, p. 650.

550 " 'All or Nothing At All' ": "The former ambassador's son had a phonograph and one record, Frank Sinatra's "All or Nothing at All," which was played until it was worn through": Lt. Cmdr. Nicholas Wells in Lynn *Republican*, n.d., JFK Political Scrapbook No. 2, JFKPP. Written and composed by Jack Lawrence and Arthur Altman, Sinatra first recorded the song with Harry James and his Music Makers band in 1939; it sold a meager eight thousand copies. When singing the song in the Palomar Ballroom in Hollywood in 1939, in fact, Sinatra was stopped and the band thrown out. The manager, Sinatra recalled, "said my singing was just plain lousy." Released again in 1943, when Sinatra was the vocalist for the popular *Your Hit Parade* radio program, the record sold more than a million copies: Kitty Kelley, *His Way: The Unauthorized Biography of Frank Sinatra* (N.Y.: Bantam, 1986), pp. 48–50.

551 "Several battalion commanders": For an account of the land campaign, see John Miller, *Cartwheel; The Reduction of Rabaul* (U.S. Army in World War II series) (Washington, D.C.: U.S. Government Printing Office, 1958).

551 " 'The eighty-footers' ": Atkinson interview.

552 "Warfield sent a 'posse' ": See Ch. 14, "Costly Errors," in Robert J. Bulkeley, *At Close Quarters: PT Boats in the United States Navy* (Washington, D.C., U.S. Government Printing Office, 1962), p. 119.

552 " 'I got confused' ": ibid.

552 " 'the biggest shit' ": John Meade interview of Nov. 6, 1990.

552 " 'tactical lessons' ": Warfield's mistake is especially difficult to understand in view of the then-current "Night Patrol and Combat Doctrine" issued by Commander Calvert, the Flotilla One commanding officer, "based on lessons learned in seven months of actual combat and patrol experience in the Southeast Solomons Area against enemy air, surface, and sub-surface craft," dated May 10, 1943. Under the heading "Number of boats on patrol," Calvert laid down that "normally, each patrol group should consist of at least two boats, but not more than three. . . . More than three boats in one formation is unwieldy to handle. The attention necessary for station-keeping lessens the efficiency of lookouts in sighting the

enemy. . . . The officer in command of the group is often forced to break radio silence in keeping his patrol together." "Tentative Motor Torpedo Boat Night Patrol and Combat Doctrine, including Tentative Torpedo Attack Doctrine for Radar Equipped Motor Torpedo Boats," Secret, FD8-1/A16, PT Boat Files, National Archives, Waltham, Mass.

553 "Between July 19": JCB, pp. 202–7.

553 " 'We had a letter' ": JPK to J. O'Leary, Aug. 16, 1943, as quoted in DKG, p. 652. Typically, JPK interpreted this as an opportunity to get his son out of the front line, though given his own reputation in Washington, he must have thought better of pulling any strings, for he added to O'Leary: "I hate to mix into any of his business for fear I'll do the wrong thing." Ibid.

554 "regulation life raft": JCB, p. 207; and Donovan, *PT 109,* p. 97.

554 " 'lousy place' ": JCB, p. 196.

554 " 'We'd been playing poker' ": Ross interview, CBSI.

555 " 'Jap air out to get' ": JCB, p. 209; and Donovan, *PT 109,* p. 100.

555 " 'operate the maximum number' ": ibid.

555 " 'all the boats' ": Ross interview, CBSI.

556 " 'getting the hell out' ": JCB, p. 231.

556 " 'My boat had already' ": Ross interview, CBSI.

556 " 'lost a couple of guys' ": ibid. Edmund Drewitch, aged 30, was injured on June 30, 1943; Maurice Kowal, twenty-one, and Leon Drawdy, 30, were wounded in action on the night of July 19, 1943: Donovan, *PT 109,* pp. 70–72 and 88–91. This left as crew: Ens. Thom, 25, and enlisted men William Johnston, 33, Patrick McMahon, 41, Charles Harris, 20, Edman Mauer, 28, Andrew Kirksey, 25, and John Maguire, 26. These had been joined by four men from Warfield's personnel pool: Raymond Starkey, 29, Gerard E. Zinser, 25, Harold Marney, 19, and Raymond Albert, 20. JCB, pp. 181, 182, 198, and 205.

557 "night blind": Paul Fay interview of June 11, 1989.

557 " 'Kennedy's boat' ": JCB, p. 221; and Hank Brantingham interview, JCBP.

557 " 'In our squadron' ": JCB, p. 221.

557 "for the Tokyo Express": ibid., p. 218.

557 " 'which we saw' ": JCB, pp. 221–24; and Brantingham interview, JCBP.

558 "how Brantingham imagined": "If the enemy is picked up by radar some distance away, every effort should be made to withhold the attack and disseminate all pertinent information to own forces," Commander Calvert laid down in his combat doctrine of May 10, 1943. "This will permit other sections to close in and will make an effective simultaneous attack possible." "Tentative Motor Torpedo Boat Night Patrol."

558 " 'The destroyers were' ": JCB, p. 220.

558 " 'ordered all boats' ": Brantingham interview, JCBP.

558 "only radar set": In Cmdr Calvert's "Night Patrol and Combat Doctrine" of May 10, 1943, it was expressly stated: "If sufficient boats

equipped with radar are available, each patrol section should employ at least one of these boats. The radar equipped boats should then be employed as section guides." "Tentative Motor Torpedo Boat Night Patrol."

558 " 'It was unheard of' ": Fred Rosen interview of Nov. 1, 1990.

559 " 'things were going along' ": Ross interview, CBSI.

559 " 'we had no idea' ": JCB, p. 231; and Harris interview, JCBP.

559 " 'shells were landing' ": "PT 162 and 109 lay to as directed. When the firing began, there was so much and over such a long stretch of coast, they thought shore batteries had opened up and retired to the Northwest, but did not regain contact with the other two boats. After the firing had ceased, they were joined by PT 169 from Division A, and after receiving radio orders to do so, took up station, but did not make contact with PT 157." "Com. MTB Rendova action report of 1–2 August 1943" (written by Commander Warfield on Aug. 5, 1943, for the Commander in Chief U.S. Fleet), JFKPOF, Box 132.

560 "an almost identical fate befell": JCB, p. 227.

560 " 'the longest minutes' ": ibid.

560 "Warfield's third group": JCB, pp. 227–28.

560 " 'My first reaction was' ": Richard E. Keresey interview, JCBP.

561 " 'They were all excited' ": James Woods interview, JCBP; and JCB, p. 229.

562 " 'If you think' ": Keresey interview, JCBP; and JCB, p. 229.

563 " 'Only the division' ": ibid.

563 " 'We didn't know' ": Ross interview, CBSI.

563 "Potter was certain": JCB, p. 227.

564 " 'it was decided to carry on' ": From Katsumori Yamashiro to JFK, Sept. 9, 1960, JFKPOF, Box 132.

564 " '*Amagiri* patrolled at' ": Katsumori Yamashiro, "Collision with Enemy Torpedo Boat," translated from *Suiko* magazine, Sept. 1960, JFKPOF, Box 132.

564 " 'During the unloading' ": ibid.

565 " 'I say definitely' ": Katsumori Yamashiro to James MacGregor Burns, April 24, 1961, JMBP.

565 "HANAMI FABRICATED STORY": *Yomiuri Weekly* (Japanese news clipping, April 1961), JMBP.

565 " 'In the case of' ": ibid.

566 " 'Of course I was' ": Hanami to James MacGregor Burns, July 1, 1959, JMBP.

566 " 'It was August 2' ": ibid.

566 " 'I had come to' ": "Kohei Hanami's Story of PT-109 Sinking," JFKPOF, Box 132.

568 " 'I don't remember' ": JCB, p. 229; and Thomas Warfield interview, JCBP.

568 " 'We had a briefing' ": Warfield interview, JCBP.

568 "Warfield had never trained": Phil Potter interview, JCBP.

568 " 'wasn't a particularly' ": JCB, p. 235.

568 " 'He lost the *109*' ": Jack E. Gibson interview, JCBP.

569 "that's number one . . .": Potter interview, JCBP.

569   " 'It was extremely difficult' ": Ross interview, CBSI.

570   " 'We were crossing' ": JCB, p. 233; and Potter interview, JCBP. "When we finished our sweep to the south and were approaching the reefs around Gizo Island, what you'd do is make a 180-degree turn, which would put Kennedy in the lead, Lowrey would stay in the center and bring me up on the aft quarter." Ibid. "Around 0215 the three [boats] were due East of Gizo Island headed South, in right echelon formation with PT 109 leading, PT 162 second and PT 169 last": "Com. MTB Rendova action report."

570   " 'ten or fifteen' ": Potter interview, JCBP.

570   " 'the destroyer rammed' ": JCB, p. 233; and Phil Potter interview, JCBP.

571   " 'recall what the heck Lowrey did' ": Potter interview, JCBP and JCB, pp. 233–34. "PT 162 [Lowrey] saw on a collision course, a warship headed Northward about 700 yards away. The PT 162 turned to fire its torpedoes, but they did not fire. The PT 162 finally turned to the Southwest upon getting within 100 yards of the warship to avoid collision. Personnel aboard the PT 162 saw 2 raked stacks, and at least 2 turrets aft, and possibly a third turret. At the time of turning, PT 109 was seen to collide with the warship, followed by an explosion and a large flame which died down a little but continued to burn for 10 or 15 minutes. The warship when it was about 3000 yards away headed towards them at high speed." "Com. MTB Rendova action report." Warfield's report made no further mention of Lowrey's *PT 162*, however, or why it failed to look for survivors from *PT 109*.

571   " 'and saw them explode' ": Potter interview, JCBP. "The PT 169 [Potter] stopped just before the warship hit PT 109, turned toward it and fired two torpedoes when abeam at 150 yards range. The destroyer straddled the PT 169 with shell fire, just after its collision with PT 109, and then circled left toward Gizo Island and disappeared. The PT 169 laid smoke screen and zigzagged to the Southeast along the reefs off Gizo Island. About 0245 a wake was seen coming up from the Northwest and on a parallel course. The PT 169 swung around to the left toward the ship (a destroyer) and fired port and starboard torpedoes at 2000 yards. The destroyer turned to its port just in time for the starboard torpedo to hit its bow and explode. The PT 169 continued its swing and retired South through Ferguson Passage at high speed for ½ mile laying smoke and zigzagging and headed for base. All its torpedoes gone." "Com. MTB Rendova action report." The phantom destroyer that

Potter hit remains a mystery, since by 0245 hours all four Japanese destroyers comprising the Tokyo Express were, unknown to Potter, safely out of the area, many miles to the north.

571   " 'We remembered seeing the fire' ": Potter interview, JCBP. However, the "Com. MTB Rendova action report" mentioned no attempt to search for survivors of *PT 109*, either by Lowrey or Potter.

572   " 'As soon as' ": Yamashiro, "Collision."

572   " 'in the early morning' ": *Asahi Shimbun*, Aug. 4, 1943.

572   "Warfield's slate": In his after-action report, Warfield not only ignored the loss of *PT 109* with all hands as well as the failure of other PT boats to search for survivors, but gave a most tendentious account of the battle, recording the sighting of no fewer than five enemy destroyers and claiming to the commander in chief that these were "attacked in Blackett Strait, five or possibly six torpedo hits scored." Worse still, Warfield overlooked many of the real tactical lessons of the fiasco. However, in his "Comments and Recommendations," para. 7, Warfield did acknowledge the fatuousness of his edict against radio communication, recommending that skippers in the future report by radio, in clear, "the type, position, course and speed of the enemy. . . . The boats making contact should continue reports of enemy position, etc., after torpedo firing and as long as the enemy is visible on radar. . . . The Mark VIII torpedo again manifested its want of capacity to inflict real damage. Enemy destroyers kept going after certain hits had been scored. Intelligence reports that 5 unexploded torpedoes are on the shore of Kolombangara Island: "Com. MTB Rendova action report." Ironically, on his recommendation, a number of medals were awarded to the division commanders for the action, despite having absconded with their radar sets and without having made any hits. Arthur Berndtson was credited, in his Silver Star citation, for "exceptionally meritorious conduct in the performance of outstanding services in combat. On the night of 1–2 August 1943 he participated as Division Comdr. in an attack in Blackett Strait against 5 enemy destroyers at Vila, Kolombangara. He made 2 probable hits on an enemy destroyer." Henry J. Brantingham was awarded the Gold Star, in lieu of a second Silver Star, for having "participated in an attack against 5 enemy destroyers in Blackett Straits, during which a total of 5 probable hits were scored." Citation list of March 8, 1950, White House Central Files, Box 722, JFKL.

Part 12: Shipwrecked

575   " 'the next morning' ": JCB, pp. 247–48, and Richard Keresey interview, JCBP.

575   " 'Bill Battle told me' ": John Iles interview of Nov. 28, 1990. The chronicler of *PT 109*, Bob Donovan, who interviewed many of the officers and men involved in the incident, considered Battle the best hope of rescuing the survivors on Aug. 2: "Ensign Battle had wanted to go back

into Blackett Strait during the day on August 2 in PT 171. He might well have found the eleven survivors while they were still clinging to the hulk of PT 109. Under the circumstances, however, he was denied permission": Robert J. Donovan, *PT 109: John F. Kennedy in World War II* (N.Y.: McGraw-Hill, 1961), p. 162.

575 " 'that Kennedy's boat' ": Alvin P. Cluster interview of Nov. 8, 1990.

575 " 'say some masses' ": John Iles interview, JCBP.

575 " 'The night *PT 109*' ": James Reed interview, JCBP.

576 " 'John F. Kennedy and his' ": Draft narrative, PBFP.

576 " 'To me that just' ": ibid. Confirmed in Paul Fay interview of Aug. 30, 1990.

577 "two-thousand-ton Japanese warship": The *Amagiri* was laid down on Nov. 28, 1928, at Ishikawajima shipyard and launched on Feb. 27, 1930. Its length was 392 ft., beam 34 ft. 8 in., and it drew 10 ft. 8 in.. A destroyer of the Fubuki class, whose weight was listed as 1,850 tons, the *Amagiri* is usually recorded as weighing 1,950 tons. (After the capsizing of the *Tomozuru* the Japanese navy apparently reverted to lighter destroyers of the 1,368-ton Ariake class.) The *Amagiri* carried a battle crew of 228 men, including 8 line officers, could make 34 knots, and was armed with 9 torpedo tubes, 10 guns, mine-laying equipment, and 12 depth charges. "First of the modern fleet destroyers, they actually led contemporary destroyer design the world over, introducing enclosed twin-gun mounts, shielded torpedo tubes, and high, all-steel bridges." ONI 222-J, "The Japanese Navy," Official U.S. Navy Reference Manual, June 1945: National Archives, Washington, D.C., Record Group 38, Office of Chief of Naval Operations, Office of Naval Intelligence, Monograph files—Japan. The *Amagiri* struck a mine and sank on April 23, 1944. *Japanese Naval and Merchant Losses During World War II*, Feb. 1947, Prepared by the Joint Army-Navy Assessment Committee: National Archives, ibid.

577 " 'striking it forward' ": "Memorandum to Commander Motor Torpedo Boat Flotilla One: Sinking of PT 109 and subsequent rescue of survivors," Aug. 22, 1943, compiled by Lieutenants (jg) B.R. White and J.C. McClure, JFKPOF, Box 132, hereafter referred to as "White Report."

577 " 'Ship at two o'clock!' ": Donovan, *PT 109*, p. 129.

578 " 'Guy named Kennedy' ": *BG*, June 21–23, 1989.

578 " 'We could see something' ": ibid.

578 " 'Then he started to' ": Charles Harris interview, JCBP.

579 " 'I would say' ": Barney Ross interview, CBSI.

580 " 'It was so dark' ": Gerard Zinser interview, JCBP.

581 " 'Please God' ": *BG*, June 21–23, 1989.

581 " 'We all lay' ": Harris interview, JCBP.

581 " 'We were waiting' ": John Maguire, quoted in *BG*, June 21, 1989.

581 " 'As the dawn' ": Ross interview, CBSI.

581 " 'We were expecting' ": ibid.

581 " 'The next morning' ": Harris interview, JCBP.

582 " 'discussed whether we' ": Ross interview, CBSI.

582 " 'that we'd drift to an island' ": Harris interview, JCBP.

582 " 'almost positive' ": Zinser interview, JCBP.

582 " 'Rather than have' ": Ross interview, CBSI.

583 " 'We had to leave' ": Harris interview, JCBP.

583 " 'We didn't know' ": Ross interview, CBSI.

583 " 'There were lots' ": Harris interview, JCBP.

584 " 'He [Kennedy] had a situation' ": Ross interview, CBSI.

584 " 'We didn't do anything' ": JCB, p. 249.

584 " 'foolish for Kennedy' ": *BG*, June 22, 1989.

584 " 'He had extraordinary' ": Zinser interview, JCBP.

584 " 'I think he felt' ": Ross interview, CBSI.

584 " 'Any average person' ": Barney Ross interview, JCBP.

585 " 'We of course' ": Ross interview, CBSI.

585 " 'Here's Kirksey!' ": Donovan, *PT 109*, p. 164.

585 " 'Of course we were' ": Ross interview, CBSI.

585 " 'Blackett St[rait]s approx' ": Donovan, *PT 109*, p. 146.

585 "Australian coastwatcher": The coastwatcher service, set up after World War I to guard Australia's almost infinite shoreline from possible attack, was probably alone responsible for more disruption and sinking of Japanese barge traffic than the vastly overrated PT boats. A colleague of Evans, working with a network of Melanesian scouts behind the Japanese lines at Munda, on New Georgia, was credited with killing over a hundred Japanese on the island, as well as sinking three barges ferrying Japanese soldiers, capturing twenty Japanese pilots, and rescuing some twenty-two American airmen: ibid., p. 118. See also Walter Lord, *Lonely Vigil: Coastwatchers of the Solomons* (N.Y.: Viking, 1977).

585 " 'object' was 'now drifting' ": JCB, p. 247. Regular reports of the drifting wreck were signaled by Evans for the following four days, until air intelligence reported it was "not worth wasting ammunition" on destroying: see Donovan, *PT 109*, pp. 149, 166, and 171.

586 " 'before he went' ": Ross interview, CBSI.

586 " 'a loser' ": Jewel Reed, interview of June 3, 1991. Ross later described himself to be "as unaggressive as a kumquat. I always tried to avoid getting into a fight. I was an only child, a spoiled brat." Ross interview, JCBP; and JCB, p. 213.

586 " 'So this is how' ": John Hersey, "Survival," *The New Yorker*, June 17, 1944.

586 " 'My trip out' ": Ross interview, CBSI.

587 " 'Harris, who was' ": ibid.

587 " 'sneaked through the' ": "White Report."

587 " 'paddled swiftly off' ": ibid.

587 " 'but again no' ": ibid.

587 " 'He had a higher' ": Ross interview, CBSI.

588 " 'There was an iron-roofed' ": Biuku Nebuchadnezar and Aaron Eroni interview, MS-84-57, JFKL (hereafter referred to as "Biuku and Eroni").

588 " 'I was thirsty' ": ibid.

588 " 'They were very scared' ": Harris interview, JCBP.

588 " 'We understood' ": Biuku and Eroni.

589 " 'Ia, mi save long' ": ibid. (The translation reads, "Yes I know him—he's living at my village, Madou.")

589 " 'They gave us some' ": Harris interview.
589 " 'The first thing' ": Biuku and Eroni.
590 " 'We laid down' ": ibid.
590 " 'to look over' ": ibid.
590 " 'He was heavy' ": ibid. "When I woke up and he [Jack] was gone, I swam back to the main island, too. Halfway back, I met the natives who had come to pick me up in the canoe. I didn't get in the canoe, I could have tipped it over, I just hung on to it.": Ross interview, CBSI.
590 " 'we hid the canoe' ": Biuku and Eroni.
590 " 'showed the two' ": "White Report."
590 " 'he said, "Biuku, I'm sorry" ' ": Biuku and Eroni.
590 " 'There's no paper' ": ibid.
591 " 'Kennedy asked us' ": ibid.
591 " 'What if the coconut' ": ibid.
591 "NAURO ISL": Donovan, *PT 109*, p. 183.
591 "intercepted the Japanese": Known afterward as the Battle of Vella Gulf, Aug. 6–7, 1943. See Samuel Eliot Morison, *History of United States Naval Operations in World War II, Vol. VI: Breaking the Bismarcks Barrier* (Boston: Little, Brown, 1950), pp. 212–20. See also E.B. Potter, *Bull Halsey.* (Annapolis, Md.: Naval Institute Press, 1985), p. 254.
592 " 'I said "Gee" ' ": Ross interview, CBSI.
592 " 'The way he put it' ": ibid.
592 " 'It was too late' ": Hersey, "Survival."
593 " 'I was always sort of' ": Ross interview, CBSI.
593 " 'You know, Jack' ": Jim Reed interview of Oct. 7, 1990.
593 " 'Ross had a terrible' ": Zinser interview, JCBP.
594 " 'I have a letter' ": Hersey, "Survival."
594 "*On His Majesty's Service*": Donovan, *PT 109*, p. 184–85.
594 " 'You've got to hand' ": ibid., p. 187.
594 " 'Hello, I'm Kennedy.' ": Lord, *Lonely Vigil*, p. 273.
594 " 'and have a cup' ": ibid.
595 " 'eleven survivors PT boat' ": Donovan, *PT 109*, p. 185.
595 " 'The reason I' ": Cluster interview.
595 "given up the search": James Woods interview, JCBP.
595 " 'on the morning' ": Col. George Hill to JFK, Oct. 21, 1957, JFKPrePres, Box 549.
596 " 'All the Americans' ": Biuku and Eroni.
596 " 'Fortunately about 2:00 P.M.' ": Hill to JFK.
596 " 'We went to Lumbari' ": Biuku and Eroni.
597 " 'I do not remember' ": "Senator's Notes," JFKPP, Box 39.
597 " 'It wasn't till . . .' ": Cluster interview.
597 " 'Three PT boats . . .' ": Donovan, *PT 109*, p. 189.
597 " 'Lieutenant Kennedy considers' ": ibid., p. 190.
598 " 'I think in the' ": Thomas Warfield interview, JCBP; and JCB, p. 250.
598 " 'The boats were' ": Biuku and Eroni.
598 " 'Lieb, if I get' ": William Liebenow, "The Incident, August 1–2, 1943," in *Knights of the Sea* (Memphis, Tenn.: PT Boats Inc., 1982), p. 100.
599 " 'Then we heard Kennedy' ": Biuku and Eroni.
599 " 'We were supposed' ": Cluster interview.
599 " 'Where the hell' ": Hersey, "Survival."
599 " 'It was an unfortunate' ": JCB, p. 262.
599 " 'We've got some food' ": Hersey, "Survival."
599 " 'The little native' ": Cluster interview.
600 " 'About midway between' ": Donovan, *PT 109*, p. 192.
600 " 'I never heard' ": Liebenow, "Incident."
600 " 'We put this little' ": Cluster interview.
601 " 'As I remember it' ": Ross interview, CBSI.
601 " 'They were hollering' ": ibid.
601 " 'Pretty soon, though' ": Cluster interview.
601 " 'much handshaking, backslapping' ": Liebenow, "Incident."
601 " 'We went back to' ": Biuku and Eroni.
601 " 'As I recall' ": JCB, p. 263.
602 " 'Ensign Thom used to' ": Harris interview, JCBP.
602 " 'Kennedy was the hero' ": ibid.
602 " 'Kennedy's friends' ": Biuku and Eroni.
602 " 'did service above' ": JFK to Clare Boothe Luce, n.d. (Aug. or Sept. 1943), Clare Boothe Luce Papers, Library of Congress. Washington, D.C.
602 " 'Sometime after we' ": Biuku and Eroni.

Part 13: Gunboat Skipper

605 " 'Admitted with abrasions' ": Medical Record, Lt. John Fitzgerald Kennedy, JFKPP, Box 11A.
605 "SHOT FROM RUSTY": *BG*, Aug. 19, 1943.
605 " 'Former Ambassador' ": *NYT*, Aug. 20, 1943.
605 " 'Of course the news' ": KK to family, Aug. 24, 1943, as quoted in DKG, p. 669.
605 " 'legitimate American hero' ": Charles Spalding interview of Aug. 29, 1990.
606 " 'Crews of two other' ": AP, Aug. 8, 1943. Quoted in JCB, p. 265.
606 " 'The injured are in' ": UPI, Aug. 8, 1943. Quoted in JCB, p. 265.
606 " 'I'll never forget' ": Alvin Cluster interview of Nov. 8, 1990.
606 " 'He was *really* skinny' ": JCB, p. 272.
606 " 'He was in this hospital' ": ibid.
607 " 'a big harp' ": JFK to parents, Sept. 12, 1943, JFKPP, Box 5.
607 " 'We only had' ": Dr. Joseph Wharton interview, JCBP; and JCB, p. 271.
607 " 'To duty' ": Medical Record. Lt. John Fitzgerald Kennedy.
607 " 'Now there was' ": Cluster interview.
608 " 'I think it was' ": ibid.
608 " 'I did all I could' ": Twenty-eight-page coast-watcher's report by Lt. A.R. Evans (1943), JCBP.
609 " 'very nearly disastrous' ": Robert J. Bulkeley, *At Close Quarters: PT Boats in the United States Navy* (Washington, D.C.: U.S. Government Printing Office, 1962), p. 135.

609 " 'suicide mission' ": JCB, p. 276.
609 " 'About this time' ": Cluster interview.
609 " 'torpedo fire' ": "It was a scandal—and that's the only word for it—about our torpedoes for the first two years of the war. I mean, it's a wonder that there weren't officers and men cashiered. . . . The torpedoes that PTs had were just abysmal, they were just terrible—old torpedoes that had been designed and built in World War I." Ibid. The unpublished official history of PT boats was more laconic: "From August of 1943 to October of 1944, PT's in the Pacific fired few torpedoes, although the boats were designed primarily for that purpose. Instead they became high speed gunboats." "An Administrative History of PT's in World War II," Office of Naval History, catalogued as "The Unpublished History of PT Boats in WWII," Operational Archives, Naval Historical Center, Washington Navy Yard, Washington, D.C., p. 136.
610 "Heavy forty-millimeter guns": JCB, p. 280.
610 "Lennie Thom, Jack's former": ibid., p. 277.
610 " 'Mauer and I' ": *BG*, June 21, 1989.
610 " 'what impressed me' ": JCB, p. 279.
610 " 'Kennedy did a fine' ": Alvin Cluster to his parents, Sept. 18, 1943, APCP.
611 " 'On the bright side' ": JFK to parents, Sept. 12, 1943, JFKPP, Box 5.
611 " 'One thing you have' ": Glen Christiansen interview, Nov. 8, 1990.
612 " 'Most of the torpedoes' ": ibid.
612 " 'Shooting dead on' ": JCB, p. 280.
612 " 'He was very determined' ": Christiansen interview.
613 " 'We asked about' ": ibid.
613 " 'Haven't heard' ": JFK to KLB, Sept. 15, 1943, KLBP.
614 " 'She was a good-looking' ": Christiansen interview.
614 " 'received a very large' ": JFK to KLB, Sept. 15, 1943, KLBP.
614 " 'Inga Binga' ": JFK to Inga Arvad n.d. (Sept. 1943), RMP.
615 " 'Dearest Inga Binga' ": JFK to Arvad, Sept. 26, 1943, RMP.
618 " 'I understand' ": JFK to KLB, Oct. 8, 1943, KLBP.
618 " 'As you can well imagine' ": JFK to KLB, Oct. 30, 1943, KLBP. "From all reports," he added, "you seem to be cutting a wide social swath or is it swathe to rhyme with suave—whatever it is you're cutting it. Figure to get out of here when the fighting in this area ceases—the pace right now is getting fairly fast as you have no doubt gathered—perhaps it won't take too long to finish it off." Ibid.
618 " 'Charlotte receiving my letter' ": JFK to KLB, Dec. 16, 1943, KLBP.
618 " 'occasionally' ": ibid., Oct. 30, 1943, KLBP.
619 " 'a publicity hand-out' ": ibid.
619 " 'I wanted to take' ": Cluster interview.
619 " 'Am now Capt' ": JFK to KLB, Oct. 30, 1943, KLBP.
619 " 'The nerve center' ": JFK to Pat Monroe, Oct. 30, 1943, JFKPOF, Box 132.
620 " 'I think up to' ": Cluster interview.

620 "Japanese planes constantly": JCB, p. 293.
620 " 'They picked up' ": JFK to parents, Nov. 1, 1943, JFKPP, Box 5.
620 " 'Don't worry about me' ": JFK to JPK, Oct. 30, 1943, JFKPP, Box 5.
621 "taken aboard Jack's *Gunboat*": PT *59* log book, as quoted in JCB, pp. 295–97.
621 " 'I remember riding' ": Alfred Wright article in *Sports Illustrated*, Dec. 10, 1962.
621 "On the night of November 5": PT *59* log book, quoted in JCB, pp. 298–300.
621 " 'The [Warrior] river had' ": Christiansen interview.
622 " 'I saw him after' ": Cluster interview.
622 " 'Mr. Cluster finally made' ": Christiansen interview.
623 " 'I think probably' ": Cluster interview.
623 " 'fine, upstanding lad' ": D. Cryley to JPK, Nov. 29, 1943, JFKPP, Box 4A.
623 " 'I think he was in pain' ": Christiansen interview.
624 " 'If I were you' ": JFK to Monroe, Oct. 30, 1943.
624 " 'I remember most of' ": Robert Rhoads interview, JCBP.
625 " 'It was miserable' ": Christiansen interview.
625 " 'The PT *59* was an old' ": Draft narrative, PBFP.
625 " 'Jeez—if one' ": Paul Fay interview of Aug. 30, 1990.
626 "promotion to full lieutenant": "Acknowledgement of Notice of Temporary Appointment," Oct. 22, 1943, Naval Records file, JFKPP, Box 11A.
626 " 'What a farce!' ": JFK to KLB, Nov. 19, 1943, KLBP.
626 "Christiansen, King, and": JCB, p. 302.
626 " 'Long John Iles' ": JFK to Monroe, Oct. 30, 1943, JFKPOF, Box 132.
626 " 'a nervous wreck' ": JFK to KLB, Nov. 19, 1943, KLBP.
626 " 'Is it true' ": JFK to KLB, Oct. 8, 1943, KLBP.
626 " 'That the pleasure of' ": JFK to KLB, Nov. 19, 1943, KLBP.
627 " 'The folks sent me' ": JFK to Robert Kennedy, Nov. 14, 1943, as quoted in Robert J. Donovan, *PT 109: John F. Kennedy in World War II* (N.Y.: McGraw-Hill, 1961) p. 216. Earlier that summer JFK had told his parents Bobby "ought to do what he wants. You can't estimate risks, some cooks are in more danger out here than a lot of flyers." JFK to Dad & Mother, May 14, 1943, JFKPP, Box 5.
627 " 'They were short' ": Christiansen interview.
627 " 'a recurrence of' ": Dr. Sara Jordan to Capt. Frederic L. Conklin, July 14, 1944, Naval Medical Records file, JFKPP, Box 11A. See also JCB, p. 302.
628 " 'a definite ulcer' ": Quoted in Report of Medical Survey for Retirement Board, Oct. 16, 1944, JFKPP, Box 11A.
628 " 'scatter like confetti' ": Cluster interview. The list of Silver Star recipients, particularly for phantom "hits" on Japanese destroyers on the night of Aug. 1, 1943, is disturbing. See Cita-

tion materials, White House Central Files, Box 722, JFKL.

628 " 'His subsequent action' ": ibid.

628 " 'this officer has demonstrated' ": Report on the Fitness of Officers, Dec. 21, 1943, JFKPP, Box 11A.

628 " 'My most vivid memory' ": *Lynn Daily Evening Item,* Nov. 22, 1988.

628 " 'out of the boats.' ": Torbert Macdonald to JFK, Dec. 7, 1943, JFKPP, Box 4B.

628 " 'His back was troubling' ": James Reed interview of Oct. 7, 1990.

629 " 'We came down to' ": Paul Fay interview of June 11, 1989.

629 " 'We'd meet up' ": ibid.

630 " 'I didn't think he' ": James Wood interview, JCBP.

630 " 'If people asked me' ": Cluster interview.

630 " 'We would argue' ": ibid.

630 " 'Most of the talk' ": Reed interview.

631 " 'He was interested' ": James Reed interview, CBSI.

631 " 'I talked to him' ": Wharton interview, JCBP.

631 " 'Most of the PT boys' ": Reed interview, Oct. 7, 1990.

631 " 'Am told it's' ": Macdonald to JFK, Dec. 7, 1943, JFKPP, Box 4B.

631 " 'chronic disc disease' ": JCB, p. 303; and Wharton interview, JCBP.

631 " 'I guess his back' ": Cluster interview.

632 " 'In accordance with' ": Commander, Motor Torpedo Boat Squadron 2, to Lt. John F. Kennedy, Dec. 21, 1943, JFKPP, Box 11.

632 " 'Would we have been' ": Cluster interview. The independence with which PT officers and men were transferred without reference to the navy's personnel bureau in Washington was noted disparagingly by the author of the unpublished history of PT boats: "For all practical purposes, the Training Center was in

complete charge of officer distribution and control. Nominally, Bupers would have been in charge of the planning and control of officer flow, but in the case of PT personnel, field rotation was determined by assignments from Melville: "Administrative History of PT's," p. 148.

637 " 'Am heading back' ": JFK to KLB, Dec. 16, 1943, KLBP.

632 "On December 21 his orders": The orders stated that "you will proceed via first available air transportation, PRIORITY FOUR, to the United States": JFK Naval Orders file, JFKPP, Box 11.

633 "set off for Espíritu Santo": The commanding officer, Receiving Station, U.S. Naval Advanced Base, Espíritu Santo, noted that JFK had "Reported 21 December 1943" (indicating that he must have flown from Guadalcanal) and that he was detatched two days later: 1st Endorsement, Dec. 23, 1943, JFK Naval Orders file.

633 "Fortunately, he found the vessel": "0920—Lieutenant John F. Kennedy reported aboard for transportation in accordance with orders of the Commanding Officer, AP0708." Dec. 23, 1943, entry, U.S.S. *Breton* (CVE23) log, Military Reference Branch, National Archives, Washington, D.C. Launched on June 27, 1942, the *Breton* was built by the Seattle-Tacoma Shipbuilding Corp. in Tacoma, Wash., commissioned in April 1943, and served with the Carrier Transport Squadron of the Pacific Fleet throughout World War II, "supplying men, material, and aircraft to units of the fleet engaged in making strikes on the enemy." *Dictionary of American Naval Fighting Ships, Vol. I* (Washington, D.C.: Navy Department, 1959). (Breton is the name of a sound in Louisiana).

633 " 'after this present fighting' ": JFK to JPK, Oct. 30, 1943, JFKPP, Box 5.

Part 14: The Home Front

637 "Once back on American soil": *"U.S.S. Breton.* You reported in this vessel for transportation on Dec. 23, 1943. Transportation completed this date." Second Endorsement, Jan. 7, 1944, JFK Naval Orders file, JFKPP, Box 11. See also Jan. 7, 1943, entry, U.S.S. *Breton* (CVE23) log, Military Reference Branch, National Archives, Washington, D.C.

637 " 'I regret that' ": JFK to Paul Fay, n.d. (Jan. 1944), PBFP, and as quoted in PBF, p. 144.

637 "She'd left Nils Blok": Inga's mother had always been troubled by Inga's relationship with Blok, and had moved to California ahead of Inga. KK, hearing of the end of the affair, wrote in Nov. 1943 to ask "what has happened to Nils? Has another husband bit the dust? You are a funny girl. I miss you lots and wonder if you are happy at the moment. I hope so. But don't make any more mistakes. You are still young and it just isn't worth it. Listen to old granny's advice." KK to Inga Arvad, Nov. 28, 1943, (V-Mail), RMP.

637 " 'Jack just looked like' ": Ronald McCoy interview, JCBP; and JCB, p. 310.

637 " 'health wrecked' ": Inga Arvad, "Consequences," (sequel to "Truth"), memoir, n.d. (1945), RMP.

637 " 'I wonder sometimes' ": Betty Coxe Spaulding interview of Dec. 19, 1991.

638 " 'Inga arranged for us' ": William G. Cahan, M.D., *No Stranger to Tears* (N.Y.: Random House, 1992). Cahan also revealed, as a doctor, a further reason why Inga enjoyed physical intercourse: namely, that it provided the only real relief for often-debilitating arthritis in her limbs, a not-uncommon phenomenon among arthritis sufferers.

639 " 'Please, please' ": KK to Arvad, Feb. 6, 1944, (V-Mail), RMP.

639 " 'by plane here' ": *BG,* Jan. 11, 1944.

639 " 'I can't tell you' ": JFK to Clare Boothe Luce, Jan. 11, 1944, Clare Boothe Luce Papers, Library of Congress, Washington, D.C.

639 "Jack's mother did not even go": Charles Spalding interview of Aug. 29, 1990.

639 " 'looked very thin' ": Charles Spalding, JFKLOH.

640 " 'He could make my mother' ": Spalding interview.
640 " 'piling up. . . .' ": JFK to Fay, Feb. 21, 1944, PBFP, and quoted in PBF, pp. 144–45.
640 " 'We found him' ": JPK to Alvin Cluster, Feb. 7, 1944, APCP.
641 " 'Yes, he told me' ": John Hersey interview of May 26, 1990.
641 "to interest *Reader's Digest*": Paul Palmer to JPK, Aug. 24, 1943; and JPK to Paul Palmer, Sept. 10, 1943, PPP.
641 " 'ventured capital' ": *BG*, Feb. 11, 1944.
642 " 'He's the boy' ": ibid.
642 " 'Come and buy' ": *BH*, Feb. 11, 1944.
643 " 'I've read accounts' ": *BG*, Feb. 13, 1944.
643 " 'There is something' ": Joe Kane to JPK, Feb. 14, 1944, as quoted in DKG, p. 700.
643 " 'Spent the week' ": JFK to Fay, Feb. 21, 1944. JFK was exaggerating, but not by much. "How a Jewish chaplain was shot by a Jap prisoner to whom he was bringing a glass of water was told yesterday at Faneuil Hall by Lieut. John F. Kennedy, USNR, grandson of Former Mayor John F. Fitzgerald, at the awarding of prizes to schoolchildren for essays on 'Religious Discrimination Must Not Exist in America.' Lt. Kennedy, who saw the incident, said two Protestant and two Jewish chaplains were working together in the South Pacific where 'a number of Jap prisoners were being brought back by our boys. One of the Japs asked for a drink of water. One of the Jewish chaplains went to give him water, and as he was performing the humanitarian act, the Jap produced a concealed gun and shot him.' " *BH*, Feb. 13, 1944.
643 " 'such delay to count' ": Chief of Naval Personnel to Lt. John F. Kennedy, Feb. 12, 1944, JFKPP, Box 11.
644 " 'I'm in the hospital' ": JFK to Fay, Feb. 21, 1944, PBFB.
644 " 'Everyone very optimistic' ": ibid.
644 " 'I don't remember' ": JCB, p. 321.
644 "Submarine Chaser Training Center": The Submarine Chaser Training Center had been founded in March 1942 "to provide men and officers properly trained for PC's and SC's, and to provide a shakedown organization which would send the ships out prepared to effectively perform their duties of escort and patrol. German subs were patrolling right off the beach, and the need for SC's was tremendous and immediate." Office of Naval History, "An Administrative History of PT's in World War II," catalogued as "The Unpublished History of PT Boats in WWII," Operational Archives, Naval Historical Center, Washington Navy Yard, Washington, D.C., p. 155. However, a shakedown detail for PTs was added in the spring of 1943 for Higgins PT boats, involving a two- later extended to three-week program familiarizing crews with their boats as well as providing operational training. By the end of 1943 the so-called Submarine Chaser Training Center became the shakedown center for *all* American PTs, taking over this responsibility from Melville, where the climate had proved

too inclement. The facility was renamed the Naval Training Center, Miami, in June 1944. Ibid., pp. 156–65.
644 "It was there": JFK reported for duty at the SCTC, Miami, on March 14, 1944. Naval Orders file, JFKPP Box 11.
644 " 'Needless to say' ": JFK to John Hersey, n.d. (March or April 1944), JHP.
645 " 'conditions here' ": ibid.
645 " 'Girls were almost' ": Nick Nikoloric interview, JCBP and JCB, p. 329.
645 " 'There is no sense' ": JFK to Fay, Feb. 21, 1944. PBFB.
646 " 'you and Teddy' ": JFK to KLB, May 3, 1944, KLBP.
646 " 'Heard from Joe' ": ibid.
646 " 'as a guest' ": Joseph Timilty interview, JCBP.
647 " 'Timilty left when' ": JFK to KLB, May 3, 1944, KLBP.
647 " 'Betram the Butler' ": ibid.
647 " 'to the hospital' ": Timilty interview, JCBP.
647 " 'limited duty' ": JCB, p. 326.
648 " 'marry an Englishman' ": KK to Arvad, Feb. 6, 1944, RMP.
648 " 'horrified' ": "Personal Reminiscences—Private," RFK Papers, quoted in DKG, p. 677.
649 " 'All the Kennedys' ": Betty Coxe Spalding interview, JCBP; and JCB, p. 318.
649 " 'driving, dominating' ": ibid.
649 " 'Heartbroken' ": "Personal Reminiscences—Private," RFK Papers, quoted in DKG, p. 677.
649 " 'Members of the Kennedy family' ": *BG*, May 4, 1944.
649 " 'I was afraid' ": ibid.
650 " 'under medical care' ": *BG*, May 5, 1944.
650 " 'Appearing wan' ": *BG*, May 6, 1944.
650 " 'The former Rose Fitzgerald' ": ibid.
650 " 'very worried' she was": KK to RFK, May 9, 1944, as quoted in DKG, p. 680.
651 " 'the marriage of' ": *BG*, May 7, 1944.
651 " 'heathen friends' ": LMT, p. 164.
651 " 'Envious must be' ": *BG*, May 7, 1944.
651 "far-from-beautiful Boston-Irish": "She was not really pretty, according to English standards, a bit plump, really, with a short neck made to look even shorter by her broad shoulders." LMT, p. 33.
651 "Kathleen's gifts and personality": These are beautifully described in LMT, pp. 32–36.
652 " 'Your plaintive howl' ": JFK to KLB, May 19, 1944, KLBP.
652 "where 'an operation' ": Lt. John F. Kennedy to chief of the Bureau of Naval Personnel, May 27, 1944, JFKPP, Box 11. Permission was granted on May 31, subject to JFK paying his own transportation. Ibid.
652 " 'Lt. Kennedy' ": Report on the Fitness of Officers, May 31, 1944, JFKPP, Box 11A.
652 " 'Those were the times!' ": Hersey interview.
652 " 'slightly disappointed' ": ibid.
652 " 'dismayed' ": ibid.
653 " 'proposed to the' ": ibid.
653 "managed to persuade": The negotiations were conducted by phone and in person, JPK afterward writing obsequiously to Paul Palmer, the associate editor of *Reader's Digest:* "I have

already thanked you about the Hersey piece, and you have demonstrated very clearly to me why it is that people really want to do things for you. . . . I think it [*Reader's Digest*] is an institution that America can feel very proud of. It really teaches a great lesson in publishing. . . . That is a feeling I have had for a great many years. . . . Thanks again and my best to the nice people who own the *Digest* and insist on nobody finding out very much about them. JPK to Palmer, June 20, 1944, PPP.

653 " 'He stopped trying' ": John Hersey, "Survival," *The New Yorker,* June 17, 1944. *Reader's Digest* carried the condensed story (including this passage), which focused almost exclusively on JFK, in its Aug. 1944 edition, pp. 75–80.

653 "Navy and Marine Corps Medal": According to wartime navy policy, the medal was "awarded to: Any person who, while serving in any capacity with the United States Navy or Marine Corps, including reserves, shall have, since December 6, 1941, distinguished himself or herself by heroism not involving actual conflict with an enemy . . . Awarded for noncombat action only." "Summary of Regulations Concerning the Issuance and Wearing of Decorations, Medals and Ribbons Now Designated for Naval Personnel, March, 1943": microfiche, National Archives. (The Silver Star medal was awarded "for combat action only." Ibid.) Admiral Halsey's temporary citation, in the case of JFK, of March 11, 1944, read: "For heroism in the rescue of three men following the ramming and sinking of his motor torpedo boat while attempting a torpedo attack on a Japanese destroyer in the Solomon Islands area on the night of August 1–2, 1943. Lieutenant Kennedy, Captain of the boat, directed the rescue of the crew and personally rescued three men, one of whom was seriously injured. During the following six days, he succeeded in getting his crew ashore, and after swimming many hours attempting to secure aid and food, finally effected the rescue of the men. His courage, endurance and excellent leadership contributed to the saving of several lives and was in keeping with the highest traditions of the United States Naval Service": Robert J. Donovan, *PT 109: John F. Kennedy in World War II* (N.Y.: McGraw-Hill, 1961), illus. of original framed citation pp. 192–93. The official, permanent citation of the president of the United States on May 19, 1944, read: "For extremely heroic conduct as Commanding Officer of Motor Torpedo Boat 109 following the collision and sinking of that vessel in the Pacific War Area on August 1–2, 1943. Unmindful of personal danger, Lieutenant (then Lieutenant, Junior Grade) Kennedy unhesitatingly braved the difficulties and hazards of darkness to direct rescue operations, swimming many hours to secure aid and food after he had succeeded in getting his crew ashore. His outstanding courage, endurance and leadership contributed to the saving of several lives and were in keeping with the highest traditions of the United States Naval Service." JFKPP, Box 11A. Later, however, there arose some controversy over the

award of such life-saving medals "for heroism not involving actual conflict with the enemy," since some recipients—such as JFK, Lennie Thom, and Barney Ross—had clearly performed their outstanding services during or in the direct aftermath of combat. On Aug. 14, 1946, the secretary of the Navy, James Forrestal, authorized the Board of Decorations and Medals to convert the award of the Navy and Marine Corps Medal into Bronze or Silver Star medals where appropriate. By this time, however, many of the "delegated authorities" that had issued the awards were no longer in existence. JFK's case was not reached until 1950. The Board noted that "on 12 March 1944, ComSoPac [Commander in Chief, South Pacific] awarded by delegated authority, the Navy and Marine Corps Medal to Lieutenant J. F. Kennedy, for *combat* services on night of August 1–2, 1943. . . . The original recommendation to ComSoPac is not in the files. . . . The permanent citation is contained in TAB (B). Since this was a life saving case *following* an attempted torpedo attack on a Jap destroyer, it can only be assumed that ComSoPac, wishing to recognize this meritorious action, awarded the Navy and Marine Corps Medal." Cmdr. A.F. Beyer, Jr., to Capt. R.L. Johnson, Feb. 27, 1950, JFKPP, Box 11A. Awards of Silver and Bronze Star medals to Arthur Berndtson, Henry Brantingham, Stuart Hamilton, and Edward Kruse, in part or in full for heroism against "five" destroyers and for having each "scored" between two and six "probable hits" on the enemy on the night of Aug. 1–2, 1943, were examined as a comparison. In consequence, given JFK's failure to make a single "hit," his medal was not converted. Ibid.

653 "ex-ambassador had harried": "The Secretary [of the Navy] has had further inquiries concerning Lieutenant Kennedy, son of former Ambassador Kennedy, who I understand is attached to Motor Torpedo Boat Squadron No. 2 in the South Pacific. The latest information he received was that Lieutenant Kennedy had been recommended on January 9, 1944 for some decoration. The Secretary would like to have this query settled if at all practicable." Capt. L.S. Perry, aide to the Secretary, to Rear-Adm. l.E. Denfeld, March 4, 1944, JFKPP, Box 11A. Confidential signals were then exchanged with Adm. Halsey in the South Pacific, and by dispatch on March 11 JFK was awarded the Navy and Marine Corps Medal "in recognition of his valorous actions," confirmed by letter the following day. Denfeld meanwhile rushed a response to Perry: "Lieutenant John Fitzgerald Kennedy, U.S.N.R., son of former Ambassador Kennedy, was awarded the Navy and Marine Corps medal for heroism by ComSoPac for the rescue of three of his crew members following collision and sinking of his command and subsequent efforts in the rescue and return to safety of his crew." March 11, 1944, JFKPP, Box 11A.

653 "Miami too late": Letter of chief of Naval Personnel to commanding officer, SCTC, Miami, Fla., May 30, 1944, JFKPP, Box 11A.

653 "caption on the picture": Viz. *The Yomiure,* Nov. 2, 1960: "John Kennedy is decorated by Fleet Adm. Nimitz for his heroic rescue of crew members of his torpedo boat which was split by a Japanese warship in the Pacific." JFKPOF, Box 132.

653 "ignore the contract": See source note for p. 755, "made a special arrangement."

653 "again and again reprint": To Robert Donovan, who approached JFK for help in writing a book of the *PT 109* story, JFK said: "Bob, this thing has been done to death. We've had myriads of reprints of the Hersey article, and that's all there is to the story." Herbert Parmet, *Jack, The Struggles of John F. Kennedy* (N.Y.: Dial Press, 1980), p. 111. When Donovan, following the Bay of Pigs disaster in 1961, pursued the book idea despite JFK's misgivings, JFK remarked of events on the night of Aug. 1, 1943: "That whole story was more fucked up than Cuba. How do we ever win wars anyway? You know the military always screws up everything." Ibid., pp. 111–12.

654 "what your story' ": Notes on "Survival," April 19, 1965, JHP.

654 "As I have said' ": JFK to Hersey, June 1944, JHP.

654 "reentered the New England Baptist Hospital": Medical Record, Lt. John Fitzgerald Kennedy, Dec. 15, 1944, JFKPP, Box 11A.

654 "On June twenty-third' ": Dr. James Poppen to Capt. Conklin, Aug. 1, 1944, JFKPP, Box 11A.

655 "lying in bed' ": Gerald Walker and Donald A. Allan, "Jack Kennedy at Harvard," *Coronet,* May 1961.

655 "That was my first' ": Kate Thom interview, JCBP; and JCB, p. 338.

655 "he had an attack' ": Medical Record, Lt. John Fitzgerald Kennedy, Dec. 15, 1944, entry of Nov. 25, 1944.

655 "As you know' ": Jordan to Conklin, July 14, 1944, JFKPP, Box 11A.

655 "Lt. Kennedy has continued' ": ibid., Aug. 1, 1944.

656 "In regard to' ": JFK to Florence Mahoney, quoted in Theodore C. Sorensen, *Kennedy* (N.Y.: Harper & Row, 1965), p. 40.

656 "I am putting in' ": JFK to Al Cluster, Sept. 2, 1944, APCP.

656 "They say it's' ": ibid.

656 "over five hundred' ": Poppen to Conklin, Aug. 1, 1944, JFKPP, Box 11A.

657 "An interesting complication' ": Clinical Notes, Aug. 4, 1944, JFKPP, Box 11A.

657 "went to see Jack' ": Joe Kane interview, RMEPP.

657 "Lt. Kennedy's Auto Stolen' ": *BG,* Aug. 9, 1944.

658 "Really good planes' ": *BG,* May 8, 1944.

658 "Ambassador Joe Kennedy' ": Timilty interview, JCBP; and JCB, pp. 286–87.

658 "in their long brotherly' ": RKRC, p. 285.

659 "Your letters' ": JPK, Jr., to JFK, Aug. 10, 1944, JFKPP, Box 4A.

659 "His venture, code-named": The *Anvil* mission was the U.S. Navy's forlorn counterpart to the U.S. Army Air Force's Operation *Aphrodite,* a wildly improbable scheme concocted in response to German secret weapon developments. The idea was to fly old air-force B-24s as unmanned bombers, guided by remote radio control and employing the latest communications technology, onto German V-bomb sites. The criminal indifference to casualties and distressing litany of failures (seventeen missions were undertaken; every single one was a failure, from Aug. 1944 to the spring of 1945) is chronicled in Jack Olsen, *Aphrodite: Desperate Mission* (N.Y.: Putnam, 1970). See also HS, pp. 244–58.

660 "Twice before takeoff": Olsen, *Aphrodite,* pp. 222 and 228–29.

660 "I'm about to go' ": HS, pp. 270–71.

660 "confided to her' ": LMT, p. 146.

660 "most of the letters' ": JPK, Jr., to JFK, Aug. 10, 1944.

660 "According to colleagues": Peter Collier and David Horowitz, *The Kennedys: An American Drama* (N.Y.: Summit Books, 1984), p. 134.

661 "forgive me, even if' ": Pat Wilson to RFK, Aug. 14, 1944, as quoted in DKG, pp. 689–90.

661 "I should be home' ": JPK, Jr., to JFK, Aug. 10, 1944.

661 "His aircraft had been": Olsen, *Aphrodite,* pp. 236–39; HS, pp. 282–83.

661 "Allied military intelligence": Allied Intelligence suspected a V-3 rocket site at Mimoyecques and was under the impression that conventional bombing had failed to halt site construction (see Olsen, *Aphrodite,* pp. 150–51). In fact, as was revealed in the official top-secret "Report by the Sanders Mission to the Chairman of the Crossbow Committee" on Feb. 21, 1945, "it has been found that Mimoyecques was intended for a very different type of weapon. It was designed to accommodate batteries of long-range guns of unorthodox design firing on a fixed line and it seems probable that London was the only target envisaged. . . . The site was finally abandoned in July, 1944." "Investigation of the Heavy Crossbow Installations in Northern France," Vols. I and III, kindly furnished to author by Mr. Rod Suddaby, Keeper of Documents, Imperial War Museum, London. Details of the German origins, design, and production failures of the ill-fated V-3 battery gun intended for Mimoyecques are given in David Irving, *The Mare's Nest* (Boston: Little, Brown, 1965), pp. 213–19 and diagram, p. 178.

662 "There's a big storm' ": *BG,* Aug. 15, 1944.

662 "Joe went out' ": RKRC, p. 301.

662 "countless messages of sympathy' ": *BG,* Aug. 15, 1944.

662 "as early as 1939' ": ibid.

662 "It was a quiet' ": *BH,* Aug. 17, 1944.

663 "Kathleen Kennedy, last of' ": *BG,* Aug. 17, 1944.

663 "MARITIME DAY SPEECH": *BG,* May 23, 1944.

663 "appalled' ": LMT, p. 175.

664 " 'back pain and leg pain' ": Clinical Record, entry of Aug. 22, 1944, JFKPP, Box 11A. To Roosevelt's secretary, Grace Tully, JPK wrote on Aug. 29, 1944: "He [Jack] is in quite bad shape and weighs as much as his twelve year old brother [Teddy]." OF 3061-3074, Box 2, FDRL.

664 " 'We were organized' ": JCB, p. 345.

664 " 'I remember Eunice' ": ibid.

664 " 'I am a Kennedy' ": KK to KLB, Nov. 29, 1944, as quoted in DKG, p. 697.

665 " 'But Kathleen handled him' ": JCB, p. 346; and Jewel Reed interview, JCBP.

665 " 'that clown' ": Jewel Reed interview of June 3, 1991.

665 " 'one of the most' ": Arthur Krock, *Memoirs: Sixty Years on the Firing Line* (N.Y.: Funk & Wagnalls, 1968), p. 348.

665 " 'Joe Jr., when he volunteered' ": Arthur Krock interview, JCBP.

665 " 'go mad' ": DKG, p. 693.

665 " 'You know how much' ": JPK to J. Calder, Sept. 26, 1944, as quoted in DKG, p. 693.

665 " 'all my plans' ": JPK to Arthur Houghton, Sept. 11, 1944, as quoted in DKG, p. 693.

666 "It was her sister Eunice": DKG, p. 696.

666 " 'So ends the story' ": ibid. On Sept. 3, 1944, troops of the 2nd British Army had liberated Brussels, with Billy Hartington—Captain Cavendish, Lord Hartington—aboard the leading tank. Hartington had subsequently written to his young bride, telling her of the reception they'd been given by the people of Belgium: "I would not have believed the human race could be capable of such emotion and such gratitude." DKG, p. 695. On Sept. 7, however, advancing forces met fierce German resistance in the northern outskirts of Antwerp, and Hartington's battalion of the Coldstream Guards encountered similar problems at Heppen near Limburg, the population having already been ordered to leave the area, while S.S. units from the nearby military camp at Beverlo prepared to give battle. "My father rode twice a day from Olmen, where we were hiding, to our farmhouse," recalled Frans Mangelschots, a witness, many years later, explaining that his father, a local farmer, "wanted to keep an eye on his farm and milk the cows." When Mangelschots arrived on Saturday, Sept. 9, he heard heavy shooting and realized the battle for Heppen had begun. "The English, on a front of 3 kilometers, captured Beringen," he later recalled. The railway marked the frontier between two elite divisions: the British Guards Armoured and the German S.S., the latter equipped with Panther tanks. "The English losses were very heavy: six tanks were left behind on the battlefield. The 3rd Company, commanded by Major Cavendish, Lord Hartington, attacked across an open field. Major Cavendish left his tank in front of our farmhouse, where the English had already lost some of their men," Frans narrated. "Major Cavendish attacked our farmhouse from the rear, and threw a handgrenade through the window, knowing the Germans were inside. (We could see from the ruins afterwards what had happened.) Major Cavendish was hit simultaneously by a bullet. When my father and I came home at three o'clock in the afternoon we found the dead body of an English officer. We could clearly see it was an officer as his uniform was quite different from that of the soldiers. He was wearing bright trousers, a bright [white] Macintosh and no beret or helmet. He had a small wound beneath his left arm—the bullet must have gone through his heart. No blood, nor scar was seen on his face. He was lying on his back, his feet against the back door of the kitchen. Clearly he was shot from inside the house. We found the body of a British soldier lying a metre away from him, and in front of the house two German bodies, and three more English. We finally found eleven English and thirty German corpses. The whole battlefield looked horrible. The scene was deserted. The neighbors—who had been permitted to stay in their bunker with a sick aunt—were still hiding, scared to death. The only living person we found in the village was the priest, hiding in his church. . . . On Sunday 10th, we came back to our farmhouse and now clearly saw how ferocious the battle had been. Two bodies were lying next to one another, a German and an English soldier, having strangled each other to death. Some had bayonets in their bodies, some even spades. It had been a hand-to-hand battle, eye to eye.' " Account by Frans Mangelschots, kindly furnished to author by Belgian historian Henriette Claessens-Heuten, Dec. 20, 1989.

666 " 'I thought so much' ": KK to KLB, Nov. 29, 1944, as quoted in DKG, p. 697.

666 "a widow in a": "I'm looking pleasant about life but it will be a long time before I get reconciled inside about this whole thing. . . . I know that there were a lot of difficulties in front of me if Billy had lived but somehow, now none of those things seem to matter. It just seems that the pattern of life for me has been destroyed. At the moment I don't fit into any design. When I'm with people I like and know well it's alright for awhile and then I just start thinking and it's no good. I'm much better down here with the [Cavendish] family and I can't face going out in London with a crowd which everyone thinks would cheer me up." KK to JFK, thanking him for his "mighty nice" letter of condolence, Oct. 31, 1944, JFKPP, Box 4A.

666 " 'Try and write' ": JFK to KLB, n.d. (Nov. 1944), KLBP.

666 " 'Am still in that' ": ibid.

667 " 'set the pace' ": Michael Grace to JFK, n.d. (Aug. or Sept. 1944), JFKPP, Box 4A.

667 " 'I would always say' ": ibid.

668 "last mistress": "Mrs. Wilson has got cracking on Joe's piece," Kathleen reported on Oct. 31, 1944, though Kathleen suspected "her's will be too personal really. I can't settle down to doing it myself as it really is difficult." KK to JFK, Oct. 31, 1944, JFKPP, Box 4A. (In fact Kathleen

wrote a most touching account of Joe Jr.'s support during the crisis surrounding her wedding, which JFK included in *As We Remember Joe*). To Arthur Krock JFK also wrote from the Chelsea Hospital on Nov. 24, 1944, soliciting an essay about Joe Jr.'s decision to vote against President Roosevelt in the 1940 Democratic convention, which Krock duly sent and which Jack duly lost, but which finally turned up—"Letter found. Essay great. Thanks very much. Best. Jack Kennedy." Telegram from Boston, Mass., JFK to Arthur Krock, Dec. 15, 1944, Box 31, AKP.

669 "Kennedy now threatened": MB, p. 257.

669 " 'a bad taste' ": ibid., pp. 257–58.

669 " 'Harry, what are you' ": Merle Miller, *Plain Speaking—An Oral Biography of Harry S Truman* (N.Y.: Putnam, 1973), p. 186.

669 " 'any part in causing' ": Walter Trohan interview, RWP.

669 " 'a gut in his body' ": ibid.

669 " 'just read in the' ": KK to JFK, Oct. 31, 1944, JFKPP, Box 4A.

669 "hernia, intravertebral disc": Clinical Record, entry of Nov. 6, 1944.

670 " 'the lack of improvement' ": ibid., entry of Nov. 13, 1944.

670 " 'This patient's abdominal' ": Report of Medical Survey for Retirement Board, Nov. 25, 1944, JFKPP, Box 11A.

670 " 'Sometime in the next' ": JFK to Paul Fay, n.d. (Nov. 1944), PBFP, p. 148.

670 " 'From a review' ": "Memo to the Surgeon General," Dec. 1, 1944, JFKPP, Box 11A.

671 " 'was not associated' ": Special Examination and Treatment Request, n.d., JFKPP, Box 11A.

671 "Admiral Dorsey": Record of the Proceedings

of the Naval Retirement Board, Dec. 27, 1944, JFKPP, Box 11A.

671 " 'subsequent to October 20' ": ibid.

671 " 'the facilities' ": JFK to Fay, n.d. (Nov. 1944), PBF, p. 148.

672 " 'Florida from one' ": Draft narrative, PBFP.

672 " 'Liking bourbon, I replied' ": ibid.

672 " 'Here I am' ": PBF, p. 151.

673 " 'I can feel Pappy's' ": ibid., p. 152.

673 " 'it was like being' ": Bob Considine column, *N.Y. Journal American*, Dec. 1, 1963.

673 " 'A lot of stories' ": KLB interview, CBSI.

674 "sent Curley twelve thousand": Kane interview, RMEPP.

674 " 'Curley knew that' ": ibid. "By 1936, Curley stood at his political peak. But the decade ended dismally for the Purple Shamrock. He lost campaigns for the U.S. Senate, mayor of Boston and governor of Massachusetts. Financially, he was ruined. He lost a lengthy lawsuit, when the state supreme court ordered him to pay the city back $42,000 for an alleged skim of an insurance settlement during his third term. Curley lived regally in office, marginally when out." Peter Holleran, *Irish America Magazine*, Oct. 1989.

674 "a second, federal": The story of Curley's arraignment on charges of using the mails to defraud is sympathetically told in Joseph F. Dinneen, *The Purple Shamrock* (N.Y.: Norton, 1949), pp. 286–97. James Michael Curley's own clownish account in his autobiography, *I'd Do It Again: A Record of All My Uproarious Years*, (Englewood Cliffs, N.J.: Prentice-Hall, 1957), was intended to be risible, and is.

674 " 'As I may have' ": JFK to KLB, Feb. 20, 1945, KLBP.

Part 15: A Hat in the Ring

677 " 'if you say another' ": Merle Miller, *Plain Speaking—An Oral Biography of Harry S Truman* (N.Y.: Putnam, 1973), p. 186.

677 "head of the federal": MB, p. 260. JPK had solicited the help of columnist Drew Pearson, who promised to "keep on plugging the idea in whatever way I can." Ibid.

677 "Reconstruction Finance Corporation": Robert Hannegan wrote to the president: "I know he is very much interested in being considered for this appointment and I recommend him to you." Ibid., p. 261.

677 "Export-Import Bank": ibid. (The potential appointment was vetoed by James Byrnes, who had attended the blackmail dinner in the White House in 1940.)

677 " 'The South was' ": JFK to KLB, Feb. 20, 1945, KLBP.

677 "at the Castle": To Arthur Krock JFK wrote extolling Castle Hot Springs and inviting him to join him. Krock declined: "I was glad to have your letter, and looked over the booklet with longing. . . . I shall miss seeing you, but I hope that you will regain your health out there and be back with us soon." Letter of Jan. 29, 1945, Box 32, AKP.

677 " 'I have gathered together' ": JFK to Harold

Tinker, Feb. 9, 1945, Harold Tinker Papers, Brown University.

678 " 'just fair' ": JFK to Paul Fay, n.d., (Feb. 1945), PBFP; and PBF, pp. 146–47.

678 " 'Red,' Jack confided to Fay, 'when': ibid., p. 152.

678 " 'I have sent quite' ": Mrs. Richardson to JFK, Feb. 7, 1945, JFKPP, Box 5.

679 " 'knew that I' ": J. Patrick Lannan interview, JCBP; and JCB, pp. 366–69.

680 " 'a whole crateful' ": ibid.

680 " 'They were a prominent' ": ibid.

681 " 'It was up' ": ibid.

681 " 'It got pretty dull' ": ibid.

681 " 'The news about Bill Coleman' ": JFK to KLB, Feb. 20, 1945, KLBP. "I know what a sock in the eyes it will be for you because I have never heard you talk so well of anyone as you did [of] Bill.": KK to JFK, Feb. 27, 1945, JFKPP, Box 4A. In one of his last letters, Coleman had described mock aerial fights in which "you climb to 12000 with another and there split off at 45 degrees to the sun, one taking a prearranged altitude advantage. Then you come at each other and scrap it out using gun cameras until either of you reach 5000 or your cylinder head temperature hits 300 degrees": William

Coleman to JFK, Naval Air Station, Melbourne, Fla., n.d. (Jan. 1945), JFKPP, Box 4B. Coleman was participating in aerial maneuvers on Jan. 24, 1945, when his joystick failed to function and he crashed into the sea. He was killed instantly. Mrs. David Wilder (formerly Mrs. William Coleman) to author, May 14, 1992.

681 " 'It was an expensive' ": Lannan interview, JCBP; and JCB, pp. 367–68.

681 " 'Went down to Phoenix' ": JFK to KLB, Feb. 20, 1945, KLBP.

682 " 'James Stewart' ". Lannan interview, JCBP; and JCB, p. 368.

682 " 'I've been out here' ": JFK to KLB, Feb. 20, 1945, KLBP.

683 " 'now seeing a bit' ": ibid.

683 " 'What you said' ": ibid.

683 " 'He was recommended' ": ibid.

683 " 'You sound like you' ": KK to JFK, Feb. 27, 1945, JFKPP, Box 4A.

683 " 'heading out of here' ": JFK to KLB, Feb. 20, 1945, KLBP.

684 " 'The period we were' ": Lannan interview, JCBP; and JCB, p. 369.

684 " 'Gee, Charlie,' ": Charles Spalding interview of Aug. 29, 1990.

684 " 'gravest mistake' ": Inga Arvad to JFK, n.d., Wed. (1942), JFKPP, Box 4A.

684 " 'That heightened feeling' ": Spalding interview.

684 "comic evening with Olivia": JCB, p. 369.

684 " 'She was blond' ": Spalding interview.

685 " 'Sorry to learn' ": J. Patrick Lannan to JFK, April 11, 1945, JPLP.

685 " 'I've got a terrific' ": James MacGregor Burns, *Roosevelt: The Soldier of Freedom* (N.Y.: Harcourt Brace, 1970), p. 600. For an account of Roosevelt's relationship with his secretary Lucy Mercer, and her presence at Warm Springs (she was spirited away once the press descended on the house) see Ted Morgan, *FDR: A Biography*, (N.Y.: Simon and Schuster, 1985), pp. 201–207 and 762–64. For a medical review of FDR's death, see Ch. 3, "Franklin D. Roosevelt: The Diagnosis of an 'Unexpected' Death" in Kenneth R. Crispell and Carlos F. Gomez, *Hidden Illness in the White House* (Durham, N.C.: Duke University Press, 1988), pp. 75–120. Roosevelt had checked into Bethesda Naval Hospital twenty-nine times under false names over the past few months, the FBI had been asked to hound anyone suspected of informing the press about the president's grave medical condition, no autopsy was performed, and all medical records were stolen and/or destroyed, leading to decades of speculation about Roosevelt's real illness and its treatment.

685 " 'was patterning himself' ": Lannan interview, JCBP.

686 " 'Any person who has' ": Eleanor Roosevelt, quoted in Hugh L'Etang, *The Pathology of Leadership* (N.Y.: Hawthorne, 1970), p. 90.

686 " 'a surprise gift of' ": *BG*, April 15, 1945.

686 " 'Boston employers, employees' ": *BG*, April 17, 1945.

686 " 'Don't you see' ": ibid.

686 "Tobin had recommended": ibid., April 29, 1945.

687 " 'Visited with his father' ": Louis Ruppel to Dr. Paul O'Leary, April 23, 1945, JFKPrePres, Box 74.

687 " 'from the point of view' ": *Chicago Herald American*, April 28, 1945.

687 " 'I haven't heard from' ": Torbert Macdonald to JFK, May 10, 1945, JFKPP, Box 4B.

687 " 'You certainly are' ": KLB to JFK, n.d. (1945), JFKPP, Box 4A.

687 " 'Haven't you' ": ibid.

688 " 'I find this rather' ": "Internal memorandum re: John Kennedy, Post War Disarmament," n.d., AMA.

688 " 'Jack felt so strongly' ": JPK to Paul Palmer, Feb. 15, 1945, PPP.

688 " 'intelligently reasoned' ": Palmer to JPK, Feb. 21, 1945, PPP.

688 " 'I have been talking' ": Edward Weeks to JFK, April 17, 1945, JFKPrePres, Box 73.

688 " 'Your Dad told me' ": Weeks to JFK, May 11, 1945, AMA.

689 " 'Charlie, I've made up' ": Spalding interview.

689 " 'It was a very beautiful' ": Lannan interview, JCBP.

689 " 'In the long run' ": Spalding interview.

690 " 'Jack didn't really' ": ibid.

690 " 'was still pretty unsure' ": DKG, p. 705.

691 " 'hated physical touching' ": Spalding interview.

691 " 'What *is* touch?' ": ibid.

692 " 'to go on with' ": Walter Millis, ed., *The Forrestal Diaries* (N.Y.: Viking Press, 1951), p. 50.

692 " 'I don't believe he' ": "Memorandum for Mr. Krock," May 26, 1945, AKP.

693 "openly contemptuous": Stassen complained that he was " 'humiliated' to find the American Secretary of State so unsure of himself in so intimate a meeting with the British Foreign Secretary." Ibid.

693 " 'I saw much of him' ": Arthur Krock, *Memoirs: Sixty Years on the Firing Line* (N.Y.: Funk & Wagnalls, 1968), p. 350.

693 " 'We had dinner together' ": Paul Fay interview of Aug. 30, 1990.

693 " 'Jack just thought' ": ibid.

693 " 'I just can't understand it' ": JCB, p. 370.

694 "There were many others": One observer was the British M.P., Robert Boothby. Traveling to Los Angeles, he met and fell passionately in love with Inga Arvad. In a whirlwind three-day romance, he proposed marriage and Inga accepted. However Inga had not reckoned on the long tentacles of the FBI. The very same 1936 photograph that had been planted at the Washington *Times-Herald* was again distributed among journalists in Los Angeles, and Inga underwent the inevitable denunciation as a Nazi spy, this time in Louella Parsons's syndicated gossip column. A scandal ensued and Boothby, who was standing for reelection in the 1945 British general election, was compelled to break the engagement. "I realized that denying the rumor would only get my future husband and myself a lot of nasty remarks from a

lot of 'bitchy' people. . . . Louella Parsons, somewhere in the morgue of the Hearst organization dug out a picture. . . . I was livid with rage, especially as Louella Parsons had told me in the Metro publicity Dept. the day before that she had written a *very nice story* about me, and I had begged her, practically on my knees not to mention anything about my Hitler interview, because of my fiance running for re-election to the British Parliament": Inga Arvad, "Consequences," (sequel to "Truth"), memoir, n.d. (June 1945), RMP; and "Memo to the Director," Mr. Ladd to J. Edgar Hoover, May 22, 1945, with enclosure, Hoover Confidential Files: Inga Arvad, FBI Records.

694 " 'It was all a little' ": Walter Johnson, ed., *The Papers of Adlai E. Stevenson, Vol. II* (Boston: Little, Brown, 1973), p. 237. See also Walter Johnson's "Edward R. Stettinius, Jr." in *An Uncertain Tradition: American Secretaries of State in the Twentieth Century,* Norman A. Graebner, ed. (N.Y.: McGraw-Hill, 1961), p. 220.

694 " 'too diffuse' ": Johnson, *Papers of Adlai E. Stevenson, Vol. II,* p. 156.

695 "His summary": ibid., p. 239.

695 " 'If the Germans lay' ": *London Times,* quoted in Brian Crozier, *This War Called Peace* (N.Y.: Universe, 1985), pp. 40–41.

695 " 'an iron curtain' ": Martin Gilbert, *Winston S. Churchill, Vol. VIII—"Never Despair": 1945–1965* (Boston: Houghton Mifflin, 1988), p. 7.

695 " 'outraged' ": Charles Bohlen, *Witness to History, 1929–1969* (N.Y.: Norton & Co., 1973), p. 215.

696 " 'Winston Churchill once' ": *N.Y. Journal American,* April 30, 1945.

697 " 'that the Soviet Foreign' ": Bohlen, *Witness, to History,* p. 214. (The Belgian foreign minister was Paul-Henri Spaak.)

697 " 'read a statement' ": Arthur H. Vandenberg, Jr., *The Private Papers of Senator Vandenberg,* (Boston: Houghton Mifflin, 1952), p. 181.

698 " 'drinking a whiskey' ": Bohlen, *Witness to History,* p. 214.

698 " 'There are three' ": *Chicago Herald American,* April, 30, 1945.

699 " 'beside his [Stalin's]' ": Andrei Gromyko, *Memoirs* (N.Y.: Doubleday, 1990), p. 104.

699 " 'Poor Gromyko can't spit' ": John Bartlow Martin, *Adlai Stevenson of Illinois* (N.Y.: Doubleday, 1976), p. 237.

699 " 'This conference' ": *N.Y. Journal American,* May 2, 1945.

699 " 'stormy sessions of' ": ibid., May 4, 1945.

699 " 'subduing Germany' ": Weeks to JFK, April 17, 1945, JFKPrePres, Box 73.

700 " 'I have delayed answering' ": JFK to Weeks, n.d., AMA.

700 " 'Diplomacy might be said' ": *Chicago Herald American,* May 3, 1945.

700 " 'It is natural' ": ibid., May 7, 1945.

701 " 'There is growing' ": ibid., May 18, 1945.

701 " 'unless the Big Three' ": ibid., May 19, 1945.

702 " 'Although at that time' ": Draft narrative, PBFP, and PBF, p. 152.

702 " 'Jack was out there' ": Elizabeth Coxe Spalding interview, JCBP.

703 " 'Cord Meyer did come' ": Charles Spalding, JFKLOH.

703 " 'I didn't think of Jack' ": E. C. Spalding interview, JCBP.

703 " 'So many of his friends' ": Spalding, JFKLOH.

703 " 'He had the bad back' ": E. C. Spalding interview, JCBP.

703 "Congressman James Michael Curley": *BG,* May 24, 1945.

704 " 'Last night he delivered' ": ibid.

704 "campaign was in part": Joe Kane interview, RMEPP. See also, inter alia, "Monster Rally, Curley for Mayor. . . . Former Police Comm. Joseph F. Timilty, Master of Ceremonies," *BG,* Nov. 5, 1945.

704 " 'The British Labor party' ": *Chicago Herald American,* May 28, 1945.

704 " 'Everyone evidently thinks' ": Robert Kennedy to JFK, June 1, 1945, JFKPP, Box 4A.

704 "finally come off the": "I have just received a very nice letter from your father in Hyannisport, which makes me very happy indeed, as he seems to like the book very much both from your end and mine." Edgar Sherrill, head of the University Press, Inc., Cambridge, Mass., to JFK, June 1, 1945, JFKPrePres, Box 74. Sadly, the University Press's correspondence with JFK was later purloined and sold privately at auction. Barry Goldman to author, 1991.

704 "Two hundred fifty copies". Mailing list for *As We Remember Joe,* Personal Secretary's Files, JFKPOF, Box 129.

704 " 'Your book' ": Louise MacColl to JFK, Condolence Mail, JFKPrePres, Box 74.

705 " 'real tribute' ": George St. John to JFK, June 7, 1945, CSA. Arthur Krock wrote: "I want to congratulate you heartily on the beautiful book about young Joe. Not only is it well edited and selected, but it is in perfect taste in every respect. I hope it brings to your parents some sense of consolation in their tremendous loss." Arthur Krock to JFK, June 4, 1945, Box 31, AKP. RFK freely used excerpts from *As We Remember Joe* in her own memoirs (RKRC) but, strangely, never commented on JFK's decision to assemble the volume.

705 " 'When two brothers' ": KLB interviews.

705 " 'read about that boy' ": JPK to George St. John, Dec. 7, 1944, as quoted in DKG, p. 693.

705 " 'If he's going' ": JPK to KK, May 1, 1945, as quoted in Arthur Schlesinger, Jr., *Robert Kennedy and His Times* (Boston: Houghton Mifflin, 1978), p. 60.

705 " 'heart swelled with pride' ": DKG, p. 703.

705 " 'We need men who' ": Millis, *Forrestal Diaries,* p. 62.

705 " 'offered him a responsible' ": JPK to R. Wilson, June 21, 1945, as quoted in DKG, p. 703. On July 14, 1945, Forrestal wrote to JPK, saying his "plans about getting overseas are still a little indefinite but in general I expect to go with Vice Admiral Cochrane of the Bureau of Ships sometime between now and the end of the month. When there is a definite date set I will advise you or send word direct to Jack and

arrange a meeting. If I go up into Germany, which I assume I will do, I would be delighted to have him go with me. He could then return to this country with me and we could develop whether one of the billets that I have in mind for him would be attractive to him.": JFP.

706 " 'Count me in' ": Lannan to JFK, May 31, 1945, JPLP.

706 " 'We arrived' ": Lannan interview, JCBP; and JCB, pp. 381–82.

706 " 'the terrific swing' ": KK to JFK, n.d. (1945), JFKPP, Box 4A.

706 " 'a few girls' ": KK to JFK, April 1, 1945, JFKPP, Box 4A.

706 " 'She was a very' ": Lannan interview, JCBP; and JCB, pp. 381–82. There was an undercurrent of anti-American hostility behind much British politeness, largely over the cost in destruction and national wealth incurred in Britain's lone fight against the Nazis before America entered the war, and compounded by the relative prosperity of American officers and GIs. "England and France have undergone common experience of foreign occupation," James Forrestal quoted a recent saying of Harold Laski, "with the difference that England was occupied by the Americans." Letter to JPK, July 14, 1945, JFP.

707 " 'We went for' ": Lannan interview, JCBP; and JCB, p. 382.

707 " 'Britishers will go' ": *N.Y. Journal American,* June 24, 1945.

708 " 'somewhat similar in philosophy' ": ibid., May 28, 1945.

708 "the 'firm belief' ": ibid., May 24, 1945.

708 " 'They were friends' ": Lannan interview, JCBP; and JCB, p. 382.

709 " 'We were very great' ": Alastair Forbes, JFKLOH.

710 " 'The first time' ": Hugh Fraser, JFKLOH.

710 " 'Kathleen was an aquaintance' ": Barbara Ward Jackson, JFKLOH.

710 "Herbert Morrison": Herbert Morrison, coalition Cabinet member and Labour Party MP, had been Home Secretary and minister of Home Security from 1942 to 1945. (After a futile attempt to wrest the prime ministership from the hands of Clement Attlee, he became deputy prime minister in the new Labour government and leader of the House of Commons in July 1945.) John P. Mackintosh, "H.S. Morrison," *The Dictionary of National Biography, 1961–1970,* E.T. Williams and C.S. Nicholls, eds. (N.Y.: Oxford University Press, 1981), p. 771.

710 " 'He wasn't predicting' ": B. W. Jackson, JFKLOH.

710 " 'He was really picking' ": Lannan interview, JCBP.

711 " 'The elder Kennedy' ": *BP,* June 29, 1945.

711 " 'we are going to win' ": *London Times,* June 5, 1945.

712 " 'the tumult and shouting' ": *N.Y. Journal American,* July 10, 1945.

712 " 'Conservatives should win' ": George Bilainkin, in his diary entry for July 5, 1945, noted that JFK's confidence that Churchill was going to win had, after touring a number of London polling stations, become "a little less firm now": George Bilainkin, *Second Diary of a Diplomatic Correspondent* (London: Sampson Low, & Marston, 1947), p. 124.

712 " 'who is leaving for Ireland' ": JPK to JFK, July 6, 1945, JFKPP, Box 4A.

712 " 'To Grosvenor House' ": Bilainkin, *Diplomatic Correspondent,* p. 128.

713 " 'Jack asked whether' ": ibid., p. 129.

713 " 'looking back on it' ": Fraser, JFKLOH.

713 "He squired his dead brother's": JCB, p. 384; and LMT, p. 195.

713 " 'really understand why' ": KK to JFK, July 29, 1943, as quoted in DKG, p. 668.

714 " 'I was in a nightclub' ": Kay Stammers interview, JCB, p. 384.

714 " 'I think he liked' ": Fraser, JFKLOH.

714 " 'Jack, were you ever' ": The Hon. Mrs. A.I. Astor, interview of Jan. 14, 1991.

714 " 'Did I love him?' ": JCB, p. 384.

715 " 'We are a Republic' ": *N.Y. Journal American,* July 29, 1945.

715 " 'as misty as' ": ibid.

716 " 'minutely' ": JPK to JFK, July 6, 1945, JFKPP, Box 4A.

716 " 'that we will pick him' ": James Forrestal to JPK, July 26, 1945, JFP, Box 89.

716 " 'I think not' ": Kenneth Harris, *Attlee* (N.Y.: Norton, 1983), p. 244.

717 " 'recognized Attlee' ": ibid., p. 248.

717 " 'England has been hit' ": *N.Y. Journal American,* July 27, 1945.

717 " 'What about the election?' ": William Douglas-Home to JFK, Mon., n.d. (1945), JFKPrePres, Box 73.

717 " 'as I have repeatedly' ": ibid.

718 " 'Jack used to talk' ": William Douglas-Home, JFKLOH.

718 " 'I mean you always' ": ibid.

718 " 'Write to me' ": Douglas-Home to JFK, Mon. n.d. (1945).

718 " 'unless France got' ": Millis, *Forrestal Diaries,* p. 77.

718 " 'The President referred to' ": ibid., p. 79.

718 " 'stories of destruction' ": James P. Forrestal Diary, entry of July 29, 1945, JFP.

719 " 'think there will be' ": JFK to KLB, Aug. 20, 1939, KLBP.

719 " 'gloomy about the influx' ": Millis, *Forrestal Diaries,* p. 79.

719 "Eisenhower later claimed": Dwight D. Eisenhower, *Crusade in Europe* (N.Y.: Doubleday, 1948), p. 444.

719 "Eisenhower would subsequently": Viz to JFK: "He [Eisenhower] mentioned that he had had only one conversation of confidence with Truman at Potsdam and Truman had mentioned then about supporting him for President in 1948 and had done so several times since." JFK to Krock, n.d. (Dec. 1951), AKP.

720 " 'We have perfected' ": Robert J. Donovan, *Crisis and Conflict* (N.Y.: Norton, 1977), p. 93.

720 " 'after about 3 August' ": ibid.

720 " 'the Russians were much' ": Millis, *Forrestal Diaries,* p. 81.

720 " 'We were impressed' ": Forrestal Diary, entry of July 30, 1945, JFP.

720 " 'The plane doors opened' ": JCB, p. 387.

721 "Hitler's aerie": Millis, *Forrestal Diaries,* p. 82.

721 " 'not to assume' ": ibid., pp. 78–79.

721 " 'that he asked' ": JFK to Krock, n.d., (Dec. 1951), enclosing copy of his notes on conversation with Eisenhower, AKP. Also, Krock to JFK, acknowledging receipt of JFK's letter, Dec. 3, 1951, AKP.

721 " 'he was quite familiar' ": Forrestal Diary, entry of July 29, 1945, JFP.

721 " 'He was sick' ": Lannan interview, JCBP; and JCB, p. 387.

722 " 'Patient flew in' ": Medical History, U.S.N. Dispensary, London, Aug. 3, 1945, JFKPP, Box 11A.

722 " 'Gastro-Enteritis' ": ibid.

722 " 'Dear Mr. Secretary' ": JFK to Forrestal, Aug. 13, 1945, JFP.

723 " 'very fine cigars' ": Forrestal to JFK, Sept. 8, 1945, JFKPrePres, Box 73.

723 " 'I hope my pessimism' ": KLB to JFK, Sept. 15, 1945, JFKPP, Box 4A. JFK had boasted to KLB of his intimacy with the Navy secretary, saying his trip had proved "extremely interesting. . . . I tried to get in a few licks for you, but it just so happened that your name never came up and I thought it might prejudice my standing if I brought it up." Quoted in David Michaelis, *Best of Friends* (N.Y.: William Morrow & Co., 1983), p. 165. (Letter missing in KLBP.)

723 " 'in the eyes of Kennedy' ": *NYT,* July 27, 1945.

724 " 'May Run If Curley' ": *BH,* Oct. 22, 1945. JFK, never overly discreet, had by this time told a number of friends of his intentions. To Lem Billings, for instance, he'd written in late August that he was working as assistant to the chairman of the Boston Community Fund. "As you can see, I'm getting ready to throw my slightly frayed belt into the political arena any time now. I'm expecting you to vote early and often." Quoted in Michaelis, *Best of Friends,* p. 165 (letter missing in KLBP). JPK also informed cronies and business contacts, such as Sir James

Calder in England, writing on Aug. 22, 1945, that JFK was becoming "quite active in the political life in Massachusetts. It wouldn't surprise me to see him go into public life to take Joe's place." Quoted in DKG, pp. 705–6.

724 " 'It will look like' ": KK to JFK, n.d., (1945), JFKPP, Box 4A.

724 " 'never forget' ": Lannan interview, JCBP.

727 " 'there is too much' ": *BG,* Sept. 17, 1945.

727 " 'in his opinion' ": *BG,* Sept. 28, 1945.

728 " 'as fine as any' ": "England, Ireland, and Germany: Victor, Neutral, Vanquished," Crosscup-Pishon Post, Sept. 11, 1945, JFKPrePres, Box 94.

729 " 'somewhat scratchy' ": Leo Damore, *The Cape Cod Years of John Fitzgerald Kennedy* (Englewood Cliffs, N.J.: Prentice-Hall, 1967), p. 87.

729 " 'I'm sending you my speech' ": JFK to Lannan, Sept. 23, 1945, JPLP.

729 " 'his suit of grey' ": Damore, *Cape Cod Years,* p. 87.

729 " 'I want you to know' ": Mike Kelleher to JFK, Oct. 19, 1945, JFKPrePres, Box 73.

730 " 'never been involved' ": Frederick L. Good, Jr., to JFK, Oct. 22, 1945, JFKPrePres, Box 73.

730 " 'Jack Kennedy always had' ": James Reed interview of Oct. 7, 1990.

730 " 'Jack could talk' ": Jewel Reed interview of June 3, 1991.

731 " 'I thought, "How nice!" ' ": ibid.

731 " 'I think Jack looked' ": James Reed interview.

732 " 'she was *gorgeous!*' ": Jewel Reed interview, JCBP.

732 " 'When he wanted' ": Jewel Reed interview, June 3, 1991.

732 "invested two thousand": JCB, pp. 411–12.

733 " 'they voted him back' ": Joseph Dinneen, *The Purple Shamrock* (N.Y.: W.W. Norton & Co., 1949), p. 291.

733 " 'The kind of administration' ": *BH,* Nov. 6, 1945.

Part 16: Election to Congress

738 " 'The first thing' ": Anonymous interview (campaign aide).

738 " 'Sometimes you read' ": Charles Bartlett, JFKLOH.

738 " 'small, wiry, always wearing' ": JCB, p. 439.

738 " 'He was with his' ": Patrick Mulkern, JFKLOH.

738 " 'I said, "Here we" ' ": ibid.

738 " 'reminded me of' ": JCB, p. 433.

738 " 'a rough diamond' ": RKRC, p. 309.

738 " 'He smoked a cigar' ": JCB, p. 400.

738 " 'In a state where' ": Joe Kane to JPK, March 3, 1944, as quoted in DKG, p. 708.

739 " 'probably one of' ": Ralph Martin and Ed Plaut, *Front Runner, Dark Horse* (N.Y.: Doubleday, 1960), p. 114.

739 " 'home of more . . .' ": JHC, p. 305.

740 " 'He was a spy' ": Joe Kane interview, RMEPP.

740 " 'So Dever went to' ": JCB, p. 429.

740 "Joe Timilty later confided": Joseph Timilty interview, JCBP.

740 " 'It was Washington's' ": Edward McLaughlin interview, JCBP; and JCB, p. 430.

741 " 'Give the kid' ": Kane to JPK, March 7, 1946, as quoted in DKG, p. 709.

742 " 'He quits' ": Kane interview, RMEPP.

742 " 'At the moment' ": Kane to JPK, March 7, 1946, as quoted in DKG, p. 709.

742 " 'still rather see Jack' ": DKG, p. 709.

742 " 'Therefore, since he would' ": JPK to Kane, March 11, 1946, as quoted in DKG, p. 710.

742 " 'Therefore, since he' ": ibid.

742 " 'Can this be done' ": Dave Powers interview of July 25, 1991.

743 " 'underneath the surface' ": Frederick L. Good, Jr., interview of Dec. 2, 1991.

744 " 'Jack didn't like' ": Cis McLaughlin interview, JCBP.

745 " 'One day he' ": Torbert Macdonald, JFKLOH.

745 " 'When he asked' ": Draft narrative, PBFP; and PBF, p. 152.

745 " 'The desk drawers' ": ibid., p. 153.

746 "God, no wonder . . .": ibid.

746 " 'authorized the circulation' ": *BG,* April 10, 1946.

746 " 'it is no secret' ": *Norwood Messenger,* April 12, 1946.

746 " 'It is not certain' ": *BH,* April 12, 1946.

746 " 'This was the poll' ": John I. Fitzgerald interview of April 26, 1991.

747 " 'Dowd asked me' ": John T. Galvin interview, JCBP; and JCB, p. 460.

747 " 'It was incredible' ": Paul Fay interview of June 11, 1989.

747 " 'Jack came in' ": Galvin interview, JCBP; and JCB, p. 460.

747 " 'I said I'd be' ": Mark Dalton, JFKLOH.

748 " 'Up in the station' ": Galvin interview, JCBP.

748 " 'Voters of the' ": "Platform," typescript, JFKPrePres, Box 96, JFKL.

748 " 'It is no answer' ": ibid.

749 " 'I stand for' ": ibid.

749 "James Michael Curley's trial": Curley's trial, along with five others, had begun on Nov. 27, 1945, after two years of postponement. "The indictment charges Curley and the others represented themselves as being an experienced and competent firm of consulting engineers with special facilities and qualifications for securing war contracts from the government. It adds the defendants had little or no experience of the sort claimed, and could not and did not produce any of the services for which they were paid." *BH,* Nov. 18, 1945. Irrefutable evidence was presented. The case went to the jury on Jan. 17, 1946, and the next day the verdict was reached. "Curley, as President of Engineers Group, Inc., and two others were found guilty, fined a thousand dollars and sentenced to from 6 to 18 months in prison. 'You are imposing a death sentence upon me [Curley was seventy-one],' Curley told the court." Ralph G. Martin, *The Bosses* (N.Y.: Putnam, 1964), p. 255.

749 "KEEP AN EYE": *BH,* April 19, 1945.

750 " 'You have to get' ": Fitzgerald interview.

751 " 'A series of' ": PBF, p. 159.

751 " 'He enjoyed' ": Fitzgerald interview.

751 " 'I would say' ": Peter Cloherty, JFKLOH.

752 " 'and see how Jack' ": KLB interviews, JCBP and JFKLOH.

752 " 'Jack had tough' ": ibid.

752 " 'Jack was closer' ": Fitzgerald interview.

752 " 'love of politics' ": KLB interviews.

753 " 'Jack had to discourage' ": ibid.

753 " 'Daddy, do you' ": Peter Collier and David Horowitz, *The Kennedys: An American Drama* (N.Y.: Summit Books, 1984), p. 150.

753 " 'been born with balls' ": ibid., p. 159.

753 " 'You must remember' ": ibid., p. 150.

753 " 'We're going to sell' ": John H. Davis, *The Kennedys: Dynasty and Disaster 1848–1984* (N.Y.: McGraw-Hill, 1984), p. 125.

753 " 'with the money' ": JMB, p. 65.

754 "newsreel . . . publicity": JPK paid RKO Radio Pictures to produce extensive film coverage for newsreels to be distributed and shown in RKO theaters throughout New England. RKO Radio Pictures to JFK, May 23–June 12, 1946, JFKPP, Box 6.

754 " 'was as invisible' ": RKRC, p. 314.

754 " 'I was very much' ": Timilty interview, JCBP.

754 " 'arranged for Jack' ": ibid.

754 " 'It was the strangest' ": DKG, p. 713.

754 " 'rainbow in the sky' ": JCB, p. 438.

754 "bribing the rival candidates": "Joe Kane paid one candidate $7,500 'to stay in or get out,' depending on how the campaign shaped up." JHC, p. 308.

754 " 'money had to be' ": Robert Neville interview of March 12, 1991.

754 " 'Neville had the' ": Daniel F. O'Brien, JFKLOH.

755 " 'the better man' ": John Galvin interview of Jan. 22, 1991.

755 "the 'very men' ": O'Brien, JFKLOH.

755 " 'The Kennedy strategy' ": Neville interview.

755 " 'There was a feeling' ": Good, Jr., interview.

755 "bought every billboard": Martin and Plaut, *Front Runner,* p. 133.

755 "special 'deal' ": Herbert Parmet, *Jack, The Struggles of John F. Kennedy* (N.Y.: Dial Press, 1980), p. 151.

755 "made a special arrangement": JCB, p. 475. John Hersey, author of the article, was not consulted (interview of May 25, 1991) or paid, and when JFK's office began handing around the article without copyright notice in the runup to the presidential election in 1960, Hersey felt compelled to ask JFK to "cease and desist" (letter of Jan. 22, 1960, JHP.) "Thank you for your gentle letter of protest," JFK replied on Jan 28, 1960. "In return for absconding with the copyright rights I hereby deed to you all reprint rights of *Why England Slept,* and all returns therefrom." JHP. This was intended as a joke, since JFK never thought *Why England Slept* would be reprinted. It was, however, in 1962— with greater commercial success than in 1940! Forgetting his bequest, JFK gave instructions that all royalties go instead to "Nazareth, Inc," a child-caring institution for homeless children, under the auspices of Cardinal Cushing, Archbishop of Boston: Correspondence in "Why England Slept" Wilfred Funk file, JFKPOF, Box 129, JFKL.

755 "100,000 copies": Mary T. Steyn to Walter Cenerazzo, May 16, 1946, JFK PrePres, Box 74.

755 " 'Christ! We had' ": Galvin interview of June 20, 1991.

755 " 'No one was ever unaware' ": Mike Neville interview, JMBP.

755 " 'Of course it was' ": Galvin interview, June 20, 1991. JFK held the Navy and Marine Corps Medal, Purple Heart medal, American Defense Service Medal, American Campaign Medal, Asiatic-Pacific Campaign Medal, World War II Victory Medal: Lieutenant John Fitzgerald Kennedy, U.S. Naval Reserve, Retired, 116071/1109, Transcript of Naval Service, Pers-E24-EPC: mew, June 19, 1961: JFKPOF, Box 132.

756 " 'Kennedy used to say' ": Galvin interview, June 20, 1991.

756 " 'He met city workers' ": Martin and Plaut, *Front Runner,* p. 136.
756 " 'We can all remember' ": KLB interviews.
756 " 'just sort of be' ": ibid.
757 " 'I don't remember' ": ibid.
757 " 'I would have given' ": Joe McCarthy, *The Remarkable Kennedys* (N.Y.: Popular Library, 1960), p. 17.
758 " 'there was no economic' ": Unidentified news cutting, April 1945, BHCL.
758 " 'Everything Jack's father' ": Martin and Plaut, *Front Runner,* p. 133.
758 " 'spent a staggering' ": ibid.
758 " 'The father's position' ": M. Neville, interview, JMBP.
758 " 'The Kennedys pulled' ": O'Brien, JFKLOH.
758 " 'Congress seat for sale' ": East Boston *Leader,* n.d., Political Scrapbook No. 1, JFKPP.
758 " 'Jawn Kennedy of Florida' ": ibid.
759 " 'Now I've seen' ": ibid.
759 " 'Edging the waterfront' ": *Look,* June 11, 1946.
759 " 'Whoops, my dear' ": Boston *Leader,* n.d., Scrapbook No. 1.
760 " 'with his amateur' ": *Look,* June 11, 1946.
760 " 'The Look article' ": East Boston *Leader,* n.d., Scrapbook No. 1.
760 " 'Because of his' ": RKRC, p. 314.
761 " 'I don't know what' ": KK to family, Feb. 22, 1944, JFKPP, Box 4A.
761 "KENNEDY IS PRESENT FAVORITE": *BH,* n.d. (May 1946), Scrapbook No. 1.
761 " 'I would say if' ": Fitgerald interview.
761 " 'I always said' ": Powers interview.
761 " 'Every guy in here' ": Martin and Plaut, *Front Runner,* p. 142.
761 " 'weeping in disgust' ": Burton Hersch, *The Education of Edward Kennedy* (N.Y.: William Morrow, 1972), p. 48.
762 " 'I never met' ": Clem Norton, JFKLOH.
762 " 'Joseph Kennedy went' ": Joseph Lee interview, JMBP.
762 " 'Then Lee did' ": ibid.
763 " 'to John F. Kennedy' ": *BP,* n.d. (May 1946), Scrapbook No. 1.
763 "paid a further huge sum": RJW, p. 399.
763 " 'It was exciting' ": KLB interviews.
764 " 'Jawn the pawn' ": East Boston *Leader,* n.d., Scrapbook No. 1.
764 " 'He was not' ": Joseph P. Healey, JFKLOH.
765 " 'Women compose' ": *BG,* Nov. 11, 1945.
765 " 'We thought there' ": John Droney, JFKLOH.
765 " 'attractive, well-mannered' ": James Colbert, *Political Parade* column, *BP,* n.d., Political Scrapbook No. 1.
765 " 'Miami candidate' ": Mulkern, JFKLOH.
765 " 'go home to Florida' ": Unidentified newspaper cutting, n.d., Scrapbook No. 1.
765 " 'I think it was' ": Fitzgerald interview.
765 " 'He hesitated a little' ": Thomas Broderick, JFKLOH.
766 " 'I was so enthused' ": ibid.
766 " 'we had, oh,' ": ibid.
766 " 'Who do I look' ": ibid.
766 " 'very, very young' ": KLB interviews. Red Fay found Bobby Kennedy even less communi-

cative at this stage in his life than did Billings: see PBF, pp. 157–58. Fay's affectionate but honest portrait of JFK, and his frank account of Bobby's earlier, taciturn personality, roused Bobby to fury and even to try and censor *The Pleasure of His Company,* much as would be the case with William Manchester's book *Death of a President* two years later. Bobby's fanatically puritan excisions and comments on the 1965 typescript have a touching pathos as he prepared to ax Fay and his wife from the Kennedy social scene. Marking the passage "As we came out of the theater that day, I would have cheerfully taken bets against the possibility that I would ever volunteer to spend an hour with Bobby again. But I would have lost. In the years since, I've spent hours, evenings, weekends and entire vacations with him—and enjoyed them all" for deletion (Fay refused to delete it), Bobby noted with *schadenfreude* that there would be no more such happy hours for Fay or his wife, Anita. Such delusions of royal grandeur, driven to hysterical heights by grief, mourning, and possessiveness over JFK's memory, were not confined to Bobby. JBKO was similarly outraged, insisted on personally vetting the manuscript and appointing Professor John Kenneth Galbraith to act on her behalf in excising all suggestions of profanity in the dead president's language, as well as any use of the names "Jackie" or "John-John." Thereafter JBKO rejected Fay's financial contribution toward the building of the John F. Kennedy Presidential Library and had Fay's name deleted from invitees to the unveiling of Britain's memorial to JFK at Runneymede. "Another family confidante says that President Kennedy's sister Eunice, is still trying to a think of a lady-like word to describe her strong reaction to the contents of Fay's book. . . . 'It's in abominable bad taste,' says one former member of the Kennedy New Frontier. 'I don't want to know that the President used slangy words like bucks instead of saying dollars. . . . It's trivia,' she added. 'It's like talking about the wart on Lincoln's nose.' " *World Journal Tribune,* Sept. 12, 1966. Years later, however, JBKO accepted an invitation to dine with Fay, apologized for her earlier childlike response, and told him his book was by far and away the most tender and amusing memoir of her first husband ever written. James Reed interview of Oct. 5, 1990.
767 " 'John F. Kennedy spoke' ": Unidentified newspaper cutting, n.d., Scrapbook No. 1.
767 " 'one of young Jack's' ": ibid.
767 "1500 WOMEN JAM": ibid.
767 " 'He really thrived on' ": Fay interview.
767 " 'dropped over to Charlestown' ": Powers interview.
768 " 'During the hectic days' ": Billy Sutton interview, *BG,* Nov. 22, 1973.
768 " 'The reviewing stand' ": Robert Lee, JFKLOH.
768 "at least five sitz": Cloherty, JFKLOH.
768 " 'He had a bad' ": Mulkern, JFKLOH.
768 " 'It was a very' ": R. Lee, JFKLOH.

769 "receiving 19,426 votes": Public Document No. 43, Office of Elections, Commonwealth of Massachusetts.

769 " 'At Cambridge more' ": *BT,* June 19, 1946.

769 " 'Remember' ": KLB interviews.

770 "YOUNG KENNEDY": Scrapbook No. 1.

770 " 'Thus the slender blonde' ": *BH,* June 19, 1946.

770 " 'John has been living' ": *BT,* June 19, 1946.

770 " 'Of course I am' ": *BH,* June 19, 1946.

770 " 'How d'you beat' ": Mike Neville, quoted in *BT,* June 23, 1945.

770 " 'the money aspect' ": *BT,* ibid.

771 " 'He was the only' ": Anthony Gallucio interview, JCBP.

771 " 'remained in the' ": *BT,* June 19, 1946.

771 " 'He was one of' ": Dalton, JFKLOH.

771 "Apart from a few": ibid.

772 " 'in 1946 if you' ": Powers interview.

772 " 'he did not seem' ": Dalton, JFKLOH.

772 " 'He was not affable' ": ibid.

773 " 'neutral' ": "The puzzle is why Curley has volunteered to remain neutral": W.E. Mullins column, *BH,* June 21, 1946. To more astute observers, there were definite signs of Curley support for the Kennedy campaign. John Cotter, Curley's political secretary in Congress, and acting congressman while Curley attended to his mayoral duties in Boston, also aspired to the seat and was considered a cofavorite along with Mike Neville in the lead-up to the primary. When Cotter suggested he had Curley's endorsement by sending out campaign literature on Curley's congressional stationery, however, the ex-ambassador was swift to act. He demanded Curley make clear he was not supporting Cotter, and Curley, in deference to their "deal" in 1944, was compelled to oblige. " 'Curley in Attack on Secretary—Says Cotter Has No Right to Use His Stationery'—Mayor Curley was drawn into the fight for the seat in Congress from which he is retiring when he declared last night that he had not authorized John F. Cotter, his Washington secretary, to use his Congressional stationery in connection with his campaign for Congress. . . . 'I did not authorize it. It is a violation of ethics and a violation of the law.' " *BP,* n.d., Scrapbook No. 1. The result was immediately noticeable to the press, who reported that Cotter "lost ground yesterday as a result of Curley's criticism of him." Ibid. Peter Cloherty, one of JFK's political secretaries, later confided that Curley's family played an active role in JFK's campaign. "As a matter of fact, Curley proclaimed to be neutral in the campaign . . . but I first met George Curley at the Bellevue Hotel in 1946. Mary Curley was also somewhat active in the campaign." Cloherty, JFKLOH. (Once the primary was over, Mayor Curley could afford to make more overt gestures, such as naming JFK to deliver the annual Independence Day Oration at Faneuil Hall.)

773 " 'nomination is tantamount' ": *BP,* n.d., Scrapbook No. 1.

773 " 'two-week vacation' ": *BH,* June 20, 1946.

773 " 'a fighting conservative' ": *BT,* June 19, 1946.

773 " 'The candidate's political' ": Billy Sutton interview, JCBP.

773 " 'Personality, religion' ": Sutton interview, *BG.* Nov. 22, 1973.

773 " 'most of the fellows' ": Fitzgerald interview.

773 " 'I do think that' ": *Boston Sunday Advertiser,* June 23, 1945.

774 " 'He asked, "What's" ' ": George Lanigan interview of March 19, 1991.

774 " 'have followed' ": J. Patrick Lannan to JFK, July 1, 1946, JPLP.

774 " 'just to tell you' ": KK to JFK, July 13, 1946, JFKPP, Box 4A.

774 " 'delivered before the' ": "Some Elements of the American Character," Independence Day Oration, July 4, 1946, JFKPrePres, Box 94.

775 " 'at home in' ": ibid.

776 " 'John F. Kennedy will' ": Unidentified newspaper cutting, n.d., Scrapbook No. 1.

776 " 'I thought Jack wouldn't' ": DKG, p. 708.

776 " 'In politics you' ": Joe Kane interview, RMEPP; and Martin and Plaut, *Front Runner,* p. 132.

776 "visited Inga Arvad": Ron McCoy interview, JCBP. Inga, having worked for some time for MGM as a screenwriter, had then become publicist for David O. Selznick: RMP.

777 " 'They were all divorcées' ": C. McLaughlin interview, JCBP.

777 " 'knocking a name' ": Charles Spalding interview of Aug. 29, 1990.

777 " 'I turned and found' ": Gene Tierney with Mickey Herskowitz, *Self Portrait* (N.Y.: Wyden Books, 1979), p. 141.

777 " 'Jack was tall' ": ibid., p. 142.

778 " 'News from the' ": Unidentified news clipping, n.d. (July 1946), Political Scrapbook #1.

778 " 'She was a' ": JCB, p. 485.

778 " 'It wasn't a' ": Elizabeth Coxe Spalding interview, JCBP; and JCB, p. 485.

778 " 'Jack told me how' ": *National Enquirer,* March 15, 1976.

778 " 'I am not sure' ": Tierney with Herskowitz, *Self Portrait,* p. 147.

779 " 'I picked him up' ": Paul Fay interview, JCBP; and JCB, p. 485.

779 " 'You can say' ": Henry James interview of Aug. 23, 1990.

779 " 'I didn't see' ": ibid.

780 " 'He was going to be' ": JCB, p. 485.

780 " 'It was going' ": Peter Cloherty interview, JCBP, and JCB, p. 486.

780 "was a poor lover": Arthur Krock interview, JCBP. "One woman said, 'I was fascinated by him at the time, but our lovemaking was so disastrous that for years later I was convinced I was frigid. He was terrible in bed' ": Ralph G. Martin, *A Hero for Our Time* (N.Y.: Macmillan, 1983), p. 56.

780 " 'He knew he was' ": Collier and Horowitz, *The Kennedys,* p. 175.

781 " 'Kennedy didn't have' ": Gallucio interview, JCBP.

781 " 'It was more' ": Cloherty interview, JCBP.

781 " 'The speeches were' ": R. Lee, JFKLOH.

781 " 'We kept moving' ": Droney, JFKLOH.

781 " 'young amateurish' ": Gallucio interview, JCBP.
781 " 'Did I ask' ": Good, Jr., interview.
782 " 'I have been hoping' ": JFK to Lannan, Sept. 12, 1946, JPLP.
782 " 'if you ever did' ": Lannan to JFK, Oct. 24, 1946, JPLP.
782 " 'Jack met me' ": Tierney with Herskowitz, *Self Portrait*, p. 152.
782 " 'The father was' ": Droney, JFKLOH.
783 " 'a very happy' ": JCB, p. 437, and Peter Cloherty interview, JCBP.
783 " 'He tried not' ": Fitzgerald interview.
783 " 'more people die' ": Powers interview.
783 " 'The great success of' ": Galvin interview, JCBP; and interview of June 20, 1991.
783 "a check for $600,000": *BG,* Aug. 12, 1946.
784 " 'It was the part' ": Powers interview.
784 " 'the stake of veterans' ": Young Democrats of Pennsylvania speech, Aug. 21, 1946, JFKPrePres, Box 94.
786 "1946 national encampment": VFW speech, Sept. 2, 1946, JFK PrePres, Box 94.
786 " 'I believe that' ": Choate School speech, Sept. 27, 1946, JFKPrePres, Box 94.
786 " 'You would have been' ": George St. John to JPK, Oct., 1946, CSA.
787 " 'The time has come' ": Radio Speech on Russia, JFKPrePres, Box 94.
787 " 'Immediately, one of' ": ibid.
787 " 'The truth is' ": ibid.
788 " 'Dante,' ": ibid.
789 " 'ultraconservative political' ": Sutton interview, JCBP.

789 " 'minding other people's' ": *Life,* March, 1946.
789 " 'the most direct-acting' ": ibid.
790 " 'he really *was*' ": JCB, pp. 353–54; and C. Mclaughlin interview, JCBP.
790 " 'thought the Kennedy family' ": Ron McCoy interview, JCBP; and JCB, pp. 142–43.
790 " 'couldn't understand' ": ibid., p. 142.
791 " 'Kennedy Favors' ": *BG,* Nov. 21, 1946.
791 " 'literally chained' ": Radio Speech on Russia.
791 " 'He was running' ": KLB interviews.
792 " 'At a Liberal' ": Harvard *Crimson,* Oct. 19, 1946.
793 "69,093 votes to 26,007": Public Document No. 43, Commonwealth of Massachusetts.
793 " 'Congratulations!' ": Lannan to JFK, Nov. 6, 1946, JPLP.
793 " 'Joe Kennedy's boy' ": Harvard *Crimson,* Oct. 19, 1946.
793 " 'big, square-shouldered' ": *BH,* Oct. 24, 1946.
793 " 'He was going' ": Mary McNeely, JFKLOH.
794 " 'The traditional parties' ": "Why I Am a Democrat" Speech, Oct. 23, 1946, JFKPrePres, Box 94.
794 " 'Do not expect' ": ibid.
794 " 'I remember that' ": JCB, p. 497.
795 " 'a small clique' ": *BG,* Nov. 21, 1946.
795 " 'By this time' ": Phyllis Brooks Macdonald interview of June 2, 1991.
795 " 'On our way home' ": ibid.
796 " 'I said,' ": ibid.
796 " 'You have my best' ": Herbert B. Swope to JFK, Nov. 6, 1946, JFKPP, Box 5.

INDEX

About the Author

NIGEL HAMILTON was born in 1944 and took an honors degree in history at Cambridge University. His first major biography, *The Brothers Mann,* was critically acclaimed both in Britain and the United States, as was *Monty,* his three-volume official biography of the legendary World War II commander Field Marshal Bernard Montgomery, which won the Whibread Prize and the Templer Medal.

For four years, while preparing this volume, Nigel Hamilton has been the John F. Kennedy Scholar and Visiting Professor in the John W. McCormack Institute of Public Affairs, University of Massachusetts at Boston. He now lives in Washington, where he is researching the second volume of *JFK.*

About the Type

This book was set in Times Roman, designed by Stanley Morison specifically for *The Times* of London. The typeface was introduced in the newspaper in 1932. Times Roman has had its greatest success in the United States as a book and commercial typeface, rather than one used in newspapers.